Health Care Law, Forensic Science, and Public Policy

Editorial Advisory Board
Little, Brown and Company
Law Book Division

Richard A. Epstein
James Parker Hall Distinguished Service Professor of Law
University of Chicago

E. Allan Farnsworth
Alfred McCormack Professor of Law
Columbia University

Ronald J. Gilson
Professor of Law
Stanford University

Geoffrey C. Hazard, Jr.
Sterling Professor of Law
Yale University

James E. Krier
Earl Warren DeLano Professor of Law
University of Michigan

Elizabeth Warren
William A. Schnader Professor of Commercial Law
University of Pennsylvania

Bernard Wolfman
Fessenden Professor of Law
Harvard University

Health Care Law, Forensic Science, and Public Policy

Fourth Edition

William J. Curran
Frances Glessner Lee Professor of Legal Medicine
Harvard University

Mark A. Hall
Professor of Law
Arizona State University

David H. Kaye
Regents Professor
Arizona State University

Little, Brown and Company
Boston Toronto London

Copyright © 1990 by William J. Curran, Mark A. Hall, and David H. Kaye

All rights reserved. No part of this book may be reproduced in any form or by any electronic or mechanical means including information storage and retrieval systems without permission in writing from the publisher, except by a reviewer who may quote brief passages in a review.

Library of Congress Catalog Card No. 90-60592

ISBN 0-316-16532-8

Fourth Edition

MV NY

Published simultaneously in Canada
by Little, Brown & Company (Canada) Limited

Printed in the United States of America

To Doris, for seeing me through four editions
— W.J.C.

To my father, for showing me the joys of an academic life
— M.A.H.

To Nancy, Miranda, and Alexander, for understanding
— D.H.K.

Summary of Contents

Contents		*ix*
Preface		*xxxvii*
Chapter 1	Perspectives in Health Law	1
Chapter 2	The Medical Sciences	31
Chapter 3	The Forensic Sciences	55
Chapter 4	Medical Proof in Litigation	201
Chapter 5	Medical and Hospital Malpractice	249
Chapter 6	Provider and Patient Access to the Health Care Delivery System	455
Chapter 7	Organization and Operation of Health Care Enterprise	583
Chapter 8	Reforming the Health Care Delivery System	665
Chapter 9	Medical-Moral Problems in a Changing World	901
Chapter 10	Public Health Regulation and the AIDS Epidemic	1129
Table of Cases		*1271*
Index		*1281*

Contents

Preface · xxxvii

Chapter 1
Perspectives in Health Law · 1

Curran, Titles in the Medicolegal Field: A Proposal for Reform · 1
  Some Medicolegal Viewpoints · 10
    On Truth · 10
    On Justice · 10
    On the Public Image of Lawyers · 11
    On the Adversary Process · 11
    On Physicians and Lawyers: How They Think · 12
    On Methods in Law and Medical Science · 13
    On Medical Practice and Technology · 15
    On Medical Opinion and Causation · 15
    On Medical Theory and Informed Consent · 15
    On Health and Disease · 16
    On Environment, Health, and Medicine · 17
    On Medical Malpractice · 18
    On Medicolegal Courses · 19
  American Society of Law and Medicine, Health Law and Professional Education · 19
  Notes: Health Law Curriculum and Periodicals · 22
  Fox, Physicians versus Lawyers: A Conflict of Cultures · 23
  Notes: Conflicts of Values in Law and Medicine · 25
  Professional Codes · 26
    National Interprofessional Code for Physicians and Attorneys · 26
    Code of Ethics for Forensic Scientists · 28

Chapter 2

The Medical Sciences 31

I. The Basic and Clinical Medical Sciences 31
   A. The Basic Sciences 31
   B. The Clinical Sciences 31
II. Medical Terms 33
   A. Introduction 33
   B. References 33
      1. Medical Dictionaries 33
      2. Medical Diagnosis, Technology, and Therapeutics 34
      3. Specialized Texts in Medicine, Epidemiology, and Other Areas 34
   C. Glossary 34
      1. Terms Referring to Areas of the Body 34
      2. Combining Forms 35
III. Medical Diagnosis and Case Management 37
      Kassirer, Our Stubborn Quest for Diagnostic Certainty: A Cause for Excessive Testing 37
      Notes: The Patient-Physician History Taking and Diagnostic Interview: A Lawyer's Viewpoint 45

Chapter 3

The Forensic Sciences 55

I. Orientation: Scope and Definition of the Field 55
      Thornton, Uses and Abuses of Forensic Science 55
      Notes: The Nature of Forensic Science 56
      Miller v. Pate 59
      Notes: The Accuracy and Impact of Forensic Science 61
      Fisher, Developing a Forensic Science Laboratory Operating Strategy 63
      Saks, Accuracy v. Advocacy: Expert Testimony Before the Bench 64

	Thornton, Uses and Abuses of Forensic Science	65
	Notes: Forensic Science in an Adversarial System	65
	Walls, Whither Forensic Science?	67
	United States ex rel. DiGiacomo v. Franzen	69
	State v. Kim	*74*
	Notes: Communicating Scientific Findings in Court	79
II.	Forensic Pathology and Toxicology	81
	Curphey, Role of the Forensic Pathologist in the Medicolegal Certification of Modes of Death	81
	Notes: Medicolegal Death Investigations	83
	People v. Yoho	*86*
	Notes: Bringing the Autopsy into the Courtroom	88
III.	Coroners and Medical Examiners	92
	O. Schultz & E. Morgan, The Coroner and the Medical Examiner	92
	Model Post-Mortem Examinations Act	93
	Note: Coroner or Medical Examiner?	96
	State v. Chambers	*96*
	Note: The Power of the State to Compel an Autopsy over Religious Objections	99
	Grad v. Kaasa	*99*
	Notes: Civil Liability for Autopsies — Confidentiality of Autopsy Reports	102
IV.	Judicial Receptivity to New Scientific Tests	103
	Frye v. United States	*103*
	Notes: The General Acceptance Standard	105
	State v. Superior Court	*106*
	Notes: *Fryed* in Arizona	*112*
	United States v. Downing	*114*

		Notes: Alternatives to the General Acceptance Standard	125
V.	Genetic Markers for Identification		126
	A.	Cell Antigens and Serum Proteins and Enzymes	126
		People v. Young	*126*
		Notes: Applying the General Acceptance Test	128
		Commonwealth v. Gomes	*129*
		Notes: The General Acceptance of Thin-Gel, Multi-System Electrophoresis of Aged or Contaminated Blood	137
		People v. Young	*137*
		Notes	143
	B.	DNA Typing	145
		People v. Wesley	*145*
		McCormick on Evidence	146
		Andrews v. State	*148*
		Notes: DNA Testing	153
VI.	Forensic Psychiatry		155
		Edwards v. State	*155*
		Notes: Determining Sanity	157
		Barefoot v. Estelle	*160*
		Notes: Predictions of Dangerousness — Other Uses of Psychiatry in the Legal System	163
VII.	Testing for Truth and Enhancing Memory		169
		Frye v. United States	*169*
		Historical Note	169
		State v. Lyon	*170*
		Notes: The Polygraph as a Lie Detector	178
		Rock v. Arkansas	*179*
		Notes: Hypnosis and Narcoanalysis for Restoring Memory and Demonstrating Veracity — Other Psychological Testimony	188

Contents xiii

Chapter 4
Medical Proof in Litigation 201

I. Lay Opinion on Medical Issues 201
    Evans v. People 201
    Notes: Lay Testimony on Medical Issues 204

II. Expert Testimony: Qualifications and Collateral Attack 207
    Sandow v. Weyerhauser Co. 207
    Lundren v. Eustermann 209
    Notes: Psychologists, Nurses, and Others as Expert Witnesses 209
    State v. Carter 210
    Smith v. Horace Williams Co. 211
    Notes: Qualifications and Collateral Attack 211
    Janus v. Hackensack Hospital 212
    Mohn v. Hahnemann Medical College 214
    Notes: The Professional Witness, Bias, etc. 216
    Sutphin v. Platt 217
    Notes: Limitations on Competency of Experts in Medical Malpractice Litigation 221

III. Basis and Content of Medical Testimony 223
    State v. Sullivan 223
    Notes: Medical Opinion and Perjury 227
    Pucci v. Rausch 227
    Blood v. Lea 228
    Notes: Reasonable Probability Standards 228
    State v. Hightower 229
    Finnegan v. Fall River Gas Works Co. 232
    Notes: Basis of Medical Opinion 233
    In re "Agent Orange" Product Liability Litigation 234

	In re Swine Flu Immunization Liability Litigation	245
	Notes: Epidemiological Studies as a Basis for Expert Opinion on Medical Issues	247

Chapter 5

Medical and Hospital Malpractice 249

I.	The Medical Profession and Medical Practice	249
	A. Medical Education	249
	B. The Medical Specialties	250
II.	Hospitals and Other Health Care Facilities and Organizations	251
	A. Major Classifications of Hospitals	251
	B. Organization of a General Hospital	253
	C. Specialty Hospitals	254
	D. Health Maintenance Organizations, Health Care Foundations, and Preferred Provider Organizations	255
III.	General Theories of Malpractice Liability	256
	Slater v. Baker and Stapleton	256
	Notes: Medical Malpractice, History and Current Status	260
	Smith v. Menet	261
	Notes: Substantive and Geographic Issues in Establishing Standards of Patient Care	266
	Lundgren v. Eustermann	267
	Thompson v. Carter	269
	Notes: Evidentiary Issues in Proving Standards of Patient Care (or the Breach of Standards) for Physicians	276
	McKellips v. St. Francis Hospital	278
	Notes: Liability for "Loss of Survival" in Medical Malpractice Cases	282

	Anderson v. Somberg	*283*
	St. Francis Regional Medical Center v. Hale	*291*
	Notes: Negligence per se, Res Ipsa Loquitur, and the "Common Knowledge Rule" in Medical Malpractice	292
	Sullivan v. O'Connor	*293*
	Notes: Liability Based Upon Contract, Guarantee, and Breach of Warranty — Fraud, Misrepresentation, and Over-Zealous Promises of Good Results of Care — Breach of Warranty	298
IV.	Informed Consent as a Basis of Liability	302
	Planned Parenthood v. Danforth	*302*
	Notes: Legal and Ethical Bases of Consent	302
	Logan v. Greenwich Hospital Assoc.	*308*
	Notes: Informed Consent as an Expression of Personal Autonomy and Medical-Consumer Choice	311
	Brenner & Gerken, Informed Consent: Myths and Risk Management Alternatives	313
	Notes: Risk Management Systems and Legal Responsibility to Obtain Informed Consent of the Patient	320
V.	Corporate Liability and Alternative Policies of Liability for Physicians, Hospitals, Health Maintenance Organizations, and Other Health Care Organizations	321
	Darling v. Charleston Community Memorial Hospital	*321*
	Notes: The Development of Hospital Liability for the Malpractice of Independent Physicians	325

	Johnson v. Misericordia Community Hospital	*326*
	Richmond County Hospital Authority v. Brown	*328*
	Jackson v. Power	*329*
	Notes: Corporate Liability of Health-Care Institutions: Various Theories	*333*
	St. Francis Regional Medical Center v. Hale	*337*
	North Miami General Hospital v. Goldberg	*338*
	Notes: Strict Liability and Warranty as a Part of Hospital Corporate Liability	*340*
	Helling v. Carey and Laughlin	*341*
	Notes: The Reasonable Prudence Rule and Strict Liability Alternatives for Physicians	*347*
	Boyd v. Albert Einstein Medical Center	*348*
	Notes: The Liability of Health Maintenance Organizations for Injury to Patients: Organizational Policies and Legal Analysis	*354*
	Wickline v. State of California	*356*
	Thompson v. Sun City Community Hospital	*357*
	Notes: Malpractice Vulnerability, "Economic Malpractice," and "Patient Dumping" As Strict Liability Torts	*357*
VI.	Defenses	*358*
	A. Standard of Care Issues	*358*
	Ouellette v. Subak	*358*
	Notes: The Error of Judgment Defense: Applications and Limitations in Medical Care and Scientific Research	*360*
	Sprowl v. Ward	*361*

		Notes: The Defense of "Schools of Thought" and "Respectable Minority Viewpoint" on Methods of Diagnosis and Treatment	363
	B.	Patient-Related Defenses: Adequate Informed Consent, Assumption of Risk, Contributory Negligence, and Other Defenses	364
		Precourt v. Frederick	*364*
		Marshall v. University of Chicago Hospitals and Clinics	*367*
		Hutton v. Craighead	*370*
		Notes: Informed Consent and Assumption of Risk as Defenses; Effect of Signed Consent Documents and Releases of Liability	372
		Fall v. White	*375*
		Notes: Contributory Negligence and Mitigation of Damages: The Obligations of Patients in Medical Care Management	378
	C.	Good Samaritan Laws and Other Immunity Defenses	380
		New York Good Samaritan Law	380
		Illinois Good Samaritan Law	380
		Arizona Good Samaritan Law	380
		Vermont Duty to Aid the Endangered Act	381
		Florida Good Samaritan Act	381
		Notes: Public Policy Concerning Immunity Defenses	383
VII.	Reform Movements in the Malpractice Field		386
	A.	Research Reports and Findings	386
		Report, The Secretary's Commission on Medical Malpractice	386
		Defense Research Institute, Medical Malpractice Position Paper	390

U.S. General Accounting
Office, Report on Medical
Malpractice: Six State
Studies Show Claims and
Insurance Costs Still Rise
Despite Reforms 392
Report, Academic Task Force
for Review of the
Insurance and Tort
Systems: Medical
Malpractice
Recommendations 396
Notes: Official Task Forces
and Investigational Bodies:
The Crisis in Medical
Malpractice 400
B. Proposals for Reform 403
AMA, A Proposed
Alternative to the Civil
Justice System for
Resolving Medical Liability
Disputes: A Fault-Based
Administrative System 403
Moore, It's Time for Reform 409
Bolt, Compensating for
Medical Mishaps — A
Model "No Fault" Scheme 411
Executive Summary: Report
of the Harvard Medical
Practice Study to the State
of New York 414
Notes: Major Proposals and
Recent Enactments
Changing the Tort System
or Installing No-Fault
Compensation Plans for
Medically Related Injuries 422
C. Judicial Responses and Constitutional Issues 427
*Kirk v. Michael Reese Hospital
and Medical Center* 427
*Smith v. Department of
Insurance* 436
Notes: Judicial Responses to
the Crisis in Medical
Malpractice: Policy Making
by Legislatures and Courts 439

Contents xix

D. Reform Movements in Theory and Practice: Alternative Dispute Resolution, Screening Procedures, Claims Handling and Loss Control, and Patient Risk Management ... 442
   Madden v. Kaiser Foundation Hospitals ... *442*
   California Contract for Medical Services, Arbitration Clause ... 448
   Blood v. Lea ... *449*
   Notes: Practical Issues in Handling of Arbitration, Screening Panel Systems, Claims and Loss Control, and Malpractice Prevention Programs ... 452

Chapter 6

Provider and Patient Access to the Health Care Delivery System ... 455

I. Providers' Rights to Practice ... 455
  A. Physician Licensure and Freedom of Practice ... 455
    Evans v. Hoyme ... *455*
    O'Faolain, Law Beyond the Grasp of Ordinary Mortals ... 457
    California Board of Medical Quality Assurance, Proposal for Revision of Section 2052 of the Medical Practice Act ... 458
    Butler, State Keeping Close Tabs on Alternative Healers ... 463
    Notes: Entry to the Medical Profession ... 463
    C. Inlander, L. Levin & E. Weiner, Medicine on Trial ... 467
    1 in 250 Malpractice Cases Leads to Doctor's Disciplining ... 468

		Lambert, New York Panel Urges Re-Testing of All Physicians	468
		Notes: Exit from the Medical Profession	469
	B.	Medical Staff Disputes and Peer Review — State Law	471
		Greisman v. Newcomb Hospital	*471*
		Notes: The Availability of Judicial Review	475
		Nanavati v. Burdette Tomlin Memorial Hospital	*478*
		Notes: The Scope of Judicial Review	482
	C.	Medical Staff Disputes and Peer Review — Antitrust Law	487
		Introductory Note: Sherman Antitrust Act, Section 1	487
		Weiss v. New York Hospital	*489*
		Notes: Medical Staff Boycotts	499
		Wilk v. American Medical Association	*502*
		Notes: The Rule of Reason and Quality of Care as a Defense — Allied Health Professionals, Professional Society Rules, and Exclusive Contracts for Hospital Ancillary Services	506
	D.	Peer Review Confidentiality and Immunity	512
		Statutes on Peer Review Committees	512
		Health Care Quality Improvement Act of 1986	513
		Notes: Confidentiality and Immunity Provisions	515
II.	Patients' Rights to Treatment		518
	A.	The Duty to Treat Paying Patients	518
		Hurley v. Eddingfield	*518*
		Wilmington General Hospital v. Manlove	*518*
		Payton v. Weaver	*521*
		Notes: Treatment Refusal and Patient Abandonment	524

Contents

B.	Handicap Discrimination and the Duty to Treat AIDS Patients	527
	Attitudes About Treating AIDS Patients	527
	School Board of Nassau County v. Arline	528
	Chalk v. United States District Court	532
	Notes: Health Care Access for AIDS Patients	536
C.	The Duty to Treat Uninsured Patients	540
	Note, Preventing Patient Dumping: Sharpening the COBRA's Fangs	540
	Thompson v. Sun City Community Hospital	542
	Consolidated Omnibus Reconciliation Act of 1985	547
	Notes: The Duty to Treat Indigent Patients	549
D.	Constitutional Rights of Access	554
	Wideman v. Shallowford Community Hospital	554
	Notes: The Constitutional Right to Treatment	558
	Andrews v. Ballard	560
	Notes: The Privacy Interest in Health Care	565
E.	The Ethics and Public Policy of Health Care Access	567
	Reinhart, Uncompensated Hospital Care	567
	McCarthy, Financing Indigent Care	571
	Cohodes, Taking a Wrong Turn	573
	Notes: Expanding Coverage of the Uninsured	574
F.	Patients' Rights	578
	Minnesota Law on Rights of Patients and Residents of Health Care Facilities	578

Notes: Patients' Bill of Rights — Nursing Homes and the Rights of the Elderly ... 581

Chapter 7
Organization and Operation of Health Care Enterprise ... 583

I. The Contemporary Scene ... 583
II. The Corporate Practice of Medicine ... 584
    Bartron v. Coddington County ... *584*
    People v. Pacific Health Corporation ... *588*
    Note, Right of Corporation to Practice Medicine ... 591
    Notes: Corporate Practice in the Modern Context — Insurance Regulation and ERISA Preemption ... 593
III. Referral Fee Prohibitions ... 600
    United States v. Greber ... *600*
    Hall, Making Sense of Referral Fee Statutes ... 603
    Notes: Referral Fees ... 608
IV. Certificate of Need, Hospital Licensure, and Private Accreditation ... 612
    Simpson, Full Circle: The Return of Certificate of Need Regulation of Health Facilities to State Control ... 612
    Irvington General Hospital v. Department of Health ... *615*
    Clifton Springs Sanitarium Co. v. Axelrod ... *617*
    Notes: Certificate of Need Coverage, Criteria, and Administrative Procedures ... 618
    Notes: Health Care Facility Licensing and Accreditation ... 622
V. Charitable Tax Exemption and the Role of the Profit Motive in Medicine ... 624
    Utah County v. Intermountain Health Care, Inc. ... *624*

		Light, Corporate Medicine for Profit	631
		Notes: The Corporate Ethos in Medicine	632
		Harding Hospital, Inc. v. United States	*633*
		Notes: The Basis for Tax Exemption — Inurement to Private Benefit and Unrelated Business Income — Hospital Reorganization	637
VI.	Antitrust Merger Law		644
		Introductory Note: Health Care Antitrust Law	644
		Hospital Corporation of America v. F.T.C.	*645*
		Notes: Hospital Mergers	649
VII.	Labor and Employment Law		652
		FHP, Inc. and Union of American Physicians and Dentists	652
		Notes: Labor Relations in the Health Care Industry	656
		Notes: Wrongful Discharge and Related Employment Issues	661

Chapter 8

Reforming the Health Care Delivery System 665

I.	The Health Care Cost Crisis		665
	A. Introduction		665
		Califano, America's Health Care Revolution: Who Lives? Who Dies? Who Pays?	665
		H. Aaron & A. Schwartz, The Painful Prescription: Rationing Hospital Care	667
		Enthoven & Kronick, A Consumer-Choice Health Plan for the 1980s	668

			Wing, American Health Policy in the 1980s	668
			Notes: Observations on Costs and Practices	669
	B.	Traditional Private Insurance		673
			Califano, America's Health Care Revolution	673
			Congressional Research Service, Health Insurance and the Uninsured	678
			Mount Sinai Hospital v. Zorek	*680*
			Notes: The Structure of Private Insurance	684
			A. Enthoven, Health Plan	688
			I. Kennedy, The Unmasking of Medicine	694
			In re Hospital Corporation of America	*695*
			Notes: The Effects of Private Insurance	697
	C.	Traditional Government Reimbursement		701
			Introductory Note: Medicare	701
			Memorial Hospital/Adair Co. Health Center v. Bowen	*703*
			Weiner, "Reasonable Cost" Reimbursement for Inpatient Hospital Services Under Medicare and Medicaid	707
			Notes: Cost-Based Medicare and Peer Review — Medicare Cost Reports and Appeal Procedures	709
	D.	Epilogue		715
			Lave & Lave, Medical Care and Its Delivery: An Economic Appraisal	715
II.	Regulatory Reforms			717
	A.	Medicare Prospective Payment		717
			Note, Medicare's Prospective Payment System: Can Quality Care Survive?	717

	Notes: Diagnosis Related Groups — Reimbursement of Capital Costs and Physician Fees	720
	Prospective Payment for Medicare Inpatient Hospital Services — Final Rule	726
	Enthoven & Noll, Prospective Payment: Will it Solve Medicare's Financial Problem?	727
	Hall, Institutional Control of Physician Behavior: Legal Barriers to Health Care Cost Containment	731
	Notes: Will DRGs Help?	736
	Mariner, Prospective Payment for Hospital Services: Social Responsibility and the Limits of Legal Standards	738
	Dolenc & Dougherty, DRGs: The Counterrevolution in Financing Health Care	742
	Notes: Will DRGs Hurt?	743
B.	The Malpractice Implications of Cost Containment	747
	Wickline v. State	747
	Notes: Economic Malpractice	755
C.	Certificate of Need Regulation	756
	Simpson, Full Circle: The Return of Certificate of Need Regulation of Health Facilities to State Control	756
	Bovbjerg, Problems and Prospects for Health Planning: The Importance of Incentives, Standards, and Procedures in Certificate of Need	757
	Irvington General Hospital v. Department of Health	762
	Clifton Springs Sanitarium Co. v. Axelrod	762

	Florida Medical Center v. Department of Health and Rehabilitative Services	762
	Havighurst & McDonough, The Lithotripsy Game in North Carolina: A New Technology Under Regulation and Deregulation	764
	Notes: The Failure of CON Regulation — The Anticompetitive Effects of CON Regulation	767
D.	Public Utility Regulation: Hospital Rate Setting and the British and Canadian Systems	773
	Hospitals as Public Utilities	773
	Schramm, State Hospital Cost Containment: An Analysis of Legislative Initiatives	773
	P. Feldstein, Health Care Economics	775
	Notes: Hospital Rate Regulation	775
	H. Aaron & W. Schwartz, The Painful Prescription: Rationing Hospital Care	779
	D. Green, Challenge to the NHS	788
	Daniels, Why Saying No to Patients in the United States Is So Hard	789
	Enthoven & Kronick, A Consumer-Choice Health Plan for the 1990s	791
	Notes: Foreign Health Care Systems	792
E.	Rationing Organ Transplants and Other Health Care Resources	794
	Thurow, Learning to Say "No"	794
	Levinsky, The Doctor's Master	796
	Eisenberg, Doctors' Decisions and the Cost of Medical Care	798

		Havighurst & Blumstein, Coping with Quality / Cost Trade-Offs in Medical Care	799
		Weinstein & Stason, Foundations of Cost-Effectiveness Analysis for Health and Medical Practice	803
		Notes: The Ethics and Economics of Health Care Rationing	808
		Besharov & Silver, Rationing Access to Advanced Medical Techniques	811
		Ellis v. Patterson	822
		Notes: The Rationing of Organ Transplants	825
III.	Competitive Reforms		829
	A.	The Role of Competition in the Health Care Sector	829
		A. Enthoven, Health Plan	829
		Fuchs, Who Shall Live? Health, Economics and Social Choice	832
		Notes: The Case in Favor of Competition	833
		Rosenblatt, Health Care Markets and Democratic Values	833
		Langwell & Moore, A Synthesis of Research on Competition in the Financing and Delivery of Health Services	841
		Notes: The Case Against Competition	843
	B.	Health Maintenance Organizations	847
		Mayer & Mayer, HMOs: Origins and Development	847
		Health Maintenance Organization Act	850
		Havighurst, Health Maintenance Organizations and the Health Planners	851
		Notes: The Development of HMOs	854

	Heinz, Medicare and HMOs: A First Look, with Disturbing Findings	858
	S. Law, Blue Cross: What Went Wrong?	860
	Enthoven, Consumer-Choice Health Plan: A National Insurance Proposal Based on Regulated Competition in the Private Sector	861
	Hellinger, Perspectives on Enthoven's Consumer Choice Health Plan	867
	Schwartz, The Inevitable Failure of Current Cost-Containment Strategies: Why They Can Provide Only Temporary Relief	870
	Notes: The Future of HMOs	873
C.	Preferred Provider Organizations	875
	Weller, "Free Choice" as a Restraint of Trade in American Health Care Delivery and Insurance	875
	Schwartz, The Preferred Provider Organization as an Alternative Delivery System	877
	Notes: Preferred Provider Organizations — State Law Issues	879
	Arizona v. Maricopa County Medical Society	*881*
	Notes: PPO Antitrust Liability	889
	Barry v. Blue Cross of California	*892*
	Notes: Antitrust and the Cost Containment Initiatives of Private Insurers	897

Chapter 9

	Medical-Moral Problems in a Changing World	901
I.	Introduction	901
II.	Termination of Treatment and Related Matters	902

A.	Defining Death and Harvesting Organs	902
	1. The Definition of Death	902
	Strachan v. John F. Kennedy Memorial Hospital	*902*
	Harvard Medical School Ad Hoc Committee to Examine the Definition of Brain Death, Report: A Definition of Irreversible Coma	906
	President's Commission for the Study of Ethical Problems in Medicine and Biomedical and Behavioral Research, Defining Death	909
	Notes: Brain Death and the Harvesting of Organs	913
	2. The Procurement of Organs	915
	State v. Powell	*915*
	Uniform Anatomical Gift Act	917
	Matas et al., A Proposal for Cadaver Organ Procurement: Routine Removal With Right of Informed Refusal	920
	Notes: Organ Donation Laws	923
B.	The Right to Refuse Life-sustaining Treatment	927
	1. Introduction	927
	Application of the President and Directors of Georgetown College	*927*
	Notes: Overview of Treatment Refusal Issues	931
	2. Patients with Clearly Expressed Wishes	934
	California Natural Death Act	934
	Notes: Living Will Acts and No Code Orders	937
	Bartling v. Superior Court	*941*
	Brophy v. New England Sinai Hospital	*948*

Notes: Suicide and the Refusal of Nutrition and Hydration — The Balancing Test and the Constitutional Right of Privacy — Provider Responsibility for Humane Treatment Withdrawal — Damages for Ignoring Treatment Refusals 955

3. Patients Without Clearly Expressed Wishes 966

In re Karen Ann Quinlan *966*

Superintendent of Belchertown State School v. Saikewicz *972*

Notes: The Role of Doctors, Courts, the Family, and Ethics Committees — Determining Incapacity 981

In the matter of Westchester County Medical Center *988*

Cruzan v. Director, Missouri Department of Health *995*

Notes: Substituted Judgment and Best Interests of the Patient 1002

4. Severely Deformed Infants 1007

Bowen v. American Hospital Association *1007*

Child Abuse and Neglect Prevention and Treatment Regulations 1009

Notes: The "Baby Doe" Cases 1010

C. Treatment Decisions for Minors and Incompetents 1014

Strunk v. Strunk *1014*

Notes: The Respective Authority of Parents and Children 1018

D. The Frontiers of Death and Dying 1024

Fletcher, Indicators of Humanhood: A Tentative Profile of Man 1024

	Notes: Higher Brain Death, Infanticide, and Animal Rights	1028
	Fletcher, The Courts and Euthanasia	1030
	Notes: Active Euthanasia and the Duty to Die	1036
III.	Issues of Human Birth	1040
	A. Reproductive Rights	1040
	Carey v. Population Services International	*1040*
	Notes: Birth Control and Population Control	1045
	B. Abortion Regulation and Funding	1047
	Webster v. Reproductive Health Services	*1047*
	Notes: Abortion Law in Flux — Abortion Funding — Other Abortion Issues	1061
	C. New Reproductive Technologies	1067
	C. M. v. C. C.	*1067*
	Notes: Artificial Insemination and In Vitro Fertilization	1073
	In the Matter of Baby M	*1078*
	Robertson, Embryos, Families, and Procreative Liberty: The Legal Structure of the New Reproduction	1088
	Notes: Surrogate Motherhood	1092
	D. Maternal-Fetal Conflict	1095
	Robertson, Procreative Liberty and the Control of Conception, Pregnancy, and Childbirth	1095
	In re A. C.	*1100*
	Notes: Fetal Rights	1109
	E. Tort Actions Arising from Procreation: Wrongful Life, Wrongful Birth, and Wrongful Conception	1113
	Curlender v. Bio-Science Laboratories	*1113*
	Turpin v. Sortini	*1119*

	Notes: Negligent Genetic Screening and Failed Sterilizations	1123

Chapter 10

Public Health Regulation and the AIDS Epidemic 1129

I.	Public Health Regulatory Policy: Issues of Individual Freedom and Compulsion	1129
	Jacobson v. Massachusetts	*1129*
	Dowell v. City of Tulsa	*1134*
	Addington v. Texas	*1139*
	Notes: Public Health Regulatory Programs: Disease Prevention and Compulsory Treatment	1142
II.	Disease and Accident Prevention: Issues of Quarantine, Prohibition, Surveillance, and Treatment	1146
	Ex Parte Company and Irwin	*1146*
	Reynolds v. McNichols	*1147*
	Notes: Public Health Regulatory Measures Regarding Sexually Transmitted Diseases: From Quarantine to Treatment	1151
	Air Line Pilots Association v. Quesada	*1153*
	Notes: Prohibitions and Affirmative Safety Actions as Regulatory Policy for Accident Prevention	1155
	Grossman v. Baumgartner	*1156*
	Notes: Prohibitions and Abatement of Public Nuisances and Other Hazards Dangerous to the Public Health	1158
III.	Drug and Alcohol Abuse and Dependence: Regulatory Policies, Treatment, and Rehabilitation	1160
	Whalen v. Roe	*1160*

	Curran, Arif, & Jayasuriya, Guidelines for Assessing and Revising National Legislation on Treatment of Drug and Alcohol-Dependent Persons	1165
	Oliphant, Drug Programs with Specifics that Don't Match Goals	1171
	Notes: Strategies for Treatment and Regulatory Programs for Drug and Alcohol Problems	1172
	National Treasury Employees Union v. Von Rabb	*1179*
	Notes: Drug Testing Programs in Government Agencies and in Private Workplaces	1190
	Hon v. Stroh Brewery Co.	*1192*
	Notes: Consumer Warnings and Product Labels for Alcoholic Beverages, Drugs, and Tobacco	1195
IV.	The AIDS Epidemic: Issues of Traditional Public Health Regulation in a New Era of Public Policy and Human Rights	1199
	U.S. Centers for Disease Control, Update: Acquired Immunodeficiency Syndrome — United States, 1981-1988	1199
	Rothman, Public Policy and Risk Assessment in the AIDS Epidemic (1987)	1207
	National Research Council, Recommendations on IV Drug Use and AIDS	1218
	Notes: The New Epidemic: AIDS Issues in Public Policy and Disease Control	1221
V.	The AIDS Epidemic: Issues of Discrimination, Confidentiality, and Disease Control	1224

World Health Organization,
Resolution on Avoidance of
Discrimination in Relation
to HIV-Infected People and
People with AIDS 1224
World Health Organization
Regional Office for Europe,
Report on International
Consultation on Health
Legislation and Ethics in
the Field of AIDS and HIV
Infection 1225
Judson & Vernon, The
Impact of AIDS on State
and Local Health
Departments: Issues and a
Few Answers 1228
Notes: AIDS Control
Programs at the National,
State, and Local Levels 1237
New York Public Health Law
Concerning AIDS
Diagnostic Testing,
Informed Consent,
Confidentiality, and
Disclosure Procedures 1240
Notes: Statutory Provisions
on Major Legal Issues in
the AIDS Epidemic 1250
*School Board of Nassau County
v. Arline* *1252*
Chalk v. U.S. District Court *1252*
Notes: AIDS Discrimination
and Legal Remedies 1252
*Glover v. Eastern Nebraska
Office of Community
Retardation* *1253*
Notes: Mandatory Testing for
HIV Infections; Obligations
of Health Care Providers
to Treat AIDS Patients and
HIV-Infected Persons 1257
*Rasmussen v. South Florida
Blood Service* *1259*

Notes: Confidentiality in the Blood Banks; Legal Liability for Blood Contaminated with HIV	1261
City of New York v. New St. Mark's Baths	*1263*
Notes: Public Health Regulatory Measures: Bathhouses, Gay Bars, and other Establishments	1265
Cordero v. Coughlin	*1266*
Notes: The AIDS Epidemic in the American Criminal Justice System	1269
Table of Cases	*1271*
Index	*1281*

Preface

As this book begins its fourth decade, we pause to reflect on the metamorphosis of health care law from a subspecialty of evidence and tort law to an immense academic and practice field whose tentacles reach into numerous interdisciplinary areas. Each of the book's four editions reflects the stages in this evolutionary growth. The first edition primarily focused on the application of medical science to law, especially in personal-injury litigation. The second edition incorporated the expansion of tort liability in medical malpractice and included a new chapter on the forensic sciences in criminal justice. The major innovation of the third edition was its recognition of the growing importance of interdisciplinary efforts in bioethics and law as a separate field of inquiry.

Now, this fourth edition brings the regulatory and reimbursement environment of health care into focus as a coequal branch of health care law. The book greatly expands its coverage of the public issues of access and cost containment, introducing a new chapter on the organization and operation of health care enterprise, and adding a new chapter on public health regulatory policy, particularly as that field is affected by the expansion in drug and alcohol abuse and the AIDS epidemic of the 1980s. We have also concentrated attention on important advances in the forensic sciences and evidentiary fields in areas not covered in previous editions.

As each of these evolutionary stages was foreshadowed in earlier editions, so this edition undoubtedly contains the seeds for the next major dimension of health care law. While we can only speculate as to this future, our guess is that just as tort law was ascendent in the 1960s, bioethics in the 1970s, and health care regulation in the 1980s, the emerging set of principles that will coalesce in health care law through the remainder of the century is to be found in fundamental issues of constitutional law. Therefore, we have attempted to anticipate future developments by coverage of discrimination in health care, the development of universal health care plans, and issues of reproductive rights and regulatory control, substance abuse and infectious disease.

Clearly, it is not possible (or, if possible, not desirable) to cover the whole book in a single course. Although the lines of division are not clear, we find it helpful to think of this field as dividing into four branches defined by the respective principles of tort, public policy, bioethics, and forensic science. Accordingly, we view this book as containing four cornerstone chapters (3, 5, 8, and 9) around which core lecture courses can be organized on medical malpractice, health care policy and regulation, bioethics and law, and forensic science and law, to be taught in law schools; schools of medicine, public health and health care administration; and courses on criminal justice. Any of the remaining chapters, standing alone, will support specialty seminar courses. We suggest the following groupings:

Medical Malpractice — We continue to view it as important to supplement the extensive core coverage in Chapter 5 with basic medical and forensic science, evidentiary and practice matters contained in Chapters 1, 2, and 4. In addition, Chapters 6, 8, 9, and 10 contain significant materials relating to the impact of regulatory policy and bioethical demands on physician and hospital liability.

Health Care Policy and Regulation — The core coverage of regulatory and reimbursement policy issues, competition in health care, and health care rationing are contained in an entirely new Chapter 8. The legal effect of these policy developments can be more fully comprehended, though, by analyzing their interplay with the organizational and financial issues addressed in Chapters 6 and 7 — issues such as access to health care, relations between hospitals and their medical staffs, health care antitrust law, and referral-fee prohibitions. Many of these topics are new to this edition.

Bioethics and Law — In Chapter 9, we have attempted to keep apace of the continual emergence of ethical and legal problems in health care practice by substantially revising these materials to update previous coverage of death, dying, and reproductive rights, and adding such new topics as surrogate parenting, conflicts between maternal and fetal interests, and genetic engineering. A course centered on these ethical issues might also contain topics from the new Chapter 10 on the AIDS epidemic, substance abuse, and public health regulation, and from Chapter 6 on equitable access to health care. More innovative still would be to incorporate materials in Chapter 8 concerning the ethics of health care cost containment programs.

Forensic Science, Medicine and Law — The expansion of coverage in Chapter 4 on the forensic sciences as well as the reorganization of evidentiary law issues in both Chapters 3 and 4 allow for use of this textbook in specialty courses and seminars in forensic science, advanced evidence law and practice, and criminal justice investigation. These chapters can be supplemented by the regulatory materials in Chapter 10 on drug and alcohol problems, an important focus of criminal law, as well as public health control.

Health care law has been enriched in the past few years with the introduction of several new and excellent texts providing the prospective teacher with both the benefit and the burden of a much wider array of choices than ever before. We offer a few observations that may aid in distinguishing this offering from others:

- If we have a political orientation, we believe it to be centrist, one that considers the merits and demerits of both conservative and liberal outlooks on issues of health care policy.
- Reflecting the varied interests and experience of each of the current editors, this text offers a uniquely detailed examination of public health regulation, the organization and operation of the health care enterprise, and recent advances in the forensic sciences and medical proof.
- A single volume of reasonable length cannot aspire to comprehensiveness in both depth and breadth of coverage. Therefore, where space constraints have necessitated a compromise we have opted for breadth, with the thought that those who desire more extensive readings may supplement this textbook with the additional professional and scientific references and legal citations contained in the editors' notes throughout the book. In seeking to provide significant coverage of every major topic in the field, we have tried to formulate the optimal mix of seminal decisions and cutting-edge developments by carefully selecting and editing main selections with an eye toward efficient presentation of a broad range of issues.
- We hope this text will serve not only as a teaching tool, but also as a continuing resource for those readers and instructors who are called upon to conduct their own research in health care law. To that end, we continue to provide substantial bibliographic notes.

This manuscript could not have been prepared without the thoughtful advice of our colleagues who commented on drafts and gave us suggestions for revision (especially Hannah Arterian-Furnish, Ira Ellman, Michael Gerhardt, Larry Gostin, Art LaFrance, Elizabeth Patterson, Jonathan Rose, and Ralph Spritzer); the diligent help of those students who were our research assistants over the past few years (Stephen A. Cushner, M.D., J.D., Holly Caldwell, Amy Gottlieb, Matt Gregory, Ann Harwood, Jeffrey Lovely, Allison Ray, Mark Siegel, and Susan Watchman); and the enduring patience of our families (who, curiously, wish to remain anonymous). We also extend our gratitude to Richard Heuser and Elizabeth Kenny at Little, Brown and Company, to Jay Boggis, also at Little, Brown, for his copyediting, and to Donna Blair, Rosalind Pearlman, and Marion Snyderman for their care and attention in preparing the manuscript.

William J. Curran
Mark A. Hall
David H. Kaye

June 1990

Health Care Law, Forensic Science, and Public Policy

CHAPTER 1

Perspectives in Health Law

Curran, Titles in the Medicolegal Field: A Proposal for Reform*
1 Am. J.L. & Med. 1 (1975)

I. *Introduction*

One of the most readily apparent weaknesses in the field of medicolegal studies has been our inability to develop consistent and lexicographically defensible descriptive titles for the field itself. The basic reason for our confusion lies in the essentially interdisciplinary character of the subject. Yet, intercommunication between the disciplines and professions which make up medicolegal relations could be greatly aided by more scholarly attention to the origin and meaning of our common terms. In this communication, I would like to offer an analysis of the historical roots of the terminology which has been applied in this field over the years and an examination of current confused usage. In the latter part of the paper I will venture proposals for a consistent terminology for the field as a whole.

II. *Historical Roots of Modern Terminology*

A. **Continental Beginnings**

Most of the descriptive titles in the medicolegal field have specific national origins. The earliest texts in the western world were Italian. They were encyclopedic scholarly works devoted to collecting the knowledge of their times in both the legal and medical areas. By contrast, most of our modern texts are little more than skill manuals outlining techniques of the field for pathologists, toxicologists, lawyers, etc. They impart little new scientific knowledge and their efforts at brief historical review generally repeat the errors of past skill-oriented texts.

The two most influential early Italian works had general titles

---

* This paper by Professor William J. Curran is reprinted by permission of the American Journal of Law and Medicine, copyright © 1975 by the American Society of Law and Medicine, Inc. It was simultaneously published in Great Britain in the journal, Medicine, Science and the Law, the official publication of the British Academy of Forensic Sciences, under the title of The Confusion of Titles in the Medicolegal Field: An Historical Analysis and a Proposal for Reform, copyright © 1975 by the British Academy of Forensic Sciences. The Academy also gives permission for reprinting.

which emphasized the *interrelationship* of the subject to both medicine and the law. The first was entitled On the Relations of Physicians, or Medical Relations. It was written by Fortunatas Fidelis and was published in Sicily in 1598. The text collected not only Roman and Italian materials and principles with their Greek influences, but also scientifically significant information and practices from the Arabic world. The other major work was published in the same period and proved to be a much more important work in the development of the academic field and the practice of legal medicine. This was the multi-volume text of Paulo Zacchias who was medical consultant to the Roman Rota, the Papal Court of Appeals, under two Popes, Innocent X and Alexander VII. Published 1621 through 1661, the text was entitled Medico-Legal Questions (Questiones Medico-Legal). It dealt exhaustively with all noteworthy previous authorities and references on a vast range of medical and legal subjects. In addition to general knowledge, it collected and outlined actual cases brought before the Papal Court and so was truly a legal as well as a medical textbook. It was the first text to use the hyphenated noun adjective "medico-legal" to describe this interdisciplinary field. The term is still in use today, though it is now so common that it is proper that the hyphen be dropped and the term be recognized as a single word.

One of the most durable terms, "forensic medicine," arose in the Germanic states in about the middle of the seventeenth century. The first formal lectures under this title are said to have been given by Johann Michaelis, a professor of pathology at the University of Leipzig, in 1650.[1] The scope of the subject was much narrower than that of the Italian encyclopedists and is essentially medical in content, not legal, and not a combination of both. The Michaelis curriculum was designed for the training of physicians employed by municipal authorities in caring for the poor, dealing with contagious diseases, and investigating deaths.

The meaning of the adjective "forensic" is a subject of some controversy. Essentially, it comes from the Latin, "forensis," or, "of the forum," referring to the common meeting place of the Roman municipality where goods were exchanged, speeches made, civic affairs transacted, and legal controversies settled. In English the word "forensic" has been given two rather distinct meanings: (1) public speaking or debating; and (2) legal or court affairs. "Forensic medicine" has come to mean that part of the medical field concerned with the presentation of medical data in courts of law.

A lack of awareness of the origins of the word "forensic" has led to many improper uses of the term. Some papers and texts refer

---

1. Ackerkenecht, Early History of Legal Medicine, 11 Ciba Symposia 1286-1290 (1950).

to "forensic lawyers," "forensic jurisprudents" or to the "forensic field" as if the word had a medical content. At least one American university has equated the term "forensic" with "police science": Indiana University has a Department of Forensic Studies which the university catalogue describes as "instruction in the methodologic problems and sciences of law enforcement."[2]

In the nineteenth century the Germanic medicolegal educators dropped "forensic medicine" and adopted a more specifically legal title which was also more purely German. This was "gerichtliche medizin" which is literally translated as "courtroom medicine" or "judicial medicine." Most British and American translators, however, have ignored its literal meaning and rendered it incorrectly as "forensic medicine."

It is from the French in the late eighteenth and early nineteenth centuries that we received the title, "médicine légale," or "legal medicine." (The French also gave the world the term, "expert," which was originally limited to special technical consultants to the French courts.) The French medicolegal subject covered primarily the same medical evidentiary matters with which the Germanic states were concerned, but it was broad enough in meaning to cover other medical areas of legal significance such as diagnosis, treatment, and rehabilitation of criminals and the criminally insane, an area of particular interest among French medicolegal practitioners.

B. Early British and American Terminology

The cycle of medicolegal terminology of the western world was completed in Great Britain when the term "medical jurisprudence" was used by Andrew Duncan, Sr. (1744-1828), a professor of the institutes of medicine at the University of Edinburgh, in 1791. Duncan's lectures were the first on the medicolegal field in the British Isles and they succeeded not only in planting the subject quite firmly in British medical education, but the title as well. The term was not original with Duncan; it could be found at the time in Continental medicolegal texts, which still tended to use academic Latin. The most influential was Michael Alberti's Systema jurisprudentiae medicae, a six-volume work published between 1733 and 1747. Duncan did not refer in his lectures to the origins of his title for the field. A perusal of his lecture notes published in Edinburgh in 1792 reveals that he used the term "Medical Jurisprudence" as an English title, but added a sub-title in Latin, "Institutiones Medicinae Legalis."[3] In the body

---

2. Indiana University, 1974-1975 University Bulletin 50 (1974).

3. Duncan, A., Heads of Lectures on Medical Jurisprudence, or Institutiones Medicinae Legales (Edinburgh: Neill and Co., 1792).

of his lectures, which he divided into four parts, he called one part "church-court matters, or questiones medico legales." Here again Dr. Duncan did not disclose the origins of his terminology, but it seems probable that he was referring to Zacchias' work which bore that title.[4] Much of Zacchias' text, though not all, was concerned with the ecclesiastical matters discussed under this title by Duncan, such as adultery, fornication, annulment of marriages, dubious sex and hermaphroditism, and the venereal diseases.

Duncan referred to his entire subject as new to the British Isles, but as a long accepted and highly respected academic field on the Continent, especially, he said, in those universities where law as well as medicine was taught. This comment seems to me to indicate that Duncan thought the subject of importance not only in medical but also in legal education, an opinion not shared in British or American legal education for many decades to come.

The British title for the field was successfully transplanted into the New World by Edinburgh graduates. The first American lectures using the title, "medical jurisprudence," were given by James S. Stringham at Columbia College of Physicians and Surgeons in 1804. Another famous early lecturer on the subject was Benjamin Rush who included "The Study of Medical Jurisprudence" as one of his sixteen brilliant "Introductory Lectures Upon the Institutes and Practice of Medicine" given at Philadelphia in 1810. It is clear that Rush was familiar with Continental European progress in the medicolegal field. His list of subject areas covered in his lectures was most exhaustive, even by modern standards, since it included what we would today call forensic psychiatry (the major emphasis of the lecture), traumatic medicine, toxicology, forensic pathology, forensic obstetrics, occupational medicine, military medicine (physical examination of recruits for the armed services), and public health regulation. The title of "medical jurisprudence" is the only credit he gave to his Edinburgh teachers. Otherwise, he referred to the "great learning" in the field in France, Germany, and Italy, observing that in Great Britain "this science has advanced with more tardy steps."[5]

The trouble with the term "medical jurisprudence" was that it was improperly used by Duncan to cover an almost exclusively *medical* field, of significance to practicing doctors, not to lawyers or to members of both professions. "Jurisprudence" was essentially an academic synonym for "law" in these centuries. Thus, it meant "medical law," a subject not even discussed by Dr. Duncan. The term is even more inappropriate in modern times. It has been used for many years in

---

4. Zacchias, P., Questiones Medico Legales (1621-1661).

5. Rush, B., Introductory Lectures Upon the Institutes and Practices of Medicine 363 (Philadelphia, 1811).

1. Perspectives in Health Law

English and American legal education *not* as a synonym for law, but in a much narrower sense of the *philosophy of law*.

As early as the first decade of the twentieth century I find that a leading American legal educator whose specialty was legal philosophy objected strenuously to the use of the term "jurisprudence" in an applied sense in medicine and other areas. In his best sardonic manner, John Chipman Gray complained:

> Jurisprudence, it is true, is often used in a sense which is difficult to defend. There are certain treatises, many of considerable merit, dealing with these facts, likely to arise in litigation, with which the members of certain professions or trades are or ought to be familiar; such books are often called treatises on Jurisprudence. Thus, works on Medical Jurisprudence are *vade mecums* for lawyers and doctors, containing a mass of useful information on poisons, parturition, etc., but without any scientific unity, or any pretension to be called "Law" at all.[6]

C. The Growth of "State Medicine"

We return to Continental Europe in the later eighteenth century to find the parallel development of another terminological area in the medicolegal field. The Germanic states had clearly made "forensic medicine" the specialty of the forensic pathologists and other physicians who served the court system. Public health regulation, however, which had been a part of the encyclopedic scope of the Italian masters, was receiving short shrift — a brief lecture or two perhaps, but little serious attention. The new scholars and activists in the public health field needed a separate academic identity as a means of breaking away from the courtroom doctors. In 1764, Wolfgang Thomas Rau coined the term "medicinischen polizey" which has been translated rather imperfectly into English as "medical police." It covered the fields of public health policy and governmental health regulation. The greatest exponent of the new and expanded subject was Johann Peter Frank (1745-1821), one of the major figures in European medical education in the late eighteenth and early nineteenth century. His finest achievement was an extraordinary six-volume treatise entitled System einer vollständigen medicinischen polizey (A Complete System of Medical Police) published from 1779 to 1817. This broad field was later called "state medicine," not only on the Continent, but in Great Britain and the United States. It encompassed three areas: (1) public health regulation; (2) public welfare medicine for the poor and chronically ill; and (3) traditional forensic or courtroom medicine. The term

---

6. Gray, J.C., The Nature and Sources of Law 129 (New York: Columbia University Press, 1909).

survived into the early decades of the twentieth century, but has now been largely discarded as the three fields have gone their separate and distinct ways.

III. Modern Usage

A. Modern European Usage: Efforts at Consolidation

In similar but seemingly independent determinations, both the British and the German medicolegal societies in the middle 1960s recommended consolidation behind the French term "legal medicine." The British proposal came in 1967 in the form of a "Memorandum of Evidence" by the British Academy of Forensic Sciences to the Royal Commission on Medical Education.[7] The proposal went on to recommend that much more material on law be added to the curriculum of British medical schools. A year later, without reference to the British report, the German Society recommended that the term "courtroom medicine" be dropped and the term "legal medicine" (Rechtsmedizin) be adopted by all university medical schools and medicolegal institutes.[8] The German report asserted that the older term was particularly unattractive to young physicians who were being recruited to the field because it implied too severe a subjugation of medical practitioners to immediate legal ends, all to the detriment of independent development of the medical aspects of the subject through research.

There seem to be indications that the change in titles may be making some progress in Germany, but I see no evidence of any such change in Great Britain where multiple terminology is still common.

B. The American Confusion

During the twentieth century, the United States, in accordance with its usual pluralistic traditions, has adopted every one of the terms discussed in these pages and has used them interchangeably, usually without the slightest notion of their origins or particular meanings.

In the first century of the American experience, the dominant term was "medical jurisprudence." The first major change in nomenclature came in 1877 at Harvard University where a separate professorship in legal medicine was established to succeed the former combination of medical jurisprudence with obstetrics. The occasion for the change was the establishment under Massachusetts law in that

---

7. Memorandum of Evidence to the Royal Commission on Medical Education, 3 Medicine, Science and the Law 104-110 (1967).

8. Schwerd, Begründung zur Aenderung der Fachbezeichnung "Gerichtliche Medizin" in "Rechtsmedizin," 65 Deutsche Zeitschrift für Gerichtliche Medizin 61-67 (1969).

year of the first medical examiner system in the United States. The Harvard emphasis for many years to come was on the field of death investigation, not on all fields of medicine related to law. One of the greatest occupants of the Harvard professorship, Alan R. Moritz, expressed his views of the scope of the field in a paper published in 1942:

> Legal medicine is ordinarily defined as the application of medical knowledge to the needs of justice. Although by definition this would appear to be a broad and scientifically heterogeneous field, the practice of legal medicine is concerned chiefly with what might be most adequately described as forensic pathology.[9]

Dr. Moritz was essentially correct in his description at that time. However, he did not go on to advocate that departments and professorships, such as his own, change their titles to "forensic pathology" and drop all illusion that they covered a broader field. On the contrary, Dr. Moritz and other forensic pathologists continued to hold to the broader terminology. As late as 1955, Dr. Moritz, in a paper in the Journal of the American Medical Association, suggested that the model course in Legal Medicine in American medical schools be concentrated upon pathology and allied forensic sciences (such as toxicology) concerned with only one medicolegal field — that of death case investigation.[10] Actually, it has been errors in nomenclature such as this that have retarded the development of all sorts of other medical applications to law and the legal systems of the United States and other countries. Curriculum developers have assumed that these legal medicine departments were dealing with all areas of medicolegal significance — which has rarely, if ever, been true. These remarks are not, however, intended as a criticism of Dr. Moritz or other forensic pathologists who have done excellent work in their own fields.

The confusion in titles of medicolegal departments in American medical schools continues unabated into the 1970s. According to my search of university catalogues during these years, there are five medicolegal departments and three recognized subdepartments now operational. Two of these eight units are entitled "legal medicine"; two are called "forensic medicine"; two are called "forensic pathology"; two are named "medical jurisprudence"; while one uses the combined title of "forensic pathology and medicine." Despite this rather classic example of almost equal treatment for the multiple and peripatetic titles of the field, we find that without exception these

---

9. Moritz, The Need of Forensic Pathology for Academic Sponsorship, 33 Archives of Pathology 382-386 (1942).

10. Moritz, Scientific Medicolegal Investigation in the Undergraduate Medical Curriculum, 158 J.A.M.A. 243-244 (1955).

units are currently limited to the death investigation field with the usual array of specialists and technicians in that area. Actually, *none* are properly titled. Even to use the title "forensic pathology" recognizes only the dominant figures in the investigation and ignores the toxicologists, the forensic chemists and serologists, etc. It seems advisable that these departments be identified by the program or service they perform rather than by a particular discipline; thus, they would be called "departments of public death investigation."

IV. *A Proposal for Reform*

It may be impractical, the vainest of follies, to suggest proper and precise usage for so polyglot a field of terminology, but I feel the attempt should be made.

For the overall aspects of the field on either side of the interface between the subject matter and the professions of law and medicine I suggest the title of "medicolegal relations."

On the medical side, I would suggest that the term "legal medicine" has the broadest application. It should include not only the evidentiary areas, but clinical medical fields related to law, law enforcement and penology, such as the treatment of criminal offenders and drug addicts in legal and correctional settings, and medicolegal-moral issues, such as abortion and euthanasia. The term "forensic medicine," on the other hand, should be *limited* to those aspects of medicine and basic medical science which are related to the investigation, preparation, preservation, and presentation of evidence and medical opinion for the courts of law and administrative, regulatory agencies. The adjective "forensic" may also be applied to those areas of the specialties in medicine and basic medical science particularly concerned with the above evidentiary matters, such as forensic pathology, forensic biochemistry, forensic toxicology, and forensic orthopedic surgery. An exception to this group is psychiatry. I would call the medicolegal relations areas of psychiatry by the title "legal psychiatry" rather than "forensic psychiatry" because it involves important aspects of clinical practice not exclusively of evidentiary significance. On the other hand, when dealing with such evidentiary areas of the subject as psychiatric examinations and reports on criminal responsibility, competency to stand trial, and the like, I would call this "forensic psychiatry."

The unfortunate title of "medical jurisprudence" should at long last be relegated to the lexicographer's scrap heap. It was incorrectly applied to the *medical* side of the field in the first place. It is now either inappropriate or too pretentious a term for the legal aspects of the subject.

On the law side, I would propose the use of "medical law" to cover legislation, court rulings, and administrative regulation of medical professional practice and medical service programs. For evidentiary matters, on the other hand, the descriptive phrase should be "medical evidence law and procedure." I would suggest the broader title, "health law," to cover the wide range of legal aspects of medicine, nursing, dentistry, and other health service fields including public health and the environment. When special aspects of the various health law fields are discussed, greater specificity can be achieved with titles such as "public health law," "nursing law," and "environmental health law."

In summary, I propose that the following set of defined terms henceforth be utilized with respect to interdisciplinary discourse in the broad field of medicolegal relations:

Environmental law: a specialty area of law, not related to *medical law,* but concerned with all legal aspects of the regulation of environmental safety and health programs.

Forensic medicine: the specialty areas of medicine, medical science and technology concerned with investigation, preparation, preservation, and presentation of evidence and medical opinion in courts and other legal, correctional, and law-enforcement settings.

Forensic pathology: a sub-specialty of pathology concerned with medicolegal autopsies and with primary emphasis on investigation, preparation, preservation, and presentation of death-case evidence in law and law-enforcement settings. The forensic pathologist may also be the operational head of a public death investigational program including other forensic medical specialists and forensic scientists.

Forensic toxicology, forensic biochemistry, forensic orthopedic surgery, etc.: other sub-specialties of medical practice fields concerned, as defined under *forensic medicine,* with producing evidence for the legal system.

Health law: a specialty area of law and law practice related to the medical and other health fields — such as dentistry, nursing, hospital administration, and environmental law.

Hospital law: a sub-specialty of *medical law* related to legal aspects of hospital administration and hospital legal liability.

Legal medicine: the specialty areas of medicine concerned with relations with substantive law and with legal institutions. Clinical medical areas — such as the treatment of offenders and trauma medicine related to law would be included herein.

Legal psychiatry: a sub-specialty of psychiatry concerned with both the clinical and the forensic aspects of psychiatry in relation to law, law enforcement, and corrections.

Medical evidence law and procedure: a sub-specialty area of *medical law* related to the utilization of medical evidence and admissibility and competency questions concerning medical fact evidence and expert medical opinion testimony and reports.

Medical law: a specialty area of law and law practice related to legal regulation of medicine and medical practice and other legal aspects of medicine.

Medicolegal relations: the broad interrelationship of the fields of medicine and law, both in regard to subject matter and professional activities of a cooperative nature.

Programs of public (medicolegal) death investigation: organized medical examiner's offices or coroner's offices programs, usually headed by a forensic pathologist, including a forensic scientific laboratory, and a faculty and staff of forensic scientists and technicians.

Public health law: a specialty area of law and law practice related to legal regulation and legal administration of public health programs.

The above set of terms has consistency and specificity for the medicolegal field. The words used are basically simple and they mean what the most common dictionary will be found to indicate they mean — a true virtue in an interdisciplinary field where jargon and exclusive usage are barriers to communication across disciplines and professions.

Some Medicolegal Viewpoints

On Truth

"To speak of telling the truth, the whole truth, and nothing but the truth to a patient is absurd."

> L.J. Henderson, The Practice of Medicine as Applied Sociology, 51 Transactions Assn. Am. Physicians 8 (1936)

" 'But what a lot of time and money,' he said [at the end of a law suit], 'it has cost to arrive at the truth.'
" 'The truth?' said Roger. 'No one in Court said anything about arriving at the truth.' "

> Henry Cecil, Friends at Court (a novel by a British barrister) (London 1956)

On Justice

"The very word *justice* irritates scientists. No surgeon expects to be asked if an operation for cancer is just or not. No doctor will be

1. Perspectives in Health Law 11

reproached on the grounds that the dose of penicillin he has prescribed is less or more than *justice* would stipulate."

Karl Menninger, M.D., The Crime of Punishment (1968)

On the Public Image of Lawyers

"There was a time, not too long ago, when lawyers were proud to work in the Justice Department. When law school graduates were happy to be paid $15,000 for the privilege of working in New York's finest firms. When partners in law firms expected to stick together for their entire careers. When attorneys tried their cases in courtrooms, not on courthouse steps. When business lawyers provided legal advice to hold big corporations together while managers, executives and directors conducted the real business of America.

"That was before the 1980s.

"Positive images of America's lawyers — never dominant in the public's mind — have faded further with the headlines of the last few years. The result, according to a wide range of observers, is that the image of lawyers today ranges somewhere between 'poor' and 'not much worse than before.'"

Kenneth Jost, Editorial; What Image Do We Deserve?, A.B.A.J. Nov. 1, 1988, p. 46.

On the Adversary Process

"For the way we administer justice is by the adversary proceeding, which is to say, we set the parties fighting."

Charles P. Curtis, It's Your Law (Cambridge, Mass. 1954)

"Finally, the lawyer reasons by analogy. . . . Inherent in much of this [law school] training is the notion, very difficult to grasp, that 'law' can usually be found on both sides of a dispute. . . ."

Martin Mayer, The Lawyers (1967)

"How odd it is that anyone should not see that all observation must be for or against some view if it is to be of any service."

Charles Darwin, More Letters of Charles Darwin (Sir Francis Darwin ed., London 1903)

"Doctors and lawyers are not alike, either by disposition, or by education, or in practice. Even though the basic objectives of our two professions are the same, namely, to serve society, the education and practice of each are worlds apart. . . .

"The adversary system squeezes the doctor into roles and settings with which he is unfamiliar and in which he is ineffective. . . . The adversary system, as effective as it may be in achieving justice, is clearly ineffective in establishing truth in medicine."

> Charles G. Guild, III, M.D., Lawyers, Doctors and Medical Malpractice: A Surgeon Reacts, in E. D. Shapiro et al., Medical Malpractice (2d ed., Institute of Continuing Legal Education 1966)

"We would have been more favorably impressed with the testimony of the doctor had he not laid so much stress on the great number of 'cases' which he had 'won' in various courts as compared with the few which he had 'lost.' We had always entertained the view that doctors neither 'win' nor 'lose' cases in which they testify as experts."

> Janvier, J. in Smith v. Horace Williams Co., 84 So. 2d 223 (La. App. 1956)

On Physicians and Lawyers: How They Think

"With its preponderance of doctors, the Health Assembly [of the World Health Organization], in exercising its authority to interpret the Constitution [of WHO], or in dealing with problems of a legal nature, has from the beginning been inclined to look for a practical solution, avoiding as much as possible legal controversy and legal niceties."

> H. B. Calderwood, The World Health Organization and Its Regional Organizations, 37 Temp. L.Q. 15-40 (1963)

"You cannot make a physician look at a question in a legal way by such a short hand process, even if it were of much importance to do so. . . . There is, moreover, this objection to the course pursued, that, by such a union of law with medicine, the physician is apt to be misled as to his duties in the court room."

> Book Review, 1 Am. L. Rev. 337 (1867), of Taylor, Medical Jurisprudence (6th Am. ed.). (The review, published anonymously, is attributed to Oliver Wendell Holmes, Jr., by Mark DeWolfe Howe in Justice Oliver Wendell Holmes, The Shaping Years, p. 270.)

"To think productively, the lawyer needs a highly developed sense of procedure."

> Martin Mayer, The Lawyers (1967)

"Medical science is made available to lawyers and the legal system through the good offices of the medical profession. There is created, therefore, in the very nature of things, a problem of communication.

"There may have been a time when doctors and lawyers had much in common, but today their environments are radically divergent and the problem of mutual understanding is a real one. The doctor is trained in a dynamic and experimental science, he is seeking truth in a physical world. He is steeped in the practical judgment, though he avoids generalization. The lawyer, on the other hand, lives within the generalities of the law. The courts apply justice through the advocacy system and seek truth through the burden of proof. When the doctor or other medical person comes into contact with the courts and lawyers, he is often mystified and is generally impatient with the conservatism of the courts in accepting the advances of science. The lawyer often does not seem to the doctor to be seeking truth, but only to place blame."

> William J. Curran, Law and Medicine (1st ed. 1960)

On Methods in Law and Medical Science

"Medical science has advanced along the same lines as any other biological discipline. It began with simple observation of facts, collection and comparison of facts, and by inductive reasoning the framing of hypotheses which gave reasonable working rules. When Hippocrates said that epilepsy was no more a 'divine' visitation than any other malady he freed the human mind to look upon human disorders as observable, natural phenomena. Hippocrates was the clinician *par excellence,* and his example has been followed by a long line of great clinicians whose field of observational research is still not closed."

> Hugh Clegg, M.D., Human
> Experimentation, 7 World Med. J. 77
> (March 1960)

"Most lawyers are Aristotelian in method, if not in philosophy. So are law students by the time they are seniors. That is to say, they work from settled principles on stated fact situations. While they are seeking the results of their deductive logic, their facts remain unchanged.

"This is not the case in science and in medicine. The scientist seeks truth within the scientific method. The physician is also an experimentalist, an empiricist. At times, however, he does not like being called a scientist, particularly when he is treating a patient. Then he may prefer the title of artisan — but still an empirical artisan.

"The failure to understand the basic difference in method between doctors and lawyers is often a stumbling block to greater cooperation between the two professions. It often leads the lawyer into error in presenting the medical issues in a legal action.

"It may seem obvious that a lawyer should understand the physician's methods as well as his conclusions. Yet, when the attorney accepts a case and prepares it for trial, he tends not to do this. If his client has a back injury, he is interested only in the doctor's conclusions in regard to that injury. He may study the basis for the physician's conclusions in regard to this case, but he rarely does anything more until the next case comes along when again he is interested only in *that* injury."

> William J. Curran, Law and Medicine
> (1st ed. 1960)

"If a doctor were called on to treat typhoid fever he would probably try to find out what kind of water the patient drank, and clean out the well so that no one else could get typhoid from the same source. But if a lawyer were called on to treat a typhoid patient he would give him thirty days in jail, and then he would think that nobody else would ever dare to drink the impure water. If the patient got well in fifteen days, he would be kept until his time was up; if the disease was worse at the end of thirty days, the patient would be released because his time was out.

"As a rule, lawyers are not scientists. They think that there is only one way to make men good, and that is to put them in such terror that they do not dare to do bad."

> Meyer Levin, Compulsion (1956)
> (taken from the defense attorney's
> closing argument to the jury)

On Medical Practice and Technology

"If physicians in general come to accept a fundamentally mechanical view of human beings, in a world that is more and more enamored of technology, the prospect for the future of medicine is extremely disquieting. To counter the fears of such a prospect, a myth has arisen in contemporary medicine that the more the machines can take over the performing of medical functions, the more the doctor will have time to deal with the patient as a human being. Thus reliance on technology is supposed to improve the doctor-patient relationships, to the benefit of both.

"These are illusions. Machines inexorably direct the attention of both doctor and patient to the measurable aspects of illness, but away from the 'human' factors that are at least equally important."

> Stanley Joel Reiser, M.D., Medicine
> and the Reign of Technology
> (Cambridge 1978)

On Medical Opinion and Causation

"It is possible that part of the difficulty in understanding the divergence of views of doctors comes about by virtue of the difference in approach to the question of causation by members of the medical and legal professions."

> Knutson, J. in Golob v. Buckingham
> Hotel, 244 Minn. 301 (1955)

"The doctor [in a particular case] is not wholly devoid of common sense or natural perception. But he does have difficulty in separating *cause* from *etiology*. . . . The medical man can say with God-like assurance that the cause for diphtheria or tuberculosis or tetanus is the body's succumbing to a pathological microbe. . . .

"Aggravation, acceleration, activation — to a doctor they are part and parcel of the natural and inevitable pathological process in cancer; they are the process. So understood, they leave little room for trauma in the causal spectrum. To aggravate aggravation, to accelerate acceleration, to make the inevitable more inevitable, are foreign to the doctor."

> Ben Small, Gaffing At a Thing Called
> Cause, 31 Tex. L. Rev. 630 (1953)

On Medical Authority and Informed Consent

"Enough has already been said to make clear that the doctor's authority over his patient is today far from absolute. The doctor knows best concept is mindlessly embraced by few doctors trained in the last decade, and by a decreasing number of laymen. The principle of informed consent has so altered the pattern of transmission of information from physician to patient that medicine's tradition of authority, physician over patient, is rapidly undergoing massive alteration. . . ."

Carleton B. Chapman, Physicians, Law, and Ethics (1984)

On Health and Disease

"The difficulty of defining disease is implied in the very structure of the word: 'dis-ease.' So many different kinds of disturbances can make a person feel not at ease and lead him to seek the aid of a physician that the word ought to encompass most of the difficulties inherent in the human condition. . . .

"The preamble of the charter of the World Health Organization attempts to convey this utopian ideal in the following words, 'Health is a state of complete physical, mental, and social well-being and not merely the absence of disease or infirmity.' Health so defined is a utopian state indeed.

"Health will be considered in the following pages from a more practical point of view, not as an ideal state of well-being achieved through complete elimination of disease, but as a modus vivendi enabling imperfect men to achieve a rewarding and not too painful existence while they cope with an imperfect world. In this light, health cannot be defined in the absolute, because different persons expect such different things from life. A Wall Street executive, a lumberjack in the Canadian Rockies, a newspaper boy at a crowded street corner, a steeplechase jockey, a cloistered monk, and the pilot of a supersonic combat plane have various physical and mental needs. The imperfections and limitations of the flesh and of the mind do not have equal importance to them. Their goals determine the kind of vigor and resistance required for success in their own lives."

Rene Dubos, M.D., Man, Medicine and Environment (1968)

"It is desirable that 'impairment' and 'disability' not be used interchangeably. The evaluation of impairment is alone a medical responsibility, while the evaluation of disability is essentially an administrative responsibility. While the uniquely medical character of the former is self-evident, the determination of disability involves review, not only of medical factors but of legal, psychological, social, and vocational considerations as well."

> Duncan W. Clark, M.D., Impairment and Disability, in Preventive Medicine (Clark and MacMahon, eds., 1967)

"The enjoyment of the highest attainable standard of health is one of the fundamental rights of every human being without distinction of race, religion, political belief, economic or social condition.

"The health of all peoples is fundamental to the attainment of peace and security and is dependent upon the fullest cooperation of individuals and States."

> World Health Organization, Preamble to the Constitution (July 1948)

"The Congress declares that the fulfillment of our national purpose depends on promoting and assuring the highest level of health attainable for every person, in an environment which contributes positively to healthful individual and family living; that attainment of this goal depends on an effective partnership, involving close intergovernmental collaboration, official and voluntary efforts, and participation of individuals and organizations. . . ."

> Findings and Declaration of Purpose, Comprehensive Health Planning Act of 1966, P.L. 89-749

"Proclaiming good health 'a fundamental human right,' Governor Rockefeller outlined tonight a program of compulsory health insurance that he will present to the [New York State] Legislature next week. . . ."

> *N.Y. Times*, Feb. 27, 1968, at 1

". . . The State [Georgia] Mental Health Committee, under the leadership of Sen. Bobby Rowan, has drawn up a 'Bill of Rights' for mental patients.

"'This will grant them a bill of rights which in my opinion will enable them to receive mental treatment without suffering the stigma that in years before was attached to mental illness,' Rowan said."

> *Atlanta Constitution*, Dec. 16, 1968, at 6

On the Environment, Health, and Medicine

" 'The environment,' as a phrase has nowadays joined the category of fighting words. Those who want to protect it face a hard-hat argument that they are elitists concerned more with esthetics than economic necessity. In fact, the human longing for natural beauty is not confined to any elite; we nearly all respond to the curve of a beach or the lift of a mountain. But in protecting the environment we care for other fundamental interests.

"Public health is one. The Environmental Protection Agency operates today, according to its officials, as virtually a public health organization. It is not hard to see why. Most of the dramatic environmental episodes in recent years have had medical consequences: the chemicals in the Love Canal, the poisoned cattle feed in Michigan that has spread its effects throughout that state, the air pollution in Los Angeles, the endangered water supplies all over the country.

" 'We complain about the cost of regulation,' one official said — 'of environmental controls. But if we don't limit the damage, what about the cost in medical bills and human suffering?' "

Anthony Lewis, International Herald Tribune, October 9, 1979

On Medical Malpractice

"Anyone can bring an action against a doctor charging him with neglect or unskilled treatment, and however trivial the charge or however right the doctor may have been in his actions, he will have to defend the case for the sake of his reputation. Sometimes it may be that the doctor is to blame, but such actions are chiefly of a vexatious nature, and not infrequently the complainers are borderline mental cases."

Douglas J. A. Kerr, M.D., Forensic Medicine: A Textbook for Students and a Guide for the Practitioner (6th ed. London 1957)

"The likelihood of being sued for malpractice is now so great that it constitutes a definite occupational hazard to the practising physician or dentist; and an increasing number of negligence actions are being brought against nurses and hospitals. Particularly during the past quarter-century there has been a tremendous increase in the number of unjustifiable malpractice suits."

Louis L. Regan, Doctor and Patient and the Law (3d ed. 1956)

"Doctors are protected by a special rule of law. They are not guarantors of cure. They do not even warrant a good result. They are not insurers against mishaps or unusual consequences. Furthermore they are not liable for honest mistakes of judgment. . . . This rule of law is such a bulwark of defense for doctors that it is almost impossible to win a malpractice case against them. . . .

"I do not know whether it is a compliment to the medical profession to say that it is almost impossible in many states to induce a doctor to testify against another doctor. That depends on whether you look at the matter from a social viewpoint and the requirements of justice, or from the viewpoint of professional loyalty and comradeship. It is not very difficult to get lawyers or accountants to testify against members of their craft. Perhaps this is because professional ostracism is applied less in those professions than in the medical profession."

Louis Nizer, My Life in Court (1961)

On Medicolegal Courses

"Medical students are customarily frightened out of their wits sometime during their training by a course in medical jurisprudence."

Louis Lasagna, M.D., The Doctors'
Dilemma (1962)

American Society of Law and Medicine, Health Law and Professional Education*
Report of the Task Force on Health Law Curricula of the
American Society of Law and Medicine (1985)

University courses addressing issues involved in the interrelationship of law and medicine date from at least the late eighteenth century in European medical schools.[1] In the United States, Benjamin Rush and others delivered lectures on "medical jurisprudence" shortly after the turn of the nineteenth century.[2] The first professorship in this field in North America was established at the College of Physicians and Surgeons in New York in 1814.[3]

---

* This excerpt is reprinted from the Report of the Task Force on Health Law Curricula of the American Society of Law and Medicine, 1985, by permission of the Society.

1. Curran, W., Titles in the Medicolegal Field: A Proposal for Reform, American Journal of Law & Medicine 1 (1): 1 (March 1975).

2. B. Rush, Sixteen Introductory Lectures to Courses of Lectures Upon the Institutes and Practices of Medicine, With a Syllabus of the Latter to Which Are Added, Two Lectures Upon the Pleasures of the Senses and of the Mind, With an Inquiry into Their Proximate Cause, Delivered in the University of Pennsylvania (Bradford & Inskeep, Philadelphia, PA) (1811).

3. Curran, W., Hamlin, R., The Medico-Legal Problems Seminar at Harvard Law School, Journal of Legal Education 8 (4): 499 (1956).

Despite these established historical roots, the subject of health law, and its teaching, is still often regarded as a novel, contemporary phenomenon without an established academic history. Such reactions might be generated, in part, by the current, highly publicized development of the field of health law. What has caused this development?

First, advances in modern biomedical technology have thrown into sharp focus some of the most critical issues that a society or an individual faces. Although the problems are not necessarily new, failure to recognize and address them is no longer possible. The most dramatic of these issues can involve choosing between life and death, between health and illness, or between a state of well-being and suffering. Second, health care has become one of the major industries of the developed world. The number of people and the amount of money involved in health care demand increasing attention. Third, there is now extensive government involvement in the development and delivery of health care. The presence of any one of these three factors would act as an impetus to legal development of an area in which it was found. When all are present, as they are in the area of health care, the evolution of the field of health law should come as no surprise. But the rapid rate of this evolution poses a challenge to educators. How does the development of health law affect the education of legal and health care professionals and, ultimately, the practice of their respective professions?

Health Law and Legal and Health Care Professionals

First, most, if not all, health care professionals will confront a variety of "health law problems" in their professional lives. They need to be equipped — by virtue of their education — to identify such problems and the means available to address them. Any professional confronted by a "health law problem" needs a broad, conceptual definition of the field involved in order to place the problem in proper perspective and to identify relevant issues. Consequently, professional education must attempt to define the field of health law. Such traditional specialties as medical jurisprudence, forensic medicine, or tort, administrative or criminal law no longer account for the entire range of knowledge encompassed by the notion of health law. Ideally, a definition of health law should be comprehensive enough to include all valid concerns of the area and detailed enough to exclude all irrelevant ones. Moreover, because health care is a universal science, and health law has aspects of both international and comparative law it is desirable to try to draft a definition which could be used in any legal jurisdiction. To this end, the Task Force has offered a conceptual model of health law, described in Chapter 2, as a map of the health care terrain that may give rise to legal issues.

Secondly, beyond an awareness of the scope of health law, legal and health care professionals require familiarity with the law's approach to defining and resolving problems. In the absence of such knowledge, decisionmakers are left with a serious gap in their resources, and the resulting decisions are likely to be needlessly flawed or ineffective. There is a need in health law decisionmaking for structures which will accommodate not only facts, judicial opinions, relevant professional judgments, and rules and principles, but also value and policy concerns. Further, these decisionmaking structures must be flexible and durable, as well as give rise to relatively predictable outcomes when applied in practice; in these respects, there may often be a need to balance theory and logic with practicality. These structures must also take into account that more than one decisionmaker can be involved: on a "vertical axis," these decisionmakers could include a government, an institution, and an individual; likewise, on a "horizontal level," the patient, his or her family, and various members of the health care team or community are potential participants. In virtually any circumstance, each of these has rights and obligations governed by law. When conflict arises between decisionmakers, how should it be resolved? The law is the ultimate civilized means of conflict resolution, but it is multifaceted and continuously evolving. What facets of the law apply, when and how should it be used, and what alternatives to use of the judicial system are available? These are questions that all legal and health care professionals face. Answering them requires a systematic understanding of legal analysis and decisionmaking. It is the aim of health law teaching to provide health care and legal professionals with the "tools" they will need both to analyze and to solve the problems and to carry out the objectives of their own professions.

Finally, because the field of health law concerns a wide variety of subjects — from physician-patient relationships to institutional structures for delivering care to social policy on pollution — it is necessarily linked with subjects taught in most professional schools. Undertaking education in the field of health law provides an exciting opportunity to realize transdisciplinary synergism. Health law principles can be taught in a variety of courses as a part of the skills and knowledge needed to address particular problems. To achieve this synergism in analyzing any problem to which health law is relevant, it is necessary to be constantly sensitive to the need to incorporate the perspectives and values not only of the relevant health care professions and of law, but those of other disciplines as well. These other disciplines include ethics, economics, theology, sociology, and anthropology. . . .

NOTES

Health Law Curriculum and Periodicals

1. For an informative symposium on the teaching of health law in law schools, see 38 J. Leg. Ed. 485 et seq. (1988). See also Annas, Health Law at the Turn of the Century, 21 Conn. L. Rev. 271 (1990). For other earlier important articles on curriculum for courses in health law, see Waddlington, Teaching Law and Medicine in the United States, J. Soc. Pub. Teach. L. 96 (1977); Spies, Weiss, and Campbell, Teaching Law in Medical Schools, 77 Surgery 793 (1975); Annas, Law and Medicine: Myths and Realities in the Medical School Classroom, 1 Am. J.L. & Med. 195 (1975). Health law is also taught in graduate schools of health services administration and hospital administration. For a report on curriculum for courses in these schools, see A. Rosoff & G. Bergwall, Teaching Health Law: A Guide on Health Law for Health Services Administration (1986). See also a symposium on the subject of health law in such schools in 6 J. Health Admin. Ed. 219 et seq. (1988).

2. There are currently many health law periodicals, sometimes combined with related subjects such as economics, public policy, and health care organization. See particularly (with their full titles): American Journal of Law and Medicine; Food, Drug and Cosmetic Law Journal; Health Law in Canada; Hospital Law; Journal of Contemporary Health Law & Policy; Journal of Health Politics, Policy, and Law; Journal of Law and Health; Journal of Health and Hospital Law; Journal of Legal Medicine; Law, Medicine and Health Care.

In the forensic sciences, see American Journal of Forensic Medicine and Pathology; American Journal of Forensic Sciences. Other references are collected in Chapter 3.

For periodicals related to personal injury litigation, see Insurance Counsel Journal; Medical Trial Technique Quarterly.

In the disability field, see Mental and Physical Disability Law Reporter. In forensic psychiatry and law, see International Journal of Law and Psychiatry (published in Canada).

For collections of health-related legislation on a worldwide basis, see International Digest of Health Legislation (published by the World Health Organization, Geneva, Switzerland).

There are also other new bibliographic and research aids in health law. LEXIS has a Health Law Library database. There is a Modern Health Care Law Digest and a Medical Malpractice Reporter.

Fox, Physicians versus Lawyers: A Conflict of Cultures*
AIDS and the Law 210-217 (H. Dalton & S. Burris eds. 1987)

The AIDS epidemic raises problems of public health policy that require physicians and lawyers to work together as never before. They must collaborate, for example, in safeguarding the privacy of persons with AIDS when their names are reported to public health agencies. Together, the two professions must assess what information is needed to monitor the epidemic, to assist science, and to protect people who have not become seropositive, and then develop strategies to preserve some privacy for persons with the disease.

Working collaboratively is no easy task for professions that have fundamentally different conceptions of their roles and their prerogatives and that increasingly regard each other as antagonists. Thus, even as the AIDS epidemic provides an opportunity for cooperation, it provides new occasions for conflict between members of the legal and medical professions. If we are to move in the direction of cooperation rather than conflict, we must understand the roots of the antagonism between the professions and the contemporary forces that threaten to deepen it.

I have observed the antagonism of physicians toward lawyers during fourteen years as a faculty member and senior manager of an academic health center — a teaching hospital and five professional schools — that is a unit of a large state university. This experience has no doubt given me a limited view of both professions. The lawyers I have observed are either public employees or private counsel retained to assist them. The physicians I work with are clinicians and scientists who are full-time faculty members at a medical school. I have recently observed physicians and lawyers concerned about AIDS while doing research on issues of public policy raised by the disease and coediting a special issue of a journal addressing the public context of the epidemic.

In this chapter, I oversimplify the relationship between physicians and lawyers in order to examine the conflict between them. In particular, I emphasize physicians' antagonism to lawyers, rather than lawyers' role in the conflict. In part I do this because I have little first-hand knowledge concerning lawyers' unguarded opinions about physicians. But it is also because — the negligence bar aside — I suspect that most lawyers are not normally antagonistic toward physicians. Physicians, on the other hand, believe they are being taken

---

* This excerpt from a chapter of the same title by Daniel M. Fox is reprinted from H.L. Dalton and S. Burris, eds., AIDS and the Law 210-217 (New Haven: Yale University Press, 1987) by permission of the Yale University Press. Text references have been omitted from this excerpt.

advantage of by lawyers who do not understand medicine or value it properly. They are, moreover, mortified because the conflict is usually displayed in public settings controlled by lawyers — court proceedings and legislative hearings. To be sure, not all physicians fall within the terms of my analysis. Some of them enjoy a role analogous to barracks or jailhouse lawyers. A few even study the law. Others relish it: I know an eminent physician, for example, who is fond of quoting in his administrative work aphorisms about the law he learned from his late father. Moreover, as I will describe at the end of the chapter, some physicians and lawyers are in fact collaborating on issues pertaining to AIDS.

The conflict between physicians and lawyers, though it is rooted in the modern history of the two professions, has become more intense in recent years as the authority most people accord to physicians has diminished. Some physicians accuse lawyers of helping to undermine public confidence in them by mindlessly pursuing malpractice litigation. Many attribute their rising premiums for malpractice insurance to the work of greedy and unscrupulous lawyers. Others assert that so-called "defensive medicine," ordering marginally useful tests and therapies to avoid being sued, has helped to increase the cost of medical care. Physicians often blame lawyers for the mass of regulations that burden them. In an astonishing display of professional bigotry, the new president of the Association of American Medical Colleges told a medical school graduating class in June 1986, "We're swimming in shark-infested waters where the sharks are lawyers."

Events during the AIDS epidemic have reinforced physicians' irritation with lawyers. Many physicians are offended that decisions about whether particular children with AIDS can attend school are made by judges after argument by lawyers. They are dismayed when an official of the U.S. Department of Justice issues a ruling about discrimination against persons with AIDS in the workplace that ignores medical opinion. Even though physicians disagree among themselves about precisely who is at risk of getting AIDS, they condemn lawyers who argue on behalf of their clients that any conceivable risk is intolerable. They routinely curse the politicians and even the public health officials who debate laws or issue regulations that, in their view, interfere with the practice of medicine; an instance in point is the guidelines for AIDS treatment centers in New York State, which require hospitals to designate a unit for AIDS patients. . . .

To most physicians, adversarial proceedings are an ineffective and irrational method for resolving conflict. Where Anglo-American lawyers presume that a person accused of a crime is innocent until proven guilty in a court of law, physicians believe it is dangerous to make any presumption before examining evidence. Similarly, most physicians do not understand the history or the logic of lawyers' claim that formalized conflict between plaintiffs and defendants in a courtroom or around a table resolves disagreements with reasonable equity and preserves social peace.

Physicians are trained to rely on two methods of addressing conflicts about data and their interpretation. The first method is the assertion of authority from the top of a hierarchy in which power is derived from knowledge. The second method is peer review — discussion to consensus among experts of roughly equal standing and attainment. Both methods, the hierarchical and the consensual, rest on the assumption that truth is best determined by experts. . . .

NOTES

Conflicts of Values in Law and Medicine

1. The Fox article spells out many of the areas of difference in approach to similar issues between lawyers and physicians. Several of the excerpts from various publications by lawyers and physicians reprinted earlier in this chapter, as *Medicolegal Viewpoints*, at 10-19, also illustrate conflicts of values in the interprofessional relations of law, medicine, and health law.

2. There are several books and periodical articles that illustrate differences (not necessarily with that intention in mind) of professional approach, ethical principles, and cultural values between lawyers and physicians. For example, in book-length treatments of the issues, see W. Curran, Law-Medicine Notes: Progress in Medicolegal Relations (1989); G. Annas, Judging Medicine (1988); I. Kennedy, Treat Me Right: Essays in Medical Law and Ethics (1988); P. Danzon, Medical Malpractice: Theory, Evidence, and Public Policy (1985); J. Katz, The Silent World of Doctor and Patient (1984); C. Chapman, Physicians, Law and Ethics (1984); B. Werthmann, Medical Malpractice Law: How Medicine is Changing the Law (1984); S. Law & S. Polan, Pain and Profit: The Politics of Malpractice (1978); W. Curran, How Lawyers Handle Medical Malpractice Cases (1976); S. Gleuck, Law and Psychiatry: Cold War or Entente Cordiale? (1966); D. Louisell & H. Williams, The Parenchyma of Law (1985). For a few, of many, periodical articles, see Rosenblatt, Conceptualizing Health Law for Teaching Purposes: The Social Justice Perspective, 38 J. Leg. Ed. 489 (1988); Bross, Should We Blame the Lawyers?, 65 Den. U.L. Rev. 102 (1987); Brennan & Carter, Legal and Scientific Probability of Causation in Cancer and Other Environmental Diseases in Individuals, 10 J. Health Pol. Poly. & Law 33 (1985); Buchanan, Medical Paternalism or Legal Imperialism: Not the Only Alternatives for Handling Saikewicz-type Cases, 5 Am. J.L. & Med. 97 (1979); Danner and Sagal, Medicolegal Causation: A Source of Professional Misun-

derstanding, 3 Am. J.L. & Med. 303 (1977); Schroeder, Legal Medicine as an Interdisciplinary Intellectual Discipline, Leg. Med. Ann. 399 (1974); Holman, The Time Lag Between Medicine and Law, 9 Lex et Scientia 102 (1972); Dukeminier, Medical Advance and Legal Lag: Hemodialysis and Kidney Transplantation, 15 U.C.L.A.L. Rev. 357 (1968); Cohn, Medical Malpractice Litigation: A Plague on Both Your Houses, 52 A.B.A.J. 32 (1966); Powers, Interprofessional Education and Medicolegal Conflict as Seen from the Other Side, 40 Am. J. Med. Ed. 233 (1965); Curran, A Problem of Consent: Kidney Transplantation in Minors, 34 N.Y.U.L. Rev. 891 (1959); Small, Gaffing at a Thing Called Cause, 31 Tex. L. Rev. 630 (1953).

Professional Codes

National Interprofessional Code for Physicians and Attorneys

Preamble

The provisions of this Code are intended as guides for physicians and attorneys in their inter-related practice in the areas covered by its provisions. They are not laws, but suggested rules of conduct for members of the two professions, subject to the principles of medical and legal ethics and the rules of law prescribed for their individual conduct.

This Code constitutes the recognition that, with the growing interrelationship of medicine and law, it is inevitable that physicians and attorneys will be drawn into steadily increasing association. It will serve its purpose if it promotes the public welfare, improves the practical working relationships of the two professions, and facilitates the administration of justice.

Medical Reports

The physicians upon proper authorization should promptly furnish the attorney with a complete medical report and should realize that delays in providing medical information may prejudice the opportunity of the patient either to settle his claim or suit, delay the trial of a case or cause additional expense or the loss of important testimony.

The attorney should give the physician reasonable notice of the need for a report and clearly specify the medical information which he seeks.

It is improper for the attorney to abuse a medical witness or to seek to influence his medical opinion. Established rules of evidence

1. Perspectives in Health Law

afford ample opportunity to test the qualifications, competence and credibility of a medical witness; and it is always improper and unnecessary for the attorney to embarrass or harass the physician.

Fees for Services of Physician Relative to Litigation

The physician is entitled to reasonable compensation for time spent in conferences, preparation of medical reports and for court or other appearances. These are proper and necessary items of expense in litigation involving medical questions. The amount of the physician's fee should never be contingent upon the outcome of the case or the amount of damages awarded.

Payment of Medical Fees

The attorney should do everything possible to assure payment for services rendered by the physician for himself or his client. When the physician has not been fully paid the attorney should request permission of the patient to pay the physician from any recovery which the attorney may receive in behalf of the patient.

Implementation of This Code at State and Local Levels

In the event similar action has not already been taken this Code should, in the public interest, be appropriately implemented at state and local levels for the purpose of improving the interprofessional relationship between the legal and medical professions.

Consideration and Disposition of Complaints

The public airing of any complaint or criticism by a member of one profession against the other profession or any of its members is to be deplored. Such complaints or criticism, including complaints of the violation of the principles of this Code, should be referred by the complaining doctor or lawyer through his own association to the appropriate association of the other profession; and all such complaints or criticism should be promptly and adequately processed by the association receiving them.

Conferences

It is the duty of each profession to present fairly and adequately the medical information involved in the legal controversies. To that end the practice of discussion in advance of the trial between the physician and the attorney is encouraged and recommended. Such discussion should be had in all instances unless it is mutually agreed that it is unnecessary.

Conferences should be held at a time and place mutually convenient to the parties. The attorney and the physician should fully disclose and discuss the medical information involved in the controversy.

Subpoena for Medical Witness

Because of conditions in a particular case or jurisdiction or because of the necessity for protecting himself or his client, the attorney is sometimes required to subpoena the physician as a witness. Although the physician should not take offense at being subpoenaed, the attorney should not cause the subpoena to be issued without prior notification to the physician. The duty of the physician is the same as that of any other person to respond to judicial process.

Arrangement for Court Appearances

While it is recognized that the conduct of the business of the courts cannot depend upon the convenience of litigants, lawyers or witnesses, arrangements can and should be made for the attendance of the physician as a witness which take into consideration the professional demands upon his time. Such arrangements contemplate reasonable notice to the physician of the intention to call him as a witness and to advise him by telephone, after the trial has commenced, of the approximate time of his required attendance. The attorney should make every effort to conserve the time of the physician.

Physician Called as a Witness

The attorney and the physician should treat one another with dignity and respect in the courtroom. The physician should testify solely as to the medical facts in the case and should frankly state his medical opinion. He should never be an advocate and should realize that his testimony is intended to enlighten rather than to impress or prejudice the court or the jury.

Code of Ethics for Forensic Scientists
American Academy of Forensic Sciences (1977)

Basic Principles

1. Every member of the American Academy of Forensic Sciences shall avoid any material misrepresentation of training, experience or area of expertise.

2. Every member of the American Academy of Forensic Sciences shall avoid any material misrepresentation of data upon which an expert opinion or conclusion is based.

Guiding Principles

1. The forensic scientist should maintain his professional competency through existing programs of continuing education.
2. The forensic scientist should render technically correct statements in all written or oral reports, testimony, public addresses, or publications and should avoid any misleading or inaccurate claims.
3. The forensic scientist should act in an impartial manner and do nothing which would imply partisanship or any interest in a case except proof of the facts and their correct interpretation.

CHAPTER 2

The Medical Sciences

I. THE BASIC AND CLINICAL MEDICAL SCIENCES

A. The Basic Sciences

Anatomy. The science of the structure of the animal body and the relation of its parts.
Bacteriology. The science dealing with bacteria.
Biochemistry. The chemistry of living organisms.
Histology. The science of the microscopic structure and composition of tissues.
Parasitology. The science of plants and animals which live upon or within another living organism (such as man) and draw nourishment therefrom.
Pathology. The science of the essential nature of disease, especially of the structural and functional changes caused by disease. The term is used as a suffix to delineate specialty areas. For example, neuropathology is the science of the nature of diseases of the nervous system.
Pharmacology. The science of drugs and their relationship to living tissue and organisms.
Physiology. The science dealing with the normal vital processes of living organisms.
Toxicology. The science dealing with poisons.

B. The Clinical Sciences

Note: The clinical sciences are generally divided into two major groups, medicine and surgery, with various subdivisions which overlap in each group.
Medicine. The branch of medical science concerned with the prevention, cure, and alleviation of disease (frequently called internal medicine).
    Allergy. The branch of medical science concerned with the hypersensitivity of the body cells to specific substances resulting in various types of reactions.

Cardiology. The branch of medicine concerned with the heart and the circulatory system.

Connective Tissue Disease. The branch of medical science concerned with any tissue connecting two cells (sometimes called collagen disease).

Dermatology. The branch of medical science concerned with the structure, function, and diseases of the skin.

Endocrinology. The branch of medical science concerned with glands and their secretions.

Gastroenterology. The branch of medical science concerned with the digestive system, including the esophagus, the stomach, the intestines, and the liver.

Hematology. The branch of medical science concerned with the blood and blood-forming tissues.

Immunology. The branch of medical science that deals with the body's reaction to foreign materials.

Infectious Disease. The branch of medical science concerned with disease capable of being transmitted by a microorganism with or without actual physical contact.

Neurology. The branch of medical science concerned with the nerves and nerve centers.

Oncology. The branch of medical science concerned with tumors of all the organs.

Pediatrics. The branch of medical science concerned with the growth and development and disease states of children.

Physical Medicine and Rehabilitation. The branch of medical science concerned with restoration of the handicapped by physical means as opposed to surgical or drug therapy.

Preventive Medicine. The branch of medical science dealing with prevention of disease as opposed to diagnosis and treatment of disease.

Psychiatry. The branch of medical science concerned with mental disorders.

Pulmonary Disease. The branch of medical science concerned with the lungs and the function of respiration.

Radiology. The branch of medical science dealing with X-rays both for diagnosis and for treatment.

Surgery. The branch of medical science concerned with all diseases, defects, and injuries amenable to operative or manual procedures.

Gynecology. The branch of medical science dealing with the reproductive system of women.

Obstetrics. The branch of medical science concerned with the care of women during pregnancy and during and after childbirth.

Ophthalmology. The branch of medical science dealing with the eye.

Orthopedics. The branch of medical science concerned with the operative or manual repair of injuries or deformities of the bones and joints.

Otolaryngology. The branch of medical science dealing with the ear, nose, throat, larynx, and trachea.

Proctology. The branch of medical science dealing with the anus and rectum.

Urology. The branch of medical science dealing with the kidney and urinary tract.

II. MEDICAL TERMS

A. *Introduction*

In order to deal effectively with the medical materials in this book, the reader should have at his side a good medical dictionary. Several of the best known dictionaries are listed below.

The glossary that follows is not a substitution for such a dictionary, but it contains frequently used prefixes, suffixes, and other terms concerning the areas of the body.

B. *References*

1. Medical Dictionaries:

Blakiston's Gould Medical Dictionary (4th ed. 1979)
Dorland's Illustrated Medical Dictionary (28th ed. 1988) (recommended)
Dorland's Pocket Medical Dictionary (24th ed. 1989) (very good, inexpensive)
Taber's Cyclopedic Medical Dictionary (16th ed. 1989) (recommended)
Mosby's Medical and Nursing Dictionary (2d ed. 1986)
Encyclopedia and Dictionary of Medicine, Nursing and Allied Health (4th ed. 1987)
R. Heister, Dictionary of Abbreviations in Medical Sciences (1989)

2. Medical Diagnosis, Technology, and Therapeutics:

Physician's Desk Reference (43rd ed. 1989) (indispensable reference for therapeutic drugs)
A. Goodman, L. Gilman, T. Rall, & F. Murad, The Pharmacological Basis of Therapeutics (7th ed. 1985) (indispensable guide to drug prescribing)
R. Collins, Atlas of Drug Reactions (1985)
J. Long, Clinical Management of Prescription Drugs (1985)
B. Bates, A Guide to Physical Examination and History Taking (4th ed. 1987)
L. Carpenito, Handbook of Nursing Diagnosis, 1989-1990 (1989)
S. Schroeder et al., Current Medical Diagnosis and Treatment (1989)
F. Fischbach, A Manual of Laboratory Tests (3rd ed. 1988)
J. Wallach, Interpretation of Diagnostic Tests: A Handbook Synopsis of Laboratory Medicine (4th ed. 1986)
B. Kozier & G. Erb, Techniques of Clinical Nursing (3rd ed. 1989)

3. Specialized Texts in Medicine, Epidemiology, and Other Areas:

D. Kreis & G. Gomez, Trauma Management (1989)
J. Jenkins & J. Loscaizo, Manual of Emergency Medicine (1986)
C. Hennekens & J. Buring, Epidemiology in Medicine (1987)
B. MacMahon & T. Pugh, Epidemiology: Principles and Methods (1970)
K. Rothman, Modern Epidemiology (1986)
R. Monson, Occupational Epidemiology (1980)
R. McCunney, Handbook of Occupational Medicine (1988)

C. Glossary

1. Terms Referring to Areas of the Body

Term	Meaning	Term	Meaning
anterior	front, forward	posterior	back, behind
caudal	tail or inferior	sagittal	long axis of the body or its parallel
cephalic	head or superior		
dorsal	back or posterior	superior	above
inferior	below	thoracic	chest
lateral	side	ventral	front or anterior
medial	middle, median plane		

II. Medical Terms

2. Combining Forms

Prefix or Suffix	Meaning (pertaining to)	Prefix or Suffix	Meaning (pertaining to)
a-; an-	not, without	ecto-	out or outside
ab-	from, absent	-ectomy	removal by cutting
acro-	extremities	-emesis	vomiting
adeno-	gland	-emia	condition of the blood
alg-; -algia	pain or suffering	encephal-	brain
am-; ambi-; amphi-	with, together, both	endo-; ento-; eso-	within or inside
angi-	blood vessel	entero-	intestine
ante-; antero-	before or in front of	epi-	upon, beside, over
arteri-	artery	-escence; -escent	beginning, condition
arthr-	joint	-esthesia	feeling or sensation, awareness
		exo-; extra-	out or outside
blast-; -blast	germ or germ cell, growth	fibro-	fiber
bronchi-	subdivision of windpipe (bronchial tube)	-form	shaped like
		-fugal; -fuge	expelling, fleeing
		gastr-	stomach, abdomen
		-genesis	originating, evolving
cardi-	heart	-genic	producing, well suited for producing
-cele	sac, cyst, tumor		
cephal-	head	-genous	produced, producing
cerebr-	brain (cerebrum)	gloss-	tongue
cervic-	neck, neck of the womb (cervix)	gon-	semen, sex; knee
		-gram; -graph	recorded or written
chondr-	cartilage		
-coccus	micro-organism	gyn-	female or woman
coccyg-	lowest end of vertebral column, tail	hem-	blood
		hemi-	half
col-	part of large intestine (colon)	hepa-	liver
		hetero-	other, different
crani-	skull	hist-	tissue
cyst-; -cyst	bladder	hydro-	water
cyt-; -cyte	cell, corpuscle	hyper-	above, excessive
		hyph-; hypo-	below, less than
		hyster-	uterus
dactyl-	finger, toe		
-dema	swelling	-ia; -iac; -ic	of or pertaining to
dent-	tooth	-iasis	pathological condition
derma-	skin	ileo-	last division of small intestine (ileum)
dextro-	right		
dis-	apart, free of	ilio-	flank, hipbone (ilium)
dura-	outer membrane covering brain and spinal cord (dura mater)	inter-	between or in the midst
		intra-; intro-	in or within
		iso-	alike, equal
dys-	ill, difficult, abnormal	-itis	inflammation

2. Combining Forms *(continued)*

Prefix or Suffix	Meaning (pertaining to)	Prefix or Suffix	Meaning (pertaining to)
laryng-	organ of voice (larynx)	ot-	ear
-lent	filled, full	oxy-	sharp, quick, keen
-lepsy	violent attack		
leuco-; leuko-	white, colorless	pan-	all, entire
		para-	beside, accessary to, abnormal, closely resembling
lip-	fat		
lith-	stone		
lumb-	back, loin	patho-;	
lymph-	fluid produced by some glands (lymph)	-pathy	disease
		ped-	child
-lysis; -lytic	loosening, breaking down	-ped; -pod	foot
		per-	through, by means of
		peri-	around, about
mamma-; mast-	breast	phago-; -phage	eating, destroying
-mania	madness	pharyng-	tube that connects mouth with esophagus (pharynx)
med-; mes-	middle		
megalo-	large, abnormally large		
mening-	membranes enfolding spinal cord (meninges)	-phasia	speech
		phlebo-	vein
		-phobia	fear or dread
meno-; mens-	menstruation	phono-	speech, voice
		photo-	light
-mentia	mind	-phyma	swelling, tumor
meta-	along with, after	plasma-; -plasm	blood substance (plasma)
-morph	shape or form, body		
myelo-	marrow		
myo-	muscle	-plegia	paralysis, stroke
		pleur-	membrane enfolding the lungs (pleura)
narco-	stupor, unconsciousness, sleep		
		pneu-	lungs, air
nas-	nose	poly-	many
necro-	dead body	post-	behind, after
nephr-	kidney	pre-; pro-	before, in front of
neur-	nerve	proct-	rectum, anus
		psych-	mind
oculo-	eye	pulmo-	lungs
-ode; -oid	like, in the form of	pur-; py-	pus
odont-	tooth		
oligo-	few, deficient	ren-	kidney
-ology	study	retro-	backward
-oma	growth, tumor, swelling	-rhage; -rhea	flow, loss
ophthalmo-	eye	rhin-	nose
-opia	vision		
-orexia	appetite	sacr-	lower part of vertebral column (sacrum)
ortho-	straight		
os-; osteo-	bone	schizo-	split
-ose; -osity; -ous	full of, like	scler-	hard
		sero-	fluid, water part of blood (serum)
-osis	disease, effect		

2. Combining Forms *(continued)*

Prefix or Suffix	Meaning (pertaining to)	Prefix or Suffix	Meaning (pertaining to)
spermat-	sperm	tropho-;	
spleno-	spleen	-trophy	nourishment, growth
spondylo-	vertebra		
-stalsis	movement		
staphylo-	genus of bacteria	-ule	small or diminutive
stomat-	mouth, small opening	-ulent	abounding in
strepto-	genus of bacteria	ur-; uria	urine
sub-	under, beneath	ureter-	tube that connects kidney with bladder (ureter)
super-; supra-	above, excess		
sym-; syn-	together, joined	urethr-	tube that connects bladder with urinary outlet (urethra)
-taxia; -taxis	movement	utero-	womb (uterus)
teno-	tendon		
-therapy	treatment		
thermo-	heat	vasc-; vaso-	vessel
thoraco-	chest (thorax)	vesi-	bladder
thrombo-	clot (thrombus)		
thyro-	thyroid gland		
-tomy	cutting	xanth-	yellow
toxi-	poison	xero-	dry

III. MEDICAL DIAGNOSIS AND CASE MANAGEMENT

Kassirer, Our Stubborn Quest for Diagnostic Certainty: A Cause for Excessive Testing*
320 New Engl. J. Med. 1489 (1989)

Absolute certainty in diagnosis is unattainable, no matter how much information we gather, how many observations we make, or how many tests we perform. A diagnosis is a hypothesis about the nature of a patient's illness, one that is derived from observations by the use of inference.[1-3] As the inferential process unfolds, our confidence as physicians in a given diagnosis is enhanced by the gathering of data that either favor it or argue against competing hypotheses. Our task is not to attain certainty, but rather to reduce the level of

---

* This article by Jerome P. Kassirer, M.D., is reprinted with permission of the New England Journal of Medicine.
Notes in this article, in accordance with medical citation style, appear on pp. 41-45, at the end of the excerpt.

diagnostic uncertainty enough to make optimal therapeutic decisions.[4-7]

Testing is a critical part of the diagnostic process. Over the past two decades, the development of new tests and procedures has increased our ability to reduce diagnostic uncertainty with progressively greater efficiency and lower risk. Until now, we have had a virtually free hand in the use of such tests, and some physicians order all the tests that may be even remotely applicable in a given clinical situation. Such a practice may comfort the patient and enhance the physician's belief that all diagnostic avenues have been pursued, but more tests do not necessarily produce more certainty. The evidence provided by each new test may argue against the most likely diagnostic hypothesis, or the test result may be falsely positive or negative.

The more information we get, the more confidence in the validity of our diagnoses we feel, even when such confidence may not be justified on the basis of the information obtained.[8,9] Of course, the more tests we perform, the higher the risk to the patient: we often find ourselves performing a cascade of risky tests when a set of results is abnormal or ambiguous.

Despite the limitations of our diagnostic procedures, we continue to test excessively, partly because of our discomfort with uncertainty. We have assiduously woven the goal of minimizing uncertainty into the fabric of clinical practice and teaching.

But here is the problem: increasingly, access to diagnostic tests will be restricted because of mounting costs. To the extent that testing is vastly overused, cutbacks will not substantially affect our degree of diagnostic confidence. If testing is restricted severely enough, however, uncertainty will increase and our confidence in our diagnostic conclusions will be eroded. If restrictions are imposed, will we be able to temper our need for the information generated by tests? Will increasing uncertainty and reduced confidence affect patient care adversely?

Excessive testing has many causes besides the quest for diagnostic certainty. Some are a function of the forces imposed on the physician by our system of patient care — for example, pressure from peers and supervisors, the convenience with which tests are ordered, the demands of the patient or family, and the desire to avoid malpractice claims.[10-18] Others stem from physicians' personal practices and whims — among them, curiosity about test results, ignorance of the characteristics of tests, financial motives, and irrational and ossified habits.[10-18] No consensus has been reached about which elements contribute most,[18] but I believe that one neglected cause, attributable to the individual physician, is the inordinate zeal for certainty. We have few data on the amount of excess testing that can be attributed to this cause, but many tests that are used in the fine-tuning of diagnostic

III. Medical Diagnosis and Case Management

certainty (such as scanning, imaging techniques, and arteriography) are expensive. Accordingly, the financial burden of attempting to attain diagnostic certainty cannot be overlooked.

Everyday experience confirms that physicians test excessively to reduce their level of uncertainty. Confirmatory venography is frequently performed in patients in whom the clinical findings are already overwhelmingly consistent with thrombophlebitis; bone marrow biopsies are carried out repeatedly until the biopsy specimen reveals the requisite percentage of plasma cells, even when the diagnosis of multiple myeloma is virtually certain. Another example is duplicate testing to assess the same anatomical finding. Redundant abdominal CT scanning is performed when ultrasonography clearly shows a dilated biliary tree; radionuclide ventricular scanning is carried out when echocardiography has already documented poor ventricular wall motion. Such tests merely confirm the results of another test. Some tests do provide somewhat different data, and certainly not all duplicate testing is redundant, but many such tests are carried out merely to confirm a diagnosis that is virtually certain. Because of this, duplicate testing has been described as a "belt and suspenders" approach — namely, one in which both are worn at the same time (Schwartz RS: personal communication).

Assessments of testing practices by clinical studies or decision analysis provide further evidence that discomfort with uncertainty drives excessive testing.[19] Although it was noted more than a decade ago that administering a battery of screening tests when a patient is admitted to the hospital only increases costs without yielding comparable benefits,[20,21] extensive testing on admission continues. The erythrocyte sedimentation rate has been acknowledged to have limited value as a screening procedure, but thousands of determinations are performed each month in hospitalized patients.[22] There are several examples in which a decision analysis found virtually no difference in value between treatment without further testing and the performance of more tests.[19,23,24] In such situations, one might expect that the discomfort and irritation associated with the tests would tip the balance away from testing, yet in each instance physicians chose to test further.[24-26]

Why are physicians uneasy with uncertainty? First, we have been taught to think categorically. When we try to think in terms of probabilities, we often falter. We disregard uncertainty or behave as if it does not exist[27]; we use inexact expressions such as "probable," "occasional," and "likely" to describe the chance nature of events, complications, and efficacies of treatment[24,28,29]; we judge the likelihood of diseases and outcomes erroneously[30-33]; and we combine data on probabilities inaccurately.[34,35] Our shunning of probability-oriented thinking is reflected in our textbooks, which are rife with absolutes and increasingly display flow charts with multiple branches that lead the reader down one of a few simplified paths toward a diagnosis. Finally, our virtual freedom to date in the use of tests and procedures has accustomed us to levels of diagnostic certainty higher than are required for optimal decision making. For some of us, ratcheting down from this level of confidence may cause substantial concern.

How should we handle uncertainty? To a large degree, the level of diagnostic certainty needed in decision making is a function of the characteristics of available therapies.[4,5,7] When a specific therapy is high in effectiveness and low in risk, one can tolerate substantial diagnostic uncertainty (and therefore avoid having to carry out many tests) — not only because the treatment cures the disease, but also because it will cause little harm to patients who do not have the disease. By contrast, any therapy that is not highly effective or that produces considerable morbidity must be given only when the level of diagnostic uncertainty is minimal. If a particular therapy combines low efficacy with high risk, one would want to give it to as few patients as possible who do not have the disease. Doing so requires substantial diagnostic certainty, for the attainment of which more testing may be justified.[5] Carried to an extreme, however, the insistence on treating only patients with a proved disease can be unduly restrictive. This approach may expose patients to a succession of invasive, even life-threatening tests when there is virtually no chance that the data to be obtained will reduce uncertainty about the diagnosis further or change the therapeutic plan.

Some may argue that optimal care requires that no restrictions be imposed on testing practices. This argument will undoubtedly fall on deaf ears, given the aggregate costs of tests and the extraordinary recent inflation in the overall cost of physicians' services. It may already be too late for us to have a large say about our future use of diagnostic tests. Nonetheless, we would do well to use fewer tests now. We should identify situations in which confirmatory tests are redundant and weed out tests and procedures that are ineffective or poorly predictive. Tests that are used in final determinations of diagnostic certainty but are only marginally effective pose more of a problem, although rigorous methods are now available with which to analyze their value.[23,36] By quantifying the degree of certainty necessary to decide whether further tests are required, such methods can enhance confidence in our choices even in the absence of a definitive diagnosis.

We must take a hard look at the ways we teach students and house staff to approach uncertainty. We should not be satisfied with descriptions of probabilities that are vague, subject to varying interpretations, and not adaptable to calculations.[24,28,29,37,38] Instead, we should be more quantitative and teach physicians how to combine numerical representations of probabilities, risks, and benefits.[39-41] Perhaps we could train ourselves to be better judges of chance events. Several efforts have been made to improve calibration in other fields,[42-46] and in some, such as weather forecasting, they have paid off, but in medicine we have no comparable experience. Many pedagogic questions of this kind are legitimate issues for further contemplation and study.

In the meantime, we must use our analytic tools to identify the circumstances in which deep cuts in our testing capacity will affect the quality of our decisions. Clinical trials, decision analyses, and clinical-efficacy projects based on literature reviews,[47] expert consensus,[48] and outcome assessments[49-52] can all serve this function. If we identify tests that have little or no influence on decision making or that simply add risk but not benefit, we should give them up. On the other hand, excessive cutbacks in testing will inevitably increase the level of diagnostic uncertainty, force physicians to treat (or not treat) inappropriately, and increase the risk to the patient.[53] We need to determine at what point the restriction of testing impedes quality. Is any increase in risk an appropriate trade-off for a monetary savings? If so, how much increased risk is worth a dollar saved? Clearly, these questions merit public debate.[54]

Our goals are several: to eliminate superfluous diagnostic tests, to preserve the tests and procedures that produce substantial incremental benefits as compared with their incremental costs and risks, and to avoid restrictions in testing so severe that they erode the quality of our decisions and our confidence in our clinical judgment. The potential rewards of this painstaking assessment are the preservation of high-quality care and the channeling of the resources saved into testing that we deem essential and into the provision of basic services.

REFERENCES

1. Barrows HS, Bennett K. The diagnostic (problem solving) skill of the neurologist: experimental studies and their implications for neurologic training. Arch Neurol 1972; 26:273-7.
2. Elstein AS, Shulman LS, Sprafka SA. Medical problem solving: an analysis of clinical reasoning. Cambridge, Mass.: Harvard University Press, 1978.
3. Kassirer JP, Gorry GA. Clinical problem solving: a behavioral analysis. Ann Intern Med 1979; 89:245-55.
4. Pauker SG, Kassirer JP. Therapeutic decision making: a cost-benefit analysis. N Engl J Med 1975; 293:229-34.

5. *Idem.* The threshold approach to clinical decision making. N Engl J Med 1980; 302:1109-17.
6. Weinstein MC, Fineberg HV, Elstein AS, et al. Clinical decision analysis. Philadelphia: W.B. Saunders, 1980.
7. Eisenberg JM, Hershey JC. Derived thresholds: determining the diagnostic probabilities at which clinicians initiate testing and treatment. Med Decis Making 1983; 3:155-68.
8. Oskamp S. Overconfidence in case-study judgments. J Consult Psychol 1965; 29:261-5.
9. Lichtenstein S, Fischhoff B. Do those who know more also know more about how much they know? Organ Behav Hum Performance 1977; 20:159-83.
10. Eisenberg JM. Doctors' decisions and the cost of medical care: the reason for doctors' practice patterns and ways to change them. Ann Arbor, Mich.: Health Administration Press, 1986: 5-79.
11. Griner PF. Use of laboratory tests in a teaching hospital: long-term trends: reductions in use and relative cost. Ann Intern Med 1979; 90:243-8.
12. Nightingale SD. Risk preference and laboratory test selection. J Gen Intern Med 1987; 2:25-8.
13. *Idem.* Risk preference and laboratory use. Med Decis Making 1987; 7:168-72.
14. Feinstein AR. The 'chagrin factor' and qualitative decision analysis. Arch Intern Med 1985; 145:1257-9.
15. Myers LP, Schroeder SA. Physician use of services for the hospitalized patient: a review, with implications for cost containment. Milbank Mem Fund Q 1981; 59:481-507.
16. Martin AR, Wolf MA, Thibodeau LA, Dzau V, Braunwald E. A trial of two strategies to modify the test-ordering behavior of medical residents. N Engl J Med 1980; 303:1330-6.
17. Griner PF, Glaser RJ. Misuse of laboratory tests and diagnostic procedures. N Engl J Med 1982; 307:1336-9.
18. Williams SV, Eisenberg JM, Pascale LA, Kitz DS. Physicians' perceptions about unnecessary diagnostic testing. Inquiry 1982; 19:363-70.
19. Hagen MD, Kassirer JP, Kopelman RI. Tripping over technology. Hosp Pract [Off] 1989; 24(2):33-5.
20. Durbridge TC, Edwards F, Edwards RG, Atkinson M. Evaluation of benefits of screening tests done immediately on admission to hospital. Clin Chem 1976; 22:968-71.
21. *Idem.* An evaluation of multiphasic screening on admission to hospital: precis of a report to the National Health and Medical Research Council. Med J Aust 1976; 1:703-5.

III. Medical Diagnosis and Case Management

22. Sox HC Jr. The erythrocyte sedimentation rate: guidelines for rational use. Ann Intern Med 1986; 104:515-23.
23. Levey AS, Lau J, Pauker SG, Kassirer JP. Idiopathic nephrotic syndrome: puncturing the biopsy myth. Ann Intern Med 1987; 107:697-713.
24. Moskowitz AJ, Kuipers BJ, Kassirer JP. Dealing with uncertainty, risks, and tradeoffs in clinical decisions: a cognitive science approach. Ann Intern Med 1988; 108:435-49.
25. Kassirer JP, Kopelman RI. Surprise! Hosp Pract [Off] 1988; 23(6):21, 25-8.
26. Detsky AS, Redelmeier D, Abrams HB. What's wrong with decision analysis? Can the left brain influence the right? J Chronic Dis 1987; 40:831-8.
27. Katz J. Why doctors don't disclose uncertainty. In: Dowie J, Elstein A, eds. Professional judgment: a reader in clinical decision making. New York: Cambridge University Press, 1988:544-65.
28. Berwick DM, Fineberg HV, Weinstein MC. When doctors meet numbers. Am J Med 1981; 71:991-8.
29. Bryant GD, Norman GR. Expressions of probability: words and numbers. N Engl J Med 1980; 302:411.
30. Dolan JG, Bordley DR, Mushlin AI. An evaluation of clinicians' subjective prior probability estimates. Med Decis Making 1986; 6:216-23.
31. Elstein AS, Holzman GB, Ravitch MM, et al. Comparison of physicians' decisions regarding estrogen replacement therapy for menopausal women and decisions derived from a decision analytic model. Am J Med 1986; 80:246-58.
32. Kassirer JP. Adding insult to injury: usurping patients' prerogatives. N Engl J Med 1983; 308:898-901.
33. Christensen-Szalanski JJJ, Bushyhead JB. Physicians' use of probabilistic information in a real clinical setting. J Exp Psychol [Hum Percept] 1981; 7:928-35.
34. Schwartz WB, Gorry GA, Kassirer JP, Essig A. Decision analysis and clinical judgment. Am J Med 1973; 55:459-72.
35. Eddy DM. Probabilistic reasoning in clinical medicine: problems and opportunities. In: Kahneman D, Slovic P, Tverksy A, eds. Judgment under uncertainty: heuristics and biases. New York: Cambridge University Press, 1982: 249-67.
36. Levey AS, Pauker SG, Kassirer JP. Occult intracranial aneurysms in polycystic kidney disease: when is cerebral arteriography indicated? N Engl J Med 1983; 308:986-94.
37. Wallsten TS, Budescu DV, Rapoport A, Zwick R, Forsyth B. Measuring the vague meanings of probability terms. J Exp Psychol [Gen] 1986; 115:348-65.

38. Wallsten TS, Fillenbaum S, Cox JA. Base rate effects on the interpretation of probability and frequency expressions. J Mem Lang 1986; 25:571-86.
39. Eddy DM. Variations in physician practice: the role of uncertainty. Health Aff (Millwood) 1984; 3(2):74-89.
40. Elstein AS. Decision making as educational subject matter. Med Decis Making 1982; 2:1-5.
41. Eisenberg JM. Doctors' decisions and the cost of medical care: the reasons for doctors' practice patterns and ways to change them. Ann Arbor, Mich.: Health Administration Press, 1986:91-125.
42. Schwartz S, Griffin T. Medical thinking: the psychology of medical judgment and decision making. New York: Springer-Verlag, 1986:56-96.
43. Freudenburg WR. Perceived risk, real risk: social science and the art of probabilistic risk assessment. Science 1988; 242:44-9.
44. Arkes HR. Impediments to accurate clinical judgment and possible ways to minimize their impact. J Consult Clin Psychol 1981; 49:323-30.
45. Hammond KR, Anderson BF, Sutherland J, Marvin B. Improving scientists' judgment of risk. Risk Anal 1984; 4:69-78.
46. Sjoberg L. Aided and unaided decision making: improving intuitive judgement. J Forecasting 1982; 1:349-63.
47. Health and Public Policy Committee. Clinical efficacy reports. Philadelphia: American College of Physicians Press, 1987.
48. Kahn KL, Kosecoff J, Chassin MR, Solomon DH, Brook RH. The use and misuse of upper gastrointestinal endoscopy. Ann Intern Med 1988; 109:664-70.
49. Ellwood PM. Outcomes management: a technology of patient experience. N Engl J Med 1988; 318:1549-56.
50. Eagle KA, Singer DE, Brewster DC, Darling RC, Mulley AG, Boucher CA. Dipyridamole-thallium scanning in patients undergoing vascular surgery: optimizing preoperative evaluation of cardiac risk. JAMA 1987; 257:2185-9.
51. Eisenberg JM, Horowitz LN, Busch R, Arvan D, Rawnsley H. Diagnosis of acute myocardial infarction in the emergency room: a prospective assessment of clinical decision making and the usefulness of immediate cardiac enzyme determination. J Community Health 1979; 4:190-8.
52. Selker HP. Electrocardiograms and decision aids in coronary care triage: the truth, but not the whole truth. J Gen Intern Med 1987; 2:67-70.
53. Fuchs VR. Has cost containment gone too far? Milbank Q 1986; 64:479-88.

54. Thurow LC. Learning to say "no." N Engl J Med 1984; 311:1569-72.

NOTES

*The Patient-Physician History Taking and Diagnostic Interview: A Lawyer's Viewpoint**

1. History

All medical examinations start with a history-taking. We have all been patients at one time or another and will remember this. The first element of the history is usually the patient's relating of his present complaint, that is, the reason for coming to the doctor at this time. It is also called the chief complaint, particularly when the patient gives more than one.

This present complaint is generally a *symptom* as reported by the patient, not the labeling of some disease as the problem. The patient no more tells the doctor "I am suffering from angina pectoris" than tells a lawyer "I have a problem in future interests." The patient relates symptoms, that is, saying, for instance, "I have a sharp pain in my chest after I walk upstairs" or "I have had dizzy spells every other day for weeks."

Most physicians are trained to record a present complaint in the exact words of the patient, that is, "a sharp pain in the chest," "a dull ache," or "a squeezing sensation." The reason for this is that it is often a great aid in diagnosis. No one knows more than the patient what type of ache or pain he has. Also, using the words of the patient helps to prevent the physician-examiner from prejudging or prediagnosing the case, from translating the words of the patient into what the physician *thinks* the symptom must be like in accord with a developing idea of what is wrong with the patient.

A lawyer should be aware of the fact that physicians generally record symptoms in the words of the patient. This gives the lawyer a check on the patient's credibility since the lawyer often asks these same questions in regard to the litigation which may be involved.

Of course, like all general rules, this rule of verbatim recording in regard to chief complaints has its limitations and exceptions. Patients vary in their ability to observe and describe their symptoms. Education, intelligence, and emotional factors all influence this proficiency. For example, for many people "pain" covers almost any kind of discomfort

---

* Prepared by one of the editors, William J. Curran.

from a mild ache or itch to a migraine. Vocabulary limitations in regard to human anatomy are also very common, particularly with regard to the internal organs. (Also, pain in the trunk area is often very difficult to localize because the brain doesn't get very clear messages about pain in these areas.)

Usually it is necessary for the physician to question the patient to get a complete picture of the present symptoms. This questioning must be skillfully applied to avoid leading the patient. Many patients will answer "yes" to any question about symptoms at this early stage of an examination. (Q. Have you a pain in your chest? A. Yes, doctor. Q. Is it a sharp pain? A. Yes, doctor, it is. Q. Does it come after exertion? A. Yes, doctor.) The doctor's questions should do no more than aid the patient (or *encourage*, which is a better word) to keep on with the story. The physician should not hurry the history and it should be conducted in quiet and privacy without interruptions.

As the story unfolds and more pieces are added, the clinical picture often becomes clearer to the physician-examiner. Here the experience, skill, patience, and devotion of the physician provide guidance in whether or not to apply more affirmative questioning to the patient in certain cases. Sometimes the patient must be encouraged to expose the story more fully. At other times, patients must be directed to talk more about a certain symptom they themselves think less important than another. On occasion, a complete story cannot be obtained from the patient, and relatives or friends must be questioned.

Complaints are usually listed in the order of their severity with the nature, quality, duration, and intermittent or cyclic character of each noted. The patient is often asked to describe a typical incident of the occurrence of the symptoms in full from before onset throughout the episode.*

Where the patient says that the present complaints arise out of a traumatic event, the physician will ask the patient to describe it in detail. The physician wants to know all about it, particularly the mechanical features and severity of any blow or fall and the exact place or places on the body where the trauma was sustained. In this questioning the doctor is trying to ascertain: (1) whether or not this trauma *was* the cause of the patient's condition; (2) whether it was a fresh cause or merely an aggravation or exacerbation of a preexisting condition. If it is the latter, physicians will continue questioning in regard to the preexisting condition, since it is *this* in particular they are interested in if they are to treat the patient.

The word *encourage* is used above in regard to aiding the patient in telling of his symptoms. The word is used advisedly. Most people

---

* C. MacBryde, Signs and Symptoms, (Blacklow 6th ed. 1983).

III. Medical Diagnosis and Case Management

don't enjoy visiting a doctor. Most don't enjoy being "patients." The first visit to the doctor is often preceded not only by the occurrence, and, generally, recurrence of certain symptoms, but by some self-diagnosing and perhaps some self-treatment as well. Of course, if the incident is severe, that is, a traumatic occasion such as a fall or automobile collision, or a very severe and prolonged pain in the left chest, there may be neither of these. However, in most cases the patient has had some recurrence of the chief symptom, and has made some guesses as to its cause. If patients are satisfied that the symptoms are logically connected with some rather mild condition, they either dismiss them or try some home-style remedy. This, of course, means delays in consulting a physician. It is only when the symptoms continue, or the symptoms are not satisfactorily explained as coming from some logical and simple source, that patients consult a doctor.

In visiting a doctor and relating his symptoms, what is the patient seeking? One might imagine that it is to find a cure for the illness, if any. In all probability, however, most patients are seeking two things: (1) an explanation of their symptoms as not serious and as caused by something they are able to understand, and (2) relief from the discomfort of these symptoms. We might also add that most patients wish to be reassured that the cause of their symptoms does not lie in any faulty action (or thoughts) of theirs, since a feeling of guilt in this regard often accompanies the discomfort due to the symptoms.†

Along with the relating of symptoms, these desires of patients often get in the way. Patients are looking for a logical answer to their symptoms, an answer which is not serious. They make either a conscious or an unconscious effort to help the doctor to find this answer. They offer their own explanations and diagnosis. The skilled physician lets the patient make these additions, but tries to keep the relating of symptoms objective and as complete as possible, encourage patients to tell their story by supporting these desires with sympathy and understanding.**

Where a legal controversy is involved in the case, other factors of conscious and unconscious desires are added. The guilt factor in particular may be exaggerated. Of course, the possibility of malingering, that is, false recounting of symptoms, exists. The patient may also, consciously or unconsciously, color not only symptoms but causal connection. This may be with the motive of defrauding an insurance company, or it may have a more complicated explanation. It may be

---

† H. Billings and J. Stoeckle, The Clinical Encounter: A Guide to the Medical Interview and Case Presentation (1989).

** J. Bates, A Guide to Physical Examination and History Taking (4th ed. 1987).

that the patient is more willing to accept a traumatic event as the cause of troubles than some other fact.

Most of the underlying motivation of patients as indicated above relates to the more-or-less "normal patient" where an organic problem exists. In a surprisingly high number of cases, however, as much as 40 percent, there will not be an organic basis for the symptoms described or exhibited by the patient. The cause may then be psychosomatic or psychoneurotic.

After completing the questioning on the present complaint and its development, the result will be a chronicle of the *present illness* based on symptoms only. Note that the present illness may extend back in time for weeks, months, or years as long as the physician determines it is the same uninterrupted illness.

At this point the physician very often has formed a tentative opinion as to what is wrong with the patient, or at least has narrowed down the possibilities quite well. This is, of course, implied when adding "present illness" to the term "present complaint," at the end of this portion of the history.

At this point, some physicians are ready to discuss treatment. Too many general practitioners fall into this class; very few specialists will stop at this point. In a complete examination, this present history will be followed by the elicitation of the *past history* as indicated in the outline.

The first procedure in the past history will be the so-called system review. Here direct questions will be asked of the patient in regard to past illness or problems regarding various parts of the body and various organs. This is usually done according to the systems of the body, that is, the nervous system, circulatory system, or cardiorespiratory system, and so forth. (Another example of this method of review will be seen in the hospital records following.) This review of the entire medical history of the patient often produces additional evidence which will aid the physician in arriving at a diagnosis. Also, it may bring out evidence of complications which will affect the method of treatment to be used in this case. Note that this review is not a mere listing of past illness; it includes any "trouble" or "problem" the patient may have had with a particular organ or member. It may, for example, reveal allergies including adverse drug reactions.

The complete history will also include questioning on the medical history of the patient's close relatives, particularly parents and siblings. This line of inquiry is most obviously aimed at revealing hereditary characteristics, but it also gives something of the environment of the patient and may aid in assessing the emotional factors in the present case. For example, if the patient's father died at 50 of a heart attack and the patient is now 50 himself, he may be seeing the physician with chest pain and fearing the same fate. If full examination fails to reveal an organic cause for the pain, it may be based in his emotional reaction at this time to having reached his father's "fatal age."

The history of the patient will continue with some further information which cannot be called either present illness history or past medical history. Here the physician fills out the total picture of the patient, listing basic living habits such as smoking, drinking, exercise, sleep, etc., eliciting something of marital history, sex habits, and social and economic background. Detail will vary with the type of present illness postulated, with the specialty area of the physician, and with whether the patient is ambulatory and being questioned in a doctor's office or is hospitalized. Hospital history-taking is almost universally more detailed than office procedures, particularly if the hospital is a teaching institution and has interns and residents to take medical histories and social service departments to compile patient social records.

The above will be the complete history of the patient. From here on physicians are finding things out for themselves.

Some further words should be said, however, before leaving the subject of the patient's history. The laity have a tendency to underestimate the significance of history-taking. They don't feel the doctor is really finding out anything until he gets up off his chair and says, "All right, take off your clothes." He then starts probing and pounding and looking through instruments and ordering diagnostic tests. The patient heaves a sigh of relief, glad to get the preliminaries over with and get down to business. Not so the physician. He now has a good impression of the diagnosis in a majority of cases. The physical examination and diagnostic tests more often confirm a tentative diagnosis than they reveal a new one. They also indicate the severity of the condition and sometimes the site of the disease in the body. They may also reveal other pathological conditions which may complicate the chief complaint of the patient.

These considerations, then, point up the importance of an adequate history skillfully obtained. In the view of most medical authorities, the art of taking good clinical histories is the key to successful diagnostic work. Most experienced lawyers will agree.

2. *Physical Examination*

The next step in the medical examination is the complete physical examination. This is again outlined in the material above. The examination there described is the general physical. For each specialty, the examination in regard to that area, organ, or system of the body will be more detailed.

It is noteworthy here that this physical examination is like the system review in that it includes all elements whether involved in the present illness or not. Sometimes, therefore, the examiner will record only results which indicate pathology or other involvement for the patient. In other words, he will record *positive* results (i.e., pathological) and ignore *negative* results (i.e., normal or nonpathological). Where this is done, it sometimes causes embarrassment later when questions are asked about results or about whether a particular part of the examination was ever performed at all. This is significant in compiling a differential diagnosis where other causes for the patient's condition are ruled out. The lack of a record of negative results often makes it impossible to rule out other possibilities than the one selected by the physician. This is obviously significant in litigation where a diagnosis is challenged.

In the discussion of the history, only very limited reference was made to the special problems of examination where legal issues are involved. In the area of the physical examination, there is particular need to call attention to the special problems involved in examinations of persons who are litigating or may be litigating claims. Many physicians who engage in this type of examination assert that they follow quite normal procedures in history-taking, but use special care in eliciting objective evidence to support — or reject — the subjective symptoms found in the history. This will, of course, be most true of physicians examining a patient-claimant for a defendant insurance company.

3. *Laboratory and Other Ancillary Tests*

The above physical examination will generally end the gathering of information at the first interview. Other diagnostic aids such as X-ray, laboratory, or other tests must await the patient's being processed through these services.

In some procedures, a tentative diagnosis, or diagnostic impression, is recorded at the end of the first interview and before the results of diagnostic tests can be added. When these are obtained a further and more final diagnosis is recorded. For legal cases, diagnostic tests are highly important. They are the most objective of evidence to support the claims of the patient. Wherever possible, such corroboration should be obtained. Unlike the system review or physical examination, negative results on these tests are routinely recorded in patient records. In asking for copies of patient records, care should be taken to obtain complete ancillary test reports, particularly the opinion as to results as written by the physician in charge of that service. The latter opinion is often listed as one of the consultations obtained in regard to the case.

4. Diagnosis

As indicated above, the case management may first contain a tentative diagnosis, or a diagnostic impression, before all ancillary test results are obtained. A final diagnosis may then be recorded, but quite often this tentative conclusion is the *only* diagnosis ever recorded before treatment begins. A final diagnosis is often not made until the patient is discharged.*

Some discussion of the elements of diagnosis may reveal the reasons for these practices. First of all, we must remember the purpose of a diagnosis. It is essentially intended as an aid to treatment. Diagnosis identifies a symptom or group of symptoms as a particular disease or other named pathological state. The specific treatment, or treatment of choice, for this condition is then applied.

Pain, dizziness, and weakness are among the most common symptoms. A skillful physician can sharpen, clarify, and localize such symptoms in the history-taking to obtain excellent diagnostic aids from them. When he has narrowed the symptoms and findings down to their basic essentials, he can list the major possibilities as to what the patient's illness may be. This is called the "differential diagnosis." The further management of the case, the use of ancillary tests, and the course of treatment involve a continuous narrowing of the list of possibilities. When the physician makes a tentative diagnosis, it enables him to begin treatment. Where he is not sure of his diagnosis, the treatment has two purposes: (1) the relief of the patient's symptoms, and (2) the narrowing of the list of diagnoses by indicating whether the patient responds to the treatment employed. If the patient's symptoms are not relieved, it is an indication that the first diagnostic impression was incorrect. Some other treatment is tried and again the results are studied. In this manner, diagnosis is often a continuous process moving right along with the treatment itself. At times, lawyers have a great deal of trouble understanding this phenomenon. They are used to the facts remaining constant throughout a logical analysis. They are unaccustomed to the process of analysis itself having an influence on the results as they go along.

5. Treatment

It can be seen, then, that medical case management is a dynamic process where diagnosis and treatment often blend into one. The essential factor here is *not* analysis, but *results*, that is, helping the patient. To help the patient, the object is first to relieve his symptoms,

---

* Schroeder, Krupp, Tierney, and McPhee, Current Medical Diagnosis and Treatment (1989).

to make him comfortable again, to restore his sense of well-being. This is an empirical approach, to use the philosophers' concept. And the truth is that very often in medicine this is all that the physician can accomplish even when he is sure of his diagnosis. There aren't as many outright "cures" in medicine as lay people imagine.

The importance of making the patient comfortable during curative or restorative treatment has its bearing on legal issues also. Attorneys representing personal injury claimants often ask the attending physician whether or not the patient suffered pain or other discomfort during the course of treatment. They are puzzled when the physician answers, "Oh, not too much pain," when the attorney is aware that because of the very nature of the injuries there must have been considerable pain and suffering. An attorney should expect this response on occasion when the question is asked so nakedly and bluntly. Many physicians consider such a question a reflection on their management of the case. The attorney should examine the patient records to see if the nurses' notes indicate pain and discomfort. He should also look at the drug sheet to see if pain-killing drugs were administered. He can then ask the physician about pain by opening the discussion with: "I suppose in this type of injury (or disease) there is normally a certain amount of pain and discomfort, doctor?" With an affirmative answer, questioning can continue in more detail about this case.

6. *Prognosis*

The trilogy of clinical case management is said to be diagnosis, treatment, and prognosis. We have discussed the first two. The last, prognosis, is the physician's estimate of how long the patient will be ill due to this present condition. Here again there are some important factors to consider in the philosophy of case management.

First of all, prognosis is *not* one of the most important features in case management to the bulk of clinical physicians who do not deal with court cases or workmen's compensation. The *treatment* of the patient is the important thing and the physician tends to watch him on a short-term basis as he responds to treatment. The physician has little need to make long-term guesses or prognoses. Second, physicians are inherently reluctant to venture guesses on a matter involving so many variables. "So much depends on the individual," they will say. Also, diseases vary in the course they run — and the variation is often substantial. Most important, however, the physician is accustomed to exercising his doubts on the shorter side, or purposely underestimating the course of a disease. He does this for the benefit of the patient and his relatives to cut down on the emotionally detrimental effect of a gloomy prediction. When a lawyer asks him

III. Medical Diagnosis and Case Management

for a more objective appraisal, he is reluctant to change his role. After all, he knows that this less optimistic view will often get back to the patient. The lawyer should make an effort to understand this attitude and to cooperate with its objectives to the extent that he can. The lawyer must also explain to the physician the legal objectives behind the need for a truthful and sober prognosis. The objectives of the law are *also* the benefit of the patient, although through his economic status in a damages award. With such an explanation and the achieving of a sympathetic understanding between the lawyer and physician, better results will be had.

CHAPTER 3

The Forensic Sciences

I. ORIENTATION: SCOPE AND DEFINITION OF THE FIELD

Thornton, Uses and Abuses of Forensic Science*
69 A.B.A.J. 288, 289-290 (1983)

In the broadest sense, forensic science is any science used in the resolution of legal conflicts. The word "forensic" comes from the Latin *forensus*, meaning "of the forum." The ancient Roman forum was the site of debates concerning governmental issues, but it also was the courthouse, where trials were held. Consequently, forensic science has come to mean the study and practice of applying natural and physical sciences to the just resolution of social and legal issues. What distinguishes it from other sciences is its use by the legal system; what distinguishes a forensic scientist from other scientists is the expectation of routine appearances in a court of law. . . .

Although forensic science historically has been identified closely with the criminal justice system, the forensic scientist now plays an increasingly active role in civil litigation and in regulatory matters. Virtually no limitation exists to the scope of physical evidence that is grist for all forensic scientists. Physical evidence may range in size from the microscopic (for example, a pollen grain) to the macroscopic (for example, a diesel truck). It may be as appalling as the lifeless body of a battered child, as intangible as the fleeting vapors of gasoline following a suspected arson fire, or as obscure as the composition of dyes in the ink of a contested will. . . .

A number of disciplines exist within the rubric of forensic science. Many of these are simply adaptations of existing disciplines — for example, forensic pathology as a specialty of pathology — although at least one subdiscipline — criminalistics — is a novel synthesis of natural and physical sciences. Its origins cannot be attributed to any single parent discipline. The American Academy of Forensic Sciences, the largest professional forensic society in the world, recognizes the following scientific disciplines: forensic pathology, forensic toxicology, forensic anthropology, forensic odontology, forensic psychiatry, questioned documents, forensic engineering, and criminalistics. . . .

---

* Reprinted with permission from the March 1983, ABA Journal, The Lawyer's Magazine, published by the American Bar Association.

NOTES

The Nature of Forensic Science

1. *Definitions and lists.* Thornton's list of forensic sciences is not exhaustive of all medicine and science as it appears in the courtroom. For example, orthopedic surgeons probably prepare more medicolegal reports and appear as witnesses in courts and before administrative agencies, such as Workers' Compensation Boards, more frequently than most of the specialists named as forensic scientists. Economists testify in antitrust, personal injury, and employment discrimination cases. Experimental psychologists who study the factors influencing the accuracy of eyewitnesses describe their general findings in criminal cases. Statisticians act as consultants and witnesses in a broad spectrum of cases. See Panel on Statistical Assessments as Evidence in the Courts, The Evolving Role of Statistical Assessments as Evidence in the Courts (S. Fienberg ed. 1988); Statistics and the Law (M. DeGroot, S. Fienberg & J. Kadane 1986 eds.).

Nevertheless, the scientists in the disciplines enumerated by the American and British Academies of Forensic Science tend to share certain distinctive professional attitudes and goals. They think of themselves not just as scientists who sometimes have information to contribute in court, but as scientists whose work is always connected with the legal system. They strive to make their disciplines more useful and more relevant to the administration of justice. In Thornton's words, "[a]ll of these disciplines have a unifying theme — the introduction of science into the legal process in an objective and impartial manner. . . ." Thornton, Uses and Abuses of Forensic Science, 69 A.B.A.J. 288, 291 (1983). Thus, one forensic laboratory's director observes that "[w]e see ourselves as different from most of the others in our circle of professional colleagues. That circle is populated by lawyers, police, administrators, an occasional pathologist, and once in a while, the press. For the most part, our nonscience peers do not speak our language and are often apathetic about our concerns." Fisher, Developing a Forensic Science Laboratory Operating Strategy, 31 J. For. Sci. 1177, 1178-1179 (1986).

While marked with a distinctive professional identity, the self-designated forensic sciences, as indicated in Fisher's remarks, are commonly part of the law enforcement apparatus. Most practitioners apply their talents in criminal investigation and in aid of police agencies and public prosecutors. This is especially true of criminalists:

> Criminalistics may be described in either a subtractive or an additive manner. In the former sense, it represents what remains other than pathology, odontology, toxicology, and the other forensic subspecialties.

> In the additive sense, criminalistics is concerned with the analysis, identification, and interpretation of hairs and fibers; bloodstains and seminal stains; firearms evidence; soil, glass and paint classifications; toolmarks; arson accelerants; explosives; serial number restoration; and virtually everything else that does not fit tidily into one of the other disciplines.

Thornton, Uses and Abuses of Forensic Science, 69 A.B.A.J. 288, 290-291 (1983).

2. *History.* Forensic medicine is by no means a 20th-century innovation. In China, the elements of toxicology were recognized long ago, and the Materia Medica of 3000 B.C. included information on aconite, arsenic, and opium. Hsi Yuan Lu (Instructions to Coroners) dealt with practically every topic in forensic medicine. This classic text first appeared in 1250 A.D. and was amended and reprinted up to the 19th century. Salgado, Forensic Medicine in the Indo-Pacific Region: History and Current Practice of Forensic Medicine, 36 For. Sci. Int. 3, 3 (1988).

Medical testimony in English criminal cases extends back into the Middle Ages, but:

> News of important advances in Italy, Germany, France and other countries crossed the Channel only, it seems, very slowly. Pathology, a sister science, did not even begin to bloom in Britain until the late 1700s. . . . For far too long the average expert medical witness in an English courtroom or inquest chamber was a busy surgeon, obliged to mount the witness box only a few times at most in his career and ill prepared for the experience. Unless he understood a foreign language, Continental lectures, books, and papers were beyond his reach. His medical education scarcely touched on the functions and duties of the expert witness, and the critical importance of useful medical testimony often escaped him — as it did the jurist and indeed the general public. When medical men did appear in court, it was to confirm the fact and more obvious circumstances of death. Very few of these witnesses understood how to search for evidence at the scene of the crime and at the autopsy table, how to record it accurately, and how to present it clearly and without equivocation. But as the eighteenth century drew to a close, concern grew within and without the medical profession that a doctor's training should include at least the fundamentals of forensic medicine. . . . Books and papers began to appear on the subject, a few universities experimented with lectures on the new specialty, and legislation recognizing the importance of the forensic expert and facilitating his work was debated.

T. Forbes, Surgeons at the Bailey: English Forensic Medicine to 1878 3 (1985).

As regards the other subfields of forensic science, however:

Forensic science is essentially a 20th century innovation. Various attempts were made earlier to use scientific evidence of one sort or another, but the results were less than satisfactory. By 1915 only three New England states and the city of New York had replaced their coroner systems with a more progressive medical examiner system. The first operational crime laboratory in the country was not established until 1923 in Los Angeles, followed by the Scientific Crime Detection Laboratory at Northwestern University in 1929, and the Federal Bureau of Investigation laboratory in 1932. Despite what one might infer from Arthur Conan Doyle's writings, England did not create a forensic laboratory until 1935. . . .

Although one might suppose that the inception of forensic science resulted from progressive attitudes of pathologists, lawyers, police administrators, or scientists, this rarely was the case. Neither physicians nor attorneys led the reform movement that resulted in the establishment of a medical examiner's office for the city of New York. Similarly, public outrage after the 1929 Valentine's Day massacre in Chicago provided the impetus for establishing that city's scientific crime detection laboratory. In fact, many of the nation's crime laboratories owe their existence not to enlightened attitudes of police administrators or other public officials but to adverse publicity or the threat of it. . . .

Thornton, Uses and Abuses of Forensic Science, 69 A.B.A.J. 288, 291 (1983).

3. *What is to come.* This book is concerned primarily with medicine as it relates to law. In the development and presentation of evidence, however, forensic medicine almost always blends with other forensic sciences. Very often, the evidence or opinion offered at trial is a conglomeration of contributions from subspecialists, some medical, some nonmedical. The lawyer must deal with the whole. Thus, this chapter provides basic information and references in the forensic sciences generally. However, it does not attempt to cover every part of forensic science. It stresses the medical areas, but it makes no attempt to cover any specific area exhaustively. The objective is to convey a flavor of and an appreciation for the way in which law, medicine, and science interact in and on the way to the courtroom.

4. *References.* General works on forensic science by or with contributions from forensic scientists themselves include Forensic Science (G. Davies 2d ed. 1985); P. De Forest, R. E. Gaensslen & H. Lee, Forensic Science: An Introduction to Criminalistics (1983); Scientific and Expert Evidence (E. Imwinkelreid 2d ed. 1981); Forensic Science Handbook (R. Saferstein ed. 1982); H. J. Walls, Forensic Science (1968), and Forensic Sciences (C. Wecht ed. 1981). Leading texts by attorneys include A. Moenssens, F. Inbau & J. Starrs, Scientific Evidence in Criminal Cases (3d ed. 1986), P. Giannelli & E. Imwinkelried, Scientific Evidence (1986), and McCormick on Evidence §§203-211 (E. Cleary 3d ed. 1984) with 1987 supplement. As with most scientific

fields, advances and changes are so rapid that papers in professional journals typically must be consulted. The American Academy of Forensic Science publishes the Journal of Forensic Science, and the British Academy of Forensic Sciences publishes Medicine, Science and the Law. See also Australian J. For. Sci.; Canadian Socy. For. Sci. J.; For. Sci. Int.; For. Sci. Socy. J.; Intl. Microform J. Leg. Med. & For. Sci.

Miller v. Pate
386 U.S. 1 (1967)

MR. JUSTICE STEWART delivered the opinion of the Court.

On November 26, 1955, in Canton, Illinois, an eight-year-old girl died as the result of a brutal sexual attack. The petitioner was charged with her murder. Prior to his trial in an Illinois court, his counsel filed a motion for an order permitting a scientific inspection of the physical evidence the prosecution intended to introduce. The motion was resisted by the prosecution and denied by the court. The jury trial ended in a verdict of guilty and a sentence of death. On appeal the judgment was affirmed by the Supreme Court of Illinois. On the basis of leads developed at a subsequent unsuccessful state clemency hearing, the petitioner applied to a federal district court for a writ of habeas corpus. After a hearing, the court granted the writ and ordered the petitioner's release or prompt retrial. The Court of Appeals reversed, and we granted certiorari to consider whether the trial that led to the petitioner's conviction was constitutionally valid. We have concluded that it was not.

There were no eyewitnesses to the brutal crime which the petitioner was charged with perpetrating. A vital component of the case against him was a pair of men's underwear shorts covered with large, dark, reddish-brown stains — People's Exhibit 3 in the trial record. These shorts had been found by a Canton policeman in a place known as the Van Buren Flats three days after the murder. The Van Buren Flats were about a mile from the scene of the crime. It was the prosecution's theory that the petitioner had been wearing these shorts when he committed the murder, and that he had afterwards removed and discarded them at the Van Buren Flats.

During the presentation of the prosecution's case, People's Exhibit 3 was variously described by witnesses in such terms as the "bloody shorts" and "a pair of jockey shorts stained with blood." Early in the trial the victim's mother testified that her daughter "had type 'A' positive blood." Evidence was later introduced to show that the petitioner's blood "was of group 'O'."

Against this background the jury heard the testimony of a chemist for the State Bureau of Crime Identification. The prosecution established his qualifications as an expert, whose "duties include blood identification, grouping and typing both dry and fresh stains," and who had "made approximately one thousand blood typing analyses while at the State Bureau." His crucial testimony was as follows:

> I examined and tested "People's Exhibit 3" to determine the nature of the staining material upon it. The result of the first test was that this material upon the shorts is blood. I made a second examination which disclosed that the blood is of human origin. I made a further examination which disclosed that the blood is of group "A."

The petitioner, testifying in his own behalf, denied that he had ever owned or worn the shorts in evidence as People's Exhibit 3. He himself referred to the shorts as having "dried blood on them."

In argument to the jury the prosecutor made the most of People's Exhibit 3:

> Those shorts were found in the Van Buren Flats, with blood. What type blood? Not "O" blood as the defendant has, but "A" — type "A."

And later in his argument he said to the jury:

> And, if you will recall, it has never been contradicted the blood type of Janice May was blood type "A" positive. Blood type "A". Blood type "A" on these shorts. It wasn't "O" type as the defendant has. It is "A" type, what the little girl had.

Such was the state of the evidence with respect to People's Exhibit 3 as the case went to the jury. And such was the state of the record as the judgment of conviction was reviewed by the Supreme Court of Illinois. The "blood stained shorts" clearly played a vital part in the case for the prosecution. They were an important link in the chain of circumstantial evidence against the petitioner, and, in the context of the revolting crime with which he was charged, their gruesomely emotional impact upon the jury was incalculable.

So matters stood with respect to People's Exhibit 3, until the present habeas corpus proceeding in the Federal District Court. In this proceeding the State was ordered to produce the stained shorts, and they were admitted in evidence. It was established that their appearance was the same as when they had been introduced at the trial as People's Exhibit 3. The petitioner was permitted to have the shorts examined by a chemical microanalyst. What the microanalyst found cast an extraordinary new light on People's Exhibit 3. The reddish-brown stains on the shorts were not blood, but paint.

The witness said that he had tested threads from each of the 10 reddish-brown stained areas on the shorts, and that he had found that all of them were encrusted with mineral pigments ". . . which one commonly uses in the preparation of paints." He found "no traces of human blood." The State did not dispute this testimony, its counsel contenting himself with prevailing upon the witness to concede on cross-examination that he could not swear that there had never been any blood on the shorts.

It was further established that counsel for the prosecution had known at the time of the trial that the shorts were stained with paint. The prosecutor even admitted that the Canton police had prepared a memorandum attempting to explain "how this exhibit contains all the paint on it."

In argument at the close of the habeas corpus hearing counsel for the State contended that "[e]verybody" at the trial had known that the shorts were stained with paint. That contention is totally belied by the record. The microanalyst correctly described the appearance of the shorts when he said, "I assumed I was dealing . . . with a pair of shorts which was heavily stained with blood. [I]t would appear to a layman . . . that what I see before me is a garment heavily stained with blood." The record of the petitioner's trial reflects the prosecution's consistent and repeated misrepresentation that People's Exhibit 3 was, indeed, "a garment heavily stained with blood." The prosecution's whole theory with respect to the exhibit depended upon that misrepresentation. For the theory was that the victim's assailant had discarded the shorts because they were stained with blood. A pair of paint-stained shorts, found in an abandoned building a mile away from the scene of the crime, was virtually valueless as evidence against the petitioner. The prosecution deliberately misrepresented the truth.

More than 30 years ago this Court held that the Fourteenth Amendment cannot tolerate a state criminal conviction obtained by the knowing use of false evidence. There has been no deviation from that established principle. There can be no retreat from that principle here.

The judgment of the Court of Appeals is reversed and the case is remanded for further proceedings consistent with this opinion. It is so ordered.

NOTES

The Accuracy and Impact of Forensic Science

1. *Laboratory proficiency.* At best, the chemist who testified for the state in Miller v. Pate merely blundered in performing or interpreting the tests. For other instances of "questionable forensic science" ex-

posed by defense experts, see Keefe, Forensic Science Services and the Criminal Justice System as Viewed by the Defense, 24 J. For. Sci. 673 (1979). Naturally, the quality of laboratories and the technicians and scientists working in them varies. See Lappas, Forensic Science Laboratories in the United States: A Survey, 18 J. For. Sci. Socy. 171 (1978). A limited number of proficiency studies, particularly in the area of forensic toxicology, have been undertaken. E.g., Peat, Finnigan & Finkle, Proficiency Testing in Forensic Toxicology: A Feasibility Study, 28 J. For. Sci. 139 (1983); Dinovo & Gottschalk, Results of a Nine-Laboratory Survey of Forensic Toxicology Proficiency, 22 Clinical Chemistry 843 (1976); cf. Miike & Hewitt, Accuracy and Reliability of Urine Drug Tests, 36 Kan. L. Rev. 641, 656 (1988) ("In a 'blind study' of fifty labs nationwide performing drug tests, there was a 35 percent false negative rate and a one percent false positive rate"). In the mid-1970s the federal Law Enforcement Assistance Administration sent known samples to many participating police laboratories for identification. The percentage of laboratories with "unacceptable" (inaccurate or incomplete) responses ranged from 1.6 percent (for a blood stained cloth) to 71.2 percent (for a semen stained cloth), depending on the nature of the sample. J. Peterson, E. Fabricant & K. Field, Crime Laboratory Proficiency Testing Research Program 251 (U.S. Dept. Justice 1978).

The absolute number of mistakes in forensic work, however, is not the relevant benchmark in assessing what forensic science has to offer the legal system. All evidence, from the reports of eyewitnesses to reliance on a person's reputation, is fallible. Is there any reason to think that scientific evidence is any worse than the more familiar modes of proof? Should courts nevertheless screen it more carefully than lay testimony? How? We explore these questions infra at §4.

2. *The impact of forensic analysis.* *Miller* highlights the powerful effect that scientific evidence can have — for better or worse — in some cases. But how many? Should more resources be invested in the scientific investigation of crime? Or did the unnamed police administrator have a strong point when he asked "Do you know how many patrol cars that gas chromatography system could buy?" Fisher, Developing a Forensic Science Laboratory Operating Strategy, 31 J. For. Sci. 1177, 1178 (1986). Empirical studies of factors that affect the disposition of cases provide few clear answers. See P. L. Bender, M. Gilliland & J. Peterson, Utilization of Forensic Sciences in Police Investigations: A Review of the Literature (U.S. Dept. of Justice 1982); J. Peterson, S. Mihajlovic & M. Gilliland, Forensic Evidence and the Police: The Effects of Scientific Evidence on Criminal Investigations 210 (U.S. Dept. of Justice 1984) ("The effect of physical evidence on clearance and conviction depends on the type of offense and the jurisdiction involved"); H. Kalven & H. Zeisel, The American Jury

139 (1966) (no experts appeared in about three-quarters of criminal trials studied and in only 3 percent of the trials did both sides employ an expert; prosecutors used experts four times as often as defense attorneys).

Fisher, Developing a Forensic Science Laboratory Operating Strategy*
31 J. For. Sci. 1177, 1178 (1986)

The police investigator sees us as a scientific resource to help prove his case. He is delighted when we can substantiate his theory of how a crime occurred and usually wants more strongly worded opinions than we often like to give. He cringes at the use of what he calls "weasel words" in laboratory reports, for example, "consistent with" and "similar to." He wants absolute statements. The concept of class characteristics is foreign to him, and he would like nothing better than reports stating that, for example, the white cotton fiber found on the victim came from the defendant and no other.

The prosecuting attorney has little appreciation for forensic scientists. After all, how many lawyers successfully made it through physical chemistry for their baccalaureate? For the most part, although there are exceptions, lawyers are intimidated by us. We are indispensible in driving under the influence (DUI) of alcohol cases, required in drug prosecutions, and downright handy in rapes, assaults and murders. Yet many will argue that forensic scientists often confuse the jury as often as they help the case.

Defense attorneys see us as extensions of the police and prosecutors. I once gave a talk to a group of public defenders in Los Angeles. . . . I explained how I saw our role as an independent, scientific evaluator of the physical evidence. The lawyers in that group laughed at me. They saw me and all government employed forensic scientists as being on the side of the prosecution and not at all unbiased.

The courts see us as a bottleneck. If your laboratories are at all similar to mine, I'm certain that at one time or another you have had a backlog in driving under the influence cases or in narcotics cases. And what happens when the laboratory begins to fall behind in those cases? The courts are likely to be in an uproar about continuances.

Administrators see us as a bottomless pit into which is continuously poured money — money to buy spectrophotometers, gas chromatographs, mass spectrometers, and other high priced laboratory equipment of that ilk. One administrator once mused to me, "Do you

---

* Copyright ASTM. Reprinted with permission.

know how many patrol cars that gas chromatography system could buy?"

Finally, the public sees forensic scientists in the most romantic terms. We are a modern incarnation of the legendary Sherlock Holmes. Quincy, the fictional TV forensic pathologist cum criminalist plays a key role in each of our institutions. The public believes that we have unlimited time and resources to expend on each and every case we examine. . . .

Saks: Accuracy v. Advocacy: Expert Testimony Before the Bench*
Technology Review, August/September 1987, at 43, 44-45

[E]xperts [are] vulnerable to the possibly distorting influence of lawyers. Long before the expert and lawyer arrive in court, a bond has formed between them. The influence of the lawyer is considerable. He or she may authorize a limited budget for analyzing the evidence and restrict the information provided to experts about the case. The attorney expects help and cooperation from experts, who know that the lawyer could hire someone else. The question is how far they are willing to be drawn out onto the forensic limb.

One prominent trial judge in Massachusetts likens the process to a seduction. The lawyer attempts to convince the experts to go as far as possible, and the experts try to resist the temptation to acquiesce. It is the lawyer's job to test the limits and the expert's job to set those limits. . . .

In contrast to what attorneys may want, experts' professional colleagues expect them to give a competent and dignified account of the field without going beyond its limits. These expectations are sometimes expressed in a code of ethics. For example, the National Society of Professional Engineers states: "Engineers shall issue public statements only in an objective and truthful manner. Engineers shall be objective and truthful in professional reports, statements, or testimony. They shall include all relevant and pertinent information in such reports, statements, or testimony." . . .

Whatever experts' perceptions of the expectations of their colleagues, the likelihood that any sanctions will be applied against those who overstep their bounds is tiny. This fact was clear in a 1983 study I did with Richard Van Duizend, then an attorney with the National Center for State Courts. We contacted the ethics and discipline committees of professional associations such as the NSPE, the American Academy of Forensic Science, and the American Medical Association.

* Reprinted with permission from Technology Review, copyright 1987.

We found that virtually no actions had been taken against members who had misrepresented the field's knowledge or drawn insupportable conclusions on behalf of one party as expert witnesses. Complaints that did surface were typically brought by attorneys complaining that the experts they hired had misrepresented their educational or professional credentials. Professional organizations are in business to ensure their members' well-being more than to police them.

Thornton, Uses and Abuses of Forensic Science*
69 A.B.A.J. 288, 292 (1983)

[C]onsider the distinction between the introduction of evidence and the introduction of an interpretation of that evidence. The two are by no means synonymous. Not infrequently, the side wishing to introduce its particular interpretation will treat itself to a scientific "smorgasbord," selecting this or that morsel for examination by the forensic scientist. The evidence will be selected or rejected with only those items that conform to the arguments of one side actually being submitted for examination. A distinct possibility exists that the results of the examination by the forensic scientist will be skewed. This is an abuse of science because the scientist is not allowed to consider all alternative interpretations of the evidence. As a result, the ethical standards of the scientist may be challenged by cogent cross-examination.

These situations represent potential sources of mischief. There is nothing necessarily unethical or mendacious about these practices, and they even might not be unfair because opposing counsel is presumed to be equally astute in reviewing the potential evidence to be introduced. Attorneys orchestrate the presentation of physical evidence and bear the responsibility for the conduct of the case in general, and it is understandable that they will wish the evidence to support the best possible case. The danger is that conflicts easily arise between scientist and lawyer — the former attempts to describe the evidence as it actually is, while the latter attempts to describe it in the most favorable light.

NOTES

Forensic Science in an Adversarial System

1. *Independence and objectivity.* Most scientists would insist that "the scientist should have no personal stake in the outcome of a civil or

---

* Reprinted with permission from the March 1983, ABA Journal, The Lawyer's Magazine, published by the American Bar Association.

criminal case. The scientist's expertise is in the application of science to a legal controversy and the proper interpretation of scientific findings. . . ." Peterson, The Team Approach in Forensic Science, Modern Legal Medicine, Psychiatry and Forensic Science 993-994 (W. Curran, A. McGarry & C. Petty eds. 1980). So too, most subscribe to the ideal of the "introduction of evidence by competent, objective scientists who constantly keep in mind the ethical responsibilities of the profession." Thornton, Uses and Abuses of Forensic Science, 69 A.B.A.J. 288, 291 (1983).

Yet Saks describes the tendency of experts to identify with the party for whom they testify or to be manipulated by that party. Inasmuch as a witness is expected to answer only those questions put to him, is it reasonable for the National Society of Professional Engineers to admonish its members to "include all relevant and pertinent information in . . . testimony"? If not, will cross-examination or opposing experts flush out the information that might not be elicited on direct examination, as Thornton's mention of "astute" opposing counsel implies? Consider the following incident:

> A convicted murderer who has served eight years of a life sentence today walked free from the Scottish Court of Criminal Appeal in Edinburgh when three judges quashed his conviction. . . . John Preece, aged 49, a former lorry driver, . . . was convicted of murdering Mrs. Helen Will, aged 54, of Mastick, Aberdeen, by a majority verdict at the High Court in Edinburgh in 1973. . . .
>
> Lord Emslie said: "At the time of the trial Dr Clift, highly qualified and experienced, appeared to be an expert witness as to whose quality, detachment and scientific reliability there was no doubt." But the court was now sure that Dr Clift's evidence that the donor of the semen was an "A" secretor was misleading. Dr Clift had kept silent although he had known that the victim, Mrs Will, was also a group "A" secretor like Mr Preece.
>
> The judge added: "This was conduct on the part of an expert witness which demonstrated a complete misunderstanding of the role of scientific witnesses in our courts and a lack of the essential qualities of accuracy and scientific objectivity which are normally to be taken for granted." . . .
>
> Lord Emslie added that Dr Richard Gregory, the Home Office scientist who had corroborated Dr Clift's evidence . . . had been to some extent influenced by his superior — Dr Clift.

Prisoner Cleared of Murder After Serving 8 Years, The Times (London), June 20, 1981, at 1, Col. 4.

2. *Selection of expert witnesses.* Many attorneys, and much of the public, believe that "an expert can be found to support almost any position." Black, A Unified Theory of Scientific Evidence, 56 Fordham L. Rev. 595, 597-598 (1988). Indeed, the chief judge of the U.S.

District Court for the Eastern District of New York is persuaded that "[a]n expert can be found to testify to the truth of almost any factual theory, no matter how frivolous, thus validating the case sufficiently to avoid summary judgment and force the case to trial." Weinstein, Improving Expert Testimony, 20 U. Rich. L. Rev. 473, 482 (1986). The availability of such testimony from "the expert-for-hire," id., is not necessarily the result of venality. "The scientific community is large and heterogeneous, and a Ph.D. can be found to swear to almost any 'expert' proposition, no matter how false or foolish." Huber, Safety and the Second Best: The Hazards of Public Risk Management in the Court, 85 Colum. L. Rev. 277, 333 (1985).

3. *Relaxing the adversarial role of the forensic expert.* In light of the widely perceived problems noted above, suggestions to reform, if not abandon, the adversary system of adjudication are not lacking. John Langbein, who maintains that the West German system of adjudication is far superior, is particularly critical of the role of experts in civil trials in the United States. Langbein, The German Advantage in Civil Procedure, 52 U. Chi. L. Rev. 823, 835-836 (1985). Court-appointed experts figure prominently in the European accusatorial systems of criminal justice. For example, court-appointed forensic medical experts in some countries usually sit in court during the whole trial, question witnesses, explain their findings and conclusions before being examined by the parties, and may discuss relevant points not raised by the parties. See Giertsen, The Doctor and the Court in Norway, 36 For. Sci. Intl. 11, 12-14 (1988). Occasionally court-appointed experts are employed in this country as well, and there is room to expand their role. See Panel on Statistical Assessments as Evidence in the Courts, The Evolving Role of Statistical Assessments as Evidence in the Courts 169-172 (S. Fienberg ed. 1989); T. Willging, Court Appointed Experts (U.S. Federal Judicial Center 1986); Weinstein, Litigation and Statistics: Obtaining Assistance Without Abuse, Toxics L. Rptr., Dec. 24, 1986, at 812, 819-20; Hand, Historical and Practical Considerations Regarding Expert Testimony, 15 Harv. L. Rev. 40 (1901).

Walls, Whither Forensic Science?*
6 Med. Sci. & L. 183 (1966)

[C]ommunication from science to law, which was never easy, is being made more difficult by [a] developing trend towards scientific results being expressed as probabilities — not just as something that

---

* This excerpt from the presidential address of Dr. H. J. Walls to the British Academy of Forensic Sciences is reprinted by permission of Medicine, Science and the Law.

might be so, but as something that has a definite numerically expressible chance of being so. The law, of course, wants yes or no, black or white, this or not this. In fact, . . . I have sometimes thought that it looks on "probability" as a dirty word. . . .

[A]ll scientific conclusions are really matters of probability. Sometimes, of course, this is so near 1 (that is, certainty) that it is for all practical purposes indistinguishable from certainty, and the residuum of "reasonable doubt" is vanishingly small. The principle, however, remains valid. For example, nothing is more conclusive than fingerprint evidence, but there is no prescriptive law of nature that prohibits two fingerprints from being identical. There is merely a descriptive one that two never *are* identical. That, of course, is quite easily explained: the number of possible different fingerprint patterns is so large that there aren't enough fingers in the whole world over many generations to give a reasonable outside chance of two identical ones turning up.

We have indeed already seen the thin edge of the wedge go in. Courts accept evidence about glass fragments in which all the scientific witness can say is that they are indistinguishable to within certain limits of accuracy, and the odds against — that is, the probability of — that happening by chance are so and so.

There is some very interesting work going on now on the characterisation of human head hair by means of the neutron activation analysis of the trace elements in it. [R]ather bold claims were made some years ago across the Atlantic that in this way a hair could practically be tied to the head from which it came. The present, much more systematic, work has shown that these claims were undoubtedly premature and over-stated, but that considerable differences between hairs from different heads do undoubtedly occur. We are not yet ready to use the results of this work routinely in evidence, but when we are they will be meaningful only if they are given as statistical probabilities. Some quite sophisticated statistical mathematics have been developed in connection with this work, and its use will enable us to give precise estimates of probability instead of, at present, vague statements such as "similar to," "could have come from the same head" and so on. And it would obviously be quite wrong not to be precise instead of vague if the known facts make that possible.

Indeed there is really no reason why in certain fields that sort of evidence should not now be used more than it is. The distribution of blood groups within the various blood-group systems which we can now determine on dried blood stains is known, at least for the population of this country. . . . Suppose . . . that a specimen of blood is grouped according to four independent systems, and that it belongs to the commonest group in each, and . . . that each of these groups occurs in half the population. Half the population is a large number of people, but when four independent systems are in question, . . . the blood could only have come from half of half of half of half of the population — that is, one-sixteenth. . . . If we could use eight systems, on the same assumption [of independence] we would have come down to one-256th part of the population. And if the groups to which the blood belongs happen to be among the rarer ones, it is quite on the cards that we can say that only one person in several thousand has this combination of groups. As a matter of fact, we do say that sort of thing now when the opportunity to do so arises. But there is no reason why we should not carry it a little farther. It should not be impossible in some cases to make an estimate of the number of persons from whom, on other evidence, the blood might have come. Suppose [there were 100 such people including the accused]. The important question then is: if the bloodstain and . . . [the accused] are of the same rare combination of groups, what is the probability of more than one person in that 100 having it? If . . . one person in 5000 in the population as a whole shows that particular combination, then . . . the probability of two people out of our 100 showing it is 1/2500 — that is, the odds against the event are 2500 to one — and the probability of more than two people out of the 100 having it is quite vanishingly small. And, obviously, the smaller the number of persons from whom the blood *might* have come, the smaller the corresponding probability. If instead of 100 it was, say, twenty, then the odds against more than one person in that twenty having the same combination of groups are over 60,000 to one. Does that sort of figure constitute proof "beyond all reasonable doubt?"

We as scientists often wonder indeed just what "beyond all reasonable doubt" really means. Can we give it a quantitative connotation? [L]aw and science would at least make a more harmonious marriage if we could put some sort of figure on "beyond reasonable doubt." Does it mean a probability of .99, or .999 or .999999 or something even higher? Should it be a higher probability in a trial for murder than in one for petty larceny? I leave the thought with you.

United States ex rel. DiGiacomo v. Franzen
680 F.2d 515 (7th Cir. 1982)

PER CURIAM.

In this appeal from the denial of a petition for a writ of habeas corpus, petitioner James G. DiGiacomo claims that he was denied a fair trial when the state was allowed to use mathematical probability to identify him as the perpetrator of a crime. We hold that the admission of the challenged testimony violated no right guaranteed by the Constitution and affirm the district court's judgment denying the petition.

I

In March 1977, James G. DiGiacomo was tried in an Illinois state court on charges of rape, deviate sexual assault, aggravated kidnapping, and battery. The principal witness against DiGiacomo was Patricia Marik, the victim of the assault. Marik testified that DiGiacomo abducted her at knife point from a tavern in Naperville, Illinois, on November 5, 1976, and ordered her to drive him to a cornfield in the country where, after a brief struggle, he forced her to have sexual intercourse with him.

In an effort to bolster Marik's identification of DiGiacomo as her assailant at trial, the state called an expert witness to testify concerning a number of hairs that had been recovered from Marik's automobile after the attack. Sally Dillon, the supervising criminologist at the Illinois Bureau of Identification, testified that she had compared the hairs found in Marik's car with a sample of DiGiacomo's hair and found them to be microscopically similar. She was then asked, over defense counsel's objection, whether she could testify as to the statistical probability of the hair found in Marik's car belonging to someone other than DiGiacomo. Dillon responded that based on a recent study she had read, "the chances of another person belonging to that hair would be one in 4500."

Several hours after beginning their deliberations, the jury, apparently confused by Dillon's testimony, submitted the following question to the court in writing: "Has it been established by sampling of hair specimens that the defendant was positively proven to have been in the automobile?" After consulting with the parties, the trial judge sent a written response to the jury in which he instructed them that it was their duty to determine the facts from the evidence presented at trial and that he could therefore provide no answer to their question. Neither side objected.

The jury later returned guilty verdicts on each of the charges, and DiGiacomo was sentenced to three concurrent terms of eight to twenty-five years for the kidnapping, rape, and deviate sexual assault, and 364 days, also concurrent, for the battery. . . .

. . . DiGiacomo filed a petition for habeas corpus in the United States District Court for the Northern District of Illinois in which he claimed that the admission of Dillon's testimony regarding the statistical likelihood of the hairs found in Marik's car belonging to him constituted a denial of due process. The district court denied the petition, and this appeal followed.

II

[A] federal court is authorized to issue a writ of habeas corpus in behalf of a person in custody under the judgment of a state court "only on the ground that he is in custody in violation of the Constitution or laws or treaties of the United States." Because the admissibility of evidence in state courts is a matter of state law, evidentiary questions are not subject to federal review . . . unless there is a resultant denial of fundamental fairness or the denial of a specific constitutional right.

In this case, DiGiacomo contends the admission of expert testimony as to the mathematical likelihood of hairs found in Marik's car belonging to him resulted in a denial of fundamental fairness in that it misled the jury into believing that the state had conclusively established that he was in the car. In support of his contention, DiGiacomo cites the Eighth Circuit's decision in United States v. Massey, 594 F.2d 676 (8th Cir. 1979).

In *Massey*, the court held that the trial judge's comments construing expert testimony with respect to comparison of hair samples in terms of mathematical probability of error, coupled with the prosecutor's emphasis upon the mathematical probabilities in his closing argument, constituted plain error . . . and required reversal of the defendant's bank robbery conviction even though no objection had been made at trial. The expert in that case had testified that three of five hairs found in a blue ski mask similar to one worn by one of the perpetrators of the robbery were microscopically similar to the defendant's hair. He was then asked by the trial judge how many people in the country might have similar hair that could not be distinguished. The expert responded that in his own experience there had been only a "couple" cases out of over 2000 in which he had been unable to distinguish hair from two different individuals. He added, however, that according to a recent study, apparently the same study on which Dillon had based her testimony, there was a one in 4500 chance of another person having the same hair. In an attempt to clarify the response, the trial judge asked the witness if this meant there was only a one in 4500 or one in 2000 chance of his identification being wrong. Although the expert's response was somewhat confusing, the prosecutor later emphasized these numbers throughout his closing argument to the jury, concluding with the statement that by itself "the hair sample would be proof beyond a reasonable doubt because it is so convincing."

In reversing the conviction, the Eighth Circuit held that not only had the Government failed to establish a proper foundation for these mathematical conclusions, but in his closing argument the prosecutor had confused the identification of the hair found in the ski cap with the identification of the perpetrator of the crime. Because of this confusion by the prosecutor and the potential for confusion already inherent in such evidence, the court concluded that plain error had been shown.

DiGiacomo contends that his case is even stronger because the record shows more than a mere possibility that the jury was confused. Here, he contends, it is apparent from the written question the jury submitted to the trial court shortly after beginning its deliberations that the jury was in fact confused by the expert testimony. The jury's confusion, which the trial judge's response wholly failed to remedy, he contends, clearly warrants the granting of federal habeas relief.

We agree that the interjection into the criminal trial process of sophisticated theories of mathematical probability raises a number of serious concerns. As one court has aptly stated, "[m]athematics, a veritable sorcerer in our computerized society, while assisting the trier of fact in the search for truth, must not cast a spell over him." People v. Collins, 68 Cal. 2d 319, 320, 66 Cal. Rptr. 497, 438 P.2d 33 (1968). While perhaps the most serious danger in admitting evidence of statistical probability in a criminal trial is the possibility that it will be used improperly, the possibility of prejudice also exists even when it is used in accordance with generally accepted principles. In a case involving the admissibility of virtually the same testimony with which we are faced here, the Supreme Court of Minnesota noted:

> Testimony expressing opinions or conclusions in terms of statistical probabilities can make the uncertain seem all but proven, and suggest, by quantification, satisfaction of the requirement that guilt be established "beyond a reasonable doubt." See Tribe, Trial by Mathematics, 84 Harv. L. Rev. 1329. . . .

State v. Carlson, 267 N.W.2d 170 (Minn. 1978). [T]he court concluded in *Carlson* that an expert's testimony regarding the mathematical probability of certain incriminating hairs belonging to someone other than the defendant was improperly received. The court went on to hold, however, that under the facts of that case the error was harmless.

Even though we share in the concern of these courts that the admission of evidence as to mathematical probability in a criminal trial may mislead and confuse the jury, we do not find on the facts before us that its admission here constituted a denial of due process. Unlike *Massey*, the prosecutor in this case did not suggest in his closing argument that the mathematical odds testified to by the expert witness made her identification of the hair specimen virtually certain. In fact, the prosecutor conceded during argument that "some people have hair like that." Furthermore, the prosecutor in this case did not confuse the issue of whether the hairs found in the car were DiGiacomo's with the issue of whether he in fact committed the crime, although DiGiacomo concedes that in this case the questions are one and the same.

Although it may be true, as the question submitted to the trial court would seem to indicate, that one or more members of the jury were nevertheless confused about the significance of the hair identification testimony, we cannot say that this confusion was caused by any error of constitutional magnitude. Generally, the admission of expert testimony is very much a matter within the broad discretion of the trial judge. The Constitution does not, and indeed, cannot guarantee that only completely reliable evidence will be placed before the jury. Although it does demand that a defendant be given a full and fair opportunity to challenge whatever evidence is admitted, DiGiacomo was afforded that opportunity here. Through his counsel, he was free to challenge Dillon's testimony if it was not true, or clarify it if it was misleading. He was also free to call his own expert if he thought Dillon's testimony was at odds with the established views of the scientific community. DiGiacomo in fact did none of these things. No attempt was made to cross-examine Dillon regarding her testimony that the hairs found in Marik's car belonged to the defendant.

Even now, DiGiacomo does not claim that Dillon was wrong in her conclusion as to the likelihood of the hair found in Marik's car belonging to someone other than him. His contention is only that she should not have been allowed to express that conclusion in terms of mathematical probability. Instead, he contends she should have stated only whether or not the hairs were similar. But to limit her testimony in this way would have robbed the state of the full probative value of its evidence. To say that the defendant's hair is merely similar to hair found in the victim's automobile is significantly different than saying that there's a one in 4500 chance of it belonging to someone else. If the expert's testimony is the latter, we know of no constitutional principle by which its admission could be held improper. While the better practice may be for the court specifically to instruct the jury on the limitations of mathematical probability whenever such evidence is admitted, we have no authority to impose such a rule upon the Illinois courts. Thus, we are unable to say that DiGiacomo's conviction resulted from a denial of any right guaranteed by the Constitution.

Of course, jury confusion by itself, even when not the product of a constitutional violation, could justify the granting of habeas relief if it resulted in a verdict that no rational trier of fact could have reached on the basis of the evidence presented. But DiGiacomo does not argue that no rational trier of fact could have found him guilty and, even if he did, the record does not support such a claim. Marik's positive identification of him as the man who had assaulted her together with the other evidence introduced by the state was more than sufficient to support a rational jury's verdict of guilty.

The district court's judgment denying the petition is affirmed.

State v. Kim
398 N.W.2d 544 (Minn. 1987)

WAHL, JUSTICE.

This appeal questions the standard that governs state appeals of pretrial orders in criminal prosecutions as well as the propriety of the trial court ruling in this case. Joon Kyu Kim is charged with accomplishing sexual penetration by use of force or coercion. . . . At a pretrial hearing, the state proferred scientific evidence in the form of blood test results linking Kim to semen found at the scene of the alleged rape and a statistical analysis of the frequency with which Kim's blood type occurred in the local male population. The trial court ruled that the blood test results and expert testimony that the test results were consistent with Kim having been the source of the semen could be admitted at trial, but ruled that the statistical population frequency evidence was to be excluded. . . .

The facts in this case, as derived from police reports, indicate the complainant reported to police that on December 10, 1984, Joon Kyu Kim, her employer, had forcible, nonconsensual sexual intercourse with her. The complainant and her husband were employed as managers of a St. Paul apartment complex owned by Kim. On the evening of December 10, 1984, the complainant told police she was home alone. She and her husband had quarreled earlier in the evening and he had left the apartment. Her husband told police that after he left the apartment, he went to talk with Kim and they discussed, among other things, his marital problems. About 10 P.M., the complainant reported, Kim showed up at her apartment and began to talk about her marital relationship, telling her she wasn't having enough sex with her husband and that he would show her how. She said Kim then grabbed her breast, but she pulled away and told him to leave. Kim grabbed her again, she told police, forced her into the bedroom and onto the bed. She said she felt very afraid. He removed his clothing and her clothing and then climbed on top of her, she stated, sucking on her breasts and penetrating her vagina with his penis until he ejaculated. She said that as he left, Kim gave her a twenty dollar bill and told her next time it would be thirty dollars. He also told her she wouldn't call the police because she "needed the job too much." The complainant contacted the police shortly after Kim left the apartment.

I. Orientation: Scope and Definition of the Field

At the time the complainant reported the incident, she turned over to police the sheet from the bed where she alleged she had been raped, a pair of panties she was wearing, a sanitary pad, a towel she had used to clean herself, and the twenty dollar bill she alleged Kim had given her. At the hospital, swab samples were taken of fluid present in the complainant's vagina. The Bureau of Criminal Apprehension Laboratory (BCA) found semen present on the bed sheet and on the vaginal swabs.

Kim was questioned by police the next day and denied having had sexual intercourse, consensual or nonconsensual, with the complainant. He admitted he had gone to her apartment that night, but stated he went there to fire her from her job as caretaker. He claimed her accusation was motivated by this firing. He pleaded not guilty to the criminal sexual conduct charges subsequently filed against him.

The trial court, on the state's motion, ordered samples of Kim's blood, saliva and hair taken for purposes of comparing his blood type with the semen found on the bed sheet and in the complainant's body.[1] Comparison samples of blood were also taken from the complainant and from her husband. The samples were tested at the BCA Lab using blood type testing (ABO system) and electrophoresis testing, a procedure that identifies distinctive enzymatic genetic markers present in the blood and bodily fluids. The tests were repeated at the Minneapolis War Memorial Blood Bank and the BCA results were replicated. The BCA Lab analyst was prepared to offer testimony that the semen found in the complainant's body and on the bed sheet was consistent with Kim's blood type and PGM reading.[2] Further, the analyst was prepared to testify that 96.4 percent of males in the Twin Cities metropolitan population, but not Kim, could be excluded on the basis of this combination of blood factors as possible sources of the semen found on the bed sheet.

Kim objected to all of the scientific evidence at the pretrial hearing. As to the statistical population frequency evidence, he argued that its prejudicial impact outweighed its probative value. The trial court excluded the statistical population frequency evidence under the rule of State v. Boyd, 331 N.W.2d 480 (Minn. 1983). This pretrial appeal followed. . . .

[W]e consider first whether the state met its burden of clearly establishing that the trial court's suppression order was erroneous. The court of appeals held that the state did not meet this burden and concluded that the trial court had properly interpreted and applied

---

1. The majority of people, including Kim, secrete their blood type in their body fluids, including semen, saliva, etc.
2. PGM is an enzyme. It is a genetic marker that may be detected in the blood by use of the electrophoresis testing process.

the rule of our decision in *Boyd* to suppress the statistical population frequency evidence. The defendant in *Boyd* was prosecuted for criminal sexual conduct in the third degree for having sexual intercourse with a 14-year-old girl, who became pregnant and gave birth as a result. We held that expert testimony that there was a 99.911 percent likelihood of paternity, based on population frequency statistics applied to interpret blood test results, must be excluded. "[T]here is a real danger," we stated, "that the jury will use the [statistical population frequency] evidence as a measure of the probability of the defendant's guilt or innocence, and that the evidence will thereby undermine the presumption of innocence, erode the values served by the reasonable doubt standard, and dehumanize our system of justice."

The state argues in this appeal that the statistical evidence it seeks to introduce against Kim can be distinguished from that [sic] we disapproved in *Boyd*. The difference between the evidence in *Boyd* — that 99.911 percent of the population, but not the defendant, could be excluded as donors — and the evidence it has proferred in this case — that 3.6 percent of the population, including the defendant, are possible donors — is the difference between inclusion and exclusion. The state contends that when statistics are stated as an exclusion figure, as in *Boyd*, the risk is greater that the jury will interpret the statistical percentage as a statement of the probability of the defendant's guilt. By contrast, when stated as an inclusion figure, the danger of such quantification is urged to be less.

The court of appeals correctly rejected this purported distinction, stating that *Boyd* "do[es] not focus on the nature of the statistics but rather on the impact of the statistics on the trier of fact." The danger we recognized in *Boyd* is that statistics on the frequency with which certain blood type combinations occur in a population will be understood by the jury to be a quantification of the likelihood that the defendant, who shares that unique combination of blood characteristics, is guilty. This danger exists as much in an inclusion as in an exclusion figure because, as the trial court noted, faced with an exclusion percentage, a jury will naturally convert it into an inclusion percentage. Because we cannot meaningfully distinguish the evidence offered in *Boyd* from that in the case now before us, we conclude that *Boyd* controls. We affirm the decision of the court of appeals and hold that the state has not clearly and unequivocally shown that the trial court order suppressing statistical population frequency evidence was erroneous.

The state next argues that if its proferred evidence cannot be distinguished from the evidence we disapproved in *Boyd*, we should modify or overrule *Boyd* but has presented no new or compelling argument. The state argues that the effect of *Boyd* is to exclude from the factfinding process reliable scientific evidence with great probative evidentiary value. The probative value of such evidence is, however, not of controlling significance in the analysis we adopted in *Boyd*. Under the Minnesota Rules of Evidence, relevant evidence may be excluded if its probative value is substantially outweighed by the danger of unfair prejudice. In *Boyd*, we clearly determined that the danger of population frequency statistics used to analyze blood test results unfairly prejudicing a defendant due to its "potentially exaggerated impact on the trier of fact" outweighed any probative value.

Boyd does not foreclose the use of expert interpretations of blood test results.[6] . . . As in *Boyd*, the expert called by the state in this case should not be permitted to express an opinion as to the probability that the semen is Kim's and should not be permitted to get around this by expressing the opinion in terms of the percentage of men in the general population with the same frequency of combinations of blood types. The expert should be permitted to testify, however, as to the basic theory underlying blood testing, to testify that not one of the individual tests excluded Kim as a source of the semen and to give the percentage of people in the general population with each of the individual blood types, and to express an opinion that scientific evidence is consistent with Kim having been the source of the semen. . . .

Affirmed.

KELLEY, JUSTICE (dissenting):

With utmost reluctance, I respectfully dissent. . . . *Carlson* is less than nine years old and *Boyd* is slightly over three. Both decisions were decided by a unanimous court. Normally, desired stability in the law is seldom enhanced by calling into question the correctness of precedents. Especially is that true when the questioned precedents are of such recent vintage. My reluctance to pen this dissent is prompted not only by that laudatory and necessary stare decisis consideration, but additionally because I joined with the remainder of the court in State v. Boyd. However, no violence is done to that laudatory and venerable doctrine of stare decisis when we re-examine a ruling that appears to be clearly wrong; nor is any valid public purpose promoted by embedding in our body of law an incorrect or outmoded decision. Further study and consideration of the issues in those two cases convinces me that both were wrongly decided.

This court in both State v. Carlson and State v. Boyd, and the majority in the instant case, relied upon an article written by Professor

---

6. The concern about the prejudicial effect of blood test evidence expressed in *Boyd* does not apply outside of the context of criminal prosecutions. Blood test results and expert explanations thereof are admissible in evidence, for example, in a paternity proceeding.

Tribe. In my opinion, the conclusions reached by Professor Tribe . . . in 1971 have since been successfully challenged by other researchers. See, e.g., Stripinis, Probability Theory and Circumstantial Evidence: Implications From a Mathematical Analysis, 22 Jurimetrics J. 59, 75-78 (1981); see also Saks and Kidd, Human Information Processing and Adjudication: Trial by Heuristics, 15 Law & Soc'y 123, 124 (1980-1981). Moreover, the assumptions upon which Tribe based his conclusions, in my opinion, have been fairly rebutted by other writers. See, e.g., Saks and Kidd, supra at 124-26, 145-51.

In a criminal case, we are concerned that no conviction shall be upheld unless guilt has been established beyond a reasonable doubt. In any system of criminal justice, a convicted person will necessarily be convicted on something less than absolute proof. Indeed, because in almost every case some doubt does exist, the law uses the expression "beyond a reasonable doubt" instead of "beyond any doubt." Thus, jurors routinely use probabilities in assessing whether the state has met its evidentiary burden. As demonstrated by Stripinis, "[i]f the probability of the accused being innocent is one in one trillion, then most people [jurors] would agree that he is 'guilty beyond a reasonable doubt.'" Thus, he points out the truism that the determination is a quantifiable solution, and that not all jurors will agree on what quantity of doubt constitutes a "reasonable doubt." The question is whether it is preferable to submit to the jury properly established scientific and mathematical probabilities of the existence of a fact to bear on its decision-making process than to ignore reality by asserting people are convicted only when absolute proof is available when, in fact, absolute proof is rarely, if ever, at hand. Therefore, I conclude with Saks and Kidd that "exclusion of mathematical guides to aid a fact finder, while avoiding some problems, exposes the fact-finding process to the heuristic biases of intuitive decision making."

I suggest that . . . the time may now have come for us to reconsider [*Carlson* and *Boyd*]. Just a few years short of the 21st century, perhaps courts should utilize those kinds of empirical, mathematical, scientific and statistical analyses used by all sorts of professional people including those in science, industry, engineering, administration, education and planning. . . . I agree with the Utah court when it said in rejecting our holding in State v. Carlson, "[We do] not share that philosophy, having a higher opinion of the jury's ability to weigh the credibility of such figures when properly presented and challenged." State v. Clayton, 646 P.2d 723, 727 n.1 (Utah 1982); see also E. Cleary, McCormick on Evidence §210, at 655 (3d ed. 1984).

In my view the specific facts of this case demonstrate the shortcomings of excluding empirical scientific evidence. The proffered evidence involves the use of population frequency statistics in conjunction with individualization typing-test results. Based upon *Boyd*, the majority sustains the court's ruling permitting introduction of the test results but excluding the population frequency statistics. I concur with one authority in this general area when he noted:

> [I]nterpretation of individualization typing results is intimately tied to population frequency statistics; without being provided the appropriate statistical information, the triers of fact have no rational basis for deciding the significance of a type-for-type match.

Sensabaugh, Biochemical Markers of Individuality, in Forensic Science Handbook 338, 403 (R. Safenstein ed. 1982). Courts of other jurisdictions addressing the issue are increasingly recognizing the necessity of providing the fact finder with both the test results and the population frequency statistics. See, e.g., Davis v. State, 476 N.E.2d 127, 135-36 (Ind. Ct. App. 1985) (noting that the approach taken by *Carlson* and *Boyd* "has been rejected by an impressive myriad of courts and commentators."); State v. Washington, 229 Kan. 47, 59, 622 P.2d 986, 995 (1981).

I agree. In my view, not to permit this evidence evinces on our part a distrust of both the abilities of the bar to demonstrate any weaknesses in analysis as well as our distrust of the ability of the jury to consider empirical scientific and mathematical statistical evidence with the same discrimination that it has to use, for example, in considering the opinion of a psychiatrist that the accused is insane.

Accordingly, even though with reluctance, I would reverse the trial court and overrule State v. Carlson and State v. Boyd.

NOTES

Communicating Scientific Findings in Court

1. *Hair individualization probabilities.* Dr. Walls' prediction that new "sophisticated statistical mathematics" will yield "precise estimates of probabilities" derived from neutron activation analysis of human hair has yet to be realized. See Cornelis, Truth has Many Facets: The Neutron Activation Analysis Story, 20 J. For. Sci. Socy. 93, 95 (1980); Comment, The Evidentiary Uses of Neutron Activation Analysis, 59 Calif. L. Rev. 997 (1971). The identifications in *DiGiacomo, Massey, Boyd,* and *Carlson,* are based on microscopic comparisons of hair samples. The studies that generated probabilities like the 1/4500 figure are Gaudette & Keeping, An Attempt at Determining Probabilities in Human Scalp Hair Comparison, 19 J. For. Sci. 599 (1974), and Gaudette & Keeping, Probabilities and Human Pubic Hair Comparison, 21 J. For. Sci. 514 (1976). Because the defendants in these

cases did not question the methodology of these studies, the opinions accept such numbers for the probability of a coincidental misidentification. These estimates, however, are easily challenged. Panel on Statistical Assessments as Evidence in the Courts, The Evolving Role of Statistical Assessments as Evidence in the Courts 64-67 (S. Fienberg ed. 1989). Thus, probability assessments for hair identification remain controversial. See Miller, Procedural Bias in Forensic Science Examinations of Human Hair, 11 L. & Human Behavior 157 (1987); Imwinkelried, Forensic Hair Analysis: The Case Against the Underemployment of Scientific Evidence, 39 Wash. & Lee L. Rev. 41 (1982). On the other hand, the probability of chance matches for many immunogenetic markers are, as Walls points out, reasonably well known. See infra at §6.

2. *Posterior probability and reasonable doubt.* Dr. Walls notes that the probability of finding two or more individuals having an incriminating trait out of 100 persons selected at random from a large population in which one out of every five thousand people has this trait is 1/2500. Cf. Finney, Probabilities Based on Circumstantial Evidence, 72 J. Am. Statistical Assn. 316 (1977). He speaks of odds of 2500 to one in favor of guilt because he presupposes that the other nonscientific evidence in the case establishes that there are only 100 individuals who could be guilty.

On the mechanics of the calculation that yields the probability of 1/2500, see, e.g., Fairley & Mosteller, A Conversation About *Collins*, 41 U. Chi. L. Rev. 242 (1974); cf. Lenth, On Identification by Probability, 26 J. For. Sci. Socy. 197 (1986). This reasoning also may be understood as an application of Bayes' rule, a formula that states how new information (like the match in blood types) alters a probability derived from previously available evidence (the prior probability). M. Finkelstein, Quantitative Methods in Law (1978); Ellman & Kaye, Probabilities and Proof: Can HLA and Blood Group Testing Prove Paternity? 54 N.Y.U.L. Rev. 1131 (1979). For a brief overview of the issues associated with this perspective on proof, see Kaye, Introduction: What is Bayesianism? in Inference and Probability in the Law of Evidence: The Limits of Bayesianism 1 (E. Green & P. Tillers eds. 1988).

From the standpoint of Bayesian decision theory, evidence that produces a very large posterior probability amounts to proof "beyond a reasonable doubt," and the minimum value of this probability depends solely on the utilities of the possible outcomes of a correct guilty verdict, a correct acquittal, a false conviction and a false acquittal. See, e.g., Kaye, Apples and Oranges: Confidence Coefficients Versus the Burden of Persuasion, 73 Cornell L. Rev. 54 (1987); Kaplan, Decision Theory and the Factfinding Process, 20 Stan. L. Rev. 1065 (1968). As to what this critical value might be, see, e.g.,

McCauliff, Burdens of Proof: Degrees of Belief, Quanta of Evidence, or Constitutional Guarantees? 35 Vand. L. Rev. 1293, 1325 (1982) (survey of judges).

3. *Virtues and vices of quantification.* Qualitative expressions such as "likely" or "rare" are subject to a broad range of interpretation, even within a single professional group. See Kong, Barnett, Mosteller & Youtz, How Medical Professionals Evaluate Expressions of Probability, 315 New Eng. J. Med. 740 (1986); D. von Winterfeldt & W. Edwards, Decision Analysis and Behavioral Research 98-99 (1986); cf. Morse, Crazy Behavior, Morals and Science: An Analysis of Mental Health Law, 51 S. Cal. L. Rev. 527, 591 (1978). Should forensic scientists be encouraged to make quantitative statements of crucial probabilities? To Dr. Walls the answer is clear: "it would obviously be quite wrong not to be precise instead of vague if the known facts make that possible." Do you agree? The opinions excerpted above reveal that some courts and commentators have serious reservations about "probability evidence." Even so, as the dissent in *Kim* indicates, Minnesota is the only state or federal jurisdiction to exclude categorically apparently well-founded, numerically expressed probabilities and population proportions. See McCormick on Evidence §210 (E. Cleary 3d ed. 1984). The criminal cases and problems associated with testimony as to such numbers are discussed in Kaye, The Admissibility of "Probability Evidence" in Criminal Trials — Part II, 27 Jurimetrics J. 160 (1987).

II. FORENSIC PATHOLOGY AND TOXICOLOGY

Curphey, Role of the Forensic Pathologist in the Medicolegal Certification of Modes of Death*
13 J. For. Sci. 163 (1968)

In a metropolitan community, figures show that 20 to 25 percent of the total deaths are currently reported [to the medical examiner's office]. Deaths from homicide rarely exceed 5 percent of the total coming to the attention of the medicolegal authorities . . . and by and large receive detailed study by the criminal investigator and the pathologist, the toxicologist, and the district attorney, as well as the medical examiner.

The importance of a complete and accurate investigation of a homicide by the forensic pathologist stands without question and must

---
* Copyright ASTM. Reprinted with permission.

always carry a high priority in the workload of any active medicolegal office. When one considers, however, that some officers see about 10 percent of their caseloads as suicides, 25 percent as accidents of all kinds, about 60 percent as natural deaths, and up to 5 percent as homicides, the forensic pathologist . . . must find some means of rendering equally good service in the study of all the types of cases he sees. . . .

Unfortunately, this is not the guiding principle in many of our offices, where the medical personnel, as well as the laboratory and clerical organization are geared to serve the high priority case of homicide at the distinct expense of the nonhomicide case. . . .

[W]hile sudden death resulting from accident, suicide, or homicide is almost invariably reported to the medical examiner, many delayed deaths of one type or another are certified by the physician and accepted for registration by the Health Department. . . . By so doing, in many instances they unwittingly deny the family their legal access to certain economic indemnities. . . . This is especially true in delayed deaths related to trauma and also in industrial or occupational hazards where the terminal stage of the disease arises directly from the hazard and is associated, for example, with certain blood dyscrasias such as aplastic anemia, or to pulmonary disease of a chronic inflammatory or neoplastic nature, or to disease of the genitourinary tract, or to hepatorenal involvement.

In such instances the physician certifying the death frequently fails to recognize the probable causal relationship and thus does not report it to the medical examiner, with the result that the economic interests of the family are either seriously impaired or totally denied because of the lack of supporting pathological evidence derived from the autopsy studies, if indeed, the case ever reaches the stage of adjudication. Added to this is vitiation of the vital statistics as to the mortality rate from the particular industrial or occupational hazard in the community, which in turn denies the Health Department the opportunity to institute preventive measures to combat the hazard. . . .

Turning now to the methods of investigation . . . , the current practice is [a multidisciplinary] approach in which the skills of the law enforcement officer, the pathologist, and the toxicologist are those most generally involved. . . .

There is, however, a group of cases of growing importance and size . . . where suicide is suspected [and where] the need arises for the behavioral scientist to become involved. . . .

[The pathologist] is frequently all too willing to . . . venture into the area of certification of the mode [rather than the cause of death] when he has little if any knowledge of human behavior vital to being able to evaluate, with any fair degree of accuracy, the mental processes of the victim that were likely to lead to a suicidal death. . . .

Perhaps the consequence of this attitude is best illustrated by a [1965] survey of the reporting of modes of death, specifically from barbituate intoxication, by 19 of the larger medicolegal offices in the nation. . . . [This survey suggests that] only five offices are properly certifying their cases of suicide, two offices their undetermined cases, and three offices their accidental deaths. . . .

NOTES

Medicolegal Death Examinations

1. *Dimensions of forensic pathology.* Dr. Curphey's paper depicts the responsibilities of the forensic pathologist and toxicologist working together in a coroner's office or the office of a chief medical examiner. Additional descriptions of the work of forensic pathologists, written especially for attorneys, include P. Giannelli & E. Imwinkelried, Scientific Evidence 679-755 (1986); Wecht, Forensic Pathology for Trial Lawyers, in Scientific and Expert Evidence 1141 (E. Imwinkelried 2d ed. 1981); Bucklin, Forensic Pathology, in Scientific and Expert Evidence 1165 (E. Imwinkelried 2d ed. 1981); Devlin, The Autopsy in Criminal Cases, in Scientific and Expert Testimony 1205 (E. Imwinkelried 2d ed. 1981). See also C. Wetli, R. Mittleman & V. Rao, Practical Forensic Pathology (1988).

Murder investigation may be the most glamorous aspect of the work, but, as Curphey emphasizes, it is merely one of many important and challenging types of investigation. See, e.g., Paul, The General Principles of Clinical Forensic Medicine and the Place of Forensic Medicine in a Modern Society, 50 Yale J. Biological Med. 405 (1977); Symposium on the Adversary System and the Role of the Forensic Scientist: "Scientific Truth" vs. "Legal Truth," 18 J. For. Sci. 173 (1973).

2. *Importance of autopsies.* The value of autopsies to accurate determinations of the causes of death has been well documented, for instance, Asnaes & Paaskeail, Uncertainty of Determining Mode of Death in Medicolegal Material Without Autopsy — A Systematic Autopsy Study, 15 For. Sci. Intl. 3 (1980); Asnaes & Paaske, The Significance of Medicolegal Autopsy in Determining Mode and Cause of Death, 14 For. Sci. Intl. 23 (1979), and the need for specialized training in forensic, as opposed to general pathology, has been noted. Eckert, The Forensic or Medicolegal Autopsy: Friend or Foe?, 9 Am. J. For. Med. & Pathology 185 (1988). The assassination of President John F. Kennedy is a glaring example of how critical an accurate and complete autopsy report can be to a medicolegal investigation. The forensic pathologists' failure to make a complete report contributed to the lingering controversy and speculation over the exact cause of the president's death. See, for instance, Wecht, A Critique of the

Medical Aspects of the Investigation into the Assassination of President Kennedy, 11 J. For. Sci. 300 (1966). For a stark comparison of postmortem protocols that illustrates the importance of the procedure, see Noguchi, Postmortem Protocols in Official Medical-Legal Investigation — A Study in Contrast (Autopsy Reports in the Assassination Deaths of President John F. Kennedy and Senator Robert F. Kennedy), 1973 Leg. Med. Ann. 21.

In addition to their obvious significance to the criminal justice system and the payment of insurance benefits, accurate determinations of death are important to the public health system. Rosenberg, Davidson, Smith et al., Operational Criteria for the Determination of Suicide, 33 J. For. Sci. 1445, 1446 (1988) ("Although the accuracy of one single [death] certificate may not appear important, collectively the enormous number of death certificates filed becomes the primary data source for mortality statistics in the United States. These data in turn affect the course of health care research, the flow of resources, and, ultimately, public health policy."); Lilienfeld, Changing Research Methods in Environmental Epidemiology, 3 Statistical Sci. 275, 277 (1988).

3. *Limits of expertise.* The opinions rendered by forensic pathologists on the cause of death can hardly be based *exclusively* on what they see or find on the autopsy table. But when they rely on facts equally accessible to the lay person, does there come a point at which they exceed the area of their expertise? Consider the following opinion rendered by Dr. Milton Helpern, then chief medical examiner for the city of New York, in a notorious case involving a mother accused of murdering her children:

> "Would you say, Dr. Helpern, that the little boy died a natural death?"
>
> This was the first time this question had been asked in public. Now, I had no evidence of a direct nature to answer that — the body was a mass of corruption and could give no clues, except to exclude massive violence to bones and tissues like an extensive fracture or gunshot wound.
>
> But I was a medical examiner, and my job was to assess deaths by a full consideration of what I knew about the whole case history. To focus narrowly on the autopsy table, like a horse with blinkers, would be pedantic and foolish. If you are searching the horizon, you don't look down the end of a fixed telescope. He asked me "Did he die a natural death?" and I knew as the whole of New York and half the United States knew, that little Eddie had been in perfect health the night before he vanished. I knew that he had been found a mile or more from his home, hidden under scrub on a waste lot. I knew his sister had vanished at the same time and had been found strangled. So what possible reason could I — or anyone else in my position — have for evading the issue. The boy had not died a natural death!

"I would not say that," I told Nicolosi, "and I base my opinion on the classification of the death, the circumstances of the death of the sister, the findings, and so on. It is a conclusion about the manner of death derived from knowledge of the circumstances of the case and of the cause of death of the sister. I would say, in my opinion, that this was not a natural death."

M. Helpern, Autopsy: The Memoirs of Milton Helpern, the World's Greatest Medical Detective 137 (1977).

Was this testimony based on expertise in forensic pathology? Was it an expert opinion that would, in the words of Federal Rule of Evidence 702, "assist the trier of fact to understand the evidence or to determine a fact in issue"? See Steinbock, Richman & Ray, Expert Testimony on Proximate Cause, 41 Vand. L. Rev. 261 (1988); Wagenaar, The Proper Seat: A Bayesian Discussion of the Position of Expert Witnesses, 12 L. & Human Behavior 499 (1988).

4. *"Psychological autopsies."* Dr. Curphey's paper stresses the need for psychological stress and suicide investigation in many cases. See also J. Selkin, The Psychological Autopsy in the Courtroom (1987); Litman, Psycho-Legal Aspects of Suicide, in Modern Legal Medicine, Psychiatry and Forensic Science 841 (W. Curran, A. McGarry & C. Petty eds. 1980); Litman, Psychological-Psychiatric Aspects of Certifying Modes of Death, 13 J. For. Sci. 46 (1968); Murphy et al., On the Improvement of Suicide Determination, 19 J. For. Sci. 276 (1974); Vorkoper & Petty, Suicide Investigation, in Modern Legal Medicine, Psychiatry and Forensic Science 171 (W. Curran, A. McGarry & C. Petty eds. 1980).

The "psychological autopsy" technique "involves interviewing family members and reviewing records — generally employment records, school records and psychiatric notes. Its purpose is to determine the probable cause of death or the person's state of mind at the time of the death." Harvey v. Raleigh Police Department, 85 N.C. App. 540, 541, 355 S.E.2d 147, 148 (1987). "[B]y reconstructing the decedent's final days behavior and communication in addition to history, personal habits, personality traits and character, [b]ehavioral science investigators develop a psychological profile through interviews with family, friends, co-workers, physicians and others. . . ." Jobes, Berman & Josselson, The Impact of Psychological Autopsies on Medical Examiners' Determination of Manner of Death, 31 J. For. Sci. 177, 178 (1986) (concluding that such investigations provide significant information in cases of equivocal deaths).

On the admissibility of these "psychological autopsies," compare Harvey (opinion of expert in "psychiatry, suicidology and police stress" who had conducted "hundreds of psychological autopsies" admissible in workers' compensation proceeding to show that depression attributable to work-related stress caused police officer's suicide) with

Thompson v. Mayes, 707 S.W.2d 951 (Tex. Civ. App. 1986) (opinion of psychologist who had conducted "psychological autopsy" of suicide victim on whether the deceased had killed his father, who had disappeared two years earlier, properly excluded). On other psychiatric aspects of homicide investigation, see Keil, The Psychiatric Character of the Assailant as Determined by Autopsy Observations of the Victim, 10 J. For. Sci. 263 (1965).

5. *References.* General texts that discuss forensic pathology and toxicology include Modern Legal Medicine, Psychiatry and Forensic Science (W. Curran, A. McGarry & C. Petty eds. 1980); Forensic Medicine: A Study in Trauma and Environmental Hazards (C. Tedeschi, W. Eckert & L. Tedeschi eds. 1977); Adelson, the Pathology of Homicide (1974); Medicolegal Investigation of Death: Guidelines for the Application of Pathology to Crime Investigation (W. Spitz & R. Fisher eds. 1973). Some of the leading British texts are Glaister's Medical Jurisprudence and Toxicology (E. Rentoul & H. Smith 13th ed. 1973); Gradwohl's Legal Medicine (Camps 3d ed. 1976); C. Polson, D. Gee & B. Knight, The Essentials of Forensic Medicine (4th ed. 1985); K. Simpson, Forensic Medicine (9th ed. 1985); Taylor's Principles and Practice of Medical Jurisprudence (A. Mant 13th ed. 1984). Many of the journals cited supra at §1 include valuable articles and reviews of new texts.

People v. Yoho
517 N.E.2d 329 (Ill. App. 1987)

JUSTICE HOPF delivered the opinion of the court:

Defendant, Carroll Yoho, and his brother, Darrell, were charged in Winnebago County with the crime of murder. The brothers were tried jointly before a jury which returned a verdict finding defendant guilty of voluntary manslaughter and not guilty of murder. Darrell Yoho was exonerated of all charges. . . .

In this court, defendant contends . . . that he was denied his right to a fair trial when the trial court allowed an autopsy photograph depicting the decedent's exposed heart within his chest cavity to be submitted to the jury for its deliberation. . . .

In the early hours of November 23, 1985, an altercation occurred between the Yoho brothers and the victim, Ron Gibson, at a tavern. . . . Several witnesses for the prosecution related seeing the altercation between the two Yohos and Ron Gibson. [They testified to the effect that in the parking lot outside the tavern Darrell beat Gibson with a cane and that defendant stabbed him repeatedly in the chest and back, while Gibson, who was unarmed, merely tried to block these blows.]

II. Forensic Pathology and Toxicology

Dr. Larry Blum, who performed the autopsy on the decedent, also testified for the State. Dr. Blum found knife wounds in the chest, in the bladder above the genitals, on the left side of the back, near the shoulder, in the left upper chest, over the left hip, on the scalp in the left parietal area, and on the penis. In addition to the knife wounds, Blum found multiple abrasions and contusions on Gibson's body as well as blunt trauma wounds. Blum described in detail the stab wound in Gibson's upper chest which punctured his heart. Blum also identified People's exhibit No. 11 as being a photograph of the internal organs of the chest, specifically showing the heart and the stab wound present in the right ventricle of the heart.

[Testimony from defense witnesses indicated that Gibson was a violent person who had provoked and threatened defendant in the tavern, then attacked him in the parking lot.]

Defendant's witness Dr. William Rouse, a general and forensic pathologist, gave an opinion as to the ability of the heart to self-seal itself upon being punctured. He also testified as to the length of time a person could continue activity depending upon the size of the hole made in the person's heart. Rouse described the hole in Gibson's heart as portrayed in People's exhibit No. 11, an autopsy photograph depicting the exposed heart within the chest cavity, to be a middle-sized wound and surmised its size three-fourths of an inch long and about one-eighth of an inch wide. Rouse estimated that a person with a wound of that size could continue functioning for a period of time as short as a minute and as long as 7 to 10 minutes. In Rouse's opinion, an individual with a wound of this size would be able to continue fighting if he had already been fighting. The doctor also opined that the wound displayed in the photograph of the heart in People's exhibit No. 11 could continue to pump some blood throughout the victim's system while he continued acting.

The court permitted People's exhibit No. 11 to go to the jury over the specific objection of counsel for the defendant. Defendant contends on appeal that permitting People's exhibit No. 11 to go to the jury for its deliberations was prejudicial and denied defendant a fair trial. At trial defendant did not contest the fact that he stabbed the decedent since his theory of defense was self-defense. Defendant maintains that, when a defendant admits to an offense, gruesome photographs of a victim are rarely admissible since they are not probative of any material fact. See People v. Lefler (1967), 38 Ill. 2d 216, 221-22, 230 N.E.2d 827 (court erred in permitting autopsy photo showing an infant's chest cavity after the breastbone portion of the ribs, lungs, heart and main blood vessels had been removed and showing the skull and portions of the brain after an area of the skull had been removed to be projected on a 44- × 26-inch screen); People v. Garlick (1977), 46 Ill. App. 3d 216, 224, 4 Ill. Dec. 746,

360 N.E.2d 1121 (court erred in allowing a gruesome, color photograph of the deceased's massive head wound).

As a physician testified concerning the stab wounds and the undisputed cause of death, defendant argues that the autopsy picture had no probative value and no purpose "other than to horrify the jurors and arouse their emotions against the defendant." [D]efendant contends that the law is adamant that a photograph of a decedent taken after autopsy is not admissible. We do not agree.

It is the function of the trial court to weigh the probative value of evidence and its potential prejudicial effect. Mindful of the prejudice that might be aroused by the introduction of a victim's photograph, courts have been strict in their requirement that a proper purpose be shown for the introduction of such an exhibit. The decision, however, of what shall be taken into the jury room rests within the sound discretion of the trial court and will not be disturbed absent a showing of prejudicial abuse.

Photographic evidence having a natural tendency to establish the facts in controversy is admissible, and it is not an abuse of discretion to allow a jury to consider photographs depicted as disgusting or gruesome. The photograph in question was a color photo roughly $3\frac{1}{2} \times 5$ inches, depicting a close-up view of the heart and its wound within what appears to be the chest cavity. It does not show the body generally, and, but for the presence of the heart and its stab wound, one would not be able to determine what exactly it represented. Thus, People's exhibit No. 11 was not of the gruesome nature as those areas displayed in the blown-up photographs in *Lefler*. Moreover, we are of the opinion that the photograph in the instant case would have materially assisted the jury in understanding both Dr. Blum's and Dr. Rouse's testimony describing the wound to the heart and the result thereof. When taken in conjunction with an evaluation of all the photographs admitted, People's exhibit No. 11 would have materially gone to a fact in controversy, i.e., defendant's claim of self-defense. Hence, the photograph's relevance outweighed any prejudice. Further, based on the record before us and the overwhelming evidence of defendant's guilt in comparison to the nature of this one contested exhibit, we can say beyond a reasonable doubt that the photograph did not contribute to the verdict of guilty and that, therefore, any error in its admission would be harmless. . . .

Affirmed.

NOTES

Bringing the Autopsy into the Courtroom

1. *Pictures of crime scenes and autopsies.* Gruesome photographs of the victims of violent crimes are common grist for the prosecutor's

II. Forensic Pathology and Toxicology

mill. The standard for the admissibility of this type of evidence is codified in Rules 402 and 403 of the federal and uniform rules of evidence, which provide that relevant evidence is admissible unless its prejudicial effect substantially outweighs its probative value. See generally McCormick on Evidence §185 (E. Cleary 3d ed. 1984). Pictures taken at the scene of the crime typically are admitted, as in *Yoho*, as long as they have some value in illustrating a pathologist's testimony as to the cause or circumstances of death. See, for instance, People v. Fierer, 151 Ill. App. 3d 649, 104 Ill. Dec. 879, 503 N.E.2d 594 (1987) (25 color photographs depicting the defendant's ex-wife as she was found with 27 stab wounds).

In Kealohapauole v. Shimoda, 800 F.2d 1463 (9th Cir. 1986), the Court of Appeals held that the due process clause was not offended when a 45-minute black and white videotape of an autopsy of a badly decomposed body found in a sugar cane field in Hawaii was shown in murder prosecution, and where:

> One of the two pathologists in the case, Dr. Woo, testified that the videotape recording was the best type of available evidence to aid in explaining his testimony to the jury that the cause of the victim's death was a blow to the head with a blunt instrument. Dr. Woo stated that the videotape best illustrated the discoloration and fracture of the victim's skull, which led to Dr. Woo's conclusion that trauma in the skull had occurred as the result of a blow to the head with a blunt instrument. Although the skull was introduced into evidence, the videotape better illustrated the discoloration as Dr. Woo stated that the stain on the skull had faded significantly since the autopsy. Dr. Woo also testified that the videotape would demonstrate the thoroughness of the pathologist's examination of the victim.

The Court of Appeals, which viewed the tape, described it as:

> in most part clinical in nature and is much clearer than the photographs introduced in evidence in showing the injury to the skull which is relied upon heavily by the pathologists in determining the cause of death. The videotape was taken in what appears to be an autopsy room, not at the scene of the crime. The autopsy procedure does not in itself cause the viewer to associate the process being watched in any way with the defendant, the scene of the crime, or the graphics of the murder. The videotape is unpleasant but not inflammatory. The portion of the videotape showing the pathologist inspecting the skull is of great probative value as it shows more clearly than the photos or the dried skull, the pathology relied upon by the doctors in making their determination of the cause of death.

The court noted also that the accused "refused to stipulate" that the death resulted from blows to the head with a blunt instrument. Would such a stipulation have led to a different result? Even if a defendant is willing to stipulate to the cause of death, the government may be allowed to introduce its more graphic and realistic proof of the event. Cf. United States v. Grassi, 602 F.2d 1192 (5th Cir. 1979), *vacated and remanded on other grounds*, 448 U.S. 902 (1980). As one state supreme court justice explained:

> Defendants — and it is their right to try — want to keep as much grisly evidence from the jury as possible so that they can disassociate themselves from those black moments when their inhumanity surfaced and deliberately caused the death of another person. A sterile courtroom scene, removed as far as possible from the facts of the killing is what they seek. However, the state has a right to try its case and to recreate the crime as it was committed. . . .

Berry v. State, 290 Ark. 238, 718 S.W.2d 447, 455 (1986) (Hickman, J., dissenting).

The *Kealohapauole* court suggested that a videotaped autopsy may be less troublesome than gruesome pictures of a crime scene, since "[t]he autopsy procedure does not in itself cause the viewer to associate the process being watched in any way with the defendant, the scene of the crime, or the graphics of the murder." Cf. Coleman v. Commonwealth, 307 S.E.2d 864, 873-874 (Va. 1983) ("an autopsy photograph by its very nature is more clinically objective and less bloody than one taken at the scene of a violent crime.").

Generally, however, the courts are more likely to balk at the admission of photographs taken during the autopsy than those of the scene. In State v. Poe, 21 Utah 2d 113, 441 P.2d 512 (1968), for instance, the defendant was convicted of murder and sentenced to die after the state used a series of color slides of an autopsy. According to the majority, to describe these slides as gruesome "would be a gross understatement. One of them, for example, depicted the deceased's head, showing the base of the skull after the skull cap and brain had been removed by the pathologist. The skin is peeled over the edge of the skull showing the empty brain cavity." Id. at 514. The court reasoned that these slides "had no probative value" because "the identity of the deceased, his death and its cause had already been established" by photographs showing the victim as he was found lying in his bed with bullet holes in his head. Opinions in other jurisdictions maintain that autopsic photographs must be "necessary" or "essential" to the state's case. E.g., Berry v. State, 290 Ark. 223, 718 S.W.2d 447, 452 (1986); People v. Fierer, 151 Ill. App. 3d 649, 104 Ill. Dec. 879, 503 N.E.2d 594 (1987); State v. Clawson, 270 S.E.2d 659, 672 (W.Va. 1980).

2. *Three problems.* Applying the principles outlined above, how should a trial court rule in the following cases:

(1) Kuntzelman is alleged to have shot and killed Wilson with a

II. Forensic Pathology and Toxicology 91

.12 gauge shotgun. Eyewitnesses have testified that Wilson died as the result of the gunshot wound inflicted by Kuntzelman. Kuntzelman does not contest the cause of death, and the major issue to be decided by the jury is whether Kuntzelman intended to shoot Wilson or merely fire over his head to scare him.

The prosecution calls as a witness the pathologist who performed the autopsy on Wilson and questions him extensively on the nature of the wound and its relation to Wilson's death. In connection with this testimony, the prosecution offers into evidence six color photographs of Wilson's body and of his organs at various stages of the autopsy. One photograph depicts the open chest cavity and internal organs of Wilson's body, and another depicts Wilson's left lung placed on a slab or table. Kuntzelman objects that these two photographs are inflammatory. See State v. Kuntzelman, 215 Neb. 115, 337 N.W.2d 414 (1983); Kuntzelman v. Black, 774 F.2d 291 (8th Cir. 1985).

(2) Bowers is charged with cruelty to a child in violation of a Georgia child abuse statute. She arrived at the home of a neighbor one morning, saying that her two-year-old daughter, Kimberly, might be dead. She said that she had struck Kimberly for wetting her pants, and that the child had fallen into an empty bathtub. The two women immediately took Kimberly to a nearby hospital. Kimberly was dead on arrival. A pathologist performed an autopsy that disclosed bruises on Kimberly's scalp, face, chest, back, and right lung; a scar on the inside of the lower lip; a fracture of the left side of her skull; a broken collar bone; a small tear in the liver; and a lacerated heart, which he determined to have caused the death. Although Bowers is willing to stipulate that the injury to the heart was the cause of death, the government proffers a color photograph of the child's lacerated heart. Bowers objects. See United States v. Bowers, 660 F.2d 527 (5th Cir. 1981).

(3) Berry is accused of capital felony murder in connection with the brutal beating of her great-aunt, Nancy Sangalli. After plea bargaining, her boyfriend testifies that he and Berry went to Sangalli's home to knock her unconscious and to steal money to finance an escape from the country. He testifies further that he struck Sangalli from behind with a crowbar taken from Berry's house, but that she did not lose consciousness. When Sangalli tried to escape, he pulled her to the floor and began hitting her. He says that Berry came in as he dragged Sangalli away. The prosecution proffers nine photographs showing the trail of blood where Sangalli was dragged, her body in a pool of blood at the scene, closeup autopsy photographs of her face, a picture of the side of the head with the hair shaved to expose the injuries, and a closeup of her shattered teeth which the medical examiner removed from her mouth. Berry objects to the admission of all these color photographs, pointing out that she never

touched the victim and that she does not contest the brutality of the murder, the cause of death, or the identity of the killer. Her defense is that she was not aware of her boyfriend's intentions until she entered her aunt's house and that she fled the jurisdiction with him because he threatened to kill her. See Berry v. State, 718 S.W.2d 447 (Ark. 1986).

III. CORONERS AND MEDICAL EXAMINERS

O. Schultz & E. Morgan, The Coroner and the Medical Examiner
7-11 (National Research Council 1928)

If there is virtue in antiquity, the coroner's office must have it. . . . It is probable that the office originated in the reign of Henry I; it is certain that it existed in 1194, and books and records show clearly that it was an office of great importance. . . .

The duties of the American coroner are not so varied as those of his medieval predecessor. [H]is chief work has to do with deaths occurring under unusual circumstances. . . .

His most important medical duty is the investigation of deaths in which an element of violence may be suspected. To such deaths have been added, by custom or specific legal enactment, those due to accident, suicide or septicemia from undetermined causes; deaths of persons who have not been attended by a duly licensed practitioner of medicine; and in certain localities deaths in which the cause, as certified by the physician, does not appear clear, the investigation in such cases being for the purpose of obtaining more accurate vital statistics. . . .

[T]he American system usually gives the coroner the assistance of a jury, and sometimes allows him to call in scientific experts. . . .

[A]s a court the coroner must decide not only the cause of death but also what person, if anybody, is responsible for it. And that is not all. As a magistrate he is to initiate steps for the apprehension of any accused. In short, he is expected to perform all these most vitally important functions of a bureau of criminal investigation up to and including the identification of the person causing the death.

Well, why not? Some office of government must perform these functions. And why not the ancient and honorable office of coroner, modernized and modernly equipped? . . . On the other hand, visualize the coroner as a poorly paid, untrained and unskilled individual, popularly elected to an obscure office for a short term, with a small staff of mediocre ability, and with inadequate equipment. . . .

III. Coroners and Medical Examiners

Model Post-Mortem Examinations Act
Handbook of the National Conference of Commissioners
on Uniform State Laws 196-202 (1954)

Preface

The purpose of the Model Post-Mortem Examinations Act is to provide a means whereby greater competence can be assured in determining causes of death where criminal liability may be involved. Experience has shown that many elected coroners are not well trained in the field of pathology, and the Act would set up in each state an Office headed by a trained pathologist, this Office to have jurisdiction over post-mortem examinations for criminal purposes. The office would in general supercede the authority of Coroner's Offices in this field.

The proposed Post-Mortem Examination Office would be controlled by an honorary commission of disinterested persons aware of the problems involved. It would be under a duty to cooperate with all law enforcement agencies in the state, to set up regional and local offices as needed, and to develop a suitable laboratory as well as to make use of other laboratories already in existence. . . .

Section 1. (Commission on Post-Mortem Examinations.)

The Commission on Post-Mortem Examinations is hereby established. The members of the Commission shall be the (Attorney General), the (Superintendent of State Police), the (State Commissioner of Public Health), the (Dean of the Medical School of the State University) (or other university), and the (Dean of the Law School of the State University) (or other university). . . .

Section 2. (Office of Post-Mortem Examinations.)

The Office of Post-Mortem Examinations is hereby established, to be operated under the control and supervision of the Commission. The Office shall be directed by a Chief Medical Examiner, and may employ such assistant medical examiners, pathologists, toxicologists laboratory technicians, regional medical examiners and other staff members. . . .

Section 3. (Chief Medical Examiner.)

The Chief Medical Examiner shall be a citizen of the United States and a physician licensed in this (or another) state who has had a minimum of two years post-graduate training in pathology. He shall be named by the Commission to serve for such term and at such salary as the (Commission) (General Assembly) may fix. . . .

Section 4. (Deaths to be Investigated.)

The Office of Post-Mortem Examinations shall investigate all human deaths of the types listed herewith:

(a) Violent deaths, whether apparently homicidal, suicidal, or accidental, involving but not limited to deaths due to thermal, chemical, electrical or radiation injury, and deaths due to criminal abortion. . . ;

(b) Sudden deaths not caused by readily recognizable disease;

(c) Deaths under suspicious circumstances;

(d) Deaths of persons whose bodies are to be cremated, dissected, buried at sea, or otherwise disposed of so as to be thereafter unavailable for examination;

(e) Deaths of inmates of public institutions not hospitalized therein for organic disease;

(f) Deaths related to disease resulting from employment or to accident while employed;

((g) Deaths related to disease which might constitute a threat to public health.)

Section 5. (Autopsies.)

Autopsies shall be conducted by the Office of Post-Mortem Examinations in cases in which, in the judgment of the Chief Medical Examiner, the public interest requires an autopsy, and in such cases an autopsy is hereby authorized. In determining whether the public interest requires an autopsy the Chief Medical Examiner shall take into account but shall not be bound by requests therefor from private persons or from public officials, except that the Prosecuting Attorney of the affected (district) (county) shall have the right to require an autopsy.

Section 6. (Cooperative Action.)

(a) All law enforcement officers and other officials shall cooperate fully with the Office of Post-Mortem Examinations in making the investigations and conducting the autopsies herein provided for. Such officials and all physicians, undertakers, embalmers and other persons shall promptly notify the Office of the occurrence of all deaths coming to their attention which under this Act are subject to investigation by the Office. . . .

(b) Any physician, undertaker or embalmer who wilfully fails to comply with this section shall be guilty of a misdemeanor. . . .

Section 7. (Laboratories.)

The Office of Post-Medical Examiner shall maintain a laboratory or laboratories. . . .

III. Coroners and Medical Examiners

Section 8. *(Rules and Regulations.)*

The Commission may promulgate rules and regulations necessary or appropriate to carry out effectively the provisions of this act.

Section 9. *(Records and Reports.)*

The Office of Post-Mortem Examinations shall keep full and complete records, properly indexed, giving the name, if known, of every person whose death is investigated, the place where the body was found, the date, cause and manner of death, and all other relevant information concerning the death, and shall issue a death certificate. The full report and detailed findings of the autopsy, if any, shall be a part of the record in each case. The Office shall promptly deliver to the (prosecuting attorney) of each (county) (district) having criminal jurisdiction over the case copies of all records relating to every death as to which further investigation may be advisable. Any (prosecuting attorney), (sheriff), (chief of police) or (enumerate other law enforcement officials) may upon request secure copies of such records or other information deemed necessary by him to the performance of his official duties. Private persons may obtain copies of such records upon such conditions and payment of such fees as may be prescribed by the Commission, provided no person with a legitimate interest therein shall be denied access thereto.

Section 10. *(Records as Evidence.)*

The records of the Office of Post-Mortem Examinations, or transcripts thereof certified by the Chief Medical Examiner, are admissible in evidence in any court of this state, except that statements by witnesses or other persons and conclusions upon extraneous matters are not hereby made admissible. The person preparing a report or record given in evidence hereunder may be subpoenaed as a witness, in any civil or criminal case, by any party to the cause.

Section 11. *(Alternative Sections.)*

(A) Section 11. (Coroners.)

The office of coroner is abolished. The duties of the coroner's office covered by this Act are transferred to the Office of Post-Mortem Examinations, and all other duties of the office are transferred to (fill in to fit the local situation).

(B) Section 11. (Duties of Coroners.)

The duties of the coroner's office covered by this Act are transferred to the Office of Post-Mortem Examinations. The coroners shall hereafter perform such duties as may be assigned to them under the rules and regulations promulgated by the Commission on Post-Mortem Examinations.

NOTE

Coroner or Medical Examiner?

The "corruption and neglect," as well as the obstacles to meaningful reform, of the English institution of the coroner are described in such works as T. Forbes, Surgeons at the Bailey: English Forensic Medicine to 1878 11-15 (1985). In this country, the 1928 National Research Council report quoted above contrasted the operation of medical examiner's programs with coroner's offices. It found that:

> The comparison is so greatly to the advantage of the medical examiner system that it is surprising that the latter, which has been in vogue in Massachusetts since 1877, has not been more generally adopted in this country. The explanation probably is that the coroner is part of a well established political scheme and the entire subject of forensic medicine is so highly technical that the layman has no proper conception of its importance. The fact that in most states the coroner's is a constitutional office, rendering it difficult to make statutory changes without making amendments to the constitution, may also be an important factor in maintaining the public inertia which prevents the replacement of an obviously bad system by a demonstrably good one.

O. T. Schultz & E. M. Morgan, The Coroner and the Medical Examiner 49 (1928).

The Model Post-Mortem Examinations Act of 1954, most of which is presented above, is a blueprint for placing the medical duties of the coroner in a medically qualified individual, and many states adopted such state- or county-wide programs. However, the enabling legislation does vary among jurisdictions. The cases that follow illustrate some of the medicolegal issues that arise in establishing or operating these programs.

State v. Chambers
477 A.2d 110 (Vt. 1984)

HILL, JUSTICE.

The defendant appeals his conviction for burying the dead body of his daughter without a burial permit, in violation of 18 V.S.A. §5211. We affirm.

The defendant's daughter, Hanna, died during the course of her

III. Coroners and Medical Examiners 97

home birth at a house in Island Pond shared by the defendant and other members of his religious community, the Northeast Kingdom Community Church. Shortly after Hanna's death, a member of the church contacted the regional medical examiner and requested a death certificate for the child. After briefly examining the baby, the examiner was unable to determine the cause of death and therefore refused to sign a death certificate. Instead, the examiner informed the state's attorney and the chief medical examiner, who decided that an autopsy should be performed. The defendant refused to allow an autopsy claiming that his religious beliefs forbade the performance of an autopsy on his child. As a result of this refusal, the defendant was unable to obtain a death certificate, which is a prerequisite for obtaining a burial permit. The defendant buried his daughter without the burial permit, in violation of 18 V.S.A. §5211.

On appeal, the defendant . . . claims: (1) his conviction, resulting from his religiously based refusal to permit an autopsy, violated his right to the free exercise of his religion protected by the First Amendment of the United States Constitution and . . . the Vermont Constitution; (2) 18 V.S.A. §5205(f), which allows the state's attorney or chief medical examiner to order autopsies, is unconstitutional because it does not contain adequate standards to guide these officials' discretion. . . .

I

We first address the defendant's argument that his conviction violated his right to the free exercise of his religion. In Wisconsin v. Yoder, 406 U.S. 205 (1972), the United States Supreme Court decided that a state may impinge upon the practice of a sincere religious belief only if the state's interest is of "sufficient magnitude to override the interest claiming protection under the Free Exercise Clause." However, before determining the importance of the state's interest, the party claiming a violation of his or her free exercise rights must show that the conduct the state is interfering with is based on a legitimate religious belief and not on "purely secular considerations." The Court pointed out that "the very concept of ordered liberty precludes allowing every person to make his [or her] own standards on matters of conduct in which society as a whole has important interests." Conduct based on "subjective evaluation and rejection of the contemporary secular values accepted by the majority . . . [has a] philosophical and personal rather than religious [basis] . . . and . . . does not rise to the demands of the Religion Clauses."

The evidence in this case does not support the defendant's claim that his conduct "is not merely a matter of personal preference, but one of deep religious conviction, shared by an organized group. . . ."

The defendant has failed to show that his church believes in the practice of burying the dead without autopsies. The record shows that the tenets of the defendant's church do not prohibit the performance of autopsies. Rather, the defendant claims only that he was opposed to this particular autopsy. Thus, the defendant's decision not to allow an autopsy was an individual one, based on this particular situation and not on a fundamental belief of the members of his church. Therefore, we hold that the defendant's conduct is not protected by the free exercise clauses of either the United States or the Vermont Constitutions.

II

The defendant next argues that 18 V.S.A. §5205(f), which authorizes the state's attorney or chief medical examiner to decide when to order an autopsy, is unconstitutional because it gives those officials unbridled discretion to order autopsies. We disagree.

This Court has held that discretion delegated by the legislature to administer a law must not be "unrestrained and arbitrary." A statute delegating to an agency or an official the duty to administer that statute is valid only if it "establish[es] a certain basic standard — 'a definite and certain policy and rule of action for the guidance of the [official authorized or] agency created to administer the law.'"

18 V.S.A. §5205(f) states that "[t]he state's attorney or chief medical examiner, if either deem it necessary and in the interest of public health, welfare and safety, or in furtherance of the administration of the law, may order an autopsy to be performed." The defendant claims that the language of this subsection provides insufficient standards to control the exercise of official discretion in ordering autopsies.

Subsection (f), however, is only one subsection of §5205. We must examine the entire section, and not just the subsection in question, to determine whether sufficient standards exist. In reading 18 V.S.A. §5205, it is clear that the legislature intended autopsies to be permitted only in those circumstances listed in 18 V.S.A. §5205(a). Section 5205(a) provides:

> When a person dies from violence, or suddenly when in apparent good health or when unattended by a physician or a recognized practitioner of a well-established church, or by casualty, or by suicide or as a result of injury or when in jail or prison, or any mental institution, or in any unusual, unnatural or suspicious manner, or in circumstances involving a hazard to public health, welfare or safety, . . . the medical examiner [shall be notified] . . . and immediately upon being notified, such medical examiner shall notify the state's attorney [who] shall thereafter be in charge of the body and shall issue such instructions covering the care or removal of the body. . . .

III. Coroners and Medical Examiners 99

When read in conjunction with §5205(a), §5205(f) contains sufficient standards to control the officials' exercise of discretion in ordering autopsies. As such, §5205(f) does not exceed constitutional limits.

The defendant contends that if §5205(f) is construed to permit autopsies only in those situations listed in §5205(a), an autopsy never should have been ordered in this case because Hanna's birth was attended by a midwife who was a "recognized practitioner" of the defendant's church. We reject this contention. Even assuming the midwife was a "recognized practitioner of a well-established church" within the meaning of §5205(a), Hanna's death could have involved a number of other situations listed in §5205(a), for which the attendance of a practitioner of a well-established church is irrelevant. For instance, §5205(a) lists death caused by violence or casualty, or death "in any unusual, unnatural or suspicious manner," as circumstances requiring the attention of the medical examiner and state's attorney (who may then decide, under §5205(f), to order an autopsy). Thus, in ordering an autopsy in this case, the state's attorney and chief medical examiner did not abuse the discretion delegated to them by §5205(f). . . .

NOTE

The Power of the State to Compel an Autopsy Over Religious Objections

Chambers rejects the argument that the Vermont statute giving the medical examiner the power to compel an autopsy is void for vagueness. It also rejects defendant's free exercise of religion claim because Chambers' church did not view autopsies as impermissible. What if Chambers had demonstrated a sincere conviction, derived (albeit idiosyncratically) from the tenets of his church? What if the organized religion that he embraced believed autopsies to be sacrilegious? See Smialek v. Begay, 104 N.M. 375, 721 P.2d 1306 (1986) (action by relatives of deceased for emotional distress and deprivation of civil rights because a body was not handled according to traditional Navajo religious beliefs); Snyder v. Holy Cross Hospital, 30 Md. App. 317, 352 A.2d 334 (1976) (injunction to prevent autopsy on religious grounds).

Grad v. Kaasa
321 S.E.2d 888 (N.C. 1984)

COPELAND, JUSTICE. . . .

[Lucille Grad sought compensatory and punitive damages for a "wrongful autopsy" conducted by Dr. Laurin Kaasa on the body of her husband, Carl Grad. Mrs. Grad's complaint alleged that Mr. Grad suffered a heart attack while playing tennis. He was rushed to a hospital where resuscitation efforts failed. An emergency room physician, unable to determine the cause of Mr. Grad's death, referred the case to the county medical examiner, Dr. Kaasa. Dr. Kaasa conducted an autopsy and determined that Mr. Grad died of a heart attack. In the process, Mr. Grad's vital organs were removed, examined, and then cremated. Dr. Kaasa did not seek plaintiff's permission to conduct the autopsy, nor did he consult Mrs. Grad or Mr. Grad's medical records to obtain information concerning the possible cause of death before conducting the autopsy. Mrs. Grad learned of the autopsy weeks later, when the death certificate was sent to her home. She was "morally opposed" to cremation and removal of human organs.

The medical examiner's answer alleged that he discussed the case with the emergency room physician, read the emergency room report and conducted an external examination of Mr. Grad's body before deciding to conduct an autopsy. Dr. Kaasa further contended that the autopsy was authorized by North Carolina law and that he is therefore entitled to immunity from liability.

The trial judge granted summary judgment.]

Defendant's forecast of the evidence tended to show that he received a proper death report and made an investigation into the cause and manner of death as required by [statute]. Following his investigation, he made a subjective determination that an autopsy was advisable and in the public interest. Defendant was acting within the scope of his office, and his forecast entitles him to summary judgment unless in her forecast of the evidence plaintiff shows by specific facts that a genuine issue of material fact exists. Plaintiff contends that a genuine issue of fact exists as to whether defendant acted maliciously or corruptly in conducting the autopsy. In support, plaintiff points to the fact that defendant was well acquainted with her but did not contact her prior to performing the autopsy. Plaintiff knew that her husband had suffered a previous heart attack and had been warned not to overexert himself. The plaintiff's forecast of evidence indicated that defendant could have obtained this information by contacting plaintiff or examining Mr. Grad's medical records. The Court of Appeals concluded that this forecast raised a genuine issue of material fact as to whether defendant acted with reckless disregard of plaintiff's rights by ordering the autopsy without first having made further reasonable investigation into the circumstances of Mr. Grad's death. Plaintiff also argues that the fact that defendant receives $200 for each autopsy he performs as medical examiner raises a genuine issue of fact on the question of whether he acted with corruption. After carefully considering the evidence, we find nothing that raises an issue of material fact as to whether plaintiff acted maliciously or corruptly.

III. Coroners and Medical Examiners

. . . There is abundant evidence in this case to support defendant's conclusion that an autopsy was necessary.

Mr. Grad had suddenly collapsed without apparent cause and had suffered extensive injuries to the head and face. The emergency room doctor had been unable to determine the cause of death. The doctor's conclusion that Mr. Grad died suddenly from a cardiac arrest merely describes the death without explaining why it occurred, and he properly notified defendant who read the emergency room report and conducted an external examination of Mr. Grad's body before ordering an autopsy. [D]efendant could not ascertain the cause of the cardiac arrest without performing an autopsy. Further, defendant testified that because of the external injuries Mr. Grad had suffered he would have conducted the autopsy even if he had known Mr. Grad had a history of heart disease. Defendant was under no legal duty to examine Mr. Grad's medical records or to ask plaintiff for permission before performing the autopsy. There is nothing in the statutes or regulations from which such a duty can be implied, and defendant's prior relationship with plaintiff did not create one. Therefore, plaintiff's forecast of the evidence does not raise an issue of material fact because, if true, it is insufficient as a matter of law to show that defendant acted with malice or corruption. The same is true of plaintiff's evidence that defendant receives $200 for each autopsy he performs as medical examiner. The simple fact that defendant is paid for his services is insufficient to show that he acted with malice or corruption. We note that the Court of Appeals' holding that plaintiff's forecast of the evidence had created an issue of material fact was based in part on the affidavit of plaintiff's expert, Dr. Edward J. Notari. In the affidavit, Dr. Notari stated that in his opinion there was ample evidence available to exclude the possibility of death by trauma, unknown circumstances or any of the other criteria enumerated in the regulations.

. . . Dr. Notari's affidavit does not raise an issue of material fact because his conclusion that the autopsy was unnecessary relates primarily to whether or not defendant was acting within the scope of his authority. That issue was decided unanimously by the Court of Appeals and [under a state rule of appellate procedure] is not [reviewable]. The fact that the autopsy was needless may be relevant to whether the performance of the autopsy was wanton, but the decision to perform the autopsy must also manifest a reckless indifference to the rights of others. Since we have already held that plaintiff's forecast does not raise an issue of material fact as to whether defendant acted corruptly or maliciously, Dr. Notari's opinion that the autopsy was unnecessary is irrelevant in determining whether defendant acted wantonly.

Based on our review of the record, we hold that plaintiff's forecast of the evidence failed to raise a genuine issue of material fact, and the Superior Court properly granted summary judgment in favor of the defendant. . . .

NOTES

Civil Liability for Autopsies

Grad recognizes a civil cause of action as against officials who authorize or conduct autopsies unnecessarily. However, medical examiners or coroners, like other government officials, typically enjoy a qualified immunity for their official acts. See also Kompare v. Stein, 801 F.2d 883 (7th Cir. 1986); Smialek v. Begay, 104 N.M. 375, 721 P.2d 1306 (1986). Is this protection desirable? The North Carolina Court of Appeals suggests that without it, medical examiners would be liable for all "mistakes" in authorizing autopsies. Cf. Model Post-Mortem Examination Act §5 (comment). Is this so? To what standard of care should officials who authorize autopsies be held?

Should there be a cause of action for "autopsy malpractice" — for performing a grossly inadequate autopsy — as well as the "wrongful autopsy" action in *Grad*? The problems of civil liability are discussed further in Dean v. Chapman, 556 P.2d 257 (Okla. 1976); Curran, Damage Suits Against Medical Examiners for Authorized Autopsies, 297 New Eng. J. Med. 1220 (1977); Lind, Caveat Prosecutor: The Pathologist and Autopsy Law, 69 Am. J. Clinical Pathology 263 (1978); Waltz, Legal Liability for Unauthorized Autopsies and Related Procedures, 16 J. For. Sci. 1 (1971).

Confidentiality of Autopsy Reports

The confidentiality afforded to autopsy and other reports of coroners or medical examiners varies among jurisdictions and depends on the details of the pertinent statutes and regulations. The value and dangers of disclosure vary from one situation to another, as in the following instances:

(a) A newspaper seeks autopsy reports containing blood-alcohol test results for use in preparing articles on the dangers of drunk driving. Herald Co. v. Murray, 136 App. Div. 2d 954, 524 N.Y.S.2d 949 (1988).

(b) A newspaper seeks autopsy reports in cases of deaths arising from encounters between police officers and minority citizens. Denver Publishing Co. v. Dreyfus, 184 Colo. 288, 520 P.2d 104 (1974).

(c) A litigant in a tort action arising from a fatal automobile accident seeks a coroner's report on the deceased's blood alcohol level. E.g., Stattner v. Caldwell, 111 Iowa 714, 727 P.2d 1142 (1986);

Hoffman v. Tracy, 67 Wash. 2d 21, 406 P.2d 323 (1965); Staples v. Glienke, 142 Wis. 2d 19, 416 N.W.2d 920 (1987).

(d) A homicide defendant seeks pretrial discovery of the report of an autopsy performed on her alleged victim. Compare People v. Preston, 13 Misc. 2d 802, 176 N.Y.S.2d 542 (1958), and People v. Cox, 24 Misc. 2d 998, 202 N.Y.S.2d 607 (1960), with State v. Petersen, 47 Wash. 2d 836, 289 P.2d 1013 (1956), and Commonwealth v. Noxon, 319 Mass. 495, 66 N.E.2d 814 (1946).

(e) A hospital seeks access to autopsy reports on patients who died while in the hospital when the attending physician was unable to certify the cause of death. Central General Hospital v. Lukash, 140 App. Div. 2d 113, 532 N.Y.S.2d 527 (1988); cf. Model Post-Mortem Examinations Act §9.

What additional information would be necessary or helpful in deciding these cases?

IV. JUDICIAL RECEPTIVITY TO NEW SCIENTIFIC TESTS

Frye v. United States
293 F. 1013 (D.C. Cir. 1923)

VAN ORSDEL, ASSOCIATE JUSTICE.

Appellant, defendant below, was convicted of the crime of murder in the second degree, and from the judgment prosecutes this appeal.

A single assignment of error is presented for our consideration. In the course of the trial counsel for defendant offered an expert witness to testify to the result of a deception test made upon defendant. The test is described as the systolic blood pressure deception test. It is asserted that blood pressure is influenced by change in the emotions of the witness, and that the systolic blood pressure rises are brought about by nervous impulses sent to the sympathetic branch of the autonomic nervous system. Scientific experiments, it is claimed, have demonstrated that fear, rage, and pain always produce a rise of systolic blood pressure, and that conscious deception or falsehood, concealment of facts, or guilt of crime, accompanied by fear of detection when the person is under examination, raises the systolic blood pressure in a curve, which corresponds exactly to the struggle going on in the subject's mind, between fear and attempted control of that fear, as the examination touches the vital points in respect of which he is attempting to deceive the examiner.

In other words, the theory seems to be that truth is spontaneous, and comes without conscious effort, while the utterance of a falsehood requires a conscious effort, which is reflected in the blood pressure. The rise thus produced is easily detected and distinguished from the rise produced by mere fear of the examination itself. In the former instance, the pressure rises higher than in the latter, and is more pronounced as the examination proceeds, while in the latter case, if the subject is telling the truth, the pressure registers highest at the beginning of the examination, and gradually diminishes as the examination proceeds.

Prior to the trial defendant was subjected to this deception test, and counsel offered the scientist who conducted the test as an expert to testify to the results obtained. The offer was objected to by counsel for the government, and the court sustained the objection. Counsel for defendant then offered to have the proffered witness conduct a test in the presence of the jury. This also was denied.

Counsel for defendant, in their able presentation of the novel question involved, correctly state in their brief that no cases directly in point have been found. The broad ground, however, upon which they plant their case, is succinctly stated in their brief as follows:

> The rule is that the opinions of experts or skilled witnesses are admissible in evidence in those cases in which the matter of inquiry is such that inexperienced persons are unlikely to prove capable of forming a correct judgment upon it, for the reason that the subject-matter so far partakes of a science, art, or trade as to require a previous habit or experience or study in it, in order to acquire a knowledge of it. When the question involved does not lie within the range of common experience or common knowledge, but requires special experience or special knowledge, then the opinions of witnesses skilled in that particular science, art, or trade to which the question relates are admissible in evidence.

Numerous cases are cited in support of this rule. Just when a scientific principle or discovery crosses the line between the experimental and demonstrable stages is difficult to define. Somewhere in this twilight zone the evidential force of the principle must be recognized, and while courts will go a long way in admitting expert testimony deduced from a well-recognized scientific principle or discovery, the thing from which the deduction is made must be sufficiently established to have gained general acceptance in the particular field in which it belongs.

We think the systolic blood pressure deception test has not yet gained such standing and scientific recognition among physiological and psychological authorities as would justify the courts in admitting expert testimony deduced from the discovery, development, and experiments thus far made.

The judgment is affirmed.

IV. Judicial Receptivity to New Scientific Tests

NOTES

The General Acceptance Standard

1. *The source of the general acceptance standard.* The rule that "the thing from which the deduction is made must be sufficiently established to have gained general acceptance in the particular field in which it belongs" is known as the *Frye* test, or the general acceptance standard. Where does this special requirement for scientific evidence come from? The trial court apparently did not apply this standard, see Starrs, A Still-Life Watercolor: Frye v. United States, 27 J. For. Sci. 684, 691-692 (1982), and nothing in the appellate court's remarks about expert testimony generally suggests that the information imparted by an expert must have attained general acceptance before it can be placed before a jury. Is the requirement justified by the fact that courts are unable to judge the validity of scientific evidence even with the aid of a qualified expert? See, for instance, United States v. Addison, 498 F.2d 741, 743-744 (D.C. Cir. 1974). By the possibility that when new techniques or theories first are introduced in court, they are likely to be understood by only one or two experts, so that the opponent of the evidence will have little chance to combat the novel evidence? Id. By the tendency of jurors to be so awed by scientific evidence that such evidence should not be put before them until it has withstood the test of time before its acceptance in the scientific community generally? See The *Frye* Doctrine and Relevancy Approach Controversy: An Empirical Evaluation, 74 Geo. L.J. 1769 (1986).

2. *The acceptance and importance of the general acceptance standard.* On the surface, *Frye* appears to have been remarkably influential. When applied faithfully, it is a more demanding standard than mere relevance (Fed. R. Evid. 401-403), "assist[ance to] the trier of fact" (Fed. R. Evid. 702) or "reasonable reliance" (Fed. R. Evid. 703). The *Frye* rule has excluded, on various occasions, polygraphy, graphology, hypnotic and drug induced testimony, voice stress analysis, voice spectrograms, ion microprobe mass spectroscopy, infrared sensing of aircraft, retesting of breath samples for alcohol content, psychological profiles of battered women, post-traumatic stress disorder as an indicator of rape, astronomical calculations, and certain types of electrophoresis of dried blood stains. See McCormick on Evidence §203, at 606 (E. Cleary 3d ed. 1984 & 1987 Supp.). Yet, many jurisdictions have disavowed *Frye* in recent decades. United States v. Downing, reprinted infra, rehearses the major arguments for and against *Frye*, and finds the traditional relevance-expert testimony analysis superior. Furthermore, even in those jurisdictions that still purport to follow *Frye*, the courts repeatedly ignore or depart from it in hard cases. Most of the scholarly commentary calls for outright rejection of the

Frye test. See id. at §203. In any event, courts applying an ordinary relevance inquiry to scientific evidence — in which the degree of acceptance among scientists is but one of several factors affecting the balance of probative value and prejudicial effect — tend to reach the same results with respect to most forms of scientific evidence as do the courts that formally adhere to *Frye*. See id. at §§204-208.

3. *The meaning of the general acceptance standard.* What was "the thing" in *Frye* that needed "to have gained general acceptance"? The link between conscious insincerity and changes in blood pressure? The ability of an expert to measure and interpret these changes? Both? By whom must "the thing" be accepted? All scientists? All forensic scientists? All scientists who have studied "the thing"? How does one prove such acceptance? The cases in this section, as well as some in succeeding portions of the chapter, agonize over such questions.

State v. Superior Court
718 P.2d 171 (Ariz. 1986)

FELDMAN, JUSTICE.

In the early morning hours of March 18, 1985, Frederick Blake was driving a car on State Route 92, south of Sierra Vista. He was stopped by Officer Hohn who had observed the vehicle meandering within its lane, and who therefore suspected Blake of driving under the influence of alcohol. Noting, also, that Blake's appearance and breath indicated intoxication, the officer had Blake perform a battery of six field sobriety tests, including the horizontal gaze nystagmus (HGN) test. Nystagmus is an involuntary jerking of the eyeball. The jerking may be aggravated by central nervous system depressants such as alcohol or barbiturates. Horizontal gaze nystagmus is the inability of the eyes to maintain visual fixation as they are turned to the side.

In the HGN test the driver is asked to cover one eye and focus the other on an object (usually a pen) held by the officer at the driver's eye level. As the officer moves the object gradually out of the driver's field of vision toward his ear, he watches the driver's eyeball to detect involuntary jerking. The test is repeated with the other eye. By observing (1) the inability of each eye to track movement smoothly, (2) pronounced nystagmus at maximum deviation and (3) onset of the nystagmus at an angle less than 45 degrees in relation to the center point, the officer can estimate whether the driver's blood alcohol content (BAC) exceeds the legal limit of .10 percent. . . .

Blake's performance of the first three standard field sobriety tests was "fair" and did not amount to probable cause to arrest Blake for

IV. Judicial Receptivity to New Scientific Tests

DUI. As a result of the HGN test, however, the officer estimated that Blake had a BAC in excess of .10 percent. Blake's performance on the last two tests strengthened his conclusion. Having also smelled a strong odor of alcohol on Blake's breath and noticed Blake's slurred speech and bloodshot, watery and dilated eyes. Officer Hohn then arrested Blake on a charge of felony DUI. Hohn then transported Blake to the police station where he administered an intoxilyzer test which showed that Blake had a BAC of .163 percent.

Blake made two motions to the trial court: to dismiss the prosecution for lack of probable cause to arrest and to preclude the admission of testimony of the HGN test and its results at trial. At the evidentiary hearing on these two motions the state presented evidence regarding the principles and use of HGN testing from Dr. Marcelline Burns, a research psychologist who studies the effect of alcohol on behavior, Sgt. Richard Studdard of the Los Angeles Police Department, and Sgt. Jeffrey Raynor and Officer Robert Hohn of the Arizona Department of Public Safety.

Dr. Burns, Director of the Southern California Research Institute (SCRI or Institute) testified that the Institute had received research contracts from the National Highway Traffic Safety Administration (NHTSA) to develop the best possible field sobriety tests. The result of this research was a three-test battery, which included the walk and turn, the one-leg stand, and the HGN. This battery could be administered without special equipment, required no more than five minutes in most cases, and resulted in 83 percent accuracy in determining BAC above and below .10 percent. Dr. Burns testified that all field sobriety tests help the police officers to estimate BAC. The HGN test is based on the known principle that certain toxic substances, including alcohol, cause nystagmus. The SCRI study found HGN to be the best single index of intoxication, because it is an involuntary response. BAC can even be estimated from the angle of onset of the involuntary jerking: 50 degrees minus the angle of the gaze at the onset of eye oscillation equals the BAC.[1] Dr. Burns testified that the HGN test had been accepted as valid by the highway safety field, including the NHTSA, Finnish researchers, state agencies such as the California Highway Patrol, Arizona Highway Patrol, Washington State Police, and numerous city agencies. Finally, the state offered in evidence an

---

1. Thus, nystagmus at 45 degrees corresponds to a blood alcohol content (BAC) of 0.05 percent; nystagmus at 40 degrees to a BAC of 0.10 percent; nystagmus at 35 degrees to a BAC of 0.15 percent; and nystagmus at 30 degrees to a BAC of 0.20 percent. At BACs above 0.20 percent, a person's eyes may not be able to follow a moving object. It should be noted however that when officers administer the test they do not necessarily measure the angle of onset; instead they look for three characteristics of high BAC: inability of smooth pursuit, distinct jerkiness at maximum deviation and onset of jerkiness prior to 45 degrees. We do not address the admissibility of quantified BAC estimates based on angle of onset of nystagmus.

HGN training manual developed by the NHTSA for its nationwide program to train law enforcement officers. Both the manual and training program were based on the Institute's studies.

Sgt. Studdard is currently a supervisor in charge of DUI enforcement for the City of Los Angeles and a consultant to NHTSA on field sobriety testing. Based on his field work administering the HGN test and his participation in double blind studies at the Institute, he testified that the accuracy rate of the HGN test in estimating whether the level of BAC exceeds .10 percent is between 80 and 90 percent. According to Studdard the margin of inaccuracy is caused by the fact that certain drugs, such as barbiturates, cause the same effects as alcohol. We take notice, however, that nystagmus may also indicate a number of neurological conditions, and the presence of any of these would also affect the accuracy of the HGN-based estimate of blood alcohol content. Both Sgt. Studdard and Sgt. Raynor, who currently administers the HGN training program for the State of Arizona, testified that the HGN test is especially useful in detecting violations where a driver with BAC over .10 percent is able to pull himself together sufficiently to pass the traditional field sobriety tests and thus avoid arrest and subsequent chemical testing.

Sgt. Raynor testified that the traditional field sobriety tests are not sensitive enough to detect dangerously impaired drivers with BAC between .10 percent and .14 percent and that the police officers thus must permit them to drive on. Sgt. Raynor also testified as to the rigor and requirements of the Arizona training and certification program.

At the close of the evidentiary hearing, the trial court concluded that HGN represented a new scientific principle and was therefore subject to the *Frye* standard of admissibility. The court ruled the HGN test did not satisfy *Frye*, was therefore unreliable, and could not form the basis of probable cause. The court granted Blake's motion to dismiss. . . .

[The Supreme Court held that the action of the police in stopping Blake and administering the HGN and other sobriety tests did not infringe his Fourth Amendment rights concerning searches and seizures, and that the district court erred in holding that *Frye* applied to evidence used to establish probable cause. It proceeded to consider whether] the test results may be admitted in evidence on the question of guilt or innocence. . . .

The HGN test is a different type of test from balancing on one leg or walking a straight line because it rests almost entirely upon an assertion of scientific legitimacy rather than a basis of common knowledge. Different rules therefore apply to determine its admissibility. It is to this question of HGN's admissibility that we now address ourselves.

IV. Judicial Receptivity to New Scientific Tests

Rules of evidence are aimed at preventing jury confusion, prejudice and undue consumption of time and trial resources. Scientific evidence is a source of particular judicial caution. Because "science" is often accepted in our society as synonymous with truth, there is a substantial risk that the jury may give undue weight to such evidence. If a technique has an "enormous effect in resolving completely a matter in controversy," it must be demonstrably reliable before it is admissible.

Before expert opinion evidence based on a novel scientific principle can be admitted, the rule of Frye v. United States requires that the theory relied on be in conformity with a generally accepted explanatory theory. The purpose of this requirement is to assure the reliability of the testimony. Because HGN is a new technique based upon scientific principles, its reliability is to be measured against the *Frye* standard. . . . Recognizing that judges and juries are not always in a position to assess the validity of the claims made by an expert witness before making findings of fact, *Frye* guarantees that reliability will be assessed by those in the best position to do so: members of the relevant scientific field who can dispassionately study and test the new theory.

If the scientific principle has gained general acceptance in the particular field in which it belongs, evidence resulting from its application is admissible, "subject to a foundational showing that the expert was qualified, the technique was properly used, and the results were accurately recorded." To determine whether the HGN test satisfies the test of general acceptance we must (1) identify the appropriate scientific community whose acceptance of the nystagmus principles and validity of the HGN test is required, and (2) determine whether there is general acceptance of both the scientific principle and the technique applying the theory. The admissibility of HGN test results under the *Frye* standard is an issue of first impression. Our search has not brought to light any reported American case law ruling on the issue.

The state argues that the relevant scientific community is that of law enforcement and highway safety agencies and behavioral psychologists. Public defender amicus contends that we should disregard these sources and argues that the HGN phenomenon requires assessment by scientists in the fields of neurology, ophthalmology, pharmacology and criminalistics. It claims that narrowing the field deprives the general scientific community of the time needed to evaluate the procedure before it is examined by the legal community. We agree that validation studies must be performed by scientists other than those who have professional and personal interest in the outcome of the evaluation.

We believe, however, that the relevant scientific community that must be shown to have accepted a new scientific procedure is often self-selecting. Scientists who have no interest in a new scientific principle are unlikely to evaluate it, even if a court determines they are part of a relevant scientific community. The HGN test measures a behavioral phenomenon: specifically the effects of alcohol on one aspect of human behavior, the movement of the eye. Thus, it stands to reason that experimental psychologists in the area of behavioral psychology would be interested in verifying the validity of the HGN test and should be included in the relevant scientific community. Similarly, the problem of alcohol's effect on driving ability is a major concern to scientists in the area of highway safety and they, too, should be included.

We disagree with the defendant's implication that those in the field of highway safety or law enforcement are necessarily biased. We believe the National Highway Traffic Safety Administration's interest in funding research to identify the drunk driver is not subject to question in this instance. The NHTSA was addressing a complex problem: every state has either a presumptive or "per se illegal" law that makes reference to BAC (typically .10 percent). Officers whose task it is to remove violators of these laws from the roads may, upon initial suspicion, administer behavioral tests, but until recently the relationship of the tests to specific BAC levels was not well documented. The purpose of NHTSA's program was to develop a test battery to assist officers in discriminating between those drivers who are in violation of these laws and those who are not. Furthermore, it is not to the advantage of law enforcement in the highway safety field to have an unreliable field sobriety test. It is inefficient to arrest and transport a driver for chemical testing, only to find that he is not in violation of the law. We believe that the work of highway safety professionals and behavioral psychologists who study effects of alcohol on behavior is directly affected by the claims and application of the HGN test, so that both these groups must be included in the relevant scientific community.

We are not forced to come to the same conclusion with respect to neurologists, pharmacologists, ophthalmologists and criminalists. Although it is true that the form of nystagmus that concerns us is the result of a neurological malfunction, we agree with Dr. Burns who testified that "the field of neurology does not concern itself specifically with alcohol effects on performance and even more specifically with field sobriety." She did state, however, that a "very small segment of the neurology community" concerns itself with the effects and has produced some literature. No argument has been made why the fields of pharmacology, ophthalmology and criminalistics (beyond those concerned with detecting violators of DUI laws) should be included in the relevant scientific community and no convincing reason

IV. Judicial Receptivity to New Scientific Tests

occurs to us. We conclude, therefore, that to determine whether the HGN test satisfies the *Frye* requirement of general acceptance the appropriate disciplines include behavioral psychology, highway safety and, to a lesser extent, neurology and criminalistics.

We now turn to the question of whether there has been general acceptance of both the HGN test and its underlying principle. The burden of proving general acceptance is on the proponent of the new technique; it may be proved by expert testimony and scientific and legal literature. We have already summarized the expert testimony presented by the state. In addition, the state submitted both scientific publications and reports of research done for the United States Department of Transportation. These are listed in Appendix A.

At the evidentiary hearing Blake presented no evidence to refute either the substance of the expert opinion testimony or the contention that it had general acceptance. Blake and public defender amicus instead argued that there is a paucity of literature and that the appropriate scientific disciplines have not yet had the opportunity to duplicate and evaluate Dr. Burns' work.

Our own research is listed in Appendix B. The literature demonstrates to our satisfaction that those professionals who have investigated the subject do not dispute the strong correlation between BAC and the different types of nystagmus. Furthermore, those who have investigated the relation between BAC and nystagmus as the eye follows a moving object have uniformly found that the higher the BAC, the earlier the onset of involuntary jerking of the eyeball. Although the publications are not voluminous, they have been before the relevant communities a considerable period of time for any opposing views to have surfaced.

Based on all the evidence we conclude there has been sufficient scrutiny of the HGN test to permit a conclusion as to reliability. The "general acceptance" requirement does not necessitate a showing of universal acceptance of the reliability of the scientific principle and procedure. Neither must the principle and procedure be absolutely accurate or certain.

We believe that the HGN test satisfies the *Frye* standard. The evidence demonstrates that the following propositions have gained general acceptance in the relevant scientific community: (1) HGN occurs in conjunction with alcohol consumption; (2) its onset and distinctness are correlated to BAC; (3) BAC in excess of .10 percent can be estimated with reasonable accuracy from the combination of the eyes' tracking ability, the angle of onset of nystagmus and the degree of nystagmus at maximum deviation; and (4) officers can be trained to observe these phenomena sufficiently to estimate accurately whether BAC is above or below .10 percent. . . .

We find that the horizontal gaze nystagmus test properly administered by a trained police officer is sufficiently reliable to be a factor in establishing probable cause to arrest a driver. . . . We further find that the horizontal gaze nystagmus test satisfies the *Frye* test for reliability and may be admitted in evidence to corroborate or attack, but not to quantify, the chemical analysis of the accused's blood alcohol content. It may not be used to establish the accused's level of blood alcohol in the absence of a chemical analysis showing the proscribed level in the accused's blood, breath or urine. [I]t is admissible, as is other evidence of defendant's behavior, to prove that he was "under the influence." . . .

NOTES

Fryed in Arizona

1. *Advisory opinions.* The trial court had dismissed the charges on the ground that the police officer's observations of HGN could not establish probable cause inasmuch as this technique for ascertaining intoxication was not generally accepted in the scientific community. What did the supreme court hold? Was the portion of the opinion deciding that the HGN test satisfies the *Frye* standard part of this holding? If not, why did the court reach this issue?

2. *Reading the scientific literature.* The literature on HGN as an indicator of alcohol cited by the state to show general acceptance of the HGN test in the scientific community consisted of seven articles or reports. The majority, four, never appeared in any scientific journal, but were published by the Department of Transportation, which presumably funded them. Another was a second-hand discussion in a looseleaf treatise for attorneys, 1 R. Erwin, Defense of Drunk Driving Cases §815A[3] (3d ed. 1985), asserting that "A strong correlation exists between the BAC and the angle of onset of [gaze] nystagmus." Only two of the seven were refereed papers in respected journals, and neither claimed that measuring the angle of the onset of nystagmus was a reliable indicator of BAC. Rashbass, The Relationship Between Saccadic and Smooth Tracking Eye Movements, 159 J. Physiol. 326 (1961) (barbiturate drugs interfere with smooth tracking eye movement); Wilkinson, Kime & Purnell, Alcohol and Human Eye Movement, 97 Brain 785 (1974) (oral dose of ethyl alcohol impaired smooth pursuit eye movement of all human subjects).

The supreme court also undertook its own, unaided study of the scientific literature on HGN and intoxication, which it summarized by listing in an appendix to its opinion the 22 papers it located. The citations there suggest that the court's study went no further than a review of abstracts from computerized databases. Indeed, one paper apparently has never been published, and only the abstract of a

IV. Judicial Receptivity to New Scientific Tests 113

conference presentation is mentioned. Some have little to do with the validity or reliability of detecting intoxication by nystagmus. E.g., Oosterveld, Meineri & Paolucci, Quantitative Effect of Linear Acceleration on Positional Alcohol Nystagmus, 45 Aerospace Med., July 1974, at 695 (G-loading brings about Positional Alcohol Nystagmus even when subject has not ingested alcohol; however when subjects ingested alcohol, no PAN was found when subjects were in supine position, even with G-force at 3). Others appear in unrefereed periodicals that can hardly be considered part of the scientific literature. E.g., Norris, The Correlation of Angle of Onset of Nystagmus With Blood Alcohol Level: Report of a Field Trial, Calif. Assn. Criminalistics Newsletter, June 1985, at 21, 22; Seelmeyer, Nystagmus, A Valid DUI Test, Law and Order, July 1985, at 29 (horizontal gaze nystagmus test is used in "at least one law enforcement agency in each of the 50 states" and is "a legitimate method of establishing probable cause").

3. *Theories or procedures used exclusively in forensic applications.* State v. Superior Court concerns a test developed specifically for use in law enforcement. Should widespread usage by law enforcement officials or police laboratory technicians demonstrate general acceptance in the requisite community? Was the Arizona court correct in treating "highway safety officials" as part of the scientific community? Arguably, the HGN test for inebriation is a special situation in this regard. Why?

With other types of "forensics-only" evidence, the courts have been more skeptical of the claims of law enforcement technicians or scientists heavily involved in the development and promotion of the methods. E.g., State ex rel. Collins v. Superior Court, 132 Ariz. 180, 199, 644 P.2d 1266, 1285 (1982); People v. Kelley, 17 Cal. 2d 24, 129 Cal. Rptr. 144, 549 P.2d 1240 (1976). So-called "voiceprint" evidence, which prompted many courts to abandon or stretch the general acceptance standard beyond recognition, supplies a shocking example of initial overenthusiasm ultimately revealed by exposure of the technique to criticism from a broader scientific community. See P. Giannelli & E. Imwinkelried, Scientific Evidence §10-3 (1986); McCormick on Evidence §207 (E. Cleary 3d ed. 1984); A. Moenssens, F. Inbau & J. Starrs, Scientific Evidence in Criminal Cases 670 (3d ed. 1986). More recently, critics of "multisystem" electrophoresis of dried blood stains suggested that this method of identifying blood serum enzymes also had been oversold to gullible courts. See infra at §6. Generating a certain sense of déjà vu, the most recent "forensics-only technique" to take the center stage is named DNA "fingerprinting" by its developers. We treat the legal issues in the forensic use of recombinant-DNA technology infra at §6.

4. *Three problems.* How should the following questions be decided in a *Frye* jurisdiction:

(a) In a homicide prosecution, several witnesses testify that before this case, tests developed specifically for and used for the first time in the case at bar — scientists believed that it was impossible to demonstrate the presence of succinylcholine chloride or its component parts in the body. However, in an effort to resolve the case at bar, a forensic toxicologist developed and performed a test to detect succinic acid, a component of succinylcholine chloride, in the body tissue. He will testify that he found this acid in abnormal amounts in the body of the victim. May he give this testimony? See Coppolino v. State, 223 So. 2d 68 (Fla. Dist. Ct. App. 1968), *appeal dismissed*, 234 So. 2d 120 (Fla. 1969), *cert. denied*, 399 U.S. 927 (1970).

(b) The state's experts are prepared to testify that the defendant is a narcotics user as shown by the Nalline test. The medical profession generally is unfamiliar with the test. See People v. Williams, 331 P.2d 251 (Cal. App. 1958).

(c) The state's expert testifies that "numerous crime laboratories" use thin-layer chromatography to detect monomethylamine nitrate, and one paper attesting to the accuracy of this technique has appeared in a scientific journal. See United States v. Metzger, 778 F.2d 1195, 1204 (6th Cir. 1985); cf. People v. Brown, 709 P.2d 440 (Cal. 1985). What if no scientific reports on the technique are in print?

(d) An impeccably conducted opinion poll of psychophysiologists shows that 61 percent think that a professionally administered polygraph test is "a useful diagnostic tool" in detecting deception. See Dowd v. Calabrese, 585 F. Supp. 430, 432 (D.D.C. 1984).

United States v. Downing
753 F.2d 1224 (3d Cir. 1985)

BECKER, CIRCUIT JUDGE.

This case presents a question of first impression in this Circuit — whether Fed. R. Evid. 702 permits a defendant in a criminal prosecution to adduce, from an expert in the field of human perception and memory, testimony concerning the reliability of eyewitness identifications. The district court refused to admit the testimony of a psychologist offered by the defendant, apparently because the court believed that such testimony can never meet the "helpfulness" standard of Fed. R. Evid. 702. We hold that the district court erred. We also hold that the admission of such expert testimony is not automatic but conditional. First, the evidence must survive preliminary scrutiny in the course of an in limine proceeding conducted by the district judge. This threshold inquiry, which we derive from the helpfulness standard of Rule 702, is essentially a balancing test, centering on two factors: (1) the reliability of the scientific principles upon which the expert testimony rests, hence the potential of the testimony to aid the jury in reaching an accurate resolution of a disputed issue; and (2) the likelihood that introduction of the testimony may in some way overwhelm or mislead the jury. Second, admission depends upon the "fit," i.e., upon a specific proffer showing that scientific research has established that particular features of the eyewitness identifications involved may have impaired the accuracy of those identifications. The district court's assessment of these factors will guide its discretion in deciding whether to admit the evidence under Fed. R. Evid. 702, which contemplates a liberal view toward the admissibility of expert testimony generally. The district court's ruling under Fed. R. Evid. 702 will be reviewable under an abuse of discretion standard. Finally, the district court retains discretionary authority under Fed. R. Evid. 403 to exclude any relevant evidence that would unduly waste time or confuse the issues at trial.

[Portions of the opinion outlining the facts and analyzing the applicability of the rules of expert testimony to psychologists testifying to the accuracy of eyewitness identifications are omitted.]

III

The conclusion that expert testimony on the perception of eyewitnesses, at least in certain cases, meets the helpfulness standard of Rule 702 does not end our analysis. On remand, the district court will still have to decide whether to admit the specific testimony proffered in this case. This exercise of the district court's discretion will be shaped by the policies of Fed. R. Evid. 702, as it impinges on the court's assessment of the scientific basis for the proffered testimony, and by the policies of Fed. R. Evid. 403. The balance of this section is devoted to a discussion of the perceived evidentiary problems posed by novel forms of scientific expertise, generally, and to an analysis of the test announced in Frye v. United States as a way of dealing with those problems. We conclude that the status of the *Frye* test under Rule 702 is somewhat uncertain, but reject that test for reasons of policy. In section IV, we set forth an alternative standard for evaluating novel scientific evidence that we believe comports with the language and policy of Rule 702. . . .

A

Courts and commentators have divided over the issue of the foundational requirements for the admission of scientific testimony. Evidence that derives from principles and techniques of uncontroverted validity is, of course, readily admissible, subject to the qualification of the proposed witness and, in some jurisdictions, to a showing that proper safeguards were employed in obtaining the evidence on the relevant occasion. Where proffered evidence arises from a novel form of scientific expertise, however, courts and commentators have taken any one of several different approaches to the question of admissibility. First, many courts impose a foundational requirement that the underlying scientific principle or technique be generally accepted in the field to which it belongs.[11]

Other courts and commentators have suggested variations on the *Frye* standard, e.g., "reasonable scientific acceptance," or alternative approaches. . . . Finally, a third group of courts and commentators reasons that the novelty of the scientific basis for expert testimony bears principally on the weight of the evidence, and that the Federal Rules of Evidence suggest, if not mandate, a generalized "relevancy" approach akin to the balancing test codified in Fed. R. Evid. 403.

As is apparent, a considerable amount of judicial and scholarly attention has been devoted to identifying when evidence resting on novel scientific principles or techniques is admissible. Because this court has never adopted a clear position on this issue, we must decide, based on the language and policies of the Federal Rules of Evidence, the appropriate test for the admissibility of novel scientific evidence.

B

Our starting point for this discussion is the seminal opinion of Frye v. United States, which had won adherents in many state and federal courts at the time of the adoption of the Federal Rules of Evidence. The *Frye* court concluded that expert testimony relating to

---

11. In [People v. McDonald, 37 Cal. 3d 351, 208 Cal. Rptr. at 251, 690 P.2d at 724 (1984)] the California Supreme Court declined to analyze the admissibility of expert testimony on eyewitness perception and memory under the standard set out in *Frye*. . . . The court apparently limited the . . . rule to those processes or devices which are surrounded by an "aura of infallibility." In contrast to such "novel" techniques, the proffered testimony was found to be unremarkable, a type of expert medical testimony to which the general acceptance standard does not apply in California. We reject the *Frye* test. As we discuss infra, however, our analysis defines "novel" scientific evidence in terms of whether judicial notice can be used to validate the scientific premises on which the evidence rests. It may well be that judicial notice will be available to the district court on remand in this case, but we leave to that court the initial determination as to the status of the science of eyewitness perception, memory, and identification. At all events, we believe that it is more useful to set forth a framework that allows courts to analyze scientific evidence generally than to declare, a priori, some technique "novel" and others not. Indeed, this dichotomization between "novel" evidence and other evidence is one avenue for possible manipulation of the *Frye* test, as some of its critics have pointed out. Concededly, however, we would expect a special foundational inquiry with respect to a particular scientific technique to be appropriate only in the early phases of its use in litigation, if at all. Indeed, the *McDonald* court might have meant to imply no more than that the state of theoretical knowledge about and empirical research relating to eyewitness perception and memory has progressed sufficiently to warrant the use of judicial notice in this context. We intimate no view on this issue, but leave it in the first instance to the district court on remand.

IV. Judicial Receptivity to New Scientific Tests

novel scientific evidence must satisfy a special foundational requirement not applicable to other types of expert testimony. [C]ourts confronted with a proffer of novel scientific evidence must make a preliminary determination through the introduction of other evidence, including expert testimony, regarding (1) the status, in the appropriate scientific community, of the scientific principle underlying the proffered novel evidence; (2) the technique applying the scientific principle; and (3) the application of the technique on the particular occasion or occasions relevant to the proffered testimony. Once a novel form of expertise is judicially recognized, this foundational requirement can be eliminated, as is done when, for example, fingerprint, ballistics, or x-ray evidence is offered.

Because the general acceptance standard set out in *Frye* was the dominant view within the federal courts at the time the Federal Rules of Evidence were considered and adopted, one might expect that the rules themselves would make some pronouncement about the continuing vitality of the standard. Neither the text of the Federal Rules of Evidence nor the accompanying notes of the advisory committee, however, explicitly set forth the appropriate standard by which the admissibility of novel scientific evidence is to be established. Although the commentators agree that this legislative silence is significant, they disagree about its meaning. . . .

. . . Arguing that *Frye* is inconsistent with the policies animating the Federal Rules of Evidence, [one] view focuses in particular on the broad scope of relevance in the federal rules. Fed. R. Evid. 401 specifically defines relevant evidence as "evidence having any tendency to make the existence of any fact that is of consequence to the determination of the action more probable or less probable than it would be without the evidence." Moreover, Fed. R. Evid. 402 provides that "[a]ll relevant evidence is admissible, except as otherwise provided by the Constitution of the United States, by Act of Congress, by these rules, or by other rules prescribed by the Supreme Court pursuant to statutory authority." Thus, because the mere relevance of novel scientific evidence does not hinge on its "general acceptance" in the scientific community, Rules 401 and 402, taken together, arguably create a standard of admissibility of novel scientific evidence that is inconsistent with *Frye*. Notwithstanding the appeal of this analysis, the notes of the advisory committee make clear that Rule 402 is limited by Fed. R. Evid. 403 and by the rules contained in Article VII of the Federal Rules of Evidence, including Rule 702. The touchstone of Rule 702 . . . is the helpfulness of the expert testimony, i.e., whether it "will assist the trier of fact to understand the evidence or to determine a fact in issue." Fed. R. Evid. 702. Thus, the rules themselves contain a counterweight to a simple relevancy analysis.

Although we believe that "helpfulness" necessarily implies a quantum of reliability beyond that required to meet a standard of bare logical relevance, it also seems clear to us that some scientific evidence can assist the trier of fact in reaching an accurate determination of facts in issue even though the principles underlying the evidence have not become "generally accepted" in the field to which they belong. Moreover, we can assume that the drafters of the Federal Rules of Evidence were aware that the *Frye* test was a judicial creation, and we find nothing in the language of the rules to suggest a disapproval of such interstitial judicial rulemaking. Therefore, although the codification of the rules of evidence may counsel in favor of a re-examination of the general acceptance standard, on balance we conclude that the Federal Rules of Evidence neither incorporate nor repudiate it. We will consider, therefore, the advantages of and the problems associated with *Frye*'s general acceptance standard.

C

The most important justification for the *Frye* test is that it provides a method by which courts can assess the reliability of novel scientific expert testimony. The general acceptance standard in effect permits the experts who know most about a procedure to form a "technical jury," whose positive assessment of the scientific status of a procedure becomes a necessary prerequisite to the admissibility of expert testimony based on the procedure. Adherents of the general acceptance standard also argue that it guarantees the existence of a coterie of experts qualified to testify about the status of a particular scientific technique and, in theory at least, promotes uniformity of decision.

The general acceptance standard also safeguards against the possible prejudicial effects of testimony based upon "an unproved hypothesis in an isolated experiment." The concern over potentially specious expert testimony assumes particular importance in the criminal context, where the general acceptance standard has had its most substantial impact. When the government seeks to introduce novel scientific evidence, for example, a possible tension between the defendant's right to a fair trial, on the one hand, and the trend toward admissibility of expert testimony embodied in the Federal Rules of Evidence, is apparent. . . . This concern is also reflected by those courts that highlight the potentially prejudicial effect on the jury arising from the "aura of special reliability and trustworthiness" of scientific expert testimony.

Notwithstanding the valid evidentiary concerns subsumed in the general acceptance standard, critics of the standard have cited two general problems with it: its vagueness and its conservatism. First, the vague terms included in the standard have allowed courts to manipulate the parameters of the relevant "scientific community" and

IV. Judicial Receptivity to New Scientific Tests

the level of agreement needed for "general acceptance." Thus, some courts, when they wish to admit evidence, are able to limit the impact of *Frye* by narrowing the relevant scientific community to those experts who customarily employ the technique at issue. Judicial interpretation of the "general acceptance" component of the test has yielded even more disparate results. One court has described "general acceptance" as "widespread; prevalent; extensive though not universal," while another has suggested that the test requires agreement by a "substantial section of the scientific community."

[Commentators] have discussed other problems that arise in applying the *Frye* test: the selectivity among courts in determining whether evidence derives from "novel" principles; the inadequacy of expert testimony on many scientific issues; an uncritical acceptance of prior judicial, rather than scientific, opinion as a basis for finding "general acceptance"; and the narrow scope of review by which some appellate courts review trial court rulings. All of these problems contribute to the "essential vagueness" of the *Frye* test.

Apart from these various difficulties in implementation, moreover, *Frye*'s general acceptance standard has been found to be unsatisfactory in other respects. Under *Frye*, some have argued, courts may be required to exclude much probative and reliable information from the jury's consideration, thereby unnecessarily impeding the truth-seeking function of litigation.[14]

In sum, the *Frye* test suffers from serious flaws. The test has proved to be too malleable to provide the method for orderly and uniform decision-making envisioned by some of its proponents. Moreover, in its pristine form the general acceptance standard reflects a conservative approach to the admissibility of scientific evidence that is at odds with the spirit, if not the precise language, of the Federal Rules of Evidence. For these reasons, we conclude that "general acceptance in the particular field to which [a scientific technique] belongs," should be rejected as an independent controlling standard of admissibility. Accordingly, we hold that a particular degree of acceptance of a scientific technique within the scientific community is neither a necessary nor a sufficient condition for admissibility; it

---

14. Less often discussed, though equally problematic, is the possibility that courts applying the *Frye* test may admit into evidence expert testimony that derives from inaccurate or unreliable principles or techniques. Ideally, a novel scientific technique will become generally accepted only after being subjected to the kind of rigorous investigation and empirical testing that we associate with the scientific method. Implicit in the *Frye* approach, therefore, is the assumption that "extensive testing of the technique will" occur within the relevant scientific community. There is no guarantee, however, that such testing will occur or will come to the attention of the court, especially in situations where the experts called upon to vouch for the validity of a technique do not fairly represent the views of the scientific community.

is, however, one factor that a district court normally should consider in deciding whether to admit evidence based upon the technique.

IV

The language of Fed. R. Evid. 702, the spirit of the Federal Rules of Evidence in general, and the experience with the *Frye* test suggest the appropriateness of a more flexible approach to the admissibility of novel scientific evidence. In our view, Rule 702 requires that a district court ruling upon the admission of (novel) scientific evidence, i.e., evidence whose scientific fundamentals are not suitable candidates for judicial notice, conduct a preliminary inquiry focusing on (1) the soundness and reliability of the process or technique used in generating the evidence, (2) the possibility that admitting the evidence would overwhelm, confuse, or mislead the jury, and (3) the proffered connection between the scientific research or test result to be presented, and particular disputed factual issues in the case.

A

In establishing the reliability of novel scientific evidence as one criterion of its admissibility under Rule 702, we join a growing number of courts that have focused on reliability as a critical element of admissibility.[16]

The reliability inquiry that we envision is flexible and may turn on a number of considerations, in contrast to the process of scientific "nose-counting" that would appear to be compelled by a careful reading of *Frye*. Unlike the *Frye* standard, the reliability assessment does not require, although it does permit, explicit identification of a relevant scientific community and an express determination of a particular degree of acceptance within that community. The district court in assessing reliability may examine a variety of factors in addition to scientific acceptance. In many cases, however, the acceptance factor may well be decisive, or nearly so. Thus, we expect that a technique that satisfies the *Frye* test usually will be found to be reliable as well. On the other hand, a known technique which has been able to attract

---

16. Indeed, the reliability of a scientific technique may be determinative even in a court that purports to follow *Frye* itself. See, e.g., United States v. Franks, 511 F.2d 25, 33 n.12 (6th Cir.) ("we deem general acceptance as being nearly synonymous with reliability. If a scientific process is reliable, or sufficiently accurate, courts may also deem it 'generally accepted.' "), *cert. denied*, 422 U.S. 1042 (1975). The notion of "deeming" general acceptance on the basis that a process is sufficiently reliable would seem, however, to be at odds with the *Frye* test, and the identification of the relevant scientific community and factual determination of general acceptance required by the test.

IV. Judicial Receptivity to New Scientific Tests

only minimal support within the community is likely to be found unreliable.[17]

Where a form of scientific expertise has no established "track record" in litigation, the court may look to other factors that may bear on the reliability of the evidence.[18] Judge Weinstein and Professor Berger have compiled a list of these factors, some of which deserve explicit mention here. For instance, a court assessing reliability may consider the "novelty" of the new technique, that is, its relationship to more established modes of scientific analysis. This consideration may be especially significant in connection with an assessment of techniques that are new to the litigation setting. The existence of a specialized literature dealing with the technique is another factor. Both of these factors bear on the likelihood that the scientific basis of the new technique has been exposed to critical scientific scrutiny. The qualifications and professional stature of expert witnesses, and the non-judicial uses to which the scientific technique are put, may also constitute circumstantial evidence of the reliability of the technique.

The frequency with which a technique leads to erroneous results will be another important component of reliability. At one extreme, a technique that yields correct results less often than it yields an erroneous one is so unreliable that it is bound to be unhelpful to a finder of fact. Conversely, a very low rate of error strongly indicates a high degree of reliability. In addition to the rate of error, the court might examine the type of error generated by a technique.[19] In a case involving the admission of voiceprint evidence, for example, the Second Circuit emphasized the fact that any shortcomings in the scientific technique or its application would result in the inability to match two voice spectrograms, rather than an erroneous conclusion that the two spectra were generated by the same voice. Finally, the district may take judicial notice of expert testimony that has been offered in earlier cases to support or dispute the merits of a particular

---

17. Unlike the *Frye* test, however, a focus on reliability does not categorically rule out, for example, the admissibility of a technique developed for use in the litigation. Cf. Coppolino v. State, 223 So. 2d 68 (Fla. Dist. Ct. App. 1968) (citing *Frye*, but upholding admission of results of test for the presence of succinylcholine chloride that had been developed specifically for use in the trial where no method for detecting the substance had theretofore been known), *appeal dismissed*, 234 So. 2d 120 (Fla. 1969), *cert. denied*, 399 U.S. 927 (1970).

18. In certain cases, however, a court might be justified in taking judicial notice of the invalidity of the underlying basis for the evidence, e.g., astrology or phrenology.

19. Of course, whenever a district court suspects that the foundational evidence as to the reliability or other aspects of a technique may not fairly reflect the true state of scientific knowledge and opinion about it, the court would have the option to consider appointing an expert to ensure a balanced view.

scientific procedure. Undoubtedly, other factors could be added to the list.

B

After assessing the reliability of the evidence, the court must also weigh any danger that the evidence might confuse or mislead the jury. It may seem paradoxical to suggest that scientific evidence based on principles bearing substantial indicia of reliability could confuse rather than assist the jury, but we do not doubt that this may be so, in some cases. One example might involve a technique which has "assume[d] a posture of mythic infallibility," among lay persons, or at least one whose shortcomings are, for some reason, unlikely to be effectively communicated to the jury. The degree to which an unwarranted "aura of reliability," attaches to scientific evidence will naturally vary with the type of evidence. The danger that scientific evidence will mislead the jury might be greater, for example, where the jury is not presented with the data on which the expert relies, but must instead accept the expert's assertions as to the accuracy of his conclusions. Cf. People v. Marx, 54 Cal. App. 3d 100, 111, 126 Cal. Rptr. 350, 356 (1975) (in support of its holding admitting bite mark comparison evidence, the court noted that "the basic data on which the experts based their conclusions were verifiable by the court"). Techniques that rely on the use of a mechanical device to produce data as well as upon the exercise of an expert's subjective judgment to draw conclusions from the data would also seem to raise at least the possibility of confusing or misleading the jury.

The trial court must then balance its assessment of the reliability of a novel scientific technique against the danger that the evidence, even though reliable, might nonetheless confuse or mislead the finder of fact, and decide whether the evidence should be admitted. We decline to specify the foundational showing required for admissibility in traditional burden of proof terms because the balancing analysis incorporates important policy elements (i.e., the likelihood that a particular type of evidence will mislead the jury) which render the determination something more than a fact-finding. Therefore, we will review district court decisions to admit or exclude novel scientific evidence by an abuse of discretion standard.[21]

We do, however, suggest some considerations that are germane to the balancing exercise. First, there is the "presumption of helpfulness" accorded expert testimony generally under Fed. R. Evid.

---

21. While we have not quantified the requisite showing, it is plain that the proponent must make more than a prima facie showing (e.g., the testimony of a single qualified expert) that a technique is reliable. . . .

IV. Judicial Receptivity to New Scientific Tests

702. We also note, however, that some caution is appropriate, especially in the criminal context, whenever proffered novel scientific evidence, if unreliable or likely to mislead, will increase the likelihood of an erroneous verdict. The trial court, in ruling upon the admissibility of this kind of evidence, should take care to ensure that any weaknesses in the proffered evidence will be fully explored before or during the trial. The extent to which the adverse party has had notice of the evidence and an opportunity to conduct its own tests or produce opposing experts are also appropriate considerations for the court.

With respect to the procedure that district courts should follow in making preliminary determinations regarding admissibility of evidence, we recognize that " 'the control of the order of proof at trial is a matter committed to the discretion of the trial judge.' " Hence, we will not prescribe any mandatory procedures that district courts must follow in every case involving proffers of scientific evidence. A few general observations in this regard are appropriate, however.

It would appear that the most efficient procedure that the district court can use in making the reliability determination is an in limine hearing. Such a hearing need not unduly burden the trial courts; in many cases, it will be only a brief foundational hearing either before trial or at trial but out of the hearing of the jury. In the course of the in limine proceeding, the trial court may consider, inter alia, offers of proof, affidavits, stipulations, or learned treatises, in addition to testimonial or other documentary evidence (and, of course, legal argument). In addition, the court may properly consider the testimony presented to other courts that have addressed the same evidentiary issue, and the opinions of those courts on the subject. If a technique has found favor with a significant number of other courts, a district court may exercise its discretion to admit the evidence through judicial notice.

C

Having generally set out the appropriate inquiry, we now turn to the facts of this case. Unfortunately the district court never addressed the reliability question because it essentially — and erroneously — concluded that expert evidence of this type could never assist the trier of fact. From the facts available on the record and otherwise, it would appear that the scientific basis for the expert evidence in question is sufficiently reliable to satisfy Rule 702. In a recent case approving the use of expert testimony on eyewitness perception and memory in certain circumstances, the California Supreme Court noted the proliferation of empirical research demonstrating the pitfalls of eyewitness identification and concluded that "the consistency of the results of these studies is impressive." People

v. McDonald, 37 Cal. 3d 351, 208 Cal. Rptr. at 245, 690 P.2d at 718 (1984). The government has not had an opportunity to make a presentation on this point, however, and we believe that the district court should make the determination in the first instance.

D

An additional consideration under Rule 702 — and another aspect of relevancy — is whether expert testimony proffered in the case is sufficiently tied to the facts of the case that it will aid the jury in resolving a factual dispute. In this regard, we hold that a defendant who seeks the admission of expert testimony must make an on-the-record detailed proffer to the court, including an explanation of precisely how the expert's testimony is relevant to the eyewitness identifications under consideration. The offer of proof should establish the presence of factors (e.g., stress, or differences in race or age as between the eyewitness and the defendant) which have been found by researchers to impair the accuracy of eyewitness identifications. Failure to make such a detailed proffer is sufficient grounds to exclude the expert's testimony.

Turning to the facts of the present case, we note that appellant made no such on-the-record proffer, but conclude that this defect is not fatal on this appeal for two reasons. First, the district court did not rely on this failure to justify its decision to exclude appellant's expert. Second, the district court conducted all proceedings concerning the admissibility of appellant's expert's testimony off the record. With the resulting undeveloped record, we simply have no way of judging whether the proffered testimony was sufficiently tied to the facts of the case. The encounters between the identification witnesses and appellant were apparently not under conditions of stress, nor so far as we know, was there a potential cross-racial identification problem. It is conceivable, however, that the off-the-record expert proffer made by the appellant was sufficiently tied to the facts of the case to satisfy Rule 702. Therefore we cannot affirm the district court's exclusion of the expert evidence on this ground, and the district court will have to explore this question of "fit" on remand. . . .

[T]he judgment of conviction will be vacated and the case will be remanded to the district court for an evidentiary hearing concerning the admissibility of appellant's proffered expert testimony. If the court determines that the expert testimony should have been admitted, it is directed to grant a new trial. If the court decides that the testimony is not admissible under Rule 702 (or should be excluded under Rule 403), then the judgment of conviction against appellant should be reinstated.

NOTES

Alternatives to the General Acceptance Standard

1. *Terminology.* As in *Downing*, courts and attorneys typically use the word "reliability" to denote that which can be relied upon without undue risk of error. In experimental science and statistics, however, "reliability" has a more restricted meaning. It refers to the reproducibility or consistency of results. A measuring instrument, say a scale, is perfectly reliable if it always gives the same reading when the same weight is placed on it.

The term "validity," on the other hand, relates to the ability of the instrument to measure that which it is supposed to measure. A scale that used the volume of an object to determine its weight would not be valid. Even a perfectly reliable volume-measuring scale would be inaccurate as applied to objects of different densities. Thus, while an unreliable instrument cannot give valid individual measurements, reliability in the technical sense of consistency does not assure accurate or correct answers. The instrument must implement (reliably) a true (valid) theory.

In these terms, the probative value of evidence derived from a scientific theory depends on (1) the validity of the theory, (2) the validity and potential reliability of the technique for applying that theory, and (3) the proper application of the technique on a particular occasion. As the cases reproduced here reveal, the validity of the theory and the technique for applying it may be established through judicial notice or the presentation of evidence, including expert testimony. In appropriate circumstances, legislative recognition or a stipulation between the parties also may demonstrate validity, but the proper application of a scientific technique on a particular occasion must be shown by case-specific information. It cannot be the subject of judicial notice. E.g., Wamser v. State, 672 P.2d 163, 164 (Alaska Ct. App. 1983).

2. *Weight.* The battle between the adherents to the general acceptance standard and its detractors will continue. See Symposium on Science and Rules of Evidence, 99 F.R.D. 187 (1983); Proposals for a Model Rule on the Admissibility of Scientific Evidence, 26 Jurimetrics J. 237 (1986). Whatever its ultimate outcome, the degree of acceptance of a principle, theory, or methodology will remain important. In addition to having some bearing — determinative or otherwise — on admissibility, it also affects the weight that the judge or jury may be disposed to place on the evidence. Parties opposing the forensic application of methods that are controversial within the scientific community or that have not had sufficient time to be accepted

as valid and potentially reliable by many scientists may well argue that these results should be viewed with considerable caution.

V. GENETIC MARKERS FOR IDENTIFICATION

A. Cell Antigens and Serum Proteins and Enzymes

People v. Young
391 N.W.2d 270 (Mich. 1986)

LEVIN, Justice. . . .

I

Defendant Jeffrey Allen Young was convicted of first-degree murder on evidence that the homicide was committed during the perpetration of a felony. The Court of Appeals affirmed.

The felony described in the information was burglary. On the earlier submission of Young's appeal to this Court, we held that . . . "the results of the blood analyses were [not] admissible at trial without a prior showing that the technique of serological electrophoresis enjoys general scientific acceptance among impartial and disinterested experts. . . ."

We declined to respond to the question "whether the results of blood analyses are admissible to *include* an accused within the class of possible perpetrators" . . . until "development of a record by the trial court at the hearing which we order to determine if serological electrophoretic analysis has achieved general scientific acceptance for reliability, by disinterested and impartial experts.". . .

We retained jurisdiction. The hearing on the admissibility of the bloodstain evidence was held in the circuit court, and the record was transmitted to us. [T]he cause was reargued.

II

Evaluating the scientific community's acceptance of the reliability of electrophoresis of dried evidentiary bloodstains presents some unusual problems. The number of scientists not working for a police agency who are familiar with electrophoresis of evidentiary bloodstains is small. If these scientists alone were considered, the community would be too small for a fair sampling of scientific opinion. There is, however, a larger number of nonforensic scientists using electrophoresis who are capable of evaluating the reliability of electrophoresis

V. Genetic Markers for Identification

of evidentiary bloodstains if presented with the information they need to fill the gaps in their own knowledge and experience. The two groups combined constitute a group of scientists large enough to make a fair determination of whether electrophoresis of evidentiary bloodstains is generally accepted by experts in the scientific community.

The prosecution has the burden of establishing this community's general acceptance of the reliability of electrophoresis of evidentiary bloodstains. In the instant case, there is disagreement within the community on three separate issues: the length of time that genetic markers, particularly erythrocyte acid phosphatase (EAP), can be accurately read in dried blood, the reliability of the thin-gel multisystem analysis, and the effects of crime-scene contaminants. The prosecution did not fulfill its burden respecting the last two issues raised by the defense.

The only prosecution witness having substantial experience with electrophoresis of evidentiary bloodstains relied on his own unpublished observations and an unpublished reliability study by the developer of the multisystem to conclude that the thin-gel multisystem analysis was reliable. A defense witness questioned both the reliability of the technique and the study. The other prosecution witnesses were unfamiliar with the thin-gel multisystem, and their conclusion about the reliability of the method was based on the absence of any study showing that it did not work. No independently conducted reliability study supported that conclusion. Another defense witness said that the scientific community would not agree on the reliability of that conclusion without better supporting evidence.

Nor have comprehensive control tests been run with respect to the effects of crime scene contaminants. Prosecution witnesses testified, on the basis of their experience with bloodstains drawn under laboratory conditions, that they can identify bacterial contamination, at least if it is of the type normally encountered. They also claimed that bacterial contamination has not affected the reliability of the electrophoresis tests they have conducted. This is, however, the type of self-verification considered inconclusive in the scientific community. The record does not indicate that any work has been done on the effects of soil and chemical contamination on the reliability of electrophoresis.

We conclude that the scientific community's general acceptance of the reliability of electrophoresis of evidentiary bloodstains has not been established in the instant case. Reliability remains in dispute and unresolved because of the questions unanswered. The questions are not likely to be answered and the reliability of electrophoresis of evidentiary bloodstains established until independently conducted validation studies on the thin-gel multisystem analysis are undertaken and comprehensive control tests evaluating the effects of different contaminants are run, and the results have been subjected to the scrutiny of the scientific community. The evidence produced by electrophoresis should, therefore, not have been admitted. . . .

If it were clear that the erroneous admission of the electrophoresis evidence did not prejudice Young, the error would be harmless. We are, however, of the opinion that but for the electrophorèsis evidence the jury may have had a reasonable doubt, and that evidence might have made the difference. We therefore remand for a new trial on the charge of second-degree murder.

NOTES

Applying the General Acceptance Test

1. *On requiring "impartiality" and "independent" verification.* Compare *Young* with *Superior Court,* supra at §4. Given the Michigan Supreme Court's requirements of "disinterested and impartial" witnesses and "independent verification," is the HGN test for intoxication generally accepted in the relevant scientific community? The *Young* court observed:

> An argument could be made that neither Grunbaum nor Sensabaugh are disinterested and impartial, and should therefore be excluded despite their expertise. Grunbaum was the leader of the team of scientists that sought to develop a bloodstain analysis system for use in crime laboratories. He brought in Brian Wraxall and Stolorow to work on the project. After expressing dissatisfaction with the multisystem being developed, he withdrew from the project and suggested that it be discontinued. The project continued and when the results were published, he claimed they included misrepresentations. An independent review group found no grounds for Grunbaum's charges, but the sponsors of the project decided not to publish its results. Arguably, Grunbaum is still seeking to vindicate his original position. Sensabaugh also is not clearly disinterested. He has been a collaborator with Brian Wraxall and a paid consultant with the Oakland Crime Laboratory. He has also contributed to a prosecution response to an amicus curiae brief in a case pending before the California Supreme Court.
>
> Nevertheless, a certain degree of "interest" must be tolerated if scientists familiar with the theory and practice of a new technique are to testify at all. The standard developed by this Court is whether the expert's "livelihood was not intimately connected with the new technique." The livelihood of Stolorow and James Kearney, the prosecution witness who directs the FBI serology laboratory, is intimately connected with the new technique. The livelihood of Grunbaum and Sensabaugh is not so intimately connected.

V. Genetic Markers for Identification

2. *On "the thing" that must be generally accepted.* Reread Frye v. United States, supra §4. Does the general acceptance standard go to anything more than the theoretical underpinnings of electrophoresis — the physics of proteins in an electric field? How much more? Often, the specificity of "the thing" that must be generally accepted seems to foreordain the outcome of the *Frye* test. The Massachusetts Supreme Judicial Court, in the case presented immediately below, described electrophoresis and its application to forensic individualization, as follows:

> Electrophoresis is the movement of charged particles through a buffered conducting medium by application of a direct current. The term isozyme is used to describe enzymically active blood proteins which can be identified by their relative mobilities in an electric field. After separation of the proteins into marker bands by application of a current, specific chemicals are applied to make the proteins visible. . . . The relative distance of the bands from a common origin is compared with known standards, and evaluated by established guidelines. The results are then compared to population studies which show the known frequency of each factor in a given population. This produces a statistic which is representative of the percentage of the population that has that group and those factors in common. "The more genetic markers identified, the smaller the population of persons who might possess a particular combination of factors." Thus, the electrophoresis procedure permits an investigator to type a blood sample with greater precision than is possible with the familiar ABO system, and results of the test may serve to establish a "strong association between the bloodstain and its possible donor or the exclusion of the criminally accused as a donor of the bloodstain."

Commonwealth v. Gomes
526 N.E.2d 1270 (Mass. 1988)

LYNCH, Justice.

Antonio Gomes was indicted for the murders in the first degree of Basilisa Melendez, Joanna Aponte Rodriguez, and Kenneth Aponte Rodriguez, and for breaking and entering a dwelling house in the night time with intent to commit a felony and making an armed assault therein. The defendant filed a motion in limine to exclude evidence of blood enzyme testing. The motion was denied after hearing, but the defendant was granted the opportunity to present further evidence on the motion. The defendant was convicted and sentenced to three consecutive life sentences on the murder charges, and to a further concurrent life term on the breaking and entering charge. We affirm.

We summarize the relevant facts as the jury could have found them. [In] 1979, Eduardo Aponte Rodriguez (Aponte) [lived with] his common law wife, Basilisa, and . . . their three children . . . at 12 Jacobs Street, Boston. . . .

[When Aponte came home on the evening of December 5, 1979] Aponte put his key into the lock but the door would not open; the door or doorlock had been broken. Part of the door fell forward and Aponte pushed the door open.

Aponte saw his wife's body lying on the floor, and exclaimed, "Oh, my God, Bassi, what have they done to you?" He told Cardoza [his landlord, who had come with him to collect the rent] to call the police. He then went out on the porch and, holding onto one of the columns, screamed, "Oh, God, please help me, please help me, God." While he was calling out for help, Aponte saw three adults emerge from nearby 24 Jacobs Street, the building where the defendant lived. They looked at him, got into an automobile parked in front of 24 Jacobs Street, and drove away.

Boston police officers . . . arrived on the scene at 6:36 P.M. [T]hey observed the bodies of Aponte's wife and two of the children. The third child, an infant, lay in a crib in another room, unharmed. Aponte's wife was covered with blood, her face and head severely battered. She had been stabbed. She was naked from the breastline down. The children had also been stabbed. One had been thrown up against the wall; the other lay tangled up with a wooden chair. One of the children had been "almost decapitated" and her throat had been cut. . . .

[A] detective . . . observed a brown paper bag in the front bedroom of the house. On the bag were some reddish stains, later determined to be blood. Inside were Christmas gifts that Aponte had bought two or three days earlier, some children's clothes. . . .

. . . Boston police criminalist Stanley Bogdan . . . collected specimens of a number of reddish stains throughout the apartment. After chemical analysis he concluded that the specimens were blood stains of human origin. He tested each specimen to determine its blood type within the ABO blood grouping system.

The mother and children all had type O blood, as did Aponte and the landlord. Aponte's friend Harry had type B. Bogdan found certain specimens to be type O. ABO tests were inconclusive as to a number of other items, including stains collected from a chair in the doorway. However, Bogdan was able to determine that the stains from the chair were consistent with a mixture of two blood types: O and A. This was consistent with two people — one with type O blood, the other with type A — bleeding at the same time in the same immediate area. Chemical analysis revealed type A blood in the following items: reddish stains from the back of a bedspread, reddish spots from the front bedroom floor, stains from the bed, stains from

V. Genetic Markers for Identification 131

the edge of the front bedroom door, stains from a hanging string of beads, and stains from the paper bag found in the front bedroom. Further tests revealed that the type A bloodstain on the paper bag was Rh positive. Bogdan sent the specimen from the paper bag to FBI agent William McInnis for additional blood grouping tests, described in detail in the body of this opinion.

The defendant's activities on the night of the murders are described as follows. At 7:00 P.M. that night the defendant was admitted to the emergency room at Boston City Hospital complaining of a stab wound to his right forearm and a bruise on his right hand. He told the treating physician that he had sustained these injuries while punching an assailant. He said that he had been stabbed. The doctor testified that the wound was of the type that would have bled.

Boston police officers . . . responded to Boston City Hospital upon report of a stabbing. They did not know about the incident at 12 Jacobs Street. [Defendant reacted to their arrival with some concern.]

. . . He did not give clear answers to the police questions and fumbled with his words. When questioned as to the particulars of how his injury had occurred, the defendant "seemed to agree with whatever was suggested to him." He was anxious to leave. . . .

The police [were unable to corroborate his story of how he came to be stabbed]. The next day, . . . police detective[s] went to the defendant's house. . . . On this occasion the defendant's account of his activities on the night of the murder differed from the account he had given at the hospital. . . . The defendant himself then raised the subject of the three murders at 12 Jacobs Street. He began to yell, "If you want my ideas on this thing next door, I'll tell you right now that those Puerto Ricans are all f——ing each other and they're doing their relatives and everything else."

[The next day] the same officers returned to speak further with the defendant. During the course of this conversation the defendant showed the officers the cut on his arm and said, "See, it's only a little scratch. [About that] report I made to the police, it never happened." The defendant said he had cut himself. Then, fifty seconds to a minute later, he said, "I didn't cut myself. I had a fight with my girl and she stabbed me." . . . The defendant again brought up the subject of the murders, saying "I hate those f——ing people anyway. [N]ow get the f—— out of my house."

[In] 1982, Boston police detective Mark Madden obtained a warrant for a sample of the defendant's blood for chemical analysis. The defendant went with the police to the hospital where the blood sample was drawn. Test results for the defendant's blood and conclusive blood-grouping results obtained two years earlier from the blood-stained paper bag were identical.

[Two months later, when] the defendant was arrested [he gave the police yet another explanation of how he had cut his arm. He also said that before going to the hospital, he heard a six o'clock news broadcast about the murders at 12 Jacobs Street. Police investigation showed that there was no such broadcast.]

After questioning the defendant was detained in a cell at . . . police headquarters. The next [evening], [a police officer] found the defendant hanging by the neck on a cord fastened to the wall of his cell, unconscious but still alive. The officer took him down and resuscitated him.

Several days later the defendant, still in his cell, engaged in a shouting argument with some recently arrested juveniles seated outside his cell. When [the officer] intervened, the defendant said to him, "Tell them what I did. Tell them why I'm here. They don't want to mess with me."

At trial the defendant offered alibi testimony from his mother and his girl friend.

1. *Admission of evidence of electrophoretic testing.* The defendant claims that the judge erroneously admitted evidence of a genetic marker analysis performed upon bloodstains on the paper bag found at the crime scene because the Commonwealth failed to establish that the procedure employed to analyse the stain — electrophoresis — is generally accepted within the relevant scientific community. There was no error. . . .

The particular electrophoretic method at issue here is known as "multisystem" electrophoresis, so-called because it entails separating a number of enzymes simultaneously on the same sample. Such a method has the advantages of saving time and requiring less bloodstain material. [Some of its developers, Wraxall and Storolow, also have] suggested that the multisystem approach provides "a substantial improvement of the resolution of the isozyme bands of [certain enzymes] compared to their respective single-system methods of conventional electrophoresis."

Both multisystem and conventional electrophoresis methods were employed in this case by FBI serologist William McInnis. McInnis received from the Boston police crime laboratory the paper bag recovered from the crime scene, on which he determined there were two bloodstains. McInnis applied the electrophoresis technique to the stains, testing for seven enzyme and protein systems, abbreviated as follows: PGM, EsD, GLO-1, EAP, ADA, AK, and Hp. With the exception of the Hp system, McInnis tested for all the systems using the multisystem approach. McInnis also performed the more traditional antigen antibody tests on the stains, testing Rh and Mn factors. As a result of these tests, in combination with testing earlier performed by the Boston crime laboratory, it was determined that one stain

V. Genetic Markers for Identification   133

exhibited identifiable types in six systems of genetic markers: ABO (type A); Rh (type D positive); Mn (type M negative); EAP (type B); ADA (type 1); Hp (type 1). Of the United States population, McInnis testified, 0.6% of whites and 1.2% of blacks would present this particular combination of genetic markers. As noted previously, a sample of the defendant's blood was taken and McInnis performed thereon ABO testing, Rh, and Mn typing, and electrophoretic analysis for the seven enzyme and protein systems. The test results corresponded identically to the results obtained from the stain on the paper bag.[6]

The defendant claims that electrophoresis may not be considered to be generally accepted in the scientific community because: the reliability of the multisystem approach is not agreed upon; there is disagreement as to the length of time that certain genetic markers can be read in dried blood; and there are questions as to the effect on the same of crime scene contaminants. We reject these claims. . . .

The Commonwealth's expert, Mark Stolorow, testified that electrophoresis, including the multisystem, is generally accepted in the forensic science community. Stolorow is serology coordinator for the Illinois Department of Law Enforcement and holds a Master of Science degree in forensic chemistry. He has testified as an expert in forensic serology over one hundred times in six states, for both prosecution and defense. As serology coordinator, he is responsible for training new serologists, proficiency testing of staff serologists in seven crime laboratories, updating staff serologists on new developments in the field of blood analysis, and evaluation and research of new equipment in the field. His achievements and experience in the field of electrophoresis are extensive.

In 1972, Stolorow participated in an electrophoresis course taught by Brian Culliford of Scotland Yard, then recognized as one of the foremost experts in the field. In 1977, Stolorow participated in a research project at the laboratory of Dr. Benjamin Grunbaum at the University of California at Berkeley. The project goal was to improve the capability of crime laboratories in electrophoretic analysis of dried bloodstains. Stolorow spent approximately six months on the project, "participating in the developmental phase . . . inventing the method that ultimately resulted from that research." Initially, Grunbaum,

---

6. Boston police department criminalist Stanley Bogdan had performed ABO and Rh testing on the sample, and determined it to be type A, Rh positive. McInnis's testing was inconclusive as to all genetic markers on one of the stains. As to the other stain, McInnis tested in the Mn system for the M factor only and none was present; since all his controls reacted properly, McInnis termed this a negative reading. However, the jury heard testimony that failure to detect the M factor does not conclusively mean M is not present; the failure may be caused by degradation in the stain. Furthermore, in addition to the seven systems noted above, McInnis employed electrophoresis to test for four additional systems — PGM, EsD, GLO-1 and AK. In these systems, he obtained inconclusive results. . . .

Stolorow, and Brian Wraxall collaborated in the development of the multisystem. While Stolorow acknowledged that studies have been published pointing out problems in the use of electrophoresis, he indicated that such studies are intended to alert those using the technique to potential pitfalls, not to call into question the technique's underlying reliability. He knew of no scientific publication that had ever refuted the reliability of electrophoresis.[8] He concluded that electrophoretic testing of dried evidentiary bloodstains "certainly has gained general acceptance in the forensic science community."

The defendant offered the testimony of Diane Juricek, Ph.D., a researcher in genetics. Dr. Juricek had performed electrophoretic testing on fresh materials, but not on dried evidentiary blood stains. She testified that electrophoresis is unreliable when applied to dried evidentiary blood because such blood not only degrades with age, but also may be subject to crime scene contaminants and adverse environmental conditions which, she claimed, may result in erroneous readings. Dr. Juricek also testified that the multisystem was unreliable because it compromises among optimum testing conditions in order to test several enzymes simultaneously. According to Dr. Juricek, the unreliability of the multisystem is illustrated by the lack of scientific publications affirming its reliability. Finally, she criticized the actual testing procedures in this case.

Also testifying as an expert for the defense was Dr. Benjamin Grunbaum, a biochemist. Grunbaum testified that electrophoresis is reliable for testing fresh blood and dried bloodstains of known origin prepared under laboratory conditions. However, Grunbaum contended that the reliability of multisystem electrophoresis for testing evidentiary bloodstains from a crime scene has never been independently verified.

A review of relevant scientific literature and court decisions reveals that, despite Grunbaum's and Juricek's criticisms, when applied properly by trained analysts cognizant of the scientific literature as to the warning signs of erroneous readings, conventional and multisystem electrophoresis are generally accepted within the scientific community. As was noted in People v. Reilly, 196 Cal. App. 3d 1127, 1148, 242 Cal. Rptr. 496 (1987), "Dr. Grunbaum stands virtually alone in his opposition to electrophoretic typing of dried bloodstain evidence." The *Reilly* court surveyed opinion of a number of experts. One of them, Dr. Edward Blake, testified that electrophoresis is generally accepted in the scientific community when performed properly, and that "[h]e was unaware of any dissension on the point until he read Dr. Grunbaum's amicus brief in [another case] and knows of no one who shares Grunbaum's views. Nor [was] he aware of any publications

---

8. The absence of published refutations attests to the technique's reliability. . . .

V. Genetic Markers for Identification

that indicate lack of reliability."[9] Another expert, Dr. George Sensabaugh, testified in *Reilly* that Doctors Grunbaum and Juricek were the only scientists he knew of who questioned the reliability of electrophoresis. He, too, knew of no publications questioning the technique's reliability. Indeed, Sensabaugh earlier had published a refutation of Juricek's assertions of unreliability . . . concluding that Juricek's analysis evidenced "a naive and often erroneous characterization of genetic typing analysis . . . [and a] . . . disregard of pertinent literature [and] distortion of context of cited works."

As to the effects of adverse environmental factors and aging on the sample, the *Reilly* court noted that Dr. Grunbaum's "criticism [as to the effects of these factors] was repeatedly qualified by noting that well trained, competent analysts who use proper procedures and are aware of the published literature warning of typing problems can account for those possibilities." . . . Thus, the above authorities indicate that, so long as the analyst is trained to recognize the signposts of adverse environmental factors, the reliability of the test is not compromised.

With the exception of . . . People v. Young, 424 Mich. 470, 391 N.W.2d 270 (1986), all courts considering the issue have held evidence of electrophoretic testing admissible. Of these, four jurisdictions have specifically held that the multisystem method is generally accepted in the relevant scientific community. We conclude, therefore, that both multisystem and conventional electrophoretic testing of dried evidentiary bloodstains are generally accepted as reliable in the relevant scientific community.

However, the defendant contends, even if the procedure is generally accepted in the scientific community, evidence of the test results nonetheless should not have been admitted because the test was not properly performed and FBI agent McInnis was not properly qualified as an expert. Testimony indicated that agent McInnis was an experienced analyst, trained in the electrophoretic technique and that he carefully conducted the genetic marker typing and used appropriate standards and controls. He was aware of typing problems described in the relevant scientific literature. Mark Storolow testified that the technique used by the FBI in this case was reliable. On this evidence there was "sufficient basis for finding, as a preliminary question of fact, that this witness was qualified to testify as an expert" and that

---

9. Appellant argues that these witnesses, particularly Dr. Baird, possess a built-in bias because their reputations and careers are built on DNA comparison work. Several courts have questioned whether a leading proponent of a particular technique could fairly and impartially testify concerning admission of the tests. Neither *Frye* nor our evidence code require impartiality. Further, the point would not appear substantial here given that unlike voiceprints, DNA comparison work has a number of uses in fields other than forensic medicine such as diagnosis and treatment of disease.

the procedures employed were performed properly and reliably. Therefore, the defendant's various attacks alleging infirmities in the performance of the testing or the skill or knowledge of the witness go only to the weight of the evidence, not to its admissibility. The evidence of electrophoretic testing was properly admitted; thereafter, any attacks on the evidence were for the jury to weigh. . . .

2. *Statistical evidence.* The defendant claims that it was error for the judge to admit McInnis' expert testimony that, in the United States, 1.2 percent of blacks present the particular combination of genetic markers found in the bloodstain. . . . The judge could find . . . that the statistical evidence presented was based on established, empirical data rather than speculation and that the evidence was more probative than prejudicial. Therefore, the evidence was properly admitted.

3. *Failure to photograph the electrophoretogram* . . . The defendant claims that the failure of the Commonwealth to photograph the electrophoretogram denied him his due process right to a fair trial. He concedes, however, that the Commonwealth provided him with FBI laboratory notes and reports. . . .[12]

> In this Commonwealth, when potentially exculpatory evidence is lost or destroyed, a balancing test is employed to determine the appropriateness and extent of remedial action. The courts must weigh the culpability of the Commonwealth, the materiality of the evidence and the potential prejudice to the defendant. . . . Where evidence is lost or destroyed, it may be difficult to determine the precise nature of the evidence. While the defendant need not prove that the evidence would have been exculpatory, he must establish "a 'reasonable possibility, based on concrete evidence rather than a fertile imagination,' that access to the [material] would have produced evidence favorable to his cause."

Applying the balancing test above, we note that the Commonwealth was culpable in some degree for failing to photograph the material. However, that culpability is mitigated to a great extent by the fact that the defendant has been provided with laboratory notes and reports of the test results from the FBI laboratory. Neither is this a case where the Commonwealth ignored or rejected a defense request to preserve evidence by special means. Rather, the Commonwealth had completed its testing over two years before the defendant's arrest, so "there was no lawyer to whom notice could have been given concerning the testing."

Furthermore, the defendant has failed to show how his case was

---

12. The defendant assumes that the Commonwealth's failure to photograph the test results is the equivalent of losing or destroying the evidence. Although this assumption is open to question, we analyze the issue as though it is correct.

prejudiced by the lack of photographs. The defendant had available agent McInnis's laboratory report and notes, from which defense counsel conducted an extensive cross-examination. Moreover, that photographs of the test results might have been useful to the defense, does not rise to a showing of "a 'reasonable possibility, based on concrete evidence . . .' that access to [a photograph] would have produced evidence favorable to his cause."

Indeed, as one commentator has remarked: "Photography of electrophoretograms of ideal samples may be reliable for the purposes of leisurely scientific appraisal, however, I know of no such proven testing of samples of varying activities as does occur in forensic samples. A single photograph of such a separation could not adequately cover the range of such activity with the sensitivity of the human eye. Photography does not necessarily represent the true picture and can lead to artifacts." Therefore, we conclude that the failure of the Commonwealth to provide a photograph of the electrophoretogram did not deprive the defendant of a fair trial. . . .

Judgments affirmed.

NOTES

The General Acceptance of Thin-gel, Multisystem Electrophoresis of Aged or Contaminated Blood

Why did the *Gomes* court differ with the *Young* court? Was the evidence on the general acceptance of thin-gel, multisystem electrophoresis of aged or contaminated blood stains different? Did the courts apply the general acceptance test differently? In what way or ways?

Does the *Gomes* opinion address and satisfy all the concerns raised in *Young*? Should the *Gomes* court have relied on judicial opinions conflicting with *Young* to ascertain the views of the pertinent scientific community? What are the implications of the fact that the multisystem, thin-gel findings in *Gomes* were replicated by a more conventional form of electrophoresis? In addressing these questions, consider the following portions of the opinion in *Young*.

People v. Young
425 Mich. 470, 391 N.W.2d 270 (1986)

At the evidentiary hearing to determine the reliability of electrophoresis of evidentiary bloodstains, the prosecution presented seven witnesses, and the defense presented two witnesses. The prosecution and defense each presented one forensic scientist having substantial experience with electrophoresis of evidentiary bloodstains. Three of the prosecution's witnesses and the other defense witness were geneticists, familiar with electrophoresis, but unfamiliar with electrophoresis of evidentiary bloodstains. The other three prosecution witnesses were technicians, two of whom were full-time employees of law enforcement agencies. Before analyzing their conclusions it is first necessary to determine whether some or all of them are "disinterested and impartial experts in the particular field."

Because a theoretical understanding is essential, the relevant scientific community is scientists not technicians. Practical experience with the process, however, is also necessary. Ideally the community would be scientists with direct empirical experience with the procedure in question.

Two of the witnesses fit this description. Dr. George Sensabaugh is an associate professor of public health at the University of California at Berkeley and a specialist in forensic science. He has also conducted electrophoresis studies of dried bloodstains. Dr. Benjamin Grunbaum is a retired biochemist from the University of California with a specialty in criminalistics, the science of identification of physical evidence in criminal cases. He has been recognized to be "a leader in the development of electrophoresis to test body-fluid enzymes for purposes of forensic identification."

Grunbaum and Sensabaugh appear to be a part of a small community of scientists doing work on electrophoresis of evidentiary bloodstains.[21] The number of scientists within this community willing to testify seems even smaller. Grunbaum, Sensabaugh, and Mark Stolorow, the police detective who did the electrophoresis in the instant case, figure prominently in the few reported cases involving electrophoresis of evidentiary bloodstains. Those cases might be described as reflecting and reporting a debate between Stolorow and Grunbaum. . . .

The precise issue in the instant case is whether electrophoresis of evidentiary bloodstains passes the general acceptance test. General acceptance of electrophoresis in other areas is not necessarily relevant. The defendant concedes that serological electrophoresis of fresh blood in paternity testing and genetics research is considered generally reliable. Electrophoresis of evidentiary bloodstains presents, however, a number of complications, particularly the electrophoresis conducted in the instant case.

The complications are the bloodstain is not fresh, it is tested by

21. Grunbaum invited Brian Wraxall and Mark Stolorow to join him at the University of California at Berkeley to develop the multisystem. Sensabaugh has collaborated with Wraxall. As the defense commented in its brief in this Court, Grunbaum and Sensabaugh "appear to be the only such (independent) scientists in the country with regard to evidentiary bloodstain electrophoresis."

V. Genetic Markers for Identification   139

thin-gel multisystem analysis, and most importantly, it has possibly been exposed to unknown contaminants.

A

Electrophoresis for paternity testing and genetics research is generally done on fresh blood. Electrophoresis of evidentiary stains is for the most part done on dried blood. . . . The important difference is that the blood is not fresh, and blood begins to degrade as soon as it leaves the body. The "crucial question is whether the marker detected in aged blood is a reliable indication of that found in fresh blood from the same person." The dispute centers on the results of the EAP test. . . .

Despite these disagreements, if the only question about the reliability of electrophoresis of evidentiary bloodstains was the survivability of degraded samples, it would be questionable whether electrophoresis evidence should be excluded where the bloodstain is less than three weeks old. The most detailed independent study discussed by the scientists suggests degraded EAP markers can be accurately read up to thirteen weeks. Before this study was written, other scientists believed EAP markers could be accurately read up to two to three weeks, which was the length of time involved in the instant case. The main support for the defense's critique of the studies are test results from too small a sample to carry much weight in the scientific community.

B

The second point of contention is the reliability of the thin-gel multisystem used in the instant case, which simultaneously analyzes three genetic markers, PGM, EsD, and GLO, on a single, thin-layer starch gel. Although other combination systems exist, the multisystem was designed by police scientists for police work; it allows the maximum amount of information to be drawn from electrophoresis of a small stain. . . .

The defense argues that the thin-gel multisystem is unreliable with respect to dried blood because the blood sample is too marginal to begin with to be accurately read after further diffusion. Once the electrophoretic separation has been conducted, a filter paper containing a chemical reagent is placed over the gel. The filter paper is meant to stain the EsD molecules, but it also soaks up PGM molecules. Grunbaum says this "compromises" the PGM test because "the PGM molecules have diffused sideways, some have disappeared . . . [and] the intensity of the PGM bands are not the same as if they were stained first, before the EsD." Grunbaum said he could "deduce from the photographs [taken of the test] that a leaching out of the PGM has occurred and you can see it very well" in the instant case. The defense argues that the multisystem "aggravates" the problem inherent in analyzing degraded samples.

The defense further argues that no independent study verifying the reliability of the thin-gel multisystem has ever been published. No prosecution witness contradicted this argument. The developer of the thin-gel multisystem, Brian Wraxall, did conduct his own blind trials,[46] but self-verification is not a sufficiently reliable procedure.

The prosecutor's response was to present witnesses who have done electrophoresis with other combination tests. Dr. Rachael Fisher and Dr. Harvey Mohrenweiser have used combination systems involving a thick-slab starch gel. Grunbaum distinguished the thick- from the thin-gel combination system. "They [those using the thick gel] slice their gel in such a way that they had several layers, like a layer cake, and they had fresh surfaces, and they stained only one for a given system. So this was not a compromising system." Testimony by at least one of the prosecution witnesses suggested there was some overlap on [the PGM and EOP] systems he used. He did not think the overlap compromised the system. . . . There was no further testimony by either side to resolve the dispute about the effect of the overlapping tests.

The prosecution also asked the scientists using the other combination tests why they believed the thin-gel multisystem was reliable. Their collective response could be summarized in the following comment by Dr. Rachael Fisher, "I have no reason to suppose it wouldn't work." They testified that they had seen no study demonstrating that the multisystem was unreliable. This line of reasoning would be adequate if the burden of establishing general acceptance of *unreliability* were placed on the defense. The burden of establishing general acceptance of *reliability* is, however, on the prosecution.

In sum, there are substantial unanswered questions respecting the reliability of Wraxall's thin-gel multisystem. Conflicting expert testimony indicates that until independent verification tests have been conducted regarding the thin-gel multisystem, general agreement in the scientific community on the reliability of that multisystem is unlikely. A specific question left unresolved is whether the filter used in the test of the EsD molecules compromises the analysis of the PGM molecules.

---

46. This study is what Sensabaugh was referring to when he said blind trials conducted between four laboratories established the reliability of the multisystem.

C

The reliability of blood degraded by dirt, gasoline, urine, sweat, and other possible crime scene contaminants is also at issue in the instant case. Electrophoresis for paternity testing and genetics research is not beset with these problems. The only scientists that have done electrophoresis of blood exposed to these contaminants are those with forensic experience.

Both witnesses for the defense, Grunbaum and Dr. Diane Juricek, testified that it is not possible to determine the reliability of electrophoresis of evidentiary bloodstains until the effects of crime scene contaminants are understood. Juricek said that for electrophoresis of evidentiary bloodstains to be accepted as reliable, scientists would have to study the effects of "common gasoline contaminants which appear on sidewalks, DDT, which can, you know, from spraying grass . . . appear. . . . There is [sic] also bacterial contamination possibilities. There are molds that could have an effect." Although Juricek would not say for certain whether the contaminants would affect the electrophoresis, she said there was a "very strong theoretical possibility" that they would. Grunbaum testified "[t]here is just no way of knowing the degree of . . . the humidity, . . . heat . . . bacterial . . . [and], chemical contamination, and . . . this is a range that goes on beyond anybody's imagination."

Both witnesses testified that the reliability of electrophoresis of evidentiary bloodstains would not be established in the scientific community until controlled studies were conducted taking into account the possible contaminants present at a crime scene. Juricek said "[y]ou would have to check all of these different factors . . . singularly and then in combination. . . ." The studies would then have to be published and "verified independently."

It appears from the record and a survey of the scientific literature that such comprehensive control studies have not been conducted.

The prosecution relies instead on inferences drawn from tests performed on dried bloodstains prepared under ideal contamination-free conditions. The only publication referred to by name was the Denault study. . . . Reliance on this study is curious given Denault's own caveat.

> [E]mphasis must be placed on the limitations of this study. It is intended as a starting point for future research. . . . Moreover, the tests were conducted on clean specimens free of impurities. It is realized that in actual practice serological evidence preserved under known and constant conditions is rare, and the specimens may be contaminated with impurities such as perspiration, urine, soil, and bacteria. These factors limit the application of the results of the study.

When questioned about the proviso, the prosecution's only expert with significant experience with evidentiary bloodstains commented, the cleanliness of the stains is not "as significant a problem as they think it is." The prosecution emphasizes that no study has shown unreliability.

Prosecution witnesses testified about their experience with contaminants. Sensabaugh, relying on his own unpublished laboratory study, said that bacterial contamination would signal itself. He said the person interpreting the test would see "new bands appearing in odd positions. . . ." Fisher also testified that bacterial contamination would result in a "different activity, different position." She suggested the contamination "will flag you. . . ."

Juricek has written, however, that bacterial contamination does not necessarily create easily excludable bizarre bands. "Many bacteria have been found to have Type 2 PGM, for example. Thus, Type 1 blood when contaminated by bacteria that have Type 2 PGM would be identified as Type 2-1 despite the use of starch gels and proper controls." The result of the PGM test in the instant case was Type 2-1.

Fisher was more willing to recognize uncertainty with respect to unknown contaminants. When asked about soil, Fisher answered, "If it is contaminated with soil, I have no idea. It depends on what is in the soil." . . . Although she followed up with the comment that "I can't conceive of anybody [having problems], unless one is going to go around sprinkling the place with rare chemicals," the testimony of another prosecution witness, Dr. Harvey Mohrenweiser, suggests that it is only fair to conclude that examiners will "catch flags" they are used to seeing. . . . The only stains he had examined were those produced in laboratories. Because these stains were not collected under sterile conditions, there could be "some bacterial contamination." Mohrenweiser and the other prosecution witnesses did not respond to the questions raised by the defense about the effect on electrophoresis of other likely crime scene contaminants such as chemicals and soil.

In sum, scientists do not agree what effect common crime scene contaminants may have on electrophoresis. They do not agree because comprehensive control tests have not been undertaken. The scientists testifying at trial had no experience with soil or chemical contamination and could only guess what effect such contaminants might engender. Although the scientists had some experience with the type of bacterial contamination found in laboratories, the bloodstains here were made during or following the commission of a crime and not under laboratory conditions. . . .

The scientific tradition expects independent verification of new procedures. When other scientists analyze and repeat the tests, they

V. Genetic Markers for Identification

counteract the dangers of biased reporting. It is scientists not responsible for the original research that confirm its validity. Although electrophoresis has been generally accepted as reliable in the scientific community for many years, Wraxall's multisystem test is a new technique. No independently conducted verification studies have been undertaken. . . .

The dangers of allowing implementation of an inadequately tested device are well-known. The paraffin test and the Dalkon Shield are two familiar examples. . . .

NOTES

1. *Other individualizing tests of bodily fluids and specimens.* The evidence in *Young* and *Gomes* included serologic tests for red blood cell antigens. Electrophoresis of the isoenzymes found in blood and other bodily fluids is but one of many methods for identifying various components of these fluids. See, e.g., United States v. Gwaltney, 790 F.2d 1378 (9th Cir. 1986); Cecka, Breidenthal & Terasaki, Direct Blood Group Typing of Forensic Samples Using a Simple Monoclonal Antibody Assay, 34 For. Sci. Intl. 205 (1987); Reguero & Arnaiz-Villena, HLA Typing of Dried Sperm, 29 J. For. Sci. 430 (1984); cf. Miyasaka, Yoshino, Sato, Miyake & Seta, The ABO Blood Grouping of a Minute Hair Sample by the Immunohistochemical Technique, 34 For. Sci. Intl. 85 (1987). These components are synthesized within a person's cells according to instructions in the cell's genetic material. Thus, the molecules identified via electrophoresis, serologic reactions, or other methods may be thought of as genetic markers. A thorough and comprehensive discussion of the many markers, genetic systems, and methods of detection can be found in R. Gaensslen, Sourcebook in Forensic Serology, Immunology, and Biochemistry (U.S. Dept. of Justice 1983). One emerging method of "DNA typing," which looks to variations in the genetical material itself, rather than its protein products, is discussed in the second part of this section.

2. *The admissibility of population statistics.* Despite earlier dicta from the Massachusetts Supreme Judicial Court "disfavoring" explicit probabilities or statistics, *Gomes* holds the population statistics on the prevalence of the incriminating isoenzymes admissible. In a footnote omitted from the opinion reproduced above, the court observed that the defense witness, Dr. Juricek, questioned the accuracy of these estimates, but held that this attack affected the weight rather than the admissibility of those numbers. Should *Frye* apply to particular tables of population frequencies and numbers deduced from these tables, or only to the method of gathering the statistics? For additional materials on "probability evidence," see supra at §I. Some technical

discussions focusing on probabilities involving genetic markers in blood are Selvin & Grunbaum, Genetic Marker Determination in Evidence Bloodstains: The Effect of Classification Errors on Probability of Non-Discrimination and Probability of Concordance, 27 J. For. Sci. Socy. 57 (1987); Gettinby, An Empirical Approach to Estimating the Probability of Innocently Acquiring Bloodstains of Different ABO Groups on Clothing, 24 J. For. Sci. Socy. 221 (1984).

3. *The government's duty to preserve scientific evidence.* The *Gomes* court holds that the Commonwealth's failure to photograph the pattern on the gel after electrophoresis did not deprive the defendant of due process of law. Why? What uses might the defense have made of such a photograph? Dr. Grunbaum testified in *Young* that he could "deduce from the photographs that a leaching out of the PGM has occurred."

When, if ever, does due process require the government to preserve trace evidence for scientific analysis by the defense? When the government knows or strongly suspects that the evidence would exonerate the defendant? Cf. Brady v. Maryland, 373 U.S. 83 (1963) (due process requires prosecution to disclose, on request, exculpatory evidence). When a reasonable investigator would want the evidence analyzed? When the government should have analyzed the evidence, but did not? See Arizona v. Youngblood, 109 S. Ct. 333 (1988) (semen stain); California v. Trombetta, 467 U.S. 479 (1984) (breath sample); Comment, The Prosecution's Duty to Preserve Evidence Before Trial, 72 Calif. L. Rev. 1019 (1984).

4. *Parentage testing.* Genetic markers provide useful and often determinative information in cases of disputed parentage. Attempts to express the outcomes of genetic testing as a "probability of paternity," however, have proved controversial. Compare Plemel v. Walter, 735 P.2d 1209 (Or. 1987), with Commonwealth v. Beausoleil, 397 Mass. 206, 490 N.E.2d 788 (1986). The latter case is criticized in Kaye, The Probability of an Ultimate Issue: The Strange Cases of Paternity Testing, 75 Iowa L. Rev. 75 (1989), and in McCormick on Evidence §211 (E. Cleary 3d ed. 1987 Supp.). The various probabilities bandied about in parentage cases can be confusing when first encountered. Accounts in legal journals and treatises, not to mention opinions, are sometimes garbled. For more precise expositions of the biostatistical analysis, see, for instance, Aickin & Kaye, Some Mathematical and Legal Considerations in Using Serological Tests to Prove Paternity, in Inclusion Probabilities in Parentage Testing 155 (R.H. Walker ed. 1983); Berry & Geisser, Inference in Cases of Disputed Paternity, in Statistics and the Law 353 (DeGroot, Fienberg & Kadane eds. 1986); Li & Chakravarti, An Expository Review of Two Methods for Calculating the Paternity Probability, 43 Am. J. Human Genetics

197-205 (1988). For a more elementary, but oversimplified discussion, see Ellman & Kaye, Probabilities and Proof: Can HLA and Blood Group Testing Prove Paternity? 54 N.Y.U.L. Rev. 1131 (1979).

B. DNA Typing

People v. Wesley
140 Misc. 2d 306, 533 N.Y.S.2d 643 (N.Y. Co. 1988)

HARRIS, J.

[T]he People move for an Order to extract blood from [defendants] for the purpose of comparing the "DNA" therein with "DNA" contained in biological evidence reasonably believed to be relevant. . . . In People v. Cameron Bailey, the defendant is charged with rape in the 1st degree; the evidence believed to be relevant is an aborted fetus. In People v. George Wesley, the defendant is charged with burglary in the 2nd degree and suspected of murder in the 2nd degree. Bloodstained clothing was retrieved from the defendant; the People propose to compare the "DNA" contained in said bloodstains with "DNA" extracted from the deceased victim and for control purposes with "DNA" to be extracted from a known blood sample of defendant Wesley.

The process sought to be used by the People is colloquially and most frequently referred to in forensic science as "DNA Fingerprinting." . . . DNA Fingerprinting is at the "cutting edge" of forensic science, just as molecular biology and genetic engineering are at the "cutting edge" of revolutionary applications in medicine and control of such genetic or genetic-influenced diseases as diabetes, diverse forms of cancer, muscular dystrophy, Down's Syndrome, and Acquired Immune Deficiency Syndrome (AIDS). . . .

[I]f DNA Fingerprinting proves acceptable in criminal courts, [it] will revolutionize the administration of criminal justice. Where applicable, it would reduce to insignificance the standard alibi defense. [E]yewitness testimony . . . has been claimed to be responsible for more miscarriages of justice than any other type of evidence, [and] DNA Fingerprinting would tend to reduce the importance of eyewitness testimony. And in the area of clogged calendars and the conservation of judicial resources, DNA Fingerprinting, if accepted, will revolutionize the disposition of criminal cases. In short, if DNA Fingerprinting works and receives evidentiary acceptance, it can constitute the single greatest advance in the "search for truth" and the goal of convicting the guilty and acquitting the innocent since the advent of cross-examination. . . .

McCormick on Evidence*
§205, at 73-75 (E. Cleary 3d ed. 1987 Supp.)

[T]he impending application of recombinant-DNA technology to determining paternity or criminal identity can be expected to produce controversy in the courtroom. DNA is a long molecule with two strands that spiral around one another, forming a double helix. Within the double helix are molecules (called nucleotide bases) that link one strand to the other, like the steps of a spiral staircase. There are four nucleotide bases, which can be referred to as A, T, G and C. The A on one strand pairs with T on the other, and the G bonds to C. The sequence of AT and GC "stairs" is the genetic code.

Rather than using cell surface antigens or serum enzymes or proteins as markers for the genes that express these molecules, it is possible to examine the DNA . . . more directly, with restriction enzymes and "DNA probes." Restriction enzymes cleave a DNA molecule whenever they encounter a certain sequence in the genetic code [of some four to eight base pairs]. . . . The sites at which a restriction enzyme will chop a length of DNA thus depends on the DNA sequence. Since the enzymes cleave DNA at characteristic locations, "digesting" a sample of DNA with the enzymes gives rise to fragments of various lengths, usually in the range from several hundred to several thousand base pairs.

The distribution of fragment lengths provides a clue as to the arrangement of the base pairs in the DNA that the enzymes digested. To see some of this distribution, two things must be done. The restriction fragments . . . must be separated by size, and at least some [fragments] must be detected. The first step is accomplished with electrophoresis . . . , which separates the [fragments], according to their size, on a thin gel. [Samples of the fragmented DNA are loaded into small holes cut into one end of a slab of agarose gel. Because DNA fragments have a negative electric charge, applying an electric field to the gel pulls all the fragments toward the positive pole. But larger fragments have more difficulty moving through the gel, so before long the smaller fragments] migrate farther along in the gel. [When the electric current is turned off, long pieces of DNA will still be near their starting point, and short pieces will be near the other end of the gel.]

The second step is accomplished with a hybridization probe, which locates specific DNA sequences. These probes are simply pieces of a single strand of DNA whose bases are in an order complementary to that of a target strand of DNA. Such a probe binds to the target DNA. With a radioactively tagged probe, the target DNA can [then]

* Reprinted with permission.

be spotted by identifying the location of the radioactive probe in the gel. Exposing appropriate film to the gel will give an image with bands at the location of the target DNA.* If the target DNA occurs in only one fragment, then only one band will appear. If it occurs in two fragments of different sizes, two bands will appear. The distance between the bands will depend on the difference in the sizes of the two fragments that contain the target DNA. If the target DNA occurs in many fragments, multiple bands will appear. The possible patterns of bands for a given probe are known as restriction fragment length polymorphisms (RFLPs). The number of such polymorphisms that might be used to differentiate among individuals is large, and RFLPs are inherited like simple Mendelian characteristics.**

Enthusiastic reports on forensic applications of RFLPs are emerging. The methodology seems to work with dried bloodstains as well as sperm, making it potentially valuable in criminal investigation. One set of probes is said to be especially discerning. Jeffreys, Wilson, and Thein describe a class of short segments of human DNA that they call minisatellite regions. Each minisatellite contains a core sequence of 10 to 15 base pairs, repeated in tandem throughout the minisatellite many times, like punctuation. The number of these repetitions within the minisatellite region varies from person to person, which leads to many different and complex banding patterns for the restriction fragments. Indeed, on the basis of their analysis of DNA from 20 unrelated British caucasians, these researchers speak of "individual-specific fingerprints of human DNA." They have applied the technique to bloodstains, semen stains, sperm found on vaginal swabs taken hours after intercourse, and to the analysis of parentage.

Although RFLPs are becoming a standard tool in genetic research, it seems doubtful that the forensic applications now qualify for admission under a general acceptance standard. In jurisdictions that do not require general acceptance, the degree of expertise demanded may limit the forensic value, particularly of the minisatellite test. Moreover, preliminary reaction to the exuberant claims of "DNA fingerprinting" indicates the adequate verification of this technique

---

* Editorial Note. In practice, after the restriction fragments are separated on the gel, they are transferred to a sheet of nylon paper-like material, which is easier to work with than the Jello-like slab. This procedure, called Southern blotting for its inventor, transfers the fragments in the same positions they occupied in the gel. The probe is applied to the nylon sheet, which is then used to expose X-ray film. Burk, DNA Fingerprinting: Possibilities and Pitfalls of a New Technique, 28 Jurimetrics J. 455, 460-461 (1988). Still more efficient procedures, which do not require blotting and radioactive probes, are becoming available. Campbell, Laser-based DNA Sequencing, 28 J. For. Sci. 266 (1988) (abstract).

** Editorial Note. See Fowler, Burgoyne, Scott & Harding, Repetitive Deoxyribonucleic Acid (DNA) and Human Genome Variation — A Concise Review Relevant to Forensic Biology, 33 J. For. Sci. 1111 (1988).

may require substantial effort. Still, molecular biology is advancing at an accelerating pace, and it may be only a matter of time before some form of DNA sequencing replaces or dramatically supplements the existing panoply of immunogenetic tests.

Andrews v. State
533 So. 2d 841 (Fla. Dist. Ct. App. 1988)

ORFINGER, J.

The issue in this case concerns the admissibility of "genetic fingerprint" evidence, by which strands of coding found in the genetic molecule of deoxyribonucleic acid (DNA) are compared for the purpose of identifying the perpetrator of a crime. The trial court admitted the evidence, and the jury convicted defendant of aggravated battery, sexual battery and armed burglary of a dwelling. Defendant also contends that his motion for mistrial should have been granted because of an improper comment by the prosecutor, and that he could not be convicted for both aggravated battery and sexual battery arising from the same incident. We conclude that the evidence was properly admitted. . . .

In the early morning hours of February 21, 1987, the victim was awakened when someone jumped on top of her and held what felt like a straight edge razor to her neck. The intruder, who the victim could only identify at trial as a strong, black male, held his hand over her mouth, told her to keep quiet and threatened to kill her if she saw his face. The victim struggled with the intruder and for her efforts was cut on her face, neck, legs and feet.

The intruder then forced vaginal intercourse with the victim, following which he stole her purse containing about $40, and then left the house. A physical examination made after the attack was reported to the police revealed the presence of semen in the victim's vagina. A crime lab analyst testified that both the victim and appellant were blood type O but that appellant, like a majority of the population, is a secretor (secretes his blood type in his saliva and other body fluids) while the victim was not. Blood type O was found in the vaginal swabs taken from the victim, though the analyst conceded that while this result could have come from the semen found in the victim's vagina, it also could have come from the victim's blood picked up by the swab. The analyst concluded that appellant was included in the population (which he stated constituted 65 percent of the male population) that could be the source of the semen.

A crime scene technician testified that on the morning following the crime one of the windows of the victim's house was open, and the screen was missing. The victim had testified that this window had

V. Genetic Markers for Identification 149

been broken previously and was held together with wire from a coat hanger. A screen was found on the ground and fingerprints were lifted from it. A fingerprint expert testified that two of the prints lifted from the screen matched appellant's right index and middle finger.

Over objection, the state presented DNA print identification evidence linking appellant to the crime. The DNA test compared the appellant's DNA structure as found in his blood with the DNA structure of the victim's blood and the DNA found in the vaginal swab, taken from the victim shortly after the attack. The test was conducted by Lifecodes Corp., a corporation specializing in DNA identity testing. Dr. Baird of Lifecodes testified to a match between the DNA in appellant's blood and the DNA from the vaginal swab, stating that the percentage of the population which would have the DNA bands indicated by the samples would be 0.0000012%. In other words, the chance that the DNA strands found in appellant's blood would be duplicated in some other person's cells was 1 in 839,914,540.

We have found no other appellate decision addressing the admissibility of DNA identification evidence in criminal cases. Although appellant primarily attacks the methods used by Lifecodes as opposed to the admissibility of DNA evidence in general, the novelty of the question requires, in our opinion, that we address both issues. . . .

We begin by confessing some uncertainty as to the standard applicable in this state governing admissibility into evidence of a new scientific technique. In the seminal case of Frye v. United States, the court [held] that expert testimony relating to novel scientific evidence must satisfy a special foundational requirement not applicable to other types of expert testimony. . . . *Frye* [requires] courts to determine: (1) the status, in the appropriate scientific community, of the scientific principle underlying the proffered novel evidence; (2) the technique applying the scientific principle; and (3) the application of the technique on the particular occasion. *Frye* is still applied in a number of jurisdictions, though it has of late come in for criticism by a number of judges and commentators as being too inflexible as well as inconsistent with modern evidence codes. . . . [It is] unclear whether that test had been accepted by the Florida courts.

[The opinion reviews the Florida cases on the admissibility of scientific evidence. It concludes that a normal relevancy approach] seems preferable to the "general acceptance" approach of *Frye* which is predicated on a "nose counting," and may result in the exclusion of reliable evidence. . . .[6]

---

6. The State correctly asserts that in this case the evidence would meet the *Frye* standard as well as the relevancy test. We have reviewed the authorities discussing the

Several witnesses testified for the State concerning the test. Dr. David E. Housman, the holder of a bachelor's degree and a Ph.D. in biology, of the Massachusetts Institute of Technology, is a professor of molecular genetics, which deals with the structure and function of the DNA molecule and has taught at several universities since 1973. He has engaged in DNA analysis for some eleven years. He has published approximately 120 papers on molecular genetics, most of which deal with DNA, and has served on advisory boards involving genetics for the National Institute of Health, the Heredity Disease Foundation, and the Tourette's Syndrome Foundation. Housman visited Lifecodes, Inc., the company which performed the instant test and examined the procedures of the company though he did not witness the instant test.

Allen Guisti is a forensic scientist employed by Lifecodes, Inc. and performed the DNA print identification tests here. He holds a Bachelor of Science degree from Yale University and has published several papers on genetics, one of which involved his own research on DNA analysis. He has performed the identification test about 200 times.

Dr. Michael Baird is the manager of forensic testing at Lifecodes. He received a doctorate in genetics from the University of Chicago in 1978. He worked as a research associate at both the University of Michigan and Columbia University in the field of blood diseases at the DNA level and joined Lifecodes at its inception in 1982. He has been the manager of forensic testing for the past year and one-half. He teaches graduate courses in DNA technology at New York Medical College and has published a number of articles on DNA testing.

[The court describes the principles and techniques of RFLP testing.] The test here was performed by Lifecodes, Inc., a licensed clinical laboratory in the State of New York. The testimony revealed that Lifecodes was founded in 1982 as a research and development laboratory, specializing in DNA paternity and identity testing and began developing DNA probes. The company currently performs forensic and paternity testing as well as testing in diagnosing genetic-type diseases. The DNA test is essentially the same for all of these purposes, with the difference being in the probe that is used.

There was extensive testimony as to the precise methods used by Lifecodes in performing the instant test. Dr. Guisti testified about each step in the process and Dr. Housman, who reviewed Dr. Guisti's results, testified that in his opinion the test was accurately and properly performed. There was also testimony that various controls were used in the testing process. For example, Dr. Baird testified that every

---

standards of admissibility to determine which of these will apply in this District, pending a definitive interpretation by our supreme court.

V. Genetic Markers for Identification

reagent and enzyme purchased by Lifecodes is tested on known DNA samples. Similar tests are performed on the gel used in the electrophoresis process. Appellant contends that this test is unreliable, because the new gel is only tested to be certain that it works the way the old gel worked and that if the old gel worked improperly, that error would be carried over to the new batch. We find no merit in this contention. In addition to the foregoing tests, control samples containing known fragment sizes are loaded in the test to monitor the electrophoresis and assure an accurate result. The evidence reveals that if the gel is not properly prepared or if it is bad, the test will ordinarily not work rather than leading to an incorrect result. Indeed, if there were any voltage fluctuations or problem with the solutions ordinarily no result is received as opposed to an erroneous result. Use of control samples is also a check, as they would also be affected by any error.

The scientific testimony indicates acceptance of the testing procedures. The probative value of the evidence is for the jury. The radiographs of the victim's and appellant's blood and the vaginal smear were exhibited to the jury, the comparison was explained, and the radiographs were admitted into evidence. Dr. Baird concluded that to a reasonable degree of scientific certainty, appellant's DNA was present in the vaginal smear taken from the victim. The State's expert witnesses were skillfully and thoroughly cross-examined, but no expert witness testified for the defense. . . .

In applying the relevancy test, it seems clear that the DNA print results would be helpful to the jury. Each of the State's witnesses was accepted by the trial court as an eminently qualified expert in the field of molecular genetics.[9] The crucial question here is whether the probative value of the testimony and test is substantially outweighed by its potential prejudicial effect. As noted in *Downing* [see supra at §4], under the relevancy approach where a form of scientific expertise has no established "track record" in litigation, courts may look to other factors which bear on the reliability of the evidence. One of these is the novelty of the technique, i.e., its relationship to more established modes of scientific analysis. DNA testing has been utilized for approximately ten years and is indicated by the evidence to be a reliable, well established procedure, performed in a number of laboratories around the world. Further, it has been used in the diagnosis, treatment, and study of genetically inherited diseases. This extensive

---

9. Blake also disagreed with the conclusions of an associate law professor, Randolph Jonakait, who has used some of his (Blake's) publications as support for a law review article criticizing the reliability of the technique as applied to bloodstain analysis. See Jonakait, Will Blood Tell? Genetic Markers in Criminal Cases, 31 Emory L.J. 833 (1982).

nonjudicial use of the test is evidence tending to show the reliability of the technique.

Another factor is the existence of specialized literature dealing with the technique. The record reveals that a great many scientific works exist regarding DNA identification. According to Dr. Baird, Lifecodes maintains a file on all scientific journal articles and publications with regard to DNA testing and he was unaware of any that argue against the test's reliability.[10]

A further component of reliability is the frequency with which a technique leads to erroneous results. . . . The testimony here was that if there was something wrong with the process, it would ordinarily lead to no result being obtained rather than an erroneous result. Further control samples are employed throughout the process which permits errors, if any, to be discovered. These factors are further indicia of reliability.

The frequency by which given DNA bands appear in the population is calculated by using an established statistical data base, employing a statistical formula known as the Hardy-Weinberg equilibria. This principle is used for determining other genetic characteristics such as blood type or Rh factors, dates back to the 1920's and has been generally accepted in the scientific community as being accurate for this calculation. Appellant contends that the data base of 710 samples is too small to be statistically significant. The only evidence in the case supports the statistical value of the randomly selected samples. The testimony reveals that as the data base expands, the probability numbers do not change statistically, and that The American Association of Blood Banks, in its book entitled Probability of Inclusion in Paternity Testing (1982) concludes that a data base of two to five hundred samples was found to provide adequate statistical results.

Admittedly, the scientific evidence here, unlike that presented with fingerprint, footprint or bite mark evidence, is highly technical, incapable of observation and requires the jury to either accept or reject the scientist's conclusion that it can be done. While this factor requires courts to proceed with special caution, it does not of itself render the evidence unreliable.

The trial court did not abuse its discretion in ruling the test results admissible in this case. In contrast to evidence derived from hypnosis, truth serum and polygraph, evidence derived from DNA

---

10. While no appellate court in this country has yet passed on the admissibility of DNA print identification in criminal cases, such evidence has been admitted in civil actions and is admitted at trials in England. Further, at least one jurist, concurring in part and dissenting in part in a capital case, wondered why the State had not done a DNA test which he said would have made the question of guilt or innocence far less murky. State v. Apanovitch, 514 N.E.2d 394, 406 (Ohio 1987).

print identification appears based on proven scientific principles. Indeed, there was testimony that such evidence has been used to exonerate those suspected of criminal activity.

Given the evidence in this case that the test was administered in conformity with accepted scientific procedures so as to ensure to the greatest degree possible a reliable result, appellant has failed to show error on this point. . . .

Finding no error, the convictions and sentences are affirmed.

NOTES

DNA Testing

1. *General acceptance of RFLPs.* *Andrews* is the first reported appellate decision on RFLP (pronounced "riflip") testing. An extensive and impressive hearing on the scientific status of the procedure and Lifecodes' laboratory protocol is summarized in People v. Wesley. In neither *Andrews* nor *Wesley* did the defense seriously contest the general acceptance and validity of the applicable principles and techniques of molecular biology and genetics. The use of suitable restriction enzymes followed by separation by gel electrophoresis and radioactive tagging of the fragments is a well established and fruitful research tool in medical genetics. Cooper, DNA Polymorphism and the Study of Disease Associations, 78 Human Genetics 299 (1988); Martin, Molecular Genetics: Applications to the Clinical Neurosciences, 238 Sci. 765 (1987); White & Lalouel, Chromosome Mapping with DNA Markers, Sci. Am., Feb. 1988, at 40.

However, the companies seeking to exploit this technology in criminal and disputed paternity cases typically use probes that have no other medical or scientific application. But see Jeffries, Wilson, Thein, Weatherall & Ponder, DNA "Fingerprints" and Segregation Analysis of Multiple Markers in Human Pedigrees, 39 Am. J. Human Genetics 11 (1986). Should a court in a *Frye* jurisdiction insist that each probe (and the estimated frequency of the incriminating pattern of RFLPs detected by that probe) be "generally accepted" by geneticists? Does it matter if geneticists and molecular biologists do not normally work with forensic sources of the DNA — dried blood, semen, or hair? Exactly what, under *Frye*, must be generally accepted? For the view that the results in *Wesley* and *Andrews* represent a "lenient" application of the general acceptance test, see Thompson & Ford, DNA Typing: Acceptance and Weight of the New Genetic Identification Tests, 75 Va. L. Rev. 601 (1989). This article also challenges the claim that false positives are not possible. Cf. Burk, DNA Fingerprinting: Possibilities and Pitfalls of a New Technique, 29 Jurimetrics J. 455 (1988); Lander, DNA Fingerprinting on Trial,

339 Nature 501 (1989); Comment, DNA Identification Tests and the Courts, 63 Wash. L. Rev. 903 (1988).

2. *Varieties of DNA Typing.* Although the courts and the press often write as if there were but one procedure for DNA typing, several techniques for detecting variations in DNA sequences are available. See Thompson & Ford, DNA Typing: Acceptance and Weight of the New Genetic Identification Tests, 75 Va. L. Rev. 601 (1989). They differ in the quantity of DNA needed for the analysis, the care required to obtain accurate results, the ease with which the test results can be interpreted, and the individualizing power of such results. The popular label "DNA fingerprinting" should be avoided in favor of more discriminating terminology. See Kaye, DNA and Paternity Probabilities, forthcoming (1990).

3. *RFLPs in Paternity Testing.* The first reported paternity case to evaluate DNA typing is In re Baby Girl S, 532 N.Y.S.2d 634 (N.Y. Co. Surrog. Ct. 1988). Here the court relies on restriction analysis, along with much other evidence, to find — in the face of the once conclusive presumption that a child born in wedlock is legitimate — that the man claiming paternity, and not the estranged husband, is the father. It holds the RFLP evidence admissible under a statute making blood tests admissible in parentage disputes. Furthermore, the court brushes aside an expert's reservations about including these results in the paternity index and, hence, the "probability of paternity."

Other courts needing to resolve questions of paternity have embraced DNA analysis with similar enthusiasm. See King v. Tanner, 539 N.Y.S.2d 617 (Westchester Co. 1989) (granting summary judgment for defendant alleged to have slandered married man by asserting that he fathered her child); Alexander v. Alexander, 537 N.E.2d 1310 (Probate Ct., Franklin Co. 1988) (permitting disinterment for "a DNA test" by an illegitimate child claiming an inheritance).

The emerging scientific literature on DNA polymorphisms in paternity testing includes Baird, Balazs, Giusti et al., Allele Frequency Distribution of Two Highly Polymorphic DNA Sequences in Three Ethnic Groups and Its Application to the Determination of Paternity, 39 Am. J. Human Genetics 489 (1986); Bolund, Recent Research on Human DNA-polymorphism, in Advances in Forensic Haemogenetics 195, 199 (B. Brinkmann & K. Henningsen eds. 1986); Oldelberg, Demers, Westin & Hossaini, Establishing Paternity Using Minisatellite DNA Probes when the Putative Father is Unavailable for Testing, 33 J. For. Sci. 921 (1988); Smouse & Chakraborty, The Use of Restriction Fragment Length Polymorphisms in Paternity Analysis, 38 Am. J. Human Genetics 918 (1986).

One might imagine that with the addition of RFLP polymorphisms to the information available from other genetic markers, the debate noted above over the presentation of the "probability of paternity" is about to become academic because the probabilities will be overwhelming. For papers indicating that some of the probabilities introduced in courts may be overstated or oversimplified, however, see Gjertson, Mickey, Hopfield et al., Assessing Probability of Paternity in DNA Systems (1989); Morris, Sanda & Glassberg, Biostatistical Evaluation of Evidence from Continuous Allele Frequency Distribution Deoxyribonucleic Acid (DNA) Probes in Reference to Disputed Paternity and Identity, 34 J. For. Sci. 1311 (1989).

VI. FORENSIC PSYCHIATRY

Edwards v. State
540 S.W.2d 641 (Tenn. 1976)

COOPER, CHIEF JUSTICE.

Petitioner, George S. Edwards, was indicted for . . . the killing of his sister. . . . The jury found petitioner guilty of murder in the second degree and fixed his punishment at ten years in the penitentiary. . . .

The record is replete with testimony, both expert and lay, on the issue of insanity. Petitioner . . . became a patient of Dr. Walker in October, 1971. The doctor testified that petitioner had a schizophrenic personality and was suffering from schizophrenia. He further testified that petitioner responded to anti-depressant drugs and his condition improved. Petitioner was still under the care of Dr. Walker at the time of the homicide in June, 1972. . . .

Lay testimony showed petitioner's personality quirks became more pronounced during the spring of 1972, particularly after petitioner quit taking his tranquilizers. . . .

[Edwards' wife] testified that petitioner . . . pulled a pistol out of a bureau drawer and, without saying a word, fired a single shot at his sister. His wife ran from the house, and the petitioner fired two shots at her, narrowly missing her. . . .

Immediately after the shooting and before the police arrived on the scene, petitioner called his mother and told her that he had shot his sister and was sorry. When the police arrived, he at first told them that his wife had shot herself. Later, he told the investigating officers that his "sister" had shot herself. He gave a third statement to the officers within fifteen minutes of the killing stating that he had killed his sister because she had sinned too much and that she was better off dead. He further stated that she was scolding him for mistreating his wife and that when he could not take it anymore, he shot her.

Following the homicide, Dr. Walker engaged the services of Dr. Garo Aivazian, Chairman of the Department of Psychiatry at the University of Tennessee Medical School, and they together evaluated the petitioner over the next several months. Both diagnosed petitioner's condition as schizophrenia. Both testified that in their opinion on the date of the shooting the petitioner was insane within the definition of the *M'Naughten* rule. Both expressed the opinion that petitioner was sane at the time of the trial. Both admitted that there were times when petitioner would know right from wrong. And, on cross-examination, Dr. Aivazian testified that petitioner was not psychotic when he first saw him on June 12, 1972, and also expressed the opinion that petitioner knew what was going on around him during the day of the homicide on June 7, 1972. There was also evidence of a history of mental illness in petitioner's family, going back several generations on both sides.

Mrs. Nona Owensby, a licensed psychological examiner employed at Central State Hospital, was called as a rebuttal witness by the state. She testified that based upon her observation of the petitioner and study of his records she was of the opinion that petitioner was not psychotic or mentally deranged at the time of the shooting, and did know right from wrong. She expressed the further opinion that petitioner was feigning mental illness in an effort to avoid criminal responsibility, and testified to observations and conversations with petitioner which led her to this belief. . . .

Petitioner insists . . . that the evidence preponderated against the jury's finding that petitioner was sane at the time of the killing. Implicit in petitioner's argument is the insistence that the testimony of the psychiatrists on this issue must be accepted over lay testimony. Petitioner also stresses the testimony of his wife and family concerning his disturbed mental condition in the days before the killing and the history of mental illness in his family, and the lack of an apparent motive for his actions.

The jury is not required to accept testimony of a psychiatrist on the issue of sanity to the exclusion of lay testimony or to the exclusion of evidence of the actions of the petitioner inconsistent with sanity. If it were, "[it] would effectively preempt our jury trial system on sanity issues and replace it with a system of trial by psychiatrists' opinions. We are unwilling, even if we had the power, to saddle society with so basic a change in our system of criminal jurisprudence."

In this state, "it is settled beyond question that the weight and value of expert testimony is for the jury and must be received with caution." This applies to the expert opinions of medical men. Where there is any conflict between expert testimony and the testimony as to the facts, the jury is not bound to accept expert testimony in preference to other testimony, and must determine the weight and credibility of each in the light of all the facts shown in case. Expert medical opinion regarding the functioning of the human body must always be more or less speculative. . . .

Petitioner's conviction is sustained. . . .

NOTES

Determining Sanity

1. *The insanity defense.* For centuries courts and legislatures have struggled with the problem of excusing criminal conduct on the part of an "insane" person. The standard the jury was asked to apply in *Edwards* was, in the words of a dissenting Justice, "the ancient and archaic M'Naghten Rule." This rule arose from an attempt by Daniel McNaghten to assassinate Robert Peel, the Prime Minister of England. Apparently believing that the Prime Minister and his political party was persecuting him, McNaughten came to London. There, he shot and killed a man riding in Peel's carriage, whom he thought was Peel, but who was in fact Peel's secretary. A jury found McNaughten "not guilty by reason of insanity," and an irate Queen Victoria summoned the House of Lords to "take the opinion of the Judges on the law governing such cases." The 15 judges of the common law courts found themselves required to answer prolix and obtuse questions on the status of criminal responsibility in England. In this politically charged atmosphere, they announced that "to establish a defence on the ground of insanity, it must be clearly proved that, at the time of the committing of the act, the party accused was labouring under such a defect of reason, from disease of the mind, as not to know the nature and quality of the act he was doing; or, if he did know it, that he did not know he was doing what was wrong." M'Naghten's Rule, 10 Cl. & F. 200, 8 Eng. Rep. 718, 722 (H.L. 1843). For discussions of and citations to the extensive literature on this rule and its more modern competitors, see A. Brooks, Law, Psychiatry and the Mental Health System 135-233 (1974); R. Moran, Knowing Right from Wrong: The Insanity Defense of Daniel McNaughton (1981); By Reason of Insanity: Essays on Psychiatry and the Law (L.Z. Freedman ed. 1983); A. Stone, Mental Health and Law: A System in Transition 218-231 (1976); Shah, Criminal Responsibility, in Forensic Psychiatry and Psychology 167 (W. Curran, A. McGarry & S. Shah eds. 1986).

Like the jury verdict in *M'Naghten*, the acquittal of John Hinckley for his attempted assassination of President Ronald Reagan provoked reflections on the status of insanity defense. The psychiatric testimony in this case, and some of the political and professional reactions to it, are discussed in A. Stone, Law, Psychiatry and Morality: Essays and Analysis 77-98 (1984).

Psychiatric evaluation is so crucial to establishing the insanity defense that "when [an indigent] defendant demonstrates to the trial judge that his sanity at the time of the offense is to be a significant factor at trial, the State must, at a minimum, assure the defendant access to a competent psychiatrist who will conduct an appropriate examination and assist in evaluation, preparation, and presentation of the defense." Ake v. Oklahoma, 463 U.S. 880, 883 (1985). On the extension of *Ake* to the provision of expert services in noncapital cases, see Expert Services and the Indigent Criminal Defendant, 84 Mich. L. Rev. 1326 (1986).

The Constitution also prevents the state from executing an insane prisoner. Ford v. Wainwright, 477 U.S. 399 (1986). The logic underlying this decision is questioned in Entin, Psychiatry, Insanity and the Death Penalty: A Note on Implementing Supreme Court Decisions, 79 J. Crim. L. & Crimin. 218 (1988). The problem of defining appropriate procedures for determining the sanity of death row inmates is pursued in Note, Ford v. Wainwright: A Coda in the Executioner's Song, 72 Iowa L. Rev. 1461 (1987).

2. *Competency.* *Edwards* also illustrates a very common use of psychiatric expertise in the criminal justice system — to assess the competency of a defendant to stand trial. Indeed, "far more persons are confined on the basis of incompetence than because they have been found not guilty by reason of insanity." A. Stone, Mental Health and Law: A System in Transition 203 (1976). Whereas the defense of insanity focuses on the ability of the defendant to have formed the requisite intent or on the desirability of punishing a person who is not considered responsible for his actions at the time of the alleged offense, competency refers to the defendant's ability to understand the subsequent legal proceedings and to participate in the defense. See id. at 199-217; Grisso & Siegel, Assessment of Competency to Stand Trial, in Forensic Psychiatry and Psychology 145 (W. Curran, A. McGarry & S. Shah eds. 1986). Questions of mental competency arise in many other areas as well, including testamentary capacity; contract formation; commission of torts; and, of course, competence to manage one's own affairs, to consent to medical treatment, to care for children, and to waive legal rights. See A. Brooks, Law, Psychiatry and the Mental Health System 971-1035 (1974); T. Gutheil & P. Appelbaum, Clinical Handbook of Psychiatry and the Law 210-303 (1982); T. Grisso, Evaluating Competencies: Forensic Assessment and Instruments (1986); R. Sadoff, Forensic Psychiatry: A Practical Guide for Lawyers and Psychiatrists (2d ed. 1988); D. Shuman, Psychiatric and Psychological Evidence 261-268, 350-364 (1986).

VI. Forensic Psychiatry 159

3. *Psychiatric opinions on ultimate issues.* The psychiatrists in *Edwards* testified that Edwards was legally insane when he shot and killed his sister.* Does psychiatric expertise extend to diagnosing insanity, as the criminal law uses the term? Should psychiatric testimony be limited to diagnoses and prognoses for psychiatrically meaningful mental diseases or conditions? See Fed. R. Evid. 704(b); A. Goldstein, The Insanity Defense 97-105 (1967); The Admissibility of Expert Witness Testimony: Time to Take the Final Leap? 42 U. Miami L. Rev. 831 (1988).

Edwards does not question the propriety of expert testimony on an "ultimate issue" like insanity or competence, but rather deals with the effect that a judge or jury must give such testimony. It applies the general rule that a jury may disbelieve expert testimony even when that testimony goes uncontradicted by other bona fide experts.**

In the case that follows, Barefoot v. Estelle, the United States Supreme Court considers psychiatric testimony introduced to satisfy a requirement in Texas for imposing capital punishment: that "there is a probability that the defendant would commit criminal acts of violence that would constitute a continuing threat to society." *Barefoot* is a mirror image of *Edwards.* The jury credited the predictions of two psychiatrists, and the convicted defendant argued that such predictions were so invalid that the jury's reliance on them deprived him of due process of law.

---

* After describing the symptoms and characteristics of schizophrenia, Dr. Parks testified that at the time of the killing the defendant was laboring under such a defect of reasoning from disease of mind as not to know the nature and quality of his act, or if he did know it, that he did not know what he was doing was wrong. Dr. Aivazian also expressed his opinion in legal as well as medical terms. He testified that "at the time of the shooting [defendant] was psychotic to a degree whereby his ability to recognize what was around him as the environment and to test the environment and its realities was impaired to a degree whereby he was not capable of deciding between right or wrong and was not capable of adhering to any decision because he could not decide between right and wrong."

** Why doesn't the appellate court place more emphasis on the opinion of the "psychological examiner" that Edwards was feigning insanity? The answer may be that this expert could provide little or no basis for her opinion and misled the trial court as to her qualifications. She began her testimony by describing herself as "the psychologist at the Forensic Services Division of Central State Psychiatric Hospital." On appeal, the state confessed that this was a "misrepresentation." It called the court's attention to a report finding, among other things, that "she exceeded her authority in testifying before courts regarding matters of probation, parole, suspension of sentence, leniency, and insanity," that "she furnished courts, attorneys for patients and district attorneys with . . . inaccurate and misleading" information on her qualifications as an expert witness, and "that she held herself out to be a psychologist . . . , tending to mislead courts before whom she gave testimony, attorneys representing patients, district attorneys, patients, and staff at FSD." But if the jury was misinformed as to this expert's qualifications, can the verdict in *Edwards* be upheld on the theory that the lay testimony as to Edwards' behavior and state of mind could have persuaded the jury that he was sane, notwithstanding the psychiatric opinions?

Barefoot v. Estelle
463 U.S. 880 (1983)

JUSTICE WHITE delivered the opinion of the Court.

I

On November 14, 1978, petitioner was convicted of the capital murder of a police officer in Bell County, Texas. A separate sentencing hearing before the same jury was then held to determine whether the death penalty should be imposed. . . .

III

Petitioner [submits] that his death sentence must be set aside because the Constitution of the United States barred the testimony of the two psychiatrists who testified against him at the punishment hearing. There are several aspects to this claim. First, it is urged that psychiatrists, individually and as a group, are incompetent to predict with an acceptable degree of reliability that a particular criminal will commit other crimes in the future and so represent a danger to the community. Second, it is said that in any event, psychiatrists should not be permitted to testify about future dangerousness in response to hypothetical questions and without having examined the defendant personally. Third, it is argued that in the particular circumstances of this case, the testimony of the psychiatrists was so unreliable that the sentence should be set aside. As indicated below, we reject each of these arguments.

A

The suggestion that no psychiatrist's testimony may be presented with respect to a defendant's future dangerousness is somewhat like asking us to disinvent the wheel. In the first place, it is contrary to our cases. If the likelihood of a defendant committing further crimes is a constitutionally acceptable criterion for imposing the death penalty, which it is, and if it is not impossible for even a lay person sensibly to arrive at that conclusion, it makes little sense, if any, to submit that psychiatrists, out of the entire universe of persons who might have an opinion on the issue, would know so little about the subject that they should not be permitted to testify. . . .

Acceptance of petitioner's position that expert testimony about future dangerousness is far too unreliable to be admissible would immediately call into question those other contexts in which predictions of future behavior are constantly made. For example, in O'Connor

v. Donaldson, 422 U.S. 563, 576 (1975), we held that a non-dangerous civil committee could not be held in confinement against his will. Later, speaking about the requirements for civil commitments, we said:

> There may be factual issues in a commitment proceeding, but the factual aspects represent only the beginning of the inquiry. Whether the individual is mentally ill and dangerous to either himself or others and is in need of confined therapy turns on the meaning of the facts which must be interpreted by expert psychiatrists and psychologists.

In the second place, the rules of evidence generally extant at the federal and state levels anticipate that relevant, unprivileged evidence should be admitted and its weight left to the fact finder, who would have the benefit of cross examination and contrary evidence by the opposing party. Psychiatric testimony predicting dangerousness may be countered not only as erroneous in a particular case but as generally so unreliable that it should be ignored. If the jury may make up its mind about future dangerousness unaided by psychiatric testimony, jurors should not be barred from hearing the views of the State's psychiatrists along with opposing views of the defendant's doctors.

Third, petitioner's view mirrors the position expressed in the amicus brief of the American Psychiatric Association (APA). . . . We are not persuaded that such testimony is almost entirely unreliable and that the factfinder and the adversary system will not be competent to uncover, recognize, and take due account of its shortcomings.

The amicus does not suggest that there are not other views held by members of the Association or of the profession generally. Indeed, as this case and others indicate, there are those doctors who are quite willing to testify at the sentencing hearing, who think, and will say, that they know what they are talking about, and who expressly disagree with the Association's point of view. Furthermore, their qualifications as experts are regularly accepted by the courts. If they are so obviously wrong and should be discredited, there should be no insuperable problem in doing so by calling members of the Association who are of that view and who confidently assert that opinion in their amicus brief. Neither petitioner nor the Association suggests that psychiatrists are always wrong with respect to future dangerousness, only most of the time. Yet the submission is that this category of testimony should be excised entirely from all trials. We are unconvinced, however, at least as of now, that the adversary process cannot be trusted to sort out the reliable from the unreliable evidence and opinion about future dangerousness, particularly when the convicted felon has the opportunity to present his own side of the case.

We are unaware of and have been cited to no case, federal or state, that has adopted the categorical views of the Association. Certainly it was presented and rejected at every stage of the present proceeding. . . .

B

Whatever the decision may be about the use of psychiatric testimony, in general, on the issue of future dangerousness, petitioner urges that such testimony must be based on personal examination of the defendant and may not be given in response to hypothetical questions. We disagree. Expert testimony, whether in the form of an opinion based on hypothetical questions or otherwise, is commonly admitted as evidence where it might help the factfinder do its assigned job. As the Court said long ago, Spring Co. v. Edgar, 99 U.S. 645, 657 (1878):

> Men who have made questions of skill or science the object of their particular study, says Phillips, are competent to give their opinions in evidence. Such opinions ought, in general, to be deduced from facts that are not disputed, or from facts given in evidence; but the author proceeds to say that they need not be founded upon their own personal knowledge of such facts, but may be founded upon the statement of facts proved in the case. Medical men, for example, may give their opinions not only to the state of a patient they may have visited, or as to cause of the death of a person whose body they have examined or as to the nature of the instruments which caused the wounds they have examined, but also in cases where they have not themselves seen the patient, and have only heard the symptoms and particulars of his state detailed by other witnesses at the trial. Judicial tribunals have in many instances held that medical works are not admissible, but they everywhere hold that men skilled in science, art, or particular trades may give their opinions as witnesses in matters pertaining to their professional calling.

Today, in the federal system, Federal Rules of Evidence 702-706 provide for the testimony of experts. The advisory committee notes touch on the particular objections to hypothetical questions, but none of these caveats lends any support to petitioner's constitutional arguments. Furthermore, the Texas Court of Criminal Appeals could find no fault with the mode of examining the two psychiatrists under Texas law. . . .

. . . Although cases such as this involve the death penalty, we perceive no constitutional barrier to applying the ordinary rules of evidence governing the use of expert testimony.

C

As we understand petitioner, he contends that even if the use of hypothetical questions in predicting future dangerousness is acceptable

VI. Forensic Psychiatry   163

as a general rule, the use made of them in his case violated his right to due process of law. For example, petitioner insists that the doctors should not have been permitted to give an opinion on the ultimate issue before the jury, particularly when the hypothetical questions were phrased in terms of petitioner's own conduct; that the hypothetical questions referred to controverted facts; and that the answers to the questions were so positive as to be assertions of fact and not opinion. These claims of misuse of the hypothetical questions, as well as others, were rejected by the Texas courts, and neither the District Court nor the Court of Appeals found any constitutional infirmity in the application of the Texas Rules of Evidence in this particular case. We agree.

IV

In sum, we affirm the judgment of the District Court. There is no doubt that the psychiatric testimony increased the likelihood that petitioner would be sentenced to death, but this fact does not make that evidence inadmissible, any more than it would with respect to other relevant evidence against any defendant in a criminal case. . . .

NOTES

Predictions of Dangerousness

1. *Validity of clinical predictions of dangerousness.* The dissenting opinion of Justice Blackmun, joined by Justices Brennan and Marshall, emphasizes that "psychiatric testimony about a defendant's future dangerousness . . . is wrong two times out of three," 463 U.S. at 916, making it "less accurate than the flip of a coin." Id. at 931. "[W]hen a person's life is at stake," they insist, "a requirement of greater reliability should prevail." Id. at 916. This figure for the accuracy of dangerousness predictions can be traced to J. Monahan, The Clinical Prediction of Violent Behavior 47-49 (1981). Monahan summarizes his metastudy as follows:

> In reviewing the research literature as of 1981 on clinical risk assessment of violence among the mentally disordered — most of it conducted on criminal or "forensic" patient populations — I [concluded]:
>
> 1. The upper bound of accuracy that even the best risk assessment technology could achieve was on the order of .33. That is, of every three disordered persons predicted by psychiatrists or psychologists to be violent, one will be discovered to commit a violent act, and two will not.

2. The best predictors of violence among the mentally disordered are the same demographic factors that are the best predictors of violence among non-disordered offender populations (e.g., age, gender, social class, history of prior violence).
3. The poorest predictors of violence among the mentally disordered are psychological factors such as diagnosis or severity of disorder, or personality traits.

Monahan, Risk Assessment of Violence Among the Mentally Disordered: Generating Useful Knowledge, 11 Intl. J.L. & Psychia. 249, 250 (1988).

Although research conducted after this 1981 review "could be seen as challenging each of these conclusions," Monahan observes that "[t]he most striking characteristic of recent risk assessment research . . . is that the research is so inconsistent. For every study that reports increases in predictive accuracy, there is another that finds clinical risk assessments no better than chance. . . ." Id. at 251-252.

The Blackmun dissent in *Barefoot* implied that a psychiatric prediction of dangerousness might even be taken as evidence of nondangerousness: "Psychiatric predictions of future dangerousness *are not accurate;* wrong two times out of three, their probative value, and therefore any possible contribution they might make to the ascertainment of truth, is virtually nonexistent. . . . Indeed, given a psychiatrist's prediction that an individual will be dangerous, it is more likely than not that the defendant will *not* commit further violence." 463 U.S. 928. However, the two-out-of-three figure should not be confused with the probative value of the evidence. To the extent that the rate of violence is higher among those people predicted to be violent than those predicted to be nonviolent, the predictions are probative. Cf. Kaye, The Validity of Tests: Caveant Omnes, 27 Jurimetrics J. 349 (1987). The two-out-of-three figure, on the other hand, is a posterior probability of nondangerousness given a prediction of dangerousness; it depends on the base rate, or prevalence, of dangerousness in the population on which predictions are made. When the prevalence of a condition is low, even an exquisitely sensitive and specific test for that condition — a test with undeniable probative value — will result in many false positive errors. As Christopher Slobogin explains:

> While it cannot be denied that mental health professionals using clinical prediction techniques are not very accurate at determining who is violence-prone, they are not nearly as inept at that task as many would suggest. In fact, knowledgeable clinicians are much better at predicting dangerousness than the random selection process suggested by the coin-flipping analogy.

To understand why this is so, it is helpful to focus at the outset on a study conducted in Massachusetts by Dr. Kozol and his associates. This investigation is chosen for illustrative purposes because it is usually cited as representative of clinical prediction at its best. Each prediction made in the study was based on independent examinations by at least five clinicians, a battery of psychological tests, and "a meticulous reconstruction of the life history [of the subject] elicited from multiple sources."

Four hundred and thirty-five male offenders evaluated in this manner were released into the community after being confined for various lengths of time. During the follow-up period, only eight percent of those predicted nondangerous (thirty-one out of 386) were found to have committed a serious assaultive act. Yet of those offenders predicted dangerous, 34.7 percent (seventeen out of forty-nine) were found to have committed such an act. More than sixty-five percent of the individuals identified as dangerous, therefore, were false positives. Given the results of this and other studies, it has become the accepted wisdom that at best only one out of every three clinical predictions of dangerousness will be correct.

On its face, this finding appears singularly unimpressive. But in evaluating what it means about the ability of mental health professionals to predict future dangerousness, one must take into account the fact that very few people commit violent acts. In the United States, for instance, only one person out of every 500 commits a seriously violent act (murder, rape, robbery, or assault) each year. Thus if one were to label a randomly selected American citizen dangerous, one would have one chance in five hundred of being right. Were Kozol and his associates able to maintain their one out of three accuracy rate when evaluating a random population, their predictions would thus be about 165 times better than chance.

Of course, most of the dangerousness studies, including Kozol's, do not involve randomly selected populations. They usually focus on male offenders, a group that has a much higher base rate for violence than the population as a whole. In Kozol's group, for example, the base rate was one out of nine; forty-eight of the 435 offenders studied committed violent acts during the time period of the study. Even so, Kozol and his associates produced predictions that were three times better than chance. Although their absolute accuracy was low, their relative accuracy could be called commendable.

Slobogin, Dangerousness and Expertise, 133 U. Pa. L. Rev. 97, 111-112 (1984).

In addition to the confusion over the meaning of the two-out-of-three figure, there are other reasons to think that "[c]ontrary to the 'nearly universal' view of academic and professional communities, the available evidence does not support the claim that predictions of future criminality are inherently or even usually inaccurate." Alshuler,

Preventive Pretrial Detention and the Failure of Interest-Balancing Approaches to Due Process, 85 Mich. L. Rev. 510, 539 (1986); Slogobin, supra, at 114-17.

2. *Legal significance of high error rates in expert predictions.* The *Barefoot* majority is painfully aware of the misgivings of many mental health professionals about their ability to make valid predictions of future dangerousness. Somewhat feebly, the Court notes that "[n]either petitioner nor the [American Psychiatric] Association suggests that psychiatrists are always wrong with respect to future dangerousness, only most of the time." 463 U.S. at 899. Hoping that "the factfinder and the adversary system will . . . be competent to uncover, recognize and take due account of its shortcomings," the Court resists any "constitutional rule barring an entire category of expert testimony." Id. Can juries "separate the wheat from the chaff"? Id. at 901 n.7. How?

If you had been arguing on behalf of Barefoot, how would you have responded to the observation that "it makes little sense, if any, to submit that psychiatrists, out of the entire universe of persons who might have an opinion on the issue, would know so little about the subject that they should not be permitted to testify"? Id. at 897. How would you counter the remark that "[t]he suggestion that no psychiatrist's testimony may be presented with respect to a defendant's future dangerousness is somewhat like asking us to disinvent the wheel"? Id. at 896.

If behavioral scientists have been unable to validate expert predictions of dangerousness, should judges or juries — with or without the benefit of mental health professionals — rely on this factor in deciding who should receive capital punishment? See Jurek v. Texas, 428 U.S. 262 (1976). Even if the constitution permits expert as well as lay predictions of dangerousness, should the general acceptance test (see §5 supra) or other evidentiary rules for scientific evidence be applied to exclude expert clinical predictions of dangerousness? See United States v. Kozminski, 821 F.2d 1186 (6th Cir. 1987) (psychologist's testimony that pressures on mentally retarded farm workers resulted in an "involuntary conversion" to dependency inadmissible without proof that the theory was scientifically recognized); Black, Evolving Legal Standards for the Admissibility of Scientific Evidence, 239 Sci. 1508, 1509-1510 (1988); Slobogin, Dangerousness and Expertise, 133 U. Pa. L. Rev. 97, 130-148 (1984).

Is there a defensible middle ground between the wholesale exclusion of predictions of dangerousness and the widespread comforting but questionable reliance on expert assessments? Should expert involvement be limited to providing "actuarial" rather than clinical predictions? Compare Faust & Ziskin, The Expert Witness in Psychology and Psychiatry, 241 Sci. 31 (1988) with Slobogin, supra. Keep in mind yet another concern with predictions of dangerousness, a concern that did not surface in *Barefoot:*

> The invidious aspect of testimony about sociopaths and their future dangerousness has to do with racial and social implications of the diagnosis of sociopath as defined by DSM-III [Am. Psychiatric Assn., Diagnostic and Statistical Manual (3d ed. 1980)] rather than with the ethics and expertise of the particular psychiatrists. The diagnostic criteria for antisocial personality in DSM-III might apply to the vast majority of those who face a death sentence as well as many black men who have grown up in inner cities. These criteria include the following characteristics . . . inability to establish consistent work behavior, lack of ability to function as a responsible parent, failure to accept social norms, e.g., holding an illegal occupation (pimping, prostitution, fencing, selling drugs), failure to honor financial obligations, failure to plan ahead, disregard for truth, and recklessness. . . .
> Whatever scientific value the diagnosis of sociopath may have, there can be little question that the urban poor and racial minorities will be swept into this diagnostic category.

A. Stone, Law, Psychiatry and Morality 110 (1984). See also Johnson, The Politics of Predicting Criminal Violence, 86 Mich. L. Rev. 1322 (1988) (reviewing The Prediction of Criminal Violence (F. Dutile & C. Foust eds. 1987)).

3. *The psychiatric testimony against Barefoot.* The psychiatrists who testified at Barefoot's trial were John Holbrook and James Grigson. Neither had examined Barefoot nor requested an opportunity to do so. Presented with a hypothetical question about Barefoot, both diagnosed him as a sociopath. Dr. Holbrook testified to "a reasonable psychiatric certainty" that there was "a probability that the Thomas A. Barefoot in that hypothetical will commit criminal acts of violence in the future." Dr. Grigson's predictions were less guarded. He declared that on a scale of one to ten for sociopaths, Barefoot was "above ten," that there was no known cure for this condition, and that there was a "one hundred percent and absolute" chance that Barefoot would commit future acts of criminal violence. 463 U.S. at 918-919.

Known to some as "Dr. Death," Dr. Grigson has testified in well over 100 death-penalty cases for the prosecution. "[H]e gives similar convincing testimony in almost every case, diagnosing the defendant as an antisocial personality (a 'sociopath' or 'psychopath'). Since sociopaths do not learn from experience and show no remorse, they are essentially untreatable people who would certainly commit further criminal violence. The jury, after hearing this psychiatrist, almost never fails to impose the death penalty." A. Stone, Law, Psychiatry and Morality 107 (1984). Does such testimony exceed the boundaries of ethical behavior for psychiatrists? See id. at 70-71, 107 (1984); *Barefoot*, 463 U.S. at 881 n.6 (dissenting opinion).

4. *Other limitations on psychiatric predictions of dangerousness.* In some circumstances the privilege against self-incrimination and the right to counsel may prevent the state from introducing clinical predictions of dangerousness. See Estelle v. Smith, 451 U.S. 454 (1981); Satterwhite v. Texas, 108 S. Ct. 1792 (1988).

5. *Other uses of psychiatric predictions of dangerousness.* The Supreme Court has held that it is not unconstitutional to keep dangerous people accused of criminal conduct in jail pending trial. See United States v. Salerno, 481 U.S. 739, 107 S. Ct. 2095, 2103-2104 (1987); Schall v. Martin, 467 U.S. 253, 264-266 (1984); Hansen, When Worlds Collide: The Constitutional Politics of United States v. Salerno, 14 Am. J. Crim. L. 155 (1987). What are the implications of *Barefoot* on the use of clinical psychiatric predictions in this context? See Alschuler, Preventive Detention and the Failure of Interest-Balancing Approaches to Due Process, 85 Mich. L. Rev. 510 (1986).

Defendants acquitted of criminal charges by reason of insanity and people never even accused of or prosecuted for crimes may be confined to mental institutions as a result of commitment proceedings. As a constitutional matter, *must* involuntary hospitalization be predicated on a finding of danger to others? See O'Connor v. Donaldson, 422 U.S. 563 (1975); A. Stone, Law, Psychiatry and Morality 111-117 (1984). Is a need for medical treatment enough? See A. Stone, Mental Health and Law: A System in Transition (1976). If the threat of harm to others is a basis for involuntary commitment, what is the burden of persuasion that the state should shoulder? See Addington v. Texas, 441 U.S. 418 (1979) (due process requires "clear and convincing evidence" for civil commitment); Jones v. United States, 463 U.S. 3043 (1983) (mere "preponderance of the evidence" enough for indefinite commitment of insanity acquittee). If the majority of predictions of dangerousness are false positives, how can the state ever meet these burdens? See Monahan & Wexler, A Definite Maybe: Proof and Probability in Civil Commitment, 2 L. & Human Behavior 37 (1978).

Other Uses of Psychiatry in the Legal System

6. *Personal injury litigation.* Psychiatric assessments have obvious application in tort suits, workers' compensation, and similar claims. E.g., Modlin, Civil Law and Psychiatric Testimony, in Forensic Psychiatry and Psychology 469 (W. Curran, A. McGarry & S. Shah eds. 1986). The use of the "psychological autopsy" to help differentiate between suicide and accident is described supra at §3.

7. *Child custody.* Psychological evaluations of children and parents

can be extremely influential when a marriage dissolves and both parents seek custody of a child, or when the fitness of parents is called into question. A survey of the Indiana Trial Lawyer's Association seeking information on the type of cases in which psychologists are employed found that "the psychologist was most frequently called upon in cases that involved children. Sixty-nine percent of the respondents had used the psychologist in a child custody case, 42 percent in cases involving child visitation rights, 27 percent in cases involving abuse of child, and 14 percent in cases involving termination of parental rights. Overall, 58 percent of the reported total of 5632 cases in which the psychologist was employed involved children." Levitt & Lawlor, Employment of the Psychologist as an Expert Witness, 1 For. Rep. 133, 135 (1988). In light of the difficulty of decisions profoundly affecting parents and children, courts may be especially willing to defer to expert judgments. See generally T. Grisso, Evaluating Competencies: Forensic Assessments and Instruments 188-267 (1986); R. Sadoff, Forensic Psychiatry: A Practical Guide for Lawyers and Psychiatrists (2d ed. 1988); D. Shuman, Psychiatric and Psychological Evidence 301-317 (1986); B. Shutz, Solomon's Sword: A Practical Guide to Conducting Child Custody Evaluations (1989); McGarry, Child Custody in Forensic Psychiatry and Psychology 247 (W. Curran, A. McGarry & S. Shah eds. 1986).

8. *Veracity of witnesses.* The courts are more chary of psychiatric or psychological opinions on the veracity of witnesses. See §7 infra.

9. *Practical references.* Some practice-oriented texts on psychiatric testimony are M. Blinder, Psychiatry in the Everyday Practice of Law (2d ed. 1982); R. Sadoff, Forensic Psychiatry: A Practical Guide for Lawyers and Psychiatrists (2d ed. 1988); D. Shuman, Psychiatric and Psychological Evidence (1986); J. Ziskin & D. Faust, Coping with Psychiatric and Psychological Testimony (4th ed. 1988) (3 volumes).

VII. TESTING FOR TRUTH AND ENHANCING MEMORY

Frye v. United States
293 F.1013 (D.C. Cir. 1923)

[See page 103.]

HISTORICAL NOTE

The defense expert in *Frye*, William M. Marston, developed the theory of a "specific lie response" while a Harvard law student. In later years, Marston created the comic strip heroine, Wonder Woman. Book Note, 94 Harv. L. Rev. 1925, 1927 n.8 (1981), citing 2 Who Was Who in America 347 (1950). Although he and others have asserted that subsequent investigations proved Frye's innocence (and hence the accuracy of the early lie detector test), this claim appears to be baseless. Starrs, "A Still-Life Watercolor": Frye v. United States, 27 J. For. Sci. 684, 690 (1982). For more on the early history of "scientific" lie detection, see D. Lykken, A Tremor in the Blood: Uses and Abuses of the Lie Detector (1981).

State v. Lyon
744 P.2d 231 (Or. 1987)

CAMPBELL, JUSTICE.

In State v. Brown, 297 Or. 404, 445, 687 P.2d 751 (1984), we held that polygraph evidence is not admissible, over proper objection, in any civil or criminal trial in this state. We reserved opinion as to the admissibility of such evidence pursuant to a preexamination stipulation. . . .

Defendant was convicted of murder in the shooting death of Mr. Terry Reiser. At defendant's trial, the court permitted the state to introduce into evidence against defendant the results of a polygraph examination administered by detective Michael Plester. Before taking the examination, defendant had received *Miranda* warnings and had read and signed a "polygraph stipulation form." Defendant had not yet been charged with the crime and was not represented by counsel when he signed the stipulation and took the examination. The results of the examination were not favorable to defendant. . . .

The issue presented in this case is one of first impression in this court. However, an impressive body of precedent from other jurisdictions is available to aid us in our resolution of this issue. Though the available authority is almost unanimous in holding that polygraph results may not be introduced into evidence upon the motion of either party, the jurisdictions appear to be almost evenly split on the question of admissibility of polygraph evidence pursuant to the parties' stipulation. The momentum does not discernibly favor either stance.

Those courts that admit polygraph evidence under stipulation typically rely upon one or the other of two basic rationales. A few courts maintain that the stipulation enhances the reliability of the polygraph by permitting the parties "to control . . . those variables deemed significant to fairness and reliability." However, most courts that permit the introduction of polygraph results pursuant to stipulation hold that by entering into the stipulation the parties waive the right to object or are estopped to object to the introduction of the proffered evidence. . . .

VII. Testing for Truth and Enhancing Memory

We noted in *Brown* that the leading case on stipulations for the admission of polygraph evidence is State v. Valdez, 91 Ariz. 274, 371 P.2d 894 (1962)....

... A number of courts have adopted the *Valdez* "qualifications" in whole or in part in concluding that polygraph results are admissible as evidence pursuant to the parties' stipulation. The imposition of these elaborate procedures and preconditions to admission appears to reflect judicial recognition that the volatile mixture of uncertain reliability and extreme persuasiveness represented by polygraph results must be handled gingerly, if at all.

At least two states that initially adopted the *Valdez* criteria later reversed field and held stipulated polygraph results inadmissible. One state that initially adopted *Valdez* later wholly abandoned the requirement of a stipulation and now admits polygraph evidence upon either party's initiative subject only to foundational requirements of the polygraph operator's expertise, the reliability of the particular testing procedure used and the validity of the tests made on the subject.

Those courts that reject the admissibility of stipulated polygraph evidence do so on the grounds (1) that the stipulation does not improve the reliability of the polygraph results, (2) that juries are likely to be unduly persuaded by the polygraph evidence, (3) that the parties can stipulate to facts but cannot by stipulation change the law regarding the admissibility of polygraph evidence, and (4) that it is logically inconsistent to hold polygraph evidence inadmissible when one party seeks to introduce it but admissible by the parties' stipulation. Even commentators who champion the general admissibility of polygraph results question the basis in logic of admitting pursuant to stipulation evidence that it is otherwise inadmissible. . . .

We find particularly instructive the experiences of two states that recently ended prolonged experiments with the *Valdez* requirements and concluded that stipulated polygraph evidence is no longer admissible in evidence.

In 1974 the Supreme Court of Wisconsin adopted the *Valdez* criteria for admission of stipulated polygraph evidence. Seven years later, the court overruled [itself] and held inadmissible polygraph evidence submitted pursuant to stipulation. The court [stated]:

> We recognize . . . that the science and art of polygraphy have advanced and that the polygraph has a degree of validity and reliability. We are, nevertheless, not persuaded that the reliability of the polygraph is such as to permit unconditional admission of the evidence. Our analysis of and our experience with the [stipulation] rule lead us instead to conclude that the . . . conditions are not operating satisfactorily to enhance the reliability of the polygraph evidence and to protect the integrity of the trial process as they were intended to do. . . .

Two years [later], North Carolina joined Wisconsin in abandoning *Valdez.* In State v. Grier, 307 N.C. 628, 300 S.E.2d 351 (1983), the North Carolina Supreme Court ended its nine-year experiment with *Valdez.* . . . The court emphasized, as the Wisconsin court had, that:

> [a]dmissibility of this evidence has not been based on the validity and accuracy of the lie detector, but rather that by consenting to the evidence pursuant to stipulation, the parties have waived any objections to the inherent unreliability of the test. The stipulation itself and the other conditions [to admissibility] were to operate as a compromise between total rejection and complete acceptance of polygraph evidence.

The court was "forced to conclude that the stipulation accomplishes little toward enhancing the reliability of the polygraph," and that subjecting admissibility to the discretion of the trial judge is not "a sufficient safeguard to ensure reliability of the polygraph test results in a particular case." The court was "also disturbed by the possibility that the jury may be unduly persuaded by the polygraph evidence," and was not convinced that the cautionary instructions required by *Valdez* sufficiently meliorated this possibility. The court concluded "that the admission by stipulation approach does not resolve some of the more perplexing problems attendant to the use of polygraph evidence," and that consequently "in North Carolina, polygraph evidence is no longer admissible in any trial."

In State v. Brown, we held that upon proper objection, polygraph test results are not admissible into evidence in any trial or other legal proceeding subject to the rules of the Oregon Evidence Code. We concluded that though "under proper conditions polygraph evidence may possess some probative value and may, in some cases, be helpful to the trier of fact," "the probative value of polygraph evidence is far outweighed by reasons for its exclusion." We conclude that the stipulation of the parties does not cure these difficulties, and that these same considerations necessitate the exclusion of polygraph evidence even when the parties stipulate to its admission.

In determining whether we will admit polygraph evidence introduced pursuant to the parties' stipulation, we first consider the terms of the stipulation and what the stipulation purports to do. We note that certain items in the stipulation form are simply not proper subjects of stipulation. That defendant, having had the operation of the polygraph explained to him by the police, "believe[s] it to be a scientifically reliable instrument and . . . stipulate[s] that it is so reliable" is testament to the officer's powers of persuasion but is not binding upon the courts of this state. Like the Alaska Supreme Court, we concluded in *Brown* that "no judgment of polygraph testing's validity or potential rate of error can be established based on available scientific evidence." The parties' stipulation to the polygraph's reli-

VII. Testing for Truth and Enhancing Memory

ability does not change this. Nor does defendant's "stipula[tion] that these results are admissible evidence" vitiate our pronouncement that "polygraph evidence shall not be admissible" over objection in Oregon's courts.

The parties may stipulate to facts. Where the admissibility of an item of evidence is conditioned upon the satisfaction of certain foundational requirements, the parties may stipulate to the satisfaction of those requirements and will be bound by that stipulation. However, they may not by stipulation change the law to render admissible that which we have concluded is not admissible. As other courts have recognized, the "stipulation" to the admissibility of polygraph results constitutes the parties' mutual waiver of the right to object to the introduction into evidence of those results. The Washington Supreme Court, in the course of adopting the *Valdez* requirements, characterized such stipulations as follows: "When there is a stipulation as in this case, the prosecution and the defense, knowing that the degree of reliability is open to question, in effect gamble that the test will prove favorable to them."

We have determined that we will not permit this gamble in Oregon's courts. Because of the importance of the institutional values implicated by the admission of polygraph results into evidence, we hold that we will not recognize a stipulation between the parties to the admissibility of polygraph evidence.

In *Brown* we were concerned with the "undue delay in administering justice that would occur if we were to allow the admission of polygraph evidence in all cases." We are not convinced that the admission of the evidence pursuant to stipulation significantly reduces the risk of such delay. We are particularly concerned with consumption of time and potential confusion of issues resulting from challenges to the accuracy of the test. Even if the stipulation at issue were read as foreclosing challenges to the qualifications of the examiner and the reliability of the polygraph test, or the introduction of opposing test results, it cannot be argued that defendant would be foreclosed from challenging the manner in which his or her test was conducted, the form of the questions asked, or inquiring into any of the myriad factors that affect the accuracy of a particular test. . . .

> [A]lthough the inquiry was far from complete, the experience of this case has amply shown that, as of now, the validity of a polygraphic test is dependent upon a large number of variable factors, many of which would be very difficult, and perhaps impossible, to assess. In a given case, the time required in order to explore and seek to adjudicate such factors would be virtually incalculable. . . . Accordingly, this court is impelled to the conclusion that the administration of justice simply cannot tolerate the burden of litigation inherently involved in such a process.

Nor is it likely that a "stipulation" that would adequately address all these factors could be drafted or, if successfully drafted, withstand judicial scrutiny. The North Carolina Supreme Court, in overturning its own prior adoption of *Valdez* and holding stipulated polygraph evidence inadmissible, stated:

> The validity of the polygraphic process is dependent upon such a large number of variable factors, many of which are extremely difficult, if not impossible, to assess, that we feel the stipulation simply cannot adequately deal with all situations which might arise affecting the accuracy of any particular test.

Of greater concern even than the possibility of undue delay is the potential for misuse and over-valuation of the polygraph evidence by the jury. We stated in *Brown:*

> Polygraph evidence may well divert the trier of fact from the direct and circumstantial evidence presented in a case to a distorted valuation of the polygraph evidence. Polygraph evidence is not just another form of scientific evidence presented by experts such as ballistics analysis, fingerprint and handwriting comparisons, blood typing and neutron activation analysis. These other tests do not purport to indicate with any degree of certainty that the witness was or was not credible. By its very nature the polygraph purports to measure truthfulness and deception, the very essence of the jury's role.

This is certainly no less true when the evidence is introduced pursuant to stipulation than when the evidence is introduced by one or other of the parties. In fact, that the parties stipulated to its introduction and to its "reliability" may only exacerbate the prejudicial impact of the polygraph evidence. Our primary considerations in reaching our conclusion in *Brown* were the probable effect of polygraph evidence upon the integrity of the trial process and our respect for the traditional role of the jury. The parties cannot by private agreement "waive" these vital institutional concerns.

A stipulation neither enhances the uncertain reliability of the polygraph examination nor blunts the prejudicial effect of polygraph results upon the jury. The same considerations that compelled us to conclude in *Brown* that polygraph results are inadmissible over the objection of either party compel us now to conclude that polygraph evidence is inadmissible for any purpose in any legal proceeding subject to the rules of evidence under the Oregon Evidence Code, and henceforth its admission, pursuant even to the parties' stipulation, is error. On retrial, the court will exclude from evidence the proffered polygraph test results. . . .

The Court of Appeals remanded the case for a new trial because of the admission of inadmissible hearsay. We agree that the conviction should be reversed and the case remanded for the reasons stated by the Court of Appeals and for the additional reasons set forth above. The decision of the Court of Appeals is affirmed. The case is remanded to the trial court for a new trial.

LINDE, JUSTICE, concurring.

While I fully concur in the court's opinion, a few words may be added to ask whether there perhaps are wider reasons for the result.

This court, like others, has rejected the use of polygraph evidence on grounds that this means of attacking or supporting the truthfulness of a person's declarations is too unreliable, too prone to error and conscious or unconscious manipulation, to have evidentiary value. The court set forth the reasons for that conclusion in Justice Jones's extensive review of the literature on polygraphy in State v. Brown. Today's decision is based on the same premises and conclusion.

These are reasons enough for the present case. Yet it seems worth raising a question whether more is involved in the widespread uneasiness about electrical lie detectors, reasons that are masked by the common law courts' characteristic professional emphasis on trial procedures and rules of evidence. In fact, the question whether more is involved than unreliability suggests itself in this case, because the holding goes beyond normal procedures for excluding unreliable evidence over an opposing party's objection and instructs courts not to admit polygraph evidence even without objection or when the parties expressly stipulate to its admission. These are extraordinary strictures against questionable evidence.

I think more is involved. I doubt that the uneasiness about electrical lie detectors would disappear even if they were refined to place their accuracy beyond question. Indeed, I would not be surprised if such a development would only heighten the sense of unease and the search for plausible legal objections.

Published accounts, not of record here, report that submission to polygraph tests is widely demanded in public as well as in private employment, not without resentment by employees. It was not only a concern about inaccuracy that caused the current Secretary of State to protest White House plans to demand such tests in a drive to discover and to inhibit unauthorized disclosures of information. In part, of course, the Secretary's protest and the resentment of many civil servants and private employees arise from the implication that their word may not be trusted; but trust, too, is not the ultimate issue.

There are many contexts in which one person — a lender, a reporter, or a careful police officer — does not take another's word about an important fact at face value without checking the credibility of the speaker and the believability of the information against other sources. The principle is familiar in the law governing warrants for a search or seizure. Sometimes a person will be required to undergo a physical examination that may contradict his verbal assertions (for instance, that he consumed no more than two beers), or without even obtaining or considering any verbal statements from him. That, too, may be resented, but it is different from a polygraph examination.

What is that difference? The heart of the matter, I suspect, is that the polygraph seeks to turn the human body against the personality that inhabits it in a way that other tests do not.

The polygraph differs in principle from other physical examinations. Tests of one's breath, blood, or urine to detect the presence of illicit substances or a communicable disease may be perceived as an insult or an infringement of one's privacy. They also may prove one a liar. But even when employed to confirm or to contradict a verbal assertion, the immediate object of the test itself is to determine an independently relevant fact, the actual condition of the organism. Whether the tested person's stated belief is proved correct or erroneous is a secondary consequence, even when it is important.

The polygraph does not independently establish any past, present, or future fact. It purports neither to replace nor to supplement the assertions of the tested person with other evidence on the matter in question. The polygraph is indifferent to what the assertions are about and whether they are factually correct. As its popular name suggests, the lie detector only purports to detect whether a person is uttering a lie.

Beyond doubt that often is a useful thing to know. There is no general right to lie, as civil, criminal, and administrative sanctions in many contexts show, although it is interesting to recall that as late as the time of Oregon's statehood it was disputed whether a defendant could be sworn to the truth as well as permitted to address the jury, and knowingly false statements do not invariably forfeit the guarantees of free expression. Doubtless, also, it often is in one's interest to be able to overcome suspicion and "prove" one's truthfulness.

Legal systems have sought truthful testimony by various means. The solemn oath to speak the truth "so help me God" invoked religious obligation and fear for one's soul. Temporal punishment for perjury was added when conscience or fear of damnation would not suffice. Both forms of admonition prompt the witness as a free agent to choose truth over falsehood and its consequences. The law also has experience with compelling disclosure by turning the human body against the human will. For five hundred years torture was a judicially administered instrument of criminal procedure to obtain confessions when reliable eyewitness testimony was lacking, because no conviction could rest only on inferences from circumstantial evidence. Even without that legal rationale (and without its accompanying legal restraints), coercion of disclosures by pain remains a widespread though officially disavowed practice. Indefensible as it is, it still is addressed to human volition, as instances of failure to break the victim's resistance show. Coercion of the will by threat or by force confirms rather than denies traditional conceptions of personality.

Of course the polygraph is not torture, no more than an electrocardiogram, for instance. Also unlike torture, however, the polygraph is unconcerned with personal choice. Purporting only to detect lies, it is as indifferent to persuading the subject to tell the truth (though it may produce that effect) as it is to the substance of the questions asked and answered. The polygraph turns its subject into an object.

So do many diagnostic tests, as I have said. The same approach also may correspond to one theory of human behavior and human relationships. But is it consistent with the theory underlying our legal and social institutions? This seems doubtful. Inconsistency of physiological lie detection with fundamental tenets about human personhood has been important in European objections to the polygraph, reflecting Christian and Kantian philosophical traditions as much as doubts of its accuracy. See, e.g., Silving, Testing of the Unconscious in Criminal Cases, 69 Harv. L. Rev. 683 (1956); Westin, Privacy and Freedom 237-39 (1967).[2]

The institution of the trial, above all, assumes the importance of human judgment in assessing the statements of disputing parties and other witnesses. The cherished courtroom drama of confrontation, oral testimony and cross-examination is designed to let a jury pass judgment on their truthfulness and on the accuracy of their testimony. The central myth of the trial is that truth can be discovered in no better way, though it has long been argued that the drama really serves symbolic values more important than reliable factfinding. One of these implicit values surely is to see that parties and the witnesses are treated as persons to be believed or disbelieved by their peers rather than as electrochemical systems to be certified as truthful or mendacious by a machine.

What would be the effect if some such machine were proved 100 percent effective? It could be the ultimate 21st-Century refinement of the medieval Anglo-Saxon oath-helpers, who, of course, were only human.[3] A machine improved to detect uncertainty, faulty memory, or an overactive imagination would leave little need for live testimony

---

2. The West German federal supreme court in 1954 held even consensual polygraph examination inconsistent with constitutional and statutory guarantees of personal dignity and free will. Professor Westin reports a 1958 papal condemnation of polygraphs as well as narco-analysis on moral grounds.

3. Oath-helpers were persons who swore on oath that they believed the oaths of a party to a suit, thus helping to prove that the assertions made by that party were true.

and cross-examination before a human tribunal; an affidavit with the certificate of a polygraph operator attached would suffice. There would be no point to solemn oaths under threat of punishment for perjury if belief is placed not in the witness but in the machine.

Compulsion to take polygraph examinations would hardly be necessary; the present somewhat pathetic urge of previously unfaithworthy prisoners and suspects to prove their statements by volunteered polygraph tests would likely be emulated by other witnesses who want to be believed. Volunteered certificates of truthfulness could be expected to spread from legal procedures to employment, credit, and more personal relationships, and their absence thereafter would appear as grounds for suspicion. Would a perfect detector enhance people's capacity to test for truth only at the cost of diminishing their common humanity?

These questions go beyond doubts of the polygraph's accuracy. I do not speculate what legal issues beyond the rules of evidence they may raise; here none has been briefed. For the present case, I am satisfied to join in the court's opinion.

NOTES

The Polygraph as a Lie Detector

1. *The varied applications of polygraphic lie detection.* Even after *Lyon*, the efforts of polygraphers to detect lies are admitted in Oregon in probation revocation hearings and administrative disciplinary hearings on state prison inmates. Wygant, And Nothing But the Truth: The Current Status of Polygraph, Ore. Bar J., Nov. 1988, at 27, 29. In the private sector, employers have used polygraphy for job screening and investigations of misconduct by employees, but very often state and now federal legislation curtails these applications of polygraphy. See Note, Lie Detectors in the Workplace: The Need for Civil Actions Against Employers, 101 Harv. L. Rev. 806 (1988).

2. *Validity of polygraphic lie detection.* The ability of polygraphers to detect lies remains controversial. No known physiological response or pattern of responses is unique to deception. Raskin, The Polygraph in 1986: Scientific, Professional and Legal Issues Surrounding Applications and Acceptance of Polygraph Evidence, 1986 Utah L. Rev. 29, 31. Consequently, the polygraph, as usually used to detect deception, is not a lie detector; it is a fear detector. Testimony of Leonard Saxe, Hearings on H.R. 1524 and H.R. 1924 Before the Subcomm. on Employment Opportunities, House Comm. on Education and Labor, 99th Cong., 1st sess., 1986, at 109. To detect deception, the polygraph operator must ensure that the subject believes that his lies can be detected (so that the subject feels fear when he speaks

falsely) and that the subject believes that his truthful statements will be recognized as such (so that he feels less fear when he speaks truthfully). In addition, other sources of anxiety that would produce responses characteristic of fear when the subject is being truthful must be eliminated. Achieving these conditions is difficult. Raskin, supra, at 31.

Nevertheless, the polygraph industry claims that the tests are very accurate, both in specific incident investigations and in job screening. The vice president of the American Polygraph Association maintains that:

> Over the past 15 years, at least 100 studies have been conducted by scholars, scientists and polygraph practitioners concerning the accuracy of the polygraph technique. Based on a responsible reading of these results, the polygraph has been shown to have an accuracy of 85-95 percent.

Testimony of Lawrence W. Talley, 1986 Hearings, supra, at 358. In contrast, the most prominent academic critic of the polygraph, insists that:

> We can summarize the available evidence as follows: When scored without knowledge of the case facts or clues based on the suspect's behavior or demeanor, the modern polygraph test can be expected to be wrong about one-third of the time. The polygraph test is strongly biased against the innocent person; truthful suspects failed the polygraph 39 percent, 49 percent and 55 percent of the time in the three scientific investigations [that meet reasonable standards of scientific research].

Lykken, Detecting Deception in 1984, 27 Am. Behav. Scientist 481, 493 (1984). For still other descriptions and differing assessments of the empirical research, see The Polygraph Test: Lies, Truth and Science (A. Gale ed. 1988); Kircher, Horowitz & Raskin, Meta-Analysis of Mock Crime Studies of the Control Question Polygraph Technique, 12 L. & Human Behavior 79 (1988); Office of Technology Assessment, U.S. Cong., Scientific Validity of Polygraph Testing: A Research Review and Evaluation — A Technical Memorandum (1983); U.S. Dept. of Defense, The Accuracy and Utility of Polygraph Testing (1984). For a review of studies of the impact of polygraph testimony on jurors, see Note, The *Frye* Doctrine and Relevancy Approach Controversy: An Empirical Evaluation, 74 Geo. L.J. 1769 (1986).

Rock v. Arkansas
483 U.S. 44 (1987)

JUSTICE BLACKMUN delivered the opinion of the Court.
The issue presented in this case is whether Arkansas' evidentiary

rule prohibiting the admission of hypnotically refreshed testimony violated petitioner's constitutional right to testify on her own behalf as a defendant in a criminal case.

I

Petitioner Vickie Lorene Rock was charged with manslaughter in the death of her husband, Frank Rock, on July 2, 1983. A dispute had been simmering about Frank's wish to move from the couple's small apartment adjacent to Vickie's beauty parlor to a trailer she owned outside town. That night a fight erupted when Frank refused to let petitioner eat some pizza and prevented her from leaving the apartment to get something else to eat. When police arrived on the scene they found Frank on the floor with a bullet wound in his chest. Petitioner urged the officers to help her husband, and cried to a sergeant who took her in charge, "please save him" and "don't let him die." The police removed her from the building because she was upset and because she interfered with their investigation by her repeated attempts to use the telephone to call her husband's parents. According to the testimony of one of the investigating officers, petitioner told him that "she stood up to leave the room and [her husband] grabbed her by the throat and choked her and threw her against the wall and . . . at that time she walked over and picked up the weapon and pointed it toward the floor and he hit her again and she shot him."

Because petitioner could not remember the precise details of the shooting, her attorney suggested that she submit to hypnosis in order to refresh her memory. Petitioner was hypnotized twice by Doctor Betty Back, a licensed neuropsychologist with training in the field of hypnosis. Doctor Back interviewed petitioner for an hour prior to the first hypnosis session, taking notes on petitioner's general history and her recollections of the shooting.[2] Both hypnosis sessions were recorded on tape. Petitioner did not relate any new information during either of the sessions, but, after the hypnosis, she was able to remember that at the time of the incident she had her thumb on the hammer of the gun, but had not held her finger on the trigger. She also

---

2. Doctor Back's handwritten notes regarding petitioner's memory of the day of the shooting read as follows:

"Pt states she & husb. were discussing moving out to a trailer she had prev. owned. He was 'set on' moving out to the trailer — she felt they should discuss. She bec[ame] upset & went to another room to lay down. Bro. came & left. She came out to eat some of the pizza, he wouldn't allow her to have any. She said she would go out and get [something] to eat he wouldn't allow her — He pushed her against a wall an end table in the corner [with] a gun on it. They were the night watchmen for business that sets behind them. She picked gun up stated she didn't want him hitting her anymore. He wouldn't let her out door, slammed door & 'gun went off & he fell & he died' [pt looked misty eyed here — near tears]" (additions by Doctor Back).

VII. Testing for Truth and Enhancing Memory   181

recalled that the gun had discharged when her husband grabbed her arm during the scuffle. As a result of the details that petitioner was able to remember about the shooting, her counsel arranged for a gun expert to examine the handgun, a single action Hawes .22 Deputy Marshal. That inspection revealed that the gun was defective and prone to fire, when hit or dropped, without the trigger's being pulled.

When the prosecutor learned of the hypnosis sessions, he filed a motion to exclude petitioner's testimony. The trial judge held a pretrial hearing on the motion and concluded that no hypnotically refreshed testimony would be admitted. The court issued an order limiting petitioner's testimony to "matters remembered and stated to the examiner prior to being placed under hypnosis." At trial, petitioner introduced testimony by the gun expert, but the court limited petitioner's own description of the events on the day of the shooting to a reiteration of the sketchy information in Doctor Back's notes.[4] The jury convicted petitioner on the manslaughter charge and she was sentenced to 10 years imprisonment and a $10,000 fine.

On appeal, the Supreme Court of Arkansas rejected petitioner's claim that the limitations on her testimony violated her right to present her defense. The court concluded that "the dangers of admitting this kind of testimony outweigh whatever probative value it may have," and decided to follow the approach of States that have held hypnotically refreshed testimony of witnesses inadmissible per se. Although the court acknowledged that "a defendant's right to testify is fundamental," it ruled that the exclusion of petitioner's testimony did not violate her constitutional rights. Any "prejudice or deprivation" she suffered "was minimal and resulted from her own actions and not by any erroneous ruling of the court." We granted certiorari, to consider the constitutionality of Arkansas' per se rule excluding a criminal defendant's hypnotically refreshed testimony.

II

Petitioner's claim that her testimony was impermissibly excluded is bottomed on her constitutional right to testify in her own defense.

---

4. When petitioner began to testify, she was repeatedly interrupted by the prosecutor, who objected that her statements fell outside the scope of the pretrial order. Each time she attempted to describe an event on the day of the shooting, she was unable to proceed for more than a few words before her testimony was ruled inadmissible. For example, she was unable to testify without objection about her husband's activities on the morning of the shooting, about their discussion and disagreement concerning the move to her trailer, about her husband's and his brother's replacing the shock absorbers on a van, and about her brother-in-law's return to eat pizza. She then made a proffer, outside the hearing of the jury, of testimony about the fight in an attempt to show that she could adhere to the court's order. The prosecution objected to every detail not expressly described in Doctor Back's notes or in the testimony the doctor gave at the pretrial hearing. The court agreed with the prosecutor's statement that "ninety-nine percent of everything [petitioner] testified to in the proffer" was inadmissible.

At this point in the development of our adversary system, it cannot be doubted that a defendant in a criminal case has the right to take the witness stand and to testify in his or her own defense. . . .

The right to testify on one's own behalf at a criminal trial has sources in several provisions of the Constitution. [The Court finds this right to be implicit in] the Fourteenth Amendment's guarantee that no one shall be deprived of liberty without due process of law . . . , the Compulsory Process Clause of the Sixth Amendment, which grants a defendant the right to call "witnesses in his favor" . . . the Sixth Amendment, [which] "grants to the accused *personally* the right to make his defense," . . . , [and] the Fifth Amendment's guarantee against compelled testimony. . . .

III

The question now before the Court is whether a criminal defendant's right to testify may be restricted by a state rule that excludes her post-hypnosis testimony. This is not the first time this Court has faced a constitutional challenge to a state rule, designed to ensure trustworthy evidence, that interfered with the ability of a defendant to offer testimony. In Washington v. Texas, 388 U.S. 14 (1967), the Court was confronted with a state statute that prevented persons charged as principals, accomplices, or accessories in the same crime from being introduced as witnesses for one another. The statute, like the original common-law prohibition on testimony by the accused, was grounded in a concern for the reliability of evidence presented by an interested party. . . .

Just as a State may not apply an arbitrary rule of competence to exclude a material defense witness from taking the stand, it also may not apply a rule of evidence that permits a witness to take the stand, but arbitrarily excludes material portions of his testimony. In Chambers v. Mississippi, 410 U.S. 284 (1973), the Court invalidated a State's hearsay rule on the ground that it abridged the defendant's right to "present witnesses in his own defense." Chambers was tried for a murder to which another person repeatedly had confessed in the presence of acquaintances. The State's hearsay rule, coupled with a "voucher" rule that did not allow the defendant to cross-examine the confessed murderer directly, prevented Chambers from introducing testimony concerning these confessions which were critical to his defense. This Court reversed the judgment of conviction, holding that when a state rule of evidence conflicts with the right to present witnesses, the rule may "not be applied mechanistically to defeat the ends of justice," but must meet the fundamental standards of due process. In the Court's view, the State in *Chambers* did not demonstrate that the hearsay testimony in that case, which bore "assurances of

VII. Testing for Truth and Enhancing Memory 183

trustworthiness" including corroboration by other evidence, would be unreliable, and thus the defendant should have been able to introduce the exculpatory testimony.

Of course, the right to present relevant testimony is not without limitation. The right "may, in appropriate cases, bow to accommodate other legitimate interests in the criminal trial process." But restrictions of a defendant's right to testify may not be arbitrary or disproportionate to the purposes they are designed to serve. In applying its evidentiary rules a State must evaluate whether the interests served by a rule justify the limitation imposed on the defendant's constitutional right to testify.

IV

The Arkansas rule enunciated by the state courts does not allow a trial court to consider whether posthypnosis testimony may be admissible in a particular case; it is a *per se* rule prohibiting the admission at trial of any defendant's hypnotically refreshed testimony on the ground that such testimony is always unreliable. Thus, in Arkansas, an accused's testimony is limited to matters that he or she can prove were remembered before hypnosis. This rule operates to the detriment of any defendant who undergoes hypnosis, without regard to the reasons for it, the circumstances under which it took place, or any independent verification of the information it produced.[13]

In this case, the application of that rule had a significant adverse effect on petitioner's ability to testify. It virtually prevented her from describing any of the events that occurred on the day of the shooting, despite corroboration of many of those events by other witnesses. Even more importantly, under the court's rule petitioner was not permitted to describe the actual shooting except in the words contained in Doctor Back's notes. The expert's description of the gun's tendency to misfire would have taken on greater significance if the jury had heard petitioner testify that she did not have her finger on the trigger and that the gun went off when her husband hit her arm.

In establishing its *per se* rule, the Arkansas Supreme Court simply followed the approach taken by a number of States that have decided that hypnotically enhanced testimony should be excluded at trial on the ground that it tends to be unreliable. Other States that have adopted an exclusionary rule, however, have done so for the testimony

---

13. The Arkansas Supreme Court took the position that petitioner was fully responsible for any prejudice that resulted from the restriction on her testimony because it was she who chose to resort to the technique of hypnosis. . . . It should be noted, however, that Arkansas had given no previous indication that it looked with disfavor on the use of hypnosis to assist in the preparation for trial and there were no previous state-court rulings on the issue.

of *witnesses,* not for the testimony of a *defendant.* The Arkansas Supreme Court failed to perform the constitutional analysis that is necessary when a defendant's right to testify is at stake.

Although the Arkansas court concluded that any testimony that cannot be proved to be the product of prehypnosis memory is unreliable, many courts have eschewed a *per se* rule and permit the admission of hypnotically refreshed testimony.[16] Hypnosis by trained physicians or psychologists has been recognized as a valid therapeutic technique since 1958, although there is no generally accepted theory to explain the phenomenon, or even a consensus on a single definition of hypnosis. See Council on Scientific Affairs, Scientific Status of Refreshing Recollection by the Use of Hypnosis, 253 J.A.M.A. 1918, 1918-1919 (1985) (Council Report).[17] The use of hypnosis in criminal investigations, however, is controversial, and the current medical and legal view of its appropriate role is unsettled.

Responses of individuals to hypnosis vary greatly. The popular belief that hypnosis guarantees the accuracy of recall is as yet without established foundation and, in fact, hypnosis often has no effect at all on memory. The most common response to hypnosis, however, appears to be an increase in both correct and incorrect recollections.[18] Three general characteristics of hypnosis may lead to the introduction of inaccurate memories: the subject becomes "suggestible" and may try to please the hypnotist with answers the subject thinks will be met with approval; the subject is likely to "confabulate," that is, to fill in details from the imagination in order to make an answer more coherent and complete; and, the subject experiences "memory hardening," which gives him great confidence in both true and false memories, making effective cross-examination more difficult. See generally M. Orne, et al., Hypnotically Induced Testimony, in Eyewitness Testimony: Psychological Perspectives 171 (G. Wells and E. Loftus,

---

16. Some jurisdictions have adopted a rule that hypnosis affects the credibility, but not the admissibility, of testimony. Other courts conduct an individualized inquiry in each case. In some jurisdictions, courts have established procedural prerequisites for admissibility in order to reduce the risks associated with hypnosis. Perhaps the leading case in this line is State v. Hurd, 86 N.J. 525, 432 A.2d 86 (1981).

17. Hypnosis has been described as "involv[ing] the focusing of attention; increased responsiveness to suggestions; suspension of disbelief with a lowering of critical judgment; potential for altering perception, motor control, or memory in response to suggestions; and the subjective experience of responding involuntarily." Council Report, 253 J.A.M.A., at 1919.

18. "[W]hen hypnosis is used to refresh recollection, one of the following outcomes occurs: (1) hypnosis produces recollections that are not substantially different from nonhypnotic recollections; (2) it yields recollections that are more inaccurate than nonhypnotic memory; or, most frequently, (3) it results in more information being reported, but these recollections contain both accurate and inaccurate details. . . . There are no data to support a fourth alternative, namely, that hypnosis increases remembering of only accurate information." Id., at 1921.

eds., 1985); Diamond, Inherent Problems in the Use of Pretrial Hypnosis on a Prospective Witness, 68 Calif. L. Rev. 313, 333-342 (1980). Despite the unreliability that hypnosis concededly may introduce, however, the procedure has been credited as instrumental in obtaining investigative leads or identifications that were later confirmed by independent evidence.

The inaccuracies the process introduces can be reduced, although perhaps not eliminated, by the use of procedural safeguards. One set of suggested guidelines calls for hypnosis to be performed only by a psychologist or psychiatrist with special training in its use and who is independent of the investigation. See Orne, The Use and Misuse of Hypnosis in Court, 27 Intl. J. Clinical & Experimental Hypnosis 311, 335-336 (1979). These procedures reduce the possibility that biases will be communicated to the hypersuggestive subject by the hypnotist. Suggestion will be less likely also if the hypnosis is conducted in a neutral setting with no one present but the hypnotist and the subject. Tape or video recording of all interrogations, before, during, and after hypnosis, can help reveal if leading questions were asked. Id., at 336. Such guidelines do not guarantee the accuracy of the testimony, because they cannot control the subject's own motivations or any tendency to confabulate, but they do provide a means of controlling overt suggestions.

The more traditional means of assessing accuracy of testimony also remain applicable in the case of a previously hypnotized defendant. Certain information recalled as a result of hypnosis may be verified as highly accurate by corroborating evidence. Cross-examination, even in the face of a confident defendant, is an effective tool for revealing inconsistencies. Moreover, a jury can be educated to the risks of hypnosis through expert testimony and cautionary instructions. Indeed, it is probably to a defendant's advantage to establish carefully the extent of his memory prior to hypnosis, in order to minimize the decrease in credibility the procedure might introduce.

We are not now prepared to endorse without qualifications the use of hypnosis as an investigative tool; scientific understanding of the phenomenon and of the means to control the effects of hypnosis is still in its infancy. Arkansas, however, has not justified the exclusion of all of a defendant's testimony that the defendant is unable to prove to be the product of prehypnosis memory. A State's legitimate interest in barring unreliable evidence does not extend to per se exclusions that may be reliable in an individual case. Wholesale inadmissibility of a defendant's testimony is an arbitrary restriction on the right to testify in the absence of clear evidence by the State repudiating the validity of all posthypnosis recollections. The State would be well within its powers if it established guidelines to aid trial courts in the evaluation of posthypnosis testimony and it may be able to show that testimony in a particular case is so unreliable that exclusion is justified. But it has not shown that hypnotically enhanced testimony is always so untrustworthy and so immune to the traditional means of evaluating credibility that it should disable a defendant from presenting her version of the events for which she is on trial.

In this case, the defective condition of the gun corroborated the details petitioner remembered about the shooting. The tape recordings provided some means to evaluate the hypnosis and the trial judge concluded that Doctor Back did not suggest responses with leading questions. Those circumstances present an argument for admissibility of petitioner's testimony in this particular case, an argument that must be considered by the trial court. Arkansas' per se rule excluding all posthypnosis testimony infringes impermissibly on the right of a defendant to testify on his or her own behalf.

The judgment of the Supreme Court of Arkansas is vacated and the case is remanded to that court for further proceedings not inconsistent with this opinion.

It is so ordered.

CHIEF JUSTICE REHNQUIST, with whom JUSTICE WHITE, JUSTICE O'CONNOR, and JUSTICE SCALIA join, dissenting.

In deciding that petitioner Rock's testimony was properly limited at her trial, the Arkansas Supreme Court cited several factors that undermine the reliability of hypnotically induced testimony. Like the Court today, the Arkansas Supreme Court observed that a hypnotized individual becomes subject to suggestion, is likely to confabulate, and experiences artificially increased confidence in both true and false memories following hypnosis. No known set of procedures, both courts agree, can insure against the inherently unreliable nature of such testimony. Having acceded to the factual premises of the Arkansas Supreme Court, the Court nevertheless concludes that a state trial court must attempt to make its own scientific assessment of reliability in each case it is confronted with a request for the admission of hypnotically induced testimony. I find no justification in the Constitution for such a ruling.

In the Court's words, the decision today is "bottomed" on recognition of Rock's "constitutional right to testify in her own defense." While it is true that this Court, in dictum, has recognized the existence of such a right, the principles identified by the Court as underlying this right provide little support for invalidating the evidentiary rule applied by the Arkansas Supreme Court.

As a general matter, the Court first recites, a defendant's right to testify facilitates the truth-seeking function of a criminal trial by advancing both the "detection of guilt" and "the protection of innocence." Such reasoning is hardly controlling here, where advancement of the truth-seeking function of Rock's trial was the sole

VII. Testing for Truth and Enhancing Memory 187

motivation behind limiting her testimony. The Court also posits, however, that "a rule that denies an accused the opportunity to offer his own testimony" cannot be upheld because, "[l]ike the truthfulness of other witnesses, the defendant's veracity . . . can be tested adequately by cross-examination." But the Court candidly admits that the increased confidence inspired by hypnotism makes "cross-examination more difficult," thereby diminishing an adverse party's ability to test the truthfulness of defendants such as Rock. Nevertheless, we are told, the exclusion of a defendant's testimony cannot be sanctioned because the defendant " 'above all others may be in a position to meet the prosecution's case.' " In relying on such reasoning, the Court apparently forgets that the issue before us arises only by virtue of Rock's memory loss, which rendered her less able "to meet the prosecution's case."

In conjunction with its reliance on broad principles that have little relevance here, the Court barely concerns itself with the recognition, present throughout our decisions, that an individual's right to present evidence is subject always to reasonable restrictions. Indeed, the due process decisions relied on by the Court all envision that an individual's right to present evidence on his behalf is not absolute and must often times give way to countervailing considerations. Similarly, our Compulsory Process Clause decisions make clear that the right to present relevant testimony "may, in appropriate cases, bow to accommodate other legitimate interests in the criminal trial process." The Constitution does not in any way relieve a defendant from compliance with "rules of procedure and evidence designed to assure both fairness and reliability in the ascertainment of guilt and innocence." Surely a rule designed to exclude testimony whose trustworthiness is inherently suspect cannot be said to fall outside this description.*

This Court has traditionally accorded the States "respect . . . in the establishment and implementation of their own criminal trial rules and procedures." One would think that this deference would be at its highest in an area such as this, where, as the Court concedes, "scientific understanding . . . is still in its infancy." Turning a blind eye to this concession, the Court chooses instead to restrict the ability of both state and federal courts to respond to changes in the understanding of hypnosis.

The Supreme Court of Arkansas' decision was an entirely permissible response to a novel and difficult question. See National

* [Note by the Chief Justice.] The Court recognizes, as it must, that rules governing "testimonial privileges [and] nonarbitrary rules that disqualify those incapable of observing events due to mental infirmity or infancy from being witnesses" do not "offend the defendant's right to testify." I fail to discern any meaningful constitutional difference between such rules and the one at issue here.

Institute of Justice, Issues and Practices, M. Orne et al., Hypnotically Refreshed Testimony: Enhanced Memory or Tampering with Evidence? 51 (1985). As an original proposition, the solution this Court imposes upon Arkansas may be equally sensible, though requiring the matter to be considered res nova by every single trial judge in every single case might seem to some to pose serious administrative difficulties. But until there is a much more general consensus on the use of hypnosis than there is now, the Constitution does not warrant this Court's mandating its own view of how to deal with the issue.

NOTES

Hypnosis and Narcoanalysis for Restoring Memory

1. *The usual rule for memories evoked under hypnosis.* Hypnotically induced memories have provoked a variety of judicial responses. Statements made while under hypnosis, offered as substantive evidence or as bearing on credibility, are almost universally inadmissible. See cases cited, P. Giannelli & E. Imwinkelried, Scientific Evidence 271 n.173 (1984). Cf. id. at 271 n. 174 (same rule for statements made under narcoanalysis). As the opinions in *Rock* recognize, however, posthypnotic testimony as to recollections enhanced or evoked under hypnosis have triggered more divergent rulings. Compare the U.S. Supreme Court's characterization of the current legal environment with the description in the Arkansas Supreme Court's opinion, Rock v. State, 288 Ark. 566, 708 S.W.2d 78, 79-80 (1986):

> While it was said in State v. Hurd that a majority of courts have held hypnotically induced testimony admissible, the cases cited for that conclusion are from the previous decade. The more recent trend is toward exclusion of such testimony. Typical of this trend is Maryland, which in 1968 permitted the testimony, treating the issue as one of weight rather than admissibility. Harding v. State, 5 Md. App. 230, 246 A.2d 302 (1968). *Harding* was the leading opinion on this point, yet in 1982 Maryland reversed its position and held that a witness who has been hypnotized may not testify to induced recollections. Polk v. State, 48 Md. App. 382, 427 A.2d 1041 (1981). . . . [E]ven in those jurisdictions that previously held post-hypnotic testimony generally admissible, there is a trend toward insisting that rigorous safeguards be observed before the hypnotically refreshed memories are admissible, and "[t]he more prevalent view is that testimony about the post-hypnotic memories is not admissible."

Although the weight of opinion now favors the per se rule, at least as applied to hypnotic subjects other than the defendant, even in these jurisdictions, untainted, prehypnotic statements are usually admissible. Indeed, this was the rule that the Arkansas courts applied in *Rock*. According to the state supreme court,

> The trial court in this case chose the course of excluding testimony induced by hypnosis and admitting testimony of the appellant based on pre-hypnotic recollection. The difficulty was determining what that recollection was, based only on a record from the pre-hypnotic session with Dr. Back, a record admittedly incomplete. In this situation the trial court limited the appellant to what she could recall without the benefit of hypnosis, as evidenced by Dr. Back's notes and enlarged by Dr. Back's memory of her discussions with appellant before she was placed in a hypnotic state. Appellant argues the court misapplied the rule employed by courts where hypnotically induced testimony is inadmissible and was too restrictive. Appellant, however, never demonstrated how the rule was violated. The rule simply limits the hypnotized subject's testimony to those matters demonstrably recalled prior to testimony. Any other testimony on the topic runs all the risks discussed earlier in hypnotically refreshed memories. Here, the court was in a difficult position as the defense supplied only partial notes of the pre-hypnotic session. Nevertheless, the appellant was allowed to testify to those items referred to in the notes and given considerable latitude in explaining them in her own words. The trial court also allowed testimony on matters Dr. Back had previously testified were covered in the pre-hypnotic session. The burden was on appellant to establish a reliable record of the testimony. She cannot now claim error because the court restricted her to the record she offered.
>
> Dr. Back testified that during the hypnotic session she took appellant back to her childhood and brought her forward to the shooting incident. Under these circumstances, in order to avoid testimony on topics covered in the sessions that were not previously preserved, the trial court could have limited appellant entirely to the notes and testimony of Dr. Back. However, to give appellant as much latitude as possible, the trial court applied that order only to the day of the shooting.

Id.

In contrast to this approach, California rigorously excludes *all* testimony of a hypnotized witness, even that which is unrelated to the hypnotic session. People v. Brown, 40 Cal. 3d 512, 709 P.2d 440, 446, 220 Cal. Rptr. 637 (1985); People v. Guerra, 37 Cal. 3d 385, 690 P.2d 635, 663-665, 208 Cal. Rptr. 162, 190-192 (1984). Exclusion of prehypnotic statements follows from the concern that the hypnotic session enhances the witness' confidence in all his recollections, thereby insulating him from meaningful cross examination. It also obviates the need to inquire into taint, but at the obvious cost of excluding sometimes untainted testimony.

2. *Limits of the* Rock *right to present evidence.* What are the implications of *Rock* for a civil litigant with hypnotically "refreshed" memories? For criminal defendants who want to introduce various kinds

of scientific evidence considered too unreliable for use by the state? In the light of *Rock*, how should the following case be decided on appeal?

> Cogburn was charged with rape for allegedly engaging in sexual intercourse with his seven-year-old daughter. He was convicted by a jury of carnal abuse and sentenced to ten years imprisonment. Prior to the trial, the defense took the deposition of Dr. Gregory S. Kaczenski. The doctor testified that he conducted a neuropsychiatric evaluation of Cogburn and an amytal interview to look for evidence of a mental disorder. The doctor stated that the amytal interview, otherwise known as administering "truth serum," lowers the inhibitions in the conscious mind and allows the person to speak freely. While under the influence of the truth serum, the doctor said that Cogburn achieved a hypnotic state and denied having sexual contact or experience with the victim. The doctor testified that, in his opinion, the test is good evidence against Cogburn having abused his daughter. The state filed a motion in limine to suppress the doctor's testimony, which was granted by the trial court.

After *Rock*, what showing must the state make to prevent an accused from introducing memories influenced by non-drug-induced hypnosis? Should the same standard be applied to all witnesses who have undergone such hypnosis? Consider the view attributed to Dr. Martin Orne, a psychiatrist at the University of Pennsylvania, whose work was cited repeatedly in all the opinions in *Rock*:

> Orne stressed that laboratory experiments have not been able to demonstrate an increase in accurate memory through hypnosis. The subject often "remembers" more after hypnosis, but much of the additional information is wrong.
>
> Nevertheless, Orne agrees that a criminal defendant should be allowed to testify after hypnosis because he is entitled to state his case and because "the judge or jury takes into account that he is putting his best foot forward."
>
> "But if you change the memory of an unbiased witness or a victim [through hypnosis], it is a catastrophe, because you can convict anyone," he said.

Stewart, Hypnotized Witnesses, Loaded Jurors, A.B.A.J., Oct. 1, 1987, at 54, 56-57.

3. *Costs of the procedural guidelines.* The majority opinion of the U.S. Supreme Court suggested that procedural safeguards along the lines suggested by Dr. Martin Orne might permit introduction of the defendant's memories induced under hypnosis. The Arkansas Supreme Court also considered these safeguards:

> One of the more significant studies . . . is that of Dr. Martin T. Orne (Orne, et al., Hypnotically Induced Testimony, In Eyewitness

Testimony: Psychological Perspectives, Wells & Loftus, edits. 1984). Orne is widely cited on this issue, and it was his guidelines for the use of hypnotic testimony that were adopted by the New Jersey court in Hurd v. State. [Yet,] Orne's current position [is that]:

> The present state of scientific knowledge is consistent with the rules of a number of state supreme courts that memories retrieved through hypnosis are sufficiently unreliable that their use is precluded as eyewitness testimony in criminal trials . . . There is no way, however, by which anyone (including an expert with extensive experience in hypnosis) can for any particular piece of information obtained in hypnosis determine whether it is an actual memory or a confabulation. For these reasons, hypnotically induced testimony is not reliable and ought not be permitted to form the basis of testimony in court. . . .

Appellant urges that if we do not allow hypnotically refreshed testimony unconditionally, we should adopt the guidelines of State v. Hurd.[1]

---

1. These safeguards are well outlined by the New Jersey Supreme Court: Whenever a party in a criminal trial seeks to introduce a witness who has undergone hypnosis to refresh his memory, the party must inform his opponent of his intention and provide him with the recording of the session and other pertinent material. The trial court will then rule on the admissibility of the testimony either at a pretrial hearing or at a hearing out of the jury's presence. In reviewing the admissibility of hypnotically refreshed testimony, the trial court should evaluate both the kind of memory loss that hypnosis was used to restore and the specific technique employed based on expert testimony presented by the parties. The object of this review is not to determine whether the proffered testimony is accurate, but instead whether the use of hypnosis and the procedure followed in the particular case was a reasonably reliable means of restoring the witness' memory.

The first question a court must consider is the appropriateness of using hypnosis for the kind of memory loss encountered. The reason for a subject's lack of memory is an important factor in evaluating the reliability of hypnosis in restoring recall. According to defendant's expert, Dr. Orne, hypnosis often is reasonably reliable in reviving normal recall where there is a pathological reason, such as a traumatic neurosis, for the witness' inability to remember. On the other hand, the likelihood of obtaining reasonably accurate recall diminishes if hypnosis is used simply to refresh a witness' memory or concerning details where there may be no recollection at all or to "verify" one of several conflicting accounts given by a witness. A related factor to be considered is whether the witness has any discernible motivation for not remembering or for "recalling" a particular version of the events. In either case, the possibility of creating self-serving fantasy is significant. . . .

Once it is determined that a case is of a kind likely to yield normal recall if hypnosis is properly administered, then it is necessary to determine whether the procedures followed were reasonably reliable. Of particular importance are the manner of questioning and the presence of cues or suggestions during the trance and the post-hypnotic period. . . . An additional factor affecting the reliability of the procedure is the amenability of the subject to hypnosis. . . .

To provide an adequate record for evaluating the reliability of the hypnotic procedure, and to ensure a minimum level of reliability, we also adopt several procedural requirements based on those suggested by Dr. Orne and prescribed by the trial court. . . . Before it may introduce hypnotically refreshed testimony, a party must demonstrate compliance with these requirements.

First, a psychiatrist or psychologist experienced in the use of hypnosis must conduct

We note that appellant has not fully complied with those guidelines, but we are not inclined to follow *Hurd* in any case. The cases which have rejected *Hurd* have noted that some of the dangers of hypnotically induced testimony are not eliminated by the *Hurd* guidelines and others are not even addressed.[2]

Of equal importance, to adopt the guidelines would further burden the pretrial process with no off-setting benefit: the guidelines require that the opposing party be notified of the intent to use hypnosis and be furnished a recording of any sessions; only a psychologist or psychiatrist experienced in hypnosis, and independent of either the state or the defense, may be used; all sessions must be recorded and the trial court in a pretrial or chambers hearing must decide a number of issues determinative of whether the induced testimony should be received, such as the presence of cues or suggestions by the hypnotist. The burden of proof is by clear and convincing evidence.

In light of the questionable probative value of such proof and the risks inherent in the means by which it is retrieved, we think it would be a serious mistake to further encumber the pretrial process with the steps outlined in *Hurd*. We agree with the comment in People v. Shirley [31 Cal. 3d 18, 181 Cal. Rptr. 243, 641, P.2d 775 (1982)]:

---

the session. . . .

Second, the professional conducting the hypnotic session should be independent of and not regularly employed by the prosecutor, investigator or defense.

Third, any information given to the hypnotist by law enforcement personnel or the defense prior to the hypnotic session must be recorded, either in writing or in other suitable form. . . .

Fourth, before inducing hypnosis the hypnotist should obtain from the subject a detailed description of the facts as the subject remembers them. . . .

Fifth, all contacts between the hypnotist and the subject must be recorded. This will establish a record of the preinduction interview, the hypnotic session, and the post-hypnotic period, enabling a court to determine what information or suggestions the witness may have received. . . .

Sixth, only the hypnotist and the subject should be present during any phase of the hypnotic session, including the prehypnotic testing and the post-hypnotic interview. . . .

2. In deciding to discard the *Hurd* approach, the *Shirley* court noted initially that it was not persuaded that the requirements adopted in *Hurd* and other cases would eliminate each of the dangers at which they were directed.

> For example, one of the requirements . . . is that all contacts between the hypnotist and the subject must be recorded for the stated purpose of enabling the trial court to determine what "cues" the hypnotist may have conveyed to the subject by word or deed; and the opinion strongly encouraged the use of videotape to make such recordings. Yet as the same opinion recognizes elsewhere, "Because of the unpredictability of what will influence a subject, it is difficult even for an expert examining a videotape of a hypnotic session to identify possible cues." If even an expert cannot confidently make that identification, it is vain to believe that a layman such as a trial judge can do so.

The court points out that certain dangers of hypnosis are not even addressed by the *Hurd* requirements recognized elsewhere in that opinion, such as the subject losing his critical judgment and crediting memories that were formerly viewed as unreliable, confusing actual recall with confabulation and the unwarranted confidence in the validity of his ensuing recollection.

On the other hand, it takes little prescience to foresee that these and related issues would provide a fertile new field for litigation. There would first be elaborate demands for discovery, parades of expert witnesses, and special pretrial hearings, all with concomitant delays and expense. Among the questions our trial courts would then be expected to answer are scientific issues so subtle as to confound the experts. Their resolution would in turn generate a panoply of new claims that could be raised on appeal, including difficult questions of compliance with the "clear and convincing" standard of proof. And because the hypnotized subject would frequently be the victim, the eyewitness, or a similar source of crucial testimony against the defendant, any errors in ruling on the admissibility of such testimony could easily jeopardize otherwise unimpeachable judgments of conviction. In our opinion, the game is not worth the candle.

4. *Significance of the hypnotic memory in* Rock. How important was the alleged memory to which Mrs. Rock was precluded from testifying? Compare the majority opinion set forth above with the Arkansas Supreme Court's analysis:

> [A]ppellant . . . was allowed to relate the substance of her version of the shooting to the jury, which she had remembered prior to hypnosis. Appellant's defense was that the shooting was an accident and this she was able to adequately relay to the jury. She testified that she and her husband were quarreling, that he pushed her against the wall, that she wanted to leave because she was frightened, and her husband wouldn't let her go. She said her husband's behavior that night was unusual, and the shooting was an accident, that she didn't mean to do it and that she would not intentionally hurt her husband.
>
> In reality nothing was excluded that would have been of much assistance to appellant, or would have enlarged on her testimony to any significant degree. . . .

Other Psychological Testimony

5. *Expert opinions on credibility.* Unlike polygraphy or narcoanalysis, hypnosis rarely is proffered as a device for verifying or extracting the truth of a witness' statements. Instead, its alleged forensic value lies in enhancing the recall of cooperative subjects. See People v. Hughes, 59 N.Y.2d 523, 453 N.E.2d 484, 466 N.Y.S.2d 255 (1983). In some cases, however, individuals with psychological training profess the ability to discern when a witness is telling the truth. The courts are reluctant to allow experts to express such opinions, whether based on clinical experience, statistical profiles, polygraphy, narcoanalysis, or hypnosis. In State v. Saldana, 324 N.W.2d 227 (Minn. 1982), for example, the Minnesota Supreme Court reversed a conviction for

rape, in part because a counselor for sexual assault victims testified that the complainant had not fantasized the event. The court explained:

> Once a victim is deemed competent, expert opinions concerning the witness' reliability in distinguishing truth from fantasy are generally inadmissible because such opinions invade the jury's province to make credibility determinations. Expert testimony concerning the reliability of a witness should be received only in "unusual cases." An example of such an unusual case is a sexual assault case where the alleged victim is a child or mentally retarded. See Commonwealth v. Carter, 9 Mass. App. 680, 403 N.E.2d 1191 (1980), *aff'd*, 417 N.E.2d 438 (Mass. 1981) (examining pediatrician may give opinion relating to the ability of a retarded child to differentiate between reality and fantasy but not concerning whether the child was telling the truth about an alleged sexual assault).

Id. at 231. Likewise, in State v. Lindsey, the Arizona Supreme Court reversed a conviction for incest because of what it deemed "direct opinion testimony on truthfulness" from the state's expert. The court remarked:

> Opinion evidence on who is telling the truth in cases such as this is nothing more than the expert's opinion on how the case should be decided. We believe that such testimony is inadmissible, both because it usurps the jury's traditional functions and roles and because, when given insight into the behavioral sciences, the jury needs nothing further from the expert. We do not invite battles of opposing experts testifying to opinions about the truthfulness of the prosecution witness as compared to that of the defense witnesses.

State v. Lindsey, 149 Ariz. 472, 720 P.2d 73 (1986). See also State v. Moran, 151 Ariz. 378, 728 P.2d 248 (1986); Lindsey v. United States, 237 F.2d 893 (9th Cir. 1956); People v. Hughes, 59 N.Y.2d 523, 453 N.E.2d 484, 466 N.Y.S.2d 255 (1983) ("when presented with scientific evidence purporting to gauge the credibility of participants or witnesses to a criminal incident, we have established a very high level of reliability, tantamount to certainty, as a predicate for its admissibility").

In addition to this general aversion to expert assessments of truthfulness, the intricate rules of evidence involving "character" and "character for credibility" affect the admissibility of expert assessments of credibility. For instance, whether or not an expert's conclusion of deception might be admissible to attack credibility, an opinion bolstering truthfulness would be inadmissible if the witness's character for credibility has not been attacked. See, e.g., State v. Kim, 645 P.2d 1330, 1339 n.14 (1982).

6. *Generalizations about eyewitnesses.* The same courts that disapprove of the psychologist or other expert's testifying to the credibility of a witness sometimes permit these experts to supply the underlying information. This testimony takes the form of generalizations derived from clinical experience or experimental studies. Such "generalized psychological testimony" is frequently offered, and in recent years an increasing number of appellate courts have deemed it admissible. Indeed, a handful of courts have even reversed convictions when trial judges excluded expert testimony as to the accuracy of eyewitness identifications. United States v. Downing, 753 F.2d 1224 (3d Cir. 1985) (government's case rested almost exclusively on the eyewitness identifications); United States v. Smith, 736 F.2d 1103 (6th Cir. 1984) (excluded testimony would have focused on "a hypothetical factual situation identical" to the facts of the case, and would have explained (1) that a witness who does not identify the defendant in a first lineup may "unconsciously transfer" his visualization of the defendant to a second line-up and thereby incorrectly identify the defendant the second time; (2) that studies demonstrate the inherent unreliability of cross-racial identifications; and (3) that an encounter during a stressful situation decreases the eyewitness' ability to perceive and remember and decreases the probability of an accurate identification); State v. Chapple, 660 P.2d 1208 (Ariz. 1983) (abuse of discretion to exclude pertinent testimony concerning: (1) the "forgetting curve," i.e., the fact that memory does not diminish at a uniform rate; (2) the fact that, contrary to common understanding, stress causes inaccuracy of perception and distorts one's subsequent recall; (3) the "assimilation factor," which indicates that witnesses frequently incorporate into their identifications inaccurate information gathered after the event and confused with the event; (4) the "feedback factor," which indicates that where identification witnesses discuss the case with each other they can unconsciously reinforce their individual identifications; and (5) the fact that studies demonstrate the absence of a relationship between the confidence a witness has in his or her identification and the actual accuracy of that identification); People v. McDonald, 208 Cal. Rptr. 236, 690 P.2d 709 (Cal. 1984) (crossracial identification and alibi defense). However, not all psychologists agree that this type of testimony is helpful. See McCloskey & Egeth, Eyewitness Identification: What Can a Psychologist Tell a Jury? 18 Am. Psych. 550, 560-562 (1983).

If the expert on eyewitness identification does not give judgments on the accuracy of the identifications at bar, what is his or her role? To identify the variables that experimenters have shown affect accuracy and to estimate their importance? Is courtroom testimony an efficient and effective way to achieve this educational mission? Consider Monahan & Walker, Social Frameworks: A New Use of Social Science in Law, 73 Va. L. Rev. 559, 559-560 (1987):

> [In] cases [involving] eyewitness identification, assessments of dangerousness, battered women, and sexual victimization, [t]he application of social science . . . does not concern legislative fact, since no rule of law is at issue. Neither does it concern adjudicative fact, since the research does not involve the parties before the court. We propose the concept of social frameworks to refer to these uses of general conclusions from social science research in determining factual issues in a specific case. . . .
>
> Currently, a social framework is typically offered by one of the parties through the oral testimony of expert witnesses for evaluation and application by a jury. [W]e present a theory that suggests a very different procedural scheme for dealing with social science used as a social framework: the research either may be offered by one of the parties in a brief or located by the trial judge; it should be evaluated by the judge according to accepted common law principles; and only then should it be conveyed to the jury, by instruction from the judge. As the same frameworks are brought to bear in an increasing number of cases, we propose that attention be given to establishing standard instructions, either by the common law process of taking them from prior cases or by creating pattern instructions.

7. *Generalizations about "rape trauma."* In addition to offering generalizations about eyewitnesses, psychologists and other experts have been asked to describe the general behavior of victims of sexual assaults. For instance, in State v. Saldana, 324 N.W.2d 227 (Minn. 1982), the prosecution sought to rebut the defendant's claim of consent with an expert who described the typical post-rape symptoms and behavior of rape victims, and gave her opinion that the complainant was a victim of rape. The Minnesota Supreme Court reversed the conviction. Concluding that "such testimony is of no help to the jury and produces an extreme danger of unfair prejudice," the court first questioned the relevance of the information: "The factual question to be decided by the jury is whether the alleged criminal conduct occurred. It is not necessary that [the victim] react in a typical manner to the incident. [The victim] need not display the typical post-rape symptoms and behavior of rape victims to convince the jury that her view of the facts is the truth." Id. Second, the Minnesota court questioned the diagnostic value of the information: "Rape trauma syndrome is not the type of scientific test that accurately and reliably determines whether a rape has occurred. The characteristic symptoms may follow any psychologically traumatic event. At best, the syndrome

describes only symptoms that occur with some frequency, but makes no pretense of describing every single case." Id. Characterizing the syndrome as "a therapeutic tool" rather than "a fact-finding tool," and reiterating that "evidence of reactions of other people does not assist the jury in its fact-finding function," the court held even the generalized testimony inadmissible.

Why is "rape trauma syndrome" testimony "of no help to the jury"? Because jurors already appreciate the range and types of normal responses to rape? Because the "syndrome" is not specific to rape, but may follow other traumatic experiences? (The medically accepted label for the diagnostic category is "post-traumatic stress disorder." E.g., Helzer, Robins & McEvoy, Post-Traumatic Stress Disorder in the General Population, 317 New Eng. J. Med. 1630 (1987).) Because the reactions do not occur "in every single case"? Because "how most people react to rape" is logically irrelevant? How convincing are these arguments of the *Saldana* court? See, e.g., Frazier & Borgida, Juror Common Understanding and the Admissibility of Rape Trauma Syndrome Evidence in Court, 12 L. & Human Behavior 101 (1988); Massaro, Experts, Psychology, Credibility and Rape: The Rape Trauma Syndrome Issue and its Implications for Expert Psychological Testimony, 69 Minn. L. Rev. 395 (1985); McCord, The Admissibility of Expert Psychological Testimony Regarding Rape Trauma Syndrome in Rape Prosecutions, 26 B.C.L. Rev. 1143 (1985).

If proof of the syndrome were allowed to show lack of consent, would the absence of the syndrome be admissible to prove that there was consent? Should a defendant be permitted to argue that the prosecution's failure to introduce evidence of post-traumatic stress disorder (PTSD) in a rape case indicates that the alleged victim really consented? See McCormick on Evidence §206, at 83 n.92.15 (1987 Supp.).

Saldana maintains that PTSD is not generally accepted in the scientific community as an indicator of rape and that expert testimony about the syndrome therefore violates the general acceptance rule announced in Frye v. United States (see supra at Section 4). Is this true? Compare Expert Testimony on Rape Trauma Syndrome: An Argument for Limited Admissibility, 63 Wash. L. Rev. 1063 (1988), with Checking the Allure of Increased Conviction Rates: The Admissibility of Expert Testimony on Rape Trauma Syndrome in Criminal Proceedings, 70 Va. L. Rev. 1657 (1984). Does the general acceptance standard even apply to this type of behavioral symptom evidence? Compare State v. Black, 745 P.2d 12 (Wash. 1987), with People v. Hampton, 746 P.2d 947 (Colo. 1987).

Many jurisdictions do not follow *Saldana*, but even when PTSD testimony is admissible in rape prosecutions, the psychological expert may be barred from offering an opinion as to whether the stress disorder diagnosed in the alleged victim resulted from rape. In the words of one state supreme court:

> We, therefore, must draw a distinction between an expert's testimony that an alleged victim exhibits post-rape behavior consistent with rape-trauma syndrome and expert opinion that bolsters the credibility of the alleged victim by indicating that she was indeed raped.

State v. McCoy, 366 S.E.2d 731, 737 (W. Va. 1988). Can this distinction be maintained in practice? What if the expert testifies that the victim was "still traumatized by this experience"? Id. Cf. State v. Lindsey, 720 P.2d 73 (Ariz. 1986) (mischaracterizing an expert's statement that "most people in the field feel that it's a very small proportion that lie" as an opinion on the credibility of a specific witness).

8. *Generalizations about sexually abused children.* Psychologists have also studied the problem of sexual abuse of children (e.g., D. Finklehor, Child Sexual Abuse: New Theory and Research (1984); R. Geiser, Hidden Victims: The Sexual Abuse of Children (1979)), the cognitive abilities of children (e.g., Children's Eyewitness Memory (S. Ceci, M. Toglia & D. Ross eds. 1987); Lewis, Stanger & Sullivan, Deception in 3-year Olds, 25 Developmental Psych. 439 (1989)), and the behavior of child witnesses (e.g., Perspectives on Children's Testimony (S. Ceci, D. Ross & M. Toglia eds. 1989); Symposium, 40 J. Soc. Issues 1 (1984)). As with PTSD, prosecutors sometimes offer expert testimony on the characteristic behavior of sexually abused children. For instance, in State v. Hall, 406 N.W.2d 503 (Minn. 1987), the defendant was found to have raped a 14-year-old who was babysitting his children. The victim testified that because the defendant threatened to kill her if she told anyone, she did not report the assault and continued to babysit the defendant's children. A clinical psychologist testified that experts are able to identify behavioral characteristics commonly exhibited by sexually abused adolescents, that one of these characteristics is a delay in reporting because of the victim's fear of being harmed, and that when the victim knows the assailant, it is not uncommon for the victim to have continued contact with the assailant. This time the Minnesota Supreme Court held that the evidence was admissible. It distinguished *Saldana* on the ground that the victim was not an adult and that the psychologist "had not examined the complainant, so she did not attempt to describe the characteristics or conditions observed in or exhibited by the complainant." Id. Nevertheless, the court cautioned that "[w]hile we hold that in cases where a sexual assault victim is an adolescent, expert testimony as to the reporting conduct of such victims and as to continued contact by the adolescent

with the assailant is admissible in the proper exercise of discretion by the trial court, . . . we do not intend to establish a categorical rule that expert testimony concerning all characteristics typically displayed by adolescent sexual assault victims is admissible."

What is the justification for allowing testimony about the "child abuse syndrome" as in *Hall*, but not about the "rape trauma syndrome"? A jury's need for the evidence? A better scientific pedigree for the evidence? An increased willingness to convict possible child abusers? May the evidence be used to prove the fact of abuse as well as to explain a child's delay in reporting the abuse or his or her retraction of an accusation? See McCormick on Evidence §206 at 82-84 (1987 Supp.). For a criticism of such testimony, see The Unreliability of Expert Testimony on the Typical Characteristics of Sexual Abuse Victims, 74 Geo. L.J. 429 (1985). For a more sympathetic response, see McCord, Expert Psychological Testimony About Child Complainants in Sexual Abuse Prosecutions: A Foray Into the Admissibility of Novel Psychological Evidence, 77 J. Crim. L. & Criminology 1 (1986).

9. *Other syndromes and profiles.* In the cases described in this section, the findings of behavioral scientists are admissible on the theory that the jurors may use this background information to evaluate the trial testimony more accurately. However, we have also seen that when psychological experts go beyond the presentation of such general knowledge and offer clinical judgments about the accuracy of a particular eyewitness, the lack of consent in an alleged rape, the credibility of a child witness, the tendency of battered women to remain with the man who abuses them, and so on, many courts will find that the testimony should be excluded. The crucial distinction, then, is between statistical, experimental, or clinical data that support a generalization about human behavior or performance, and the expert's application of these data or this generalization to a specific person. It has been argued that the former testimony should be admissible because it provides a useful "social framework" for evaluating the trial evidence, Monahan & Walker, Social Frameworks: A New Use of Social Science in Law, 73 Va. L. Rev. 559 (1987), but that once the expert supplies these generalizations, "the jury needs nothing further from the expert." State v. Lindsey, 149 Ariz. 472, 720 P.2d 73 (1986).

Other examples of such testimony include "profiles" of certain types of offenders — characteristics statistically associated with an offense. May the prosecution prove that a defendant fits the "profile" of a rapist, arsonist, a drug courier, or the like? Consider rule 404(b) of the federal and uniform rules of evidence:

> Evidence of other crimes, wrongs or acts is not admissible to prove the character of a person in order to show that he acted in conformity

therewith. It may, however, be admissible where such evidence is probative of any other fact that is of consequence to the determination of the action, such as proof of motive, opportunity, intent, preparation, plan, knowledge, identity, modus operandi, or absence of mistake or accident.

See State v. Hester, 760 P.2d 27, 33-34 (Idaho 1988); People v. Walkey, 223 Cal. Rptr. 132, 137-139 (App. 1986); McCormick on Evidence §206, at 635-636 (E. Cleary 3d ed. 1984). May the defendant prove that he does not fit the incriminating profile? See State v. Cavallo, 443 A.2d 1020 (N.J. 1982); McCormick on Evidence §206, at 636 (E. Cleary 3d ed. 1984).

CHAPTER 4

Medical Proof in Litigation

I. LAY OPINION ON MEDICAL ISSUES

Evans v. People
12 Mich. 27 (1863)

CAMPBELL, JUSTICE. Evans, the plaintiff in error, was convicted of manslaughter in killing one Coban Balch. Error is brought on two grounds: *First.* That the information is insufficient to sustain the conviction; and *Second.* That evidence was received which was inadmissible. . . .

The remaining ground of error alleged is, that one John Hendershot, not being shown to possess any special qualifications, was allowed to answer a question involving an inquiry of medical science, having an important bearing upon the cause of Balch's death. It had been shown that he died of erysipelas, claimed by the prosecution to have resulted from the injuries inflicted by Evans. The defense had introduced medical witnesses, whose evidence tended to prove the existence of that disease in an epidemic form in Balch's neighborhood, previous to his visit to Grand Rapids, where he died two days after the assault upon him. Hendershot was called as a rebutting witness, and was asked, under objection, whether there was "any case of erysipelas about the neighborhood of the residence of the deceased, before his coming to Grand Rapids, in February last"; the witness answered, "No, sir; neither before nor since; no sickness within five or six miles of Coban Balch's residence during the month of February, nor until after that time."

There can be no doubt of the importance of these various inquiries, inasmuch as they were aimed at explaining the causes of the death of Balch, and showing how far Evans was responsible for it. It becomes essential, therefore, to consider whether this question was admissible under the circumstances, and also how far the form of the answer may affect the legality of its reception.

If the question was improper, it is because it is supposed to involve obtaining an opinion which no one has a right to give in evidence without an especial knowledge of diseases in general, or of the particular disease named, not supposed to be possessed except by those whose study or attention has been turned in that direction.

It is not always easy to determine the propriety of receiving or rejecting testimony concerning matters involving, apparently, to a greater or less extent, medical or other scientific investigation. There are many cases where it is difficult to determine whether the facts to be examined are to be considered beyond the range of ordinary intelligence. And the decisions are by no means clear or satisfactory upon the distinctions. The principles on which the authorities rest are more consistent than the attempts to apply them.

The primary rule, concerning all evidence, is, that personal knowledge of such facts as a court or jury may be called upon to consider, should be required of all witnesses, where it is attainable. It is also an elementary rule that, where the court or jury can make their own deductions, they shall not be made by those testifying. In all cases, therefore, where it is possible to inform the jury fully enough to enable them to dispense with the opinions or deductions of witnesses from things noticed by themselves, or described by others, such opinions or deductions should not usually be received. But experience has shown that many cases exist, in which it is impossible, by any description, however graphic, to explain things so as to enable any one but the witness himself to see or comprehend them, as they would have been seen or comprehended could the jury have occupied his position of observation. In such cases, the witness must give his own impressions and conclusions, or his narrative is useless; adding, however, as full explanations as the nature of the case will admit, so that his capacity and truthfulness may be tested as far as practicable. Examples of this kind frequently occur, when it becomes necessary to inquire into mental condition and disposition, into the existence of passion or emotion, attention or inattention, vigor or weakness, affection or aversion, or any other matter in which we usually form our opinions without stopping to analyse the reasons for them, or notice their elements. Similar instances occur where witnesses attempt to describe natural phenomena, as degrees of light and darkness, the measurement of distances by the eye, changes of heat and cold, and the like. The principle which allows persons who understand matters of science or skill to give their opinions and deductions from facts exhibited or described to them, rests upon the same foundation. In all these cases, the witness is allowed to testify to a result, because, without such evidence, the jury cannot be supposed able to arrive at a knowledge of it, and therefore such aid is indispensable. And it also follows, that no witness can be permitted to offer such testimony, unless he appears to be qualified in some degree, at least, to furnish the means of aiding the jury in arriving at a true result. The greatest difficulty encountered in determining questions of competency of testimony, on subjects connected more or less with medical science, is in ascertaining how far it is safe to suppose unprofessional observers are able to form a reliable judgment. There are some simple disorders, which all persons are familiar with. Others require the very highest degree of medical skill to distinguish them from disorders having some resembling appearances or symptoms. In some cases, too, although inquiries arise concerning the existence of health or disease, it does not become important to have accurate information as to the precise character of such disorders as may exist. In the view of evidence now entertained by the best authorities, it is settled that a jury should be allowed to have placed before them all the means of knowledge which can be had without involving the danger of leading them to form conclusions not based on solid truth, and not reliable as reasonably certain. If a witness is competent to form an opinion which the jury could not, or which an ordinary witness could not, it would be absurd to reject his aid. But, on the other hand, a scientific witness, when he testifies to matters within the comprehension of ordinary witnesses, stands on the same footing with them as to all such testimony, and as to those matters can only give his opinions where any other observer might.

Thus, when it was held by some authorities that, upon questions touching the mental capacity of a particular person, only physicians and subscribing witnesses could give their opinion, the inquiry was not made one of science merely, and the scientific expert was put on the same footing, on questions not purely medical, with ordinary witnesses having no scientific knowledge, and whose powers of observation were those possessed by any one in like circumstances; and the recognition of this equality has led to the modern sensible doctrine, that similar opinions are receivable from all who have, by personal observation, had means of forming a judgment concerning the condition of the party. The value of any such opinion depends, like all other testimony, on the honesty and sagacity of the witness, and on his means of observing and judging.

Such opinions being constantly formed and acted upon by all men in their daily intercourse, are among the most familiar means of safety in business transactions. But there may be, in addition to appearances which all intelligent men understand, peculiar symptoms and conditions understood only by medical men or other experts; and as to these peculiarities, the testimony of such experts becomes admissible beyond that of others.

What is thus true of mental capacity may become equally true in regard to other matters involving some questions of skill. Circumstances may make whole communities familiar with diseases not generally known elsewhere, and reasonably competent to manage ordinary cases of such diseases, and to recognize their symptoms. Such is often the case from necessity in new countries; and the same necessity leads to a more general knowledge of the extent to which a neighborhood has suffered from any prevailing sickness than is usual in populous towns. And it often happens that some persons having no general skill become very familiar with particular subjects.

It would be very unwise to exclude such evidence, merely because the range of the witness's knowledge is limited. There are as many grades of knowledge and ignorance in the professions as out of them. The only safe rule in any of these cases is, to ascertain the extent of the witness's qualifications, and, within their range, to permit him to speak. Cross-examination, and the testimony of others, will here, as in all other cases, furnish the best means of testing his value.

The circumstances of the case, therefore, must be looked at to determine the admissibility, not only of the question put to Hendershot, but also of his answer. As he was not examined concerning his knowledge of erysipelas, or of diseases generally, he could not be asked such a question, if the issue materially required from the witness any such knowledge. The inquiry before the jury was whether the erysipelas, of which Balch died, was dependent on a wound, or was wholly or in part derived from other causes. It was attributed by the defense to his previous exposure to an epidemic.

The exact nature, as well as the existence of such epidemic was thus directly in controversy. This question, therefore, could not properly be put to any one not having some knowledge of the disease; and, as the record stands, was erroneously allowed.

But Hendershot's answer, denying the existence of any disease whatever in that vicinity, stands on a different footing. The difference between health and any sickness whatever can hardly be regarded as open only to medical knowledge; and his contradiction of the medical testimony is a contradiction of common facts, and not of science. The value of such a sweeping assertion is not to be determined in this Court.

The testimony was not incompetent. There was no error in the proceedings, and the judgment must be affirmed.

The other Justices concurred.

NOTES

Lay Testimony on Medical Issues

1. Why was the disease involved in the instant case, erysipelas, so clearly known to lay people in the community in 1863? First, epidemic communicable diseases that resulted in death for so many in these years were tracked by word of mouth in their progress through a neighborhood and across a city. Second, erysipelas was easily identified by a ghastly red skin eruption or rash called, at the time, "St. Anthony's Fire." The disease was systemic throughout the body. For a graphic picture of the public reactions to an epidemic moving through a community, see A. Camus, The Plague (1947).

2. The evidentiary rules governing the scope of what areas of opinion on medical and scientific issues a lay person may be allowed

I. Lay Opinion on Medical Issues

to testify are very broadly expressed and not very informative. For example, Rule 701 of the Federal Rules and the Uniform Rules of Evidence provide:

> If a witness is not testifying as an expert, his testimony in the form of opinions or inferences is limited to those opinions or inferences which are (a) rationally based on the perceptions of the witness, and (b) helpful to a clear understanding of the testimony or the determination of a fact in issue.

Many of the situations where lay persons are allowed to answer questions that include opinion or inference on medical/scientific facts or conditions turn out, when more closely examined, to be matters wherein the lay person is actually quite experienced and often rather expert, although not by formal education or an academic degree. Such circumstances will exist when the lay person is an experienced police officer, a lay nurse, a pastoral counselor, or a mother who has cared for a severely handicapped child for many years.

Other situations will present rather common physical and mental conditions that are important to a question in litigation, and where the lay person was the only available observer at the time. For example, may a lay person testify on the following:

a. That a person was "ill" or in "good shape"? See Wilson v. Liberty National Life Ins. Co., 331 So. 2d 617 (Ala. 1976), where the court allowed a widow to state that her husband had been in "good shape" asserting such a statement to be a statement of fact rather than an expression of opinion. See also Stanley v. Ford Motor Co., 374 49 A.D. 2d 979, N.Y.S. 2d 370 (3d Dept. 1975), wherein the court held a lay person could testify as to a person's general strength, vigor, or feebleness and illness as well as comparative condition from day to day; accord, Philip v. Steward, 207 Va. 214, 148 S.E.2d 784 (1966). Heiting v. Heiting, 64 Wis. 2d 110, 218 N.W.2d 334 (Wis. 1974), held that a "close relative or associate" could testify as to objective symptoms of one alleged to be suffering physical distress. See also National Life Ins. & Accident Co. v. Whetlock, 198 Okla. 561, 180 P.2d 647 (1947); Graham v. Police & Firemen's Ins. Assn., 10 Wash. 2d 288, 116 P.2d 352 (1941); Equitable Life Assurance Socy. of the U.S. v. Bomar, 106 F.2d 640 (6th Cir. 1939); Daniels v. Bloomquist, 138 N.W.2d 868 (Iowa 1965); Tyron v. Casey, 416 S.W.2d 252 (Kan. City Ct. App. 1967); Life & Casualty Ins. Co. of Tenn. v. Rivera, 420 S.W.2d 788 (Tex. Civ. App. 1967); Dickson v. Minnesota Mut. Life Ins., 562 S.W.2d 925 (Tex. Civ. App. 1978); Kentucky Central Life Ins. Co. v. Fannin, 575 S.W.2d 76 (Tex. Civ. App. 1978).

b. That a person was in pain? Any lay observer who has a

reasonable opportunity to see and observe may testify regarding an observation of a person apparently in pain, see generally Wright v. Graniteville Co., 221 S.E.2d 777 (S.C. 1976); Tyron v. Casey, 416 S.W.2d 252 (Mo. App. 1967); Mielke v. Dobrydnio, 138 N.E. 561 (Mass. 1923); Haney v. Town of Rainelle, 125 W. Va. 397, 25 S.E.2d 207 (Tenn. 1943); American Enka Corp. v. Sutton, 391 S.W.2d 643 (Tenn. 1965); Granite State Ins. Co. v. Martin, 480 S.W.2d 326 (Ark. 1972); Southern Pac. Transp. Co. v. Peralez, 546 S.W.2d 88 (Tex. Civ. App. 1976); Holt v. City of Statesville, 241 S.E.2d 362 (N.C. App. 1978); 90 A.L.R.2d 1071 (1963). However, this view is not universally held; see Brown v. Rogers, 313 A.2d 547 (Md. App. 1974), wherein the court held a mother incompetent to testify as to whether her daughter appeared to be in pain during a hospital stay.

c. That a person was intoxicated? Gensemer v. Williams, 419 F.2d 1361 (3d Cir. 1970), permitted lay testimony but required that facts upon which the opinion rested be established. See also Esquivel v. Nancarrow, 450 P.2d 399 (Ariz. 1969), wherein the court required only that the lay witness have sufficient time to observe the subject. For similar holdings, see Burke v. Tower East Restaurant, 37 App. Div. 2d 836, 326 N.Y.S.2d 32 (2d Dept. 1971); State v. Cummings, 206 S.E.2d 781 (N.C. App. 1974); Miles v. West, 580 P.2d 876 (Kan. App. 1978); Allison v. Davies, 318 N.E.2d 1034 (Ill. Dec. 1978).

3. Keeping in mind what you have learned from the above situations, what rulings on admissibility of opinions by "lay persons" would you make on the following?

   a. That a wound on the body was caused by gunshot?
   b. That death was caused by a gunshot wound?
   c. That a person was hallucinating due to a drug overdose?
   d. That the "white powder" found at the scene was LSD? Was heroin?
   e. That the victim was "knocked unconscious"?
   f. That a disability is permanent?
   g. That a claimant was "faking" an alleged injury and consequent physical disability?
   h. That a person was unable to walk? Unable to talk? Unable to see?

4. Lay opinion on mental condition is much more readily admitted than opinion on "more scientific" aspects of physical condition and disability. This practice is historically based upon the ready admission of lay opinion on "soundness of mind" in testamentary and contractual mental capacity. This attitude has had an impact on the scope of psychiatric testimony on these same issues. See Curran, The Psychiatrist as Expert Witness, in Forensic Psychiatry and Psychology (Curran, McGarry & Shah eds. 1986).

5. Have psychiatrists any greater expertise than lay people in

predicting future conduct, especially dangerous or violent conduct, on the part of mentally ill persons? Psychiatrists have recently joined in the effort to deny any special expertise of psychiatrists on these and other issues viewed as "ultimate questions" for the jury. See the American Bar Association, Criminal Justice Mental Health Standards, §7.3.9 (2d ed. 1986). These standards were adopted on the basis of recommendations of a committee composed of lawyers and mental health professionals. See also Ennis & Litwack, Psychiatry and the Presumption of Expertise: Flipping Coins in the Courtroom, 25 Calif. L. Rev. 37 (1978); Ewing, "Dr. Death" and the Case for an Ethical Ban on Psychiatric and Psychological Predictions of Dangerousness in Capital Sentencing Cases, 8 Am. J.L. & Med. 407 (1983). The Supreme Court has disagreed with the position of a total ban on psychiatric opinion testimony in predictions of future dangerous conduct. See Barefoot v. Estelle, reprinted in Chapter 3 at 160 and notes following. For other aspects of psychiatric testimony, see the section on Forensic Psychiatry in Chapter 3.

II. EXPERT MEDICAL TESTIMONY: QUALIFICATIONS AND COLLATERAL ATTACK

Sandow v. Weyerhaeuser Co.
449 P.2d 426 (Or. 1969)

HOLMAN, JUSTICE. This is an action under the Jones Act for damages for personal injuries sustained by plaintiff in the course of his employment as a seaman aboard defendant's vessel. Plaintiff received a judgment for $5,000 general damages. Thereafter the trial court ordered a new trial unless the plaintiff filed a remittitur of all the judgment in excess of $750. Plaintiff appealed.

The basis for the remittitur was that the verdict was excessive for the superficial cut on the forehead suffered by plaintiff. Plaintiff testified that he had felt depressed, that he had suffered blackouts and dizziness, and had experienced suicidal feelings. The trial court took the consideration of these complaints from the jury because there was no evidence that they were caused by the injury to plaintiff's head. Plaintiff offered the testimony of a clinical psychologist to the effect that plaintiff's depression was caused by the injury. The trial court refused to admit the testimony on the ground that the witness was not qualified to give such testimony because he was not medically trained. . . . The evidence showed plaintiff suffered a cut 2 inches in length which left a scar that the trial judge could not see from a distance of five feet. In the absence of testimony connecting plaintiff's complaints with the superficial injury to his head, we cannot say the trial judge erred in concluding that the judgment exceeded any rational appraisal.

The principal question to be decided in this case is whether the trial court erred in refusing to admit in evidence the opinion of a clinical psychologist that the superficial injury to plaintiff's head caused the emotional disturbance of which he complained. Had the opinion been admitted it would have furnished a basis for allowing the jury to consider whether plaintiff's depression was the result of the accident.

To warrant the use of expert opinion testimony, inferences being drawn must be so related to some science, profession, business or occupation that is sufficiently technical that a lay juror cannot be expected to be equally well qualified to form a worthwhile judgment. Ritter v. Beals et al., 225 Or. 504, 525, 358 P.2d 1080 (1961); Welter, Adm'x. v. M & M Woodworking Co., 216 Or. 266, 278-279, 338 P.2d 651 (1959). Obviously, the question upon which the witness's opinion was sought was one which the average juror, unaided, would not have the skill to decide.

In addition, the witness must have such skill, knowledge or experience in the field or calling in question as to make it appear that his opinion or inference-drawing would probably aid the trier of the facts in his search for the truth. [citations omitted.]. . .

The majority of the available case law indicates that a properly-qualified clinical psychologist is competent to testify concerning a person's mental and emotional condition despite his not having medical training. Though we find no cases which hold that psychologists are competent to testify as to the causative factors of a given mental or emotional condition, the accepted literature in the field of psychology states that such factors are within their expertise.

We hold that clinical psychology has become established and recognized as a profession whose members possess special expertise in the field of mental and emotional disorders and that a psychologist who is a diplomate in clinical psychology of the American Board of Examiners in Professional Psychology, who is a member of the American Psychological Association and who is licensed to practice psychology in Oregon is qualified to express an opinion such as the one offered by the witness in question. The law does not require that in order to qualify as an expert the witness be better qualified than anyone else. It only requires that he have sufficient expertise to make it probable that he will aid the jury in its search for the truth. Therefore, the trial court erred in refusing the expert testimony offered and the refusal was necessarily prejudicial. The judgment of the trial court is reversed and the case is remanded for a new trial.

Lundgren v. Eustermann
370 N.W.2d 877 (Minn. 1985)

[See opinion at page 267 of Chapter 5.]

NOTES

Psychologists, Nurses, Pharmacists, and Others as Expert Witnesses

1. The majority of American case law agrees that a properly qualified psychologist is competent to testify about a person's mental and emotional condition despite a lack of medical training. However, several courts are still hesitant to allow psychologist testimony as to the organic or causative factors of a given mental or emotional condition. Much of the literature in the field of psychology states that such diagnostic activities are within the profession's expertise; see Ziskin, Coping with Psychiatric and Psychological Testimony (3d ed. 1981); Perlin, The Legal Status of the Psychologist in the Courtroom, 5 J. Psychia. & L. 41 (1977). Most recently, see Kennedy, The Psychologist as Expert Witness in Forensic Psychiatry and Psychology (Curran, McGarry & Shah eds. 1986).

2. The *Lundgren* case illustrates the refusal of some courts to allow psychologists (and other nonphysicians) to testify on the standard of patient care for physicians, even in areas of clear expertise by those other disciplines. The Supreme Court of Alabama came to the same conclusion in excluding a psychologist's testimony in a medical malpractice case, citing with approval the finding in *Lundgren*. See Bell v. Hart, 516 So. 2d 562 (Ala. 1987). A more liberal view on the admission of opinion evidence of nonphysicians (a pharmacist and a toxicologist) is found in the Supreme Court of Mississippi. See Thompson v. Carter, 518 So. 2d 609 (Miss. 1987) reprinted in Chapter 5 at 269.

3. Nurses are frequent witnesses in court, usually in relation to their observations of patients under their care in hospitals, clinics, and at home. In these situations they generally report on the patient's comfort, discomfort, or pain while receiving medications, recuperating from operations, etc. The testimony of registered or professional nurses is usually preferred in these situations to the observations of practical nurses or nursing orderlies.

Nurses may also be called as expert witnesses regarding standards of nursing care in malpractice cases against nurses. See C. Northrop & M. Kelly, Legal Issues in Nursing (1987); A. Rhodes & R. Miller, Nursing and the Law (1984). Should nurses be admitted as expert witnesses on the standards of care determined of physicians when the nurses have observed the care being given? In a quite provocative discussion, an experienced nursing authority indicated that such testimony should be allowed, at least in special circumstances, where the nurses are quite knowledgeable, due to practical experience, of accepted standards of medical clinical care. See Eccard, Revolution in White: New Approaches in Treating Nurses as Professionals, 30 Vand. L. Rev. 839, 865 (1977). The testimony of a nurse anesthetist was admitted as an expert opinion on anesthesia standards of care by a physician. See Cornfield v. Tangen, 262 N.W.2d 684 (Minn. 1977).

4. Courts have had to determine the competence of many other medical care professionals and allied health care specialists under various circumstances. The following cases, some mentioned above, are illustrative. In most instances, the courts admit opinion evidence when the practitioner has special knowledge due to education and/or practical experience. See Ornoff v. Kuhn, 549 A.2d 728 (D. Ct. D.C. 1988) (hematologist); Thompson v. Carter 518 So. 2d 609 (Miss. 1987) (psychologist and toxicologist); Stevens v. Smallman, 590 S.W.2d 674 (1979) (chiropractor); Alexander v. Mt. Carmel Med. Cent., 560 Ohio St. 2d 155, 383 N.E.2d 564 (1978) (podiatrist); Ory v. Libersky, 40 Md. App. 151, 389 A.2d 922 (1978) (rescue squad technician); De Falco v. Long Island College Hosp., 393 N.Y.S.2d 859 (N.Y. Sup. 1977) (chemist).

State v. Carter
217 La. 547, 46 So. 2d 897 (1950)

HAWTHORNE, JUSTICE. . . . During the course of his examination he was asked the following question by counsel for the defendant.

Q. Doctor, if an autopsy revealed there was an acute right cardiac dilatation, contusions, discoloration around the fold in neck and base of skull from ear to ear, would that, could that be from a disease, such as heart trouble?

Counsel for the State objected to the question on the ground that the doctor had qualified as a general practitioner and not as a heart specialist. The court sustained the objection, and the witness was not permitted to answer the question. Counsel for defendant thereupon reserved a bill of exception. . . .

It will be observed that the only objection to the question made by counsel for the State and sustained by the court was that the witness was not a heart specialist. The fact that the witness was not a heart specialist might affect the weight to be given to his testimony, but it certainly did not affect its admissibility. . . .

II. Expert Medical Testimony

Smith v. Horace Williams Co.
84 So. 2d 223 (La. App. 1956)

JANVIER, JUDGE. . . . When Dr. Salatich was placed on the stand, his qualifications as an expert orthopedist were questioned and the District Judge on several occasions stated that he hoped that this Court would advise him as to whether Dr. Salatich should be considered an expert.

Although Dr. Salatich conceded that he had never been admitted to the American Board of Orthopedic Surgery and had twice been unable to pass the second examination of that Board, and that the third time the Board had refused to permit him to take the examination because he did not devote himself exclusively to that specialty, it appears that he graduated from the medical college of the Louisiana State University in 1939, and that since that time he has practiced his profession, specializing in orthopedic surgery. He stated that he is recognized as an Orthopedist in Charity Hospital, Hotel Dieu, Lakeshore Memorial Hospital, and Metairie Memorial Hospital, and as a consultant at the Southern Baptist Hospital. He also stated that until the time of its "deactivation" he "worked on the Independent Unit Orthopedic Division" of Charity Hospital, having been appointed "Chief of Orthopedics."

It is regrettable that the doctor has not been admitted to membership in the American Board of Orthopedic Surgery, but that fact in our opinion would not justify refusal to accept his testimony as an expert in that specialty to which he has devoted himself since his graduation in medicine, though it might affect the weight which should be given to his opinions when contradictory to opinions of those who have qualified for admission in that well recognized group of specialists. The doctor himself, by his own efforts to gain admission, has evidenced the desirability of being recognized by that group.

We would have been more favorably impressed with the testimony of the doctor had he not laid so much stress on the great number of "cases" which he had "won" in various courts as compared with the few which he had "lost." We have always entertained the view that doctors neither "win" nor "lose" cases in which they testify as experts. . . .

NOTES

Qualifications and Collateral Attack

1. The *Carter* and *Smith* decisions represent the traditional view in the United States on medical qualifications, with only rare exceptions. Steinberg v. Indemnity Ins. Co. of North America, 364 F.2d

266 (5th Cir. 1966); Baerman v. Reisinger, 363 F.2d 309, 124 U.S. App. D.C. 180 (D.C. Cir. 1966); Katsetos v. Nolan, 368 A.2d 172 (Conn. 1976). See generally 31 A.L.R.3d 1163 (1978).

Many years ago Dr. Hubert Winston Smith assessed the situation very well: "Courts have plodded along, quite willing to recognize any holder of an M.D. degree as a universal expert on science. This naivete is surprising, for the same judge who rules a general practitioner competent on his qualifying or voir dire examination will take the train for the Mayo Clinic if he stands in personal need of specialized surgery." Smith, Scientific Proof and Relations of Law and Medicine, 23 B.U.L. Rev. 143, 147 (1943).

2. The practical result of the above is that an attorney is able to bring his action and get to a jury even though he may not be able to obtain the best possible medical testimony. This may well be a salutary rule. Obtaining expert medical testimony is often very difficult, even though the attorney's case is quite meritorious. Medical specialists tend to congregate in the larger cities and not all are willing to appear in court, particularly as nontreating witnesses called only to evaluate a case for one side or another.

3. It is generally stated that the opinion of a treating physician should be accorded greater weight than that of an examining physician who has seen the patient only briefly and chiefly for the purpose of evaluation rather than treatment. Also, of course, treating physicians are allowed much greater range in their testimony about subjective symptoms ("I had great pain.") than examining physicians who are limited to objective observations and the results of diagnostic testing. The rationale for the greater breadth of testimony, otherwise objectionable as hearsay, has been that the patient is motivated to tell the truth in order to receive proper treatment. Is this motivation affected by knowledge at the time of a potential law suit or worker's compensation claim? See Horsley & Carlova, Testifying in Court: A Guide for Physicians (2d ed. 1983).

Janus v. Hackensack Hospital
131 N.J. Super. 535, 330 A.2d 628 (1974)

LEONARD, PRESIDING JUDGE. . . . We consider first defendants' contention that the trial judge committed reversible error in prohibiting defense counsel from cross-examining plaintiff's medical experts as to their experience and background in testifying in medical malpractice cases in the past.

Primarily they complain of the judge's action with regard to the cross-examination of Dr. Tuby. On direct examination this witness, who was licensed to practice medicine in New York in 1930, gave his educational and medical background. He testified to his experience

II. Expert Medical Testimony

as a surgeon which terminated in 1959. Since that time he stated that

> . . . my work consisted mainly of examining injured people, since that was my specialty, traumatic surgery, for lawyers, rendering medical reports of my findings and coming to court to testify when requested.
> I also reviewed medical files for attorneys throughout the United States with regard to whether there was malpractice on the part of either the doctor or a hospital.
> I would render these reports to the attorneys and if the case had merit and they required my services at trial, I would testify in these cases.
> Also I have spent many years teaching attorneys medicine and by invitation I have addressed the medical-legal societies throughout the United States, Canada and Puerto Rico, to attorneys, and have written books on medicine for attorneys.

On cross-examination by the attorney for Hackensack he also stated that he had not been treating patients for some time and had co-authored two legal-medical articles for lawyers.

The first question propounded to Dr. Tuby on cross-examination by the attorney for defendant doctors was, "How many times have you testified in malpractice cases in the last ten years?" Plaintiff's objection was sustained and the jury instructed that they were to "ignore any implications from that question." Defense counsel then asked "Have you ever testified as ———? The court interrupted, excused the jury and requested defense counsel to make an offer of proof.

Counsel replied that he desired to ask the doctor how many times he had testified in court in the last ten years, the number of times he testified for plaintiffs or defendants, and the various medical specialties upon which he had held himself out to be an expert during that period.

Following this colloquy between counsel and court the judge ruled that "all questioning along that line is excluded. Any further reference by you to that subject in your cross-examination will result in the imposition of sanctions by the court." Defendant objected to the ruling. . . . The judge reiterated his previous ruling, stating that he did not believe such an inquiry to be "relevant or material in terms of the evaluation of his testimony." Excerpts of the cross-examinations contained in these transcripts have been included in appellants' transcript as a part of that proffer. They reveal that in the last ten years Dr. Tuby has testified in malpractice cases on a great number of occasions and in various states. He has appeared exclusively for plaintiffs and has given expert opinion on numerous medical specialties. . . .

In evaluating the issue presented herein, we must be mindful of the fact that one of the three main functions of cross-examination is to shed light on the credibility of the direct testimony. In this respect the test of relevancy is whether the examination will aid the judge or jury to a useful extent in appraising the credibility of the witness and assessing the probative value of the direct testimony. McCormick, Evidence, §29 at 54-55 (1954), cited with approval in Lawlor v. Kolarsick, supra, 92 N.J. Super. at 314. . . .

As previously noted, the issues of malpractice, causal connection and damages were strongly contested. Credibility of the competing medical witnesses was a paramount factor to be first determined by the jury in resolving the controversy. Under these circumstances, and in the light of the previously discussed legal principles, we conclude that the action of the trial judge in preventing the full cross-examination of Dr. Tuby, and impliedly of Dr. Tesler, constituted a mistaken exercise of his discretion which amounted to "clear error and prejudice" to defendants. It was clearly capable of producing an unjust result, R. 2:10-2, and accordingly mandates a reversal and the granting of a new trial. . . .

Mohn v. Hahnemann Medical College
515 A.2d 920 (Pa. Super. 1986)

POPOVICH, JUDGE. . . .

Hahnemann Hospital complains that the trial court committed reversible error in allowing its expert witness (Dr. Urbach) to be cross-examined with regard to his receipt of fees for medical-legal cases other than the one being tried. . . .

It is entirely proper to inquire of an expert witness what his fees are for testifying in the case on trial. . . . [citations omitted.] But none of the reported cases go to the length that was permitted here, and in overruling the appellant's objection the court abused its discretion. The earnings of the expert witness from other services performed for the defendant were a purely collateral matter and the testimony thereon was not admissible to affect his credibility.

As properly characterized by Mohn in his brief to us, the case reduced itself to a "battle of experts" on the issues of negligence and causation. The jury, after hearing from all sides, and being instructed by the court on the law, returned a verdict in favor of Mohn and his wife (for her loss of consortium claim) in the amount of $1,776,000.00 and $1,175,000.00, respectively. Pursuant to Pa. R. Civ. P. 238, damages for delay were added and the verdicts were molded to $2,440,175.33 for Mohn and $1,614,417.80 for his wife. Post-verdict motions were filed and denied. After the verdict was reduced to judgment, this appeal followed. . . .

II. Expert Medical Testimony 215

When Dr. Urbach was asked if [his previously admitted] ledger cards produced were *all* of medico-legal cases, he answered that it depended on counsel for the plaintiff's definition of the term. Counsel's offer that he considered the instant suit such a case was rejoined with an example by the doctor that a bill for whom a person became sick on the job and necessitated a pacemaker was included in his ledger cards. As it was, the bill was paid by an attorney after the implant surgery and the patient's return to work.

To counsel for the plaintiffs' question as to whether he had tabulated the figures for any of the years represented by the ledger cards, the doctor stated he had not done so. Counsel then advised the doctor that during the morning session of the trial, his (counsel's) secretary had added the amounts starting with the year 1979. At this point, defense counsel's objection to the admission of such figures was overruled, and plaintiffs' counsel was permitted to read the five yearly tabulations collated from the cards, i.e., for 1979 the amount was $54,652; for 1980 the figure was $59,832; for 1981 the total was $108,636; for 1982 the calculation was $124,507; and for 1983 (up until the trial date) the breakdown came to $55,165.

No one disputes that *Zamsky* approves of cross-examining an expert as to the amount of his compensation for testifying in the case on trial. This same thinking has been extended to permit inquiry into a physician's personal friendship with a party to a suit or a party's attorney so as to expose his interest in or bias towards either side of the lawsuit. Downey v. Weston, 451 Pa. 259, 301 A.2d 635 (1973). In this regard, we find proper the trial court's allowance of the plaintiffs' query about the existence of the financial relationship between Dr. Urbach and defense counsel's firm, which spans approximately twelve (12) years and is still extant as evidenced by some thirty (30) cases in which the two are still actively involved.

We do not believe, however, that the case law in this jurisdiction would condone the type of extensive disclosure of an expert's fee generating cases, especially since they were not related to the case at bar (except tangentially) nor were all of them, to coin a phrase utilized by the parties, "medico-legal" cases. There must be, and is, a point beyond which inquiry is/will be held to be prejudicial, too intrusive and only serving to divert the case into collateral matters. The inquiry should not be allowed into these other cases. . . . At bar, as discussed by counsel for the defense, the plaintiffs, in their closing argument, and the trial court, in its charge, characterized Dr. Urbach as a "hired gun" who peddles his expertise randomly and generates a large amount of revenue in the process.

It is true, as made mention of in the trial court's opinion to us, that Dr. Urbach should be required to "lift his visor so that the jury could see who he was, what he represented, and what interest, if any, he had in the *results of the trial,* so that the jury could appraise his credibility." Goodis v. Gimbel Brothers, 420 Pa. 439, 445, 218 A.2d 574, 577 (1966) (Musmanno, J.) (Emphasis added). However, we do not think this encompasses the emptying of one's pockets and turning them inside out so that one's financial worth can be open to scrutiny.

Credibility was the question, and the permissible bounds of assailing it were exceeded when the expert's total income, unrelated (quoting from the trial court's own citation of *Goodis*) to the "results of the trial," was exposed to the jury. See *Zamsky,* supra. Consistent therewith, we conclude that, under the facts of this case, the nexus between Dr. Urbach's compensation for *all* services rendered (which included work for private and governmental agencies, patients and other law firms) from 1979 to 1983, *exclusive of those received for work performed for defense counsel's law firm,* and his credibility on the witness stand is tenuous at best. See *Downey,* supra.

Although a trial court is vested with the authority to set the perimeters of cross-examination, it is subject to having its decision reviewed and reversed if found to be the product of an abuse of discretion. See Grzywacz v. Meszaros, 417 Pa. 51, 208 A.2d 237 (1965). We so find and hold that the challenged evidence was erroneously admitted and prejudicial to the hospital, given the rather large verdict awarded and the hospital's admitted reliance on Dr. Urbach as a vital witness to its case on the question of liability. In this situation, we need not consider the other alleged trial errors.

Judgment reversed and the case remanded for a new trial. Jurisdiction is not retained.

NOTES

The Professional Medical Witness, Bias, etc.

1. As illustrated in the above cases, American courts, which rely heavily upon the willingness of the medical experts to testify, often chastise those physicians who testify frequently or make a considerable part of their income as courtroom experts. Consider the innuendo inherent in the following observation in an appellate court opinion given over 60 years ago:

> The professional expert, whose testimony we relate above, frequently appeared in court as a witness in personal injury cases, and the inference from his evidence is that he made the giving of testimony in such actions a business. One of the evils in the trial of personal injury cases is padding the claim with evidence of the professional medical expert. When considering a motion for a new trial, based on excessive verdict, ordinarily but little weight should be given to such testimony. Murphy v. Pennsylvania R.R., 216, 140 A. 867, 869 (Pa. 1927).

2. When does a medical expert witness become a "professional" expert? The witness in the *Murphy* case, supra, was before the court again in Nickolls v. Personal Finance Co., 185 A. 286 (Pa. 1936), and in the latter case it was asserted he had been a witness before the courts for 30 years. In both cases he was treated as a "professional." Does this label depend on the number of appearances? The number of times the expert appears for one side or one client? See Wilson v. Stilwell, 141 Mich. 587, 309 N.W.2d 898 (1981), where the court ruled that experts may be found biased if they commonly testify for only one type of party. See also Lineberry v. Schull, 695 S.W.2d 132 (Mo. App. 1985). Is the term "professional witness" an unjust and unreasonable label to place upon medical and other scientific people who are sufficiently capable, experienced, and willing to appear in court as expert witnesses? See Weatherly v. Miskle, 655 S.W.2d (Mo. App. 1983); Sears v. Butishauser, 102 Ill. 2d 132 (1984).

3. Inquiry into the existence and amount of compensation is proper, but is generally limited, as indicated in the Mohn case, to the litigation at hand. See Calderon v. Sharky, 70 Ohio St. 218, 436 N.E.2d 1008 (1982). Witnesses compelled to testify as court-appointed experts are allowed reasonable compensation at their usual fee levels, but these cannot exceed statutorily imposed limits. See In re Machuca, 113 Misc. 2D 1044, 451 N.Y.S.2d 338 (1982).

4. May an expert medical witness be impeached by offering rebuttal testimony to the effect that the witness is not expressing an opinion that conforms to commonly expected medical opinion in the particular field? See Carver v. Orange County, 444 So. 2d 452 (Fla. App. 5 Dist. 1983). See also In re Swine Flu Immunization Products Liability Litigation, reprinted at page 245 in this chapter, and notes following that opinion.

Sutphin v. Platt
720 S.W.2d 455 (Tenn. 1986)

FONES, JUSTICE.

The issue presently before this Court is whether the requirement of Tennessee's Medical Malpractice Review Board and Claims Act of 1975, T.C.A. §29-26-101 et seq., that a medical expert witness be a licensed practitioner in Tennessee or a contiguous state violates the due process and/or equal protection rights of a party proferring a medical expert from a non-contiguous state. Because there is a conceivable rational basis for the contiguous state limitation upon the competency of medical expert witnesses, we uphold this requirement as reasonably related to legitimate state interests in medical malpractice actions and, thus, consistent with constitutional mandates.

In 1976, plaintiff's decedent entered under the care of defendant doctors for treatment of a gastro-intestinal problem that had plagued the decedent from the mid-1960's. Defendants recommended that the patient undergo corrective surgical procedures which were performed at Northside Hospital in Johnson City, Tennessee on July 20, 1976. Although the patient's post-operative recovery appeared to be progressing satisfactorily, complications arose, ultimately culminating with the patient's death from respiratory failure less than one month after his surgery.

In 1981, plaintiff filed a complaint alleging that defendants' deviation from normal medical standards proximately caused the patient's death. Defendants countered with a Motion for Summary Judgment supported by affidavits, including the sworn opinion of a surgeon licensed in Tennessee that defendants had responded to the post-operative complications within the community standards of Johnson City physicians. Plaintiff then filed the affidavit of a Florida physician, which asserted that the patient's death proximately resulted from defendants' post-operative negligence.

Defendants challenged the sufficiency of the Florida doctor's affidavit because of its failure to comply with the requirements of T.C.A. §29-26-115(b).[1] This objection was based on the affiant's failure to state that he had practiced medicine within the year preceding the date of the injury presently at issue or that he was licensed to practice in Tennessee or a contiguous state. After oral argument, the trial judge agreed with defendants' contentions and held the Florida physician's affidavit inadmissible. The trial judge then granted defendants' motion for summary judgment because plaintiff had failed to provide evidence sufficient to sustain her burden of going forward on issues in which she was saddled with the burden of proof by T.C.A. §29-26-115(a).[2]

---

1. T.C.A. §29-26-115(b) reads:

    No person in a health care profession requiring licensure under the laws of this state shall be competent to testify in any court of law to establish the facts required to be established by subsection (a) unless he was licensed to practice in the state or a contiguous bordering state a profession or specialty which would make his expert testimony relevant to the issues in the case and had practiced this profession or specialty in one of these states during the year preceding the date that the alleged injury or wrongful act occurred. This rule shall apply to expert witnesses testifying for the defendant as rebuttal witnesses. The court may waive this subsection when it determines that the appropriate witnesses otherwise would not be available.

2. T.C.A. §29-26-115. Claimant's burden in malpractice action — Expert testimony — Presumption of negligence — Jury instructions. — (a) In a malpractice action, the claimant shall have the burden of proving by evidence as provided by subsection (b):

    (1) The recognized standard of acceptable professional practice in the profession and the specialty thereof, if any, that the defendant practices in the community in which he practices or in a similar community at the time the alleged injury or wrongful

II. Expert Medical Testimony

Plaintiff subsequently sought to challenge the contiguous state limitation upon the competency of medical expert witnesses as a deprivation of her due process and/or equal protection rights guaranteed by the federal constitution. After notifying the Attorney General pursuant to T.R.C.P. 24.04,[3] oral argument was heard on the constitutionality of T.C.A. §29-26-115(b). The trial judge ultimately agreed with defendants and the Attorney General, rejecting plaintiff's constitutional challenge. The case comes to this Court on direct appeal, the sole issue being the constitutionality of a state statute. We affirm.

Plaintiff attacks Tennessee's contiguous state limitation upon the competency of medical experts to testify in a medical malpractice action as an arbitrary and irrational legislative pronouncement that denies her due process and equal protection under the federal constitution. There is no question that these two clauses of the Fourteenth Amendment have been, and continue to be, applied to protect individuals from irrational legislation. [citations omitted.]. . .

The statute presently at issue imposes a limitation upon the competency of a witness to testify in a civil tort action. No attempt is made to argue that the right to present an expert witness in a state tort action is a fundamental right. Similarly, this Court has previously held that medical malpractice victims are not a suspect class. Harrison v. Schrader, 569 S.W.2d 822, 825 (Tenn. 1978). Thus, the contiguous state limitation upon the competency of medical experts to testify in a medical malpractice action must be reviewed under the rational basis test. Under that test if any state of facts can reasonably be conceived to justify the classification, or if it is a fairly debatable question, the statute must be upheld. Harrison v. Schrader, supra; Swain v. State, 527 S.W.2d 119 (Tenn. 1975).

When compared to most tort claims based upon negligence, a plaintiff alleging medical malpractice must prove several unique elements. One such element is the geographic component to the relevant standard of care. In order to prove that a doctor has been negligent in most jurisdictions, as in Tennessee, a plaintiff must show that the defendant failed to act with ordinary and reasonable care when compared to the customs or practices of physicians from a particular

---

action occurred;

(2) That the defendant acted with less than or failed to act with ordinary and reasonable care in accordance with such standard; and

(3) As a proximate result of the defendant's negligent act or omission, the plaintiff suffered injuries which would not otherwise have occurred.

3. T.R.C.P. 24.04. Notice to Attorney General When Statute, Rule or Regulation is Questioned

When the validity of a statute of this state or an administrative rule or regulation of this state is drawn in question in any action to which the State or an officer or agency is not a party, the court shall require that notice be given the Attorney General, specifying the pertinent statute, rule or regulation.

geographic region. King, The Standard of Care and Informed Consent Under the Tennessee Malpractice Act, 44 Tenn. L. Rev. 225, 256 (1977).

This geographic component to the relevant standard of care evolved out of a recognition that medical customs or practices varied depending on the particular area in which the physician practiced. King, Standard of Care, 44 Tenn. L. Rev. at 257. Traditionally, the relevant geographic area was strictly defined. The plaintiff was required to introduce evidence concerning the standard of care in the strict locality where the defendant worked. Floyd v. Walls, 26 Tenn. App. 151, 168 S.W.2d 602 (1941). However, in light of a modern trend towards the national standardization of medical practices, especially in specialties, courts and legislatures have gradually expanded the relevant geographic area for proving the medical standard of care. See, Waltz, The Rise and Gradual Fall of the Locality Rule in Medical Malpractice Litigation, 18 De Paul L. Rev. 408 (1969). Indeed, the Tennessee Legislature has adopted a somewhat broadened definition of the geographic component to the medical standard of care, requiring proof of "[t]he recognized standard of acceptable professional practice . . . in the community in which [the defendant] practices or in a similar community. . . ." T.C.A. §29-26-115(a)(1).

Another unique element in a medical malpractice action concerns the limitations upon the competency of a witness to opine as to whether the defendant's actions complied with the relevant standard of care. When a medical malpractice claim involves complex issues beyond the common knowledge of laypersons, medical expert testimony must be proffered. Bowman v. Henard, 547 S.W.2d 527 (Tenn. 1977). In addition, the Tennessee Legislature has imposed a geographical limitation upon the competency of a proffered medical expert: the physician must have been licensed to practice in Tennessee or a contiguous state for the one year previous to the date of the injury at issue. T.C.A. §29-26-115(b).

In attempting to sustain her burden of proving this geographic qualification upon the competency of medical experts to be unconstitutionally arbitrary and irrational, the plaintiff asserts that the contiguous state limitation is "beyond the implicit requirement of [T.C.A. §29-26-115(a)(1)] that the expert be familiar with the standard of care in the same or similar community." Plaintiff's Brief, p. 11, quoting King, Standard of Care, 44 Tenn. L. Rev. at 267. In other words, the plaintiff argues that as long as the proffered expert is able to show that he has knowledge of the customs or practices in medical communities similar to the one in which the defendant practices, it is irrelevant whether the expert is licensed to practice in Kentucky or Alaska.

This Court would be remiss if we did not admit that plaintiff's argument has some logic. Our present responsibility, however, is not to interpret the "implicit requirement[s]" of T.C.A. §29-26-115(a)(1). Rather, we must emphasize our limited duty when reviewing the constitutionality of a statute under the rational basis test. If we are able to conceive of a rational basis for the legislation reasonably related to a legitimate state interest, our inquiry can go no further. We believe that a rational basis for the contiguous state limitation exists.

There is an undeniable legitimate state interest in assuring that doctors charged with negligence in this State receive a fair assessment of their conduct in relation to community standards similar to the one in which they practice. The Tennessee Legislature may believe that physicians licensed to practice in Tennessee or, since a couple of Tennessee's major medical centers are close to the state border, a contiguous state are most qualified to render an opinion on the standard of care to which Tennessee's doctors must conform. In other words, it is conceivable that the risk of inaccurate assessment of the defendant's conduct in relation to customs or practices in a similar community are reduced if the expert is from Tennessee or a contiguous state. We believe that this possible reduction in inaccurate expert testimony is reasonably related to the legitimate state interest in ensuring fair trials.

In our opinion, any doubt as to the constitutionality of T.C.A. §29-26-115(b) was laid to rest by a provision within the statute itself. The act vests the trial judge with the authority to waive the contiguous state limitation upon a proper showing that an appropriate witness would not otherwise be available. The statute, therefore, contains a "safety valve" for those situations in which a party is unable to locate a qualified expert within the state or one of our bordering states. The rights of a party who proffered a non-contiguous expert along with evidence of local unavailability are not presently at issue. The record does not reveal why no hardship showing was made in the present case.

In conclusion, we hold that there is a rational basis for the contiguous state limitation upon the competency of medical expert witnesses that is reasonably related to legitimate state interests and, thus, uphold T.C.A. §29-26-115(b) as constitutional. The order of the trial judge is affirmed. Costs are adjudged against plaintiff.

NOTES

Limitations on Competency of Experts in Medical Malpractice Litigation

1. The *Sutphin* opinion is the only decision by the highest court of a state reviewing and upholding a statutory limitation on the competency of expert witnesses in medical malpractice cases. It is not

clear that the statute would have survived constitutional scrutiny without the "safety valve" provision. Other state legislatures have enacted similar and even stricter limitations (only physicians practicing in the same state deemed competent to testify on medical practice standards in that state) and have not allowed discretion in the trial judge to admit out-of-state practitioners to offer opinions. See, for example, Fla. Stat. §768-45.

2. What offer of proof should a trial judge require of a party attempting to present an expert from a state not contiguous to Tennessee? Would it be enough that a "diligent search" had been made for an expert within the nearby states? What more could be expected of the parties? Would evidence of a "conspiracy of silence" against a plaintiff suing a Tennessee physician in a small community be acceptable? How is a "conspiracy of silence" proved?

3. The Tennessee Supreme Court did not discuss the most common argument made for this type of restrictive statute. This is the allegation that attorneys may seek "hired guns" from out-of-state to appear in medical malpractice cases for exorbitant fees. The type of statute reviewed in the *Sutphin* case is usually sponsored by state medical societies and other medical defense organizations. Are these statutes the most effective method of dealing with inaccurate or fraudulent testimony in cases involving scientific, medical, or other technical subjects?

4. Various organizations have been formed to provide medical and other scientific expert evaluations for the courts. These organizations place advertisements in periodicals and newsletters addressed to trial attorneys offering to provide expert medical evaluations and testimony, charging a referral fee for such services. In a recent medical malpractice case in Virginia, a physician from out of state who was then medical director for a large insurance company (Aetna Life and Casualty Insurance) and formerly a professor of medicine at the University of Missouri for 18 years testified on behalf of the plaintiff. In cross-examination, the defense attempted to bring out that the witness had been employed in this case by a company called Professional Medical Witnesses, Inc. The corporation identifies physicians willing to examine clinical records and to testify in malpractice cases all over the country. The organization pays a separate fee to the expert for review of records. Another fee is paid for appearance in court and is not contingent on the outcome of the case. The trial court excluded all questions concerning the corporation and its arrangement with the witness allowing only questions concerning how much he was paid. The Virginia Supreme Court reversed and ordered a new trial observing, "The defendant doctors were entitled to attempt to persuade the jury that Dr. Culley was a 'doctor for hire' who was part of a nationwide group that offered themselves as witnesses on

behalf of medical malpractice plaintiffs. Once the jury was made aware of this information, it was for the jury to decide what weight, if any, to give to Culley's testimony. This was a classic case of an effort to establish bias, prejudice, or relationship." Henning v. Thomas, 366 S.E.2d 109, 113 (Va. 1988).

III. BASIS AND CONTENT OF MEDICAL TESTIMONY

State v. Sullivan
24 N.J. 18, 130 A.2d 610 (1957), *cert. denied*, 355 U.S. 840 (1957)

[Defendant, a general practitioner, was convicted of perjury in falsifying medical testimony at the murder trials of certain persons known as the "Trenton Six." The basis of the conviction was the differing testimony between the first trial when all six were convicted and the second, three years later, when four of the six were acquitted. Dr. Sullivan's testimony was a report of an examination made of the prisoners at the request of the state at the time when they had given confessions. It was used by the state to show the voluntary nature of the confessions. By a 4 to 3 vote, this court affirmed certain of the counts of the perjury indictment.]

WACHENFELD, JUSTICE. . . . The defendant's position is that it is practically impossible to convict a doctor of perjury. Apart from epistemological problems concerning the imperfections of the senses and the consequent relativity of all knowledge, it is urged Sullivan testified only as to medical opinions and beliefs which, no matter how erroneous, cannot attaint him in the absence of conclusive proof that they were not actually entertained. Defendant says the only direct or reliable proof on the issues raised by the present indictment would be his admission or confession almost tantamount to guilt.

Additionally, it is said that if contradictions exist between defendant's statements at the two murder trials, the State failed in its obligation to demonstrate the second testimony was false rather than the first.

These contentions make it important to recognize that much of Sullivan's testimony dealt with findings resulting from his examinations of the accused prisoners. To this extent, he was describing physical manifestations, exclusive of their supposed cause or psychic effect. The existence of the symptoms to which he testified is fundamentally a matter of fact, readily subject to independent verification or disproof. Most of the alleged findings were the direct product of observation and not the result of scientific tests or research. The police officers in attendance as well as Dr. Corio are, therefore, qualified to refute the truthfulness of the defendant's testimony in this respect because they had the same opportunities for observation. [Citations omitted.]

Admittedly, Dr. Sullivan also gave evidence in the form of medical opinions based on his physical findings. We now refer to his own diagnosis of the individual prisoners as totally divorced from his answers to purely hypothetical questions. Vide, Beam v. Kent, 3 N.J. 210, 215 (1949). It is argued these opinions can be proven false only by direct evidence in the form of an admission, but we cannot agree. The evidence presented was more than sufficient to satisfy the rule as to quantum of proof which requires at least the testimony of one witness supported by strong corroborating circumstances to obtain a conviction. [Citations omitted.]

To hold that a "confession" by a doctor is an indispensable prerequisite to proving he wilfully and corruptly gave false opinion testimony would place an intolerable and impossible burden on the State in its prosecution and would subject the entire judicial process, both civil and criminal, to the spectre of fraudulent testimony freely given with complete immunity and without fear of subsequent prosecution. We hold high regard for the competence and integrity of the medical profession, but we must reluctantly recognize that, like any other profession, it occasionally harbors members whose ethics are not compatible with the lofty and established standards of the group. . . .

In general, Sullivan's statements at the second trial varied violently from those he delivered at the first. Indubitably realizing he had been called upon because of his race and special qualifications as a physician to verify the good faith of the accused's confessions and their voluntariness, he manifested in his sworn statement to the police and in the testimony he first gave that there was nothing seriously amiss physically or mentally with the murder defendants which would disqualify the confessions they had made.

On his subsequent appearance three years later, his answers were radically different. Then, in effect, he stated all of the murder defendants, for one reason or another, were totally incapable of understanding the serious consequences of their confessional act, and that their physical and mental conditions were such as to negative the voluntariness of their statements.

Defendant asserts a doctor is entitled to change his professional views, and we cannot quarrel with this academic observation. We, however, are concerned with the actualities of judicial proceedings, and unless such change is upon valid grounds and for good reason, there is a justifiable inference that its motivation is corrupt. When witnesses for the State directly controvert the existence of the facts upon which the new opinions are allegedly predicated, this inference

III. Basis and Content of Medical Testimony

may, under the circumstances, ripen into a reflection of guilt sufficient to be considered by a jury or a judge. . . .

WEINTRAUB, JUSTICE. (dissenting). . . . I do not quarrel with the abstract proposition that an opinion, as distinguished from a statement of fact, may be perjurious. But we should recognize the inherent dangers of injustice when a medical opinion is thus assailed. It is commonplace for experts to differ in equal numbers. It would be absurd to suggest that the testimony of any two will suffice to convict another who differs with them. The point is that the issue is not whether a defendant's *opinion* is false, but whether his *belief* in his opinion is false, and it is the falsity of his *belief* in that opinion which must be demonstrated. Proof that others hold a contrary opinion evidences disagreement and nothing more.

It may indeed be difficult to prove such a case. But that is exactly as it should be. The badge of criminality should be richly deserved. We do not sacrifice individuals for some prophylactic benefit to society. On the contrary we surround men accused of crime with assurances against unfairness because we conceive that justice to the individual is the only defensible course.

This case is made still more unusual by the circumstances that the testimony charged to be false was given on cross-examination and on redirect. I agree that a departure from or an addition to direct testimony may be perjurious. But it would seem elementary that in such circumstances a charge of perjury should not be sustained unless a corrupt motive is evident. Cross-examination is rightly extolled as "the greatest legal engine ever invented for the discovery of truth," 5 Wigmore, Evidence (3d ed. 1940), §1367, p. 29. Its purpose is to achieve departures from direct, both departures which are literal and departures which arise in ultimate effect from the development of additional facts or views. I am sure no one would subscribe to a caveat to every witness that if he deviates from his direct testimony he will thereby sign his own commitment. . . .

A *medical opinion* is a conclusion from *facts.* If a physician swears to the truth of those *facts,* proof by qualified observers that the facts were otherwise may well suffice to sustain perjury charged with respect to the testimony as to such facts. Where the *medical opinion* is charged to be perjurious, conflicting *medical opinions* of others may prove the *medical opinion* to be erroneous, but cannot prove that the defendant's belief in his opinion was false; at least I cannot conceive hypothetically a case in which they could. Whether perjury charged to reside in an *opinion* may be made out by proving the falsity of the *facts* which the physician swore he observed and relied upon, is difficult to consider in a vacuum. The prudent course there would be to charge perjury as to the factual observations rather than in the opinion. . . .

The cross-examination of Dr. Sullivan was fantastic. On direct he repeated the testimony as to Cooper which suggested the possibility that marijuana had been used. Since Dr. Sullivan was a physician, the trial judge properly permitted some cross-examination along the line whether what he observed was consistent with the use of the narcotic, and of course the answer was in the affirmative. Then followed an amazing performance, wholly beyond the direct examination. Dr. Sullivan was queried hypothetically as to the effects of various drugs, etc., and what could conceivably cause this, that, or the other, without any foundation in the direct examination. That course having been permitted by the trial judge over the State's objection, defense attorneys worked in relays upon the witness, traversing the course time and again, and propounding one hypothesis upon another. A direct examination of 15 printed pages was followed by 298 printed pages further interrogation.

Dr. Sullivan dutifully answered myriads of questions as to whether A *could* cause B, giving what seems to have been the only conceivable answer, to wit, that A could cause B. Although, of course, Dr. Sullivan did not author the questions, and could answer only in terms of *possibilities* any question which was so framed, yet the trial court chided him because he did not answer in terms of *probabilities*. The prosecutor on redirect appeared also to seek answers in terms of probabilities when manifestly the witness could not answer in those terms without assuming facts not within his personal knowledge. Thus when the prosecutor returned to the subject of Cooper and marijuana, and Dr. Sullivan repeated that what he observed could have been caused by the narcotic but that he could not say that it was, the trial court said to the witness, "you are professionally trained," "You are a trained man," and for the third time admonished him:

"Wait a minute. Let me finish. What was the condition that you found Ralph Cooper, or any one of these defendants in when you examined them? I don't want possibilities, because anything relating to human affairs may be possible. I want reasonable probabilities, and you ought to be able to tell me what you found."

The prosecutor pressed the inquiry for some 25 additional pages and finally obtained the answer he here charged to be perjurious, "I say it could have been — it was caused by marijuana."

In short, although offered as a pure fact witness, Dr. Sullivan was converted into an expert and asked to express opinions which manifestly could not rest solely upon his own factual observations. He thus was called upon either to guess or to use factual information acquired from other sources. Hence, when asked at the second trial to explain why he had not testified to certain views at the first trial, he answered that no one had put the questions, and that whereas he then testified to factual observations, he was now asked to give opinions and diagnoses. . . .

NOTES

Medical Opinion and Perjury

1. As a perjury conviction of an expert medical witness, the Sullivan case continues, after a diligent search, to be unique in American court annals. It is used to open this section of the chapter as an important reminder of the truth of its finding, however. It can be dangerous to repeat the old cliche that an expert can *never* be convicted of perjury for opinion evidence.

2. The attitude noted in the dissent in *Sullivan* regarding the physician's "opinion" and whether it is somehow protected from prosecution for perjury may be compared with the oft-stated rule that a physician is not liable in malpractice for "a mere error of judgment." This type of defense is reviewed in Chapter 5 at 358-361.

Pucci v. Rausch
2d 187 N.W.2d 138 (Wis. 1971)

[This was an action to recover damages for alleged personal injuries sustained when plaintiff's automobile was struck by a vehicle driven by defendant.]

HALLOWS, CHIEF JUSTICE. . . . On cross-examination of Dr. Peterson, he was asked whether his opinion was not "a little bit speculative." Dr. Peterson countered that "Everything in medicine is speculative; there is nothing that is not speculative." He was ordered to answer yes or no or I don't know, and he answered "I don't know." In the light of this answer the court struck his testimony. It is plain from reading the record that the two attorneys and the court were on a semantic merry-go-round with the doctor and there was a lack of communication between the legal profession and the medical profession over the legal formula in which an acceptable medical opinion should be expressed.

The term "medical certainty" is misleading if certainty is stressed to mean absolute certainty or metaphysical certainty. Medicine is not based upon such certitude but rather upon the empirical knowledge and experience in the area of cause and effect. The term "medical probability" more accurately expresses the standard. The standard requires a conviction of the mind or that degree of positiveness that the doctor has in his opinion, which is based upon his knowledge of medicine and the case facts, that his belief is correct to a reasonable medical probability. Other doctors may differ, but whether his opinion corresponds with that of another member of the medical profession does not go to admissibility of his opinion but to the weight the trier of the facts should give to his opinion. See Puhl v. Milwaukee Automobile Ins. Co. (1959), 8 Wis. 2d 343, 353, 99 N.W.2d 163. . . .

We think the trial court acted hastily in striking the doctor's testimony and it was error to do so. The doctor was testifying to a reasonable medical certainty based upon medical probabilities although he used the word "speculative" in a broad sense to negate absolute certitude. It is clear from the record the doctor intended by his word that his opinion was to a reasonable medical probability and that was his conception of medical certainty. . . .

Affirmed.

Blood v. Lea
530 N.E.2d 344 (Mass. 1988)

[See opinion reprinted in Chapter 5 at 449.]

NOTES

Reasonable Probability Standards

1. The minimum degree of certainty with which a medical expert must speak varies according to the subject matter of the case and according to the jurisdiction. In Parker v. Employers Mutual Liability Insurance Co., 440 S.W.2d 43 (Tex. Ct. App. 1969), the court distinguished between the "reasonable medical probability" test and the more demanding "reasonable medical certainty" standard, declaring that the latter is required only where the proponent is offering medical records containing opinion or diagnosis. Under the Federal Rules of Evidence, Rule 702, it was held that admission of expert testimony does not depend on the relative certainty of the subject matter but on the assistance given by the expert testimony to the trier of fact in understanding evidence or determining the facts in issue. Taenzler v. Burlington Northern, 608 F.2d 796 (8th Cir. 1979). See generally Hullverson, Reasonable Degree of Medical Certainty, 31 St. Louis U.L.J. 577 (1987); Howard, Proving Causation with Expert Opinion: How Much Certainty is Enough?, 74 Ill. B.J. 580 (1986).

2. Many courts find it necessary to examine the meaning behind the words used in medical testimony much the same as the court in Pucci v. Rausch. Invariably the problems of semantics intrude on such an analysis. See Thrailkill v. Montgomery Ward and Co., 670 S.W. 2d 582 (Tex. App. 1 Dist. 1984). Some courts have rejected the use of "verbal formulas" altogether. See Redmon v. Sooter, 1 Ill. App. 3d 406, 272 N.E.2d 200 (1971). Frustrated with the burden of constant interpretation, the Pennsylvania court, in McMahon v. Young, explained:

The issue is not merely one of semantics. There is a logical reason for the rule. The opinion of a medical expert is evidence. If the fact finder chooses to believe it, he can find as fact what the expert gave as opinion. For a fact finder to award damages for a particular condition to a plaintiff, he must find as a fact that the condition was legally caused by the defendant's conduct. Here, the only evidence offered was that it was "probably caused," and that is not enough. Perhaps in the world of medicine nothing is absolutely certain. Nevertheless, doctors must make decisions in their own profession every day based on their own expert opinions. Physicians must understand that it is the intent of our law that if the plaintiff's medical expert cannot form an opinion with sufficient certainty so as to make a medical judgment, there is nothing on the record with which a jury can make a decision with sufficient certainty so as to make a legal judgment.

McMahon v. Young, 442 Pa. 484, 486, 276 A.2d 534 (1971).

3. The *Blood* decision involves medical malpractice, but it follows the general rule in evidence law that an opinion concerning causation based upon "probability" is enough to support a finding. The distinction between an expression of "probability" and one of "possibility" is frequently relied upon by courts to determine an acceptable degree of medical certainty. See Ratterlee v. Bartlett, 707 P.2d 1063 (Kan. 1985); Gideon v. Johns-Manville Sales Corp., 761 F.2d 1129 (1985); Dallas v. Burlington Northern, Inc., 689 P.2d 273 (Mont. 1984).

4. Are the courts losing sight of the real issue in preferring qualitative over quantitative descriptions? Does the logical interpretation of "medical uncertainty" take into account a statistical framework? See generally The Evolving Role of Statistical Assessments as Evidence in the Courts (Feinberg ed. 1989); Eggleston, Evidence, Proof and Probability (2d ed. 1983); Black, Evolving Standards for Admissibility of Scientific Evidence, Science 1508 (Mar. 25, 1988). For further discussion, see Notes on Communicating Scientific Findings in Court, at 79 of Chapter 3.

State v. Hightower
121 S.E. 616 (N.C. 1924)

STACY, JUSTICE. . . . Mere opinion evidence was wholly rejected by the early English courts as being insufficient to support an absolute judgment or to hold a witness for perjury. Hence it was not received as evidence at all. "It is no satisfaction for a witness to say that he 'thinketh' or 'persuadeth himself,' " was the reason assigned for its exclusion by Coke. And in S. v. Allen, 8 N.C., p. 9, Henderson, J., said: "The law requires that he who deposes to a fact should have the means of knowing it. Grounds of conjecture and opinions are not sufficient." But the law in this respect has been the subject of considerable growth and development, both in England and in this country. The history of this development, beginning with its original exclusion and leading up to the admission of such evidence, with illustrations from the decisions of the courts, is given by Wigmore in his valuable work on the subject of Evidence. In this connection he refers to the practice of admitting opinion evidence by experts based upon observation or investigation, and concludes that such evidence by experts of conceded skill and experience may be received without in the first instance requiring the facts observed or discovered to be stated to the court and jury, such disclosures being more properly a matter for cross-examination. We quote from section 1922.

> It has already been seen, in reviewing the history of the doctrine, that in the beginning the disparagement of opinion rested on grounds totally different from those now received. It was objected to because, as a mere guess, the belief of one having no good grounds, it lacked the testimonial qualification of observation; hence, a *mere* opinion, as soon as it appeared to be such, must be rejected. In a few jurisdictions the modern doctrine has been confused with the earlier one, and it is laid down as a general rule that opinions must be accompanied with the facts on which they are based — usually with the exception that expert witnesses are exempted from this rule.
>
> Now, in no respect is this rule sound. In the first place, then, there is no principle and no orthodox practice which requires a witness having personal observation to state in advance his observed data before he states his inferences from them; all that needs to appear in advance is that he had an opportunity to observe and did observe, whereupon it is proper for him to state his conclusions, leaving the detailed grounds to be drawn out on cross-examination. Any other rule cumbers seriously the examination, and amounts in effect to changing substantially the whole examination into a voir dire — an innovation on established methods which is unwarranted by policy.

He further says (section 675): "All opinions or conclusions are in a sense hypothetical. But does it follow that, when the opinion comes from *the same witness* who has learned the premises by actual observation, those premises must be stated beforehand, hypothetically or otherwise, by him or to him? For example, the physician is asked, 'Did you examine the body?' 'Yes.' 'State your opinion of the cause of death.' Is it here necessary that he should first state in detail the facts of his personal observation, as premises, before he can give his opinion? In academic nicety, yes; practically, no; and for the simple reason that on cross-examination each and every detail of the appearances he observed will be brought out, and thus associated with his general conclusion as the grounds for it, and the tribunal will understand that the rejection of these data will destroy the validity of his opinion. In the opposite case, where the witness has not had

III. Basis and Content of Medical Testimony

personal observation of the premises, they are not to be got from him on cross-examination, because he had no data of personal observation; and that is precisely the reason why they must be indicated and set out in the question to him, for thus only can the premises be clearly associated with the conclusion based upon them.

"Through failure to perceive this limitation, courts have sometimes sanctioned the requirements of an advanced hypothetical statement even where the expert witness speaks from personal observation."

We are disposed to adopt the conclusions reached by Mr. Wigmore in his work on Evidence, though the numerical weight of authority may be otherwise, and a very satisfactory statement of what we conceive the law to be will be found in People v. Youngs, 151 N.Y., p. 218. There, opinion evidence of experts was received without first requiring the observations upon which such opinions were based to be given in evidence. This was affirmed on appeal, it being the subject of exception, and the reviewing Court, speaking to the question, said:

> It appears by the record that certain medical experts were called as witnesses by the prosecution, who testified that they made a personal examination of the defendant with reference to his sanity, and were then asked whether in their opinion he was sane at the time of such examination. These questions were objected to by the defense as incompetent, but the objection was overruled, and there was an exception. It is now urged that these experts should not have been permitted to express an opinion without first stating the facts upon which such opinion was based. The testimony of experts is an exception to the general rule, which requires that the witness must state facts and not express opinions. In such cases the opinion of the witness may be based upon facts so exclusively within the domain of scientific or professional knowledge that their significance or force cannot be perceived by the jury, and it is because the facts are of such a character that they cannot be weighed or understood by the jury that the witness is permitted to give an opinion as to what they do or do not indicate. In such cases it is the opinion of the witness that is supposed to possess peculiar value for the information of the jury. Of course, all the facts or symptoms upon which the opinion is based may be drawn out also, either upon the direct or cross-examinations. It is undoubtedly the better practice to require the witness to state the circumstances of his examination, and the facts, symptoms or indications upon which his conclusion is based, before giving the opinion to the jury. But we think that it is not legal error to permit a medical expert, who has made a personal examination of a patient for the purpose of determinining his mental condition, to give his opinion as to that condition at the time of the examination, without in the first instance disclosing the particular facts upon which the opinion is based. The party calling the witness may undoubtedly prove the facts upon which the opinion is based, and, as we have already observed, that is doubtless the safer practice. It may also be true that the court, in the exercise of a sound discretion, may require the witness to state the facts before expressing the opinion, and in all cases the

opposite party has the right to elicit the facts upon cross-examination. But the precise question here is whether the court committed an error in permitting the witness to give the opinion before the facts upon which it was founded were all disclosed, and we think that when it is shown that a medical expert has made the proper professional examination of the patient in order to ascertain the existence of some physical or mental disease, he is then qualified to express an opinion on the subject, though he may not yet have stated the scientific facts or external symptoms upon which it is based.

Applying these principles to the instant case, we think the better practice would have been for Latham and Coursey to have stated the facts or to have detailed the data observed or discovered by them, before drawing their conclusions or giving their opinions in evidence, but we shall not hold it for legal or reversible error that such was not required as a condition precedent to the admission of their opinions in evidence before the jury. S. v. Felter, 25 Ia. 75; S. v. Foote, 58 S.C. 218. Speaking of a similar question, in Commission v. Johnson, 188 Mass. 385, Bradley, J., said: "By this form of examination no injustice is done, for whatever reasons, even to the smallest details, that an expert may have for his opinion can be brought out fully by cross-examination." . . .

[Reversed on other grounds.]

Finnegan v. Fall River Gas Works Co.
34 N.E. 523 (Mass. 1893)

HOLMES, JUSTICE. In the opinion of a majority of the court, the exceptions must be sustained. The evidence for the plaintiff tended to show that his intestate was killed by inhaling gas while he was in the cellar of a building of the defendant, in pursuance of his duty as an employee of the Water Board of the city of Fall River, for the purpose of reading a water meter. There was no evidence how the gas got into the cellar, nor any evidence of the defendant's negligence, beyond the facts that the gas was there, and that the ventilation of the cellar was stopped up. But it appears that the defendant, by taking water, voluntarily entered into a relation, the result of which, as it knew, was to require some one to enter its premises in order to read the water meter. It was bound to use reasonable care to prevent the place thus necessarily entered by the deceased from being a death trap. The jury might have found that it knew or ought to have known of the presence of gas in the cellar in quantities that might be dangerous, and that it might have prevented the accumulation by opening the ventilator, or might have put the meter in a different place. We are of the opinion that they might have found the defendant guilty of negligence towards the deceased. See Smith v. Boston Gas Light Co., 129 Mass. 318.

We must take it that there was a perceptible smell of gas when the deceased entered the cellar, but that he was acting under a certain stress of duty. We cannot say that the jury would not have been warranted in finding that the risk did not appear to be great, and in fact would not have been great if the ventilation had been open, and that, in view of the exigency, the deceased could take such risk as was manifest without losing the protection of the law. Pomeroy v. Westfield, 154 Mass. 462, 465.

There was evidence for the jury, whatever may be thought of its weight, that the deceased had a period of conscious suffering before death. One of the doctors testified to that effect. To be sure, he had not had any experience of this kind of asphyxiation personally, or with patients, but his general competency as an expert seems not to have been questioned; and, although it might not be admissible merely to repeat what a witness had read in a book not itself admissible, still, when one who is competent on the general subject accepts from his reading as probably true a matter of detail which he had not verified, the fact gains an authority which it would not have had from the printed page alone, and, subject perhaps to the exercise of some discretion, may be admitted. . . .

NOTES

Basis of Medical Opinion

1. Some jurisdictions still do not agree with the reasoning in *Hightower*, especially where the underlying facts will not be established by the same expert whose opinion is in question. It should also be noted that while medical testimony often is more meaningful and persuasive if its basis is fully stated, in other situations, only confusion results. The Federal Rules of Evidence state: "The expert may testify in terms of opinion or inference and give his reasons therefor without prior disclosure of the underlying facts or data, unless the court requires otherwise. The expert may in any event be required to disclose the underlying facts or data on cross-examination." Federal Rules of Evidence, Rule 705. See generally Inker, A Practical Guide to Using Expert Testimony Under The Federal Rules of Evidence, 31 Prac. Law 21 (1985). See also Rossi, Modern Evidence and the Expert Witness, 12 Litigation 18 (1985); Younger, Expert Witnesses, 48 Ins. Coun. J. 267 (1981).

2. Like so many other opinions by Mr. Justice Holmes, *Finnegan* is terse to the point of being laconic, and yet it has become a classic statement around which rally those who feel expertise validates evi-

dence that is otherwise hearsay. Holmes reiterated his view in a later case, where he stated, "An expert may testify to value although his knowledge of details is derived from inadmissible sources, because he gives the sanction of his general experience." National Bank of Commerce v. New Bedford, 56 N.E. 288, 290 (Mass. 1900). Construed in its broadest sense, the "inadmissible sources" that Holmes refers to may be not only treatises, but medical facts and conclusions of others. For a recent and comprehensive review, see Carlson, Policing the Basis of Modern Expert Testimony, 39 Vand. L. Rev. 577 (1986). See also Graham, Expert Witness Testimony and the Federal Rules of Evidence: Insuring Adequate Assurance of Trustworthiness, 1986 U. Ill. L. Rev. 43.

3. It is axiomatic that the basis of any medical expert opinion includes the witnesses' general knowledge, including formal medical education, post-doctoral training, and clinical expertise. The recitation of this background is generally presented and explained early in the witnesses' testimony and is rarely objected to on hearsay or other grounds. General medical education is adequate to support most expert medical opinion, subject to cross-examination. Specialized training, or the buttressing of an expert's opinion, with references to learned treatises, or recent research findings, is not essential, but obviously increases the weight of authority of the opinion. See Bellardini v. Krikorian, 537 A.2d 700 (N.J. Super. App. Div. 1988); Matter of Lou, R., 131 Misc. 2d 138, 499 N.Y.S.2d 846 (1986); Jeffries v. Marzano, 696 P.2d 1087 (Or. 1985).

In re "Agent Orange" Product Liability Litigation
611 F. Supp. 1223 (D.C.N.Y. 1985)

WEINSTEIN, CHIEF JUDGE.

I. Introduction

Defendants, seven chemical companies, have moved to dismiss or in the alternative for summary judgment. Plaintiffs are Vietnam veterans and members of their families who have opted out of the class previously certified by the court pursuant to Rule 23(b)(3) of the Federal Rules of Civil Procedure. In re "Agent Orange" Product Liability Litigation, 100 F.R.D. 718 (E.D.N.Y.), *mandamus denied,* 725 F.2d 858 (2d Cir.), *cert. denied,* — U.S. — , 104 S. Ct. 1417, 79 L. Ed. 2d 743 (1984). They allege that as a result of the veterans' exposure to Agent Orange, a herbicide manufactured by the defendants, they suffer from various health problems.

Defendants contend that they are entitled to judgment dismissing

III. Basis and Content of Medical Testimony

the claims asserted against them because of each plaintiff's conceded inability to identify the individual manufacturer of the Agent Orange to which a given veteran was exposed, inapplicability of any alternative theory of liability that would overcome that inability, the government contract defense, and inability of any plaintiff to prove that his or her injuries were caused by Agent Orange.

Plaintiff Vietnam veterans do suffer. Many deserve help from the government. They cannot obtain aid through this suit against private corporations. . . .

After settling with members of the class on May 7, 1984, defendants moved on July 24, 1984 for summary judgment in the opt-out cases and a number of cases brought by civilians. On December 10, 1984, the court heard oral argument on defendants' motion. Defendants offered overwhelming proof that no causal connection exists between exposure to Agent Orange and development of miscarriages or birth defects. In response, the veterans' wives and children produced no evidence sufficient to create an issue of material fact on causation. See also In re "Agent Orange" Product Liability Litigation, 603 F. Supp. 239 (E.D.N.Y. 1985) (dismissing claims of wives and children against government).

The court adjourned consideration of the opt-out veterans' claims against the chemical companies to allow plaintiffs' counsel time to produce evidence of causation. Counsel produced the affidavit of Dr. Barry M. Singer and 189 accompanying affidavits on January 24, 1985. At that time, the court, at the request of plaintiffs' counsel, allowed plaintiffs fifteen days to produce additional affidavits; the court's order stated that "no further extensions [would] be granted." See Order dated January 24, 1985. Nevertheless, on March 12, 1985, without leave for late filing, counsel produced a second affidavit by Dr. Singer with 93 accompanying affidavits. On that day, counsel also produced a general affidavit by Dr. Samuel S. Epstein with 15 accompanying affidavits. . . .

III. Facts

In support of their contention that Agent Orange did not cause the various ailments that allegedly afflict the veteran plaintiffs, defendants rest upon a number of epidemiological studies. As this court has indicated in extensive and repeated recorded colloquy with counsel and in prior opinions, e.g., In re "Agent Orange" Product Liability Litigation, 597 F. Supp. 740, 777-95 (E.D.N.Y. 1984), all reliable studies of the effect of Agent Orange on members of the class so far published provide no support for plaintiffs' claims of causation. See also In re "Agent Orange" Product Liability Litigation, 603 F. Supp.

239 (E.D.N.Y. 1985) (granting summary judgment against the veterans' wives and children in their case against the government for failure to show causation).

A. Epidemiological Studies

Epidemiological studies rely on "statistical methods to detect abnormally high incidences of disease in a study population and to associate these incidences with unusual exposures to suspect environmental factors." Dore, "A Commentary on the Use of Epidemiological Evidence in Demonstrating Cause-in-Fact," 7 Harv. Envtl. L. Rev. 429, 431 (1983). In their study of diseases in human populations, epidemiologists use data from surveys, death certificates, and medical and clinical observations. Id.

A number of sound epidemiological studies have been conducted on the health effects of exposure to Agent Orange. These are the only useful studies having any bearing on causation.

All the other data supplied by the parties rests on surmise and inapposite extrapolations from animal studies and industrial accidents. It is hypothesized that, predicated on this experience, adverse effects of Agent Orange on plaintiffs might at some time in the future be shown to some degree of probability.

The available relevant studies have addressed the direct effects of exposure on servicepersons and the indirect effects of exposure on spouses and children of servicepersons. No acceptable study to date of Vietnam veterans and their families concludes that there is a causal connection between exposure to Agent Orange and the serious adverse health effects claimed by plaintiffs. Chloracne and porphyria cutanea tarda are the only two diseases that have been recognized by Congress as having some possible connection to Agent Orange exposure, but no proof has been shown of any relationship of these diseases to these plaintiffs. . . .

The studies to date conclude that there is as yet no epidemiological evidence that paternal exposure to Agent Orange causes birth defects and miscarriages. See, e.g., Erickson, Mulinare, et al., "Vietnam Veterans' Risks for Fathering Babies with Birth Defects," 252 J.A.M.A. 903-12 (1984); J. D. Erickson, J. Mulinare, et al., Vietnam Veterans' Risks for Fathering Babies with Birth Defects, published by the U.S. Department of Health and Human Services, Public Health Service, Centers for Disease Control (August, 1984) ("CDC study"); J. W. Donovan, et al., Case-control Study of Congenital Anomalies and Vietnam Service (Birth Defects Study): Report to the Minister for Veterans' Affairs, January 1983, published by Australian Government Publishing Service, Canberra (1983) ("Australian study"); Donovan,

III. Basis and Content of Medical Testimony

MacLennan and Andena, "Vietnam service and the risk of congenital anomalies," 140 Med. J. of Australia, 394 (March 31, 1984). . . .

In a comprehensive epidemiological examination of 96 categories of birth defects occurring among subsequently conceived offspring of American servicemen who served in Vietnam, the authors of the CDC study concluded: "This study provides strong evidence that Vietnam veterans, in general, have not been at increased risk of fathering babies with the aggregate of the types of defects studied here." CDC study at 2. The CDC study further concluded: "At present, *no adverse human reproductive effects have been shown to be related to exposure to phenoxy herbicides and dioxin.*" Id. at 67 (emphasis supplied).

The conclusions of the Australian study are similarly negative:

> There is no evidence that Army service in Vietnam increases the risk of fathering children with anomalies diagnosed at birth.

Donovan, MacLennan and Andena, "Vietnam service and the risk of congenital anomalies," 140 Med. J. of Australia 394 (March 31, 1984). See also CDC study at 6-7 (number of offspring of Vietnam veterans with serious birth defects no greater than the population at large); cf. House Rep. No. 98-592 on Veterans' Dioxin and Radiation Exposure Compensation Standards Act, reprinted in 1984 U.S. Code Cong. & Admin. News 4449, 4453 ("insufficient credible scientific evidence" that veterans exposed to Agent Orange are experiencing higher incidence of medical problems). . . .

Epidemiological studies addressing the effect of Agent Orange exposure on veterans' health have not furnished support for plaintiffs' claims. They have been negative or inconclusive.

The Air Force study is the most intensive examination to date of Agent Orange effects on exposed veterans. See Air Force Health Study, An Epidemiologic Investigation of Health Effects in Air Force Personnel Following Exposure to Herbicides (February 24, 1984) (Ranch Hand II Study — 1984 Report). This study utilized 1,024 matched pairs of men for analysis. Id. at v. Essentially all those who had participated in the fixed wing spraying and who could be located were studied. The conclusion was negative. . . .

A comprehensive study by the Centers for Disease Control may be available after mid-1989. See Centers for Disease Control, Protocol for Epidemiologic Studies of the Health of Vietnam Veterans (November 1983). But cf. McIntyre, "End to Dioxin Study Fund Asked," Newsday, May 1, 1985, at 25, col. 1 (White House scientist Alvin L. Young, a toxicologist, recommends that no further research on dioxin should be funded, "because research has failed to show it causes cancer or birth defects in humans."). . . .

Two recently-released studies fail to establish any causal connection. A comparison of New York State Vietnam veterans with veterans of that era who did not serve in Vietnam revealed no increased incidence of disease. Lawrence, et al., Mortality Patterns of New York State Vietnam Veterans, 75 AJPH 277 (1985). The authors note that the long induction period involved in some of the diseases suggests the need for further study, but conclude:

> Overall, these studies show no remarkable disease differences between Vietnam veterans and other veterans of that era. To the extent that Vietnam service may be indicative of dioxin-contaminated herbicide exposure, we find no suggested association with cause of death.

Id. at 279.

The comprehensive three-part Australian study is similarly negative. Australian Veterans Health Studies, *The Mortality Report* (1984). In 1980, the government of Australia commissioned the Commonwealth Institute of Health to conduct a series of scientific studies of the health of Vietnam veterans and their families. The Commission undertook a retrospective cohort study of mortality among former national servicemen of the Vietnam era, which is reported in Part I of the Report. Australian forces that served in Vietnam were exposed at least as heavily as United States forces to Agent Orange. See Tr. at 479 (San Francisco Hearings, August 24, 1984).

This study sought to determine whether death rates among Vietnam veterans were higher than among comparable non-veterans for all causes of death combined. The study included 46,166 subjects: 19,209 veterans who served in Vietnam or Vietnam waters for over 90 days and did not die prior to two years of service, and 26,957 non-veterans. Information about the study subjects was obtained through death registers, medical certificates, and military and non-military records. The follow-up rate was high, and the authors conclude that the data used was of "high quality." "Executive Summary," at vii.

The study found the death rate among study subjects — both veterans and non-veterans — "statistically significantly lower than expected for Australian males, taking age and calendar year into account." Id. Mortality among veterans was not higher than that among non-veterans in a statistically significant sense, except among Veterans who were members of The Royal Australian Engineers. Id. at viii. Part III of the Report offers several possible explanations for this discrepancy, none of them attributable to Agent Orange. See Part III, "The Relationship Between Aspects of Vietnam Service and Subsequent Mortality Among Australian National Servicemen of the Vietnam Conflict Era," at 41-46 (1984).

III. Basis and Content of Medical Testimony

With respect to specific causes of death, the Report found no statistically significant difference in death rates from cancer among veterans and non-veterans. . . .

Plaintiffs cite a number of studies conducted on animals and industrial workers as evidence of a causal link between exposure to TCDD and the development of various hepatotoxic, hematotoxic, genotoxic, and enzymatic responses. None of these studies do more than show that there may be a causal connection between dioxin and disease. None show such a connection between plaintiffs and Agent Orange.

Plaintiffs also rely on several depositions and affidavits by experts. As indicated below, to the extent that these experts rely on available epidemiological studies, the studies supply no basis for an inference of causation. There is simply no other reliable data on which an expert can furnish reliable testimony. Thus, no expert tendered by plaintiffs would be permitted to testify under Rules 702 and 703 of the Federal Rules of Evidence.

B. Expert Affidavits

Even most of plaintiffs' experts express doubt about causation, except for some ill-defined possible "association" as compared with associations with any specific other products or natural carcinogens; none supports the conclusion that present evidence permits a scientifically acceptable conclusion that Agent Orange did cause a specific plaintiff's specific disease. . . .

1. Dr. Singer's Affidavit

Plaintiffs submitted two affidavits on causation by Dr. Barry M. Singer. Their wording is virtually identical. Dr. Singer's affidavits were accompanied by 282 "affidavits" by individual veteran plaintiffs. The latter are form statements, signed by either the plaintiff or his attorney, or both. A representative set of statements is attached as Appendix "A" to this opinion.

The forms typically allege that the plaintiff "saw spraying of Agent Orange, entered defoliated areas and consumed local food and water." The forms then describe the plaintiff's diagnosed medical problems and refer to an attached "checklist" for a description of alleged Agent Orange related symptoms. . . .

The checklists allow the individual to identify any or all of a number of symptoms which they attribute to their exposure to Agent Orange in Vietnam. In addition to general symptoms such as fatigue, space is provided in which to indicate specific skin, skeletal-muscular, gastro-intestinal, visual and behavioral disorders, as well as to identify any tumors as malignant or nonmalignant. Finally, the checklist asks for information about the individual's offspring. A perusal of the checklists reveals that plaintiffs believe they suffer most frequently from "behavioral" disorders: memory loss, increased irritability, anger and anxiety, insomnia, confusion, depression, and tremors.

The final part of the form affidavits describes the individual's medical history, and asks for a description of tobacco, alcohol, and drug use. This portion also alleges no exposure to any toxic chemical besides Agent Orange.

Dr. Singer, who is board certified in internal medicine, hematology, and oncology, reaches a number of conclusions based on his review of the numerous form affidavits with their attached checklists. He bases his opinion on his medical background, a review of the literature on the biomedical effects of Agent Orange, and an examination of the individual affidavits. He apparently did not examine any medical records or any plaintiffs. In discussing his conclusions, the numbers from his two separate affidavits will be combined.

Dr. Singer notes at the outset that 2,4-D, 2,4,5-T, and 2,3,7,8-tetrachlorodibenzo-p-dioxin ("dioxin") "are potent and toxic agents *capable of inducing* a wide variety of adverse effects both in animals and in man." Singer Aff. ¶5 (emphasis supplied). See also In re "Agent Orange" Product Liability Litigation, 597 F. Supp. at 778 (dioxin one of most powerful poisons known). Dr. Singer then analyzes the various ailments suffered by the individual affiants. . . .

As a review of Dr. Singer's affidavit reveals, he attributes some 37 separate diseases, disorders, and symptoms — including baldness and diarrhea — to exposure to Agent Orange. He mentions only two doubtful examples of chloracne and none of porphyria cutanea tarda, the two afflictions Congress considered worthy of a statutory presumption of service connection, although not without reservations. See House Report, supra, reprinted in 1984 U.S. Code Cong. & Admin. News 4449, at 4453 ("insufficient credible scientific evidence" that veterans exposed to Agent Orange suffer increased adverse health effects).

Stripped of its verbiage, Dr. Singer summarizes his overall conclusion by stating that *if* the affiants are telling the truth and *if* there is no cause for their complaints other than Agent Orange, then Agent Orange must have caused their problems. Dr. Singer states:

> *Assuming the truth of the affidavits* submitted, *and absent any evidence of pre-existing, intervening, or superseding causes for the symptoms and diseases* complained of in these affidavits, it is my opinion to a reasonable degree of medical probability (that is, more likely than not) that the medical difficulties described by the affiants were proximately caused by exposure to Agent Orange.

(Emphasis supplied).

III. Basis and Content of Medical Testimony 241

Put differently, Dr. Singer's analysis amounts to this: the affiants complain of various medical problems; animals and workers exposed to extensive dosages of TCDD have suffered from related difficulties; therefore, assuming nothing else caused the affiants' afflictions, Agent Orange caused them. . . .

As section IV.A.3 will show, Dr. Singer's conclusory allegations lack any foundation in fact. His analysis, in addition to being speculative, is so guarded as to be worthless.

2. Dr. Epstein's Affidavits

Plaintiffs belatedly submitted affidavits by Dr. Samuel S. Epstein. He has been specially trained in the fields of pathology, bacteriology, and public health. He is currently Professor of Occupational and Environmental Medicine at University of Illinois Medical Center in Chicago. Among his 239 publications are a number of articles on the effects of exposure to 2,3,7,8-tetrachlorodibenzo-paradioxin ("TCDD"). His credentials clearly suffice to qualify him as an expert pursuant to Rule 702 of the Federal Rules of Evidence.

Dr. Epstein submitted a general or master affidavit on the scientific literature on causation. This 65-page affidavit is substantially identical to an earlier brief submitted by plaintiffs dated September 18, 1984 in opposition to the motion for summary judgment — some time before Dr. Epstein was retained on February 27, 1985. Dep. of Dr. Epstein at 14 (April 11, 1985). An extensive deposition of Dr. Epstein dated April 11, 1985 adds nothing of a substantive nature to the affidavit, but consists of a devastatingly successful showing of his lack of knowledge of the medical and other background of those on whose behalf he submitted affidavits. . . .

Dr. Epstein also submitted fifteen individual affidavits of causation. In reaching conclusions with respect to the individual plaintiffs, he says that he generally relied upon their military service records, Veterans Administration medical records, and interview questionnaires, symptomology checklists, and affidavits completed by plaintiffs. See Attachments to Dr. Epstein's Deposition submitted as Appendix A to Defendants' Supplemental Memorandum in Opposition to Plaintiffs' Motion for Partial Summary Judgment and Reply Memorandum in Further Support of Defendants' Motion to Dismiss and/or for Summary Judgment, Dep. at 474 ff. Each affiant-plaintiff states in general terms that he was exposed to Agent Orange.

In sum, Dr. Epstein attributes some fourteen different diseases and afflictions to exposure to Agent Orange of fifteen plaintiffs. Dr. Epstein's affidavits, even if considered timely, are insufficient to oppose the motion for summary judgment. All of the diseases in the cases he relies upon are found in the general population of those who were never exposed to Agent Orange. There is no showing that the incidence of the diseases relied upon are greater in the Agent Orange-exposed population than in the population generally. It must be borne in mind that these are fifteen cases not taken at random but deliberately selected because of their claims from a population of 2,600,000 who served in Vietnam.

IV. Law

A. Legal Standards Governing Expert Opinion

1. Admissibility of Epidemiological Studies

In a mass tort case such as Agent Orange, epidemiologic studies on causation assume a role of critical importance. Cf. In re Swine Flu Immunization Products Liability Litigation, 508 F. Supp. 897, 907 (D. Colo. 1981) ("[w]here . . . the exact organic cause of a disease cannot be scientifically isolated, epidemiologic data becomes highly persuasive."), *aff'd sub nom.* Lima v. United States, 708 F.2d 502 (10th Cir. 1983). Confronted with the reality of mass tort litigation, courts have been forced to abandon their traditional reluctance to rely upon epidemiological studies. Dore, "A Commentary on the Use of Epidemiological Evidence in Demonstrating Cause-in-Fact," 7 Harv. Envtl. L. Rev. 429 (1983).

2. Admissibility of Expert Opinion Under Rule 702

Rule 702 of the Federal Rules of Evidence provides for opinion testimony by experts "if scientific, technical or other specialized knowledge will assist the trier of fact to determine a fact in issue" and the witness is "qualified as an expert by knowledge, experience, training or education." . . .

(a) Admissibility of Dr. Singer's Testimony

(i) *Qualifications as an Expert.* Federal Rule 702 embodies a liberal policy towards qualification as an expert. The court makes the determination based on the witness' actual qualifications and knowledge of the subject matter and not his title. Mannino v. International Manufacturing Co., 650 F.2d 846, 851 (6th Cir. 1981). Thus, it is not determinative that Dr. Singer is not an epidemiologist.

It is disturbing that Dr. Singer has shown no great interest in the subject of critical importance in this case. He does not belong to any epidemiological societies. Cf. Kubs v. United States, 537 F. Supp. 560, 562 (E.D. Wisc. 1982) (peer review important). Apparently his only publication after eighteen years of practice is a co-authored article addressing leukemia therapy — a subject far removed from the population-based studies Dr. Singer purports to rely upon in his affidavit. See Black and Lilienfeld, supra, at 775 (arguing that a medical doctor should be allowed to testify on toxic tort causation "only if he could demonstrate knowledge of epidemiology."). He does, nevertheless, have a distinguished record as practitioner and teacher. In keeping with the spirit of rule 702, Dr. Singer will be considered an expert although obviously he would not be held in the same esteem on the critical issue of causation and the effects of toxic substances as Dr. Epstein or some of the other experts relied upon by plaintiffs and defendants.

(b) Admissibility of Dr. Epstein's Testimony

Dr. Epstein's affidavits and deposition demonstrate that his testimony would meet the standards of Rule 702. He is clearly a highly qualified expert in the field, his testimony meets the helpfulness requirement, and his analytical technique — inference from epidemiological data and medical records — is acceptable. Just as in the case of Dr. Singer's testimony, however, compliance with Rule 702 does not guarantee admissibility under Rules 703 and 403.

3. Rule 703

Rule 703 of the Federal Rules of Evidence attempts to delimit the bases upon which an expert may rely in testifying to those "reasonably relied" upon "by experts in the field." It provides:

> The facts or data in the particular case upon which an expert bases an opinion or inference may be those perceived by or made known to him at or before the hearing. If of a type reasonably relied upon by experts in the particular field in forming opinions or inferences upon the subject, the facts or data need not be admissible in evidence.

Neither Dr. Singer nor Dr. Epstein based his conclusions on observations. But cf. Dep. of Dr. Epstein at 16 ("I had some conversations with the clients" — none of whom is apparently involved in the opt-out cases now before the court); documents at Dep. 474 ff. Rather, each one relied almost wholly upon the specific anecdotal written information supplied by the plaintiffs and upon general studies and literature.

The trial court must decide whether this data is of a type reasonably relied upon by experts in the field. . . . The trial court's examination of reasonable reliance by experts in the field requires at least that the expert base his or her opinion on sufficient factual data, not rely on hearsay deemed unreliable by other experts in the field, and assert conclusions with sufficient certainty to be useful given applicable burdens of proof. . . .

4. The Requirement of "Sufficient Basis"

Courts excluding expert opinion as not based on data reasonably relied upon in the field often note that the expert's conclusions are speculative or unfounded in fact. This was the approach of Judge Skelly Wright in Merit Motors, Inc. v. Chrysler Corp., 569 F.2d 666 (D.C. Cir. 1977), a complex antitrust case. To establish the requisite antitrust injury plaintiffs relied almost exclusively on their expert's report which set forth a theory of "inherent" economic effect. Id. at 671. Judge Wright, for the court, approved the trial court's grant of summary judgment, finding that the expert had made "unsupported assumptions about the elasticities of demand in various markets and that he virtually ignore[d] the impact of the dominant forces in the automobile market: General Motors and Ford." . . .

Courts are particularly wary of unfounded expert opinion when causation is the issue. In Tabatchnick v. G.D. Searle & Co., 67 F.R.D. 49 (D.N.J. 1975), the court refused to allow the testimony of plaintiff's expert that an oral contraceptive caused certain adverse neurological effects. The expert relied in part on the notion that the symptoms stopped when plaintiff discontinued use of the pill, yet the testimony had been that the symptoms continued for some time. Id. at 55. Labelling the expert's opinion a "bare conclusion," the court admonished that careful screening of expert testimony on causation was "especially important when the subject is emotionally charged, as it is here." . . .

As these cases illustrate, the testimony of Doctors Singer and Epstein is insufficiently grounded in any reliable evidence. Framing Dr. Singer's testimony as a hypothetical does not defeat the need for an adequate basis. Cunningham v. Rendezvous, Inc., 699 F.2d 676, 678 (4th Cir. 1983). The conclusions Doctors Singer and Epstein reach are also insufficient as a basis for a finding of causality because they fail to consider critical information, such as the most relevant epidemiologic studies and the other possible causes of disease.

Central to the inadequacy of plaintiffs' case is their inability to exclude other possible causes of plaintiffs' illnesses — those arising out of their service in Vietnam as well as those that all of us face in military and civilian life. For example, the largest number of plaintiffs considered by Dr. Singer suffer from symptoms such as exhaustion, depression, sleep disturbances, anxiety and anger. He concludes that these symptoms are "compatible with" exposure to dioxin. As scientific literature establishes, such symptoms are also frequently identified with Vietnam stress syndrome due to battle and other military stresses. DeFazio, "Dynamic Perspectives on the Nature and Effects of Combat Stress" in Stress Disorders Among Vietnam Veterans: Theory, Research and Treatment 23 (C. Figley, ed. 1978); Shatan, "Stress Disorders Among Vietnam Veterans: The Emotional Content of Combat

Continues" in id. 43 (both articles on file as subject to court's judicial notice). The onset of stress syndrome may be delayed and the symptoms may persist for decades. DeFazio, supra, at 34-35. Dr. Singer in no way rules out stress syndrome as the cause of plaintiffs' neurological symptoms. . . .

Dr. Singer's failure to discuss the individual plaintiffs' medical histories and personal habits is endemic to his analysis. He does not consider alternative possible causes of illness, even when those potential causes are admitted by the plaintiffs themselves in their affidavits. . . .

A false aura of scientific infallibility, coupled with low probative value, increases resistance to admitting evidence since it multiplies the hazards of misleading a jury. . . .

From this review of the relevant law, several clear principles emerge. Although summary judgment is a drastic procedural device, courts in the Second and other Circuits follow the edicts of Rule 56(e) and do not allow mere conclusory allegations that a factual dispute exists to defeat a motion for summary judgment. This general prohibition extends to the use of conclusory allegations by experts. . . .

[Motion granted.]

In re Swine Flu Immunization Products Liability Litigation
508 F. Supp. 967 (1981)

FINESILVER, DISTRICT JUDGE.

This case[1] brings into sharp focus various medical viewpoints and theories as to the causation and etiology of Guillain-Barre syndrome ("GBS"),[2] a neurologic disorder. Specifically, it involves the question whether the swine flu vaccine caused plaintiff, Joseph Lima, a thirty-

---

1. The case is brought under the Federal Tort Claims Act ("FTCA"), 28 U.S.C. §§1346(b), 2671 et seq., in conjunction with the National Influenza Immunization Program of 1976 ("Swine Flu Act"), Public Law 94-380 (Aug. 12, 1976), 42 U.S.C. §247b(j)-(l). The Swine Flu Act makes recovery from the United States the exclusive remedy for damages resulting from an innoculation. It further establishes the FTCA as the vehicle for asserting such claims. For the history of the Swine Flu Act and the litigation it has generated, see, Hunt v. United States, 636 F.2d 580, and Hollar v. United States, # 79-1282, 636 F.2d 580 (D.C. Cir. 1980); Sparks v. Wyeth Laboratories, 431 F. Supp. 411 (W.D. Okl. 1977), aff'd per curiam, #77-1407 (10th Cir. Dec. 22, 1978) (unpublished opinion); Alvarez v. United States, 495 F. Supp 1188 (D. Colo. July 31, 1980).

2. GBS is discussed in greater detail below. Several cases have addressed the issue of causation between the swine flu vaccine and GBS. See, e.g., Alvarez, supra; Thompson v. United States, No. 79-1017 (E.D. Va. Nov. 6, 1980); Schultz v. United States, No. 78-0259 (S.D. Cal. Oct. 17, 1980).

three year old Denver microbiologist, to contract GBS during the winter of 1976-1977. The vaccination was administered pursuant to the mass immunization program of 1976 which sought to prevent a projected swine flu epidemic. . . .

Conclusion

While there was a conflict in the medical testimony concerning the causal connection between the immunization and plaintiff's GBS, we believe that plaintiff has failed to sustain his burden of proof. It is not probable that the vaccine was a contributing factor in his neurologic illness.

The theories advanced by the experts who testified on plaintiff's behalf are speculative and are not generally supported in the medical literature. On the other hand, the opinions of Drs. Ringel and Lisak comport with the present state of medical knowledge. They are in accord with the widely accepted epidemiologic studies. Where, as here, the exact organic cause of a disease cannot be scientifically isolated, epidemiologic data becomes highly persuasive. The epidemiologic data in the instant case does not support plaintiff's allegations of causation. In addition, the viral infection suffered by Mr. Lima immediately prior to his hospitalization is a medical event which is known to precede GBS. Its presence and the length of time between the vaccination and onset of diagnosable neurologic symptoms make it less probable that the vaccine was a contributing factor in plaintiff's GBS. . . .

The evidence in this case does not persuade us that plaintiff's GBS began until the beginning of March 1977, sixteen weeks following his inoculation. Additionally, we are of the view that Mr. Lima's generalized weakness in the winter of 1976-1977 was not related to the vaccine or initial symptoms of GBS. Finally, we are of the view that the most credible and soundest medical opinions were expressed by Drs. Ringel, Lisak and Kohler. Additionally, their education, clinical experience and research in the area entitle their opinions to great weight.

In sum, we find and conclude that plaintiff has failed to establish by a preponderance of the evidence that the swine flu vaccine was a contributing factor, or a proximate cause, of his Guillain-Barre syndrome.

Order

It is hereby ordered that this action be dismissed with prejudice. The Clerk of the Court is directed to enter judgment in favor of defendant, United States, and against plaintiff, Joseph Lima.

Each party is to pay his or its own costs.

NOTES

Epidemiological Studies as a Basis for Expert Opinion on Medical Issues

1. The *Agent Orange* case and the *Swine Flu Immunization* case are trial-court examples of highly sophisticated applications of epidemiological studies designed to support, or deny, causal relationships in medical cases of disease or toxic reactions in human beings. See particularly Dore, A Commentary on the Use of Epidemiological Evidence in Demonstrating Cause-in-Fact, 7 Harv. Envtl. L. Rev. 429 (1983). See also Black & Lilienfeld, Epidemiological Proof in Toxic Tort Litigation, 52 Ford. L. Rev. 732 (1984). For a contrary view of epidemiological studies, see Hall & Silbergeld, Reappraising Epidemiology: A Response to Mr. Dore, 7 Harv. Envtl. L. Rev. 441 (1983). See also Hoffman, the Use of Epidemiology in the Courts, 120 Am. J. Epi. 190 (1984).

2. In both of the above cases, the judges sitting as finders of fact rejected opinion testimony for plaintiffs after examining, quite extensively, the basis for the opinions in epidemiological studies. The key element in rejecting much of the opinion testimony in each case was its "unreliability." Why have the tests for admissibility and reliability become so rigorous in these kinds of cases? See Carlson, Collision Course in Expert Testimony: Limitations on Affirmative Introduction of Underlying Data, 36 U. Fla. L. Rev. 234 (1984). See also Arnolds, Federal Rule of Evidence 703: The Back Door is Wide Open, 20 Forum: Tort and Ins. Prac. Section, A.B.A.1 (1984).

3. For a highly detailed account of the Agent Orange litigation, the trial before Judge Weinstein, and the aftermath of the trial including the settlement agreement, see P. Schuck, Agent Orange on Trial: Mass Toxic Disasters in the Courts (1987). On the background of the development of the use of Agent Orange in Vietnam, see Young, Agent Orange: The Bitter Harvest (1980). See also Wilcox, Waiting for an Army to Die: The Tragedy of Agent Orange (1983).

4. In a reversal of policy, the Secretary of Veterans Affairs declared some veterans with soft-tissue sarcoma, alleged to be caused by Agent Orange, as eligible for disability payments. N.Y. Times, May 19, 1990, at 10.

5. An appreciation of the issues in the evidentiary use of epidemiological findings will be aided by a basic understanding of epidemiological methods as applied to medical matters. See particularly Hennekens & Buring, Epidemiology in Medicine (1987); A. Monson, Occupational Epidemiology (1980). Litigation in this area also involves complex and subtle analysis of statistical probability and the burden of proof. On the evidentiary application of statistical methods, see

Note, Proof of Cancer Causation in Toxic Waste Litigation: The Case of Determining versus Indeterminacy, 61 So. Cal. L. Rev. 2075 (1988); Brennan, Causal Chains and Statistical Links: The Role of Scientific Uncertainty in Hazardous Substance Litigation, 73 Cornell L. Rev. 469 (1988); Ginsberg, Use and Misuse of Epidemiological Data in the Courtroom: Defining the Limits of Inferential and Particularistic Evidence in Mass Tort Litigation, 12 Am. J.L. & Med. 423 (1986); Gold, Causation in Toxic Torts: Burdens of Proof, Standards of Persuasion, and Statistical Evidence, 96 Yale L.J. 376 (1986); Brennan & Carter, Legal and Scientific Probability of Causation in Cancer and Other Environmental Disease in Individuals, 10 J. Health Pol., Poly. & L. 33 (1985). See also Schwartzbauer & Shindell, Cancer and the Adjudicative Process: The Interface of Environmental Protection and Toxic Tort Law, 14 Am. J.L. & Med. 1 (1988).

6. Another approach to establishing causation in toxic tort litigation involves the use of quantitative risk assessment. Specific risk assessments are generally based on responses to toxic chemicals by laboratory animals, and they are used to estimate the probability of diseases in humans where epidemiologic studies are unavailable or of insufficient power to detect low levels of risk. The method involves four sequential statistical determinations: (1) hazard identification; (2) dose-response assessment; (3) human exposure assessment; and (4) final risk characterization. For a symposium of articles describing the methodology, see 236 Science 267 (1986). The method is also frequently used to form the basis of government regulatory decisions. Given that risk assessments generally involve exposures to chemicals producing a low probability of disease, how likely are they to be useful in establishing causation based on a standard of "reasonable medical certainty" or "more probable than not"? Note Judge Weinstein's comment in the *Agent Orange* case about the different levels of proof necessary to justify regulation as opposed to compensation in tort. For a discussion of the methodology of risk assessment and its role in toxic tort litigation, see Dore, The Law of Toxic Torts 26.02-26.08 (1988). See also Leape, Quantitative Risk Assessment in Regulation of Environmental Carcinogens, 4 Harv. Envtl. L. Rev. 86 (1980). For a judicial review of the application of the method in the Food and Drug Administration, see Public Citizen v. Young, 831 F.2d 1108 (1987). See also a report of the National Research Council, Risk Assessment in the Federal Government: Managing the Process (1983). See also Huber, Safety and the Second Best: The Hazards of Public Risk Assessment in the Courts, 85 Colum. L. Rev. 277 (1985).

CHAPTER 5

Medical and Hospital Malpractice

I. THE MEDICAL PROFESSION AND MEDICAL PRACTICE

A. Medical Education

Professional medical education in the United States today is of uniformly good quality. The medical student spends four years in medical school training to become an M.D. In 39 states the graduate is then required to spend one year in internship before being eligible for a license. For specialty practice, postgraduate training is much more extended.

As with all professional training, the medical student must achieve proficiency in two areas: theory and practice. While legal education has been accused of emphasizing the former and almost ignoring the latter, the medical schools have been moving into the hospitals more and more every year. At present, medical education is roughly divided into two years of basic medical science and two years of clinical science. The latter, generally referred to as a clinical clerkship, has assumed such importance in hospital training that many are now advocating that it should absorb the internship phase of medical training, leaving hospital residency training for specialization as the major area of postgraduate study.

The basic content of a medical education is set out in Chapter 2, where the basic and clinical sciences are defined. Many medical schools today are in the process of restructuring the curriculum to provide for a basic core curriculum and to allow for more flexibility in the balance of the program — more electives are permitted, patient care is introduced earlier in the program, and less factual information is pressed upon the student. There appears to be a trend to teach more behavioral science along with the basic and clinical sciences. Also, more medical schools are adding courses in the medical humanities (history, ethics, law, and literature) and in medical economics and health policy subjects. It is hoped that this new approach will prepare the physician better for the broader role that today's society expects.

B. The Medical Specialties

The practice of medicine today is divided between general practitioners and specialists, with the ratio of specialists to generalists rising each year. Lawyers will, of course, deal with both groups. However, expert witnesses and consultants are predominantly specialists. It is essential that lawyers differentiate between the specialties and make use of them properly.

There is no legally instituted method by which competent specialists can be recognized. Each state requires a license or registration to practice medicine, but the standards for registration are minimal and the license is merely a general authorization to practice in any area of medicine. Specialization is regulated by the profession itself through the mechanism of the American Specialty Boards. There are currently 23 specialty boards with various subdivisions approved by the Council on Medical Education of the American Medical Association. Each board requires one year of internship and three to seven years of approved training and practice. The candidate must then pass an examination in order to be certified as a specialist in any given area of practice. The boards do not confer any legal status on the doctor. The primary function of the specialty boards is to determine the competence of candidates and certify those who qualify, and to improve general standards of graduate medical education and the facilities for specialty training. The boards are listed below with appropriate abbreviations. By and large, they correspond to the clinical sciences defined in Chapter 2. It should be noted that upon certification all diplomates of the American Specialty Boards must agree to devote at least 90 percent of their practice to the appropriate specialty area.

American Board of Allergy and Immunology (AI)
American Board of Anesthesiology (AN)
American Board of Colon and Rectal Surgery (CRS)
American Board of Dermatology (DS)
American Board of Emergency Medicine (EM)
American Board of Family Practice (FP)*
American Board of Internal Medicine (M)
American Board of Neurological Surgery (NS)
American Board of Nuclear Medicine (Nu M)
American Board of Obstetrics and Gynecology (OG)
American Board of Ophthalmology (OP)

---

* This Board was formed in 1969 after many years of effort in seeking recognition. It is not a specialty in the same sense as the other boards since it is composed of general practitioners treating all family members in community practice.

American Board of Orthopedic Surgery (OS)
American Board of Otolaryngology (OT)
American Board of Pathology (P)
  This board issues certificates in special divisions, one of which is Forensic Pathology.
American Board of Pediatrics (Pd)
American Board of Physical Medicine and Rehabilitation (PMR)
American Board of Plastic Surgery (PIS)
American Board of Preventative Medicine (Pr M)
American Board of Psychiatry and Neurology (PN)
  This board also certifies in Child Psychiatry.
American Board of Radiology (R)
American Board of Surgery (S)
American Board of Thoracic Surgery (TS)
American Board of Urology (U)

Biographical data on physicians is readily available in two major sources. The first is the American Medical Directory published biennially by the American Medical Association. This is a general listing of all physicians licensed to practice medicine. There is also a Directory of Medical Specialists published by A. M. Marquis. This service lists all diplomates of the American Specialty Boards and gives more comprehensive information than does the general directory. It also publishes the requirements for each specialty board and the names and addresses of corresponding officers for each board. Other important source books for information on practitioners and organizations in the health field are the directories of the American College of Physicians and the American College of Surgeons, the Health Care Directory, the Directory of Women Physicians in the United States, and the Medical and Health Information Directory.

II. HOSPITALS AND OTHER HEALTH CARE FACILITIES AND ORGANIZATIONS

A. Major Classifications of Hospitals

Hospitals may be described in different ways, but the most commonly accepted classifications are by clinical purpose and by ownership or control.* Over 90 percent of all American hospitals are short-term care (also called acute care) institutions with patients' stays of under,

---

* See generally Hospital Organization and Management (3d ed. J. Rakich & K. Darr, 1983); E. Garrett, Hospitals: A Systems Approach (1973); A. Southwick, The Law of Hospitals and Health Care Organizations (2d ed. 1988).

usually considerably under, 30 days in length. The remainder provide chronic care for special classes of patients such as those suffering from cancer, tuberculosis and other respiratory diseases, and mental illness. Currently, there are a total of about 1,267,000 hospital beds in the nation's hospitals, which have registered decreases in total numbers in every year since 1965.† There also have been decreases in the daily census of inpatients in all hospitals since 1964. Fluctuations in the general economy have relatively less impact on hospital-service demands than on most other goods and services. The portion of the gross national product devoted to health care, including hospital services, has increased in each year of the last two decades.

In terms of clinical purpose, the great majority (80 percent) of all hospitals offer general medical and surgical services and are short-term care institutions. The remainder are specialized hospitals offering either short-term or chronic care or both. The American Hospital Association (AHA) uses a somewhat different classification. The AHA provides statistics on "community hospitals" which it describes as all nonfederal, short-term, general and specialized hospitals that are located in communities and that offer services to the general public; at the end of the late 1980s, there were approximately 5600 community hospitals in the country. The AHA also publishes extensive data on all hospitals of the country each year. The National Center for Health Statistics, a federal agency, also annually publishes considerable statistical data.

Hospital ownership and control is usually described in four subgroups: federal hospitals, county and municipal hospitals, voluntary or nonprofit (charitable) hospitals, and private, proprietary hospitals. In the past, the hospitals in the latter three subgroups were nearly all independent units with their own governing bodies or boards, thus earning the earlier description of a "cottage industry." In recent years, however, cooperative efforts have become much more common in all of the categories. The voluntary hospitals are developing a great variety of shared-service plans. Mergers of voluntary hospitals are also taking place at a growing rate. Among the proprietaries, a revolution has been taking place in organization and management. Corporate financing now dominates the field and the category tends to be known more accurately as "investor-owned hospitals." Management groups now operate large chains of proprietary institutions located in many states, thus providing the advantages of joint ownership and improved

---

† AHA, Hospital Statistics (1988). Much of the data contained in this section has been drawn from this publication, an annual periodical on hospital administration and operation. See also the AHA Guide to the Health Care Field, published annually, and the AHA Directory of Shared Service Organizations for Health Care Institutions, revised periodically since 1974.

II. Hospitals and Other Health Care Facilities

managerial skills and policies spread over a variety of health care facilities.

At present, about 50 percent of American hospitals are in the nonprofit subgroup, 38 percent are government controlled, and 12 percent are in the private, proprietary category.

B. *Organization of a General Hospital*

General hospitals in the voluntary, nonprofit subgroup and general hospitals in the private, proprietary category usually have at least two large clinical services, the medical department and the surgical service. A large percentage also have obstetrical services although, with the declining birth rate, such departments have been decreasing in number quite consistently in recent years. There have also been decreases in some other types of services such as intensive cardiac care units, X-ray therapy, and abortion services. Among the services recently increasing in number have been rehabilitation outpatient services, neonatal intensive care units, patient representative programs, speech pathology, and genetic screening. As might be expected, the varieties of services and programs correlate closely with the size of the general hospitals; the larger the hospital the more likely it is to provide the additional facilities, expenditures, skilled personnel, and expanded services.

The voluntary general hospitals operate under nonprofit or charitable corporate charters. They are commonly governed by boards of trustees or directors drawn from their local communities. Management is shared with a chief executive officer or director and the medical staff, which usually has its own bylaws.** In most hospitals, there is a joint conference committee with members from the medical staff and the administration. Under the director will be gathered the administrative and housekeeping functions, and most auxiliary medical services: nursing, pharmacy, laboratory, and recordkeeping services. The medical staff organizes and governs all types of physicians providing care to patients in the hospital.†† These usually include the attending physicians, who regularly carry responsibility for patient care; consultant physicians, who are specialists on call to advise the regular staff physicians; and visiting or courtesy staff doctors, who

---

** A group of attorneys representing the American Hospital Association (and the American Academy of Hospital Attorneys) and the American Medical Association (with the Society of Medical Association Counsel) produced a set of guidelines regarding shared responsibilities of hospital administration and medical staffs. See The Report of the Joint Task Force on Hospital-Medical Staff Relationships, Chicago, AHA-AMA, February 1985.

†† For a useful and colorful description of hospital structures and their complex interrelationships, see D. Smith & A. Kaluzny, The White Labyrinth (1975).

may only occasionally refer a patient and attend the patient in the institution. A teaching hospital will also have interns and residents who are receiving postgraduate training and providing a substantial amount of the care in such institutions. Private, proprietary hospitals have many of the same features except they have their own governing structures. Most voluntary community hospitals have "open staff privileges" since they invite qualified doctors in their geographic areas to join their staffs. Some voluntary hospitals, particularly teaching institutions, have closed medical staffs wherein membership is strictly limited. Proprietary hospitals also tend to have closed medical staffs. Specialized hospitals generally have closed staffs because of their limited range of clinical services. Also, the larger teaching hospitals, often university affiliated, tend to have restricted or closed staffs composed entirely of specialty-qualified physicians.

C. Specialty Hospitals

There are a variety of hospitals in this category offering specialized treatment and care. There are children's hospitals offering mainly short term or acute care of a general nature and there are specialized hospitals for orthopedic diseases and disabilities offering both short-term and longer stay. The majority of specialized institutions, however, deal with chronic disease patients. These include the mental hospitals, the institutions for severely retarded persons, tuberculosis hospitals, alcoholism and drug dependency hospitals, and cancer disease hospitals. Some 40 years ago, psychiatric hospitals accounted for about 50 percent of *all* hospital beds in this country. The number of large public hospitals and their psychiatric beds for inpatients have been declining rapidly in recent decades and currently there are vigorous "deinstitutional" programs in every state in this country. On the other hand, smaller nongovernmental psychiatric wards in general hospitals have been increasing in number considerably in the last 20 years or so. For example, the number of short-term psychiatric hospitals increased from 64 in 1965 to 231 in 1987.* Another area of dramatic decline has been the tuberculosis hospitals. In 1925, tuberculosis was the largest single cause of death in the United States. In 1947 there were still 411 tuberculosis hospitals with over 70,000 beds in this country. By 1978 there were only 15 hospitals specializing in tuberculosis and other respiratory illnesses with only 2783 beds. In 1987, there were fewer than 10 hospitals in this category with about 1000 beds.

* Hospital Statistics 8 (1987).

D. Health Maintenance Organizations, Health Care Foundations, and Preferred Provider Organizations

The newest and most aggressively supported form of health care delivery in this country is that provided through what are generally called health maintenance organizations (HMOs). These programs require a single subscription fee and in return offer members a comprehensive range of health care services including walk-in medical (sometimes dental and other) services and hospitalization. Various HMOs have different operational and management systems, different medical staff organizations, and hospitals which are either owned by the HMO or offer services to HMO subscribers under contracts with the HMO central structure. The primary advantages for subscribers are the comprehensiveness of the services offered under the plans and the single annual premium for all services rendered under the plan. The programs stress outpatient services, ambulatory care, preventive care and consultation, and early diagnosis and treatment, thus the title of "health maintenance." The first such program was begun in 1929 by the Ross-Loos Clinic in Los Angeles. National attention was focused on the field with the expansion of the Kaiser Foundation Health Plans in the 1950s and 1960s. The federal government backed the development strongly under the Health Maintenance Organization Act of 1973 which was further amended in 1976. The growth of the HMO plans in the 1970s and 1980s was phenomenal; from 1971 to 1986, the number of fully operational HMOs increased from 33 to 623 with the enrollment of subscribers increasing from 3.6 million people to 25.7 million people.†

In later years, other alternative forms of health care delivery have been formed including Preferred Provider Organizations (PPOs) and Health Care (or Independent Practice) Foundations. The PPOs are the fastest growing groups in the country since they are organized particularly to offer a competitively superior system (in terms of efficiency and cost) to third-party payers. The Health Care Foundations are usually structured by independent practitioners, often associated with a state or local medical society, as a counteraction to the HMOs and PPOs. The Foundations offer prepaid health insurance with a wide range of choice of community-based physicians. Some HMOs have also used large panels of community-based physicians. These organizational variations have blurred the distinctions between these basic forms of health care delivery. The systems are further explained in Chapter 8.III.C.

For those people not involved in any of these systems, the largest sources of prepaid health insurance are the Blue Cross and Blue

† U.S. Dept. of H.H.S., Health, United States, 1987, 170 (1988).

Shield plans that finance care largely through local independent practitioners and community hospitals. There are about 95 Blue Cross plans (for hospital care) and about the same number of Blue Shield plans (for physicians and, in some systems, for psychologists and other allied health professionals).* Private insurance companies also provide health care policies paying for hospital and physician services, usually on a fee-for-service basis.

III. GENERAL THEORIES OF MALPRACTICE LIABILITY

Slater v. Baker and Stapleton
95 Eng. Rep. 860 (K.B. 1767)

Special action upon the case, wherein the plaintiff declares that the defendant Baker being a surgeon, and Stapleton an apothecary, he employed them to cure his leg which had been broken and set, and the callous of the fracture formed; that in consideration of being paid for their skill and labour, &c. they undertook and promised, &c.; but the defendants not regarding their promise and undertaking, and the duty of their business and employment, so ignorantly and unskilfully treated the plaintiff, that they ignorantly and unskilfully broke and disunited the callous of the plaintiff's leg after it was set, and the callous formed, whereby he is damaged. The defendants pleaded not guilty, whereupon issue was joined, which was tried before the Lord Chief Justice Wilmot, and a verdict found for the plaintiff, damages 500*l*. The substance of the evidence for the plaintiff at the trial was, first a surgeon was called, who swore that the plaintiff having broken both the bones of one of his legs, this witness set the same; that the plaintiff was under his hands nine weeks; that in a month's time after the leg was set, he found the leg was healing and in a good way; the callous was formed; there was a little protuberance, but not more than usual: upon cross examination he said he was instructed in surgery by his father, that the callous was the uniting the bones, and that it was very dangerous to break or disunite the callous after it was formed.

John Latham an apothecary swore he attended the plaintiff nine weeks, who was then well enough to go home; that the bones were well united; that he was present with the plaintiff and defendants, and at first the defendants said the plaintiff had fallen into good hands; the second time he saw them all together the defendants said

---

* Medical and Health Information Directory, Ch. 9, (4th ed. 1988).

III. General Theories of Malpractice Liability

the same; but when he saw them together a third time there was some alteration; he said the plaintiff was then in a passion, and was unwilling to let the defendants do any thing to his leg; he said he had known such a thing done as disuniting the callous, but that had been only when a leg was set very crooked, but not where it was straight.

A woman called as a witness, swore, that when the plaintiff came home he could walk with crutches; that the defendant Baker put on to the plaintiff's leg an heavy steel thing that had teeth, and would stretch or lengthen the leg; that the defendants broke the leg again, and three or four months afterwards the plaintiff was still very ill and bad of it.

The daughter of the plaintiff swore, that the defendant Stapleton was first sent for to take off the bandage from the plaintiff's leg; when he came he declined to do it himself, and desired the other defendant Baker might be called in to assist; when Baker came he sent for the machine that was mentioned; plaintiff offered to give Baker a guinea, but Stapleton advised him not to take it then, but said they might be paid all together when the business was done; that the third time the defendants came to the plaintiff, Baker took up the plaintiff's foot in both his hands and nodded to Stapleton, and then Stapleton took the plaintiff's leg upon his knee, and the leg gave a crack, when the plaintiff cried out to them and said, "You have broke what nature formed"; Baker then said to the plaintiff, you must go through the operation of extension, and Stapleton said, We have consulted and done for the best.

Another surgeon was called, and swore, that in cases of crooked legs after they have been set, the way of making them straight is by compression, and not by extension, and said he had not the least idea of the instrument spoken of for extension: he gave Baker a good character, as having been the first surgeon of St. Bartholomew's Hospital for 20 years, and said he had never known a case where the callous had deossified.

Another surgeon was called, who swore, that when the callous is formed to any degree, it is difficult to break it, and the callous in this case must have been formed, or it would not have given a crack, and said extension was improper; and if the patient himself had asked him to do it, he would have declined it; and if the callous had not been hard, he would not have done it without the consent of the plaintiff; that compression was the proper way, and the instrument improper: he said the defendant Baker was eminent in his profession. Another surgeon was called, who swore, that if the plaintiff was capable of bearing his foot upon the ground, he would not have disunited the callous if he had been desired by him, but in no case whatever without consent of the patient: if the callous was loose, it was proper to make the extension, to bring the leg into a right line. A servant of the plaintiff swore the plaintiff had put his foot upon the ground three or four weeks before this was done.

The counsel for the defendants at the trial, for Baker, relied upon the good character which was given him, and objected there was no evidence to affect the other defendant Stapleton the apothecary; but the Lord Chief Justice thought there was such evidence against both the defendants as ought to be left to the jury, as the nodding, the advising Baker not to take the guinea offered to him by the plaintiff; besides, the apothecary first proposed sending for Baker: the plaintiff was in no pain before they extended his leg, and he only sent to Stapleton to have the bandage taken off. The Lord Chief Justice asked the jury whether they intended to find the damages against both the defendants? and they found 500*l.* against them jointly, and he said he was well satisfied with the verdict.

It was now moved that the verdict ought to be set aside, because the action is upon a joint contract, and there is no evidence of a joint undertaking by both the defendants: the plaintiff sends for Stapleton to take off the bandage, who declines doing it, and says, I do not understand this matter, you must send for a surgeon; accordingly Mr. Baker is sent for, who enters upon the business as a surgeon unconnected with Stapleton, who, it does not appear, ever undertook for any skill about the leg, so the jury have found him guilty without any evidence. That Baker has been above 20 years the first surgeon in St. Bartholomew's Hospital, reads lectures in surgery and anatomy, and is celebrated for his knowledge in his profession as well as his humanity; and to charge such a man with ignorance and unskilfulness upon the records of this Court is most dreadful. All the witnesses agreed Mr. Baker doth not want knowledge, therefore this verdict ought not to stand. 2dly, it was objected that the evidence given does not apply to this action, which is upon a joint contract; the evidence is, that the callous of the leg was broke without the plaintiff's consent; but there is no evidence of ignorance or want of skill, and therefore the action ought to have been trespass vi & armis for breaking the plaintiff's leg without his consent. All the surgeons said they never do any thing of this kind without consent, and if the plaintiff should not be content with the present damages, but bring another action of trespass vi & armis, could this verdict be pleaded in bar? The Court, without hearing the counsel for the plaintiff, gave judgment for him.

CURIA. — 1st, it is objected, that this is laid to be a joint undertaking, and therefore it ought to be proved, and we are of opinion that it ought: the question therefore is, whether there is any evidence of a joint undertaking? We are of opinion there is; Mr. Stapleton declines acting alone, but in concurrence with Mr. Baker attends the plaintiff every time any thing is done, and assists jointly with Mr.

Baker. This appears in evidence, and is sufficient, for there is no occasion to prove an express joint contract, promise, or undertaking. When an offer is made to Baker of a guinea, Stapleton says, You had better be paid all at last: they both attended plaintiff together every time, and Stapleton said, We have consulted and done for the best: when the plaintiff complained of what they had done, Stapleton considered himself as one of the persons to join in the cure of the leg, for he put his hand on the knee when Baker nodded, and then the bone cracked; he is the original person aiding in this matter, and there is no ground for this objection. When we consider the good character of Baker, we cannot well conceive why he acted in the manner he did; but many men very skilful in their profession have frequently acted out of the common way for the sake of trying experiments. Several of the witnesses proved that the callous was formed, and that it was proper to remove plaintiff home; that he was free from pain, and able to walk with crutches. We cannot conceive what the nature of the instrument made use of is: why did Baker put it on, when he said that plaintiff had fallen into good hands, and when plaintiff only sent for him to take off the bandage? It seems as if Mr. Baker wanted to try an experiment with this new instrument.

2dly, it is objected, that this is not the proper action, and that it ought to have been trespass vi & armis. In answer to this, it appears from the evidence of the surgeons that it was improper to disunite the callous without consent; this is the usage and law of surgeons: then it was ignorance and unskilfulness in that very particular, to do contrary to the rule of the profession, what no surgeon ought to have done; and indeed it is reasonable that a patient should be told what is about to be done to him, that he may take courage and put himself in such a situation as to enable him to undergo the operation. It was objected, this verdict and recovery cannot be pleaded in bar to an action of trespass vi & armis to be brought for the same damage; but we are clear of opinion it may be pleaded in bar. That the plaintiff ought to receive a satisfaction for the injury, seems to be admitted; but then it is said, the defendants ought to have been charged as trespassers vi & armis. The Court will not look with eagle's eyes to see whether the evidence applies exactly or not to the case, when they can see the plaintiff has obtained a verdict for such damages as he deserves, they will establish such verdict if it be possible. For any thing that appears to the Court, this was the first experiment made with this new instrument; and if it was, it was a rash action, and he who acts rashly acts ignorantly: and although the defendants in general may be as skilful in their respective professions as any two gentlemen in England, yet the Court cannot help saying, that in this particular case they have acted ignorantly and unskilfully, contrary to the known rule and usage of surgeons.

Judgment for the plaintiff per totam Curiam.

NOTES

Medical Malpractice, History and Current Status

1. Most of the decisions in this volume are quite modern. The above case, however, would not be considered "recent" even by the most traditional Property Law teacher. Yet, it raises a surprising number of the problems in contemporary medical malpractice.

2. Does the *Slater* case sound in negligence or in battery? Was there a failure to obtain adequate informed consent to the operative procedure? Was the procedure experimental in nature? Under current rules of medical ethics and medical practice could the modern counterparts of Baker, the surgeon, and Stapleton, the apothecary, join together in treating the patient for one fee?

3. Surgeon Baker was a leader in his profession at St. Bartholomew's Hospital, then, as well as now, one of the best hospitals in Great Britain. The court was loath to call into question his skill or his humanity. To do so was considered, as the court observed, "most dreadful." The challenge to skill and personal reputation of dedicated medical people is still one of the most painful aspects of all medical malpractice claims. Is it not a very important part of the various efforts to reform the cause of action and to move to a no-fault system of medical accident compensation?

4. On the history of medical malpractice, see C. Chapman, Physicians, Law and Ethics (1984). See also King, Medicine 100 Years Ago: The Doctor and the Law, 257 J.A.M.A. 2204 (1984); Shapiro, Medical Malpractice: History, Diagnosis, and Prognosis, 22 St. Louis U.L. Rev. 469 (1978). On various aspects of historical importance in shaping medical negligence doctrines and their relationship to medical care standards, see Schwartz & Kamesar, Doctors, Damages and Deterrence, 298 New Eng. J. Med. 1282 (1978); Mechanic, Some Social Aspects of the Medical Malpractice Dilemma, 1975 Duke L.J. 1179. For perspective on the development of the medical profession in America, see P. Starr, The Social Transformation of American Medicine (1982). For a social as well as a legal perspective on the pressures and demands of medical malpractice litigation on the political and legal systems in the United States, see S. Law & S. Polan, Pain and Profit: The Politics of Malpractice (1978).

5. Do malpractice actions help to encourage better medical and hospital care of patients? Some responsible commentators have indicated in important testimony that legal actions and the threat of actions have an adverse effect on physicians' attitudes and on health care generally. See the statement of Dr. George Northrop before the Secretary's Commission on Medical Malpractice,

> As a physician, I live in an aura of fear, fear of suit. Fear contributes to hostility and rarely contributes to constructive action. Medical organi-

zations are trying their best to overcome their deficiencies, but in my opinion, malpractice litigation is not the incentive to improvement. It places medicine in an adversary position and hostilities often result. . . . It may be hard to believe but we are a frightened profession. The doctor feels put upon. . . .

HEW, Report of the Secretary's Commission on Medical Malpractice (1973). More recently, see Sanders, Confronting Professional Liability: A Roundtable Discussion on Medical Risk Management, 70 Minn. Med. 142 (1987). For a different viewpoint, see Jost, The Necessary and Proper Role of Regulation to Assure the Quality of Health Care, 25 Houston L. Rev. (1988).

6. For many decades, lawyers and physicians in Great Britain and Canada prided themselves on their avoidance of what they called "the American problem" (or "the American disease") of increasing medical malpractice litigation and high malpractice insurance premiums. During the 1980s, however, the malpractice climate changed for the worse in both of these nations. See Miller, Medical Malpractice Litigation: Do the British Have a Better Remedy? 11 Am. J. L. & Med. 433 (1986); Korcok, Medical Malpractice: The Growing Crisis, Can. Med. Assoc. J. 641 (1986). See also a comparative review of the American, British, and Swedish legal systems in their handling of medical malpractice litigation. M. Rosenthal, Dealing With Medical Malpractice: The British and Swedish Experience (1988).

7. There are several useful texts on medical malpractice. For a superb review of the character, current status, and problems in malpractice litigation with clear and complete statistical analysis, see P. Danzon, Medical Malpractice: Theory, Guidance and Public Policy (1985). For a comprehensive text that is periodically supplemented with new statutory and case-law developments, see D. Louisell & H. Williams, Medical Malpractice, 2 vols. (2d ed. 1986). See also S. Pegalis & H. Wachsman, American Law of Medical Malpractice, 3 vols. (1980). More recently, a monthly periodical reviews case law and law review articles on medical malpractice; see Medical Malpractice Reports (1987). For a briefer but quite authoritative text addressed to law students, see J. King, The Law of Medical Malpractice, Nutshell Series (2d ed. 1986). On hospital malpractice liability, see A. Southwick, The Law of Hospital and Health Care Administration (2d ed. 1988).

Smith v. Menet
530 N.E.2d 277 (Ill. App. 2 Dist. 1988)

JUSTICE INGLIS delivered the opinion of the court:
This is a medical malpractice action brought by plaintiff, William Smith, against defendants, Paul Menet and Glen Ellyn Clinic. A jury

returned a verdict in favor of plaintiff and assessed damages at $630,000, which amount was reduced by 33% for comparative negligence to $422,100. Defendants timely appealed. We reverse. . . .

Defendants contend that the evidence failed to sustain plaintiff's burden of proof. Defendants argue that in order to succeed on his complaint, plaintiff had to prove that Dr. Menet's treatment of plaintiff fell below acceptable medical standards. Defendants argue that plaintiff's expert witness only testified that Dr. Menet's treatment of plaintiff fell below good medical care. Defendants further argue that good medical care is a higher standard than acceptable medical care. . . .

In the instant case, the following colloquy occurred:

Q: Based upon your review of these materials, Doctor, and mindful of the factual dispute that's in this case and assuming for the purpose of this question that Dr. Menet did not recommend further diagnostic studies to Bill Smith following the two X-rays that were taken at Glen Ellyn Clinic and told him that the abnormality shown on those films was old scar tissue, do you have an opinion, based upon a reasonable degree of medical certainty and as a Board-certified and practicing specialist in the field of internal medicine, as to whether or not Dr. Menet's conduct fell within the standard of good medical care in attending Mr. Smith? . . .

BY THE WITNESS:
A: Yes, sir, I do have an opinion.

BY MR. SCHROEDER:
Q: And what is that opinion?
A: That further evaluation was indicated on the visit of April 5th, 1984, and that not to do further evaluation to try to come to a diagnosis of the X-ray abnormality was below the standard of care. . . .

The issue thus presented to this court is if the question of whether a doctor's conduct falls within "the standard of good medical care" is equivalent to asking whether a doctor possessed and applied the knowledge and used the skill and care that is ordinarily used by reasonably well-qualified doctors in similar circumstances. The problem with the question as phrased to plaintiff's expert is the use of the term "good."

"Highest degree of skill" and "best possible care" are phrases which have been rejected as setting a standard which is too high. (Newell v. Corres (1984), 125 Ill. App. 3d 1087, 1094, 81 Ill. Dec. 283, 466 N.E.2d 1085, Northern Trust Co. v. Skokie Valley Community Hospital (1980), 81 Ill. App. 3d 1110, 1126-27, 37 Ill. Dec. 153, 401 N.E.2d 1246.) The question is whether "good medical care" similarly sets the standard too high. The word "good" has on several

III. General Theories of Malpractice Liability

occasions been used to define the standing of doctors with which the defendant doctor is to be compared. (E.g., Newell v. Corres (1984), 125 Ill. App. 3d 1087, 1094, 81 Ill. Dec. 283, 466 N.E.2d 1085 ("the standard of care against which such a defendant's conduct is measured is not the highest degree of skill possible, but the reasonable skill which a *physician in good standing* in the community would use in a similar case") (emphasis added); Cassady v. Hendrickson (1985), 138 Ill. App. 3d 925, 934, 93 Ill. Dec. 494, 486 N.E.2d 1329 ("defendant doctor is held to that degree of skill, knowledge, and *care exercised by a good practitioner* in the same or similar community") (emphasis added).) However, exactly what "good" means or the connotation that it conveys is a function of how it is used. This is borne out by looking to Webster's, which variously defines "good" as:

> *1 good . . . 1 a* (1): having a favorable or auspicious character: PROSPEROUS, BENEFICIAL . . . (4): favorably affecting one's interests: leading to or attended by a favorable or prosperous outcome . . . *b* (1): adapted to the end designed or proposed: satisfactory in performance: free from flaws or defects: USEFUL, SUITABLE, FIT . . . (2): not impaired: SOUND . . . (8): certain to elicit or produce a specified result . . . *f* (1): conforming to the needs or requirements of the case: ADEQUATE, SUFFICIENT, SATISFACTORY . . . (4): better than average but short of excellent . . . *2 c* (1): having or demonstrating the qualities or skills requisite or appropriate in a specified capacity or occupation (a [good] doctor) . . .
> *2 good . . . 1 a:* something that possesses desirable qualities, promotes success, welfare, or happiness, or is otherwise beneficial. . . .

(Webster's Third New International Dictionary 978 (1971).) "Standard of good medical care" is thus not as precise as the IPI instruction. And, when "good" is interpreted to mean better than average it contradicts the applicable standard as set forth in Northern Trust Co. v. Skokie Valley Community Hospital (1980), 81 Ill. App. 3d 1110, 1126-27, 37 Ill. Dec. 153, 401 N.E.2d 1246. Consequently, we find that asking whether defendant's conduct fell within the "standard of good medical care" was improper. . . .

In accordance with the foregoing analysis, we reverse the judgment of the trial court and remand for a new trial.

Reversed and remanded.

DUNN, J., concurs.

JUSTICE NASH, dissenting:

. . . If considered on the merits, I would . . . find that the use of the phrase "good medical care" in qualifying plaintiff's expert witness to give an opinion does not require reversal in this case.

The jury was instructed as to the requisite standard of care by which defendant's conduct was to be measured by an instruction combining Illinois Pattern Jury Instructions, Civil, Nos. 105.01 and 105.02 (2d ed. 1971) (hereinafter IPI Civil 2d), as follows:

> In treating a patient, a doctor who holds himself out as a specialist and undertakes service in a particular branch of medical, surgical or other healing science, must possess and apply the knowledge and use the skill and care which reasonably well-qualified specialists in the same field, practicing in the same locality or in similar localities, ordinarily would use in similar cases and circumstances. A failure to do so is a form of negligence called malpractice.

Defendants do not now question the correctness of the instruction given by the trial court. They urge, however, that the standard of care expressed in the instruction has been equated to that of "acceptable medical standards," citing Gorman v. St. Francis Hospital (1965), 60 Ill. App. 2d 441, 208 N.E.2d 653; and Alton v. Kitt (1982), 103 Ill. App. 3d 387, 59 Ill. Dec. 132, 431 N.E. 2d 417, and that plaintiff's medical expert incorrectly defined the standard of care applicable to defendant as that of "good medical care," a higher standard than is required.

I would note first that plaintiff's expert, Dr. Golomb, at no time sought to define the applicable standard of care in the trial of the case. To the contrary, the witness declined to do so when plaintiff's counsel inquired of him whether Dr. Menet's failure to do further evaluation of decedent after his April 5, 1984, visit was medical negligence. The witness responded, "Well, you're defining it. You asked me if it was below the standard of care and I've stated it is." The reference to "good" medical care, to which defendants now object with specificity, arose in this case only during the qualifying questioning of the expert witness by plaintiff's counsel in which he inquired, "[D]o you have an opinion, based upon a reasonable degree of medical certainty and as a Board-certified and practicing specialist in the field of internal medicine, as to whether or not Dr. Menet's conduct fell within the standard of *good medical care* in attending Mr. Smith." (Emphasis added.) The witness responded that it was his opinion Dr. Menet's conduct was below the standard of care, and he related the basis for his opinion as reflected in defendant's conduct.

I do not share the hypertechnical concern of my colleagues that by this exchange the jury was led to consider that the standard of care to be applied was anything more or less than that stated in the instruction given by the trial court. Use of the word "good" in the context applied here does no violence to the court's instruction and does not suggest defendants should be held to any higher standard of care than expressed by that instruction. Reference in the opinion to the dictionary definitions of "good" is unnecessary, and perhaps misleading, as the jury was not so instructed and could only have

III. General Theories of Malpractice Liability

tested defendant's conduct on the standard set forth in the court's instruction.

As noted in the comment to IPI Civil 2d No. 105.01, the court in Holtzman v. Hoy (1886), 118 Ill. 534, 536, 8 N.E. 832, stated that the medical standard of care requires the skill "which a *good* physician would bring to a similar case under like circumstances." (Emphasis added.) (IPI Civil 2nd No. 105.01, Comment, at 319.) This court stated the rule in Olander v. Johnson (1930), 258 Ill. App. 89, as follows:

> The duty which a physician and surgeon owes his patient is to bring to the case at hand that degree of knowledge, skill, and care which a good physician and surgeon would bring to a similar case under like circumstances. While this rule, on the one hand, does not exact the highest degree of skill and proficiency attainable in the profession, it does not contemplate merely average merit. (Holtzman v. Hoy, 118 Ill. 534, 8 N.E. 832; 21 R.C.L. Physicians and Surgeons, sec. 27.) To this extent he is liable and no further. He is not required to possess the highest, but reasonable skill. The burden of proof is upon the plaintiff in an action for malpractice to show the want of such care, skill, and diligence and also to show that the injury complained of resulted from failure to exercise those requisites. (McKee v. Allen 94 Ill. App. 147; Goodman v. Bigler, 133 Ill. App. 301; 21 R.C.L. Physicians and Surgeons, sec. 49.)

258 Ill. App. 89, 95.

I have no quarrel with the settled rule that the standard of care against which a medical defendant's conduct is to be measured is that "reasonable skill which a physician in good standing in the community would use in a similar case" (Newell v. Corres (1984), 125 Ill. App. 3d 1087, 1094, 81 Ill. Dec. 283, 466 N.E.2d 1085), and it is not measured against the highest degree of skill possible, or a best possible care standard (125 Ill. App. 3d 1087, 1094, 81 Ill. Dec. 283, 466 N.E.2d 1085; Northern Trust Co. v. Skokie Valley Community Hospital (1980), 81 Ill. App. 3d 1110, 1126-27, 37 Ill. Dec. 153, 401 N.E.2d 1246). However, that is not the question presented in this case. The standard of care to be applied was correctly stated in the instructions to the jury. Use of the phrase "good medical care" in qualifying the expert witness was clearly not intended to elevate the requisite standard of care and would be considered as equivalent to the phrase "acceptable medical standards" which defendant offers as a short description of the standard of care. In the cases noted herein, the courts commonly use language such as "good standing," "good medical practice," "physicians in good practice," and "good practitioner" in describing the medical standard of care and, in my view, that is all that occurred here. "Good" medical care in this context means no more than the application of the skill and knowledge which a reasonably well-qualified practitioner in the field would have used. When the expert witness responded that defendant's conduct was below the requisite standard of care, and the jury was instructed as it was, no untoward prejudice to defendants could have followed from the form of the question to which they now object.

For these reasons I would affirm the judgment of the circuit court.

NOTES

Substantive and Geographic Issues in Establishing Standards of Patient Care

1. The *Smith* opinion indicates the care that most courts take in requiring a clear and unambiguous statement of the substantive requirements for the standard of patient care in medical negligence cases. Nearly all jurisdictions have accepted the concepts of "ordinary, reasonable care" or care such as that rendered by the "average, reasonable physician." As it is sometimes put, the practitioner is safe from malpractice if he or she is "not too far out in front and not too far behind" fellow practitioners in the same field. Is there a difference between "acceptable practice" and "good practice"? See 18 A.L.R. 4th 603 (1982). See also Keeton, Medical Negligence: The Standard of Care, 10 Tex. Tech. L. Rev. 351 (1979); King, In Search of a Standard of Care for the Medical Profession: The "Accepted Practice" Formula, 28 Vand. L. Rev. 1213 (1975).

2. The criterion of the "average reasonable physician" is usually accompanied by a requirement that the action (or inaction) of the defendant practitioner be judged in a clinical medical setting similar to the conditions of practice of the defendant. The common wording in this regard is that the defendant be judged "under the same or similar circumstances." This requirement is taken to mean that the case is governed by the clinical resources available at the time. The defendant cannot be faulted for a failure to perform diagnostic tests or to apply treatment techniques with respect to facilities or equipment not reasonably available where and when the defendant is in practice. See 51 A.L.R. 4th 205 (1987). See also Hardy v. Brantley, 471 So. 2d 358 (Miss. 1985).

3. Does this same limitation to reasonably available clinical resources apply in cases of hospital negligence? Must all hospitals that are accredited (by national hospital groups) have available a certain level of technical facilities and equipment for various hospital functions? See cases and notes in the later sections of this chapter concerning corporate liability of hospitals and statutory requirements in many states for hospital-based risk management programs.

III. General Theories of Malpractice Liability

4. What are the legal duties of consulting specialists and laboratory-based physicians to the patient? Has a hospital pathologist a duty to transmit results of diagnostic tests directly to the patient, or only to the patient's attending physician (an oncologist)? See a detailed examination of prevailing standards of practice for consultants in community hospitals and large teaching institutions in Mahannah v. Hirsch, 237 Cal. Rptr. 140 (Cal. App. 1987).

5. The standard of care of physicians may also be affected by geographic availability of modern medical facilities for hospitalization, diagnostic technologies, and biomedical research opportunities. Under the common law, these geographic considerations should be taken into account as part of the "circumstances" of the particular case. However, quite early on in the American courts, a protective standard was applied to impose a much more sweeping significance to geographic location of a physician's practice. The so-called "locality rule" was established under which physicians could be judged *only* in regard to the prevailing clinical (or substantive) standards of physicians practicing in the same community or, in a relaxed version, in a "similar" community to that in which the defendant practiced at the time of the clinical event. This rule severely limited the opportunity of the plaintiff to obtain expert testimony favorable to the plaintiff's side in malpractice cases. In the past 20 years or so, the courts have moved away from this rule, particularly for specialists who are now nationally accredited by the American Medical Specialty Boards. The trend is also toward a national standard for accredited hospitals. See the leading case, Shilkret v. Annapolis Emergency Hosp., 349 A.2d 245 (Md. 1975). See also King & Coe, The Wisdom of the Strict Locality Rule, 3 U. Balt. L. Rev. 221 (1975); Nations & Surgent, Medical Malpractice and the Locality Rule, 14 S. Tex. L.J. 129 (1973). See also 99 A.L.R.3d 1133 (1980). More recently, see the review in Hansbrough v. Kasyak, 490 N.E.2d 181 (Ill. App. 1986).

The statutory reforms adopted in many jurisdictions in the middle and late 1970s and on into the 1980s reinstated the locality rule, or a state-wide version of geographic limitation, in several states where court decisions had moved to a national standard. The statutory changes have also usually included limitations on the competency of expert medical witnesses, requiring that the experts be practitioners licensed in the home state or, in others, in the home state or geographically contiguous states. For example, see Sutphin v. Platt, reprinted in Chapter 4, at 217.

Lundgren v. Eustermann
370 N.W.2d 877 (Minn. 1985)

SIMONETT, JUSTICE.
In this case we conclude that plaintiffs' expert, a licensed con-

sulting psychologist, is not qualified to give opinions in a medical malpractice action on the standard of care required of the defendant medical doctor. We reverse the contrary ruling of the court of appeals. . . .

To establish the foundation necessary to qualify a witness as an expert on whether a physician has exercised that degree of care required of a physician in administering Thorazine, the witness must have both the necessary schooling and training in the subject matter involved, plus practical or occupational experience with the subject. *Cornfeldt*, 262 N.W.2d at 692. Ordinarily, this foundation is best supplied if the expert witness is also a physician, especially a physician in the same area of practice, but this need not always be so. At least some courts have allowed a variety of cross-overs on medical expert testimony in malpractice actions if the proposed expert's knowledge and experience of the specialty or profession in question is apparent. See 1 D. Louisell & H. Williams, Medical Malpractice §11.30, p. 11-92, n.23. In any event, theoretical expertise is not enough. There must also be some practical knowledge or experience. Thus, in *Swanson* we refused to let an internist testify to the standard of care required of an orthopedist in the treatment of an arm fracture, not because the witness was an internist, but because the witness lacked experience and expertise in treating fractures. What is required, we said, is "a practical knowledge of what is usually and customarily done by physicians under circumstances similar to those which confronted the defendant." *Swanson*, 281 Minn. at 137-38, 160 N.W.2d at 668, quoting Pearce v. Linde, 113 Cal. App. 2d 627, 629, 248 P.2d 506, 508 (1952), quoting Sinz v. Owens, 33 Cal. 2d 749, 753, 205 P.2d 3, 5 (1949). In *Cornfeldt*, to give another example, we intimated that a nurse anesthetist might have been a competent expert witness on the standard of care for the defendant anesthesiologist "[i]f he [the nurse anesthetist] otherwise had sufficient scientific and practical experience." 262 N.W.2d at 697.

In this case the expert witness was not a physician but a psychologist. He has admirable qualifications as a psychologist, with extensive training and experience in the areas of psychology and pharmacology, including a doctorate in biopsychology. Dr. Rucker has also done consultant work for drug companies and has engaged in research and laboratory studies on the psychopharmacologic aspects of drug dependence. He has read books and journals, attended lectures, and trained graduate students, and he may well have the requisite scientific knowledge to testify about the nature of Thorazine, its dangers and uses. What the witness lacks, however, is practical experience or knowledge of what physicians do. He himself has never prescribed Thorazine for a patient. It is one thing to study Thorazine in the laboratory and to discuss it in the classroom, but it is quite

III. General Theories of Malpractice Liability   269

another thing to prescribe the drug for a patient under the circumstances of a family medical practice. Dr. Rucker does not know how physicians themselves customarily use Thorazine in treatment of their patients. In his response to defendant's interrogatories, Dr. Rucker concedes, "I have not worked with physicians in the Mankato area who have dealt with the question of when and under what circumstances to prescribe thorazine to their patients. I have received a small but continuing flow of information about prescription practices in Minnesota from students . . . , from other Licensed Consulting Psychologists in the state, and from people for whom such drugs have been prescribed."

Clearly, plaintiffs' expert does not have the practical knowledge and experience contemplated by the medical witness rule. We hold, as a matter of law, that Dr. Rucker was not competent to give an opinion on the standard of medical care required of Dr. Eustermann nor to give an opinion on whether Dr. Eustermann had departed from that standard, much less to characterize the degree of that departure. . . .

Reversed.

Thompson v. Carter
518 So. 2d 609 (Miss. 1987)

PRATHER, JUSTICE, for the Court:

At issue in this appeal are two evidence questions addressing the conditions under which (1) a "package insert" accompanying a pharmaceutical product may be introduced into evidence, and (2) the admissibility of a non-physician's expert testimony on the issue of a physician's standard of care with respect to the use and administration of pharmaceutical drugs.

In this medical malpractice action, Lynette Inez Thompson contended she developed Stevens Johnson Syndrome as a result of Dr. Robert Carter's negligent prescribing of the drug Bactrim. From a directed verdict in the Circuit Court of Harrison County, Thompson appeals, assigning as error:

1) The court erred in refusing to admit into evidence the package insert relative to the drug Bactrim.
2) The court erred in refusing to admit the testimony of Michael P. Hughes, a pharmacologist and toxicologist, on the issues of liability and causation.
3) The court erred in sustaining appellee's motion for a directed verdict.

This Court reverses. . . .

A. Was the Package Insert Inadmissible Hearsay?

Pursuant to congressional directives, the Food and Drug Administration (FDA) has developed a regulatory procedure to inform the medical profession about prescription drugs. 21 C.F.R. §1, 201; 50 Fed. Reg. 51108 (1985) The "package insert" distributed with the drug by the pharmaceutical manufacturer is the basis of this system of notification concerning composition, dosage, indications, contraindications, potential side effects, and adverse reactions of drugs. The package insert information is based upon data the manufacturer has submitted to the FDA as proof that the drug is safe and effective for the uses the manufacturer wishes to market the drug. Jennings, The RX Label Basis for all Prescribing Information, FDA Papers (Nov. 1967) 14-15. The insert advises the physician, based upon the manufacturer's testing results, of (1) the conditions under which the drug should be prescribed, (2) the disorders it is recommended to relieve, (3) the precautionary measures which should be observed, and (4) warning of adverse effects that may result. A compilation of these package inserts on drugs, referred to as the Physicians' Desk Reference, is annually distributed to the medical profession.

Under the common law scheme of hearsay exceptions, market quotations, tabulations, lists, directories and other published compilations generally used and relied upon by the public or by persons in particular occupations were excepted from the rule against hearsay. [Citations omitted.]

Applying this rule of evidence to the instant case, the Court notes the testimony of Dr. Robert Carter, the defendant, identifying the package insert accompanying a pharmaceutical drug as "one source of reference" and "one source of information." He relied upon this package insert for information of adverse affects, or contraindications, of the drug Bactrim.

Further, Dr. Carter identified the Physicians' Desk Reference as "a good reference with some authority" and that it represented the standard of care "in the local area" of Biloxi with respect to the administration of the drug Bactrim at the time Lynette Thompson was treated by him. Carter used and relied upon the information contained in the Bactrim package insert in his practice and particularly for the treatment of Lynette Thompson. Although Dr. Carter testified that other medical publications and information were used and relied upon by him in his practice, that testimony does not diminish the admissibility of the package insert after identification by Dr. Carter of its acceptance by him as one source of information and by the medical profession in the Biloxi area as a standard of care in the administration of drugs.

The package insert is a compilation of information concerning pharmaceutical drugs and is generally relied upon by the public as well as physicians prescribing the drug. Therefore, we hold that the package insert, properly identified, was admissible by virtue of the above described exception to the hearsay rule.

B. For What Purposes May the Package Insert Be Admitted into Evidence?

Other jurisdictions have allowed package inserts into evidence to serve a variety of purposes. See, Dixon, Drug Product Liability, §7.02 (1986). One of the strongest cases to date in favor of allowing package inserts into evidence was Ohligschlager v. Proctor Community Hospital, 55 Ill. 2d 411, 303 N.E.2d 392 (1973), in which the court allowed the manufacturer's instructions regarding the use of a drug to establish the professional standards ordinarily established by expert testimony.

It is suggested by some writers in this field of pharmaceutical drugs[2] that caution should be exercised by courts in accepting the manufacturer's test results as conclusive. Notwithstanding the government regulations in this field, the package insert is a marketing or merchandising procedure to promote sales. Drug manufacturers have had to answer for alleged dilution of warnings by over-promotion in sales programs. Magee v. Wyeth Laboratories, Inc., 214 Cal. App. 2d 340, 29 Cal. Rptr. 322 (1963); Love v. Wolf, 226 Cal. App. 2d 378, 38 Cal. Rptr. 183 (1964); Sanzari v. Rosenfeld, 34 N.J. 128, 167 A.2d 625 (1961).

Likewise, independent researchers have reached contradictory results to drug manufacturers and have recommended different dosages. Updated information gained from a broader base usage of a drug is not always reflected in the original insert until a new distribution of the drug or new publications of the Physicians' Desk Reference. Text writers suggest that antibiotic drugs[3] represent an exception to set dosages. This rationale is explained by the assertion that as bacteria become more resistant to drugs, the dosage may be increased. A doctor's experiences offers a basis for varying dosages.

With these considerations in view, this Court is persuaded by the reasoning of the Idaho Supreme Court in Julien v. Barker, 75 Idaho 413, 272 P.2d 718 (1954). In Julien v. Barker the Court held:

> [The package insert] is not conclusive evidence of standard or accepted practice in the use of the drug by physicians and surgeons, nor that a

---

2. Marden G. Dixon and Frank C. Woodside, Drug Product Liability, Vol. 1: The Physicians Responsibility and Liability. (New York: Matthew Bender & Company, 1987), pp. 7-6, 7-7.

3. Ibid pp. 7-12.

departure from such directions is negligent. But it is prima facie proof of a proper method of use, given by the maker, which must be presumed qualified to give directions for its use and warnings of any danger inherent therein.

Id. 272 P.2d at 724.

This Court agrees that the package insert in the instant case should not be taken as conclusive evidence of the physician's standard of care, nor should a departure from the directions contained in the package insert be considered to establish a prima facie case of negligence. However, this Court holds the package insert contains prima facie proof of the proper method of use of Bactrim and, for those purposes, was admissible at trial. See, Nolan v. Dillon, 261 Md. 516, 276 A.2d 36, 49 (1971); Salgo v. Leland Stanford Jr. University Board of Trustees, 154 Cal. App. 2d 560, 317 P.2d 170, 180 (1957). The package insert can be given weight as authoritative published compilation by a pharmaceutical manufacturer. It is some evidence of the standard of care, but it is not conclusive evidence. The prescribing physician can be permitted to rebut this implication and explain its deviation from the manufacturer's recommended use on dosage. The holding will shift the burden of persuasion to the physician to provide a sound reason for his deviating from the directions for its use, and will require corroborative evidence to determine whether the physician met or violated the appropriate standard.

IV. Did the Court Err by Excluding the Testimony of Michael P. Hughes?

At trial, appellant offered Michael P. Hughes as an expert witness in the fields of Pharmacology and Toxicology. Mr. Hughes testified that he had received a bachelor's degree from Millsaps College with major in chemistry and minor in biology and a master's degree in both Pharmacology and Toxicology. In the process of obtaining his degrees, he had taken five or six courses in Pharmacology and between eight and ten courses in Toxicology. After completing his graduate degree programs, Mr. Hughes became coordinator of the Regional Poison Control Center for the entire State of Mississippi. As coordinator for the Poison Control Center, which is located at the University of Mississippi Medical Center, Mr. Hughes was often consulted by physicians for suggested treatment of poisoning victims and other types of adverse reactions to various compounds or drugs. Mr. Hughes further testified he was on the teaching staff at the University of Mississippi Medical School and taught Pharmacology and Toxicology to both dental and medical students. Additionally Hughes had taken training to render emergency medical care as an "emergency medical technician."

III. General Theories of Malpractice Liability

Mr. Hughes testified that by virtue of his education and work experience, he was familiar with the drug Bactrim and its indications as well as its contra-indications. Likewise, he was familiar with Stevens Johnson Syndrome and its causes.

The trial court found that Hughes was qualified to testify as an expert witness as to causation in the field of Pharmacology and Toxicology, but was not qualified to testify concerning the standard of care to which physicians are required to conform with respect to the use and administration of drugs.

Pharmacology is defined as "The science that deals with drugs, their sources, appearance, chemistry, actions, and uses." Steadman's Medical Dictionary, p.952 (3rd ed. 1972). Toxicology is "a science that deals with poisons and their effect on living organisms, with substances otherwise harmless that prove toxic under particular conditions, and with the clinical, industrial, legal or other problems involved." Webster's Third New International Dictionary, p.2419 (1961).

Appellant had no other expert witness to testify concerning causation or standard of care with respect to use and administration of drugs. A proffer of Mr. Hughes' testimony was offered which, if admitted, would have made a prima facie case. After the proffer, the trial court granted Carter's motion for directed verdict on the grounds that Thompson failed to establish the standard of care by an expert possessing a medical degree.

A. Was Hughes Qualified to Testify Concerning Causation?

In Sonford Products Corp. v. Freels, 495 So. 2d 468 (Miss. 1986), this Court reversed a circuit judge's order which disallowed a toxicologist from testifying as an expert witness in a workmen's compensation proceeding. Because he was not a medical doctor or a licensed physician, the toxicologist was not allowed to testify concerning the "medical causation" between the decedent's employment and his fatal condition.

The key to the *Sonford* decision was the Court's recognition that " 'medical causation' is no more than causation in fact." Id. at 472. The Court held further:

> It is this Court's opinion that Dr. Verlangieri is qualified to give an opinion regarding such "cause in fact" and should not be disqualified from testifying because his degree is a Ph.D. instead of an M.D. The Commission's inquiry should be whether the witness is in fact qualified — by knowledge, skill, experience, training or education — not by what degree he holds. It is certain and probable that Ph.D. biochemists and

toxicologists are at least equally competent to testify as to the cause and effect of chemicals in our environment as medical doctors.

495 So. 2d at 473, see also, Mississippi Farm Bureau Mutual Ins. Co. v. Garrett, 487 So. 2d 1320, 1325-27 (Miss. 1986).

The *Sonford* rationale concerning causation would apply equally to the present case. A pharmacologist/toxicologist would be at least equally competent to testify concerning what effect a certain drug would have on the human body.

B. Was Hughes Qualified to Testify Concerning Medical Standard of Care?

The issue under this question is whether an expert witness, called to establish the standard of care in pharmaceutical litigation for physicians, must possess a medical degree. This Court holds that he does not. What is necessary is that the witness possess medical knowledge, however obtained.

Generally, if scientific, technical, or other specialized knowledge will assist the trier of fact to understand the evidence or to determine a fact in issue, an expert witness may testify thereto in opinion form or otherwise. [Citations omitted.]

A witness may qualify as an expert based on his knowledge, skill, experience, training, education, or a combination thereof. Qualification as an expert does not necessarily rest upon the educational or professional degree a witness possesses. *Sonford*, 495 So. 2d at 473. Hall v. Hilbun, 466 So. 2d at 873. See also, Rule 702, Mississippi Rules of Evidence, effective January 1, 1986. Simply put, before one may testify as an expert, that person must be shown to know a great deal regarding the subject of his testimony. As a pharmacologist/toxicologist, Hughes was an expert in the area in which his testimony was offered. Mississippi Farm Bureau Mut. Ins. Co. v. Garrett, 487 So. 2d 1320 (Miss. 1986).

Other jurisdictions have held likewise. In Cornfeldt v. Tongen, 262 N.W.2d 684 (Minn. 1977) a chief nurse anesthetist was not allowed to provide expert testimony relative to the use of anesthesia because he was not licensed to practice medicine. The Minnesota Supreme Court held the nurse was competent to testify notwithstanding the lack of a medical degree if he otherwise had sufficient scientific and practical experience about the matter to which he would have testified. Id. at 697. . . . See also, Smith v. St. Therese Hospital, 106 Ill. App. 3d 268, 62 Ill. Dec. 141, 435 N.E.2d 939 (1982); Mellies v. National Heritage, Inc., 6 Kan. App. 2d 910, 636 P.2d 215 (1981).

The instant record reflects that Michael P. Hughes, who taught medical students and advised and counseled physicians as to drug use

III. General Theories of Malpractice Liability

and administration, through his skill, knowledge, training, and education, knew the standard of care to which physicians adhered when prescribing Bactrim. Therefore, this Court holds that he was qualified to deliver expert testimony, notwithstanding his lack of a medical degree, on the issue of a physician's standard of care in the use and administration of this drug.

This is not to say that every pharmacologist or toxicologist is qualified to testify as an expert to establish the physicians' standard of care. Only if the witness possesses scientific, technical or specialized knowledge on a particular topic will he qualify as an expert on that topic. This witness qualified as an expert and should have been permitted to testify as to a physician's standard of care in issue here.

V

The proffer of Hughes' testimony suggested that Hughes, had he been permitted to testify, would have opined a departure from the standard of care in the use and administration of drugs in the following respects:

> [That] the Defendant departed from the standard of care as established by recognized pharmacological literature in prescribing Bactrim to the Plaintiff; . . . that the Defendant violated the standard of care because Bactrim was not the drug of choice to treat acute pyelonephritis and in fact that said drug was contraindicated; . . . that after prescribing Bactrim though contraindicated, the Defendant should have conducted various urine tests to determine whether there were crystals of the sulfur developing in her urine, whether her kidneys were properly functioning and the level of protein and sugar in the urine; . . . that the administration of Bactrim and the failure of the Defendant to properly monitor Plaintiff's condition after the administration of same were approximately contributing causes of the onset of the Stevens-Johnson syndrome. . . .

Because Ms. Thompson was unable to produce an expert witness with a medical degree to establish the standard of care for physicians prescribing Bactrim, the trial judge directed a verdict in favor of Dr. Carter. This Court has now determined that the trial judge should have admitted the package insert into evidence and should have admitted the expert testimony of Hughes. Had this additional evidence been admitted in the complainant's proof, a prima facie case would have been met sufficient to have withstood a motion for directed verdict.

For failure to admit the package insert, properly identified, and the exclusion of the expert testimony of Hughes, the case must be remanded for a new trial. Hardy v. Brantley, 471 So. 2d 358, 373-

74 (Miss. 1985); Hall v. Hilbun, 466 So. 2d 856, 880 (Miss. 1985). Reversed and Remanded for a New Trial.

WALKER, C.J., ROY NOBLE LEE and DAN M. LEE, P.JJ., and GRIFFIN, J., dissent.

DAN M. LEE, PRESIDING JUSTICE, dissenting: [Dissent omitted.]

NOTES

Evidentiary Issues in Proving Standards of Patient Care (or the Breach of Standards) for Physicians

1. The American courts are split on the issue of the competency of nonphysicians to testify on the standards of patient care required of medical practitioners. The *Lundgren* case expresses the more restrictive viewpoint. The Alabama Supreme Court followed the *Lundgren* reasoning in denying admissibility of expert opinions from two other allied medical specialists, one a pharmacist, the other a toxicologist. See Bell v. Hart, 516 So. 2d 562 (Ala. 1987).

2. The *Thompson* case illustrates the more liberal rule allowing expert opinion testimony from a broad range of nonphysicians when there is convincing evidence of knowledge and/or experience concerning the particular medical practice standards involved before the court. This approach is in keeping with the general law of expert opinion testimony in the federal courts, and also in most states following similar rules of admissibility. See Carlson, Policing the Basis of Modern Expert Testimony, 39 Vand. L. Rev. 577 (1986). See also Oleinick, Expert Witnesses Under Rule 702: Circuit Court Attitudes Towards Qualifications of Experts During the Period 1971-1972, 8 Envtl. L. 753 (1978). In accord, see Pratt v. Stein, 444 A.2d 674 (Pa. Super. 1982).

3. Counsel on both sides in medical malpractice litigation utilize published professional standards and guidelines to prove the "accepted practice" in a particular clinical situation. In previous years, most of the offered publications were textbooks written by "recognized authorities" in the particular field. Most of the appellate court reviews involved attempts by plaintiffs' attorneys to put these textbooks into evidence in lieu of, or supplementary to, the testimony of expert witnesses called to provide opinion evidence on the standard of care and its violation by the defendant physician. See, for example, Jones v. Bloom, 200 N.W.2d 196 (Mich. 1972); Gridley v. Johnson, 476 S.W.2d 475 (Mo. 1972). See also Student Note, Admissibility of Medical Treatises in Iowa: Expert Witnesses in Hardback Covers, 56 Iowa L. Rev. 1028 (1971). The most common use of treatises and articles from medical journals on standards of patient care has, however, been in cross-examining experts who have already given direct

testimony on the applicable standard. Most commonly, the courts require that such witnesses accept the textbook or periodical article (or its authors) as "authoritative" before they may be cross-questioned on matters contained in the publications. See Fed. R. Evid., Rule 803 (18); Rule 902 (6). See also Bivens v. Detroit Osteopathic Hosp., 258 N.W.2d 527 (Mich. App. 1977); Ciaccio v. Housemann, 411 N.Y.S.2d 524 (Sup. Ct. 1978).

4. In more recent years, parties have sought to utilize and to admit into evidence officially adopted standards and guidelines as much more authentic and reliable evidence of widely known and accepted criteria of "accepted practice" in the particular field. The famous *Darling* case in Illinois (reprinted at 321 of this chapter) led the way in this trend by its reliance on the published standards of the Joint Commission on Accreditation of Hospitals (now the Joint Commission on the Accreditation of Healthcare Institutions).

Since that time, courts have utilized these standards and several other sets of professional and organizational guidelines to support efforts to prove relevant standards of patient care. See Fed. R. Evid., Rule 703.

Another type of guideline for clinical practice is provided by the requirements of the Federal Food and Drug Administration concerning advice to physicians on the proper use of prescription drugs. These requirements apply to the so-called "package inserts" prepared by pharmaceutical companies and distributed as a part of the packaging of their proprietary drug products. The system is well described in the *Thompson* case above. As indicated in the opinion, the information included in the package inserts is gathered, along with other information and pictures of the tablets or other drug products, in a periodical handbook, The Physicians' Desk Reference, published annually by Edward R. Barnhart, Medical Economics Co., Inc., Oradell, NJ. The 1990 annual is the 44th edition of the periodical. As the witness, Dr. Carter, testified in *Thompson,* the PDR provides "one source" of the accepted standards of drug prescribing. The classic case admitting the package insert as evidence of the relevant standard of care in prescribing that particular drug was Salgo v. Leland Stanford University, 317 P.2d 170, (Cal. App. 1957). See also Stafford v. Nipp, 502 So. 2d 702 (Ala. 1987). One jurisdiction has held the package insert not only admissible, but *"essential* in determining the possible lack of care of a doctor where the issue involved is injury from the administration of a drug" (emphasis supplied). Mueller v. Mueller, 221 N.W.2d 39, 43 (S.D. 1974).

5. A recent federal appeals court decision seems to have gone somewhat further in ruling that the package insert and the PDR concerning the drug Tobramycin (Eli Lilly and Co.) was, if accompanying expert testimony, to be accorded as "relevant and probative

evidence of the medical standard of care for selecting, administering and monitoring the drug." Furthermore, these documents were admissible as prima facie evidence of the standard of care and of personal notice by the physicians of the content of the standard set forth in the documents. See Garvey v. O'Donoghue, 530 A.2d 1141, 1146 (D.D. App. 1987).

The Supreme Court of Utah recently rejected a requested instruction that the "package insert" was *prima facie* evidence of the applicable standard of care, holding that the package guidelines of Marcaine (and the PDR provisions) were "some evidence that the finder of fact could consider along with expert testimony on the standard of care." However, the court noted that the manufacturer's package insert had not recommended against the particular use involved in the case but had expressly reserved making a recommendation pending further results of clinical research. See Ramon v. Farr, 770 P.2d 131, 136 (Utah 1989).

McKellips v. St. Francis Hospital
741 P.2d 467 (Okla. 1987)

HODGES, JUSTICE.

On June 3, 1986, the United States Court of Appeals for the Tenth Circuit certified the following two questions of law to this Court pursuant to the Uniform Certification of Questions of Law Act, 20 O.S. 1981 §1602:

> I. In a medical malpractice action under Oklahoma law, absent evidence that the patient more likely than not would have survived with proper treatment, may a plaintiff establish causation under the loss of chance doctrine by presenting evidence that the alleged negligence lessened the chance of survival?
>
> II. If the loss of chance doctrine is recognized in Oklahoma, is expert testimony that "unquestionably [the deceased's] chances would have been significantly improved" sufficient under that doctrine to create a question for the jury, notwithstanding the expert cannot quantify the increased chance of survival?

A review of the decisional law which sets forth the traditional causation standard to be applied in ordinary negligence actions in Oklahoma, as well as decisions from other jurisdictions which reevaluate the use of that standard in reference to a medical malpractice claim where a defendant has negligently breached an undertaking to prevent a certain harm, and adopt the loss of chance doctrine in those limited situations, persuade this Court to answer both questions in the affirmative. . . .

III. General Theories of Malpractice Liability

An evolving trend has developed to relax the standard for sufficiency of proof of causation ordinarily required of a plaintiff to provide a basis upon which the jury may consider causation in the "lost chance of survival" cases. . . .

We think in those situations where a health care provider deprives a patient of a significant chance for recovery by negligently failing to provide medical treatment, the health care professional should not be allowed to come in after the fact and allege that the result was inevitable inasmuch as that person put the patient's chance beyond the possibility of realization. Health care providers should not be given the benefit of the uncertainty created by their own negligent conduct. To hold otherwise would in effect allow care providers to evade liability for their negligent actions or inactions in situations in which patients would not necessarily have survived or recovered, but still would have a significant chance of survival or recovery.

Today's pronouncement adopts the loss of a chance doctrine in Oklahoma in a limited type of medical malpractice case where the duty breached was one imposed to prevent the type of harm which a patient ultimately sustains and because of the inherent nature of such a case a plaintiff is unable to produce evidence of causation sufficient to meet the traditional rule of causation. We note that our decision today does not change the traditional principles of causation in the ordinary negligence case and this new rule applies only in those limited situations as presented here. . . .

II

With regard to the second certified question concerning whether expert testimony must be expressed in terms of percentage probabilities under the loss of a chance approach adopted herein to allow the causation issue to go to the jury, we hold percentage probability testimony is not required. In the instant case testimony that "unquestionably [the deceased's] chances would have been significantly improved" is sufficient to take the case to the jury even in the absence of testimony which quantifies the increased chance of survival. We find it unnecessary to require a precise percentage increment of chance of recovery or survival to create a jury question on causation.

However, statistical evidence combined with evidence linking the probabilities to the patient in the case should be considered by the jury in apportioning damages. We believe it is better to limit probabilistic proof to the damage issue. Once the issue of causation goes to the jury upon proof of the defendant's conduct increased the risk of harm or death by substantially decreasing the chance of recovery or survival, it is the jury's task, not the medical expert's, to determine whether the defendant's negligence was a cause in fact of the patient's injury. *Thompson,* 688 P.2d at 614-16. It is within the jury's province to make the determination whether a health care provider's failure to use reasonable care increased the risk of the harm he undertook to prevent by substantially decreasing the chance of recovery or survival, and upon such finding of fact the jury may determine that the tortious act of malpractice was in turn a substantial factor in causing a patient's injury or death.

III

It is necessary in answering the certified questions posed for us to address apportionment of damages. We note that in medical malpractice cases where application of the loss of chance doctrine is appropriate, damages must be limited to only those proximately caused from a defendant's breach of duty. Otherwise, the traditional principles of causation would be distorted. We specifically point to the language of the Supreme Court of Washington in Herskovits v. Group Health Co-op., 664 P.2d at 479:

> Causing reduction of the opportunity to recover (loss of chance) by one's negligence, however, does not necessitate a total recovery against the negligent party for all damages caused by the victim's death. Damages should be awarded to the injured party or his family based only on damages caused directly by premature death, such as lost earnings and additional medical expenses, etc.

The above discussion of damages does not however offer a clear method as to how the damage award should be adjusted. We do not believe a court should rely solely on a jury's common sense to discount the damage award to reflect the uncertainty of causation. One commentator has suggested a meaningful method of valuing damages in the loss of chance cases which we find instructive. J. King, Causation, Valuation, and Chance in Personal Injury Torts Involving Preexisting Conditions and Future Consequences, 90 Yale L.J. 1353 (1981). This method is advantageous as it is simple to apply and accomplishes a more predictable result. Under this method statistical evidence with regard to the decedent's reduction of his chance to recover or survive is utilized to determine the amount of damages recoverable. Although we found in Part II above that statistical evidence is not necessary to create a causation issue for the jury, statistical data relating to the extent of the decedent's chance of survival is necessary in determining the amount of damages recoverable after liability is shown. Statistical evidence, however, merely provides a base estimate and is not in itself sufficient to make the damage determination. Facts relevant to the particular patient should also be weighed in determining the net reduced figure used to represent the patient's loss of survival chance attributable to the defendant's negligence.

The amount of damages recoverable is equal to the percent of chance lost multiplied by the total amount of damages which are ordinarily allowed in a wrongful death action. After consideration of the statistical evidence of the original and diminished chance of survival presented by both sides as well as other factors which are peculiar to the individual decedent, the jury should select from the figures presented or choose appropriate figures to find the percentage of original chance of survival in absence of negligence and the percentage of diminished chance resulting from the defendant's negligence in order to determine the net reduced figure. The percentages and net reduced figure should be found and added by the jury through a general verdict. Okla. Const. art. 7, §15; 12 O.S. 1981 §588; Smith v. Gizzi, 564 P.2d 1009 (Okla. 1977). The trial court should then multiply the total amount of damages by the net reduced figure to determine the final damage award.

To illustrate the method in a case where the jury determines from the statistical findings combined with the specific facts relevant to the patient the patient originally had a 40% chance of cure and the physician's negligence reduced the chance of cure to 25%, (40% − 25%) 15% represents the patient's loss of survival. If the total amount of damages proved by the evidence is $500,000, the damages caused by defendant is 15% × $500,000 or $75,000.

We believe this method of valuation constitutes the proper view for determining damages in a medical malpractice action where the loss of chance doctrine is applied.

Accordingly, we find if defendants in the present case are found liable the award of damages must be reduced to reflect the probability that defendants caused the death, and recovery is permitted only for the percent of chance lost times the total amount of damages which are ordinarily allowed. This approach provides a fair method of apportioning the damages to account for the decedent's pre-existing condition. An award of *all* damages for the underlying injury, i.e., death, is precluded.

Conclusion

In summary, we hold in medical malpractice cases involving the loss of a less than even chance of recovery or survival where the plaintiff shows that the defendant's conduct caused a substantial reduction of the patient's chance of recovery or survival, irrespective of statistical evidence, the question of proximate cause is for the jury. We further hold if a jury determines the defendant's negligence is the proximate cause of the patient's injury, the defendant is liable for only those damages proximately caused by his negligence which aggravated a pre-existing condition. Consequently, a total recovery for all damages attributable to death are not allowed and damages should be limited in accordance with the prescribed method of valuation.

Questions answered.

DOOLIN, C.J., and LAVENDER, OPALA, ALMA WILSON and KAUGER, JJ., concur.

SUMMERS, J., concurs in result.

HARGRAVE, V.C.J., and SIMMS, J., dissent.

NOTES

Liability for "Loss of Chance of Survival" in Medical Malpractice Cases

1. The *McKellips* opinion provides useful instruction on issues of damages calculation. Most of the judicial argument on "loss of chance of survival" has related to clinical situations where the expert opinion on prognosis supports a chance of survival of less than 50 percent. The current trend supports liability in these situations, although on a discounted basis for a percentage of the total future loss. Does such a ruling violate the general requirement that future damages must be more probable than not? See, for example, Werner v. Hetrick, A.2d 643 (Md. 1987).

Some cases involving evidence of a failure to diagnose or other negligence resulting in lost chance of survival have actually reduced the burden of proving causation to a level of "substantial possibility." The classic case in this group is Hicks v. U.S., 368 F.2d 626 (4th Cir. 1966). Later commentators have quarrelled with the broad interpretation of the *Hicks* doctrine, pointing out that the expert opinion before the court supported a firm prognosis of survival. See Wolfstone and Wolfstone, Recovery of Damages for the Loss of a Chance, 28 Med. Trial Tech. Q. 121 (1982); King, Causation, Valuation, and Chance in Personal Injury Torts Involving Preexisting Conditions and Future Consequences, 90 Yale L.J. 1353 (1981). See also 54 A.L.R. 4th 10 (1987). For a plaintiffs' trial attorney's experiences in cases involving lost-chance of survival, see R. Shandell, The Preparation and Trial of Medical Malpractice Cases §10.02 (1981 and supplements).

2. Most, but not all, of the "loss of chance of survival" cases involve a failure to diagnose cancer promptly when a thorough examination would have revealed the condition. Current policies in hospitals and health maintenance organizations to reduce costs of medical care may militate against early diagnosis of many conditions

when the potential "yield" of the tests in positive findings of disease are low compared to the unit cost of the diagnostic testing. If policy decisions in cost containment render some "missed diagnoses" as statistically inevitable, should the health care provider be liable under the "lost chance" doctrine? See Student Note, Increased Risk of Harm: A New Standard for Sufficiency of Evidence of Causation in Medical Malpractice Cases, 65 B.U.L. Rev. 275 (1985). See also Calabresi, The Problem of Malpractice — Trying to Round Out the Circle, in The Economics of Medical Malpractice (C. Rosenthal ed. 1978). Policy issues concerning cost containment in health care are dealt with in other chapters of this text. See particularly Chapter 8. On health maintenance organizations, see Chapter 8.III.B. On the implications of cost-containment on malpractice liability, see Chapter 8.II.B.

3. No court has as yet upheld a lost-chance of survival ruling in a case involving negligent failure to diagnose AIDS. Does the doctrine apply to this new disease entity? See Herman, AIDS: Malpractice and Transmission Liability, 58 U. Colo. L. Rev. 63 (1986/1987).

Anderson v. Somberg
338 A.2d 1 (N.J. 1975)

PASHMAN, JUSTICE.

These negligence-products liability actions had their inception in a surgery performed in 1967 on the premises of defendant St. James Hospital (Hospital). Plaintiff was undergoing a laminectomy, a back operation, performed by defendant Dr. Somberg. During the course of the procedure, the tip or cup of an angulated pituitary rongeur, a forceps-like instrument, broke off while the tool was being manipulated in plaintiff's spinal canal. The surgeon attempted to retrieve the metal but was unable to do so. After repeated failure in that attempt, he terminated the operation. The imbedded fragment caused medical complications and further surgical interventions were required. Plaintiff has suffered significant and permanent physical injury proximately caused by the rongeur fragment which lodged in his spine.

Plaintiff sued: (1) Dr. Somberg for medical malpractice, alleging that the doctor's negligent action caused the rongeur to break; (2) St. James Hospital, alleging that it negligently furnished Dr. Somberg with a defective surgical instrument; (3) Reinhold-Schumann, Inc. (Reinhold), the medical supply distributor which furnished the defective rongeur to the hospital, on a warranty theory and (4) Lawton Instrument Company (Lawton), the manufacturer of the rongeur, on a strict liability in tort claim, alleging that the rongeur was a defective product. In short, plaintiff sued all who might have been liable for his injury, absent some alternative explanation such as contributory negligence.

Dr. Somberg testified that he had not examined the rongeur prior to the day of surgery. He inspected it visually when the nurse handed it to him during the operation, and manipulated its handles to make certain it was functional. The doctor stated that he did not twist the instrument and claimed that the manner in which the instrument was inserted in plaintiff's body precluded the possibility of twisting. He noted the absence of one of the rongeur's cups when he withdrew the instrument from plaintiff's spinal canal, but his efforts to retrieve the fragment proved of no avail.

Dr. Graubard, a general surgeon, testified as an expert witness for plaintiff. He stated that the rongeur was a delicate instrument, a tool not to be "used incorrectly or with excessive force or to be used against hard substances." He claimed that a twisting of the instrument might cause it to break at the cups. Dr. Graubard stated that a "rongeur used properly and not defective would not break."

The deposition of the operating room supervisor of defendant hospital, Sister Carmen Joseph, was read into the record. She was responsible for visually examining and sterilizing all instruments prior to surgery. The rongeur in question was used about five times a year, and had been used about 20 times before this operation. She did not know who had taken out the rongeur for this operation; she had not worked the day of plaintiff's operation.

The hospital's purchasing agent testified that the rongeur had been purchased from the distributor, Reinhold, about four years prior to plaintiff's surgery and was received in a box bearing the name of the manufacturer, Lawton. The owner of Reinhold testified that the rongeur was not a stock item and had to be specially ordered from Lawton upon receipt of the hospital purchase order. The box was opened at Reinhold's warehouse, to verify that it was a rongeur and it was then forwarded to the hospital.

Defendant Lawton called a metallurgist, a Mr. John Carroll, as an expert witness. He testified that an examination of the broken rongeur revealed neither structural defect nor faulty workmanship. He said that the examination (conducted at an optical magnification 500 times normal size) revealed a secondary crack near the main crack but he could not suggest how or when that crack formed. Mr. Carroll offered an opinion as to the cause of the instrument's breaking: the instrument had been strained, he said, probably because of an improper "twisting" of the tool. The strain, however, could have been cumulative, over the course of several operations, and the instrument could conceivably have been cracked when handed to Dr. Somberg and broken in its normal use.

In short, when all the evidence had been presented, no theory for the cause of the rongeur's breaking was within reasonable contemplation save for the possible negligence of Dr. Somberg in using the instrument, or the possibility that the surgeon had been given a defective instrument, which defect would be attributable to a dereliction of duty by the manufacturer, the distributor, the hospital or all of them. . . .

In the ordinary case, the law will not assist an innocent plaintiff at the expense of an innocent defendant. However, in the type of case we consider here, where an unconscious or helpless patient suffers an admitted mishap not reasonably foreseeable and unrelated to the scope of the surgery (such as cases where foreign objects are left in the body of the patient), those who had custody of the patient, and who owed him a duty of care as to medical treatment, or not to furnish a defective instrument for use in such treatment can be called to account for their default. They must prove their nonculpability, or else risk liability for the injuries suffered.

This case resembles the ordinary medical malpractice foreign-objects case, where the patient is sewn up with a surgical tool or sponge inside him. In those cases, res ipsa loquitur is used to make out a prima facie case. Martin v. Perth Amboy General Hospital, 104 N.J. Super. 335, 342, 250 A.2d 40 (App. Div. 1969); Gouid v. Winokur, 98 N.J. Super. 554, 237 A.2d 916 (Law Div. 1968), aff'd 104 N.J. Super. 329, 250 A.2d 38 (App. Div. 1969), certif. den. 53 N.J. 582, 252 A.2d 157 (1969); Annotation, "Malpractice — Res Ipsa Loquitur," 82 A.L.R.2d 1262; Annotation, "Malpractice — Foreign Object Left In Patient," 10 A.L.R.3d 9; cf. Williams v. Chamberlain, 316 S.W.2d 505 (Mo. 1958) (breaking of hypodermic needle did not make out prima facie case). . . .

The imposition of the burden of proof upon multiple defendants, even though only one could have caused the injury, is no novelty to the law, as where all defendants have been clearly negligent. Summers v. Tice, 33 Cal. 2d 80, 199 P.2d 1 (1948). As against multiple defendants where there is no evidence as to where culpability lies, the rule is not generally available, according to Prosser, because it might impose an equal hardship on an innocent defendant as on an innocent plaintiff. Prosser notes exceptional special cases, as where defendant owes a special responsibility to plaintiff, and in those instances the burden of proof can in fact be shifted to defendants. Prosser, Torts (4 ed. 1973), pp. 243-244, 231, 223. The facts of this case disclose just such a special responsibility, and require a shifting of the burden of proof to defendants.

We hold that in a situation like this, the burden of proof in fact does shift to defendants. All those in custody of that patient or who owed him a duty, as here, the manufacturer and the distributor, should be called forward and should be made to prove their freedom from liability. The rule would have no application except in those instances where the injury lay outside the ambit of the surgical procedure in question; for example, an injury to an organ, when that organ was itself the object of medical attention, would not by itself make out a prima facie case for malpractice or shift the burden of proof to defendants. Farber v. Olkon, 40 Cal. 2d 503, 254 P.2d 520, 524 (1953).

Further, we note that at the close of all the evidence, no reasonable suggestion had been offered that the occurrence could have arisen because of plaintiff's contributory negligence, or some act of nature; that is, there was no explanation for the occurrence in the case save for negligence or defect on the part of someone connected with the manufacture, handling, or use of the instrument. (Any such proof would be acceptable to negative plaintiff's prima facie case.) Since all parties had been joined who could reasonably have been connected with that negligence or defect, it was clear that one of those parties was liable, and at least one could not succeed in his proofs.

In cases of this type, no defendant will be entitled to prevail on a motion for judgment until all the proofs have been presented to the court and jury. The judge may grant any motion bearing in mind that the plaintiff must recover a verdict against at least one defendant. Inferences and doubts at this stage are resolved in favor of the plaintiff. If only one defendant remains by reason of the court's action, then, in fact, the judge is directing a verdict of liability against that defendant.

The holding of the Court in this matter will, according to the dissenters, remove from the judicial process "any semblance of rationality" and reduce it to "trial by lot, or by chance." The objections which they raise, however, hardly justify this resplendently apocalyptic rhetoric.

The dissenters are concerned with the possibility that there will be cases in which a foreign object is left in the body of the plaintiff after surgery — a fact which bespeaks tortious conduct on the part of somebody — and all persons who might reasonably have been liable for the injury are before the court, but none of the parties, in fact, acted tortiously. They express dismay that in such cases, which they anticipate will be "many," juries will be obliged to act contrary to their oaths and that liability will be imposed on wholly innocent parties.

Once stated in simple language, free of the epithets with which the dissenters have clothed it, the objection largely evaporates. Almost by definition, one or more of the defendants are liable. Identifying the responsible party is merely a matter of elimination. To instruct the jury that it must return a verdict against one or more of the defendants is simply requiring it to determine upon the evidence

III. General Theories of Malpractice Liability

which defendants, if any, have exculpated themselves. For the jury under these circumstances to conclude that no defendant is liable would be a contradiction in logic. Certainly this procedure neither compels jurors to violate their oaths nor leads to random and haphazard imposition of liability as alleged by the dissent.

The dissenters also accuse the Court of deliberately and perversely ignoring the fact — known, they assert, by everyone associated with the case — that not all conceivable defendants are before the trial court. The accusation is, of course, true. Anyone with a moderately fertile imagination could conceive of other persons whose conduct might have caused the injury. Indeed, as the dissenters are at pains to note, two witnesses did speculate that another doctor might have damaged the rongeur within the preceding four years, and, while none of the witnesses or parties have thus far suggested the possibility, the Court on its motion might note that it is also conceivable that some unknown enemy of Mr. Anderson might have slipped into the hospital prior to the operation and deliberately damaged the instrument or that some unknown disgruntled employee of Rheinhold-Schumann or Lawton Instrument might have done so.

Nevertheless, the fact remains that involvement by any person other than the defendants actually before the court below has never been asserted as anything other than pure and undisguised speculation. None of the defendants introduced any evidence to actually support the claim of responsibility by other persons; they made no effort to join additional parties.[5] It would be exceedingly unjust to deny plaintiff compensation simply because an imaginative defendant can conceive of other possible parties. On the record presently before the Court, the contention of the dissent, that the Court is "visiting liability . . . upon parties who are more probably than not totally free of blame," is, at best, an exercise in judicial hyperbole.

A wholly faultless plaintiff should not fail in his cause of action by reason of defendants who have it within their power to prove nonculpability but do not do so. See Broder, "Res Ipsa Loquitur in Medical Mal-Practice Cases," 18 De Paul L. Rev. 421, 422-23 (1969). In this case, the balance of equities requires no less.

The judgment of the Appellate Division is hereby affirmed, and the cause remanded for trial upon instructions consonant with this opinion.

JACOBS, J., concurs in the result but votes to affirm on the majority opinion rendered in the Appellate Division.

---

5. On remand, defendants will have the opportunity to engage in discovery so as to identify possible additional defendants and will have the benefit of our liberal joinder rules. R. 4:8-1, R. 4:29-1(a), R. 4:30.

For affirmance: CHIEF JUSTICE HUGHES and JUSTICES JACOBS, SULLIVAN and PASHMAN — 4.

For reversal: JUSTICES MOUNTAIN and CLIFFORD, and JUDGE COLLESTER — 3.

MOUNTAIN, J., dissenting.

This Court has reached an extraordinary result in a very remarkable way. As I shall hope to make clear, the structure of argument as presented in the Court's opinion is rested upon an assumed factual premise which does not exist. In part because of this, the concluding and most significant part of the argument suffers from the defect of visiting liability, in a wholly irrational way, upon parties who are more probably than not totally free of blame. I respectfully dissent.

During the course of the Court's opinion there appear statements to the effect that all those who might have been in any way responsible for plaintiff's injury are before the court. Hence, the argument continues, a process of selection properly undertaken by the finder of fact cannot fail to implicate the true culprit or culprits. Indeed, as I read the opinion, the entire argument is made to rest upon this premise: each and every person who may have brought about the imperfection in the surgical instrument or who may have caused the injury by its misuse is before the court; it remains only to identify him.

And yet we know — and everyone who has been associated with this case has always known — that this assumption is not in fact true. The only four defendants in the case are: the surgeon, Dr. Harold Somberg, who performed the operation; St. James Hospital, the medical facility in which the operation took place; Lawton Instrument Co., which manufactured the rongeur; and Rheinhold-Schumann, Inc., the distributor which sold it to the hospital. There is no other defendant in the case. And yet the record is replete with testimony that other surgeons — perhaps as many as twenty — have used the rongeur during the four years that it has formed part of the surgical equipment of the hospital, and that any one or more of them may perfectly well have been responsible for so injuring the instrument that it came apart while being manipulated in plaintiff's incision; or that it may have been weakened to near breaking point by cumulative misuse, entirely by persons not now before the court. In the face of this uncontroverted proof that the surgical instrument had been used upon approximately twenty earlier occasions and possibly by the same number of different surgeons, in the hands of any of whom it may have been fatally misused, how then can it be said that the wrongdoer is surely in court! There is a far greater likelihood that he is no party to this litigation at all and that his identity will never be established.

I of course agree with the Court that it is most unfortunate that this plaintiff should go uncompensated. Every humanitarian instinct

III. General Theories of Malpractice Liability

impels the hope that when an unconscious patient is injured in some unforeseen and unforeseeable way, due reparation will be forthcoming. It is to the manner in which the Court would seek to fulfill this hope that I object.

As the opinion of the Court has been careful to point out, (P. 8), plaintiff's claims against the surgeon, Dr. Somberg, and against the hospital sound in negligence;[3] his claims against the manufacturer and distributor, on the other hand, are stated as arising from alleged breach of warranty or as resting upon a theory of strict liability in tort. At the conclusion of the plaintiff's case it had become apparent that with respect to his negligence claims he was entitled to invoke the doctrine of res ipsa loquitur.[4] The fracture of the rongeur in the wound bespoke negligence on the part of someone, the instrument was at the time within the control of a defendant and the injury was clearly not attributable to any fault or neglect on the part of the plaintiff. Rose v. Port of New York Authority, 61 N.J. 129, 136, 293 A.2d 371 (1972); Kahalili v. Rosecliff Realty, Inc., 26 N.J. 595, 605-607, 141 A.2d 301 (1958).

The opinion takes the view that at this point the burden of proof shifted to defendants. This, as is apparently conceded, has not hitherto been the law of this State. "The operation of this rule of evidence

---

3. Not presented for consideration under the pleadings and not touched upon by the parties or any of the courts before which this case has come is the issue of whether a hospital *at its peril* puts into the hands of a surgeon a defective instrument, such as everyone seems to agree was the condition of the rongeur here, no matter how that defect came about. The state of the law in New Jersey thus remains open as to whether strict liability in tort might be available against the hospital here, see generally Johnson v. Sears, Roebuck Co., 355 F. Supp. 1065 (E.D. Wis. 1973); Note, Torts — Strict Liability — Hospitals May be Strictly Liable for Administrative Services, 41 Tenn. L. Rev. 392 (1974); cf. Magrine v. Spector, 100 N.J. Super. 223, 255-41, 241 A.2d 637 (App. Div. 1968) (Botter, J.S.C., dissenting); Farnsworth, "Implied Warranties of Quality in Non-Sales Cases," 57 Colum. L. Rev. 653 (1957); or whether, in appropriate circumstances, a court might recognize an absolute duty of some other origin under which a hospital would be required to furnish a surgeon with a non-defective instrument.

4. It has hitherto been the generally accepted rule that the doctrine of res ipsa loquitur has no application to cases involving alleged breach of warranty. "The doctrine of res ipsa loquitur relates to cases involving negligence and has no application to an alleged breach of warranty." Trust v. Arden Farms Co., 50 Cal. 2d 217, 324 P.2d 583, 586 (1958). Nevertheless the manner in which inferences of defective manufacture may be drawn from factual circumstances in breach of warranty or strict tort liability cases is not very different from the way in which inferences of negligence may be drawn where res ipsa loquitur properly applies. "The doctrine of res ipsa loquitur, frequently resorted to in negligence cases, is not applicable as such in the field of warranty, although the usual resort to circumstantial evidence in attempting to establish a breach of warranty indicates some of the same thinking found in res ipsa loquitur cases." State Farm Mut. Auto. Ins. Co. v. Anderson-Weber Inc., 252 Iowa 1289, 110 N.W.2d 449, 452 (1961). This similarity was noted by this Court in Corbin v. Camden Coca-Cola Bottling Co., 60 N.J. 425, 436, 290 A.2d 441 (1972), holding that a res ipsa charge in a products liability case resting upon strict tort liability would not, at least in that case, be deemed reversible error.

[res ipsa loquitur] does not shift the burden of persuasion [citing authorities]." Bornstein v. Metropolitan Bottling Co., 26 N.J. 263, 269, 139 A.2d 404, 408 (1958). Nevertheless this alteration in the law may be entirely reasonable and justified — at least if limited to this kind of medical malpractice case. 1 Louisell & Williams, Medical Malpractice sec. 15.02 et seq. In any event the argument as to the procedural effect to be given the rule of res ipsa has well been called "a tempest in a teapot." 2 Harper & James, The Law of Torts (1956) sec. 19.11, p. 1104. Parenthetically, it may be pointed out that the duty of explanation on the part of a surgeon, when unforeseen injury occurs, is always inherent in the relationship between physician and patient. 1 Louisell & Williams, Medical Malpractice, supra, sec. 15.01. Thus far, as to the negligence claims, I might be persuaded to agree with the Court.

But certainly no farther. At this point the *effect* to be given a shift in the burden of proof becomes the crucial issue. The authorities which have adopted or espoused the view that res ipsa shifts the burden of proof have, as far as I can discover, understood this to mean that upon such a shift taking place, a defendant becomes obliged to offer evidence explaining his own conduct or throwing light upon the circumstances attending plaintiff's injury, which will be of sufficient probative force to establish his lack of fault by a preponderance of the evidence. The fact finder will then be called upon to decide whether the defendant's proofs have met this test or whether they have fallen short.

The view expressed by the Court in this case as to the effect of shifting the burden of proof appears to be something quite different. Under this new rule it is no longer enough that a defendant meet the standard described above. His role is no longer simply that of one who may hope to succeed if his proofs justify a verdict. Rather he now finds himself one of a band of persons from among whom one or more *must* be singled out to respond in damages to the plaintiff's claim. He is now a member of a group who must collectively, among themselves, play a game of *sauve qui peut* — and play it for rather high stakes. With all due respect I submit that at this point there has been complete departure from the rule of reason; the argument is now stripped of all rational basis.

Note, first, the role the jury is being called upon to play. The judge will give to the jury two potentially contradictory instructions. First the jurors will be told to arrive at a verdict by a preponderance of the evidence, each defendant having the burden of exculpating himself. Then a further direction will be given that they *must* bring in a verdict against some one or more of the defendants. But suppose the members of the jury cannot agree that the evidence will sustain a verdict against *any* defendant. What then! Each juror has taken an oath — no small matter — to reach a verdict only "according to the evidence." What does he now do? Presumably he poses his problem to the judge. And upon seeking the aid of the court, what further instructions is he to be given?

What is to be the posture of the judge if he is thereafter called upon to rule upon a motion for judgment notwithstanding the verdict or for a new trial, and it is perfectly clear to him that the verdict could not be supported by the evidence and was rendered only in response to the compulsion of this proposed charge? I leave the answers to these questions to those jurors and judges who must in the future act under the shadow of this decision.

Consider further the hypothesis last suggested, that a jury does undertake, despite a failure of adequate proof, to carry out the mandate of this instruction. How is a verdict to be reached? The absence of sufficient evidence upon which a verdict might justly rest, coupled with the compulsion to reach a verdict against *someone*, removes from the case any semblance of rationality. It then becomes a mere game of chance. There being no rational guide, each jury may proceed as the whimsy of the moment dictates. Thus we have trial by lot, or by chance — no more a rational process than were trial by ordeal or trial by combat. And yet it is the very essence of the judicial process that a determination reached by a court shall be the result of a rational study and analysis of applicable fact and law.

Nor can it be seriously contended that in following the course outlined by the Court there would not be instances — perhaps many — where liability would be visited upon wholly innocent persons. I cannot concur in a decision announcing a rule of law which invites such a result. "It is, of course, generally accepted as axiomatic in a society dedicated to the values of individualism, that no person shall be made to answer for an event, unless his responsibility for it has been convincingly proved by due process of law. [Fleming, Developments in the English Law of Medical Liability, 12 Vand. L. Rev. 633, 646 (1959).]" Finally it may be asked whether a trial such as is here projected may in any true sense be termed either a trial by jury or an exercise of the judicial process, as those concepts are generally understood.

I would vote to reverse the judgment of the Appellate Division and to reinstate the judgment of the trial court.

CLIFFORD, J., and JUDGE COLLESTER join in this dissenting opinion.

St. Francis Regional Medical Center v. Hale
752 P.2d 129 (Kan. App. 1988)

[See opinion at page 337 in this chapter.]

NOTES

Negligence per se, Res Ipsa Loquitur, and the "Common Knowledge Rule" in Medical Malpractice

1. The three evidentiary rules noted above are often confused, or used interchangeably, in American courts in medical malpractice litigation. Are the rules clearly distinctive one from the other? For a case-by-case comparison, see Note, 9 A.L.R.3d 1315 (1977). See also D. Louisell & H. Williams, Medical Malpractice, §14.01 et seq. (1988). For a recent review of the application of these rules in cases of multiple medical defendants, see Note, 67 A.L.R.4th 544 (1989).

2. Res ipsa loquitur as an evidentiary rule allowing plaintiffs to "get to the jury" without offering expert testimony of a violation of the applicable standard of care has a long history in medical malpractice litigation. See W. Prosser & P. Keeton, Law of Torts (5th ed. 1984) p.257 et seq. The most liberal applications of the rule have, since the beginning, been found in California. See the classic early case of Ybarra v. Spangard, 208 P.2d 445 (Cal. App. 1949). Another expansive view of the availability of res ipsa loquitur and the "common knowledge rule" can be found in Pennsylvania. See, for example, Jones v. Harrisburg Polyclinic Hosp., 437 A.2d 1134 (Pa. 1981), and an excellent student note on the case, 21 Duq. L. Rev. 547 (1983). For a contrary view, see Baker v. Chastain, 389 So. 2d 932, 935 (Ala. 1980), where the Supreme Court of Alabama expressed great reluctance to apply res ipsa loquitur or any other rule of evidence that would relax the plaintiff's requirement of producing expert testimony in medical malpractice cases.

3. In earlier years, it was often alleged by legal commentators that the liberal application of res ipsa loquitur and similar rules was designed to aid plaintiffs with legitimate claims who were confronted with "the conspiracy of silence" on the part of physicians refusing to appear as expert witnesses. In more recent times, the attitudes of commentators in both legal and medical journals have all but totally reversed. These rules are now often described as unfair to defendant physicians. See particularly the Report of the Secretary's Commission on Medical Malpractice (1973), and recommendations of the Commission reprinted at 386-390 in this chapter. Many of the statutory reforms adopted in the legislatures in the mid-1970s and mid-1980s included modifications of the res ipsa loquitur doctrine in order to establish "greater fairness" in medical malpractice litigation. See references and discussion later in this chapter at 439-441. A particularly outspoken expression of the modern view is found in Priest v. Lindig, 583 P.2d 173, 175 n.7 (Alaska 1976), where the court asserted that the legislative history of the Alaska statute abolishing res ipsa loquitur

in medical malpractice cases was intended to counteract "the *intolerable* rule of law [of res ipsa loquitur] resulting in astronomically high malpractice insurance rates" (emphasis added). For examples of other recent commentaries on these rules, see Seidelson, Res Ipsa Loquitur: The Big Umbrella, 25 Duq. L. Rev. 387 (1987); Eaton, Res Ipsa Loquitur and Medical Malpractice in Georgia: A Reassessment, 17 Ga. L. Rev. 33 (1982).

4. The *St. Francis* case is also noted above for its refusal to apply a "common knowledge" rule to find negligence in a hospital in a situation of nosocomial infection. Are there differences of legal policy in applying these evidentiary rules to the general duties of hospitals and hospital administration (the board of trustees and the chief executive officers)? See further discussion in this chapter at 334-335.

5. There have been numerous applications of the evidentiary rules noted above in clinical situations where physicians have failed to utilize commonly known and accepted techniques of diagnosis, particularly the taking of X-rays in cases of suspicion of bone fractures. Most of the cases apply a res ipsa loquitur rule, but others apply a "common knowledge" doctrine or even negligence per se. Later cases have applied these rules to inappropriate use of radiology. In Deutsch v. Skein, 597 S.W.2d 141 (Ky. 1980), a physician was found negligent per se in ordering radiology and other invasive tests on a pregnant woman, causing damage to the fetus.

6. How can physicians and hospitals avoid application of these doctrines? Should diagnostic tests be done, and other precautionary procedures be performed for protection against malpractice suits?

Sullivan v. O'Connor
296 N.E.2d 183 (Mass. 1973)

KAPLAN, JUSTICE.

The plaintiff patient secured a jury verdict of $13,500 against the defendant surgeon for breach of contract in respect to an operation upon the plaintiff's nose. The substituted consolidated bill of exceptions presents questions about the correctness of the judge's instructions on the issue of damages.

The declaration was in two counts. In the first count, the plaintiff alleged that she, as patient, entered into a contract with the defendant, a surgeon, wherein the defendant promised to perform plastic surgery on her nose and thereby to enhance her beauty and improve her appearance; that he performed the surgery but failed to achieve the promised result; rather the result of the surgery was to disfigure and deform her nose, to cause her pain in body and mind, and to subject her to other damage and expense. The second count, based on the same transaction, was in the conventional form for malpractice, charging that the defendant had been guilty of negligence in performing the surgery. Answering, the defendant entered a general denial.

On the plaintiff's demand, the case was tried by jury. At the close of the evidence, the judge put to the jury, as special questions, the issues of liability under the two counts, and instructed them accordingly. The jury returned a verdict for the plaintiff on the contract count, and for the defendant on the negligence count. The judge then instructed the jury on the issue of damages.

As background to the instructions and the parties' exceptions, we mention certain facts as the jury could find them. The plaintiff was a professional entertainer, and this was known to the defendant. The agreement was as alleged in the declaration. More particularly, judging from exhibits, the plaintiff's nose had been straight, but long and prominent; the defendant undertook by two operations to reduce its prominence and somewhat to shorten it, thus making it more pleasing in relation to the plaintiff's other features. Actually the plaintiff was obliged to undergo three operations, and her appearance was worsened. Her nose now had a concave line to about the midpoint, at which it became bulbous; viewed frontally, the nose from bridge to midpoint was flattened and broadened, and the two sides of the tip had lost symmetry. This configuration evidently could not be improved by further surgery. The plaintiff did not demonstrate, however, that her change of appearance had resulted in loss of employment. Payments by the plaintiff covering the defendant's fee and hospital expenses were stipulated at $622.65.

The judge instructed the jury, first, that the plaintiff was entitled to recover her out-of-pocket expenses incident to the operations. Second, she could recover the damages flowing directly, naturally, proximately, and foreseeably from the defendant's breach of promise. These would comprehend damages for any disfigurement of the plaintiff's nose — that is, any change of appearance for the worse — including the effects of the consciousness of such disfigurement on the plaintiff's mind, and in this connection the jury should consider the nature of the plaintiff's profession. Also consequent upon the defendant's breach, and compensable, were the pain and suffering involved in the third operation, but not in the first two. As there was no proof that any loss of earnings by the plaintiff resulted from the breach, that element should not enter into the calculation of damages.

By his exceptions the defendant contends that the judge erred in allowing the jury to take into account anything but the plaintiff's out-of-pocket expenses (presumably at the stipulated amount). The defendant excepted to the judge's refusal of his request for a general charge to that effect, and, more specifically, to the judge's refusal of

III. General Theories of Malpractice Liability

a charge that the plaintiff could not recover for pain and suffering connected with the third operation or for impairment of the plaintiff's appearance and associated mental distress.

The plaintiff on her part excepted to the judge's refusal of a request to charge that the plaintiff could recover the difference in value between the nose as promised and the nose as it appeared after the operations. However, the plaintiff in her brief expressly waives this exception and others made by her in case this court overrules the defendant's exceptions; thus she would be content to hold the jury's verdict in her favor.

We conclude that the defendant's exceptions should be overruled.

It has been suggested on occasion that agreements between patients and physicians by which the physician undertakes to effect a cure or to bring about a given result should be declared unenforceable on grounds of public policy. See Guilmet v. Campbell, 385 Mich. 57, 76, 188 N.W.2d 601 (dissenting opinion). But there are many decisions recognizing and enforcing such contracts, see annotation, 43 A.L.R.3d 1221, 1225, 1229-1233, and the law of Massachusetts has treated them as valid, although we have had no decision meeting head on the contention that they should be denied legal sanction. Small v. Howard, 128 Mass. 131; Gabrunas v. Miniter, 289 Mass. 20, 193 N.E. 551; Forman v. Wolfson, 327 Mass. 341, 98 N.E.2d 615. These causes of action are, however, considered a little suspect, and thus we find courts straining sometimes to read the pleadings as sounding only in tort for negligence, and not in contract for breach of promise, despite sedulous efforts by the pleaders to pursue the latter theory. See Gault v. Sideman, 42 Ill. App. 2d 96, 191 N.E.2d 436; annotation, supra, at 1225, 1238-1244.

It is not hard to see why the courts should be unenthusiastic or skeptical about the contract theory. Considering the uncertainties of medical science and the variations in the physical and psychological conditions of individual patients, doctors can seldom in good faith promise specific results. Therefore it is unlikely that physicians of even average integrity will in fact make such promises. Statements of opinion by the physician with some optimistic coloring are a different thing, and may indeed have therapeutic value. But patients may transform such statements into firm promises in their own minds, especially when they have been disappointed in the event, and testify in that sense to sympathetic juries.[2] If actions for breach of promise

---

2. Judicial skepticism about whether a promise was in fact made derives also from the possibility that the truth has been tortured to give the plaintiff the advantage of the longer period of limitations sometimes available for actions on contract as distinguished from those in tort or for malpractice. See Lillich, The Malpractice Statute of Limitations in New York and Other Jurisdictions, 47 Cornell L.Q. 339; annotation, 80 A.L.R.2d 368.

can be readily maintained, doctors, so it is said, will be frightened into practising "defensive medicine." On the other hand, if these actions were outlawed, leaving only the possibility of suits for malpractice, there is fear that the public might be exposed to the enticements of charlatans, and confidence in the profession might ultimately be shaken. See Miller, The Contractual Liability of Physicians and Surgeons, 1953 Wash. L.Q. 413, 416-423. The law has taken the middle of the road position of allowing actions based on alleged contract, but insisting on clear proof. Instructions to the jury may well stress this requirement and point to tests of truth, such as the complexity or difficulty of an operation as bearing on the probability that a given result was promised. See annotation, 43 A.L.R.3d 1225, 1225-1227.

If an action on the basis of contract is allowed, we have next the question of the measure of damages to be applied where liability is found. Some cases have taken the simple view that the promise by the physician is to be treated like an ordinary commercial promise, and accordingly that the successful plaintiff is entitled to a standard measure of recovery for breach of contract — "compensatory" ("expectancy") damages, an amount intended to put the plaintiff in the position he would be in if the contract had been performed, or, presumably, at the plaintiff's election, "restitution" damages, an amount corresponding to any benefit conferred by the plaintiff upon the defendant in the performance of the contract disrupted by the defendant's breach. See Restatement: Contracts §329 and comment a, §§347, 384(1). Thus in Hawkins v. McGee, 84 N.H. 114, 146 A. 641, the defendant doctor was taken to have promised the plaintiff to convert his damaged hand by means of an operation into a good or perfect hand, but the doctor so operated as to damage the hand still further. The court, following the usual expectancy formula, would have asked the jury to estimate and award to the plaintiff the difference between the value of a good or perfect hand, as promised, and the value of the hand after the operation. (The same formula would apply, although the dollar result would be less, if the operation had neither worsened nor improved the condition of the hand.) If the plaintiff had not yet paid the doctor his fee, that amount would be deducted from the recovery. There could be no recovery for the pain and suffering of the operation, since that detriment would have been incurred even if the operation had been successful; one can say that this detriment was not "caused" by the breach. But where the plaintiff by reason of the operation was put to more pain than he would have had to endure, had the doctor performed as promised, he should be compensated for that difference as a proper part of his expectancy recovery. It may be noted that on an alternative count for malpractice the plaintiff in the *Hawkins* case had been nonsuited; but on ordinary principles this could not affect the contract claim, for it is hardly a defence to a breach of contract that the promisor acted innocently and without negligence. The New Hampshire court further refined the *Hawkins* analysis in McQuaid v. Michou, 85 N.H. 299, 157 A. 881, all in the direction of treating the patient-physician cases on the ordinary footing of expectancy. See McGee v. United States Fid. & Guar. Co., 53 F.2d 953 (1st Cir.) (later development in the *Hawkins* case); Cloutier v. Kasheta, 105 N.H. 262, 197 A.2d 627; Lakeman v. LaFrance, 102 N.H. 300, 305, 156 A.2d 123.

Other cases, including a number in New York, without distinctly repudiating the *Hawkins* type of analysis, have indicated that a different and generally more lenient measure of damages is to be applied in patient-physician actions based on breach of alleged special agreements to effect a cure, attain a stated result, or employ a given medical method. This measure is expressed in somewhat variant ways, but the substance is that the plaintiff is to recover any expenditures made by him and for other detriment (usually not specifically described in the opinions) following proximately and foreseeably upon the defendant's failure to carry out his promise. . . . This, be it noted, is not a "restitution" measure, for it is not limited to restoration of the benefit conferred on the defendant (the fee paid) but includes other expenditures, for example, amounts paid for medicine and nurses; so also it would seem according to its logic to take in damages for any worsening of the plaintiff's condition due to the breach. Nor is it an "expectancy" measure, for it does not appear to contemplate recovery of the whole difference in value between the condition as promised and the condition actually resulting from the treatment. Rather the tendency of the formulation is to put the plaintiff back in the position he occupied just before the parties entered upon the agreement, to compensate him for the detriments he suffered in reliance upon the agreement. . . .

For breach of the patient-physician agreements under consideration, a recovery limited to restitution seems plainly too meager, if the agreements are to be enforced at all. On the other hand, an expectancy recovery may well be excessive. The factors, already mentioned, which have made the cause of action somewhat suspect, also suggest moderation as to the breadth of the recovery that should be permitted. Where, as in the case at bar and in a number of the reported cases, the doctor has been absolved of negligence by the trier, an expectancy measure may be thought harsh. We should recall here that the fee paid by the patient to the doctor for the alleged promise would usually be quite disproportionate to the putative expectancy recovery. To attempt, moreover, to put a value on the condition that would or might have resulted, had the treatment succeeded as promised, may sometimes put an exceptional strain on the imagination of the fact finder. . . .

There is much to be said, then, for applying a reliance measure to the present facts, and we have only to add that our cases are not unreceptive to the use of that formula in special situations. We have, however, had no previous occasion to apply it to patient-physician cases.

The question of recovery on a reliance basis for pain and suffering or mental distress requires further attention. We find expressions in the decisions that pain and suffering (or the like) are simply not compensable in actions for breach of contract. The defendant seemingly espouses this proposition in the present case. True, if the buyer under a contract for the purchase of a lot of merchandise, in suing for the seller's breach, should claim damages for mental anguish caused by his disappointment in the transaction, he would not succeed; he would be told, perhaps, that the asserted psychological injury was not fairly foreseeable by the defendant as a probable consequence of the breach of such a business contract. See Restatement: Contracts, §341, and comment a. But there is no general rule barring such items of damage in actions for breach of contract. It is all a question of the subject matter and background of the contract, and when the contract calls for an operation on the person of the plaintiff, psychological as well as physical injury may be expected to figure somewhere in the recovery, depending on the particular circumstances. . . .

In the light of the foregoing discussion, all the defendant's exceptions fail: the plaintiff was not confined to the recovery of her out-of-pocket expenditures; she was entitled to recover also for the worsening of her condition, and for the pain and suffering and mental distress involved in the third operation. . . .

Plaintiff's exceptions waived.
Defendant's exceptions overruled.

NOTES

Liability Based Upon Contract, Guarantee, and Breach of Warranty

1. The application of a contractual theory of liability in medical malpractice is rare, and, as illustrated in the instant case, the courts usually impose a very high standard for proving a contractual breach. The concept of "abandonment" of a patient wherein a physician or hospital totally neglects a patient, or fails to give any care or attention to a patient for an extended period of time, may sound in negligence, but also can be said to be bottomed on the contractual obligation to attend the patient properly and continuously until care in the particular illness is no longer needed. In this respect, the physician has failed to provide the personal professional services demanded under the contract of medical care. The application of a breach of contract

theory to abandonment situations is most likely to be successful when the failure to attend the patient is intentional and quite prolonged, indicating a complete breakdown in the physician-patient relationship. See J. King, The Law of Medical Malpractice (Nutshell Series) (2d ed. 1986) pp. 23-29. See also generally B. Werthmann, Medical Malpractice Law — How Medicine is Changing the Law (1984).

2. Many personal injury actions against physicians and hospitals alleging breach of contract are thinly disguised attempts to avoid application of unfavorable aspects of tort actions for negligent medical care. For example, these efforts will include seeking a longer statute of limitations, avoidance of doctrines of sovereign or charitable immunity, and avoidance of evidentiary requirements to produce expert medical testimony concerning deviation from an accepted standard of care. Most of the appellate court reviews have denied the strategy and applied the tort-law requirements. Several statutory reforms in the mid-1970s that defined "medical malpractice" and imposed shorter statutes of limitations include both tort and contract actions under the broad definition of "medical malpractice." See the references and discussion of statutory reforms later in the chapter at 403-427.

3. The *Sullivan* case involves an allegation of contractual guarantee of a particular result in plastic surgery. Other cases in surgery have involved alleged failures to achieve sexual sterilization. Several jurisdictions have denied recovery for alleged guarantees in such situations in the absence of an express written guarantee negotiated prior to the surgery. See Coleman v. Garrison, 349 A.2d 8 (Del. 1975); Herrera v. Roessing, 533 P.2d 60 (Colo. 1975). Other states have achieved the same policy by statute. See Ariz. Rev. Stat. §12.672(B) (1976); Ind. Code Ann. §16-9.5-1-4 (Burns Supp. 1987); Mich. Comp. Laws Ann. §566.132(g) (West Suppl. 1987).

Do the same judicial policies apply to allegations of guarantee of results in dental surgery? See Ferlito v. Cecola, 419 So. 2d 102 (1982); Burns v. Wannemaker, 315 S.E.2d 179 (S.C. 1984).

4. As a practical matter, most plastic surgeons (and surgeons performing sterilization procedures as well) currently follow a standard practice of providing patients with a written statement (or contract) which they require the patient to sign under which the surgeon specifically denies a guarantee of results and asserts only that the surgeon will use his professional skills in the accepted manner. After signing such a document, can the patient claim not to have understood its plain language? Is such a document similar to a covenant not to sue? Are there legal policy reasons to discourage such agreements *not* to offer guarantees of a particular result?

5. Under the English and American common law, a physician owes the same obligation of quality of care (average reasonable care) to patients who are not expected or asked to pay for services (so-

called "charitable care") as to paying patients. To this extent, the "contract" for personal services requires no financial consideration and is considered both legally and ethically binding on the physician or hospital. It must be clear, however, that absent a statutory obligation, the physician is free to deny entering into a physician-patient relationship with any particular patient.

In a few instances, patients have brought suit against physicians wherein the existence of a valid physician-patient relationship was highly doubtful. In the strangest case of all, a plaintiff brought a malpractice action against a medical school professor who had given a lecture attended by the plaintiff. The plaintiff spoke to the professor after the lecture and described the condition. The professor "advised" surgery to correct the condition; nothing more was said, and no financial agreement for a professional consultation at the professor's office was ever arranged. An appellate court dismissed the action, holding that no physician-patient relationship was established and the professor/physician owed no professional duty to the plaintiff. The court went on to support a policy of general discussion of medical issues in such situations without legal obligation in order to encourage a free-flowing and informal dissemination of medical information. See Rainer v. Grossman, 107 Cal. Rptr. 469 (Cal. App. 1973).

6. The application of the rule indicated above depends in most instances on the beginning of the rendering of any type of medical care, regardless of financial consideration. On this basis, at least in theory, the voluntary physician who acts to provide any degree of emergency care is obliged to render quality of care equal to that afforded paying patients. Because physicians have been afraid of the implications of this common law rule, the 50 states have all enacted "good samaritan laws" that reduce the obligation of volunteer physicians in emergency situations. See discussion later in this chapter at 380-384.

Fraud, Misrepresentation, and Over-Zealous Promises of Good Results of Care

7. Closely related to the contract and guarantee situations represented by the *Sullivan* case are those situations where a physician is accused of fraudulent statements or intentional misrepresentation of the results that can be expected from treatment. Most of these cases involve unethical practices and criminal activities by charlatans who are not licensed physicians or are persons who have had medical licenses revoked in the past for improper practices. There are many alleged "doctors" who set up practices in regard to such areas as weight loss, hair restoration, and cancer cures. The most well known action in this field was the prosecution of a chiropractor "faith healer"

III. General Theories of Malpractice Liability

for murder in the case of a young child with cancer in her eye. The District Attorney of Los Angeles brought a murder charge under the murder-felony rule and obtained a guilty verdict from a jury.

An intermediate appellate court upheld the murder conviction, but the California Supreme Court reversed, asserting that the felony involved, grand theft, was not usually associated with personal danger to human life and so could not support the felony-murder rule applied in the trial court. See People v. Phillips, 414 P.2d 353 (Cal. App. 1966). The case did not end at this point, however. The District Attorney persisted and in a second jury trial the defendant chiropractor was convicted of second-degree murder. On appeal, the intermediate appellate court upheld the conviction on grounds that the defendant maliciously caused the child's death by fraudulently discouraging the parents from seeking proper treatment. People v. Phillips, 270 Cal. App.2d 381, 75 Cal. Rptr. 720 (Cal. Appl. 1969), *cert. denied*, 396 U.S. 1021 (1970). For a review of the background of the case see W. Curran, Law-Medicine Notes — Progress in Medicolegal Relations 161-164 (1989).

8. Some cases do not involve frankly criminal conduct, but do involve overzealous assurances to patients, before or after treatment, or both. The allegations may contain statements as mild as "you will be fine," or "you will return to normal," or "you will improve considerably." Do such statements constitute a guarantee of cure or good result? See cases collected in D. Louisell & H. Williams, Medical Malpractice §§2.04, 8.11 (1988). In order to sustain liability for fraud, the plaintiff would be required in these situations to prove that the statements of reassurance were made with malice and were knowingly false, due to the obvious existence of medical clinical findings indicating clearly that poor results were inevitable beforehand, or were clearly evident after the fact of treatment. See also Ficarra, Medical Negligence Based on Bad Faith, Breach of Contract, or Mental Anguish, 1980 Leg. Med. Ann. 187-206.

Breach of Warranty

9. Physicians do not generally sell products to patients and so are rarely vulnerable to law suits for breaches of sales warranties, express or implied by law. Physicians who prescribe drugs or use therapeutic devices perform "services" related to these products, but do not become merchants of sale. Actions for breach of warranty would therefore be available only against the manufacturers. In some instances, however, a surgeon may actually design a particular therapeutic device, or may aid the manufacturer as a "design consultant." In such situations, if the design were found defective, could the surgeon be joined in an action against the manufacturer on a neg-

ligence basis? On the basis of an implied warranty of fitness for the purpose involved? See Bruner & Drinker, The Physician, the Manufacturer, and Medical Devices, 23 Med. Trial Tech. Q. 307 (1977); Watrous, Liability for Medical Appliances in Medical Malpractice Suits: The Fly in the Ointment, 10 Tex. Tech. L. Rev. 405 (1979).

10. Under what circumstances can a hospital be held liable for breach of warranty in regard to patient care? Does a hospital "sell" any products to its patients? See the examination of liability theories in Section V of this chapter.

IV. INFORMED CONSENT AS A BASIS OF LIABILITY

Planned Parenthood of Central Missouri v. Danforth
428 U.S. 52 (1976)

[The central issues in the case involved the constitutionality of portions of a Missouri statute controlling and regulating abortions. Herein we reprint a footnote observation by Justice Blackmun concerning the meaning of the legal concept of informed consent.]

MR. JUSTICE BLACKMUN delivered the opinion of the Court. . . . One might well wonder, offhand, what informed consent of a patient is. The three Missouri federal judges who comprised the three-judge District Court were not concerned and we are content to accept, as the meaning, the giving of information to the patient as to just what would be done and as to its consequences. To ascribe more meaning than this might well confine the attending physician in an undesired and uncomfortable straitjacket in the practice of his profession.

NOTES

Legal and Ethical Bases of Consent

1. Do you find Justice Blackmun's definition adequate? The Justice deals only with the "informed" portion of the term, not the "consent." When confined to describing "what would be done and its consequences," is the physician giving the patient a choice? The context fits surgical operations most closely where the surgeon is attempting to describe his already selected procedures.

2. James Ludlam, a leading hospital defense lawyer, in his AHA handbook, Informed Consent (1978), quotes the above definition in his first few pages. He seems particularly impressed with Justice Blackmun's reluctance to over-define the term, thus constricting the

IV. Informed Consent as a Basis of Liability   303

therapeutic discretion of the physician. Ludlam lists what he considers serious problems for physicians as a result of court decisions on informed consent:

- basic change in the role of the physician,
- uncertainty of definition of terms of the physician's responsibility,
- inability to predict whether the courts will ultimately find that the physician has fulfilled his duty,
- inability of the physician to be able to determine in advance whether he has "properly documented" his professional responsibility to inform, and
- ethical concerns with the willingness of courts to allow patients to make the "wrong medical" decision.

Do you agree with Ludlam's view? Can greater certainty about responsibility and about the adequacy of written consent forms prepared by physicians and hospitals be provided? See the various reform efforts in this field later in this chapter.

3. Informed consent is also considered an ethical requirement either as a part of the fiduciary duty of the physician or as a part of the "autonomy" of the patient. See a thoughtful review by a psychiatrist (psychoanalyst) teaching in a law school for many years, J. Katz, The Silent World of Doctor and Patient (1984). For a detailed review of developments in the medical, ethical, and legal aspects of the subject, see R. Faden & T. Beauchamp, A History and Theory of Informed Consent (1986). For other ethical analysis, see S. Bok, On Lying (1978); Ramsey, The Patient as a Person: Explorations in Medical Ethics (1970); A. Dyck, On Human Care (1978). Not all physicians have agreed with the more expansive ethical views on the requirements of informed consent. See Inglefinger, Informed (but Uneducated) Consent, 287 New Eng. J. Med. 465 (1970); Shaw, Dilemmas of Informed Consent, 289 New Eng. J. Med. 885 (1973). At least one medical editor of an important medical journal has endorsed eloquently the ethical and legal objectives of informed consent. See Rennie, Informed Consent by "Well-Nigh Abject" Adults, 303 New Eng. J. Med. 916 (1980). Another physician writing on medical ethics has been favorably impressed by the legal requirements of informed consent in improving the interrelationships of patients and doctors. See C. Chapman, Physicians, Law, and Ethics (1984). See also R. Burt, Taking Care of Strangers: The Rule of Law in Doctor-Patient Relations (1979). For a classic review of the subject by a medical sociologist, see B. Barber, Informed Consent in Medical Therapy and Research (1980). For a sensitive discussion of medical duties to patients, see E. Pellegrino, Humanism and the Physician

(1979). See also President's Commission for the Study of Ethical Problems in Medicine and Behavioral Research, Making Health-Care Decisions: A Report on the Ethical and Legal Implications of Informed Consent in the Patient-Practitioner Relationship (Wash. D.C. 1982).

4. It has long been a tenet of Anglo-American law that a mentally competent adult is the master of his or her own body, and unpermitted touching, or dangerous intrusion upon or into the human body, was a trespass; battery if intentional, negligence if unintentional. In the United States, in relation to medical malpractice actions, the classic judicial formulation was expressed by Justice Cardozo in Schoendorff v. Society of New York Hospital, 106 N.E. 93 (N.Y. 1914). The movement away from characterizing failure to obtain an *adequately informed consent* as battery on the part of the physician has been gradual, but is now very strong and nearly complete. In the great majority of American jurisdictions, the action is based in negligence. See Note, 38 A.L.R. 4th 900 (1985).

The only exceptions where a battery action may still be brought are situations where the procedure is forced upon the patient without any consent, or where the consent is fraudulently obtained and the fraud relates to the character of the touching. An example of the latter is a seemingly permitted touching and examination of a woman for medical purposes wherein the actual purposes are related to sexual abuse. Some recent statutory reforms have required the application of a negligence theory in informed consent cases. In one court review, however, the statutory removal of a cause of action for battery in all informed consent situations was found overly broad and unconstitutional. See Rubino v. Fretias, 638 F. Supp. 182 (D. Ariz. 1986).

For a highly detailed and authoritative examination of the legal and practical requirements of informed consent of patients and research subjects in a wide variety of situations, see F. Rozovsky, Consent to Treatment: A Practical Guide (2d ed. 1990).

5. The trend of the American courts since 1972 has been toward a standard of disclosure of the risks of medical treatment most commonly known as the "reasonable prudence" or "materiality rule." The classic expression of this rule is found in Canterbury v. Spence, 464 F.2d 772 (D.C. Cir. 1972), *cert. denied*, 409 U.S. 1064. In this case, the Court broke away from the traditional application of a professional standard or custom applied in all other areas of medical malpractice and applied a patient-oriented standard requiring disclosure of risks that would be "material" to a patient's decision whether or not to undergo the treatment or procedure. This case was quickly followed by quite similar decisions in two other widely separate jurisdictions. See Cobbs v. Grant, 502 P.2d 1 (Cal. 1972); Wilkinson v. Vesey, 295 A.2d 676 (R.I. 1972). As is clear from a reading of the *Canterbury* opinion, the Court was greatly influenced in developing

its position by a comprehensive law review article, Waltz & Scheuneman, Informed Consent to Therapy, 64 N.W.U.L. Rev. 628 (1970).

There are differences in language among the three leading cases noted above in their descriptions of the scope of disclosure required. The *Wilkinson* case is read by some commentators as demanding a fuller disclosure of risks because of the statement that the physician is bound to explain "all the known material risks peculiar to the proposed procedure." Later cases in these jurisdictions and others have not, however, drawn significant differences in the application of the criteria expressed in the opinions. It should be noted that there are limitations on the duty to disclose: (1) the physician need not disclose discomforts and risks which should be obvious to persons of average intelligence and education; and (2) the physician need not disclose risks so remote as not to be material to a reasonable evaluation of the risks and benefits involved in the procedure. For an examination these limitations, see the discussion in this chapter at §VI.

6. The movement following the *Canterbury* approach in regard to the standard for disclosure of information has now reached the point where most newly examined cases call it the majority rule in American jurisdictions. For a recent case adopting the *Canterbury* opinion and providing a detailed summary of the history of the law of informed consent since 1972, see Largey v. Rothman, 540 A.2d 504 (N.J. 1988). The *Canterbury* rule is identified under at least three different descriptive titles: "the materiality rule," "the prudent patient rule," and "the layperson rule." The more traditional approach is known as "the professional standard." See D. Louisell & H. Williams, Medical Malpractice §22.11 (1988). For a recent defense of "the professional standard," with a rather stubborn commitment not to change the rule, see a recent opinion in the Supreme Court of Maine, Ouellette v. Mehalic, 534 A.2d 1331 (Me. 1988). There was an earlier and quite confusing case in Maine where a divided Supreme Court seemed to move very close to a "prudent patient rule" in an opinion holding that a general practitioner had a duty to disclose alternative, more conservative forms of treatment when he referred the patient to a surgeon for an operation on a dislocated clavicle (collarbone). See Jacobs v. Painter, 530 A.2d 231 (Me. 1987). One of the authoritative texts on the law of informed consent still asserts that "the professional standard" constitutes the majority rule in American jurisdictions. See F. Rozovsky, Consent to Treatment: A Practical Guide at §1.16.1 (2d ed. 1990).

7. Another variation on the *Canterbury* approach occurred in Truman v. Thomas, 611 P.2d 902 (Cal. 1980), wherein a physician's failure to urge a patient to accept a Pap smear during a routine gynecological examination and to explain to her the dangers of undetected cervical cancer was found a violation of the California version

of *Canterbury* in Cobbs v. Grant, noted earlier. The decision was reached by a 5 to 4 majority with the majority opinion by Chief Justice Bird. The four-justice minority, with the opinion by Justice Clark, found the result an "intolerable burden" on physicians. It was asserted that since the physician-patient relationship is based upon trust, this case would force a "hard-sell approach" upon the doctor, thus jeopardizing the trust relationship.

8. Are the basic requirements for informed consent any different when the procedure suggested is experimental? When the patient is a subject in a formal clinical investigation of a new drug or a new therapeutic procedure? See discussion of Karp v. Cooley at 373.

9. One of the more controversial aspects of "the professional standard" for determining the scope of disclosure of information to patients has been the existence of a "therapeutic privilege" to withhold information — permanently, or for a period of time until the patient is believed by the doctor to be emotionally "ready" to receive it — in the best interests of the patient. Under the practice, the physician is allowed discretion concerning what and when to disclose "disturbing" information directly to the patient; a full disclose is usually made to a relative or close associate who is regularly attending the patient. The *Canterbury* case severely criticized the scope of this privilege as too loosely expressed to be applied. What is left of the privilege under *Canterbury*? To what situations would it apply in practice? For an imaginative evaluation of the privilege, see Somerville, Therapeutic Privilege: Variation on the Theme of Informed Consent 12 L. Med. & Health Care 4 (1984). In her article, Prof. Somerville offers a diagrammatic expression of the *Canterbury* rule as adopted in Canada in two decisions: Reibl v. Hughes, (1980) 114 D.L.R. (3d) 1 (S.C.C.); Hopp v. Lepp, (1980) 112 D.L.R. (3d) 67 (S.C.C.). For diagrams, see 307.

What are the differences in the two diagrammatic models? In suggesting the differences, the author asserts,

> One can imagine the possible scope of disclosure of information required for obtaining informed consent as starting at zero percent and ending at one hundred percent of the information relevant to the particular situation. If this is represented in diagrammatic form, one can imagine the scope of information disclosed starting at the narrow end and gradually increasing as one moves from a subjective physician standard, to a reasonable physician standard, to a reasonable patient standard, to a subjective patient standard (Diagram 1). One can then superimpose on this model factors which may extend the scope of the disclosure otherwise required (for example, the patient's questions). Similarly, one can take into account other factors which may restrict the "normal" scope of the disclosure, that is, the patient's waiver (an informed and voluntary refusal of information) and therapeutic privilege (Diagram 2). [Id. at 6.]

IV. Informed Consent as a Basis of Liability   307

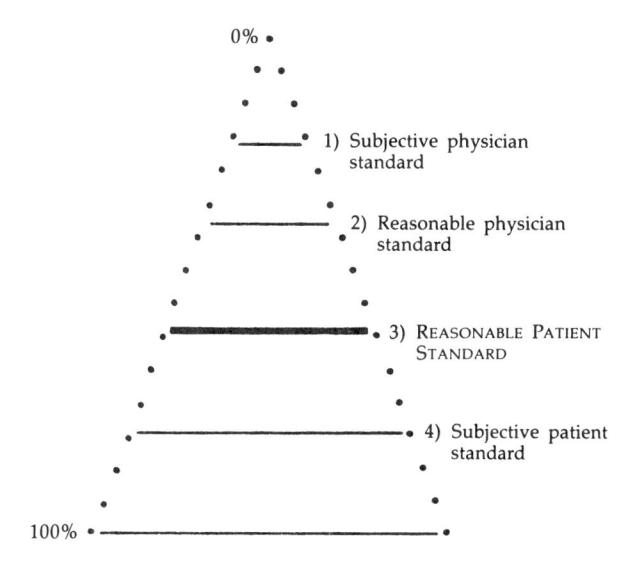

Diagram 1
Possible Standards for Scope of Disclosure

0%

1) Subjective physician standard
2) Reasonable physician standard
3) REASONABLE PATIENT STANDARD
4) Subjective patient standard

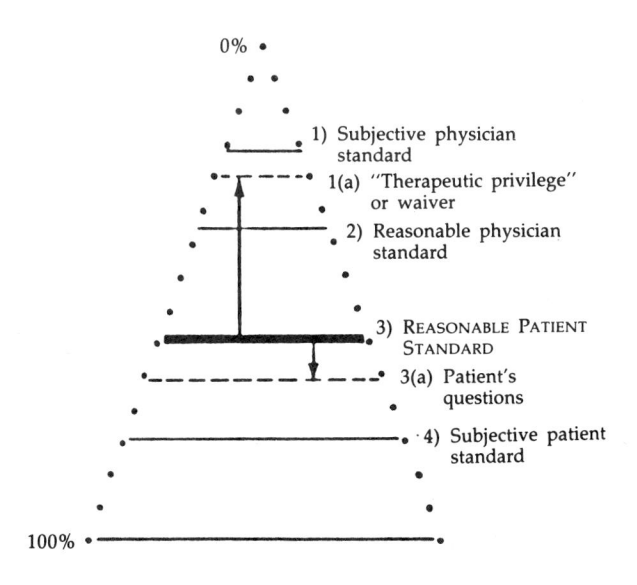

100%

Diagram 2
Variations of the Normally Required Scope of Disclosure

0%

1) Subjective physician standard
1(a) "Therapeutic privilege" or waiver
2) Reasonable physician standard
3) REASONABLE PATIENT STANDARD
3(a) Patient's questions
4) Subjective patient standard

100%

Logan v. Greenwich Hospital Association
465 A.2d 294 (Conn. 1983)

SHEA, J. In this medical malpractice action the trial court directed a verdict for the defendant hospital and for one of the three doctors whom the plaintiff had named as defendants. The jury returned a verdict for the other two defendant doctors. The plaintiff has appealed, claiming error in the direction of the verdicts and in the charge to the jury. The principal issue raised involves the propriety of the court's instruction that the duty of a physician to advise a patient of possible alternatives in obtaining an informed consent to a contemplated operative procedure does not require the disclosure of a more hazardous alternative. We find error in this instruction and order a new trial limited to the absence of informed consent theory of the complaint. . . .

I

The plaintiff's first claim of error involves the charge upon the absence of informed consent as alleged in the complaint, particularly with respect to the duty of a physician to advise a patient of feasible alternatives.[1] The court instructed the jury that the duty to give a patient all information material to the decision to undergo an operation includes the obligation to advise of feasible alternatives. The charge continued: "Now the duty to warn of alternatives exists only when there are feasible alternatives available. *An alternative that is more hazardous is not a viable alternative.*" (Emphasis added.) The plaintiff excepted to the italicized sentence of the charge as removing from the patient the decision of which alternative procedure was the least dangerous. The same charge was repeated in response to a

---

1. This portion of the charge was as follows:

   The theory of informed consent imposes a duty upon a doctor which is completely separate and distinct from his responsibility to skillfully diagnose and treat the patient's ills. A physician is bound to disclose all known material risks peculiar to the proposed procedure. Materiality is defined as the significance a reasonable person in what the physician knows, or should know, in his patient's position would attach to the disclosed risk or risks in deciding whether to submit or not to submit to the renal biopsy. It is the duty of the physician to give a patient whose situation otherwise permits it all information material to the decision to undergo the proposed procedure. And this duty also includes a duty of a physician to advise of feasible alternatives. Now, the duty to warn of alternatives exists only when there are feasible alternatives available. An alternative that is more hazardous is not a viable alternative. The burden is on the plaintiff to show not only an unjustified failure to disclose the risk of a proposed procedure, but also that such failure was the proximate cause of the plaintiff's injury.

IV. Informed Consent as a Basis of Liability

request of the jury, after they commenced deliberations, for a further definition of the standard of care. Again the plaintiff excepted to that part of the instructions. . . .

The incongruity of making the medical profession the sole arbiter of what information was necessary for an informed decision to be made by a patient concerning his own physical well-being has led to various judicial and legislative attempts within the last decade to define a standard tailored to the needs of the patient but not unreasonably burdensome upon the physician or wholly dispensing with the notion that "doctor knows best" in some situations. While the essential ambivalence between the right of the patient to make a knowledgeable choice and the duty of the doctor to prescribe the treatment his professional judgment deems best for the patient has not been fully resolved, the outline has begun to emerge.

In a trilogy of cases decided in 1972 the traditional standard of customary medical practice in the community was abandoned by three jurisdictions as the criterion for informed consent in favor of a judicially imposed standard designed to provide a patient with information material to his decision upon a course of therapy. [Citations omitted.]

Despite the possibility of legislative revision, we are persuaded that criticism of the professional standard as expounded in *Canterbury* is well-founded and we, therefore, shall follow the lay standard of disclosure.

This standard was the basis for the charge given by the trial court upon informed consent. As we have noted, the plaintiff takes issue only with the single sentence of that charge which declares "[a]n alternative that is more hazardous is not a viable alternative." During the trial there was considerable testimony about the hazards of the needle biopsy, which had resulted in puncturing the plaintiff's gall bladder, as compared to an open biopsy requiring general anesthesia and a surgical incision. Philip Roen, a urologist called by the plaintiff, testified that the alternative of an open biopsy should have been discussed with the plaintiff with disclosure of the risks attending any surgical procedure conducted under general anesthesia. Three doctors presented by the defendants testified that an open renal biopsy was not a viable alternative to a needle biopsy. Another witness for the defendants, Malcolm Galen, a physician, testified that an open biopsy was more hazardous than a needle biopsy, but that he did inform his patients that the alternative of an open biopsy was available with its attendant risks, though he advised against it. It was conceded that an open biopsy alternative was never discussed with the plaintiff who, with the benefit of hindsight, testified that she would have chosen that procedure if she had known of it.

The instruction that an alternative which is more hazardous is not viable and, therefore, need not be mentioned to the patient has the effect of limiting the physician's duty to disclosure of only the least hazardous procedure available, presumably the one contemplated. The issue then becomes, not whether the patient has been informed of viable alternatives, but whether the doctor has recommended the least dangerous of them, because those which are more hazardous need not be discussed. This instruction, therefore, wholly relieves physicians of any obligation to discuss alternatives with their patients and substitutes merely a duty to recommend the safest procedure. It is incompatible, therefore, with the view which the trial court expressed in the remainder of the charge that the patient must be provided with sufficient information to allow him to make an intelligent choice.

The defendants have not attempted to defend or to cite any authority in support of the proposition that if an alternative is more hazardous it need not be disclosed, although its source appears to have been one of their requests to charge.[5] They contend (1) that there was overwhelming evidence that an open kidney biopsy was not a viable alternative to a closed needle biopsy; (2) that, because of the plaintiff's previous education and employment as a medical assistant to a physician, she was far more sophisticated in medicine than most patients; and (3) that the questioned sentence of the charge did not sufficiently distort the total effect of the charge, which was otherwise favorable to the plaintiff, so as to be prejudicial. We disagree. The plaintiff did produce at least one doctor who testified that an open biopsy was a viable alternative and the jury could reasonably have believed him rather than the several experts who testified for the defendants. The jury could also have found that the plaintiff had insufficient medical knowledge to be aware of the open biopsy procedure as a viable alternative for her. It is true, of course, that "a charge to the jury is to be judged in its entirety and harmful error cannot be predicated on detached sentences or portions of the charge unless it is reasonably probable that the jury could have been misled by them." Vandersluis v. Weil, 176 Conn. 353, 360, 407 A.2d 982 (1978). Although we are reluctant to find reversible error because of a single sentence of a lengthy charge, we are unable to avoid the conclusion that the error was probably harmful. The major focus of the testimony on the issue of informed consent was the relative hazard involved in each of the two medical procedures. In advising the jury

---

5. The requests to charge of the defendants Bogdan and Newberg included this statement, citing the note at 88 A.L.R.3d 1044. We have examined that annotation, but are unable to find anything in support of the proposition in question.

that more hazardous alternatives were not viable and could be withheld from the patient, the trial court invited them to decide the issue of informed consent simply by comparing the risks of the two procedures. The jury could well have understood that, if they concluded that an open biopsy was more hazardous than the needle biopsy performed, there was no duty to inform the plaintiff of that alternative. Such a misunderstanding would have been wholly inconsistent with the view we have adopted requiring that all viable alternatives be disclosed even though some involve more hazard than others. . . .

NOTES

Informed Consent as an Expression of Personal Autonomy and Medical-Consumer Choice

1. The *Canterbury* decision and its progeny since 1972 are an expression of much more than a rule that makes expert testimony concerning the professional standards of medical practice on consent "unacceptable." They are in essence a political statement, an acceptance of a "market theory" concerning the availability and delivery of medical and other health services. The *Logan* opinion reprinted above from the Supreme Court of Connecticut makes what is to this point the most specific formulation of a consumer-choice model. In this application, the attending doctor is required to review with the patient and allow choice of alternatives the physician personally believes too hazardous to offer or to deliver. Does such a requirement violate the physician's Hippocratic Oath not to do or offer to do harm to the patient? Is the Court "saved" from this criticism by the fact that the less hazardous procedure actually resulted in harm to the patient (due to the puncture of the gall bladder)? What does the Court mean by "feasible alternatives"?

2. An expansive and very well expressed viewpoint concerning a patient's right to know "the full picture" of what the physician knows, including uncertainties and ambiguities in the physician's own thinking, can be found in J. Katz, The Silent World of Doctor and Patient (1984). See also a symposium of articles expressing different positions concerning the ideas of Professor Katz in his book: Symposium, 9 W. New Engl. L. Rev. 1-226 (1987).

3. The concept of "full disclosure" of information "material" to a patient's decision should encompass more than merely a detailed litany of direct clinical risks of the proposed procedure. (Although the case law and most law-review commentary concentrates virtually exclusively on these factors.) The information given to patients should

also indicate the *relative benefits* of the proposed procedures and potential or feasible alternatives, such as differences in the quality of life to be expected from the various alternatives, the chances of going back to work at the same job (as a skilled carpenter, a professional ski instructor, a championship tennis player, etc.), and even a greater or lesser life-expectancy for a 35-year old patient.

Under a "market theory" model, the patient is also entitled to information about the costs of the proposed procedure as compared to potential or feasible alternatives, as well as the costs of after-care over a short or long period of time. The literature of cost-benefit analysis offers substantial support for the availability and utility of such data in health care consumer choice. See, for example, M. Weinstein & H. Fineberg, Clinical Decision Analysis (1980); K. Warner & B. Luce, Cost-Benefit Analysis and Cost-Effectiveness Analysis in Health Care: Principles, Practice and Potential (1982).

5. One of the great figures in the field of sociology, the late Talcott Parsons, expressed his views about the various models being formulated to describe the requirements of the physician-patient relationship. He described a "market model" where the patient is a "consumer" and decisions are essentially economic; a "bureaucratic association" where the health care system or governmental agency controls obligations and benefits; and a "democratic association" where all members of the health care system are equal. Prof. Parsons rejected each of these approaches and concluded,

> Adopting, as I have, the fashionable term "model" but without excessive commitment to it; it seems to me that none of the three models just reviewed, . . . provides a fully adequate framework for the social organization in which health services can appropriately be fitted. . . . I suggest that the conventional lines of conflict between seller and buyer and between employer and employee will not prove to be the key to analyzing the organizational structure in which health care is provided. . . . Indeed, I wish to suggest a distinct type, that of the *collegial association*, is the most appropriate and the most likely to have a strong prospect of survival in the field of purveying of professional services; and that this is not to be identified, in any facile fashion, with the market model, the bureaucratic model, or the democratic model.

Parsons, Epilogue, a chapter in The Doctor-Patient Relationship in the Changing Health Scene: Report of an International Conference. DHEW Pub No. (NIH) 78-183 (F. Gallagher ed. 1978). In the "collegial association model," Parsons supported the concept of the various parties in the health care system (patients, families, doctors, hospitals, etc.) accepting and supporting each other's special roles and expertise, and allowing separate but cooperative spheres of influence and decisionmaking. Do you find the Parson's approach a more acceptable and accurate description of the current-day social interactions in the health care system than the other models he described?

6. The Connecticut Court in *Logan* indicated it was adopting the *Canterbury* approach on requirements of disclosure, but the opinion does not go on to examine the remainder of the *Canterbury* opinion wherein that court adopted an objective test for proximate causation concerning the response of the plaintiff after receiving a more adequate explanation of risks and benefits of the suggested procedure and alternatives. Under Canterbury, as noted earlier in this chapter, the plaintiff must act prudently and will not be allowed recovery based merely on the self-serving presumption that he or she would not have consented to the procedure had the further information been disclosed. Such a theory of recovery would reward the patient for a "hindsight denial" of consent. Is that not what occurred in the *Logan* case? See further references on the issues of "proximate cause" in informed consent at pages 372-374.

Brenner & Gerken, Informed Consent: Myths and Risk Management Alternatives*
Risk Management and Quality Assurance: Issues and Interactions
(Chapman-Cliburn ed. 1986)

The evolving doctrine of informed consent is often cited as a major contributor to the increasing number of malpractice claims: Growing concern over the complex issue of "full disclosure" has provoked heated debate among health care and legal professionals. Although the doctrine is considered a component of good medical practice (conscientious communication with the patient), it is also seen as a perversion of the medical process, draping the provider-patient relationship in the trappings of legalism. In this context, every patient is a potential adversary, and communication is reduced to the provider's effort to avoid litigation. Also, some providers have difficulty accepting the patient's right (and responsibility) to participate in and ultimately to control the decision-making process, especially when the patient's choice contradicts the provider's.

Within such a setting, the doctrine of informed consent is an enigma for most risk management personnel. Many have experienced the anxiety of searching through a medical record for the right form when a patient has experienced an adverse outcome. Every risk man-

---

* This article appears as a chapter in Risk Management and Quality Assurance: Issues and Interactions (Chapman-Cliburn ed. 1986). It is reprinted by permission of the Quality Review Bulletin of which this publication was a special issue.
   This article follows medical rather than legal citation style. References appear at 319, following the main text of the article.

ager can testify to both the relief at finding a completed consent form and the panic at finding an inadequate consent form or none at all. The relief quickly turns to frustration when a patient complains that he did not understand the form, was forced into signing it, and would never have undergone the procedure had he known that a bad outcome could occur. It is not surprising that hospital personnel often think of the informed consent doctrine as conceived by expensive lawyers, implemented by irrational courts, and exploited by ungrateful patients.

Although these attitudes may be familiar, the informed consent doctrine is a powerful, rational concept that advances many of the goals of concerned risk managers. To demonstrate the doctrine's rationality and utility, the following discussion focuses on a series of "myths" that have arisen in bringing the doctrine from the courtroom to the hospital.

Eight Myths

Myth 1: Informed consent involves moral, ethical, and legal issues. An early landmark case in the evolution of informed consent is Schloendorff v. Society of New York Hospitals. This case involved the removal of a fibroid tumor from a patient's abdomen without her consent during a purportedly diagnostic procedure. In the *Schloendorff* decision, Justice Cardozo made an observation quoted in almost every treatise on informed consent: "Every human being of adult years and sound mind has a [legal] right to determine what shall be done with his own body."[1] This sentiment was further expressed in a report by the President's Commission for the Study of Ethical Problems in Medicine and Biomedical and Behavioral Research, Making Health Care Decisions: The Ethical and Legal Implications of Informed Consent in the Patient-Practitioner Relationship.[2] The report states that even if no legal doctrine of informed consent existed, the moral imperative of preserving the individual's right to choose what happens to his or her body would mandate faithful compliance with the principle of informed consent. The report further ascribes importance to the patient's right to make the "wrong" decision regardless of the medical practitioner's recommendations.

Although both Justice Cardozo and the President's Commission correctly identified the moral, ethical, and legal issues in informed consent, it would be a mistake to conclude that the concerns of health care professionals are only of a moral, ethical, or legal nature. Informed consent raises issues of quality as well. Evidence suggests that proper informed consent has direct impact on the quality of health care services; informed consent is a determinant of health care outcomes. . . .

IV. Informed Consent as a Basis of Liability

Myth 2: Signing the form constitutes the entire informed consent process. In essence, informed consent consists of the physician communicating important information to his patient and the patient consenting to the treatment. The physician must then record that such an exchange has occurred. Frequently, health care professionals confuse the record with the communication itself. The record of the physician-patient exchange is not a substitute for the communication but serves as written evidence of the communication. A physician should not only conscientiously discuss consent-related matters with every patient but should also keep a written record.

Under good risk management procedures, physicians should include in their progress notes any comments concerning the informed consent process. These notes can be simple: "I advised the patient of the procedure's material risks and of alternatives. The patient appeared alert, seemed to understand what I had to say, and felt comfortable with my advice." Such comments indicate that the practitioner did discuss the form and the procedure with the patient. In countless lawsuits involving informed consent, plaintiffs state, "I signed the form, but I didn't understand it, and the doctor never talked to me." Although often attributed to patients with "short memories," such comments further substantiate the need for adequate documentation.

Evidence in the medical literature suggests that consent forms do not contain meaningful information. Grundner applied two standard readability tests, the Fry Readability Scale and the Flesch Readability Formula, to five surgical consent forms. He found that "the readability of all five was approximately equivalent to that of the material intended for upper-division undergraduate and graduate students. Four of the five forms were written at the level of a scientific journal, and the fifth at the level of a specialized academic magazine." Grundner concluded that, since few consent forms could pass readability tests, "thousands of persons may be undergoing surgery each year on the basis of inadequate consent."[6] Grundner's study supports the conclusion that risk management of informed consent must focus less on the form of the process and more on its content.

Myth 3: All risks of the procedure need to be disclosed. A common misunderstanding about informed consent is the belief that if an undisclosed risk materializes, the physician will be liable to the patient for damages. The courts have long held that not all risks need to be disclosed. Risks that are obvious or that stand a statistically insignificant chance of materializing need not be disclosed. . . .

Myth 4: The physician needs to provide the patient with thorough knowledge on the procedure to be performed. One common misconception concerning informed consent is that the patient needs comprehensive knowledge of the procedure. In reality, a patient needs to receive essential, comprehensible information. In Cobbs v. Grant, the court stated that "the patient's interest in information does not extend to a lengthy polysyllabic disclosure on all possible complications. A minicourse in medical science is not required; the patient is concerned with the risk of death or bodily harm, and the problems of recuperation."[8]

Practitioners should be aware of the level to which disclosure is necessary for and desired by their patients. This level is a function of the patient's capacity to understand the significant consequences of a procedure rather than the technology used in performing it. For example, in a thoracic outlet procedure, it is much more important to tell the patient that pain and/or a winged scapula are potential complications rather than to discuss different technical aspects of removing the sixth rib.

Myth 5: The informed consent process consists solely of advising the patient of the procedure's risks. Although this myth adequately states one component of proper informed consent, it omits another essential element. In fact, the physician must advise patients of not only the risks involved in the procedure but also any appropriate alternative forms of treatment. This aspect of the informed consent doctrine is frequently neglected when providers advise patients only of the risks involved.

The requirement that alternatives be discussed originates with the courts' reasoning that the informed consent process consists of providing the patient with a variety of choices. The presentation of choices is the most salient aspect of the consent process; although the presentation of risk alone may contain implicit suggestions of alternatives, the patient must also be given the full array of therapeutic alternatives, even if one alternative is to do nothing. As the court in *Canterbury* stated,

> it is the prerogative of the patient, not the physician, to determine for himself the direction in which his interests [or peril] seem to lie. To enable a patient to change his course of direction understandably, some familiarity with the therapeutic alternatives and their hazards becomes essential.[7]

Myth 6: Informed consent is absolute: it applies to all patients, all the time. A frequent objection physicians make to informed consent is that some patients will react hysterically to disclosure of any risk, making such disclosure antitherapeutic. This provocative exception to the informed consent doctrine is the principle of "therapeutic privilege." Most states recognize, in one form or another, the physician's right to withhold information if disclosure would harm the patient's well-being. However, there is evidence to suggest that the therapeutic privilege is overused by physicians and applied to situations in which it is not necessary. In general, physicians overestimate the extent to which people find information troublesome. In medical training, there is a bias toward nondisclosure which is evident in studies comparing patients' desires for information with the physicians' perceptions of that desire. For example, while only 13% of physicians say they would give "a straight statistical prognosis" to patients with advanced lung cancer, 85% of the public wishes to have that sort of information.[3]

The physician should take several precautions when relying on the therapeutic privilege to withhold pertinent information from the patient. First, this decision should be discussed, in detail, with a relative or close friend of the patient. Second, the physician should consult the patient's family physician and/or psychiatrist. Third, the medical record should carefully reflect why information was withheld from the patient and should fully identify the friends, relatives, and/or practitioners who were consulted.

Myth 7: A physician who fails to obtain proper informed consent will always be found liable for complications arising from the procedure. One cause of the anxiety surrounding informed consent is the false belief that inadequate disclosure will inevitably lead to liability for patient injury. The patient is only entitled to compensation if there is a cause-and-effect relationship between the inadequate disclosure and the complication. For a patient to prove such a relationship, he or she must establish two crucial elements: that the complications resulted from an undisclosed material risk of the procedure: and that, had the risk been disclosed, the patient would have refused to undergo the procedure. These two elements of proof significantly reduce the likelihood of liability when the physician has disclosed the risks of death and serious bodily injury. Since a patient must establish a relationship between inadequate disclosure and an unfavorable health outcome, the question must inevitably be asked: If the patient consented to treatment after being advised of the risk of death or serious bodily harm, would the patient have refused treatment if an additional, lesser risk were also disclosed?

The true impact of this requirement can be appreciated by analyzing the courts' approach to cause-and-effect relationships in informed consent. The majority of courts have held that a patient must establish a cause-and-effect relationship objectively; in other words, the patient would generally have refused the procedure had the risk been disclosed. The courts recognize that some patients feel and express idiosyncratic responses to insignificant complications. The objective cause-and-effect relationship is required to protect the physician from litigation that results solely from such idiosyncratic responses. Some patients will react to slight fevers, insignificant rashes, mild pain, or short extensions of hospitalization. Courts do not recognize such claims of inadequate consent even if the complications were not disclosed. As the court in Canterbury v. Spence stated, "Better it is, we believe, to resolve the causality issue on an objective basis: in terms of what a prudent person in a patient's position would have decided if suitably informed of all perils bearing significance."[7]

Myth 8: Informed consent requires disclosing only the risks of performing a procedure. A new twist was added to the informed consent doctrine in the California case of Truman v. Thomas, after which commentators began speaking of the "doctrine of informed refusal." In *Truman*, the plaintiff's physician recommended that she undergo a Papanicolaou smear. When the plaintiff refused, the physician failed to advise her of the risks associated with not having the test. After she died from cervical cancer, her estate filed a wrongful death action, claiming the physician had an obligation to inform her of the importance of this diagnostic procedure. The California Supreme Court upheld the estate's cause of action.[9]

The *Truman* case presents a slight variation from the informed consent doctrine; it is also the judicial expression that physicians need to communicate with patients about all aspects of care that have an impact on their health and life. The courts reasoned that Truman had a right to know that her refusal to undergo a Papanicolaou smear posed a significant risk to her health and survival. The risks from her refusal threatened her well-being as much as risks from very dangerous procedures. The *Truman* decision allows us to say, with some degree of confidence, that physicians need to tell their patients that treatment of disease often poses risks of harm; that failure to treat certain conditions also poses such risks; and that modern medicine does not always have a simple or clear answer to the complex trade-offs a patient faces when deciding to consent or not consent to treatment. The physician must present information concerning these choices simply and comprehensibly to assure that the choice made is the patient's, not the provider's. The consent doctrine's profound expansion in Truman v. Thomas arises from the court's unwillingness to constrict the need for consultation between patient and provider when a patient is considering a procedure or treatment. . . .

Conclusion

Informed consent continues to be a complex issue. Practitioners and risk managers must constantly assess the fine line between advising the patient of possible risks and giving the patient hope and reassurance. Although evaluating the doctrine may be difficult, the health care professional should be guided by the principle of Cobbs v. Grant, that "good medicine makes good law."[8] As Gutheil et al recently noted:

> Ideally, the clinical utility of informed consent lies in bridging the gap between either of the two fantasies — helpless ignorance or omnipotent certainty — and a more complicated reality. To achieve this goal, however, physicians must stop thinking of informed consent as a formality . . . and enter into it with their patients as a process of mutual discovery. Informed consent as we envision it here is not an empty gesture toward liability reduction, but an interaction between physician and patient, a dialogue intended not only to satisfy their legal requirement, but to do more as well. The real clinical opportunity offered by informed consent is that of transforming uncertainty from a threat . . . into the very basis on which an alliance can be formed.[11]

Most health care practitioners view malpractice liability as an unrelenting series of negative events constantly exposing them to trouble. This fear and misunderstanding contribute to the perception of every patient as a potential adversary. From this, providers have developed a view of informed consent as a means of protecting themselves from claims and litigation.

When the doctrine is carefully examined, it appears that the fears of health care professionals may be overstated. Perhaps more importantly, these fears have generated responses that are counterproductive to both the physician and the patient. If practitioners can take the time to talk to, listen to, communicate with, and express concern for their patients, they will simultaneously be protecting themselves and helping those whom they, as concerned health care professionals, are committed to help.

REFERENCES

1. Schloendorff v. Society of N.Y. Hosps., 211 N.Y. 125, 105 N.E. 92 (1914).
2. President's Commission for the Study of Ethical Problems in Medicine and Biomedical and Behavioral Research: Making Health Care Decisions: The Ethical and Legal Implications of Informed Consent in the Patient-Practitioner Relationship. Washington, DC, 1982.
3. Andrews LB: Informed consent statutes and the decision making process. *J. Leg. Med.* 5:164-217, June 1984.
4. Steel K., et al.: Iatrogenic illness on a general medical service at a university hospital. *N. Engl. J. Med.* 304:638-642, Mar 12, 1981.
5. Donabedian A: The Methods and Findings of Quality Assessment

and Monitoring: An Illustrated Analysis. Ann Arbor, Mich: Health Administration Press, 1985.
6. Grundner TM: On the readability of surgical consent forms. *N. Engl. J. Med.* 302:900-902, Apr 17, 1980.
7. Canterbury v. Spence, 464 F.2d 722 (D.C. Cir. 1972), *cert. denied*, 409 U.S. 1064 (1972).
8. Cobbs v. Grant, 8 Cal. 2d 229, 104 Cal. Rptr. 505, 502 P.2d 1 (1972).
9. Truman v. Thomas, 165 Cal. Rptr. 308, 611 P.2d 902 (1980).
11. Gutheil TG, Bursztajn H, Brodsky A: Malpractice prevention through the sharing of uncertainty: Informed consent and therapeutic alliance. *N. Engl. J. Med.* 311:49-51, Jul 5, 1984.

NOTES

Risk Management Systems and Legal Responsibility to Obtain Informed Consent of Patient

1. The article reprinted above represents advice to hospital-based risk managers in regard to informed consent issues. Do you agree with each of the myths described? The risk managers and quality-assurance personnel in hospitals, health maintenance organizations, and other health care institutions are often given responsibility to ensure that the hospital and its medical staff have installed an effective program of informed-consent procedures. The courts often describe the obtaining of the patient's informed consent as a "nondelegable duty" of the attending physician. If so, what is the responsibility of the hospital? The traditional view is that the hospital has no duty (and no legal liability) for a privately practicing physician's (or surgeon's) violation of the duty of proper disclosure of information to obtain a valid informed consent. See the leading case, Fiorentino v. Wenger, 277 N.E.2d 296 (N.Y. 1967). See also more recent cases in accordance with *Fiorentino:* Krame v. St. Anthony Hosp. Systems, 738 P.2d 75 (1987); Alexander v. Gosner, 711 P.2d 347 (1986); Cox v. Haworth, 283 S.E.2d 392 (N. Car. 1981).

Despite the general rule, may a hospital incur legal liability for informed consent by adopting administrative policies placing duties upon employees such as nurses to impart information to patients? By requiring detailed and uniform consent documents for certain regularly performed clinical procedures? See Campbell v. Pitt County Mem. Hosp., Inc. 352 S.E.2d 902 (N. Car. 1987). See also J. Orlikoff & A. Vanagunas, Malpractice Prevention and Liability Control in Hospitals (1988).

2. Most hospitals and many other health care institutions (HMOs and nursing homes) employ patient advocates or patient representa-

tives who deal directly with patient complaints and misunderstandings. These professionals often become involved in problems of informed consent wherein they seek to help to solve problems of patient miscommunication. See N. Hogan, Humanizing Health Care: The Task of Patient Representatives (1980). Nurses also become involved in informed consent problems. See Bille, The Nurses' Role in Informed Consent, 6 Quality Rev. Bull. 25 (1980). Do nurses, patient representatives, risk managers, or other hospital personnel have obligations to intervene in a patient-care situation where they become aware that a patient has misunderstood what the doctor has proposed to do in a clinical procedure? Where a doctor seems to have negligently or deliberately misled a patient? See Hardy, When Doctrines Collide: Corporate Negligence, Respondent Superior, and Hospital Liability When Employees Fail to Speak Up, 61 Tulane L. Rev. 85 (1986).

V. CORPORATE LIABILITY AND ALTERNATIVE POLICIES OF LIABILITY FOR PHYSICIANS, HOSPITALS, HEALTH MAINTENANCE ORGANIZATIONS, AND OTHER HEALTH CARE ORGANIZATIONS

Darling v. Charleston Community Memorial Hospital
211 N.E.2d 253 (Ill. 1965), *cert. denied*, 383 U.S. 946 (1966)

MR. JUSTICE SCHAEFER: . . . On November 5, 1960, the plaintiff, who was 18 years old, broke his leg while playing in a college football game. He was taken to the emergency room at the defendant hospital where Dr. Alexander, who was on emergency call that day, treated him. Dr. Alexander, with the assistance of hospital personnel, applied traction and placed the leg in a plaster cast. A heat cradle was applied to dry the cast. Not long after the application of the cast plaintiff was in great pain and his toes, which protruded from the cast, became swollen and dark in color. They eventually became cold and insensitive. On the evening of November 6, Dr. Alexander "notched" the cast around the toes, and on the afternoon of the next day he cut the cast approximately three inches up from the foot. On November 8 he split the sides of the cast with a Stryker saw; in the course of cutting the cast the plaintiff's leg was cut on both sides. Blood and other seepage were observed by the nurses and others, and there was a stench in the room, which one witness said was the worst he had smelled since World War II. The plaintiff remained in Charleston Hospital until November 19, when he was transferred to Barnes Hospital in St. Louis and placed under the care of Dr. Fred

Reynolds, head of orthopedic surgery at Washington University School of Medicine and Barnes Hospital. Dr. Reynolds found that the fractured leg contained a considerable amount of dead tissue which in his opinion resulted from interference with the circulation of blood in the limb caused by swelling or hemorrhaging of the leg against the constriction of the cast. Dr. Reynolds performed several operations in a futile attempt to save the leg but ultimately it had to be amputated eight inches below the knee.

The evidence before the jury is set forth at length in the opinion of the Appellate Court and need not be stated in detail here. The plaintiff contends that it is established that the defendant was negligent in permitting Dr. Alexander to do orthopedic work of the kind required in this case, and not requiring him to review his operative procedures to bring them up to date; in failing, through its medical staff, to exercise adequate supervision over the case, especially since Dr. Alexander had been placed on emergency duty by the hospital, and in not requiring consultation, particularly after complications had developed. Plaintiff contends also that in a case which developed as this one did, it was the duty of the nurses to watch the protruding toes constantly for changes of color, temperature and movement, and to check circulation every ten to twenty minutes, whereas the proof showed that these things were done only a few times a day. Plaintiff argues that it was the duty of the hospital staff to see that these procedures were followed, and that either the nurses were derelict in failing to report developments in the case to the hospital administrator, he was derelict in bringing them to the attention of the medical staff, or the staff was negligent in failing to take action. Defendant is a licensed and accredited hospital, and the plaintiff contends that the licensing regulations, accreditation standards, and its own bylaws define the hospital's duty, and that an infraction of them imposes liability for the resulting injury.

The defendant's position is stated in the following excerpts from its brief:

> It is a fundamental rule of law that only an individual properly educated and licensed, and not a corporation, may practice medicine. . . . Accordingly, a hospital is powerless under the law to forbid or command any act by a physician or surgeon in the practice of his profession. . . . A hospital is not an insurer of the patient's recovery, but only owes the patient the duty to exercise such reasonable care as his known condition requires and that degree of care, skill and diligence used by hospitals generally in that community. . . . Where the evidence shows that the hospital care was in accordance with standard practice obtaining in similar hospitals, and Plaintiff produces no evidence to the contrary, the jury cannot conclude that the opposite is true even if they disbelieve the hospital witnesses. . . . A hospital is not liable for the torts of its nurse committed while the nurse was but executing the orders of the

V. Corporate Liability and Alternative Policies of Liability

patient's physician, unless such order is so obviously negligent as to lead any reasonable person to anticipate that substantial injury would result to the patient from the execution of such order. . . . The extent of the duty of a hospital with respect to actual medical care of a professional nature such as is furnished by a physician is to use reasonable care in selecting medical doctors. When such care in the selection of the staff is accomplished, and nothing indicates that a physician so selected is incompetent or that such incompetence should have been discovered, more cannot be expected from the hospital administration.

The basic dispute, as posed by the parties, centers upon the duty that rested upon the defendant hospital. That dispute involves the effect to be given to evidence concerning the community standard of care and diligence, and also the effect to be given to hospital regulations adopted by the State Department of Public Health under the Hospital Licensing Act (Ill. Rev. Stat. 1963, chap. 111½, pars. 142-157.), to the Standards for Hospital Accreditation of the American Hospital Association, and to the bylaws of the defendant.

As has been seen, the defendant argues in this court that its duty is to be determined by the care customarily offered by hospitals generally in its community. Strictly speaking, the question is not one of duty, for ". . . in negligence cases, the duty is always the same, to conform to the legal standard of reasonable conduct in the light of the apparent risk. What the defendant must do, or must not do, is a question of the standard of conduct required to satisfy the duty." (Prosser on Torts, 3rd ed. at 331.) "By the great weight of modern American authority a custom either to take or to omit a precaution is generally admissible as bearing on what is proper conduct under the circumstances, but is not conclusive." 2 Harper and James, The Law of Torts, sec. 17.3, at 977-78. Custom is relevant in determining the standard of care because it illustrates what is feasible, it suggests a body of knowledge of which the defendant should be aware, and it warns of the possibility of far-reaching consequences if a higher standard is required. (Morris, Custom and Negligence, 42 Colum. L. Rev. 1147 (1942); 2 Wigmore, Evidence, 3rd ed. secs. 459, 461.) *But custom should never be conclusive.* As Judge Learned Hand said, "There are, no doubt, cases where courts seem to make the general practice of the calling the standard of proper diligence; We have indeed given some currency to the notion ourselves. . . . Indeed in most cases reasonable prudence is in fact common prudence; but strictly it is never its measure; a whole calling may have unduly lagged in the adoption of new and available devices. It never may set its own tests, however persuasive be its usages. Courts must in the end say what is required; there are precautions so imperative that even their universal disregard will not excuse their omission." The T.J. Hooper, (2d cir. 1932,) 60 Fed. 2d 737, 740.

In the present case the regulations, standards, and bylaws which the plaintiff introduced into evidence, performed much the same function as did evidence of custom. This evidence aided the jury in deciding what was feasible and what the defendant knew or should have known. It did not conclusively determine the standard of care and the jury was not instructed that it did.

"The conception that the hospital does not undertake to treat the patient, does not undertake to act through its doctors and nurses, but undertakes instead simply to procure them to act upon their own responsibility, no longer reflects the fact. Present-day hospitals, as their manner of operation plainly demonstrates, do far more than furnish facilities for treatment. They regularly employ on a salary basis a large staff of physicians, nurses and interns, as well as administrative and manual workers, and they charge patients for medical care and treatment, collecting for such services, if necessary, by legal action. Certainly, the person who avails himself of 'hospital facilities' expects that the hospital will attempt to cure him, not that its nurses or other employes will act on their own responsibility." (Fuld J., in Bing v. Thunig, (1957) 2 N.Y.2d 656, 143 N.E.2d 3, 8.) The Standards for Hospital Accreditation, the state licensing regulations and the defendant's bylaws demonstrate that the medical profession and other responsible authorities regard it as both desirable and feasible that a hospital assume certain responsibilities for the care of the patient.

We now turn to an application of these considerations to this case. The defendant did not object to the instruction on the issues, which followed Illinois Pattern Jury Instruction 20.01. Nor did it move to withdraw any issues from the jury. Under section 68 of the Civil Practice Act, an entire verdict is not to be set aside because one asserted ground of recovery was defective or inadequately proven, if one or more of the grounds is sufficient, unless a motion to withdraw the issue in question was made. (Ill. Rev. Stat. 1963, chap. 110, par. 68(4).) Therefore we need not analyze all of the issues submitted to the jury. Two of them were that the defendant had negligently: "5. Failed to have a sufficient number of trained nurses for bedside care of all patients at all times capable of recognizing the progressive gangrenous condition of the plaintiff's right leg, and of bringing the same to the attention of the hospital administration and to the medical staff so that adequate consultation could have been secured and such conditions rectified; . . . 7. Failed to require consultation with or examination by members of the hospital surgical staff skilled in such treatment; or to review the treatment rendered to the plaintiff and to require consultants to be called in as needed."

We believe that the jury verdict is supportable on either of these grounds. On the basis of the evidence before it the jury could reasonably have concluded that the nurses did not test for circulation in the leg as frequently as necessary, that skilled nurses would have promptly recognized the conditions that signalled a dangerous impairment of circulation in the plaintiff's leg, and would have known that the condition would become irreversible in a matter of hours. At that point it became the nurses' duty to inform the attending physician, and if he failed to act, to advise the hospital authorities so that appropriate action might be taken. As to consultation, there is no dispute that the hospital failed to review Dr. Alexander's work or require a consultation; the only issue is whether its failure to do so was negligence. On the evidence before it the jury could reasonably have found that it was. . . .

Judgment Affirmed.

NOTES

The Development of Hospital Liability for the Malpractice of Independent Physicians

1. The most significant medical malpractice case of the 1960s was undoubtedly the *Darling* case. It greatly influenced the new standards of the Joint Committee on the Accreditation of Hospitals in 1971 and virtually became the official philosophy of the American Hospital Association. See Southwick, The Hospital's New Responsibility, 17 Cleve.-Mar. L. Rev. 146 (1968); Copeland, Hospital Responsibility for Basic Care Provided by Medical Staff Members: "Am I My Brother's Keeper?," 5 N. Kent. L. Rev. 27 (1978). In the courts, see particularly the interpretation offered by the Nevada Supreme Court:

> Today in response to demands of the public, the hospital is becoming a community health center. The purpose of the community hospital is to provide patient care of the highest possible quality. To implement this duty of providing competent medical care to patients, it is the responsibility of the institution to create a workable system whereby the medical staff of the hospital continually reviews and evaluates the quality of care being rendered within the institution. The staff must be organized with a proper structure to carry out the role delegated to it by the governing body. All powers of the medical staff flow from the board of trustees, and the staff must be held accountable for its control of quality. The concept of corporate responsibility for the quality of medical care was forcibly advanced in Darling v. Charleston Community Memorial Hospital. . . . The role of the hospital vis-à-vis the community is changing rapidly. The hospital's role is no longer limited to the furnishing of physical facilities and equipment where a physician treats his private patients and practices his profession in his own individualized manner.

Moore v. Board of Trustees of Carson-Tahoe Hospital, 495 P.2d 605 (Nev. 1972).

2. The AMA's reaction to the *Darling* decision was immediate and negative. In its comment on the case in 12 Citation 82 (1965) it said, "The effect of this decision is unfortunate since it appears to place a hospital in a position where it must exercise control over the practice of medicine by physicians on its attending staff in order to avoid liability. This is apt to encourage control of the practice of medicine by persons who are not licensed physicians. The decision is also unfortunate because it is apt to discourage the adoption of high standards which are intended to improve the level of hospital care, but which may now be misinterpreted as a basis for liability."

3. The *Darling* case is frequently referred to as a landmark decision in the field of hospital liability because it placed at least some degree of direct responsibility on the hospital for the maintenance of an acceptable standard of care of patients. Rapp, Darling and Its Progeny: A Radical Approach Toward Hospital Liability, 60 Ill. B.J. 883 (1972); Walkup & Kelly, Hospital Liability: Changing Patterns of Responsibility, 14 Cal. Trial Law. Assn. J. 41 (1975); Comment, The Hospital and the Staff Position — An Expanding Duty of Care, 7 Creighton L. Rev. 249 (1974); Symposium on Darling v. Charleston Community Memorial Hospital, 11 Forum 727 (1976); Lisko, Hospital Liability Under Theories of Respondeat Superior and Corporate Negligence, 47 U. Mo. Kan. City L. Rev. 171 (1978). See also Hackler, Expansion of Health Care Provider's Liability: an Application of Darling to Long-Term Health Care Facilities, 9 Conn. L. Rev. 462 (1977); Note, 14 A.L.R.3d 873 (1978).

4. For more recent applications of the rulings in *Darling*, see Schoening v. Grays Harbor Community Hospital, 698 P.2d 593 (Wash. App. 1985), wherein a hospital was held liable for a failure to provide monitoring and supervision of an attending independent physician who allowed a patient to deteriorate seriously under the observation of employed staff nursing personnel. See also 12 A.L.R.4th 57 (1982). Is a hospital liable for the negligence of medical staff physicians in their office practice prior to hospitalization of a patient? See Pedroza v. Bryant, 677 P.2d 166 (Wash. 1984) wherein liability could be imposed on the hospital if it had actual or constructive notice of the negligence of the physician and failed to take action to protect the interests of the hospitalized patient.

Johnson v. Misericordia Community Hospital
301 N.W.2d 156 (Wis. 1981)

COFFEY, JUSTICE.

This is a review of a decision of the court of appeals affirming

V. Corporate Liability and Alternative Policies of Liability

a judgment of the circuit court for Milwaukee County, the judgment was entered in favor of the plaintiff-respondent, James Johnson, pursuant to a jury verdict finding the defendant-petitioner, Misericordia Community Hospital (Misericordia), Milwaukee, negligent in granting orthopedic surgical privileges to Dr. Lester V. Salinsky. . . .

In summary, we hold that a hospital owes a duty to its patients to exercise reasonable care in the selection of its medical staff and in granting specialized privileges. The final appointing authority resides in the hospital's governing body,[27] although it must rely on the medical staff and in particular the credentials committee (or committee of the whole) to investigate and evaluate an applicant's qualifications for the requested privileges.[28] However, this delegation of the responsibility to investigate and evaluate the professional competence of applicants for clinical privileges does not relieve the governing body of its duty to appoint only qualified physicians and surgeons to its medical staff and periodically monitor and review their competency.[29] The credentials committee (or committee of the whole) must investigate the qualifications of applicants. The facts of this case demonstrate that a hospital should, at a minimum, require completion of the application and verify the accuracy of the applicant's statements, especially in regard to his medical education, training and experience.[30] Additionally, it should: (1) solicit information from the applicant's peers, including those not referenced in his application, who are knowledgeable about his education, training, experience, health, competence and ethical character; (2) determine if the applicant is currently licensed to practice in this state and if his licensure or registration has been or is currently being challenged; and (3) inquire whether the applicant has been involved in any adverse malpractice action and whether he has experienced a loss of medical organization membership or medical privileges or membership at any other hospital.[31] The investigating committee must also evaluate the information gained through its inquiries and make a reasonable judgment as to the approval or denial of each application for staff privileges. The hospital will be charged with gaining and evaluating the knowledge that would have been acquired had it exercised ordinary care in investigating its medical staff applicants and the hospital's failure to

---

27. Wis. Adm. Code, secs. H24.02(1)(a), 24.04(1) and 24.04(1)(d). See also: The Joint Commission on Accreditation of Hospital Standards in the American Hospital Association Manual, pp. 54-56 (hereinafter referred to as AHA Manual).

28. Wis. Adm. Code, secs. H24.04(1)(d) and 24.04(1)(k); AHA Manual, pp. 55-56.

29. Wis. Adm. Code, secs. H24.02(1), 24.02(1)(e) and 24.04(1)(d).

30. See: AHA Manual, p. 94, suggesting that the application form require this information.

31. Id.

exercise that degree of care, skill and judgment that is exercised by the average hospital in approving an applicant's request for privileges is negligence. This is not to say that hospitals are *insurers* of the competence of their medical staff, for a hospital will not be negligent if it exercises the noted standard of care in selecting its staff.

The decision of the Court of Appeals is affirmed.

Richmond County Hospital Authority v. Brown
361 S.E.2d 164 (Ga. 1987)

[The plaintiff was injured in an automobile accident and was taken to the defendant University Hospital emergency department. He was treated therein by two physicians. The plaintiff alleges negligence on the part of the two physicians resulting in serious further injury and disability. The two physicians were employed by an intermediary corporation, Coastal Emergency Services, Inc., which in turn contracted with University Hospital to offer all physician services in the emergency department. The trial court granted summary judgment against both University Hospital and Coastal Emergency Services, Inc., on the basis that no agency was established between these corporations and the physicians who were otherwise independent contractors. The Court of Appeals agreed with the summary judgment in regard to actual agency, but ordered a trial on the issue of ostensible agency as to the hospital. The summary judgment was affirmed in regard to Coastal Emergency Services Inc.]

GREGORY, J.

Across the nation the ostensible agency doctrine has been widely applied to certain hospital/doctor arrangements. In particular it has been applied to emergency room settings. See the citations listed by the Court of Appeals in *Brown*, supra, at 896, 354 S.E.2d 632. See also, Butler and Laszlo, "Hosp. Liability for Physician Negligence in Ga.: A Realistic Approach," 37 Mercer L. Rev. 817 (Winter 1986). We note too that the result we reach today was anticipated by Judge Murphy in Stewart v. Midani, 525 F. Supp. 843(4) (1981). The history and development of this law will not be set out here but we observe it has been well considered by Justice Leibson in Paintsville Hosp. Co. v. Rose, 683 S.W.2d 255 (Ky. 1985). See also, Adamski v. Tocoma Gen. Hosp., 20 Wash. App. 98, 579 P.2d 970 (1978).

The argument is made by University Hospital and in briefs of a number of amici that a physician is licensed to practice medicine, exercises special knowledge and skill, and therefore may not be controlled in these functions by another. Thus, they maintain, Drs. Fowler and Willoughby cannot in any event be agents of the hospital for the performance of their professional duties. The tortured application of this view through the years is analyzed in the Court of Appeals' opinion. There may have been a time when all the world knew hospitals were mere structures where physicians treated and cared for their patients. In such a society one would be hard pressed to show that he justifiably relied on the hospital to care for his illness or injury through doctors employed for that purpose. But the situation has evolved. Most modern hospitals hold themselves out to the public as providing many health related services including services of physicians. A patient is likely to look to the hospital, not just to a particular doctor he comes into contact with through the hospital. That is what the Browns contend in this case. If they can prove the hospital represented to Isiah Brown that its emergency room physicians were its employees and that he therefore justifiably relied on the skill of the doctors but suffered injury due to the legal insufficiency of their medical services, the hospital may be held liable therefor. Capan v. Divine Providence Hospital, 287 Pa. Super. 364, 430 A.2d 647 (1981).

It should be noted that the doctrine can seldom apply to the customary situation in which a patient consults his own doctor who then has him admitted to a hospital where the doctor renders negligent medical services. In such a case there is no representation or holding out by the hospital to the patient. The hospital does not furnish him a doctor. He obtains his own.

Judgment affirmed.

All the Justices concur, except MARSHALL, C.J., dissents.

Jackson v. Power
743 P.2d 1376 (Alaska 1987)

BURKE, JUSTICE.

This case presents an issue of first impression in this state, concerning health care delivery in hospital emergency rooms. The question that we must resolve is whether a hospital may be held vicariously liable for negligent health care rendered by an emergency room physician who is not an employee of the hospital, but is, instead, an independent contractor. We hold that the hospital in this case had a non-delegable duty to provide non-negligent physician care in its emergency room and, therefore, may be liable. . . .

Jackson's final point is that the trial court erred in refusing to rule, as a matter of law, that FMH, as a general acute care hospital, has a non-delegable duty to provide non-negligent physician care in its emergency room. In essence, Jackson's position is that when a hospital undertakes to operate an emergency room as an integral part of its health care enterprise, public policy dictates that it not be allowed to insulate itself from liability by shunting that responsibility onto another.

FMH, on the other hand, argues that a hospital does not have a non-delegable duty to guarantee safe treatment in its emergency room. Physicians, not hospitals, FMH asserts, have a duty to practice medicine non-negligently. Thus, according to FMH, a hospital cannot be held to have delegated away a duty it never had.

The trial court ruled that "[t]here cannot be a non-delegable duty if there is no contractual relationship." Since it was unclear from the evidence whether or not there was any contractual relationship between ERI and FMH, the court denied Jackson's motion for summary judgment. Initially, we note the trial court's erroneous characterization of the issue. By holding that there can be no "non-delegable duty if there is no contractual relationship," the court confused the question of the existence of a duty with the issue of whether a duty is non-delegable. The flaw in this reasoning is self-evident. As FMH points out, a party cannot be held to have delegated away a duty it never had. Thus, the threshold question is whether FMH had a duty to provide emergency room care. Only if it did, is it necessary to determine what that duty entailed.

FMH is licensed as a "general acute care hospital."[11] As such, it is required to comply with state regulations designed to promote "safe and adequate treatment of individuals in hospitals in the interest of public health, safety and welfare." AS 18.-20.060. These regulations provided, at the time of Jackson's accident, that an acute care hospital *shall* "insure that a physician is available to respond to an emergency at all times." Former 7 AAC 12.110(c)(2).[12] Thus, at a minimum, the law imposed a duty on FMH to provide emergency care physicians on a 24-hour basis.

FMH, however, voluntarily assumed a much broader duty. At the time of Jackson's accident, FMH was accredited by the Joint Committee on the Accreditation of Hospitals (JCAH).[13] In order to receive and maintain accreditation,[14] FMH had to comply with the

---

11. A general acute care hospital is a "facility which provides hospitalization for inpatient medical care of acute illness or injury and obstetric care." 7 AAC 12.100.

12. In 1983, this regulation was amended to provide that "[a] general acute care hospital *must* provide . . . [among other services not relevant here] emergency care services." 7 AAC 12.105 (emphasis added).

13. The JCAH was formed in the early 1950's by the American College of Surgeons, the American College of Physicians, the American Hospital Association, and the American Medical Association. Its purpose was to establish minimum hospital standards for patient care. For details of the program, see Dornette, The Legal Impact on Voluntary Standards in Civil Actions Against the Health Care Provider, N.Y.L. Sch. L. Rev. 925, 925-28 (1977); Holbrook & Dunn, Medical Malpractice Litigation: The Discoverability and Use of Hospitals' Quality Assurance Committee Records, 16 Washburn L.J. 54, 57 (1976).

14. Hospitals voluntarily seek accreditation for financial and professional prestige reasons. First, accreditation by the JCAH means the hospital qualifies to participate in the federal Medicare and Medicaid programs. Accreditation by JCAH is deemed

V. Corporate Liability and Alternative Policies of Liability

JCAH's standards promulgated in the Accreditations Manual For Hospitals, Emergency Services. Standard I mandates that all accredited hospitals implement a well defined plan for emergency care based on community need and the capability of the hospital. The JCAH standards also mandate, among other things, that: (1) FMH's emergency room be directed by a physician member of the active medical staff (Standard II); (2) FMH's emergency room be integrated with other units and departments of the hospital (Standard III); (3) that emergency care be guided by written policies and procedures; and (4) that the quality of care be continually reviewed, evaluated and assured through establishment of quality control mechanisms (Standard V).

Additionally, FMH's own bylaws provided for the establishment and maintenance of an emergency room. Article X, section 1(d)(1)(b) of FMH's Medical Bylaws provides for an emergency room as one of the services of the hospital. Article XI, section 3(e) provides for the creation of an emergency room committee which is required among other things to:

a) formulate rules and regulations for the continuous coverage of the emergency room; and
b) supervise the clinical work in that department.

Based upon the above, it cannot seriously be questioned that FMH had a duty to provide emergency room services and that part of that duty was to provide physician care in its emergency room. Having so determined, we must next ascertain whether FMH's duty to provide physician care in the emergency room is non-delegable. That is, we must determine whether, having assumed the duty to staff an emergency room, FMH should be allowed to avoid responsibility for the care rendered therein by claiming that the physicians it provides are not its employees. We conclude that it cannot.

Our principal decision on non-delegable duty is [Alaska Airlines v. Sweat,] 568 P.2d 916. In that case, Sweat sued Alaska Airlines for injuries sustained in an air crash while traveling aboard a Chitina Air Service plane. Id. at 922. Chitina had been engaged under a contract with Alaska Airlines to service a portion of Alaska Airlines' regularly scheduled routes. Id. at 921, 922. Alaska Airlines contended that Chitina was an independent contractor and therefore it was not liable

---

substantial compliance with the Medicare conditions of participation. 42 U.S.C. §1395bb (1982); 42 C.F.R. §405.1901(d) (1986). See generally, Dornette, supra n.13 at 927, Holbrook & Dunn, supra n.13, at 58. Second, JCAH accreditation is often a prerequisite to obtaining approval of internship and residency programs. See generally, American Medical Association Directory of Accredited Residencies 3 (1975-76), quoted in Dornette, supra n.13, at 928. Finally, the institution's reputation and standing in the community is affected by whether it receives JCAH accreditation. See Holbrook & Dunn, supra n.13.

for Chitina's negligence. Id. at 923. The trial court found Alaska Airlines vicariously liable based on Restatement (Second) of Torts §428. Id. On appeal, we affirmed the trial court's decision on the alternative ground that Alaska Airlines owed a common law nondelegable duty of safety to its passengers. Id. at 925. . . .

We have little trouble concluding that patients, such as Jackson, receiving treatment at a hospital emergency room are as deserving of protection as the airline passengers in *Sweat*. Likewise, the importance to the community of a hospital's duty to provide emergency room physicians rivals the importance of the common-carriers' duty for the safety of its passengers. We also find a close parallel between the regulatory scheme of airlines and hospitals. Undoubtedly, the operation of a hospital is one of the most regulated activities in this state. Besides the license,[15] and certificate of need,[16] requirements mentioned above, a hospital must comply with state regulations promulgated to control its activities, AS 18.20.070, 7 AAC 12.610; adopt a state approved risk management program "to minimize the risk of injury to patients," AS 18.20.075; and undergo "annual inspections and investigations" of its facilities, AS 18.20.080. Failure to comply with these statutory requirements can lead to suspension or revocation of the hospital's license. AS 18.20.050.

The hospital regulatory scheme and the purpose underlying it (to "provide for the development, establishment, and enforcement of standards for the care and treatment of hospital patients that promote safe and adequate treatment" AS 18.20.010), along with the statutory definition of a hospital, (an institution devoted primarily to providing diagnosis, treatment or care to individuals, AS 18.20.130(3)), manifests the legislature's recognition that it is the hospital as an institution which bears ultimate responsibility for complying with the mandates of the law. It is the hospital that is required to ensure compliance with the regulations and thus, relevant to the instant case, it is the hospital that bears final accountability for the provision of physicians for emergency room care. We, therefore, hold that a general acute care hospital's duty to provide physicians for emergency room care is non-delegable. Thus, a hospital such as FMH may not shield itself from liability by claiming that it is not responsible for the results of negligently performed health care when the law imposes a duty on the hospital to provide that health care.

We are persuaded that the circumstances under which emergency room care is provided in a modern hospital mandates the rule we adopt today. Not only is this rule consonant with the public perception of the hospital as a multifaceted health care facility responsible for

---

15. See AS 18.20.020.
16. See AS 18.07.031.

the quality of medical care and treatment rendered, it also treats tort liability in the medical arena in a manner that is consistent with the commercialization of American medicine. Finally, we simply cannot fathom why liability should depend upon the technical employment status of the emergency room physician who treats the patient. It is the hospital's duty to provide the physician, which it may do through any means at its disposal. The means employed, however, will not change the fact that the hospital will be responsible for the care rendered by physicians it has a duty to provide.

This holding is necessarily limited. We do not change the standard of care with which a physician must comply, nor do we extend the duty which we find non-delegable beyond its natural scope. Our holding does not extend to situations where the patient is treated by his or her own doctor in an emergency room provided for the convenience of the doctor. Such situations are beyond the scope of the duty assumed by an acute care hospital. Rather our holding is limited to those situations where a patient comes to the hospital, as an institution, seeking emergency room services and is treated by a physician provided by the hospital. In such situations, the hospital shall be vicariously liable for damages proximately caused by a physician's negligence or malpractice.

In the instant case, Jackson came to FMH as an institution seeking emergency room services. Dr. Power was a physician FMH had a non-delegable duty to provide. FMH is, therefore, vicariously liable as a matter of law for any negligence or malpractice that Dr. Power may have committed. Accordingly, the trial court's ruling on this issue must be reversed. Jackson is entitled to partial summary judgment on the issue of FMH's vicarious liability. . . .

For the reasons outlined above, the trial court's denial of summary judgment on Jackson's theories of enterprise liability and apparent authority are affirmed. However because we hold that FMH has a non-delegable duty to provide non-negligent physician care in its emergency room, the trial court's denial of summary judgment on the theory of non-delegable duty, is reversed and remanded with instructions to enter partial summary judgment on the issue of FMH vicarious liability in favor of Jackson.

Affirmed in part; reversed in part; and remanded.

NOTES

Corporate Liability of Health Care Institutions: Various Theories

1. The three cases gathered above provide a spectrum of judicial theories applied to determine corporate responsibilities for injuries

to patients in health care institutions. The *Misericordia* case is generally recognized as the leading case establishing corporate negligence liability, especially in regard to responsibilities clearly identified with the duties of the chief operating officers and the governing boards of the institutions.

The court in *Misericordia*, however, was able to rely heavily on already established legislative policies in placing responsibilities on governing boards and organized medical staffs of licensed hospitals in Wisconsin. The type of statutory duties found in Wisconsin have been adopted widely across the United States, particularly since the mid-1980s, as a part of hospital risk management programs. See A. Southwick, The Law of Hospital and Health Care Administration ch. 13 (2d ed. 1988). On the structure of hospital risk management programs, see J. Orlikoff & A. Vanagunas, Malpractice Prevention and Liability Control for Hospitals (1988); G. Kraus, Health Care Risk Management (1986); G. Troyer & S. Salman, Handbook of Health Care Risk Management (1985); E. Richards & K. Rathbunn, Medical Risk Management (1983). On the legal responsibilities of organized medical staffs to monitor and discipline physicians practicing in hospitals, see W. Isele, The Hospital Medical Staff: Its Legal Rights and Responsibilities (1984).

2. The most celebrated of the earlier cases wherein a hospital was held liable for failures to monitor competence in its medical staff arose from the litigation against Dr. John Nork in Sacramento County, California. This physician was sued in over 60 law suits filed in the county between 1972 and 1973. The hospital was the Mercy Hospitals of Sacramento. The trial court found that the hospital had no actual knowledge of Dr. Nork's failures to render safe and effective treatment, and it had complied with then-existing requirements of the Joint Commission on Accreditation of Hospitals. Nevertheless, Superior Court Judge Goldberg found the hospital responsible, asserting: "I have reached the conclusion that the hospital is liable with great reluctance, because I am sure that the Sisters of Mercy have done everything within their power to run a proper institution. But they, like every hospital governing board, are corporately responsible for the conduct of their medical staff." Gonzales v. Nork, No. 228566, Cal. Sup. Ct., Nov 27, 1973; *rev'd on other grounds*, 131 Cal. Rptr. 717 (Cal. App. 1976), *rev'd and remanded*, 573 P.2d 458, 240 (Cal. 1978). See an extended excerpt from Judge Goldberg's unreported original 200-page opinion in S. Law & S. Polan, Pain and Profit: The Politics of Malpractice (1978). The acceptance of hospital corporate liability by an appellate court in California came in Elam v. College Park Hospital, 183 Cal. Rptr. 156, *modified*, 133 Cal. App. 3d 94a (1982). See also Curran, A Further Solution to the Malpractice Problem: Corporate Liability of Hospitals, 310 New Eng. J. Med. 704 (1984).

3. The *Misericordia* case involved a small hospital with a very small medical staff. The statutes applied and the judicial positions adopted by the Court have been said to be more properly applicable to larger, more comprehensive hospitals meeting the description of "the modern-day scientific research center" described in the opinion. Must all licensed hospitals have the financial resources and the medical manpower to meet the requirements laid out in *Misericordia*? A student note in the Wisconsin Law Review greeted the *Misericordia* decision with considerable concern over issues of this nature in the state. See Note, Johnson v. Misericordia Community Hospital: Corporate Liability of Hospitals Arrives in Wisconsin, 1983 Wis. L. Rev. 453. The Note describes the decision as "overbroad" and as creating "an overgeneralized view of the structure of Wisconsin's health care industry." Id. 471-472. It is asserted that hospitals in large cities such as Milwaukee and Madison may be of the character described in the judicial ruling, but for smaller hospitals, economic constraints are likely to make compliance difficult. The Note concludes, "The Wisconsin Supreme Court in *Johnson* thus failed to recognize that all hospitals are not large, sophisticated medical centers." Id. at 472. See also Hollowell, Does Hospital Corporate Liability Extend to Medical Staff Supervision?, 32 Defense L. Rev. 202 (1983).

4. Do hospitals have *moral obligations* to safeguard their patients, even from harm from their own freely chosen physicians? Do such moral obligations also apply to patients' wishes for particular forms of treatment, or to patients' refusal of treatment? Hospital organizations suggest that health care institutions should adopt general policy statements indicating what they consider proper areas of responsibility for their institutions. See Kapp, Can Hospitals Have Moral Objections?, 17 Hastings Cent. Rep. 43 (1987). See also AHA, Values in Conflict: Resolving Ethical Issues in Hospital Care, Report of the Special Committee on Bioethics (1985); Miles, Singer & Seigler, Conflicts Between Patient's Wishes to Forgo Treatment and the Policies of Health Care Facilities, 321 New Eng. J. Med. 48 (1989).

5. The *Brown* case illustrates the application of ostensible or apparent agency to hospital responsibility for emergency care physicians. The clinical situation of emergency care was quite similar in the *Darling* case which began the movement toward corporate negligence.

Would the *Darling* case have been as significant as a turning point in the law if the court had merely applied an ostensible agency doctrine? See Classen, Hospital Liability for Independent Contractors: Where Do We Go From Here?, 37 Def. L.J. 75 (1988); Lisko, Hospital Liability Under Theories of Respondent Superior and Corporate Negligence, 47 U. Mo. Kansas City L. Rev. 171 (1978). For a symposium of articles on the *Darling* case, see 11 Forum 727 (1976). See also Hackler, Expansion of Health Care Provider's Liability: An Application of Darling to Long-Term Care Facilities, 9 Conn. L. Rev. 462 (1977). See also 12 A.L.R.4th 57 (1982).

6. The *Jackson* case examines a range of theories that have been suggested to expand the legal liability of hospitals for injuries to patients. The applications of a nondelegable duty represents a means of preventing health care institutions from shielding themselves from liability by using independent physicians or contract services. The comparison to airlines does suggest enterprise liability, and even a *dangerous enterprise* liability. Are there other departments or functions of a hospital that are comparable to the emergency department in carrying a nondelegable duty? What are the characteristics of such a duty? Would an X-ray department fit such a definition? See Beeck v. Tucson Gen. Hosp., 500 P.2d 1153 (Ariz. App. 1972). See also D. Louisell & H. Williams §16.09 (1989).

7. None of the alternative policies of liability described in the cases collected above actually change the level of the standard of care required. None of the recent developments in hospital liability impose a "highest degree of care" standard upon health care institutions as is often applied to hotels and inns. Are there departments of hospitals where such a standard should be applied? Court decisions have imposed a "highest degree of care" standard on retail pharmacists and on hospital-based pharmacists in compounding medications under a physician's prescription. See Morgan, Pharmacists Liability, 33 Med. Trial Tech. Q. 315 (1987); Greenfield & Hirsh, Pharmacists Liability in Tort, 29 Med. Trial Tech. Q. 434 (1983). See also Vandall, Applying Strict Liability to Pharmacists, 18 U. Toledo L. Rev. 1 (1986); Crumley, Professional Liability of Pharmacists, 22 Def. L. Rev. 471 (1973). There is, of course, less opportunity in recent years for the application of this doctrine since a large part of the prescription drug market involves prepackaged products.

8. Law reform concerning emergency care has taken a very different course in the state legislatures from what is evidenced in judicial attitudes found in the cases reported above. In regard to liability, legislatures have quite uniformly answered affirmatively the medical community's requests for a *reduced standard of care* for voluntarily undertaken emergency care. All 50 states have enacted so-called "Good Samaritan Laws" that either substantially reduce the standard of care required, or grant a direct immunity from malpractice suits as long as the physicians (and often nurses) acted in "good faith" to render gratuitous emergency or first-aid care. Traditionally, such statutes did not apply to hospital emergency care, even when the hospital was caring for charity patients. However, later case law and statutory reforms have now begun to extend an immunity or reduced standard of care to in-hospital emergency care. The most far-reaching statutory change took place in Florida in 1988 when the legislature

provided a substantial immunity for emergency care given to patients admitted directly to the emergency service of a hospital or trauma center. The statute grants immunity from a malpractice suit unless the injury resulted from a "reckless disregard" for the life or health of the patient. Fla. Stat. §768.13. See the statute set out in full at 381-382.

St. Francis Regional Medical Center v. Hale
782 P.2d 129 (Kan. App. 1988)

RULON, Judge:

Ralph and Esther Hale (defendants) appeal from the district court's grant of summary judgment to St. Francis Regional Medical Center, Inc., (plaintiff) on defendants' counterclaim alleging negligence. Finding no error, we affirm. . . .

In the present case, the district court ruled that expert testimony was necessary to establish standard of care, deviation from standard of care, and causation. The district court apparently reasoned that without that proof, the Hales would be unable to prove the essential elements of their negligence case and entered summary judgment in favor of the hospital. We agree.

In order to maintain a cause of action, the Hales need to establish three elements: (1) a duty on the part of the hospital to protect Esther from the contraction of the staph infection and subsequent problems; (2) failure on the part of the hospital to perform the duty; and (3) Esther's contraction of the infection and subsequent problems must have proximately resulted from the hospital's failures. See Mellies v. National Heritage, Inc., 6 Kan. App. 2d 910, Syl. ¶1, 636 P.2d 215 (1981).

The Hales contend on appeal that "[a]s a matter of public policy and common sense, the testimony of an expert is unnecessary to prove that *physicians* must be responsible for removing all harm-producing foreign objects which they knowingly place inside a patient's body during an operation." (Emphasis supplied.) Appellants, however, have no cause of action against a physician. Dr. Newby, the physician performing the initial surgery is not a party to this appeal. Therefore, the Hales must establish the elements of their cause of action as to St. Francis.

The Hales assert that the hospital is liable for (1) its failure to provide safe and sanitary operating and recuperating facilities; (2) the failure of nurses to notify physicians of the swelling and infection, (3) the failure of the records to show the use of metal hemoclips, (4) its failure to culture, x-ray, and diagnose the infection at an earlier date; and (5) its failure to properly treat the infection after it was discovered. However, the Hales offered no expert testimony regarding the hospital's standard procedure or duty in these particular areas. Appellants rely upon the lay person's understanding of standard hospital procedure and the duties of a hospital versus the duties of the treating physician and staff nurses.

The Hales assert the "common knowledge" exception is applicable to this case:

> There is a common knowledge exception to the rule requiring expert medical testimony in malpractice cases. This common knowledge exception applies if what is alleged to have occurred in the diagnosis, treatment, and care of a patient is so obviously lacking in reasonable care and the results are so bad that the lack of reasonable care would be apparent to and within the common knowledge and experience of mankind generally. [Citations omitted.]

In the present case, the hospital's duty is not so obvious as to fall within the common knowledge exception. The doctor was primarily responsible for the initial surgery. The hospital, however, is the only defendant and the hospital's duty to Esther needs to be established by competent medical experts. See Chandler v. Neosho Memorial Hospital, 223 Kan. at 5, 574 P.2d 136.

Nor does the cause of a staph infection appear so obvious that a lack of reasonable care by the hospital would be apparent to a lay person and within common knowledge and experience generally. Esther's treating physicians were unsure of the cause. Expert evidence is needed to establish whether some failure of the hospital proximately caused Esther to contract the infection. See *Mellies*, 6 Kan. App. 2d 910, Syl. ¶4, 636 P.2d 215.

In the district court, the Hales' claims failed for lack of evidence because no expert testimony established the essential elements of their case. The district court's determination that expert testimony was necessary to establish the hospital's standard of care, deviation from standard of care, and causation was correct.

Affirmed.

North Miami General Hospital v. Goldberg
520 So. 2d 630 (Fla. App. 3d Dist. 1988)

SCHWARTZ, CHIEF JUDGE.

The plaintiff recovered a money judgment against the North Miami General Hospital upon a jury's conclusion that she had sustained an injury caused by a manufacturing defect in a piece of equipment the hospital employed during an operation. We reverse on the ground

V. Corporate Liability and Alternative Policies of Liability

that no strict liability claim lies against a hospital in these circumstances.

When Ms. Goldberg awoke from a routine operation conducted at North Miami, she had sustained burns at the places on her body where an electro-surgical grounding pad had been used during the surgery. She went to trial against North Miami to recover damages for those injuries.[1] The evidence revealed that the burns could have been caused in but one of two ways: either the surgical nurse had, in preparing the pad, negligently failed to apply protective jelly in the prescribed manner, or an undiscoverable[2] manufacturing defect in the pad had resulted in an excessive electrical charge to the plaintiff's body. The case was submitted to the jury on the issues of (a) the alleged active negligence of the hospital's nurse, and (b) over the defendant's specific objection, strict liability, under which the hospital would be liable if the injury were caused by a defect in the pad. In answer to special interrogatories, the jury found in favor of the hospital on the negligence claim, but that it was liable under the strict liability theory.

The underlying basis of the strict liability doctrine, which is expressed in section 402(A) of the Restatement (Second) of Torts (1965) as adopted in Florida by West v. Caterpillar Tractor Co., 336 So. 2d 80 (Fla. 1976), is that those who profit from the sale or distribution of a particular product to the public, rather than an innocent person injured by it, should bear the financial burden of even an undetectable product defect. . . .

This model plainly does not fit a health care provider like North Miami General with respect to a piece of equipment it employs in treating its patients. Surely, while Ms. Goldberg was injured by a defect in the pad and is therefore entitled to recover against its manufacturer, it was not transferred or disposed of to her by the hospital. Indeed, the hospital is properly regarded as itself a consumer of the product which merely employs it in performing its actual function of providing medical services. [Citations omitted.]

In accordance with this approach, it has been widely held that strict liability may not be invoked by a patient against a hospital or physician in the use of a defective medical implement. Hector v. Cedars-Sinai Medical Center, 180 Cal. App. 3d 493, 225 Cal. Rptr. 595 (1986) (hospital not strictly liable for defective pacemaker); *Sil-*

---

1. The plaintiff also initially joined the manufacturer and the distributor of the grounding pad, but these parties were dismissed because of the plaintiff's inability to effect jurisdiction over them.

2. There was no evidence that the defect could have been detected by the hospital in the exercise of reasonable care and therefore no claim of negligence in this regard. The sole issue raised as to the hospital's liability with respect to the pad itself was the theory of strict liability.

verhart, 20 Cal. App. 3d at 1022, 98 Cal. Rptr. at 187 (hospital not strictly liable for defective surgical needle broken in plaintiff during surgery); *Magrine,* 94 N.J. Super. at 228, 227 A.2d at 539 (dentist not strictly liable for defective needle broken in plaintiff's gum during treatment); Probst v. Albert Einstein Medical Center, 82 A.D.2d 739, 440 N.Y.S.2d 2 (1981) (hospital not strictly liable for defective spinal rod broken after surgical implantation); see also Annot., Application of Rule of Strict Liability in Tort to Person or Entity Rendering Medical Services, 100 A.L.R.3d 1205 (1980). See generally Annot., Liability of Hospital or Medical Practitioner Under Doctrine of Strict Liability in Tort, or Breach of Warranty, for Harm Caused by Drug, Medical Instrument, or Similar Device Used in Treating Patient, 54 A.L.R.3d 258 (1973). As the law is summarized in 2 Am. Prod. Liab. 3d §16:83 (1987):

> Hospitals are not ordinarily engaged in the business of selling products or equipment used in the course of their primary function of providing medical services, and strict liability will not be imposed where an injured party alleges that professional services connected with the use of a product, rather than the product itself, were defective, or where the professional services could not have been rendered without using the product.

We agree with and follow these authorities in holding that the trial court erroneously submitted the strict liability issue to the jury. . . .

NOTES

Strict Liability and Warranty as a Part of Hospital Corporate Responsibility

1. The two cases reprinted above illustrate recent judicial responses to efforts to impose a theory of strict liability or warranty of safety in regard to the general environment of a hospital, or to a hospital's use of therapeutic equipment and devices. As these opinions indicate, the great majority of courts have refused such interpretations. There are exceptions, however. See, for example, a case in the Alabama Supreme Court involving the breaking of a suturing needle during surgery. A portion of the needle lodged in the patient's body. A majority of the Court held that the hospital was a "seller of goods," namely the needle, under the Uniform Commercial Code in Alabama, and liable under a theory of an implied warranty of fitness for the particular purpose, despite the fact that the hospital made no charge to the patient for the needle. See Skelton v. Druid City Hosp. Bd., 459 So. 2d 818 (Ala. 1984).

In an earlier case in the Supreme Court of Wisconsin, the court

V. Corporate Liability and Alternative Policies of Liability   341

was asked to apply strict liability to a clinical situation of cardiac arrest during a lung biopsy under general anesthesia. The court rejected application of the argument that a medical care provider stands in "substantially the same position" as other sellers of goods. In rejecting strict liability, the court concluded,

> Although there may be general dissatisfaction with our present tort medical injury compensation system, moving from the malpractice concept — even with its many problems — to a strict liability system at the present time appears to be a dubious move. Strict liability has been far from a panacea in products cases, and there has been reluctance to advocate the extension of the principle to medical services. . . .
>
> We have no doubt that concepts of tort liability will continue to change and that service industries including the medical profession may be affected by such change. However, at this time the consequences of the step the plaintiffs urge cannot be predicted with sufficient clarity to permit that step to be taken.

Hoven v. Kelble, 256 N.W.2d 379, 390 (Wis. 1976).

2. Hospitals and other health care institutions make special efforts to avoid hospital-related patient infections and cross-infections of patients and hospital staff. These efforts at prevention of "nosocomial infections" are usually, at least in larger hospitals, placed under the direction of a physician specialist in communicable disease and infection control, assisted by a broadly representative committee on hospital infection control. These efforts are also combined with comprehensive programs of patient care quality assurance, risk management, and malpractice prevention. See particularly Hughes, Nosocomial Infection Surveillance in the United States: Historical Perspective, 8 Infection Control 430 (1987); Haley, The Role of the Infectious Disease Physician in Hospital Infection Control, 63 Bull. N.Y. Acad. Med. 597 (1987); Condon, Does Infection Control Control Infection?, 123 Arch. Surg. 250 (1988); Larson, Nosocomial Infection Rates as an Indicator of Quality, 26 Med. Care 676 (1988); Bradford, Ambulatory Care Infection Control Quality Assurance Monitoring, 16 Am. J. Infect. Control 21A (1988).

3. The concerns of hospitals for nosocomial infection has been aggravated in recent years by the problems of AIDS and hepatitis infection. See further discussion of these issues in Chapter 10.V.

Helling v. Carey and Laughlin
519 P.2d 981 (Wash. 1974)

HUNTER, ASSOCIATE JUSTICE.

This case arises from a malpractice action instituted by the plaintiff (petitioner), Barbara Helling.

The plaintiff suffers from primary open angle glaucoma. Primary open angle glaucoma is essentially a condition of the eye in which there is an interference in the ease with which the nourishing fluids can flow out of the eye. Such a condition results in pressure gradually arising above the normal level to such an extent that damage is produced to the optic nerve and its fibers with resultant loss in vision. The first loss usually occurs in the periphery of the field of vision. The disease usually has few symptoms and, in the absence of a pressure test, is often undetected until the damage has become extensive and irreversible.

The defendants (respondents), Dr. Thomas F. Carey and Dr. Robert C. Laughlin, are partners who practice the medical specialty of ophthalmology. Ophthalmology involves the diagnosis and treatment of defects and diseases of the eye.

The plaintiff first consulted the defendants for myopia, nearsightedness, in 1959. At that time she was fitted with contact lenses. She next consulted the defendants in September, 1963, concerning irritation caused by the contact lenses. Additional consultations occurred in October, 1963; February, 1967; September, 1967; October, 1967; May, 1968; July, 1968; August, 1968; September, 1968; and October, 1968. Until the October 1968 consultation, the defendants considered the plaintiff's visual problems to be related solely to complications associated with her contact lenses. On that occasion, the defendant, Dr. Carey, tested the plaintiff's eye pressure and field of vision for the first time. This test indicated that the plaintiff had glaucoma. The plaintiff, who was then 32 years of age, had essentially lost her peripheral vision and her central vision was reduced to approximately 5 degrees vertical by 10 degrees horizontal.

Thereafter, in August of 1969, after consulting other physicians, the plaintiff filed a complaint against the defendants alleging, among other things, that she sustained severe and permanent damage to her eyes as a proximate result of the defendants' negligence. During trial, the testimony of the medical experts for both the plaintiff and the defendants established that the standards of the profession for that specialty in the same or similar circumstances do not require routine pressure tests for glaucoma upon patients under 40 years of age. The reason the pressure test for glaucoma is not given as a regular practice to patients under the age of 40 is that the disease rarely occurs in this age group. Testimony indicated, however, that the standards of the profession do require pressure tests if the patient's complaints and symptoms reveal to the physician that glaucoma should be suspected.

The trial court entered judgment for the defendants following a defense verdict. The plaintiff thereupon appealed to the Court of Appeals, which affirmed the judgment of the trial court. Helling v.

V. Corporate Liability and Alternative Policies of Liability

Carey, No. 1185-41918-1 (Wn. App., filed Feb. 5, 1973). The plaintiff then petitioned this Court for review, which we granted.

In her petition for review, the plaintiff's primary contention is that under the facts of this case the trial judge erred in giving certain instructions to the jury and refusing her proposed instructions defining the standard of care which the law imposes upon an ophthalmologist. As a result, the plaintiff contends, in effect, that she was unable to argue her theory of the case to the jury that the standard of care for the speciality of ophthalmology was inadequate to protect the plaintiff from the incidence of glaucoma, and that the defendants, by reason of their special ability, knowledge and information, were negligent in failing to give the pressure test to the plaintiff at an earlier point in time which, if given, would have detected her condition and enabled the defendants to have averted the resulting substantial loss in her vision.

We find this to be a unique case. The testimony of the medical experts is undisputed concerning the standards of the profession for the specialty of ophthalmology. It is not a question in this case of the defendants having any greater special ability, knowledge and information than other ophthalmologists which would require the defendants to comply with a higher duty of care than that "degree of care and skill which is expected of the average practitioner in the class to which he belongs, acting in the same or similar circumstances." Pederson v. Dumouchel, 72 Wash. 2d 73, 79, 431 P.2d 973 (1967). The issue is whether the defendants' compliance with the standard of the profession of ophthalmology, which does not require the giving of a routine pressure test to persons under 40 years of age, should insulate them from liability under the facts in this case where the plaintiff has lost a substantial amount of her vision due to the failure of defendants to timely give the pressure test to the plaintiff.

The defendants argue that the standard of the profession, which does not require the giving of a routine pressure test to persons under the age of 40, is adequate to insulate the defendants from liability for negligence because the risk of glaucoma is so rare in this age group. The testimony of the defendant, Dr. Carey, however, is revealing as follows:

Q: Now, when was it, actually, the first time any complaint was made to you by her of any field or visual field problem?
A: Really, the first time that she really complained of a visual field problem was the August 30th date. [1968]
Q: And how soon before the diagnosis was that?
A: That was 30 days. We made it on October 1st.
Q: And in your opinion, how long, as you nor I have the whole

history and analysis and the diagnosis, how long had she had this glaucoma?
A: I would think she probably had it ten years or longer.
Q: Now, Doctor, there's been some reference to the matter of taking pressure checks of persons over 40. What is the incidence of glaucoma, the statistics, with persons under 40?
A: In the instance of glaucoma under the age of 40, is less than 100 to one percent. The younger you get, the less the incidence. It is thought to be in the neighborhood of one in 25,000 people or less.
Q: How about the incidence of glaucoma in people over 40?
A: Incidence of glaucoma over 40 gets into the two to three per cent category, and hence, that's where there is this great big difference and that's why the standards around the world has been to check pressures from 40 on.

The incidence of glaucoma in one out of 25,000 persons under the age of 40 may appear quite minimal. However, that one person, the plaintiff in this instance, is entitled to the same protection, as afforded persons over 40, essential for timely detection of the evidence of glaucoma where it can be arrested to avoid the grave and devastating result of this disease. The test is a simple pressure test, relatively inexpensive. There is no judgment factor involved, and there is no doubt that by giving the test the evidence of glaucoma can be detected. The giving of the test is harmless if the physical condition of the eye permits. The testimony indicates that although the condition of the plaintiff's eyes might have at times prevented the defendants from administering the pressure test, there is an absence of evidence in the record that the test could not have been timely given.

Justice Holmes stated in Texas & Pac. Ry. v. Behymer, 189 U.S. 468, 470, 23 S. Ct. 622, 623, 47 L. Ed. 905 (1903): "What usually is done may be evidence of what ought to be done, but what ought to be done is fixed by a standard of reasonable prudence, whether it usually is complied with or not."

In The T. J. Hooper, 60 F.2d 737, on page 740 (2d Cir. 1932), Justice Hand stated: "[I]n most cases reasonable prudence is in fact common prudence; but strictly it is never its measure; a whole calling may have unduly lagged in the adoption of new and available devices. It never may set its own tests, however persuasive be its usages. *Courts must in the end say what is required; there are precautions so imperative that even their universal disregard will not excuse their omission.*" (Italics ours.)

Under the facts of this case reasonable prudence required the timely giving of the pressure test to this plaintiff. The precaution of

V. Corporate Liability and Alternative Policies of Liability

giving this test to detect the incidence of glaucoma to patients under 40 years of age is so imperative that irrespective of its disregard by the standards of the ophthalmology profession, it is the duty of the courts to say what is required to protect patients under 40 from the damaging results of glaucoma.

We therefore hold, as a matter of law, that the reasonable standard that should have been followed under the undisputed facts of this case was the timely giving of this simple, harmless pressure test to this plaintiff and that, in failing to do so, the defendants were negligent, which proximately resulted in the blindness sustained by the plaintiff for which the defendants are liable.

There are no disputed facts to submit to the jury on the issue of the defendants' liability. Hence, a discussion of the plaintiff's proposed instructions would be inconsequential in view of our disposition of the case.

The judgment of the trial court and the decision of the Court of Appeals is reversed, and the case is remanded for a new trial on the issue of damages only.

HALE, C.J., and ROSELLINI, STAFFORD, WRIGHT and BRACHTENBACH, J.J., concur.

UTTER, ASSOCIATE JUSTICE (concurring).

I concur in the result reached by the majority. I believe a greater duty of care could be imposed on the defendants than was established by their profession. The duty could be imposed when a disease, such as glaucoma, can be detected by a simple, well-known harmless test whose results are definitive and the disease can be successfully arrested by early detection, but where the effects of the disease are irreversible if undetected over a substantial period of time.

The difficulty with this approach is that we as judges, by using a negligence analysis, seem to be imposing a stigma of moral blame upon the doctors who, in this case, used all the precautions commonly prescribed by their profession in diagnosis and treatment. Lacking their training in this highly sophisticated profession, it seems illogical for this court to say they failed to exercise a reasonable standard of care. It seems to me we are, in reality, imposing liability, because, in choosing between an innocent plaintiff and a doctor, who acted reasonably according to his specialty but who could have prevented the full effects of this disease by administering a simple, harmless test and treatment, the plaintiff should not have to bear the risk of loss. As such, imposition of liability approaches that of strict liability.

Strict liability or liability without fault is not new to the law. Historically, it predates our concepts of fault or moral responsibility as a basis of the remedy. Wigmore, Responsibility for Tortious Acts: Its History, 7 Har. L. Rev. 315, 383, 441 (1894). As noted in W. Prosser, The Law of Torts §74 (3d ed. 1964) at pages 507, 508:

"There are many situations in which a careful person is held liable for an entirely reasonable mistake. . . . in some cases the defendant may be held liable, although he is not only charged with no moral wrongdoing, but has not even departed in any way from a reasonable standard of intent or care. . . . There is 'a strong and growing tendency, where there is blame on neither side, to ask, in view of the exigencies of social justice, who can best bear the loss and hence to shift the loss by creating liability where there has been no fault.'" (Footnote omitted.) Tort law has continually been in a state of flux. It is "not always neat and orderly. But this is not to say it is illogical. Its central logic is the logic that moves from premises — its objectives — that are only partly consistent, to conclusions — its rules — that serve each objective as well as may be while serving others too. It is the logic of maximizing service and minimizing disservice to multiple objectives." Keeton, Is There a Place for Negligence in Modern Tort Law?, 53 Va. L. Rev. 886, 897 (1967).

When types of problems rather than numbers of cases are examined, strict liability is applied more often than negligence as a principle which determines liability. Peck, Negligence and Liability Without Fault in Tort Law, 46 Wash. L. Rev. 225, 239 (1971). There are many similarities in this case to other cases of strict liability. Problems of proof have been a common feature in situations where strict liability is applied. Where events are not matters of common experience, a juror's ability to comprehend whether reasonable care has been followed diminishes. There are few areas as difficult for jurors to intelligently comprehend as the intricate questions of proof and standards in medical malpractice cases.

In applying strict liability there are many situations where it is imposed for conduct which can be defined with sufficient precision to insure that application of a strict liability principle will not produce miscarriages of justice in a substantial number of cases. If the activity involved is one which can be defined with sufficient precision, that definition can serve as an accounting unit to which the costs of the activity may be allocated with some certainty and precision. With this possible, strict liability serves a compensatory function in situations where the defendant is, through the use of insurance, the financially more responsible person. Peck, Negligence and Liability Without Fault in Tort Law, supra at 240, 241.

If the standard of a reasonably prudent specialist is, in fact, inadequate to offer reasonable protection to the plaintiff, then liability can be imposed without fault. To do so under the narrow facts of this case does not offend my sense of justice. The pressure test to measure intraocular pressure with the Schiotz tonometer and the Goldman applanometer takes a short time, involves no damage to the patient, and consists of placing the instrument against the eyeball.

V. Corporate Liability and Alternative Policies of Liability

An abnormally high pressure requires other tests which would either confirm or deny the existence of glaucoma. It is generally believed that from 5 to 10 years of detectable increased pressure must exist before there is permanent damage to the optic nerves.

Although the incidence of glaucoma in the age range of the plaintiff is approximately one in 25,000, this alone should not be enough to deny her a claim. Where its presence can be detected by a simple, well-known harmless test, where the results of the test are definitive, where the disease can be successfully arrested by early detection and where its effects are irreversible if undetected over a substantial period of time, liability should be imposed upon defendants even though they did not violate the standard existing within the profession of ophthalmology.

The failure of plaintiff to raise this theory at the trial and to propose instructions consistent with it should not deprive her of the right to resolve the case on this theory on appeal. Where this court has authoritatively stated the law, the parties are bound by those principles until they have been overruled. Acceptance of those principles at trial does not constitute a waiver or estop appellants from adapting their cause on appeal to such a rule as might be declared if the earlier precedent is overruled. Samuelson v. Freeman, 75 Wash. 2d 894, 900, 454 P.2d 406 (1969).

FINLEY and HAMILTON, JJ., concur.

NOTES

The Reasonable Prudence Rule and Strict Liability Alternatives for Physicians

1. The *Helling* decision, with its judicially created standard of care unsupported by any expert medical testimony, met with an immediate storm of criticism in the legal and medical literature. The concurring opinion by Justice Utter, with two other justices also concurring, advocating an even further step into strict liability, upset the insurance industry even more, causing many medical malpractice insurance underwriters to feel that "the deluge" of expanded legal liability had reached revolutionary levels of social and political policy. The decision was credited with having considerable influence on the development of the medical malpractice insurance crisis of the mid-1970s, especially the withdrawal of many insurance carriers from the field. See Senate Subcommittee on Health Report on the Continuing Medical Malpractice Insurance Crisis (December 1975). See also Charfoos, *Helling*: The Law of Medical Malpractice Rewritten, 2 Ohio N.L. Rev. 692 (1975); Wechsler & Classe, Helling v. Carey: Caveat Medicus (Let the Doctor Beware), 48 J. Am. Opto. Assn. 1526 (1977).

2. The Washington legislature moved promptly in an effort to remove the "reasonable prudence rule" derived from the *T. J. Hooper* case and to replace it in malpractice cases with the traditional standard. However, the legislature did not succeed, according to the stubborn judges on the Washington Supreme Court. See Gates v. Jensen, 595 P.2d 919 (Wash. 1979). In that decision, again a case involving glaucoma, the court was faced with the remedial statute, Wash. Rev. Code §4.24.290 (1975), which stated: "In any civil action for damages based on professional negligence against . . . a member of the healing arts . . . the plaintiff . . . shall be required to prove . . . that the defendant or defendants failed to exercise that degree of skill, care and learning possessed by other persons in the profession." The court held that by using the word "possessed," the legislature had not abrogated the ruling of the *Helling* case. The majority pointed out that the original bill had contained the word "practiced." It was amended during its course of passage. The majority held that the "possessed" standard was "much broader than the one embodied in the original bill and allowed ample scope for the application of the limited *Helling* rule." Only two judges in the nine-judge bench dissented on this issue, observing that they felt that the legislature had intended to abrogate the *Helling* rule of "reasonable prudence" and that the court's holding in *Gates* was "absolutely contrary to the mandate of the legislature." See generally Reuter, *Helling* Doctrine Buried, 7 Leg. Aspects Med. Pract. 25 (1979). The Supreme Court of Washington was determined, however, to consolidate its position, no matter what criticism it received. In 1983, in Harris v. Groth, 663 P.2d 113 (Wash. 1983), the Court explicitly abrogated the "average practitioner" standard and adopted the "reasonable prudence" rule for all health-care providers.

3. The *Helling* decision, despite the publicity it has received, has not begun a judicial trend in the direction of the "reasonable prudence" rule being adopted in other courts. In fact, according to one authority, the trend is in the contrary attitude toward "affording greater weight, probably even conclusive weight, to professional standards." See King, The Law of Medical Malpractice, Nutshell Series, 52 (2d ed. 1986).

4. The interest in a much more broadly applicable no-fault compensation system to replace the current tort liability approach to medical care injuries has not quieted down in the late 1980s. See our discussion of no-fault reforms at 422-426.

Boyd v. Albert Einstein Medical Center
547 A.2d 1229 (Pa. Super. 1988)

OLSZEWSKI, JUDGE:

This is an appeal from the trial court's order granting summary

V. Corporate Liability and Alternative Policies of Liability 349

judgment in favor of defendant/appellee, Health Maintenance Organization of Pennsylvania (hereinafter HMO). Appellant asserts that the trial court erred in granting the motion for summary judgment when there existed a question of material fact as to whether participating physicians are the ostensible agents of HMO. For the reasons stated below, we reverse the grant of summary judgment.

The facts, as averred by the parties in their pleadings and elicited through deposition testimony, reveal that at the time of her death, decedent and her husband were participants in the HMO. HMO is a medical insurance provider that offers an alternative to the traditional Blue Cross/Blue Shield insurance plan.[1] Decedent's husband became eligible for participation in a group plan provided by HMO through his employer. Upon electing to participate in this plan, decedent and her husband were provided with a directory and benefits brochure which listed the participating physicians. Restricted to selecting a physician from this list, decedent chose Doctor David Rosenthal and Doctor Perry Dornstein as her primary care physicians.

In June of 1982, decedent contacted Doctor David Rosenthal regarding a lump in her breast. Doctor Rosenthal ordered a mammogram to be performed which revealed a suspicious area in the breast. Doctor Rosenthal recommended that decedent undergo a biopsy and referred decedent to Doctor Erwin Cohen for that purpose. Doctor Cohen, a surgeon, is also a participating HMO physician. The referral to a specialist in this case was made in accordance with the terms and conditions of HMO's subscription agreement.[2]

On July 6, 1982, Doctor Cohen performed a biopsy of decedent's breast tissue at Albert Einstein Medical Center. During the procedure, Doctor Cohen perforated decedent's chest wall with the biopsy needle, causing decedent to sustain a left hemothorax. Decedent was hospitalized for treatment of the hemothorax at Albert Einstein Hospital for two days.

In the weeks following this incident, decedent complained to her primary care physicians, Doctor David Rosenthal and Doctor Perry Dornstein, of pain in her chest wall, belching, hiccoughs, and fatigue. On August 19, 1982, decedent awoke with pain in the middle of her chest. Decedent's husband contacted her primary care physicians, Doctors Rosenthal and Dornstein, and was advised to take decedent

---

1. "A Health Maintenance Organization is an organized system of health care which provides or arranges for a comprehensive array of basic and supplemental health care services. These services are provided on a prepaid basis to voluntarily enrolled members living within a prescribed geographic area. Responsibility for the delivery, quality and payment of health care falls to the managing organization — the HMO." Physicians Office Coordinator Training Manual citing HMOs An Alternative to Today's Health Care System. A Towers, Perrin, Forster, and Crosby Background Study, December 1975.

2. Doctor Rosenthal admitted in his deposition that HMO limited specifically the doctors to whom decedent could have been referred. Deposition, p. 70.

to Albert Einstein hospital where she would be examined by Doctor Rosenthal. Upon arrival at Albert Einstein emergency room, decedent related symptoms of chest wall pain, vomiting, stomach and back discomfort to Doctor Rosenthal. Doctor Rosenthal commenced an examination of decedent, diagnosed Tietz's syndrome,[3] and arranged for tests to be performed at his office where decedent underwent x-rays, EKG, and cardiac isoenzyme tests.[4] Decedent was then sent home and told to rest.[5]

During the course of that afternoon, decedent continued to experience chest pain, vomiting and belching. Decedent related the persistence and worsening of these symptoms by telephone to Doctors Rosenthal and Dornstein, who prescribed, without further examination, Talwin, a pain medication. At 5:30 that afternoon decedent was discovered dead in her bathroom by her husband, having expired as a result of a myocardial infarction. . . .

Appellant's complaint and new matter aver that HMO advertised that its physicians and medical care providers were competent, and that they had been evaluated for periods of up to six months prior to being selected to participate in the HMO program as a medical provider. The complaint further avers that decedent and appellant relied on these representations in choosing their primary care physicians. The complaint then avers that HMO was negligent in failing to "qualify or oversee its physicians and hospital who acted as its agents, servants, or employees in providing medical care to the decedent nor did HMO of Pa. require its physicians, surgeons and hospitals to provide adequate evidence of skill, training and competence in medicine and it thereby failed to furnish the decedent with competent, qualified medical care as warranted." Paragraph 39, plaintiff's amended complaint. Finally, appellant's new matter avers that HMO furnished to its subscribers documents which identify HMO as the care provider and state that HMO guarantees the quality of care. Plaintiff's new matter, paragraph 18.

---

3. Tietze's Syndrome is an inflammatory condition affecting the costochondral cartilage. It occurs more commonly in females, generally in the 30 to 50 age range. Deposition of Doctor Rosenthal, p. 48.

4. HMO avers that decedent was returned to the doctor's office for testing because it was more comfortable and convenient for her. Appellant, however, asserts that the tests were performed in the doctor's office, rather than the hospital, in accordance with the requirements of HMO whose primary interest was in keeping the medical fees within the corporation.

5. Appellant contends that Doctor Rosenthal acted negligently in ordering the tests to be performed in his office when decedent exhibited symptoms of cardiac distress. The safer practice, avers appellant, would have been to perform the tests at the hospital where the results would have been more quickly available. Appellant further contends that, despite Doctor Rosenthal's diagnosis of Tietze's Syndrome, the nature of the tests he ordered indicates that he was concerned about the possibility of a heart attack.

V. Corporate Liability and Alternative Policies of Liability 351

Appellant's theory of recovery before the trial court was primarily one of vicarious liability under the ostensible agency theory. See Capan v. Divine Providence Hospital, 287 Pa. Super. 364, 430 A.2d 647 (1980). In granting defendant HMO's motion for summary judgment, the trial court found that plaintiff/appellant had failed to establish either of the two factors on which the theory of ostensible agency, as applied to hospitals in *Capan,* is based. On appeal, appellant contends that the evidence indicates that there exists a question of fact regarding whether HMO may be held liable under this theory. . . .

The group master contract provides that HMO "operates a comprehensive prepaid program of health care which provides health care services and benefits to Members in order to protect and promote their health, and preserve and enhance patient dignity." Group master contract, Form HMOPA/GM-6 (5/83) of record [hereinafter group master contract]. HMO was incorporated in 1975 under the laws of Pennsylvania and converted from a non-profit to a for-profit corporation in 1981. Training manual of record at 1. HMO is based on the individual practice association model (hereinafter IPA), which means that HMO is comprised of participating primary physicians who are engaged in part in private practice in the HMO service area. Id. Under the plan, IPA contracts with HMO to provide medical services to HMO members. Id. at 1-2. IPA selects its primary and specialist physicians and enters into an agreement with them obligating the physician to perform health services for the subscribers of HMO. Primary physician agreement of record at 1.

The primary physician's role is defined as the "gatekeeper into the health care delivery system." Document entitled Role of the Primary Physician of record at 1. "An HMO member must consult with his primary physician before going to a specialist and/or the hospital." Id.; Group master contract at II B. If the primary physician deems it necessary, he arranges a consultation with an HMO participating specialist, which constitutes a second opinion. Role of the Primary Physician at 1. "Basically, with the primary physicians 'screening' the members' illnesses, excessive hospitalization and improper use of specialists can be reduced." Id.

Member-patients use a physician directory and choose a conveniently located office of a participating primary physician. HMO members will only receive reimbursement from non-participating providers when the condition requiring treatment was of an immediate nature. Determinations of immediacy are made by the HMO quality assurance committee. In any event, persons desiring emergency non-provider benefits must notify HMO or their primary physician of the emergency within forty-eight hours and must give written proof of the occurrence within ninety days after service is rendered. . . .

Primary physicians are paid through a mechanism termed "capitation." Capitation is an actuarially determined amount prepaid by HMO to the primary physician for each patient who has chosen his office. Revised attachment AA to primary physician agreement. The dollar amount is based upon a pre-determined rate per age group. The primary physicians are paid 80 percent of the capitation amount and the remaining 20 percent is pooled by IPA and goes back into a pooled risk-sharing fund as a reserve against specialty referral costs and hospital stays. Each primary care office has its own specialist fund and hospital fund established by allocating a pre-determined amount each month for each member who has chosen that primary care office. The surplus from the specialist fund is returned to the primary care office. The hospital fund, however, is governed by a hospital risk/incentive-sharing scheme which anticipates a number of inpatient days per members per year. If the actual hospital utilization is less than anticipated, the HMO and IPA each receive 50 percent of the savings. IPA must place the savings in the Special IPA risk-sharing account and must use the fund to offset losses resulting from unanticipated physician costs. Attachment B to primary physician agreement. If utilization is greater than anticipated, IPA is responsible for 50 percent of the loss up to the amount of uncommitted funds in the Special IPA risk sharing account. Id. . . .

HMO asserts that because the theory of ostensible agency has been applied in Pennsylvania only to the relationship between hospitals and independent contractor physicians, the theory is not appropriate in the instant situation. We emphasize, however, that when this Court introduced the concept of ostensible agency to this Commonwealth in *Capan,* supra, we based that decision in large part upon "the changing role of the hospital in society [which] creates a likelihood that patients will look to the institution" for care. Id. 287 Pa. Super. at 368, 430 A.2d at 649. Because the role of health care providers has changed in recent years, the *Capan* rationale for applying the theory of ostensible agency to hospital is certainly applicable in the instant situation. . . .

We find that the facts indicate an issue of material fact as to whether the participating physicians were the ostensible agents of HMO. HMO covenanted that it would "[provide] health care services and benefits to Members in order to protect and promote their health. . . ." Group master contract at 1. "HMOPA operates on a direct service rather than an indemnity basis." Id. Appellant paid his doctor's fee to HMO, not to the physician of his choice. Then, appellant selected his primary care physicians from the list provided by HMO. Regardless of who recommended appellant's decedent to choose her primary care physician, the fact remains that HMO pro-

V. Corporate Liability and Alternative Policies of Liability

vides a limited list from which a member must choose a primary physician. Moreover, those primary physicians are screened by HMO and must comply with a list of regulations in order to honor their contract with HMO. See discussion and footnote 8, supra.

Further, as mandated by HMO, appellant's decedent could not see a specialist without the primary physician's referral. As HMO declares, the primary physician is the "gatekeeper into the health care delivery system." Document entitled Role of the Primary Physician of record at 1. "An HMO member must consult with his primary physician before going to a specialist and/or the hospital." Id. Moreover, appellant's decedent had no choice as to which specialist to see. In our opinion, because appellant's decedent was required to follow the mandates of HMO and did not directly seek the attention of the specialist, there is an inference that appellant looked to the institution for care and not solely to the physicians; conversely, that appellant's decedent submitted herself to the care of the participating physicians in response to an invitation from HMO. See comment (a), Restatement (Second) Agency §267.

Summary judgment should be granted only where there is not the slightest doubt as to the absence of a triable issue of fact. *Thompson*, supra, 370 Pa. Super. at 120, 535 A.2d at 1180, citing Chandler v. Johns-Manville Corp., 352 Pa. Super. 326, 507 A.2d 1253 (1986); Long John Silver's, Inc. v. Fiore, 255 Pa. Super. 183, 386 A.2d 569 (1978). Based on the foregoing, we find that there is an issue of material fact as to whether the participating physicians were the ostensible agents of HMO. We conclude, therefore, that the trial court erred when it granted HMO's motion for summary judgment on the ground that the participating physicians were not the ostensible agents of HMO.

The order granting summary judgment is reversed and the case remanded for proceedings consistent with this opinion. Jurisdiction is relinquished.

McEwen, J., concurs with opinion.

McEwen, Judge, concurring.

I concur in the result reached by the majority since the author, after a very careful analysis of the issues presented in this appeal, reaches the quite basic principle that issues of material fact may not be resolved by summary judgment.

I write only because it appears to me that the learned trial court improperly resolved by summary judgment the basic factual issue of whether the literature, in which HMO "guaranteed" and "assured" the quality of care provided to its subscribers, had been distributed to appellant or to other subscribers of HMO.

It might also be mentioned that while the court was understandably uncertain as to the theories upon which plaintiff was proceeding,[1] it appears that the amended complaint of plaintiff does contain factual averments supporting a breach of warranty claim. See: Alpha Tau Omega Fraternity v. University of Pennsylvania, 318 Pa. Super. 293, 298, 464 A.2d 1349, 1352 (1983) ("Pennsylvania is a fact-pleading state."). Accord: Smith v. Brown, 283 Pa. Super. 116, 119, 423 A.2d 743, 745 (1980).

NOTES

The Liability of Health Maintenance Organizations for Injury to Patients: Organizational Policies and Legal Analysis

1. Even though health maintenance organizations in a wide variety of structural forms have been involved in health care finance and delivery in the United States for over 20 years, very few opportunities seem to have been presented for an appellate judicial review of the medical malpractice liability of such organizations. In earlier years, most of the court cases at trial and in appellate judicial review have involved HMO-owned and operated hospitals where liability issues have not been argued to be distinguishable from other hospitals. The *Boyd* case, however, raised novel questions because of the particular structure of the HMO involved. On organization of HMOs and their systems of health care delivery, see discussion and references in Chapter 8.III.B. See also Stewart, Vicarious Liability of Health Maintenance Organizations for the Acts of Independent Physician Contractors, 2 Med. Malpractice Rep. 114 (1989).

2. Despite the fact that the HMO involved in *Boyd* was an "open panel" of community-based physicians rather than the more common structure of a "closed panel" of a smaller number of employed physicians working within HMO-owned facilities, many other features of an HMO organization were present, including the use of general practitioners as "gatekeepers" and the payment of general practitioners on a capitation basis rather than on individual fee-for-service charges. What features of the HMO's operational structure led the

---

1. The trial court noted in its opinion that "the gravamen of plaintiff's complaint is that HMO of PA guaranteed or warranted the quality of care provided. . . . Plaintiff's theory of recovery . . . is not entirely clear. A reading of the complaint suggests Plaintiff is proceeding upon grounds of corporate liability. However, in his answer to the motion of HMO of PA for summary judgment, plaintiff contends HMO of PA is vicariously liable through ostensible agency."

V. Corporate Liability and Alternative Policies of Liability

court in *Boyd* to determine that medical malpractice liability for the negligence of the independent medical practitioners was legally justified?

3. The issue of a guarantee or warranty of quality of patient care by HMOs is raised in *Boyd.* What was the basis for such a claim? Do HMOs as a class of health care provider offer a different type of health care service to subscribers from that offered by other providers? Is there a difference in the "promises made" by HMOs for quality of patient care from those made by other alternative forms of health care delivery? See Gilman & Bucco, Alternative Delivery Systems: An Overview, 1 Topics in Health Care Finance 3 (1987).

An earlier study of the 15 largest HMOs in the United States found that these organizations were generally self-insured regarding malpractice and had installed quite detailed programs of malpractice prevention and physician monitoring, often under the direction of a medicolegal department. See Curran & Moseley, The Malpractice Experience of Health Maintenance Organizations, 7. N.W.U.L. Rev. 69 (1975).

4. On the opposite side of the coin to the concept that HMOs may be making promises to "maintain" a patient's current (or expected) level of health, and to offer some higher level of quality of care, is the claim that HMOs and other alternative systems of health care delivery such as preferred provider organizations (PPOs) have installed better systems of cost control. These systems are designed, for example, to reduce the need for hospitalization and the use of expensive and unnecessary diagnostic tests. Do these cost-containment systems present dangers of compromise of the quality of health care? See Chapter 8.III.B. See also Morreim, Cost Containment and the Standard of Medical Care, 75 Cal. L. Rev. 1719 (1987). Do patients and third-party payer organizations who contract with alternative systems *expect* that the care offered will be at least as high as in traditional systems? Should the courts expect standards of quality to be essentially the same ("ordinary, reasonable care") no matter what the organizational structure or fundamental goals of the delivery system may be? Questions of this type are suggested in the article by Morreim cited above. The author observes,

> The current legal insistence upon an essentially uniform standard of basic medical care arises largely from the fiduciary nature of the physician-patient relationship. The enormous importance of the patient's interest in good health care, combined with his increased dependency during serious illness and his general inability to meet his own medical needs, renders him highly vulnerable to the physician's superior knowledge, skill, and consequent power in the relationship. The patient must be able to repose confidence in his physician, believing that the latter will be not only professionally competent but also devoted to his interests.

Otherwise, it would be difficult for the patient to generate the trusting cooperation so essential to good health care. To permit physicians routinely to balance their patients' interests against others' economic welfare could devastate this fiduciary relationship. And yet as we have seen, the pressures upon the medical community to contain costs are inescapable.

Id. at 1727. For a recent field investigation, see Hillman, Pauly & Kerstein, How Do Financial Incentives Affect Physicians' Clinical Decisions and the Financial Performance of Health Maintenance Organizations?, 321 New Eng. J. Med. 86 (1989). For a detailed further review of issues of economic incentives and quality of care, see Chapter 8 of this text.

5. Another recent appellate court case involved an "open panel" HMO in Pennsylvania. The HMO utilized general practitioners as "gatekeepers" to specialist services. The HMO "signed on" both general practitioners and specialists to their lists of accepted practitioners whose services the HMO would include in their program. The names of specialists were not released to subscribers. Only the general practice "gatekeepers" kept the names and referred patients on to these specialists.

The plaintiff sued the HMO for negligence of a specialist and presented evidence of the physician's poor record of malpractice claims. The HMO owned no treatment facilities and contracted with all of the physicians without any investigation of their qualifications or their malpractice claims history. The "signing on" of physicians for participation was done through mail solicitation by the HMO. The HMO contended it was not responsible for the negligence of the specialist (or of the general practitioner who made the referral) because both types of physicians were independent contractors whose standards were not under the supervision or control of the HMO, as would be the case in a hospital. In effect, the HMO was asserting that it could rely on the fact that each of the physicians was properly licensed to practice medicine in the state and that any supervision of the specialist was the duty of the hospital wherein the alleged negligent care was received. Should the court accept this defense? See Harrell v. Total Health Care, Inc., — N.W.2d — (Mo. App. 1989). Should PPOs be treated differently? See discussion in Chapter 8.III.C.

Wickline v. State of California
688 P.2d 605 (Ariz. 1984)

[See opinion in Chapter 8 §II B.]

V. Corporate Liability and Alternative Policies of Liability 357

Thompson v. Sun City Community Hospital
688 P.2d 605 (Ariz. 1984)

[See opinion in Chapter 6 §4 C.]

NOTES

Malpractice Vulnerability, "Economic Malpractice," and "Patient Dumping" as Strict-Liability Torts

1. *Wickline* and further review in Chapter 8.III.B, analyze the implications of cost containment-motivated clinical decisions on malpractice liability. The issue is also raised in "patient dumping" situations, such as the *Sun City* case noted earlier. Do these novel features of clinical decision making create new kinds of malpractice tort liability that could be called "economic malpractice"?

2. Does the COBRA legislation on the federal level reprinted in Chapter 6.II.B establish an action in strict liability for harm resulting from an inappropriate transfer? Under COBRA, the law of the jurisdiction where the transfer and harm occurred applies. Does this rule require application of all of the state's reform legislation on medical malpractice? See Reid v. Indiana Osteopathic Med. Cent., 709 F. Supp. 853 (S.D. Ind. 1989).

3. There is a common assumption that the patient is unable to make decisions about care during an emergency, due either to an excess of pain and anxiety and a lack of clear knowledge of the extent of the danger in the emergency, or due to the patient's unconscious or comatose state at the time of the emergency. Should the patient's consent play a role in emergency care? In decisions in regard to transfer to another facility? See Kellerman & Ackerman, Interhospital Patient Transfer: The Case for Informed Consent, 319 New Eng. J. Med. 643 (1988).

4. Does an emergency care physician incur obligations to patients beyond the rendering of needed emergency care? In a controversial California case, an emergency care doctor treated a child under conditions in which it was alleged he should have recognized signs of child abuse as a cause of the child's injuries. The doctor treated the child and did not object to the return of the child to the parents. Later, the child was further abused by the parents. The court held that the emergency care physician could be found to have "caused" the later injuries due to the alleged failure (under a California statute) to report the parents to proper authorities as suspected child abusers. See Landeros v. Flood, 17 551 P.2d 389 (Cal. 1976). For further

examination of the legal obligations of emergency care physicians and other emergency personnel, see the discussion of recent reforms in the Good Samaritan Laws at 380-385 of this chapter.

VI. DEFENSES

A. *Standard of Care Issues*

Ouellette v. Subak
391 N.W.2d 810 (Minn. 1986)

KELLEY, JUSTICE.

The father of a child born with brain damage brought this negligence action on behalf of the child and himself against two medical general practitioners. The trial court refused to give the doctors' requested jury instructions that physicians are not responsible for an honest error in judgment. A Hennepin County jury by special verdict found the doctors negligent and awarded $1 million in damages. Following denial of their post trial motions and entry of judgment on the verdict, the doctors appealed. Holding that the trial court erred when it refused to give the so-called "honest error in judgment" instruction, the court of appeals reversed and remanded for a new trial on all issues. Both parties petitioned this court for further review. Both petitions were granted. For the purpose of this opinion, the Ouellettes will be denominated appellants and the physicians, respondents.

The complaint charged the two physicians with negligence in permitting a prolonged pregnancy, failing to timely induce labor or recognize increased risks of injury to the fetus, and ignoring signs of fetal distress. In defense, the physicians alleged: (1) they neither erred in their diagnosis nor treatment of the pregnancy; (2) if they did err, it was not negligence, but an honest error in professional judgment, and (3) any alleged negligence was not the cause of Kristian's condition.

1. The trial court refused to give the "honest error in judgment" instruction found in the last sentence of 4 Minn. Dist. Judges Assn., Minnesota Practice, JIG II, 425 G-S (2d ed. 1974). This was done notwithstanding one of respondents' defenses was that even had they erred in handling Mrs. Ouellette's pregnancy, the error was not negligence but an honest error in judgment. The portion of the JIG II, 425 G-S instruction omitted reads:

> A [physician] is not a guarantor of a cure or a good result from his treatment and he is not responsible for an honest error in judgment in choosing between accepted methods of treatment.

VI. Defenses

The court of appeals ruled that elimination of the "honest error in judgment" instruction rendered the trial court's instruction insufficient to state the standard of care applicable to a physician. . . .

We agree with the majority of the court of appeals that if the respondents were entitled to the "honest error in judgment" instruction, the trial court's refusal to give it in this case was prejudicial error. Here the standard of care was crucial. The respondent physicians were receiving conflicting information. Their physical observations and tests, made periodically during the course of the pregnancy, conflicted with the presumed date of conception, and therefore the EDC. Determination of whether to allow the pregnancy to continue or terminate depended upon an exercise of their judgment at a time when a reasonable doubt existed as to the stage of the pregnancy and what should be done. Failure to give the requested instructions deprived the physician of the right to have the conduct evaluated in that light, and likewise deprived their counsel of the right to argue the issue before the jury.

Moreover, we reject, in part at least, appellants' invitation to follow a few courts that have rejected the "honest error" rule claiming it to be potentially misleading (see, e.g., Wall v. Stout, 310 N.C. 184, 311 S.E.2d 571 (1984)); or claiming it presumably conflicts with ordinary care language suggesting a disjunctive standard of care for a physician (Teh Len Chu v. Fairfax Emergency Medical Associates, Ltd., 223 Va. 383, 290 S.E.2d 820 (1982)); or claiming the language "confuses" the jury by implying only bad faith errors are actionable (Logan v. Greenwich Hospital Association, 191 Conn. 282, 465 A.2d 294 (1983), Magbuhat v. Kovarik, 382 N.W.2d 43 (S.D. 1986)). In Kinning v. Nelson, 281 N.W.2d 849, 853 (Minn. 1979), we recently rejected some of those very same arguments. . . .

Professionals are hired for their judgment and skill. If there is a lack of skill (the knife slips for a doctor or a statute of limitations is missed by a lawyer), we have a straight-forward enough malpractice claim. But if the claim involves a question of professional judgment, a choice of strategies or treatment, there may be a need, as we explained in Staloch v. Holm, 100 Minn. 276, 111 N.W. 264 (1907), to caution the trier of fact in applying the standard of care to the professional's conduct. The instruction that a doctor "is not responsible for an honest error in judgment in choosing between accepted methods of treatment," is an attempt to meet this problem, but the instruction, because it tries to set out the *Staloch* rationale in shorthand fashion, tends to be subjective and, perhaps on occasion, misleading.

Upon reflection we now conclude the time has come to hold that in professional malpractice cases the mostly subjective "honest error in judgment" language is inappropriate in defining the scope of the professional's duty toward those the professional serves. In our view, henceforth, in a medical negligence case, preferably the jury should be instructed as follows: A doctor is not negligent simply because his or her efforts prove unsuccessful. The fact a doctor may have chosen a method of treatment that later proves to be unsuccessful is not negligence if the treatment chosen was an accepted treatment on the basis of the information available to the doctor at the time a choice had to be made; a doctor must, however, use reasonable care to obtain the information needed to exercise his or her professional judgment, and an unsuccessful method of treatment chosen because of a failure to use such reasonable care would be negligence.

Notwithstanding that conclusion, it does not follow that the court of appeals erred in remanding this case for a new trial. An extremely close issue existed whether the respondents' prenatal judgment not to terminate the pregnancy was due to failure to exercise reasonable care. In the light of the facts of this case, had the jury been given even the modified instruction that we today propose eliminating the "honest error" language, the verdict might well have been different. This is particularly true because of the existence of controverted causation issues. Therefore, we agree with the court of appeals that failure to sufficiently inform the jury on professional liability rules was prejudicial, requiring a new trial.

NOTES

The Error of Judgment Defense: Applications and Limitations in Medical Care and Scientific Research

1. The error of judgment defense is probably the most common of all requests for instruction made on behalf of physician defendants in medical malpractice litigation. Nevertheless, it is often difficult to define and confusing to apply in individual cases.

2. As pointed out in the *Ouellette* opinion, the trend in American case law is to apply the error of judgment rule only when no actual negligence can be proved; that is, where the physician's choice of a differential diagnosis, or of an initial course of treatment, was clinically justified under the circumstances of the case at the time. In this respect, the rule can be called a "best judgment" rule, or a "choice of treatments" concept, just as well as an "error of judgment" rule. See King, The Law of Medical Malpractice 65-75 (Nutshell Series) (2d ed. 1986).

3. In many situations where a negligent diagnosis is alleged to have resulted in delay of proper treatment, the litigation will also involve a proximate causation issue over the "lost chance" of a correct

VI. Defenses

diagnosis and a timely, successful treatment. See cases and discussion of these problems at 278-283 earlier in this chapter.

4. Are there also important legal issues of error of judgment in biomedical research? Recent investigations in the federal Congress have charged biomedical scientists with fraud in conducting federally funded research projects. Prominent academic researchers have answered these Congressional inquiries in guest editorials published in the New York Times and have asserted that the investigations have confused fraud with honest scientific error. In an editorial entitled, "In Science, Error Isn't Fraud," Robert E. Pollack, Dean of Columbia College, asserted that, "Published error is at the heart of any real science. We scientists love to do experiments that show our colleagues to be wrong, and, if they are any good, they love to show us to be wrong in turn. By this adversarial process science reveals the way nature works." He concluded his article by saying, "If we as a country make science a field for only those who enjoy a good lawsuit, we will shut the door on our future as a technologically serious nation." Id. New York Times, May 2, 1989, at A25.

There is an important contribution to issues of error, misconduct, and fraud in biomedical research by a committee of the Institute of Medicine, National Academy of Sciences. See Report of a Study on the Responsible Conduct of Research in the Health Sciences, 37 Clinical Research 179 (1989). See also Russell, A Perspective on the Debate Over Scientific Misconduct, 37 Clin. Research 177 (1989).

Sprowl v. Ward
441 So. 2d 898 (Ala. 1983)

SHORES, JUSTICE.

Darrell Sprowl, plaintiff, appeals from a judgment entered on a jury verdict against him in this dental malpractice case. We affirm.

The facts are essentially undisputed. Sprowl, after suffering from a toothache for several weeks, made an appointment with Dr. Ward. After an initial examination and X-rays, Dr. Ward diagnosed Sprowl's problem and advised Sprowl that it could be treated by either a root canal or extraction of the affected tooth. Sprowl elected to have Dr. Ward perform the root canal. The initial X-rays revealed that there was a big amalgam filling which was pin-retained in the tooth. The presence of this filling gave Dr. Ward reason to be concerned about the use of a rubber dam during the root canal procedure. A rubber dam is specifically designed for use during this operation to prevent debris from falling into the patient's mouth and being swallowed. The rubber dam is held in place by a clamp which is actually placed around the affected tooth. The clamp adheres very tightly and could damage or fracture a weak tooth or an amalgam filling. In this case, Dr. Ward made the decision, without consulting Sprowl, not to use the rubber dam, because of the risk of fracturing the filling or tooth, which would cause additional expense and discomfort to the patient.

In the course of the root canal procedure, Dr. Ward allowed a dental file, which is a metal, spiral-shaped file about one-and-one-quarter inches long, to drop into Sprowl's mouth and be swallowed. Sprowl ultimately passed the file, apparently without physical injury.

Dr. Ward was the only expert to testify at the trial. He admitted that the file slipped from his fingers and was swallowed by Sprowl. He also admitted that if he had used a rubber dam during the procedure, Sprowl would not have ingested the dental file. However, there was no evidence that Dr. Ward acted below the applicable standard of care in failing to use a rubber dam. . . .

Dr. Ward explained that there are circumstances under which the use of the rubber dam may be harmful. It was his opinion that the use of the dam in Sprowl's case might cause the filling to fracture and cause economic hardship to Sprowl. Excerpts from a text on endodontics, recognized by Dr. Ward to be one of the leading authorities on the subject, were admitted into evidence. A portion of this text listed various alternative ways of using the rubber dam. Sprowl argues that Dr. Ward was negligent in failing to use one of these alternatives once he realized that the traditional method would do damage.

The decision to use one method of treatment as opposed to others, where there is reasonable doubt as to the proper course, is not a breach of duty. McTyeire v. McGaughy, 222 Ala. 100, 130 So. 784 (1930). Dr. Ward, based on his expert knowledge and skill, made the decision to forego the use of the dam in this case. Under these facts and according to the expert testimony presented, the decision not to use a dam was a "method of treatment." Under these circumstances, the jury was authorized to hold that Dr. Ward was not liable for his good faith decision to use one method over another, where there was evidence that the decision was made using reasonable care, and the method chosen was proper according to the standards followed in his field by dentists in the same general neighborhood.

The evidence shows that Dr. Ward was not mishandling the dental file at any time. The file slipped from his fingers by accident. The question of whether Dr. Ward had breached any duty to the patient in this regard was also properly submitted to the jury. We will not disturb the verdict in the absence of a showing that it is against the great weight of the evidence or manifestly unjust. Osborne v. Cobb, 410 So. 2d 396 (Ala. 1982).

VI. Defenses

NOTES

The Defense of "Schools of Thought" and "Respectable Minority Viewpoint" on Methods of Diagnosis and Treatment

1. The *Sprowl* opinion illustrates the application of the defense that the dentist or physician honestly and properly (without negligence) chose one method among several "schools of thought" concerning the management of the patient's clinical care. The issue, as in the previous cases in this section, is the use of clinical judgment. As it has been stated in other cases, "In treating a patient, a physician is permitted to choose between two or more methods of treatment. In making the choice, the physician must use his judgment. The judgment must be based upon scientific knowledge and his experience. He is not free to guess or take needless risks with the patient's well being." See Fall v. White, 449 N.E.2d 628, 635 (Ind. App. 4 Dist. 1983).

2. The application of the "schools of thought" defense can present sensitive issues of language and meaning. Great care must be taken by defendants in requesting jury instructions in accordance with the concept. Appellate courts have frequently reversed trial court verdicts for the defendant when such an instruction does not make it clear that the defendant must exercise due care and must follow an accepted, non-negligent standard of care in exercising medical judgment. One version of the precautionary instruction on alternative methods of treatment states that where the defendant does not select the alternative which was most commonly utilized, the choice that was actually made must represent at least a "respectable minority viewpoint." This does not mean that the chosen method is "acceptable" to one expert witness who testified at the trial; the method must represent a group of physicians whose methods are respected and found to be within the boundaries of the state of the art in the field. See Rogers v. Meridian Park Hosp., 763 P.2d 400 (Or. App. 1989); D'Angelis v. Zakato, 55 A.2d 431 (Pa. Super. Ct. 1989); Chumbler v. McClure, 505 F.2d 489 (6th Cir. 1974).

3. It should also be recognized that a physician or other health care provider is expected to follow reasonable standards of care at the time of the patient's treatment. Changes in "schools of thought" after the events in question cannot affect the proper standard that the provider should have followed at the earlier time. Care must be taken to monitor the opinions of "medical experts" who are asked to evaluate medical care, which may have taken place from two to ten years beforehand. Should an "expert" be allowed to testify who was not in practice or in training many years before, when the alleged negligent care took place?

4. The "schools of thought" defense should not be confused with an earlier and quite traditional reference to "schools of medicine." This phrase was developed to distinguish separate types of medical practitioners who went through different schooling and training under different scientific foundations or philosophies. These were, most commonly, the allopathic school (today's M.D. degree), the homeopathic school (now merged with the allopathic system), the osteopathic school, and the chiropractic school. Under most of the earlier judicial applications, each of these schools was recognized as offering distinct systems of medical care. Thus, each was entitled to develop separate standards of care concerning which only practitioners of that school could testify as experts. In later years, these distinctions have often been blurred both generally and in specific types of patient care management, especially as between the majority group of allopathic physicians and the minority group of osteopaths. In several states, one medical licensing board examines and monitors practice of both allopathic and osteopathic medicine.

Issues of a similar nature are raised when the defendant is a practitioner from among other health professionals such as nurses, podiatrists, hematology technicians, physiotherapists, etc. Usually, such practitioners are held only to ordinary, reasonable standards of care within their own professional group. There are exceptions, however, wherein such practitioners may be held to standards of care usually applied to physicians. See for example, Thompson v. Brett, 245 So. 2d 751 (La. App. 1971).

B. *Patient-Related Defenses: Adequate Informed Consent, Assumption of Risk, Contributory Negligence, Release of Liability, and Other Issues*

Precourt v. Frederick
481 N.E.2d 1144 (Mass. 1985)

O'CONNOR, J.

In Harnish v. Children's Hosp. Medical Center, 387 Mass. 152, 155 (1982), we said that "a physician owes to his patient the duty to disclose in a reasonable manner all significant medical information that the physician possesses or reasonably should possess that is material to an intelligent decision by the patient whether to undergo a proposed procedure." . . .

The plaintiffs commenced this action in April, 1980, alleging that the defendant, Albert R. Frederick, Jr., a physician, negligently prescribed for the plaintiff Wilfred Precourt a drug called Prednisone, and that, as a result, Precourt developed severe damage to the bones

VI. Defenses

of both his hips. Precourt sought damages for his personal injuries, and his wife, Elizabeth, sought damages for her loss of consortium. After our decision in *Harnish,* supra, the plaintiffs amended their complaint to allege, in addition to negligence, that, although Frederick knew or reasonably should have known that the use of Prednisone presented a risk of the type of hip damage that Precourt sustained, Frederick nevertheless prescribed Prednisone for Precourt without informing him of that risk. The trial judge denied Frederick's motions for directed verdicts, but the jury found for Frederick on the counts alleging negligence. The jury found for Precourt on his lack of informed consent claim, and they awarded Precourt $800,000 and Elizabeth $200,000. Frederick moved for judgment notwithstanding the verdicts or for a new trial. The judge denied Frederick's motion, although he conditioned his denial of a new trial of Elizabeth's claim on her remitting $100,000, which she thereafter did. Frederick appealed from the judgments for the plaintiffs and from the denial of his motion for judgment notwithstanding the verdict, and we transferred the case to this court on our own motion. Frederick challenges the denial of his motions and he challenges various aspects of the judge's charge to the jury as well. We do not reach the latter challenges because we hold that the evidence was legally insufficient to warrant submission of the case to the jury. We reverse the judgments for the plaintiffs. . . .

In order for the jury properly to have determined whether Frederick failed to disclose to Precourt information that Frederick should reasonably have recognized as material to Precourt's decision, therefore, the jury had to have information about both the severity of aseptic necrosis and the likelihood that it would occur after the use of Prednisone. See Smith v. Shannon, 100 Wash. 2d 26, 33 (1983) ("The determination of materiality is a 2-step process. Initially, the scientific nature of the risk must be ascertained. i.e., the nature of the harm which may result and the probability of its occurrence. . . . The trier of fact must then decide whether that probability of that type of harm is a risk which a reasonable patient would consider in deciding on treatment"); LaCaze v. Collier, 434 So. 2d 1039, 1046 (La. 1983) ("Materiality is, in essence, the product of the risk and its chance of occurring. A severe consequence, ordinarily of interest to the patient, would not require disclosure if the chance of the consequence occurring was so remote as to be negligible. Likewise, no disclosure would be required of a very minor consequence even though the probability of occurrence was high. At trial, once the severity and probability of risk is presented, the trier of fact may determine materiality without the further aid of expert testimony"); Winkjer v. Herr, 277 N.W.2d 579, 588 (N.D. 1979) ("There is no need to disclose risks of little consequence, those that are extremely remote, or those that are common knowledge as inherent in the treatment"); Beauvais v. Notre Dame Hosp., 120 R.I. 271, 276 (1978) (in affirming the granting of a directed verdict for the defendant physician in a case involving the doctrine of informed consent, the court said: "While it is clear that defendant failed to disclose the classic hazards of spinal anesthesia, no evidence regarding the severity or likelihood of those risks was presented so that a jury could determine the materiality of those risks to a reasonable person in plaintiff's position. See Wilkinson v. Vesey, 110 R.I. at 627-28 . . .").

In this case, there was no evidence of the likelihood that a person would develop aseptic necrosis after taking Prednisone or that Frederick knew or should have known that the likelihood was other than negligible. Therefore, as a matter of law, the plaintiffs failed to show that Frederick recognized or reasonably should have recognized that the undisclosed risk was material to Precourt's decision. Characterization of Precourt's Prednisone dosage as "high" and the course of treatment as "long," in combination with the evidence that the probability of aseptic necrosis increases as the exposure to Prednisone increases, does not permit the inference that Frederick reasonably should have recognized that the possibility that Precourt would develop aseptic necrosis was material to Precourt's decision. Nor is such an inference made possible by the evidence of Precourt's preexisting medical condition or by the evidence that aseptic necrosis is one of the most prominent musculoskeletal complications of Prednisone, or that the risk was "high." "High" is a relative word. It could mean one in ten, but it could just as well mean one in a million.

The evidence did not warrant a finding that Frederick violated a duty he owed to Precourt. A contrary result is not required by the testimony of the expert witnesses with respect to their essentially legal conclusion that Frederick "should have" made a disclosure that he did not make. Also, no different result is compelled by Precourt's testimony that before the second operation Frederick told him that he had "everything to gain and nothing to lose." Precourt could not reasonably have taken that statement literally to mean that the proposed surgery was free of risk.

We continue to adhere to the views we expressed in *Harnish,* supra at 154-156, that self-determination by the patient is an important value worthy of society's protection, but that there must be a reasonable accommodation between the patient's right to know, fairness to physicians, and society's interest that medicine be practiced in this Commonwealth without unrealistic and unnecessary burdens on practitioners. As we said in *Harnish,* supra at 156, "[t]he obligation to give adequate information does not require the disclosure of all risks of a proposed therapy." We also observed in *Harnish,* supra at 155, that "[t]he remotely possible risks of a proposed treatment may be almost without limit," and we at least implied, as we now hold, that a physician is not required to inform a patient of remote risks. The development of our law concerning the distinction between risks that as a matter of law may be considered remote, and those that may be left to the determination of a fact finder, must await future cases. It is clear, however, that when, as in this case, the evidence does not permit the jury to draw an inference that the physician knew or reasonably should have known that the probability that a particular risk would materialize was other than negligible, the evidence is insufficient to warrant a finding that the physician violated his duty of disclosure.

Judgments reversed.

Marshall v. University of Chicago Hospitals and Clinics
520 N.E.2d 740 (Ill. App. 1987)

BILANDIC, J.

Plaintiff brought a medical malpractice action against the defendant hospitals because she got pregnant with her fifth child approximately 11 months after elective surgical sterilization by tubal ligation. Plaintiff's original complaint alleged that because of the negligent tubal ligation, she became pregnant. When the negligent count was dropped, plaintiff filed an amended complaint alleging that the defendants failed to inform her that there was a 1 percent chance of failure of tubal ligation to prevent future pregnancies. She further alleged that had she known the failure rate of 1 percent, she would not have undergone that procedure. This is the sole basis for the alleged malpractice.

The jury returned a verdict of $20,000 for the plaintiff. The trial court denied defendants' post-trial motion for judgment *n.o.v.* or for a new trial. Defendants appeal.

In May 1976, while pregnant with her fourth child, plaintiff was receiving prenatal care at the defendant hospitals. She was a borderline diabetic, was financially strapped, experiencing marital difficulties, and consequently did not want to have any more children. On May 13, 1976, she discussed the relative merits of various forms of birth control with a resident physician at the defendant hospitals. Plaintiff informed the resident physician that she was not interested in birth control pills because she used them before and they made her sick. She also told him that she became pregnant while using a contraceptive cream.

The resident physician testified that he explained the merits of the various options and gave the plaintiff a brochure entitled "Voluntary Sterilization for Women" to read and discuss with her husband. The three-page brochure consisted of information taken from the Planned Parenthood Association. It stated that tubal ligation is a "virtually certain" form of birth control and should be regarded as permanent because it was rarely possible to repair tubes surgically if a woman wanted to have more children. Plaintiff testified that she understood "virtually certain" to mean she would never get pregnant again.

On May 13, 1976, plaintiff also signed a "Consent for Non-Therapeutic Sterilization" which consisted of one page with information on the front and back. The first page states in part:

> The risk of failure must be recognized but the percentage of pregnancy subsequent to sterilization is small.

Plaintiff's signature appeared on the other side of the document. She testified that she never saw the side with the risk of failure information. The resident physician testified that the risk of failure was explained to the plaintiff and that she was given an opportunity to ask questions.

On May 29, 1976, at about 3:30 A.M., plaintiff was admitted to the defendant hospitals to deliver her fourth child and gave birth approximately an hour later. The surgeon testified that he saw the plaintiff after the delivery, explained the tubal ligation procedure and failure rate, and obtained another written consent form. The explanation took 10 to 15 minutes and plaintiff was given an opportunity to ask questions. She was not mentally impaired in any way. Plaintiff testified that she never read the consent form.

The tubal ligation was performed at about 8 A.M. on May 29, 1976, about 3½ hours after delivery and about 1½ hours after signing the consent form.

Approximately 11 to 12 months after the tubal ligation, plaintiff got pregnant with her fifth child. She delivered that child on January 17, 1978, at Michael Reese Hospital. Immediately after the birth of that child, she had another tubal ligation performed at Michael Reese.

Plaintiff testified that had she known there was a failure rate of 1 percent, she would not have undergone the tubal ligation the first time, but would have instead gone back on birth control pills even though they made her sick.

Plaintiff's complaint against the defendants was filed on May 26, 1978, just prior to the expiration of the two-year statute of limitation and approximately four months after she had undergone a second tubal ligation at another hospital. The principal issue on appeal is whether the trial court erred in denying defendant's motion for judgment *n.o.v.* or, in the alternative, for a new trial.

VI. Defenses 369

I

Initially, defendants contend that plaintiff failed to present any expert testimony or other evidence that the standard of care required disclosure of a 1 percent risk of failure.

Plaintiff did not present her own expert. Instead, plaintiff subpoenaed defendants' expert and called the surgeon as an adverse witness. Both testified in plaintiff's case in chief. . . .

Plaintiff's trial counsel posed the following question, and the following answer was given:

> *Q:* But, Doctor, based upon a reasonable degree of medical certainty, would you consider it a deviation from the standard of care that was present in Cook County, Illinois in 1976 to merely give a patient a consent form to sign for a tubal ligation without explaining anything to her about its context?
> *A:* Yes.

There was conflicting evidence regarding the information given to the plaintiff and the explanations made to her prior to surgery. Applying the *Pedrick* standard, the trial court properly refused to direct a verdict for the defendants and properly denied defendants' motion for judgment *n.o.v.* based on the issue of the standard of care.

II

However, plaintiff is also required to prove that the failure to meet the standard of care was the proximate cause of her injury. That burden of proof is equally applicable to allegations of a lack of informed consent as to negligent performance of a medical procedure. . . .

It was not enough for plaintiff to subjectively assert at trial that, had she known that tubal ligation was only 99 percent effective, she would have chosen instead the 90 percent effective birth control pills that made her sick. Rather, as stated in St. Gemme v. Tomlin (1983), 118 Ill. App. 3d 766, 769, 455 N.E.2d 294, *appeal denied* (1984), 96 Ill. 2d 571, it was incumbent upon plaintiff to prove by "objective" evidence that a reasonable person, in possession of the allegedly omitted information, would have rejected the treatment in question:

> "The patient-plaintiff may testify on this subject but the issue extends beyond his credibility. Since at the time of trial the uncommunicated hazard has materialized, it would be surprising if the patient-plaintiff did not claim that . . . treatment. Subjectively he may believe so, with the 20/20 vision of hindsight, but we doubt that justice will be served by placing the physician in jeopardy of the patient's bitterness

and disillusionment. Thus *an objective test* is preferable: *i.e., what would a prudent person in the [plaintiff's] position have decided if adequately informed of all significant perils."* [Citation.] (Emphasis added.)

The record in this case contained no objective evidence that "a reasonably prudent person in plaintiff's position" would have refused the tubal ligation. The only reasonable inference from the objective evidence is that a reasonable person in plaintiff's position would not have refused the tubal ligation under the circumstances. Moreover, it is a demonstrable, irrefutable conclusion from the undisputed facts that after her last daughter was born and she was now well aware of the risk of failure, plaintiff still elected to have another tubal ligation four months prior to filing this action.

We therefore conclude that plaintiff failed to meet her burden of proof on the issue of proximate cause. The trial court erred in denying defendants' motion for judgment *n.o.v.* Accordingly, the judgment in favor of the plaintiff is reversed and judgment is entered in favor of the defendant hospitals.

Affirmed in part; reversed in part.

Hutton v. Craighead
530 So. 2d 101 (La. App. 4 Cir. 1988)

Plaintiff, Yvonne Hutton, sued defendants, Dr. Claude Craighead and his insurer Hartford Insurance Co. . . .

On September 29, 1980, Ms. Hutton consulted with Dr. Craighead concerning gastro-gastrostomy surgery for weight loss. This procedure entails a partial stapling of the stomach so that it is divided into a very small pouch connected to a larger pouch by a small tube with an opening of 1.5 centimeters. The purpose of the procedure is to reduce food intake, which results in weight loss. . . .

Ms. Hutton consented to the gastro-gastrostomy operation by reading and signing a consent form, which was unquestionably in compliance with the requirements of LSA-R.S. 40:1299.40. (See Appendix.) In LaCaze v. Collier, 434 So. 2d 1039 (La. 1983), the Louisiana Supreme Court concluded that the statutory language has superseded the jurisprudential rules defining consent to medical treatment. Therefore, under the statute, when a patient consents in writing to medical treatment pursuant to Louisiana's Uniform Consent Law, no other evidence "shall be admissible to modify or limit" the consent except evidence proving "the consent was induced by misrepresentation." Leiva v. Nance, 506 So. 2d 131, 132 (La. App. 4th Cir. 1987).

The statute further provides that the nature and purposes of the surgical procedure to be undergone by the patient must be set out in general terms in a valid consent form. If any of the following enumerated risks — death, brain damage, quadriplegia, paraplegia, the loss or loss of function of any organ or limb, of disfiguring scars — are associated with the procedure, it must also be stated in the consent form.

When, as in the instant case, a consent form which complies with the statutory requirements was signed by the plaintiff, the written consent is presumed to be valid in the absence of proof that the execution of the form was induced by misrepresentation. Id. at 133. A five-judge panel of this court has recently held that the use of the statutory language in the written form, "coupled with the patient's right to ask questions concerning his treatment and to have them answered to his satisfaction before signing a consent form, is sufficient to indicate informed consent to medical treatment." Hondroulis v. Schuhmacher, 521 So. 2d 534 (La. App. 4th Cir. 1988).

Ms. Hutton claims, however, that Dr. Craighead induced her to consent to the surgery by a misrepresentation of material facts as to the nature and purpose of the procedure. Specifically, Ms. Hutton alleges that Dr. Craighead misrepresented the following three facts: (1) That the surgery would obviate the need for her to exercise will power in controlling her eating habits, (2) That she would lose about 80 pounds and (3) That the doctor had had personal success with this procedure in weight reduction.

Because of the presumption that a written consent is valid in the absence of proof that the consent was induced by misrepresentation, we have examined the record and determined no misrepresentations of material fact which would vitiate consent were made.

On appeal, Ms. Hutton argues that she was misled concerning the benefits of the surgery because she understood that she would not have to exercise any willpower to lose the weight she wanted to lose. . . . Ms. Hutton is a licensed practical nurse; we can assume that she is more aware than the average person of bodily processes. We can also presume that she recognizes the inexorable calories in/ calories out equation that results in weight gain or weight loss. That she was able to defeat the system by continuing to eat until the small pouch was stretched out to the size of a normal stomach cannot be attributed to misrepresentation by the surgeon.

Ms. Hutton argues in her second point that she was led to believe she would lose 80 pounds. This argument should not be considered because the consent form Ms. Hutton signed specifically states "there can be no guarantee expressed or implied either as to the result of treatment or as to cure." Hence, evidence is not admissible as to expressed or guaranteed results of treatment. Leonhard v. New Orleans East Orthopedic Clinic, 485 So. 2d 1008 (La. App. 4th Cir. 1986), Writ denied, 489 So. 2d 919 (La. 1986).

We also find no merit in Ms. Hutton's third argument that she would not have undergone the surgery had she not believed Dr. Craighead had personally had success with the gastro-gastrostomy procedure. The record reveals that Ms. Hutton was aware that the surgery she elected was a new procedure. Therefore, even if she knew of Dr. Craighead's reputation as an accomplished surgeon, she could not have thought he was experienced at this particular procedure. Furthermore, the surgery was performed correctly.

Considering the evidence in the case at bar, we find no support for the plaintiff's claim that consent was induced by material misrepresentation. We realize that Ms. Hutton did not achieve the results she sought when she agreed to the surgery and that she suffered for more than a year with a wound infection. It is understandable that a jury would sympathize with her. Yet, the burden of proof borne by the plaintiff is clear, and there is no evidence of misrepresentation to support the jury verdict. Therefore, we find that the evidence before the trier of fact in this case does not furnish a reasonable basis for the decision in this case. Canter v. Koehring Co., 283 So. 2d 716, 724 (La. 1973). Since we find that the jury verdict is manifestly erroneous, we reverse. . . .

NOTES

Informed Consent and Assumption of Risk as Defenses; Effect of Signed Consent Documents and Releases of Liability

1. The three cases reprinted above illustrate most of the major issues in considering informed consent and assumption of risk defenses in medical malpractice. The many authoritative textbooks and law-review articles cited earlier in this chapter at 302-304 and 311-313 provide background on the doctrine of informed consent. The most useful of the texts in advising physicians and other health care providers concerning the content of disclosure requirements is F. Rozovsky, Consent to Treatment: A Practical Guide (2d ed. 1990). See also Haligan, The Standard of Disclosure by Physicians to Patients: Competing Models of Informed Consent, 41 La. L. Rev. 9 (1980); Schueyer, Informed Consent and the Danger of Bias in the Formulation of Medical Disclosure Practices, 1976 Wis. L. Rev. 124.

2. The Massachusetts decision in *Precourt* was reached after that state had adopted the *Canterbury* rule in the *Harnish* case noted in the opinion. Is the *Precourt* determination of remoteness of risk consistent with the *Canterbury* opinion's criteria? Is any risk too remote for disclosure when it is specifically mentioned in the manufacturer's package insert? See discussion of issues of standard of care and package insert information at 277-278 of this chapter.

3. When the physician informs the patient about "material" risks

and benefits of a proposed procedure, the patient is, in effect, being asked to assume the disclosed risks (of a non-negligent nature) in order to achieve the potential benefits. The classic judicial recognition of an assumption of risk came in the Federal Circuit Court decision in Karp v. Cooley, 493 F.2d 408 (5th Cir. 1974) applying Texas law. The case involved an experimental procedure, the first attempt to implant a totally mechanical heart into a human patient. The surgeon was the famous Dr. Denton Cooley of Houston, Texas. The court held that the plaintiff, Haskell Karp, was adequately informed of the experimental nature of the procedure and its risks. There was a detailed discussion with the patient conducted by Dr. Cooley in the presence of the patient's wife, a religious adviser, and the hospital's assistant administrator. The discussion was followed by the signing of a consent form specifically designed for this procedure. A directed verdict for the defendant on the issue of informed consent was sustained by the appellate court.

4. In experimental medicine, despite a huge volume of activity involving patients and research subjects, there have been very few law suits either under a negligence theory or based on inadequacy of informed consent. Most of the field of clinical investigation is now very closely regulated by the Federal Food and Drug Administration and by the National Institutes of Health in its Office of Protection from Research Risks. Particular attention is given to prior approval of written informed consent documents. These documents are reviewed by interdisciplinary ethical review committees (called "institutional review boards") located in hospitals, other medical research centers, and in universities where research is conducted using human subjects. See particularly Levine, Ethics and Regulation of Clinical Investigation (2d ed. 1986). For further background, see B. Barber, Informed Consent in Medical Therapy and Research (1980); G. Annas, L. Glanz & B. Katz, Informed Consent to Human Experimentation (1977); B. Gray, Human Subjects in Medical Experimentation (1975); Fried, Medical Experimentation: Personal Integrity and Social Policy (1974).

5. The past two decades have witnessed an explosion of public policy interest in issues of human experimentation. Much of the concern has been over the rights and welfare of certain "disenfranchised" groups.

Useful articles on issues relating to the involvement of children in medical research include Shivers, Informed Consent and the Child in Nontherapeutic Human Experimentation, 32 Med. Trial Tech. Q. 33 (1985); Langer, Medical Research Involving Children: Some Legal and Ethical Issues, 35 Baylor L. Rev. 1 (1984); Furlow, Consent of Minors to Participate in Nontherapeutic Research, 1980 Leg. Med. Ann. 261.

On fetal research, see Clapp, State Prohibition of Fetal Experimentation and the Fundamental Right of Privacy, 88 Col. L. Rev. 1073 (1988); Fletcher & Ryan, Federal Regulations for Fetal Research: A Case for Reform, 15 L. Med. & Health Care 128 (1987).

On research involving mentally disabled subjects, see Roth, Informed Consent in Psychiatric Research, 39 Rutgers L. Rev. 425 (1987); Dickens, Ethical Issues in Psychiatric Research, 4 Intl. J. Law & Psychia. 271 (1981).

Finally, the AIDS epidemic has focused attention on the vulnerability of research subjects in this field and on the urgency to develop both therapeutic drugs and vaccines. See Levine, Has AIDS Changed the Ethics of Human Subject Research?, 16 L. Med. & Health Care 167 (1988).

6. Another aspect of remoteness of risk is presented in the *Marshall* case. The requirement of proximate causation is applied in order to deny liability when a "prudent person" would have consented to the procedure even with knowledge of risk information that was not disclosed. The same concept of remoteness has been applied in vaccine cases where the risk of the product is extremely remote and the risk of contracting the disease in the community if not vaccinated is considerably higher. See Cunningham v. Chas. Pfizer & Co., 532 P.2d 1377 (Okla. 1974).

7. Not all aspects of assumption of the risk of a medical procedure are related to informed consent. In some situations, the patient may independently refuse some aspect of the care or some alternative that the physician feels advisable or even necessary for the patient's welfare. In such situations, the physician is justified in withdrawing from the case and in referring the patient elsewhere. Among the most common of these situations confronting American hospitals is the refusal of blood transfusions on religious grounds. In a recent case in the Washington Supreme Court the patient's voluntary refusal of blood was found to be an express assumption of risk. The patient and her husband signed a release of liability for any harm resulting from the refusal. The court held the document of release from liability as valid and not against public policy since it did not release liability for any negligent conduct. Shorter v. Drury, 695 P.2d 116 (Wash. 1985). Should releases of liability by hospitalized patients (or research subjects) be against public policy? See generally Tunkl v. Regents of the U. of Cal., 383 P.2d 441 (Cal. 1963); Note 6 A.L.R.3d 704 (1984).

8. The last case reprinted above, the *Hutton* case, provides an important example of judicial interpretation of one of the numerous legislative reforms adopted in recent years designed to make the rules of informed consent "fairer" for health care providers. The types of reforms include the following (1) statutes that return the state law on disclosure requirements for consent to a "professional standard"; (2) statutes denying recovery for any guarantee of cure or specific

VI. Defenses

good result unless documented in writing; (3) statutes creating a presumption of informed consent, as in Louisiana in the *Hutton* case, when the patient signs a written consent document meeting certain specified standards, and (4) statutes, as in Texas and Hawaii, that establish administrative bodies to subscribe actual "lists" of risks that must be disclosed in certain procedures.

Fall v. White
449 N.E.2d 628 (Ind. App. 4 Dist. 1983)

[This case involved a claim for medical malpractice arising out of alleged negligence by physicians in not caring for the plaintiff adequately before his death by a heart attack and by not warning him adequately to change his lifestyle and reduce his physical activity.]

MILLER, J.

... [The plaintiff, Mrs. Fall,] also asserts the trial court erred in giving instruction number ten which reads:

> The patient, as well as the physician, has the duty to exercise reasonable care; the physician has a duty to his patient to exercise reasonable care in forming his diagnosis and rendering treatment while the patient has a duty to exercise reasonable care in providing the physician with accurate and complete information and following his instructions for further care or further diagnostic tests. If Max L. Fall failed to exercise reasonable care in providing Dr. White with accurate and complete information regarding his condition or in following instructions given him by Dr. White for further care or tests and such failure on Max Fall's part directly contributed to causing his death, then your verdict should be against the plaintiff, Lula M. Fall and in favor of the defendant doctor.

Fall objects to this contributory negligence instruction which informed the jury Max had the duty of exercising reasonable care both in providing his doctor with complete and accurate information and in following his doctor's instructions. Fall claims contributory negligence was not an issue in the lawsuit, and further, the instruction was a misstatement of the law and not supported by the evidence. First, we note that part G of a May 15, 1981, pretrial order enumerated the contested issues of fact which included "[w]hether acts or omissions on the part of the decedent proximately contributed to his death." Additionally, a preliminary instruction (reread as final instruction) also addressed the subject of Max's negligence as a defense and stated: "The defendants have the burden of proving this claim by a preponderance of the evidence." Finally, Fall herself tendered an instruction, given with only slight modification, which instructed the jury:

The defendant claims that Max Fall was guilty of contributory negligence which caused or contributed to his death. Defendant has the burden of proof on this issue.

Before you can find that Max Fall was guilty of contributory negligence, you must first find that he failed to act in a way that a reasonably prudent person would have acted under the same or similar circumstances and that such failure was a direct cause of his death.

In determining the question of whether or not Max Fall exercised the care of a reasonably prudent person, you may consider his prior medical history, his experiences with Dr. White, and the care, advice and treatment given to him along with all of the other evidence *and circumstances* in this case. (Emphasized language added by trial court.)

Under the foregoing circumstances, it is apparent contributory negligence was an issue at the trial.

With respect to Fall's claim there was no evidence of contributory negligence, we find evidence in the record Max failed to submit to the blood lipid profile — a test which Dr. White ordered after explaining to Max his heart problem on March 29, 1973, nor did he return to Dr. White, as instructed, for further evaluation. Other evidence disclosed that Max was cautioned at the March 29 examination to report immediately to a hospital if he experienced chest pains. However, on the morning of his death he complained of chest pains both before he began working and while working. In the latter situation, he rested for a few minutes and commenced working again.[3] Dr. White's deposition revealed he asked Max at the March 29 office visit if he had been having any chest pains and Max answered in the negative. Yet according to Mrs. Fall, Max complained frequently of chest pains so severe he thought he would die. Thus, contrary to Fall's assertion, there is evidence in the record both of Max's failure to follow his doctor's instructions and his failure to give complete and accurate information.

Regarding the legal correctness of the instruction, Fall does not complain of the language which instructs that a patient may be contributorily negligent if he fails to follow the physician's instructions. This principle of law is well established in this jurisdiction. Jones v. Angell, (1883) 95 Ind. 376; Young v. Mason, (1893) 8 Ind. App. 264, 35 N.E. 521; 23 I.L.E. Physicians & Surgeons §18 (1970). She does object to the portion of the instruction which states "[A] patient has a duty to exercise reasonable care in providing the physician with accurate and complete information." She claims in her brief:

> A patient does not have a duty to advise the doctor. That is to say, a patient has the right to expect his physician to make inquiry of

---

3. This evidence was gleaned from an accident report of the investigating police officer (Fall's Exhibit Number 7) who obtained the information from the homeowner where Max was working on April 11, 1973.

VI. Defenses

him. Under this instruction, it would appear that a patient has a duty to spontaneously advise his physician of his complete medical background.

Frequently, if not usually, patients are not learned enough to know what facts are of critical importance and which are not. They rely on their doctor to ask them what he needs to know in order to properly care for them.

Appellant's brief p. 71. However, Fall goes on to concede that:

[i]f Max Fall had been asked a question and failed or refused to give an answer, that might constitute negligence on his part. If contributory negligence was [sic] an issue in this case, such conduct might even have constituted a defense.

Id.

In addressing this issue we would first note, as conceded by Fall, that the principle of contributory negligence is applicable in malpractice actions. It has been explained thusly: "The creation of the relation of physician and patient gives rise to reciprocal that he failed to cooperate in his treatment by providing such information within his own knowledge." Skar v. Lincoln, supra, at 260.

We acknowledge a patient does not have a duty to diagnose his own condition as he can reasonably expect the physician to ask the proper questions. However, we disagree with Fall's contention that the court's instructions commanded the jury to find Max contributorily negligent if he failed to spontaneously advise his physician of his complete medical background. Rather, the instruction in question required only that a patient has a duty to exercise *reasonable care* in providing medical information and the jury was further instructed that Max's standard of conduct was that of a reasonably prudent person under like or similar circumstances. These instructions conform to the rule of contributory negligence in medical malpractice actions set out by our supreme court in Memorial Hospital of South Bend, Inc. v. Scott, (1973) 261 Ind. 27, 300 N.E.2d 50:

The general rule on the issue of the plaintiff's contributory negligence is that the plaintiff must exercise that degree of care that an ordinary reasonable man would exercise in like or similar circumstances. Bain, Admx. v. Mattmiller (1938), 213 Ind. 549, 13 N.E.2d 712. Contributory negligence is conduct on the part of the plaintiff, contributing as a legal cause to the harm he has suffered, *which falls below the standard to which he is required to conform for his own protection.* Restatement Second of Torts §463. (Emphasis in original.)

Id. at 36, 300 N.E.2d at 56.[4] Based on the foregoing, we find the

---

4. In Memorial Hospital of South Bend, Inc. v. Scott, supra, at 36, 300 N.E.2d

jury was properly instructed on contributory negligence.[5] . . .

NOTES

Contributory Negligence and Mitigation of Damages: The Obligations of Patients in Medical Care Management

1. In a physician-patient relationship, it is not only the doctor who owes a duty to the patient. The patient also has certain responsibilities to the doctor: to give an honest and complete medical history, to follow reasonable advice of the doctor, to inform the doctor of any unexpected matters occurring in a contemplated course of treatment, and to make it known whether he or she clearly understands a contemplated course of action and what he or she is expected to do. D. Louisell & H. Williams, Medical Malpractice, §8.02 (1989). If a physician breaches the duty, the patient clearly has the right to bring an action against the doctor if harm results. If the patient also breaches important duties, however, it may serve either to negate the patient's ability to recover from the physician (contributory negligence), or reduce the amount of recovery (mitigation of damages). Some states allow comparative negligence recovery, in which the degree of negligence of the physician is compared to the degree of fault of the patient, so that the patient's negligence may reduce the amount of ultimate recovery. Morganstein v. House, 547 A.2d 1180 (Pa. 1988); Suria v. Shiffman, 67 N.Y.2d 87, 499 N.Y.2d 913 (1986);

---

at 56, the court noted: "[A] departure from the general rule is required where the plaintiff is suffering from physical infirmities which impair his ability to function as an 'ordinary reasonable man.'" In the case before us, there is no claim that Max suffered from any physical infirmity rendering him unable to function as an "ordinary reasonable man."

5. We also recognize that failure to disclose could, under certain factual circumstances, preclude a finding of negligence on the part of the doctor. Amdur v. Zim Israel Navigation Co., (S.D.N.Y. 1969), 310 F. Supp 1033; Tangora v. Matanky, (1974) 231 Cal. App. 2d 468, 42 Cal. Rptr. 348; Johnson v. St. Paul Mercury Insurance Co., (1969) La. App., 219 So. 2d 524, 36 A.L.R.3rd 1349. In *Johnson*, for example, a hospital doctor was called upon to treat a 2½ year old child who, some nineteen hours earlier, had ingested aspirin. This latter fact was not revealed to the doctor by the child's parents although the father was asked specifically by the doctor whether the child had taken any aspirin, cough syrup or any other medication before he was brought to the hospital. Consequently, the doctor did not administer a test to determine the presence of aspirin and proceeded to diagnose and treat the illness as a typical case of croup. From the expert testimony the court was able to determine 1) there was no reason to believe the doctor could have discovered the problem other than being alerted to its possibility and, 2) he exercised the degree of skill ordinarily employed under similar circumstances by the members of his profession in good standing in the community and used reasonable care and diligence, along with his best judgment in the application of his skill to the case. With these findings, the court concluded the doctor was free of negligence in all respects.

McGuire v. Sifers, 681 P.2d 1025 (Kan. 1984). See also D. Louisell & H. Williams, supra, §18.18.

2. The principal case demonstrates that a patient may be contributorily negligent in failing to follow the physician's instructions or in providing an incorrect medical history. See also MacKey v. Greenview Hosp., Inc., 587 S.W.2d 249 (Ky. Ct. App. 1979); Davila v. Bodelson, 704 P.2d 1119 (N.M. 1985); Ziegert v. South Chicago Community Hosp., 425 N.E.2d 450 (Ill. App. 1981); 33 A.L.R.4th 790 (1984). There are other ways that a patient could be contributorily negligent. For example, a patient's leaving the hospital against the advice of a physician or a patient's failure to return for an examination as directed may also be cause for a contributory negligence defense. See 100 A.L.R.3d 723 (1980). In situations where a patient seeks to leave a hospital against medical advice, the patient is often requested to sign a document acknowledging that the departure is against advice. The document also often contains a release of liability for any injury resulting from the premature departure from the hospital. On the general subject of patients' responsibility in medical matters, see a recent comparative international study, Osinga, The Patient's Responsibilities in Medical Care and Treatment (World Health Organization, European Office: Copenhagen 1989).

3. Any negligence of the patient which occurs after the physician's treatment ordinarily does not qualify as contributory negligence which bars or limits recovery. Rather, it may serve to mitigate the damages, on the principle that the plaintiff cannot aggravate his own damages in order to increase his recovery. See Quinones v. Public Admin. of County of Kings, 373 N.Y.S.2d 224 (App. Div. 1975); Bird v. Pritchard, 291 N.E.2d 769 (Ohio App. 1973); Blair v. Eblen, 461 S.W.2d 370 (Ky. Ct. App. 1970).

The plaintiff is only required to take reasonable steps to mitigate his damages: a patient does not have to submit to a dangerous operation or to a course of treatment where the outcome is uncertain. Robins v. Katz, 391 N.W.2d 495 (Mich. App. 1986); Dodds v. Stellar, 175 P.2d 607 (Cal. App. 1946). Damages may also be mitigated by the value of any benefit conferred on the patient by the tortious act. Barnette v. Potenza, 79 Misc. 2d 51, 359 N.Y.S.2d 432 (1974); Maben v. Rankin, 358 P.2d 681 (Cal. 1961). In this respect, issues of public policy are presented by a failed surgical procedure for sterilization. Should the fact that the plaintiff safely delivered a healthy child (but unplanned due to the failed sterilization) require reduction of her total damages due to the value of the expected "benefits" of the bringing up of the child? Should recovery of damages be allowed at all under such circumstances? See Flowers v. District of Columbia, 478 A.2d 1073 (D.C. App. 1984); Sherlock v. Stillwater Clinic, 260 N.W.2d 169 (Minn. 1977); Anon. v. Hosp., 33 Conn. Supp. 126, 366 A.2d 204 (1976).

C. Good Samaritan Laws and Other Immunity Defenses

New York Good Samaritan Law
N.Y. Educ. Law §6527(2)

Notwithstanding any inconsistent provision of any general, special or local law, any licensed physician who voluntarily and without the expectation of monetary compensation renders first aid or emergency treatment at the scene of an accident or other emergency, outside a hospital, doctor's office or any other place having proper and necessary medical equipment, to a person who is unconscious, ill or injured, shall not be liable for damages for injuries alleged to have been sustained by such person or for damages for the death of such person alleged to have occurred by reason of an act or omission in the rendering of such first aid or emergency treatment unless it is established that such injuries were or such death was caused by gross negligence on the part of such physician. Nothing in this subdivision shall be deemed or construed to relieve a licensed physician from liability for damages for injuries or death caused by an act or omission on the part of a physician while rendering professional services in the normal and ordinary course of his practice.

Illinois Good Samaritan Law
Ill. Ann. Stat. Ch. 91, §2a

Any person licensed pursuant to this Act or any person licensed to practice the treatment of human ailments in any other state or territory of the United States, except a person licensed to practice midwifery, who in good faith provides emergency care without fee at the scene of a motor vehicle accident or in case of nuclear attack shall not, as a result of his acts or omissions, except wilful or wanton misconduct on the part of such person, in providing such care, be liable for civil damages.

Arizona Good Samaritan Law
Ariz. Rev. Stat. §32-1471

A physician or surgeon or a registered nurse, graduate nurse, or a professional nurse as defined in §32-1601, licensed to practice as such in this state or elsewhere, or a licensed ambulance attendant, driver or pilot as defined in §41-1831, or any other person who renders emergency care at a public gathering or at the scene of an emergency occurrence gratuitously and in good faith shall not be liable for any civil or other damages as the result of any act or omission by such person rendering the emergency care, or as the result of any act or failure to act to provide or arrange for further medical treatment or care for the injured persons, unless such person, while rendering such emergency care, is guilty of gross negligence.

Vermont Duty to Aid the Endangered Act
Vt. Stat. Ann. tit. 12, §519

(a) A person who knows that another is exposed to grave physical harm shall, to the extent that the same can be rendered without danger or peril to himself or without interference with important duties owed to others, give reasonable assistance to the exposed person unless that assistance or care is being provided by others.

(b) A person who provides reasonable assistance in compliance with subsection (a) of this section shall not be liable in civil damages unless his acts constitute gross negligence or unless he will receive or expects to receive remuneration. Nothing contained in this subsection shall alter existing law with respect to tort liability of a practitioner of the healing arts for acts committed in the ordinary course of his practice.

(c) A person who willfully violates subsection (a) of this section shall be fined not more than $100.00.

Florida Good Samaritan Act
Fla. Stat. §768.13

(1) This act shall be known and cited as the "Good Samaritan Act."

(2)(a) Any person, including those licensed to practice medicine, who gratuitously and in good faith renders emergency care or treatment at the scene of an emergency outside of a hospital, doctor's office, or other place having proper medical equipment, without objection of the injured victim or victims thereof, shall not be held liable for any civil damages as a result of such care or treatment or as a result of any act or failure to act in providing or arranging further medical treatment where the person acts as an ordinary reasonably prudent man would have acted under the same or similar circumstances.

(b)1. Any hospital licensed under chapter 395, any employee of such hospital working in a clinical area within the facility and providing patient care, and any person licensed to practice medicine who in good faith renders medical care or treatment necessitated by a sudden, unexpected situation or occurrence resulting in a serious medical condition demanding immediate medical attention, for which the patient enters the hospital through its emergency room or trauma center, shall not be held liable for any civil damages as a result of such medical care or treatment unless such damages result from providing, or failing to provide, medical care or treatment under circumstances demonstrating a reckless disregard for the consequences so as to affect the life or health of another.

2. The immunity provided by this paragraph does not apply to damages as a result of any act or omission of providing medical care or treatment:

   a. Which occurs after the patient is stabilized and is capable of receiving medical treatment as a nonemergency patient, unless surgery is required as a result of the emergency within a reasonable time after the patient is stabilized, in which case the immunity provided by this paragraph applies to any act or omission of providing medical care or treatment which occurs prior to the stabilization of the patient following the surgery; or

   b. Unrelated to the original medical emergency.

3. For purposes of this paragraph, "reckless disregard" as it applies to a given health care provider rendering emergency medical services shall be such conduct which a health care provider knew or should have known, at the time such services were rendered, would be likely to result in injury so as to affect the life or health of another, taking into account the following to the extent they may be present;

   a. The extent or serious nature of the circumstances prevailing.

   b. The lack of time or ability to obtain appropriate consultation.

   c. The lack of a prior patient-physician relationship.

   d. The inability to obtain an appropriate medical history of the patient.

   e. The time constraints imposed by coexisting emergencies.

4. Every emergency care facility granted immunity under this paragraph shall accept and treat all emergency care patients within the operational capacity of such facility without regard to ability to pay, including patients transferred from another emergency care facility or other health care provider pursuant to Pub. L. No. 99-272, s. 9121. The failure of an emergency care facility to comply with this subparagraph constitutes grounds for the department to initiate disciplinary action against the facility pursuant to chapter 395.

VI. Defenses

(c) Any person who is licensed to practice medicine and who is performing screening services while acting as a staff member or with professional clinical privileges at a nonprofit medical facility, other than a hospital licensed under chapter 395, shall not be held liable for any civil damages as a result of care or treatment provided gratuitously in such capacity as a result of any act or failure to act in such capacity in providing or arranging further medical treatment, if such person acts as a reasonably prudent person licensed to practice medicine would have acted under the same or similar circumstances.

(3) Any person, including those licensed to practice veterinary medicine, who gratuitously and in good faith renders emergency care or treatment to an injured animal at the scene of an emergency on or adjacent to a roadway shall not be held liable for any civil damages as a result of such care or treatment or as a result of any act or failure to act in providing or arranging further medical treatment where the person acts as an ordinary reasonably prudent man would have acted under the same or similar circumstances.

NOTES

Public Policy Concerning Immunity Defenses

1. So-called Good Samaritan Laws of the voluntary, good-faith variety have been enacted in all 50 states. They generally cover physicians licensed in the state or elsewhere, and often cover nurses as well. Prior to the enactment of the laws, opinion surveys among physicians indicated that a large percentage of doctors would not stop at the scene of an accident because of fear of a malpractice suit should they not be able to prove they rendered "reasonable, ordinary care" at the scene. See Pulse of Medicine, Med. Tribune, Aug. 28, 1961, at p. 23. See also Gray & Sharpe, Doctors, Samaritans and the Accident Victim, 11 Osgood Hall L.J. 1 (1973). The attitude of physicians had been built up over a period of time as a result of popular-press articles and medical journal commentary warning doctors of their vulnerability in such situations. In fact, there had been no recorded malpractice suits against physicians who rendered emergency care on a voluntary basis at accident scenes, in theaters, or other situations. The Governors of New York in 1962 and Illinois in 1963 vetoed Good Samaritan Laws as unnecessary because they were unable to find any actions in the United States against physicians for rendering voluntary emergency care. The Secretary's Commission on Medical Malpractice in its Report in 1973 reached a similar conclusion. See the Report and recommendations later in this chapter at 386. See also Curran, The Not-So-Good Samaritan Laws, 270 New

Eng. J. Med. 1003 (1964); Hessell, Good Samaritan Laws: Bad Legislation, 2 J. Leg. Med. 40 (1974). See also Comment, Good Samaritan Statutes: Time for Uniformity, 27 Wayne L. Rev. 217 (1980).

2. The provisions collected above from New York, Illinois, Arizona, and Florida are illustrative of the voluntary, gratuitous care variety enacted all across the country. See statutes collected in D. Louisell & H. Williams, Medical Malpractice §21.01 et seq. (1989). The exception to the voluntary care approach was the Vermont law set out above, enacted with the support of the state's medical community, which created an affirmative duty to render reasonable assistance. See Franklin, Vermont Requires Rescue, 25 Stan. L. Rev. 51 (1972). See also Levmore, Waiting for Rescue: An Essay on the Evolution and Incentive Structure of the Law of Affirmative Obligations, 72 Va. L. Rev. 879 (1986). The enactment of state laws in this field was encouraged by the Federal Government's Highway Emergency Medical Services Program, which provided financial incentives to states to enact such laws covering highway automobile accident scenes.

3. Later statutes have extended immunity protection to emergency medical technicians as well as physicians who render emergency care outside a hospital as part of an organized community emergency service, even if the service does attempt to make charges to the patient for the service. See Mich. Comp. Laws §691.1502 (West 1987); Hawaii Rev. Stat. §663-1.5 (c) (1985).

4. Case law as well as statutory reforms in a few states have also extended varying degrees of immunity to hospital-based situations where physicians have voluntarily rushed to a patient's bedside to aid in an emergency such as a cardiac arrest. In California, immunity was applied when a resident physician (in training) who was not a member of the hospital's emergency service or panels answered a call for assistance in emergency. McKenna v. Cedars of Lebanon Hosp. 155 Cal. Rptr. 631 (Cal. App. 1979). See also Markman v. Kotler, 382 N.Y.S.2d 522 (N.Y. App. Div. 1976). See Note, 39 A.L.R.3d 222 (1981).

5. The most dramatic of the legislative reforms granting immunity in emergency care situations in hospitals where payment for care is expected is the statute reprinted above from Florida. It was enacted by a Special Session of the Legislature called specifically to deal with the malpractice crisis. The law covers emergency care for patients admitted directly to emergency departments and relates to clinical services up to the point where the patient's condition is stabilized. The public policy expressed in the statute is obviously more detailed and sophisticated than the earlier versions of such laws. The standard of "reckless disregard" would seem intended to offer an extensive degree of immunity not found in other Good Samaritan laws.

VI. Defenses

6. There are several other immunity doctrines, mainly statutory, which have been enacted across the United States to encourage physician and hospital peer review programs to monitor and discipline health care providers to improve the quality of health care services. The peer review immunities usually apply to retaliatory actions by physicians who have been disciplined. They provide immunity from slander and libel actions and other law suits under conditions where the members of peer review committees, witnesses, and hospital administrators have acted in good faith to carry out the objectives of quality assurance and risk management programs. Such immunity provisions have been enacted by most states and in 1986 a Federal "Shield Law" was enacted to provide a more national protection for peer review programs in the states. See Health Care Quality Improvement Act of 1986, Pub. L. 99-660. The Act also contains authorization to establish a National Practitioner Data Bank to contain extensive information on physicians, and other health care providers, all over the country who have been disciplined or who have lost hospital staff privileges for conduct indicating unacceptable quality standards of care or for violations of ethical or moral standards in professional practice.

The most serious challenge to these peer review programs in recent years has come from the Federal Antitrust Laws when the physicians subject to disciplinary action have countered that the physicians and health care institutions have acted against them for anticompetitive reasons rather than in good-faith attempts to seek improved quality of care. The Supreme Court of the United States reversed a Circuit Court holding that a state "shield law" had provided a complete immunity from antitrust violations. See Patrick v. Burget, 486 U.S. 94, 108 S. Ct. 1658 (1988); also Taylor, The Antitrust Treatment of Peer Review. For further exploration of these issues, see Chapter 6.I.D.

7. Governmental immunity of public medical facilities and charitable immunity of not-for-profit hospitals and other programs have been declining steadily in the states over the past two decades. Only a few states now still provide full immunity in either area. Several states do, however, still provide statutory financial limits for law suits of medical or hospital malpractice against public hospitals or private charitable health care institutions. See D. Louisell & H. Williams, Medical Malpractice §§17.04, 17.57 (1988). The Federal Government removed sovereign immunity from federal health facilities and personnel in 1946 in the Federal Tort Claims Act. The statutory defense of "discretionary action" under the Tort Claims Act is not applied to the professional clinical decisions or actions of federally employed physicians and other health care personnel. See Jackson v. Kelly, 557 F.2d 735 (10th Cir. 1977).

VII. REFORM MOVEMENTS IN THE MALPRACTICE FIELD

A. Research Reports and Findings

Report, The Secretary's Commission on Medical Malpractice
HEW Dept. Pub. No. (OS) 73-88 (1973)

[The Commission made the following key recommendations after over two years of investigation including seven public hearings in different cities throughout the country. An appendix to the Report contains highly valuable research results on studies conducted under contract from the Commission. See Appendix, HEW Pub. No. (OS) 73-89.]

Defensive Medicine — The Commission finds that defensive medicine is the alteration of modes of medical practice, induced by the threat of liability, for the principal purposes of forestalling the possibility of lawsuits by patients as well as providing a good legal defense in the event such lawsuits are instituted.

The Commission recommends that over-utilization of health-care resources by any provider should be aggressively attacked by physician-directed regulatory efforts. Hospital utilization committees should be mandatory in every hospital, and their efficiency should be subject to statistical analysis and review by physician-directed supervisory groups.

In order to encourage physicians to render the highest possible quality care and to reduce the practice of unwarranted defensive medicine the Commission recommends that medical and osteopathic organizations exert maximum moral suasion over physicians who avoid professional responsibilities on the basis of fear of malpractice liability.

Good Samaritans — The Commission finds that there is no factual basis for the commonly-asserted belief that malpractice suits are likely to stem from rendering emergency care at the scene of accidents.

The Commission recommends that widespread publicity be given to this fact in order to allay the fears of physicians, nurses, and other health-care providers in this regard and to encourage the rendering of aid in non-hospital emergency situations.

Qualified Immunity — The Commission recommends that the states enact legislation to provide qualified immunity to hospitals and members of hospital rescue teams while they are attempting to resuscitate any person who is in immediate danger of loss of life, provided good faith is exercised.

The Commission recommends that the states enact legislation designed to provide qualified immunity to physicians and other health-care personnel who respond to emergencies arising from unexpected complications that arise in the course of medical treatment rendered by other physicians or other health-care personnel.

The Commission recommends that all physicians who regularly practice in hospitals be encouraged, through continuing medical education, to become proficient in cardiac arrest and cardiopulmonary resuscitation techniques.

Patient Injuries — The Commission finds that patient injuries, real or imagined, are prime factors in the malpractice problem.

Legal Doctrines — The Commission finds that some courts have applied certain legal doctrines for the purpose of creating or relieving the liability of health professionals. The Commission further finds that such special doctrines, or the application thereof, are no longer justified.

Informed Consent — The Commission finds that the doctrine of informed consent is subject to abuse when it imposes an unreasonable responsibility upon the physician.

Res Ipsa Loquitur — The Commission finds that the doctrine of res ipsa loquitur in its classical sense performs a useful purpose in common law, but that it should be applied differently in medical malpractice cases than in other types of tort litigation.

Application of Legal Doctrines — The Commission recommends that legal doctrines relating to the liability of health professionals should be applied in the same manner as they are applied to all classes of defendants, whether they be favorable or unfavorable to health professional defendants. Such doctrines would include (a) the application of the discovery rule under the statute of limitations; (b) the terms of the statute of limitations; (c) the application of the doctrine of res ipsa loquitur to injuries arising in the performance of professional services; (d) the rule allowing liability based on oral guarantee of good results, and (e) the doctrine of informed consent to treatment.

Contingent Fee — The Commission recommends that courts adopt appropriate rules and that all states enact legislation requiring a uniform graduated scale of contingent fee rates in all medical malpractice litigation. The contingent fee scale should be one in which the fee rate decreases as the recovery amount increases.

Legal Aid — The Commission recommends that public legal assistance mechanisms be established, or expanded where they already exist, to assure adequate legal representation to persons with small malpractice claims.

Medical-Legal Cooperation — The Commission recommends that the professions of law and medicine seek to improve their level of understanding and cooperation, specifically in the area of malpractice litigation to facilitate the handling of claims in the most equitable manner.

Expert Testimony — The Commission recommends that organized medicine and osteopathy establish an official policy encouraging members of their professions to cooperate fully in medical malpractice actions so that justice will be assured for all parties; and the Commission encourages the establishment of pools from which expert witnesses can be drawn.

Ad Damnum — The Commission recommends that the states enact legislation eliminating inclusion of dollar amounts in *ad damnum* clauses in malpractice suits.

Nationwide Standards — The Commission recommends that a feasibility study be made regarding the establishment of uniform national procedures for examining and licensing health professionals and the establishment of uniform standards of practice.

Injury Prevention — The Commission recommends the development of intensified medical injury prevention programs for every health-care institution in the nation, such programs to be predicated on the following:

1. investigation and analysis of the frequency and causes of the general categories and specific types of adverse incidents causing injuries to patients;
2. development of appropriate measures to minimize the risk of injuries and adverse incidents to patients through the cooperative efforts of all persons involved in the providing of patient care in such institutions.

Patients' Rights — The Commission recommends that hospitals and other health-care facilities adopt and distribute statements of patients' rights in a manner which most effectively communicates these rights to all incoming patients.

Informed Consent — The Commission finds that there is a generally recognized right of a patient to be told about the danger inherent in proposed medical treatment. That right is consistent with the nature of the doctor-patient relationship and with fundamental fairness. A much greater degree of communication between health-care providers and patients is really good, basic medical practice and should be encouraged.

The Commission finds that the law relating to the nature of information which the health-care provider must supply to obtain valid consent for treatment is presently in flux. Adoption of uniform standards requiring full disclosure of material risks would eliminate much confusion as to the basis and nature of informed consent. Under such standards, both patient and doctor would gain a clearer understanding of their respective rights and obligations.

The Commission recommends that a responsible member of the patient's family be given appropriate explanations where the physician is justifiably reluctant to explain such matters directly to the patient because of his concern that the explanation itself is likely to have an adverse effect on the patient.

VII. Reform Movements in the Malpractice Field

Grievance Mechanisms — The Commission recommends that all health-care institutions establish a patient grievance mechanism capable of dealing with patient care problems.

The Commission recommends that, to the extent possible, patient grievance mechanisms be established to deal with patient care problems in non-institutional settings.

The Commission recommends that the Secretary require, as a condition of receiving Medicaid and Medicare payments, that all health-care institutions establish a patient grievance mechanism capable of dealing with direct patient-care problems.

The Commission recommends the initiation of research programs to determine the best way to utilize patient grievance mechanisms to deal with problems involving patient care, including all health-care providers: hospitals, nursing homes, HMO's, clinics, and private practitioners, and also all levels of regulation — Federal, State, and professional.

Screening Panels — The Commission recognizes the value of local efforts to mediate medical malpractice disputes, and therefore recommends continuous experimentation with voluntary mediation devices. The Commission also recommends that persons other than attorneys and members of the profession involved in the disputes be included as members of any mediation board or panel.

Imposed Arbitration — The Commission recommends more widespread use of imposed arbitration as an alternative mode for resolving small medical malpractice disputes, providing the arbitration mechanisms have the following characteristics and do not preempt contractual arbitration agreements:

1. Arbitration statutes enacted by the States should be designed to give jurisdiction over all parties, plaintiffs and defendants, involved in a specific medical malpractice case.
2. State arbitration laws should set a maximum monetary limit for invoking the jurisdiction of the arbitration board, with cases demanding higher amounts being handled through the present jury system.
3. Arbitration panels should include some persons who are neither attorneys nor persons involved in the delivery of health-care services.
4. There should be the right of trial *de novo* subsequent to arbitration in the highest level jury court in the State.
5. The State arbitration statute should provide economic and legal sanctions, in order to discourage subsequent trials *de novo* of questionable merit, (e.g. evidentiary rules, presumptions, taxation of court costs).
6. A fairly detailed synopsis of each arbitration decision should be made and published in order to establish precedents,

provide information necessary to evaluate and improve the arbitration system, and provide adequate feedback information to the health-care system.
7. Although the Commission has recommended that the results of formal arbitration proceedings be published, publicity focused on the names of parties involved in disputes should be avoided or minimized.

Alternative Compensation Systems — The Commission recommends that the Federal Government fund one or more demonstration projects at the State or local level in order to test and evaluate the feasibility of possible alternative medical injury compensation systems.

The Commission finds that further study is warranted and essential for better definition of the event for which compensation should be paid and for developing a method of financing whatever new system is recommended.

Defense Research Institute, Medical Malpractice Position Paper
6 Def. Research Rep. 3 (1974)

[The following are the key provisions in a series of recommendations of the Institute, a defense bar organization, produced by a special committee headed by George I. Meisel, Esq., of Cleveland, later redrafted and amended in consultation with Institute staff, and endorsed as a Position Paper by the four leading defense attorney organizations: The Defense Research Institute, the International Association of Insurance Counsel, The Federation of Insurance Counsel, and the Association of Insurance Attorneys.]

Summary of Proposals

Retention of Adversary-Jury System. Retention of the adversary-jury system is favored as being based upon a principle fundamental to our society and its legal system — one who negligently causes injury to another should fairly and adequately compensate him for that injury. The basic principles of the liability reparations system are sound, the system can be improved without resorting to untested changes and improvements should be effected at the local level. A claimant's right to recover general damages should be preserved in all claims and no single segment of society, such as the medical and health care professions, should be immune from responsibility for negligent conduct.

Medical Malpractice Insurance. Efforts by the private insurance industry to make medical malpractice coverage available have produced favorable results and should be encouraged. More companies should unite their efforts in underwriting, rate-making, rate reduction and group medical organization plans. The private insurance industry is providing active competition among insurers for acceptable medical malpractice business; the resultant benefits include premium reduction and promotion of measures assuring higher standards of care.

Safety and Loss Control. The defense bar encourages further cooperative efforts among the insurance industry, medical personnel, institutions, medical societies and hospital societies to reduce risks and improve loss experience. The insurance industry can contribute greatly to the development of safety and loss control programs; and medical societies and hospital staffs should conduct educational programs aimed at improving procedures, thus reducing risks of medical malpractice.

Legal Doctrines. The various jurisdictions should be permitted to determine their own statutory and common law rules, as they find desirable, in light of their particular needs. The defense bar favors judicial restraint and reasonable application of statutory and common law rules.

Licensing, Controls and Discipline. Recent trends toward maintenance of high professional standards and reduction of malpractice risks — through controls and discipline at the hospital staff, medical and hospital society and state-licensing board levels — should be encouraged and strengthened.

Physician-Patient Relationship. The supply of physicians should be increased and each physician should have the necessary time to practice medicine properly and to develop rapport and an understanding, personalized relationship with his patients. Increased use of paramedical personnel is valuable if personnel are properly trained and supervised, if the proper relationship between physician and patient is maintained and if necessary state legislation is enacted permitting proper licensing and definition of responsibilities.

Public Image of Medicine. Efforts should be made to correct the frequently distorted public image of physicians and to educate the public to medical facts of life, such as:

a) despite recent spectacular advances, medical science is limited in its capacity to effect perfect results and cannot be expected to perform miracles;

b) a bad medical result is not an indication of actionable negligence; and

c) exaggerated malpractice claims and recoveries add to the cost of medical care.

Court Congestion and Delay. Where the problem of court congestion and delay exists, it should be attacked. While the incidence of malpractice cases is relatively small (and thus not a serious cause of congestion and delay) responsible measures should be adopted to relieve this problem in areas where it exists.

Arbitration. Arbitration proposals designed to have special and limited application to disputes between hospitals and physicians and between physicians and plaintiffs should be discouraged and rejected. Malpractice claims should be given no favored status. Arbitration should be encouraged and promoted for small claims of all types (including malpractice claims) and when applicable should be binding on the plaintiff as well as the defendants. Insurance carriers may find it effective to use arbitration, on a voluntary basis, to determine relative responsibilities among multiple defendants.

Screening Panels. The establishment of medical-legal screening panels should be left to local option. Where successful results have been reported with such panels, they have been confined to less populous areas. Reports from metropolitan areas, where such medical-legal panels have been established, indicate that they have not been used.

Contingent Fee Regulation. If contingent fees are to be allowed, they should be regulated by court control, according to the following program:

1) the amount of any contingent fee should be strictly regulated by local court rule or legislation;
2) every retainer on a contingent basis should be in writing in a fixed format and signed by the client;
3) a retainer statement should be filed with the appropriate judicial authority by a retained attorney within a fixed number of days from the date of the written contingent fee retainer;
4) there should be strict control of the division of fees between attorneys based only upon work performed;
5) upon completion of the claim or suit, an attorney should file an itemized closing statement with the proper judicial authority, with a copy to be delivered to the client.

Elimination of Ad Damnum. The dollar demand ad damnum should be eliminated. Any pleading demanding relief in the form of unliquidated damages should make only a prayer for general relief stating that the amount claimed is within the court's minimum and maximum jurisdictional limits.

U.S. General Accounting Office, Report on Medical Malpractice: Six State Case Studies Show Claims and Insurance Costs Still Rise Despite Reforms
GAO/HRD-87-21 (1986)

[The following is the Executive Summary of the six-state survey of medical malpractice conducted by the GAO in 1986. Separate publications were also issued concerning each of the six states.]

VII. Reform Movements in the Malpractice Field

Purpose

Did actions taken by states since the mid-1970's to address medical malpractice insurance problems reduce insurance costs, the number of claims filed, and the average amount paid per claim? Representative John Edward Porter and Senator John Heinz, Chairman, Senate Special Committee on Aging, asked GAO to do work in selected states to address this question. GAO did work in Arkansas, California, Florida, Indiana, New York, and North Carolina.

Background

During the mid-1970's, the unavailability and increasing cost of medical malpractice insurance prompted 49 states to enact various reforms. GAO obtained views of organizations representing physicians, hospitals, insurers, and lawyers in the six selected states on perceived malpractice insurance problems — such as the cost and availability of insurance, number of claims filed, and size of malpractice awards/settlements — actions taken to deal with them, the results of these actions, and the need for federal involvement. GAO also surveyed nonfederal hospitals in each state about the sources, coverage limits, and costs of their malpractice insurance. GAO requested leading insurers in each state to provide data for physicians and hospitals regarding the cost of malpractice insurance, the frequency of claims, the average amount paid per claim, and the cost to investigate and defend against malpractice claims. For comparison, we obtained country-wide claims data from the St. Paul Fire and Marine Insurance Company, the largest malpractice insurer in the United States.

Results In Brief

Reforms to deal with medical malpractice problems can focus on changing the tort system, changing the way public bodies and peer groups regulate health care providers, changing the way the insurance industry is regulated, and developing realistic consumer expectations about the health care delivery system. Most of the changes made by the six states to respond to the crisis of the mid-1970's focused on tort reforms designed to assure the availability and to reduce the cost of malpractice insurance.

Officials of the interest groups GAO surveyed in California and Indiana said that the changes to the tort laws of their states had helped to moderate upward trends in the cost of insurance, and the average amount paid per claim. Representatives from the groups surveyed in Arkansas, Florida, New York, and North Carolina generally believed the tort law changes in their states had little effect. GAO identified no studies undertaken in the six states to determine the impact of any specific reforms.

While it is possible that the reforms which focused on changing the tort laws moderated upward trends in some states, GAO data showed that since 1980, insurance costs for many physicians and hospitals increased dramatically, as did the number of malpractice claims filed and the average amounts paid.

Although Florida and New York enacted further tort law changes in 1985 and 1986, both also enacted measures that focused on improved identification and disciplining of physicians with malpractice histories and increased oversight of malpractice insurance rates. However, it is too early to assess the effects of these measures for resolving malpractice problems.

GAO's Analysis

Since the mid-1970's the six states have taken a variety of actions designed to assure the availability of malpractice insurance and to reduce the cost of insurance. Table 1 summarizes the status, as of August 1986, of the major tort reforms in each state.

Cost of Insurance

From 1980 to 1986, the cost of malpractice insurance increased in each of the six states — often much more than the consumer price

Table 1. Summary of Tort Reforms Enacted in Selected States

Tort Reforms	AR	CA	FL	IN	NY	NC
Ad damnum	1	1	1	2	1	1
Arbitration		1	1		1	
Attorney's fees		2[a]	2	2	1	
Awarding costs	1		1		1	1
Collateral source		2	2	1	1	
Expert witness			1			
Limits on liability		2[a]	1	2		
Patient compensation fund			4	2		4
Periodic payment	1	2	1	1	1	
Pretrial screening panel	3		1	2	1	
Res ipsa loquitur		1	1			
Statute of limitations	1	1	1	2	1	1
Special statute of limitations for minors	1	1		2	1	1
Standards of care	1		1			1

Legend:
1 = Provision exists
2 = Provision found constitutional by highest state court
3 = Provision repealed or allowed to expire
4 = Provision exists in statute, but not implemented

[a] The U.S. Supreme Court declined to review the decision of the highest state court.

VII. Reform Movements in the Malpractice Field   395

index and the medical care index, which increased 41 and 65 percent, respectively. The greatest increases were experienced by physicians in New York, Florida, and North Carolina. For example, malpractice insurance costs for an obstetrician increased 345 percent in New York, 395 percent in Florida, and 547 percent in North Carolina.

Although North Carolina experienced among the highest percentage increases, insurance rates for North Carolina physicians were still considerably lower than those for physicians in New York, California, and Florida. In January 1986, for example, premiums for obstetricians in North Carolina were $16,904 compared to $35,133, $42,928, and $59,537 for obstetricians in New York, California, and Florida, respectively.

Nationally, from 1983 to 1985, hospitals experienced a 76-percent increase in annual costs per bed for malpractice insurance. For the six states, rates of increase from 1983 to 1985 in annual costs per hospital bed ranged from 33 percent in New York to 141 percent in North Carolina.

Frequency of Claims

Country-wide, from 1980 to 1984, the frequency of claims reported against physicians and hospitals insured by the St. Paul Company increased 56 and 71 percent, respectively.

Claims reported against physicians increased in each of the six states. Indiana experienced the largest percentage increase — 92 percent. The frequency of claims reported against hospitals increased in five of the six states, but the frequency of claims against Arkansas hospitals was the same in 1980 and 1984. North Carolina experienced the largest percentage increase — 27 percent.

Average Paid Claims

Country-wide, from 1980 to 1984, the average paid claim against physicians and hospitals insured by the St. Paul Company increased 102 and 137 percent, respectively.

The average paid claim against physicians increased significantly in Arkansas, California, Florida, New York, and North Carolina. Except for New York, however, where the average paid claim increased 124 percent — from $46,789 in 1980 to $104,810 in 1984 — all increases were less than the country-wide average.

The average paid claim against hospitals increased in Arkansas, California, and North Carolina (data were not available for Florida hospitals). The largest percentage increase was experienced by North Carolina hospitals — 183 percent. Although the average paid claim against New York hospitals decreased slightly, it was still much higher than the other three states. For example, in 1984 the average paid claim was $88,917 in New York compared to $18,345 in Arkansas.

The average paid claim by primary insurers for physicians in Indiana decreased from $23,801 in 1980 to $19,510 in 1984 but increased for hospitals from $7,146 in 1981 to $11,244 in 1984. The number of paid claims by the Indiana Patient's Compensation Fund, which is responsible for paying claims between $100,000 and $500,000, rose from 11 to 36 and the amount paid increased from $3.9 million to $11.7 million between 1980 to 1985.

Perceived Effect of Reforms

Four of the six groups GAO surveyed in Indiana believed that the state's $500,000 statutory cap on malpractice awards had a major effect on decreasing the size of awards/settlements. Also, three of six groups surveyed believed Indiana's pretrial screening process had a major effect on decreasing the number of claims that go to trial. Several officials in Indiana and California believed that their state's comprehensive malpractice legislation has helped to moderate upward trends in the cost of malpractice insurance and size of awards. However, Indiana officials were concerned that the increasing number and size of payments from the state Patient's Compensation Fund may adversely affect the Fund's solvency.

Role of the Federal Government

Many officials and organizations GAO contacted indicated that medical malpractice insurance was a problem that should be dealt with at the state level. There was little support for federal involvement.

Recommendations

GAO is making no recommendations.

Report, Academic Task Force for Review of the Insurance and Tort Systems: Medical Malpractice Recommendations
(1987)*

[The following is the Summary of Recommendations and the Major Findings of the Academic Task Force set up by the Florida state legislature to examine insurance and tort law issues. The members of the Task Force were not drawn from among the various

---

* The extracts from the Report of the Task Force for Review of the Insurance and Tort Systems are reprinted with permission.

VII. Reform Movements in the Malpractice Field

interest groups in the field; they were the presidents of three of the major universities in the state (Florida State University, University of Florida, and University of Miami) and two prominent businessmen. The major findings are taken from an earlier report of the Task Force: Preliminary Fact-Finding Report on Medical Malpractice (1987)]

1. The Task Force recommends adoption of the Prompt Resolution of Meritorious Medical Negligence Claims Plan which includes the following provisions:

   a) Claims against physicians and denials of such claims must be preceded by reasonable investigation and accompanied by an expert's written opinion;
   b) Incentives should be provided for claimants and health care providers to submit claims to a binding arbitration proceeding to determine the amounts of economic damages, non-economic benefits not to exceed $250,000 and reasonable attorneys' fees.
   c) If the defendant refuses to submit the claim to arbitration, the plaintiff should retain all existing rights to a jury trial.
   d) If the plaintiff refuses to submit a claim to arbitration, plaintiff's non-economic damages at trial should be limited to $350,000.

2. The Task Force recommends adoption of legislation allowing physicians and hospitals to participate in a no-fault plan limited to birth-related neurological injuries.

3. The Task Force recommends that the Legislature not adopt a plan that would eliminate recovery for all non-economic damages and the right to jury trial while requiring the claimant to prove fault.

4. The Task Force recommends rejection of a plan that would limit recovery of non-economic damages to $100,000 in all tort cases, including claims for medical negligence, in an attempt to solve Florida's medical malpractice problems.

5. The Task Force recommends substantially strengthened regulation of health care providers by the state of Florida. This more robust professional regulation must include not only a commitment by the Legislature to provide more resources, but also an improved administrative structure that will enable the state agency to pursue vigorously its obligation to discipline physicians whose incompetence results in medical malpractice.

6. The Task Force recommends that a separate division, to be known as the Division of Medical Quality, be created within the Department of Professional Regulation to discipline and license health care providers. This division should be funded, entirely or in part, by increases in professional licensing fees for health care providers.

7. The Task Force recommends that legislation be enacted that requires the state health care regulatory division to assume greater responsibility for medical professional discipline and quality assurance at the local level. The division should establish local quality assurance boards to identify health care provider competency and disciplinary problems at their source and to coordinate with peer review and quality assurance programs conducted by local medical societies and hospitals.

8. The Task Force recommends adoption of the Premium Impact Equity Plan. This plan provides for equity payments for those physicians who can demonstrate affirmatively that high medical malpractice premiums are creating genuine financial difficulties. The plan would be financed solely by a small tax on all medical malpractice insurance premiums.

9. The Task Force recommends rejection of any risk class compression plan requiring a state operated (or other mandatory) insurance pool.

10. The Task Force recommends rejection of any proposal which uses existing tax revenues or any other general revenues to subsidize high medical malpractice insurance premiums. . . .

Major Findings

The major findings of the Academic Task Force regarding Florida's medical malpractice situation are as follows:

1. *Affordability.* The cost of medical malpractice liability insurance has increased dramatically during the last eight years, with the largest share of this increase coming during the past two years. The extent of the problem of affordability varies greatly among medical specialties and between south Florida physicians and those in the remainder of the state.
2. *Availability.* At the current time, the availability of liability insurance for physicians does not pose a serious problem in Florida.
3. *Cause of Price Increases.* The primary cause of increased malpractice premiums has been the substantial increase in loss payments to claimants.
4. *Profitability.* During the period 1977 through 1985, medical malpractice insurers have been slightly more profitable than the property-liability insurance industry as a whole. For the same time period, the profitability of the property-liability insurance industry was slightly less than that of American industrial and financial corporations. The profitability of insurance companies varies dramatically from year to year.

VII. Reform Movements in the Malpractice Field 399

5. *Market Structure.* The medical malpractice insurance market in Florida is highly concentrated, but so far this market concentration does not appear to have contributed to the problem of affordability of liability insurance.
6. *Impact of Underwriting Cycle.* The rate of price increases during the period 1983 through 1987 was disproportionately dramatic because of the insurance underwriting cycle. Over the course of an entire underwriting cycle, however, it is the increase in paid claims which causes higher premiums.
7. *Risk Classes.* The practice of dividing Florida physicians into risk classes by specialty, and into two different geographic areas, for rating and pricing purposes contributes to current affordability problems for high risk specialty practitioners, particularly those in South Florida.
8. *Frequency of Claims Payments.* The frequency of claims payments in Florida has increased 4.6 percent per year since 1975, but only 1.8 percent when adjusted for the increase in population.
9. *Amounts of Claims Payments.* The average cost of paid claims has increased at a compound rate of 14.8 percent per year since 1975. The increase in the size of loss payments is a substantially more important factor in the overall increase in paid claims than is the increasing frequency of paid claims.
10. *Geographic Variations in Claims Payments.* The frequency of paid claims per capita is twice as great in Dade and Broward Counties as in the rest of the state. The severity of claims also is greater in South Florida than in the remainder of the state, but the difference is not nearly so dramatic.
11. *Variations Among Medical Specialties.* There are considerable variations both in frequency and in severity of paid claims among medical specialties. Obstetrics and gynecology account for 13.6 percent of all paid claims, while specialties such as endocrinology, psychiatry and thoracic surgery each account for less than 2 percent of all paid claims. The largest average claims payments (1986) are in pediatrics, neurosurgery and thoracic surgery, with the average claim payment for pediatrics exceeding $350,000.
12. *Multiple Claims.* Nearly one-half of the amount of paid claims during the period 1975-1986 was accounted for by physicians with two or more paid claims. Physicians with two or more paid claims during this eleven year period are not necessarily "bad doctors."
13. *Changes in the Law.* During the past thirty years, there has been a national trend toward expanded legal liability for medical malpractice. The research conducted for this report

does not reveal any major pro-plaintiff development in medical liability rules of law in Florida during the past two decades, but overall changes in the environment of the legal system appear to benefit plaintiffs.

14. *Attorneys' Fees and Other Litigation Costs.* Attorneys' fees and other litigation costs represent approximately 40 percent of the total incurred costs of insurance carriers, with claimants receiving 43.1 percent of the total incurred costs. The total amount of attorneys' fees is divided approximately equally between plaintiffs' attorneys and defense attorneys. During the past eleven years, the average legal cost of defending a malpractice claim has increased at an annual compound rate of 17 percent.

15. *Possible Explanations for Increased Claims Frequency.* Increased claims frequency probably results both from a greater number of injuries occurring as a result of medical maloccurrences and from a much greater likelihood that injured plaintiffs will file claims. Any increase in the aggregate number of medical injuries in Florida likely results from the greater number of contacts between physicians and patients as the number of Florida residents and physicians both increase, and does not imply any increase in the frequency of medical maloccurrences per physician.

16. *Professional Regulation of Medical Care.* The Department of Professional Regulation disciplines a relatively low percentage of physicians with multiple paid claims.

NOTES

Official Task Forces and Investigational Bodies:
The Crises in Medical Malpractice

1. The Reports reprinted above and the recommendations of these groups provide a representative spectrum of findings and recommendations for reform as a result of the crises over medical malpractice litigation, insurance premiums, and insurance availability in recent years. There have been roughly two publicly recognized crises, one in the mid-1970s and the other in the mid-1980s. The crisis of the mid-1970s is easier to mark in time — at 1975 — and in its primary impact: a precipitous rise in insurance premiums and a decrease in the availability of insurance carriers willing to sell malpractice insurance. The efforts of state legislatures in the mid-1970s were to deal first with the most serious problem (insurance availability) and to enact more specific reforms after that. The specific reforms tended to follow from the recommendations of the Secretary's

Commission summarized above, since that was the only available national study on the subject at that time. Many states conducted their own investigations and made their own reports. Nearly all of the reports recommended statutory reforms in the tort system related to medical malpractice litigation and the installation of screening devices to eliminate clearly unmeritorious claims, but only one state, New York, recommended the more radical solution of a general no-fault compensation system. See Report, N.Y. Governor's Advisory Panel on Medical Malpractice (1976). On the responses throughout the 50 states in the mid-1970s, see Curran, The Malpractice Insurance Crisis: Short-Term and Long-Term Solutions, 293 New Eng. J. Med. 24 (1975); Comment, An Analysis of the State Legislative Responses to the Medical Malpractice Crisis, Duke L.J. 241 (1977); Redish, Legislative Response to the Medical Malpractice Insurance Crisis: Constitutional Implications, 55 Tex. L. Rev. 759 (1977). The first state to enact major reforms in the tort system was Indiana, where the legislation was proposed by Governor Bowen who was a physician. The Indiana legislation had considerable influence on legislative draftsmen in other states during the 1970s. See Note, The Indiana Malpractice Act: Legislative Surgery on Patients' Rights, 10 Valparaiso U.L. Rev. 303 (1976). For a later view of issues in the Indiana legislation, see Hurlbut, Constitutionality of the Indiana Medical Malpractice Act, Revisited, 19 Valparaiso L. Rev. 493 (1985). For a detailed analysis of the impact of the reforms enacted in the 1970s, see Sloan, State Responses to the Insurance "Crisis" of the 1970s: An Empirical Assessment, 9 J. Health Pol. Poly & L. 629 (1985). See also Priest, The Current Insurance Crisis and Modern Tort Law, 96 Yale L.J. 1521 (1987).

2. The report of the Defense Research Institute was the major response of medical malpractice defense lawyers and insurance legal counsel during the crisis of the mid-1970s. The defense lawyers were quite conservative in viewpoint. They did not wish to scrap the adversary system or trial by jury. Also, defense groups did not recommend radical changes in common law doctrines. Even more enlightening, perhaps, was their rejection of more rapid disposition of claims through arbitration and their lukewarm support of screening panels. Can you explain the rationale behind the different policy positions taken by the defense attorneys? Do these views differ greatly from those of plaintiffs' attorney organizations?

3. The report of the six-state survey of medical malpractice by the GAO was one of four studies done by that agency in 1986. The others were Medical Malpractice: No Agreement on the Problems and Solutions (GAO/HRD-50, 1986); Medical Malpractice: Insurance Costs Increased but Varied Among Physicians and Hospitals (GAO/HRD-86-112, 1986). See also another related report, Medicare: Re-

views of Quality of Care at Participating Hospitals (GAO/HRD 1986). These reports provided important data and also opinion surveys among interested parties in the field. A later report was also important in providing specific data on insurance carrier experience with malpractice claims in the mid-1980s. See Medical Malpractice: Characteristics of Claims Closed in 1984 (GAO/HRD 1987). For other governmental reports on malpractice, see Report of the Task Force on Medical Liability and Malpractice, Dept. H.H.S., Wash., D.C. (1986); Report of the Tort Policy Working Group on the Causes, Extent and Policy Implications of the Current Crisis in Insurance Availability, U.S. Office of the Attorney General, Wash., D.C. (1986).

4. The recommendations of the Academic Task Force in Florida are brief, but quite significant since they came after numerous legislative attempts in Florida, most recently in 1985 and 1986, to deal comprehensively with the malpractice crisis in that state. During the middle and later 1980s, Florida had the highest premiums for malpractice insurance in the country, especially in South Florida. See Medical Malpractice: Case Study in Florida (GAO/HRD 1986). The recommendations were concentrated on three issues: (1) restoring some "cap" on non-economic damages, since the Florida Supreme Court had declared an earlier "cap" to be unconstitutional; (2) special relief for obstetricians through a no-fault compensation plan; and (3) greater regulatory supervision of physicians somewhat based on "the bad-apple theory" that a relatively small number of below-standard physicians were responsible for a disproportionate number of the malpractice claims in the state. There was, however, disagreement on the "bad apple" theory, as is evidenced by the findings noted above. The concentration of claims among physicians could be due to other causes, not related to negligence. The Task Force also recommended improvement in the processing of claims through a "prompt resolution" system described in Recommendation 1. Much of the background data to support the Task Force's recommendations were contained in the major findings reprinted above. The research group that worked with the Task Force was based at the University of Florida. Much of the research work of the Task Force is summarized in a quite comprehensive article: Nye, Gifford, Webb & Dewar, The Causes of the Medical Malpractice Crisis: An Analysis of Claims Data and Insurance Company Finances, 76 Geo. L.J. 1495 (1988).

The Governor of Florida called a special session of the legislature in early 1988 and the legislature adopted the recommendations of the Academic Task Force as well as other features sought by other interested groups. The preamble to the new reforms specifically refers to the work of the Task Force. Special "E" Session, Medical Incidents — Quality Assurance and Tort Reform, Fla. Sess. Laws, ch. 1 (west 1988).

B. Proposals for Reform

American Medical Association, A Proposed Alternative to the Civil Justice System for Resolving Medical Liability Disputes: A Fault-Based, Administrative System*
(1988)

[The following is the Executive Summary of the Report of the American Medical Association/Specialty Society Medical Liability Project.]

The American Medical Association (AMA), 31 national medical specialty societies and the Council of Medical Specialty Societies have joined together to create the Medical Liability Project to propose a fair and efficient system of resolving medical liability disputes. Specifically, we propose a system in which such disputes would be adjudicated by an expert administrative agency. This agency can be either a modification of the current state licensing board or a new agency. This Medical Board would also have the power to take appropriate action to identify and rehabilitate or discipline physicians whose practice patterns pose a threat to patients. Because of the radical nature of our proposal, we recommend that it be tried as an experiment in one or more states.

We have endeavored to create a system that is fair and equitable to patients and physicians alike. Medical liability is only a part of the much larger and more important issues concerning the quality of medical care being provided by physicians. Accordingly, in addition to changes in the legal standards for determining medical liability, the proposal includes specific provisions designed to enhance the state medical board's credentialing and disciplinary functions. The administrative scheme proposed in this Report recognizes that physicians, patients and the public have distinct interests which must be respected and evenly balanced in any reasonable attempt to solve the medical liability crisis.

Part I: The Administrative Alternative to the Current Medical Liability System and Improved Credentialing and Disciplinary Processes

A. Rationale for the Alternative

Our proposal arises out of two basic facts. First, the current judicial system for determining professional liability does not com-

---

* This excerpt from the report of the American Medical Association proposal is reprinted herein with permission of the American Medical Association.

pensate a significant number of patients who have been injured by medical negligence. Individuals who have claims which do not involve a substantial potential recovery have difficulty enlisting the services of private attorneys. Thus, the existing system imposes barriers to the courts which preclude plaintiffs from receiving any compensation for injuries caused by medical negligence.

Second, the current tort system, which relies heavily upon juries, is not optimally suited for resolving medical negligence issues. Under the current system, there have been consistent increases in the size of damage awards, especially for non-economic damages. By their magnitude, these awards are threatening the availability and affordability of insurance coverage and health care in many geographic areas in the United States and in many medical specialties. Moreover, juries have tended to award plaintiffs significantly greater amounts in malpractice cases than in cases which concern identical injuries not involving physicians. In addition, the use of juries can be a time-consuming and inefficient way to resolve medical liability disputes. Currently, less than half of the total dollars spent on malpractice insurance ever reach the injured patient.

Because the existing judicial system is not entirely fair either to patients or physicians and is not an effective or efficient method of medical liability dispute resolution, it is reasonable to consider whether an alternative could be developed which would be fairer and more efficient. However, the system of trial by jury has strong historical roots in this country and there are significant constitutional and political limitations on the range of alternatives to the civil justice system that can be implemented even on a limited basis. In particular, there must be a meaningful quid pro quo provided to patients in order to justify withdrawing their claims from the jury system — as there is in no-fault automobile and workers compensation systems.

The Medical Liability Project does not suggest a general rejection of the tort system, nor does it advocate the abandonment of traditional tort reform. However, the Project has concluded that a persuasive case can be made for employing on an experimental basis an administrative alternative to the tort system for resolving medical liability disputes. The Medical Liability Project therefore proposes that in one or more states broad authority to handle medical liability disputes be granted to an existing medical disciplinary board or to a new agency so that an administrative system of medical liability compensation can be established. This Medical Board would provide several advantages to patients. The most important of these is that the system should permit more injured parties to be compensated than does the current system. At the same time, windfall damage awards would be eliminated, medical liability disputes would be resolved more quickly and efficiently, and certainty and predictability of compensation for medical liability would be increased.

B. The Claims Resolution Function

The administrative system for adjudicating medical liability can be divided into three parts: (1) the pre-hearing and initial hearing stage; (2) the final decision of the Board; and (3) judicial review. The proposed system would provide a significant benefit to patients by making available to any patient who has a claim of reasonable merit an experienced attorney from the Medical Board's general counsel's office who will litigate the claim on behalf of the patient free of charge.

Under proposed pre-hearing procedures, claims reviewers from the Medical Board will quickly evaluate claims and dismiss those without merit. For claims with merit, the claims reviewers will submit the matter to an expert in the same field as the health care provider. The expert will review the claim and make a judgment as to whether it has merit. The claims reviewer also will assist the patient in evaluating the claim and any settlement offers.

If the claim is not settled, it will be assigned to one of the Medical Board's hearing examiners. In order to encourage reasonable and timely settlements, blind settlement offers by the parties will be required prior to a hearing. A party would be subject to sanctions if the outcome of the case is not an improvement over a settlement offer that the party has rejected. The hearing examiner also will oversee expedited discovery and ensure that the parties have valid expert evidence available to support their case. At the hearing itself, the examiner will have broad authority to conduct the proceedings, including authority to call an independent expert to provide assistance in deciding the case. The hearing examiner will be required to render a written decision within 90 days of the hearing. In that decision, the hearing examiner will determine whether the health care provider is liable for the claimant's injury and, if so, will determine the size of the damage award.

The hearing examiner's decision will be subject to review by the Medical Board. The Board will have discretion to award fees and costs incurred in an appeal if the appeal presented no substantial question. The Medical Board will hear these cases as an appellate body in panels of three members. The Medical Board will make a full independent determination whether the health care provider's conduct was inadequate and caused the claimant's injury. Appeal from the Medical Board's decision will be to the intermediate appellate court of the state, where the review will be limited to whether the Board acted contrary to statute or the Board's own rules.

This proposed scheme will provide experienced and expert personnel at every level in the decision-making process. Over time, they should be better able than a jury to evaluate medical negligence claims. In addition, the involvement of the Board will increase the ability of the decision-making process to be consistent in both liability determinations and the size of damage awards. The proposed administrative system also should be able to resolve disputes more quickly than the current system and thereby save both plaintiffs and defendants the substantial expense incurred in litigating cases for years in court.

In addition to acting as an adjudicator of medical liability claims, the Medical Board also will develop rules and substantive guidelines to complement the statutory standards. The Board will have administrative authority to initiate rulemaking and to solicit public comments. A rule promulgated by the Board will have the force of law and will be subject to judicial review by an appellate court to determine if it is arbitrary, capricious or in excess of the Medical Board's authority.

C. The Performance Monitoring Function

1. In conjunction with its expanded authority to handle medical liability claims, the Board's performance monitoring function will be strengthened. Specifically, all settlements and awards based on medical liability will be reported to the Board's investigative branch. This does not mean that every or even many liability determinations will lead to disciplinary actions. What it means is that every liability determination will give rise to an initial screening of the physician's practices as reported to the Medical Board. The primary purpose of this endeavor, as with all performance monitoring, will be education and rehabilitation. Thus, our proposal is intended to enhance the Board's ability to discover physicians who are impaired, lacking appropriate medical skills or otherwise unable to provide acceptable medical care.

2. In conjunction with the proposals for monitoring physician performance by the Medical Board, our proposal calls for enactment of three categories of changes designed to further strengthen physician credentialing. First, reporting requirements will be increased by requiring hospitals and other health care institutions to conduct periodic physician performance reviews (a modified version of those required by the Joint Commission on the Accreditation of Healthcare Organizations) and to report to the Medical Board any conclusion that a physician's performance has been substandard. Insurers will be required to report cancellations and failures to renew for reasons that are not class based. All physicians will be required to report instances of suspected incompetence, impairment, or drug or alcohol dependence to the hospital credentials committee or other credentialing entity. In order to facilitate physician reporting, the state will provide immunity to physicians who report suspected problems in good faith. All of these reporting requirements are designed to increase substantially the amount of information available on physician performance.

Second, this information must be maintained in a form that is accessible to those who conduct professional review activities under the proposed system. To facilitate this process, the Medical Board will create and maintain a clearinghouse (or utilize the one established pursuant to the Health Care Quality Improvement Act of 1986) for reports from insurers, reports from hospitals and other entities and disciplinary actions taken by other states. Much of the information that will be collected under this proposal overlaps with the required reporting under current federal law. The licensing board will review this information, on a routine basis, every two years. Immediate review is required in the event of certain negative reports. The Board will also have authority to conduct an on-site review of the medical practices of all physicians against whom a medical liability determination (or settlement) has been made where there is reason to believe that the physician's practices pose a threat to patient health. In addition, certain credentialing entities, such as hospitals, will be required to check with the clearinghouse in connection with credentialing and privilege reviews.

Finally, the Project calls for the furtherance of quality assurance/risk prevention goals by requiring all physicians to complete a number of continuing medical education "credit hours" per year. A certain percentage of these hours must be directly relevant to clinical practice. In addition, all physicians will be required to participate in a risk management program. This change is designed to ensure that physicians maintain and enhance their professional skills.

In addition to the settlements and awards that are automatically reported, performance complaints — from hospitals, physicians, the public or employees of the Medical Board — will be sent to a claims reviewer at the Board for investigation. As with claims of medical liability, the claims reviewer will evaluate these complaints and, if appropriate, make a recommendation to the Board's general counsel's office to pursue complaints that appear meritorious. A member of the general counsel's office will then make a decision whether to initiate a disciplinary charge. Once a disciplinary charge is initiated, a member of the general counsel's office will prosecute the charge before a hearing examiner who, after an appropriate due process proceeding, will make a decision as to what, if any, action is appropriate. The examiner's action is subject to review by the Board, which is required to provide notice of any disciplinary action to credentialing entities, insurers and other state Medical Boards.

D. The Structure of the Board

In order to perform the complex and sensitive functions outlined above, the existing Medical Boards will be restructured or a new agency will be created. Membership on the Board will have to become full time, probably for a five year term. Members will be selected by the governor — from a list of nominees selected by a nominating committee — and approved by the legislature. The Project recommends a seven person Board, of which at least two but no more than three members are physicians. It is also crucial that the Medical Board members be widely recognized as experienced and neutral, and that they be committed to attempting a bold new approach to the problems of medical negligence. To ensure the Board's quality, all of its employees, from claims reviewers to hearing examiners, must be selected and retained on the basis of their ability and commitment to resolving claims efficiently and fairly.

Proper implementation of the administrative model also will require that substantial issues of funding be addressed. With respect to the increased funding requirements of the Board itself, because of the substantial benefits to the public and expected lower overall costs, use of general revenues will be necessary and appropriate. In addition, the state could make an initial assessment against insurance companies, which provide medical liability insurance within the state, or physicians and other health care providers.

Part II: The Legal Elements of Medical Liability

In order to ensure that the administrative model of medical liability passes constitutional muster, it will be necessary to codify the liability rules to be applied by the Medical Board under the administrative system. It will not be enough simply to incorporate by reference existing common law standards. The statute establishing the Medical Board will have to define specifically the standards under which a claim for medical liability is established, although as noted previously, the Board will be expected to exercise its rulemaking authority to fill in the interstices of the statute. The need for codification of the rules governing medical liability provides an opportunity to revise existing rules in a way that furthers the patient's interests in fair compensation, the physician's interest in predictable awards and the public's interest in standards of liability and damages that can be consistently and efficiently applied. Set forth below is a summary of the most important proposed rules of medical liability.

The rules governing standard of care based on custom and locality would be abolished in favor of a standard that focuses on whether the challenged actions fall within a range of reasonableness, to be determined by reference to the standards of a prudent and competent practitioner in the same or similar circumstances. The hearing examiner would be required to consider a variety of factors in determining the range of reasonableness, including the expertise of and means available to the health care provider, the state of medical knowledge, the availability of facilities and access to transportation and communications facilities. With respect to proof of liability, the statute also would set standards for evidentiary matters such as the qualifications of experts, the use of manufacturer's instructions on drugs and medical devices and the use of medical literature.

A significant modification in the causation standard is also proposed. Traditionally, recovery has been denied unless the physician was at least 50 percent responsible for the patient's loss. The causation standard would be modified to allow recovery if the physician's negligence was a "contributing factor" in causing the injury. Damages under this standard would be apportioned according to the physician's degree of fault.

The informed consent doctrine would be codified under the current "minority" rule which requires that the adequacy of the disclosure should be measured from the perspective of the reasonable patient. The privilege to withhold information (for therapeutic reasons) and standards for determining individual responsibility for disclosure also would be included in the statutory "informed consent" doctrine.

In the area of damages, non-economic damages (and punitive damages) would be capped at an amount that is tied to a percentage of the average annual wage in the state. Special damages would be awarded under a series of guidelines designed to ensure that those damages represent a realistic "replacement cost." For example, in determining the "lost income" of an unemployed minor, the hearing examiner would be required to award damages based on the average annual income in the state multiplied by the average work life expectancy, absent clear and convincing proof that the loss would be greater or smaller.

The rule of joint and several liability would be abolished so that defendants would be liable for damages only in proportion to their actual liability. In addition, any award of future damages, where the present value of such damages exceeds $250,000, would be made in accordance with a periodic payment schedule. Finally, damages generally would be reduced by collateral source payments.

Moore, It's Time for Reform*
71 A.B.A.J. 38 (1985)

[The following article summarizes briefly the main objectives of a bill to establish a "contract-style" no-fault compensation plan to

---

* This article, by Representative W. Hansen Moore, Republican, U.S. Congress, is reprinted with permission of the American Bar Association.

apply to certain federally supported health programs. The measure was introduced in the 99th Congress by Representative Hansen Moore, Republican of Louisiana; Representative Richard Gephardt, Democrat of Missouri; Representative Edward Madigan, Republican of Illinois, and Representative John Porter, Republican of Illinois.]

My career as a trial lawyer in Baton Rouge, La., and now as a public servant interested in health care matters convinces me that litigation of medical malpractice claims is not in the best interest of plaintiffs, defendants or, most important, the public. I believe a large number of lawyers share this view.

Some Collect Nothing

The adversarial system consumes large amounts of resources in fees for lawyers and expert witnesses and for operation of the courts. Outcomes are fortuitous. Success or failure often turns on the skills of the lawyer (which may not be a fortuity to members of the bar but is to the public), the attractiveness of the plaintiff, the perceived wealth of the defendant and a host of other such extraneous factors. A few "fortunate" victims win large recoveries that far exceed their economic losses, but only after they fight for years. Others who may equally deserve compensation collect nothing.

Litigation is traumatic for all participants. It forces physicians to deny fault they might be willing to accept under other circumstances, and it destroys the special trust that is at the core of the physician-patient relationship.

The tort system has caused physicians to become wary of their patients and to practice defensive medicine. Some have abandoned their practice, and others have abjured complex procedures. Premiums for malpractice coverage are increasing because the number of claims and the size of malpractice awards are rising. All Americans pay these increased costs.

There is broad agreement that the current system is failing to serve the persons whom it is supposed to serve, both plaintiffs and defendants. As lawyers, we must recognize that we are driving a system that benefits perhaps ourselves more than those we serve. The relevant question is not whether the system should be reformed, but what those reforms should be.

Fair Compensation

Our proposal is intended to modify the tort system as it affects medical malpractice, to make it less adversarial and to provide fair compensation to more victims in a more efficient and humane manner.

A health care provider would have the option after an adverse outcome to make a commitment to pay the victim's net economic loss. If the provider did so, the patient would receive prompt payment when he most needs it, and he would be spared the risk, trauma and delay of litigation. In exchange, the patient would be precluded from pursuing a malpractice claim in tort and thus would lose any claim for non-economic loss.

Our proposal will remove many cases from the current system of litigation and reduce transaction costs and amounts paid for pain and suffering. We believe the savings would be sufficient to compensate more injured patients for their economic loss and still produce net savings of malpractice costs. Simultaneously, our proposal provides a more rational and fairer remedy to all injured patients and not just those who are lucky enough to recover under the current system. For these reasons, we believe this proposal should be adopted.

Bolt, Compensating for Medical Mishaps — A Model "No-Fault" Scheme*
139 New L.J. 109 (1989)

[The following article presents a summary of the recent proposal by the British Medical Association for a no-fault compensation system to replace the current tort-law system in Great Britain.]

The medical profession has long been dissatisfied with the working of the tort system as it applies to cases of medical negligence. It is regarded as being unfair in that, effectively, it is available only to those patients who are either very wealthy or eligible for legal aid. It is intolerably slow, often awarding compensation between five and ten years after the date of the injury complained of. It customarily provides lump sums, disregarding both the provision of the NHS and the Social Services and the possibility that the needs of the victim will change with time. And, since it depends upon proof of negligence, it denies compensation to 75 per cent of litigants and to all those patients, comparably damaged, who cannot possibly allege that their injury results from failure to discharge the duty of care.

For these reasons, long before there was any important increase in Defence Society subscriptions, the Council of the British Medical Association set up a Working Party, in 1983, to look into the possibility of no fault compensation.

Evidently, the urgency of the issue has increased with the rapid rise in Defence Society subscriptions which has taken place over the last three years. One of the three Defence Societies which protect

* This article by David Bolt, C.B.E., F.R.C.S., chairman of the British Medical Association's Working Party on No Fault Compensation, is reprinted with permission of the New Law Journal.

all medical practitioners in the United Kingdom has, this year, abandoned the time honoured system of charging a uniform rate to all doctors, in favour of differential premiums for specific fields of practice. Since the heaviest drain on their resources arises from brain damaged infants, the current premium paid by obstetricians is in excess of £1,000 a year and, already, the Royal College of Obstetricians & Gynaecologists has evidence of premature retirement by senior obstetricians and of the decline in the numbers of young doctors entering the speciality. It seems probable that this trend will extend to the speciality of anaesthesia in the near future.

While it is not clear that a no fault system will necessarily reduce the financial burden of doctors, their considerations clearly increase the need for early exploration of the possibilities. But it should be emphasised that the primary concern of the medical profession is to identify an arrangement which is fairer to patients than the present one. In the profession's view, any process for compensating patients for medical injury should depend upon need, not upon the necessity of proving negligence.

Strictly, the "no fault" label is misleading. It is not intended to imply that a medical mishap may not be due to fault but the proposal is desired to relieve the patient of the necessity to prove culpability in order to obtain compensation. Many mishaps are due to circumstances which, while clearly involving error, do not involve negligence. It is inevitable that any professional person will react strongly to the suggestion that he has been negligent in relation to the care that he has provided to those for whom he is responsible, while freely admitting error in their management.

The profession is unhappy that a hint that litigation is being contemplated, inevitably immediately alters the proper relationship between doctor and patient from a caring one into an adversarial one. It is anxious that this should be eliminated in as many cases as possible.

In the BMA's view, eligibility for compensation, under a no fault scheme, should not be conditional upon the individual giving an undertaking not to proceed through the courts, if he chooses to do so. Nor should subsequent application be rejected merely because he has unsuccessfully sought damages.

Compensation would be confined to physical injury and would not be available for problems resulting from progress of the underlying disease. Compensation would not be available for injury resulting from diagnostic error, judged reasonable by a panel of experts, nor for the recognised complications of any procedure competently performed for valid indications.

Compensation would be available for the results of infection, except where the infection resulted from operation upon tissues already infected, upon tissues of reduced viability, from prolonged catheterisation or drainage, a year or more after the implantation of a prosthesis or in patients with a defective immune system.

Compensation would not be available from injury resulting from the use of drugs, provided the programme was within the recommendations laid down by manufacturers. In the view of the Association, intrinsic defects in drugs, licensed for use in the treatment of patients, is [sic] a matter for the manufacturers. Compensation would be available for injury resulting from extraneous accidents, such as equipment failure, mishaps in patient handling and the like.

To exclude trivia, a minimum period of disability would be necessary before claims could be made. Compensation would concentrate upon reimbursement of identifiable financial loss, taking account of other sources of reimbursement, such as National Insurance. Earnings would be made good up to a ceiling, probably twice the national average wage. Such costs as domestic help for housewives or care at home beyond that provided by the Social Services and special educational needs would be met. Where a mishap led to death, dependants would become the responsibility of the fund, after taking account of other pension rights, as long as need continued. The same principle would apply in the case of brain-damaged patients, including infants. Lump sum payments would be restricted to such events as permanent damage to an organ or function, which did not affect the capacity to earn a living and to recognition of pain and suffering. The sums available would not, of course, match those sometimes available through litigation.

Paying for "No Fault"

It is clearly difficult to estimate the likely cost of such a scheme. The King's Fund paper published last year, Medical Negligence: Compensation and Accountability suggested that to operate a system resembling the Swedish one, which is the nearest to the BMA proposals currently in operation, would cost £50 million for England alone, implying about £75 million a year for the whole of the United Kingdom. This may well be an underestimate but it is difficult to assess the figure very accurately, as it is unlikely that either the Health Authorities or the Defence Societies have records of all the mishaps which would justify compensation. At the present time, when compensation depends upon litigation, many eligible mishaps are probably completely unreported.

Government Approval

The medical profession is fully aware that much of the cost of its proposals would fall upon doctors. But it is hoped that the Health

Authorities would share the burden. At present, in accordance with Government practice, they do not insure against such risks, with the result that when confronted with successful litigation, they sometimes need to find sums in excess of a million pounds, in damages and costs, out of current strained budgets.

Clearly, the Health Authorities could not take part in such a scheme without Government authority. But for the present, ministers are categorical in their rejection of no fault compensation. We hope that they may be persuaded to relax their opposition and investigate the likely costs. It is in the public interest that the issue should be fully ventilated, even if it proved impossible to implement in the final event.

It is certainly not the wish of the profession to see the strained resources of the National Health Service diverted into financing a no fault scheme. It may be that no fault compensation is not a realisable objective in the present financial climate and that the best which can be achieved will be a reform of the tort system to reduce its delays and widen its availability to those with limited financial resources who fall outside the legal aid scheme. But this would be in the view of the medical profession, very much a second best given the large number of the victims of medical mishap who cannot possibly allege negligence in relation to the care that they have received.

Executive Summary, Report of the Harvard Medical Practice Study to the State of New York*
(1990)

Introduction

The Harvard Medical Practice Study, carried out under contract to the State of New York, was designed to inform the policy debate now going on in New York and elsewhere about how society can best deal with its medical injuries and malpractice. To do so, we had to understand and isolate the key issues and assumptions that divide the protagonists of the current tort system, a reformed tort system, and no-fault alternatives. We have not prejudged the feasibility of any such no-fault program for injured patients, nor have we endorsed the criticisms that are made about present day malpractice litigation. Rather, we believe we have provided relevant empirical data that will permit informed judgments and sound policy-making concerning this complex area.

The Study had four principal components:

* Reprinted by permission.

VII. Reform Movements in the Malpractice Field

1. A population based measure of the incidence of injuries resulting from medical interventions, which we called "adverse events," and a determination of the percentage of such events that resulted from fault or negligence of the physician or other provider.
2. A determination of the percentage of adverse events, both negligent and non-negligent, that led to claims and suits. In addition, we obtained information about the numbers of claims and suits by patients in whose hospital records we found no evidence of injury.
3. Measures of the costs of medical expenses, lost wages, and lost household production to the victims of medical injuries and to their families, and their compensation for such losses under current arrangements.
4. Estimates of the degree to which variations in the threat of litigation affected the incidence of adverse events.

The following summarizes some of our methods and major findings.

1. The Incidence of Adverse Events

The hospital medical record review was key to estimating the incidence of adverse events associated with medical management. The record review focused on two critical issues: causation and negligence. We asked, "Was the patient's condition attributable to medical management rather than to the disease under treatment (causation)? Was negligence involved?"

In addition to establishing causation and negligence, we determined where injuries occurred, the types of injury and then the magnitude of disability experienced.

The review was conducted by teams of trained medical record administrators and nurses for the screening phase, and board-certified physicians for the physician-review phase.

Methods were devised to resolve the logistic problems that arose because of the infrequency of adverse events: we found efficient and reliable ways to sift through thousands of medical records to find the few that indicated the patient disability caused by medical management. We also developed ways to deal with the methodologic problems that arose: the medical record administrators had to make valid judgments regarding the presence of screening criteria and physicians had to make valid and reliable judgments about whether a patient's injury resulted at least in part from medical management, and, if so, whether management failed to meet a standard of medical care.

In order to make our results generalizable to the entire population of hospital discharges in New York, we drew a probability sample of more than 31,000 hospital records. Our ability to obtain such a sample was made possible by the availability of the Statewide Planning and Research Cooperative System (SPARCS) data system. The basic sampling design of the Study was an implicitly stratified, systematic, two-stage cluster sample of discharges. We first selected hospitals with probabilities proportional to the number of non-psychiatric discharges and then secured the cooperation of all 51 hospitals selected. Records within hospitals were selected with three different sampling frequencies determined by patient age and diagnosis-related group (DRG). Using SPARCS information on patient discharges, we drew a sample with a distribution that conformed closely to the population on important hospital and patient characteristics.

We analyzed 30,121 (96 percent) of the 31,429 records selected for the study sample. After preliminary screening, physicians reviewed 7,743 records, from which a total of 1,133 adverse events were identified that occurred as a result of medical management in the hospital or required hospitalization for treatment. Of this group, 280 were judged to result from negligent care. Weighting these figures according to the sample plan, we estimated the incidence of adverse events for hospitalizations in New York in 1984 to be 3.7 percent, or a total of 98,609. Of these, 27.6 percent, 27,179 cases, or 1.0 percent of all hospital discharges, were due to negligence.

Physician confidence in the judgments of causation of adverse events spanned a broad range, but only 1.3 percent of all discharges were in the close-call range (defined as a confidence in causation of just under or just over 50-50). An even smaller fraction, 0.7 percent of discharges were close-call negligent adverse events, but they constituted a larger proportion of total negligent adverse events.

The majority of adverse events (57 percent) resulted in minimal and transient disability, but 14 percent of patients died at least in part as a result of their adverse event, and in another 9 percent the resultant disability lasted longer than 6 months. Based on these figures, we estimated that about 2,500 cases of permanent total disability resulted from medical injury in New York hospitals in 1984. Further, we found evidence that medical injury contributed at least in part to the deaths of more than 13,000 patients in that year. Many of the deaths occurred in patients who had greatly shortened life expectancies from their underlying diseases, however. Negligent adverse events resulted, overall, in greater disability than did non-negligent events and were associated with 51 percent of all deaths from medical injury.

Risk Factors

The risk of sustaining an adverse event increased with age. When rates were standardized for DRG level, persons over 65 years had

VII. Reform Movements in the Malpractice Field

twice the chance of sustaining an adverse event of those in the 16-44 years group. Newborns had half the adverse event rate of the 16-44 years group. The percent of adverse events resulting from negligence was increased in elderly patients. We found no gender differences in adverse event or negligence rates. Although the rates were higher in the self-pay group than in the insured categories, the differences were not significant. Blacks had higher rates of adverse events and adverse events resulting from negligence, but these differences overall were not significant. However, higher rates of adverse events and negligent events were found in hospitals that served a higher proportion of minority patients. At hospitals that cared for a mix of white and minority patients, blacks and whites had nearly identical rates.

Adverse event rates varied 10-fold between individual hospitals, when standardized for age and DRG level. Although standardized adverse event and negligence rates for small hospitals (fewer than 8,000 discharges/year) were less than for larger hospitals, these differences were not significant. Hospital ownership (private, non-profit, or government) also was not associated with significantly different rates of adverse events. The fraction of adverse events due to negligence in government hospitals was 50 percent higher than in non-profit institutions, however, and three times that in proprietary hospitals. These differences were significant. The standardized rate of adverse events in upstate, non-MSA hospitals was one-third that of upstate metropolitan hospitals and less than one-fourth that in New York City. These differences were highly significant. The percent of adverse events due to negligence was not significantly different across regions. Non-teaching hospitals had half the adverse event rates of university or affiliated teaching hospitals, but university teaching hospitals had rates of negligence that were less than half those of the non-teaching or affiliated hospitals.

The Nature of Adverse Events

Nearly half (47 percent) of all adverse events occurred in patients undergoing surgery, but the percent caused by negligence was lower than for non-surgical adverse events (17 percent vs. 37 percent). Adverse events resulting from errors in diagnosis and in non-invasive treatment were judged to be due to negligence in over three-fourths of patients. Falls were considered due to negligence in 45 percent of instances.

The high rate of adverse events in patients over 65 years occurred in three categories: non-technical postoperative complications, complications of non-invasive therapy, and falls. A larger proportion of adverse events in younger patients was due to surgical failures. The operating room was the site of management for the highest fraction of adverse events, but relatively few of these were negligent. On the other hand, most (70 percent) adverse events in the emergency room resulted from negligence.

The most common type of error resulting in an adverse event was that involved in performing a procedure, but diagnostic errors and prevention errors were more likely to be judged negligent, and to result in serious disability.

The more severe the degree of negligence the greater the likelihood of resultant serious disability (moderate impairment with recovery taking more than six months, permanent disability, or death).

2. *Litigation Data*

We estimated that the incidence of malpractice claims filed by patients for the study year was between 2,967 and 3,888. Using these figures, together with the projected statewide number of injuries from medical negligence during the same period, we estimated that eight times as many patients suffered an injury from negligence as filed a malpractice claim in New York State. About 16 times as many patients suffered an injury from negligence as received compensation from the tort liability system.

These aggregate estimates understate the true size of the gap between the frequency of malpractice claims and the incidence of adverse events caused by negligence. When we identified the malpractice claims actually filed by patients in our sample and reviewed the judgments of our physician reviewers, we found that many cases in litigation were brought by patients in whose records we found no evidence of negligence or even of adverse events. Because the legal system has not yet resolved many of these cases, we do not have the information that would permit an assessment of the success of the tort ligitation system in screening out claims with no negligence.

Confining our analysis to the adverse events that involved strong or certain evidence of negligence, however, we estimate that 12,859 injuries from medical negligence did not lead to malpractice claims. Of these injuries, 22 percent (2,833) occurred in patients under age 70 years who suffered moderate or greater incapacity. Our projections suggest that if this group of patients had litigated, the malpractice claims frequency for year 1984 would have increased by 75 percent.

3. *Economic Consequences of Medical Injury*

Having documented from the medical records survey which patients were injured, and from the litigation survey which patients filed tort suits, we used the patient survey to determine from the patients themselves what losses they suffered as a result of these injuries and what compensation they received from non-tort sources. For that

VII. Reform Movements in the Malpractice Field

purpose we divided our patient sample into five categories — worker, homemaker, child, retired, and disabled — and assembled data about lost wages and fringe benefits, medical costs, lost household production, and levels of physical and functional impairment. Our data for that final category have not been analyzed for this Report.

We faced two major difficulties in this survey. First, we had to locate, in 1989, people who had been hospitalized in 1984 in order to interview them about their experience since 1984. In fact, we were successful in finding and interviewing 71 percent of all injured patients, a response rate which is quite respectable for a survey of this type.

Our second problem was how to disentangle the effects of the adverse event itself from those that were properly attributable to the underlying illness, which itself would naturally be expected to entail considerable medical costs, time off work, and inability to perform normal household tasks. Two different strategies were devised for this purpose. One was to interview a control group of uninjured patients who were matched with our "experimental" group on the relevant dimensions, thus permitting econometric analysis of the precise difference which the iatrogenic injury made in the aggregate economic experience of the two groups. While we have collected all the data for the two groups, we have not completed this analysis for purpose of presentation in this Report.

Instead our primary focus has been on an alternative method — estimating the compensable losses that might be paid under a hypothetical no-fault plan in which each patient's experience was assessed individually (as would have to be done in a real no-fault program), and then totaled. For that purpose we had to make a number of assumptions about program design: two important ones are noted here. First, all financial losses and compensation received during the first six months from hospital admission were deleted. These short-term losses are likely reimbursed from other sources (e.g., sick pay for time off work). Further, this reduces the number of cases in which disentangling the effect of the injury from the underlying illness may be very difficult. Second, we assumed that a no-fault patient compensation scheme would involve a second insurer, standing behind primary sources of general medical or disability insurance.

Our key findings with respect to these two criteria were that the bulk of disabilities were of short duration — e.g., 42 percent of absences from work lasted for less than a month and 76 percent lasted less than six months. However, the average economic losses were much larger in the smaller number of more serious or fatal disabilities. With respect to these longer-lasting disabilities, more than 85 percent of the medical bills were covered by some form of health insurance, but only 20 percent of the lost earnings, and no detectable portion of lost household production.

Our ultimate finding is that the present discounted value of the net compensable losses (past and future) suffered by patients injured in New York hospitals in 1984 amounted to $894 million (in 1989 dollars). These compensable losses consisted of $285 million in lost wages and fringe benefits, $103 million in uninsured medical costs, and $506 million in lost household production (the latter having been valued at the market wages earned by the working women in our patient cohort).

To provide some perspective for these figures, the malpractice premiums paid by New York doctors and hospitals in 1988 amounted to $850 million. When one includes the amount spent by self-insured hospitals and the health care organizations, the total malpractice insurance burden is over $1 billion. However, these tort costs incorporate two major factors not reflected in our estimate. One is damage for pain and suffering, which typically are not compensated under no-fault programs. The other component is administrative and legal expenses which definitely would be a significant factor over and above the patient's economic losses. The administrative share of claims costs in no-fault workers compensation is usually estimated to be around 20 percent, though we believe it would be somewhat higher for no-fault patient compensation.

Since the sample of injured and interviewed patients in our different categories was rather small despite the relatively large sample of 31,000 hospitalizations, the confidence intervals surrounding our point estimates are large: the figures might be as much as 50 percent less or 100 percent more than those presented. On the other hand, the estimate of net wage losses and medical costs — these being the items typically covered by a no-fault scheme, and even then not in full fault — totalled just $335 million. Thus, there is considerable room within the current tort "envelope" to adjust even for an outcome at the highly improbable outer limit of these confidence estimates.

4. Malpractice Litigation and Deterrence

We examined the presumed deterrent effects of the tort system in two ways — a series of physician surveys as well as an econometric study that compared the rates of adverse events and negligent adverse events, on the one hand, with the threat of a claim on the other.

The physician surveys revealed that the overall perceived risk of being sued in a given year was 20 percent, approximately 3 times the actual risk of being sued. The perceived risk of suit for negligent care was about 60 percent, a figure substantially greater than the actual risk of litigation from injuries caused by negligence. Additionally, perceived risk was significantly greater for high-risk specialties such as obstetrics, orthopedics, and neurosurgery and for physicians in Nassau and Suffolk counties, lending credence to the responses.

VII. Reform Movements in the Malpractice Field

Physicians who perceived themselves to be at greater risk of suit said that in the past ten years they had ordered more tests and procedures and reduced their practice scope more than had their colleagues with perceived risk.

The tort system's deterrence signal to physicians appeared mixed. For example, physicians often considered the *severity* of punishment to depend on whether a case went to trial or whether the media publicized it. The evidence was not clear, however, on whether the severity of the punishment and the actual transgression were related: most physicians perceived their suits as having arisen from circumstances beyond their control. Many seemed to believe that the threat of the tort system was too broad and lacked specificity.

Although physicians believed they practiced medicine defensively, they did not report long-term changes in their practice patterns as the result of a specific suit. Thus, it was not clear whether defensive medicine resulted from the malpractice environment or from other factors such as advances in the science and technology of medicine, changes in societal expectations as to what constitutes an appropriate level of care, or changes in Peer Review Organization (PRO), state and hospital requirements, or a combination of factors.

Another important finding concerned physician attitudes about iatrogenic injury and negligence. Physicians tended to equate a finding of negligence with a judgment of incompetence. Thus, although willing to admit that all doctors make mistakes, physicians were often unwilling to label substandard care as negligent and were opposed to compensation for iatrogenic injury.

The final part of our study examined the relationship between variations in claims rates and variations in cost and in injury rates in the sample of study hospitals. We found some evidence that total cost per discharge was greater in hospitals that faced higher claims rates, although the relationship that we estimated was sensitive to how we specified the relationship. Even conceding that there is an effect on cost, however, does not tell us whether the effect is good or bad. On the one hand, greater efforts to prevent injuries or ameliorate the consequences of those that occur may well require greater resources. On the other hand, additional resources in response to a greater threat may simply represent wasteful defensive medicine and not contribute to a reduction in patient injuries.

The important test, therefore, is whether hospitals that face higher claims rates actually do exhibit lower injury rates. We find no evidence that they do, but the precision of our estimates is not good, and we cannot rule out the possibility that there are in fact substantially reduced rates of injuries at the hospitals in our sample with higher claims rates. More specifically, the point estimate relating injuries to claims is actually positive in most specifications and never close to significantly negative. However, the confidence intervals around the coefficient include values that would demonstrate substantial deterrence.

We illustrate how our data cannot rule out a substantial deterrent effect by choosing one of the relationships we estimated, that for the probability that an adverse event is negligent, controlling for a number of other hospital characteristics. The point estimate of the claims variable is slightly positive; however, if we reduce the point estimate by approximately one standard error, it shows substantial deterrence. In quantitative terms, the reduced estimate would suggest that, other things equal, hospitals in the highest quartile of claims rates would have about 24 percent fewer negligent events (conditional upon an adverse event) as those in the lowest quartile.

Moreover, there may be a bias in our results toward showing no deterrent effect. Our goal was to determine whether there is a negative relationship between claims rates and injuries, but hospitals and physicians that have higher injury rates may have more claims filed against them. This possible positive relationship between injuries and claims would tend to mask any true deterrent effect. We have tested for this bias and do not find any evidence of it, but our test could simply be failing to detect it.

Finally, even if we had been able to conclude that our data ruled out all but a negligible deterrent effect, we could not conclude that abolishing the tort system would have no effect on injury rates. All the hospitals in our sample faced some threat of a claim if an injury occurred, and the most we could hope to learn was the effect on injury rates of variation in that threat. Abolishing the tort system could reduce that threat to zero (depending on what, if anything replaced it), and we cannot learn from our data what the effect of that might be.

NOTES

Major Proposals, Research Studies, and Recent Enactments Changing the Tort System or Installing No-Fault Compensation Plans for Medically-Related Injuries

1. The proposals included in the reports and articles reprinted above provide a broad review of the current scene in the United States and the United Kingdom, another common law jurisdiction applying similar general rules of tort liability for medical negligence. In addition to examining these proposals of a more radical nature, most of the American states have enacted various patchwork adjustments and reforms in tort law, evidence law, and insurance regulation, and in regulation of health care providers. Many of these reforms

VII. Reform Movements in the Malpractice Field 423

have been reviewed earlier in this chapter, and several more will be examined in this section. For a comprehensive examination of reforms enacted in the 1980s and commentary on the effectiveness of these reforms in reducing the crisis in medical malpractice insurance and litigation, see Kapp, Solving the Medical Malpractice Problems: Difficulties in Defining What Works, 17 L. Med. & Health Care 156 (1989). For an analysis of research efforts to determine the effectiveness of recent reforms, see Danzon, The Frequency and Severity of Medical Malpractice Claims: New Evidence, 49 L. & Contemp. Prob. 57 (1986). For a recent review of the economic impact of legislative reform on medical malpractice insurance, see Sloan & Bovbjerg, Medical Malpractice: Crises, Response and Effects, Research Bulletin, Health Ins. Assoc. of America, Wash., D.C. (1989). Research projects supported by the Robert Wood Johnson Foundation over the past few years in areas such as legislative reform and risk management should produce important new data and proposals as results are published. In the latter part of 1989, the insurance industry began to reduce premiums for medical malpractice. An article in a leading financial newspaper asserted that the crisis in insurance premium rates was over. The cover story had the headline: Medical Malpractice: End of a Nightmare. See Henriques, Just What the Doctor Ordered, 69 Barron's, October 2, 1989, at 8.

2. The proposal of the American Medical Association and the medical specialty groups is probably the most novel of the many comprehensive measures that have been presented in recent years. Surprisingly, the Association does not propose a no-fault plan, the objective of many medical groups in the past, but a major modification of a fault-based system. The new AMA plan is a complex format of claims negotiation with features of a workers' compensation system combined with traditional labor negotiation methods. The role of plaintiffs' lawyers directly retained by malpractice claimants is unclear under the plan and is probably discouraged in favor of the use of system-retained legal counsel. As indicated in the summary, the plan is integrated with a medical care quality assurance program and a physician licensing, monitoring, and disciplining function in the state medical licensure agencies.

Why has the AMA determined to advocate such a complete plan? Why has the Association decided to support retention of a fault-based system? Two major reasons have been expressed: (1) the number of claims for injuries related to medical care may be expected to increase under a no-fault system by as much as ten to twenty fold over current levels; and (2) the AMA believes that, from an ethical viewpoint, professional people should continue to be responsible for their negligent performance (or lack of proper attention) resulting in patient injury. See Special Task Force on Professional Liability and Insurance,

Professional Liability in the '80s (Chicago: AMA 1985). The AMA was greatly impressed with the results of a California study some years ago indicating that a no-fault system would result in very substantial increases in medical care related claims. See Calif. Med. Assoc. and Calif. Hosp. Assoc., Report on the Medical Insurance Feasibility Study (San Fran. 1977). See also Mills, Medical Insurance Feasibility Study, 128 West. J. Med. 363 (1978). A new study has been undertaken to gather similar data in New York State. See Pilot Study, Medical Care and Medical Injuries in the State of New York (Boston: Harv. Med. Practice Group 1987).

How would the AMA's new proposal be greeted by plaintiff's attorneys? By health care public interest groups? According to a public media report at the time the plan was announced, neither of these groups responded favorably. The Association of Trial Lawyers of America called the plan "bizarre and unconstitutional." Public Citizen Health Research, Inc. responded that the proposal was "reckless and dangerous" to the welfare of medical patients. See Highlight Note, 1 Med. Malpractice Rep. 178, 180 (1988).

3. One of the most serious problems for no-fault proposals in the medical malpractice field is the definition of a compensable event or incident related to the medical care involved. The broader (or vaguer) the definition, the more "events" that would be compensated under the plan. Vagueness would also increase litigation (and delay recoveries) related to coverage of the system. The more inclusive definition would put pressure on the system to reduce awards of compensation to quite low levels. What would be the premium rates for a no-fault system? Who would pay the premiums? Should a national health insurance system of a universal coverage include a compensation system for medical care "injuries"? See particularly Abraham, Medical Liability Reform: A Conceptual Framework, 260 J.A.M.A. 68 (1988); Tancredi, Designated Events: A No-Fault Approach to Medical Malpractice, 10 Law, Med. & Health Care 200 (1982).

4. In an effort to explore the feasibility of a no-fault sytem for medically related injuries (or iatrogenic injury), the California Hospital Association and the California Medical Association commissioned a study to determine the extent of "potentially compensable events" of medical injury occurring in California hospitals. See Calif. Med. Assn. & Calif. Hosp. Assn., Medical Insurance Feasibility Study (D. Mills ed. 1977).

More recently, the Department of Health of the State of New York contracted with a group at Harvard University to reexamine the kinds of issues first explored in the Mills study in California. The study, in some areas, came to conclusions similar to those in the Mills study but provides considerably more investigation of a wide range of issues. The Executive Summary of the Report is reprinted above.

VII. Reform Movements in the Malpractice Field   425

Does the Report support a public policy of movement to a no-fault system?

5. The brief article by Representative Moore outlines the Alternative Medical Liability Act (also called, in other versions, the Medical Offer and Recovery Act) submitted to the Federal Congress in 1985 and 1986. The plan would apply to all beneficiaries of federal health care programs in the states and would be intended, according to the proponents, as a model for general adoption in the states. It is designed to encourage a prompt settlement of economic damages due to medical injury and to avoid payment of non-economic "pain and suffering" damages. The federal proposals arise mainly out of contractual plans developed by Professor Jeffrey O'Connell. See particularly O'Connell, Neo-No Fault Remedies for Medical Injuries: Coordinated Statutory and Contractual Alternatives, 45 J. Law & Contemp. Prob. 125 (1986). One of the attractions of the contractual model of no-fault compensation is that it seeks to avoid the problems of defining a "compensable event" since the parties, when arranging their contract, would agree in advance what injuries or bad outcomes would be compensated by the physician.

What would be the attitude of practicing lawyers to the Moore-Gephardt bill? The American Bar Association conducted an opinion poll that was published in the same issue as the Moore article reprinted above. The opinion survey indicated that the majority of practitioners (60 percent) opposed the legislation. Among plaintiff's lawyers, opposition was even higher (78 percent opposed). Among defense lawyers, a majority (55 percent) also opposed the plan. See Reskin, Lawyers Oppose Medical Malpractice Bill, 71 A.B.A.J. 40 (1985).

6. The article by David Bolt summarizes the objectives of the British Medical Association's plan for a no-fault compensation system for medical malpractice in Great Britain. As described in the article, the plan is not entirely no-fault in character. Adverse drug reactions are not covered and "diagnostic error" which is found "reasonable" is also not compensated. The plan is fairly closely modeled after the medical no-fault plan currently operating in Sweden. That plan also does not compensate for adverse drug reactions, but these injuries are covered under another Swedish no-fault plan related to pharmaceutical adverse reactions. For a review of the Swedish no-fault plan system and a comparison to British and American tort-law systems, see M. Rosenthal, Dealing with Medical Malpractice: The British and Swedish Experience (1988). On the no-fault system for pharmaceutical drug reactions, see a recent symposium surveying 10 years of experience: Report of a Symposium, The Swedish Pharmaceutical Insurance Program, Swedish Drug In. Assoc., Stockholm (1989). See also M. Dukes & B. Swartz, Responsibility for Drug-Induced Injury (1988). There is also a no-fault system for medical malpractice in

New Zealand. This plan, however, is not limited to medically-related injuries. It is a very comprehensive, general compensation plan, originally a workers' compensation program, that covers virtually all accidental injury in that country. For a description of the plan, see Unintentional Injury: New Zealand's Accident Compensation Scheme (ISBMO-477-04617-7) (Wellington, N.Z. 1988).

7. In the United States at present, no-fault compensation systems have begun to be enacted on the federal level and in a few states, but they have been quite specialized to deal with particularly difficult problems in the tort-law field. On the federal level, the Congress in 1986 enacted a compensation plan for children who have severe reactions to immunizations against childhood diseases. See National Childhood Vaccine Injury Act of 1986; Vaccine Compensation Amendments of 1987. Pub. L. 100-203. The state of North Carolina also adopted a compensation plan in 1986 for vaccine-related injuries. See N.C. Gen. Stat. §130A-42 et seq. (1987); Pub. L. No. 100-203. The first report of a recovery under the Act before the U.S. Claims Court has now been published. The court adopted the report of a special master for a recovery of $312,983 in damages, plus attorney's fees of $27,631. Reddish v. Secretary of the Dept. of HHS, 18 Ct. Cl. 379 (1989).

The North Carolina program, like the federal legislation, covers injuries received from legally required childhood disease immunizations. The North Carolina law adds a feature not found in the federal legislation. It provides an immunity from a no-fault product liability suit for damages against physicians or others administering the vaccines or against the manufacturer on a product liability basis, but the law allows the state attorney general, after compensation is paid by the state, to bring a subsequent suit for negligence against the manufacturer or others to recover the states payment under the plan.

The other no-fault laws enacted cover very strict neurological birth injuries wherein the child is totally and permanently disabled. These laws, enacted in Virginia in 1987 and in Florida in 1988, are intended to protect obstetricians from malpractice suits where the tort-law damages would be very high (estimated at $2 to $6 million). Both states place responsibility for the programs in the state workers' compensation systems and make periodic payments for the care and maintenance of the children throughout life with a payment for lost income potential after the age of 18. See Va. Code Ann. §2-5002 et seq. (1987); 1988 Fla. Sess. Law Serv., ch. 88-1, §60 et seq. (west). Both laws apply to live births only. They compensate for neurological damage sustained during labor, delivery, or resuscitation immediately after birth due to oxygen deprivation or mechanical mishap. They do not cover handicap due to fetal congenital or developmental abnormalities.

C. Judicial Responses and Constitutional Issues

Kirk v. Michael Reese Hospital and Medical Center
513 N.E.2d 387 (Ill. 1987)

WARD, J.

The five causes consolidated in this appeal arise from one personal injury action. The plaintiff, James D. Kirk, filed a six-count complaint in the circuit court of Cook County against six defendants, five of whom are involved in this appeal. The defendants moved to dismiss the plaintiff's third amended complaint for failure to state a cause of action; the trial court dismissed the action against five of the defendants. On the plaintiff's appeal from the dismissal, the appellate court reversed the dismissals of the five counts and remanded for further proceedings.

The plaintiff was injured August 1, 1978, while a passenger in a car driven by Daniel McCarthy when the car struck a tree. McCarthy had been a psychiatric patient at Michael Reese Hospital and Medical Center (hereafter Michael Reese), where he was treated by Dr. Irving H. Tracer and Dr. Henry K. Fine. The plaintiff alleges that Dr. Tracer was rendering medical treatment to McCarthy in the capacity of an agent, servant, or employee of Dr. Fine. The plaintiff alleges that Dr. Tracer, Dr. Fine, or their agents ordered prescription drugs in treating McCarthy. The drug Thorazine, which is manufactured by the defendant SmithKline Beckman Corp. (hereafter SmithKline), had been prescribed and McCarthy also had been given Prolixin Decanoate, which is manufactured by the defendant E. R. Squibb & Sons, Inc. (hereafter Squibb), on the day he was discharged from the hospital. McCarthy, following his discharge from Michael Reese, consumed an alcoholic drink. Later in the day, Kirk was a passenger in the car driven by McCarthy and was injured when the car left the roadway and struck a tree in Chicago Heights.

In count I of the plaintiff's third amended complaint, he seeks recovery from Michael Reese on the theory that the hospital negligently failed to adequately warn McCarthy that the prescribed drugs administered would diminish his physical and mental abilities. Counts II and III seek recovery from Drs. Tracer and Fine, respectively, on the theory that the physicians knew or should have known that the drugs would diminish McCarthy's mental abilities and that they negligently failed to warn McCarthy. Counts IV and V, both of which seek recovery against Michael Reese, as well as Squibb and SmithKline, respectively, are based on a strict liability theory and allege that the drugs were in an unreasonably dangerous condition because the manufacturers failed to adequately warn of the drugs' dangerous propensities, that is, that the drugs would diminish the physical and mental abilities of the user, McCarthy. Count VI seeks recovery from McCarthy for his alleged negligence in operating the car. The trial court, after memoranda were filed and numerous arguments were heard, granted the motions of the hospital, two doctors, and two drug companies to dismiss. The trial court also denied the plaintiff's oral motion to file a fourth amended complaint. Count VI against McCarthy was not dismissed and is not involved in this appeal.

The appellate court, with one justice dissenting, reversed and remanded the dismissed counts for trial. (136 Ill. App. 3d 945, 91 Ill. Dec. 420, 483 N.E.2d 906.) The appellate court, considering whether the defendants owed a duty to the plaintiff as but a single issue, held that the doctors, hospital, and drug manufacturers each had a duty to adequately warn McCarthy of the adverse effects of the drugs, which duty, the court stated, was implicitly extended to cover members of the public who may be injured as a proximate cause of the failure to adequately warn (136 Ill. App. 3d 945, 952, 91 Ill. Dec. 420, 483 N.E.2d 906). Too, the appellate court held the hospital was open to liability on a strict liability theory for failure to warn McCarthy of the effects of the prescribed drugs. As stated, the five defendants filed petitions for leave to appeal; their petitions were initially denied, but upon reconsideration, they allowed and consolidated for review. Briefs *amici curiae* have been filed by five organizations. The Illinois Trial Lawyers Association, as *amicus*, supports the plaintiff's arguments that the appellate court decision should be affirmed. Another *amicus*, the Pharmaceutical Manufacturers Association, supports the arguments of defendants SmithKline and Squibb. The Illinois Hospital Association and Metropolitan Chicago Healthcare Council, in a joint *amicus* brief, support Michael Reese's views and particularly argue against liability being imposed toward the hospital under strict liability principles. The Illinois Association of Defense Trial Counsel generally argues to reverse the appellate court's decision and specifically supports the drug manufacturers' views. . . . Section 402A of the Restatement (Second) of Torts (1965), which this court has previously followed (Suvada v. White Motor Co. (1965), 32 Ill. 2d 612, 210 N.E.2d 182), would subject a seller or manufacturer of a product to liability if the product is sold "in a defective condition unreasonably dangerous" to an ultimate user or consumer who is injured by the product. It is recognized that a failure to warn of a product's dangerous propensities may serve as the basis for holding a manufacturer strictly liable in tort. (Hammond v. North American Asbestos Corp. (1983), 97 Ill. 2d 195, 206, 73 Ill. Dec. 350, 454 N.E.2d 210; Woodill v. Parke Davis & Co. (1980), 79 Ill. 2d 26, 29, 37 Ill. Dec. 304, 402 N.E.2d 194; Restatement (Second) of Torts sec.

402A, comment *j* (1965).) A prescription drug may be deemed unreasonably dangerous because of the absence of an adequate warning accompanying the product as the product may be "unavoidably unsafe" without such warning. Restatement (Second) of Torts sec. 402A, comment *k* (1965); Lawson v. G. D. Searle & Co. (1976), 64 Ill. 2d 543, 550-51, 1 Ill. Dec. 497, 356 N.E.2d 779.

The plaintiff asserts that, while the class of persons to whom the warning is required to be given may be very limited, the class of persons to whom the duty is owed includes the public generally. He contends also that the appellate court holding does not abolish or diminish the "learned intermediary" doctrine. The plaintiff, although he argued at the trial proceedings that the pharmaceutical companies owed a duty to warn the patients who use the drugs, now accepts Squibb's and SmithKline's position that adequate warnings are to be given to physicians only and not to the public generally. Our appellate court has previously adopted the learned intermediary doctrine (Mahr v. G. D. Searle & Co. (1979), 72 Ill. App. 3d 540, 28 Ill. Dec. 624, 390 N.E.2d 1214 (applying Texas law); Hatfield v. Sandoz-Wander, Inc. (1984), 124 Ill. App. 3d 780, 80 Ill. Dec. 122, 464 N.E.2d 1105 (applying Indiana law); Eldridge v. Eli Lilly & Co. (1985), 138 Ill. App. 3d 124, 92 Ill. Dec. 740, 485 N.E.2d 551), but this court had not directly considered the issue. The rule, as adopted in numerous jurisdictions, provides that manufacturers of prescription drugs have a duty to warn prescribing physicians of the drugs' known dangerous propensities, and the physicians, in turn, using their medical judgment, have a duty to convey the warnings to their patients. . . .

The rationale for the doctrine was stated in a holding concerning Thorazine, one of the drugs involved here, in Stone v. Smith, Kline & French Laboratories (11th Cir. 1984), 731 F.2d 1575, 1579:

> "We cannot quarrel with the general proposition that where *prescription* drugs are concerned, the manufacturer's duty to warn is limited to an obligation to advise the prescribing physician of any potential dangers that may result from the drug's use. This special standard for prescription drugs is an understandable exception to the Restatement's general rule that one who markets goods must warn foreseeable ultimate users of dangers inherent in his products. See Restatement (Second) of Torts, Section 388 (1965). Prescription drugs are likely to be complex medicines, esoteric in formula and varied in effect. As a medical expert, the prescribing physician can take into account the propensities of the drug as well as the susceptibilities of his patient. His is the task of weighing the benefits of any medication against its potential dangers. The choice he makes is an informed one, and individualized medical judgment bottomed on a knowledge of both patient and palliative. Pharmaceutical companies then, who must warn ultimate purchasers of

dangers inherent in patent drugs sold over the counter, in selling prescription drugs are required to warn only the prescribing physician, who acts as a 'learned intermediary' between manufacturer and consumer." (Emphasis in original.)

731 F.2d 1575, 1579-80, quoting Reyes v. Wyeth Laboratories (5th Cir. 1974), 498 F.2d 1264, 1276, *cert. denied* (1974), 419 U.S. 1096, 95 S. Ct. 687, 42 L. Ed. 2d 688.

The drug manufacturer generally communicates warnings relating to prescription drugs to the medical profession through package inserts, the Physician's Desk Reference, "Dear Doctor" letters, detailmen, and through other measures. (Sterling Drug, Inc. v. Yarrow (8th Cir. 1969), 408 F.2d 978; Mahr v. G. D. Searle & Co. (1979), 72 Ill. App. 3d 540, 562, 28 Ill. Dec. 624, 390 N.E.2d 1214; Parke-Davis & Co. v. Stromsodt (8th Cir. 1969), 411 F.2d 1390.) The doctor, functioning as a learned intermediary between the prescription drug manufacturer and the patient, decides which available drug best fits the patient's needs and chooses which facts from the various warnings should be conveyed to the patient, and the extent of disclosure is a matter of medical judgment. (Hatfield v. Sandoz-Wander, Inc. (1984), 124 Ill. App. 3d 780, 788, 80 Ill. Dec. 122, 464 N.E.2d 1105; Eldridge v. Eli Lilly & Co. (1985), 138 Ill. App. 3d 124, 127, 92 Ill. Dec. 740, 485 N.E.2d 551; Jones v. Irvin (S.D. Ill. 1985), 602 F. Supp. 399, 402.) As such, we believe the learned intermediary doctrine is applicable here and that there is no duty on the part of manufacturers of prescription drugs to directly warn patients. Certainly, if the manufacturer of a prescription drug has no duty to directly warn the user of a drug of possible adverse effects, it has no duty to warn a nonuser as Kirk.

The plaintiff also argues that the warnings given to the two doctors here were inadequate, thus making the prescription drugs "unreasonably dangerous." This contention, however, is premature and puts the cart before the horse. As we determined in Winnett v. Winnett (1974), 57 Ill. 2d 7, 10, 310 N.E.2d 1, whether a product is unreasonably dangerous for its intended uses "is simply not a relevant consideration unless plaintiff is a person entitled to the protections afforded by the concepts of strict-tort-liability actions against manufacturers." It is recognized that a legal duty is imposed under strict liability upon those in the original production chain of a product to the benefit of those individuals to whom injury from a defective product may reasonably be foreseen. . . .

We believe the facts alleged in counts IV and V against Squibb and SmithKline demonstrate on their face that plaintiff would never be entitled to recover. As such, it cannot be said that Squibb and SmithKline should have reasonably foreseen that their drugs would

VII. Reform Movements in the Malpractice Field 431

be dispensed without warnings by the physicians, that the patient would be discharged from the hospital, drink alcohol, drive a car, lose control of his car, hit a tree, and injure the passenger, Kirk, on the same day. This sequence would be triggered by an element that we have determined that the pharmaceutical companies did not have to foresee under the circumstances shown here: that the drugs would be dispensed without the warnings that the two companies provided to the physicians. As this court has noted, "[s]trict liability is not the equivalent of absolute liability. There are restrictions imposed upon it." (Woodill v. Parke Davis & Co. (1980), 79 Ill. 2d 26, 37, 37 Ill. Dec. 304, 402 N.E. 2d 194; see also Coney v. J. L. G. Industries, Inc. (1983), 97 Ill. 2d 104, 111, 73 Ill. Dec. 337, 454 N.E.2d 197.) The trial court properly dismissed the two strict liability counts against Squibb and SmithKline. . . .

Turning to the portions of the complaint charging Michael Reese, the plaintiff posits liability in counts I, IV, and V against the hospital on two theories: strict liability and negligence. Under the strict liability counts, the plaintiff alleges that the products — the prescription drugs — were made unreasonably dangerous through the hospital's alleged failure to warn the patient, McCarthy, of their possible adverse effects. The plaintiff correctly states that strict tort liability may be imposed upon sellers and those in the chain of distribution, as well as manufacturers, for their role in placing a defective product into the stream of commerce. (Crowe v. Public Building Com. (1978), 74 Ill. 2d 10, 13, 23 Ill. Dec. 80, 383 N.E.2d 951; Cunningham v. MacNeal Memorial Hospital (1970), 47 Ill. 2d 443, 266 N.E.2d 897.) The plaintiff bases his strict liability count against the hospital on the hospital's role in the chain of distribution, "standing between the manufacturer and the doctor," and also as the supplier of the prescription drug to McCarthy. For the reasons discussed concerning the pharmaceutical companies, we believe there is no duty here to this nonpatient, nonuser of the product, and, as such, Kirk is not a plaintiff entitled to protection under strict liability principles. . . . We believe the trial court properly dismissed this strict liability count against the hospital.

As for the negligence count against the hospital, the plaintiff's complaint alleges that Michael Reese had a duty, in prescribing the two drugs, to adequately warn McCarthy of adverse effects the drugs may have on his ability to safely operate an automobile. The hospital contends that it had no duty to warn McCarthy of the adverse effects of the drug because such a warning is a medical question within the discretion of the treating physician, who, the hospital says, bears this responsibility. The hospital also argues that its duties should not be extended to unknown, nonpatient, third parties.

Kirk makes no allegations that Drs. Fine or Tracer, the defendant physicians, were agents or employees of Michael Reese, which would postulate liability on a respondeat superior basis. Absent a principal-agent relationship, the alleged misconduct of a physician may not be imputed to the hospital, unless it had reason to know that malpractice would occur. (Pickle v. Curns (1982), 106 Ill. App. 3d 734, 738-39, 62 Ill. Dec. 79, 435 N.E.2d 877.) Nor does the complaint allege that the hospital, through one of its agents or employees, was negligent in administering the drugs prescribed to McCarthy by, for example, providing the wrong quantity or type of drug. (Ohligschlager v. Proctor Community Hospital (1973), 55 Ill. 2d 411, 420, 303 N.E.2d 392.) The extent of warnings to patients concerning prescription drugs, as we have previously noted, is within the discretion of the physician. As such, the alleged negligent acts specified in the complaint are matters within the duty of care owed by the treating physician, rather than the hospital.

Recognizing the physician's duty, the plaintiff also argues that the hospital has an independent duty to warn, which is "based on ordinary principles of professional malpractice," and that that duty is extended to third parties. With this contention, then, the plaintiff is arguing that a third party with no patient/hospital or patient/physician relationship be allowed to bring a cause of action based on the alleged negligent treatment of another.

Holding the hospital liable for all harmful acts committed by patients who have been released would be an unreasonable burden on the institution. Too, a court's determination of duty reflects the policy and social requirements of the time and community. (Mieher v. Brown (1973), 54 Ill. 2d 539, 544-45, 301 N.E.2d 307; Green, Foreseeability in Negligence Law, 61 Colum. L. Rev. 1401, 1423 (1961); Prosser, Palsgraf Revisited, 52 Mich. L. Rev. 1, 15 (1953).) It has been recognized that " 'duty' is not sacrosanct in itself, but is only an expression of the sum total of those considerations of policy which lead the law to say that the plaintiff is entitled to protection." (W. Prosser & W. Keeton, The Law of Torts sec. 53, at 358 (5th ed. 1984).) Our State's public policy concerning malpractice actions and health care professionals was recently discussed in Bernier v. Burris (1986), 113 Ill. 2d 219, 100 Ill. Dec. 585, 497 N.E.2d 763. This court observed that the legislature's goal in enacting a comprehensive medical malpractice law, in which one provision prohibited punitive damages in actions for "healing art malpractice" or medical malpractice, was to reduce damages generally against the medical profession. (113 Ill. 2d 219, 246, 100 Ill. Dec. 585, 497 N.E.2d 763.) In upholding the provision that limited attorney fees in successful medical malpractice actions, we observed that "[t]he goals of the legislation . . . were to reduce the burden existing in the health professions as a result of the perceived [medical] malpractice crisis." (113 Ill. 2d

VII. Reform Movements in the Malpractice Field 433

219, 252, 100 Ill. Dec. 585, 497 N.E.2d 763; see also Mega v. Holy Cross Hospital (1986), 111 Ill. 2d 416, 428, 95 Ill. Dec. 812, 490 N.E.2d 665.) We believe that public policy and social requirements do not require that a duty be placed upon the hospital to warn the patient of the dangers of using the drug, prescribed by his physician, that would be extended to third-party nonpatients who have no patient-hospital relationship or a special relationship with a patient.

In determining that a duty existed, the appellate court relied partially on Renslow v. Mennonite Hospital (1977), 67 Ill. 2d 348, 10 Ill. Dec. 484, 367 N.E.2d 1250, a decision that the hospital contends does not support the expanded duty of care imposed by the appellate court. *Renslow*, it would appear, is the only medical malpractice action in which this court recognized that a nonpatient third party with no patient-hospital or patient-doctor relationship was allowed to maintain a cause of action against a hospital and doctor. In *Renslow*, a child not conceived at the time negligent acts were committed against its mother by a doctor and hospital employees was allowed to sue for that negligence directed against its mother. A wrong against one person may invade the protected rights of one who has a special relationship with the first party, as the law recognizes a limited area of transferred negligence. (Renslow v. Mennonite Hospital (1977), 67 Ill. 2d 348, 357, 10 Ill. Dec. 484, 367 N.E.2d 1250; see also Hoffmann v. Blackmon (Fla. App. 1970), 241 So. 2d 752.) The transfer of duty is limited by a court's policy decision that the duty to act with reasonable care should be transferred to the third-party plaintiff. This duty, however, arises from a *special relationship* between either the defendant and the other party or the third-party plaintiff and the other party. The duty in *Renslow* was based primarily on the injury's being a direct result of alleged negligence to the infant's mother, which was found to have invaded the protected rights of the child, who was intimately related to the mother. Obviously, that type of relationship does not exist between McCarthy, the patient who allegedly received negligent care, and Kirk, the passenger in his car.

As we stated in Teter v. Clemens (1986), 112 Ill. 2d 252, 258, 97 Ill. Dec. 467, 492 N.E.2d 1340, "[t]he basis for liability in a negligence action is not the mere fact of injury but that an injury has been caused by fault." The negligence count against the hospital failed to state a cause of action because it lacks the first essential element in a negligence claim: a recognized duty of care owed by the defendant to the particular plaintiff. The trial court properly dismissed this count.

Much of our discussion of the negligence count against the hospital is applicable to the counts against the two doctors. The plaintiff says the treating physicians had a duty to warn their patient, McCarthy, that the drugs could diminish his physical and mental abilities and that that duty runs in favor of those in the reasonably foreseeable field of danger, which included Kirk. The plaintiff also contends that it was reasonably foreseeable that a patient who is given a drug that diminishes his driving abilities will later have a car accident. Thus, the plaintiff argues, the circumstances of this case give rise to a common law duty to warn, running from the doctors to those in the general public who may reasonably be expected to come in contact with the patient on the day he is released. Dr. Tracer acknowledges that he had a duty to warn his patient about adverse effects that may result from taking a prescription drug. He argues, however, that physicians do not owe a general duty to unknown nonpatients who are injured by the physician's alleged negligent treatment of a patient. Dr. Tracer also asserts that the public policy of this State prohibits such a broad duty being imposed against treating physicians. Both doctors also say that the events alleged in the plaintiff's third amended complaint that resulted in Kirk's injury were not reasonably foreseeable. The third amended complaint specifically alleges that Dr. Tracer rendered medical treatment to McCarthy in the capacity of agent/servant or employee of Dr. Fine and is thus based on a *respondeat superior* theory. Dr. Fine argues that the trial court properly dismissed the plaintiff's claim based on *respondeat superior* for failure to state a cause of action and also because the complaint alleges a superseding, intervening cause of plaintiff's injuries, McCarthy's alleged negligent driving.

With the exception of *Renslow*, discussed previously with reference to the hospital, the plaintiff has not cited any holding in which this court has extended a physician's duty of care beyond the patient. In *Renslow*, this court recognized that the defendant doctor's duty to the mother could be transferred to her child based on the "intimate relationship" between the two. (67 Ill. 2d 348, 357, 10 Ill. Dec. 484, 367, N.E.2d 1250.) There is no patient-doctor relationship here between the two defendant doctors and Kirk, nor is there a special relationship present as in *Renslow* between the patient and the plaintiff. . . .

There is no allegation here that the plaintiff was negligently released from the hospital, and there is no allegation that McCarthy had dangerous propensities of which the hospital and physicians were aware. . . .

It is true, as the plaintiff points out, that several jurisdictions (Welke v. Kuzilla (1985), 144 Mich. App. 245, 375 N.W.2d 403; Davis v. Mangelsdorf (Ariz. App. 1983), 138 Ariz. 207, 673 P.2d 951; Gooden v. Tips (Tex. App. 1983), 651 S.W.2d 364; Wharton Transport Corp. v. Bridges (Tenn. 1980), 606 S.W.2d 521; Watkins v. United States (5th Cir. 1979), 589 F.2d 214; Freese v. Lemmon

VII. Reform Movements in the Malpractice Field 435

(Iowa 1973), 210 N.W.2d 576; Kaiser v. Suburban Transportation System (1965), 65 Wash. 2d 461, 398 P.2d 14, *modified* (1965), 65 Wash. 2d 461, 401 P.2d 350) have held that a physician's relationship with the patient was sufficient to impose a duty to protect unidentifiable, unknown third parties who are endangered by a patient. Other jurisdictions have limited the scope of the physician's duty to warn to situations in which there is, apart from the patient, a specifically identifiable potential victim, rather than holding that a duty exists to the public generally. (See, e.g., Furr v. Spring Grove State Hospital (1983), 53 Md. App. 474, 454 A.2d 414; Cairl v. State (Minn. 1982), 323 N.W.2d 20; Anthony v. United States (S.D. Iowa 1985), 616 F. Supp. 156.) We consider that the preferable view, and the one consistent with this court's holdings and with legislation based on social and public policy, is that a plaintiff cannot maintain a medical malpractice action absent a direct physician-patient relationship between the doctor and plaintiff or a special relationship, as present in *Renslow*, between the patient and the plaintiff. See also Pelham v. Griesheimer (1982), 92 Ill. 2d 13, 21, 64 Ill. Dec. 544, 440 N.E.2d 96 (a third-party nonclient who brings a negligence action against an attorney must prove that the primary purpose and intent of the attorney-client relationship itself was to benefit or influence the third party).

Dr. Tracer points out that the most effective way to fulfill the duty required by the appellate court's decision is through continued confinement of the patient, which he says would thwart drug therapy that enables psychiatric patients to return to the community to lead normal, productive lives. The plaintiff contends, however, that Dr. Tracer has falsely portrayed the burden of the physician's duty under the appellate court's decision. All that is necessary for a physician to extinguish his potential liability, in the plaintiff's view, is for the physician to tell the patient that the drug will diminish his physical and mental abilities, that he should not drive for a designated time period, and that he should not consume alcohol. The plaintiff overlooks that the appellate court decision explicitly extends the duties of the doctors — and, for that matter, all the defendants — beyond the patient to the general public. Such a broad duty extended to the general public would expand the physician's duty of care to an indeterminate class of potential plaintiffs. Our General Assembly, as we discussed previously, has very recently enacted major medical malpractice legislation to reduce the burden of litigation against health care professionals.

Other contentions of the plaintiff need not be considered because the first essential of a negligence action — the existence of a recognized duty — has not been met.

For the reasons stated, the judgment of the appellate court is reversed as to all counts and the judgment of the trial court is affirmed.

Smith v. Department of Insurance
507 So. 2d 1080 (Fla. 1987)

PER CURIAM.

This is an appeal from a circuit court judgment holding constitutional substantially all of chapter 86-160, Laws of Florida, known as the "Tort Reform and Insurance Act of 1986." The appellants are Robert P. Smith, Jr., with the Academy of Florida Trial Lawyers; Cigna Insurance Group, representing nine insurance companies; the American Insurance Association, National Association of Independent Insurers, and Alliance of American Insurers, representing 240 insurance companies transacting business in the State of Florida; and State Farm Insurance Companies. The appellees are the State of Florida, Department of Insurance; the Florida Medical Association, Inc., and the Florida Railroad Association, together with Florida Power and Light Company. This appeal comes directly to us under the provisions of article V, section 3(b)(5), Florida Constitution, having been certified by the First District Court of Appeal as an issue of great public importance requiring immediate resolution by this Court. We have accepted jurisdiction. . . .

The 1986 Tort Reform and Insurance Act is the legislative solution to a commercial insurance liability crisis which the legislature found existed. For various reasons, both the insurance industry and the trial lawyers' bar challenge the act's constitutionality. The legislature, to ensure that the public and reviewing courts fully understood the reasons and purpose for enacting this legislation, set forth, in the preamble of the act, detailed legislative findings, including the following: (1) "that there is in Florida a financial crisis in the liability insurance industry, causing a serious lack of availability of many lines of commercial liability insurance"; (2) "that professionals, businesses, and governmental entities are faced with dramatic increases in the cost of insurance coverage"; (3) "the absence of insurance is seriously adverse to many sectors of Florida's economy"; (4) "that if the present crisis is not abated, many persons who are subject to civil actions will be unable to purchase liability insurance, and many injured persons will therefore be unable to recover damages for either their economic losses or their noneconomic losses."

VII. Reform Movements in the Malpractice Field

Limitation on Noneconomic Damages in the Amount of $450,000

Section 59 places a $450,000 limitation on damages for noneconomic losses, defined as damages "to compensate for pain and suffering, inconvenience, physical impairment, mental anguish, disfigurement, loss of capacity for enjoyment of life, and other nonpecuniary damages." Smith and the Academy argue that the cap on noneconomic damages is contrary to article I, section 21 of the Florida Constitution:

> The courts shall be open to every person for redress of any injury, and justice shall be administered without sale, denial or delay.

It is uncontroverted that there currently exists a right to sue on and recover noneconomic damages of any amount and that this right existed at the time the current Florida Constitution was adopted. The right to redress of any injury does not draw any distinction between economic and noneconomic damages nor does article I, section 21 contain any language which would support the proposition that the right is limited, or may be limited, to suits above or below any given figure.

The parties agree that the seminal case on the right of access to the courts is Kluger v. White, 281 So. 2d 1 (Fla. 1973). They disagree, however, as to its application. In *Kluger*, we addressed the question of whether the legislature could restrict the right by establishing a minimum threshold of $550 for economic damages below which the injured plaintiff would have no right to sue. Our answer was no and our holding there is directly controlling here.

> [W]here a right of access to the courts for redress for a particular injury has been provided by statutory law predating the adoption of the Declaration of Rights of the Constitution of the State of Florida, or where such right has become a part of the common law of the State pursuant to Fla. Stat. §2.01, F.S.A., the Legislature is without power to abolish such a right without providing a reasonable alternative to protect the rights of the people of the State to redress for injuries, unless the Legislature can show an overpowering public necessity for the abolishment of such right, and no alternative method of meeting such public necessity can be shown.

Id. at 4. There is no relevant distinction between the issue in *Kluger* and the issue here. In *Kluger*, the legislature attempted to unconstitutionally restrict the right of redress at the bottom of the damages spectrum; here, it attempts to restrict the top of the spectrum. Neither restriction is permissible unless one of the *Kluger* exceptions is met; i.e., (1) providing a reasonable alternative remedy or commensurate benefit, or (2) legislative showing of overpowering public necessity for the abolishment of the right *and* no alternative method of meeting such public necessity.

Appellees urge that *Kluger* is distinguishable in light of Lasky v. State Farm Insurance Co., 296 So. 2d 9 (Fla. 1974), and Chapman v. Dillon, 415 So. 2d 12 (Fla. 1982). In *Lasky*, we upheld a statutory provision which denied recovery for pain and suffering and similar intangible items of damages unless the plaintiff was able to meet a $1,000 medical expense threshold. We did so, however, because the legislature had provided such plaintiffs with an alternative remedy and a commensurate benefit. First, the vehicular no-fault insurance statute required that all motor vehicle owners obtain insurance or other security to provide injured persons with minimum benefits. This was essentially a contractual arrangement; if the defendant vehicle owner failed to purchase the required insurance, the defendant's immunity was nullified and the plaintiff retained the right to sue below the threshold. Second, under the no-fault insurance statute, any given vehicle owner was as likely to be sued as to sue and giving up the right to sue was compensated for by obtaining the right not to be sued. Thus, unlike here, the legislation we upheld in *Lasky* provided a reasonable trade off of the right to sue for the right to recover uncontested benefits under the statutory no-fault insurance scheme *and* the right not to be sued. Here, the benefits of a $450,000 cap on noneconomic damages run in only one direction because the potential plaintiffs and defendants stand on different footing. For example, a medical patient or the client of a lawyer obtains no compensatory benefit from a cap placed on noneconomic damages because of the unlikeliness of negligence by a patient or client. . . .

Appellees also argue, and the trial court below agreed, that the legislature has not totally abolished a cause of action, it has only placed a cap on damages which may be recovered and, therefore, has not denied the right to access the courts. This reasoning focuses on the title to article I, section 21, "Access to courts," and overlooks the contents which must be read in conjunction with section 22, "Trial by jury." Access to courts is granted for the purpose of redressing injuries. A plaintiff who receives a jury verdict for, e.g., $1,000,000, has not received a constitutional redress of injuries if the legislature statutorily, and arbitrarily, caps the recovery at $450,000. Nor, we add, because the jury verdict is being arbitrarily capped, is the plaintiff receiving the constitutional benefit of a jury trial as we have heretofore understood that right. Further, if the legislature may constitutionally cap recovery at $450,000, there is no discernible reason why it could not cap the recovery at some other figure, perhaps $50,000, or $1,000, or even $1. None of these caps, under the reasoning of appellees, would "totally" abolish the right of access to the courts. At least one of the appellees candidly argues that there is no constitutional bar to completely abolishing noneconomic damages by requiring potential injured victims to buy insurance protecting themselves against economic loss due to injury as an alternative remedy. That particular issue is not before us but we note that if it were permissible to restrict the constitutional right by legislative action, without meeting the conditions set forth in *Kluger*, the constitutional right of access to the courts for redress of injuries would be subordinated to, and a creature of, legislative grace or, as Mr. Smith puts it, "majoritarian whim." There are political systems where constitutional rights are subordinated to the power of the executive or legislative branches, but ours is not such a system. . . .

Rationality only becomes relevant if the legislature provides an alternative remedy or abrogates or restricts the right based on a showing of overpowering public necessity and that no alternative method of meeting that necessity exists. Here, however, the legislature has provided nothing in the way of an alternative remedy or commensurate benefit and one can only speculate, in an act of faith, that somehow the legislative scheme will benefit the tort victim. We cannot embrace such nebulous reasoning when a constitutional right is involved. Further, the trial judge below did not rely on — nor have appellees urged before this Court — that the cap is based on a legislative showing of "an overpowering public necessity for the abolishment of such right, and no alternative method of meeting such public necessity can be shown." *Kluger*, 281 So. 2d at 4.

It is so ordered.

NOTES

Judicial Responses to the Crisis in Medical Malpractice: Policy Making by Legislatures and Courts

1. The three cases reprinted above provide examples of responses of the appellate courts to legislative efforts to deal with the medical malpractice crisis or with aspects of the crisis. The *Kirk* opinion indicates the acceptance by the Illinois Supreme Court of the policy change established by the state legislature. The opinion indicates, in several areas of tort law, a conscious effort to limit the extent of physician and hospital liability.

This decision in Illinois is particularly significant because the Illinois Supreme Court in the past had been one of the leading proponents of the expansion of liability principles. The two major cases identified with this earlier position, the *Darling* case in 1965 (at 321 of this chapter) and the *Renslow* case in 1977 were, in fact, relied upon by the plaintiff in the *Kirk* case and application of these opinions to the present situation was denied in the opinion of Justice Ward.

The importance of this appeal was not lost on the health care organizations and bar groups in Illinois. As indicated in the opinion, amicus curiae briefs were filed by five organizations: the Illinois Hospital Association, the Metropolitan Chicago Healthcare Council, the Pharmaceutical Manufacturers Association, the Illinois Association of Defense Trial Council, and the Illinois Trial Lawyers Association. The first four all filed briefs favoring reversal. The last, the plaintiffs' counsel group in Illinois, was the only organization supporting the plaintiff in the case. The Pharmaceutical Manufacturers Association, a national organization representing American pharmaceutical companies, was appearing to argue for limitation of the liability of the two pharmaceutical companies involved in the litigation. The decision of the intermediate appellate court which would have expanded liability had received wide publicity in medical and legal circles.

2. The *Smith* case in Florida illustrates what is probably a majority viewpoint of the appellate judiciary on the constitutional validity of arbitrary "caps" on malpractice awards. The field is still quite unsettled, however, with a bewildering number of opinions on all sides of the issues raised by the statutes. With the decision in Fein v. Permanente Medical Group, 695 P.2d 665 (Cal. 1985), upholding a "cap" of $250,000 on non-economic damages in that key state, it seemed that the trend might be in the direction of upholding the statutory limitations. This did not occur, however, and several courts quickly struck down statutes similar to that in California. See a student note tracing developments in the mid-1980s: Note, the Constitutionality of Recent Efforts to Limit Personal Injury Damages, 13 West. State L. Rev. 595 (1986). See also Note, A.L.R.3d 583 (1987).

The legislative interest in installing "caps" continued, however, stimulated by a study by the Rand Corporation of the effects of the various reforms upon closed claims. The study found that only two changes in the law made any difference in either the frequency or severity (total dollar amount) of paid claims by the insurance industry. These were "caps" on awards and repeal of the collateral source rule. In the 1980s, as indicated in the article by Professor Kapp, these two reforms were favored by the state legislatures. See P. Danzon, The Frequency and Severity of Medical Malpractice Claims, Rand Corporation, Santa Monica, Cal. (1983). See also Danzon, The Frequency and Severity of Medical Malpractice Claims: New Evidence, 49 L. & Contemp. Prob. 57 (1986).

The *Smith* opinion indicated that the "cap" could not be supported because the plaintiffs were not given anything of value in return for the loss of the opportunity to recover a larger damages award. What *benefits* for injured patients might the Florida court accept in order

VII. Reform Movements in the Malpractice Field 441

to find a "cap" constitutional? The new legislation in Florida enacted in 1988, based upon the recommendations of the Academic Task Force (see report at 396), suggests an arbitration plan voluntarily accepted by plaintiffs with built-in benefits and a "cap." If both parties voluntarily accept arbitration, the result is binding and non-economic damages are limited to $250,000. The arbitration hearing is also limited to the examination of "the defendant's obligation to pay damages," not an examination of fault issues. If the defendant refuses arbitration, but the plaintiff accepts, the case may go to trial without limitation of damages and the defendant, if the case is won by the plaintiff, must pay attorney's fees up to 25 percent of the award reduced to current value. If the defendant accepts arbitration, but the plaintiff refuses, the case may go to trial with a limitation of non-economic damages of $350,000. The statute makes a specific public-policy finding on the latter limitation as follows:

> The Legislature expressly finds that such conditional limit on non-economic damages is warranted by the claimant's refusal to accept arbitration, and represents an appropriate balance between the interests of all patients who ultimately pay for medical negligence losses and the interests of those patients who are injured as a result of medical negligence.

1988, Fla. Sess. Law Serv. ch. 1 §56(4)(a) (West). Does the new approach to a legislative "cap" answer the Florida Supreme Court's objections in the *Smith* decision?

3. The legislative limitations on awards enacted during the 1970s and 1980s relating to non-economic damages have been "arbitrary"; that is, they have not allowed any exceptions for special circumstances. Would a statutory limit with a built-in "safety valve" allowing the fact-finder to avoid the limit in special circumstances be more *apt* to pass constitutional muster? The "cap" enacted in Massachusetts in 1986 on non-economic damages is $500,000 unless the fact-finder determines that there was substantial or permanent loss or impairment of bodily functions, or other special circumstances, such as to warrant a finding that the limitation would deprive the plaintiff of "just compensation." 1986 Mass. Acts, ch. 351, §26.

4. In a recent opinion, the Virginia Supreme Court went against the tide in upholding a $750,000 limitation on *all damages* recoverable in medical malpractice. The plaintiff suffered brain damage in an operative procedure on the jaw and was paralyzed on the left side. The jury verdict was $2,750,000. The Supreme Court, in a split decision with a vigorous dissent, upheld the general limitation of damages, citing the legislature's finding of a serious crisis in medical malpractice and malpractice insurance in the state. See Etheridge v. Medical Center Hospitals, 376 S.E.2d 525 (Va. 1989).

D. Reform Movements in Theory and Practice: Alternative Dispute Resolution, Screening Procedures, Claims Handling and Loss Control, and Patient Risk Management

Madden v. Kaiser Foundation Hospitals
552 P.2d 1178 (Cal. 1976)

TOBRINER, JUSTICE. Defendants appeal from an order denying enforcement of an arbitration provision in a medical services contract entered into between the Board of Administration of the State Employees Retirement System (hereafter board) and defendant Kaiser Foundation Health Plan. Plaintiff, a state employee who enrolled under the Kaiser plan, contends that she is not bound by the provision for arbitration. The instant appeal presents the issue whether an agent or representative, contracting for medical services on behalf of a group of employees, has implied authority to agree to arbitration of malpractice claims of enrolled employees arising under the contract. . . .

When plaintiff first enrolled under the Kaiser plan in 1965, it did not contain an arbitration provision. On April 1, 1971, however, the Kaiser Foundation Health Plan, anticipating the inclusion of an arbitration provision, mailed to all subscribers a brochure which, in describing the terms and benefits of the plan, stated that claims involving professional liability and personal injury must be submitted to arbitration. Shortly thereafter, on May 28, 1971, the Kaiser Foundation Health Plan and the board amended their contract in several respects and included a provision for binding arbitration of "any claim arising from the violation of a legal duty incident to this Agreement."[2]

On August 1, 1971, plaintiff underwent a hysterectomy at the Kaiser Hospital in Los Angeles. During the surgery, her bladder was perforated; blood transfusions were required; plaintiff thereafter contracted serum hepatitis.[3]

Plaintiff filed a malpractice complaint against Kaiser and the blood banks. Kaiser moved to stay the action and compel arbitration. Opposing this motion, plaintiff filed a declaration stating that because

---

2. The arbitration agreement stated that it was retroactive to April 1, 1971, the date of the Kaiser brochure advising subscribers of the arbitration clause. Since plaintiff's claim arose after May 28, 1971, we need not consider whether the agreement can be retroactively effective to require arbitration of claims arising before it was finally approved.

3. Defendants California Transfusion Services and American Red Cross supplied the blood, which was stored at the Kaiser facility for use when necessary. These defendants do not claim to be covered by the arbitration provision in the Kaiser contract and are not parties to this appeal.

VII. Reform Movements in the Malpractice Field

of absence from work by reason of illness she had not received the April 1971 brochure, that she was not aware of the execution of the arbitration agreement in May of 1971, and thus had no knowledge that the Kaiser plan, at the time of her operation, required arbitration of malpractice claims.

By order of April 22, 1974, the trial court denied the motion to stay the action and compel arbitration. Kaiser appeals from that order. . . .

2. *The Board, as Agent for the Employees, Had Implied Authority to Provide for Arbitration of Malpractice Claims*

Government Code sections 22774, 22790 and 22793 authorize the board to negotiate contracts for group medical plans for state employees. In negotiating such agreements and amendments the board acts as the agent or representative of the employees. . . .

We shall explain that although the courts in the past regarded arbitration as an unusual and suspect procedure, they now recognize it as an accepted method of settlement of disputes. Since Civil Code section 2319 grants an agent the authority to do whatever is "proper and usual" to carry out his agency, the board enjoyed an implied authority to agree to arbitration of malpractice claims of enrolled employees.

This preliminary doctrinal recitation sets the stage for the principal issue of this appeal: whether the board, as agent of the employees, had implied authority to agree to a contract which provided for arbitration of all disputes, including malpractice claims, arising under that contract. That issue turns on the application of Civil Code section 2319, which authorizes a general agent "To do everything necessary or proper and usual . . . for effecting the purpose of his agency." For the reasons explained below, we conclude that arbitration is a "proper and usual" means of resolving malpractice disputes, and thus that an agent empowered to negotiate a group medical contract has the implied authority to agree to the inclusion of an arbitration provision.

In Crofoot v. Blair Holding Corp. (1953) 119 Cal. App. 2d 156, 183-184, 260 P.2d 156, 170, Justice Peters summarized the evolution of legal attitudes toward arbitration. "Arbitration has had a long and troubled history. The early common law courts did not favor arbitration, and greatly limited the powers of arbitrators. But in recent times a great change in attitude and policy has taken place. Arbitrations are now usually covered by statutory law, as they are in California. Such statutes evidence a strong public policy in favor of arbitrations, which policy has frequently been approved and enforced by the courts." Subsequent decisions confirm the self-evident fact that arbitration has become an accepted and favored method of resolving disputes (Ware v. Merrill Lynch, Pierce, Fenner & Smith, Inc. (1972) 24 Cal. App. 3d 35, 43, 100 Cal. Rptr. 791; Federico v. Frick (1970) 3 Cal. App. 3d 872, 875, 84 Cal. Rptr. 74; Roberts v. Fortune Homes, Inc. (1966) 240 Cal. App. 2d 238, 244, 49 Cal. Rptr. 429), praised by the courts as an expeditious and economical method of relieving overburdened civil calendars (Player v. Geo. M. Brewster & Son, Inc. (1971) 18 Cal. App. 3d 526, 534, 96 Cal. Rptr. 149).

The transformation of legislative and judicial attitudes toward arbitration has encouraged a dramatic development in the use of this procedure. A 1952 study estimated that "aside from personal injury cases and cases in which the government is a party, more than 70 percent of the total civil litigation is decided through arbitration rather than by the courts" (Mentschikoff, The Significance of Arbitration — A Preliminary Inquiry (1952) 17 Law & Contemp. Prob. 698). In the following decades arbitration further expanded its role to encompass in certain circumstances disputes requiring evaluation of personal injury claims: California and many other states now require arbitration of uninsured motorist claims (see Ins. Code, §11580.2), and proposals for no-fault automobile insurance frequently provide for arbitration (see Judicial Council of Cal., Study of the Role of Arbitration in the Judicial Process (1973) pp. 71-73). . . . The agent today who consents to arbitration follows a "proper and usual" practice "for effecting the purpose" of the agency; he merely agrees that disputes arising under the contract be resolved by a common, expeditious, and judicially-favored method.

The matter becomes even clearer if we narrow our focus to arbitration of disputes arising under group contracts. In collective bargaining agreements, which, like the present contract, are negotiated by elected representatives on behalf of a group of employees, arbitration has become a customary means of resolving disputes. . . .

Finally, we observe the growing interest in and use of arbitration to cope with the increasing volume of medical malpractice claims. (See Judicial Council Study, op. cit., supra, pp. 70-71 and references there cited.) Butler, Arbitration: An Answer to the Medical Malpractice Crisis (Sept.-Oct. 1975) 9 Beverly Hills Bar J. 41; Henderson, op. cit., supra, 58 Va. L. Rev. 947; Note, Rx for New York's Medical Malpractice Crisis (1975) 11 Colum. J.L. & Soc. Prob. 467, 500-503.[9] The authority of an agent to agree to the arbitration of such claims

---

9. In 1975 the Legislature enacted Code of Civil Procedure section 1295, which specifies the language which must be used in an arbitration provision inserted into an individual medical services contract. Although this enactment does not apply to the case at bar, it evidences legislative acknowledgment of arbitration as a means of resolving malpractice disputes.

VII. Reform Movements in the Malpractice Field

finds an illustration in our decision in Doyle v. Giuliucci (1965) 62 Cal. 2d 606, 43 Cal. Rptr. 697, 401 P.2d 1. In *Doyle*, the father of an injured minor entered into a contract with the Ross-Loos Medical Group which provided for arbitration of tort and contract claims arising under the contract. In an unanimous opinion authored by Chief Justice Traynor, we held that the minor was bound by the provision of the agreement to submit her malpractice claim to arbitration. "[T]he power to enter into a contract for medical care that binds the child to arbitrate any dispute arising thereunder," we stated, "is implicit in a parent's right and duty to provide for the care of his child." (P. 610, 43 Cal. Rptr. p. 699, 401 P.2d p. 3.) Rejecting the contention that the arbitration clause unreasonably limited the minor's rights, we replied, "The arbitration provision in such contracts is a reasonable restriction, for it does no more than specify a forum for the settlement of disputes." (Ibid.)[10]

We do not believe *Doyle* can be distinguished from the instant case because it involves a parent contracting on behalf of a child instead of an agent contracting on behalf of its principal. Both parent and agent serve as fiduciaries with limited powers, and if, as *Doyle* holds, the implied authority of a parent includes the power to agree to arbitration of the child's malpractice claims, we perceive no reason why the implied authority of an agent should not similarly include the power to agree to arbitration of the principal's malpractice claims.

We therefore conclude that an agent or other fiduciary who contracts for medical treatment on behalf of his beneficiary retains the authority to enter into an agreement providing for arbitration of claims for medical malpractice.[11]

---

10. Plaintiff seeks to distinguish *Doyle*. She points out that in *Doyle* the minor did not question the authority of her father to agree to arbitration until after the arbitrators had rendered an award. Plaintiff asserts that unlike the minor in *Doyle*, she presented her objection to arbitration at the earliest opportunity. In other words, plaintiff claims that the minor in *Doyle* failed to prevail *only* because she was dilatory in objecting to arbitration. But nothing in our opinion in *Doyle* suggests that our decision rested upon any theory that the minor had not raised her contention in a timely fashion; the opinion clearly holds that the fiduciary acted within his authority in entering into the initial arbitration agreement.

11. Amicus suggests that we should fashion a new rule to the effect that no arbitration provision in a group insurance policy will bind the beneficiary absent proof of the beneficiary's *actual* knowledge of that provision. In the present case, Kaiser provided plaintiff with a brochure describing the Kaiser plan, including the arbitration provision. Apart from plaintiff's own testimony, neither the Board nor Kaiser have any way of proving whether or not plaintiff read all or part of that brochure. The orderly administration of the plan would be impossible if it were to depend on such proof. Amicus acknowledges as much; it does not maintain that no provision of the Kaiser plan can be enforced against a beneficiary who enrolls without actual knowledge of that provision; it would, instead provide only that arbitration provisions cannot be enforced without actual knowledge. But amicus' proposal for a special rule which discriminates against enforcement of arbitration clauses would be viable only if arbitration were an extraordinary procedure, and one especially disadvantageous for the

3. The Principles that Govern Contracts of Adhesion Do Not Bar Enforcement of the Arbitration Amendment

Contending that the Kaiser contract is one of adhesion, plaintiff argues that the courts should refuse to enforce its arbitration clause on the ground that the clause is inconspicuous, unexpected, and disrupts the members' reasonable expectation that a malpractice claim will be adjudicated by trial by jury. We explain our reason for concluding that the principles governing adhesion contracts do not cover the present case. . . .

In the characteristic adhesion contract case, the stronger party drafts the contract, and the weaker has no opportunity, either personally or through an agent, to negotiate concerning its terms. (See Steven v. Fidelity & Casualty Co., supra, 58 Cal. 2d 862, 882, 27 Cal. Rptr. 172, 377 P.2d 284; Kessler, Contracts of Adhesion — Some Thoughts About Freedom of Contract (1943) 43 Colum. L. Rev. 629, 632.) The Kaiser plan, on the other hand, represents the product of negotiation between two parties, Kaiser and the board, possessing parity of bargaining strength. Although plaintiff did not engage in the personal negotiation of the contract's terms, she and other public employees benefitted from representation by a board, composed in part of persons elected by the affected employees, which exerted its bargaining strength to secure medical protection for employees on more favorable terms than any employee could individually obtain.

In many cases of adhesion contracts, the weaker party lacks not only the opportunity to bargain but also any realistic opportunity to look elsewhere for a more favorable contract; he must either adhere to the standardized agreement or forego the needed services. (See, e.g., Tunkl v. Regents of University of California, supra, 60 Cal. 2d 92, 32 Cal. Rptr. 33, 383 P.2d 441.) Plaintiff, on the other hand, enjoyed the opportunity to select from among several medical plans negotiated and offered by the board, some of which did not include arbitration provisions, or to contract individually for medical care. . . .

To support her contract of adhesion argument, plaintiff points to Tunkl v. Regents of University of California, supra, 60 Cal. 2d 92, 32 Cal. Rptr. 33, 383 P.2d 441; that decision, however, serves instead to illuminate by contrast the nonoppressive character of the contract in the present case. In *Tunkl*, defendant hospital presented to all incoming patients a document entitled "Conditions of Admission," which provided that the patient *release* the hospital from liability for negligent or wrongful acts. We observed that the "would-be patient

---

beneficiary — propositions which we have rejected in *Doyle* and other cases cited in this opinion.

VII. Reform Movements in the Malpractice Field

is in no position to reject the proffered agreement, to bargain with the hospital, or in lieu of agreement to find another hospital." (60 Cal. 2d at p. 102, 32 Cal. Rptr. at p. 39, 383 P.2d at p. 447.) Thus, the patient had no realistic choice but to assent to a standardized agreement under which he waived his right to recover for negligently inflicted injuries.

As we have explained, plaintiff, in contrast to *Tunkl*, benefitted from the board's assertion of equal power on her behalf, enjoyed the opportunity to choose from among alternative medical plans, and waived no substantive right. We conclude that *Tunkl* is not controlling in the instant setting; the principles of adhesion contracts, as elucidated and applied in *Tunkl* and the other cases we have cited, do not bar enforcement of terms of a negotiated contract which neither limit the liability of the stronger party nor bear oppressively upon the weaker. Accordingly, such principles do not bar enforcement of the arbitration amendment against plaintiff Madden.

4. *Enforcement of the Arbitration Provision Does Not Violate Constitutional or Statutory Protections of the Right to Trial by Jury*

Plaintiff further contends that the arbitration provision in the Kaiser contract fails because it does not expressly waive the parties' constitutional right to jury trial. But to predicate the legality of a consensual arbitration agreement upon the parties' express waiver of jury trial would be as artificial as it would be disastrous.

When parties agree to submit their disputes to arbitration they select a forum that is alternative to, and independent of, the judicial — a forum in which, as they well know, disputes are not resolved by juries. Hence there are literally thousands of commercial and labor contracts that provide for arbitration but do not contain express waivers of jury trial. Courts have regularly enforced such agreements; in Charles J. Rounds Co. v. Joint Council of Teamsters No. 42, supra, 4 Cal. 3d 888, 95 Cal. Rptr. 53, 484 P.2d 1397, for example, we unanimously affirmed an order compelling an employer to submit a contract dispute to arbitration, although the arbitration provision did not expressly waive the employer's right to trial by jury. Relying on this consistent pattern of judicial decision, contracting parties, such as Kaiser and the board in the case at bar, continue to draft arbitration provisions without express mention of any right to jury trial. Before today no one has so much as imagined that such agreements are consequently invalid; to destroy their viability upon an extreme hypothesis that they fail expressly to negative jury trials would be to frustrate the parties' interests and destroy the sanctity of their mutual promises.

5. Plaintiff Cannot Avoid Arbitration with Kaiser by Joining Other Parties as Defendants in Her Malpractice Suit

Plaintiff contends that a stay of her action with respect to Kaiser will lead to piecemeal and protracted litigation because she has also named as defendants the two blood banks. We agree that plaintiff may properly join the blood banks as parties defendant (Landau v. Salam (1971) 4 Cal. 3d 901, 95 Cal. Rptr. 46, 484 P.2d 1390), but that right does not empower her to avoid her duty to arbitrate any dispute with Kaiser. . . .

We conclude that the trial court erred in denying Kaiser's motion to compel arbitration and in refusing to stay the action against Kaiser. The trial court's refusal to stay the action as to the blood bank defendants is not challenged on appeal, but the trial court may wish to reconsider its order with respect to those defendants in light of our disposition of Kaiser's appeal.

The order of April 22, 1974, denying Kaiser's motion to stay further proceedings and compel arbitration is reversed, and the cause remanded for further proceedings consistent with the views expressed herein. The appeal from the order of May 22, 1974, denying Kaiser's petition for reconsideration, is dismissed.

WRIGHT, C.J., and MCCOMB, SULLIVAN, CLARK and FILES, JJ., concur.

MOSK, JUSTICE (dissenting) [omitted.]

California Contract for Medical Services, Arbitration Clause
Cal. Civ. Code tit. 9.1 §1295

(a) Any contract for medical services which contains a provision for arbitration of any dispute as to professional negligence of a health care provider shall have such provision as the first article of the contract and shall be expressed in the following language: "It is understood that any dispute as to medical malpractice, that is as to whether any medical services rendered under this contract were unnecessary or unauthorized or were improperly, negligently or incompetently rendered, will be determined by submission to arbitration as provided by California law, and not by a lawsuit or resort to court process except as California law provides for judicial review of arbitration proceedings. Both parties to this contract, by entering into it, are giving up their constitutional right to have any such dispute decided in a court of law before a jury, and instead are accepting the use of arbitration."

(b) Immediately before the signature line provided for the individual contracting for the medical services must appear the following in at least 10-point bold red type:

"NOTICE: BY SIGNING THIS CONTRACT YOU ARE AGREEING TO HAVE ANY ISSUE OF MEDICAL MALPRACTICE DECIDED BY NEUTRAL ARBITRATION AND YOU ARE GIVING UP YOUR RIGHT TO A JURY OR COURT TRIAL. SEE ARTICLE 1 OF THIS CONTRACT."

(c) Once signed, such a contract governs all subsequent open-book account transactions for medical services for which the contract was signed until or unless rescinded by written notice within 30 days of signature. Written notice of such rescission may be given by a guardian or conservator of the patient if the patient is incapacitated or a minor.

(d) Where the contract is one for medical services to a minor, it shall not be subject to disaffirmance if signed by the minor's parent or legal guardian.

(e) Such a contract is not a contract of adhesion, nor unconscionable nor otherwise improper, where it complies with subdivisions (a), (b) and (c) of this section.

Blood v. Lea
530 N.E.2d 344 (Mass. 1988)

[The plaintiff appeals from a final judgment rendered after a medical malpractice review panel found the evidence presented at the hearing to be inadequate to raise a legitimate question of liability appropriate for a trial in court.]

ABRAMS, J.

. . . *The tribunal's determination.* The plaintiffs argue that the tribunal erred in its determination that the evidence presented was not sufficient to raise a legitimate question of liability appropriate for judicial inquiry. The plaintiffs correctly state that the tribunal must use the same standard that a judge would use "in ruling on a defendant's motion for directed verdict." Little v. Rosenthal, 376 Mass. 573, 578 (1978). "The applicable standard is comparable to that applied to a defendant's motion for a directed verdict, and appraisal of the *weight* and *credibility* of the evidence is *impermissible*" (emphasis added). Gugino v. Harvard Comm. Health Plan, 380 Mass. 464, 468 (1980).[5] "A plaintiff's offer of proof as to negligence will prevail

---

5. Contrary to the defendant's argument, the tribunal's function is not to "evaluate" the evidence in the full sense of that term. Little v. Rosenthal, 376 Mass. at 578 and

before a malpractice tribunal . . . (1) if a doctor-patient relationship is shown, (2) if there is evidence that the doctor's performance did not conform to good medical practice, and (3) if damage resulted therefrom." Kapp v. Ballantine, 380 Mass. 186, 193 (1980).

The plaintiffs' offer of proof consisted of defendant Dr. Lea's office records; the discharge summary, labor and delivery summary and labor progress sheet from defendant Emerson Hospital; an opinion letter from Dr. Saul Lerner[6]; and a report from Dr. Martin Feldman.[7]

The doctor-patient relationship and hospital-patient relationship are clear from the records, and the defendants do not dispute the relationship each had with the plaintiffs. Thus, the remaining issues for the tribunal were whether Dr. Lea and the hospital fell below the standard of good medical practice and whether damage resulted.

The plaintiffs offered a letter from Dr. Saul Lerner, a physician practicing obstetrics and gynecology in Worcester and professor of obstetrics and gynecology at the University of Massachusetts Medical Center. In the course of the letter, Dr. Lerner detailed the requirements of good medical practice in a case of pregnancy-induced hypertension and intrauterine growth retardation, including prompt diagnosis, fetal assessment, early intervention, and heightened alertness to the warning signs of fetal stress at delivery, and he specified how the defendants failed to meet those requirements.

In his letter, Dr. Lerner concluded that the "baby was in danger all of the last month of the pregnancy . . . [and that the] baby was further compromised by the failure of staff and physician to recognize the significance of the ominous fetal monitoring patterns being displayed immediately following admission to the hospital. This delay in rescuing the fetus from its dangerous predicament probably contributed to the damage to this baby's brain."

The defendants attack Dr. Lerner's letter on several grounds. They make much of the word "probably" in the last sentence of Dr. Lerner's letter, asserting that it does not sufficiently support the allegation of a causal link between the malpractice and the injury. A medical expert's assessment of a "probable" causal link between an alleged negligent act and an alleged injury is sufficient basis for consideration by a trier of fact. Berardi v. Menicks, 340 Mass. 396, 402 (1960). The defendants assert that Dr. Lerner's opinion is based on surmise and conjecture. We do not agree. Doctor Lerner's opinion

---

n.4. Its function is limited to the determination of the sufficiency of the plaintiff's offer of proof, if that offer can be substantiated at trial, and does not include an assessment of the credibility of potential witnesses.

6. The letter was accompanied by a four and one-half page document detailing Dr. Lerner's qualifications and expertise in the field of obstetrics.

7. The report from Dr. Feldman merely recited the condition of Richard E. Blood, Jr., at the time of the hearing.

VII. Reform Movements in the Malpractice Field   451

is based on the medical information in the records of Dr. Lea and Emerson Hospital. Doctor Lerner's opinion is not mere "speculation," but rather an opinion based on records before the tribunal. See Girard v. Crawford, 13 Mass. App. Ct. 916 (1982). The defendants suggest that, in light of Dr. Lerner's expertise, he held the defendants to too high a standard. That argument goes to the weight of the evidence, not to its sufficiency.

The documents offered by the plaintiffs, taken in the light most favorable to them, and with all permissible inferences, are sufficient to permit a reasonable fact finder to find that the defendants' acts or omissions caused the injury to the plaintiffs. The tribunal's decision in favor of the defendants therefore is in error.

The composition of the tribunal. In view of our decision on the sufficiency of the plaintiffs' offer of proof, we need not pass on the composition of the tribunal. Nevertheless, because the issue has been fully argued, we express our opinion. . . .

General Laws c. 231, §60B, requires that the medical member of the tribunal be chosen from a list which "consist[s] only of physicians who practice medicine outside the county where the defendant practices or resides or if the defendant is a medical institution . . . outside the county where said institution . . . is located." The plaintiffs assert that the medical member of the tribunal convened in their case practices in Middlesex County as does Dr. Lea. Emerson Hospital is located in Middlesex County. The plaintiffs claim that the tribunal therefore lacked "jurisdiction" to hear this matter. We do not agree.

The statute requires a physician member on the tribunal so that he or she may lend expertise in medical matters and assist in screening out nonmeritorious claims. See Paro v. Longwood Hosp., 373 Mass. 645, 657 (1977). The physician member's place of practice or residence does not affect his or her expertise or the ability of the tribunal to fulfil its function of screening out nonmeritorious claims. "Jurisdiction concerns and defines the power of courts, encompassing the power to inquire into facts, apply the law, make decisions, and declare judgment." Police Comm'r of Boston v. Municipal Court of the Dorchester Dist., 374 Mass. 640, 662 (1978). In our view, the geographical area in which the physician member of the panel resides or practices is more akin to venue than to jurisdiction. Venue, of course, may be waived. Paige v. Sinclair, 237 Mass. 482, 484 (1921).

The plaintiffs, who knew of the physician member's identity before the hearing date, failed to object to the composition of the tribunal prior to the hearing. Absent an objection, the place of residence or place of practice of the physician member is not "sufficient ground to deny the existence of a jurisdiction which was intended by the Legislature to be given." Commonwealth v. New York Cent. & H.R.R.R., 206 Mass. 417, 428 (1910). Therefore, we deem the plaintiffs' failure to note their objection in a timely fashion a waiver of their objection. The judge correctly denied the motion to strike the tribunal's determination on the ground of "jurisdiction."

Conclusion. The judgment dismissing the plaintiffs' individual claims is vacated. The matter is remanded to the Superior Court, where the tribunal's decision is to be struck, and, in substitution therefor, a determination shall be entered that the offer of proof by the plaintiffs is sufficient to raise a legitimate question of liability appropriate for judicial inquiry.

So ordered.

NOTES

Practical Issues in Handling of Arbitration, Screening Panel Systems, Claims and Loss Control, and Malpractice Prevention Programs

1. A great deal happened behind the scenes in the health care system as a result of the malpractice insurance crisis of the mid-1970s. Because of the withdrawal of many private insurers from the field, and greatly increased premium rates by those companies that stayed, a number of large hospital groups and medical centers reluctantly moved to self-insurance plans or organized their own "captive" insurance companies, often located in jurisdictions outside the United States. These moves saved hundreds of thousands of dollars in premium costs for many health care systems and hospitals that, prior to 1975, had relatively low levels of malpractice claims.

2. As a result of moving to self-insurance, many health care systems, especially HMOs and medical groups with prepaid health plans, installed alternative dispute resolution procedures and other more efficient claims handling programs. At that time, the greatest amount of experience with the use of arbitration as a built-in feature of an HMO plan was to be found in California. Some HMOs in California had made arbitration available for subscribers for over two decades. See a study done in these years of HMO practices in California and in other parts of the country: Curran & Mosely, The Malpractice Experience of Health Maintenance Organizations, 70 N.W.U.L. Rev. 69 (1975).

3. As the landmark opinion in the *Madden* case indicates, California's largest HMO, the Kaiser Foundation, had moved to installing arbitration as a required feature of its prepaid health plan. Some California hospitals also later installed such provisions in their admission forms. Most of the programs in the United States for binding arbitration of medical malpractice involve contractual agreements with health care program subscribers. Court challenges to these agreements

VII. Reform Movements in the Malpractice Field   453

have been made in other states. See Guardano v. Long Is. Plastic Surg. Group, 607 F. Supp. 136 (E.D.N.Y. 1982); Morris v. Metriyakool, 344 N.W.2d 736 (Mich. 1984); Miner v. Walden, 101 Misc. 2d 814, 422 N.Y.S.2d 335 (1979). See generally Henderson, Contractual Problems in Enforcement of Agreements to Arbitrate Medical Malpractice, 58 Va. L. Rev. 947 (1972).

4. Arbitration plans have been a common feature of statutory reforms in medical malpractice all during the 1970s and 1980s. See the recently enacted arbitration system in Florida described at 397 of this chapter. The constitutionality of the most widely known statutory system was upheld in an important decision by the Supreme Court of Michigan. See Morris v. Metriyakool, supra, note 3 above. In Michigan, unlike other states, the legislation *requires* hospitals to offer a voluntary arbitration procedure to all admitted patients. For recent reviews of the practical application of arbitration in the malpractice field, see Terry, The Technical and Conceptual Flaws in Medical Malpractice Arbitration, 30 St. L.U.L.J. 571 (1986); Saunders, The Quest for Balance: Public Policy and Due Process in Medical Malpractice Arbitration Agreements, 23 Harv. J. Legis. 267 (1986).

5. The adoption of screening panel systems to eliminate "frivolous" or otherwise nonmeritorious medical malpractice claims has, along with arbitration, been the most frequently installed program of alternative dispute resolution. The screening panels, since they get the parties together for an early review of the claim, are quite useful in encouraging settlement. They are also used, like other pretrial conference techniques, to sort out the parties and to eliminate the indiscriminate joining of parties as defendants who have had no relationship to the matter or no legal responsibility for the patient's care. The *Blood* case from Massachusetts illustrates issues in the practical operation of a claims-screening system. In the earlier years of its operation, the defendants won dismissal in the great majority of reviews by the tribunals. In later years, however, as plaintiffs' counsel learned how to use the system, the plaintiffs began to receive larger numbers of meritorious findings to the point that at present the majority of findings by the Massachusetts screening tribunals are favorable to plaintiffs. As a practical matter, as the *Blood* case indicates, the plaintiff must produce at least one credible expert opinion that the defendant or defendants breached the applicable standard of care. For reviews of experience in other states, see White, Are the New State Malpractice Laws Working to Protect You?, 8 Leg. Aspects Med. Prac. 40 (1980). See also Comment, Constitutional Challenges to Medical Malpractice Boards, 46 Tenn. L. Rev. 607 (1979). For a review of practice issues in the New Jersey system, see Vasily v. Cole, 413 A.2d 954 (N.J. Super. 1980).

6. Some states, notably California and Florida, have utilized other

methods to discourage nonmeritorious malpractice claims. Both states have installed a mandated certification by the plaintiff's counsel that the claim has been thoroughly investigated and at least one qualified expert medical evaluation has been obtained that agrees with the contention that negligence of a health care provider has caused the plaintiff's injury. See Cal. Civ. Code §411.30; Fla. Stat. §455.242. Does such a requirement eliminate the need for a screening panel mechanism?

7. Another of the important results of the movement to self-insurance has been the establishment in health care organizations, hospital chains, and individual hospitals of internally operated malpractice claims handling loss control and patient risk prevention. These functions are usually grouped together in what are called "risk management programs." These programs work closely with health care quality assurance programs and patient representative or advocacy programs. There was very little activity in this field before the malpractice insurance crisis of 1975. Over the years since that time, most health care institutions have formed such programs. They are now required, along with quality assurance, by the health care institutional accrediting bodies. Risk management systems are required by statute in several states. There is a professional organization of risk managers, the American Society of Healthcare Risk Managers, an affiliate of the American Hospital Association. There are some useful texts in the field; see J. Orlikoff & A. Vanagunas, Malpractice Prevention and Liability Control for Hospitals (1988); G. Kraus, Health Care Risk Management (1986); G. Troyer & S. Salman, Handbook of Health Care Risk Management (1985); E. Richards & K. Rathbunn, Medical Risk Management (1983); G. Brown, Risk Management for Hospitals: A Practical Approach (1979); Risk Management Manual: A Guide to Safety, Loss Control, and Malpractice Prevention for Hospitals, Fed. Amer. Hospitals (1977). For a description of some of the basic philosophies and practices of risk management programs, see Brenner & Gerken supra 313.

CHAPTER 6

Provider and Patient Access to the Health Care Delivery System

I. PROVIDERS' RIGHTS TO PRACTICE

A. Physician Licensure and Freedom of Practice

Evans v. Hoyme
105 N.W.2d 71 (S.D. 1960)

RENTTO, J. This proceeding was brought to enjoin the defendant, Ellis Hoyme, a reflexologist residing in Big Stone City, from holding himself out as qualified to engage in the diagnosis and treatment of human ills and from engaging in or offering to engage in their treatment. The trial court granted the injunction and he appeals from the judgment.

Hoyme had lived in Big Stone City about two and a half years before the trial of this matter. During that time he had treated some 350 to 400 people administering close to 10,000 treatments in all. Briefly stated, the practice of reflexology as disclosed by the record, is based on the theory that the human body has defined nerve zones and that the nerves from these zones have their endings in designated areas of the feet. Those who follow this practice claim that an ailment involving one of the nerve zones can be relieved by rubbing that area of the feet where the nerve endings from the affected zone are concentrated. These are known as reflex areas. It is their claim that the treatment improves the circulation of the blood to the ailing zone by destroying congestive deposits of calcium which have formed in its reflex areas.

The statute on which this proceeding is based . . . says that:

> No person shall in any manner engage in, offer to engage in, or hold himself out as qualified to engage in the diagnosis or treatment of any human ill, unless such person is the holder of a legal and unrevoked license or certificate issued under the laws of South Dakota authorizing such person to practice the healing art. . . .

There is no provision in our law for the certification or licensing of reflexologists. To qualify as such Hoyme studied a few books, pamphlets and charts concerning it and on a few occasions observed others practice it. . . .

455

In applying this statute we must honor these definitions which the legislature has provided in the act in question:

> "Human ill" shall include any human disease, ailment, deformity, injury or unhealthy or abnormal physical or mental condition of any nature;
>
> "Diagnosis" shall include the use professionally of any means for the discovery, recognition or determination of character of any human ill;
>
> "Treatment" shall include the use of drugs, surgery, including appliances, manual or mechanical means, or any other means of any nature whatsoever, for the cure, relief, palliation, adjustment or correction of any human ill as defined herein. . . .

Concerning the activities of Hoyme the trial court found as follows:

IV

For some 2 (two) years last past, the defendant has maintained an office on Main Street in Big Stone City, South Dakota. This office apparently consisted of one room divided by a curtain across it. The front part was a waiting room, and behind the curtain was a reclining chair for the customers and a stool for the defendant. There [were] no signs in or about the office.

V

[T]he usual and customary procedure was to ask the patient what troubled the particular customer, and from such customer's own report or opinion, the defendant learned what ailment the person claimed to have. After learning what the customer thought ailed him, the defendant usually said: "I might be able to help you, I have helped others." . . .

VIII

The customers of the defendant were, in no manner misled, it was patently apparent to each that the defendant limited his treatment to kneading and massaging the customer's feet below the ankle bones. . . . There is no proof what-so-ever that the defendant claimed to be a physician or surgeon or publicly professed to assume the duties of a physician or surgeon, nor that he prescribed or furnished medicine for any human ailment, or treated any human ailment by surgery, or attempted to do either of such things. . . .

On this factual basis the court concluded "That the defendant, Ellis Hoyme, has held himself out as qualified to engage in the diagnosis and treatment of human ills and did engage in and offer to engage in the treatment of human ills without being the holder of a legal and unrevoked license . . . to practice any healing art. . . ."

The ailments of which the witnesses complained to Hoyme included an injured shoulder, stomach trouble, foot trouble, nervousness, heart trouble, kidney stones and arthritis. Clearly, these are included in the term human ills as used in this act. . . . We think it follows that in administering to these people as the court found he did, he was engaged in the treatment of human ills within the meaning and purpose of this statute. . . .

Affirmed.

O'Faolain, Law Beyond the Grasp of Ordinary Mortals*
The Irish Times, Aug. 19, 1986

While all the rest of us were gathering seaweed and watching our cows and giving the baby a bottle, smart men in towns organised themselves into self-protecting associations, called the professions. That is why you can't go into a chain store to buy a pair of reading glasses — the opticians have the business of you and your spectacles all sewn up.

That is why you have to go to a doctor, and pay him money, and then to the chemist, and pay him money, if you want something to get rid of your cough — from time immemorial the bodies of the populace have been supporting at least those two professions.

You cannot, just because you are a brilliant natural teacher, open a school. You can't be a freelance midwife, whatever your gifts. Once, years and years ago and lost in the mist of time, you could do all those things. But that was before man realised that the best way to protect his income was to build a mystique around certain functions.

The first thing you do is set up a group of your fellow-functionaries to decide on entry to your profession, thus limiting it to those who can jump through all the hoops. Then you design the hoops so that only people of your own background can jump them. Then you put letters after the names of the hoop-jumpers. Then you get a headquarters, with a president and a committee and over time you build up as much pomp as you can get away with, so as to impress outsiders with your importance.

You fix a scale of fees. You set up a system for throwing people out — this is known as keeping up the standards of your profession. And you're away. For the rest of your life you can go to dress-dances with your peers, secure in the knowledge that you control access to something that other people need — education, health, medicine or — above all — justice. . . .

To us, any contact with the law is experience, that is, it is felt, it is emotional. To lawyers the law is a subject, a field of study. The gap between subjectivity and objectivity means the client and the

* Nuala O'Faolain is a columnist with The Irish Times.
Reprinted with permission.

lawyer don't understand each other from the start. But the gap can be to some extent bridged, and I would have thought it was part of the wider duty of lawyers to the society in which they live, to grasp every means of educating us.

Unfortunately, lawyers don't remember, if they ever knew, what it is like to be just once-in-a-lifetime in a court, not knowing why your case is going this way or that, helpless, as the professionals work it all out. The Bar Council isn't in the business of writing pamphlets, sending speakers to schools, or using the mass media to demystify as much as they can. Why should they? They're doing fine as they are. Anyway, at heart they think it is too mysterious to demystify.

In this they are succumbing to their own myth. Doctors are much the same. Doctors don't really believe that the rest of us need to know or are capable of understanding what it is they do. They haven't the time, anyway, to sit down with patients and explain why, how and for what purpose they're about to cut you open. They haven't time to hang about just to explain that your aged mother's medication has been changed and that's why she suddenly doesn't recognise you.

This leads to the blinding realisation that if there were more doctors, more consultants, of course each one wouldn't be so busy. They would have time to have as complete a relationship as possible with each patient. But if there were that many doctors they all couldn't be rich! They'd merely make a living. Similarly, if there were enough barristers for each to care about each client, if they weren't double-booked into another court, or due at another consultation, then there would be so many barristers that they'd be poor too! And you can't have that.

The whole point of a profession is to keep the value of the expertise as high as possible, as difficult to acquire as possible, and as remote from common understanding as possible. So successfully have the professions pulled this off, that people think it is human nature that doctors and barristers should have money, and be treated with far greater deference than, say, food-producers are, or child-rearers, or policemen.

Of course, it is felt to be bad manners to mention these things.

California Board of Medical Quality Assurance, Proposal for Revision of Section 2052 of the Medical Practice Act*
3-5, 8-9 (1982)

The following report is the result of over two years of study by the Board of Medical Quality Assurance on the impact of the current

* Editors' Note: This statute reads: "Any person who practices . . . any system

I. Providers' Rights to Practice   459

language of Section 2052 of the Business and Professions Code. This section defines the practice of medicine, giving physicians exclusive right to practice all forms of diagnosis and treatment of all physical and mental conditions. Although the section exempts other licensed health professions from this exclusive control of health care in limited ways, it is unlawful for an unlicensed person to offer or provide health care of any sort.

Because section 2052 is so all-encompassing, other health occupations must seek legislative exemptions to add to their scopes of practice. As health care science and technology expand, and as lower-level occupations assume more and more complex tasks, there has been an increasing awareness by many that the existing system of regulation is inflexible and cumbersome. In addition, there is a growing movement among consumers to seek alternative types and sources of care which generally are not available from physicians and other licensed professions and occupations. . . .

As in every other state in the nation, California law has long identified a specific set of activities as constituting the practice of medicine, and has maintained standards for entitlement to practice those activities in the law. [T]he statute, commonly known as the Medical Practices Act, . . . assumes that certain activities are so inherently dangerous to the public health that only individuals who have met high standards of education and training can safely do them. Few would disagree with these points.

However, certain other implicit assumptions forming the basis for the present system of physician licensure may not be as readily accepted. Among these are the following:

1. That *all* activities which can be done by physicians under current law are necessarily threatening to public health, safety or welfare and require regulation by the state.
2. That only physicians are competent to perform those activities.
3. That all physicians are competent to perform all activities which the law permits.
4. That only by licensing physicians and other health practitioners can the public be protected.
5. That licensure does indeed assure the public of the competence of licensed practitioners to practice safely and effectively.

---

or mode of treating the sick or afflicted in this state or who diagnoses, treats, operates for or prescribes for any ailment, blemish, deformity, disease, disfigurement, disorder, injury or other physical or mental condition of any person without a medical license is guilty of a misdemeanor."

The first of these assumptions (that everything subsumed under the current definition of the practice of medicine is inherently dangerous) is patently illogical. The specific language of Section 2052 of the Business and Professions Code includes the following phrases: "*Any* person who practices . . . *any* system or mode of treating . . . *any* ailment, blemish, deformity, disease, disfigurement, disorder, injury, or other physical or mental condition of *any* person . . ." (emphasis added). In reality, the range of activities which can be shown to pose real or potential threat to the public health and safety is less broad than the Medical Practices Act defines.

The Board of Medical Quality Assurance concluded in June, 1982 that there are four major activity groups which are of such high potential public hazard that they require stringent legal controls. These include surgery and penetration of the human skin and tissues; determining the need for and using ionizing radiation; prescribing dangerous drugs; and instrumentation of bodily orifices beyond the mouth, anus and vagina. . . .

This leads to the second questionable assumption: that only physicians are competent to practice the broad range of activities currently subsumed as the practice of medicine. There is no question that medical education in the present century has achieved an admirable level of excellence. Likewise, no one would seriously question that physicians are the most capable of making the most complex decisions about health care. On the other hand, there are those who question whether the majority of decisions about common health related conditions requires the level of education, skill and judgement that a physician brings to decision making. Clearly there are many "medical" decisions that the average layperson can make: minor cuts and scrapes should be washed; ice reduces pain and swelling of a minor bruise, etc.

The third assumption is that all physicians are competent to perform all the activities which the law permits. This assumption is arrived at inductively by noting that physicians are licensed generically, rather than by specialty, and that the law does not specify that only certain physicians may perform certain activities. In fact, medical science has become so complex and there are so many formal and informal controls on practice no physician is able to do all things the law allows. Hospitals, insurers, peer review organizations, specialty boards, and individual ethics all contribute to assuring that physicians practice within the bounds of their areas of competence, but the law does not require them to do so.

The case for the fourth assumption, that licensure is necessary to protect the public, requires more complex analysis. Throughout the past century a system of formal and informal mechanisms has emerged for assuring the competence of practitioners of healing arts. These mechanisms include the development of widespread standards for practitioner education, including private and public organizations which accredit educational institutions. . . . Once a practitioner has completed educational requirements and passed an examination, there are still other mechanisms which contribute to assuring competence and public safety. Health care facilities establish high standards for practitioners to gain staff privileges. Malpractice insurers develop complex actuarial data on which to base the rates they charge for coverage of practitioners. National, state and local professional associations promulgate codes of ethics and standards of practice for their members. Internalized ethical standards and the spectre of public or professional notoriety further serve to minimize substandard care. Finally, the self-adjusting nature of market economics may provide certain assurances that the flagrantly incompetent will not remain in practice for long.

None of these mechanisms provides any guarantee that the marginally competent will be prevented from practicing. Unfortunately, as will be shown later, neither does licensure. It can be argued that most of the mechanisms which contribute to assuring initial and continued competence of health practitioners would continue to operate in the absence of licensure. It also can be argued that licensure does not significantly add to the efficacy of those mechanisms. This, then, leads to the fifth assumption upon which the present statute rests, and with which some may argue: that licensure assures the competence of practitioners.

While licensure ratifies the judgements implicit in the successful completion of professional education and passing a comprehensive examination, it does not add any significant assurances of competence to these mechanisms. What licensure *does* add is a means to take legal action against those who practice incompetently or unethically in spite of their success in surmounting the obstacles to entry into practice. While California leads the nation in disciplining physicians, only a small fraction of bad practice ever leads to disciplinary action. . . .

Historically, the foremost advocates of licensure have been the members of health professions themselves, not the citizens they serve. It has been said that the reasons for state regulation have had less to do with meeting the goals and objectives described above, than with being responsive to the aspirations of the professional associations. While the professional associations used public protection to justify the need for licensure, the more immediate motivations appear to have been gaining control of health care delivery, eliminating competition, restricting supply, acquiring the mantle of orthodoxy and assuring desirable levels of reimbursement. . . .

Seen from the consumer's perspective, licensure also has meant that choices have been limited to selecting between a small number of primary practitioners: physicians, osteopaths, chiropractors and in a few states, naturopaths and homeopaths. Most other licensed professions work under the direction or supervision of physicians and rarely have independent access to patients. The boundaries of orthodox medicine are formally defined, in part, by the mechanisms of licensure: scope of practice, education requirements and standards of practice. Even if a consumer cannot find a licensed practitioner who will provide certain techniques, a nonphysician is prevented from offering them. For example, consumers seeking access to homebirth or midwives, orthomolecular medicine, therapeutic massage and other "unorthodox" health practices generally have been forced to seek out unlicensed practitioners. . . .

The effect of this regulatory approach is to prevent people from employing unlicensed practitioners to provide services which they may wish to receive, and which they believe may help them. The state assumes the role of a benevolent, but nonetheless paternalistic, gatekeeper for access to practitioners and techniques. . . .

State governments use a number of methods to regulate health occupations. These include licensure, certification, title licensure and registration. Each term has a different meaning in various states, but for the purpose of this paper, the definitions . . . are: Licensure: comprises use of educational, experience and other requirements, plus a state examination to determine competence, and specifies a scope of practice exclusive to the group. Certification: may or may not include a state exam, education or experience standards; often relies on examinations or other standards established by private agencies or associations, which the state accepts and endorses. May or may not include an exclusive scope of practice. Title licensure: permits anyone to practice an activity or scope of practice, but only licensed individuals may use a specific title. Registration: may impose few or no entry requirements to practice. Often consists of nothing more than maintaining a list of individuals who are "holding themselves out" as practicing a specified occupation.

The HEW . . . urges states to impose the least restrictive level of credentialing which is consistent with the potential hazardousness of an occupation. For example, if an occupation such as Physical Therapy Aide works only under direct supervision, does not prescribe, diagnose or do invasive procedures, it is inappropriate to require them to be licensed. If regulation is needed at all, registration probably would provide adequate public protection by limiting scope of practice, setting standards for supervision, and providing a legal basis for disciplining aides who exceed their limits. . . .

Butler, State Keeping Close Tabs on Alternative Healers
San Francisco Chronicle, Oct. 7, 1985, at 4

Tessy Elman, a nutritionist and "energy balancer," is scheduled to go on trial this morning . . . for the unlicensed practice of medicine. . . . In September 1984, an undercover investigator . . . visited Elman at the Nutritional Balancing Center offices in downtown Palo Alto, complaining of being sluggish and out-of-balance. Using a system based on ancient Chinese medicine and applied kinesiology, Elman conducted "muscle testing" by holding the investigator's arm and asking the woman to press against the pressure. To Elman, the tests revealed "subtle energies of the body," and she recommended mineral supplements and vitamins. . . .

"This lady seems like a snake oil salesman to me," said Deputy District Attorney John Schon, who will prosecute the case. . . . "This is a bunch of malarkey that people are paying good money for. The gullible public needs protection." . . .

"I don't practice medicine. I do nutritional counseling and energy balancing," said Elman, whose only previous legal difficulty was for gathering crayfish without a permit. "I'm not trying to do what a doctor does. My goal is not to make people believe in this. It's to provide a service to people who want it." . . .

In November 1983, a medical board staff report recommended decriminalizing most of the alternative practitioners by narrowing the definition of medical practice to include only diagnosis, surgery, the use of drugs and X-rays and penetration of the body. "We drafted legislation and frightened the heck out of organized medicine," Rowland said. "But the legislation was way too controversial for anybody to carry."

NOTES

Entry to the Medical Profession

1. During the 19th century, snake oil salesmen and other quacks roamed the countryside preying on the gullible public with unfounded promises of miracle cures. To eliminate such practices, around the turn of the century every state began to license medical practitioners. The typical Medical Practice Act makes it a criminal offense to practice medicine without a physician's license and establishes the grounds for revocation or suspension of a license. The job of medical licensure and discipline is entrusted to a Board of Medical Examiners, which usually consists predominantly of physicians.

Some alternative practitioners such as osteopaths, chiropractors, and podiatrists, to name a few, have likewise been successful in petitioning the legislature for recognition and protection through professional licensure and self-regulation. As these materials demonstrate, however, this patchwork of licensing provisions does not include a number of other alternative healing arts that consumers evidently desire.

2. The prosecution of energy balancer Tessy Elman resulted in a conviction and small fine. How far can the definition of medical practice be stretched? The various exotic and peripheral ministrations successfully attacked under medical licensure statutes range from the sublime to the absurd. Magnetism, mental suggestion, faith healing, color wave therapy, nutritional advice, reflexology, massage, hypnotism, tattooing, and electrical hair removal all have been held to constitute medical practice. Note, Restrictions on Unorthodox Health Treatment in California, 24 U.C.L.A.L. Rev. 647 (1977); Hall, Institutional Control of Physician Behavior, 137 U. Penn. L. Rev. 431, 453 (1988) (collecting cases). What about friendly advice from the local grocer on what to eat to avoid indigestion and heart burn? Pinkus v. MacMahon, 29 A.2d 885 (N.J. 1943) ("Clearly [the grocer] attempted to diagnose the 'physical condition' of the witnesses and to . . . prescribe for such condition"). See also Stetina v. Medical Licensing Bd., 513 N.E.2d 1234 (Ind. App. 1987) (nutritional advice illegal); Foster v. Georgia Bd. of Chiropractic Examiners, 359 S.E.2d 877 (Ga. 1987) (same). The courts have finally drawn the line at ear piercing and other cosmetic procedures such as hair removal. See Hicks v. Arkansas State Med. Bd., 260 Ark. 31, 537 S.W.2d 794 (1976) (ear piercing "is not as serious as the normal anatomical change wrought by surgery [and] it is not a corrective undertaking").

The licensing laws have been invoked in recent decades to attack the centuries-old tradition of nurse midwives assisting in home birth, a practice that has experienced recent revival in light of the medical establishment's escalated use of surgical and technological intervention in normal hospital deliveries. See Bowland v. Municipal Court, 556 P.2d 1081 (Cal. 1976) (conviction of lay midwives for unlicensed practice of medicine); Note, Regulation of Midwives as Home Birth Attendants, 30 B.C.L. Rev. 477 (1989); Note, Choice in Childbirth: Parents, Lay Midwives, and Statutory Regulation, 30 St. Louis U.L.J. 985 (1986).

3. Do reflexology and the examples cited in the previous note present the same threat to public safety as the forms of quackery that existed at the turn of the century? Was there any confusion in *Evans* and in the California energy-balancer prosecution over who the real doctors were? Not all such cases are as innocuous, however. One recent prosecution of a religious healer found that, by prescribing

I. Providers' Rights to Practice

extended fasts lasting over six weeks, he caused severe and permanent disabilities that, in at least one case, led to a person's death. Board of Med. Quality Assur. v. Andrews, 260 Cal. Rptr. 113 (Cal. App. 1989).

4. Do these cases have a constitutional dimension? Drawing from the Supreme Court's protection in the abortion cases of "the woman's right to receive medical care in accordance with her . . . physician's best judgment," Doe v. Bolton, 410 U.S. 179, 197 (1973), some courts have found that "the decision to obtain or reject medical treatment . . . is protected by the right of privacy." Andrews v. Ballard infra at p.560 (overturning decision of Board of Medical Examiners that acupuncture constitutes the practice of medicine). But see p.565. On the other hand, it is generally conceded that licensing or banning a school of practice is within the state's police power and does not interfere with any right to practice or receive medical treatment. E.g., State v. Hoffman, 733 P.2d 502, 505 & n.4 (Utah 1987); Bowland v. Municipal Court, 556 P.2d 1081 (Cal. 1976); State v. Kuhwald, 389 A.2d 1277, 1281 (Del. 1978). Is it possible to reconcile these cases by distinguishing between the regulation of schools of practice versus individual procedures?

Out of a sensitivity to first amendment rights, state codes often contain explicit exemptions for unorthodox treatment regimens that occur within a religious context (such as Christian Science or Jehovah's Witnesses). E.g., Cal. Health & Safety Code §2063 ("Nothing in this chapter shall be construed so as to . . . interfere in any way with the practice of religion"). A recent California case ruled, however, that this exemption ceases when "the conduct and the treatment goes beyond prayer and reliance on divine intervention." It enjoined the "Religious School of Natural Hygiene" from prescribing extended fasts as a means for curing a variety of physical ailments by ridding the body of toxins. Board of Med. Quality Assurance v. Andrews, 260 Cal. Rptr. 113 (Cal. App. 1989).

5. Over thirty categories of health professionals are licensed in the United States. Council of State Governments, State Regulation of the Health Occupations and Professions (1987). This proliferation of licensing is not limited to the medical professions. "After reviewing the roster of those who must receive official permission to function, a cynic might conclude that virtually the only people who remain unlicensed in at least one of the United States are clergymen and university professors, presumably because they are nowhere taken seriously." Gellhorn, The Abuse of Occupational Licensing, 44 U. Chi. L. Rev. 6 (1976).

The patchwork system of medical licensure creates many interprofessional turf battles. For example, in Connecticut State Medical Society v. Connecticut Board of Examiners of Podiatry, 546 A.2d

830 (Conn. 1988), the physician licensure agency sued the podiatrist licensure agency to establish the monumental proposition that podiatry is restricted to treatment of the foot and therefore does not include ailments of the ankle. See also Bordie v. State Bd. of Med. Examiners, 427 A.2d 104 (N.J. App. 1981) (radiologists v. chiropractors); Washington State Nurses Assoc. v. Board of Med. Examiners, 605 P.2d 1269 (Wash. 1980) (nurses v. doctors); Hill v. Highland Park Gen. Hosp., 263 N.W.2d 362 (Mich. App. 1977) (dentists v. oral surgeons); Paravecchio v. Memorial Hosp., 742 P.2d 1276 (Wy. 1987) (dentists vs. anesthesiologists).

6. Most states require M.D.s to graduate from an AMA accredited medical school (or, for foreign medical graduates, an internship in an AMA approved residency program). As a result, medical licensure essentially cedes to the medical profession control of how many doctors can enter practice, since the AMA can control the size of medical school classes through the accreditation process. M. Friedman, Capitalism and Freedom 149 (1962); Note, The American Medical Association: Power, Purpose, and Politics in Organized Medicine, 63 Yale L.J. 937 (1954).

Allowing the medical profession to control entry into its own market creates the anticompetitive risk that the AMA will act out of economic self-interest to maintain artificial shortages. Barriers of entry into service professions tend automatically to drive up prices by creating a supply shortage because, in contrast with manufacturing industries, the capacity of existing suppliers is inherently limited by the number of hours in the day. See p.500 infra; Rose, Occupational Licensing: A Framework for Analysis, 1979 Ariz. St. U.L.J. 189. Perhaps this explains in part why only in the United States doctors earn six times more than the average worker.

7. The medical profession suffered much criticism during the 1960s for causing physician shortages, particularly in rural areas. Since then, however, shortages have been largely alleviated. Assisted by federal funding, American medical schools have doubled their graduates to 16,000 per year. In addition, liberalized state licensing laws and federal immigration policy have allowed a dramatic growth in foreign medical graduates. Consequently, the number of doctors now stands at about 240 per 100,000 population, in contrast with the 1960s level of 140. Noether, Effect of Government Policy Changes on the Supply of Physicians, 29 J.L. & Econ. 23 (1986).

Rather than shortages, we now hear complaints about a physician "glut." See Harris, How Many Doctors are Enough?, 5 Health Affairs at 73 (Winter 1986); Rose, Who Said We Have Too Many Doctors?, N.Y. Times, June 29, 1986 at F2; Inglehart, The Future Supply of Physicians, 314 New Eng. J. Med. 860 (1986). Whether more doctors will help or hurt turns on one's view of whether competition actually exists in health care markets, a question explored at greater length in Chapter 8.III.A. Perversely, it has been documented that "more doctors per capita means . . . *higher* prices . . . '[b]ecause physicians can and do determine the demand [and prices] for their own services to a considerable extent.' " A. Enthoven, Health Plan 27 (1980). For a contrasting view, see McCarthy, The Competitive Nature of the Primary-Care Physician Services Market, 4 J. Health Econ. 93 (1985). See also Sloan & Feldman, Competition Among Physicians, in Competition in the Health Care Sector: Past, Present and Future (W. Greenberg ed. 1978). See generally Schwartz, Sloan & Mendelson, Why There Will be Little or no Physician Surplus, 318 New Eng. J. Med. 892 (1988); Inglehart, How Many Doctors do We Need?, 254 J.A.M.A. 1785 (1985).

C. Inlander, L. Levin & E. Weiner, Medicine on Trial*
18-19 (1988)

This book provides what amounts to a profound indictment of many aspects of the way medicine is practiced in America, and of many of those who practice it. We show the range and depth of medical mistakes in this country, and our documentation provides evidence that most medical mistakes are rooted in individual incompetence, misplaced emphasis, poor skills, greed, and the failure of the medical profession to acknowledge its weaknesses and correct them. We demonstrate how the medical profession has systematically allowed known incompetents to practice, making mistake upon mistake, threatening life upon life.

Our data were studiously and carefully accumulated; . . . for the most part, the evidence we present comes from the medical literature itself — from physicians, medical educators, medical researchers, and experts in the field of medicine. We cite studies from the world's most respected medical journals, health publications, and books.

What is appalling to us is that the facts we've found have been available to the profession for years. It's been right in front of their eyes, and yet they did not see. . . . And all the while the experts have gone unheeded, medical consumers have suffered. Unsuspecting consumers have been battered by drunk or doped-up doctors. Their ills have been misdiagnosed by poorly trained physicians. They have had procedures performed on them on the basis of incorrect test

---

* Charles B. Inlander and Ed Weiner are President and Senior Editor, respectively, of the People's Medical Society. Lowell S. Levin is on the faculty of the Yale University School of Medicine.

results. . . . The list of indignities is almost as long as the list of patients.

1 in 250 Malpractice Cases Leads to Doctor's Disciplining
Arizona Republic, Aug. 28, 1985, at B12

Doctors are placed on probation or have their licenses revoked or suspended in no more than one of every 250 cases of medical malpractice, a study by a Ralph Nader-founded health group estimated Tuesday. The study by the Public Citizen Health Research Group found that state medical boards took such disciplinary action against 563 physicians in 1983, a year when there were up to an estimated 310,000 cases of medical malpractice.

"The bottom line is that there is frightfully little discipline of doctors in this country in comparison with the number that need to be disciplined," said Dr. Sidney Wolfe, director of the private group, which tracks health concerns. "Every so often, we hear the American Medical Association say we should discipline doctors, but they haven't pushed for any significant reforms," Wolfe said. "They are more interested in protecting doctors from lawsuits and big insurance premiums than protecting the public from malpractice."

Lambert, New York Panel Urges Re-Testing of All Physicians
N.Y. Times, Feb. 26, 1988, at 1

All 50,000 physicians in New York State would have to be reexamined to retain their licenses under a plan unanimously agreed on by a state medical panel formed by Governor Cuomo. If the new regulatory system is adopted, it would make New York the first state to monitor and discipline all physicians under its jurisdiction on a regular basis. Supporters predicted that the plan, disclosed yesterday, would create a national trend of reviewing physicians to raise the quality of medical care, prevent malpractice and bolster public confidence in the profession. The American Medical Association has expressed serious reservations about the plan, questioning whether recertification would improve medical care.

The move to review physicians results from what medical critics say is the profession's lack of self-policing and the reluctance of physicians to criticize or act against deficient colleagues. . . . Under the proposal, physicians seeking to renew their licenses every nine years would be offered a choice of taking an examination, undergoing a peer review or having their patient records evaluated. The requirement could also be met by recertification from a medical specialty board. . . . Under the current system, physicians file a pro forma registration every three years. They are subject to government review only if a complaint is lodged with the state's Office of Professional Medical Conduct.

NOTES

Exit from the Medical Profession

1. Medical Practice Acts typically authorize disciplinary action for "unprofessional conduct," which is defined to include a number of specific actions such as patient abandonment, incapacitating substance abuse, inappropriate prescriptions, fee splitting, and aiding unlicensed persons in the practice of medicine. In addition, these acts usually contain a general proscription of "unethical" and "incompetent" practice. See 14 State Health Legislation Report 1 (1986) (survey of physician discipline statutes).

2. The Medical Practice Acts' reference to professional ethics is usually taken as incorporating the AMA's Principles of Medical Ethics as grounds for discipline. These ethical principles in the past have banned advertising, corporate practice, and association with "unscientific" practitioners such as chiropractors. Thus, Boards of Medical Examiners have been accused of using their authority more to police the economics and organization of medical practice than for patient welfare. While the antitrust laws have required the AMA to cease from using *private* ethics codes to encourage such practices (see pp.502 and 510-511), individual Boards of Medical Examiners apparently remain free to enforce the *legal codifications* of these ethical restraints, within the bounds of the constitution. (One constitutional restraint, the right to free speech, limits the ability to ban advertising. Note, 50 U. Mo. K.C.L. Rev. 82 (1981).)

3. Most Boards of Medical Examiners lack adequate staff to conduct extensive investigations of unprofessional conduct. Therefore, they have tended to rely on local medical societies to report and document disciplinary cases. See generally R. Derbyshire, Medical Licensure and Discipline in the United States (1969); Cohen, Professional Licensure, Organizational Behavior, and the Public Interest, 51 Milbank Mem. Fund Q. 73 (1973). What is the justification for entrusting medical discipline to the profession itself? Are there any conceivable alternatives to this structure? See S. Gross, of Foxes and Hen Houses: Licensing and the Health Professions (1984).

4. For documentation of laxness in medical discipline, see Derbyshire, Medical Ethics and Discipline, 228 J.A.M.A. 59 (1974). There

has been some recent improvement on this score, however. Kusserow, Handley & Yessian, An Overview of State Medical Discipline, 257 J.A.M.A. 820 (1987).

While states have not undertaken the wholesale reform of medical licensing suggested by the California report or the New York Times article, several have made important improvements prompted by the medical malpractice crisis. Illustrative are the District of Columbia Health Arts Practice Reform Act of 1976, D.C. Code §§2-123, 2-124 and a recent reform of Maryland's Board of Physician Quality Assurance, Md. Code Ann. art. 14 §200, which provide for a broader representation of community interests among Board members and establish more rigorous investigative systems. See Jost, The Necessary and Proper Role of Regulation to Assure the Quality of Health Care, 25 Hous. L. Rev. 525 & n.331 (1988) (discussing consumer members on state medical boards).

5. Much of the law relating to medical discipline is procedural. Courts have been sensitive to protecting physicians' due process rights because of the severe consequence of license revocation. For a recent example, see In re Magee, 362 S.E.2d 564 (N.C. App. 1987) (due process violated by inadequate notice of grounds for refusing license reinstatement). One frequently-litigated issue has been bias among board members. In Withrow v. Larkin, 421 U.S. 35 (1975), the Court held that there is no constitutional bar to a board of medical examiners conducting a license revocation hearing after it had previously conducted the investigation into the initial charge. However, Gibson v. Berryhill, 411 U.S. 564 (1973) disqualified an entire board of optometry composed solely of optometrists in independent practice, as being per se biased against optometrists who work for chain stores. Nevertheless, the Court upheld as facially valid a similar arrangement that gave *majority* membership to independent optometrists. Friedman v. Rogers, 440 U.S. 1 (1979). For further reading on this and other aspects of medical licensure and discipline, see F. Grad & N. Marti, Physicians' Licensure and Discipline (1979) (comprehensive analysis and assessment of statutes, cases, and regulations); Forgotson, Roemer & Newman, Licensure of Physicians, 1967 Wash. U.L.Q. 249 (same); 7 L. & Human Behavior Nos. 2/3, Sept. 1983 (well-regarded symposium on professional regulation, with a focus on medicine); Gaumer, Regulating Health Professionals: A Review of the Empirical Literature, 62 Milbank Mem. Fund Q. 380 (1984); Vodicka, Medical Discipline, Parts I & II, 233 J.A.M.A. 1106, 1427 (1975); Parts III-V, 234 J.A.M.A. 327, 642, 1062 (1975); Parts VI, VII, 235 J.A.M.A. 302, 651, 1051 (1976) (extensive summary of case law); D. Young, The Rule of Experts: Occupational Licensing in America (1987) (comprehensive review of the literature on the economics of occupational licensing).

I. Providers' Rights to Practice

B. Medical Staff Disputes and Peer Review — State Law

Greisman v. Newcomb Hospital
192 A.2d 817 (N.J. 1963)

In 1958, the plaintiff graduated from the Philadelphia College of Osteopathy with the degree of doctor of osteopathy. He served an internship, took the full medical boards in New York, and was given an unqualified license to practice medicine and surgery in that state. Thereafter, he was admitted to practice in Michigan, Florida and New Jersey. His New Jersey admission by the State Board of Medical Examiners constituted an unrestricted license to practice medicine and surgery within the borders of our State. See N.J.S.A. 45:9 — 11 et seq.; Falcone v. Middlesex Co. Medical Soc., 34 N.J. 582, 170 A.2d 791 (1961). In July 1959, he began the general practice of medicine in the City of Vineland and, in November 1959, he opened an office in Newfield which is in the Vineland metropolitan area. Until January 1962 he also engaged in the practice of medicine from his home in Vineland. He is the only licensed physician in Newfield, is the plant physician for a Newfield company engaged in heavy industrial work and for an additional company engaged in the making of glassware, and is the school physician for Newfield's public school as well as for a Catholic school in the same community. He states that he is the only osteopathic physician fully licensed to practice general medicine and surgery in the metropolitan Vineland area which is said to have a population approximating 100,000; the defendants state that there is another osteopathic physician practicing in Vineland but the suggested variance is of no real significance here.

In 1961, the plaintiff sought to file an application for admission to the courtesy staff of the Newcomb Hospital which is located in Vineland about a mile from his home. The hospital was incorporated in 1921, is operated as a general hospital, and is the only hospital in the Vineland metropolitan area. Its certificate of incorporation sets forth the purposes for which it was formed including, first, the care of sick and injured persons residing in Vineland, second, the care of sick and injured persons residing in the vicinity of Vineland, and thereafter the care of such "other sick or injured persons as the facilities of the hospital will permit." The hospital is a nonprofit corporation and its governing body is a Board of Trustees consisting of not less than 15 members. It solicits and receives funds annually in the form of charitable contributions and has received funds from the Ford Foundation. Several years ago it constructed a new building, the cost being borne almost entirely by public subscription. It receives funds from the City of Vineland for the treatment of indigent patients from within the city, and funds from the County of Cumberland for the treatment of indigent patients from other areas in the county. It receives tax exemptions available to nonprofit corporations operated for charitable and like purposes. It is eligible for federal funds under the Hill-Burton Act.

Despite suitable requests, the Newcomb Hospital refused to permit the plaintiff to file any application for admission to its courtesy staff. In taking that course it did not question his personal or professional qualifications nor did it purport to exercise a discretion in the process of administrative screening and selection. It rested entirely on a provision in the hospital bylaws which sets forth that an applicant for membership on the courtesy staff must be a graduate of a medical school approved by the American Medical Association and must be a member of the County Medical Society. The American Medical Association has long rejected schools of osteopathy, though the original supporting reasons have been largely dissipated. See Falcone v. Middlesex Co. Medical Soc., supra, 34 N.J., at p.585, n.1, 170 A.2d at p.793; cf. Report of the Committee for the Study of Relations Between Osteopathy and Medicine, 158 A.M.A.J. 736 (1955); Special Report of the Judicial Council, 177 A.M.A.J. 774 (1961), 178 A.M.A.J. 226 (1961); Report of the Judicial Council, 184 A.M.A.J. 356 (1963). Admittedly, the plaintiff is not a graduate of a medical school approved by the American Medical Association and, because of his schooling, his application to the County Medical Society was never acted upon. The school he graduated from is an accredited school of osteopathy, has been approved as in good standing by the New Jersey State Board of Medical Examiners, and has long given the full traditional medical course as well as osteopathic teaching. . . .

The Law Division found that the Newcomb Hospital did not confine itself to any specialized branch of medicine and had assumed the position and status of the only general hospital open to the public within the convenient accessibility of the inhabitants of the metropolitan area of Vineland, including Newfield; that the plaintiff had suffered economic and other harm because he was not permitted to admit his patients to the hospital or to serve them professionally once they were admitted, or to use the emergency room services of the hospital; that his patients suffered restriction in their choice of physicians or hospital facilities because of the plaintiff's inability to attend them professionally at the hospital, and that this was not minimized by the fact that the plaintiff was permitted to visit them at the hospital without, however, any opportunity to read their charts or prescribe for them. . . .

The defendants contend that the Newcomb Hospital is a private rather than a public hospital, that it may in its discretion exclude physicians from its medical staff, and that no legal ground exists for judicial interference with its refusal to consider the plaintiff's application for membership. . . . Broad judicial expressions may, of course, be found to the effect that hospitals such as Newcomb are private in nature and that their staff admission policies are entirely discretionary. They are private in the sense that they are nongovernmental but they are hardly private in other senses. Newcomb is a nonprofit organization dedicated by its certificate of incorporation to the vital public use of serving the sick and injured, its funds are in good measure received from public sources and through public solicitation, and its tax benefits are received because of its nonprofit and nonprivate aspects. It constitutes a virtual monopoly in the area in which it functions and it is in no position to claim immunity from public supervision and control because of its allegedly private nature. Indeed, in the development of the law, activities much less public than the hospital activities of Newcomb, have commonly been subjected to judicial (as well as legislative) supervision and control to the extent necessary to satisfy the felt needs of the times. See Munn v. Illinois, 94 U.S. 113, 24 L.Ed. 77 (1877); German Alliance Ins. Co. v. Lewis, 233 U.S. 389, 34 S. Ct. 612, 58 L. Ed. 1011 (1914); Nebbia v. New York, 291 U.S. 502, 54 S. Ct. 505, 78 L. Ed. 940 (1934).

During the course of history, judges have often applied the common law so as to regulate private businesses and professions for the common good; perhaps the most notable illustration is the duty of serving all comers on reasonable terms which was imposed by the common law on innkeepers, carriers, farriers and the like. See Falcone v. Middlesex Co. Medical Soc., supra, 34 N.J., at p.594; Messenger et al. v. Pennsylvania R.R. Co., 36 N.J.L. 407 (Sup. Ct. 1873), *aff'd*, 37 N.J.L. 531 (E. & A. 1874). In the *Messenger* case Chief Justice Beasley, speaking for the former Supreme Court, noted that a railroad, though a private corporation, is engaged in a "public employment," that it "owes a duty to the community" and that under considerations of public policy it must be held under obligation to serve without discrimination. On appeal, Justice Bedle, speaking for the Court of Errors and Appeals, expressed the view that although railroad corporations are private, they hold their property "as a quasi-public trust," and that as trustees they must conduct their operations in such manner so as to insure to every member of the community the equal enjoyment of the means of transportation.

Implemented by specific legislation, the supervision of private businesses and professions for the public good has gone far beyond the early common law fields. In Munn v. Illinois, supra, a state's imposition of maximum charges for the storage of grain in warehouses was sustained in an opinion which stressed that the private property was devoted "to a public use" and was therefore subject to public regulation (94 U.S., at p.130, 24 L. Ed., at p.86); in German Alliance

Ins. Co. v. Lewis, supra, a state's fixing of fire insurance rates was upheld on the ground that the business of insurance was "so far affected with a public interest" as to justify its regulation (233 U.S., at p.406, 34 S. Ct., at p.617, 58 L. Ed., at p.1020); and in Nebbia v. New York, supra, a state's extensive regulation of its milk industry was upheld in an opinion by Justice Roberts which frankly recognized that there is no closed class or category of businesses affected with a public interest, that the phrase means no more than that an industry, for adequate reason, is subject to control for the public good, and that "upon proper occasion and by appropriate measures the state may regulate a business in any of its aspects" (291 U.S., at pp. 536-537, 54 S. Ct., at p.516, 78 L. Ed., at pp. 956-957). . . .

It is evident that . . . similar policy considerations apply with equal strength and call for a declaration that . . . Dr. Greisman is entitled to have his application evaluated on its own individual merits without regard to the bylaw requirement rejected by the Law Division. His personal and professional qualifications are not in dispute here, he lives in Vineland, has an office in Newfield in the Vineland metropolitan area, has an unrestricted license to practice medicine and surgery, and is engaged in the general practice of medicine. All he seeks, at this juncture, is simply permission to file his application for membership on the courtesy staff of the Newcomb Hospital and have it considered to the end that, if he is passed on favorably in accordance with the hospital's valid bylaws, he and his patients, as such, will have hospital facilities when needed.

The Newcomb Hospital is the only hospital in the Vineland metropolitan area and it is publicly dedicated, primarily to the care of the sick and injured of Vineland and its vicinity and, thereafter to the care of such other persons as may be accommodated. Doctors need hospital facilities and a physician practicing in the metropolitan Vineland area will understandably seek them at the Newcomb Hospital. Furthermore, every patient of his will want the Newcomb Hospital facilities to be readily available. It hardly suffices to say that the patient could enter the hospital under the care of a member of the existing staff, for his personal physician would have no opportunity of participating in his treatment; nor does it suffice to say that there are other hospitals outside the metropolitan Vineland area, for they may be too distant or unsuitable to his needs and desires. All this indicates very pointedly that, while the managing officials may have discretionary powers in the selection of the medical staff, those powers are deeply imbedded in public aspects, and are rightly viewed . . . as fiduciary powers to be exercised reasonably and for the public good.

It must be borne in mind that we are not asked to pass on a discretionary exercise of judgment but only on the validity of the bylaw requirement. Therefore, we need not concern ourselves with any of the larger issues relating to discretionary limits or the general lengths to which a hospital may go in conditioning staff admissions on the approval of outside bodies. Viewed realistically, our proper concern here is whether the hospital had the right to exclude consideration of the plaintiff, solely because he was a doctor of osteopathy and had not been admitted, because of his osteopathic schooling, to his County Medical Society. . . . In this day there should be no hesitancy in rejecting as arbitrary, the stand that a doctor of osteopathy, though fully licensed by State authority and reputably engaged in the general practice of medicine and as the local school and plant physician, is nonetheless automatically, and without individual evaluation, to be considered unfit for staff membership at the only available hospital in the rather populous metropolitan area where he resides and practices. The public interest and considerations of fairness and justness point unerringly away from the hospital's position and we agree fully with the Law Division's judgment rejecting it.

Hospital officials are properly vested with large measures of managing discretion and to the extent that they exert their efforts toward the elevation of hospital standards and higher medical care, they will receive broad judicial support. But they must never lose sight of the fact that the hospitals are operated not for private ends but for the benefit of the public, and that their existence is for the purpose of faithfully furnishing facilities to the members of the medical profession in aid of their service to the public. They must recognize that their powers, particularly those relating to the selection of staff members, are powers in trust which are always to be dealt with as such. While reasonable and constructive exercises of judgment should be honored, courts would indeed be remiss if they declined to intervene where, as here, the powers were invoked at the threshold to preclude an application for staff membership, not because of any lack of individual merit, but for a reason unrelated to sound hospital standards and not in furtherance of the common good.

Affirmed.

NOTES

The Availability of Judicial Review

1. Access to a hospital is essential for most physicians to carry on a practice. Hospitals, on the other hand, are coming under increasing legal and economic pressure to monitor who joins the medical staff. From the intersection of these two competing interests springs a powerful flow of litigation, second only to malpractice in the health care field.

The principal focus of these notes will be the common law fairness theory. However, there are many other causes of action potentially available to excluded physicians. Pursued below in Section I.C. are challenges under the federal antitrust laws. State antitrust statutes and common law unfair competition theories are another hook for the same hat. Under tort law, excluded physicians can allege defamation (e.g., Maimon v. Sisters of the Third Order, 491 N.E.2d 779 (Ill. App. 1986)), civil conspiracy, (Nashville Mem. Hosp. v. Brinkley, 534 S.W. 2d 318 (Tenn. 1976)), or tortious interference with contract; see Hall, Institutional Control of Physician Behavior, 137 U. Penn. L. Rev. 431, 460-462 (1988). Under contract law, courts usually require hospitals to adhere to their bylaws when reviewing the credentials of existing medical staff members. Gianetti v. Norwalk Hosp., 557 A.2d 1249 (Conn. 1989); Berberian v. Lancaster Osteopathic Hosp., 149 A.2d 456 (Pa. 1959). But see Munoz v. Flower Hosp., 507 N.E.2d 360 (Oh. App. 1985). Several states create statutory causes of action. E.g., N.Y. Pub. Health Law §2901-c(1) (McKinney 1985). Finally, civil rights statutes may protect against discrimination based on suspect classifications. E.g., Doe v. St. Joseph's Hosp., 788 F.2d 411 (7th Cir. 1986) (action stated under Title VII); contra, Diggs v. Harris Hosp., 847 F.2d 270 (5th Cir. 1988) (no Title VII action exists where physician is independent contractor). For general surveys, see Groseclose, Hospital Privilege Cases: Braving the Dismal Swamp, 26 S.D.L. Rev. 1 (1981); Hein, Hospital Staff Privileges and the Courts: Practice and Prognosis, 32 Fed. Ins. Counsel Q. 157, 172 (1984); Kessenick, Physicians' Access to the Hospital: An Overview, 14 U. San. Fran. L. Rev. 43, 54 (1979).

2. Care must be taken to distinguish the *common law* fairness theory articulated in *Greisman* from *constitutional* due process and equal protection. While the content of the doctrines may (or may not) be the same, their origins are distinctly different. See Applebaum v. Board of Directors, 163 Cal. Rptr. 831, 836 (Cal. App. 1980). Only public hospitals, that is, those *owned* by state or municipal authorities, are subject to the Constitution; it is well settled that the extensive involvement of private hospitals with public funding and regulation is not sufficient to constitute state action. Blum v. Yaretsky, 457 U.S. 991 (1982).

A constitutional theory that has not succeeded, even at public hospitals, is the *substantive* due process argument that "all licensed physicians have a constitutional right to practice their profession. It is not incumbent on the state to maintain a hospital for the private practice of medicine." Hayman v. City of Galveston, 273 U.S. 414, 417 (1926).

3. The *Greisman* public-facility theory has not won uniform acceptance. The following are a sampling of cases pro and con: Pro

judicial review — Silver v. Castle Mem. Hosp., 497 P.2d 564, *cert. denied*, 409 U.S. 1048 (1972); Bricker v. Sceva Speare Mem. Hosp., 281 A.2d 589 (N.H.), cert. denied, 404 U.S. 995 (1971); Davidson v. Youngstown Hosp. Assn., 250 N.E.2d 892 (Oh. App. 1969). Contra judicial review — Pepple v. Parkview Mem. Hosp., 536 N.E.2d 274 (Ind. 1989); Barrows v. Northwestern Mem. Hosp., 525 N.E.2d 50 (Ill. 1988); Hottentot v. Mid-Maine Med. Cent., 549 A.2d 365 (Me. 1988); Wood v. Hilton Head Hosp., 356 S.E.2d 841 (S.C. 1987); Lakeside Community Hosp. v. Levenson, 710 P.2d 727, 728 (Nev. 1985); Hoffman v. Garden City Hosp., 321 N.W.2d 810 (Mich. App. 1982). See generally Nodzenski, Medical Staff Decisions in Private Hospitals: The Role of Due Process, 18 Loy. U.L.J. 951 (1987); Comment, Medical Staff Membership Decisions: Judicial Intervention, 1985 U. Ill. L. Rev. 473; Note, Judicial Review of Private Hospital Activities, 75 Mich. L. Rev. 445 (1976); Comment, Denial of Hospital Staff Privileges: Hearing and Judicial Review, 56 Iowa L. Rev. 1341 (1971); Annot., Exclusion of or Discrimination Against Physician or Surgeon by Hospital, 37 A.L.R.3d 645 (1971).

4. Consider the validity of the following objection to the quasi-public facility theory:

> It is far from clear today why hospitals are under any greater obligation than typical employers to account to the courts for the fairness with which they screen applicants for professional positions or why health care professionals deserve any special legal help in surmounting marketplace barriers to their pursuit of a livelihood. The due process requirements that common-law courts have required private hospitals to observe in allocating staff privileges are in fact anomalous and find weak support in the common-law ground in which they are rooted.

Havighurst, Doctors and Hospitals: An Antitrust Perspective on Traditional Relationships, 1984 Duke L.J. 1071, 1099-1100.

5. In examining how faithful this body of law is to the common carrier/inn keeper precedent on which it is based, consider whether excluded physicians should be able to demand judicial review of the fairness of a private hospital's decision even if they (and their patients) have the choice of several other hospitals in town, or should the public-facility theory apply only where hospitals exercise monopoly power in their local markets? Rosenberg v. Holy Redeemer Hosp., 506 A.2d 408 (Pa. Super. 1986) (the latter); Barrows supra, 525 N.E.2d 50 (Ill. 1988) (same). Given that 80 percent of all municipalities in the United States with an acute care hospital have only one, and 90 percent have only two, usually with similar medical staff membership, is it appropriate to overlook this technicality in those locations where there is effective competition?

6. Note that the common law public service duties of common

carriers were owed to their *customers,* not to their employees. As *Greisman* recognizes, then, excluded doctors have cause to complain only by virtue of their control over patient admissions to hospitals. Consequently, should the public-facility doctrine apply to doctors such as anesthesiologists and consulting specialists who do not admit patients? No one appears to have considered this issue.

7. It is fascinating to speculate what other applications might exist for a doctrine as novel as this. Consider, for instance, whether private hospitals owe common law fairness duties to their *employed* physicians. Ezekial v. Winkley, 572 P.2d 32 (Cal. 1977) (yes). If so, do these duties extend to employment *applicants?* To *nurse* employees? Cruz, The Duty of Fair Procedure and the Hospital Medical Staff: Possible Extension in Order to Protect Private Sector Employees, 16 Cap. U.L. Rev. 59 (1986) (arguing yes, but only for existing employees).

And what about possible duties extending to *patients?* For instance, could this doctrine be used by a woman in labor to demand that her husband be allowed to attend the birth? Hulit v. St. Vincent's Hosp., 520 P.2d 99 (1974) (holding no, but only after finding that hospital rule was "reasonable" and "fair"); McMahon, Judicial Review of Internal Policy Decisions of Private Nonprofit Hospitals: A Common Law Approach, 3 Am. J.L. & Med. 149 (1977) (arguing yes). One case has extended the quasi-public-facility theory to physician (as opposed to hospital) services, holding that a patient refused service by the only practice group in town after lodging a complaint against one of the doctors in the group may maintain an action alleging an arbitrary refusal to serve.

Finally, if there are no holds barred, note that common carriers were subject to strict liability for accidents and to common law judicial scrutiny for the reasonableness of their rates! See generally D. Moore, Law of Carriers (1914); B. Wyman, Public Service Corporations (1911).

Nanavati v. Burdette Tomlin Memorial Hospital
526 A.2d 697 (N.J. 1987)

POLLOCK, J.

This appeal arises out of the revocation of the staff privileges of Suketu H. Nanavati (Dr. Nanavati) as a cardiologist at Burdette Tomlin Memorial Hospital (the hospital). . . .

The background of this case is a dispute between Dr. Nanavati and Dr. Robert Sorensen, who at the time was the chief of cardiology, chairman of the Department of Medicine, and a member of the Board of Governors at the hospital. The dispute originated over the allocation of the reading of electrocardiograms (ECGs or EKGs), which,

I. Providers' Rights to Practice 479

at $5 per reading, produced an annual income of approximately $75,000. Burdette Tomlin is the only hospital in Cape May County, and when he was granted staff privileges, Dr. Nanavati was the only board-certified cardiologist in the county. Before the arrival of Dr. Nanavati in 1979, Dr. Sorensen, an internist, enjoyed a virtual monopoly on reading ECGs. Dr. Nanavati was allowed to read ECGs one day each week, but when he requested an additional day, Dr. Sorensen rejected his request. The rejection stimulated Dr. Nanavati into criticizing Dr. Sorensen, who retaliated. As the discord between the two doctors escalated, Dr. Nanavati allegedly committed a series of violations of the hospital's bylaws. On August 2, 1982, the medical staff executive committee "voted unanimously to act toward the revocation of Dr. Nanavati's medical staff privileges." That action marked the beginning of lengthy proceedings before the hospital authorities and before federal and state courts in this state.

Pursuant to the hospital bylaws, the chairman of the medical staff executive committee requested the hospital executive committee to take corrective action. The executive committee forwarded the request to the chief of the Department of Medicine, who appointed an ad hoc committee to investigate the matter. The charges against Dr. Nanavati were captioned as "Acts of Disruptive Behavior" and "Failure to Cooperate with Hospital Personnel Regarding the Use of Facilities Especially During the Summer Months and the Emergent Admissions Procedures."

Underlying these charges is the contention that Dr. Nanavati caused disruption in violation of a bylaw provision requiring a staff doctor to

> be of a temperament and disposition that will enable him to work in harmony with his colleagues on the Medical Staff; with the professional, technical, and other personnel in the hospital, and with the administration, accepting criticism without resentment and offering it in a spirit and manner that is constructive and devoid of offense and malice. . . .

The further allegation is that Dr. Nanavati violated a bylaw provision that a staff member "must enjoy the reputation of being an ethical and conscientious practitioner and must strictly abide by the Code of Ethics. . . ." At no time has the hospital questioned Dr. Nanavati's technical competence.

On August 23, 1982, the ad hoc committee "found against Dr. Nanavati on all charges and specifications" and recommended as the only appropriate punishment "his discharge from the Medical Staff of Burdette Tomlin Memorial Hospital, together with the permanent deprivation of Burdette Memorial Hospital privileges." The executive committee of the medical staff affirmed that finding, and Dr. Nanavati appealed to an ad hoc committee of the medical staff, which unanimously found against him and recommended that he be dismissed from the staff of the hospital. In November, the hospital administrator advised Dr. Nanavati of the revocation of his staff privileges.

Dr. Nanavati immediately filed an action in the Chancery Division, which found that the proceedings had not been conducted in accordance with the hospital's bylaws, enjoined the revocation of Dr. Nanavati's privileges, and remanded the matter for further proceedings to be conducted in accordance with the hospital's bylaws. The Board of Governors thereupon appointed a hearing committee, which recommended on April 15, 1983, "that the action of the medical staff in dismissing Dr. Nanavati be affirmed." Two weeks later, on April 29, the Board affirmed the hearing committee's recommendation. . . .

[On appeal] the Chancery Division independently reviewed the record by a preponderance-of-the-evidence standard. The court determined that Dr. Nanavati's staff privileges should not be revoked on the ground of disharmony, absent a showing of actual interference with patient care, and concluded that the record did not support any such showing. Consequently, the court issued a permanent injunction against revocation of his privileges.

Although the Appellate Division affirmed the trial court's finding that the hospital proceedings were invalid, it disagreed with other portions of the trial court's opinion and held that the trial court, in reviewing the revocation of hospital staff privileges, should not have made independent findings of fact, but should have determined whether the hospital's decision was supported by sufficient credible evidence. In addition, the Appellate Division ruled that mere disharmony, although an insufficient ground by itself, is a relevant consideration in revocation proceedings. . . .

We granted Dr. Nanavati's petition for certification to determine the appropriate standard of review of the decision by a hospital to terminate a physician's staff privileges and to determine further whether actual interference with patient care is required in order to terminate those privileges. . . .

Twenty-five years ago we rejected the notion that decisions of private hospitals concerning staff privileges were beyond judicial review. Greisman v. Newcomb Hosp., 192 A.2d 817. By analogy to private businesses affected by the public interest, we ruled that courts should intervene when a hospital denied staff membership "for a reason unrelated to sound hospital standards and in furtherance of the common good." In reaching that conclusion, we also declared that "reasonable and constructive exercises of judgment should be honored. . . ." Thus, courts should sustain a hospital's standard for granting staff privileges if that standard is rationally related to the

I. Providers' Rights to Practice

delivery of health care. A decision is so related if it advances the interests of the public, particularly patients; the hospital; or those who are essential to the hospital's operations, such as doctors and nurses.

Although not quite so deferential when reviewing individual decisions denying staff privileges, courts still apply a relaxed standard of review to those decisions. The test for judicial review of such a decision is whether it is supported by "sufficient reliable evidence, even though of a hearsay nature, to justify the result."

We have previously explained the difference between the two tests by analogy to judicial review of administrative actions. Setting a standard for admission to staff privileges is roughly analogous to the kind of policy decision reflected in administrative rulemaking. Carrying forward the analogy, a hospital's use of that standard to decide a particular case is like quasi-judicial agency action. . . . Underlying the more relaxed standard is our growing awareness that courts should allow hospitals, as long as they proceed fairly, to run their own business. That sense is tempered by the recognition that doctors need staff privileges to serve their patients, and that the public interest requires that hospitals treat doctors fairly in making decisions about those privileges. . . .

In prior cases, we have considered the denial of privileges to new applicants. . . . Although we have not previously decided a case involving the *revocation* of privileges, . . . [n]onetheless, the standard of judicial review should remain the same. . . .

[I]f a hospital is to care for its patients, the staff, particularly doctors and nurses, must work together. As important as cooperation is to other corporations, it is even more critical in a modern hospital, where no single doctor cares for all the needs of any one patient. Hospital doctors depend on their colleagues, nurses, technicians, and other employees for total patient care. . . . Consequently, a hospital may adopt a bylaw providing that the inability of a doctor to work with nurses and other doctors is a ground for denying or terminating staff privileges. . . .

Doctors, like other people, have quirks, and some doctors are more disagreeable than others. The mere fact that a doctor is irascible, however, does not constitute good cause for termination of his or her hospital privileges. McElhinney v. William Booth Memorial Hosp., 544 S.W.2d 216, 218 (Ky. 1977). Nor should allegations of "disharmony" ever be used as a ruse to deny or terminate staff privileges because of a doctor's race, religion, color, or gender. Likewise, a doctor should not be cut off from staff membership merely because he or she has criticized hospital practices and other doctors. . . . A hospital need not wait for a disruptive doctor to harm a patient before terminating his or her privileges. Nonetheless, more should be required than general complaints of a physician's inability to cooperate with others. To constitute disruptive behavior meriting termination of staff privileges, hospital authorities should present concrete evidence of specific instances of misbehavior, such as unjustified altercations with other doctors or nurses, violations of hospital routines or rules, breaches of professional standards, or the commission of some other act that will adversely affect health care delivery. . . .

The judgment of the Appellate Division is affirmed as modified, and the cause is remanded to the hospital.

NOTES

The Scope of Judicial Review

1. As *Nanavati* indicates, it is helpful to divide the scope of judicial review into two components — procedural and substantive — and, further, to divide substantive review into (a) the rationale for the general membership criteria contained in the bylaws and (b) the evidence supporting the application of the bylaws to an individual physician. The primary focus of these notes is on issue 2(a): the substantive validity of general criteria.

2. Why might a hospital want to exclude a doctor? More doctors, after all, mean more patients. If it is in a hospital's economic interest to exclude only bad doctors, why should we bother to scrutinize the hospital's decision at all?

3. Concerning the particular ground for discipline sustained in *Nanavati*, see Springer & Casale, Hospitals and the Disruptive Health Care Practitioner — Is the Ability to Work with Others Enough to Warrant Exclusion?, 24 Duq. L. Rev. 377 (1985); Hollowell, Physicians' Disruptive Behavior: Grounds for Discipline, 11 L. Med. & Health Care 25 (Feb. 1983). It has been held arbitrary to deny initial privileges on the grounds that the candidate did not graduate from a medical school approved by the American Medical Association, Fritz v. Huntington Hospital, 39 N.Y.2d 92, 348 N.E.2d 547 (1976); was not a member of the local medical society (when membership was denied to black physicians), Foster v. Mobile County Hospital, 398 F.2d 227 (5th Cir. 1968); or did not submit adequate personal and professional references, although he was licensed to practice in the state, Rao v. Board of County Commissioners, 80 Wash. 2d 695, 497 P.2d 591 (1972). See generally Annot., 37 A.L.R.3d 645 (1971).

4. Is *Nanavati* consistent with the following frequently quoted standard of review?

> No court should substitute its evaluation of such matters for that of the Hospital Board. . . . Human lives are at stake, and the governing

board must be given discretion in its selection so that it can have confidence in the competence and moral commitment of its staff. The evaluation of professional proficiency of doctors is best left to the specialized expertise of their peers, subject only to limited judicial surveillance. . . . In short, so long as staff selections are administered with fairness, geared by a rationale compatible with hospital responsibility, and unencumbered with irrelevant considerations, a court should not interfere.

Sosa v. Board of Managers, 437 F.2d 173 (5th Cir. 1971).

5. In *Greisman*, the hospital did not attempt to defend its exclusion of osteopaths on the basis of a quality-of-care rationale. If it had, what justification would suffice? Is it necessary to establish *poor* quality of care, or only a relative *difference* in the quality of care? Which of the following exclusionary policies do you think are valid?

- a) A hospital limits staff membership to licensed physicians (M.D.'s or D.O.'s), which necessarily excludes other licensed health professionals such as clinical psychologists, podiatrists, nurse midwives and chiropractors. Shaw v. Hospital Auth., 614 F.2d 946 (5th Cir. 1985) (constitutionally permissible to exclude podiatrists).
- b) A tertiary care hospital limits staff membership to specialists who are board eligible or board certified, which necessarily excludes osteopaths and other general practitioners. Limmer v. Samaritan Health Serv., 710 P.2d 1077 (Ariz. App. 1985) (valid); Silverstein v. Gwinnett Hosp. Auth., 861 F.2d 1560 (11th Cir. 1988) (same); Armstrong v. Board of Directors, 553 S.W.2d 77 (Tenn. 1977) (invalid).
- c) A Christian Science hospital excludes physicians who do not practice according to its religious beliefs. Cf. Watkins v. Mercy Med. Ctr., 520 F.2d 894 (9th Cir. 1975) (Catholic hospital may refuse to have abortions performed on premises, but may not exclude abortionists from staff).
- d) A hospital excludes osteopaths because they are trained under a different medical philosophy. Hayman v. City of Galveston, 273 U.S. 414, 417 (1926) (sufficient to pass constitutional muster); Stern v. Tarrant County Hosp. Dist., 778 F.2d 1052 (5th Cir. 1985) (en banc) (same).

It may assist you in answering these questions to employ an equal protection type of analysis by asking what level of scrutiny do physician exclusion decisions warrant — minimum "rational basis," strict "compelling interest," or intermediate "substantial basis" scrutiny?

6. The debate in physician exclusion cases usually turns on whether the decision was motivated by the public interest in quality of care

or by the existing doctors' interest in limiting competition. But what about the *hospital's* interest? Is it ever allowed to exclude a physician to advance its private economic interest, so long as that interest does not conflict with the public interest? For example, most hospitals grant exclusive privileges to a select group of radiologists, anesthesiologists, and pathologists ("hospital-based physicians"). One reason for doing so is that hospitals can then capture some of the profits generated by these physicians' services. This reason appears neutral with respect to the public's interest. Yet courts sustaining exclusive contract arrangements usually refer only to public-interest justifications such as efficiency in department operation and ease of monitoring performance, suggesting that the more honest explanation would not suffice. Cases are collected and discussed in Belmar v. Cipolla, 475 A.2d 533, 540 (N.J. 1984); Annot., Validity and Construction of Contract Between Hospital and Physician, 74 A.L.R.3d 1268 (1974).

In another context, however, courts have been more explicit about the validity of self-interested hospital motives. Courts have held that a hospital has a "right to take reasonable measures to protect itself" against exposure to joint and several liability with a doctor by requiring all medical staff members to carry a certain level of malpractice insurance. Holmes v. Hoemako Hosp., 573 P.2d 477 (1977). See Annot., 7 A.L.R.4th 1238 (1977); Bernstein, Medical Staff Privilege Disputes, 58 Hospitals, Apr. 16, 1984, at 85, 88 (this requirement "is for the protection of the facility's assets, not necessarily for protection of the patient").

7. Another difficult exclusionary policy is presented by hospitals that close their medical staffs entirely, limiting membership to only the existing physicians. The ostensible reason for closure is overcrowding, but what is to prevent an overcrowded hospital from expanding? Are there any possible bad motivations for hospital closure? Two recent cases that attempt to sort out these problems are Desai v. St. Barnabas Med. Cent., 510 A.2d 662 (N.J. 1986); and Berman v. Valley Hosp., 510 A.2d 673 (N.J. 1986) (closely scrutinizing rationale for closing medical staff: closing staff is a permissible response to genuine overcrowding, but cannot be used to favor incumbent physicians).

8. With the mounting pressure for improved efficiency in medical treatment, it is widely predicted that hospitals will begin employing utilization criteria in the credentialing process to screen out wasteful doctors. E.g., Cantrell & Flick, Physician Efficiency and Reimbursement: A Case Study, Hosp. & Health Servs. Admin., Nov/Dec 1986, at 43. Will a body of law premised on excluding physicians for poor quality accommodate physician exclusion for *excessive* quality? See Hall, Institutional Control of Physician Behavior: Legal Barriers to Health Care Cost Containment, 137 U. Penn. L. Rev. 431, 518-527 (1988) (probably, but only if medical staff bylaws can be amended).

9. It is important to realize who controls medical staff membership criteria. The JCAH accreditation standards require that the criteria be contained in the medical staff bylaws, rather than in the hospital bylaws. The medical staff bylaws are controlled jointly by the staff and the hospital board. Hospitals therefore may not unilaterally change the credentialing process or impose new substantive criteria on a reluctant medical staff. St. John's Hosp. Med. Staff v. St. John Regional Med. Cent., 245 N.W.2d 472 (S.D. 1976) (overturning hospital's unilateral amendment to medical staff bylaws).

The distinction between medical staff bylaws and hospital bylaws reflects a fundamental division of authority between medical and financial matters within all hospitals, HMOs, and other health care institutions. This division of responsibilities makes it difficult for governing bodies to influence changes in patient care procedures that are necessary to respond to pressures for quality assurance or cost control. See Hall, supra, 137 U. Penn. L. Rev. at 528-532; Southwick, The Hospital as an Institution — Expanding Responsibilities Change Its Relationship with the Staff Physician, 9 Cal. W.L. Rev. 429 (1973).

10. Much of the case law on medical staff disputes is procedural in nature. See, for instance, Gill v. Mercy Hosp., 245 Cal. Rptr. 304 (Cal. App. 1988); Silver v. Castle Mem. Hosp., 497 P.2d 571 (Haw. 1972), *cert. denied*, 409 U.S. 1048 (1973); Ascherman v. San Francisco Med. Soc., 114 Cal. Rptr. 681 (1974). Physician credentialing usually proceeds through several stages: investigation by a departmental or hospital-wide credentialing committee, vote by the medical staff as a whole and/or its executive committee, consideration of the medical staff recommendation by the hospital board, and an evidentiary review hearing if the board's decision is negative. Courts require that an excluded physician, whether an applicant or an existing staff member, be given notice of the charges, an opportunity to present evidence, and the right to confront and cross-examine opposing witnesses. The decision makers in this quasi-adjudicatory hearing may not be exposed to ex parte communication and must not have prejudged the merits. Much of this law is codified in the Health Care Quality Improvement Act of 1986 (quoted and discussed in Section I.D), which imposes fair procedure requirements as a condition for conferring an immunity on those who participate in the hospital peer review process. The major respects in which this act differs from the case law are: (1) it allows the challenged physician representation by counsel; (2) it provides that a transcript be made of the hearing; and (3) it disqualifies from the hearing panel anyone who is in "direct economic competition" with the physician. 42 U.S.C. §11112(b). Observe, though, that this act's procedural steps are not mandatory; they only create a safe harbor that establishes one, nonexclusive manner in which a hospital can qualify for immunity.

What problems do these requirements present for a small rural hospital? See A. Southwick, The Law of Hospital and Health Care Administration 618 (2d ed. 1988) ("in hospitals having a relatively small medical staff the risk of bias and partiality increases. A hearing panel composed of persons from outside the hospital may then be necessary"); H.R. Rep. No. 903, at 6393-6394 ("The Committee recognizes that in many cases . . . it may not be feasible to find physicians who are of the same specialty as the respondent but who are not in direct economic competition. Nevertheless, the Committee expects the professional review body to make every reasonable effort to find appropriate [reviewers], even if this requires bringing in reviewers from out of town or using physicians of a different specialty").

On procedural requirements generally, see Comment, Medical Staff Decisions in Private Hospitals: The Role of Due Process, 18 Loy. U. Chi. L.J. 951 (1987); Comment, Procedural Due Process Rights of Physicians Applying for Hospital Staff Privileges, 17 Loy. U. Chi. L.J. 453 (1986); Cray, Due Process Considerations in Hospital Staff Privilege Cases, 7 Hastings Const. L.Q. 217 (1979); Note, Denial of Hospital Staff Privileges: Hearing and Judicial Review, 56 Iowa L. Rev. 1351 (1971). Compare Board of Curators v. Horowitz, 435 U.S. 78 (1978) (formal hearing not required to dismiss a medical student).

11. One of the cutting-edge issues of peer review is whether it is possible to accomplish its objectives without going through the process of conducting extensive fact-finding proceedings within the medical staff, thus exposing the hospital to substantial headaches (not to mention legal liability). Consider, for instance, the practicality and legality of the following techniques:

1) Write the bylaws to include a greatly expanded list of objective criteria, so that it is easier to disqualify physicians at the outset.
2) For hospital-based physicians with exclusive contracts, such as radiologists and anesthesiologists, to make staff privileges turn on contract renewal, so that their conduct is evaluated only in the context of contract negotiations.
3) Contract with individuals outside the hospital to conduct the credentialing review. See p.500 infra.
4) Restrict the medical staff's role solely to the assessment of clinical technique; make all other evaluations (such as whether a doctor complies with hospital rules or is a financial drain) at the level of the hospital administration.

12. Canadian courts have also become active in this area. The leading case is Abouna v. Foothills Provincial General Hosp., [1978] 2 W.W.R. 130. See F. Rozovsky, Canadian Hospital Law.

C. Medical Staff Disputes and Peer Review — Antitrust Law

INTRODUCTORY NOTE

Sherman Antitrust Act, Section 1

Physicians frequently challenge medical staff membership decisions under federal antitrust laws, contending that exclusion from the hospital constitutes a concerted refusal to deal, which is pejoratively known as a group boycott. Health care boycott cases are emerging with such force and prominence that antitrust analysis can no longer be reserved to the litigation specialist. Health care lawyers must have a working understanding of this area of the law in order to advise their clients effectively on how to plan their activities in advance to minimize antitrust exposure. See Miller, Teaching Antitrust to Health Law Students: Peer Review as a Case Study, 38 J. Leg. Educ. 545 (1988).

The primary basis for these suits is section 1 of the Sherman Act, 15 U.S.C. §1:

> Every contract, combination . . . or conspiracy in restraint of trade or commerce among the several States, or with foreign nations, is declared to be illegal.

The three elements of a section 1 action, evident from the face of the statute, are (1) concerted, as opposed to unilateral, action; (2) restraint of trade; and (3) interstate commerce. A general overview of these three elements may be helpful to the uninitiated reader prior to tackling the principal cases.

Conspiracy. No Sherman Act section 1 violation exists if the challenged activity is unilateral in nature, that is, if it is the action of a single entity. The theory underlying section 1 is that competitive harm exists only when two or more economic actors collude to subvert the forces of competition. When a single hospital excludes a physician, concerted action is not readily apparent, even though many individual doctors and administrators within the hospital participate in the exclusion decision. The Supreme Court has clearly held that "[t]he officers of a single firm are not separate economic actors pursuing separate economic interests, so agreements among them do not suddenly bring together economic power that was previously pursuing divergent goals. Coordination within a firm is as likely to result from an effort to compete as from an effort to stifle competition." Copperweld Corp. v. Independence Tube Corp., 467 U.S. 752, 769 (1984). This reasoning is referred to as the intra-enterprise conspiracy rule: ordinarily, no conspiracy can exist within a single business enterprise.

There is an exception to this intra-enterprise conspiracy rule, however. A combination or conspiracy may exist within a single enterprise if one or more of its members is motivated by an outside economic interest that is separate from the firm's. In such a situation, it is no longer the case that the various corporate actors are pursuing a single economic purpose, and, therefore, the potential for harmful collusion exists even within a single firm. For instance, suppose a malpractice insurance company owned and operated by obstetricians were to deny coverage to a doctor who happened to work with midwives. There would be no conspiracy if the company simply thought the doctor posed an excessive risk, but a conspiracy would exist if the corporate actors were motivated by an outside interest unrelated to the concerns of insurance, namely to suppress competition from midwives.* Likewise, the threshold issue in hospital exclusion cases is whether the economic interest that existing medical staff members have in competition with applicants (and with each other) results in the concerted behavior required to invoke Sherman Act §1.

Unreasonable Restraint of Trade. If concerted action is present, then the core substantive question becomes whether the challenged conduct results in an unreasonable restraint of trade. This is a complex and difficult inquiry, one that is incapable of completely accurate summation. Nevertheless, some preliminary analysis is useful before encountering the case law. First, observe that the language of the Sherman Act provides no useful guidance; it prohibits "*every* contract . . . in restraint of trade," which, taken literally, is an impossibility since every contract *in fact* restrains trade, at least to some small extent (by precluding the contracting parties from dealing with someone else for the subject matter of the contract). Therefore, courts have found it necessary to add a judicial gloss to the statute so that it prohibits only *unreasonable* restraints of trade. This generates what is known as the "rule of reason" test of illegality: a restraint is illegal only if its anticompetitive harms outweigh its procompetitive benefits. Such a finding often requires a complex, lengthy, and expensive inquiry. To avoid engaging in this burdensome undertaking in every case, the courts have crafted what is known as the "per se rule" of illegality: certain restraints are automatically illegal if it is clear from their general nature that they are anticompetitive in the vast majority of situations. The primary example of per se illegality is horizontal price fixing, that is, price fixing among competitors.

In the context of medical staff disputes, plaintiffs attempt to

---

* These facts are suggested by Nurse Midwifery Assocs. v. Hibbett, 549 F. Supp. 1185 (M.D. Tenn. 1982). However, a later decision in this case dismissed the section 1 count, finding that the sixth circuit does not follow the independent personal stake exception to the intra-enterprise conspiracy rule. 689 F. Supp. 799 (M.D. Tenn. 1988).

invoke the rule of per se illegality for medical staff exclusion decisions by characterizing these decisions as group boycotts, that is, an agreement among the medical staff not to deal with the plaintiff. Unfortunately for litigants and for students of health care antitrust, "there is more confusion about the scope and operation of the *per se* rule against group boycotts than in reference to any other aspect of the *per se* doctrine." L. Sullivan, Law of Antitrust 229-230 (1977). Despite several Supreme Court precedents declaring boycotts per se illegal, "exactly what types of activity fall within the forbidden category is . . . far from certain." Northwest Wholesale Stationers Inc. v. Pacific Stationary and Printing Co., 472 U.S. 284, 294 (1985). In this case, the Court explained that "the mere allegation of a concerted refusal to deal does not suffice because not all concerted refusals to deal are predominantly anticompetitive." Therefore, "a plaintiff seeking application of the *per se* rule must present a threshold case that the challenged activity falls into a category likely to have predominantly anticompetitive effects." Id. at 297. How this general directive might apply to medical staff disputes is the second principal issue explored in the following section.

Interstate Commerce. In order for federal antitrust jurisdiction to attach, a restraint must have a substantial effect on interstate commerce. This requirement will have the least importance in these materials, but it too has been controversial in this body of law. See p.501 infra.

Weiss v. York Hospital
745 F.2d 786 (3rd Cir.), *cert. denied*, 470 U.S. 1060 (1984)

BECKER, CIRCUIT JUDGE.

I. Introduction and General Background

This antitrust case arises from the refusal to grant hospital staff privileges to a physician. The plaintiff, Malcolm Weiss, is an osteopath[2] who was denied staff privileges at York (Pennsylvania) Hospital. Dr. Weiss brought this suit, both individually and as representative of the class of all osteopathic physicians in the York Medical Service Area

---

2. Dorland's Illustrated Medical Dictionary defines Osteopathy as:

a system of therapy . . . based on the theory that the body is capable of making its own remedies against disease. . . . It utilizes generally accepted physical, medicinal and surgical methods of diagnosis while placing chief emphasis on the importance of normal body mechanics and manipulative methods of detecting and correcting faulty structure. Osteopathic physicians signify their degree as D.O.

(York MSA), against York Hospital ("York"), the York Medical and Dental Staff, and ten individual physicians who served on the York Medical Staff Executive Committee and the York Judicial Review Committee. York is controlled by, and, at the time Dr. Weiss applied for staff privileges, was exclusively staffed by doctors who graduated from allopathic medical schools.[3]

The gravamen of Weiss' lawsuit is that, although allopaths (hereinafter referred to as medical doctors or M.D.s) and osteopaths (D.O.s) are equally trained and qualified to practice medicine,[4] his application for staff privileges at York hospital was turned down solely because of his status as an osteopath. . . . In Weiss' submission, this scheme to exclude D.O.s from York Hospital was motivated by a desire to restrict the ability of D.O.s to compete with M.D.s, thereby increasing the profits of the M.D.s. [The jury found that the medical staff, but not the hospital, violated section 1 of the Sherman Act.] . . .

II. The Facts

A. Hospital Services in the York MSA

There are two providers of in-patient hospital services in the York MSA: York, which is run by M.D.s, and Memorial Hospital ("Memorial"), which is run by D.O.s. York is by far the larger of

---

3. Allopathy is defined as a system of remedial treatment in which it is sought to cure a disease by producing, through medicines, a condition incompatible with the disease. See Funk & Wagnalls New Standard Dictionary of the English Language (1942). Allopathy constitutes the common or "regular" system of medical practice. Allopathic doctors signify their degree as M.D.

4. At trial Dr. Merle S. Bacastow, an M.D. and the Vice-President of Medical Affairs at York, testified that at least since the mid-1960's there has been no difference in terms of medical training and ability to provide medical care between graduates of osteopathic medical schools and graduates of allopathic medical schools. This observation is born out by the fact that osteopaths and allopaths are equally qualified for state licensure to practice medicine and surgery within the Commonwealth of Pennsylvania. . . . See also Blackstone, The A.M.A. and The Osteopaths: A Study of the Power of Organized Medicine, 22 Antitrust Bulletin 405, 408-14 (1977). Professor Blackstone concludes that in general D.O.s receive somewhat shorter, less expensive, and less specialized training than today's highly specialized M.D.s. He states that this difference may justify limitations on the privileges of osteopaths that are similar to limitations imposed upon general practice M.D.s and family practitioners, but that it would not seem to justify the total exclusion of osteopaths. See id. at 411; Kissam, Webber, Bigers, and Holzgraefe, Antitrust and Hospital Privileges: Testing the Conventional Wisdom, 70 Calif. L. Rev. 595, 641 n.218 (1982) [hereinafter cited as Antitrust and Hospital Privileges]; Dolan & Ralston, Hospital Admitting Privileges and the Sherman Act, 18 Houston L. Rev. 707, 728 (1981) ("Osteopaths undergo training regimens quite similar to that of M.D. practitioners, except that greater emphasis is placed on family practice and on some manipulative practices. Regardless of the situation thirty years ago, it is highly unlikely that any significant qualitative difference between the two groups exists today."); [Ed. note: See also Enders, Federal Antitrust Issues Involved in the Denial of Medical Staff Privileges, 17 Loyola U. Chi. L.J. 331 (1986)].

I. Providers' Rights to Practice

the two, with approximately 450 beds and 2,500 employees. Memorial has 160 beds. The testimony at trial established that York had a market share of 80 percent of the patient-days of hospitalization in the York MSA.

In addition to York's overall market dominance, testimony at trial established that certain complex, highly technical "tertiary care" services and facilities are, for a number of reasons, only available at York. Included among the services offered only at York are therapeutic radiology, open heart surgery, cardiac catheterization, renal dialysis, neo-natal intensive care, short-term acute psychiatric care, monitored stroke treatment, audiology, burn care, cardiopulmonary laboratory, cardiopulmonary rehabilitation, electroencephalography, genetic counseling, prosthetic service, speech therapy, computerized axial tomography (CAT scan), and infusion aspirator. . . .

[I]n early 1976, Weiss and another osteopath named Dr. Michael Zittle, both of whom were engaged in family practice in the York MSA, applied for staff privileges at York. Dr. Weiss informed representatives of the York medical staff that if York excluded him because of his osteopathic training he would institute legal action.

The York medical staff considered the applications and Weiss' threat of legal action, and in November of 1976 amended its bylaws to permit admission of osteopaths at York. Dr. Weiss contends that the amendment of the bylaws was purely cosmetic, and that since 1976 the York medical staff has engaged in a deliberate covert policy of discrimination against osteopaths. . . .

D. Doctor Weiss' Application for Staff Privileges

In 1976 Doctors Weiss and Zittle applied for staff privileges in York's Family Practice Department. In accordance with the procedures outlined above, the Family Practice Department Credentials Committee and the chairman of the Family Practice Department considered the applications. On January 17, 1977, the department recommended that they be accepted. The Medical Staff Credentials Committee then reviewed the applications and also recommended acceptance. The Medical Staff Executive Committee, however, did not approve either application. Instead, it took the unusual step of deciding to conduct a further investigation. The Committee made extensive oral and written inquiries concerning the professional competence and moral character of both Weiss and Zittle. No such survey had ever been conducted by the hospital before. Ultimately the investigation turned up some questions about Dr. Weiss' personality. The investigation also raised some glimmer of a question about Dr. Weiss' medical competence, but the sole "evidence" that was adduced was hearsay, often second or third level hearsay. Nevertheless, the Medical Staff

Executive Committee, apparently based on this "new evidence," decided not to recommend Weiss for staff privileges.

On June 30, 1977, the hospital Board of Directors considered the recommendations of the various committees which had considered Weiss' and Zittle's applications. The Board voted to approve Zittle's application and deny Weiss' application. . . . The Credentials Committee's written report is revealing in both its assessment of the "evidence" against Weiss, and in its frank recognition of the "controversy" at York over the admission of D.O.s to staff privileges:

> The Committee invited Dr. Weiss to discuss the reactivation of his application and to direct certain questions to him. He was told of the developments in the past and precisely how his application has been handled and of the problems that had arisen. He was specifically told that almost everybody with whom we spoke acknowledged him to be an intelligent, competent, conscientious physician whose care of his patients in the Hospital was quite competent. He was told that the Chairman of his Department suggested that he probably was the best general practitioner. However, almost everyone to whom we spoke acknowledged that he has had personality problems in the past which have caused him to have difficult interpersonal relations with other members of the staff. He was told that because of this personality problem, his application was rejected. It was further explained to him that because of the controversy that accompanied the application of osteopaths to the York Hospital, it was felt that acceptance of his application would jeopardize that endeavor. We explained to Dr. Weiss that his admission to the staff would be met in some instances with outright hostility and in others with indifference and it was a matter of real concern to the Committee how he would react to this sort of reception. . . .

IV. *The Sherman Act Claims*

We now turn to the substantive-law questions presented by this appeal. . . .

A. Section 1 of the Sherman Act

In order to establish a violation of section 1 of the Sherman Act, 15 U.S.C. §1 (1982), a plaintiff must establish three elements: (1) a contract, combination, or conspiracy; (2) restraint of trade; and (3) an effect on interstate commerce. Each of these three elements has been the subject of extensive analysis by the courts, and we now turn to a discussion of that caselaw and its application to the facts of this case, taking the elements up in turn.

I. Providers' Rights to Practice

1. Proof of an Agreement: Is There a Sufficient Number of Conspirators?

In order to establish a violation of section 1, a plaintiff must prove that two or more distinct entities agreed to take action against the plaintiff. Before the district court, Weiss contended that the hospital and its medical staff were legally distinct entities and therefore capable of conspiring in violation of section 1. He also asserted that the doctors who joined together to form the medical staff were separate economic entities who competed against each other so that, as a matter of law, the medical staff was a "combination" of doctors within the meaning of section 1. Finally, Weiss argued that even if the individual doctors who made up York's medical staff were deemed by the court to be the equivalent of "officers or employees" of the hospital and therefore ordinarily not capable of conspiring with the hospital, nevertheless the doctors were acting for their own benefit in discriminating against osteopaths, and therefore fell within an exception to the ordinary rule that "officers or employees of the same firm do not provide the plurality of actors imperative for a §1 conspiracy." Copperweld Corp. v. Independence Tube Corp., 467 U.S. 752 (1984).

The district court concluded, and instructed the jury, that the medical staff was an "unincorporated division" of the hospital, and as such the two were legally a "single entity" incapable of conspiring. . . . However, . . . the district court held the defendant medical staff liable to the plaintiff class under section 1. On the question who conspired with the medical staff, the court stated only: "The York Hospital Medical and Dental Staff conspired with another person or entity to deny or impede reasonable, fair, equal, and full access to staff privileges at York Hospital by osteopathic physicians other than Plaintiff Weiss."

We agree with the plaintiffs that, as a matter of law, the medical staff is a combination of individual doctors and therefore that any action taken by the medical staff satisfies the "contract, combination, or conspiracy" requirement of section 1. . . .

Antitrust policy requires the courts to seek the economic substance of an arrangement, not merely its form. The "substance" of an arrangement often depends on the economic incentive of the parties. The York medical staff is a group of doctors, all of whom practice medicine in their individual capacities, and each of whom is an independent economic entity in competition with other doctors in the York medical community. Each staff member, therefore, has an economic interest separate from and in many cases in competition with the interests of other medical staff members. Under these circumstances, the medical staff cannot be considered a single economic entity for purposes of antitrust analysis. . . . In substance, the medical staff is a group of individual doctors in competition with each other and with other physicians in the York MSA, who have organized to regulate the provision of medical care at York hospital. Where such associations exist, their actions are subject to scrutiny under section 1 of the Sherman Act in order to insure that their members do not abuse otherwise legitimate organizations to secure an unfair advantage over their competitors. . . .

Finally, we deal with the plaintiff's assertion that the district court erred in charging the jury that the hospital could not conspire with its medical staff. The district court found that the medical staff was an unincorporated division of the hospital, and as such the court determined that the two could not conspire. Although we do not necessarily agree with the district court's characterization of the medical staff as an unincorporated division of the hospital, we agree with its basic conclusion that, with respect to the issues in this case, the hospital could not, as a matter of law, conspire with the medical staff. The medical staff was empowered to make staff privilege decisions on behalf of the hospital. As such, with regard to these decisions, the medical staff operated as an officer of a corporation would in relation to the corporation. Although the members of the medical staff had independent economic interests in competition with each other, the staff as an entity had no interest in competition with the hospital. Accordingly, we conclude that the district court correctly charged the jury that there could not be a conspiracy between the hospital and the medical staff.[29]

2. *Proof of Restraint of Trade*

a. Introduction

Read literally, Section 1 prohibits every agreement "in restraint of trade." In United States v. Joint Traffic Assn., 171 U.S. 505, 19 S. Ct. 25, 43 L. Ed. 259 (1898), the Supreme Court recognized that Congress could not have intended a literal interpretation of the word "every," and since Standard Oil Co. of New Jersey v. United States, 221 U.S. 1, 31 S. Ct. 502, 55 L. Ed. 619 (1911), courts have analyzed most restraints under the so-called "rule of reason." As its name suggests, the rule of reason requires the factfinder to decide whether, under all the circumstances of the case, the restrictive practice imposes an unreasonable restraint on competition.[52]

---

29. [Excerpted from earlier in the opinion.] We note however that exoneration of York Hospital on the section 1 claims does not necessarily result in the dismissal of the action as to York. The medical staff . . . does not exist independent of the hospital, and therefore the hospital may be liable to pay any award of money damages in favor of the plaintiffs and against the staff . . . on a respondeat superior theory of liability. We leave this question to another day.

52. Justice Brandeis provided the classic statement of the rule of reason in Board

The courts have also, however, applied a rule of per se illegality to certain types of business practices. The development of per se rules has resulted from a recognition that the case-by-case approach inherent in the rule of reason has significant costs, and that certain types of business practices almost always have anticompetitive effects without offsetting pro-competitive effects. In applying the per se rules, a court eschews the ordinary evaluation of the effect of the challenged practice, and concentrates instead on the question whether the practice falls within one of the categories of practices condemned by the per se rule. In this case, the plaintiffs argued that the actions of the defendants were the equivalent of a boycott, or as it is sometimes called, a concerted refusal to deal, and thus illegal per se. We now turn to that inquiry.

b. Is Defendants' Exclusionary Conduct the Equivalent of a Concerted Refusal to Deal ("Boycott")?

The jury found that the defendants had engaged in a policy of discrimination against Dr. Weiss and the other D.O.s in the York MSA by applying unfair, unequal, and unreasonable procedures in reviewing their applications. In addition, the district court concluded that this unfair, unreasonable, and unequal treatment "could reasonably be anticipated [by the defendants] to cause osteopathic physicians to refrain from applying for staff privileges at the York Hospital." The question before us is whether these actions should properly be characterized as a "group boycott" or "concerted refusal to deal," in which case they are illegal per se under section 1. If the defendants' actions cannot be so characterized, the rule of reason analysis would apply and the outcome of the case could be different. We conclude that the defendants' actions, as found in the district court, are the equivalent of a concerted refusal to deal.

The classic example of a concerted refusal to deal is the situation in which businesses at one level of production or distribution, e.g., retailers, use the threat of a boycott to induce businesses at another level, e.g., manufacturers, not to deal with competitors of the retailers. As Professor Sullivan has observed, "The boycotting group members, in effect, say to their suppliers or to their customers, 'If you don't

---

of Trade of City of Chicago v. United States, 246 U.S. 231, 238, 38 S. Ct. 242, 244, 62 L. Ed. 683 (1918):

> The true test of legality is whether the restraint imposed is such as merely regulates and perhaps thereby promotes competition or whether it is such as may suppress or even destroy competition. To determine that question the court must ordinarily consider the facts peculiar to the business to which the restraint was imposed; its condition before and after the restraint and its effect; the nature of the restraint and its effect, actual or probable. The history of the restraint, the evil believed to exist, the reason for adopting the particular remedy, the purpose or end sought to be attained, are all relevant facts.

stop dealing with non-group members, we will stop dealing with you.' If continued trade with group members is more important to a supplier or customer than is trading with non-group members, this threat will be effective." L. Sullivan, Handbook of the Law of Antitrust §83, at 230 (1977).

In this case York is a provider of hospital services; for the purpose of our analysis, the equivalent of the manufacturer in the example of a classical boycott. Similarly, the M.D.s are the equivalent of the retailers in the example, in the sense that physicians require access to a hospital in order to effectively treat patients. The difficulty with this analogy, at first blush, is that there is no evidence that the M.D.s have used coercion for the purpose of inducing York to exclude their competitors, the D.O.s. Upon closer analysis, however, the absence of coercion is irrelevant. A boycott is not illegal under the antitrust laws because of opposition to the use of coercion, but because it involves the use by businesses of an existing relationship with a supplier to exclude competition. In the paradigm case, coercion is necessary to induce the supplier not to deal with the competitors. In this case, because of the M.D.s' control over York's admission decisions, no coercion is necessary. The underlying antitrust violation is the same: a group of firms at one level of distribution, i.e., the doctors' level, have used their existing relationship with a supplier to exclude their competitors from dealing with the supplier.

We recognize that the facts of this case do not precisely fit into the mold of the classical refusal to deal. The refusal to deal is less than total insofar as York admitted Dr. Zittle and a number of other osteopaths. Arguably then, what is at issue is not a boycott but mere discrimination, which sounds less like a per se antitrust violation. However, given the evidence of the different standards applied to osteopaths and M.D.s and the second class citizenship afforded D.O.s upon admission to staff privileges at York, and in view of the adverse impact of these factors upon D.O. applications for York staff privileges, we are satisfied that the restrictive policy is, in purpose and effect, sufficiently close to the traditional boycott, that the characterization is appropriate.

The Medical Staff is, however, entitled to exclude individual doctors, including osteopaths, on the basis of their lack of professional competence or unprofessional conduct. If York's policy toward D.O.s could be viewed as a form of industry self-regulation of this type, the rule of reason, rather than a per se rule, would be applicable. See generally L. Sullivan, Handbook of the Law of Antitrust §§86-88 (1977). We recognize, therefore, that in many cases involving exclusion from staff privileges, courts will, more or less openly, have to utilize a rule of reason balancing approach. This case is different, however, because York has not contended that osteopaths as a group

I. Providers' Rights to Practice

are less qualified than M.D.s. See supra note 4. In the absence of such a contention, or another legitimate explanation for the discrimination, we conclude that a per se rule should be applied, since the effect of the practice is identical to that of the traditional boycott, and plainly anticompetitive.

Congruent with the foregoing discussion, the Supreme Court has adopted an exception to application of the per se rule of illegality where the case involves a learned profession and where the restriction is justified on "public service or ethical norm" grounds. Thus unlike most cases where characterization of some activity as a classical boycott ends the inquiry, here, because the medical profession is involved, the rule of reason analysis may still control, as a "built-in" exception. We now turn to a discussion of this potential "escape hatch" to see if it can extricate the defendants from the "cut" of the per se rule.

c. The "Learned Profession" Exception

In Goldfarb v. Virginia State Bar, 421 U.S. 773, 788 n.17, 95 S. Ct. 2004, 2013 n.17, 44 L. Ed. 2d 572 (1975), in which the Supreme Court made clear that the medical profession is not exempt from the antitrust laws, the Court stated that the "public service aspect, and other features of the professions, may require that a particular practice, which could properly be viewed as a violation of the Sherman Act in another context, be treated differently." See also National Society of Professional Engineers v. United States, 435 U.S. 679, 696, 98 S. Ct. 1355, 1367, 55 L. Ed. 2d 637 (1978). In Arizona v. Maricopa County Medical Society, 457 U.S. 332, 348-49, 102 S. Ct. 2466, 2475-2476, 73 L. Ed. 2d 48 (1982), the Court partially explained this exception by stating that conduct which is normally subject to per se condemnation under section 1 will instead be subject to rule of reason analysis where the challenged conduct is "premised on public service or ethical norms." Id. In *Maricopa*, because the defendants did not attempt to justify their price fixing arrangements on either of these grounds, but instead attempted to argue that the maximum price levels were pro-competitive, the Court held that the per se rule controlled and consequently found that the defendants' conduct violated section 1.

In this case the defendants have offered no "public service or ethical norm" rationale for their discriminatory treatment of D.O.s. Indeed, their defense at trial was that they did not discriminate against D.O.s. Since the jury believed otherwise, we conclude that the per se rule governs this case. . . .[61]

---

61. Several circuit court opinions have held the rule of reason analysis, not the per se rule of illegality, controls in boycott cases involving the learned professions. We believe these cases are readily distinguishable from the instant case. In Wilk v. American

3. Substantiality of Effect on Interstate Commerce

In order to violate section 1 of the Sherman Act, a defendant's actions must relate to trade or commerce "among the several States." There are two ways to satisfy this requirement: the proscribed conduct may itself be "in interstate commerce," or the conduct may be a purely intrastate activity that has a "substantial and adverse effect" on interstate commerce. See, e.g., McLain v. Real Estate Bd. of New Orleans, Inc., 444 U.S. 232, 246, 100 S. Ct. 502, 511, 62 L. Ed. 2d 441 (1980); Hospital Building Co. v. Trustees of Rex Hospital, 425 U.S. 738, 743, 96 S. Ct. 1848, 1851, 48 L. Ed. 2d 338 (1976); Cardio-Medical Associates v. Crozer-Chester Medical Center, 721 F.2d 68, 71 (3d Cir. 1983).

The district court focused its evidentiary inquiry on the effect on interstate commerce of the defendants' conduct and found the requisite "substantial and adverse" effect. . . .[65] We therefore affirm the finding of a "substantial and adverse" impact on interstate commerce in this case. . . .

Medical Assn., 719 F.2d 207 (7th Cir. 1983), *cert. denied*, — U.S. — , 104 S. Ct. 2399, 81 L. Ed. 2d 355 (1984), a case involving the refusal of M.D.s to deal with chiropractors, the Seventh Circuit stated: "boycotts are illegal per se only if used to enforce agreements that are themselves illegal per se — for example price fixing agreements." Id. at 221 (quoting Marrese v. American Academy of Orthopaedic Surgeons, 706 F.2d 1488, 1495 (7th Cir. 1983). Since the court could find no per se illegal purpose for the A.M.A.'s medical ethics principle 3, which in essence provided that M.D.s should not associate with chiropractors, it concluded that the rule of reason analysis governed in that case. We believe that the Seventh Circuit was correct in utilizing a rule of reason analysis in the Wilk case because the defendants were plainly asserting a "public service or ethical norm" justification for their concerted refusal to deal with chiropractors. In Virginia Academy of Clinical Psychologists v. Blue Shield of Va., 624 F.2d 476, 484-85 (4th Cir. 1980), the Fourth Circuit stated: "Because of the special considerations involved in the delivery of health services, we are not prepared to apply a per se rule of illegality to medical plans which refuse or condition payments to competing or potentially competing providers." [A] "medical necessity" justification was apparently raised by the defendants, and in our view that would have been sufficient to bring the defendants within the purview of *Maricopa*'s exception for conduct based on "public service or ethical norms." Finally, in Kreuzer v. American Academy of Periodontology, 735 F.2d 1479 (D.C. Cir. 1984), the D.C. Circuit Court held that the rule of reason analysis governed a section 1 challenge to a rule promulgated by the American Academy of Periodontology (AAP) that limited membership in the AAP to licensed dentists who practice periodontics exclusively, and who do not practice other forms of dentistry. The court labeled the effect of the AAP's rule a "group boycott" but concluded that "[w]hen a conspiracy of this sort is alleged in the context of one of the learned professions, the nature and extent of its anticompetitive effect are often too uncertain to be amendable to per se treatment." Id. at 1492. . . .

65. At trial the plaintiff presented evidence demonstrating that York's business activities had a substantial effect on interstate commerce. York's gross patient revenue for an average year was approximately 50 million dollars. The testimony indicated that York made substantial purchases of drugs and equipment in interstate commerce. In addition York routinely treated out-of-state patients and billed them at their out-of-state residences. Finally, the overwhelming majority of patient bills were paid by third party payors (i.e., private insurance companies and federal and state insurers) many of whom are located outside Pennsylvania. . . .

V. Conclusion

In summary, we reach the following conclusions. First, we find that the district court's decision that the medical staff violated Sherman Act section 1 as to the plaintiff class is supported by sufficient evidence, and we therefore will affirm the district court on this point. [W]e also agree that the issuance of an injunction by the district court in this case was proper.

NOTES

Medical Staff Boycotts

1. *Weiss* ruled that all physicians participating in a medical staff credentialing decision are engaged in a conspiracy as a matter of law. Granted that some physicians on the York Hospital medical staff have an independent interest in competition with Dr. Weiss, is this true of neurosurgeons, pathologists, or specialists who are not engaged in a general practice? The Health Care Quality Improvement Act of 1986, discussed in Section I.D, suggests not, for it confers an immunity on the peer review process where, inter alia, the participants "are not in direct economic competition with the physician involved." 42 U.S.C. §11112(b)(3)(A).

Even for those doctors who potentially are in direct competition — in Dr. Weiss' case, say general and family practitioners — should the court find a conspiracy as a matter of law? Individual doctors might in fact ignore their competitive interests in making a staffing decision. Indeed, following *Weiss*, at least two district courts have gone to the other extreme, holding as matter of law that there was *no* conspiracy because no evidence was presented on summary judgment that medical staff physicians acted out of their personal economic interests. Friedman v. Delaware County Mem. Hosp., 672 F. Supp. 171 (E.D. Pa. 1987); Kaczanowski v. Medical Cent. Hosp. of Vt., 612 F. Supp. 688 (D. Vt. 1985). In another case, the court found no conspiracy between a hospital and its medical staff after observing that "a mere potential or indirect motive would be too speculative a basis from which to infer an independent personal stake. Furthermore, the [doctor] would have to possess the power to institute the anti-competitive policy for his corporation." Nurse Midwifery Assocs. v. Hibbett, 689 F. Supp. 799, 804 (M.D. Tenn. 1988).

In contrast with its holding as a matter of law that a conspiracy existed *within* the medical staff, *Weiss* held that the medical staff cannot, as a matter of law, conspire *with the hospital*. But if members of the medical staff conspire with each other by virtue of their independent stake in the decision, why not with the hospital as well? Compare

Bolt v. Halifax Hosp. Med. Cent., (11th Cir. — F.2d — (1990) ("a hospital and the members of its medical staff are all legally capable of conspiring with one another" because they are legally separate entities); Oltz v. St. Peter's Community Hosp., 861 F.2d 1440 (9th Cir. 1988) (medical staff physicians conspired with hospital where their "interests were sufficiently independent so that the collaborated conduct . . . [with the hospital] coalesced economic power previously directed at disparate goals").

Professors Blumstein and Sloan offer an inviting solution to this problem: "[H]ospitals concerned about antitrust exposure could avoid liability by . . . using outside professional consultants for quality assurance." Blumstein & Sloan, Antitrust and Hospital Peer Review, 51 L. & Contemp. Probs. 7, 92 (1988). "[Medicare] Peer Review Organizations ("PRO's") might be authorized to perform such quality assurance services, and PRO's enjoy their own independent statutory immunity from the antitrust laws. Even if non-PRO external reviewers are employed, however, the . . . lack of competitive status with staff physicians would remove such peer-review activities from coverage under section 1 of the Sherman Act. No capacity to conspire would exist." Id. at 77.

2. What was the precise nature of the boycott alleged in *Weiss:* (a) that the existing medical staff threatened to boycott the hospital if it admitted Dr. Weiss, a secondary boycott, or (b) that the medical staff boycotted Dr. Weiss directly by not allowing him in, a primary boycott? This characterization problem may turn on who is conceived to control the admission decision, the hospital or the medical staff. What position did the court take?

The *Weiss* court struggles to fit the exclusion of Dr. Weiss within existing boycott precedent, which is addressed largely to secondary boycotts. Admittedly, boycott law is opaque and unresolved, but shouldn't this case be even easier than existing analogies if it concerns a *primary* boycott? Perhaps there are few existing such cases because only in the professions are market competitors entrusted with the authority to police entry into the market. See Section I.A. supra.

3. In support of the court's per se rule, consider the anticompetitive effects of excluding competitors from professional as opposed to manufacturing markets. In the manufacturing industries, reducing the number of competitors is considered potentially harmful because this makes it easier for those who remain to collude. See Chapter 7.VI. concerning hospital mergers. In the service professions, however, an underlying cartel is not needed to restrict output (and, thereby, to raise prices). Because there is a natural limit on the number of hours a day that a doctor is capable of working, exclusion *automatically* tends to create the conditions of artificial shortage that generate monopoly power. By contrast, manufacturing firms are usually con-

sidered capable of expanding their production capacity geometrically to meet pent up demand.

4. In order for the court to apply a per se rule of illegality, it first characterized the medical staff's decision as a class-based exclusion of all osteopaths not premised on any quality-of-care justification. How strong is the evidence for this characterization? Consider that the medical staff did amend its bylaws to allow in osteopaths, and it in fact extended privileges to Dr. Zittle, a D.O. who applied at the same time as Dr. Weiss. Consider also the stated justification relating to Dr. Weiss' personality.

5. Although the interstate commerce requirement is rarely controversial in antitrust law generally, the health care antitrust cases are deeply split on this issue. Some courts, like *Weiss*, find the issue worth only passing mention given the substantial amount of supplies, equipment, and reimbursement that any hospital receives from out of state. Other courts balk at the jurisdiction stage, based on two lines of reasoning. First, they ask whether the challenged activity itself (that is, the exclusion decision) rather than the defendant's overall operation affects interstate commerce. Second, they look for a net decrease in interstate commerce rather than a mere shift in its source or destination. They reason that exclusion of a single practitioner will simply force the patients to another hospital in the same state or to another doctor at the same hospital. Representative of these stricter jurisdictional views are Mitchell v. Frank R. Howard Mem. Hosp., 853 F.2d 762 (9th Cir. 1988); Sarin vs. Samaritan Health Cent., 813 F.2d 755 (6th Cir. 1987); Seglin v. Esau, 769 F.2d 1274 (7th Cir. 1985); and Furlong v. Long Island College Hosp., 710 F.2d 922, 926 (2d Cir. 1983). The tension between these two lines of cases remains a significant unresolved matter.

6. How would you advise a hospital to structure its credentialing process to minimize antitrust exposure if it were faced with the question of whether to extend admitting privileges to a clinical psychologist (assuming it has a psychiatric department)?

7. Plaintiffs have rarely succeeded in hospital exclusion cases. *Weiss* is unique in applying a per se rule because the stated justification for hospital privilege decisions is almost always related to quality of care. When exclusions *are* premised on quality, the *Weiss* court concedes that the Rule of Reason applies. The Supreme Court appeared to endorse this view in F.T.C. v. Indiana Fedn. of Dentists, 476 U.S. 447 (1986), a case concerning a group of dentists who refused on quality-of-care grounds to submit dental X-rays to insurance companies. The dentists claimed that their cooperation would lead to the denial of necessary care because X-rays, standing alone, are an insufficient basis for claims verification. Despite the group boycott characterization of this activity, the Court reviewed it under the Rule of

Reason. Cf. NCAA v. Board of Regents, 468 U.S. 85 (1984) (refusing application of the per se rule to restrictive policies regarding televising college football games because "horizontal restraints on competition are essential to the existence of intercollegiate athletics"). See generally, Blumstein & Sloan supra, 51 L. & Contemp. Prob. at 53-75.

Even under a Rule of Reason analysis, however, the hospital and its medical staff are far from being home free. Due to the potential difficulty of prevailing at the summary judgment stage, defendants might still have to face the enormous costs of a complex litigation. We turn, then, to the questions of (1) how courts should frame the Rule of Reason when quality-of-care justifications are proffered and (2) what level of scrutiny those justifications should receive. While the following case does not fit precisely within the context of hospital exclusion, it concerns boycott activity designed to keep an entire class of medical professionals from practicing.

Wilk v. American Medical Association
671 F. Supp. 1465 (N.D. Ill. 1987), *aff'd*, 895 F.2d 352
(7th Cir. 1990)

GETZENDANNER, DISTRICT JUDGE:

This antitrust case is on remand for a new trial from the Court of Appeals, Wilk v. AMA, 719 F.2d 207 (7th Cir. 1983) ("*Wilk*"). . . . The plaintiffs . . . are licensed chiropractors. In a complaint filed in 1976, plaintiffs charged the defendants with violating Section 1 . . . of the Sherman Act, 15 U.S.C. §1. . . . The defendants [are] the American Medical Association ("AMA"), the American Hospital Association ("AHA"), . . . the Joint Commission on Accreditation of Hospitals ("JCAH"), [and] the American Academy of Orthopaedic Surgeons ("AAOS"). . . .

At the first trial, the plaintiffs' principal claim was that the defendants engaged in a conspiracy to eliminate the chiropractic profession by refusing to deal with the plaintiffs and other chiropractors. Plaintiffs claimed that the boycott was accomplished through the use of Principle 3 of the AMA's Principles of Medical Ethics ("AMA's Principles") which prohibited medical physicians from associating professionally with unscientific practitioners. Principle 3 provided as follows:

> A physician should practice a method of healing founded on a scientific basis; and he should not voluntarily professionally associate with anyone who violates this principle.

It was the plaintiffs' contention that the AMA used Principle 3 to achieve a boycott of chiropractors by first calling chiropractors "un-

I. Providers' Rights to Practice

scientific practitioners," and then advising AMA members and other medical societies that it was unethical for medical physicians to associate with chiropractors. The other defendants, plaintiffs claimed, joined the boycott and the result was a conspiracy in restraint of trade in violation of Section 1 of the Sherman Act. The jury returned a verdict for the defendants and against the plaintiffs. That judgment was reversed on appeal and the case was remanded.

The *Wilk* Court clarified the principal legal issues in the case. The Court held that the legality of the defendants' conduct under Section 1 must be adjudged under the rule of reason articulated in Chicago Board of Trade v. United States, 246 U.S. 231, 238, 38 S. Ct. 242, 244, 62 L. Ed. 683 (1918). The Court rejected the plaintiffs' argument that the defendants' conduct was a per se violation of Section 1, holding that "a canon of medical ethics purporting, surely not frivolously, to address the importance of scientific method gives rise to questions of sufficient delicacy and novelty at least to escape per se treatment." . . .

Next, the Court held that if the plaintiffs met their burden of showing that the effect of Principle 3 and the implementing conduct had been to restrict competition rather than to promote it, the defendants could then come forward to show:

> (1) that they genuinely entertained a concern for what they perceive as scientific method in the care of each person with whom they have entered into a doctor-patient relationship; (2) that this concern is objectively reasonable; (3) that this concern has been the dominant motivating factor in defendants' promulgation of Principle 3 and in the conduct intended to implement it; and (4) that this concern for scientific method in patient care could not have been adequately satisfied in a manner less restrictive of competition.

719 F.2d at 227. This was called the "patient care defense." . . .

In view of the length of this opinion, I shall summarize my principal findings. The AMA and its officials . . . instituted a boycott of chiropractors in the mid-1960s by informing AMA members that chiropractors were unscientific practitioners and that it was unethical for a medical physician to associate with chiropractors. The purpose of the boycott was to contain and eliminate the chiropractic profession. This conduct constituted a conspiracy among the AMA and its members and an unreasonable restraint of trade in violation of Section 1 of the Sherman Act. . . .

[Facts]

In the early 1960s the AMA became concerned that medical physicians were cooperating with chiropractors. . . . As early as September 1963, the AMA's objective was the complete elimination of the chiropractic profession. In November of 1963, the AMA authorized the formation of the Committee on Quackery under the AMA's Department of Investigation. [T]he Committee's primary goal was to contain and eliminate chiropractic. . . . In 1967, the AMA Judicial Council issued an opinion under Principle 3 specifically holding that it was unethical for a physician to associate professionally with chiropractors. "Associating professionally" would include making referrals of patients to chiropractors, accepting referrals from chiropractors, providing diagnostic, laboratory, or radiology services for chiropractors, teaching chiropractors, or practicing together in any form. . . .

In 1980 the AMA adopted a completely revised version of the principles of medical ethics. Principle 3 finally was eliminated. The new principles provided that a medical physician "shall be free to choose whom to serve, with whom to associate, and the environment in which to provide medical services." . . .

As the hospital standard-setting organization, JCAH has the power to define and regulate the activities which take place in hospitals and to eliminate or frustrate competition from nonmedical physician health care providers. From before 1958, JCAH had standards which provided that the hospital medical staff shall be limited to fully licensed physicians. . . . Throughout the early 1970s, JCAH staff responded to several inquiries from hospitals and others about the role of chiropractors in hospitals by stating that the Commission would withdraw and refuse accreditation of a hospital that had chiropractors on its medical staff or that granted privileges to chiropractors. . . .

In 1983 the AMA participated in the revision of the JCAH accreditation standards for hospitals. The revision process started in 1982 with recommendations from the JCAH staff and the JCAH Standard-Survey Procedures Committee that each hospital, through its governing body, be permitted to decide for itself, under applicable state law, which licensed health care providers would be allowed hospital privileges and membership on the medical staff. . . .

[The court found that these changes in AMA and JCAH policies came only in response to this litigation and did not support the absence of a boycott. The court then concluded that the boycott clearly was an unreasonable restraint of trade because there were no substantial procompetitive benefits.]

[Legal Analysis]

I now consider whether the AMA has established the *Wilk* patient care defense. . . . I conclude that the AMA has established the first element of genuine concern. The next element is whether the concern for scientific method in patient care is objectively reasonable. . . .

I. Providers' Rights to Practice

At the time the Committee on Quackery was operating, there was a lot of material available to the Committee that supported its belief that all chiropractic was unscientific and deleterious. . . . There also was some evidence before the Committee that chiropractic was effective — more effective than the medical profession in treating certain kinds of problems such as workmen's back injuries. . . . The Committee did not follow up on any of these studies or opinions. Basically the Committee members were doctors who, because of their firm belief that chiropractic had to be stopped and eliminated, volunteered for service on the committee. . . .

The AMA acknowledges that, after the Committee on Quackery disbanded, chiropractic improved (and the AMA takes partial credit for it). . . . Thus the AMA's own evidence suggests that at some point during the boycott there was no longer an objectively reasonable concern that would support a boycott of the entire chiropractic profession.

The plaintiffs clearly want more from the court. They want a judicial pronouncement that chiropractic is a valid, efficacious, even scientific health care service. I believe that the answer to that question can only be provided by a well designed, controlled, scientific study. . . . No such study has ever been done. In the absence of such a study, the court is left to decide the issue on the basis of largely anecdotal evidence. I decline to pronounce chiropractic valid or invalid on anecdotal evidence. . . . Taking into account all of the evidence, I conclude only that the AMA has failed to meet its burden on the issue of whether its concern for the scientific method in support of the boycott of the entire chiropractic profession was objectively reasonable throughout the entire period of the boycott. This finding is not and should not be construed as a judicial endorsement of chiropractic.

The next element of the patient care defense is whether the AMA's concern about scientific method has been the dominant motivating factor in the defendants' promulgation of Principle 3 [and] the conduct undertaken and intended to implement Principle 3. The AMA has carried its burden on this issue. While there is some evidence that the Committee on Quackery and the AMA were motivated by economic concerns — there are too many references in the record to chiropractors as competitors to ignore — I am persuaded that the dominant factor was patient care and the AMA's subjective belief that chiropractic was not in the best interests of patients.

The final question is whether this concern for scientific method in patient care could have been adequately satisfied in a manner less restrictive of competition. It would be a difficult task to persuade a court that a boycott and conspiracy designed to contain and eliminate a profession that was licensed in all fifty states at the time the

Committee on Quackery disbanded was the only way to satisfy the AMA's concern for the use of scientific method in patient care. The AMA presented no evidence that a public education approach or any other less restrictive approach was beyond the ability or resources of the AMA or had been tried and failed. The AMA obviously was not successful in defeating the licensing of chiropractic on a state by state basis, but that failure does not mean that they had to resort to the highly restrictive means of the boycott. The AMA and other medical societies have managed to change America's health-related conduct by what appears to be good public relations work and there has been no proof that a similar campaign would not have been at least as effective as the boycott in educating consumers about chiropractic and the AMA's concern for scientific method. . . .

Order

Based on the findings of fact and conclusions of law set forth in this opinion, an injunction shall issue against defendant AMA [but not the other defendants, whom the court found acted independently and therefore were not part of the conspiracy]. . . . FORM OF INJUNCTION: The AMA, its officers, agents and employees, and all persons who act in active concert with any of them and who receive actual notice of this order are hereby permanently enjoined from restricting, regulating or impeding . . . the freedom of any AMA member or any institution or hospital to make an individual decision as to whether or not that AMA member, institution, or hospital shall professionally associate with chiropractors, chiropractic students, or chiropractic institutions. . . .

NOTES

The Rule of Reason and Quality of Care as a Defense

1. Does *Wilk* effectively mandate chiropractors' access to hospitals? What if a hospital excluded all allied health professionals because it stakes its reputation on providing the *most* highly advanced, scientifically based, and technologically sophisticated medicine available, or because it believes that its competitive position will be enhanced if it restricts itself to a single, well-identified school of practice? In other words, must quality-of-care concerns relate to *poor* quality, or is it sufficient to demonstrate that an alternative practitioner's school of practice isn't quite *as* good or is merely different?

The answer depends in part on whether quality of care is considered as an *excuse* for anticompetitive conduct or instead whether it supports a *procompetitive* justification. If quality concerns serve as a

I. Providers' Rights to Practice

positive justification, then any enhancement of quality factors into the balance. However, if quality concerns are raised to excuse an otherwise anticompetitive restraint, it would appear that only demonstrably poor quality serves as a defense.

There presently is no clear answer to this query. Indeed, the law is in a state of complete confusion. As summarized in *Weiss* supra, the Supreme Court rejected in Goldfarb v. Virginia State Bar, 421 U.S. 773 (1975), the then-prevailing notion that the "learned professions" might be exempt from antitrust. However, the Court dropped a puzzling footnote 17 in which it stated that the "public service aspect, and other features of the professions, may require that a particular practice, which could properly be viewed as a violation of the Sherman Act in another context, be treated differently." See page 497 supra. The Court has never adequately explained footnote 17. Although on its face, the footnote appears to suggest a patient care excuse is available, the Court appeared to repudiate this notion in National Society of Professional Engineers v. United States, 435 U.S. 679 (1978). There, a professional society of engineers sought to defend an ethical canon against competitive bidding based on the public safety concerns raised by the prospect of inferior engineering work. The Court rejected this defense, holding:

> Contrary to its name, the Rule [of Reason] does not open the field of antitrust inquiry to any argument in favor of a challenged restraint that may fall within the realm of reason. Instead, . . . the inquiry is confined to a consideration of the impact on competitive conditions. [T]he purpose of the analysis is to form a judgment about the competitive significance of the restraint; it is not to decide whether a policy favoring competition is in the public interest, or in the interest of the members of an industry. [T]hat policy decision has been made by the Congress.

Nevertheless, the Court in dictum continued to give lip service to a patient care defense in Arizona v. Maricopa County Medical Society, 435 U.S. 679, 696 (1978), reprinted in Chapter 8.III.C, and it appeared to give at least passing reference to a patient care defense in F.T.C. v. Indiana Federation of Dentists, 476 U.S. 447 (1986), although in both cases it had little difficulty in finding the doctors' actions illegal.

One possible manner in which to reconcile these various rulings is to observe, first, that a patient care defense will, at a minimum, take the case out of the per se category. Otherwise, *National Society* and *Indiana Federation*, which were treated as Rule of Reason cases, probably would have been per se decisions on their facts. Beyond this, there may still be room to give a sensitive, balancing consideration to patient care concerns, as the court did in *Wilk*, if the action in question appears to be a legitimate ethical rule and not a naked restraint motivated by economic considerations. The Supreme Court has never clearly allowed this, but all of the cases it has considered so far have concerned rather obviously anticompetitive actions. But see Greaney, Quality of Care and Market Failure Defense in Antitrust Health Care Litigation, 21 Conn. L. Rev. 605 (1989) (no patient care defense should be allowed except in narrowly defined circumstances of "market failure").

In any event, it is clear that quality of care concerns can be considered under the Rule of Reason at least in the form of procompetitive justifications for a restraint, which is quite possible in staffing decisions made by hospitals:

> Under the rule of reason, an exclusion based on quality of care is defensible [ ] because quality is a major competitive variable in the health care industry. . . . Quality, instead of price, is a major factor patients and physicians use to select a hospital. Therefore, where an exclusion improves the overall quality of a hospital, the restriction is procompetitive and quality of care may be asserted as a defense.

Note, Denial of Hospital Privileges to Non-Physicians: Does Quality of Care Justify a Potential Restraint of Trade?, 19 Ind. L. Rev. 1219, 1232-1233 (1986) ["*Quality of Care Note*"]. See also Havighurst, Doctors and Hospitals, An Antitrust Perspective on Traditional Relationships, 1984 Duke L.J. 1071, 1095 ("[T]he self-policing activities of a medical staff are upheld only because they promote competition and efficiency, and not because they are in some other sense 'in the public interest.' . . . Antitrust law does not, as a general rule, tolerate competitor collaboration simply because it serves worthy purposes, professional or otherwise"); Kauper, The Role of Quality of Health Care Considerations in Antitrust Analysis, 51 L. & Contemp. Prob. 273 (1988). Why, then, is a Catholic hospital allowed to exclude abortionists? (Possibly because of overriding First Amendment interests.)

2. The *Wilk* court's highly stylized version of the Rule of Reason is far from universally accepted. Consider the relative merits of the following alternative formulations advanced by commentators and other courts:

(a) *The purpose-based version:*

> [H]elpful lines between legal and illegal privilege decisions can be drawn . . . by requiring, for proof of an antitrust violation, that there be convincing evidence that the privilege decision has been motivated by a dominant anticompetitive purpose. . . . [This] would give notice to hospitals that they remain free to base privilege decisions on any arguable quality of care concern that they choose to pursue.

Kissam, et al., supra, 70 Calif. L. Rev. at 669-670. See also Kissam, Antitrust Boycott Doctrine, 69 Iowa L. Rev. 1165, 1222 (1984).

I. Providers' Rights to Practice

(b) *The quick-look version:*

To ensure that hospitals have reasonable freedom of action, a court, once it is satisfied that the hospital and not the medical staff has made a particular staffing or privileges decision, should refrain from closely scrutinizing the action taken. . . . Thus, summary judgment or a directed verdict would be appropriate if documentary evidence and affidavits showed that the hospital's action reflected its [own] corporate concerns. . . . Under this test, a court would not concern itself . . . with whether the ostensible motives for the actions taken were the real motives or whether the adverse effect of the hospital action on competition among practitioners was outweighed by its actual contribution to fulfilling the hospital's objectives.

Havighurst, Doctors and Hospitals: An Antitrust Perspective on Traditional Relationships, 1984 Duke L.J. 1071, 1133-1134, 1157. See also Havighurst, Professional Peer Review and the Antitrust Laws, 36 Case W. L. Rev. 1117 (1986).

(c) *The due process version:*

If a hospital decides, following a hearing which meets the requirements of due process, to terminate a physician's staff privilege for reasons valid under the antitrust laws, and those reasons are supported by substantial evidence, no factual question remains as to section 1 claims [and the case may be dismissed before trial].

Pontius v. Children's Hosp., 552 F. Supp. 1352, 1372 (W.D. Pa. 1982). See also Silver v. N.Y. Stock Exch., 373 U.S. 341 (1965). Contra Miller v. Indiana Hospital, 843 F.2d 139 (3d Cir. 1988).

(d) *The Rebuttable Presumption of Invalidity Version:*

The historical institutional relationships within the hospital dictate a precautionary prophylactic approach [to certain, "cartel-behavior" staffing decisions. . . .] These [ ] decisions [should] be subject to the rule requiring defendants to establish an overriding procompetitive justification. [I]n attempting to satisfy [this] burden . . . a defendant hospital would have to show that its procompetitive justification is not just theoretically but factually demonstrable.

Blumstein & Sloan, Antitrust and Hospital Peer Review, 51 L. & Contemp. Prob. 7, 81-82 (1988).

3. Note that both *Weiss* and *Wilk* deal with class-based exclusions of an entire practitioner group. How do the antitrust considerations differ for the exclusion of individuals? See Quality of Care Note, supra, 19 Ind. L. Rev. at 1228-1237 (arguing for relaxed scrutiny of individual exclusions because they receive greater procedural protection and have a much smaller impact on the market); Health Care

Quality Improvement Act of 1986 infra at 513 (immunizing individual but not class-based exclusions).

Allied Health Professionals, Professional Society Rules, and Exclusive Contracts for Hospital Ancillary Services

4. Both *Wilk* and *Weiss* manifest the traditional medical establishment's longstanding hostility to competing schools of practitioners that are founded on less scientific theories of medicine. Chiropractors and osteopaths are only two among the many allied health professions that are engaged in active struggles to achieve professional recognition and hospital access. Similar challenges have been mounted by podiatrists, clinical psychologists, nurse anesthetists, and midwives. See, e.g., Oltz v. St. Peter's Community Hosp., 861 F.2d 1440 (9th Cir. 1988) (finding antitrust violation in hospital's termination of nurse anesthetist's contract); Cooper v. Forsyth County Hosp. Auth., 789 F.2d 278 (4th Cir. 1986) (refusing to entertain a suit by podiatrists).

An important indirect effect of this antitrust pressure has been to force a favorable revision of the JCAH accreditation standards. Prior to 1984, JCAH standards were read as prohibiting hospitals from extending staff privileges to practitioners other than doctors and dentists. However, in that year, the JCAH adopted an amendment that allowed hospitals to "include other licensed individuals permitted by law and by the hospital to provide patient care services independently." For a survey of these developments, see Quality of Care Note, supra, 19 Ind. L. Rev. at 1224-1228; Note, Health Professionals' Access to Hospitals: A Retrospective and Prospective Analysis, 34 Vand. L. Rev. 1161 (1981).

In some states, allied health professionals have won their contest in the state legislature with statutory enactments that require hospitals to grant them equal consideration in extending clinical privileges. Representative is D.C. Code Ann. §32-1307, which requires individual, nondiscriminatory consideration of the credentials of podiatrists, psychologists, nurse anesthetists, nurse midwives, and nurse practitioners. See also Ohio Rev. Code Ann. §3701.35.1(B). For a comprehensive list of similar state provisions, see Hospitals, May 16, 1984, at 23; Dooley v. Barberton Citizens Hosp., 465 N.E.2d 58, 61 n.1 (Ohio 1984) (citing to 14 state codes).

5. *Wilk* also represents a line of cases that address the validity of professional society and accreditation rules. The most prominent of these is American Medical Association vs. F.T.C., 94 F.T.C. 980, 1015 (1979), *enforced*, 638 F.2d 443 (2d Cir. 1980), *aff'd by an equally divided Court*, 455 U.S. 676 (1982), which invalidates ethical prohibitions against advertising and certain physician contractual arrangements. See also F.T.C. v. Indiana Fedn. of Dentists, 476 U.S. 447

(1986) (striking dentist society refusal to cooperate with insurance company's claims verification process); Kreuzer v. American Academy of Periodontology, 735 F.2d 1479 (D.C. Cir. 1984) (reviewing requirement limiting dentists' practice to periodontics only); Koefoot v. American College of Surgeons, 652 F. Supp. 882 (N.D. Ill. 1986). The year 1983 saw extensive academic commentary on this topic: Havighurst & King, Private Credentialing of Health Care Personnel: An Antitrust Perspective, 9 Am. J.L. & Med. 131, 263 (1983); Jost, The Joint Commission on Accreditation of Hospitals: Private Regulation of Health Care and the Public Interest, 24 B.C.L. Rev. 835 (1983); Kissam, Government Policy Toward Medical Accreditation and Certification: The Antitrust Laws and Other Procompetitive Strategies, 1983 Wisc. L. Rev. 1.

6. Another related line of cases are those concerning health insurance company limitations on reimbursement. Chiropractors, for instance, would be severely affected if Blue Cross/Blue Shield refused to pay for their services. However, if Blue Cross/Blue Shield merely determines on its own the terms under which it is willing to do business and separately reaches an agreement with individual providers, there is no horizontal conspiracy — or is there? Law professor Sylvia Law, in her influential study Blue Cross: What Went Wrong? (2d ed. 1976), explains that providers historically have dominated the Blues and used them to enforce their economic interests. This complication, which creates possible grounds for finding the requisite multiplicity of actors, has caused the courts endless difficulty in sorting out the conduct of various Blue Cross/Blue Shield plans around the country. See Chapter 8.III.C.

7. Finally, hospital/physician arrangements are sometimes characterized as per se illegal "tie-ins," that is, attempts to force consumers to purchase an unwanted item when they buy another item they want. For instance, hospitals that limit anesthesiology services exclusively to in-house physicians, rather than opening them up to the independent medical community at large, have been accused of tying these services to their surgery services. So far, such challenges have failed, not because the tie-in characterization is inapplicable but because the particular hospital lacks the requisite market power to force the sale on the patient. Jefferson Parish Hosp. Dist. v. Hyde, 466 U.S. 2 (1984); Collins v. Associated Pathologists, Ltd., 844 F.2d 473 (7th Cir. 1988); Classen, *Jefferson Parish* and Its Progeny, 75 Ky. L.J. 441 (1987). For a succinct analysis of the underlying economic issues, see Lynk, Restraint of Trade through Hospital Exclusive Contracts: An Economic Appraisal of Legal Theory, 9 J. Health Pol. Poly. & L. 269 (1984).

8. For general review of antitrust challenges to staff privileges decisions, see 89 A.L.R. Fed. 419 (1988), in addition to the numerous

secondary sources cited in the notes and cases of this section and of Chapters 7.VII (hospital mergers) and 8.III.C. (PPOs).

D. Peer Review Confidentiality and Immunity

Statutes on Peer Review Committees
Arizona Revised Statutes

§36-445. *Review of Certain Medical Practices*

The governing body of each licensed hospital shall require that physicians admitted to practice in the hospital organize into committees or other organizational structures to review the professional practices within the hospital for the purposes of reducing morbidity and mortality and for the improvement of the care of patients provided in the institution. Such review shall include the nature, quality and necessity of the care provided and the preventability of complications and deaths occurring in the hospital.

§36-445.01. *Confidentiality of Information; Conditions of Disclosure*

All proceedings, records and materials prepared in connection with the reviews provided for in §36-445, including all peer reviews of individual health care providers practicing in and applying to practice in hospitals and the records of such reviews, shall be confidential and shall not be subject to discovery except in proceedings before the board of medical examiners, or the board of osteopathic examiners, or in actions by an individual health care provider against a hospital or its medical staff arising from discipline of such individual health care provider or refusal, termination, suspension or limitation of his privileges. No member of a committee established under the provisions of §36-445 or officer or other member of a hospital's medical, administrative or nursing staff engaged in assisting the hospital to carry out functions in accordance with that section or any person furnishing information to a committee performing peer review may be subpoenaed to testify in any judicial or quasi-judicial proceeding if such subpoena is based solely on such activities. . . . In any legal action brought against a hospital licensed pursuant to this chapter claiming negligence for failure to adequately do peer review, representatives of the hospital are permitted to testify as to whether there was peer review as to the subject matter being litigated. The contents and records of the peer review proceedings are fully confidential and inadmissible as evidence in any court of law.

I. Providers' Rights to Practice

Health Care Quality Improvement Act of 1986
Title 42, United States Code

§11101

The Congress finds the following:

(1) The increasing occurrence of medical malpractice and the need to improve the quality of medical care have become nationwide problems that warrant greater efforts than those that can be undertaken by any individual State.

(2) There is a national need to restrict the ability of incompetent physicians to move from State to State without disclosure or discovery of the physician's previous damaging or incompetent performance.

(3) This nationwide problem can be remedied through effective professional peer review.

(4) The threat of private money damage liability under Federal laws, including treble damage liability under Federal antitrust law, unreasonably discourages physicians from participating in effective professional peer review.

(5) There is an overriding national need to provide incentive and protection for physicians engaging in effective professional peer review.

§11111

(a)(1) If a professional review action . . . meets all the standards specified in section 11112(a) of this title, . . . any person who participates with or assists . . . with respect to the action, shall not be liable in damages under any law of the United States or of any State (or political subdivision thereof) with respect to the action. The preceding sentence shall not apply to damages under any law of the United States or any State relating to the civil rights of any person or persons. . . .

(c) . . . Subsection (a) of this section shall not apply to State laws . . . if the State by legislation elects such treatment.

§11112

(a) For purposes of the protection set forth in section 11111(a) of this title, a professional review action must be taken — (1) in the reasonable belief that the action was in the furtherance of quality health care, (2) after a reasonable effort to obtain the facts of the matter, (3) after adequate notice and hearing procedures are afforded to the physician involved or after such other procedures as are fair to the physician under the circumstances, and (4) in the reasonable belief that the action was warranted by the facts. . . . A professional review action shall be presumed to have met the preceding standards, . . . unless the presumption is rebutted by a preponderance of the evidence.

(b) A health care entity is deemed to have met the adequate notice and hearing requirement of subsection (a)(3) with respect to a physician if the following conditions are met: . . . (3) If a hearing is requested on a timely basis . . . , (A) the hearing shall be held . . . before a panel of individuals who are appointed by the entity and are not in direct economic competition with the physician involved; . . . (C) in the hearing the physician involved has the right (i) to representation by an attorney [ ], (ii) to have a record made of the proceedings, . . . (iii) to call, examine, and cross-examine witnesses, [and] (iv) to present [relevant] evidence regardless of its admissibility in a court of law. . . .

A professional review body's failure to meet the conditions described in this subsection [b] shall not, in itself, constitute failure to meet the standards of subsection (a)(3).

§11113

In any suit brought against a defendant, to the extent that a defendant has met the standards set forth under section 11112(a) of this title and the defendant substantially prevails, the court shall, at the conclusion of the action, award to a substantially prevailing party defending against any such claim the cost of the suit attributable to such claim, including a reasonable attorney's fee, if the claim, or the claimant's conduct during the litigation of the claim, was frivolous, unreasonable, without foundation, or in bad faith. . . .

§11115

Except as specifically provided . . . , nothing in this subchapter shall be construed (a) as changing the liabilities or immunities under law; . . . (b) as requiring health care entities to provide clinical privileges to any or all classes or types of physicians or other licensed health care practitioners; . . . [or] (c) as affecting, or modifying any provision of Federal or State law, with respect to activities of professional review bodies regarding nurses, other licensed health care practitioners, or other health professionals who are not physicians. . . .

§11151

(a) In this title: . . . (9) The term "professional review action" means an action or recommendation . . . which is based on the competence or professional conduct of an individual physician (which conduct affects or could affect adversely the health or welfare of a patient or patients).

NOTES

Confidentiality and Immunity Provisions

1. Virtually every state has a peer review confidentiality statute similar to Arizona's. The constitutionality of one such statute was upheld in Eubanks v. Farrier, 267 S.E.2d 230 (Ga. 1980), in which the court observed that the statute represents a legislative balance "between the competing public concerns of fostering medical staff candor, on the one hand, and impairing medical malpractice plaintiffs' access to evidence, on the other hand." Id. at 232. Recently, however, the Kentucky Supreme Court struck down the application of its peer review confidentiality statute to a patient's malpractice action as being in violation of that state's prohibition on laws which "relate to more than one subject" and laws whose subject is not expressed in their title. Sweasy v. King's Daughters Mem. Hosp., 771 S.W.2d 812 (Ky. 1989).

In general, these statutes produce a constant stream of litigation over which hospital committees and which records they cover. Consider, for instance, whether the privilege extends to the proceedings of ethics committees. See Merritt, The Tort Liability of Hospital Ethics Committees, 60 S. Cal. L. Rev. 1239 (1987). Answers to these questions depend on the variability of statutory wording in each state. For a sampling of recent decisions, see Gallagher v. Detroit-Macomb Hosp. Assn., 431 N.W.2d 90 (Mich. App. 1988) (statute protects hospital "incident report"); John C. Lincoln Hosp. v. Superior Court, 768 P.2d 188 (Ariz. App. 1989) (statute does not cover "incident report" because it contains no committee deliberations, only factual information); Humana Hosp. Desert Valley v. Superior Court, 742 P.2d 1382 (Ariz. App. 1987) (statute protects files of new applicants as well as reviews of existing staff members); Klarfeld v. Salsbury, 355 S.E.2d 319 (Va. 1987) (statute does not apply to proceedings before a malpractice screening panel); Sanderson v. Bryan, 522 A.2d 1138 (Pa. Super. 1987) (confidentiality not limited to proceedings concerning only the plaintiff patient's case; extends to deliberations over doctor's treatment of other patients). See generally AHA, Immunity for Peer Review Participants in Hospitals (1989); Comment, The Medical Review Committee Privilege: A Jurisdictional Survey, 67 N.C.L. Rev. 179 (1988); Rowland, Enforcing Hospital Responsibility through Self-Evaluation and Review Committee Confidentiality,

9 J. Leg. Med. 377 (1988); Butler, Records and Proceedings of Hospital Committees Privileged Against Discovery, 28 S. Tex. L. Rev. 97 (1987); Comment, Peer Review Committee Minutes and Memoranda: Non-Discoverable at All Costs?, 1 J.L. & Health 249 (1986-1987); Comment, Medical Peer Review Protection in the Health Care Industry, 52 Temple L.Q. 5552 (1979); Hall, Hospital Committee Procedures and Reports: Their Legal Status, 1 Am. J.L. & Med. 245 1978; Note, 53 U. Mo. K.C. L. Rev. 663 (1985); Annot., 81 A.L.R.3d 944 (1977); Annot., 60 A.L.R. 4th 1273 (1988); Bertolet, Hospital Liability §15.02 (5th Ed. 1987).

A few decisions have recognized a common law privilege protecting internal hospital review records even in the absence of such statutes. See Bredice v. Doctor's Hosp., 50 F.R.D. 249 (D.D.C. 1970), *aff'd*, 479 F.2d 920 (D.C. 1973); Comment, Criticizing the Self-Criticism Privilege, 1987 U. Ill. L. Rev. 675.

2. In addition to the state confidentiality laws and the federal immunity statute, several states have passed their own "shield laws" that are designed to provide a degree of legal immunity for hospital peer-review committees, hospital staffs, and witnesses. E.g., Or. Rev. Stat. §§441.030-441.055; Ariz. Rev. Stat. §36-445.02. See Leonard, Codifying a Privilege for Self-Critical Analysis, 25 Harv. J. Leg. 113, 119 (1988) (collecting citations).

3. Precisely which medical staff disputes does the federal immunity cover? A helpful guide is to check (carefully) how many of the cases in this chapter it would have precluded. Realize, for instance, that by virtue of the definition of professional review action, "actions against a class of physicians do not fall within the purview of this legislation." H.R. Rep. No. 903, 99th Cong., 2d Sess. at 21 (1988) p.21.

How effective do you think the federal immunity will be even for those disputes that it does cover, considering the showing that must be made to enjoy the immunity? See Austin v. McNamara, 731 F. Supp. 934 (C.D. Cal. 1990) (undertaking extensive analysis of facts, proceedings, and evidence before finding immunity); Curran, Medical Peer Review of Physician Competence and Performance: Legal Immunity and the Antitrust Laws, 316 New Eng. J. Med. 597, 598 (1987) ("the shield for physicians now contains a plethora of gaping holes through which many a guided missile can reach its human target"); Havighurst, Professional Peer Review and the Antitrust Laws, 36 Case W. L. Rev. 1117, 1161 (1986) ("the new act does more to complicate than to simplify litigation"); Note, 29 Wm. & Mary L. Rev. 609, 632 (1988) (the act "will reduce litigation expenses and encourage better peer review"); Note, The Health Care Quality Improvement Act of 1986: Will Physicians Find Peer Review More

Inviting?, 74 Va. L. Rev. 1115 (1988) ("the Act should remove the threat of litigation"); Bierig & Portman, The Health Care Quality Improvement Act of 1986, 32 St. Louis U.L.J. 977 (1989); Colantonio, The Health Care Quality Improvement Act of 1986 and its Impact on Hospital Law, 91 W. Va. L. Rev. 91 (1988).

4. Another potential defense, one that is applicable under the federal antitrust laws, is known as the "state action exemption." In Parker v. Brown, 317 U.S. 341 (1943), the Supreme Court held that the antitrust laws do not apply to activity engaged in or required by the states. For instance, it would be spurious to charge a state Board of Medical Examiners with an antitrust violation for revoking a physician's license. The state action defense potentially exists with respect to physician discipline even at *private* hospitals if state law mandates and "actively supervises" the private peer review process.

This contention was the subject of the Supreme Court's most noted health care law decision of the 1987 term, Patrick v. Burgett, 486 U.S. 94, 108 S. Ct. 1658, 100 L. Ed. 2d 83 (1988). *Patrick* involved a doctor who was forced to resign from the staff of the only hospital in town in retaliation for refusing to join the group practice that composed a majority of the medical staff. The Ninth Circuit relied on the Parker v. Brown state action exemption in overturning a damage award of more than $2 million that had "sent shock waves through the ranks of medical and hospital organizations." Curran, supra at 598. However, the Supreme Court reversed and reinstated the verdict, holding that private hospital credentialing decisions in Oregon are not sufficiently supervised by the state to bring them within the protection of this defense. The Court observed that Oregon so far has not recognized a common law right of judicial review of credentialing decisions.

Although *Patrick* was initially read as closing the door to state action exemption in medical staff disputes, it left open the small crack of a possibility that this defense might be available in another state whose common law differs. However, it does not appear that even a *Greisman* common law theory of judicial review would meet the Court's objection that "[the courts do no] more than to make sure that some sort of reasonable procedure was afforded and that there was evidence from which it could be found that plaintiff's conduct posed a threat to patient care." *Patrick*, 108 S. Ct. at 1665. So far, subsequent federal decisions have been in accord with this reading of *Patrick*. Pinhas v. Summit Health Ltd., 880 F.2d 1108 (9th Cir. 1989) (the "limited form of [judicial] review [in California] is similar to the standards applied by the Oregon courts that the Supreme Court found insufficient to constitute active supervision"); Shahawy v. Harrison, 875 F.2d 1529 (11th Cir. 1989) (same, for Florida).

II. PATIENTS' RIGHTS TO TREATMENT

A. *The Duty to Treat Paying Patients*

Hurley v. Eddingfield
59 N.E. 1058 (Ind. 1901)

BAKER, J. The appellant sued appellee for $10,000 damages for wrongfully causing the death of his intestate. The court sustained appellee's demurrer to the complaint, and this ruling is assigned as error.

The material facts alleged may be summarized thus: At and for years before decedent's death appellee was a practicing physician at Mace, in Montgomery county, duly licensed under the laws of the state. He held himself out to the public as a general practitioner of medicine. He had been decedent's family physician. Decedent became dangerously ill, and sent for appellee. The messenger informed appellee of decedent's violent sickness, tendered him his fee for his services, and stated to him that no other physician was procurable in time, and that decedent relied on him for attention. No other physician was procurable in time to be of any use, and decedent did rely on appellee for medical assistance. Without any reason whatever, appellee refused to render aid to decedent. No other patients were requiring appellee's immediate service, and he could have gone to the relief of decedent if he had been willing to do so. Death ensued, without decedent's fault, and wholly from appellee's wrongful act. The alleged wrongful act was appellee's refusal to enter into a contract of employment. Counsel do not contend that, before the enactment of the law regulating the practice of medicine, physicians were bound to render professional service to every one who applied. The act regulating the practice of medicine provides for a board of examiners, standards of qualification, examinations, licenses to those found qualified, and penalties for practicing without license. The act is a preventive, not a compulsive, measure. In obtaining the state's license (permission) to practice medicine, the state does not require, and the licensee does not engage, that he will practice at all or on other terms than he may choose to accept. Counsel's analogies, drawn from the obligations to the public on the part of innkeepers, common carriers, and the like, are beside the mark. Judgment affirmed.

Wilmington General Hospital v. Manlove
174 A.2d 135 (Del. 1961)

SOUTHERLAND, CHIEF JUSTICE.

This case concerns the liability of a private hospital for the death

II. Patients' Rights to Treatment

of an infant who was refused treatment at the emergency ward of the hospital. . . .

There is no real conflict of fact as to what occurred at the hospital. The parents took the infant into the reception room of the Emergency Ward. A nurse was on duty. They explained to the nurse what was wrong with the child, that is, that he had not slept for two nights, had a continuously high temperature, and that he had diarrhea. Mr. Manlove told the nurse that the child was under the care of Dr. Hershon and Dr. Thomas, and showed the nurse the medicines prescribed. The nurse explained to the parents that the hospital could not give treatment because the child was under the care of a physician and there would be danger that the medication of the hospital might conflict with that of the attending physician. The nurse did not examine the child, take his temperature, feel his forehead, or look down his throat. The child was not in convulsions, and was not coughing or crying. There was no particular area of body tenderness.

The nurse tried to get in touch with Dr. Hershon or Dr. Thomas in the hospital and at their offices, but was unable to do so. She suggested that the parents bring the baby Thursday morning to the pediatric clinic.

Mr. and Mrs. Manlove returned home. Mrs. Manlove made an appointment by telephone to see Dr. Hershon or Dr. Thomas that night at eight o'clock. At eight minutes past three o'clock in the afternoon the baby died of bronchial pneumonia. . . .

Defendant answered [the complaint] denying negligence and averring that, pursuant to its established rules and community practice, plaintiff was advised by its employee that it was unable to accept the infant for care. . . .

The holding of the court below may be summarized as follows: 1. The hospital is liable for refusal to furnish medical treatment in an emergency because it is a quasi-public institution, being the recipient of grants of public funds and of tax exemptions. 2. There was some evidence of an apparent emergency because (1) of death following in a few hours, and (2) of the child's symptoms as recited by the nurse. Hence the court denied the [defendant's summary judgment] motion. The hospital appeals. We take a somewhat different view of these questions from that of the learned judge below.

First, as to the status of the defendant hospital . . . [w]e are compelled to disagree with the view that the defendant has become a public (or quasi-public) hospital. It is admitted (although the record does not show it) that it is privately owned and operated. We find no dissent from the rule that such a hospital is a private hospital, and may, at least in the absence of control by the legislature, conduct its business largely as it sees fit. . . .

Moreover, the holding that the receipt of grants of public money requires the hospital to care for emergency cases, as distinguished from others, is not logical. Why emergency cases? If the holding is sound it must apply to all the hospital services, and that conclusion, as we shall see, is clearly unsound. . . .

What, then, is the liability of a private hospital in this respect? Since such an institution as the defendant is privately owned and operated, it would follow logically that its trustees or governing board alone have the right to determine who shall be admitted to it as patients. No other rule would be sensible or workable. Such authority as we have found supports this rule.

"A private hospital owes the public no duty to accept any patient not desired by it, and it is not necessary to assign any reason for its refusal to accept a patient for hospital service." 41 C.J.S. Hospitals §8, p.345. To the same effect is 26 Am. Jur. "Hospitals and Asylums," p.593. In Birmingham Baptist Hospital v. Crews, 229 Ala. 398, 157 So. 224, 225, it appeared that after giving a child emergency treatment for diphtheria the hospital refused her admission because its regulations did not permit the admission of patients with contagious diseases. . . .

The above authorities announce a general rule governing the question of admissions to a private hospital. Does that rule apply to the fullest extent to patients applying for treatment at an emergency ward? . . . It may be conceded that a private hospital is under no legal obligation to the public to maintain an emergency ward, or, for that matter, a public clinic. . . . But the maintenance of such a ward to render first-aid to injured persons has become a well-established adjunct to the main business of a hospital. If a person, seriously hurt, applies for such aid at an emergency ward, relying on the established custom to render it, is it still the right of the hospital to turn him away without any reason? In such a case, it seems to us, such a refusal might well result in worsening the condition of the injured person, because of the time lost in a useless attempt to obtain medical aid. Such a set of circumstances is analogous to the case of the negligent termination of gratuitous services, which creates a tort liability. Restatement, Law of Torts, "Negligence," §323. . . .

[W]e are of opinion that liability on the part of a hospital may be predicated on the refusal of service to a patient in case of an unmistakable emergency, if the patient has relied upon a well-established custom of the hospital to render aid in such a case. . . . Applying this rule here, we inquire, was there an unmistakable emergency? Certainly the record does not support the view that the infant's condition was so desperate that a layman could reasonably say that he was in immediate danger. The learned judge indicated that the fact that death followed in a few hours showed an emergency; but with this we cannot agree. It is hindsight. And it is to be noted that

II. Patients' Rights to Treatment

the attending physician, after prescribing for the child one morning before, did not think another examination that night or the next morning was required. If this case had gone to the jury on the record here made, we would have been required to hold that it was insufficient to establish liability. We cannot agree that the mere recitation of the infant's symptoms was, in itself, evidence of an emergency sufficient to present a question for the jury. Before such an issue could arise there would have to be evidence that an experienced nurse should have known that such symptoms constituted unmistakable evidence of an emergency. . . .

The possibility that the case might turn on additional evidence respecting the matters we have touched upon was not considered either by the court or counsel. In the circumstances we think the case should go back for further proceedings. We should add, however, that if plaintiff cannot adduce evidence showing some incompetency of the nurse, or some breach of duty or some negligence, his case must fail. Like the learned judge below, we sympathize with the parents in their loss of a child; but this natural feeling does not permit us to find liability in the absence of satisfactory evidence.

For the reasons above set forth the order denying summary judgment is affirmed, without approving the reasons therefor set forth in the court's opinion.

Payton v. Weaver
182 Cal. Rptr. 225 (Cal. App. 1982)

GRODIN, ASSOCIATE JUSTICE.

Occasionally a case will challenge the ability of the law, and society, to cope effectively and sensitively with fundamental problems of human existence. This is such a case. Appellant, Brenda Payton, is a 35-year-old black woman who suffers from a permanent and irreversible loss of kidney function, a condition known as chronic end stage renal disease. To stay alive, she must subject herself two or three times a week to hemodialysis (dialysis), a process in which the patient's circulatory system is connected to a machine through which the blood is passed. . . .

Brenda has other difficulties. Unable to care for her children, she lives alone in a low-income housing project in West Oakland, subsisting on a $356 per month Social Security check. She has no family support; one brother is in prison and another is a mental patient. She confesses that she is a drug addict, having been addicted to heroin and barbiturates for over 15 years. She has alcohol problems, weight problems and, not surprisingly, emotional problems as well.

Despite these difficulties Brenda appears from the record to be a marvelously sympathetic and articulate individual who in her lucid moments possesses a great sense of dignity and is intent upon preserving her independence and her integrity as a human being. At times, however, her behavior is such as to make extremely difficult the provision of medical care which she so desperately requires.

The other principal figure in this case is respondent John C. Weaver, Jr., a physician specializing in kidney problems. He conducts his practice through respondent Biomedical Application of Oakland, Inc. (BMA), which operates an outpatient dialysis treatment unit on the premises of respondent Providence Hospital.

Dr. Weaver began treating Brenda in 1975 when, after the birth of Brenda's twin daughters, her system rejected a transplanted kidney. He has been treating her ever since. To her, "Dr. Weaver is and was and still is the man between me and death . . . other than God, I don't think of nobody higher than I do Dr. Weaver."

On December 12, 1978, Dr. Weaver sent Brenda a letter stating he would no longer permit her to be treated at BMA because of her "persistent uncooperative and antisocial behavior over . . . more than . . . three years, . . . her persistent refusal to adhere to reasonable constraints of hemodialysis, the dietary schedules and medical prescriptions . . . the use of barbiturates and other illicit drugs and because all this resulted in disruption of our program at BMA."

In the latter part of 1978, Brenda applied for admission to the regular dialysis treatment programs operated by respondents Alta Bates and Herrick hospitals, and was refused.

For several months Dr. Weaver continued to provide Brenda with necessary dialysis on an emergency basis, through Providence. On April 23, 1979, he again notified her by letter that he would no longer treat her on an outpatient basis. This letter led to Brenda's filing of a petition for mandate to compel Dr. Weaver, BMA, and Providence to continue to provide her with outpatient dialysis services. . . .

The trial court, after a lengthy evidentiary hearing, found that . . . Brenda's behavior . . . affect[ed] not only Dr. Weaver but the other patients and the treating staff as well. Dialysis treatment is typically provided to several patients at a time, all of them connected to a single dialysis machine. There was evidence that Brenda would frequently appear for treatment late or at unscheduled times in a drugged or alcoholic condition, that she used profane and vulgar language, and that she had on occasion engaged in disruptive behavior, such as bothering other patients, cursing staff members with obscenities, screaming and demanding that the dialysis be turned off and that she be disconnected before her treatment was finished, pulling the dialysis needle from the connecting shunt in her leg causing blood to spew, and exposing her genitals in a lewd manner. The trial court

II. Patients' Rights to Treatment

found that during the times she has sought treatment "her conduct has been disruptive, abusive, and unreasonable such as to trespass upon the rights of other patients and to endanger their rights to full and adequate treatment," and that her conduct "has been an imposition on the nursing staff." . . .

Discussion

We begin our analysis by considering the trial court's conclusion that Dr. Weaver and the clinic with which he is associated have no present legal obligation to continue providing Brenda with dialysis treatment. . . . Brenda relies upon the general proposition that a physician who abandons a patient may do so "only . . . after due notice, and an ample opportunity afforded to secure the presence of other medical attendance." (Lathrope v. Flood (1901) 6 Cal. Unrep. 637, 639, 63 P. 1007, 1008, *revd. on other grounds* (1902) 135 Cal. 458, 67 P. 683; see also Capps v. Valk (1962) 189 Kan. 287, 369 P.2d 238; McGulpin v. Bessmer (1950) 241 Iowa 1119, 43 N.W.2d 121, 125; Johnson v. Vaughn (Ky. App. 1963) 370 S.W.2d 591, 596.)

The trial court found, however, that Dr. Weaver gave sufficient notice to Brenda, and discharged all his obligations in that regard, and that finding, also, is amply supported. Dr. Weaver supplied Brenda with a list of the names and telephone numbers of all dialysis providers in San Francisco and the East Bay, and it is apparent from the record that nothing would have pleased him more than to find an alternative facility for her, but there is no evidence that there is anything further he could have done to achieve that goal under the circumstances. . . . It appears that Dr. Weaver has behaved according to the highest standards of the medical profession, and that there exists no basis in law or in equity to saddle him with a continuing sole obligation for Brenda's welfare. The same is true of the clinic, the BMA. . . .

It does not necessarily follow that a hospital, or other health care facility, is without obligation to patients in need of continuing medical services for their survival. While it has been said that "[a] private hospital owes the public no duty to accept any patient not desired by it, and it is not necessary to assign any reason for its refusal to accept a patient for hospital service," it is questionable whether a hospital which receives public funding under the Hill-Burton Act (42 U.S.C. §291), and perhaps from other sources, can reasonably be said to be "private" in that sense. Rather, where such a hospital contains a unique, or scarce, medical resource needed to preserve life, it is arguably in the nature of a "public service enterprise," and should not be permitted to withhold its services arbitrarily, or without reasonable cause. (Cf. Gay Law Students Assn. v. Pacific Tel. & Tel. Co. (1979) 24 Cal. 3d 458, 482-483, 156 Cal. Rptr. 14, 595 P.2d 592;

see also James v. Marinship Corp. (1944) 25 Cal. 2d 721, 731, 155 P.2d 329; Tunkl v. Regents of University of California (1963) 60 Cal. 2d 92, 98-100, 32 Cal. Rptr. 33, 383 P.2d 441; Tobriner and Grodin, The Individual and the Public Service Enterprise in the New Industrial State (1967) 55 Cal. L. Rev. 1247, passim). And, while disruptive conduct on the part of a patient may constitute good cause for an individual hospital to refuse continued treatment, since it would be unfair to impose serious inconvenience upon a hospital simply because such a patient selected it, it may be that there exists a collective responsibility on the part of the providers of scarce health resources in a community, enforceable through equity, to share the burden of difficult patients over time, through an appropriately devised contingency plan.

This argument was not presented to the trial court, however, and the record is not adequate to support relief on that ground as a matter of law.

NOTES

Treatment Refusal and Patient Abandonment

1. Despite the reluctance of the *Manlove* court to find a duty to treat, it is considered a breakthrough case in being the first to articulate some basis for requiring hospitals to treat patients in emergency situations. *Manlove* thus paved the way for other courts to make more definitive findings of liability for the refusal of emergency care based on a reliance theory. E.g., Stanturf v. Sipes, 447 S.W.2d 558 (Mo. 1969) (hospital may be liable for refusing to treat frostbite victim who could not post $25 deposit); Mercy Med. Cent. v. Winnebago County, 206 N.W.2d 198 (Wis. 1973) ("It would shock the public conscience if a person in need of medical emergency aid would be turned down at the door of a hospital"); Chandler v. Hospital Auth., 548 So. 2d 1384 (Ala. 1989) (in its formal admissions policy, hospital explicitly assumed duty to treat emergency patients) (extensive discussion of case law). See generally Rothenberg, Who Cares? The Evolution of the Legal Duty to Provide Emergency Care, 26 Hous. L. Rev. 21, 31-42 (1989).

Why couldn't these courts have found liability more straightforwardly under a malpractice theory? The answer turns on the existence *vel non* of a patient/physician relationship. Malpractice occurs only in the context of an established treatment relationship. Where the gravamen of the complaint is a refusal to treat, then, by definition, no such relationship has been created. Thus, it is only before doctors have entered into a patient/physician relationship that they enjoy the protection of the "no duty" rule. Thereafter, abandonment law de-

II. Patients' Rights to Treatment

termines the conditions under which a provider can properly sever a treatment relationship.

2. What if the nurse in *Manlove* had taken the infant's temperature, would that have sufficed to cross the intangible "treatment relationship" line? Or what if a doctor had been present and had advised the parents to go home, take some aspirin, and call in the morning? See O'Neill v. Montefiore Hosp., 202 N.Y.S.2d 436 (App. Div. 1960) (phone call from nurse to doctor was "sufficient to permit inference that the emergency ward undertook to provide medical attention for the deceased"); Lyons v. Grether, 239 S.E.2d 103 (Va. 1977) (scheduling appointment sufficed); Hamil v. Bashline, 307 A.2d 57 (Pa. Super. 1973) (telling patient to come to hospital and then attempting to administer an EEG established a physician/patient relationship); Annot., What Constitutes Physician-Patient Relationship for Malpractice Purposes, 17 A.L.R.4th 132 (1982).

3. The parents in *Manlove* apparently were able and willing to pay for their child's care. (Likewise, Brenda Payton's treatment was covered by Medicare, which has a special program for kidney disease.) Nevertheless, *Manlove* has had its greatest impact on the development of the duty to treat *indigent* patients, the subject of a following section. Few hospitals turn away paying patients with any frequency. However, *Manlove* has the potential for taking on renewed importance in the context of the AIDS epidemic. One survey at Johns Hopkins found that over 5 percent of the patients treated in the emergency room tested positive for AIDS infection. Is it permissible for a hospital to refuse emergency AIDS patients based on the assertion that it lacks the expertise and facilities to handle the disease? See the following section for further discussion.

4. Can *Hurley* be reconciled with *Manlove*? Isn't it just as likely for doctors as for hospitals that, in life-threatening situations, patients rely on a holding out and custom of their family physician to render treatment? Despite *Hurley*'s age, it is still considered to state the established law. See Childs v. Weis, 440 S.W.2d 104 (Tx. Ct. Civ. App. 1969) ("a physician is not to be held liable for arbitrarily refusing to respond to a call of a person even urgently in need of medical or surgical assistance"); Annot., 17 A.L.R.4th 132 (1982); Note, 7 U.C. Davis L. Rev. 246 (1974).

"Even the Hippocratic Oath, by which every doctor is morally bound, assumes a pre-existing relationship of patient and physician, which relationship in its inception is basically contractual and wholly voluntary." Agnew v. Parks, 343 P.2d 118, 123 (Cal. App. 1959). However, Principle VI of the AMA Code of Medical Ethics allows doctors the freedom to turn down patients only in *non*emergency situations: "A physician shall . . . , except in emergencies, be free to choose whom to serve." See May, Medical Ethics: Code and Covenant or Philanthropy and Contract?, 5 Hastings Center Rep. 29 (Dec. 1975); Dyck, On Human Care (1977).

5. Does it matter why Dr. Eddingfield refused to treat Mr. Hurley? In Walker v. Pierce, 560 F.2d 609 (4th Cir. 1977), the court upheld an obstetrician's policy of not accepting low-income patients unless they agreed to submit to sterilization following the delivery of their third child: "We perceive no reason why Dr. Pierce could not establish and pursue the policy which he publicly and freely announced. Nor are we cited to judicial precedent or statute inhibiting this personal economic philosophy." What if Dr. Pierce were the only obstetrician in town? There are scattered reports of some doctors refusing to treat any lawyers, their families, or employees. See Hiser v. Randolph, 617 P.2d 774 (1980) (refusal to treat based on personal animosity and because plaintiff's husband was a lawyer). Assuming doctors acted in concert, could such a boycott be challenged under the antitrust laws?

6. Does it matter under the abandonment doctrine why the doctor wants to discontinue treatment? Again, apparently not. Any reason for abandonment will suffice — a desire to leave practice or to take a vacation, for instance — so long as the patient has an adequate opportunity to arrange for substitute care. To assure that there is no question concerning the adequacy of notice and the availability of substitute care, prudent physicians usually take affirmative steps to arrange for a substitute when they cannot attend a patient themselves. See generally, Comment, The Action of Abandonment in Medical Malpractice Litigation, 36 Tulane L. Rev. 834 (1962); Annot., Liability of Physician Who Abandons Case, 57 A.L.R.2d 432 (1958).

The practice of arranging for a substitute gives rise to the following dilemma: What if, as in *Payton*, there is no available substitute? For instance, suppose a physician wishes to abandon a patient who can no longer pay, but for this very reason no other physician is available to take the case. Is abandonment in these circumstances legal if the physician gives the patient some advance notice, or is the doctor stuck? The case law is not clear on these questions, see Ricks v. Budge, 64 P.2d 208 (Utah 1937) (physician may not abandon patient without notice and at a critical stage in treatment even though the patient refused to pay overdue bills), but they may take on central importance in an era of sharply rising health care costs coupled with constrained reimbursement. See generally Chapter 8 of this text.

7. As *Payton* reflects, some states, following Greisman v. Newcomb Hospital supra at p.471, have accepted the quasi-public facility characterization of hospitals that was rejected by *Manlove*. This being so, is the *Payton* court's speculation correct that, at least for hospitals, the duty to treat paying patients extends beyond emergency care? It would be ironic indeed to insist on physician access but deny patient

access. Nevertheless, this remains a largely unanswered question in the common law. However, one recent decision found a common law duty to treat when the sole physician practice group in town refused a patient who had filed a complaint against one of the doctors in the group. Leach v. Drummond Med. Group, 192 Cal. Rptr. 650 (Cal. App. 1983).

8. Regardless of whether the *common law* contains a duty to treat nonemergency patients, there are numerous *statutory* grounds for preventing hospital discrimination against paying patients. State and local law frequently prevent discrimination in all places of public accommodation. Some statutes apply only to specified categories of discrimination; see, for instance, Lyons v. Grether, 239 S.E.2d 103 (Va. 1977) (duty to treat the blind), while others broadly require "full and equal accommodations" for all customers. Cal. Civ. Code §51. These statutes clearly apply to hospitals, but the case is less clear for doctors' offices. Compare Leach v. Drummond Med. Group, 192 Cal. Rptr. 650 (Cal. App. 1983) (statute reaches a group physician practice), with Rice v. Rinaldo, 119 N.E.2d 657 (Oh. App. 1951) (dental office does not constitute a place of public accommodation, for purposes of race discrimination law).

In addition to these statutes, the JCAH's hospital accreditation standards require impartial access to treatment without regard to race, creed, sex, or national origin. Under federal law, nondiscriminatory admission policies are required of tax-exempt hospitals, of those that have received federal grants and loans under the Hill-Burton Hospital Construction Act, and, most sweeping, of any hospital that receives any federal funds through Medicare or Medicaid. 42 U.S.C. §§2000d et seq. (Title VI of the Civil Rights Act of 1964); Civil Rights Restoration Act of 1987, P.L. 100-259; United States v. Baylor Univ. Med. Cent., 736 F.2d 1039 (5th Cir. 1984); Wing, Title VI and Health Facilities: Forms Without Substance, 30 Hastings L.J. 137 (1978). As explored in the following section, a person's physical condition is included in the prohibited bases for discrimination.

B. Handicap Discrimination and the Duty to Treat AIDS Patients

Attitudes About Treating AIDS Patients

"The treatment of AIDS patients places greater burdens on hospitals than the treatment of most other patients. People with AIDS tend to be hospitalized frequently, often for long periods. . . . AIDS patients also require almost twice as much nursing care as patients with other terminal illnesses. As a result, institutional pressures to prohibit or severely limit the hospitalization of people with AIDS are strong. In addition, many private hospitals strive to avoid the 'stigma' of being characterized as AIDS hospitals, fearing that other patients will not be referred to them."

Banks, The Right to Medical Treatment, in Aids and the Law: A Guide for the Public 179-180 (H. Dalton et al. eds. 1987).

"A prominent heart surgeon has refused to operate on patients infected with the AIDS virus and says that he finds it disturbing that all hospitals do not insist on virus tests before surgery. The surgeon, Dr. Dudley W. Johnson, . . . said he recently refused to perform bypass surgery on two such patients. . . . 'We are dealing with a procedure that has a high blood profile,' he said. 'There is blood all over the place. There is an absolute danger from needle sticks.' . . . Dr. Johnson said he knew of no doctor ever contracting AIDS from a patient. 'I want to keep it that way,' he said."

N.Y. Times, March 13, 1987, at 11.

"One hospital in Maryland . . . will neither treat nor employ individuals testing positive [for AIDS exposure]. Fully 35 percent of physicians surveyed in Sacramento, California stated they will not treat individuals [exposed to the AIDS virus]."

Perkins, Health Benefits: How the System Is Responding to AIDS, Clearinghouse Rev. (Dec. 1988).

School Board of Nassau County v. Arline
480 U.S. 273 (1987)

JUSTICE BRENNAN delivered the opinion of the Court.

Section 504 of the Rehabilitation Act of 1973, 87 Stat. 394, as amended, 29 U.S.C. §794 (Act), prohibits a federally funded state program from discriminating against a handicapped individual solely by reason of his or her handicap. This case presents the questions whether a person afflicted with tuberculosis, a contagious disease, may be considered a "handicapped individual" within the meaning of §504 of the Act, and, if so, whether such an individual is "otherwise qualified" to teach elementary school.

I

From 1966 until 1979, respondent Gene Arline taught elementary school in Nassau County, Florida. She was discharged in 1979 after suffering a third relapse of tuberculosis within two years. After she was denied relief in state administrative proceedings, she brought suit in federal court, alleging that the School Board's decision to dismiss her because of her tuberculosis violated §504 of the Act . . . [which] reads in pertinent part:

> No otherwise qualified handicapped individual . . . shall, solely by reason of his handicap, be excluded from participation in, be denied the benefits of, or be subjected to discrimination under any program or activity receiving Federal financial assistance. . . .

29 U.S.C. §794. In 1974 Congress expanded the definition of "handicapped individual" for use in §504 to read as follows:

> [A]ny person who (i) has a physical or mental impairment which substantially limits one or more of such person's major life activities, (ii) has a record of such an impairment, or (iii) is regarded as having such an impairment.

29 U.S.C. §706(7)(B). The amended definition reflected Congress' concern with protecting the handicapped against discrimination stemming not only from simple prejudice, but from "archaic attitudes and laws" and from "the fact that the American people are simply unfamiliar with and insensitive to the difficulties confront[ing] individuals with handicaps." S. Rep. No. 93-1297, p.50 (1974), U.S. Code Cong. & Admin. News 1974, p.6400. To combat the effects of erroneous but nevertheless prevalent perceptions about the handicapped, Congress expanded the definition of "handicapped individual" so as to preclude discrimination against "[a] person who has a record of, or is regarded as having, an impairment [but who] may at present have no actual incapacity at all." Southeastern Community College v. Davis, 442 U.S. 397, 405-406, n.6 (1979).[4] . . .

Petitioners concede that a contagious disease may constitute a handicapping condition to the extent that it leaves a person with "diminished physical or mental capabilities," Brief for Petitioners 15, and concede that Arline's hospitalization for tuberculosis in 1957

---

4. See id., at 39 ("This subsection includes within the protection of sections 503 and 504 those persons who do not in fact have the condition which they are perceived as having, as well as those persons whose mental or physical condition does not substantially limit their life activities and who thus are not technically within clause (A) in the new definition. Members of both of these groups may be subjected to discrimination on the basis of their being regarded as handicapped"); id., at 37-39, 63-64; see also 120 Cong. Rec. 30531 (1974) (statement of Sen. Cranston).

demonstrates that she has a record of a physical impairment, see Tr. of Oral Arg. 52-53. Petitioners maintain, however, Arline's record of impairment is irrelevant in this case, since the School Board dismissed Arline not because of her diminished physical capabilities, but because of the threat that her relapses of tuberculosis posed to the health of others.

We do not agree with petitioners that, in defining a handicapped individual under §504, the contagious effects of a disease can be meaningfully distinguished from the disease's physical effects on a claimant in a case such as this. Arline's contagiousness and her physical impairment each resulted from the same underlying condition, tuberculosis. It would be unfair to allow an employer to seize upon the distinction between the effects of a disease on others and the effects of a disease on a patient and use that distinction to justify discriminatory treatment.[7] . . .

Allowing discrimination based on the contagious effects of a physical impairment would be inconsistent with the basic purpose of §504, which is to ensure that handicapped individuals are not denied jobs or other benefits because of the prejudiced attitudes or the ignorance of others. By amending the definition of "handicapped individual" to include not only those who are actually physically impaired, but also those who are regarded as impaired and who, as a result, are substantially limited in a major life activity, Congress acknowledged that society's accumulated myths and fears about disability and disease are as handicapping as are the physical limitations that flow from actual impairment. Few aspects of a handicap give rise to the same level of public fear and misapprehension as contagiousness. Even those who suffer or have recovered from such noninfectious diseases as epilepsy or cancer have faced discrimination based on the irrational fear that they might be contagious.[13] . . . We conclude

---

7. The United States argues that it is possible for a person to be simply a carrier of a disease, that is, to be capable of spreading a disease without having a "physical impairment" or suffering from any other symptoms associated with the disease. The United States contends that this is true in the case of some carriers of the Acquired Immune Deficiency Syndrome (AIDS) virus. From this premise the United States concludes that discrimination solely on the basis of contagiousness is never discrimination on the basis of a handicap. The argument is misplaced in this case, because the handicap here, tuberculosis, gave rise both to a physical impairment and to contagiousness. This case does not present, and we therefore do not reach, the questions whether a carrier of a contagious disease such as AIDS could be considered to have a physical impairment, or whether such a person could be considered, solely on the basis of contagiousness, a handicapped person as defined by the Act.

13. Senator Humphrey noted the "irrational fears or prejudice on the part of employers or fellow workers" that make it difficult for former cancer patients to secure employment. 123 Cong. Rec. 13515 (1977). See also Feldman, Wellness and Work, in Psychosocial Stress and Cancer 173-200 (C. Cooper ed. 1984) (documenting job discrimination against recovered cancer patients); S. Sontag, Illness as Metaphor 6 (1978) ("Any disease that is treated as a mystery and acutely enough feared will be felt to

that the fact that a person with a record of a physical impairment is also contagious does not suffice to remove that person from coverage under §504.

IV

The remaining question is whether Arline is otherwise qualified for the job of elementary school teacher. To answer this question in most cases, the District Court will need to conduct an individualized inquiry and make appropriate findings of fact. Such an inquiry is essential if §504 is to achieve its goal of protecting handicapped individuals from deprivations based on prejudice, stereotypes, or unfounded fear, while giving appropriate weight to such legitimate concerns of grantees as avoiding exposing others to significant health and safety risks.[16] The basic factors to be considered in conducting this inquiry are well established. In the context of the employment of a person handicapped with a contagious disease, we agree with amicus American Medical Association that this inquiry should include:

> [findings of] facts, based on reasonable medical judgments given the state of medical knowledge, about (a) the nature of the risk (how the disease is transmitted), (b) the duration of the risk (how long is the carrier infectious), (c) the severity of the risk (what is the potential harm to third parties) and (d) the probabilities the disease will be transmitted and will cause varying degrees of harm.

In making these findings, courts normally should defer to the reasonable medical judgments of public health officials. The next step in the "otherwise-qualified" inquiry is for the court to evaluate, in light of these medical findings, whether the employer could reasonably accommodate the employee. . . . Because of the paucity of factual findings by the District Court, we, like the Court of Appeals, are unable at this stage of the proceedings to resolve whether Arline is "otherwise qualified" for her job. . . .

---

be morally, if not literally, contagious. Thus, a surprisingly large number of people with cancer find themselves being shunned by relatives and friends . . . as if cancer, like TB, were an infectious disease"); Dell, Social Dimensions of Epilepsy: Stigma and Response, in Psychopathology in Epilepsy: Social Dimensions 185-210 (S. Whitman & B. Hermann eds. 1986) (reviewing range of discrimination affecting epileptics); Brief for Epilepsy Foundation as Amicus Curiae 5-14 ("A review of the history of epilepsy provides a salient example that fear, rather than the handicap itself, is the major impetus for discrimination against persons with handicaps").

16. A person who poses a significant risk of communicating an infectious disease to others in the workplace will not be otherwise qualified for his or her job if reasonable accommodation will not eliminate that risk. The Act would not require a school board to place a teacher with active, contagious tuberculosis in a classroom with elementary school children.

We remand the case to the District Court to determine whether Arline is otherwise qualified for her position. The judgment of the Court of Appeals is Affirmed.

[Dissenting opinions of CHIEF JUSTICE REHNQUIST and JUSTICE SCALIA omitted.]

Chalk v. United States District Court
840 F.2d 701 (9th Cir. 1988)

POOLE, CIRCUIT JUDGE. . . .

Petitioner Chalk has been teaching hearing-impaired students in the Orange County schools for approximately six years. In February 1987, Chalk was hospitalized with pneumocystis carinii pneumonia and was diagnosed as having AIDS. On April 20, after eight weeks of treatment and recuperation, he was found fit for duty and released to return to work by his personal physician, Dr. Andrew Siskind. The Department, however, placed him on administrative leave pending the opinion of Dr. Thomas J. Prendergast, the Director of Epidemiology and Disease Control for the Orange County Health Care Agency. On May 22, Dr. Prendergast informed the Department that "[n]othing in his [Chalk's] role as a teacher should place his students or others in the school at any risk of acquiring HIV[3] infection."

Chalk agreed to remain on administrative leave through the end of the school year in June. On August 5, . . . [the Department] informed him that if he insisted on returning to the classroom, it would file an action for declaratory relief. Chalk refused the offer. On August 6, the Department filed an action in the Orange County Superior Court, and Chalk filed this action in the district court seeking a preliminary and permanent injunction barring the Department from excluding him from classroom duties. . . .

Chalk's motion for a preliminary injunction ordering his reinstatement was denied by the district court, and Chalk brought this appeal. After hearing oral argument, we issued an order reversing the district court and directing it to issue the preliminary injunction. . . .

Chalk bases his claim on section 504 of the Rehabilitation Act of 1973. . . . As the district court recognized, the Supreme Court recently held that section 504 is fully applicable to individuals who suffer from contagious diseases. School Bd. of Nassau County v. Arline, [480] U.S. [273], 107 S.Ct. 1123, 94 L. Ed. 2d 307 (1987).[6] . . .

---

3. HIV (Human Immunodeficiency Virus) is the viral agent that causes AIDS.

6. The district court ruled that Doe was handicapped within the meaning of the Act, and the Department does not contest that ruling on appeal. See *Arline*, 107 S. Ct. at 1127-30 & n.7. The Department stipulated that it was a program receiving Federal financial assistance and thus subject to the Act.

II. Patients' Rights to Treatment

In its opinion, the Court addressed the question which is of central importance to this case: under what circumstances may a person handicapped with a contagious disease be "otherwise qualified" within the meaning of section 504? Relying on its earlier opinion in Southeastern Community College v. Davis, 442 U.S. 397, 99 S. Ct. 2361, 60 L. Ed. 2d 980 (1979), the Court said:

> An otherwise qualified person is one who is able to meet all of a program's requirements in spite of his handicap. In the employment context, an otherwise qualified person is one who can perform "the essential functions" of the job in question. When a handicapped person is not able to perform the essential functions of the job, the court must also consider whether any "reasonable accommodation" by the employer would enable the handicapped person to perform those functions. Accommodation is not reasonable if it either imposes "undue financial and administrative burdens" on a grantee, or requires a "fundamental alteration in the nature of [the] program."

Arline, 107 S. Ct. at 1131 n.17 (citations omitted). . . .

Chalk submitted in evidence to the district court, and that court accepted, more than 100 articles from prestigious medical journals and the declarations of five experts on AIDS, including two public health officials of Los Angeles County. Those submissions reveal an overwhelming evidentiary consensus of medical and scientific opinion regarding the nature and transmission of AIDS. AIDS is caused by infection of the individual with HIV, a retrovirus that penetrates chromosomes of certain human cells that combat infection throughout the body. Individuals who become infected with HIV may remain without symptoms for an extended period of time. When the disease takes hold, however, a number of symptoms can occur, including swollen lymph nodes, fever, weight loss, fatigue and night sweats. Eventually, the virus destroys its host cells, thereby weakening the victim's immune system. When the immune system is in a compromised state, the victim becomes susceptible to a variety of so-called "opportunistic infections," many of which can prove fatal.

Transmission of HIV is known to occur in three ways: (1) through intimate sexual contact with an infected person; (2) through invasive exposure to contaminated blood or certain other bodily fluids; or (3) through perinatal exposure (i.e., from mother to infant). Although HIV has been isolated in several body fluids, epidemiologic evidence has implicated only blood, semen, vaginal secretions, and possibly breast milk in transmission. Extensive and numerous studies have consistently found no apparent risk of HIV infection to individuals exposed through close, non-sexual contact with AIDS patients.

Based on the accumulated body of medical evidence, the Surgeon General of the United States has concluded:

There is no known risk of non-sexual infection in most of the situations we encounter in our daily lives. We know that family members living with individuals who have the AIDS virus do not become infected except through sexual contact. There is no evidence of transmission (spread) of AIDS virus by everyday contact even though these family members shared food, towels, cups, razors, even toothbrushes, and kissed each other.

U.S. Public Health Service, Surgeon General's Report on Acquired Immune Deficiency Syndrome at 13 (1986) (hereinafter Surgeon General's Report). . . . These conclusions are echoed by such medical authorities as the United States Centers for Disease Control, the American Medical Association and the Institute of Medicine of the National Academy of Sciences. . . .

Nonetheless, the district judge expressed skepticism about the current state of medical knowledge. He was troubled that there might be something yet unknown to science that might do harm. He said:

Now, here, according to present knowledge, the risk probably is not great because of the limited ways that medical science believes the disease is transmitted. But, of course, if it is transmitted the result is horrendous. It seems to me the problem is that we simply do not know enough about AIDS to be completely certain. The plaintiff has submitted massive documentation tending to show a minimal risk. . . . But in any event, the risk is small — risk of infection through casual contact. . . . The incubation period is reported to be seven years. We have been studying this only for six. And I do not in any sense mean to be an alarmist. I — I reiterate, I think the risk is small. The likelihood is that the medical profession knows exactly what it's talking about. But I think it's too early to draw a definite conclusion, as far as this case is concerned, about the extent of the risk.

This language demonstrates that the district court failed to follow the legal standards set forth in *Arline* and improperly placed an impossible burden of proof on the petitioner. Little in science can be proved with complete certainty, and section 504 does not require such a test. As authoritatively construed by the Supreme Court, section 504 allows the exclusion of an employee only if there is "a *significant* risk of communicating an infectious disease to others." *Arline*, 107 S. Ct. at 1131 n.16 (emphasis added).[11] In addition, *Arline* admonishes courts that they "should defer to the reasonable medical judgments of public health officials." Id. at 1131. The district judge ignored these admonitions. Instead, he rejected the overwhelming consensus

---

11. Where there is a significant risk, *Arline* further requires a court to determine if any reasonable accommodation will eliminate that risk. Id. As no significant risk is posed here, this is not a case involving the standards or limits of accommodation and we do not reach those issues.

of medical opinion and improperly relied on speculation for which there was no credible support in the record.

That Chalk demonstrates a strong probability of success on the merits is supported by the three published opinions brought to our attention dealing with AIDS discrimination under section 504.* In Thomas v. Atascadero Unified School Dist., 662 F. Supp. 376 (C.D. Cal. 1987), the court granted a preliminary injunction prohibiting the school district from excluding a child with AIDS from the classroom, despite the child's involvement in a biting incident. . . . In Ray v. School Dist. of DeSoto County, 666 F. Supp. 1524 (M.D. Fla. 1987), the court followed *Thomas* and granted a preliminary injunction prohibiting the district from excluding three seropositive[13] brothers from the classroom. . . .

The third case, District 27 Community School Bd. v. Board of Educ., 130 Misc. 2d 398, 502 N.Y.S.2d 325 (Sup. Ct. 1986), concerned the New York City Board of Education's policy of determining on a case-by-case basis whether the health and development of children with AIDS permitted them to attend school in an unrestricted setting. Two school districts challenged the policy, seeking an injunction prohibiting the Board from admitting any child with AIDS into the classroom. After a five-week trial, the court upheld the policy in an exhaustive opinion. One of the central conclusions was that the transmission of the AIDS virus in the classroom setting was "a mere theoretical possibility" and that exclusion of AIDS victims on that basis would violate section 504. . . .

In denying the preliminary injunction, the district court concluded that Chalk's injury was outweighed by the fear that his presence in the classroom was likely to produce. . . . Here, however, there is no evidence of any significant risk to children or others at the school. To allow the court to base its decision on the fear and apprehension of others would frustrate the goals of section 504. "[T]he basic purpose of §504 [is] to ensure that handicapped individuals are not denied jobs or other benefits because of the prejudiced attitudes or ignorance of others." *Arline,* 107 S. Ct. at 1129. The Supreme Court recognized in *Arline* that a significant risk of transmission was a legitimate concern which could justify exclusion if the risk could not be eliminated through reasonable accommodation; however, it soundly rejected the argument that exclusion could be justified on the basis of "pernicious mythologies" or "irrational fear." Id. at 1129-30 & n.12. . . .

---

* [Ed. Note:] See also Raytheon Co. v. Calif. Fair Employment & Housing Comm., 261 Cal. Rptr. 197 (Cal. App. 1989) (employer violated state antidiscrimination law in discharging AIDS-infected employee).

13. "Seropositive" denotes persons who have tested positive for the HIV virus, but who have not yet exhibited symptoms of AIDS.

Nonetheless, we recognize that the parties and the district court will have to deal with the apprehensions of other members of the school community, as well as with the inexorable progress of Chalk's disease. Although the time frame is unpredictable, given the current state of medical knowledge, the course of petitioner's condition is reasonably certain. Chalk's immune system will deteriorate over time, leaving him increasingly susceptible to opportunistic infections. These infections do not cause AIDS, nor do they increase the risk of transmission of the AIDS virus, but some of them may themselves be communicable to others in a classroom setting. The district court is in the best position, guided by qualified medical opinion, to determine what reasonable procedures, such as periodic reports from petitioner's doctors, will best give assurance to the Department, the community and the court that no significant risk of harm will arise in the future from Chalk's continued presence in the classroom. . . .

Reversed and remanded.

NOTES

Health Care Access for AIDS Patients

1. How do *Arline* and *Chalk* apply to the right to medical care? Primarily, the issue is whether hospitals and nursing homes, which receive substantial federal funding, violate §504 by refusing to treat patients infected with AIDS or by treating them differently from other patients. Although the risk to medical personnel is remote, there are a number of documented cases of AIDS infections through accidental needle sticks and the like. More frightening still, the Center for Disease Control has reported three cases of AIDS infection through mere skin contact with infected blood. Cotton, The Impact of AIDS on the Medical Care System, 260 J.A.M.A. 519 (1988). On the other hand, the risk is still quite slight compared with other forms of hospital contagion. For instance, an estimated 100 hospital workers die each year from hepatitis, another blood-borne infection. Comment, AIDS Discrimination in Medical Care, 63 Wash. L. Rev. 701 (1988). For additional sources discussing the risk to medical personnel and incidents of discrimination, see AIDS Infection Among Health-Care Workers, 259 J.A.M.A. 2817 (1988); Gramelspacher & Siegler, Do Physicians Have a Professional Responsibility to Care for Patients with HIV Disease?, 4 Issues L. & Med. 383 (1988); 63 Wash. L. Rev. 701 supra; Marcus et al., Surveillance of Health Care Workers Exposed to Blood from Patients Infected with HIV, 319 New Eng. J. Med. 1118 (1988); New York City Commission on Human Rights, Report on Discrimination Against People with AIDS (Aug. 1987); Perkins &

II. Patients' Rights to Treatment

Boyle, AIDS and Poverty: Dual Barriers to Health Care, Clearinghouse Rev., March 1986, at 1283, 1284.

2. *Chalk*, like *Arline*, addresses a person who is both contagious and physically suffering from disease. Therefore, neither squarely resolves whether a "seropositive" or "asymptomatic" AIDS patient — that is, one whose blood has tested positive for exposure to the AIDS virus but who has not yet exhibited any of the AIDS symptoms — is handicapped within the meaning of §504. The U.S. Department of Justice, Office of Legal Counsel, answered "yes" in an opinion memorandum dated Sept. 27, 1988. The DOJ reasoned that mere exposure to the AIDS virus constitutes a handicap because of the resulting physical impairment to the immune system, which limits the major life activities of procreation and sex. The only court to address this question so far reached a similar result, but on even broader grounds. In Doe v. Centinela, No. CV 87-2514 (C.D. Cal., June 10, 1988), the court found §504 applicable to a patient excluded from a drug rehabilitation program because he tested positive for exposure to the AIDS virus. The court reasoned:

> There is no dispute that defendant . . . treated [plaintiff] as limited in his ability to learn how to deal with a dependency problem in the LifeStarts program. It did so on the footing that noncommunicability is an essential eligibility requirement. No matter what else *Arline* may fairly be read to hold, it clearly states that discrimination based solely on fear of contagion is discrimination based on a handicap when the impairment has that effect on others [that is, when the impairment causes others to treat the person as if he were handicapped].

Id. Most commentators agree that AIDS infection alone is a handicap, based on the strong language concerning perception of handicap and protection of contagiousness that Justice Brennan craftily worked into his opinion. See Note, Asymptomatic Infection with the AIDS Virus as a Handicap, 88 Colum. L. Rev. 563 (1988); Leonard, AIDS in the Workplace, in AIDS and the Law: A Guide for the Public (Yale AIDS Law Project, H. Dalton, S. Burris & eds. 1987). See generally, Legal, Medical, and Governmental Perspectives on AIDS as a Disability (D. Rapaport & J. Parry eds. 1987).

There is at least some difference of opinion, however. "The Court in *Arline* expressly limited its holding to individuals who have a history of actual physical impairment. . . . In cases to come, the Court may find itself forced to cling to the peg of physical or mental impairment. The problem is one of scope. The mere fact that an employer irrationally dislikes an employee is not enough to provide protection under traditional discrimination law. Only if the irrational dislike is based upon certain recognized and disapproved stereotypes, such as those involving race or gender, does the law intervene."

Parmet, AIDS and the Limits of Discrimination Law, 15 L. Med. & Health Care 61, 66-67 (1987).

3. Even if the federal statute is considered unclear on the protection of mere contagiousness, state and local laws in several jurisdictions have been construed to apply to AIDS carriers. See O'Connor, Defining "Handicap" for Purposes of Employment Discrimination, 30 Ariz. L. Rev. 633, 672 (1988) (cataloguing all state laws); Lewis, Acquired Immunodeficiency Syndrome: State Legislative Activity, 258 J.A.M.A. 2410 (1987); Wasson, AIDS Discrimination Under Federal, State and Local Law After *Arline*, 15 Fla. St. U.L. Rev. 221 (1987); AHA, AIDS and the Law: Responding to the Special Concerns of Hospitals 9 (1987); National Gay Rights Advocates, AIDS and Handicap Discrimination: A Survey of 50 States (Sept. 1986).

4. After establishing the threshold issue of handicapped status, the inquiry shifts to whether an AIDS patient (either a sufferer or a carrier) is "otherwise qualified" for hospital admission and what reasonable accommodations the hospital must make. See generally Hentoff, The Rehabilitation Act's Otherwise Qualified Requirement and the AIDS Virus, 30 Ariz. L. Rev. 571 (1988).

5. The *Chalk* court gave little credence to the school system's concerns about the incorrect fears of the school children and their parents, even though such fears are understandable on at least a human, emotional level. But can such concerns always be dismissed so easily? In *Chalk*, these fears may not have had a substantial effect on the school's viability. By contrast, suppose that a restaurant were forced to employ an AIDS-infected chef or waiter, or a hospital were forced to employ an AIDS-infected nurse. Conceivably, the institution might have to shut its doors. However, if other institutions have to follow suit, perhaps customers will have no choice.

6. Section 504 is usually raised in the context of institutional discrimination, but could it not apply with equal force to *individuals* who receive federal funding? If so, this would be the *only* source of law that constrained a doctor's freedom to choose patients. Surprisingly, then, this issue seems to have avoided careful examination. Doctors, like hospitals, receive substantial funds from Medicare and Medicaid. It might be objected that, at least under Medicare, the payments in theory are made to the patient and only assigned to the doctor by private agreement, but the direct link between Medicare funds and doctors' reimbursement nevertheless should be sufficient to establish "federal financial assistance." Frazier v. Board of Trustees, 765 F.2d 1278, 1298 (1985) (supplier of respiratory care services to hospital is covered by §504 despite lack of direct reimbursement from government because supplier's income was "linked to the hospital's receipt of Medicare and Medicaid funds"). Another possible escape hatch for doctors is the exclusion for "contracts of insurance" con-

II. Patients' Rights to Treatment

tained in the regulations under §504. Medicare Part B, which covers physician fees, is more akin to an insurance plan than Part A because it is funded in part by subscribers' voluntary payment of a monthly premium. Compare United States v. University Hosp., 575 F. Supp. 607, 613 (E.D.N.Y. 1983) (hospital payments "are not funded by beneficiaries' premium payments, but by a payroll tax"). However, this insurance exception is not contained in the statute and therefore may not be valid; in any event, it has received a rather narrow construction, and it would not apply to Medicaid. See United States v. Baylor Hosp., 736 F.2d 1039, 1048-1049 (5th Cir. 1984).

Apart from the *law* on this question, the AMA's Council on Ethical and Judicial Affairs has stated that "a physician may not *ethically* refuse to treat a patient whose condition is within the physician's current realm of competence solely because the patient is seropositive." 259 J.A.M.A. 1360 (1988). It reconciles this position with the general "no duty" rule explored above by observing that doctors are not free to engage in "invidious discrimination," and by likening an epidemic to a medical emergency. See also AIDS: The Responsibility of Health Professionals, Hastings Cent. Rep. (April/May 1988) (symposium collecting several articles); Annas, Not Saints, But Healers: The Legal Duties of Health Care Professionals in the AIDS Epidemic, 78 Am. J. Pub. Health (1 July 1988). One author argues that "we must nurture the ethical duty to treat by shifting the costs of an occupational HIV accident from the worker to the government through a compensation plan . . . similar to workers' compensation." Brennan, Ensuring Adequate Health Care for the Sick: The Challenge of AIDS as an Occupational Disease, 1988 Duke L.J. 29, 66. Do you agree?

7. Should hospitals and physicians insist on AIDS testing for all patients so they know which ones to treat with extra precaution, or should they treat all patients as if they might have AIDS? See Henry et al., HIV Antibody Testing, 259 J.A.M.A. 1819 (1988) (surveying current hospital practices and policies). Chapter 10 contains an extensive discussion of the many additional legal issues arising from the AIDS crisis.

8. A related issue of AIDS discrimination — one that falls within a different body of substantive law — is whether private insurance companies are free to exclude high-risk groups from their coverage in order to avoid the high cost of AIDS treatment (which is estimated in some cities to average $150,000 per case). Insurers have attempted to screen out likely AIDS patients by mandating HIV antibody testing of insurance applicants or questioning applicants about their lifestyle. A few states have prohibited HIV testing by insurers, a restraint that has faced mixed results in the courts. See American Council of Life Ins. v. District of Columbia, 645 F. Supp. 84 (D.D.C. 1986) (upholding

insurance regulation); Health Insurance Assn. of America v. Corcoran, 531 N.Y.S.2d 456 (Sup. 1988) (finding regulation null and void). See generally Schatz, The AIDS Insurance Crisis: Underwriting or Overreaching, 100 Harv. L. Rev. 1782 (1982); Clifford & Iuculano, AIDS and Insurance: The Rationale for AIDS-Related Testing, 100 Harv. L. Rev. 1806 (1987); Note, AIDS Antibody Testing and Health Insurance Underwriting, 59 Ohio St. L.J. 1059 (1989).

9. The application of handicapped discrimination law to AIDS and other diseases will take on considerably more importance if Congress passes the currently pending Americans With Disabilities Act, which would extend §504 to private businesses.

10. For additional discussion of the right of AIDS patients to receive care, see Symposium, AIDS and the Rights and Obligations of Health Care Workers, 48 Md. L. Rev. 1 (1989); Banks, AIDS and the Right to Health Care, 4 Issues in L. & Med. 151 (1988); Gerry, Section 504 of the Rehabilitation Act, HIV and AIDS, 4 Issues in L. & Med. 175 (1988); 10 J. Leg. Med., No. 1 (1989) (symposium on "The Medical Profession and AIDS"); 4 Issues in L. & Med., No. 3 (1988) (same); Spece, AIDS: Due Process, Equal Protection, and the Right to Treatment, 4 Issues in L. & Med. 283 (1988).

C. The Duty to Treat Uninsured Patients

Note, Preventing Patient Dumping: Sharpening the Cobra's Fangs*
61 N.Y.U.L. Rev. 1186-1187, 1193-1195 (1986)

— Neurosurgeons in a private hospital refused to see a thirty-six-year-old uninsured man who had suffered head injuries in a fight. The patient went into a coma before being transferred to Highland Hospital, Oakland, California's primary public health care center, where doctors discovered he had a fractured skull. He died without regaining consciousness.

— A private hospital admitted a pregnant woman who was in the early stages of labor after she paid a $250 deposit on a $1,500 bill for a normal birth. Subsequent tests revealed that the woman needed a caesarean section. Upon learning that the woman and her husband had no health insurance, the hospital demanded "cash up front" for the $4,000 procedure. The couple could not pay in advance but offered to pay in installments. Refusing the couple's offer, the hospital told the woman, who was by this time in mid-labor, to go to a public hospital. She gave birth six hours later.

* Reprinted with permission of the New York University Law Review.

II. Patients' Rights to Treatment

— After an uninsured man received severe burns over ninety-five percent of his body, his doctor requested he be admitted to approximately forty hospitals with burn centers. All of these hospitals refused treatment, and at least one-half of the hospitals based their refusal on the man's lack of insurance.

— A man with a knife wedged against his spine was transferred from an emergency room because he did not have insurance. The transferring hospital refused to take the knife out unless he paid $1,000 cash in advance.[4]

These are but a few examples[5] of a phenomenon known as "patient dumping," which occurs when a hospital that is capable of providing the needed medical care (the transferring hospital) sends a patient to another facility (the receiving hospital) or simply turns the patient away because the patient is unable to pay. Because treating uninsured patients is expensive, hospitals have an economic incentive to dump them.[8] Consequently, public hospitals care for the majority of the uninsured. . . .

The first factor contributing to the patient dumping problem is an increase in the number of uninsured people in the United States. The number of people under sixty-five without health insurance increased from twenty-nine million in 1979 to thirty-five million in 1984. This dramatic increase is due, in part, to federal and state reductions in the Medicaid program. Over one million people were cut from the Medicaid program between 1981 and 1985. Because of these federal cuts, Medicaid covered less than forty percent of the poor in this nation in 1984 — compared to seventy percent when the program began in 1965. These Medicaid reductions coincide with a marked increase in patient dumping.

Second, widespread cost containment efforts by the federal government [discussed in Chapter 8] have contributed to the patient dumping problem. . . .

The health care cost containment fever is not restricted to the federal government. Hospitals have also caught the competitive fever. Many now offer discounts to large buyers of health care services, mainly employers, and view charity care as an inefficient giveaway.

---

4. Annas, Your Money or Your Life: 'Dumping' Uninsured Patients from Hospital Emergency Wards, 76 Am. J. Pub. Health 74, 74 (1986).

5. See, e.g., Demkovich, Hospitals That Provide for the Poor Are Reeling from Uncompensated Costs, 16 Nat'l J. 2245, 2245 (1984) (after woman told doctor that she had lost health insurance, doctor sent her "in mid-labor" to county hospital); Dowell, Indigent Access to Hospital Emergency Room Services, 18 Clearinghouse Rev. 483, 483 (1984) (hospital refused emergency treatment to 15-day-old infant because his uninsured mother could not pay $54 emergency room fee).

8. See Schiff, Ansell, Schlosser, Idris, Morrison & Whitman, Transfers to a Public Hospital — A Prospective Study of 467 Patients, 314 New Eng. J. Med. 552, 556 (1986). . . .

In the new era of competition with a price-driven marketplace, cost-shifting to subsidize charity care is impractical and bad business. "As economic pressures on hospitals grow and hospital managers are encouraged — or forced — to act like businessmen concerned primarily with profit margins, more and more patients will be denied access to urgently needed care simply because they cannot pay for it."[69]

Health care cost containment is also spurred by the concerns of employers, the major purchasers of private insurance. American businesses pay $77 billion per year for employee health insurance. Frustrated with the high costs of health care, employers are holding hospitals accountable for costs. This pressure further limits the hospitals' ability to shift costs to subsidize charity care and bad debts, thus increasing the incentives to dump patients who cannot pay.

The changes in Medicare and Medicaid, as well as private sector cost containment initiatives, make it increasingly difficult for the uninsured to receive needed emergency medical care.

Thompson v. Sun City Community Hospital
688 P.2d 605 (Ariz. 1984)

FELDMAN, JUSTICE.

Michael Jessee, plaintiff's son, was injured on the evening of September 4, 1976. Jessee was 13 years old at the time of this accident. He was rushed by ambulance from the place of the accident (Wittman, Arizona) to the Boswell Memorial Hospital operated by Sun City Community Hospital, Inc. (Boswell) in Sun City. Among Jessee's injuries was a transected or partially transected femoral artery. The injury was high in the left thigh and interrupted the flow of blood to the distal portion of the leg. Upon arrival at the emergency room at 8:22 P.M., Jessee was examined and initially treated by Dr. Steven Lipsky, the emergency room physician. Fluids were administered and blood was ordered. The leg injury prompted Dr. Lipsky to summon Dr. Alivina Sabanas, an orthopedic surgeon. She examined Jessee's leg and determined that he needed surgery. Dr. Jon Hillegas, a vascular surgeon, was consulted by phone.

At some time after 9:30 P.M. Jessee's condition "stabilized" and the decision was made to transfer him to County Hospital. . . . Dr. Hillegas told Dr. Lipsky that Jessee could be transferred when "sta-

---

69. See Relman, Economic Considerations in Emergency Care: What Are Hospitals For?, 312 New Eng. J. Med. 372, 372 (1985). An American Hospital Association survey in 1984 found that 15% of hospitals established explicit limits on charity care, 84% increased their billing and collection efforts, and 10% reduced staffing or hours of operation to cut costs.

bilized." A witness for the plaintiff testified that "The doctor at Boswell [apparently Dr. Lipsky] said [to Ada Thompson], 'I have the shitty detail of telling you that Mike will be transferred to County. . . .'" A Boswell administrator testified that emergency "charity" patients are transferred from Boswell to County whenever a physician, in his professional judgment, determines that "a transfer could occur."

Thus, at 10:13 Jessee was discharged from the Boswell emergency room, placed in an ambulance, and taken to County. The doctors who attended to him at County began administering fluids and ordered blood. They testified that Jessee's condition worsened but that he was eventually "stabilized" and taken to surgery at about 1:00 A.M. Jessee underwent abdominal surgery and, immediately thereafter, surgery to repair his torn femoral artery. He survived but has residual impairment of his left leg. His mother, as guardian ad litem, brought a malpractice action against Boswell and the physicians. . . .

In any case such as this there are two types of causation questions. The first, relating to the question of breach of duty, pertains to the cause for the transfer to another hospital. Was the patient transferred for medical or other reasons? The second question relates to the cause of injury and is concerned with whether the transfer, with its attendant movement and delay, caused a new or additional injury or aggravated any injury which already existed. The first question was answered by defense counsel in chambers, prior to any testimony being taken in the case:

> We admit and stipulate that the plaintiff in this case was transferred from Boswell to County Hospital for financial reasons. There is no question about it.

This stipulation was prompted by a record which clearly indicates that the transfer was made because the type of insurance available for the patient did not satisfy the hospital's financial requirements for admission. Thus, as soon as he became "medically transferable," Jessee was transferred because he lacked the necessary financial standing and not because surgery at County Hospital could be performed more quickly or by a more skilled surgeon. . . .

[T]he trial court instructed the jury that "the hospital may properly determine a patient's eligibility according to its own rules . . . and may transfer a patient to another appropriate hospital if the patient is medically transferable . . . [i.e.,] when in the judgment of the staff or emergency physician the patient may be transferred without subjecting the patient to an unreasonable risk of harm to his life or health." Under these instructions, the jury found for the defendants.

Plaintiff claims that under the facts of the case at bench, these instructions misstate the law to be applied in Arizona. . . .

The Standard of Care

The Hospital

In this state, the duty which a hospital owes a patient in need of emergency care is determined by the statutes and regulations interpreted by this court in Guerrero v. Copper Queen Hospital, 112 Ariz. 104, 537 P.2d 1329 (1975). Construing the statutory and regulatory scheme governing health care and the licensing of hospitals as of 1972, we held that it was the "public policy of this state" that a general "hospital may not deny emergency care to any patient without cause." Id. at 106, 537 P.2d at 1331.

In *Guerrero*, we referred primarily to former A.R.S. §36-405(A) in construing the statutes governing the licensing of hospitals [which required that "general hospitals shall provide facilities for emergency care."] . . . [Subsequently,] the Director of Health Services was required to adopt regulations for the licensure of health care facilities. As guidelines for minimum requirements, the director was mandated to use the standards of the Joint Commission for Accreditation of Hospitals (JCAH). . . . The emergency services section of the JCAH states that:

> no patient should arbitrarily be transferred if the hospital where he was initially seen has means for adequate care of his problem.

JCAH, Accreditation Manual for Hospitals 69 (1976). The "Patient's Rights" section of the JCAH manual makes it clear that the financial resources of a patient are among the "arbitrary" considerations within the contemplation of the above language:

> no person should be denied impartial access to treatment or accommodations that are available and medically indicated, on the basis of such considerations as . . . the nature or the source of payment for his care.

Id. at 23.

. . . Our holding in *Guerrero* is reinforced by A.R.S. §41-1837(A). This statute is of particular relevance in understanding the entire legislative scheme bearing on the issue of emergency care. It reads as follows:

> A. When an indigent emergency medical patient is received by an emergency receiving facility . . . , the county shall be liable . . . to

II. Patients' Rights to Treatment

the facility for the reasonable costs of all medical services rendered to such indigent by the facility until such patient is transferred by the county to the county hospital, or some other facility designated by the county.

The quoted statute was in effect in 1975 when we decided *Guerrero* and is still in effect. It provides the answer to a serious problem. Charging hospitals with a legal duty to render emergency care to indigent patients does not ignore the distinctions between private and public hospitals. Imposition of a duty to render emergency care to indigents simply charges private hospitals with the same duty as public hospitals under a statutory plan which permits reimbursement from public funds for the emergency care charges incurred at the private hospital.

This legislative and regulatory history provides no reason to retreat from or modify *Guerrero*. We therefore affirm its holding that, as a matter of public policy, licensed hospitals in this state are required to accept and render emergency care to all patients who present themselves in need of such care. The patient may not be transferred until all medically indicated emergency care has been completed. This standard of care has, in effect, been set by statute and regulation embodying a public policy which requires private hospitals to provide emergency care that is "medically indicated" without consideration of the economic circumstances of the patient in need of such care.[3] Thus, the word "cause" used in the quoted portion of *Guerrero* refers to something other than economic considerations. See Hiser v. Randolph, 126 Ariz. 608, 611, 617 P.2d 774, 777 (App. 1980). Interpreting the standard of care in accordance with the public policy defined in *Guerrero*, we hold that reasonable "cause" for transfer before completion of emergency care refers to medical considerations relevant to the welfare of the patient and not economic considerations relevant to the welfare of the hospital. A transfer based on the forbidden criterion of economic considerations may be for the convenience of the hospital but it is hardly "medically indicated."[4]

---

3. Although the *Guerrero* decision was based on statutory grounds rather than the common law doctrine enunciated in Wilmington General Hospital v. Manlove, 54 Del. 15, 174 A.2d 135 (1961), this court noted that the public policy concerns embodied in the Arizona statutory scheme are consistent with . . . *Manlove*. [T]he court of appeals' reliance on Harper v. Baptist Medical Center-Princeton, 341 So. 2d 133 (Ala. 1976) [which reached a contrary result] is misplaced. *Harper* does indeed present a factual situation nearly identical to the case at bench. However, in Alabama a private hospital has no duty to provide care to an emergency patient. Birmingham Baptist Hospital v. Crews, 229 Ala. 398, 157 So. 224 (1934). . . .

4. Trial testimony of several physicians that transfer based on the indigence of an emergency patient was a common practice among private hospitals in the Phoenix area in 1976 is, therefore, only probative of a negligent custom. See Helling v. Carey, 83 Wash. 2d 514, 517, 519 P.2d 981 (1974). Once Boswell stipulated that the transfer

Given the duty imposed in Arizona — that a general hospital may not deny emergency care to any person without valid cause — there are three possible defenses a hospital may raise in an appropriate fact situation: (1) that the hospital is not obligated (or capable) under its state license to provide the necessary emergency care, (2) there is a valid medical cause to refuse emergency care, (3) there is no true emergency requiring care and thus no emergency care which is medically indicated.

Neither of the first two defenses are at issue under the facts of this case. The third is more troublesome. Many people who enter the doors of an emergency room do not truly require "emergency care." The statutes and regulations do not apply to those who go to an "emergency room"; they apply to those in need of "emergency care." What constitutes an emergency is a matter of some disagreement. There are various definitions; the need for immediate attention seems to be the common thread. Ordinarily it is for the jury to determine the actual question of the duration of an emergency and the treatment modalities that are a necessary component of emergency care.

Given the stipulation that Boswell ordered the transfer of Jessee to County Hospital because of financial reasons, the relevant inquiries in the case at bench did not relate to "stabilization" and "transferability," but rather to the nature and duration of the emergency. The question was whether, before transfer, the hospital had rendered the emergency care medically indicated for this patient. The facts of this case indicate that emergency surgery was indicated for Jessee. Dr. Hillegas testified that "once the diagnosis is made, you should move on with definitive treatment," and that "you want to repair the arterial injury just as soon as you can." Dr. Lipsky knew Jessee needed surgery. Dr. Sabanas believed Jessee needed emergency surgery. Dr. Krigsten, an orthopedic surgeon called to testify on behalf of Dr. Sabanas, believed it would have been advantageous for two surgical teams to have worked simultaneously on Jessee at County Hospital in order to promptly revasculate the leg. Plaintiff's experts were even more insistent on the need for emergency surgery. Thus, the judge's view that the patient's condition was one requiring emergency care which included surgery to repair a transected artery was clearly supported by the evidence in addition to the defendant's concessions on this issue. Given this view of the case it was error for the trial judge to refuse plaintiff's request for a peremptory instruction on the issue of the hospital's breach of its duty of care. The undisputed

---

was based upon plaintiff's lack of economic resources, proof of professional custom to establish the standard of care was irrelevant because that custom embraced an erroneous view of the applicable legal standard. . . .

II. Patients' Rights to Treatment

evidence established that the patient was transferred for financial reasons while emergency care was medically indicated. As a matter of law this was a breach of the hospital's duty. Thus, the only question before the jury on the issue of the hospital's liability was whether its breach of duty was a cause of some compensable damage.

The Physicians

The duty of care owed by a physician to a patient is different from the hospital's duty. No statute requires the physician to provide services . . . Hiser v. Randolph, 126 Ariz. at 611, 617 P.2d at 777. . . . The trial court directed a verdict in favor of the vascular surgeon, Dr. Hillegas. The court of appeals found no error. We agree. Plaintiff argues, however, that the vascular surgeon breached his duty in failing to come to the hospital to attend Jessee, and is liable under the principles set forth in Hiser v. Randolph, supra. We disagree. In *Hiser* the hospital did not have a physician on duty in the emergency room. Several local physicians were "on call" to come to the emergency room to render emergency care. By assenting to the hospital bylaws, rules and regulations these physicians "personally became bound" to come to the emergency room when called. The doctor in *Hiser* was called to the emergency room to treat a patient in a diabetic coma and flatly refused to fulfill his obligation.

In the case at bench, physicians were on duty and present at Boswell to care for emergency patients; specialists were "on call," prepared to come to the hospital and treat patients who needed specialized attention. Dr. Hillegas was one of the latter. Unlike the hospital in *Hiser,* Boswell did not request this physician to come. To the contrary, Boswell's refusal to admit Jessee would have made Dr. Hillegas' arrival at the hospital an empty gesture. We find no error in the directed verdict in favor of Dr. Hillegas. . . .

The judgments in favor of defendants Hillegas and Lipsky are affirmed. The judgment in favor of Boswell is reversed and the case remanded for further proceedings.

Consolidated Omnibus Reconciliation Act of 1985 ("COBRA")
42 U.S.C. §1395dd

(b) (1) If any individual (whether or not eligible for benefits under [Medicare]) comes to a hospital and the hospital determines that the individual has an emergency medical condition or is in active labor, the hospital must provide either —

    (A) within the staff and facilities available at the hospital, for such further medical examination and such treatment as may be required to stabilize the medical condition or to provide for treatment of the labor, or

(B) for transfer of the individual to another medical facility in accordance with subsection (c) of this section. . . .

(c)(1) . . . The hospital may not transfer the individual unless —

(A)(i) the individual (or a legally responsible person acting on the individual's behalf) requests that the transfer be effected, or (ii) a physician . . . has signed a certification that, based upon the reasonable risks and benefits to the patient, and based upon the information available at the time, the medical benefits reasonably expected from the provision of appropriate medical treatment at another medical facility outweigh the increased risks to the individual's medical condition, and in the case of labor, to the unborn child, from effecting the transfer; and

(B) the transfer is . . . to a medical facility . . . in which the receiving facility — (i) has available space and qualified personnel for the treatment of the individual, and (ii) has agreed to accept transfer of the individual and to provide appropriate medical treatment; . . .

(d)(1) If a hospital knowingly and willfully, or negligently, fails to meet the requirements of this section, such hospital is subject to termination of its provider agreement under [Medicare]. . . .

(2) (A) A participating hospital that knowingly violates a requirement of this section is subject to a civil money penalty of not more than $50,000 for each such violation. . . .

(3) (A) Any individual who suffers personal harm as a direct result of a participating hospital's violation of a requirement of this section may, in a civil action against the participating hospital, obtain those damages available for personal injury under the law of the State in which the hospital is located, and such equitable relief as is appropriate. . . .

(e) In this section:

(1) The term "emergency medical condition" means

(A) a medical condition manifesting itself by acute symptoms of sufficient severity (including severe pain) such that the absence of immediate medical attention could reasonably be expected to result in —

(i) placing the patient's health in serious jeopardy,

(ii) serious impairment to bodily functions, or

(iii) serious dysfunction of any bodily organ or part, or

(B) with respect to a pregnant woman who is having contractions

(i) that there is inadequate time to effect a safe transfer to another hospital before delivery, or

(ii) that transfer may pose a threat to the health or safety of the woman or the unborn child. . . .

(3) (A) The term "to stabilize" means, with respect to an emergency medical condition, to provide such medical treatment of the condition as may be necessary to assure, within reasonable medical probability, that no material deterioration of the condition is likely to result from the transfer of the individual from a facility, or with respect to an emergency medical condition described in Paragraph (1)(B), to deliver (including the placenta).

NOTES

The Duty to Treat Indigent Patients

1. To better understand the distinct nature of the theory of the *Thompson* case — the duty to treat emergency patients regardless of the ability to pay — consider whether Jessee had a case for abandonment. (Answer: no, because he wasn't abandoned; he was transferred.) Also, consider whether he had a case for malpractice. (Answer: maybe, if the doctors were negligent in assessing whether he was "medically transferable," but the jury found for the defendants on this question.) In effect, then, the doctors were held strictly liable for incorrectly assessing the likelihood that a transfer would result in permanent impairment of his leg.

2. Why is patient-dumping so prevalent if Medicaid programs exist to care for the poor?

> The fact that many low-income families have no public coverage is rarely understood by the public. Although the view that all poor people receive public medical assistance may be generally accepted, in fact only about one-half of those classified as poor under Federal guidelines are covered by Medicaid. . . . Moreover, eligibility for Medicaid is tied to particular family composition requirements, such as being a single parent with children; a couple without children, no matter how poor, is typically ineligible for Medicaid. One Commission witness told how her $53-a-week salary, the only source of support for herself and her children, was too high to allow her to qualify for public medical assistance. She became eligible only when the cost of hospitalization forced her income down. . . . The Commission also learned of an Atlanta couple, with one child, who were unable to afford needed care. The husband, an automobile mechanic by trade, had been unable to find work after being laid off. They had virtually no income but were ineligible for Medicaid because they were married.

President's Commission, Securing Access to Health Care 154-156 (1983).

3. Many states explicitly require treatment of all emergency patients despite the ability to pay. E.g., Cal. Health & Safety Code §§1317, 1799.10; Ill. Ann. Stat. ch. 111 1/2, §86; N.Y. Pub. Health Law §2805-b. See Waxman & Dorn, States Take the Lead in Preventing Patient Dumping, 22 Clearinghouse Rev. 136 (1988); Relman, Texas Eliminates Dumping, 314 New Eng. J. Med. 578 (1986); Summary of State Emergency Care: Statutes and Case Law, 18 Clearinghouse Rev. 494 (1984). Federal law has long required the same for Hill-Burton and tax-exempt hospitals. See 553 and 636 infra.

Given the overlay of state statutory and common law duties, and given the fact that the overwhelming trend in modern state caselaw prohibits hospitals from refusing emergency care, what was the need for federal enactment of the COBRA antidumping statute? If federal intervention is necessary, is it appropriate to use Medicare participation to penalize hospitals for not treating non-Medicare patients? See Hall, The Unlikely Case In Favor of Patient Dumping, 28 Jurimetrics 389 (1988) (arguing that this redundant enactment is a cosmetic measure that detracts attention from the much larger problem of providing for the nonemergency medical needs of the uninsured); contra, Rothenberg, supra, 26 Hous. L. Rev. at 51-75 (COBRA goes long way toward remedying defects of common law).

For further discussion of the private right of action that COBRA creates, see Reid v. Indianapolis Osteopathic Medical Hosp., 709 F. Supp. 853 (S.D. Ind. 1989) (action is subject to state law cap on medical malpractice damages, but not to medical review panel screening requirement); Thorton v. Southwest Detroit Hosp., 895 F.2d 1131 (6th Cir. 1989) (emergency patient hospitalized for 21 days clearly "stabilized"); McClurg, Your Money or Your Life: Interpreting the Federal Act Against Patient Dumping, 24 Wake Forest L. Rev. 173 (1989).

4. What constitutes an emergency? *Thompson* clarifies that a hospital does not have the duty to treat every patient who stumbles through the emergency room doors, but does its definition provide sufficient guidance? Is it consistent with *Manlove's* definition? Compare Hill v. Ohio County, 468 S.W.2d 306 (Ky. 1970) (active labor does not constitute "unmistakable emergency"). A portion omitted from Payton v. Weaver supra held that a hospital is obliged to provide kidney dialysis only where the patient is in need of "immediate lifesaving treatment." 182 Cal. Rptr. 225 (Cal. App. 1982). The Alabama cases cited in footnote 3 of *Thompson* have been read to hold *not* that there is no duty to treat emergency patients, but that no true emergency existed, that is, no immediately threatened loss of life or limb. K. Wing, The Law and the Public's Health 234-237 (2d ed. 1985).

If there is an emergency, how far does the duty to treat extend? Do hospitals have to perform bypass surgery after they halt a heart

II. Patients' Rights to Treatment

attack? As quoted above, COBRA, the federal antidumping statute, requires only "stabilizing" care, and only for those patients in "serious jeopardy." Does this stop "patient dumping?" See Joyner v. Alton Ochsner Med. Found., 230 So. 2d 913 (La. App. 1970) (auto accident victim did not "require immediate admission" after stabilizing care was rendered, despite "multiple deep facial lacerations, a possible head injury, traumatic damage to the teeth and multiple bruises and contusions of the body, resulting in considerable loss of blood"). See generally Wing & Campbell, The Emergency Room Admission: How Far Does the "Open Door" Go?, 65 U. Det. L. Rev. 119 (1985); Hall, supra, 28 Jurimetrics at 392-393 ("In the great majority of cases, the federal standard will do nothing to prevent patient dumping. . . . Even for those patients who do require stabilization prior to transfer, the federal law will result only in a delay in the transfer").

5. Do the Arizona statute and regulations cited in *Thompson* mandate emergency treatment of their own force, or does the court create a common law duty based on the public policy that emanates from the statute? If the latter, how clear is the perceived public policy? Hospital licensing statutes, which the *Thompson* court noted require hospitals to maintain emergency rooms, also require hospitals to maintain surgery suites, pathology services, and a cafeteria. Does that mean these too must be offered for free? As for the JCAH standard, is discrimination based on the *source* of payment the same as discrimination based on the *absence* of payment?

At one level, the theory of liability makes little practical difference since, under one theory or another, hospitals cannot turn away emergency patients. At another level, the theory of liability might be critical to the question of what constitutes an emergency and how far the duty to treat extends. Thompson, after all, did receive stabilizing (life-saving) emergency care; he complained only of the failure to render the full range of emergency medical care and to restore full function of his leg. Review the *Manlove* theory of liability and how that court defined the scope of the duty to treat. Do you think it would have (or should have) reached the same result under *Thompson*'s facts? See Fabian v. Matzko, 344 A. 2d 569 (Pa. Super. 1975) (no duty to treat woman who sustained severe brain hemorrhage because "appellant did not rely on a policy of rendering emergency care . . . and thus did not waste valuable time").

The Guerrero v. Copper Queen Hospital case discussed in *Thompson* is notable in that it allowed a nonresident Mexican family to enforce the duty to treat against a border town hospital owned by a local mining company. In 1985, Copper Queen Hospital had nearly $900,000 in uncollectible accounts. Arizona Republic, July 26, 1985, at C1.

For general commentary on this line of cases, see Enfield & Sklar,

Patient Dumping in the Hospital Emergency Room: Renewed Interest in an Old Problem, 13 Am. J.L. & Med. 561 (1988); Comment, Medical Indigence and Economic Scarcity: Are Egalitarian Access to Care and Cost Control Mutually Inconsistent Goals?, 33 Loy. L. Rev. 113 (1987); Curran, Economic and Legal Considerations in Emergency Care, 312 New Eng. J. Med. 374 (1985); Dougherty, The Right to Health Care: First Aid in the Emergency Room, 4 Pub. L. Forum 101 (1984); Fine, Opening the Closed Doors: The Duty of Hospitals to Treat Emergency Patients, 24 Wash. J. Urb. & Contemp. L. 123 (1983); Comment, To Treat or Not to Treat: A Hospital's Duty to Provide Emergency Care, 15 U.C. Davis L. Rev. 1047 (1982); Annot., 35 A.L.R.3d 841 (1971). Further information on the "patient dumping" phenomenon can be found in Dallek & Waxman, "Patient Dumping": A Crisis in Emergency Medical Care for the Indigent, 19 Clearinghouse Rev. 1413 (1986); Reed, Cawley & Anderson, The Effect of a Public Hospital's Transfer Policy on Patient Care, 315 New Eng. J. Med. 1428 (1986); Himmelstein et al., Patient Transfers: Medical Practice as Social Triage, 74 Am. J. Pub. Health 494 (1984); Wing, American Health Policy in the 1980s, 36 Case W. Res. L. Rev. 608, 679-681 (1986).

6. Do you think the existence of the statute cited in *Thompson* that allows private hospitals to recoup from the county the expenses of indigent treatment was critical to the outcome of the case? Statutes like this have been the subject of increasing enforcement litigation against local governments. See Saxton v. Gem County, 750 P.2d 950 (Idaho 1988) (county statutorily required to pay physician fees for emergency treatment); Sioux Valley Hosp. Assoc. v. Yankton County, 424 N.W.2d 379 (S.D. 1988) (county must pay for emergency hospitalization of indigent); Middlesex Mem. Hosp. v. Town of North Haven, 535 A.2d 1303 (Conn. 1988) (no town liability where income eligibility not clearly established).

Concerning the obligation of local governments to provide for the health care needs of the indigent, see generally Dowell, State and Local Government Legal Responsibility to Provide Medical Care for the Poor, 3 J.L. & Health 1 (1989) (comprehensive collection of statutory and case law authority); Bovbjerg & Kopit, Coverage and Care for the Medically Indigent: Public and Private Options, 19 Ind. L. Rev. 857 (1986); Brown & Cousineau, Effectiveness of State Mandates to Maintain Local Government Health Services for the Poor, 9 J. Health Pol. Poly. & L. 223 (1984); Note, 20 Wake Forest L. Rev. 317 (1984); Brown, Public Hospitals on the Brink: Their Problems and Their Options, 7 J. Health Pol. Poly. & L. 927 (1983).

7. Hospital responsibility for *emergency* treatment of the poor is more or less taken for granted. Far more controversial is the role private hospitals should play in providing charity care generally. Is

there any source of law that requires a hospital to accept a nonpaying patient for hernia repair, hip-replacement, or other serious conditions that are disabling but not life-threatening?

As described more fully below in Chapter 7.V, in 1969 the government rescinded its position that required tax exempt hospitals to provide a reasonable level of general charity care in order to maintain their favored tax status. The Supreme Court rejected a challenge to this ruling based on lack of standing. Simon v. Eastern Kentucky Welfare Rights Organization, 426 U.S. 26 (1976). However, state taxing authorities have shown a renewed interest in the level of general charity care for purposes of hospital exemption from property and other local taxation.

8. A second source of federal law for a non-emergency indigent care duty is the Hill-Burton Hospital Construction Act of 1946, which has pumped billions of dollars into financing hospital construction, largely in rural and southern areas of the country. The Act requires that Hill-Burton hospitals (those that have received construction funding) must provide a "reasonable amount" of free services for patients unable to pay. For decades, this charity care requirement was not monitored or enforced. However, as a result of intensive public-interest group pressure in the courts and before the regulators, HEW issued regulations in the 1970s that codified and quantified the charity care obligation: Hill-Burton hospitals must provide 3 percent of their care to indigent patients for 20 years after receiving assistance. See AHA v. Schweiker, 721 F.2d 170 (7th Cir. 1983); Cook v. Ochsner Found. Hosp., 555 F.2d 968 (5th Cir. 1977); Rohrer, The Political Development of the Hill-Burton Program: A Case Study in Distributive Policy, 12 J. Health Pol. Poly. & L. 137 (1987); Dowell & Freifeld, Hill-Burton Uncompensated Care: HHS Administrative Decisions and Remedies, 19 Clearinghouse Rev. 133 (1985); Blumstein, Court Action, Agency Reaction: The Hill-Burton Act as a Case Study, 69 Iowa L. Rev. 1227 (1984); Wing, The Community Service Obligation of Hill-Burton Health Facilities, 23 B.C.L. Rev. 577 (1982); Curran, Medical Charity for the Poor — Hill-Burton and the Hospitals, 287 New Eng. J. Med. 498 (1972); Annot., 11 A.L.R. Fed 683 (1972).

This victory for indigent patients represents the apex of the broad-based drive of welfare rights groups in the 1970s to fight for increased medical benefits for their clients. See Rosenblatt, Health Care Reform and Administrative Law: A Structural Approach, 88 Yale L.J. 243 (1978); Law, Health Care and Social Change, 19 Clearinghouse Rev. 419 (1985); section II.F infra. However, the explicit Hill-Burton obligations have provided little relief, according to one report, because the government has been lax in monitoring. Dowell, Hill-Burton: The Unfulfilled Promise, 12 J. Health Pol. Poly. & L. 153 (1987) (noncompliance is "widespread"). Note, however, the possibility of some private monitoring: failure to provide hospital patients the required notice of the hospital's Hill-Burton obligation may provide a defense to a collection suit on a hospital bill. See Cooper Med. Cent. v. Boyd, 430 A.2d 261 (N.J. App. Div. 1981).

D. Constitutional Rights of Access

Wideman v. Shallowford Community Hospital
826 F.2d 1030 (11th Cir. 1987)

HILL, CIRCUIT JUDGE:

This case presents the novel question of whether a county government's alleged practice of using its emergency medical vehicles to transport patients only to certain county hospitals which guarantee the payment of the county's medical bills violates a right protected by the federal constitution. We hold that such a practice, even if proved, would not violate any established constitutional right; therefore, the plaintiffs have failed to state a claim under 42 U.S.C. §1983.

I. Background

The facts underlying this case are undeniably tragic. On April 12, 1984, Toni Wideman, who at the time was four months pregnant, began experiencing abdominal pain. She called her obstetrician, Dr. John Ramsey, who instructed her to come immediately to Piedmont Hospital. Ms. Wideman called the 911 emergency telephone number in DeKalb County and requested an ambulance to take her to Piedmont. Three employees of the DeKalb County Emergency Medical Service (EMS) responded to this call. Ms. Wideman claims that she again informed the EMS employees to take her to Piedmont where her doctor was waiting, but they refused and, instead, took her against her wishes to Shallowford Community Hospital. After a substantial delay, during which the attending physician at Shallowford spoke by phone with Dr. Ramsey, Ms. Wideman was transferred to Piedmont. At that point, however, Dr. Ramsey was unable to stop her labor, and Ms. Wideman gave birth to a premature baby, named Ebony Laslun Wideman, who survived for only four hours.

Toni Wideman and her husband subsequently filed this action under 42 U.S.C. §§1983, 1985 and 1988 seeking damages for the wrongful death of their child. Specifically, they alleged that a conspiracy existed between Shallowford Hospital and DeKalb County, whereby the County had a policy and practice of using its emergency medical vehicles to transport patients only to hospitals such as Shallowford which guaranteed the payment of the County's emergency medical bills. Piedmont Hospital supposedly had no such agreement

II. Patients' Rights to Treatment

with DeKalb County. The plaintiffs claimed that this conspiracy deprived them of their federal constitutional right to essential medical treatment and care. . . .

It seems that both parties, as well as the district court, have assumed that the alleged policy violates a cognizable constitutional right, which the plaintiffs characterize as their right to the provision of essential medical treatment and services by the County.[3] However, because section 1983 provides a remedy only for violations of rights secured by the Constitution or federal laws, the proper resolution of this case requires us first to determine whether the Constitution grants a right to medical care and treatment in these circumstances.

III. Existence of a Constitutional Right to Essential Medical Care

A

Beginning from the broadest prospective, we can discern no general right, based upon either the Constitution or federal statutes, to the provision of medical treatment and services by a state or municipality. If such a right exists at all, it must derive from the fourteenth amendment's due process clause, which forbids a state to deprive anyone of life, liberty or property without due process of law. The due process clause, however, has traditionally been interpreted as protecting certain "negative liberties," i.e., an individual's right to be free from arbitrary or discriminatory action taken by a state or municipality. This circuit has recognized the "well established notion that the Constitution limits the actions the states can take rather than mandating specific obligations." Bradberry v. Pinellas County, 789 F.2d 1513, 1517 (11th Cir. 1986). The Constitution is "a charter of negative rather than positive liberties." Jackson v. City of Joliet, 715 F.2d 1200, 1203 (7th Cir. 1983), *cert. denied*, 465 U.S. 1049, 104 S. Ct. 1325, 79 L. Ed.2d 720 (1984). "[I]t tells the state to let people alone; it does not require the federal government or the state to provide services. . . ." Bowers v. DeVito, 686 F.2d 616, 618 (7th Cir. 1982).

Two Supreme Court decisions dealing with access to abortions also support our conclusion that there is no general right to medical care or treatment provided by the state. In Maher v. Roe, 432 U.S.

---

3. The constitutional right alleged by the plaintiffs arguably may be characterized as the much more specific right to the medical care and services of their choice. Ms. Wideman was provided with medical care in this case; indeed, she was rushed to a hospital in an ambulance provided by the County. Her claim appears to be that she should have been able to direct the ambulance wherever she wanted to go. For purposes of our analysis, however, we shall consider the plaintiffs' alleged constitutional right as they have characterized it.

464, 97 S. Ct. 2376, 53 L. Ed.2d 484 (1977), two indigent women brought suit challenging a Connecticut regulation prohibiting the funding of abortions that were not medically necessary. The plaintiffs argued under the fourteenth amendment that the state regulation impinged on their constitutional right to an abortion, as recognized in Roe v. Wade, 410 U.S. 113 (1973). The Court upheld the state regulation, concluding that *Roe* did not declare an unqualified constitutional right to an abortion; rather, that case declared a woman's right to be protected from unduly burdensome interference with her freedom to decide whether to terminate her pregnancy. Significantly, in reaching this result, the Court noted that "[t]he Constitution imposes no obligation on the States to pay the pregnancy-related medical expenses of indigent women, or indeed to pay any of the medical expenses of indigents." Maher, 432 U.S. at 469 (footnote omitted).

The Court's subsequent decision in Harris v. McRae, 448 U.S. 297 (1980), reinforced the constitutional distinction between requiring the state to provide medical services and prohibiting the state from impeding access to such services. The plaintiffs in *Harris* challenged the constitutionality of the Hyde amendment, which denied public funding for certain medically necessary abortions, as violating their due process liberty interest in deciding whether to terminate a pregnancy. The Supreme Court held that although the liberty protected by the due process clause prohibits unwarranted government interference with freedom of choice in the context of certain personal decisions, "it does not confer an entitlement to such funds as may be necessary to realize all the advantages of that freedom." Harris, 448 U.S. at 317-18. The court concluded that the limitation on governmental power implicit in the due process clause does not translate into an affirmative obligation on the part of government to fund abortions or other medically necessary services. Id. at 318. More recently, the Court has interpreted *Maher* and *Harris* as standing for the proposition that, "[a]s a general matter, the State is under no constitutional duty to provide substantive services for those within its border." Youngberg v. Romeo, 457 U.S. 307, 317 (1982). Several court of appeals decisions have addressed the issue of whether a state or municipality has a duty under the fourteenth amendment to provide various protective services to its citizens. Almost without exception, these courts have concluded that governments are under no constitutional duty to provide police, fire, or other public safety services. . . .

B

That there exists no such general right to the provision of medical care and services by the state, however, does not end our inquiry.

II. Patients' Rights to Treatment

Both the Supreme Court and various circuit courts have indicated that the existence of a "special custodial or other relationship" between an individual and the state may trigger a constitutional duty on the part of the state to provide certain medical or other services. In these special circumstances, the state's failure to provide such services might implicate constitutionally protected rights. For example, the Supreme Court has held that the eighth amendment prohibition against cruel and unusual punishments, applicable to the states via the fourteenth amendment, requires states to provide medical care for those whom it is punishing by incarceration. Estelle v. Gamble, 429 U.S. 97, 103, 97 S. Ct. 285, 290, 50 L. Ed.2d 251 (1976). The Court concluded that "deliberate indifference" to the serious medical needs of prisoners violates the eighth amendment and therefore states a cause of action under section 1983. Similarly, the Court has held that an involuntarily committed mental patient retains certain constitutionally protected substantive liberty interests under the fourteenth amendment. Youngberg v. Romeo, 457 U.S. 307, 315-19 (1982). The state defendants in that case conceded, and the Court accepted, the fact that mental patients have a clear fourteenth amendment right "to adequate food, shelter, clothing, and medical care." Courts have also recognized the existence of a special relationship imposing a duty on a state or municipality to provide care and treatment for persons in its custody in situations less extreme than permanent incarceration or institutionalization. [I]n City of Revere v. Massachusetts General Hosp., 463 U.S. 239 (1983), the Supreme Court held that the due process clause requires "the responsible government or governmental agency to provide medical care to persons . . . who have been injured while being apprehended by the police." . . .

Following this rationale, a constitutional duty can arise only when a state or municipality, by exercising a significant degree of custody or control over an individual, places that person in a worse situation than he would have been had the government not acted at all. Such a situation could arise by virtue of the state affirmatively placing an individual in a position of danger, effectively stripping a person of her ability to defend herself, or cutting off potential sources of private aid. See Walker, 791 F.2d at 511; Estate of Gilmore, 787 F.2d at 722. The key concept is the exercise of coercion, dominion, or restraint by the state. The state must somehow significantly limit an individual's freedom or impair his ability to act on his own before it will be constitutionally required to care and provide for that person.

In the present case, we conclude that DeKalb County did not exercise a degree of coercion, dominion, or restraint over Ms. Wideman sufficient to create a "special relationship," thus imposing on the County a constitutional duty to provide her with the medical treatment she alleges was necessary. The County did not force or otherwise coerce her into its ambulance; it merely made the ambulance available to her, and she entered it voluntarily. Ms. Wideman's physical condition at the time might have required her to seek immediate medical help, and that need might have induced her to make use of the service provided by the County, hoping that she could convince the EMS employees to take her where she wanted to go. Her physical condition, however, cannot be attributed to the County. Clearly, the County did not cause the medical emergency Ms. Wideman faced. Neither did her condition arise while she was in the County's custody or control. Therefore, the county was under no affirmative constitutional duty to provide any particular type of emergency medical service for her. . . . Because the Constitution does not require municipalities to provide any emergency medical services at all, it would be anomalous indeed to hold them liable for providing limited services which happen to be less extensive than a particular citizen may desire. . . .

The judgment of the district court is affirmed.

NOTES

The Constitutional Right to Treatment

1. In holding that the state had no special obligation by virtue of having custody of Ms. Wideman, does the court mean to say that the ambulance service was free to take her anywhere, or nowhere at all? Would the court have been on firmer ground if it had assumed a special obligation existed once Ms. Wideman was in the ambulance, but held that the obligation was discharged by taking her to *a* hospital, in other words, by holding that, if there is a constitutional right to health care, it does not include the right to *designate* one's hospital of choice? See footnote 3 in the case. See generally Curran, The Constitutional Right to Health Care, 320 New Eng. J. Med. 788 (1989).

2. The Supreme Court subsequently employed an analysis similar to that in *Wideman* in holding that no constitutional violation occurred in a case where a child was left with permanent brain damage when a state social services agency failed to intervene aggressively enough in a case of reported child abuse despite repeated warnings of severe beatings by the father. The Court reaffirmed "that the Due Process Clauses generally confer no affirmative right to governmental aid," and it reasoned that the state agency had not assumed a "special relationship" with the child by virtue of having made some ineffectual efforts to protect him since the agency did nothing to make him more vulnerable to the danger. DeShaney v. Winnebago County Department of Social Services, 109 S. Ct. 998 (1989). See also Archie

II. Patients' Rights to Treatment

v. Racine, 847 F.2d 1211 (7th Cir. 1988) (en banc) (Section 1983 action not maintainable for city rescue service's negligent failure to dispatch ambulance; no constitutional right to treatment exists).

3. An early, highly influential decision addressing the constitutional right to treatment in the context of state institutionalization is Judge Frank Johnson's remarkable order taking direct charge over the administration of Alabama's state mental hospital because of its persistent failure to provide any meaningful form of treatment. Wyatt v. Stickney, 325 F. Supp. 781 (M.D. Ala. 1971); 344 F. Supp. 373 (M.D. Ala. 1972). See also O'Connor v. Donaldson, 422 U.S. 563 (1975) (civil commitment to psychiatric hospital invalid without treatment); Comment, Wyatt v. Stickney and the Right of Civilly Committed Mental Patients to Adequate Treatment, 86 Harv. L. Rev. 1282 (1973). In Thomas S. v. Morrow, 781 F.2d 367 (4th Cir. 1986), the court found a constitutional duty to provide "clinically adequate community mental health services" in order to assure the availability of a least restrictive means of treatment for patients who would otherwise have to be involuntarily committed.

4. In Maher v. Roe, 432 U.S. 464, 469-470 (1977), discussed in the principal case, the Court identified another possible source of a constitutional duty to treat: "The Constitution imposes no obligation on the States to pay . . . any of the medical expenses of indigents. But when a State decides to alleviate some of the hardships of poverty by providing medical care, the manner in which it dispenses benefits is subject to constitutional limitations." For example, in Memorial Hospital v. Maricopa County, 415 U.S. 250 (1974), the Court struck down a durational residency requirement imposed on county health service eligibility as infringing on the right to travel. Also, a state might be subject to an equal protection attack for funding some procedures but not others. What level of scrutiny should such decisions be subjected to? See Mariner, Access to Health Care and Equal Protection of the Law: The Need for a New Heightened Scrutiny, 12 Am. J.L. & Med. 345 (1986) (arguing for an intermediate level of scrutiny).

5. Harris v. McRae, the abortion funding case discussed in *Wideman*, also addressed a *non*constitutional theory for compelling government funding of health care. States that participate in Medicaid are, generally speaking, required to fund most medically necessary forms of treatment. See Beal v. Doe, 432 U.S. 438, 444 (1977). Although Harris v. McRae found this statutory requirement to be inapplicable to abortions, in other cases the medical necessity mandate has proved to be an effective tool for obtaining Medicaid coverage. See infra p.822 (liver transplants must be covered); Rush v. Parham, 625 F.2d 1150 (5th Cir. 1980) (sex change operation must be funded in certain circumstances); Gosfield, Medical Necessity in Medicare and

Medicaid, 51 Temple L.Q. 229 (1978); Note, State Restrictions on Medicaid Coverage of Medically Necessary Services, 78 Colum. L. Rev. 1491 (1978).

Andrews v. Ballard
498 F. Supp. 1038 (S.D. Tex. 1980)

McDonald, District Judge.

Introduction

This is a challenge to the constitutionality of . . . the Texas Medical Practice Act as applied to the practice of acupuncture, and Rules . . . of the Texas State Board of Medical Examiners . . . [that] generally provide that only licensed physicians can practice acupuncture in the state of Texas. The plaintiffs are 46 residents of Harris County, Texas, who seek acupuncture treatment. They maintain that the constitutional right of privacy, protected by the Due Process Clause of the Fourteenth Amendment, encompasses the decision to obtain or reject medical treatment. . . .

Acupuncture Theory and Practice

Before proceeding to the merits of this action, it may prove useful to review the theory and practice of acupuncture. Acupuncture, one branch of traditional Chinese medicine, has been practiced for 2,000 to 5,000 years. It consists of the insertion and manipulation of very fine needles at specific points on or near the surface of the skin. The needles . . . may be used to affect the perception of pain (acupuncture analgesia) or to treat certain diseases or dysfunctions (acupuncture therapy).

The traditional Chinese explanation of how acupuncture works relies heavily on concepts unfamiliar to the Western scientific community. According to traditional Chinese theory, the basic energy or force of life, which flows through all living things, is called "Ch'i." When this force flows through the human body, it travels along twelve primary and two secondary channels or meridians. It is along these channels that the acupuncture points lie. Ch'i, traditional Chinese theory teaches, has two aspects to it: Yin, the negative aspect, and Yang, the positive aspect. The twelve primary channels through which Ch'i flows are divided accordingly into six Yin and six Yang channels and paired. For each Yin channel, there is a Yang channel.

Despite the reference to them as "negative" and "positive," as Yin and Yang are two aspects of the same force, one is no more desirable than the other. In fact, it is a basic tenet of traditional

II. Patients' Rights to Treatment

Chinese theory that Yin and Yang must be in balance for Ch'i to flow freely and for all living things, therefore, to function properly. Thus, the theory teaches that it is when Yin and Yang are out of balance that the body is susceptible to pain and illness. Acupuncture treatment is designed to correct this imbalance. The skilled acupuncturist, by placing and manipulating the needles in the proper points, brings Yin and Yang back into balance. This allows Ch'i to flow freely and the body's natural defenses to combat disease and pain.[17]

. . . Whatever the best explanation is for how acupuncture works, one thing is clear: it does work. All of the evidence put before this Court indicates that, when administered by a skilled practitioner for certain types of pain and dysfunctions,[21] acupuncture is both safe and effective.

The Right of Privacy

In order to evaluate the plaintiffs' claim, it is first necessary to determine whether the interest they seek to protect is of constitutional dimension. The plaintiffs contend that they have a constitutional right, encompassed by the right of privacy, to decide to obtain or reject medical treatment. That right, they say, protects their decision to obtain acupuncture treatment.

"The Constitution," of course, "does not explicitly mention any right of privacy. In a line of decisions, however going back . . . as far as Union Pacific R. Co. v. Botsford, 141 U.S. 250, 251 (1891), the (United States Supreme) Court has recognized that a right of personal privacy, or a guarantee of certain zones of privacy, . . . does exist." Roe v. Wade, 410 U.S. 113, 152 (1973). . . . One such interest is "the interest in independence in making certain kinds of important decisions." Whalen v. Roe, 429 U.S. 589, 599-600 (1977).

---

17. Much of this can be expressed in more familiar terminology. "Everything is basically electrical," says the World Book Encyclopedia, Vol. 6, at 147 (1980). "All matter consists of atoms." It contains electrons, "negative particle(s) of electricity," and protons, "positive particle(s) of electricity. These tiny particles always have equal, but opposite, charges of electricity." Id. (Emphasis deleted.) They are, in other words, in balance.

The World Book Encyclopedia goes on to say that "the brain continually" sends "small waves of electricity" through the body. Id., Vol. 2, at 460b. It is not unreasonable to assume that the disruption of those waves could adversely affect the body. Nor is it illogical to conclude that the form of those waves could be altered by the insertion into the skin and manipulation of tiny metal needles.

21. According to the undisputed testimony of Dr. Kroening, Doctor of Traditional Chinese Medicine Yee-Kung Lok, and assistant acupuncturist Peter Lok, the ailments effectively treated by acupuncture include migraine headaches, arthritis, cataracts, trigeminal neuralgia, whiplash, asthma, and certain types of pain, paralysis, and respiratory diseases.

[A]mong the decisions that an individual may make without unjustified government interference are personal decisions "relating to marriage, procreation, contraception, family relationships, and child rearing and education" Roe v. Wade, supra, 410 U.S. at 152-153 [citations omitted].

Carey v. Population Services International, supra, 431 U.S. at 684-685. . . . [These decisions] meet two criteria. First, they [are] "personal decisions." Id. They [ ] primarily involve one's self or one's family. Second, they [are] "important decisions." Id. at 684. They [ ] profoundly affect one's development or one's life. . . .

The decision to obtain or reject medical treatment, no less than the decision to continue or terminate pregnancy, meets both criteria. First, although decisions "relating to marriage, procreation, contraception, family relationships, and child rearing and education," often involve and affect other individuals as directly as they do one's self, decisions relating to medical treatment do not. They are, to an extraordinary degree, intrinsically personal. It is the individual making the decision, and no one else, who lives with the pain and disease. It is the individual making the decision, and no one else, who must undergo or forego the treatment. And it is the individual making the decision, and no one else, who, if he or she survives, must live with the results of that decision. One's health is a uniquely personal possession. The decision of how to treat that possession is no less personal in nature.

Second, it is impossible to discuss the decision to obtain or reject medical treatment without realizing its importance. The decision . . . is, for some, the difference between a life of pain and a life of pleasure. It is, for others, the difference between life and death. . . . One's health is perhaps one's most valuable asset. The importance of decisions affecting it cannot be overstated.

Thus, the decision to obtain or reject medical treatment, presented in the instant case as the decision to obtain acupuncture treatment, is both personal and important enough to be encompassed by the right of privacy. This should come as no surprise. . . . Chief Justice Burger, while a Circuit Judge for the District of Columbia, included the choice of "refusing medical treatment even at great risk" among those encompassed by the right of privacy. Application of President and Directors of Georgetown College, Inc., 331 F.2d 1010, 1017 (D.C. Cir. 1964) (dissenting opinion). And Justice Douglas, in Doe v. Bolton, 410 U.S. 179, 213 (1973) (concurring opinion), stated that the "right of privacy" included "the freedom to care for one's health and person." . . .

Finally, to the knowledge of this Court, since Roe v. Wade, supra, thirteen different courts in ten different jurisdictions have, in the absence of controlling decisions, directly addressed the question of

II. Patients' Rights to Treatment

whether the right to privacy encompasses the decision to obtain or reject medical treatment. Wensel v. Washington [slip op., reprinted at 385 A.2d 1148, 1154 (D.C. 1978)]; Matter of Quinlan, 355 A.2d 647, 662-663 (N.J. 1976); Price v. Sheppard, 307 Minn. 250, 239 N.W.2d 905, 910-912 (1976); Superintendent of Belchertown State School v. Saikewicz, 373 Mass. 728, 370 N.E.2d 417, 424 (1977); Rutherford v. United States, 438 F.Supp. 1287, 1298-1301 (W.D. Okl.), *reversed on other grounds*, 442 U.S. 544 (1979), *reversed*, 616 F.2d 455 (10th Cir. 1980);[34] People v. Privitera, 23 Cal.3d 697, 153 Cal. Rptr. 431, 439, 591 P.2d 919, 927 (1979) (Bird, C.J., dissenting); Satz v. Perlmutter, 362 So. 2d 160, 162-163 (Fla. Dist. Ct. App. 1978); Rennie v. Klein, 462 F. Supp. 1131, 1144-1145 (D.N.J. 1978); Rogers v. Okin, 478 F. Supp. 1342, 1365-1366 (D. Mass. 1979); In re Eichner, 73 A.D.2d 431, 456-460, 423 N.Y.S.2d 517, 537-540 (1980).

Of these, all but two, see Wensel v. Washington and People v. Privitera[36] responded in the affirmative. Thus, this Court is merely joining the clear trend of modern authority in acknowledging that the decision to obtain or reject medical treatment, consisting in the instant case of the decision to obtain acupuncture, is protected by the right of privacy. . . .

There can be little doubt that the articles and rules challenged in the present case "impos[e] a burden on" and "significantly interfere[] with," the decision to obtain acupuncture treatment. [Cit. omitted] Plaintiff John Walter testified that he was unable to find a single licensed physician in the state of Texas who was skilled in the practice of acupuncture. . . .

---

34. Rutherford v. United States, supra, a class action by terminal cancer victims seeking to obtain laetrile treatment, is still being litigated. In the most recent opinion issued, the Tenth Circuit ruled against the plaintiffs, stating that, "the decision by the patient whether to have a treatment or not is a protected right, but his selection of a particular treatment, or at least a medication, is within the area of governmental interest in protecting public health." Rutherford v. United States, 616 F.2d at 457 (10th Cir. Feb. 19, 1980), *rehearing denied* (April 28, 1980). This distinction is a difficult one to support, particularly where, as with laetrile, to deny the particular treatment involved may be to deny the decision to have treatment. The court gave no explanation for it. . . .

36. People v. Privitera, supra, like Rutherford v. United States, supra, involved a challenge to laws limiting access to laetrile. Unlike the court in the latter case, however, the majority in Privitera refused to acknowledge that the right of privacy encompasses the decision to obtain or reject medical treatment. In so doing, it relied heavily on the recognition in Roe v. Wade, supra, 410 U.S. at 153-154, 93 S. Ct. at 726-727, that the right of privacy is not absolute. Privitera, supra, 153 Cal. Rptr. at 434, 591 P.2d 922. That recognition, however, says nothing about whether the right of privacy encompasses a particular decision. Although not absolute, the right of privacy includes the decision "whether or not to terminate . . . pregnancy." Roe v. Wade, supra, 410 U.S. at 153, 93 S. Ct. at 727. It similarly includes the decision whether or not to obtain medical treatment. . . .

The Offered Justifications

The fact that the articles and rules in question effectively deprive the plaintiffs of their right to decide to obtain acupuncture treatment does not necessarily, as has been discussed, render them constitutionally infirm. The right of privacy is not absolute. Roe v. Wade, supra, 410 U.S. at 154. It may be overcome if the articles and rules being challenged are both motivated by a "compelling state interest" and "narrowly drawn to express only" that interest. Id. at 155. In the present case, the plaintiffs concede that the former requirement is met. Roe v. Wade establishes that the State's "interest in preserving and protecting the health of the (patient)" may be a "compelling" one. The question here is whether the State's regulations meet the latter requirement. To do so, they must be "necessary," Shapiro v. Thompson, 394 U.S. 618, 634 (1969), to the protection of the patient's health. . . .

The defendants argue that the limitation of the practice of acupuncture to licensed physicians serves the State's interest in preserving the patient's health in [two] ways. The first is that it protects against misdiagnoses. Neither patients nor nonphysicians in general, the defendants contend, are as skilled as physicians in diagnosing injuries and illnesses. Thus, the argument goes, it is entirely possible that an individual suffering from cancer would obtain acupuncture treatment for the related pain and that the cancer would continue to spread, undetected by both the patient and the acupuncturist, until it was too late. . . . That limitation is not, however, "necessary," to prevent such occurrences. The State merely need require that patients consult physicians prior to obtaining acupuncture treatment. At least one state does precisely that. California law provides that acupuncture "not be performed on a person without prior diagnosis or referral from a licensed physician." . . .

The [second] way in which the challenged articles and rules theoretically protect the patient's health is by assuring that any complications which may arise during acupuncture treatment will be remedied as quickly as possible. However safe acupuncture is, the defendants say, it is always possible that something will go wrong. . . . There are clearly "less drastic means" [ ] the State could take to avoid the danger involved here. It could require acupuncturists to pass courses in emergency medical treatment. It could require acupuncturists to make arrangements to have emergency medical treatment readily available. Or, if it truly considered the presence of a physician essential, it could enact regulations requiring acupuncturists to assure that their patients have ready access to a physician. . . .

Conclusion

The plaintiffs have a constitutional right, encompassed by the right of privacy, to decide to obtain acupuncture treatment. The challenged articles and rules effectively deprive them of that right and are not necessary to serve the State's interest in protecting the patient's health. That being so, they cannot stand.

NOTES

The Privacy Interest in Health Care

1. The *Andrews* court's treatment of the case law is somewhat misleading because virtually all of the favorable precedents it cites concern the right to *refuse* medical treatment, a topic discussed in Chapter 9. While litigation over the right to *receive* medical treatment has been less common, the clear predominance of the case law is *against Andrews*, as best illustrated by the series of cases described below that refuse to upset a ban on the use of laetrile as a cancer therapy. Is there any meaningful distinction, though, between the right to refuse and the right to receive treatment? See p.318 supra; Suenram v. Society of Valley Hosp., 383 A.2d 143, 148 (N.J. Super. 1977) (drawing on informed consent cases and *Quinlan* to find a constitutional right to use laetrile). If not, which body of case law should fall? Or should the constitutional right to control treatment be restricted to especially sensitive forms of health care? See Aden v. Younger, 129 Cal. Rptr. 535, 546 (Cal. App. 1976) (concerning restrictions on the use of electroshock therapy and psychosurgery, "we need not decide whether the decision to undergo medical treatment is deserving of constitutional protection in and of itself because the right to privacy so clearly includes privacy of the mind").

2. The leading decision upholding the constitutionality of a ban on laetrile is People v. Privitera, 153 Cal. Rptr. 431 (1979), discussed in footnote 36 of the main case, which found that the constitutional privacy interest is restricted to matters involving family and childbirth. Bowers v. Hardwick lends support to this distinction by observing that there is "no connection between family, marriage, or procreation on the one hand and homosexual activity on the other." 478 U.S. 186 (1986).

The leading federal decisions on laetrile are contained in the series of decisions in Rutherford v. U.S., discussed in footnote 34, which upheld the FDA's ban. The Supreme Court's decision mysteriously reached this result on statutory grounds without mentioning the constitutional issue, even though it was clearly a part of the rulings below, 442 U.S. 544 (1979), but on remand the 10th circuit directly disposed of the constitutional objection based on the distinction noted in footnote 34 above. Do you agree with the *Andrews* court's criticism of this distinction?

In general, there has not yet been a satisfactory resolution of these issues, although courts have continued to reject a constitutional privacy interest in health care in a variety of circumstances. See Whalen v. Roe, 429 U.S. 589 (1977) (enforcing restrictions on prescription practices for dangerous drugs); Lemmon v. State Bd. of Med. Examiners, 417 A.2d 568, 573 (N.J. Super. 1980) (upholding ban of heroin use for terminal cancer patients); Pharmaceutical Socty. v. Lefkowitz, 586 F.2d 953 (2d Cir. 1978) (enforcing generic drug substitution requirement); Hartz v. Bensinger, 461 F. Supp. 431 (E.D. Pa. 1978) (rejecting argument that "unrestricted [therapeutic] use of marijuana is every person's constitutional birthright"). See generally, Brant & Graceffa, Rutherford, Privitera and Chad Green: Laetrile's Setbacks in the Courts, 6 Am. J.L. & Med. 151 (1980); Patterson, Health Care Choice and the Constitution: Reconciling Privacy and the Public Health, 42 Rutgers L. Rev. 1 (1989) (a particularly thorough and thoughtful analysis of the topic); Note, Laetrile: Statutory and Constitutional Limitations on the Regulation of Ineffective Drugs, 127 U. Pa. L. Rev. 233 (1978); Cooper, Therapeutic Use of Marijuana and Heroin: The Legal Framework, 35 Food, Drug & Cosmetics L.J. 68 (1980); Merriken & Overcast, Governmental Regulation of Heart Transplantation and the Right to Privacy, 11 J. Contemp. L. 481 (1985); Blumstein, Rationing Medical Resources: A Constitutional, Legal, and Policy Analysis, 59 Tex. L. Rev. 1345 (1981); Blumstein, Constitutional Perspectives on Governmental Decisions Affecting Human Life and Health, 40 L. & Contemp. Prob., Autumn 1976, at 231.

3. Do you agree with the following sentiment expressed by the dissent in People v. Privitera?

> To require the doctor to use only orthodox "state sanctioned" methods of treatment under threat of criminal penalty for variance is to invite a repetition in California of the Soviet experience with "Lysenkoism."[5]
> The mention of a requirement that licensed doctors must prescribe [and] treat within "state sanctioned alternatives" raises the spector of medical stagnation at best, statism, paternalistic Big Brother at worst. It is by the alternatives to orthodoxy that medical progress has been

---

5. Soviet geneticist T. D. Lysenko, controversial dictator of "communistic" biology during the Stalin period, stultified the science of genetics in the U.S.S.R. for at least a generation. He imposed the "state sanctioned alternative," the curious idea that environmentally acquired characteristics of an organism could be transmitted to the offspring through inheritance. Thus, the Stalinist concept of ideological conformity politically implanted in genetics paralyzed this important branch of Soviet science.

made. A free, progressive society has an enormous stake in recognizing and protecting this right.

E. The Ethics and Public Policy of Health Care Access

Reinhardt, Chapter 1 in Uncompensated Hospital Care: Rights and Responsibilities*
(T. Sloan, J. Blumstein, & J. Perrin eds. 1986)

While honest economists long ago despaired of developing an overarching theory of distributive justice, political philosophers continue to hammer away at the problem. The several distinct theories of distributive justice emerging from these efforts are elegant in their internal logic, and eminently stimulating even to a skeptic. In the end, however, that literature fails as a guide towards a universally acceptable principle of justice. On the contrary, it persuades one that there cannot possibly be such a principle. For however tight the internal logic of any particular philosopher's theory of justice may be, that logic is ultimately anchored on some overarching value for which that author claims primacy on purely subjective grounds. Collectively, the political philosophers writing on the subject teach us that justice, like beauty, rests in the eye of the beholder.

Libertarian philosophers, for example, elevate individual liberty to the status of the single, overriding social value to which all other values are subordinate, and which can never justly be traded off against any subordinate value. Implicit in the libertarian's concept of "liberty" is the tenet that the individual is entitled to dispose of his or her possessions as he or she sees fit. Extreme versions of the theory — articulated, for example, in Robert Nozick's Anarchy, State, and Utopia (1974) — hold that any governmental infringement on this presumed property right is ipso facto unjust. Thus, to tax one person's wealth in order to finance another person's health care is unjust, as is a policy that compels physicians or privately owned facilities to render health care to designated individuals. In the libertarian's credo, it is the health care provider's right to determine whom to serve and whom not to serve, and also what price to exact for health services rendered. Health care providers must find this a comforting credo.

Diametrically opposed to the libertarian credo are the various theories of distributive justice espoused by egalitarian philosophers. Egalitarian philosophers elevate "equal respect for all individuals" or "equality of opportunity" to the overriding value of a just society to

---

* Reprinted with permission of Johns Hopkins University Press.

which all other values — among them individual liberty — are deemed subordinate. Equality of opportunity, argue these philosophers, requires as a minimum that all members of society have equal access to certain basic commodities, access to which determines an individual's range of opportunities and measure of self-respect. Health care, along with food, shelter, and education, is among these basic commodities.

The entitlements implicit in the egalitarian tenet seem rather open-ended, and as recent history in this country has shown, they certainly are. Egalitarians, however, do not glibly ignore resource constraints. They merely argue that, in the face of such constraints, need, rather than ability to pay, should be the basis for rationing. Clearly this theory of justice implies redistribution of the sort libertarians consider coercive and hence unjust.

One's own predilections aside, it is certainly no more logically compelling to let equal opportunity triumph completely over individual liberty than it is to do the reverse. Indeed, outside the ivory tower any prevailing sense of justice is apt to be an amalgam in which each of the pure theories is somewhat compromised. While purist philosophers may deplore such compromises, policymakers must not only countenance them but actively lead in forging the amalgam.

A remarkable and unique feature of American health policy has been its attempt to accommodate simultaneously both the egalitarian and the libertarian theories of justice in their extreme purity. No other nation in the industrialized West has been quite so bold, or quite so naive, as to attempt that feat. Ironically, no other nation finds itself, in the mid-1980s, with the unsolved problem of uncompensated indigent care at the center stage of its health policy debate. There appears to be a causal link between schizoid thinking on the ethical plane and impotence at the level of policy.

Throughout the postwar period, and possibly even earlier, our policies on the distribution of health care have been firmly rooted in the egalitarian credo: it has been a widely shared notion that health care in the United States should be distributed on the basis of medical need rather than ability to pay. Furthermore, with appeal to the overarching principle of "equal respect for all individuals," it has generally been held (at least in public debate) that the nation should aim for equality in the *process* of health care — that there should be equality in the so-called amenities accompanying the delivery of health care, including the travel and wait time during access and the degree of free choice among providers. Politicians of all ideological stripes have supported these tenets (at least none has openly questioned them), and health care providers have endorsed them as well.

Cynics may argue that no one seriously entertained these lofty maxims and that they were recited by politicians mainly for public consumption. Some glaring remaining inequalities in access to health care may be cited to buttress that case. But a fair reading of health legislation during the 1960s and 1970s should persuade even a skeptic that public policy in those years was motivated by a genuine desire to move the country closer to an egalitarian distribution of health care. By the end of the 1970s, few policy analysts and even fewer public officials still questioned the proposition that access to all medically necessary and technically feasible health care on equal (process) terms is one of an American citizen's basic rights.

The pursuit of an egalitarian health care system is, of course, not a uniquely American phenomenon. Most other industrialized nations have shared that goal, and some of them seem to have been rather more successful than have we in approaching it. A uniquely American phenomenon, however, has been the endeavor to extract an *egalitarian* distribution of health care from a delivery system still firmly grounded in *libertarian* principles.

To be sure, our health care delivery system does not measure up in all respects to a libertarian's dream. Some individual liberties are being compromised by government for the sake of quality control, and even the staunchest defenders of the libertarian credo, America's physicians, have from time to time enlisted the government's coercive power to protect their economic turf through occupational licensing. We share such infringements with other modern societies. But in no other modern society espousing egalitarian principles for the distribution of health care have physicians and hospitals been quite so free as they have in the United States to organize their facilities as they see fit, to practice medicine as they see fit, and to price their services as they see fit. In these realms, libertarian principles have prevailed, and every legislative attempt to compromise them for the sake of cost control or greater equity in distribution has, until very recently, been beaten back successfully, with overt appeals to the libertarian credo. "If you want an egalitarian distribution of health care," providers have said, "we endorse it heartily, and we shall do our best to bring it about — but for a fee, and we want that fee to be reasonable as we define that term."

Libertarian and egalitarian purists wrestle with one another in any democratic society. The politician's task, as noted earlier, is to fashion from this struggle a sustainable social compromise. It is on that count that American health policy has performed poorly relative to other democracies. For, in seeking to cater to both extremes among notions of distributive justice, American policymakers have bestowed upon the nation a maze of public health programs that make a Rube Goldberg contraption appear streamlined by comparison.

There has been extraordinarily generous public health insurance coverage for some services and for some individuals — replete with completely free choice of providers by patients and with virtually open-ended reimbursement formulas for providers. One would be hard put, for example, to identify another Western democracy in which the government reimbursed as passively as has ours the synthetic depreciation expenses created by the mere swapping of hospital ownership. Yet, attempts to curb that flow of public funds into private treasuries have always been decried and, until very recently, rejected as an intolerable, regulatory infringement on private liberties.

Congressional respect for this peculiar conception of "liberty" naturally carried the danger of turning any federal health program into a fiscal hemorrhage. Too timid to prevent that outcome through controls on providers, our politicians have pursued the next logical policy to contain public health budgets: they simply have left glaring gaps in health insurance coverage, particularly for the near poor and the unemployed (whose health insurance coverage typically ceases with employment). As the Medical Tribune reported in 1982 under the headline "Food Budget Paying Doctor":

> One of the hardest things about the current recession is facing patients who have lost jobs and can't pay their medical bills. "I experience a feeling of guilt [reports a family physician]; I've got groceries and my home. Some of our patients no longer have money for either." . . . A survey by this newspaper at the American Association of Family Practitioners annual meeting suggests that this experience reflects those of many — and perhaps most — primary physicians today in this country as they confront the impact of a nationwide 10 percent unemployment rate, peaking at 15 percent and 20 percent in some localities. (November 10, 1982, pp. 1, 15)

One may protest the injection of anecdotal evidence into august policy analysis and quibble over the aggregate statistical significance of such stories. But the fact remains, once again, that one would be hard put to identify any other industrialized society today that would still visit upon an unemployed worker's family, already down on its luck in so many material and emotional ways, the added anxiety and potential real hardship of going without health insurance coverage. It happens only in America.

It has become fashionable to attribute our long-standing failures in this area to a streak of meanness in the American character. Having lived both outside and inside this nation, I do not accept that interpretation. The special genius of nations who have long settled these problems lies not in their citizens' superior character, but lies, as noted, in a political process capable of forging a more stable ethical foundation for their health care systems. In all of these nations, the providers of health care enjoy fewer liberties than do their American counterparts. But in addition, a good many of these countries — for example, the United Kingdom, West Germany, France, Switzerland,

and Holland — have been rather more tolerant of some degree of tiering in their health systems than have the champions of egalitarianism in the United States.

Perhaps the time has come for Americans, too, to debate more openly — and without the customary rancor and slander — just what are the essential ingredients of a just health care system. . .

Conclusion

In its best aspects, the American health care system is arguably the best in the world. In its worst aspects, it is arguably among the worst, certainly in the industrialized world. One manifestation of the worst is the perennial problem of uncompensated indigent care, a hot potato no one seems willing to hold any longer. That problem is uniquely American.

It has been the central thesis of this essay that the problem of uncompensated indigent care springs not so much from meanness in the American spirit as from our ill-fated attempts during the past several decades to guarantee too many entitlements to too many actors in health care. In this connection, one thinks instinctively of the entitlements granted individuals in their role as patients. There may have been, indeed, a few too many of those. But one should also think of the extraordinary entitlements American policymakers have traditionally granted the providers of health care, entitlements that have, on occasion, bordered on handing providers the key to the public treasury.

As policy analysts and policymakers address themselves to the problem of uncompensated indigent care, they would do well to fold into their deliberations a review of the nation's presumed health care entitlements *all around.*

McCarthy, Financing Indigent Care: Short- and Long-term Strategies*
259 J.A.M.A. 75 (1988)

Historically, most indigent care has been financed in three ways: cost shifts to insured patients, public insurance programs such as Medicaid, and state and local appropriations to public hospitals and other providers. In the past decade, however, cost-containment efforts in the public and private sectors, coupled with increased competition in the health care industry, have disrupted traditional ways for fi-

---

* Copyright 1988, American Medical Association. Reprinted by permission.
Carol M. McCarthy, Ph.D., J.D., is President of the American Hospital Association.

nancing indigent care at the very time such care is most needed. Changes in Medicare reimbursement methods and commercial insurance practices have made it extremely difficult for hospitals to subsidize indigent care through cost shifts to other payers. At the same time, the ranks of the uninsured have swelled. Medicaid coverage of the poor has plummeted from 65 percent to 38 percent, and to below 25 percent in many states. Within the employed population, in 1985 there were 17 million uninsured workers — 3.1 million more than in 1982. Nearly three fourths of the uninsured employed had annual incomes of less than $10,000.

In the wake of these changes, hospitals have provided increasing amounts of unsponsored care — that is, uncompensated care less state and local government tax appropriations. Although the proportion of unsponsored care compared with total costs is greatest for public general hospitals, unsponsored care has increased throughout the hospital industry, with volunteer hospitals providing the largest amount. Public hospitals and other providers serving large numbers of the uninsured are experiencing severe financial strain.

Clearly, there is a compelling need to shore up these historical financing mechanisms and to build some new ones. There is no single, or simple, solution, however. The medically indigent are a diverse and growing group, uninsured for many different reasons. The American Hospital Association's (AHA) Special Committee on Care for the Indigent (on which I served prior to assuming the presidency of the AHA) found that an enduring solution will require many bold private and public sector initiatives to expand the number of people who can be covered through adequate private health insurance and to extend public programs to finance care for the rest.

Private Sector Approaches

More than half of the uninsured live in families of full-time, steadily employed workers and another third are in families employed at least part-time or intermittently. Much of the insurance gap, therefore, can and should be closed through expansions in private insurance. Insurers, employers, and providers should develop alternative sources of affordable insurance, particularly for small employers, and should work together to develop financing and delivery systems that reduce per capita costs.

To make this happen, however, we will need strong positive and negative incentives from the government. . . . States could encourage formation of multiple-employer insurance arrangements, risk pools, pools for persons who cannot afford to pay insurance premiums, and other approaches to spread the risk and lower the cost of private insurance.

II. Patients' Rights to Treatment

Such incentives could help bolster private insurance coverage of the medically indigent. However, they may not be enough. For this reason, the AHA supports federally mandated insurance for employees. Such a mandate would have to be carefully designed to minimize regulatory intrusion and economic dislocations and would need to provide for widely available, affordable insurance; gradual, phased-in mandates; and significant tax relief and other subsidies. If provision of health insurance is to be a condition of doing business, government must make it possible for this condition to be met.

Public Sector Approaches

Although private sector initiatives will be an essential component of any comprehensive solution to the indigent care crisis, the private sector cannot compensate for the erosion in public programs. The deterioration of Medicaid is a major cause of the indigent care crisis and therefore Medicaid reform must be part of the solution.

Over the years, Medicaid has largely evolved from a primary insurance program for the poor to a supplemental insurance program for individuals already receiving coverage under Medicare. By 1983, the elderly, the blind, and the disabled accounted for three fourths of all Medicaid expenditures. Medicaid reform ultimately will require a reorganization of the program, a strengthened federal role in financing it, and implementation of new delivery and payment mechanisms. . . .

The American health care system is undergoing a period of tremendous change. Increased competition and public and private cost-containment efforts are producing many desirable results, but they also have placed an increasing number of the uninsured in serious jeopardy. We cannot permit this to happen. Public and private sector solutions can and must be found.

Cohodes, Taking a Wrong Turn: Mandated Employment-Based Health Insurance*
24 Inquiry 5-6 (1987)

No one can say that creativity is dead in America. The legislative process provides a continuous view of creativity at its best and its worst. An example of creativity run amok is a proposal emerging in Congress to mandate employers to provide their employees with health insurance coverage. In the words of one observer, these types of proposals constitute a "cowardly, backdoor approach to national health insurance."

* Reprinted with permission of the Blue Cross/Blue Shield Association.

Even bad ideas can emerge from good intentions. Congress's involvement in mandating incremental extensions of health insurance coverage to various subgroups of the population has dramatically increased in the last three years. Linked with a diagnosis of the problem of the uninsured that tells that between two-thirds and three-fourths of the uninsured have some relationship to the place of employment, the idea of tying health insurance to the place of employment has a natural surface appeal. Closer examination indicates that the consequences of enactment of such a proposal would yield a very different outcome than intended.

Although it is true that most of the uninsured have some tie to the place of employment, it is not at all clear that the solution to the problem of the uninsured lies with mandating employer-based health insurance. The experience to date with mandates has much to say about the success of future mandates. Mandates are costly. Mandating health insurance coverage carries with it a double-edged problem.

First is the direct cost increase of purchasing health insurance for employees. Labor costs go up and the ability to compete declines. Smaller firms would be particularly hard hit. The secondary impact on the labor market would be analogous to an increase in the minimum wage. Unemployment would likely rise, employers would substitute part-time for full-time employees, and the decision to hire marginal employees might not be made. It is unlikely that worker productivity would rise sufficiently to offset the unit cost increases that would result.

The problem of the uninsured is primarily a problem of low income. Inability to pay, not lack of health insurance product availability, is the problem. In a number of communities around the country, affordable health insurance products have been targeted to the small-employer market. The results have been fairly uniform. Some purchases are made, but mostly the market chooses not to buy — affordability is the issue. At any non-zero price, health insurance is too costly. Mandating health insurance coverage for employees of small employers may be tantamount to mandating employer bankruptcy.

NOTES

Expanding Coverage of the Uninsured

1. The foregoing materials are intended to contrast with the discussion of patients' *legal* rights by providing a glimpse of the divergent views on the *moral* and *policy* dimensions of access to health care. In further consideration of the moral argument, do you think

II. Patients' Rights to Treatment

every person has an ethical right to health care regardless of the ability to pay? Our society recognizes such a right for education, food, and housing; health care would seem just as essential. But see Sade, Medical Care as a Right: A Refutation, 285 New Eng. J. Med. 1288 (1973); Szasz, The Right to Health, 57 Geo. L.J. 734 (1969).

Precisely how far a right to health care extends depends on one's "theory of justice." Possibilities include (from greater to lesser): (a) a right to equal health; (b) a right to equal medical treatment; (c) a right to a decent minimum level of medical treatment; or (d) a right to be free from discrimination in the purchase of health care. Most of us would agree in principle to (c) and then debate what constitutes a "decent minimum," but our society currently fails to provide even this. The United States is the only industrialized country other than South Africa without some form of universal health care coverage for the poor. See generally President's Commission, Securing Access to Health Care (1983); N. Daniels, Just Health Care (1985); Bayer, Ethics, Politics, and Access to Health Care: A Critical Analysis of the President's Commission, 6 Cardozo L. Rev. 303 (1984); Arras, Retreat from the Right to Health Care: The President's Commission and Access to Health Care, 6 Cardozo L. Rev. 321 (1984).

2. Recognizing a moral right to health care, the inquiry then shifts to the difficult policy question of how we should go about securing that right. Currently, the treatment source of last resort for the millions of uninsured is the municipal hospital emergency room, but this system is clearly inadequate and cost-escalating because it provides no care until hospitalization is required. A compelling example is the extreme costs and human tragedy that result from underweight premature infants born to mothers who receive no prenatal care during their pregnancies. In most cases, providing this inexpensive care through public clinics would save the tens of thousands of dollars required for neonatal intensive hospital care. Among the other defects of the municipal hospital system are that it often bypasses rural areas, and individual localities bear the costs disproportionately depending on local economic and demographic variables. Blendon et al., Uncompensated Care by Hospitals or Public Insurance for the Poor, 314 New Eng. J. Med. 1160 (1986).

3. The ready solution to the inadequacies of the status quo appears to be expansion of government programs designed for the poor, primarily Medicaid. Apart from the political obstacles, however, consider whether Medicaid eligibility can be structured easily to cover the situation of the minimum wage worker, the seasonal worker, or the recently unemployed worker, many of whom do not fit our traditional definition of indigency yet cannot afford health insurance: "The uninsured are very heterogeneous. They are largely poor or near poor, but a majority are employed or are dependents of workers.

Many are only temporarily uninsured. . . . Those without coverage do not form a stable grouping in the way that larger workplace groups do, but rather constitute a shifting, residual category. . . ." Bovbjerg, Insuring the Uninsured through Private Action: Ideas and Initiatives, 23 Inquiry 403 (1986).

4. Recognize that McCarthy, author of the second article, represents the views of the AHA, an institution with a distinct stake in the question of who should fund indigent care. Are private hospitals, which provide approximately 5 percent of their care on an uncompensated basis, doing all that they can? See Chapter 7.V for further debate.

5. This is an area of active legislative ferment. A number of states are implementing risk pools for the uninsured — which provide an opportunity, but no funding, to purchase insurance — or are providing direct subsidies to hospitals. The latter programs are funded in states with hospital rate regulation by authorizing a rate add-on to cover the expense of caring for uninsured members of the community. Other states are beginning to look toward a hospital use tax to fund indigent care. Massachusetts recently passed the most ambitious legislation to date by enacting a program that seeks to provide universal coverage to everyone in the state by 1992. This enactment imposes a heavy tax on employers with more than five workers that do not offer insurance as a fringe benefit, and it provides insurance to the unemployed at discounted, sliding scale rates adjusted for income level. Sager, Prices of Equitable Access: The New Massachusetts Health Insurance Law, 18 Hastings Cent. Rep. 21 (June/July 1988). See generally Dowell, State Health Insurance Programs for the Uninsured Poor, 23 Clearinghouse Rev. 141 (1989).

On the federal level, employers with group health insurance are required to enable their discharged workers to continue to purchase the insurance at group rates. 29 U.S.C. §10001; Somers, COBRA: An Incremental Approach to National Health Insurance, 5 J. Contemp. Health L. & Pol. 141 (1989); Gregory, COBRA: Congress Provides Partial Protection Against Employer Termination of Retiree Health Insurance, 24 San Diego L. Rev. 77 (1987). The much further-reaching federal proposal sponsored by Senator Edward Kennedy, which is referenced in the Cohodes commentary, is still pending before Congress as of this writing. It would require all employers to provide a minimum package of health care benefits to employees (and their families) who work 17.5 hours a week. Minimum Health Benefits for All Workers Act, §1265, 100th Cong., 1st Sess. (1987). Do these measures adequately cover all of the trouble spots?

6. An alternative to patching the holes in the current crazy quilt of private and public insurance programs is to institute a national health insurance, which would cover everyone by displacing all the

existing sources of coverage, or at least by drawing them all together in a comprehensive, interlocking system that left no one out. Most other western industrialized nations have some system of national health insurance, but initiatives in this country have consistently been rejected, largely due to medical profession and hospital industry opposition to "socialized medicine." See generally, P. Starr, The Social Transformation of American Medicine (1982). Nevertheless, the topic periodically resurfaces in public and political debate. Most recently, see Enthoven & Kronick, A Consumer-Choice Health Plan for the 1990s: Universal Health Insurance in a System Designed to Promote Quality and Economy, 320 New Eng. J. Med. 29, 94 (1989); Himmelstein et al., A National Health Program for the United States: A Physicians' Proposal, 320 New Eng. J. Med. 102 (1989); Relman, Universal Health Insurance: Its Time Has Come, 320 New Eng. J. Med. 117 (1989). However, we are unlikely to witness any radical change in the foreseeable future: "inertia surrounding universal health insurance is the product of a long tradition of equivocation . . . [that] is likely to prevail because of the power of special-interest groups in American life, the failure to agree on a workable solution, the weakness of resolve of our political leaders, and the lack of widespread discontent in the general population." Levey & Hill, National Health Insurance — The Triumph of Equivocation, 321 New Eng. J. Med. 1750, 1751 (1989).

7. Most of the debate to date has focused on insurance coverage for acute care, the most pressing need. However, a looming crisis is the availability of insurance for long-term care of chronic illness, care such as that rendered in nursing homes. Two developments are accelerating the rate at which long-term care is increasing its portion of the nation's health care budget. First, as the baby boom generation begins to age, a much greater portion of the population will enter old age where the need for long-term care is most prevalent. Second, as medical science conquers specific infections and learns techniques for overcoming life-threatening traumas, more people are living to suffer from more slowly degenerating illnesses such as heart disease, arthritis, and Alzheimer's disease.

Private insurance coverage for the expenses of nursing homes and home health care traditionally has been limited to the short-lived after effects of acute sickness. Medicare and Medicaid, the public programs for the elderly and the poor, likewise have grossly inadequate coverage for on-going nursing care. The appropriate structure and the sources of financing for long-term care insurance will be one of the most pressing public health policy issues through at least the turn of the century. See generally S. Sullivan & M. Lewin, The Economics and Ethics of Long-Term Care and Disability (1989); K. Davis & D. Rowland, Medicare Policy: New Directions for Health and Long-

Term Care (1986); Somers, Insurance for Long-Term Care, 317 New Eng. J. Med. 23 (1987); Kapp, Financing Long-Term Care for the Elderly: Am I Your Parents' Keeper?, 13 L. Med. & Health Care 188 (1985).

8. The book in which Reinhardt's piece appears is the product of a highly-regarded conference on approaches to resolving the problem of the uninsured. For additional reading, see Thorpe et al., Including the Poor: The Fiscal Impacts of Medicaid Expansion, 261 J.A.M.A. 1003 (1989) (expanding Medicaid to cover everyone below the federal poverty line would cost between $9 billion and $35 billion); Wilensky, Filling the Gaps in Health Insurance, 7 Health Affairs 133 (Summer 1988); Comment, Medical Indigence and Economic Scarcity: Are Egalitarian Access to Care and Cost Control Mutually Inconsistent Goals?, 33 Loy. L. Rev. 113 (1987); Bovbjerg & Kopit, Coverage and Care for the Medically Indigent: Public and Private Options, 19 Ind. L. Rev. 857 (1986); Wilensky, Viable Strategies for Dealing with the Uninsured, 6 Health Affairs at 36 (Spring 1987), and other articles in the same issue; Iglehart, Medical Care of the Poor — A Growing Problem, 313 New Eng. J. Med. 59 (1985); Perkins, The Effects of Health Care Cost Containment on the Poor: An Overview, 19 Clearinghouse Rev. 831, 847-848 (1985).

For a thorough account of health services coverage on Indian reservations, see Comment, Health Care for Indigent American Indians, 20 Ariz. St. L.J. 1105 (1989).

F. Patients' Rights

Minnesota Law on Rights of Patients and Residents of Health Care Facilities
Minn. Stat.

§144.651

It is the intent of the legislature and the purpose of this section to promote the interests and well being of the patients and residents of health care facilities. No health care facility may require a patient or resident to waive these rights as a condition of admission to the facility. Any guardian or conservator of a patient or resident or, in the absence of a guardian or conservator, an interested person, may seek enforcement of these rights on behalf of a patient or resident. It is the intent of this section that every patient's civil and religious liberties including the right to independent personal decisions and knowledge of available choices, shall not be infringed and that the facility shall encourage and assist in the fullest possible exercise of these rights.

II. Patients' Rights to Treatment

For the purposes of this section, "patient" means a person who is admitted to an acute care inpatient facility for a continuous period longer than 24 hours, for the purpose of diagnosis or treatment bearing on the physical or mental health of that person. "Resident" means a person who is admitted to a non-acute care facility including extended care facilities, nursing homes, and board and care homes for care required because of prolonged mental or physical illness or disability, recovery from injury or disease, or advancing age. It is declared to be the public policy of this state that the interests of each patient and resident be protected by a declaration of a patient's bill of rights which shall include but not be limited to the following:

(1) Every patient and resident shall have the right to considerate and respectful care;

(2) Every patient and resident can reasonably expect to obtain from his physician or the resident physician of the facility complete and current information concerning his diagnosis, treatment and prognosis in terms and language the patient can reasonably be expected to understand. In cases in which it is not medically advisable to give the information to the patient or resident the information may be made available to the appropriate person in his behalf;

(3) Every patient and resident shall have the right to know by name and specialty, if any, the physician responsible for coordination of his care;

(4) Every patient and resident shall have the right to every consideration of his privacy and individuality as it relates to his social, religious, and psychological well being;

(5) Every patient and resident shall have the right to respectfulness and privacy as it relates to his medical care program. Case discussion, consultation, examination, and treatment are confidential and should be conducted discreetly;

(6) Every patient and resident shall have the right to expect the facility to make a reasonable response to his requests;

(7) Every patient and resident shall have the right to obtain information as to any relationship of the facility to other health care and related institutions insofar as his care is concerned;

(8) Every patient and resident shall have the right to expect reasonable continuity of care which shall include but not be limited to what appointment times and physicians are available;

(9) Every resident shall be fully informed, prior to or at the time of admission and during his stay, of services available in the facility, and of related charges including any charges for services not covered under medicare or medicaid or not covered by the facility's basic per diem rate;

(10) Every patient and resident shall be afforded the oppor-

tunity to participate in the planning of his medical treatment and to refuse to participate in experimental research;

(11) No resident shall be arbitrarily transferred or discharged but may be transferred or discharged only for medical reasons, for his or other residents' welfare, or for nonpayment for stay unless prohibited by the welfare programs paying for the care of the resident, as documented in the medical record. Reasonable advance notice of any transfer or discharge must be given to a resident;

(12) Every resident may manage his personal financial affairs, or shall be given at least a quarterly accounting of financial transactions on his behalf if he delegates this responsibility in accordance with the laws of Minnesota to the facility for any period of time;

(13) Every resident shall be encouraged and assisted, throughout his period of stay in a facility, to understand and exercise his rights as a patient and as a citizen, and to this end, he may voice grievances and recommend changes in policies and services to facility staff and outside representatives of his choice, free from restraint, interference, coercion, discrimination or reprisal;

(14) Every resident shall be free from mental and physical abuse, and free from chemical and physical restraints, except in emergencies, or as authorized in writing by his physician for a specified and limited period of time, and when necessary to protect the resident from injury to himself or to others;

(15) Every patient and resident shall be assured confidential treatment of his personal and medical records, and may approve or refuse their release to any individual outside the facility, except as otherwise provided by law or a third party payment contract;

(16) No resident shall be required to perform services for the facility that are not included for therapeutic purposes in his plan of care;

(17) Every resident may associate and communicate privately with persons of his choice, and send and receive his personal mail unopened, unless medically contraindicated and documented by his physician in the medical record;

(18) Every resident may meet with representatives and participate in activities of commercial, religious, and community groups at his discretion; provided, however, that the activities shall not infringe upon the right to privacy of other residents;

(19) Every resident may retain and use his personal clothing and possessions as space permits, unless to do so would infringe upon rights of other patients or residents, and unless medically contraindicated and documented by his physician in the medical record;

(20) Every resident, if married, shall be assured privacy for visits by his or her spouse and if both spouses are residents of the

facility, they shall be permitted to share a room, unless medically contraindicated and documented by their physicians in the medical record; and

(21) Every patient or resident shall be fully informed, prior to or at the time of admission and during his stay at a facility, of the rights and responsibilities set forth in this section and of all rules governing patient conduct and responsibilities.

NOTES

Patients' Bills of Rights

1. The 1975 Minnesota law was the first enacted patients' bill of rights in the United States. It is based on the American Hospital Association's Bill of Rights (1972), which gave great impetus to the patients' rights movement of the 1970s. See p.553 supra. The AHA adoption arose largely from earlier efforts in the neighborhood health centers affiliated with larger general hospitals, especially in urban black and Hispanic communities.

A number of other states have adopted bills of rights for hospital patients, some by statute, others by administrative regulations of the licensing agencies. Rather than enact a general bill of rights, some states require that each facility provide its own policy statement, following certain guidelines as to coverage. Colorado requires each hospital of over 50 beds to operate its patients' grievance mechanism around a program of patient representatives. The Massachusetts law on patients' rights is unusual because it creates duties for both the hospital and the attending physician. The JCAH Accreditation Manual for Hospitals contains a bill of rights that creates duties for both the hospital and the patient.

To what extent is the Minnesota bill of rights simply a restatement of common law? To what extent does it contain bold new declarations? Are its statements legally enforceable or purely hortatory?

2. What created the need for these numerous specific protections, and why do you suppose they contain so much stress on treating patients with dignity and as individuals? See Annas, The Hospital: A Human Rights Wasteland, 4 Civil Liberties Rev. 9 (1974). For further discussion of these issues, see G. Annas, The Rights of Patients (1989); Rozovsky, The Canadian Patient's Book of Rights (1980).

3. Over half of the general hospitals of over 200 beds have patient representatives or advocates on their staffs to handle patient complaints and to encourage more considerate, personalized care for all patients. For a thorough review of the philosophy and operations of patient representative programs, see Hogan, Humanizing Health Care: The Task of Patient Representatives (1980).

Nursing Homes and The Rights of the Elderly

4. A major patients' rights development occurred at the end of 1987 with Congress's enactment of a comprehensive set of federal protections for nursing home patients. P.L. No. 100-203, 101 Stat. 1330-39 (1987), to be codified at 42 U.S.C. §1395x. The law requires nursing homes that participate in Medicare or Medicaid to: comply with detailed staffing and training requirements, guarantee patient privacy, give notice of roommate changes or discharge from the home, establish a grievance process, allow patients to select their own attending physician and to participate in planning their treatment, and refrain from unnecessary use of physical or chemical restraints.

5. Because elderly patients are particularly susceptible to abuse and because increasing portions of our health care facilities are devoted to their care, the legal rights of the elderly is emerging as a separate topic of special importance. Other aspects of this topic are explored below in the materials on Medicare in Chapter 8.II.A and on Death and Dying in Chapter 9.II. See also M. Kapp, Legal Aspects of Health Care for the Elderly: An Annotated Bibliography (1988); M. Kapp, H. Pies & A. E. Doudera, Legal and Ethical Aspects of Health Care for the Elderly (1985); Kapp, Health Care Delivery and the Elderly, 17 Cumb. L. Rev. 437 (1987).

CHAPTER 7

Organization and Operation of Health Care Enterprise

I. THE CONTEMPORARY SCENE

A generation ago, practically the only legal representation hospitals and doctors required, aside from malpractice defense, was occasional tax advice. It was common for even large hospitals to rely solely on sporadic pro bono counsel, often from lawyer members of their governing boards. These idyllic days passed quickly with the onset of Medicare/Medicaid. Health care law is now a flourishing practice area that requires sophistication in subjects as diverse as antitrust, administrative law, and securities regulation.

This transformation in the legal climate has resulted from the strong winds of economic and organizational change buffeting the health care delivery system. What was once a tranquil service industry dominated by religious orders is now a dynamic sector of the economy driven by a new-found entrepreneurial fervor. "Merger," "diversification," "joint venturing," and "strategic planning" are the buzz words that fill today's health care trade press. Doctors are investing in surgery clinics and urgent care centers that perform traditional hospital functions. Hospitals are expanding into long-term, out-patient, and psychiatric/substance abuse care — services historically the province of others. Blue Cross/Blue Shield, hospital chains, and large employers are experimenting with novel forms of insurance and health care delivery such as health maintenance organizations ("HMOs") and preferred provider organizations ("PPOs"). All manner of health care firms are reorganizing their corporate structures, diversifying into nonmedical service lines, and entering into unconventional business arrangements.

The result of this cauldron of activity, aside from a never-ending stream of new acronyms, is a tremendous surge in legal work. Each of these innovative ventures must be examined against the backdrop of both traditional legal doctrine and new forms of health care regulation. This chapter is intended to provide a sampling of the sorts of issues modern health care attorneys must contend with at the cutting edge of their practice field. We cannot hope to convey the universe of law relevant to the multitude of organizational and operational activities of health care business, so we will set aside the areas of doctrine that have more general applicability — such as corporations, securities, and contract law — and focus instead on several doctrinal areas of unique importance to health care.

II. THE CORPORATE PRACTICE OF MEDICINE AND THE BUSINESS OF INSURANCE

Bartron v. Coddington County
2 N.W.2d 337 (S.D. 1942)

SMITH, J.

The central question of law to be determined is whether certain exhibited bargains between Codington County and the Bartron Clinic, a corporation for profit, pursuant to which such corporation furnished medical and surgical services, and medicines to the county indigent, are illegal and unenforceable.

The "Bartron Clinic" was incorporated in February of 1929, "to conduct and operate a general medical and surgical hospital and clinic and employ duly licensed physicians, surgeons, nurses, students, and other persons to carry on the business of said corporation." Its 750 shares of capital stock were originally issued and held by duly licensed physicians and surgeons, and by nurses and other employees of the corporation. During the period of time at issue in these causes, only 28 of its shares were held by Joyce H. Williams, a lay person. The remaining shares were held by Dr. Bartron and Dr. Brown until 1936, and thereafter by Dr. Bartron. Joyce H. Williams was secretary of the corporation and served on its board of directors. . . .

Except for some minor services of an intern, all of the professional services involved herein were performed by duly licensed physicians and surgeons employed at fixed salaries by the corporation, and all charges therefor accrued to and were made by the corporation. The corporation owned all equipment used by the doctors and maintained the supply of drugs furnished patients. The corporation did not hold a license to practice medicine and surgery, nor to operate a pharmacy.

On January 3, 1933, the county and the corporation executed and delivered two contracts in writing wherein the corporation agreed to furnish hospitalization, medical and surgical services and medicine to the county for its poor persons. . . .

The court [below] found that there was not in connection with the organization of the Bartron Clinic, or at any time thereafter, any purpose or intent whatsoever on the part of Dr. Bartron or anybody else connected with said corporation to place the actual control of the practice of medicine with any person other than duly licensed physicians; that there was not at any time throughout the existence

II. The Corporate Practice of Medicine

of said corporation any control, or effort to exercise control, as to the actual practice of medicine on the part of anybody other than a licensed physician and no interference, or attempted interference, by anybody other than a licensed physician, with the actual practice of medicine; that the actual purpose and intent of Dr. Bartron in promoting the organization of said corporation was to establish what amounted to a system of profit sharing, whereby the prominent and leading employees of said hospital and clinic business would have some actual interest in the success thereof.

[This case] originated as a claim before the county commissioners in aggregate amount of $3,649.63 for medicine supplied the county indigent between January 1, 1938 and September 1, 1938. . . . The court found that the professional services were actually rendered by duly licensed physicians, except for a small item for intern's services, and that the medicines were prescribed by such physicians in treatment of the county poor, and that all of this was done pursuant to directions and orders of the county commissioners.

The court concluded as a matter of law . . . that it is unlawful and contrary to public policy for a corporation to practice medicine or surgery and to operate a pharmacy or sell medicine without a license as required by the statutes of South Dakota. These conclusions are challenged here by appropriate assignments of error. . . .

When conduct opposed to the public interest is made the subject of a bargain the courts ordinarily refuse to accord a party thereto a remedy predicated thereon. . . . While decision has rarely turned on the naked issue of public policy, the expressions of the courts indicate a current of opinion, to which there are but few dissentients, that such practice contravenes the public interest and is contrary to public policy.

The leading case is that of In re Cooperative Law Co., 198 N.Y. 479, 92 N.E. 15, 16, 32 L.R.A., N.S. 55, 139 Am. St. Rep. 839, 19 Ann. Cas. 879. The Court said:

> The practice of law is not a business open to all, but a personal right, limited to a few persons of good moral character, with special qualifications ascertained and certified after a long course of study, both general and professional, and a thorough examination by a state board appointed for the purpose. . . . The relation of attorney and client is that of master and servant in a limited and dignified sense, and it involves the highest trust and confidence. It cannot be delegated without consent, and it cannot exist between an attorney employed by a corporation to practice law for it, and a client of the corporation, for he would be subject to the directions of the corporation, and not to the directions of the client. There would be neither contract nor privity between him and the client, and he would not owe even the duty of counsel to the actual litigant. The corporation would control the liti-

gation, the money earned would belong to the corporation, and the attorney would be responsible to the corporation only. His master would not be the client but the corporation, conducted it may be wholly by laymen, organized simply to make money and not to aid in the administration of justice which is the highest function of an attorney and counsellor at law. The corporation might not have a lawyer among its stockholders, directors, or officers. Its members might be without character, learning or standing. There would be . . . no stimulus to good conduct from the traditions of an ancient and honorable profession, and no guide except the sordid purpose to earn money for stockholders. The bar, which is an institution of the highest usefulness and standing, would be degraded if even its humblest member became subject to the orders of a money-making corporation engaged not in conducting litigation for itself, but in the business of conducting litigation for others. *The degradation of the bar is an injury to the state.* . . .

Debasement of the learned professions is in fact inimical to the public welfare. The public is the ultimate beneficiary of its professional social organisms, and of the private, as well as of the unselfish public, exercise of the skills and talents of its professional practitioners. Although the members of the legal profession in their individual capacities as officers of the courts of justice sustain a relationship to the public without parallel in the medical professions, in all other respects the services of the two professions are of equal importance to the public, and debasement of the one, in our opinion, would constitute no less a public evil than would the degradation of the other.

These professions, as they exist in our social structure, rest upon a foundation of sturdy, sterling human character which, in turn, has been and is being shaped and moulded by the impact of traditional ideals and points of view. The licensing statutes with their emphasis on character and professional conduct evidence a fixed public desire and will not only to foster, but to develop and reinforce, these basic attributes of its professional servants. . . .

We are therefore persuaded that that which tends to debase the learned professions is at war with the public interest and is therefore contrary to public policy.

Does practice of the learned professions by a profit corporation functioning through duly licensed practitioners tend to debase the professions?

We pause to emphasize the word "tend" because the learned trial court has found that the Bartron Clinic was innocent of any unethical intention or practice, and that its licensed officers and employees controlled its professional activities. Our present concern is with the tendency of the challenged conduct. Though the exhibited instance of that conduct has accomplished no evil, if its inherent

II. The Corporate Practice of Medicine

tendency be at war with public interest, it is contrary to public policy. Moore v. Hyde, supra.

Because of the rights with which the law invests a stockholder in a corporation for profit, recognition of such a means of conducting a professional business involves yielding the right of participation in control of its policies and in its earnings to lay persons. A share in the fees of professional men would come to the owners of capital stock as a matter of right in the form of dividends. The stockholder's right to vote his stock would provide him with an instrumentality to be used for shaping policy. Ownership of stock would ordinarily qualify him to serve as a director or officer of the company. Lay ownership of stock would be ultimately assured by the incidental rights of transfer and succession. The object of such a company would be to produce an earning on its fixed capital. Its trade commodity would be the professional services of its employees. Constant pressure would be exerted by the investor to promote such a volume of sales of that commodity as would produce an ever increasing return on his investment. To promote such sales it is to be presumed that the layman would apply the methods and practices in which he had been schooled in the market place. The end result seems inevitable to us, viz., undue emphasis on mere money making, and commercial exploitation of professional services. To universalize the use of this method of organizing the professions, or to permit such a use to become general, would ultimately wipe out or blight those characteristics which distinguish the business practices of the professions from those of the market place. Such an ethical, trustworthy and unselfish professionalism as the community needs and wants cannot survive in a purely commercial atmosphere....

That such is the tendency of the profit corporation when used to conduct a professional practice is not a matter of mere fancy or conjecture. It is a matter of common knowledge that this form of organization has been tried in the field of dentistry and resulted in such unethical and commercial practices as induced the Legislature of this and many other states to pass statutes expressly prohibiting its use.

Being convinced that the practice of the learned professions by a profit corporation tends to the commercialization and debasement of those professions, we are of the opinion that such a mode of conducting the practice is in contravention of the public interest and is against public policy. It follows that we are of the view that insofar as the bargains of the Bartron Clinic and Codington County dealt with medical and surgical services, they were illegal. [As a result, the court refused to order the county to pay for medical services it had received, but the court did allow the clinic to keep funds previously paid.]

People v. Pacific Health Corporation
82 P.2d 429 (Cal. 1938)

PER CURIAM. This is an appeal from a judgment in quo warranto against defendant holding its activities violative of the California Medical Practice Act. . . .

The facts are stipulated. Defendant Pacific Health Corporation, Inc., is a corporation organized under the general corporation law of the state of California, with its principal place of business in San Francisco. Upon application of persons in good health, the defendant issues a contract by the terms of which defendant undertakes to pay for services rendered by physicians, hospitals, ambulance and medical laboratories under certain circumstances, and the applicant pays the required sum or premium therefor. When a contract holder becomes sick or is injured, defendant advises him from whom these services are to be obtained, that is, the physician, hospital or ambulance available to him. After the services are rendered, defendant pays the charges. Defendant keeps a list of physicians and surgeons approved by it, and to obtain the benefits of the service the contract holders must, save as to emergency expenses not exceeding $50, accept a doctor from the list.

Defendant is a stock corporation, operated for profit. It advertises its service and solicits the public for purchase of its contracts, paying commissions to its soliciting agents. The money collected from contract holders is paid into the general fund, and this, together with the capital and surplus, is invested. The charges for medical services are paid out of the general fund and income from investments.

Upon these facts the lower court concluded that defendant was illegally engaged in the practice of medicine, in excess of its corporate rights, powers and franchises. It was ordered that defendant be excluded from such practice, and that its articles of incorporation be amended to conform to the decree. We are in accord with the court's conclusion.

The issue presented herein is not new, and has been considered in this state by recent cases which are controlling. It is an established doctrine that a corporation may not engage in the practice of such professions as law, medicine or dentistry. Painless Parker v. Board of Dental Examiners, 216 Cal. 285, 14 P.2d 67. . . . This doctrine is not challenged by defendant, which seeks to distinguish its activities from those previously held to constitute illegal practice of medicine. It is stated that defendant does not itself undertake to perform medical service, but merely to furnish competent physicians. . . . Defendant's theory is that the doctors are independent contractors, and that this fact absolves it of the charge of practicing medicine.

We are unable to agree that the policy of the law may be

circumvented by technical distinctions in the manner in which the doctors are engaged, designated or compensated by the corporation. The evils of divided loyalty and impaired confidence would seem to be equally present whether the doctor received benefits from the corporation in the form of salary or fees. And freedom of choice is destroyed, and the elements of solicitation of medical business and lay control of the profession are present whenever the corporation seeks such business from the general public and turns it over to a special group of doctors. . . .

To avoid this result, defendant launches into a discussion of the effect of an adverse decision upon other [health care] organizations and activities. [W]e are told that a decision against defendant will outlaw all fraternal, religious, hospital, labor and similar benevolent organizations furnishing medical services to members, . . . [organizations] which have been tacitly approved for generations. But a most obvious and, to us, a fundamental distinction must be made between defendant and these other institutions. . . . In almost every case the institution is organized as a nonprofit corporation or association. Such activities are not comparable to those of private corporations operated for profit and, since the principal evils attendant upon corporate practice of medicine spring from the conflict between the professional standards and obligations of the doctors and the profit motive of the corporation employer, it may well be concluded that the objections of policy do not apply to nonprofit institutions. This view almost seems implicit in the decisions of the courts and it certainly has been the assumption of the public authorities, which have, as far as we are advised, never molested these organizations.

The other question raised by defendant's proffered materials is whether the time has come, as indicated by the movement for health insurance and group medicine, to reverse the long settled policy against corporate medical practice and declare it legal and proper. A simple answer would be that the few extracts from the opinions of writers which we find in the briefs furnish us with no evidence whatsoever of a widespread change in social viewpoint sufficient to repudiate the existing law of practically all the states. All that we have before us is the proof of a controversy, which has raged for years, between medical men, sociologists and others, as to the future course of medical practice. The desirability of present methods and the suggested reforms, including various kinds of insurance and group treatment, are hotly debated. (See 25 Cal. L. Rev. 91, 93.) Public policy may change, and doubtlessly where statutes do not cover the field, the court may follow such changes, but the court must, in such case, declare the public policy, the social view of people generally, and not merely its own private choice among hopelessly conflicting views of desirable reform of settled practices or principles in this field. In the present circumstances there can be no true declaration by this court that a change in social viewpoint now requires the abandonment of the rule against corporate practice of medicine. Such a drastic change should come from the legislature, after the full investigation and debate which legislative organization and methods permit. Though certainly aware of the controversy, and with presumed knowledge of our decisions preventing corporate practice (see supra), the legislature thus far has not acted, and until it does we deem it proper to follow the existing law. . . .

The judgment is affirmed.

EDMONDS, Justice (dissenting).

This case presents only two questions for decision: (1) Does the plan followed by the appellant in providing health service for its contract holders violate the provisions of the Medical Practice Act, and (2) If not, is its plan violative of public policy? I find nothing in the act which expressly or by implication prohibits a corporation from hiring a physician regularly licensed to practice in this state to care for its employees or members, and I see no reason for holding that the plan contravenes public policy.

The decision to the contrary relies upon . . . Painless Parker v. Board of Dental Examiners, 216 Cal. 285, 14 P.2d 67. . . . The Painless Parker Case involved the unlawful practice of dentistry by a corporation in violation of the Dental Practice Act, a statute substantially different from the Medical Practice Act in that it expressly prohibited the practices there involved. There can be no doubt, and appellant concedes, that within certain constitutional limitations the legislature may declare that the employment of physicians by lay persons or corporations constitutes the practice of medicine. The Dental Practice Act did so declare. The Medical Practice Act contains no such provision. . . .

Respondent and amici curiae appearing on its behalf urge that the plan of the appellant violates public policy. But if the policy were as contended by respondent it would be clearly stated in the pertinent statutes. This the legislature has not seen fit to do. In recent years the subjects of health insurance and group medicine have been the frequent source of discussion and investigation, and both lay and professional opinion concerning them is sharply divided. The need for some such service, particularly in the lower income brackets, is conceded by all parties to the controversy. The courts, in the absence of legislation, should not on the ground of public policy place a stumbling block in the way of working out this problem. It is not a proper function of the courts to thus block the natural growth of social and economic processes. . . .

The judgment should be reversed.

We concur: WASTE, C.J.; HOUSER, J.

II. The Corporate Practice of Medicine

Note, Right of Corporation To Practice Medicine*
48 Yale L.J. 346 (1938)

Efforts to obtain adequate medical care at reasonable cost have stimulated extensive experimentation with methods of medical organization. The result has been widespread development of such diversified types as private group clinics, employee health associations, county physician bureaus, health insurance plans, and medical co-operatives. Many of the sponsors of these systems have attempted to take advantage of the corporate form in order to achieve limited liability and continuity of existence. Groups of physicians have incorporated to operate their own clinics; laymen have formed corporations, hiring physicians to treat patients for profit; and aggregations of prospective patients have organized nonprofit co-operative corporations. Yet the legal existence of these corporate types has been jeopardized at one time or another by attempted application of the principle that corporations may not practice the learned professions. . . .

While numerous state statutes directly forbid the corporate practice of law, express prohibition of the corporate practice of medicine is rare. Instead, denial of the right of some corporations to practice medicine has been based upon those statutes in every state which outlaw performance of the healing art by unlicensed persons. The obvious inability of a corporate entity to meet the educational and character requirements prerequisite to a license is said to inhibit a corporation from practicing medicine. To bolster this interpretation of the statutes, courts have commonly resorted to arguments of public policy. Since the judiciary do not possess an intrinsic power to regulate the medical profession as they do the legal, the validity of this viewpoint is necessarily dependent upon the soundness of the courts' inference that state licensing statutes automatically forbid utilization of the corporate power.

Courts which profess to deny all corporations the right to have any connection with medical activities have apparently misconstrued the purpose of the state licensing statutes. These statutes are designed to preserve the public health by excluding from practice persons with inadequate ability, morality, and training. Since the diagnosis and treatment of disease are obviously purely personal functions, a corporation can perform them only through the medium of doctors. But the mere fact that a corporation employs physicians, or is operated by physicians, provides no valid basis for requiring the corporation itself to be licensed. As long as the doctors are properly licensed and their professional activities are not interfered with by unlicensed persons, the purpose of the statutes is fully effected, for no one

---

* Reprinted by permission of the Yale Law Journal.

without proper qualifications is then directly or indirectly administering to the public. This is true even though laymen may be entrusted with considerable control over administrative details. Only when lay officers or directors exercise substantial supervision over the professional activities of the physicians employed is there ground for arguing that the corporation is enabling unlicensed persons to practice medicine. Thus the real issue is not whether corporations generally are unlicensed to practice medicine, but whether in each individual case physicians are *actually* controlled in their purely professional functions by unlicensed persons in such a manner as to nullify the purpose of the licensing statutes. . . .

Even in states following the [*Pacific Health*] decision, numerous corporations engage unchallenged in activities which have all the indicia of corporate practice of medicine as defined by the same courts. It is common knowledge that private hospitals, sanitariums, fraternal organizations, educational institutions, and industrial concerns all administer medical services to their constituents through staffs of physicians hired and paid on a full or part time basis. Similarly, salaried physicians undertake part time contract practice on behalf of various companies, particularly railroads, to treat passengers and employees. The explanation for such discrimination may be that the social utility of these types of corporate medical service has long been tacitly recognized; nevertheless, the fact remains that some corporate forms have been permitted in the face of the same state licensing statutes which are so rigorously invoked against others.

Since the legal construction of state licensing statutes is by no means inexorable, their varying application to certain corporate forms is probably attributable to the judges' evaluation of social policy arguments against corporate medical practice. Impairment of the intimate doctor-patient relationship and commercialization of the medical profession are the two general social policy objections most commonly cited by the courts. The first evil will result, it is feared, from possible restrictions upon the patient's freedom of choice of physician and from a division of the physician's loyalty between patient and corporate employer. If the old-fashioned family doctor is used as the norm, this objection might assume serious proportions. But when the challenged corporate forms are compared with the many types of corporate medical service already accepted, any distinguishing basis must be fanciful indeed. Furthermore, consistency would require that the same charge be levelled against non-corporate forms such as county, municipal, and private partnership clinics. And even if the choice of doctors should be unusually restricted within a particular corporate scheme, many patients might prefer that scheme to other types of private group medical services or to receiving inadequate or no medical treatment whatsoever. As a matter of fact, however, this broad objection is made in disregard of the actual functionings of many of the various plans, for the patient is commonly encouraged to select one of the doctors on the organization's panel and thereafter consult him as a family physician. Moreover, insulation of the doctor from administrative and economic cares and elimination of the patient's concern over cost may actually enhance the relationship between patient and physician.

More plausible is the second social objection to the corporate furnishing of medical service. It is feared that the profession may be commercially exploited by laymen who, not being amenable to ethical standards, are free to engage in high pressure solicitation of patients and sharp competitive advertising. But the fact that this fear may at times be well-grounded should not justify resort to the drastic measure of barring corporate medical service entirely. A more sensible solution is for the state to combine its recognized regulatory powers over corporations and professions in order to curb objectionable professional activity. And even without special regulation, the state can undoubtedly hold contract physicians to the same standard of ethics as private practitioners. Moreover, the opposition of the American Medical Association to this type of corporate medical practice assures a zealous and vigilant supervision by a body dutybound to report to the state injurious professional activity.

. . . Some courts persist in trying to solve such cases by repeating generalizations which are meaningless in the abstract. A more realistic judicial approach would disregard the corporate form as such and inquire instead whether the actual setup is so provocative of abuses that the only solution is to deny the corporation existence altogether. However, the public interest in furthering experiments in medical care may suffer much by trusting to haphazard decisions by tribunals ill-fitted to investigate intricate specific cases. The surer method of achieving the benefits of corporate medical organization without possible attendant evils would be by enactment of legislation specifically authorizing the corporate form but carefully regulating its activities so as to insure the highest response to professional ethics by the corporation as an entity and by its physicians.

NOTES

Corporate Practice in the Modern Context

1. A frequently quoted argument for the corporate practice prohibition appears in Dr. Allison, Dentist, Inc. v. Allison, 196 N.E. 799, 800 (1935): "The qualifications [to practice a profession] include personal characteristics such as honesty, guided by an upright conscience and a sense of loyalty to clients or patients. . . . These

requirements are spoken of generically as that good moral character which is a prerequisite to the licensing of any professional man. No corporation can qualify. It can have neither honesty nor conscience."

Does this line of reasoning differ in form or substance from the following argument?

- The actions of drivers hired by a corporation are attributed to the corporation.
- An eyesight examination is required for a driver's license.
- Corporations cannot take an eye exam.
- Therefore, a corporation that hires drivers is guilty of driving without a license.

2. As the *Pacific Health* dissent observes, the corporate practice doctrine is founded on two distinct bases: the medical practice act and common law public policy. As the *Pacific Health* majority illustrates, however, courts rarely draw this distinction. *Bartron* is one court that did. In another portion of the opinion, the court, influenced by the Yale Note, rejected the literal terms of the Medical Practice Act as a basis for a corporate practice challenge. In doing so, it stands almost alone. See also N.M. Atty. Gen. Opin. No. 87-39 (July 30, 1987).

3. Addressing corporate practice from a common law public policy perspective, how far should the courts go in striking down private contractual arrangements? Many of the original and leading cases address situations of apparent quackery in the peripheral medical professions (dentistry, optometry, etc.). *Pacific Health*, for example, cites to one of a whole series of "Painless Parker" cases in various states involving a dentist who changed his first name from Edgar Randolph, for obvious commercial reasons. See Laufer, Ethical and Legal Restrictions on Contract and Corporate Practice of Medicine, 6 Law & Contemp. Probs. 521, 526 (1939). *Bartron*, however, applies a rigidly prophylactic rule despite the completely upright behavior of the individual doctors. Are there any countervailing harms to banning corporate practice, or should the courts lean as far as possible in the direction of a pristine practice setting? In 1979, the Federal Trade Commission permanently enjoined the AMA from enforcing *ethical* prohibitions against corporate practice. The FTC reasoned that there were illegal anticompetitive effects stemming from the profession's control of the economic and organizational aspects of medical practice. American Medical Assoc., 94 F.T.C. 980, 1015 (1979), *aff'd by equally divided court*, 455 U.S. 676 (1982).

4. How great a concern is the threat of divided loyalty, that is, the responsibility an employed physician owes to the employer as well as to the patient? Is the loyalty any greater than that owed by one physician *partner* to another? Than that owed by a physician to other

patients? Is it not possible to serve two masters so long as they do not impose inconsistent duties?

5. And what of the commercialization concern, that is, the fear that introduction of a profit motive will debase the profession? Clearly a profit motive exists in medical practice regardless of the organizational form of practice. Doctors are the highest paid profession in the country.* What additional concerns are introduced by *incorporating* a profitable practice? Consider whether there isn't a form of hypocrisy or self-interest in keeping only outsiders from sharing in medicine's rich rewards. See Veatch, Ethical Dilemmas of For-Profit Enterprise in Health Care, in Institute of Medicine, The New Health Care for Profit 125, 130-134 (1983); Note, The Corporate Practice of Medicine Doctrine: An Anachronism in the Modern Health Care Industry, 40 Vand. L. Rev. 445 (1987).

6. As *Pacific Health* indicates, many accepted forms of corporate practice are accommodated because of their nonprofit, charitable nature. For other accommodation techniques, see People v. John H. Woodbury Dermatological Institute, 84 N.E. 697, 699 (N.Y. 1908) (implicit authorization for corporate practice contained in hospital licensure statutes); Rush v. City of St. Petersburg, 205 So. 2d 11, 15 (Fla. App. 1967) (no corporate practice by employed intern due to absence of direct physician/patient relationship); and Willcox, Hospitals and the Corporate Practice of Medicine, 45 Cornell L. Q. 432, 486 (1960) (despite *Pacific Health*, some courts distinguish independent contractors).

7. The arrangement that *Pacific Health* struck down appears structurally similar to what is now known as a Health Maintenance Organization ("HMO") (specifically, the individual practice association ("IPA") form of HMO). The corporate practice prohibition is recognized as one of the major stumbling blocks in HMO development. Developments, The Role of Prepaid Group Practice in Relieving the Medical Care Crisis, 84 Harv. L. Rev. 887, 960-961 (1971). It is therefore puzzling that the federal HMO Act initially did not include this body of state law in its pre-emption provision when enacted in 1973. Comment, The Corporate Practice of Medicine Doctrine: An Anachronism in the Modern Health Care Industry, 40 Vand. L. Rev. 445, 481 (1987). Although individual state HMO acts frequently provide

---

* "Lore holds that physicians are frequently more noble, altruistic and charitable than the patients they treat. If ever that belief was true, it no longer is. At the last annual meeting of the American Heart Association in Dallas, Robert Swank, an economist from the Johns Hopkins Medical School, released a study showing that when a physician's income drops, his blood pressure zooms and stays elevated for five years. Swank . . . found that for each 1 percent drop in income, the number of doctors with elevated blood pressure rose 2.5 percent the next year. In short, physicians are as vulnerable economically and reactive physically as the rest of us." Parade, Feb. 15, 1987, at 4.

protection from this doctrine (see, for instance, Ga. Code Ann. §33-21-28(c) (Michie)), nevertheless corporate practice prohibitions have remained a significant inhibiting factor because of the spotty coverage of the state acts. Welch, HMO Enrollment: A Study of Market Forces and Regulations, 8 J. Health Pol., Poly. & Law 743, 755 (1984). However, 1988 amendments to the federal act significantly broadened its preemptive provision to strike all state laws that "impose requirements that would inhibit" HMOs. 42 U.S.C. §300e-10(a)(1)(E).

8. Practice formats such as that invalidated in *Bartron* involving exclusive physician ownership of a group practice are now permitted by professional corporation ("PC") laws widely adopted during the 1960s. Dunn, Professional Corporations: Their Development and Present Status with Respect to the Practice of Medicine, 24 U. Fla. L. Rev. 625 (1972); Note, Professional Corporations: Analysis Under Tax Reform Act and Survey of State Statutes, 58 Geo. L.J. 487 (1970); Malone, Professional Corporations — A Current Appraisal, 23 Ark. L. Rev. 215 (1969). A PC essentially allows physicians and other licensed professionals (lawyers included) to enjoy the tax benefits of corporate organization while practicing in substance as a partnership. (Note, though, that 1982 and 1986 tax reform legislation has substantially restricted PC pension and retirement benefits, the major tax advantage.) See Philipps, McNider & Riley, Origins of Tax Law: The History of the Personal Service Corporation, 40 Wash. & Lee L. Rev. 433 (1983). Do these laws change the public policy recognized in *Bartron*? See Sloan v. Metropolitan Health Council, 516 N.E.2d 1104, 1107 (Ind. App. 1987) (dictum) ("We believe that the Professional Corporation Act . . . totally abolished [the] public policy [prohibiting a corporation to practice medicine], if, indeed, it ever existed") (holding that an HMO may be held vicariously liable for the malpractice of its employed physicians).

9. The conflict between the corporate practice prohibition and the need for organizational experimentation, a dominant theme in both *Pacific Health* and the 1938 Yale Note, has an eerie resonance with present day circumstances. This theme is finding renewed currency as the corporate practice doctrine is coming under increasing attack in today's health care environment. Hall, Institutional Control of Physician Behavior, 137 U. Penn. L. Rev. 431, 516 (1988); Rosoff, The Business of Medicine: Problems with the Corporate Practice Doctrine, 17 Cumb. L. Rev. 485 (1987); Note, The Corporate Practice of Medicine Doctrine: An Anachronism in the Modern Health Care Industry, 40 Vand. L. Rev. 445 (1987); Comment, The Corporate Practice of Medicine Doctrine: An Outmoded Theory in Need of Modification, 8 J. Leg. Med. 465 (1987). Do you agree with *Pacific Health* that we must await legislative action?

10. Following the 1930s and 1940s, the corporate practice of

II. The Corporate Practice of Medicine

medicine doctrine entered a period of relative quiescence in the courts. It still continued to thrive, though, in state attorney general opinions during the 1950s. Activity at even that level has slackened noticeably over the past two decades, leading one to consider whether the doctrine hasn't been quietly defused. However, in Professor Rosoff's apt metaphor, corporate practice prohibitions survive as "legal landmines, remnants of an old and nearly forgotten war, half-buried on a field fast being built up with new forms of health care organizations. Occasionally, usually at the instigation of those who resist the change now taking place, one is detonated, with distressing results." 17 Cumb. L. Rev. at 499. Instances of recent application include Morelli v. Ehsan, 737 P.2d 1030 (Wash. App. 1987) (corporate practice doctrine bars enforcement of medical clinic partnership agreement by a lay partner/business manager); Garcia v. Texas State Board of Medical Examiners, 384 F. Supp. 434 (W.D. Tex. 1974) (no constitutional infirmity in preclusion of HMO form of operation). Consider also the following prediction of the doctrine's reemergence:

> The doctrine has a long history of suppressing needed innovation in times of industry upheaval. During the 1930s, when prepaid group practices (now known as HMOs) were being developed in response to severe gaps in insurance coverage, the corporate practice doctrine was a major obstacle that took decades to remove. During the 1950s, when hospitals felt an increasing need to employ hospital-based specialists in response to the technological transformation of medical care, numerous state attorney general opinions struck down their initiatives. During the 1980s and 1990s there will be tremendous pressure to search for more cost conscious organizational forms and relationships. These changes will raise combined threats of commercialization and professional subordination, concerns that will be a powerful stimulus to professional opposition. This opposition will surely invoke the corporate practice doctrine to preserve independence from the institution.

Hall, supra, 137 U. Penn. L. Rev. at 510.

Insurance Regulation and ERISA Preemption

1. Another inhibition to experimentation in health care delivery comes from insurance laws, which restrict organizational activity in a regulatory rather than a prohibitory fashion. Every state heavily regulates the business of insurance by prescribing the financial structure of the company, the terms of insurance policies, the manner of soliciting clients, and the prices charged. See generally Symposium: Insurance Regulation, 1969 Wisc. L. Rev. 1019; R. Jerry, Understanding Insurance Law (1987). For obvious reasons, innovative health care ventures are wary of getting tangled in this web of regulation. For example, until Congress enacted the protective Health Mainte-

nance Organization Act in 1973, state insurance laws were used in past generations to frustrate the development of prepaid group practice. See Developments, The Role of Prepaid Group Practice in Relieving the Medical Care Crisis, 84 Harv. L. Rev. 887, 918 (1971); Chapter 8.III.B. One court enjoined the operation of an abortion referral agency on the grounds that charging clients a single fee for all expenses constitutes the unauthorized business of insurance. State v. Abortion Information Agency, 330 N.Y.S.2d 927 (App. Div. 1971), *aff'd*, 334 N.Y.S.2d 174 (1972). In the future, as hospitals, doctors, and employers begin to devise novel health care delivery systems that blur the traditional distinctions between provider and payer, the question of precisely what activity constitutes the business of insurance under state law will assume renewed importance. For instance, when you come to the on Preferred Provider Organizations in Chapter 8.III.C, consider whether they constitute the business of insurance.

2. The definition of the business of insurance is even more significant under federal law, but in ways that cut in opposite directions. A health care venture might very much desire the insurance label because of a federal statute, known as the McCarran-Ferguson Act, 15 U.S.C. §1011 et seq., that immunizes insurance from prominent federal laws such as antitrust and securities regulation. Another federal law known as ERISA (the Employment Retirement Income Security Act of 1974), 29 U.S.C. §1001 et seq., which regulates pension plans and employee benefits, potentially goes even further by exempting *employee* insurance from all state law. However, that sweeping protection from regulatory authority is limited by a "savings clause" that reinstates regulatory authority over the business of insurance, 29 U.S.C. §1144(b)(2)(A). Conveniently, but perhaps curiously, the extent of both the protective McCarran-Ferguson immunity provision and the ERISA savings clause are governed by the same definition of what constitutes the business of insurance. As discussed in the leading decision:

> Cases interpreting the scope of the McCarran-Ferguson Act have identified three criteria relevant to determining whether a particular practice falls within that Act's reference to the "business of insurance": "first, whether the practice has the effect of transferring or spreading a policyholder's risk; second, whether the practice is an integral part of the policy relationship between the insurer and the insured; and third, whether the practice is limited to entities within the insurance industry."

Metropolitan Life Ins. Co. v. Massachusetts, 471 U.S. 724 (1985). This definition pinpoints only the most central core of insurance practice — risk spreading — and only when that practice relates directly to the insured. These two limitations exclude a broad array of important activities, thereby exposing them to ERISA preemption.

II. The Corporate Practice of Medicine

In Group Life & Health Ins. Co. v. Royal Drug Co., 440 U.S. 205 (1979), the Court held that an insurance company's setting the amount it is willing to pay a health care provider does not constitute the business of insurance because it fails to meet either prong of the test. Similarly, in Union Labor Life Ins. Co. v. Pireno, 458 U.S. 119 (1982), the Court excluded from the business of insurance the process of verifying insurance claims because it occurs only after risk has been transferred. In its most recent pronouncement, the Court held that a common law cause of action for bad faith and breach of contract in the denial of an insurance claim is pre-empted by ERISA, since the payment of reimbursement does not meet the rigid McCarran-Ferguson definition of the business of insurance. Pilot Life Ins. Co. v. Dedeaux, 481 U.S. 41 (1987). See generally Irish & Cohen, ERISA Preemption: Judicial Flexibility and Statutory Rigidity, 19 U. Mich. J.L. Ref. 109, 111 (1985) (collecting citations to other articles); Annot., 87 A.L.R. Fed. 797 (1988); Casenote, 36 U.Kan. L. Rev. 611 (1988).

3. From this juncture, the effect of ERISA preemption is limited only by the bounds of one's imagination. In one case, the court held that states may not require employers to provide all employees a minimum level of health insurance coverage. Standard Oil v. Agsalud, 633 F.2d 760 (9th Cir. 1980), *aff'd mem.*, 454 U.S. 801 (1981). In another, the court struck down a state requirement that health insurers offer employees the opportunity to purchase continued health insurance benefits for six months after employment ends. St. Paul Elec. Workers Welfare Fund v. Markman, 490 F. Supp. 931 (D. Minn. 1980). See also Taylor v. Blue Cross/Blue Shield, 684 F. Supp. 1352 (E.D. La. 1988) (ERISA preempts state law requiring payment within 30 days). One commentator has argued that ERISA preempts state laws that prohibit discrimination in the amount health insurance pays to different health care practitioners. Note, ERISA Preemption of State-Mandated Provider Laws, 1985 Duke L.J. 1194. Another article makes a case for preemption of tort actions against insurance companies that cause the premature discharge of hospital patients. Macaulay, Health Care Cost Containment and Medical Malpractice: On a Collision Course, 21 Suffolk L. Rev. 91 (1986). See generally Law & Ensminger, Negotiating Physicians' Fees: Individual Patients or Society?, 61 N.Y.U.L. Rev. 1, 80-81 (1986) ("in this judicially constructed Alice in Wonderland world, any state seeking to regulate insurers' arrangements with physicians or providers must be prepared to litigate claims of ERISA preemption").

4. Another important aspect of ERISA preemption is its effect of inducing employer self-insurance. In *Metropolitan Life*, supra, the Court explained that the insurance savings provision is limited by a proviso that prohibits states from deeming a benefit plan to be

insurance. 29 U.S.C. §1144(b)(2)(B). The effect of this "deemer clause" is that self-funded insurance plans are entirely exempt from state regulation. Children's Hosp. v. Whitcomb, 778 F.2d 239 (5th Cir. 1985); Moore v. Provident Life and Accident Ins. Co., 786 F.2d 922 (9th Cir. 1986). But see Northern Group Servs. v. Auto Owners Ins. Co., 833 F.2d 85 (6th Cir. 1987) (regulation of self-insurers preempted only where the federal interest in uniformity outweighs the state interest in regulation).

Consequently, the number of employees covered by self-insured health care plans has grown dramatically in recent years: "During the past 10 years, the percentage of large employers who self-insure for medical care has risen from 19 percent to 40 percent, and some estimates place the current percentage even higher. Large employers enjoy several advantages if they self-insure, and thus fall under ERISA preemption. For example, they are exempt from State-mandated benefit laws, State taxes on insurance premiums, and required participation in assigned-risk pools." Congressional Research Service, Health Insurance and the Uninsured 10 (June 1988). This preemption for self-insured employers also frustrates state efforts to target employers with solutions to the uninsured and underinsured problems addressed in Chapter 6.II.E. See Dawson v. Whaland, 529 F. Supp. 626 (D.N.H. 1982). See generally Dechene, Application of Coverage and Mandatory Benefits Requirements to ERISA Health Benefits Plans, 21 J. Health & Hosp. L. 321 (1988); Note, ERISA's Deemer Clause and the Question of Self-Insureds: What's a State to Do?, 67 Wash. U.L.Q. 291-303 (1989).

III. REFERRAL FEE PROHIBITIONS

United States v. Greber
760 F.2d 68 (3rd Cir.), cert. denied, 474 U.S. 988 (1985)

WEIS, Circuit Judge.

In this appeal, defendant argues that payments made to a physician for professional services in connection with tests performed by a laboratory cannot be the basis of Medicare fraud. We do not agree and hold that if one purpose of the payment was to induce future referrals, the Medicare statute has been violated. . . .

Defendant is an osteopathic physician who is board certified in cardiology. In addition to hospital staff and teaching positions, he was the president of Cardio-Med, Inc., an organization which he formed. The company provides physicians with diagnostic services, one of which uses a Holter-monitor. This device, worn for approximately 24 hours, records the patient's cardiac activity on a tape. A computer operated by a cardiac technician scans the tape, and the data is later correlated with an activity diary the patient maintains while wearing the monitor.

Cardio-Med billed Medicare for the monitor service and, when payment was received, forwarded a portion to the referring physician. The government charged that the referral fee was 40 percent of the Medicare payment, not to exceed $65 per patient.

Based on Cardio-Med's billing practices, counts 18-23 of the indictment charged defendant with having tendered remuneration or kickbacks to the referring physicians in violation of [the Medicare fraud statute]. . . . The proof as to the Medicare fraud counts was that defendant had paid a Dr. Avallone and other physicians "interpretation fees" for the doctors' initial consultation services, as well as for explaining the test results to the patients. There was evidence that physicians received "interpretation fees" even though defendant had actually evaluated the monitoring data. Moreover, the fixed percentage paid to the referring physician was more than Medicare allowed for such services.

The government also introduced testimony defendant had given in an earlier civil proceeding. In that case, he had testified that ". . . if the doctor didn't get his consulting fee, he wouldn't be using our service. So the doctor got a consulting fee." . . .

I. Medicare Fraud

The Medicare fraud statute was amended by P.L. 95-142, 91 Stat. 1183 (1977). Congress, concerned with the growing problem of fraud and abuse in the system, wished to strengthen the penalties to enhance the deterrent effect of the statute. To achieve this purpose, the crime was upgraded from a misdemeanor to a felony. . . .

A particular concern was the practice of giving "kickbacks" to encourage the referral of work. Testimony before the Congressional committee was that "physicians often determine which laboratories would do the test work for their medicaid patients by the amount of the kickbacks and rebates offered by the laboratory. . . . Kickbacks take a number of forms including cash, long-term credit arrangements, gifts, supplies and equipment, and the furnishing of business machines."

To remedy the deficiencies in the statute and achieve more certainty, the present version of 42 U.S.C. §[1320a-7b(b)] was enacted. It provides:

> whoever knowingly and willfully offers or pays any remuneration (including any kickback, bribe or rebate) directly or indirectly, overtly or covertly in cash or in kind to induce such person — . . . to purchase,

lease, order, or arrange for or recommend purchasing . . . or ordering any . . . service or item for which payment may be made . . . under this title, shall be guilty of a felony.

The district judge instructed the jury that the government was required to prove that Cardio-Med paid to Dr. Avallone some part of the amount received from Medicare; that defendant caused Cardio-Med to make the payment; and did so knowingly and willfully as well as with the intent to induce Dr. Avallone to use Cardio-Med's services for patients covered by Medicare. The judge further charged that even if the physician interpreting the test did so as a consultant to Cardio-Med, that fact was immaterial if a purpose of the fee was to induce the ordering of services from Cardio-Med.

Defendant contends that the charge was erroneous. He insists that absent a showing that the only purpose behind the fee was to improperly induce future services, compensating a physician for services actually rendered could not be a violation of the statute.

The government argues that Congress intended to combat financial incentives to physicians for ordering particular services patients did not require.

The language and purpose of the statute support the government's view. Even if the physician performs some service for the money received, the potential for unnecessary drain on the Medicare system remains. The statute is aimed at the inducement factor.

The text refers to "any remuneration." That includes not only sums for which no actual service was performed but also those amounts for which some professional time was expended. "Remunerates" is defined as "to pay an equivalent for service." Webster Third New International Dictionary (1966). By including such items as kickbacks and bribes, the statute expands "remuneration" to cover situations where no service is performed. That a particular payment was a remuneration (which implies that a service was rendered) rather than a kickback, does not foreclose the possibility that a violation nevertheless could exist. . . .

We conclude that the more expansive reading is consistent with the impetus for the 1977 amendments and therefore hold that the district court correctly instructed the jury. If the payments were intended to induce the physician to use Cardio-Med's services, the statute was violated, even if the payments were also intended to compensate for professional services.*

---

* Ed. Note: For commentary on *Greber*, see; Comment, The Medicare-Medicaid Anti-Fraud and Abuse Amendments: Their Impact on the Present Health Care System, 36 Emory L.J. 691 (1987); Comment, United States v. Greber and its Effect on the Medicare and Medicaid Programs, 75 Ky. L.J. (1987); Comment, United States v. Greber: A New Era in Medicare Fraud Enforcement?, 3 J. Contemp. Health L. &

Hall, Making Sense of Referral Fee Statutes†
13 J. Health Pol., Poly. & Law 623 (1988)

Someone uninitiated to the intricacies of health care financing would find it startling to learn that it is potentially a felony punishable by five years imprisonment for a rural hospital to recruit a badly needed specialist to the community, for a doctor to discount his services by waiving insurance deductibles and coinsurance, or for a health care institution to pay its doctors a bonus as a reward for efficient practice. A case can be made that each of these activities falls within the literal terms of the broadly worded Medicare and Medicaid referral fee statute. Enticing a physician to join the medical staff necessarily involves implicit or explicit incentives to refer the physician's patients to that hospital.[2] Price discounts can be characterized as payments to refer one's patients to one's self for treatment.[3] And efficiency bonuses can induce doctors to admit patients to a particular hospital or encourage them to direct patients to a particular insurance plan. . . .

Because these and other absurd applications of the referral fee concept are within a plausible reading of the federal referral fee statute, the statute has been a constant thorn in the side of the health care industry since the 1977 enactment of its current form. . . . However, some relief is now in sight. The federal government has finally agreed to clarify precisely what this statute does and does not prohibit by . . . "specifying payment practices that shall not be treated as a criminal offense under [the referral fee statute]." . . .

The action DHHS is most likely to take in response to the directive from Congress is to create discrete safe harbors by identifying a limited list of specific transactions that are exceptions to the referral fee prohibition. . . . [However,] a purely transactional approach provides little guidance for novel, unanticipated business arrangements because it tends to resort to arbitrary distinctions and compromises that are not predictable based on any *a priori* principles.

[A] preferred approach would be for DHHS to craft its referral fee regulations based on a definitional model — one that seeks to redefine the essence of prohibited referral fees in a more limited

---

Policy 309 (1987); and Roble & Mason, The Legal Aspects of Health Care Joint Ventures, 24 Duquesne L. Rev. 464-467 (1985).

† Reprinted with permission.

2. Comment, The Medicare-Medicaid Anti-Fraud and Abuse Amendments: Their Impact on the Present Health Care System, 36 Emory L.J. 691, 727-31 (1987) (hereinafter "Emory Comment").

3. Letter from Inspector General of DHHS to Assistant Attorney General, Criminal Division, U.S. Department of Justice (April 17, 1985), reprinted in, Medicare and Medicaid Guide (CCH) ¶35,105 (hereinafter "OIG/DOJ Correspondence").

manner before applying that definition to individual cases. . . . Past interpretations of referral fee statutes suggest two definitional approaches: interpreting these statutes according to their purposes and prohibiting only fees that are unearned.

Purposes of the referral fee prohibition. Health care attorneys have sometimes sought refuge in an analytical tool that the law customarily uses to shape the meaning of language: construing statutory text according to the purposes of the prohibition. Referral fee statutes are intended to prevent three abuses: ordering unnecessary services, increasing charges for needed services, and influencing with financial considerations the decision of where best to refer a patient. To illustrate with the most common target of referral fee prosecutions, a clinical laboratory kickback to doctors who order tests might induce doctors to order unnecessary tests, increase a lab's billings for tests that are necessary, or persuade doctors to send tests to an inferior lab. A common mode of legal analysis is to reason that a particular practice does not violate referral fee statutes if the practice does not conflict with any of the three mentioned purposes, even though the practice falls within the literal language of these sweeping prohibitions.[12]

For example, in correspondence with the Department of Justice concerning the federal referral fee statute, the DHHS has taken the position that the waiver of insurance deductibles and copayments should not be prosecuted because this practice does not result in any increased costs to the government. Likewise, hospital efficiency incentive plans do not increase costs to the government because Medicare now pays hospitals a flat fee per patient that does not vary based on the ordering behavior of physicians. Indeed, such plans reduce costs in the long run by encouraging more efficient practice patterns.

Ultimately, this analysis is not likely to provide much relief. First, in the waiver case just cited, the Department of Justice rejected the DHHS position. Reasoning that there were subtle effects of waiving deductibles and copayments that might result in increased program costs — primarily, that relieving patients from any financial responsibility for their care will make it somewhat more likely that Medicare will be billed for unnecessary treatment.[13] . . . Indeed, almost by

---

12. See, e.g., American Hospital Association, Office of Legal and Regulatory Affairs, Medicaid-Medicare Antifraud and Abuse Amendments: Application to Hospital Activities Under the Medicare Prospective Payment System (Legal Memorandum No. 2) 5-6 (1985).

13. OIG/DOJ Correspondence, supra note 3. But see West Allis Mem. Hosp. v. Bowen, 660 F.2d 936, 939 (E.D. Wisc. 1987), *reversed on other grounds*, 852 F.2d 251 (7th Cir. 1988) (questioning validity of this position).

III. Referral Fee Prohibitions

definition, any arrangement that possesses some referral incentive will have some tendency to increase utilization.

Moreover, "it should be noted that the law does not make increased cost to the government the sole criterion of corruption."[14] Any incentive plan that has a referral aspect in a literal sense will always conflict with at least one of the stated purposes — namely, the potential to influence *where* a patient is referred. Thus, other authorities have viewed as "irrelevant" the fact that the challenged activity "may not have involved an increase in cost."[16] . . .

Observing that any referral incentive entails some chance of increasing costs and influencing the choice of care is not to contend that all referral incentives should be banned. . . . My point is that inflationary and provider-selection incentives are so pervasive that it is impossible to fashion a limiting rule based on their absence.

Earned versus unearned fees. A superior definitional model can be found in state law interpretations of fee splitting statutes. These interpretations have regularly grappled with the problem of subsidiary referral motivations that underlie payments for legitimate services. A classic situation is the rental of hospital space and equipment to in-house pharmacies and radiologists in exchange for a percentage of their gross receipts. Since hospital pharmacies and radiologists obtain their patients from the hospital, these rental payments have the clear potential to induce referrals. California courts and attorney general opinions analyzing this situation under the state's felony statute have developed a penetrating distinction between earned and unearned referral fees. Fees incidentally related to a referral are nevertheless valid if they are fully earned by legitimate nonreferral services — that is, if they do not exceed the fair market value of necessary services bargained for at arm's length:

> When called upon to apply or interpret [the referral fee prohibition], opinions of the [California attorney general] and of the courts concluded that only those arrangements were illegal wherein the consideration paid for the referral was not commensurate with the services rendered or expenses incurred by the receiver, but that no violation occurred where the fee paid reasonably approximated their true value.[17]

---

14. U.S. v. Ruttenberg, 625 F.2d 173, 177 n.9 (7th Cir. 1980).

16. State v. Abortion Information Agency, Inc., 330 N.Y.S.2d 927, 929 (N.Y. App. Div. 1971), *aff'd*, 334 N.Y.S.2d 174 (1972) (upholding an injunction against an abortion agency's negotiating discounts in hospital charges). See Mast v. State Board of Optometry, 139 Cal. App. 2d 78, 91, 293 P.2d 148 (1956) ("an excessive charge is not an element of the offense").

17. 65 Cal. Atty. Gen. Op. 252, 254 (1982).

Thus, reasonable percentage-of-revenue terms for internal hospital franchises are commonly accepted, despite the result that the franchise holder pays the hospital precisely in proportion to the amount of business received from hospital patients. Blank v. Palo Alto-Stanford Hospital Center held that a radiologist paying a hospital two-thirds of his receipts does not constitute fee splitting because "the evidence sustains the conclusion that the portion of the fees received was commensurate with the expenses . . . incurred by the hospital in connection with furnishing the diagnostic facilities. . . . Under these circumstances there is no illegality."[19]

Indeed, the analysis could hardly be otherwise. Referral incentives are fundamental to the financial foundation on which the superstructure of traditional medical practice has been erected. Inherent in a fee-for-service method of payment is an incentive to order more treatment — that is, to refer one's patient to oneself. Yet fee-for-service reimbursement, like earned fee splitting, survives a referral fee attack because the fees are (by definition) "for service," not for referral.

Potentially, the earned/unearned distinction neatly resolves the complication of secondary referral incentives that has plagued legitimate business practices. For instance, if a physician purchases an ownership interest in a health care institution to which he refers patients, his receipt of a share of the profits does not constitute a referral fee if the profit distributions are a fair reflection of the value of his capital investment rather than a reflection of the value of his referrals.[20] . . .

The reliability of the earned/unearned distinction is cast in doubt, however, by a number of imprecise interpretations of referral fee statutes that appear to treat as irrelevant the earned nature of the fee. Currently, the most widely discussed instance is Greber v. United States. In that case the federal government successfully prosecuted the owner of a cardiology diagnostic laboratory for violating the federal statute by paying "interpretation fees" to referring physicians, ostensibly as compensation for evaluating the diagnostic data produced by the lab tests. The court rejected the defense's contention that "compensating a physician for services actually rendered could not be a violation of the statute," reasoning in terms that appear to reject outright the earned/unearned distinction.

The *Greber* court's approach is far too searching in its attempt to ferret out any form of referral inducement. The same reasoning might be used to attack the basis of every traditional third-party

---

19. 44 Cal. Rptr. 572, 580 (Cal. Dist. Ct. App. 1965).
20. Hall, Institutional Control of Physician Behavior, 137 U. Penn. L. Rev. 431, 493 (1988).

III. Referral Fee Prohibitions

might be used to attack the basis of every traditional third-party reimbursement system, both governmental and private. Fee-for-service and cost-based reimbursement, in the words of the *Greber* decision, present just as strong a "potential for unnecessary drain on the Medicare system," despite the fact that "the physician performs some service for the money received." However, close attention to the facts of the *Greber* case suggest that the decision may not be as ominous as its reasoning portends. There are strong indications that the "interpretation services" were a bogus front to disguise what was in reality a true kickback scheme. Thus, there is good reason to suspect that the court would not have reached the same result if in fact the fee had been fully earned by legitimate services in a fully disclosed, arm's length relationship.

A helpful way to characterize the controversy is to consider whether an objective or a subjective test should be used to determine the referral nature of a fee. Decisions emphasizing the earned nature of the fee look to the value of and need for the services that generate the fee as an objective test of the claim that the fee is in consideration of only those services. Decisions that consider the earned aspect irrelevant tend to emphasize a state-of-mind test for detecting referral fees. They search for an "intent" to induce referrals and consider irrelevant the presence of nominally legitimate services. An objective test is preferable. Just as it would be inappropriate to determine tax liability based solely on whether a transaction was structured with an eye toward minimizing taxation, the subjective expectation of producing more health care business should not be determinative in referral fee cases.

Fortunately, other authorities suggest that a more measured attitude still prevails despite the *Greber* court's overboard reasoning.[29] One is the Health Care Financing Administration (HCFA) ruling on durable medical equipment (DME) suppliers, companies that rent (or sell) for home use equipment such as hospital beds and respirators. Some DME suppliers pay the respiratory therapist who is treating the patient a fee for setting up, maintaining, and instructing the patient in the use of oxygen equipment. Despite the potential for inducing the therapist's referral of the patient to the DME supplier, HCFA's

---

29. Another helpful example is the recent California Attorney General opinion that ruled that a cardiology lab's payment to referring physicians of a fee for "preparing an evaluation report of the referred patient's test data violates" the California referral fee prohibition. Although the opinion relied on *Greber*, it emphasized repeatedly as an apparently critical part of its analysis the supposition that "no legitimate reason . . . exist[s] for the report to be prepared as part of the referral." 70 Cal. Atty. Gen. Opin. 65 (1987). See also United States v. Lipkis, 770 F.2d 1447, 1449 (9th Cir. 1985) (upholding kickback conviction in a case where clinical lab paid for "collecting specimens, spinning down blood, supplying forms and stickers, and carrying insurance" where the "fair market value of these services was substantially less than the compensation" paid).

final ruling stated that it would judge DME payments on a case-by-case basis using factors that essentially replicate an earned/unearned determination.[30]

On balance, the earned/unearned distinction appears to retain a central place in the analysis of referral fee prohibitions. Those decisions that have considered the rendering of services irrelevant have done so in situations where the services were a subterfuge or where the fee paid for the services was excessive. In such cases, it is entirely appropriate to characterize part or all of the fee as being in consideration for a referral. But absent such subterfuge, the pursuit of a legitimate business objective should result in an innocent characterization.

NOTES

Referral Fees

1. There are three sources of referral fee prohibitions. The most threatening is the federal Medicare/Medicaid anti-fraud and abuse statute discussed in the principal readings. Many states also directly criminalize referral fees. California's statute has received the most discussion: "[R]eceipt or acceptance, by any [physician] of any rebate, refund, commission . . . or other consideration, whether in the form of money or otherwise, as compensation or inducement for referring patients . . . to any person . . . is unlawful . . . and is punishable [as a felony]." Cal. Bus. & Prof. Code §650 (West Supp. 1987). Third, state medical practice acts frequently enumerate fee splitting as one of the grounds for revocation or suspension of a physician's license to practice. A typical statute allows disciplinary action by the board of medical examiners for "division of fees . . . received for professional services with any person for bringing or referring a patient." D.C. Code Ann. §2-1326(d)(8),(9) (1981).

2. Do the evil incentives inherent in referral fees differ fundamentally from those inherent in conventional fee-for-service reimbursement set according to usual, customary, and reasonable rates? Might not the ability to generate more income under traditional insurance influence a physician to refrain from referring a patient to a more competent doctor, to render unnecessary services to that patient, or to charge too much for necessary services? Consider the

---

30. Intermediary Letter No. 85-2, supra note 6. HCFA looks to factors that indicate if there is a legitimate reason for employing therapists to perform these services, factors such as whether the supplier needs to and regularly does use therapists to install and service its equipment in all cases, whether other suppliers in the area use therapists for this purpose, and whether there are unique reasons that prevent the supplier from using its own employees. Id.

III. Referral Fee Prohibitions

following from the prestigious Institute of Medicine's influential report on For-Profit Enterprise in Health Care 153 (B. Gray ed. 1986):

> All compensation systems — from fee-for-service to capitation or salary — present some undesirable incentives for providing too many services, or too few. No system will work without some degree of integrity, decency, and ethical commitment on the part of professionals. Inevitably, we must presume some underlying professionalism that will constrain the operation of unadulterated self-interest.

Medical economist Mark Pauly contends that "it is possible for fee splitting to offer incentives which actually improve patient welfare" by counteracting a general practitioner's temptation not to refer patients to specialists. The Ethics and Economics of Kickbacks and Fee Splitting, 10 Bell J. Eco. 344 (1974). Professor Frankford argues that prohibiting only certain forms of referral fees will distort health care financial arrangements and will concentrate more influence within medical institutions. He continues: "laws like the [Medicare fraud and abuse statute] are absolutely incapable of logically defining, much less policing against, inflated prices. [T]hey fail even to create a language for comprehensible debate. They simply obfuscate the issues." Frankford, Creating and Dividing the Fruits of Collective Economic Activity: Referrals Among Health Care Providers, 89 Colum. L. Rev. 1861, 1937 (1989).

Dr. Arnold S. Relman, editor of the New England Journal of Medicine, has responded:

> The situation is different when physicians seek income beyond fee for service and make business arrangements with other providers of services to their patients. Such arrangements introduce a new and unnecessary conflict, which strains the physician's fiduciary commitment to the patient. Unlike the conflicts of interest in the fee-for-service system, these new arrangements are usually not fully disclosed to the patient, and therefore are more difficult to control.

Relman, Dealing With Conflicts of Interest, 313 New Eng. J. Med. 749, 750 (1985).

Do the rule of necessity and the absence of disclosure justify felony imprisonment? For a rebuttal to Relman, see Hall, supra 137 U. Pa. L. Rev. at 498-499.

3. The referral fee regulations proposed by the DHHS in fact follow a transactional model that creates safe harbors only for already recognized practices, but in doing so the regulations rely heavily on the fair market value concept. E.g., 42 C.F.R. §1001.952(a) (proposed) (protecting a physician's return "from an investment obtained for fair market value"); id. at §1001.952(b) (protecting hospital space rental charges that are "consistent with fair market value in arms-length

transactions"). However, the proposed regulations allow only hospitals (not doctors) to waive copayments and deductibles, and they do not address efficiency incentive plans. 54 Fed. Reg. 3088 (Jan. 23, 1989).

For an additional analysis of the effect of the Medicare fraud and abuse statute on contemporary business arrangements, see Comment, Curing the Health Care Industry: Government Response to Medicare Fraud and Abuse, 5 J. Contemp. Health L. & Pol. 175 (1989); Hyman & Williamson, Fraud and Abuse: Regulatory Alternatives in a "Competitive" Health Care Era, 19 Loy. U.L.J. 1133 (1988).

4. The First and Ninth Circuits, by recently adopting the same broad interpretation of the federal statute as *Greber,* set back the hopes of those who initially read that decision as aberrational. United States v. Bay State Ambulance and Hosp. Rental Service, 874 F.2d 20 (1st Cir. 1989); United States v. Kats, 871 F.2d 105 (9th Cir. 1989). However, the First Circuit made a conviction at least marginally more difficult by requiring a showing that there be a "primary" rather than merely "incidental" purpose to induce referrals.

5. Another source of law relevant to the practice of waiving coinsurance and deductibles discussed above are insurance fraud statutes. To illustrate, a dentist who normally charges $100 for a procedure that is reimbursed at 80 percent by dental insurance may agree to waive the $20 copayment required of the patient.

> Thus, the argument goes, the dental plan should only be responsible for 80 percent of $80, or $64, and the dentist by submitting a billing to the insurance carrier for $100 is "overbilling" the carrier by misrepresenting the practitioner's true fee. . . . The fraud or misrepresentation would be based upon the recitals in the specific claim form furnished to the carrier by the dentist. . . . Arguably, for example, a claim which states a total fee has *actually been charged* to a patient is evidence that the amount recited has in fact been charged to the patient. . . . [However], in states where the practice has been found not to violate state law, the conclusion is generally based on the rationale that the term 'usual and reasonable' fee is ambiguous.

Oregon Atty. Gen. Opin No. 5415 (Jan. 18, 1983). See Parrish v. Lamm, 758 P.2d 1356 (Colo. 1988) (upholding constitutionality of statute that makes it a misdemeanor to "abuse health insurance" by routinely waiving deductibles and co-payments).

6. A related development is the recent emergence of state and federal laws prohibiting physicians from referring patients to institutions (such as hospitals or clinical laboratories) in which they have an ownership interest, in essence, a prohibition of *self*-referral fees. A government study reported that, on average, physicians own or invest in 25 percent of the labs to which they refer patients, and that

III. Referral Fee Prohibitions

physicians with an ownership interest refer their patients 45 percent more than the norm. N.Y. Times, April 29, 1989, at 1. Another study found that, after a physician clinic converted from an hourly wage form of compensation to paying its doctors a percentage of the gross charges they generated, the number of lab tests immediately shot up by 23 percent and total charges per month grew 20 percent. Hemenway et al., Physicians' Responses to Financial Incentives, 322 New Eng. J. Med. 1059 (1990).

With respect to these self-interested referrals, some states require merely disclosure to the patient of the doctor's financial conflict of interest (e.g., Cal. Bus. & Prof. Code §654.2; Wash. Rev. Code §19.68.010), but a few state statutes prohibit physician self-referrals altogether (e.g., Mich. Comp. L. Ann. §400.604). A federal bill championed by Representative Stark would have prohibited such referrals outright for many Medicare and Medicaid services, H.R. 939, 101st Cong. 1st Sess. (1989), but as passed it was diluted to prohibit only referrals to certain clinical labs, with further study to follow. 42 U.S.C. §1395 nn. Commenting on these developments, Hall supra, 137 U. Penn. L. Rev. at 499 n.242 contends: "These restrictions are sensible in the traditional fee-for-service system where rendering more services leads to collecting more fees. Under the [new] prospective payment systems [discussed in Chapter 8], however, it is counterproductive to discourage self-referrals because payment incentives reach physicians only if the physician is brought within the economics of the institution. Discouraging self-referrals therefore . . . insulat[es] physicians from the incentives inherent in their own medical enterprises." See generally, Morreim, Conflicts of Interest: Profits and Problems in Physician Referrals, 262 J.A.M.A. 390 (1989); Iglehart, The Debate over Physician Ownership of Health Care Facilities, 321 New Eng. J. Med. 198 (1989); McDowell, Physician Self-Referral Arrangements: Legitimate Business or Unethical "Entrepreneurialism," 15 Am. J.L. & Med. 61 (1989).

7. Another related development, discussed at greater length in Chapter 8.II.A, is a 1986 federal prohibition of payments to *reduce* services, what might be called a prohibition of *anti*referral fees. 42 U.S.C. §1320a-7a(b). This law is an outgrowth of a new form of hospital reimbursement under Medicare that pays hospitals a fixed, predetermined amount for each patient instead of the actual costs of treatment. This "prospective payment system" is intended to encourage more efficient treatment and shorter lengths of stay. In response to this new system, several hospitals adopted a physician incentive plan that paid each doctor a percentage of the profits the hospital earns from the doctor's Medicare patients, in order to encourage more efficient treatment patterns. A similar form of profit-sharing is widespread in the HMO industry. HMOs frequently share

with their doctors a portion of the savings generated by avoiding referrals to hospitals or outside specialists. The federal prohibition of efficiency incentives is scheduled to extend to HMOs as well beginning April 1, 1991. See generally Hall supra, 137 U. Penn. L. Rev. at 485; U.S. General Accounting Office, Physician Incentive Payments by Hospitals Could Lead to Abuse, Report to the Chairman, Subcommittee on Health, House Committee on Ways and Means (No. HRD-86-103) (July 1986); Dechene, Physician Incentive Programs: Are They Legal, 4 Health Span, Jan. 1987, at 3; Comment, Abusing the Patient: Medicare Fraud and Abuse and Hospital-Physician Incentive Plans, 20 U. Mich. J.L. Reform 279 (1986); Emory L.J. supra, vol. 36, pp. 732-735.

IV. CERTIFICATE OF NEED, HOSPITAL LICENSURE, AND PRIVATE ACCREDITATION

Simpson, Full Circle: The Return of Certificate of Need Regulation of Health Facilities to State Control*
19 Ind. L. Rev. 1025-27, 1043-1048, 1066, 1071, 1087 (1986)

Certificate of need (CON) programs are . . . [state] regulatory mechanisms providing for review and approval by health planning agencies of capital expenditures and service capacity expansion by hospitals and other health care facilities. Their primary purpose is to discourage unnecessary investment in health care facilities and to channel investment into socially desirable uses. At the beginning of 1986, forty-two states and the District of Columbia had statutes authorizing such programs. . . .

State certificate of need programs generally operate in the following manner. A health care facility covered by the program must submit a permit application to an official state health planning agency before undertaking those capital expenditures and other projects subject to review. . . . Review criteria include consideration of community need, financial feasibility, expected quality of care, less costly alternatives, and accessibility of the project to underserved and indigent populations. [A] local organization conducts a public meeting at which interested persons may comment on the proposal. It then

---

* Reprinted by permission of the Indiana Law Review.
James B. Simpson is Director, Legal Resources Program, Western Consortium for Public Health, San Francisco, Cal.

IV. Certificate of Need

conveys its recommendation to approve or deny the project to the state health planning agency. The state agency conducts an administrative adjudicatory hearing on the application and renders a formal decision as to the need for the project. Administrative and judicial appeals may follow, and often do when multiple applicants compete to serve an identified community need. The ultimately successful applicant is awarded a "certificate of need" entitling it to proceed with its project.

Federal Involvement

Over the years, federal control over state health planning and certificates of need has waxed and waned. . . . In 1975, Congress passed the National Health Planning and Resources Development Act of 1974[6] (NHPRDA or Act). The Act provided substantial funding for state and local health planning activities and effectively required states to adopt certificate of need laws conforming to federal standards. . . . In a few years most states had programs resembling the federal model.

With the advent of the Reagan administration in 1980, federal support for certificate of need fell on hard times. The administration entered office with an anti-regulatory platform and a strong interest in using market incentives rather than regulatory controls to restrain the rising costs of health programs. [As a result, in 1987 Congress repealed NHPRDA]. . . .

Consequently, state certificate of need programs have begun to diverge from the federal model and from each other. Some states have entirely repealed their certificate of need laws. Others have increased the scope and forcefulness of their regulatory controls. The vast majority of states have modified their programs in recent years by streamlining the review process and narrowing the range of health care facilities and projects subject to review. . . . [Nevertheless, the previous NHPRDA provisions are the best vantage point for an overview of a typical state's CON coverage.]

NHPRDA Coverage. . . .

1. NHPRDA Coverage of Facilities

[T]he health care facilities subject to certificate of need review include: hospitals, . . . skilled nursing facilities, intermediate care facilities, kidney disease treatment centers including freestanding he-

---

6. Pub. L. No. 93-641, 88 Stat. 2225 (1975) (codified as amended at 42 U.S.C. §§300k-300n-6 (1982)).

modialysis units, and ambulatory surgical facilities. [Specifically excluded are "the offices of private physicians or dentists, whether for individual or group practice."][84] . . .

2. Projects Subject to Review. . . .

The Act required states to review "new institutional health services," . . . defined by regulation as:

1. Construction, development, or establishment of a new health care facility; . . .
2. Capital expenditures by or on behalf of a health care facility . . . in excess of [$600,000, (or $400,000 for equipment), adjusted for inflation each year];
3. Increases in health care facility . . . bed capacity, bed category changes, and bed relocations; and
4. New clinically-related health services offered in or through a health care facility [that have not been offered on a regular basis during the prior twelve months]. . . .

The Department of Health and Human Services has never specified the services that fall within the term "health services," except to indicate that the term refers to clinical services. It has stated, somewhat unhelpfully, that "[a]ny service is covered if it is included in the scope of coverage developed by the state." Additionally, it has never clarified whether increases in the volume, intensity, or type of clinical services provided in a department constitute a new service, or whether only a new department or cost center would be covered. . . .

Many states have raised their thresholds above the maximum federal level (which would be $736,200 in states taking full advantage of the threshold inflator). This practice appears most common in the western states, where Alaska and California have capital thresholds set at one million dollars for certain specified projects and general purpose thresholds in several other states are at similar levels. Five other states have thresholds exceeding the federal level. Colorado's two million dollar threshold is the highest in the country. . . .

A state elevating its capital and other expenditure thresholds to levels at or above one million dollars greatly increases the temptation to health care facilities to attempt to evade certificate of need review by artifically dividing projects into two or more stages, each costing less than the threshold. When the expenditure threshold is $100,000, the risks of evasion of certificate of need by dividing, for example, a $198,000 project into two $99,000 stages are not likely to be worth

---

84. 42 C.F.R. §§123.401, 404.

IV. Certificate of Need

the benefit to the facility. But with a five million dollar threshold, project division could permit a project costing nearly ten million dollars to escape planning agency scrutiny. In response to this problem, several states have adopted statutory prohibitions on project division undertaken for the purpose of avoiding certificate of need review. . . .

A number of states have adopted a new approach to coverage of health service additions. These states cover additions of a small number of specified new health services regardless of their capital or operating cost, and all other new services only if their capital or operating costs exceed a threshold. For example, . . . Ohio covers additions of heart, lung, liver, and pancreas transplant programs without regard to cost and other new services only if their annual operating costs exceed $297,500. . . .

The Future of Certificate of Need

. . . Whether or not federal funding continues, it appears that a substantial number of states will retain certificate of need programs, at least in the near future. It should be apparent that certificate of need regulation continues to satisfy a wide range of state policy roles. However, it also appears that in the absence of federal requirements, a significant number of states will abandon the program in favor of efforts to promote more competitive health service markets.

Irvington General Hospital v. Department of Health
149 N.J. Super. 461, 374 A.2d 49 (1977)

Irvington General Hospital submitted an application for a certificate of need in November 1973. It sought permission to construct an addition to the hospital and to add . . . 19 medical/surgical beds.

After several delays attributable both to the Department [of Health] and the applicant, hearings were held in September and October 1975. The hearing officer recommended that the application be approved. . . .

Between the time of the hearing and the time when the Health Care Administration Board considered the hearing officer's recommendation, the Board reclassified 150 long-term care beds at Clara Maas Hospital as medical/surgical beds, thereby creating an excess of medical/surgical beds in Essex County, the county in which Irvington General Hospital is located. [O]n May 6, 1976 the Board remanded this application to the hearing officer, instructing him to make additional findings of fact "particularly pertinent to the current effect of the reclassification of the beds in the area."

The remand hearing was held, and thereafter the hearing officer recommended that the application be denied solely on the ground that Department of Health statistics now showed an excess of medical/surgical beds in the county. . . .

We agree with plaintiff's contention that the Board erred in giving conclusive weight to the[se] Department of Health statistics. [T]he Legislature has required the Health Care Administration Board to take into account several factors:

> (a) the availability of facilities or services which may serve as alternatives or substitutes, (b) the need for special equipment and services in the area, (c) the possible economies and improvement in services to be anticipated from the operation of joint central services, (d) the adequacy of financial resources and sources of present and future revenues, (e) the availability of sufficient manpower in the several professional disciplines, and (f) such other factors as may be established by regulation.

It is clear, therefore, that in light of those established considerations and the general policy of providing the highest quality health care, it is not sufficient for the Board to consider only the number of beds available in the area, particularly where the area designated by the Department as the "area to be served" may not, in fact, coincide with the area for which the services will, in fact, be provided. Total reliance upon bed statistics would permit the Board to make its decision solely on the basis of the first factor noted in N.J.S.A. 26:2H-8: "the availability of facilities, or services which may serve as alternatives or substitutes." It would permit the Board to ignore the remaining factors, notably, in this case, the second one: "the need for special . . . services in the area."

The extensive record compels the conclusion that Irvington General Hospital primarily serves the population of the Town of Irvington. That town has the largest density of citizens over 65 of any municipality in this State. Testimony of various experts establishes that the elderly patients who make up the largest portion of the Hospital's population have a greater need than other patients for the support of relatives and friends during their illnesses, and that the knowledge that they and their families are secure is a significant factor in their successful medical treatment.

The testimony also shows that public transportation to other hospitals in Essex County is poor and that many elderly patients are at least reluctant to go to those hospitals because they are located in high crime areas. Moreover, their elderly spouses and friends are unable to visit them at other locations because of the lack of transportation and threats to their safety. . . .

[W]e believe that the Board, in deciding whether to grant a certificate of need, may not, as it did here, rely solely on bed need statistics. Unquestionably, it must also take into account all of the factors set out in N.J.S.A. 26:2H-8 and must, if appropriate, recognize and accept a need for special services in any local area smaller than the larger health care area established by the Department.

Because the Board failed to make those considerations a remand is required. On remand we direct that the Board take into account an additional factor: At the time of the original hearing the Department statistics showed that Essex County needed 73 more medical/surgical beds. By the time of the remand hearing 150 beds at Clara Maas Hospital had been reclassified to medical/surgical. That fact created an excess of beds in the county. The reclassification had been made upon application by Clara Maas suggested by the Department. We cannot tell from the record when the Clara Maas application was made. If, in fact, it was made after the application by Irvington General, we direct that the Irvington General application be considered first, since it was submitted first. In other words, on remand the Irvington General application should be considered as if the Clara Maas application had not yet been determined. . . .

Clifton Springs Sanitarium Co. v. Axelrod
115 App. Div. 2d 949, 497 N.Y.S.2d 525 (1985)

Petitioner Hospital, with the benefit of private grant monies, purchased a trailer which it installed on its grounds approximately eight feet from its principal hospital building. A connecting walkway and extended electrical service were provided from the hospital building to the trailer. The trailer was then leased to a staff radiologist, Dr. Steven Braff, who rented and installed in the trailer a Computerized Axial Tomography Scanner (CAT scanner) with which he performed CAT scans on in-patients of petitioner Hospital, as well as on in-patients of other area hospitals. Dr. Braff also provided service to out-patients in the area. Eventually, Dr. Braff purchased his own CAT scanner.

. . . After a hearing, the Administrative Law Judge concluded that petitioner was operating a CAT scanner without obtaining a Certificate of Need (CON) from respondents [the Department of Health], as required by Article 28 of the Public Health Law. Respondents adopted these conclusions and ordered petitioner to terminate its lease with Dr. Braff for the trailer insofar as it provided for CAT scanning services on its in-patients, discontinue permitting its in-patients to be CAT scanned in the trailer, and levied monetary sanctions. We reverse. . . .

The conclusions of the Administrative Law Judge that the trailer was a part of the Hospital or that the trailer itself constituted a hospital, that the scanning services being provided were "Hospital" services, and that the Hospital "controlled" the operation of the CAT scanner are without support in the record.

The record demonstrates that the trailer, purchased with private funds, is not part of the Hospital and was not constructed in accordance with hospital codes. Only the covered walkway was constructed to code. The CAT scanner is the property of Dr. Braff, not the Hospital, and the lease does not require him to perform CAT scans on Hospital in-patients. The rent for the trailer is constant and not related to the number of scans performed on in-patients of petitioner Hospital. Dr. Braff bills patients directly, purchases his own supplies, and employs his own staff. The record further indicates that, at the time of the hearing, in-patients of petitioner Hospital comprised only 20 percent of the population to which Dr. Braff was providing CAT scanning services. The evidence does not support the conclusion that CAT scanning services were provided by petitioner Hospital.

The central issue posed is whether the CAT scan services are provided by a hospital or a private physician. The former requires a Certificate of Need (CON) approval by the Department of Health; the latter does not. Respondents have not demonstrated that the CAT scanning service provided by Dr. Braff is a Hospital service or is in any way controlled by the Hospital. State regulations do not require private physicians to obtain CONs and the effect of respondents' order is to arbitrarily impose a requirement on the Hospital which the law does not impose. Indeed, efforts in recent years to bring privately owned equipment used on hospital in-patients within the State's CON requirements has consistently failed to obtain legislative approval. There is nothing in the present statutory scheme to prohibit a private physician from establishing a private CAT scanning service, nor is it illegal for a hospital to facilitate such action on the part of a physician. . . .

Determination unanimously annulled on the law with costs.

NOTES

Certificate of Need Coverage, Criteria, and Administrative Procedures

1. These materials cover the specifics of certificate of need coverage, from the perspective of a hospital administrator or lawyer who needs to know the details of coverage and the process for application in order to make effective planning decisions. Chapter 8.II.C. addresses CON laws from the more critical health policy perspective of a legislator considering whether this regulatory system is a workable means of constraining society's health care expenditures.

2. Other decisions (in addition to *Irvington*) that reject numerical

IV. Certificate of Need

bed-need guidelines include Charter Medical v. HCA Health Servs., 542 N.E.2d 82 (Ill. App. 1989); Meadowbrook Nursing Home v. Axelrod, 517 N.Y.S.2d 625 (App. Div. 1987); Roanoke Mem. Hosp. v. Kenley, 352 S.E.2d 525 (Va. App. 1987); Oak Park Manor v. State CON Review Board, 500 N.E.2d 895 (Oh. App. 1985); Department of Health and Rehabilitative Services v. Johnson and Johnson Home Health Care, 447 So. 2d 361 (Fla. App. 1984). But see State Health Coordinating Council v. General Hospitals of Humana, 660 S.W.2d 906 (Ark. 1983), *cert. denied,* 467 U.S. 1205 (*"Humana"*) (bed-need formula is mandatory); Appeal of New Hampshire Catholic Charities, 546 A.2d 1085 (N.H. 1988) (error to approve application for 85 nursing home beds based on factors of marginal importance when predetermined bed need was for only 82 beds); Yankton v. South Dakota Dept. of Health, 432 N.W.2d 68 (1988) (enforcing agency's bed-need formula despite contrary evidence of waiting lists and high occupancy rates).

3. The doctor's office exemption has proven to be quite a large loophole. See also Finger Lakes HSA v. St. Joseph's Hospital, 442 N.Y.S.2d 219 (App. Div. 1981) (injunction denied against CAT scanner in medical office building adjacent to and owned by hospital); Women's Med. Ctr v. Finely, 469 A.2d 65 (N.J. App. 1983) (abortion clinic). For instance, the exemption has been used frequently to purchase magnetic resonance imagers (MRIs) without CON approval. Boulware v. State Dept. of Human Resources, 737 P.2d 502 (Nev. 1987). MRIs are highly sophisticated diagnostic scanning devices that cost up to $3 million installed. Although they originally were found only in major medical centers, three-fourths of MRIs are now located outside the hospital setting, largely because of the CON laws. Hospitals, Sept. 20, 1987 at 18, 21. See Steinberg, Sisk & Locke, X-Ray CT and Magnetic Resonance Imagers: Diffusion Patterns and Policy Issues, 313 New Eng. J. Med. 859 (1985).

A number of states have attempted to close this loophole by extending CON laws to outpatient facilities intended primarily to treat inpatients. E.g., Radiological Society v. New Jersey State Dept. of Health, 506 A.2d 755 (N.J. Super. 1986).

4. The coverage of new health care services is another CON provision that challenges creative hospital managers who choose to test the limits of what constitutes a "new service." Does the designation of an existing wing of beds as a psychiatric unit require a CON where the hospital previously treated an occasional psychiatric patient? See Charter Southland Hospital v. Hospital Corporation of America, 480 So. 2d 591 (Ala. Civ. App. 1985) (no) (dictum); St. Francis/St. George Hospital v. Blue Cross, 1983 WESTLAW 5323 (Ohio App. 1983) (no CON required for conversion of long-term beds to alcohol treatment); SHPA v. Mobile Infirmary Assn., 533 So. 2d 255 (Ala. App. 1988)

(consolidation of existing fragmented rehabilitation services into a separate unit does require CON).

5. Health care facilities have found various other inventive techniques for circumventing the CON laws. One is suggested by *Irvington's* willingness to "recognize and accept a need . . . in a [ ] local area smaller than the larger health care area established by the Department." For instance, a hospital company in an overbedded metropolitan area may try to carve out an unserved area in the affluent, growing suburbs. The success of this technique turns on whether the suburbs are considered to be within the service area of the existing "downtown" hospitals. States vary in their methodologies for defining service areas. Without entering into the full complexities of service area gerrymandering, consider what the policy implications are of (a) refusing local hospital facilities to newly emerging communities; (b) locating new construction in affluent white suburbs at the cost of patient census at older, city-center hospitals.

Another technique for circumventing numerical bed-need limitations is for an existing hospital to construct a new facility that "replaces" older beds, sometimes in an entirely different location. This technique of trading in old beds for new has created a lively market in the sale of older hospitals. In some cases, the replaced capacity consists of only "paper beds," that is, licensed bed capacity that has long since been taken out of operation to make room for other uses and services. These and other circumvention techniques are discussed extensively in Comment, Certificate of Need for Health Care Facilities: A Time for Re-Examination, 7 Pace L. Rev. 491, 512-526 (1987).

6. *Irvington* required the earlier CON application to be considered first. But what if both applications were filed at approximately the same time? In such circumstances, courts require the applications to be considered in a comparative hearing, which seeks to determine not only whether there is a need for the service or facility, but, if so, who among many hospitals will best serve that need. Huron Valley Hosp. v. Michigan State Health Facilities Commission, 312 N.W.2d 422 (Mich. App. 1981); Bio-Medical Applications v. Dept. of Health and Rehab. Servs., 370 So. 2d 19 (Fla. App. 1979); Appeal of Behavior Science Institute, 436 A.2d 1329 (N.H. 1981).

Comparative hearings can turn into surprisingly complex affairs that last for weeks. Once one application is filed, it is usually followed by several other competing ones that are batched together in the same review cycle. In the experience of one of your authors, these contests quickly degenerate into disputes over trivia such as who has the superior parking lot design or who is cutting down the most trees. See, for instance, In re Health Care and Retirement Corp., 364 S.E.2d 150 (N.C. App. 1988).

IV. Certificate of Need

The administrative and legal burdens of CON even in unopposed applications can be considerable. "For example, the CON application filed by a group of Connecticut hospitals for an [MRI] was over 1400 pages, and the required supplement exceeded 1700 pages. From conception until final approval, Greenwich Hospital's noncontroversial and unopposed request for a CON to replace its telephone system took one year, and that period was 'brief' only because the hospital agreed to waive its right to a hearing." Comment, Certificate of Need for Health Care Facilities: A Time for Re-examination, 7 Pace L. Rev. 491, 509 (1987).

7. Among the controversial procedural disputes that arise in CON litigation are

(a) whether states are authorized to impose a moratorium on CONs for certain types of services — United Hospital Center v. Richardson, 328 S.E.2d 195 (W. Va. 1985) (moratorium invalid);

(b) whether expiration of the statutory period for the agency to review an application results in the application being "deemed approved" automatically — Platte County Medical Center v. Missouri Health Facilities Review Commn., 734 S.W.2d 608 (Mo. App. 1987) (deemed approved); Myers v. State, 503 N.E.2d 451 (Ind. App. 1987) (same); Benedictine Sisters Benevolent Association v. Petterson, 299 N.W.2d 738 (Minn. 1980) (contra);

(c) whether competing hospitals have standing to challenge the grant of an application — Community Care Centers v. Missouri Health Facilities Review Comm., 735 S.W.2d 13 (Mo. App. 1987) (no standing); Dolan, Who Has Standing to Appeal Certificate-of-Need Decisions?, 1978 Utah L. Rev. 155;

(d) whether completion of the project pending appeal of a CON moots the controversy. *Humana* supra, 660 S.W.2d 906 (Ark. 1983) (not mooted; hospital required to abandon $7 million partially completed building); Tulsa Area Hospital Council v. Oral Roberts Univ., 626 P.2d 316, 324 (Okla. 1981) (Opala, J., dissenting) (moot);

(e) whether an approved project can be moved to a new site without further approval. Appeal of Rehabilitation Associations of New England, 556 A.2d 1183 (N.H. 1989) (yes).

See generally, J. Simpson & T. Bogue, Guide to Health Planning Law: Topical Digest of Case Law (1985).

NOTES

Health Care Facility Licensing and Accreditation; the Measurement of Quality

1. Certificate of need laws are only the most recent form of health care facility regulation. Since the mid-century, virtually every state has regulated the operation of hospitals, nursing homes, and similar facilities through licensure statutes and regulations. Space does not permit an exploration of this body of law. However, it is possible to observe in brief that state licensing authorities typically do not inquire into the quality per se of a hospital's services. Instead, hospital licensure provisions typically read like a gigantic building code for the hospital industry, specifying a host of architectural, safety, and sanitation minutia as a condition for issuing or renewing an operating permit. See S. Jonas et al., Health Care Delivery in the United States (2d ed. 1981); Lander, Licensing of Health Care Facilities, in Legal Aspects of Health Care Policy (R. Roemer & G. McKray eds. 1980); A. Somers, Hospital Regulation: The Dilemma of Public Policy (1969).

2. An emerging area of importance on the facilities licensing horizon is the coverage of freestanding emergency centers ("FECs"), colloquially known as "Doc-in-Boxes." These storefront medical clinics cater to no-wait, no-appointment medical needs of an urgent nature, short of life-or-limb threatening conditions. They provide a more convenient and sometimes less expensive alternative to hospital emergency rooms for conditions such as broken legs, bad cuts, and sudden illnesses. There is an argument that FECs are nothing more than glorified doctors' offices, which traditionally have not been covered by facilities licensing laws. However, states are beginning to amend their statutes to cover these and other novel delivery arrangements such as ambulatory surgery clinics. See Primary Care Physicians Group v. Ledbetter, 634 F. Supp. 78 (N.D. Ga. 1978) (striking FEC license law as unconstitutionally overbroad and vague); Note, Freestanding Emergency Centers: Regulation Through Classification, 36 U. Fla. L. Rev. 465 (1984); Comment, Freestanding Emergency Centers: Regulation and Reimbursement, 11 Am. J. L. & Med. 105; Entin, Emergicenters: A Health Care System in Evolution, 5 J. Leg. Med. 399 (1984); Zaremski & Fohrman, The Emergicenter: Has its Time Arrived?, 11 L. Med. & Health Care 4 (1983).

3. Private accreditation of hospitals and other health care facilities overlaps to a significant extent the function performed by state licensure. The Joint Commission on Accreditation of Healthcare Organizations (formerly, "of Hospitals") ("JCAH" or "JCAHO") is a private association that imposes detailed organizational and procedural standards for the structure and operation of each department

IV. Certificate of Need 623

of a hospital. JCAH, Accreditation Manual for Hospitals. The JCAH wields enormous power and influence because virtually no hospital of respectable size risks the business consequences of jeopardizing its accreditation status. Although the JCAH is composed of many constituent health care organizations, it is effectively dominated by the medical profession, whose representation is much stronger than that of the hospital industry.

Traditionally, the JCAH has addressed itself exclusively to the organizational and structural aspects of what goes into a hospital's operation — whether bylaws are properly drafted, whether there are the proper committees, the hospital's staffing ratio, the adequacy of plant and equipment, documentation and monitoring processes, etc. — rather than attempting any direct assessment of the quality of the hospital's actual output. Recently, however, the JCAH has announced that it intends to include outcome criteria as part of its accreditation procedures. Precisely how it intends to do so is still unknown. It faces two difficulties: finding an objective measure of the quality of care and determining what factors should be taken into account to adjust for expected variations in outcome according to different population groups and different levels of care. See Schroeder, Outcome Assessment 70 Years Later: Are We Ready? 316 New Eng. J. Med 160 (1987); O'Leary, The Joint Commission Looks Ahead, 258 J.A.M.A. 951 (1987).

Many states essentially delegate their licensing function to the JCAH by incorporating its standards by reference. Similarly, the federal Medicare program automatically deems all JCAH-accredited hospitals to be fit for Medicare participation. Is it a wise public policy to allow private accreditation to largely displace government licensing? See Jost, The Joint Commission on Accreditation of Hospitals: Private Regulation of Health Care and the Public Interest, 24 B.C.L. Rev. 835 (1983) (critical of JCAH role); Cospito v. Heckler, 742 F.2d 72 (3rd Cir. 1984) (finding no constitutional infirmity in JCAH role). For a survey of legal issues relating to private accreditation and certification, see American Board of Medical Specialties, Legal Aspects of Certification and Accreditation (D. Langsley, ed. 1983); supra 511.

4. "Approaches to the appraisal of health care quality generally fall into three broad categories: evaluation of structure, evaluation of process, and evaluation of outcome or end results. Structural indicators include not only physician aspects of facilities and equipment, but also characteristics of the organization and qualifications of its health professionals. Process measures pertain to the activities of health professionals in the care of patients. Outcome measures may be stated in terms of health or in terms of patient or family satisfaction." Institute of Medicine, For-profit Enterprise in Health Care 127 (1986). See also Donabedian, The Quality of Care: How Can it Be Assessed?,

260 J.A.M.A. 1743 (1988); Symposium, 7 Health Affairs, Spring 1989. Which appraisal method does hospital licensure primarily employ? JCAH accreditation? Malpractice litigation? Licensure revocation? Peer review committees such as quality assurance and utilization review? See generally Furrow, The Changing Role of the Law in Promoting Quality in Health Care, 26 Hous. L. Rev. 147 (1989); Jost, The Necessary and Proper Role of Regulation to Assure the Quality of Health Care, 25 Hous. L. Rev. 525 (1988).

V. CHARITABLE TAX EXEMPTION AND THE ROLE OF THE PROFIT MOTIVE IN MEDICINE

Commenting on the perhaps anomalous tax-exempt status of "voluntary" hospitals, one authority has observed,

> The voluntary [that is, charitable nonprofit] hospital, like the government hospital, generally enjoys exemption from the federal income tax and from state and local property taxes. This has been true historically and it is true today. Any general repeal of the exemptions is most unlikely in the near future, despite the criticism of some respected authorities who see the exemptions as "mindless subsidies" of the industry which could be carried out much more effectively in other ways. [Ed. Note: See, for instance, Clark, Does the Nonprofit Form Fit the Hospital Industry?, 93 Harv. L. Rev. 1416 (1980).] The complexities of current tax law are such, however, that even in a basically exempt industry the law impinges on many aspects of hospital operations and can be manipulated one way or another with resulting impact in hospital developments. It thus constitutes a *de facto* type of public regulation.

A. Somers, Hospital Regulation: The Dilemma of Public Policy 38 (1969).

Utah County v. Intermountain Health Care, Inc.
709 P.2d 265 (Utah 1985)

DURHAM, Justice:

Utah County seeks review of a decision of the Utah State Tax Commission reversing a ruling of the Utah County Board of Equalization. The Tax Commission exempted Utah Valley Hospital, owned and operated by Intermountain Health Care (IHC), and American Fork Hospital, leased and operated by IHC, from ad valorem property taxes. At issue is whether such a tax exemption is constitutionally

V. Charitable Tax Exemption

permissible. We hold that, on the facts in this record, it is not, and we reverse. . . .

IHC's policy with respect to all of its hospitals is to make charges to patients for hospital services whenever it is possible to do so. Hospital charges are paid either by patients, by private insurance companies such as Blue Cross and Blue Shield, or by governmental programs such as Medicare and Medicaid. IHC and its individual hospitals also are the recipients of private bequests, endowments, and contributions in amounts not established in the record.

[T]he charitable exemption granted by article XIII, section 2 of the Utah Constitution (1895, amended 1982), . . . provides in pertinent part: "[P]roperty . . . used exclusively for either religious worship or charitable purposes, . . . shall be exempt from taxation. . . ."

The power of state and local governments to levy property taxes has traditionally been limited by constitutional and statutory provisions such as those at issue in this case that exempt certain property from taxation. These exemptions confer an indirect subsidy and are usually justified as the quid pro quo for charitable entities undertaking functions and services that the state would otherwise be required to perform. A concurrent rationale, used by some courts, is the assertion that the exemptions are granted not only because charitable entities relieve government of a burden, but also because their activities enhance beneficial community values or goals. Under this theory, the benefits received by the community are believed to offset the revenue lost by reason of the exemption. . . .

An entity may be granted a charitable tax exemption for its property under the Utah Constitution only if it meets the definition of a "charity" or if its property is used exclusively for "charitable" purposes. Essential to this definition is the element of gift to the community. . . . A gift to the community can be identified either by a substantial imbalance in the exchange between the charity and the recipient of its services or in the lessening of a government burden through the charity's operation. . . .

Because the "care of the sick" has traditionally been an activity regarded as charitable in American law, and because the dissenting opinions rely upon decisions from other jurisdictions that in turn incorporate unexamined assumptions about the fundamental nature of hospital-based medical care, we deem it important to scrutinize the contemporary social and economic context of such care. We are convinced that traditional assumptions bear little relationship to the economics of the medical-industrial complex of the 1980's. Nonprofit hospitals were traditionally treated as tax-exempt charitable institutions because, until late in the 19th century, they were true charities providing custodial care for those who were both sick and poor. The hospitals' income was derived largely or entirely from voluntary charitable donations, not government subsidies, taxes, or patient fees.[7] The function and status of hospitals began to change in the late 19th century; the transformation was substantially completed by the 1920's. "From charities, dependent on voluntary gifts, [hospitals] developed into market institutions financed increasingly out of payments from patients." The transformation was multidimensional: hospitals were redefined from social welfare to medical treatment institutions; their charitable foundation was replaced by a business basis; and their orientation shifted to "professionals, and their patients," away from "patrons and the poor." . . .

Also of considerable significance to our review is the increasing irrelevance of the distinction between nonprofit and for-profit hospitals for purposes of discovering the element of charity in their operations. . . . Through the creation of holding companies, nonprofit hospitals have grown into large groups of medical enterprises, containing both for-profit and nonprofit corporate entities. . . . The emergence of hospital organizations with both for-profit and nonprofit components has increasingly destroyed the charitable pretentions of nonprofit organizations: "The extension of the voluntary hospital into profit-making businesses and the penetration of other corporations into the hospital signal the breakdown of the traditional boundaries of voluntarism. Increasingly, the polycorporate hospitals are likely to become multihospital systems and competitors with profit-making chains, HMO's and other health care corporations." Id. at 438.

The foregoing discussion of the economic environment in which modern hospitals function is critical to our analysis in this case because it is an analysis which is generally not present in any of the cases relied upon by the dissenting opinions. Those cases, in our view, do not take into account the revolution in health care that has transformed a "healing profession" into an enormous and complex industry, employing millions of people and accounting for a substantial proportion of our gross national product. . . .

Having discussed the standards for the application of Utah's constitutional exemption for property used for charitable purposes, and the economic and historic context in which we conduct this review, we now examine the record respecting the two hospitals ("the defendants") whose eligibility has been challenged by Utah County.

---

7. Paul Starr, The Social Transformation of American Medicine at 150 (1982). "Voluntary" hospitals, like public hospitals (which evolved from almshouses for the dependent poor), performed a "welfare" function rather than a medical or curing function: the poor were housed in large wards, largely cared for themselves, and often were not expected to recover. See id. at 145, 149, 160. Early voluntary hospitals had paternalistic, communal social structures in which patients entered at the sufferance of their benefactors, "had the moral status of children," and received more moralistic and religious help than medical treatment. Id. at 149, 158.

V. Charitable Tax Exemption 627

[C]urrent operating expenses for both hospitals are covered almost entirely by revenue from patient charges. Although a substantial donation to capital was identified in the case of Utah Valley Hospital, there was no demonstration of the impact of that donation on the current support, maintenance, and operation of that hospital in the tax year in question in this lawsuit. The evidence was that both hospitals charge rates for their services comparable to rates being charged by other similar entities, and no showing was made that the donations identified resulted in charges to patients below prevailing market rates. . . . The Tax Commission in this case found as follows: "The policy of [IHC's hospitals] is to collect hospital charges from patients whenever it is reasonable and possible to do so; however, no person in need of medical attention is denied care solely on the basis of a lack of funds." The record also shows that neither of the hospitals in this case demonstrated any substantial imbalance between the value of the services it provides and the payments it receives apart from any gifts, donations, or endowments. The record shows that the vast majority of the services provided by these two hospitals are paid for by government programs, private insurance companies, or the individuals receiving care. Collection of such remuneration does not constitute giving, but is a mere reciprocal exchange of services for money. Between 1978 and 1980, the value of the services given away as charity by these two hospitals constituted less than one percent of their gross revenues. Furthermore, the record also shows that such free service as did exist was deliberately not advertised out of fear of a "deluge of people" trying to take advantage of it. Instead, every effort was made to recover payment for services rendered. Utah Valley Hospital even offered assistance to patients who claimed inability to pay to enter into bank loan agreements to finance their hospital expenses.

The defendants argue that the great expense of modern hospital care and the universal availability of insurance and government health care subsidies make the idea of a hospital solely supported by philanthropy an anachronism. We believe this argument itself exposes the weakness in the defendants' position. It is precisely because such a vast system of third-party payers has developed to meet the expense of modern hospital care that the historical distinction between for-profit and nonprofit hospitals has eroded. . . .

The dissent of Justice Stewart suggests that the fact that "ability to pay" is not a criterion for admission to IHC's facilities is dispositive of the question of "charitable purpose," regardless of the actual amount of free care provided therein. This argument overlooks the fact that for-profit institutions may well implement similar policies, either for public relations reasons or by virtue of regulations mandated by their receipt of federal- or state-funded payments. . . .

Because the vast majority of their services are paid for, the nonprofit hospitals in this case accumulate capital as do their profit-seeking counterparts. . . . A large portion of the profits of most for-profit entities is used for capital improvements and new, updated equipment, and the defendant hospitals here similarly expend their revenues in excess of operational expenses. There can be no doubt, in reviewing the references in the record by members of IHC's administrative staff, that the IHC system, as well as the two hospitals in question, has consistently generated sufficient funds in excess of operating costs to contribute to rapid and extensive growth, building, competitive employee and professional salaries and benefits, and a very sophisticated management structure. While it is true that no financial benefits or profits are available to private interests in the form of stockholder distributions or ownership advantages, the user entity in this case clearly generates substantial "profits" in the sense of income that exceeds expenses. This observation is not intended to imply that an institution must consume its assets in order to be eligible for tax exemption — the requirement of charitable giving may obviously be met before that point is reached. However, there is a serious question regarding the constitutional propriety of subsidies from Utah County taxpayers being used to give certain entities a substantial competitive edge in what is essentially a commercial marketplace. . . .

In summary, after reviewing the facts in this case in light of the factors we have identified, we believe that the defendants in this case confuse the element of gift to the community, which an entity must demonstrate in order to qualify as a charity under our Constitution, with the concept of community benefit, which any of countless private enterprises might provide. We have no quarrel with the assertion that Utah Valley Hospital and American Fork Hospital meet great and important needs of persons within their communities for medical care. Yet this meeting of a public need by a provision of services cannot be the sole distinguishing characteristic that leads to an automatic property tax exemption. "[T]he usefulness of an enterprise is not sufficient basis for relief from the burden of sharing essential costs of local government." In re Marple Newton School District, 39 Pa. Commw. 326, 336, 395 A.2d 1023, 1028, (1978). Such a "usefulness" rule would have to be equally applied to for-profit hospitals and privately owned health care entities, which also provide medical services to their patients. We note, for example, that the increasing emphasis on competition in health care services is resulting in significant expansion of the activities and roles of health care providers generally, including hospitals, both for-profit and nonprofit. Laboratory services, pharmaceutical services, "birthing" centers, and outpatient surgical units are becoming common adjuncts to traditional hospital care. It would be impossible to justify a distinction, within

V. Charitable Tax Exemption

the constitutional boundaries of "charitable" activities, between outpatient surgical services, for example, provided on property owned by an IHC hospital and those provided on privately owned property, where both are identical and are remunerated at the same rate. . . .

Neither can we find on this record that the burdens of government are substantially lessened as a result of the defendants' provision of services. The record indicates that Utah County budgets approximately $50,000 annually for the payment of hospital care for indigents. Furthermore, the evidence described two instances within a three-month period where, after a Utah County official had declined to authorize payment for a person in the emergency room, Utah Valley Hospital refused to admit the injured person on the basis of that person's inability to pay. The county official was told in these instances to either authorize payment or to "come and get" the person. Such behavior on the hospital's part is inconsistent with its argument that it functions to relieve government of a burden. Likewise, as we have pointed out, there has been no showing that the tax exemption is a significant factor in permitting these defendants to operate, thereby arguably relieving government of the burden of establishing its own medical care providers. In fact, government is already carrying a substantial share of the operating expenses of defendants, in the form of third-party payments pursuant to "entitlement" programs such as Medicare and Medicaid. . . . If nonprofit hospitals, which charge fully for their services, were to be made tax exempt under the "burden" theory, for-profit hospitals logically ought to be treated in the same manner since both provide the public with the same service. . . .

We cannot find, on this record, the essential element of gift to the community, either through the nonreciprocal provision of services or through the alleviation of a government burden, and consequently we hold that the defendants have not demonstrated that their property is being used exclusively for charitable purposes under the Utah Constitution. . . .

HALL, C.J., and DAVID SAM, District Judge, concur.

STEWART, Justice (dissenting):

. . . The Court's holding is without precedent either in Utah or elsewhere in the United States. . . . The Supreme Court of Nebraska in Evangelical Lutheran Good Samaritan Society v. Gage County, 181 Neb. 831, 151 N.W.2d 446, 449 (1967), stated that hospitals operated as nonprofit institutions "are universally classed as charitable institutions." The cases which suport that proposition are legion. . . .

[I]n City of Richmond v. Richmond Memorial Hospital, 202 Va. 86, 116 S.E.2d 79, 82 (1960), which construed a Virginia constitutional provision similar to Article XIII, Section 2 of the Utah Constitution, [t]he Virginia Supreme Court stated:

Whether these hospitals are "conducted not for profit, but exclusively as charities," within the meaning of the constitutional provision, depends not upon the number of patients who are treated free of charge, but the nature of the institutions, and the purpose of their operations. The nature of these institutions, the purpose and use to which they are put, all combine to show that they are operated "exclusively as charities." . . .

The legal concept of charity does not require, as the majority apparently requires, that a hospital incur a deficit to qualify as a charitable institution. Charitable hospitals need not be self-liquidating. . . . More importantly, there is in fact a very substantial imbalance between the total cost of the hospital care given and the revenues of the hospital in this case, which is so apparent from the record as to be undeniable.

The basic facts are not disputed. Both hospitals render wholly free patient services in substantial amounts. In addition, they subsidize the cost of hospital services to the poor, the elderly, and workers whose hospital bills are paid only in part by worker's compensation. During the years 1978-80, Utah Valley Hospital rendered wholly free services to indigents in the amount of $200,000, and in each of those years the amount increased substantially over the preceding year. During the same period, the hospital subsidized services rendered to Medicare, Medicaid, and worker's compensation patients in the amount of $3,174,024. The corresponding figures for American Fork Hospital were $39,906 in indigent care and $421,306 for subsidization of Medicare, Medicaid, and worker's compensation benefits. . . .

The majority argues that for-profit hospitals also have bad debts. That is, of course, true, but it completely evades the central point. Unlike for-profit hospitals, Utah Valley and American Fork have a policy against turning away indigent patients. . . .

HOWE, Justice (dissenting):

I dissent. The views of the majority on charitable hospitals are without precedent in the jurisprudence of this country. The majority introduces confusion and mischief into an area of the law that has been well settled in this state for at least 50 years and strips from all nonprofit hospitals the exemption they have had over that span of time. The result will be that each hospital seeking an exemption must demonstrate ultimately to this Court the extent of its almsgiving. . . .

The annotation at 37 A.L.R.3d 1223 contains cases spanning from the last century to the present time where the issue of paying patients was raised, but in which it was held not disqualifying as a charity. Courts long ago fully considered and firmly rejected the notion now advanced by the majority that the charitable character of a hospital is determined by the quantity of its almsgiving. They do not cite a single case where an exemption was denied for insufficiency in quantity of free care. . . .

In Harvard Community Health Plan, Inc. v. Board of Assessors of Cambridge, 384 Mass. 536, 427 N.E.2d 1159 (1981), a nonprofit health clinic that provided prepaid comprehensive health care services for its subscribers sought a charitable exemption on its building. The court remarked:

> However, we recognize too that major changes in the area of health care, especially in modes of operation and financing, have necessitated changes as well in definitional predicates. The term "charitable," as applied to health care facilities, has been broadened since earlier times, when it was limited mainly to almshouses for the poor. As a result, the promotion of health, whether through the provision of health care or through medical education and research, is today generally seen as a charitable purpose. A. Scott [Trusts §§368, 372]; G. T. Bogert, Trusts & Trustees §374 (rev. 2d ed. 1977). Such a purpose is separate and distinct from the relief of poverty, and no health organization need engage in "almsgiving" in order to qualify for exemption.

Id., 384 Mass. at 542-43, 427 N.E.2d at 1163 (citations omitted).

Light, Corporate Medicine for Profit
255 Scientific American 38 (1986)

A new era in American health care can be said to date from 1968. In that year Thomas F. Frist and Jack C. Massey — the former a Nashville doctor and the latter the man who had made Kentucky Fried Chicken into a national chain — formed the Hospital Corporation of America (HCA). . . . HCA soon began acquiring [hundreds of] additional hospitals, and it is now the country's largest investor-owned hospital chain. . . . Today about a third of the country's acute-care hospitals belong to multi-unit systems. Investor-owned corporations have also established themselves in many other areas of health care, ranging from primary-care clinics to specialized referral centers. It is in the guise of for-profit chains, however, that the corporate presence in health care provokes the most debate.

The juxtaposition of the commercial ethos familiar in fast-food chains with hospital care challenges traditional images of medicine as the embodiment of humane service and even charity. The investor-owned chains have elicited a number of specific criticisms . . . : commercial considerations could undermine the responsibility of doctors toward their patients, conceivably leading to unnecessary tests and procedures or — given other financial incentives — to inadequate treatment. Critics of for-profit chains also suspect they drive up the cost of health care, reduce its quality, neglect teaching and research and reject those who cannot pay for treatment. . . . The failings of the for-profit hospitals are not theirs alone, however. Those hospitals are only the purest expression of a commercialism that has come to pervade American medicine.

NOTES

The Corporate Ethos in Medicine

The ongoing debate over the relative merits of the proprietary versus the voluntary form of organization in health care has produced the following stimulating literature: Institute of Medicine, For-Profit Enterprise in Health Care (B. Gray ed. 1986); P. Starr, The Social Transformation of American Medicine, Chapter 5 (1982); Relman & Reinhardt, Debating For-Profit Health Care and the Ethics of Physicians, 5 Health Affairs, Summer 1986, at 2; Schlesinger, Marmor & Smithey, Nonprofit and For-Profit Medical Care: Shifting Roles and Implications for Health Policy, J. Health Pol., Poly. & Law 427 (1987); Marmor, Schlesinger & Smithey, A New Look at Nonprofits: Health Care Policy in a Competitive Age, 3 Yale J. Reg. 313 (1986); Relman, The New Medical-Industrial Complex, 303 New Eng. J. Med. 963 (1980).

The following exchange gives a glimpse of the highly charged nature of this debate:

> Nonprofit hospitals . . . receive billions of dollars annually in subsidies from the rest of us taxpayers through various tax exemptions. Our research showed that nonprofit hospital chains did not provide benefits to society that justified this multibillion dollar gift. When compared with for-profits, the nonprofit hospital chains had the same prices and the same level of access for patients with no or low levels of health insurance. Moreover, they had higher costs, more employees, less efficient use of beds, and much older capital than for-profits. The net result was that the nonprofits performed less and cost much more — billions of dollars more!

Herzlinger, An Author Replies, 65 Harv. Bus. Rev., March-April 1987, at 135, replying in support of Herzlinger & Krasker, Who Profits from Nonprofits?, 65 Harv. Bus. Rev. at 93 (Jan.-Feb. 1987) (nonprofits "do more to maximize the welfare of the physicians who are their main consumers").

Uwe Reinhardt, a leading health economist, responds: "[T]his study is a truly shoddy statistical analysis. . . . The author's bias for privatization screams out from every page of the study. I'm concerned

V. Charitable Tax Exemption 633

by the apparent attempt to propagate personal bias in the guise of science." N.Y. Times, April 2, 1987, p. 32, col. 3.

Harding Hospital, Inc. v. United States
505 F.2d 1068 (6th Cir. 1974)

PHILLIPS, Chief Judge.

The sole issue presented in this appeal is whether Harding Hospital, Inc. (the Hospital) qualified under 501(c)(3) of the Internal Revenue Code of 1954 as an organization exempt from federal income taxes during the years 1966, 1967 and 1968. The District Court determined, inter alia, that the Hospital was not operated exclusively for charitable purposes and denied the exemption. We affirm.

I . . .

The Hospital, a nationally recognized psychiatric institution, treats mental and nervous diseases. It utilizes a method of treatment known as milieu therapy in which a patient's total environment is controlled on an around-the-clock basis and structured toward rehabilitation.

The Hospital was originally a corporation for profit. In December 1961, its articles of incorporation were amended to adopt its present name and to qualify under Ohio law as a corporation not for profit. . . . Before amending its articles of incorporation, the Hospital had a contract with a medical partnership composed of seven doctors. This medical partnership performed all the psychiatric treatment on ninety to ninety-five per cent of the patients admitted to the Hospital. Immediately after the Hospital's change in status in 1962, the medical partnership was incorporated as the Harding-Evans Medical Associates, Inc. (the Associates).

Starting in 1962, and for the years in question, the Hospital entered into contracts with the Associates whereby the Associates provided medical supervision in the Hospital, teaching and supervision in the residency and other training programs, and medical service to the Hospital's indigent patients without a charge or at a reduced rate. For these services, the Hospital paid the Associates an annual amount of $25,000. This amount was raised to $35,000 as of July 1, 1968. Further, the agreement provided that the Associates were to pay the Hospital $1000 per month as rental for facilities, equipment and business office services. This rental was increased to $35,000 per year as of January 1, 1965. It subsequently was lowered to $15,000 per year as of July 1, 1968, at the same time that the amount which the Hospital paid the Associates for medical supervision was increased from $25,000 to $35,000.

Since 1963, individuals not connected with the Associates have constituted a majority of the Board of Trustees of the Hospital. During the years in question, the Board consisted of nine members, only two of whom had any connection with the Associates of the Hospital prior to the 1961 reorganization.

The Harding-Evans Foundation (the Foundation) was set up in 1959 and is an entity separate from the Hospital and the Associates. The Foundation is a tax exempt organization, the principal activity of which is to provide a residency program in the field of psychiatry for the physicians. The Foundation collects charitable funds and expends them on the residency training program at the Hospital.

II

Since the early days of federal income tax law, corporations organized and operated exclusively for charitable, religious, educational and certain other purposes have been accorded exemption from the tax. Act of Oct. 3, 1913, c. 16, II, G, 38 Stat. 172. The exemption is conferred in recognition of the benefit which the public derives from the activities of such organizations. See, e.g., Trinidad v. Sagrada Orden, 263 U.S. 578, 581, 44 S. Ct. 204, 68 L. Ed. 458 (1924); St. Louis Union Trust Co. v. United States, 374 F.2d 427, 432 (8th Cir. 1967).

> [T]he Government is compensated for the loss of revenue (caused by the exemption) by its relief from financial burden which would otherwise have to be met by appropriations from public funds, and by the benefits resulting from the promotion of the general welfare.

H. Rep. No. 1860, 75th Cong., 3d Sess., p.19 (1939-1 Cum. Bull. (Part 2) 728, 742). . . .

Section 501(a) of the Code provides that the following organizations, which are listed in 501(c)(3), are exempt from federal income taxation:

> Corporations . . . organized and operated exclusively for religious, charitable, scientific, testing for public safety, literary, or educational purposes, or for the prevention of cruelty to children or animals, no part of the net earnings of which inures to the benefit of any private shareholder or individual, no substantial part of the activities of which is carrying on propaganda, or otherwise attempting, to influence legislation, and which does not participate in, or intervene in (including the publishing or distributing of statements), any political campaign on behalf of any candidate for public office.

In the context of the present case, this section essentially imposes three requirements for exemption: 1) the corporation must be organized and operated exclusively for charitable purposes; 2) no part of its net earnings may inure to the benefit of a private individual

V. Charitable Tax Exemption

or shareholder; and 3) it cannot engage in certain lobbying and political activities. The Government stipulated that the Hospital did not offend the third requirement for exemption. . . .

The Commissioner's standards relative to when a hospital is exempt under 501(c)(3) are set forth in Rev. Rul. 56-185, 1956-1 Cum. Bull. 202, which provides in pertinent part:

> In order for a hospital to establish that it is exempt as a public charitable organization within the contemplation of section 501(c)(3), it must, among other things, show that it meets the following general requirements: . . . .
> 2. It must be operated to the extent of its financial ability for those not able to pay for the services rendered and not exclusively for those who are able and expected to pay. . . .
> 3. It must not restrict the use of its facilities to a particular group of physicians and surgeons, such as a medical partnership or association, to the exclusion of all other qualified doctors. Such limitation on the use of hospital facilities is inconsistent with the public service concept inherent in section 501(c)(3) and the prohibition against the inurement of benefits to private shareholders or individuals. . . .
> 4. Its net earnings must not inure directly or indirectly to the benefit of any private shareholder or individual. This includes the use by or benefit to its members of its earnings by way of a distribution of profits, the payment of excessive rents or excessive salaries, or the use of its facilities to serve their private interests. . . .

The Commissioner modified Rev. Rul. 56-185, especially the second numbered paragraph thereof, in Rev. Rul. 69-545, 1969-2 Cum. Bull. 117. There the Commissioner held that Hospital A as described therein qualified as a tax exempt charitable hospital even though it did not provide free or reduced rate services to indigents other than emergency care. Rev. Rul. 69-545 provides in part:

> In the general law of charity, the promotion of health is considered to be a charitable purpose. Restatement (Second), Trusts, sec. 368 and sec. 372; IV Scott on Trusts (3rd ed. 1967), sec. 368 and Sec. 372. A nonprofit organization whose purpose and activity are providing hospital care is promoting health and may, therefore, qualify as organized and operated in furtherance of a charitable purpose. If it meets the other requirements of section 501(c)(3) of the Code, it will qualify for exemption from Federal income tax under section 501(a).
> Since the purpose and activity of Hospital A, apart from its related educational and research activities and purposes, are providing hospital care on a nonprofit basis for members of its community, it is organized and operated in furtherance of a purpose considered "charitable" in the generally accepted legal sense of that term. The promotion of health, like the relief of poverty and the advancement of education and

religion, is one of the purposes in the general law of charity that is deemed beneficial to the community as a whole even though the class of beneficiaries eligible to receive a direct benefit from its activities does not include all members of the community, such as indigent members of the community, provided that the class is not so small that its relief is not of benefit to the community. Restatement (Second), Trusts, sec. 368, comment (b) and sec. 372, comments (b) and (c); IV Scott on Trusts (3rd ed. 1967), sec. 368 and sec. 372.2. By operating an emergency room open to all persons and by providing hospital care for all those persons in the community able to pay the cost thereof either directly or through third party reimbursement, Hospital A is promoting the health of a class of persons that is broad enough to benefit the community.

The fact that Hospital A operates at an annual surplus of receipts over disbursements does not preclude its exemption. By using its surplus funds to improve the quality of patient care, expand its facilities, and advance its medical training, education, and research programs, the hospital is operating in furtherance of its exempt purposes. . . . Revenue Ruling 56-185 is hereby modified to remove therefrom the requirements relating to caring for patients without charge or at rates below cost. . . .

III

Applying the above principles to the present case, we proceed to determine if the District Court was correct in holding that the Hospital "was operated almost exclusively for the benefit of the members of the . . . Associates and was not operated exclusively for charitable purposes." 358 F. Supp. at 814. . . . Based on the five factors set forth below, we hold that the Hospital was not entitled to tax exemption under 501(c)(3) during the years in question. We do not single out any one or combination of these factors as the consideration crucial to our holding. We conclude only that all these factors, as they occurred in the aggregate in this case, require denying the appellant Hospital the tax exemption for the years in question.

1) There is insufficient evidence that the appellant Hospital for the years in question "held itself out to the public even in a limited way as a charitable institution." Sonora Community Hospital, supra, 46 T.C. at 526. Insofar as the record reveals, the only significant charitable donations which the Hospital received during the years in question, if any, were contributions of Hospital notes held by the Associates.

2) The Hospital did not have a specific plan or policy for the treatment of charity patients during the years in question. Rather, as its Medical Director admitted, practically all patients presented themselves as paying patients and only when their funds were exhausted did the Hospital treat them on a charitable basis. . . .

3) Since the doctors who were members of the Associates treated between ninety and ninety-five per cent of the patients admitted to

the Hospital, they derived substantial benefit from the existence and operation of the Hospital. This was the primary source of the doctors' professional income. Although the Hospital did not pay over any of its net earnings to the Associates, except for the annual sum for supervision, this virtual monopoly by the Associates of the patients permitted benefits to inure to the Associates within the intendment of the statute. Sonora Community Hospital, supra, 46 T.C. at 526; 6 Mertens, Law of Federal Income Taxation, 34.13, at 63-64 (1968 ed.).

4) Associates also benefitted from the agreement with the Hospital whereby the Associates paid $35,000 annually as rental for office space, equipment, and business office services. See the fourth requirement of Rev. Rul. 56-185. The $35,000 amount was reduced to $15,000 as of July 1, 1968. . . .

The Hospital introduced the testimony of an appraiser who indicated, in sum, that the $35,000 figure was a fair rental for the office space. That essentially meant that the Associates were not adequately compensating the Hospital for the use of the equipment and business office services (including secretarial assistance). Further, when the annual rental was reduced to $15,000, the Associates were not adequately compensating the Hospital for office space alone.

5) The Associates also received a private benefit from the agreement whereby the Hospital paid an annual sum of either $25,000 or $35,000 to the Associates for hospital supervision. . . .

On the basis of these five factors, the judgment of the District Court is affirmed.

NOTES

The Basis for Tax Exemption

1. In reviewing these materials, it may be helpful to distinguish among three different bases for charitable status: (1) relief of poverty; (2) promotion of health; and (3) provision of hospital facilities.

2. The 1969 revenue ruling extending federal tax exemption to hospitals that provide charity care only in the emergency room was premised on a view that "[t]hanks to Medicare, Medicaid, and numerous other public and private mechanisms for financing care for the indigent and medically indigent, in a few years free hospital care will approach the vanishing point." A. Somers, supra, at 41. See Godfrey, Federal Income Tax Exemption for Private Hospitals, 36 Fordham L. Rev. 747 (1968). The materials in Chapter 6.II.C and E explore whether this optimism was well founded. Regardless, the IRS further liberalized its free care policy in 1983, ruling that even free emergency services are unnecessary if an emergency room isn't needed in the community or if the hospital is a specialized one that

offers limited treatment (for instance, eye hospitals or cancer hospitals). Rev. Rul. 83-187. See Milligan, Provision of Uncompensated Care in American Hospitals: The Role of the Tax Code, 31 Cath. Law. 7 (1987). The IRS maintains a similar position with respect to nursing homes. Rev. Rul. 72-124.

3. Rumblings of possible legislative change have emanated from Washington:

> [Congressman Stark], a key member of a Congressional tax-writing committee, said today that the Federal tax exemption for nonprofit hospitals was probably unwarranted because they generally did not provide substantial amounts of charitable care. [T]he American Hospital Association rejected Mr. Stark's criticism. "It is government's responsibility to take care of the poor and the needy. . . . In return for their tax exemption, nonprofit hospitals provide a means to state and local government to provide for the poor." . . . Mr. Stark, a Democrat, said it was unlikely that Congress would revoke the tax exemption for nonprofit hospitals. But he said such hospitals should be required to demonstrate the benefits they provide to the community through charitable care.

New York Times, July 15, 1987, at A21.

4. Attempts by poor patients to challenge the federal position fail for lack of standing. See, for instance, Eastern Kentucky Welfare Rights Organization v. Simon, 426 U.S. 26 (1976). It is for this reason that state tax exemption has assumed much greater prominence in the past few years. For an overview of state law, see Perkins & Dowell, Developments Regarding the Charitable Tax Exemption of Hospitals, 19 Clearinghouse Rev. 472 (1985). The following treatises cover tax exemption generally under both federal and state law: Exempt Organization Reporter (CCH); Tax Exempt Organizations (PH); A. Southwick, The Law of Hospital and Health Care Administration, Chapter 5 (2d ed. 1988); B. Hopkins, The Law of Tax-Exempt Organizations (5th ed. 1987); M. Phelan, Nonprofit Enterprises: Law and Taxation (1985); Bromberg, The Charitable Hospital, 20 Cath. U.L. Rev. 237 (1970). Federal tax law is further discussed in the sources cited throughout these notes. There is also an extensive practitioner-oriented literature in trade journals such as Hospitals and Healthcare Financial Management.

5. The *Utah County* holding reflects a distinctly minority view. It has recently been rejected in Vermont, Medical Center Hospital v. City of Burlington, 566 A.2d 1352 (Vt. 1989) (exemption upheld despite only 1 percent free care), and in Tennessee, Downtown Hosp. Assoc. v. Tennessee State Board of Equalization, 760 S.W.2d 954 (Tenn. App. 1988). See also West Allegheny Hospital v. Board of Property Assess., 455 A.2d 1170 (Pa. 1982); Hall & Colombo, The Charitable Status of Nonprofit Hospitals: Toward a Donative Theory

V. Charitable Tax Exemption

of Tax Exemption (forthcoming); Mancino, Income Tax Exemption of the Contemporary Nonprofit Hospital, 32 St. Louis U.L.J. 1015 (1988).

However, denials of tax exemption based on a low volume of free care have occurred more frequently for *non*hospital health care enterprises. See, e.g., Highland Park Hospital v. State, 507 N.E.2d 1331 (Ill. App. 1987) (immediate care center and laboratory denied exemption); Grand Prairie Hospital Authority v. Dallas County Appraisal Dist., 730 S.W.2d 849 (Tex. App. 1987) (medical office building denied exemption); Share v. Commissioner, 363 N.W.2d 47 (Minn. 1985) (HMO denied exemption). Likewise, federal tax policy is also much more demanding on HMOs. The IRS originally took the position that they were private membership organizations and therefore did not serve the community at large. The tax court rejected this absolute stance in Sound Health Assoc. v. Commnr., 71 Tax Ct. 158 (1978), but the service still takes a narrow view of when HMOs meet the community benefit and no-private-inurement standards. See id. (HMO granted exemption, but only because it had a plan for reduced-fee treatment of indigent patients and its board was composed of community leaders); G.C.M. 38894 (Sept. 9, 1982) (outlining requirements for HMO exemption). The Service is likewise more demanding of nursing homes than hospitals, by forbidding them to discontinue care for patients whose funds run out. Is there any reason to distinguish between the charitable status of inpatient versus outpatient health care services, or hospital versus other institutional services?

Inurement to Private Benefit and Unrelated Business Income

6. The private benefit prohibition in §501(c) is the greatest danger to tax exempt status: "*no* part of the [hospital's] net earnings [may] inure[ ] to the private benefit of *any* private shareholder or individual" (emphasis added). Short of compelling cases such as *Harding Hospital*, what hospital business arrangements potentially threaten total loss of tax exemption? Consider the validity of each of the following activities under recent IRS position statements:

(a) In order to attract physicians to an understaffed, rural area, a hospital guarantees physicians a minimum annual income of $60,000 for the first two years. See General Counsel Memorandum 39498 (Jan. 28, 1986) ("may constitute" private inurement, depending on reasonableness and necessity of the amount in the individual case). Compare General Counsel Memorandum 39598 (Dec. 8, 1986) (rental of medical office building space at less than fair market value threatens exempt status).

(b) A hospital acts as a general partner with physicians in a venture to construct and operate a medical office building; in doing so, it contributes substantial capital and places its assets at risk. See General Counsel Memorandum 39546 (possibly valid, but requires a highly individualized determination); Hopkins & Beckwith, The Federal Tax Law of Hospitals: Basic Principles and Current Developments, 24 Duquesne L. Rev. 691, 731-733 (1985); Myre, Significant Tax Issues in Hospital Related Joint Ventures, 75 Ken. L.J. 559 (1987); Note, The Participation of Charities in Limited Partnerships, 93 Yale L.J. 1355 (1984).

(c) Instead of hiring an administrative staff, a hospital contracts with an outside firm for all of its management services in exchange for 15 percent of net profits. See Bromberg & Teplitzky, Tangling with Tax Law, 57 Hospitals, March 1, 1983, at 69, 78 ("management contracts based on a percentage of hospital *net* earnings [as opposed to a flat fee or a percentage of *gross* revenues] should be avoided at all costs").

(d) A hospital compensates an exclusively-retained radiologist with 50 percent of the radiology department's net profits. Bromberg & Teplitzky, supra, at 78 ("On its face, such a method could be regarded as inurement. . . . Nevertheless, in the last 20 years, the IRS has not, to our knowledge, challenged such compensation arrangements."); Rev. Rul. 69-383 (valid, if arm's-length).

7. A related concern is to what extent hospitals generate "unrelated business income," that is, income from activities that are not connected with their exempt functions. There are two consequences to earning such income:

(1) Even if earned at relatively low levels, it is subject to tax, a so-called "unrelated business income tax" (UBIT). I.R.C. §§511-513.

(2) If such income constitutes a substantial portion of the entity's receipts, it may threaten the entire exemption. See, for instance, General Counsel Memorandum 39684 (Sept. 28, 1984) (hospital subsidiary that provided purchasing and data processing services to nonexempt hospitals lost exemption because of "substantial, nonexempt commercial purpose").

8. The major decision applying the unrelated business income tax to hospital operations is Carle Foundation v. United States, 611 F.2d 1192 (7th Cir. 1980). It sets forth the general rule that income from health services to *non*hospital patients is unrelated to the insti-

tution's exempt function. Thus, for instance, a nonprofit hospital's pharmacy sales to outpatients are taxable, even if sold to patients of physicians on the medical staff with offices in the hospital's own building, because these are not hospital patients. Why is it necessary to define the hospital's exempt function so narrowly? Why not conceive of the hospital's purpose as providing health care services generally to the community at large? For a criticism of this position, see Colombo, Are Associations of Doctors Tax Exempt? Analyzing Inconsistencies in the Tax Exemption of Health Care Providers, 9 Va. Tax Rev. 469 (1990). The Service exempts pharmacy and laboratory sales to nonpatients only in "unique circumstances" where the hospital is the only available source for the service to nonhospital patients. Rev. Rul. 85-110. See also Hi-Plains Hospital v. U.S., 670 F.2d 528 (5th Cir. 1982) (laboratory services for physicians' private patients produce related income if the services are necessary to attract doctors to underserved rural area).

9. The statute (I.R.C. §513(a)) excludes from its definition of "unrelated trade or business" that which is "carried on . . . by the organization primarily for the convenience of its . . . members, patients, or employees." Thus, for instance, it might be argued that sales by hospital gift shops and cafeterias, and receipts by the hospital parking garage, are not taxable because of their convenience function. The Service peculiarly has refrained from this straightforward reasoning and instead has held such receipts not taxable under a much more strained rationale: they are directly related to the hospital's exemption function (and therefore need not fall within the convenience exception) because gift shop and cafeteria sales encourage doctors to remain on the premises during their breaks so that they are more available for emergency calls, and parking lots serve the therapeutic function of encouraging visitors. Rev. Ruls. 69-463 (revenue from medical office building); 69-267 (gift shop); 69-268 (cafeteria); 69-269 (parking lot).

Could the exception for convenience to members be used to undermine the holding of *Carle Foundation* by arguing that pharmacy sales to doctors' office patients are for the convenience of the "members" of the hospital's medical staff? St. Luke's Hospital v. United States, 474 F. Supp. 85, 92-93 (W.D. Mo. 1980) (yes). The Service has refused to accept this view, however, reasoning that, in the context of nonprofit institutions, "members" has a different meaning. Rev. Rul. 85-109. For further discussion of these issues, see Comment, Unrelated Trade or Business Income and Hospitals, 19 Loy. U.L.J. 1318 (1988); Janich & Sor, When is an Activity "Substantially Related" to a Health Care Institution's Tax-exempt Purpose? [Parts I & II], 20 Hosp. Law 145, 193 (1987); Hopkins & Beckwith, supra, 24 Duquesne L. Rev. at 714-717; Bromberg, Tax Problems of the Hospital, in Representing Health Care Facilities 179-182 (Strickler & Ballard eds. 1981).

10. Hospitals sometimes find it efficient to operate certain internal functions such as laundry services on a shared, cooperative basis with other hospitals. Considerable attention has been given to whether such supporting enterprises are themselves tax exempt. Ordinarily, the answer would be no because, while laundry services within a hospital clearly are related to the hospital's function, standing alone they do not constitute a charitable enterprise. However, code section 501(e) provides a special exemption for "cooperative hospital service organizations" that perform the following services for tax-exempt hospitals: "data processing, purchasing, warehousing, billing and collection, food, clinical, industrial engineering, laboratory, printing, communications, record center, and personnel." Owing to effective lobbying from commercial laundries, laundry services are notably absent from this list, though. HCSC-Laundry v. U.S., 450 U.S. 1 (1981).

Hospital Reorganization

11. According to one account, a third of U.S. hospitals have undergone corporate restructuring since 1979. Alexander & Orlikoff, Hospital Corporation Restructuring Gains Widespread Acceptance, Trustee, Jan. 1987, at 16. The predominate pattern is to segregate various hospital functions into separate entities, some for-profit and some nonprofit, all under the auspices of a parent holding company. The following structure (discussed in G.C.M. 39508 infra) is representative:

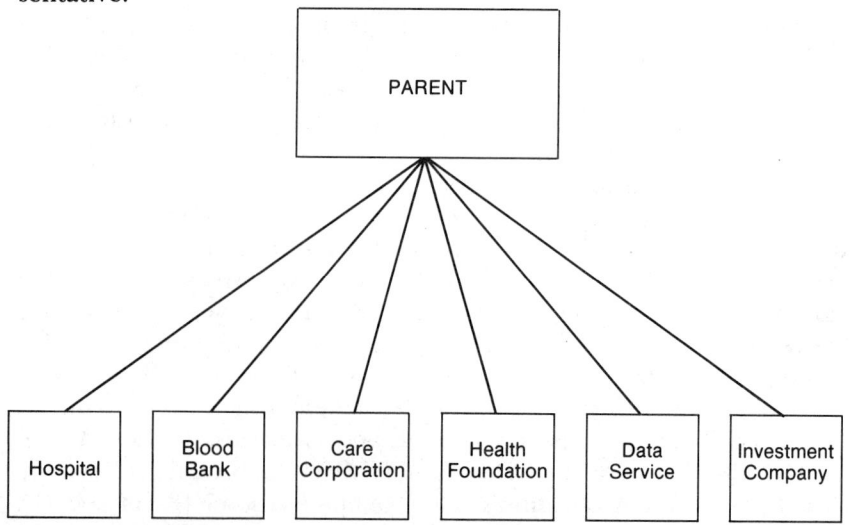

Figure 7.1 Reorganized Hospital System Chart

V. Charitable Tax Exemption   643

The wave of hospital reorganizations has been prompted by a variety of complex and sometimes conflicting regulatory and economic forces. For example, a medical office building (MOB) might be developed through a separate corporation in order to avoid threatening a hospital's exempt status. On the other hand, it might be more advantageous to operate an MOB in-house in order to shelter its revenues as related income. Tax laws are not the only relevant considerations. Hospitals must also consider the impact of certificate of need regulation and government reimbursement under Medicare or Medicaid. For further consideration, see AHA, Tax Advisory Group, 22 J. Health & Hosp. L. 3 (1989); Mancino, Income Tax Exemption of the Contemporary Nonprofit Hospital, 32 St. Louis U.L.J. 1015 (1988); Hopkins & Beckwith, supra, 24 Duquesne L. Rev. at 734-736; Beautyman & Thallner, Does Hospital Restructuring Make Sense Today?, 20 Hosp. Law 121 (1987); Squires, Corporate Restructuring of Tax-Exempt Hospitals: The Bastardization of the Tax-Exempt Concept, 14 L. Med. & Health Care 66 (1986); McCoy, Health Care and the Tax Law: Reorganizations, Structural Changes, and Other Contemporary Problems of Tax-Exempt Hospitals, 44 N.Y.U. Instit. Fed. Tax., ch. 58; Hoch, Corporate Reorganization: Nonprofit Tax-Exempt Hospitals, 11 Topics in Health Care Financing 1 (Fall 1984); General Counsel Memorandum 39508 (May 28, 1986); General Counsel Memorandum 39598 (Dec. 8, 1986).

12. As a review problem, analyze under federal tax law the situation described in the following newspaper article:

> Since 1984, Day Kimball Hospital, on the outskirts of the old mill town of Putnam, Conn., has provided most of the health care for the largely rural northwestern corner of the state. These days, corporate offshoots of the hospital are providing something else: a commercial cleaning business for schools and factories, a computerized billing service for doctors in the area, and a catering business that uses the hospital's kitchen at off-hours to prepare food for wedding receptions and parties. . . . To counter a continuing decline in patient admissions and stricter limits on payments for hospital care from insurers and Government programs, such as Medicare, hospitals are reorganizing to spawn an array of new ventures to generate more income. . . . The most common change, officials said, has been the creation of a parent or holding company, with the nonprofit hospital becoming a separate subsidiary to preserve its tax-exempt status and other business ventures grouped into separate divisions, which pay taxes on any profits that flow to the corporate parent and back to the hospital.

N.Y. Times, Jan. 25, 1987, at 1.

Other examples the article cites are athletic clubs, day care centers, and frozen food for the elderly. If these new ventures were undertaken in-house, would any qualify as related income? What are the potential tax risks of engaging in these businesses through separate subsidiaries? (Suppose physicians were allowed to participate as investors and the hospital contributed substantial capital to get the venture off the ground.) Would any of these ventures be able to qualify for tax exemption independently? Does the answer depend on how much of their services they give away for free?

VI. ANTITRUST MERGER LAW

INTRODUCTORY NOTE

Health Care Antitrust Law

Until the 1980s, the health care industry was remarkably complacent about the antitrust laws. Physicians openly threatened boycotts to enforce their interests; hospitals had few qualms about dividing markets with each other; and the AMA ruled supreme over the economics and organization of medical practice. No one thought to challenge this conduct because it was considered that the learned professions did not engage in the type of trade that is subject to antitrust scrutiny, that health care is an inherently local enterprise not subject to federal jurisdiction, and that lofty considerations of ethical practice and quality of care removed health care decision making from base concerns of economic efficiency.

However, Supreme Court decisions over the past decade have systematically upset these assumptions. In Goldfarb v. Virginia State Bar, 421 U.S. 773, 787 (1975), the Court held that there was no antitrust exemption for professionals: "The nature of an occupation, standing alone, does not provide sanctuary from the Sherman Act." In Hospital Building Company v. Trustees of Rex Hospital, 425 U.S. 738 (1976), the Court held that hospital activities can meet the interstate commerce prerequisite to antitrust jurisdiction. And in American Medical Association v. Federal Trade Association, 455 U.S. 676 (1982), the Supreme Court upheld without opinion an injunction against the AMA's using its code of professional ethics to ban physician advertising and certain physician contractual arrangements. 94 F.T.C. 701 (1979), *enforced*, 638 F.2d 443 (2d Cir. 1980).

The result of exposing an entire industry that antitrust law once essentially bypassed has been an explosion of litigation and counseling. Health care antitrust cases are popping up all over the landscape faster than dandelions after a spring rain. National Health Lawyers Association, Antitrust Law Survey 1984-1986 (50 to 60 pending cases);

VI. Antitrust Merger Law   645

ABA Section of Antitrust Laws, Compendium of Antitrust/Health Care Cases (1986) (digesting 205 cases decided by Sept. 1984). Law firms are creating new health care practice groups, and old antitrust litigators have found an area of revival in an otherwise sluggish specialty.

Antitrust liability is a frightening prospect to physicians and hospital administrators. Violations can be privately enforced in civil damage actions brought by injured plaintiffs in which malpractice insurance rarely covers the exposure or defends the action; defendants face the possibility of treble damages; and losing defendants must pay the plaintiff's attorney fees. Enforcement authority is also lodged in the Federal Trade Commission, which is empowered to bring civil injunction actions, and in the Department of Justice, which, in addition, may prosecute criminal violations.

It is not possible in the course of this survey text to cover the entirety of a field as complex as health care antitrust.* Nevertheless, materials in this chapter and elsewhere expose the uninitiated reader to some basic principles governing the more prominent areas of antitrust litigation. Chapter 6.I.C examines group boycott law in the context of physician exclusion from hospital medical staffs. Chapter 8.III.C contains a discussion of the price-fixing ramifications of structuring Preferred Provider Organizations and other insurance innovations. The following materials explore antitrust merger doctrine as applied to various health care ventures.

Hospital Corporation of America v. Federal Trade Commission
807 F.2d 1381 (7th Cir.), *cert. denied*, 481 U.S. 1038 (1986)

POSNER, Circuit Judge. Hospital Corporation of America ["HCA"], the largest proprietary hospital chain in the United States, asks us to set aside the decision by the Federal Trade Commission that it violated section 7 of the Clayton Act, as amended, 15 U.S.C. §18,† by the acquisition in 1981 and 1982 of two corporations, Hospital Affiliates

---

* For a more comprehensive overview of health care antitrust, see Symposium, Antitrust and Health Care, 51 L. & Contemp. Prob., No. 2 (Spring 1988); ABA Health Care Committee, Section of Antitrust Law, The Antitrust Health Care Handbook (1988); Miles & Philip, Hospitals Caught in an Antitrust Net: An Overview, 24 Duquesne L. Rev. 489-689 (1985), and the following symposia: XIV Am. J.L. & Med., Nos. 2 & 3 (1988); 51 Law & Contemp. Prob., No. 2 (1988); Antitrust Bull., Summer 1984; and St. Louis U.L.J., April 1982.

† [Ed. note: "No person engaged in commerce shall acquire . . . the stock . . . or assets of another person engaged also in commerce, . . . where . . . the effect of such acquisition may be substantially to lessen competition, or to tend to create a monopoly."]

International, Inc. and Health Care Corporation. Before these acquisitions (which cost Hospital Corporation almost $700 million), Hospital Corporation had owned one hospital in Chattanooga, Tennessee. The acquisitions gave it ownership of two more. In addition, pursuant to the terms of the acquisitions it assumed contracts, both with four-year terms, that Hospital Affiliates International had made to manage two other Chattanooga-area hospitals. So after the acquisitions Hospital Corporation owned or managed 5 of the 11 hospitals in the area. . . .

If all the hospitals brought under common ownership or control by the two challenged acquisitions are treated as a single entity, the acquisitions raised Hospital Corporation's market share in the Chattanooga area from 14 percent to 26 percent. This made it the second largest provider of hospital services in a highly concentrated market where the four largest firms together had a 91 percent market share compared to 79 percent before the acquisitions. . . .

The Clayton Act allows Hospital Corporation to seek judicial review of the Commission's order in any circuit in which it does business, see 15 U.S.C. §21(c), and for unexplained reasons it has chosen this circuit. . . . Our only function is to determine whether the Commission's analysis of the probable effects of these acquisitions on hospital competition in Chattanooga is so implausible, so feebly supported by the record, that it flunks even the deferential test of substantial evidence. . . .

[T]he ultimate issue is whether the challenged acquisition is likely to facilitate collusion. In this perspective the acquisition of a competitor has no economic significance in itself; the worry is that it may enable the acquiring firm to cooperate (or cooperate better) with other leading competitors on reducing or limiting output, thereby pushing up the market price. . . . There is plenty of evidence to support the Commission's prediction of adverse competitive effect in this case; whether we might have come up with a different prediction on our own is irrelevant.

The acquisitions reduced the number of competing hospitals in the Chattanooga market from 11 to 7. . . . The reduction in the number of competitors is significant in assessing the competitive vitality of the Chattanooga hospital market. The fewer competitors there are in a market, the easier it is for them to coordinate their pricing without committing detectable violations of section 1 of the Sherman Act, which forbids price fixing. This would not be very important if the four competitors eliminated by the acquisitions in this case had been insignificant, but they were not; they accounted in the aggregate for 12 percent of the sales of the market. As a result of the acquisitions the four largest firms came to control virtually the whole market,

VI. Antitrust Merger Law

and the problem of coordination was therefore reduced to one of coordination among these four.

Moreover, both the ability of the remaining firms to expand their output should the big four reduce their own output in order to raise the market price (and, by expanding, to offset the leading firms' restriction of their own output), and the ability of outsiders to come in and build completely new hospitals, are reduced by Tennessee's certificate-of-need law. Any addition to hospital capacity must be approved by a state agency. The parties disagree over whether this law, as actually enforced, inhibits the expansion of hospital capacity. . . . At least the certificate of need law would enable [colluders] to delay any competitive sally by a noncolluding competitor. Or so the Commission could conclude (a refrain we shall now stop repeating). . . .

All this would be of little moment if, in the event that hospital prices in Chattanooga rose above the competitive level, persons desiring hospital services in Chattanooga would switch to hospitals in other cities, or to nonhospital providers of medical care. But this would mean that the Chattanooga hospital market . . . includes hospitals in other cities plus nonhospital providers both in Chattanooga and elsewhere; and we do not understand Hospital Corporation to be challenging the Commission's market definition, which is limited to hospital providers in Chattanooga. Anyway, these competitive alternatives are not important enough to deprive the market share statistics of competitive significance. Going to another city is out of the question in medical emergencies; and even when an operation or some other hospital service can be deferred, the patient's doctor will not (at least not for reasons of price) send the patient to another city, where the doctor is unlikely to have hospital privileges. Finally, although hospitals increasingly are providing services on an out-patient basis, thus competing with nonhospital providers of the same services (tests, minor surgical procedures, etc.), most hospital services cannot be provided by nonhospital providers; as to these, hospitals have no competition from other providers of medical care.

In showing that the challenged acquisitions gave four firms control over an entire market so that they would have little reason to fear a competitive reaction if they raised prices above the competitive level, the Commission went far to justify its prediction of probable anticompetitive effects. Maybe it need have gone no further. . . . But it did. First it pointed out that the demand for hospital services by patients and their doctors is highly inelastic under competitive conditions. This is not only because people place a high value on their safety and comfort and because many of their treatment decisions are made for them by their doctor, who doesn't pay their hospital bills; it is also because most hospital bills are paid largely by insurance companies or the federal government rather than by the patient. The less elastic the demand for a good or service is, the greater are the profits that providers can make by raising price through collusion. . . .

Second, there is a tradition, well documented in the Commission's opinion, of cooperation between competing hospitals in Chattanooga. Of course, not all forms of cooperation between competitors are bad. See, e.g., Broadcast Music, Inc. v. Columbia Broadcasting System, Inc., 441 U.S. 1, 99 S. Ct. 1551, 60 L. Ed. 2d 1 (1979). But a market in which competitors are unusually disposed to cooperate is a market prone to collusion. The history of successful cooperation establishes a precondition to effective collusion — mutual trust and forbearance. . . . Hospitals routinely exchange intimate information on prices and costs in connection with making joint applications to insurers for higher reimbursement schedules. Such cooperation may be salutary but it facilitates collusion and therefore entitles the Commission to worry even more about large horizontal acquisitions in this industry than in industries where competitors deal with each other at arm's length.

Third, hospitals are under great pressure from the federal government and the insurance companies to cut costs. One way of resisting this pressure is by presenting a united front in negotiations with the third-party payors — which indeed, as we have just said, hospitals in Chattanooga have done. See also United States v. North Dakota Hospital Assn., 640 F. Supp. 1028 (D.N.D. 1986). The fewer the independent competitors in a hospital market, the easier they will find it, by presenting an unbroken phalanx of representations and requests, to frustrate efforts to control hospital costs. This too is a form of collusion that the antitrust laws seek to discourage. . . .

All these considerations, taken together, supported — we do not say they compelled — the Commission's conclusion that the challenged acquisitions are likely to foster collusive practices, harmful to consumers, in the Chattanooga hospital market. Section 7 does not require proof that a merger or other acquisition has caused higher prices in the affected market. All that is necessary is that the merger create an appreciable danger of such consequences in the future. . . .

But of course we cannot just consider the evidence that supports the Commission's prediction. We must consider all the evidence in the record. We must therefore consider the significance of the facts, pressed on us by Hospital Corporation, that hospital services are complex and heterogeneous, that the sellers in this market are themselves heterogeneous because of differences in the services provided by the different hospitals and differences in the corporate character of the hospitals (some are publicly owned, some are proprietary, and some are private but nonprofit), [and] that the hospital industry is undergoing rapid technological and economic change, that the payors for most hospital services (Blue Cross and other insurance companies, and the federal government) are large and knowledgeable. . . .

The first fact is the least impressive. It is true that hospitals provide a variety of different services many of which are "customized" for the individual patient, but the degree to which this is true seems no greater than in other markets. . . . Different ownership structures might reduce the likelihood of collusion but this possibility is conjectural and the Commission was not required to give it conclusive weight. The adoption of the nonprofit form does not change human nature. . . . Nonprofit status . . . may make management somewhat less beady-eyed in trying to control costs. . . . But no one has shown that it makes the enterprise unwilling to cooperate in reducing competition. . . .

The concentration of the buying side of a market does inhibit collusion. . . . But as a practical matter Blue Cross could not tell its subscribers in Chattanooga that it will not reimburse them for any hospital services there because prices are too high. As a practical matter it could not, if the four major hospital owners in the city, controlling more than 90 percent of the city's hospital capacity, raised their prices, tell its subscribers that they must use the remaining hospitals — whose aggregate capacity would be completely inadequate and, for reasons discussed earlier, could not readily, or at least rapidly, be expanded — if they want to be reimbursed. . . .

The Commission's order is affirmed and enforced.

NOTES

Hospital Mergers

1. As illustrated by *HCA* and the *AMA* case mentioned above, the Federal Trade Commission has been a major impetus to extending antitrust scrutiny to the health care industry. See Costilo, Antitrust Enforcement in Health Care, 313 New Eng. J. Med. 901 (1985); Lerner, Federal Trade Commission Antitrust Activities in the Health Care Services Field, 29 Antitrust Bull. 205 (1984). A similar challenge to a hospital merger resulted in another divestiture order in American Medical International, 104 F.T.C. 177 (1984). The Department of Justice is also actively involved through its direct enforcement powers under the antitrust laws. E.g., United States v. National Medical Enterprises, Trade Cases (CCH) ¶67,640 (E.D. Cal. 1987) (hospital divestiture consent decree). It is now common to seek the approval of these agencies before undertaking a wide variety of new health care ventures.

2. Merger analysis is not restricted to hospitals. The Department of Justice announced its intention to challenge a proposed merger of two general surgery practice groups comprising ten physicians. Letter from Charles F. Rule, Assistant Attorney General, to William L. Trombetta, dated Aug. 28, 1987. Merger analysis is also relevant to the formation of a variety of joint ventures and alternative delivery systems, such as those discussed in Chapters 7.V and 8.III.C. See Thompson & Scott, Antitrust Considerations and Defenses in Reorganizing for Multi-Institutional Activities, 26 St. Louis U.L.J. 465 (1982). Consider, for instance, the applicability of the *HCA* analysis to a sole community hospital's formation of a joint venture with its medical staff to construct and operate an ambulatory surgery clinic and a freestanding emergency center.

3. Market share statistics are the primary focus of a merger analysis. The case is often won or lost based on how the market is defined. This fact is vividly portrayed by the contrasting outcomes in two simultaneous government challenges to hospital mergers in Rockford, Illinois, and Roanoke, Virginia, each of which would result in reducing the number of competitors in town from three to two. The court that allowed the merger to go forward found that the hospitals competed in a 14-county region surrounding Roanoke, Virginia and, therefore, that this merger had no threatening effect on market concentration, United States v. Carilion Health System, 1989-2 Trade Cas. (CCH) ¶68,859 (4th Cir. 1989), whereas in the Rockford case the court permanently enjoined the merger, finding (after 16 pages of analysis) that the relevant market consisted primarily of three counties. United States v. Rockford Mem. Corp., 717 F. Supp. 1251, 1261-1278 (N.D. Ill. 1989), *aff'd*, 1 Trade Cas. ¶68,978 (7th Cir. 1990). These different outcomes probably are attributable more to the vagaries of the fact-finding process than to any major differences in the actual hospital markets in these two locations. See U.S. v. Rockford Mem. Corp., 1 Trade Cas. (CCH) ¶68,978 (7th Cir. 1990) (Posner, J.) ("People want to be hospitalized near their families and homes, in hospitals in which their own, local doctors have hospital privileges. . . . It is always possible to take pot shots at a market definition . . . and the defendants do so with vigor and panache. Their own proposal, however, is ridiculous — a ten-county area in which it is assumed . . . that Rockford residents . . . will be searching out small, obscure hospitals in remote rural areas"). See generally Morrisey, Sloan & Valvona, Defining Geographic Markets for Hospital Care, 51 L. & Contemp. Prob. 165 (1988); Baker, The Antitrust Analysis of Hospital Mergers and the Transformation of the Hospital Industry, 51 L. & Contemp. Prob. 93 (1988); Blair & Fesmire, Antitrust Treatment of Hospital Mergers, 2 U. Fla. J.L. & Pub. Poly. 25 (1989); Schramm & Renn, Hospital Mergers, Market Concentration and the Herfindahl-Hirschman Index, 33 Emory L.J. 869 (1984).

VI. Antitrust Merger Law

The second aspect of market determination is defining the relevant product. Although HCA did not contest the issue, how was the product market defined in the principal case and how might it have differed? Compare United States v. Carilion Health Serv. supra: "Because patients or their doctors can choose to have problems treated either in a hospital or in an outpatient clinic or doctor's office in a significant number of cases, the court finds that [the product market includes outpatient care]. . . . The hospitals consist of a cluster of product markets, each with a different degree of substitutability between inpatient and outpatient services"; *Rockford* supra (Posner, J.) ("For many services provided by acute-care hospitals, there is no competition from other sorts of providers. . . . Hospitals can and do distinguish between the patient who wants a coronary bypass and the patient who wants a wart removed from his foot; these services are not in the same product market merely because they have a common provider."). See also Cruz, Product and Geographical Market Measurements in the Merger of Hospitals, 91 Dickinson L. Rev. 497, 527 (1986) ("the 'cluster' approach seems to be unfair to hospitals by excluding non-hospital providers from the market"); Robinson v. Magovern, 521 F. Supp. 842, 878-885 (W.D. Pa. 1981) (medical staff exclusion case that defined the product market as "adult open heart surgery" and the geographic market as a 16-county area centered on Pittsburgh that extended into Ohio and West Virginia); the lower court opinions in Jefferson Parish Hosp. Dist. v. Hyde, 466 U.S. 2 (1984).

4. Observe that market share statistics are not the sole consideration. The DOJ recently declined to oppose the merger of the only two hospitals in Danville, Illinois, and the only three hospitals in Portsmouth, Ohio, citing the poor financial health of the hospitals involved and the lack of local opposition. Rule, Antitrust Enforcement and Hospital Mergers: Safeguarding Emerging Price Competition, Remarks Delivered in Washington D.C., January 21, 1988, reprinted in 21 J. Health & Hosp. L. 125 (1988). Arguing against the result in these cases, see Blackstone & Fuhr, Hospital Mergers and Antitrust: An Economic Analysis, 14 J. Health Pol., Poly. & L. 383 (1989).

5. Elsewhere we learn that price competition historically has been virtually nonexistent in the health care industry due primarily to the prevalence of insurance. See Chapter 8.I infra. If these inherent market conditions allow hospitals and doctors to *unilaterally* raise their prices at will, why are we even concerned about the threat of price *collusion*? Commissioner Calvani's extensive analysis in the FTC's *HCA* opinion provides three answers: First, hospitals might collude to foreclose *quality* competition as well as *price* competition. Second, as Judge Posner recognizes, pressures for health care cost containment (explored at length in Chapter 8) have forced on the industry an increasing degree of price competition in recent years. See Chapter

8.III.A. Third, "whatever price competition exists in a market, . . . the antitrust laws will endeavor to protect this competition, if, for nothing else, the hope that price competition will be enhanced." 106 F.T.C. at 484.

6. Judge Posner's opinion briefly touches on another issue of controversy in hospital mergers: Whether there is any reason to be less suspect of nonprofit than for-profit hospitals. What does Posner say in his dictum? For technical, statutory reasons, there is an unresolved jurisdictional dispute over whether Clayton Act §7 even applies to nonprofit entities. See United States v. Carilion Health Serv., 707 F. Supp. 840 (W.D. Va. 1989) (holding no); contra, *Rockford Mem.* supra. This debate is essentially moot, however, since Sherman Act §1, which does apply to nonprofits, is generally thought to contain the same standards of merger legality as Clayton Act §7. Nevertheless, the nonprofit/for-profit controversy remains vital at a level of determining on the merits the likelihood of anticompetitive results from the merger of nonprofit hospitals. On this score, the lower court in *Carilion Health Servs.* supra (in analysis apparently affirmed by the Fourth Circuit) concluded that the hospitals' "nonprofit status weighs in favor of the merger's being reasonable." However, in the companion, *Rockford* case, the court reasoned to the contrary:

> [T]he defendants contend that they have no incentive to act anticompetitively because . . . monopoly profits garnered by a not-for-profit company cannot be distributed to anyone, let alone corporate decisionmakers. Instead, any excess of revenues over expense must be farmed back into the firm's operation. . . . The court rejects the defendants' narrow view as to the motivation behind anti-competitive action. . . . The not-for-profit decisionmaker may desire more money for a new piece of equipment or to hire a new specialist or for a better office, salary or title, or just to keep the firm afloat in particularly lean or dangerous times. . . . Simply put, decisionmakers need not be solely interested in the attainment of profit to act anti-competitively.

717 F. Supp. 1284. See generally Baker supra; Kopit & McCann, Toward a Definitive Antitrust Standard for Nonprofit Mergers, 13 J. Health Pol. Poly. & L. 638 (1988).

VII. LABOR AND EMPLOYMENT LAW

FHP, Inc. and Union of American Physicians and Dentists
274 N.L.R.B. 1141 (1985)

[The National Labor Relations Act ("NLRA"), 29 U.S.C. §151 et seq., establishes a comprehensive regulatory scheme, administered

VII. Labor and Employment Law

by the National Labor Relations Board ("NLRB"), to protect employees' rights to form a union, to require their employer to bargain with the union in good faith and honor collective bargaining agreements, and to strike if they are dissatisfied with the terms or conditions of their employment.

Physician efforts to unionize must clear a critical hurdle, however. The Supreme Court has interpreted the NLRA as excluding from its protections "managerial employees," those who assist management in determining and implementing policy. NLRB v. Bell Aerospace, 416 U.S. 267 (1974). In NLRB v. Yeshiva University, 444 U.S. 672 (1980), the Court determined in a 5-to-4 vote that this exclusion applies to professional employees — in that case, university professors — who serve on important committees and heavily influence hiring decisions. In Delphic dictum, however, the Court cautioned that not all employed professionals are ipso facto managers: "employees whose decisionmaking is limited to the routine discharge of professional duties in projects to which they have been assigned cannot be excluded from coverage. . . . Only if an employee's activities fall outside the scope of the duties routinely performed by similarly situated professionals will he be found aligned with management." 444 U.S. at 690. The following decision examines what this ruling might mean for the various administrative duties typically assigned to physicians within medical institutions.]

The Employer operates a health maintenance organization (HMO) which provides health care in seven clinics in Los Angeles and Orange Counties, California. As a nonprofit corporation, the organization's board of directors is the single body controlling the direction of the enterprise. The HMO's chief of staff sits on the board of directors and presides over the organization's provider division headed by a provider director. [T]he provider division is organized into a departmental structure consisting of seven departments of physicians — family practice, pediatrics, surgery, ophthalmology, radiology, obstetrics-gynecology; and optometry — and separate departments of dentistry and licensed clinical social workers. Physicians report directly to the heads of the departments in which they practice.

. . . The Employer maintains six standing and various ad hoc committees consisting of physicians and dentists employed at the HMO. [A]ny full-time physician or dentist may be called on to serve on one or more committees, each of which has rotating memberships. During the year before the representation hearing, 38 out of approximately 70 full-time physicians and dentists served on committees, and more than half of those currently employed so served over the past 5 years. The functions of these committees are as follows:

Peer Review Committee: This committee reviews the quality of care provided by individual physicians and health care providers. . . .

Every FHP physician is reviewed by the committee within 6 months of his employment and annually each year thereafter. Any significant critical finding is the basis for further investigation by the committee and, depending on the nature of the finding, may be the basis for awarding an incentive pay increase or taking disciplinary action, including suspension and termination. The committee makes recommendations concerning protocol changes to department heads. Department heads have never overruled the committee's protocol recommendations.

Physician and Therapeutics Committee: This committee develops and maintains a medication formulary, hears testimony and reviews literature concerning new medications, and monitors the prescribing practices of new physicians. Excessive prescribing by a physician of 10 specific drugs for which there is a less expensive generic equivalent leads to the filing of a report by the committee in the physician's personnel records. This action, depending on the severity of the offense, may lead to discipline, including termination.

Advisory Committee on Provider Work Environment: This committee meets biweekly to examine work environment issues with the objective of recommending changes in the organization's annual compensation package. The committee also develops plans to improve the utilization of the organization's support staff and facilities, such as increases in the nurse-to-doctor ratio. Its recommendations are regularly implemented.

Emergency Services Committee: The organization's capacity to respond to medical emergencies is the subject of this committee's evaluations and recommendations. . . .

Patient Services Committee: This committee investigates all reports raising issues concerning the organization's legal liability. The committee meets biweekly, and findings of medical malpractice are referred to both the provider director and the Peer Review Committee for physician discipline.

Advisory Committee to the Board of Directors: Chaired by the chief of staff and staffed by physicians of 2 or more years of service, this committee meets on a quarterly basis to chart the direction of the HMO. Each member of the committee represents a department or group of health care providers at FHP and provides a report for the chief of staff to present to the board of directors at their quarterly meetings concerning issues of wages, benefits, and working conditions. . . .

In NLRB v. Yeshiva University, supra, the Supreme Court defined managerial employees as those who "formulate and effectuate management policies by expressing and making operative the decisions of their employer" through "taking or recommending discretionary actions that effectively control or implement employer policy." 444 U.S.

at 682-683. Based on its findings that the faculty of Yeshiva University through their committee service exercised authority beyond strictly academic areas to matters such as faculty hire, tenure, sabbaticals, terminations, and promotions and that the overwhelming majority of faculty committee recommendations were followed, the Court held that the faculty members exercised managerial authority and therefore did not constitute a unit appropriate for collective bargaining. We find, contrary to the Acting Regional Director's report, that the full-time staff physicians and dentists of FHP, like the faculty of Yeshiva University, possess and exercise authority to formulate and effectuate management policies.

As professional employees, staff physicians may also be managerial if their activities on behalf of their employer fall outside the scope of decision-making routinely performed by similarly situated health care professionals and that is primarily incident to their treatment of patients.[4] Here, the functions of staff committees are by no means all-encompassing in terms of discharging the organization's total managerial agenda. To be sure, the committees are not involved, for example, in setting base salaries or formulating premiums to be charged FHP subscribers. These decisions are made at the corporate level. Similarly, hiring decisions are made not on the basis of any of the standing or ad hoc committee recommendations, but by the provider director on the basis of departmental need and the recommendations of the recruiting division, the department chairmen, and area chiefs. Nonetheless, the record convincingly demonstrates that many of the decisions made at the committee level, which include managing the organization's protocol system, overseeing its medical records system, setting its medicinal prescription policy, reviewing and modifying the benefits and working conditions of its staff, establishing procedures and staff training for medical emergencies, and minimizing the institution's risk of medical malpractice liability, lie at the core of the health maintenance organization's operations. Accordingly, we conclude that the committees perform managerial functions within the meaning of the *Yeshiva* decision.

In his Decision and Direction of Election, the Acting Regional Director concluded that, because stipulated managers and supervisors who serve on the Employer's committees are representatives of management, the participation of staff physicians and dentists is "primarily advisory or related to the quality of patient care in the clinics based on their professional experience." We find that the Acting Regional Director erred in this determination. [A]lthough the record is less than clear on the effectiveness of recommendations of the Advisory

---

4. See Montefiore Hospital, 261 NLRB 569 (1982); Sutter Community Hospitals, 227 NLRB 181, 193 (1976).

Committee to the board of directors, the operation of other committees within the organization is clearly more than advisory. In instances where personnel action such as retraining, more intense monitoring, or discipline of physicians is at issue, the committees may either take action directly or instruct the provider director to do so. In other instances, where the committees' action takes the form of recommendations to department heads or management, such as concerning protocol changes or employee compensation, the recommendations are regularly if not always followed. The committee unit itself establishes the Employer's practice in developing a formulary, evaluating both patient care and cost-related concerns. On the basis of these facts, we conclude that the full-time staff physicians and dentists, in their capacity as committee members, effectively formulate and effectuate the policies of the Employer. We therefore find that they are excluded from coverage under the Act as managerial employees.

NOTES

Labor Relations in the Health Care Industry

1. Although the disturbing specter of a physician strike is as yet uncommon, labor union activity in the health care sector is rapidly increasing. Becher, Structural Determinants of Union Activity in Hospitals, 7 J. Health Pol., Poly. & L. 889 (1983) (one-fourth of hospitals currently unionized; expected to increase to two-thirds by 1990). Most of this activity involves nonprofessionals such as hospital maintenance workers, and nonphysician health professionals such as nurses, but even among physicians there is a marked increase in unionizing:

> Complaining of inadequate wages, poor working conditions and callous management, an unlikely group of workers in Minnesota is threatening to unionize: doctors. Thousands of doctors in Minnesota are rebelling against something that is happening throughout the country: the challenge to their authority and attempts to cut their incomes by health maintenance organizations and other corporate-like healthcare delivery systems that provide a range of services for one set fee. . . .
> Unthinkable not long ago, such working-class sentiment illustrates doctors' rising frustration over the dramatic changes sweeping the health care industry that are eroding their authority and income. [W]ith these systems cutting doctors' fees and tightening their control over the type of treatment patients receive and where they get it, doctors' anger is mounting. . . .
> To deal with that problem, the Minnesota Medical Society passed

a resolution last month, asking the American Medical Association to seek Government permission to form a union.

Johnson, Doctors' Dilemma: Unionizing, N. Y. Times, July 13, 1987, at D1. See also Marcus, Trade Unionism for Doctors: An Idea Whose Time Has Come, 311 New Eng. J. Med. 1508 (1984).

2. It is important to realize that the NLRA covers only employees. This limitation would seem to exclude independent physicians on a hospital medical staff from the NLRA's protections — or would it? See p.328 supra; Craver, The Application of Labor and Antitrust Laws to Physician Unions, 27 Hast. Lab. L.J. 55 (1975).

Despite this limitation, physician unionizing is still of pressing importance due to the great increase in physician employment projected in the near future. According to one account, "already, almost 50 percent of all physicians are salaried," Relman, The Future of Medical Practice, 3 Health Affairs, Summer 1986, at 5, and it is widely predicted that this percentage will increase in coming decades, both within HMOs and within hospitals.

3. Generally speaking, the dispute over the federal labor law status of managerial professionals in the health care industry has not yet spilled over into the courts. One state court decision addressed this issue as a matter of local law and found that psychiatrists employed at a state mental hospital were sufficiently involved in the hospital's budgetary process and policy committees to constitute managerial employees. Penn. Assoc. of State Mental Hosp. Physicians v. Commonwealth, 554 A.2d 1021 (Pa. Cmwlth. 1989).

The NLRB's other major decision in this area is *Montefiore Hospital*, cited in *FHP* at n.4. Remarkably, that decision reached the opposite conclusion with respect to physicians employed by a hospital, holding that they do not enjoy sufficient autonomy to fall within the managerial employee exception. The Board reached this result despite the numerous committees that hospital physicians sit on and despite the fact that hospitals are generally viewed as providing physicians much greater autonomy than HMOs. (An even greater irony is that these physicians were members of the teaching faculty at *Yeshiva University's* medical school!!) The Board explained:

> [I]n the health care context the Board must evaluate the facts of each case to determine whether decisions alleged to be managerial or supervisory are incidental to the professional's treatment of patients. [The hospital contends] that the doctors' managerial status is shown by their participation in departmental operations, committee service, and the residents training program. . . . [However, department] chairmen make every major administrative decision with respect to the operation of their departments that is not dictated from above. Staff doctors have some input, but this is only in the form of recommendations which,

for the most part, the chairmen or their designees evaluate. For example, unlike the faculty in some universities, the staff does not vote on hiring decisions. . . . Medical procedures and policies are discussed and adopted at staff meetings, but the record does not show that these become management directives to any significant extent; rather what little the record offers tends to show that the policies become general guidelines, implementation of which is, to a large extent, the individual doctor's professional decision. . . . In short, the department chairman . . . does not rubber-stamp the staff's recommendation. Rather, as one departmental supervisor testified: "[The chairman's] decisions take into account the will of the staff." . . . [Moreover, adopting medical policy] do[es] not necessarily fall outside the professional duties primarily incident to patient care.

261 N.L.R.B. at 570-72. Is the Board's reasoning consistent with *FHP?* Is it consistent with what courts in other contexts have to say about the voice that physicians have in hospital staffing decisions? See Chapter 6.I.C.

4. "If the *FHP* reasoning becomes the accepted approach, . . . [physicians may] refuse to participate on staff committees. Both the health care institutions and the public at large would then be deprived of the invaluable input and expertise of these physicians." Wanger, Unionization by Salaried Physicians and the Managerial-Employee Exclusion: The Need for a Modified Approach, 15 L. Med. & Health Care 144, 149 (1987).

A second criticism that has been leveled against this field of law is that tests for employee control drawn from hierarchical work environments such as manufacturing industries are ill-suited to determining labor policy in collegial professional groups. See Rabban, Distinguishing Excluded Managers from Professionals Under the NLRA, 89 Colum. L. Rev. 1775 (1989); Angel, Professionals and Unionization, 66 Minn. L. Rev. 383 (1982); Comment, Reexamining the Managerial Employee Exclusion, 56 N.Y.U.L. Rev. 694 (1981).

5. One advantage physicians seek by unionizing is protection from the antitrust laws, by virtue of the antitrust exemption for labor activities. 15 U.S.C. §17. (Otherwise, every employee strike over wages would constitute per se price fixing.) Subsequent sections of these materials describe the antitrust difficulties physicians face when they organize into groups to negotiate with insurance companies, HMOs, and PPOs over reimbursement rates. See Chapter 8.III.C. As a result, doctors have begun to label their negotiating groups "unions." The flaw in this tactic is that doctors are not employees of insurance plans; they are, at best, independent contractors. Therefore, "if doctors think that by calling it a union they can engage in collective price-setting like steelworkers, they will find out they are wrong." Meyer, Antitrust Russian Roulette, Am. Med. News, Feb. 3, 1989, at 1, 32

(quoting Charles Rule, head of the Justice Departments antitrust division). See AMA v. U.S., 317 U.S. 519 (1943) (rejecting labor exemption claim made by physicians who boycotted an HMO).

6. The courts have sustained the NLRB's somewhat strained theory that employed hospital residents and interns may not unionize because they are primarily students, not employees. Physicians National Housestaff Assoc. v. Fanning, 642 F.2d 492 (D.C. Cir. 1980); Cedars-Sinai Medical Ctr. v. Cedars-Sinai Housestaff, 223 N.L.R.B. 251 (1976); Casenote, 56 Notre Dame Law. 314 (1980). In another case, the court refused a nurse's union under the "supervisory employee" exclusion because nurses oversee nurse's aids. NLRB v. Beacon Light Christian Nursing Home, 825 F.2d 1076 (6th Cir. 1987). What policy considerations justify this strict attitude against unions in the health care industry?

7. Until 1974, nonprofit hospitals, which constitute the bulk of the industry, were not covered by the NLRA. In that year, however, Congress amended the act with provisions directed specifically to all hospitals. 29 U.S.C. §§152, 158, 169, 183. In doing so, Congress expressed a concern that union activity not disrupt patient care. Specifically, both the Senate and the House stated that "due consideration should be given by the Board to preventing proliferation of bargaining units in the health care industry" because too many unions within a single institution would pose an excessive risk of crippling, repetitive strikes. 1974 U.S. Code Cong. & Ad. News 3950. This "nonproliferation" directive has been a constant thorn in the side of the NLRB in its numerous attempts to determine the appropriate scope of hospital bargaining units. See, for example, NLRB v. HMO International, 678 F.2d 806 (9th Cir. 1982) (improper to exclude vocational nurses from RN's union) (noting the "nearly perfect record of reversals of the NLRB by the Court of Appeals in review of health care bargaining units").

Normally, the NLRB determines the appropriate bargaining unit according to a "community of interests" test, that is, whether there is such a close community of interests between, say, RNs and vocational nurses to include them both in the same union. However, in response to a series of reversals holding that this test did not give sufficient weight to the nonproliferation mandate, the NLRB adopted a "disparity-of-interests" test, which created a presumption in favor of the largest possible unit that does not include employees with clearly disparate interests. St. Francis Hospital II, 271 N.L.R.B. 948 (1984). See also, NLRB v. St. Francis Hospital of Lynwood, 601 F.2d 404 (9th Cir. 1979). Other circuits, however, have criticized or refused to enforce the disparity-of-interests test. NLRB v. Walker County Medical Center, 722 F.2d 1535, 1539 n.4 (11th Cir. 1984); International Brotherhood of Electrical Workers, Local Union No. 474 v.

NLRB, 814 F.2d 697 (D.C. Cir. 1987). Regardless, the NLRB has stuck to its guns. 126 Lab. Rel. Ref. Man. 1361 (1987) (reaffirming disparity test on remand from D.C. Cir.). In order to resolve all the confusion, the NLRB, which is notorious for deciding all policy issues in adjudication, took the extraordinary step of initiating a rulemaking proceeding to define the proper approach to health care unit determinations. Its final regulations allow up to eight separate bargaining units: RNs, physicians, other professionals, technicians, clerical, maintenance, security guards, and others. 29 C.F.R. §103.30, 54 Fed. Reg. 16336 (April 21, 1989). These rules generated intense opposition from health care management, which perceives that carving units into smaller divisions greatly increases the ease of unionizing. However, AHA v. NLRB, 899 F.2d 651 (7th Cir.), held that a division into eight units does not constitute proliferation.

8. Patient care concerns manifest themselves in the labor law field in two other ways. First, the rules on when and where employee union organizers can distribute union literature in hospitals are particularly restrictive due to the concern for maintaining a "tranquil atmosphere." Generally, such solicitation activity is limited to non-working hours and non-patient-care areas. NLRB v. Baptist Hospital Inc., 442 U.S. 773 (1979). See Manchester Health Center Inc. v. NLRB, 861 F.2d 50 (2d Cir. 1988) (permissible to limit union solicitation to non-patient areas of hospital); Asociacion Hosp. Del Maestro, Inc. v. NLRB, 842 F.2d 575 (1st Cir. 1987) (hospital rule prohibiting employees from wearing union insignia anywhere on premises is overbroad); Comment, 28 Vill. L. Rev. 622 (1983); Note, Am. J.L. & Med. 105 (1980). Second, the NLRA requires a ten-day notice prior to striking or picketing a hospital, out of the obvious concern over avoiding disruption of care. 29 U.S.C. §158(g). However, the NLRB and the courts have limited this requirement to *authorized* strikes of a *recognized* union, excluding wild-cat strikes by unrepresented employees. See East Chicago Rehab. Center v. NLRB, 710 F.2d 397 (7th Cir. 1983); Recent Developments, 59 Wash. L. Rev. 947 (1984) (criticizing this limitation).

9. A final area of controversy is whether unionized health care workers can press demands related to the quality of medical care in addition to demands that affect only workers' economic situation. See Hoffman, Housestaff Activism: The Emergence of Patient-Care Demands, 7 J. Health Pol., Poly. & L. 421 (1982). Generally, the answer is no. Good Samaritan Hospital & Health Center, 265 N.L.R.B. 618, 626 (1982) (the workers' "energies were not an effort to improve their lot as employees. . . . As such, their criticisms and recommendations related to disputes outside the objectives of the mutual aid or protection provisions of the National Labor Relations Act."). Is this position consistent with the health care labor policy reflected in the previous notes?

10. For general discussions of labor law issues in the health care industry, see A. Rutkowski, Labor Relations in Hospitals; R. Miller, The Impact of Collective Bargaining on Hospitals (1979); Stapp, Ten Years After: A Legal Framework of Collective Bargaining in the Hospital Industry, 2 Hofstra Lab. L.J. 63 (1984); Comment, Labor Relations in the Health Care Industry, 54 Tul. L. Rev. 416 (1980); Vernon, Labor Relations in the Health Care Field, 70 Nw. U.L. Rev. 202 (1975); Comment, National Labor Relations Act — History and Interpretation of the Health Care Amendments, 60 Marq. L. Rev. 921 (1977). Determining the appropriate bargaining unit has been the subject of particularly voluminous commentary. For a sampling, see also Note, NLRB Guidelines for Determining Health Care Industry Bargaining Units, 78 Ky. L.J. 143 (1990); Wiethoff, The Prospects for Multifacility Bargaining Units in the Health Care Industry, 13 Emp. Rel. L.J. 322 (1987).

NOTES

Wrongful Discharge and Related Employment Issues

1. In contrast with the *public* law rights of *groups* of health care employees, the law has also been concerned with the *private* law rights of *individual* doctors and nurses. By convention, the former set of issues is labeled "labor law" and the latter "employment law." The prime example of an employment law dispute is an action for "wrongful discharge." In such cases, the primary issue is whether the so-called rule of "at-will employment" has been abrogated or eroded. Classic contract law implies that an employment arrangement with no fixed ending date can be terminated entirely at the will of the employer — for any cause or no cause. Recent years have seen a rapid erosion of the at-will rule. For some reason, these wrongful discharge cases seem to crop up with surprising frequency in the hospital industry. For instance, in Wagenseller v. Scottsdale Memorial Hospital, 710 P.2d 1025 (1985), a nurse alleged she was fired in retaliation for refusing to engage in lewd antics during a rafting trip with other hospital employees (including "a parody of the song 'Moon River,' which allegedly concluded with members of the group 'mooning' the audience"). The court held that firing for this reason is contrary to public policy since it penalizes conduct that arguably contravenes statutes concerning public indecency. Other courts have limited the "at will" rule by finding implicit promises of job tenure in employee manuals. See, for instance, Duldulao v. Saint Mary of Nazareth Hospital Center, 505 N.E.2d 314 (Ill. 1987); Hobson v. McLean Hospital Corp., 522 N.E.2d 975 (Mass. 1988). For a contrasting view, see Hinson v. Cameron, 742 P.2d 549 (Okla. 1987) (refusing to allow claim based on hospital's employee handbook); Riley

v. Warm Springs State Hospital, 748 P.2d 455 (Mont. 1987) (similar). Also, observe that municipal hospitals may be subject to constitutional as well as contractual restrictions in their employment decisions. Vinyard v. King, 728 F.2d 428 (10th Cir. 1984).

2. The public policy exception to at-will employment is applied most frequently in "whistleblower" cases, those where an employee is fired in retaliation for reporting, for example, workplace safety problems to the proper authorities. E.g., McQuary v. Bel Air Convalescent Home, 684 P.2d 21 (Or. App. 1984) (threatening to report abuse of patients to state authorities). Compare Rozier v. St. Mary's Hosp., 411 N.E.2d 50 (Ill. App. 1980) (notifying newspaper of patient mistreatment does not constitute protected whistleblowing). See generally, AHA Office of General Counsel, The Wrongful Discharge of Employees in the Health Care Industry (1987). One area in which the public policy limitation on grounds for discharge has unique importance to health care institutions is whether employees may be fired for exercising conscientious objection to assisting in particular medical procedures, such as abortions or termination of life support. The leading case, Pierce v. Ortho Pharmaceutical Corp., 417 A.2d 505 (N.J. 1980), held that such terminations are permissible since the employee's objection is a purely private one that has no basis in public policy (as long as the medical procedure is consistent with the law). However, legislatures have been somewhat more sympathetic. Most states have "conscience clause" statutes that expressly prohibit discharge for refusal to perform abortions. E.g., Mo. Ann. Stat. §197.032. A federal statute known as the "Church Amendment" enforces a similar prohibition against institutions that receive certain forms of federal health care funding. 42 U.S.C. §300a-7. In one state, the conscience clause statute extends broadly to moral objections that relate to "any phase of patient care." Ill. Ann. Stat. 111 1/2 §5303. See generally, Davis, Defining the Employment Rights of Medical Personnel Within the Parameters of Personal Conscience, 3 Det. Col. L. Rev. 847 (1986). Feliu, Discharge of Professional Employees: Protecting Against Dismissal for Acts Within a Professional Code of Ethics, 11 Colum. Hum. Rts. L. Rev. 1249 (1980).

3. Another statute of importance to health care employment relations is the prohibition of discrimination against employees on the basis of race, color, religion, sex, or national origin contained in Title VII of the Civil Rights Act of 1964. See generally Martin, Discrimination in the Health Care Profession, 7 Med. Law 133 (1988); Harstein, EEO Issues in the Health-Care Field: A Roundup of Recent Developments, 12 Emp. Rel. L.J. 241 (1986). Under an expansive concept of what constitutes an employment relationship, some courts have extended Title VII to apply to hospital medical staff membership decisions. Doe v. St. Joseph's Hospital, 788 F.2d 411 (7th Cir. 1986);

VII. Labor and Employment Law

Pardazi v. Cullman Medical Center, 838 F.2d 1155 (11th Cir. 1988). But see Diggs v. Harris Hospital, 847 F.2d 270 (5th Cir. 1988) (no Title VII action exists where physician is independent contractor).

Title VII cases sometimes raise issues unique to the health care setting. In Backus v. Baptist Medical Center, 570 F. Supp. 1191 (E.D. Ark. 1981), the court found that business necessity justifies a hospital in restricting male nurses from labor and delivery work. Similarly, the court found in Carswell v. Peachford Hospital, 27 F.E.P. 698 (1981), that the potential for patient disturbance allowed a psychiatric hospital to terminate a nurse who insisted on wearing "Bo Derek" beads in her hair.

Also of interest under Title VII is the 1978 amendment that includes pregnancy as an aspect of prohibited gender considerations. In Hayes v. Shelby Memorial Hospital, 726 F.2d 1543 (11th Cir. 1984), the court required a hospital to reassign a pregnant X-ray technician rather than discharge her out of concern for the effects of fetal exposure to radiation. For further reading on this problem, see Furnish, Beyond Protection: Relevant Difference and Equality in the Toxic Work Environment, 31 U. Cal. Davis 1 (1988) (collecting citations to other articles).

4. A final area of importance springs from physicians' recurrent challenges to the enforcement of covenants not to compete contained in their employment contracts. Physicians who join a practice group are usually required to abide by restrictive covenants that prevent them from practicing in the same geographic area for a certain period of time once they leave the group, in order to protect the group's interest in its established patients. However, covenants not to compete in this and other employment contexts are viewed with suspicion by the courts because they tend to contravene public policies in favor of free trade and the right to work. Nevertheless, these covenants are upheld if they are reasonable as to (1) duration, (2) geographic scope, and (3) the range of activities covered, and if they are not otherwise contrary to the public interest. See Karpinski v. Ingrasci, 320 N.Y.S.2d 1 (1971) (restriction of defendant from practice of dentistry is overbroad where his employer practiced only oral surgery); Karlin v. Weinberg, 390 A.2d 1161 (N.J. 1978) (extensive discussion of various factors that determine legality of restrictive covenants); Getty, Enforceability of Noncompetition Covenants in Physician Employment Contracts, 7 J. Leg. Med. 235 (1986) (collecting and discussing cases).

The issue of greatest relevance in the medical context is whether it contravenes the public interest to restrain the practice of a physician whose services are much needed in the community. For example, in Dick v. Geist, 693 P.2d 1133 (Idaho App. 1985), the court refused to enforce a restrictive covenant that would have excluded the two doctors who rendered 90 percent of the neonatal care in the community. See also Ellis v. McDaniel, 596 P.2d 222 (Nev. 1979) (refusing enforcement against the only orthopedic surgeon within 200 miles); Irdell Digestive Disease Clinic v. Petrozza, 373 S.E.2d 449 (N.C. App. 1988) (refusing to enforce covenant that would leave only one gastroenterologist in the local area). Another line of cases has reasoned, though, that the public interest is equally well served even if the doctor is forced to treat patients in another part of the state. Willman v. Beheler, 499 S.W.2d 770 (Mo. 1973); Canfield v. Spear, 254 N.E.2d 433 (Ill. 1969) ("the health of persons elsewhere is just as important").

CHAPTER 8

Reforming the Health Care Delivery System

I. THE HEALTH CARE COST CRISIS

A. Introduction

Califano, America's Health Care Revolution:
Who Lives? Who Dies? Who Pays?*
3-4, 58 (1986)

A revolution in the American way of health is under way, and it's likely to be as far-reaching as any economic and social upheaval we have known.

The revolution promises to be bruising and bloody. At stake are who gets how much money out of one of America's top three industries, who suffers how much pain how long, and who gets the next available kidney, liver, or heart: in short, who lives and who dies — and who decides.

The revolutionary forces at work are profound. In science, our genius for invention is serving up incredible diagnostic, surgical, and biomedical breakthroughs that blur the lines between life and death and hold the promise of remarkable cures and the threat of unacceptable costs. In demography, the graying of America presents a burgeoning population of elderly citizens who consume the most expensive high-tech medicine and who already strain our capacity to provide adequate medical, nursing-home, and home health care. In law and religion, our judges, ethicists, and moral theologians are confounded by the Pandora's box of medical discoveries that insists they reexamine questions as fundamental as when life begins and ends.

Against the backdrop of these extraordinarily powerful currents, other major forces are moving and shaking the health care system. Fed up with the waste and inefficiency of our health industry, the

---

* Reprinted by permission of the author and Touchstone Books/Simon & Schuster.

biggest buyers of health care — governments and corporations — are mounting aggressive efforts to change the way doctors, hospitals, and other providers are used and paid, and to reshape financial incentives that encourage patients to seek unnecessary care. These forces are sparking a sweeping social and cultural shift in how our people view hospitals, doctors, and medical machines, and how individuals see their responsibilities to take care of their own health.

In business, Lee Iacocca, fighting off Chrysler's collapse, was jolted into action by the fact that Blue Cross/Blue Shield was the company's biggest single supplier, that health care was one-tenth the cost of a Chrysler K-Car. To fight rising costs and spur competition, large corporations are embracing health maintenance organizations, which they once derided as socialistic.

In politics, leaders as diverse as President Ronald Reagan — who discovered that Medicare was growing at a faster clip than Social Security — and Senator Edward Kennedy — who realized that even his cradle-to-grave national health plan could not afford to cover the costs of long-term care for the nation's elderly — are pressing for significant changes in our health care system.

Within the medical industry itself, for-profit health care chains are growing rapidly and using spectacular high-tech superstars like artificial-heart surgeon William DeVries to advertise their wares. The billion-dollar merger fever spreading among the nation's large for-profit hospital chains and medical supply companies in 1985 portends the medical mega-empires ahead.

With such potent scientific, demographic, political, and economic forces afoot, the ferment and turmoil throughout the health care industry have reached the high pitch of revolution. . . .

Health has become one of America's biggest businesses. It is the nation's second-largest employer, after education, and third-largest industry in consumer spending, behind only food and housing.

The health industry's piece of the gross national product in 1984 was $387 billion, 10.6 percent. That means Americans broke the billion-dollar-a-day barrier in money they spent on health care in 1984. . . .

The numbers are so big we tend to lose perspective. We pay for health care in everything we purchase. . . . Some 15 cents of every federal tax dollar went to the health industry in 1984. For years, government health programs — not defense or Social Security — have been the fastest-rising segment of the federal budget. For millions of workers, the cost of health insurance premiums and health care, not income taxes, has been the major cause of the rapidly widening gap between total compensation and cash taken home. The fastest-rising cost of doing business has been health care and health insurance premiums, not labor or raw materials.

H. Aaron & W. Schwartz, The Painful Prescription: Rationing Hospital Care*
7, 113, 118 (1984)

With some important exceptions, the norm for hospital care in the United States approximates the maxim "if it will help, do it." The system of third-party payment that dominates hospital reimbursement in the United States encourages the provision to most patients of all care that promises to yield benefits, regardless of cost. Most American patients are insulated from the financial consequences of most hospital episodes. Most American physicians gain financially from providing additional care, and medical ethics preclude only the delivery of care that will do harm, not of care that is unreasonably expensive. Hospital administrators seek facilities of high enough quality to satisfy the professional goals of their staffs. Thus care in the United States is usually close to what would be provided if cost were no object and benefit to patients were the sole concern. . . .

If Americans could be confident that the expected incremental benefit of all medical care they buy exceeds the incremental cost of those services, the growth in medical expenditures, like similar past increases in spending on automobiles, television, and computers, would be a measure of the superior capacity of new commodities to satisfy consumer wants. But the system of third-party reimbursement precludes such rosy interpretations. Because care is essentially free when demanded, incentives encourage the provision of all care that produces positive benefits whatever the cost. Combined with scientific ingenuity, this system has led not only to dramatic advances in diagnosis and therapy but also to the use of technologically sophisticated and costly methods to provide medical care that is sometimes of slight value. Small increases in the certainty of diagnoses often come at great cost. . . .

Take, for instance, the use of the CT scanner for a patient who has unexplained dizziness or headaches that the doctor feels are almost certainly caused by tension. Because the likelihood of finding a treatable lesion by means of a scan is low, the cost of the many studies required to find the one patient with a lesion is high. Moreover, as new noninvasive methodologies, such as CT scanners, have replaced risky or painful techniques, the pool of patients who are candidates for study has expanded. Doctors are no longer forced to weigh the risk and discomfort of invasive procedures against the potential gain

---

* Henry Aaron is a Senior Fellow at the Brookings Institution. William Schwartz is a Professor of Medicine at Tufts University.
Reprinted by permission of the Brookings Institution.

of information; consequently, any return greater than zero becomes medically justified.

Enthoven & Kronick, A Consumer-Choice Health Plan for the 1990s*
320 New Eng. J. Med. 29 (1989)

The health care economy of the United States is a paradox of excess and deprivation. We spend about 11.5 percent of the gross national product (GNP) on health care, much more than any other country. And whereas other countries have stabilized the share of their GNP that is spent on health, ours has accelerated in recent years. Inflation-adjusted per capita spending for health care grew by 4 percent per year from 1970 to 1980, and by 4.6 percent per year from 1980 to 1986. The Health Care Financing Administration (HCFA) recently projected that according to present trends, health care spending would reach 15 percent of the GNP by 2000. These growing expenditures are adding greatly to deficits in the public sector, threatening the solvency of some industrial companies, and creating heavy burdens for many people.

At the same time, roughly 35 million Americans have no financial protection from the expenses of medical care — no insurance or other coverage, public or private. This number is substantially higher than it was 10 years ago, as increasing numbers of employers find ways to avoid supplying coverage for employees and their dependents. Millions more have inadequate coverage that leaves them vulnerable to large financial risks. And uncounted millions have coverage that excludes preexisting medical conditions. Our present system of financing health care systematically denies coverage to many who need it most. Health insurers want to insure those who are the least likely to need medical care and to protect themselves and their policy holders from the costs associated with the care of the very sick.

Wing, American Health Policy in the 1980s**
36 Case W. Res. L. Rev. 608, 620 (1986)

National health expenditures ["NHEs"] have been dramatically and steadily increasing for at least forty years, in both absolute and relative terms. In 1950, essentially the eve of the technological rev-

---

* Alain Enthoven and Richard Kronick are on the Faculty of the Graduate School of Business, Stanford University.

** Kenneth W. Wing is Professor of Law at the University of Puget Sound. Reprinted by permission.

olution in modern medicine, Americans were spending $12.7 billion annually for their health care, 4.4 percent of the nation's GNP. What followed was several decades of continually increasing growth. NHEs increased at an average annual rate of over 8 percent per year through the 1960s, accelerated to an average annual growth rate of 12 percent after the implementation of Medicaid and Medicare and through the mid-1970s, and grew by an average rate of over 13 percent from 1975 to 1983.

Thus, as early as 1972, with NHEs "only" $94 billion and demanding 7.9 percent of the GNP, annual health expenditures were described as "staggering" and "unbelievable," and projections into the future were inspiring predictions of "crisis" from a wide range of health policy critics. Nonetheless, each year the unbelievable became the believable as the mathematics of compounded percentage increases pushed NHEs over $200 billion in 1979 and quickly over $300 billion by 1982 and, each year, to even greater proportions of the GNP.

NOTES

Observations on Costs and Practices

Health care spending remains at crisis proportions. After a brief respite during 1984, health care inflation has resumed its steep upward climb. "Spending for medical care has doubled since the beginning of the decade, reaching $500 billion in 1987. On average, $1,987 was spent on health care for every person in the United States." Levit & Freeland, National Health Care Spending, 7 Health Affairs, No. 5, at 124, 125 (Winter 1988). The latest projections are $661 billion in 1990, with the inflation rate continuing at 10 to 14 percent through 1995.

Curiously, though, public opinion surveys show a persistent lack of concern about health care spending. Blendon & Altman, Public Attitudes about Health-Care Costs, 311 New Eng. J. Med. 613 (1984) ("Only 14 percent of the public think that our society is spending too much for health care, and 53 percent think we are not spending enough"); Gabel, Cohen & Fink, Americans' Views on Health Care, 8 Health Affairs 103 (Spring 1989) (9 percent say too much, and 54 percent too little). Do these survey results properly distinguish between how *much* is spent and how *well* it is spent?

Who is to say that the enormous resources we devote to medical treatment are really excessive? After all, isn't your health the most important thing in life? The answer may depend on distinguishing between health and health care. Consider whether increased spending on food, shelter, pollution control, and other preventive measures might not advance the goal of health more productively than one more X ray, an additional day in the hospital, or another prescription drug.

At least among health care policy analysts, there is agreement that something must be done to halt health care inflation or to allocate our spending in a different manner. This consensus is important to stress because the unanimity of informed opinion is easily obscured by the heat of the debate over what exactly should be done. Following, then, are some additional pointed facts and opinions. (Be careful to distinguish between the two.)

> Medicine, like many other American institutions, suffered a stunning loss of confidence in the 1970s. Previously, two premises had guided government health policy: first, that Americans needed more medical care — more than the market alone would provide; and second, that medical professionals and private voluntary institutions were best equipped to decide how to organize those services. . . . In the 1970s this mandate ran out. The economic and moral problems of medicine displaced scientific progress at the center of public attention. Enormous increases in cost seemed ever more certain; corresponding improvements in health ever more doubtful. The prevailing assumptions about the need to expand medical care were reversed: The need now was to curb its apparently insatiable appetite for resources. In a short time, American medicine seemed to pass from stubborn shortages to irrepressible excess, without ever having passed through happy sufficiency.

P. Starr, The Social Transformation of American Medicine 379 (1982).

> [A]bout half the patients treated in hospital emergency rooms are not urgently in need of care; many could receive better care at lower cost in a setting expressly designed for routine ambulatory care. Estimates of the percentage of hospital days that are inappropriate have ranged as high as 20 percent. Surveys in hospitals have indicated that 50-65 percent of the antibiotics that are ordered are not indicated at all or are being given incorrectly. . . . Laboratory tests and X-rays merit particular scrutiny, since the increase in their use has been especially dramatic. . . . Reports of the Food and Drug Administration suggest that of the 75 million chest X-rays done in 1980, at a cost of nearly $2 billion, nearly one-third were unnecessary because they were unlikely to either detect disease or affect its outcome.

President's Commission for the Study of Ethical Problems in Medicine and Biomedical Behavioral Research, Securing Access to Health Care 187 (1983).

> Americans are four times more likely to have bypass operations than Western Europeans with the same symptoms. According to studies, . . . at least 60 percent, and perhaps 80 percent, of the 250,000 Americans who undergo coronary bypass surgery each year [at a cost

of about $25,000 each] gain no increase in life span beyond what they would have achieved through medical management of their conditions. . . . Medical experts estimate that at least half of the 900,000 C[aesarean] sections performed in 1986 were unnecessary. The cost of these excess operations came to $728 million — for poor quality medicine.

J. Califano, The Health-Care Chaos, New York Times Magazine, March 20, 1988, at 44, 45, 56.

A survey of 1000 eleven-year-old schoolchildren in New York City [during the 1960s] found that 65 percent had undergone tonsillectomy. The remaining children were sent for examinations to a group of physicians and 45 percent were selected for tonsillectomy. Those rejected were examined by another group of physicians and 46 percent were selected for surgery. When the remaining children were examined again by another group of physicians, a similar percent were recommended for tonsillectomy, leaving only sixty-five students. At that point, the study was halted for lack of physicians.

Eddy, Variations in Physician Practice: The Role of Uncertainty, 3 Health Affairs, Summer 1984, at 84-85.

Uncomplicated heart attack provides a concrete illustration of the difference between conservative and elaborate practice styles. Prevailing practice in the United States is to keep a patient in the hospital for three weeks, initially in an intensive coronary care unit. More conservative practice has shown patients can safely be discharged after one week. Most conservative of all are British studies which show that patients can be treated entirely at home with as good or better health outcomes. All these practice styles apparently achieve equally good results. Many similar examples could be given.

Weller, "Free Choice" as a Restraint of Trade, 69 Iowa L. Rev. 1351, 1391 (1984).

On the whole, doctors earn more money than any other occupational group in our society. According to American Medical Association (AMA) figures, the average net income of American physicians was over $106,000 in 1983 [and reached $145,000 in 1988]. Furthermore, the average physician's income exceeds that of other workers. By conservative estimate, over the past decade doctors have earned more than six times as much as the average American worker.

Law & Ensminger, Negotiating Physicians' Fees: Individual Patients Or Society?, 61 N.Y.U.L. Rev. 1, 4 (1986).

Forty-four percent of the residents of Brownsville [Texas] receive their health care in Mexico. [T]wo-thirds of the residents of San Elizario, a small town 20 miles southeast of El Paso, cross to Mexico when they are sick. . . . Hospital administrators in that part of Texas estimate that nearly 75 percent of the residents do not have health insurance. Most of those, in turn, do not qualify for Medicaid because . . . only those who earn 34 percent or less than the national poverty level are entitled to such funds in Texas, and even they are disqualified if they have assets totaling more than $1,500, including a home or car.

New York Times, Oct. 17, 1988, at A1.

It is fast becoming a tradition for both popular and scholarly articles to begin with a litany of figures contrasting spiraling costs with appallingly bad American health indices. The nation now spends a larger portion of its total gross national product on health care than does any other country in the world. . . . [By contrast], the infant death rate in the United States . . . exceed[s] that of fourteen other industrial countries. . . . American males have a shorter life expectancy than the males of nineteen other industrial countries. . . . Unless the system of providing health care is improved, the health of Americans will become even less satisfactory, despite massive increases in costs.

Sylvia Law, Blue Cross: What Went Wrong? 1 (2d ed. 1976).

Have the benefits been worth the cost? Has all this spending yielded a substantial improvement in the health of the American people? We really don't know. Data on life expectancy suggest that there has been some recent improvement. But once a reasonable minimum level of care is provided, factors other than medical care — diet, lifestyle, heredity, environment — appear to have much more effect on health and longevity than does more or less medical care. Above a reasonable minimum, the availability of more medical care resources appears to have little or no effect on many indicators of health status.

A. Enthoven, Health Plan xvi (1980).

Awe-inspiring medical technology has combined with egalitarian rhetoric to create the impression that contemporary medicine is highly effective. Undoubtedly, during the last generation, a limited number of specific procedures have become extremely useful. But where they are not monopolized by professionals as tools of their trade, those which are applicable to widespread diseases are usually very inexpensive and require a minimum of personal skills, materials, and custodial services from hospitals. In contrast, most of today's skyrocketing medical expenditures are destined for the kind of diagnosis and treatment whose effectiveness at best is doubtful.

I. Illych, Medical Nemesis 15 (1977).

Eighty-nine percent of Americans say they believe the nation's health care system needs fundamental change. . . . [Polls taken in three countries] showed that only 10 percent of those surveyed in the United States said their health system functioned "pretty well," as against 56 percent in Canada and 27 percent in Britain. . . . The president of the Louis Harris organization . . . added, "If I look at it with an American hat on, what it confirms is all of one's worst fears about the American system. We have the most expensive, the least well-liked, the least equitable and, in many ways, the most inefficient system."

N.Y. Times, Feb. 15, 1989, at A8. See Blendon & Taylor, Views on Health Care: Public Opinion in Three Nations, 8 Health Affairs 149 (Spring 1989).

B. Traditional Private Insurance

Califano, America's Health Care Revolution
40-47, 126-128 (1986)*

Prior to the 1930s there was virtually no health insurance in the United States. Americans personally paid more than 90 percent of their hospital and doctors' bills. What coverage existed aimed at replacing some part of wages lost due to illness or accident. There was little sentiment for health insurance, partly because, unlike Europe, America had no tradition of broad social insurance schemes, and partly because the need was not perceived as acute. Physicians' charges were low and hospitals still provided lots of charitable care. . . .

In the 1920s hospital costs began to rise, particularly those for extended stays. By 1929 illnesses requiring hospitalization accounted for 50 percent of all medical expenditures. Then the Great Depression struck and people went to hospitals only in dire emergencies. Many patients couldn't pay their bills. Between 1929 and 1930, average hospital receipts plummeted from more than $200 per patient to less than $60.

Spurred by the ravages of the depression, potential patients and hospital administrators began to look for some way to pay and be paid. And health insurance became an industry within the health industry.

It started in 1929 in Dallas, Texas. Baylor University Hospital initiated an insurance plan for 1,250 schoolteachers. Each teacher paid fifty cents a month and received up to twenty-one days of hospital care each year. Other Dallas hospitals soon offered competing plans, and the idea spread to cities across America.

Three years later, in 1932, a community-wide plan was developed in California. Under it, participating hospitals in a given area agreed

---

* Reprinted by permission of the author and Touchstone Books/Simon & Schuster.

to provide services to subscribers, who paid their premiums to the plan rather than to individual hospitals. The community-wide concept eliminated any competition among the participating hospitals; there was no need for each to provide its own plan. Hospitals in other areas embraced such plans and marketed them on a not-for-profit basis. They became known as Blue Cross plans. By 1937 these noncompetitive plans had 800,000 subscribers, while competing plans set up by individual hospitals had only 125,000. In 1938 the American Hospital Association began vigorously promoting noncompetitive community-wide Blue Cross plans; by 1940 membership ballooned to six million.

These Blue Cross plans covered only hospitalization and offered a single community rate, regardless of the risk related to specific groups and individuals. Participating hospitals guaranteed to provide the stipulated services to members of Blue Cross plans. Organized and administered by community groups and hospitals, these not-for-profit plans were exempt from taxes.

Initially, commercial insurers were wary of health insurance because of the difficulty of establishing actuarial principles that would ensure a profit. As Blue Cross plans succeeded, however, commercial insurers began to offer coverage, in 1934 for hospitalization, in 1939 for surgery. Commercial insurers did not use a single community-wide risk rate; they calculated rates based upon their experience related to differences in age and health. Typically, commercial policies offered cash payments to individual subscribers, rather than paying hospitals directly, as Blue Cross did. The cash patients received from these commercial insurance plans could be used to pay doctors as well as hospitals. By 1940 commercial insurers covered 3.7 million people.

The American Medical Association did not object to commercial insurers paying cash to patients, who in turn paid doctors. But the association initially resisted any health plans that paid physicians directly, considering such plans corrosive of the doctor-patient relationship.

Blue Cross plans, which covered only hospitalization and not doctors' bills, began to look for ways to compete with commercial insurers. At the same time, physicians were seeking ways to take the steam out of proposals in some states, like California, for mandatory government health insurance to cover doctors' and hospital bills. Working together in the late 1930s and early 1940s, Blue Cross organizations and physicians established Blue Shield plans to complement Blue Cross hospitalization with coverage of physicians' services. In the beginning, these plans offered subscribers cash payments for doctors' hospital fees only. Eventually, physicians' services of all sorts were covered and the AMA eased its objection to direct payments to doctors.

I. The Health Care Cost Crisis

Both Blue Cross and Blue Shield were captives of the doctors and hospitals. Through their state and local medical societies and their dominance of the boards of directors of the Blues, doctors controlled the scope of coverage and the amounts they and the hospitals were paid. Portrayed as a public service, Blue Shield was also a minimum income security program for doctors. Participating doctors had to accept the amounts the plans set as full payment only for low-income subscribers; they were free to levy additional charges on others. Doctors who chose not to participate could charge Blue Shield subscribers at any income level whatever they wished for a particular service. The patients then had to make up the difference between the doctors' charge and what Blue Shield paid.

The commercial plans were initially independent of doctors and hospitals. They frequently contested the unfair advantage of Blue Cross and Blue Shield plans that physicians controlled. But at this stage, commercial insurers were not about to jeopardize their business by getting involved with what doctors or hospitals charged. Within a short time, commercial plans perceived themselves as more closely aligned with the doctors and hospitals whose bills they paid than with the patients who bought their insurance.

The patients, who were the consumers of health care, were dazzled by the magic of the medicine men and grateful for some protection. Before these consumers realized what was happening, or anybody took much notice, the health insurance sector of the health care industry was harnessed to minimize competition, control prices, direct usage, and ease bill collection for doctors and hospitals. In the case of Blue Cross and Blue Shield, the hospitals and the doctors controlled rates, coverage, and payment; in the case of commercial plans that paid patients directly, there were no limits on charges by hospitals or doctors.

Big Corporate America and Big Union America were not paying much attention to these developments either. After all, what did the employment relationship have to do with health insurance benefits in a world where child labor protection laws were barely making it through Congress and union organizing was a dirty, often violent business that threatened the lives of men like UAW president Walter Reuther?

World War II changed all that. Price and wage controls were strictly enforced and observed. As pressure mounted for pay increases, the War Labor Board held the line on wages, but it did permit increases in fringe benefits in amounts equivalent to 5 percent of wages. Health insurance became a premier fringe benefit. Employers began to use group health insurance to attract scarce labor, and unions began to regard such insurance as a way to supplement income. The tax laws provided added stimulus: unlike wages and most other fringe benefits, employer contributions to group health insurance policies were tax-deductible business expenses, were explicitly exempted from employees' taxable income, and were not subject to the payroll taxes shared by employers and employees. The number of Americans enrolled in group hospital plans bolted from seven million in 1942 to twenty-six million by the end of the war.

Corporate employers tended to prefer commercial insurers to Blue Cross and Blue Shield because the commercial insurers based their rates on the age and health of the particular group covered. For most corporations, this meant lower rates. Commercial insurers also offered more flexibility and variety in types of coverage, and they were quick to work out arrangements so that the employer could take full credit with its employees for providing the benefits. Eventually, as the corporate group insurance market expanded, Blue Cross and Blue Shield began adjusting their plans for employers in an attempt to compete with commercial insurance companies. . . .

As employers negotiated health care packages with unionized employees, commercial insurers surpassed Blue Cross in hospitalization coverage. Because the focus of employer-employee insurance was expensive catastrophic care, the insurance benefits first bargained for were tilted decidedly toward hospital care. As unions gained power, however, big corporations agreed to coverage for outpatient physician care, prescription drugs, and laboratory tests. In the early rounds of bargaining, corporations insisted that employees pay some part of the health insurance premiums and doctors' and hospital bills.

Then the large unions mounted a major effort to reduce payments by employees toward their health insurance premiums and health care bills.

The big event came in 1959. A 116-day United Steelworkers strike ended with a settlement that required the steel companies to pay the entire premium for health insurance. In 1961 General Motors, Ford, and Chrysler accepted similar health care schemes in their negotiations with the United Automobile Workers. The three auto companies agreed to pay the full cost of hospital, surgical, and medical insurance premiums for employees and their dependents. Throughout the 1960s and 1970s, business and labor kept extending health insurance coverage and benefits and eliminating worker incentives to seek efficient care and physician incentives to hold down fees and hospitalization.

Without appreciating the full implications, big business and big labor signaled the fall from grace of deductible plans, under which the employee paid a certain amount of doctors' or hospital bills before the insurance company took over the payments, and of co-payment plans, under which the employee paid a share (usually 20 percent) of each doctor's or hospital bill. The first-dollar coverage plans, as they became known, rendered the cost of the doctor or hospital irrelevant to any patient they insured.

First-dollar coverage plans spread like an infectious flu through a crowded elementary school — not only among union employees, but among nonorganized white-collar workers as well. By and large, employers could not easily give greater benefits to union employees than to nonunion workers. Companies without unions wanted to stay that way, and one method was to provide good wages and generous fringe benefits, to convince employees that they had all the advantages of being organized, without the need to pay union dues. Moreover, as corporate and individual income and payroll taxes increased, deductible, nontaxable health care benefits became better than money. The employment relationship became the source of health care benefits for virtually all working Americans and their families.

To a great extent, the health industry was insulated from the competing demands of food, clothing, shelter, and recreation on a family budget. Its cost was hidden in the products consumers bought — from cars and radios to food, clothing, and shelter themselves. Families blanketed in the rich first-dollar coverage plans thought they never had to pay for doctors or hospitals. . . .

Such was the stage set for the government as it debated in the early 1960s whether to enact some kind of national health plan. About 60 percent of our citizens, 110 million Americans, were at least partially insulated from hospital and doctors' bills; many didn't have to pay much or anything. Our biggest corporations and unions had, with little or no appreciation of the ramifications, granted to doctors, hospital administrators, medical laboratories, and pharmaceutical manufacturers the power to tell the patients what services, tests, and drugs to buy, regardless of cost. The steel and auto workers, other big unions, and the Fortune 500 — the tough streetfighters of labor and business — had been kidnapped by the health care industry without so much as a whimper. They didn't even know what had happened until it was too late. . . .

[Today,] the commercial insurers, the Blues, and the self-insured corporations provide widely varying kinds of insurance coverage to about 175 million Americans. Many people are covered by more than one policy, and many are covered for only part of a year. Virtually all have some sort of hospitalization coverage, including about 50 million through HMOs, fraternal and community organizations, cooperatives, and plans administered directly by employers or labor unions. The total number of people with hospital and surgical coverage has grown steadily but slowly since 1977 at 1.5 to 2 percent per year, with a slight dip in 1981 as unemployment rates rose. But the Blues' share of the market has been steadily declining. Since 1950 the Blues coverage of individuals with hospitalization insurance has slipped from 50 to just over 40 percent.

As with so much of the health care industry, the health insurance business is in turmoil. There has been competition among insurers for some time, but insurers are now vying with hospital chains and clinics, HMOs, and preferred providers that offer services (including claims administration) directly to big corporations, and with former big customers that self-insure. Of special significance, over the long haul, is the changing relationship between insurers and government and corporate purchasers of insurance and administrative services, who are insisting that the insurance industry act as their agents.

Until the 1980s, the Blues and the commercial insurers — despite their occasional protestations and marketing rhetoric — acted as though their bread was buttered by health care suppliers, notably the doctors and hospitals, paying them whatever they charged. . . . During my tenure as Secretary of HEW I announced my intention to develop a regulation that would require the boards of Blue Cross and Blue Shield to have a majority of members who were not providers of health care. . . . The Blues declared war on the regulation, took their case to their friends on Capitol Hill, and prevented the issuance of a final order for the duration of my time in office. Although no regulation was ever issued, by 1982 the Blues had voluntarily, if reluctantly, adopted policies requiring nonprovider majorities on their boards.

These battles helped break up the intimate relationship between the commercial insurers and Blues and the doctors and hospitals. The metamorphosis of the insurers into energetic advocates of those who pay the bills is likely to be achieved in the private sector, motivated particularly by big business. In 1984 more and more corporations insisted that their insurer — commercial or Blues, whether acting as the insurer or just administering a self-insured plan — represent their interests. The big companies are demanding that their group insurers review health care utilization patterns, monitor physicians and hospitals, and discipline those providers who exceed standards established for reasonable testing, drug prescriptions, admissions, or lengths of stay. If the commercial insurers and the Blues want to keep their corporate business, they're beginning to realize, they must respond to those who pay their bills.

Congressional Research Service, Health Insurance and the Uninsured
17-22 (1988)

It is important to establish certain basics about how health insurers evaluate and select risks and price their products in order to understand why private insurance does not cover all Americans. In what follows, some basic generalizations and definitions set the stage for examining health insurance, primarily as it is provided through the workplace, which is the major source of health insurance in this country. . . .

Various terms are used in the health insurance industry to describe how insurers determine rates. There are two basic methods of calculation: community-rating and experience-rating.

Under community-rating, insurers aggregate into one "community" individuals or a number of groups, such as employers, for the purpose of providing insurance. Generally speaking, a community-rated plan charges the same rate to all members or classes of members (e.g., single versus family enrollees) in the community, spreading the costs for the entire group evenly over its members. Community-rating with adjustments based on such demographic factors as age and sex is common. Such a rating system has the advantage of allowing an insurer to apply a single rate to a large number of people, thus simplifying the process of determining premiums and, more importantly, averaging the costs of poor health risks. . . .

Under experience-rating, the past claims experience of a particular group, such as the members of an employer plan, is used to determine the premium rate for that group. Experience-rating is used for groups that meet certain size requirements and is not used where groups are so small that experience is likely to be unreliable. This procedure can allow rates to be set closer to the expected claims experience of a particular group than under community-rating.

Experience-rating and community-rating spread costs differently. Experience-rating, in its purest form, charges a unique rate to a group of enrollees. Community-rating is similar in concept, but rates are based on the experience of all individuals and groups in the community. As a result, groups of enrollees with lower-than-average costs will be paying for part of the insurance for groups of enrollees with high-than-average costs. . . .

An insurer who had a monopoly would have no problem charging a community rate to employers. However, in a competitive environment, insurers try to provide the most attractive rates to increase their market share. Experience-rated plans can offer employers with lower-than-average costs the same benefits as a community-rated plan for a lower rate. In this manner, experience-rating can draw the low-risk groups out of the community-rated plans.

This process can leave a community-rated plan with fewer low-cost enrollees, thereby pushing up the average cost for groups left in the community. As the average premium for community-rated groups increases, experience-rated plans can attract increasing numbers of groups with lower-than-average risks. The ultimate effect is to leave the community-rated plan with high-cost enrollees and upwardly spiraling rates. In order to remain competitive, insurers that once used only community-rating [such as Blue Cross/Blue Shield] now use experience-rating for large groups (such as large employers) and have modified their community-rating practices to set rates far closer to the actual experience of the groups they are insuring. Though there are still major components of the insurance industry that community-rate, insurers generally use experience-rating to attract and retain low-risk groups.

Mount Sinai Hospital v. Zorek
271 N.Y.S.2d 1012 (Civ. Ct. 1966)

EDWARD J. GREENFIELD, JUDGE.

One of the most celebrated trials of our literature was the confrontation of Portia and Shylock as they struggled with the problem of the removal of a pound of flesh. Now, once again, the removal of a pound of flesh, or more properly several pounds, has created a weighty legal problem for resolution by the Court.

The hopes, despairs, and conflicts of our time, and ultimately every crisis, custom and social neurosis find reflection in the matters brought before the courts, the great mirror of our society. While not of the same magnitude as wars, depressions or the disasters of nature, the problem of obesity has persistently troubled part of mankind, but even more of womankind, ever since man first eked out more than the marginal subsistence required for bare survival, accumulated the luxury of a surplus food supply, and began to live to eat instead of eating to live.

With the plump and fleshy females portrayed by Rubens no longer in vogue, having been supplanted by the ideal of the lithe and willowy high-cheekboned model, the plight of those women whose rotundity does not conform to the ideal has been accentuated. The plaintiff cry

> O! that this too too solid flesh would melt
> Thaw and resolve itself into a dew

is re-echoed today by the plump and portly, and has evoked a burgeoning and varied response from Elizabeth Arden, reducing pills, milk farms, steam baths and slenderizers to No-Cal and the Drinking Man's Diet.

Grace, felicity and beauty are qualities ardently sought after — but aesthetic considerations aside, excess avoirdupois also creates problems of health, vigor, longevity, hygiene and a general state of well-being that call for the arts of the medical practitioner. Obesity is definitely a medical problem. The correlation between overweight and a shortened lifespan has been amply demonstrated. What a chal-

I. The Health Care Cost Crisis

lenge to a medical Michelangelo, to liberate from beneath mountains of flesh the slender, sylphlike creature yearning to be free!

Doctor John J. Bookman was one who rose to the challenge. Among his patients was Jane Zorek, the wife of the defendant and third-party plaintiff in this action. Mrs. Zorek was 5'2", but could not exactly be described as petite, for she had weighed well over 200 pounds. The doctor had been treating her for a number of medical problems arising from her obesity — including abscesses, cysts, and skin grafts. In 1962, when this had caused sebaceous gland trouble, he had her hospitalized. In the hospital she was put on a rigid reducing diet restricted to 800 calories a day and lost 7½ pounds. The third-party defendant, Associated Hospital Service of New York, with whom Mr. Zorek had a family Blue Cross contract, on that occasion paid the expenses of Mrs. Zorek's hospital stay without a murmur of protest.

Out of the hospital, Mrs. Zorek was unable to maintain her weight loss, and was plagued by recurring boils and cysts. Hence, in May of 1963, Doctor Bookman again concluded that hospitalization was required and had her admitted to the plaintiff Mount Sinai Hospital. This time she was put on what is known as the "Duncan Regime" — a rigid starvation diet, in which the patient receives no calories at all, only fluids, vitamins and minerals. During her three weeks stay in the hospital on this stringent program, Mrs. Zorek lost 17½ pounds without adverse effects.

When pressed by the hospital for payment, Mr. Zorek looked to his Blue Cross policy with Associated Hospital Service of New York for reimbursement. AHS, however, this time refused payment, contending that obesity was not within the coverage of the contract, and that Mrs. Zorek's hospital confinement was not necessary for treatment of her condition. This lawsuit then followed.

While on the trial AHS argued that obesity is neither a disease nor an injury, it is clear that Blue Cross coverage is not limited only to those calamities, since the policy spells out the "condition, disease, ailment or accidental injury" which is *excluded* from coverage, it should be plain that there *is* coverage for hospitalization resulting from any condition, disease, injury or ailment which is not excluded. While it is debatable whether or not obesity is an illness or ailment, certainly it is a "condition", and the test of coverage must be determined on other grounds.

The policy provides:

> Such Hospital Service shall be available to a Subscriber, following his admission to a hospital and during the time he is confined herein as a registered bed patient and while he is under the treatment of a physician, *when such hospital confinement is necessary for his proper treatment.* . . .

However, there shall be available only such items of Hospital Service as are necessary and consistent with the diagnosis and treatment of the *condition* for which such hospitalization is required. (Italics supplied)

Under Exclusions appear the following:

A. Hospital Service Shall Not Be Provided: . . .
   5. For a hospital stay or that portion of a hospital stay which is primarily for custodial, convalescent or sanitarium type care or for a rest cure.

Associated Hospital Service, the third-party defendant, argues that hospital confinement was not necessary for proper treatment of Mrs. Zorek's obese condition, and that the care rendered to her during her stay in the hospital was convalescent or sanitarium type care which the contract excludes. . . .

The words "necessary for proper treatment" call into play the exercise of judgment. "Proper" in whose eyes? The patient's, the treating physician's, the hospital's, an AHS administrator's, or a court's looking back on the events sometime afterwards? Although no cases have been brought to the Court's attention directly dealing with this problem, this Court concludes that the applicable standards of judgment as to the treatment prescribed must be those of the treating physician.

Only the treating physician can determine what the appropriate treatment should be for any given condition. Any other standard would involve intolerable second-guessing, with every case calling for a crotchety Doctor Gillespie to peer over the shoulders of a supposedly unseasoned Doctor Kildare. The diagnosis and treatment of a patient are matters peculiarly within the competence of the treating physician. The diagnosis may be insightful and brilliant, or it may be wide of the mark, but right or wrong, the patient under his doctor's guidance proceeds upon his theories and sustains expenses therefor. Can a hospitalization insurer rightfully decline to pay for the expenses incurred on the theory that subsequent events may have proved the diagnosis or the recommended treatment to have been wrong?

Once the treating doctor has decided on the treatment, we may of course review his judgment, as to whether or not hospital confinement was necessary for the particular treatment prescribed. The doctor who orders hospital confinement for the removal of a simple splinter or the lancing of a boil has almost certainly exceeded the bounds of proper medical judgment in providing for his patient. The doctor who orders hospitalization for major surgery clearly is correct in concluding that hospital confinement is necessary for that treatment, even though he may be in egregious error in deciding that major

I. The Health Care Cost Crisis 683

surgery is called for. Once the treating doctor has decided on a course of treatment for which hospitalization is necessary, his judgment cannot be retrospectively challenged.

A gall-bladder or a liver condition may be treated by a radical operation or by allowing a healthy regimen and the healing passage of time to work the miracle of regeneration. Who can say with certainty which course of treatment is correct? But if the operation is decided on, can there be a denial of Blue Cross coverage because alternative courses of treatment were available?

In this case doctors might differ as to what treatment should have been given to Mrs. Zorek for obesity and related disorders. The doctor who treated her concluded the appropriate treatment for the condition would be not further home dieting, or intensive exercise, or sanitarium care, but the Duncan regime. Other doctors might disagree as to prescribing the Duncan regime, but they were not treating Mrs. Zorek. . . .

The Duncan regime is a recognized medical treatment for obesity. While there is some controversy about it, and not all doctors would choose to resort to that treatment, many reputable doctors do. Doctor Bookman chose that treatment here. He having determined, within the scope of his medical competence, that the treatment was necessary, the sole question remaining is whether hospitalization was necessary for the treatment decided on.

AHS contends that what was done for Mrs. Zorek in the hospital demonstrates that hospitalization was not necessary. Apart from restricting her intake of food and administering vitamins, the patient was permitted to continue ambulatory and was weighed daily. All these things, AHS contends, were in the nature of custodial care and could have been done at home or in any sanitarium or rest home. Looking back, Mrs. Zorek's stay was indeed uneventful. However, we must measure the necessity for hospitalization by the prospective potentialities for danger inherent in a treatment, and not by fortuitous actuality.

Dr. Bookman testified that the Duncan regime was a dangerous course of treatment, and because of the dangers involved called for careful supervision at all times. The patient's blood pressure, temperature, and body fluids had to be continuously checked to be certain that proper chemical balance was maintained, and he insisted much more than mere custodial care would be required. Indeed, severe shock and even death are known to have ensued for persons following the Duncan regime even under carefully supervised conditions, since the changes which occur may be sudden and drastic. Even the medical expert who testified for Blue Cross stated that while he personally would not recommend the Duncan regime, the reason he would not do so is because of its inherent danger. In fact, he said, it would be foolishness to place someone on a Duncan diet outside of a hospital with facilities for 24 hour supervision and a well-trained medical staff.

Fortunately, there were no adverse developments or complications for Mrs. Zorek during her hospital stay. The possibilities were ever-present however, and in any sensible society penalties are not to be imposed where common-sense precautions are taken. The Court concludes that not only was hospitalization necessary once the Duncan regime was decided upon, but that it would have been medically irresponsible to have had anything less. Certainly we must presume that a busy metropolitan hospital complex like Mount Sinai was not going to make one of its much sought-after beds available for three weeks for a person who merely was seeking a "rest cure", and the kind of enforced diet she could otherwise get on a milk farm. It was medical necessity and not cosmetic vanity which dictated the hospital stay. . . .

It is the holding of this Court in construing the Blue Cross contract that when multiple courses of treatment are available, whether for the obese, the alcoholic, or the addicted, if the treating physician chooses that treatment for which hospitalization is required, and rejects those treatments which can be adequately administered in a rest home or sanitarium, then, absent a specific contractual exclusion, there is full coverage for the hospital stay. . . .

The amount of the hospital bill in this case attributed to Mrs. Zorek's treatment for obesity came to $557.90, for which sum the plaintiff, Mount Sinai Hospital, is entitled to judgment.*

NOTES

The Structure of Private Insurance

1. It is widely accepted that "the main cause of the unnecessary and unjustified increase in costs is the complex of irrational economic incentives inherent in the system of . . . what are called 'third-party payors.'" A. Enthoven, Health Plan 16 (1980). This is why most

---

* [Editors' note: For another court moved to literary heights by this issue, see Zuckerberg v. Blue Cross & Blue Shield, 464 N.Y.S.2d 678, 683 (1983), *rev'd* 487 N.Y.S.2d 595 (1985) (requiring Blue Shield to pay for a course of nutritional cancer therapy of unproven benefit that the plaintiff obtained in Mexico): "A possible path was opened, had it not been taken, what then? At least, it was tried.

> For of all sad words of tongue or pen,
> The saddest are these: 'It might have been!'

(Maud Muller, by John Greenleaf Whittier, Stanza 53)."]

solutions to the health care spending crisis focus on reforms to our existing health insurance system. An informed study of these reforms, then, requires some understanding of the traditional financing system. For another account in a similar vein to Califano's, see S. Law, Blue Cross: What Went Wrong? (2d ed. 1976). See also R. Fein, Medical Care, Medical Costs: The Search for a Health Insurance Policy (1986); Havighurst, The Questionable Cost-Containment Record of Commercial Health Insurers, in Health Care in America (H. Frech & R. Zechhauser eds. 1988).

2. Have we now come full circle in the evolving structure of health insurance?

> Several large private hospital chains have expanded into health insurance, a move that many experts predict will significantly alter the health care industry. . . . Barely a year old, hospital chain insurance already has about a million subscribers over all, according to company officials. "What we are seeing is a major structural change in the health care delivery system in the U.S.," said Royce Diener, chairman of American Medical International of Beverly Hills, a chain of 129 hospitals, whose year-old Amicare health insurance plan has 400,000 subscribers.
>
> The companies' insurance costs less when subscribers use their hospitals, clinics and physicians. Company officials say this gives patients rather than doctors control over where they get care, while critics . . . say the companies are trying to fill their hospital beds. In many hospitals, in the United States, less than half the beds are occupied.

Tolchin, Private Hospitals are now Offering Health Insurance, N.Y. Times, July 5, 1985, p.1, col. 5.

3. The inevitable effect of competition in the health insurance industry is to force identifiable, high-risk individuals such as the elderly and disabled into rating groups that price the product out of the affordable range, and, of course, the poor cannot afford health insurance at any price. These two gaps in the private insurance market were at least partially filled in 1965 by the federal government's enactment of Medicare (for the elderly and disabled) and Medicaid (for the poor), as more fully described below in Section I.C.

4. The *Zorek* court appears quite absolute in its statement that "only the treating physician can determine what the appropriate treatment should be for any given condition." What term do we usually apply to the incentives created by allowing the one who is paid (or, here, a member of its medical staff) to be the sole judge of the necessity of its services? In case there is any confusion on this point, realize that three weeks of hospitalization at Mount Sinai Hospital would no longer cost $557.90; now, this would buy about *one day's* hospitalization. Should this fact change the outcome?

Other courts, while reaching the same result as *Zorek*, have softened somewhat its absolutism. Shumake v. Travelers Ins. Co., 383 N.W.2d 259, 263 (Mich. 1985) (The terms "necessarily incurred" and "required" in an insurance contract are ambiguous, and a physician is generally better equipped than lawyers to determine what is medically necessary); Carrao v. Health Care Serv. Corp., 454 N.E.2d 781, 788 (Ill. App. 1983) ("the insured is justified in relying on the good faith judgment of his treating physician as to the medical necessity of services prescribed"); Van Vactor v. Blue Cross Assoc., 365 N.E.2d 638, 643 (Ill. App. 1977) (because of ambiguity of "medically necessary," "there was sufficient evidence to warrant [the trial court's conclusion] that the insured was justified in relying on the good faith judgment of his treating physician"). See generally J. Appleman, Insurance Law and Practice §705.35 (1981) ("coverage will be found where the treating physician determined that such hospitalization was necessary"); Kalb, Controlling Health Care Costs by Controlling Technology: A Private Contractual Approach, 99 Yale L.J. 1104, 1117 (1990) (collecting cases).

5. *Zorek* suggests that complete autonomy of physician judgment is only a presumption that applies in the "absen[ce of] a specific exclusion" of coverage for the procedure. One way in which insurance companies typically seek to limit physician discretion is to exclude payment for "experimental" procedures. Zuckerberg v. Blue Cross & Blue Shield, 487 N.Y.S.2d 595 (1985) (upholding such an exclusion as applied to nutritional cancer therapy obtained in Mexico). What if an insurance policy states that only Blue Cross may determine medical necessity and its decisions are final? Several cases have relied on such language to distinguish the decisions cited above. Sarchett v. Blue Shield of Cal., 233 Cal. Rptr. 76, 83 (Cal. 1987) ("it is unlikely that any insurer could permit the subscriber free selection of a physician if it were required to accept without question the physician's view of reasonable treatment and good medical practice"); Lockshin v. Blue Cross of Northeast, Ohio, 434 N.E.2d 754, 756 (Oh. App. 1980) ("a function, basic to the insurer, is the right . . . 'to determine whether . . . [a] claim should be allowed or rejected'"). But see Weissman v. Blue Cross of Western New York, Inc., 457 N.Y.S.2d 392, 396 (Buffalo City Ct. 1982) (granting summary judgment for plaintiff's claim that it is unconscionable for Blue Cross to exercise sole judgment over medical necessity), *rev'd.*, 482 N.Y.S.2d 659, 660 (Erie Co. Ct. 1984) (finding triable issues of fact on unconscionability claim). See generally Annot. 75 A.L.R. 4th 763 (1990).

6. A related body of law addresses whether state Medicaid programs may limit reimbursement for care they deem medically unnecessary. See 711 and 822 infra. In one recent decision, the court

held that Medicaid must cover AZT treatment for both early and advanced stages of AIDS, even though FDA approval of the drug is limited to the latter. The court reasoned that "it would be improper . . . to interfere with a physician's judgment of medical necessity" based on FDA drug-labeling requirements because "FDA approved indications [are] not intended to limit or interfere with the practice of medicine; . . . the package insert is only informational." Weaver v. Reagan, 886 F.2d 194, 198 (8th Cir. 1989).

7. Would it constitute the unlicensed practice of medicine for Blue Cross to use nonphysician personnel such as nurses to make medical necessity determinations? See Hall, Institutional Control of Physician Behavior, 137 U. Penn. L. Rev. 431, 460-467 (1988) (arguing no). Even if insurers hire doctors to review insurance claims (as they often do), could a patient denied reimbursement allege that second guessing his doctor's judgment constitutes tortious interference with the doctor/patient relationship? See Hall at 474, n.151 ("Such review does not prohibit performance of the procedure; it only imposes a financial burden on the patient. While this is interference to some degree, . . . the insurer's only alternative is to submit to the conflict of interest inherent in allowing the physician who is paid to be the sole judge of the necessity of the service.") Compare Association of American Physicians and Surgeons v. Weinberger, 395 F. Supp. 125 (N.D. Ill. 1975) (three-judge court), *aff'd mem.* 423 U.S. 975 (1975) (medical necessity review under Medicare does not unduly interfere with physicians' judgment), with American Med. Assoc. v. Weinberger, 395 F. Supp. 515 (1975) (contra). See also the discussion of medical necessity review under Medicare at 710 infra.

Insurance company medical necessity review has also led to substantial awards for bad faith denial of reimbursement. Aetna Life Ins. Co. v. Lavoie, 470 So. 2d 1060 (Ala. 1984) ($3.5 million punitive damage award), *vacated on other grounds,* 475 U.S. 813 (1986); Hughes v. Blue Cross of Northern Calif., 245 Cal. Rptr. 273 (Cal. App. 1988) (use of overly restrictive definition of medical necessity justifies an $850,000 bad faith award).

8. Note that the federal ERISA statute (the Employment Retirement Income Security Act), discussed in Chapter 7.II, preempts this body of state law as it applies to disputes arising under health insurance that is provided through the workplace. Pilot Life Ins. Co. v. Dedeaux, 481 U.S. 41 (1987) (employee has no action for bad faith denial of coverage).

9. Understanding more of the structure of private insurance, we now turn in the following section to a study of the effects of this structure on the perceptions and behavior of (1) patients, (2) doctors, (3) hospitals, and (4) employers/insurers.

A. Enthoven, Health Plan
xviii-xix, 1-3, 9-10, 12, 18-19, 21-26, 32, 93-95, 111-113 (1980)*

[Effect on Patients]

The economic effect of health insurance is, of course, to reduce the cost of covered services to the insured consumer. Instead of paying the full cost to the economy of a service, the insured consumer pays some fraction of that cost, possibly even zero. Thus any economic restraint on the would-be patient, and any restraint on his or her doctor that comes from knowing that the patient will have to pay the cost of care, is greatly attenuated or even eliminated when the patient is insured.

Data from Harvard University economists Martin Feldstein and Amy Taylor, illustrate this point. Although average hospital cost per patient day increased from $15.62 in 1950 to $151.53 in 1975, the net cost to the consumer in constant 1967 dollars remained virtually unchanged, at about $11.

The large increase in cost of services with no increase in cost to the consumer when he receives the services has, of course, meant large increases in insurance premiums. The question naturally arises, then, of why the increase in premiums has not produced more consumer resistance and, perhaps, decisions to buy less costly insurance covering less costly benefits. The answer is that most people have their premiums paid, in large part or in total, by employer or government and have no choice in the matter. In 1974 the benefits of 68 percent of the workers in those private-industry health plans covering more than twenty-five workers were paid for entirely by the employer. Similarly, the hospital-insurance part of Medicare is paid for largely by payroll taxes; the physician-service part, heavily subsidized by general tax revenues. Medicaid benefits are fully paid by federal and state governments. So most people are quite unaware of the costs of their health insurance. . . .

[Effect on Doctors]

Most doctors in the United States are paid on the basis of "fee for service," essentially a piece-work basis, rather than some other arrangement, such as a monthly retainer fee for providing comprehensive care or an all-inclusive charge per case. In the fee-for-service system, doctors charge separately for each service performed. If they

---

* Alain Enthoven is on the faculty of the Graduate School of Business, Stanford University.
Copyright © 1980, Addison-Wesley Publishing Co., Inc., Reading, Massachusetts. Reprinted by permission.

do more services, they charge more. This, of course, gives them an incentive to do more, even if more yields a negligible benefit to the patient. Typically, the doctor is both the advisor to the patient on the need for services and the provider to the patient of physician services. (The doctor may also advise and provide lab tests, X-rays, injections, and other services.) The conflict of interest should be apparent. As the element of uncertainty in medical practice is quite large, the physician has wide latitude to recommend more services that might do some good. And, of course, the insured patient has little or no financial incentive to question the need for more services. In prescribing more for an insured patient, the doctor can usually feel that he or she is acting in the patient's best interest. It is the combination of insured patients and fee-for-service doctors that is an especially potent force for increased spending.

The incentives in the fee-for-service system also reward more costly types of care rather than less costly care. Doctors are paid more per hour for doing new technologic procedures than for such services as examining and advising patients.

Alvin Thompson, M.D., gave the following example in his September 1978 valedictory address as President of the Washington State Medical Society:

> We must think about the effect of financial incentives on what we do. I am a gastroenterologist and an endoscopist. Suppose a patient comes in complaining of diarrhea. If I do a colonoscopy examination, many third party payers will readily pay nearly $400. That is ten times the forty dollars I might receive if I just talked with the patient for an hour to find out what he was doing that was causing the diarrhea. Yet, from the point of view of his health, listening might be a better way for me to spend the hour. We must ask ourselves whether such incentives are leading us to do more costly procedures than would be best for our patients.

Dr. Blumberg also found that the structure of fees provides strong financial incentives to care for patients in the hospital rather than in the office. . . . In 1974 an internist saw an average of 2.47 patients per hour when caring for patients in the office, 3.69 per hour, or 49 percent more, when seeing patients on hospital rounds. Yet the fee for a follow-up visit in the hospital was 34 percent higher than for a follow-up visit in the office. The net result was that the doctor's revenue per hour when working in the hospital was twice that realized when working in the office. The differential in net revenue is even greater because the physician does not need to use as much office staff and overhead for a hospital visit. . . .

To observe that financial incentives play an important role in the use of medical services is not to imply that they are the only, or even the most important, factor. Physicians are concerned primarily with curing their sick patients, regardless of the cost. That ethic has been instilled in them through years of arduous training. Many take a failure to cure a sick patient as a personal defeat. When we are sick, we want our doctors to be concerned with curing us and nothing else. Physicians and other health professionals are also motivated by a desire to achieve professional excellence and the esteem of their peers and the public. But their use of resources is inevitably shaped by financial incentives. Physicians who survive and prosper must ultimately do what brings in money and curtail those activities that lose money. . . .

[Effect on Hospitals]

The physicians' impact on hospital costs cannot be characterized merely as one of neutrality based on ignorance. Paul Ellwood, M.D., President of InterStudy, put it this way: "Hospitals don't have patients. Hospitals have doctors, and doctors have patients. Therefore, hospitals compete for doctors." And they compete in costly ways such as providing house staff (resident physicians) to do much of the work and to eliminate the inconvenience of night or weekend visits. Hospitals also compete for doctors by offering them the use of the latest and most complex equipment, the use of convenient offices at subsidized rental rates, and even guarantees of a certain income. All of these costs are passed on to the third-party payors. . . .

[The Role of Insurers and Employers]

Most medical bills are paid for by "third-party payors," insurance companies and government agencies that pay the bills after the care has been given and the costs incurred. And they are powerless to control costs. Most consumers' insurance gives them free choice of doctor and hospital and little or no incentive to seek out a less costly doctor or style of care. Their personal insurance premium will be the same whether they go to the most economical or the most extravagant doctor. This system embodies many cost-increasing incentives and virtually no rewards for economy. . . .

Why have we chosen a financing system with such perverse consequences? The reasons are many and complex. Some are historical accidents. One important factor has been the medical profession's insistence on the principles of *fee-for-service* payment and *"free choice of doctor"* in every insurance plan. Fee for service is advantageous for doctors, both economically and in ensuring their independence. Free-

I. The Health Care Cost Crisis

dom of choice of doctor is important to doctors and patients. But insurance with "free choice of doctor" effectively rules out economic competition among doctors. The insured patient has little reason to care about medical costs. Medicare and Medicaid were made to conform to these principles.

Other factors have reinforced the system of insured fee for service. In effect, the *tax laws* put the control of health insurance for employees and their families into the hands of employers by making employer contributions to health insurance tax-free. Employers and unions have used this control to make themselves the workers' benefactors. For the most part, they have chosen to offer employees a single health insurance plan with "free choice of doctor" rather than a menu of competing alternative health plans, each associated with a limited set of doctors. . . .

Private insurers usually do not have a strong incentive to control costs, because of the way they set their premiums. Most premiums, at least for large employee groups, are set on the basis of what is called "experience rating." This means that the premium is set equal to the actual health care costs experienced by the insured group, plus an additional amount for administrative cost and profit. In some cases the premium is set in advance. If it turns out not to have been enough to cover costs, the insurer may include the overrun in the next year's premium. . . .

Moreover, both insurers and employers are reluctant to take any actions that would upset employees. This might occur if either refused to pay a bill or antagonized a patient's doctor. Such action might appear to be an attempt to evade a contractual obligation. The potential savings in any individual case are likely to appear small compared with the potential cost of contesting a claim submitted by either an employee or physician. . . .

If one plan is to be offered, almost inevitably it will be a "free choice of doctor" plan. Employers and unions are understandably reluctant to attempt to restrict employee choices of doctor. "Company store medicine" is not popular in the United States. The effect is that the employee can elect the most costly doctor at no economic penalty. Employers who offer such insurance are, in effect, saying to the most costly providers that their costs will be paid, almost no matter what they are. . . .

Most people think of the need for medical care as an insurable event, very similar to insured hurricane or automobile collision damage. You are either sick or well. If you are sick, you go to the doctor. The doctor diagnoses your illness, applies the standard treatment, and sends the bill for his or her "usual, customary, and reasonable fee," all or most of which is paid by your insurance company. Our entire Blue Cross-Blue Shield and commercial insurance system was built on that view of the problem. Medicare and Medicaid, the public insurance systems for the elderly and poor, were built on the same model. The consequence is a financial disaster. Our society has accepted the casualty insurance model for health care financing, only to find that it contributes to excessive and excessively costly care. . . .

Many people seem to think that medical care is like mechanical engineering — that for each medical condition there is a "best treatment," a "professional standard." It is up to the doctor to know that treatment and to use it. People do not fully understand the great uncertainties that pervade medical care and the variety of acceptable treatments. They think of medical care as mostly treatment for acute life-threatening conditions, as if it were accurately represented by the television dramas about the emergency room. Based on these misconceptions, we have applied to medical care a financing system that was developed for casualty (fire and collision) insurance.

The ideal case for casualty insurance is one in which the damage is caused by an act of God and the cost of repair can be determined objectively. In such a case the financial incentives inherent in insurance do not play a significant role in either the incidence of damage or the cost of repair. Insurance of houses against hurricane damage or fires caused by lightning does not bring on more storms. Collision insurance for automobiles fits the model tolerably, but much less well. Most people do not drive less carefully just because they have insurance. But those who do have insurance are likely to demand more and better repairs than those who do not — because someone else is paying the bill. Still, ordinarily, having your collision-damaged car repaired is not an open-ended task.

Medical insurance hardly fits the model at all. The element of judgment and choice in the decision to seek care and in the amount of care provided is too great. Caring for a patient can be open-ended, especially if he or she has a chronic disease. Uncertainty pervades medical diagnosis and treatment. In most cases there is not one correct or standard treatment. There may be several accepted therapies. Most medical care is not a matter of life and death, but rather of darker or lighter shades of grey concerning the quality of life. In view of this, it should not be surprising that the institutional arrangements for providing care, including the financial incentives facing the doctor, are very important. The casualty insurance model does not fit medical care at all well, because making more care free to the patient and remunerative to the doctor leads to more, and more costly, care being demanded and provided. . . .

Of course, in many cases the diagnosis is clear-cut. But in many others there is a great deal of *uncertainty* in each step of medical care. Doctors are confronted with patients who have symptoms and syndromes, not labels with their diseases. A set of symptoms can be associated with any of several diseases. The chest pains produced by a gall bladder attack and by a heart attack can be confused by excellent doctors. Diagnostic tests are not 100 percent reliable. Consider a young woman with a painless lump in her breast. Is it cancer? There is a significant probability that a breast X-ray (mammogram), will produce a false result; that is, it will say that she does have cancer when she does not, or vice versa. There is less chance of error if a piece of the tissue is removed surgically (biopsy) and examined under a microscope by a pathologist. But even pathologists may reach different conclusions in some cases. . . .

Of course, in many cases there is a clearly indicated treatment. But for many other medical conditions there are *several possible treatments*, each of which is legitimate and associated with different benefits, risks, and costs. Consider a few examples.

A forty-year-old laborer's chronic lower-back pain sometimes requires prolonged bed rest and potent pain medication. One doctor may recommend surgery; another, hoping to avoid the need for surgery, may recommend continued bed rest and traction followed by exercises. Whether one treatment is "better" than the other depends in part on the interpretation of the diagnostic tests (how strong the evidence is of a surgically correctable condition), but also in considerable part on the patient's values and the surgeon's judgment (how large a surgical risk the patient is willing to accept for the predicted likelihood of improvement).

As another common example with more than one treatment, consider a young woman with abnormal uterine bleeding, a nuisance but not a serious health hazard. One doctor may recommend a hysterectomy, whereas a second may advise that a dilatation and curettage be done as the first course of therapy, a third may feel that hormonal treatment is indicated, and a fourth may recommend no treatment. Any of the four might make sense, depending on the circumstances. There is no formula for calculating "the best" treatment, no clear dividing line between a "necessary" and an "unnecessary" operation. . . .

When thinking about medical care, then, we should think in terms of a variety of legitimate treatments for each condition, with their relative merits in a particular case depending on the unique circumstances and values of the people involved. We should remember that there is pervasive uncertainty and that medicine is more an art based on judgment than a science based on calculation. Medical care deals more with the quality of life than with the quantity (length) of life. The "product" does not come in standard units. Medical care is a matter of subtle and complex judgments about more versus less, and more may often not be better.

I. Kennedy, The Unmasking of Medicine*
1-4, 11-14, 17 (1981)

Six years ago, the American Psychiatric Association took a vote and decided homosexuality was not an illness. So, since 1974 — at least to the A.P.A. — it has not been an illness. How extraordinary, you may think, to decide what illness is by taking a vote. What exactly is going on here? . . .

"Illness", you insist, is a technical term, a term of scientific exactitude. Whether someone has an illness, is ill, is a matter of objective fact. . . .

. . . Obviously we all agree that someone with an inflamed appendix is ill, as is someone who cannot breathe very well, even when resting. Equally, we agree that someone with, say, leprosy or cancer is ill. . . . We all agree that these are illnesses because we accept two propositions. The first is that there is a normal state in which the appendix is not inflamed and breathing is easy while resting. Second, it is appropriate to judge someone who deviates from this norm as ill. Only if we examine both of these will we understand what is involved in the meaning of the word "illness".

Take the first of the two propositions, that there must be a deviation from the normal state. . . . The point is clear. What is the normal state against which to measure abnormality is a product of social and cultural values and expectations. It is not some static, objectively identifiable fact. As views and values change, so the norm will change. So, if illness has as its first criterion some deviation from the norm, some abnormality, it too will vary and change in its meaning. . . .

Let me explain what follows from this. The treatment of illness is for doctors. A social institution has grown up defined and managed by doctors, the role of which is to persuade us that our preoccupations must be related to them, and them alone (since they alone have competence). We appear, perforce, naked both physically and emotionally. However willing we may be, and however well intentioned the doctor, it is hard to overstate the power which this vests in the doctor. It is hard to overstate how such a social arrangement may undermine the notion of individual responsibility and of course, ultimately, individual liberty. . . .

If you remain unconvinced of the view I am advancing, consider Mrs. Jones. Married at nineteen, she is now thirty-five. She stays at home all day, while her husband is at work and their children are at school. She has grown to dread and despise the tedium of her life.

---

* Professor Ian Kennedy is on the Faculty of Law, King's College, London. Reprinted with permission.

She finds her husband boring. She feels trapped. She has ambivalent emotions towards her children. Life, she feels, is passing her by. She finds herself crying most days. She decides to visit her doctor. She has diagnosed herself as needing help and chosen the doctor in the absence of other obvious candidates as the appropriate provider. She may not think of herself as ill. Indeed, in previous times she may have consulted her priest although not thinking of herself as sinful or in danger of perdition. Her doctor tells her that she is anxious and depressed, something she already knew. The doctor can then confer on her the status of ill, if he so chooses, by offering to treat her through the use of his medical expertise. He will provide anti-depressants or tranquillisers. . . . This is not to say that the doctor's role is sinister or conspiratorial. In some large part the doctor acts as a socialiser quite unwittingly. His education has trained him to see illness and to try to ease pain, even if by so doing he merely drives the cork deeper into the bottle so making uncorking that much more explosive. . . .

In conclusion, I am not saying that we should abandon the use of the word "illness". I am merely urging that we understand what it involves. Since the diagnosis of illness always calls for a judgement, it is right for us all to consider when it is properly to be applied and who should apply it. We should consider what limits may properly be placed by us on the power of doctors to manipulate the concept. I am not suggesting that we take a vote. But we must make it our business to ensure that the judgements arrived at reflect the considered views of all of us. Each diagnosis is an ethical decision. . . . This is captured in the World Health Organisation's definition of health as "not the mere absence of disease, but total physical, mental and social well-being".

In re Hospital Corporation of America
106 F.T.C. 455, 457-459 (1984), *aff'd,* 807 F.2d 1381 (7th Cir.),
cert. denied, 481 U.S. 1038 (1986)

[The following is an excerpt from a decision enjoining the merger of two hospital companies in the Chattanooga area because the merger would tend to create a substantial reduction in competition. This is the Commission's preliminary discussion of the economic forces that operate within the health care industry.]

[I]t is important to have a fundamental understanding of the role of physicians and third-party payors in the health care transaction.

The role of the physician is a market response to the extremely high cost to consumers of health care information and expertise. As a result of the patient's grossly imperfect information concerning proper diagnosis and treatment, and the doctor's much greater knowledge, the doctor decides what diagnoses, treatments, and so forth the patient will have. The physician orders tests, prescribes drugs and courses of treatment, and so forth, and most important for our analysis, decides whether and when a patient will be admitted to and discharged from a hospital, along with the battery of tests and procedures he receives while there. The patient simply cannot decide these things for himself; the doctor is his repository of information and expertise and thus plays the critical role in determining the nature and extent of hospital and other health services the patient will receive.

In addition to a lack of information about how to diagnose and treat himself, the patient has perhaps even less perfect information about the occurrence and extent of future illness and injury. For the most part, neither the doctor nor the patient can control frequency or intensity of disease or injury. For example, the typical patient cannot anticipate or prevent being in an automobile accident or developing cancer. Likewise, the doctor cannot determine the type or intensity of diagnosis and treatment until a problem develops, to the extent that he can determine the severity of a problem within a short period of time at all. The uncertainty associated with the nature and extent of potential health problems is thus enormous, and the uncertainty about the cost associated with diagnosis and treatment of such contingent events is equally high. As a result, the patient cannot plan financially for the treatment of his health problems; he may be healthy for the rest of his life and have to spend no money on health care whatsoever, or he may receive an injury so serious that he could not possibly hope to pay for his treatment with his annual salary. What is the logical market response to this dilemma? Health insurance.

Insurance is a response to uncertainty, and spreads the risk of financial loss occasioned by treatment of disease or injury over both the people who turn out to have little need for health care and those who turn out to have a great need. By paying an insurance premium in a world where the future need for health care is uncertain, a potential patient eliminates the risk of not having the money he needs to pay for diagnosis and treatment, particularly of serious illnesses or injuries, should health care and of particular interest to us, hospital care, be needed. . . .

With respect to our analysis, there is one extremely important effect on the hospital services market of third-party payment: The extent to which a patient is insured determines the extent to which he is sensitive to the price of hospital care. If he is fully insured, once he becomes ill his interest lies in receiving the best quality care possible, including the highest quality comforts and surroundings if he is in the hospital, no matter what the costs. Who, then, is concerned about price? We would expect third-party payors and their customers,

I. The Health Care Cost Crisis

the world of potential patients and employers who pay insurance premiums, to be interested in minimizing the costs of insurance. Of course, the government and taxpayers, who insure many of the elderly and under-privileged through the Medicare and Medicaid programs, should be interested as well. There is one wrinkle, however. When hospital prices rise, the increased payments made by an insurance company are spread over all its subscribers, both patients and non-patients (*i.e.*, prospective patients); premiums rise less than proportionally to the increase in hospital prices. Thus, not every significant increase in hospital prices will bring a significant market reaction from insurance consumers. . . .

We are thus confronted in this case with a very peculiar market indeed. Because of the uncertainty of illness and injury and the grossly imperfect information available to consumers of hospital services, patients generally rely on physicians to determine the nature and extent of the medical care they receive and on third-party payors to provide the financial assurances that such care will be paid for.

NOTES

The Effects of Private Insurance

1. Professor Havighurst has correctly observed that "the extensive anecdotal evidence of inefficient spending on unnecessary services is not conclusive [of whether we are spending too much on health care], because some . . . wasteful spending is an inevitable cost of having third-party financial protection (public or private), which all agree is desirable and necessary to some measure. Although some of that inefficiency could certainly be eliminated by tighter administrative controls, the various costs of those controls might add up to more than the savings they would achieve." The Professional Paradigm of Medical Care: Obstacle to Decentralization, 30 Jurimetrics (Summer 1990). The impossibility of *empirical* verification of inefficiency in the medical system makes the preceding *structural* analysis of systemic flaws in the health care market even more important. It is because the incentives flowing from traditional forms of insurance have an irrational effect on health care spending decisions that we know the market is not determining the proper level and distribution of health care resources. In other words, the severe defects in the functioning of ordinary market forces gives us strong theoretical grounding for concluding that health care resources are both *over* allocated and *mis*allocated. A second point of significance in understanding the various forms of market failure is that this understanding helps us to better appreciate the precise nature of the reforms that will be

necessary to produce a more satisfactory allocation of health care resources.

2. Would a properly functioning health care delivery system eliminate just unnecessary care, that is, care that provides no benefit at all? Thurow, Learning to Say "No," 311 New Eng. J. Med. 1569 (1984) ("Instead of stopping treatments when all benefits cease to exist, physicians must stop treatments when marginal benefits are equal to marginal costs."); Schwartz, The Inevitable Failure of Current Cost-Containment Strategies, 257 J.A.M.A. 220 (1987) ("even if all useless care were gradually eliminated, we could anticipate only a temporary respite from rising costs. . . . Long-term control of the rate of increase in expenditures thus requires that we curb the development and diffusion of clinically useful technology").

3. Traditional insurance is usually referred to as "third-party, fee-for-service" reimbursement. Do these two characteristics have a unitary or separate effect? Free choice of provider is the third characteristic of traditional insurance. The anomaly that "free choice" has been used to restrain competition is explored in the excellent article by Charles Weller, "Free Choice" as a Restraint of Trade in American Health Care Delivery and Insurance, 69 Iowa L. Rev. 1351 (1984), excerpted below in Chapter 8.III.C.

4. Two additional views on the effects of insurance:

In his Preface on Doctors that accompanies his play The Doctor's Dilemma, George Bernard Shaw wrote: "That any sane nation . . . should . . . give a surgeon a pecuniary interest in cutting off your leg, is enough to make one despair of political humanity. But that is precisely what we have done. And the more appalling the mutilation, the more the mutilator is paid. Scandalized voices murmur that . . . operations are necessary. They may be. It may also be necessary to hang a man or pull down a house. But we take good care not to make the hangman and the house breaker the judges of that." See Relman, The Future of Medical Practice, 5 Health Affairs, Summer 1983, at 7.

A practicing surgeon in Manhattan recently confessed: "When I finished my [medical] training some years ago, the surgeon who directed my department was routinely allowed $800 from Medicare for a commonly performed surgical procedure. This was considered top dollar for such a procedure but was entirely commensurate with his skill and reputation. Acting upon the advice of my predecessors, . . . I began to bill $1,000 in order to 'up' my profile for the same procedure — and, to my surprise, I began receiving higher fees than my former chief despite my nearly novice status. Neither I nor the American Medical Association complained about these arrangements." Sislowitz, Doctors' Faustian Deal, N.Y. Times Jan. 7, 1988, p. 23.

5. The seminal analysis of medical uncertainty as the justification

for health insurance is Arrow, Uncertainty and the Welfare Economics of Medical Care, 53 Am. Econ. Rev. 941 (1963). Compare P. Starr supra at 226-227 (uncertainty justifies some form of insurance, but not the particular forms that have developed).

6. Underscoring the judgmental nature of medical care, medical epidemiologist John Wennberg's pathbreaking research has uncovered tremendously wide variation in the rate with which common medical procedures are used in similar localities. "[A] child in Rumford, Maine, has fifteen times the probability of being hospitalized with a diagnosis of pediatric pneumonia as does a child living in Portland." Caper, Variations in Medical Practice: Implications for Health Policy, 3 Health Affairs at 110 (Summer 1984). The cited journal contains several articles devoted to this topic that provide an excellent entry point to the literature. See also J. Eisenberg, Doctors' Decisions and the Cost of Medical Care (1986) (Chapter 1); Wennberg, Freeman & Culp, Are Hospital Services Rationed in New Haven or Over-Utilised in Boston?, The Lancet, Vol. I 1987, at 1185.

7. The phenomenon of a market for medical services controlled by doctors (described in the F.T.C. opinion) is referred to in economic jargon as "supplier-induced demand" — the seller, not the buyer, makes the purchasing decision. The phenomenon that the costs of an individual patient's treatment decisions are borne by the community at large is known as a "free rider" problem — the patient takes a free ride on the insurance premiums paid by other members of the community.

8. "Many institutional providers of health services are nonprofit and have no incentive to improve efficiency. Instead, to attract physicians and patients they have tended to maximize their quality of care by making available a full range of diagnostic and therapeutic services. This augmented service and quality rivalry may be an important source of inefficiency in the system, akin to the service rivalry that occurred in regulated airline markets. . . . In health markets, such quality one-upmanship has . . . resulted in overemphasis on utilization of new and expensive technology at the expense of improvements in existing technology. Unlike other industries . . . , intense rivalry in medicine has raised, not lowered hospital costs." Alpert & McCarthy, Beyond *Goldfarb:* Applying Traditional Antitrust Analysis to Changing Health Markets, 29 Antitrust Bull. 165, 170 (1984). The phrase "technological imperative" has emerged as an enduring label for this phenomenon. See generally V. Fuchs, Who Shall Live?: Health Economics and Social Change (1974).

9. "Since . . . third-party payors have proved to be so powerless to control costs, one wonders what people thought *would* control cost in such a system. One of the main answers is deductibles and coinsurance. Make the patient pay the first $200 of each year's medical

bills and 25 percent of the cost above that, and he will be cost-conscious and go to the doctor only when necessary. . . . This principle has been applied in most health insurance in the United States." A. Enthoven, Health Plan 32-33 (1980). The principle has not worked well. See Siu et al., Inappropriate Use of Hospitals in a Randomized Trial of Health Insurance Plans, 315 New Eng. J. Med. 1259 (1986) ("In plans with cost sharing for all services, 22 percent of admissions and 34 percent of hospital days were classified as inappropriate, as compared with 24 percent of admissions and 35 percent of hospital days in the plan under which care was free to the patient. . . . Our data show that . . . cost sharing did not selectively reduce inappropriate hospitalization."). What aspect of the economics of medical markets could account for this failure?

10. Further market anomalies and distortions are created by the tax treatment of employer-provided health insurance: "Under current law, employer contributions toward employee health benefits are not included in the employee's taxable income. . . . [Consequently], the tax law provides a discount (before administrative expenses) of roughly 35 percent [prior to 1986 tax reform] for all health services purchased through an insurance plan. . . . The Congressional Budget Office estimates that the exclusion will reduce federal revenues by $21.4 billion in fiscal year 1982 and by $41.4 billion in fiscal year 1986. . . . The tax subsidy for employer-paid health benefits distorts demand for insurance and medical care in two ways. First, it induces the purchase of more comprehensive insurance than would otherwise be purchased, which in turn extends third-party payment's distorting effect on the demand for medical care. Second, it causes consumers to undervalue insurer cost-containment efforts, since any saving in premium that results from such efforts and is paid out as increased wages becomes taxable income." Havighurst, Competition in Health Services: Overview, Issues and Answers, 34 Vand. L. Rev. 1117, 1146 n.46 (1981).

"The effects of the employer exclusion vary greatly across income groups. Because marginal tax rates increase with income, the government subsidy provided for a given health insurance fringe benefit also increases with income. For example, people in the 40 percent tax bracket (rather than the 20 percent bracket) save $40 (not $20) in taxes when they receive $100 worth of health insurance in lieu of cash. To this must be added the fact that although health insurance is very important, it is less important than food or shelter. Lower-income workers may prefer to have more cash to pay for food and housing even if it means taking a chance on being inadequately protected against the expense of an illness. Thus, the employer exclusion provision gives a larger subsidy to those with a smaller need for financial protection and exacerbates the tendency of lower-income people to be less well insured than those with higher incomes." President's Commission, Securing Access to Health Care 169 (1983). This effect was lessened, but not eliminated, by the 1986 tax reform.

C. Traditional Government Reimbursement

INTRODUCTORY NOTE

Medicare

State and federal government programs directly finance some 40 percent of our nation's health care budget.[1] The largest of these programs are Medi*care*, the federal program that *cares* for the aged and disabled, and Medic*aid*, the federally-*aided* state program for the poor. They were enacted in 1965 as titles XVIII and XIX (respectively) of the Social Security Act.[2] Medicare is available, regardless of wealth or income, to anyone 65 or over who is also eligible for social security retirement or disability benefits.[3] Medicaid is available primarily to the "categorically needy," that is, those low-income individuals eligible for welfare under Aid to Families with Dependent Children (single parents) or Supplemental Security Income (aged, blind, and disabled). Individual states may choose to extend Medicaid eligibility to the noncategorically needy as well.

Because of the wide variation in state Medicaid program design,[4] these materials focus on the federal Medicare program.[5] Medicare is governed by the Health Care Financing Administration (HCFA), within the Department of Health and Human Services (DHHS). HCFA delegates much of the front-line, day-to-day work to "fiscal intermediaries" — private insurance companies that contract with HCFA to handle Medicare claims administration.

Medicare is divided into two parts. Part A covers institutional

---

1. This is in addition to indirect federal support through tax exemptions. See 700 supra.

2. 42 U.S.C. §§1395 and 1396. The leading tool for in-depth Medicare/Medicare research is the CCH treatise on the subject. An excellent source for current working knowledge of these programs is the public interest law journal Clearinghouse Review, which regularly publishes articles by the National Health Law Program. See also R. Buchanan & J. Minor, Legal Aspects of Health Care Reimbursement (1984).

3. Medicare also covers anyone suffering from kidney failure.

4. See Cromwell, Hurdle, & Schurman, Defederalizing Medicaid: Fair to the Poor, Fair to Taxpayers?, 12 J. Health Pol. Poly. & L. 1 (1987).

5. Further reading on current issues relating to Medicaid can be found in the Summer 1987 issue of J. Health Pol. Poly. & L.; P. Hayes, Evaluating State Medicaid Reforms (1985); D. Freund, Medicaid Reform: Four Studies of Case Management (1984); and T. Grannemann & M. Pauly, Controlling Medicaid Costs: Federalism, Competition and Choice (1983).

health care services — primarily hospitalization, but also some nursing home, home health, and hospice services. Part B coverage, known as "supplementary medical insurance," extends primarily to outpatient care and physician services. Part A coverage extends to all eligible persons[6] and is supported by a dedicated trust fund financed by an earmarked payroll tax. Part A recipients may (and virtually all do) also purchase Part B's supplemental coverage by paying a monthly premium of roughly $30. This premium covers only one fourth of Part B's costs, however; the remainder comes from general taxes.

These materials address the structure of Medicare provider reimbursement rather than the particulars of patient eligibility. Unable to study profitably the intricacies of both parts of Medicare, we will restrict our focus primarily to Part A hospital reimbursement. The design of Part A is tremendously influential on hospital behavior because Medicare accounts for 25 to 30 percent of hospital revenues, and its reimbursement system is widely copied by state Medicaid programs, which account for another 10 to 15 percent of revenues.

Historically, Part A reimbursed hospitals *100 percent* of their *costs* of treating Medicare patients.[7] Although retrospective, cost-based reimbursement has been largely replaced by a new "prospective payment system" (which we will study in Section II.A.), cost-based reimbursement nevertheless is the initial object of our study for two reasons. Medicare still reimburses major segments of the institutional health care industry on a cost basis, primarily, specialty facilities such

---

6. However, the coverage that Part A provides is increasingly limited, forcing patients to pay a growing portion of the costs of their care out of pocket. For instance, Medicare patients must pay a deductible of $565 per year and are charged a substantial daily copayment for hospitalization that extends beyond two months. These various payments, in addition to expenditures under Part B for unreimbursed physician services and medications, can amount to thousands of dollars annually for seriously ill patients, to the extent that mean out-of-pocket expenses of medical care as a percentage of income was about the same (15 percent) in 1984 as it had been before Medicare was enacted.

To prevent these hidden costs from reaching catastrophic levels, Congress enacted the Medicare Catastrophic Protection Act of 1988, H.R. 2470, which eliminated this hospitalization copayment requirement and capped out-of-pocket expenses for physician services at roughly $1500. However, this legislation produced a fire-storm of opposition from the middle and upper class elderly who bore the brunt of the program's costs through a hefty tax surcharge imposed only on Medicare recipients. As a result, this legislation was repealed by an overwhelming vote the following year.

7. By contrast, Part B reimburses physicians *80 percent* of their *charges*. Patients are responsible for the remaining 20 percent, unless physicians take "assignment" from Medicare, that is, agree to accept the Medicare portion as payment in full. Requiring physicians to take assignment under Medicare or Medicaid is an issue of intense current controversy. Dukakis v. Massachusetts Medical Society, 815 F.2d 790 (1st Cir. 1987); Law & Ensminger, Negotiating Physicians' Fees: Individual Patients or Society?, 61 N.Y.U.L. Rev. 1, 41-56 (1986). "Last year, 16 states introduced mandatory assignment bills, but only two — Rhode Island and Vermont — saw their enactment." American Medical News, Feb. 5, 1988, at 3.

as psychiatric and children's hospitals and long-term facilities such as nursing homes and home health agencies. More importantly, it is helpful to understand the defects of the prior system in order to appreciate the need for a replacement.

Memorial Hospital/Adair County Health Center v. Bowen
829 F.2d 111 (D.C. Cir. 1987)

BUCKLEY, CIRCUIT JUDGE:

The Secretary of Health and Human Services issued two decisions denying a rural hospital in Oklahoma full reimbursement for pharmacy services rendered to Medicare patients in 1979 and 1980. The Secretary's decisions are based on findings of Medicare's Provider Reimbursement Review Board, which found Memorial's pharmacy costs to be unreasonable. The hospital, Memorial Hospital/Adair County Medical Center, disagreed with the Board's conclusions and filed complaints challenging the two decisions. . . .

I. Background

In 1983 Congress changed the method of reimbursing hospitals for costs incurred in caring for Medicare patients. . . . Under the new system the Department of Health and Human Services ("HHS" or "Department") reimburses medicare health care providers, including hospitals like Memorial, according to standard national rates for particular therapies.

This case arises under the Medicare reimbursement scheme previously in effect. In Part A of the Social Security Act, 42 U.S.C. §§1395c-1395i (1982) (the "Act"), Congress permitted the Secretary of HHS to consider cost audits before approving hospital applications for Medicare reimbursement. Section 1395f(b) of the Act states:

> The amount paid to any provider of services . . . [shall be] the reasonable cost of such services. . . .

The regulation further defines "reasonable cost" in a broad fashion:

> The costs of providers' services vary from one provider to another and the variations generally reflect differences in scope of services and intensity of care. The provision in title XVIII of the Act for payment of reasonable cost of services is intended to meet the actual costs, however widely they may vary from one institution to another. This is subject to a limitation where a particular institution's costs are found to be substantially out of line with other institutions in the same area

which are similar in size, scope of services, utilization, and other relevant factors.

42 C.F.R. §405.451(c)(2) (1985).

In addition to this regulation, section 2103 of the Secretary's Provider Reimbursement Manual . . . states that "[t]he prudent and cost-conscious buyer not only refuses to pay more than the going price for an item or service, he also seeks to economize by minimizing cost." . . .

Two weeks before it was ready to open in 1977, Memorial's administrator requested Oklahoma State Health Department personnel, then under contract with the Secretary, to " 'survey' [Memorial's] facilities to determine whether . . . Medicare standards are satisfied. This team found [Memorial's] pharmacy to be very deficient in pharmacy services." When Memorial's administrator asked how that deficiency could be corrected,

> [t]he surveyor told him to come to Oklahoma City (Doctors Hospital of Oklahoma) to observe an acceptable pharmacy operation. He observed a contract pharmacy, HPI [Hospital Pharmacies, Inc.], for the first time. He requested HPI to . . . provide a proposal for operating [his] pharmacy.

HPI's proposal offered Memorial's patients the most advanced of three commonly used methods for administering medications. Some hospitals keep a stock of drugs in each ward or floor, permitting nurses to retrieve and administer supplies without supervision by a pharmacist. According to Memorial, that system "poses a threat to patient safety . . . [and] can result in decreased care to patients and financial loss to hospitals employing this procedure." Other hospitals use a second method. They store drugs in a pharmacy where a pharmacist places each patient's medications in prescription containers and distributes them to nurses for dispensation. These may contain large quantities of medication for use over several days. In [the third method, called an "intravenous admixture" program], an HPI pharmacist would prepare each single dose for each patient and, whenever prescribed, mix drugs in intravenous solutions for particular patients under sterile conditions ("intravenous" or "IV admixture"). In exchange Memorial would compensate HPI an amount equal to forty-five percent of the gross inpatient billings of the pharmacy department, less five percent of said billings to cover bad debts. . . .

Memorial did not advertise or request competitive bidding. Memorial nevertheless accepted HPI's [third] proposal.

At the end of fiscal year 1979, Memorial requested reimbursement for that portion of HPI's charges relating to pharmacy services for Medicare patients. The Act entrusts the initial determination of the reimbursement a hospital may receive to an intermediary agency or organization appointed by the Secretary. See 42 U.S.C. §1395h (1982). The Secretary appointed Blue Cross of Oklahoma ("Blue Cross"), a private insurer, as intermediary to audit Memorial's Medicare reimbursement claim for 1979. Using a cost-per-patient-per-day ("per diem") method of accounting, Blue Cross compared Memorial's total pharmacy costs and those of "peer" hospitals. All the hospitals in this peer group had between forty-six and sixty patient beds, were located in Oklahoma, and used drug-dispensation methods different from those HPI furnished Memorial's patients. For instance, not one of the peer hospitals operated an intravenous admixture program similar to Memorial's.

The intermediary found Memorial's 1979 pharmacy costs "substantially out-of-line with the hospitals in the peer group." It then decided to reduce Memorial's claimed cost figures to the highest per diem cost figures of any hospital in the peer group, and adjusted the result by an inflation factor. This calculation resulted in an approved reimbursement that was $30,000 short of Memorial's 1979 claim. . . . Blue Cross had calculated that the total costs of pharmacy services per diem were $18.03 at Memorial and approximately $12.42 at the costliest peer group hospital, Tahlequah. None of the hospitals in the peer group, however, employed a pharmacist to prepare intravenous drug solutions. Instead they all relied on nurses to perform that task. . . .

On cross motions for summary judgment, the district court presented the issue as "whether a hospital whose total costs are unexceptional is thereby entitled to reimbursement under the Medicare Act . . . for the extraordinary expenses of a single costly state-of-the-art service it elects to operate." Rejecting all arguments Memorial presented to the Board, the district court concluded that the Board's decisions were not "irrational," in part because

> subsidizing a hospital's elevated aspirations for one of its services by way of disproportionate reimbursements (possibly to the neglect of other services in the same hospital, and the disappointment of other hospitals competing for the same limited government funds) is at variance with the statutory purpose. The Medicare Act vests broad power in the Secretary to control costs of medical care subject to reimbursement which health care providers should not be allowed to circumvent by artful accounting at reimbursement time. . . .

II. *Discussion*

It should be self-evident that one objective of section 405.451(c)(2) is to ensure that apples are compared with apples, and that the apples to be compared are the services provided by a particular institution. . . .

The Board denied Memorial reimbursement of actual per diem pharmacy costs that were in excess of the highest per diem pharmacy costs in the 1979 and 1980 peer hospital groups, even though none of the comparison hospitals used a pharmacist-supervised intravenous admixture program that accounted for most of Memorial's purportedly excessive costs. The Board thus interpreted the phrase "similar . . . size, scope of services, utilization, and other relevant factors" to permit it to limit its comparison to the category of "pharmacy services." The Board did not consider intravenous admixture, a part of pharmacy services, a relevant category of comparison.

We reject this approach. Under the regulations at issue, intermediaries must arrive at truly comparable bases for comparison in determining whether the actual costs of a particular provider are out of line. It was incumbent on Blue Cross in this case to come up with an appropriate basis for determining whether the costs allocated to pharmacist-supervised intravenous admixture were reasonable in light of the costs incurred by other providers offering that service. This Blue Cross failed to do. . . .

Memorial [also] contends that as HPI absorbed the overhead costs associated with its pharmacy services, Memorial's total compensation to HPI could not be compared fairly with the pharmacy costs reported by the peer group hospitals because they did not take overhead into account. The Board responds that in this case it was permissible for the intermediary to rely solely on the peer group's direct costs because any "cost measurement variations are reasonably compensated for by using the highest per diem in the peer group study."

We find these explanations unacceptable. Section 405.451(c)(2) clearly requires that the costs to be compared be truly comparable; that is to say, that they be comprised of the same basic elements. The cost of any service provided by a complex institution, fairly measured, will reflect both direct costs and the overhead costs allocable to the service; and this applies to Memorial as well as to the members of the peer group. Even though the billings from HPI to Memorial do not distinguish between direct and indirect expenses, surely it is not beyond the capacity of accounting and health care professionals to find a reasonable basis for making such an allocation.

As Board member Dudgeon demonstrated in his dissent, the intermediary could and therefore should have divided Memorial's pharmacy costs into two parts for purposes of comparison; namely, the costs attributable to its intravenous admixture program and those attributable to the remainder of its pharmacy services. Thus, on remand, the intermediary should be required to make such a division so that Memorial's pharmacy costs may be compared with those incurred by peer groups offering comparable IV and other pharmacy services. The intermediary, in turn, should require the members of each of the peer groups, and Memorial as well, to provide information as to both the direct and overhead costs of the services in question. . . .

So ordered.

Weiner, "Reasonable Cost" Reimbursement for Inpatient Hospital Services Under Medicare and Medicaid*
3 Am. J.L. & Med. 1 (1977)

From 1950 to 1960, hospital semiprivate room charges increased at an average annual rate of 6.6 percent. . . . In contrast, from 1965 to 1970, the average annual rate of increase was 13.9 percent. Hospital cost per adjusted patient day increased at an annual rate of 7.5 percent from 1963 to 1965, and 12.7 percent from 1965 to 1970. . . . This rapid escalation in the costs of and charges for hospital services is related in significant part to the creation in 1965 of the Medicare and Medicaid programs (Titles XVIII and XIV of the Social Security Act). . . . Both programs, through legislative action and subsequent administrative implementation, required reimbursement for inpatient hospital services on the basis of "reasonable cost."

"Reasonable cost" reimbursement, or reimbursement based on a provider's cost, means simply that the payment made to a hospital for services rendered to Medicare or Medicaid patients is calculated to reimburse the hospital for its expenses, or costs, incurred in providing such services. As will be described below, the definition of "cost" is a critical element in the use of such a methodology. Suffice it to say here that because the approach, as originally employed, contained a guarantee that costs incurred by a hospital would be recouped, hospitals had a clear incentive to expand services and increase costs to meet anticipated new demand, and had no incentives under the reimbursement methodology to control costs. The methodology itself was inherently inflationary in its impact on the payment obligations of the Medicare and Medicaid programs. It substantially increased the pressure to increase costs that was a function of the expanded entitlement to health care created by the programs themselves.

The decision to base Medicare and Medicaid reimbursement on "reasonable cost" reflected Congressional concern that hospitals would

---

* Chairman, Massachusetts Rate Setting Commission.
Copyright © 1977, American Society of Law & Medicine, Boston, Mass. Reprinted with permission.

be unwilling to participate voluntarily in those programs unless adequate reimbursement were assured. The approach did succeed in attracting the voluntary participation of most American hospitals. But the introduction of the Medicare and Medicaid programs stands as an example of the fiscal dangers inherent in a program that rapidly measures entitlement to services without, at the same time, taking strong measures to contain the cost impact of that expansion. . . .

The initial HEW regulations defining "reasonable cost" under section 1861(v) chose not to emphasize the *reasonableness* of costs but rather the determination of whether the costs fell into defined *allowable* categories. The regulations provided, in effect, for full reimbursement of all costs falling within these defined categories. . . . The only limit on the magnitude of a cost item appears to be an exclusion from allowability if "a particular institution's costs are found to be *substantially out of line* with other institutions in the same area which are similar in size, scope of services, utilization, and other relevant factors." However, no adequate criteria were adopted further defining "substantially" for these purposes or providing a method for determining what might constitute a "similar" institution.

In adopting such provisions, then, HEW effectively abdicated all responsibility for evaluating — or assisting the hospitals in determining for themselves — the necessity of efficiency of costs incurred by hospitals. The regulations stood as a promise to hospitals that if they accepted patients under these public programs they would receive all costs *they* chose to incur in providing that care. . . . The benefits to hospitals from the approach to "reasonableness" taken in the regulations were buttressed by the liberality of the definition of "cost." Indeed, in operation the Medicare regulations provided for a "cost-plus" formula, with the most prominent "plus" factors being the rather generous depreciation provisions and an "allowance in lieu of specific recognition of other costs."

One must question, of course, why there should be a need for "plus" factors in an industry dominated by non-profit institutions. The answer, in the author's opinion, is that hospitals could use the additional revenues generated by the "plus" factors to generate capital funds. . . . The concept is at variance with the more traditional notion of depreciation as a cost attendant in the use of an asset, intended to reimburse for the wearing away in value of the asset. . . . Depreciation was allowed on assets originally financed with federal or other public funds, despite the fact that the hospital incurred no cost in acquiring the asset. Finally, depreciation was allowed on assets in use at the time the hospital entered the program, even though the assets may have been fully depreciated on the hospital's books or fully depreciated with respect to other third party payors.

The other major "plus" factor reflecting the hospitals' efforts to generate capital funds through "cost" reimbursement appears in the "allowance in lieu of specific recognition of other costs in providing and improving services." The regulations, as promulgated, provided for an allowance, in addition to all other categories of reimbursable cost, equal to 2 percent of allowable costs (excepting interest and the instant allowance itself). This allowance [for a "return on equity capital"] was wholly unanticipated by Congress, was not contemplated in the actuarial projections underlying the original cost estimates of the programs, and generally had little basis to justify itself. It had the effect of providing hospitals with a reserve, a "profit" as it were, which was directly correlated with the level of *spending*, not efficiency, of the facility. Therefore, not only were the Medicare reimbursement principles unconducive to hospital efficiency, but the 2 percent allowance presented a positive incentive to increased inefficiency. The more the hospital spent, the greater the "plus" it received.

In summary, the formula for reasonable hospital cost reimbursement developed for Medicare represented a guarantee to hospitals not only that their "actual" patient-related costs would be reimbursed in full but that they would receive significant payments even above actual cost, in the form of accelerated depreciation amounts and the 2 percent allowance. As a result, following the inception of Medicare, the net income of hospitals rose substantially. As indicated earlier, especially with the nonprofit hospitals, this excess revenue would find its way back into operations, generally through capital expenditures, and thereby generate a constantly escalating cost in a hospital's operations.

NOTES

Cost-Based Medicare and Peer Review

1. The cost-based nature of traditional Medicare reimbursement, in combination with other factors such as expansion in coverage and the increase in elderly population, caused Medicare expenditures to rise 10-fold in its first fifteen years. Early 1980 projections of the Medicare trust fund's insolvency warned of $100 billion deficits by 1990.

2. One commentator has provided this historical sketch:

In setting up Medicare, Congress and the administration were acutely concerned to gain the cooperation of the doctors and hospitals. Consequently, they established buffers between the providers of health care and the federal bureaucracy. Under Part A of Medicare, the law allowed groups of hospitals . . . the option of nominating "fiscal intermediaries" . . . to provide reimbursements, consulting, and auditing services. The federal government was to pay the bills. As expected, the overwhelming majority of hospitals and other institutions nominated Blue Cross. . . . As a result, the administration of Medicare was lodged in the private insurance systems originally established to suit provider interests. And the federal government surrendered direct control of the program and its costs. . . .

> Why? . . . Some observers have said that Medicare officials feared a hospital boycott if they did not give in. The officials themselves explain their position differently. Their feeling . . . [was that] there's a real difference in launching a program with the help of the hospitals as opposed to against them. To an administrator, that difference makes all the difference in the world.

P. Starr, The Social Transformation of American Medicine 375 (1982). The intermediaries are now much less favorable to providers than this excerpt suggests. Largely through intensive government monitoring and selective contracting, Blue Cross plans and other insurance companies serving as intermediaries have begun to pursue HCFA's policies more aggressively.

3. Sacred Heart Hospital v. United States, 616 F.2d 477 (Ct. Cl. 1980), is a case similar to *Memorial Hospital*. There, the court upheld a hospital's claim for respiratory therapy services that were ten times costlier than neighboring hospitals, reasoning that the costs were justified since the quality and quantity of its services were so superior to peer hospitals. See also JIGC Nursing Home Co. v. Bowen, 667 F. Supp. 949 (E.D.N.Y. 1987) (lengthy discussion of flaws in peer group audit procedures). These cases illustrate the difficulty of controlling the amount spent *per service*, but limiting the *number* of services proves even more problematic. The facts of *Sacred Heart* provide a good illustration of the effects of cost-based reimbursement on the intensity of service: "Prior to 1963, . . . the [respiratory therapy] department, as such, consisted of a non-certified therapist and a technician who were trained to administer oxygen. . . . [Since then], the department has grown to eight full time, board certified anesthesiologists, nine trained technicians, two therapists and two registered therapists." 616 F.2d at 479.

4. The very first section of the Medicare statute, by prohibiting any federal "supervision or control over the practice of medicine," 42 U.S.C. §1395, foreshadows the fiscal problems that were to follow. This guarantee of physician autonomy has made it difficult for the government to protest the necessity of the medical services it pays for. See, e.g., AMA v. Weinberger, 395 F. Supp. 515 (N.D. Ill. 1975) (questioning validity of a second opinion requirement for hospitalization). Nevertheless, the government has enjoyed somewhat greater success than the private insurance industry in this regard. Compare

I. The Health Care Cost Crisis

the cases discussed at 686 supra with Goodman v. Sullivan, 891 F.2d 449 (2d Cir. 1989) (Medicare may refuse to pay for medically necessary MRI scan); Medical Society v. Toia, 560 F.2d 535, 538-539 (2d Cir. 1977) (upholding second opinion requirement); Cowan v. Myers, 232 Cal. Rptr. 299, 304 (Cal. App. 1986) (same); Home Health Care v. Heckler, 717 F.2d 587, 590-591 (D.C. Cir. 1983) (upholding prudent buyer concept); Association of Am. Physicians and Surgeons v. Wineberger, 395 F. Supp. 124 (E.D. Ill.), *aff'd mem.* 423 U.S. 975 (1975) (upholding peer review). See generally, Gosfield, Medical Necessity in Medicare and Medicaid, 51 Temple L.Q. 229 (1978); Note, State Restrictions on Medicaid Coverage of Medically Necessary Services, 78 Colum. L. Rev. 1491 (1978).

5. Medicare uses the mechanism of physician peer review, that is, doctors monitoring themselves, to reconcile the need for judging medical necessity with the principle of noninterference. Medicare peer review has evolved through three stages of development: utilization review, Professional Standards Review Organizations ("PSROs"), and Peer Review Organizations ("PROs"). Since the outset of the program, Medicare has required hospital medical staffs to maintain an ongoing internal review of the necessity of treatment, a process known as utilization review. See 42 C.F.R. §405.1305; Mellette, The Changing Focus of Peer Review Under Medicare, 20 U. Rich. L. Rev. 315, 326 (1986). Hospital utilization review committees are composed of physicians practicing at the hospital who audit selected patient records for signs of waste and overutilization and require responsible physicians to explain their excesses. The committee refers any cases of unnecessary care to government representatives for denial of payment and possible disciplinary sanctions.

Medicare utilization review has proven to be a thorough failure. It is pursued vigorously only where hospital overcrowding presents a pressing need for rationing. See, e.g., Suckle v. Madison Gen. Hosp., 362 F. Supp. 1196, 1199 (W.D. Wisc. 1973), *aff'd*, 499 F.2d 1364 (7th Cir. 1974) (utilization review committee active in enforcement "[b]ecause the hospital's facilities were then unequal to the demands upon them"). Otherwise, utilization review committees have been extremely lax. The conflict of interest of those conducting the review accounts for this failure. Reviewing physicians take their responsibilities lightly because of the realization that potentially they are subject to the same scrutiny by those whom they discipline.

In order to eliminate this internal conflict of interest, utilization review was supplemented in 1972 with newly created external review bodies called Professional Standards Review Organizations ("PSROs"). Blum, Gertman & Rabinow, PSROs and the Law (1977); A. Gosfield, PSROs: The Law and the Health Consumer (1975). A single PSRO was established to review cases from all hospitals in each locality.

PSROs also failed, although less disastrously. The modest savings they produced were offset by the considerable costs of the program. Congressional Budget Office, The Effect of PSROs on Health Care Costs: Current Findings and Future Evaluations (1979). The efficiency gains were modest because the cost saving goals of PSROs were severely compromised by the conflicting mandate to enhance quality of care. Coping with Quality/Cost Trade-Offs in Medical Care: The Role of PSROs, 70 N.W.U.L. Rev. 6 (1975). This is illustrated by an anecdote in the popular press reporting the standard-setting process under PSROs:

> They'd get a group of doctors together and ask something like, "How long are you guys keeping patients in the hospital for gallbladders?" . . . If one doctor said 6 days, and another said 8, and a third said 12, they'd put down 12 as the standard. There was no attempt to be parsimonious, only catch the very small percentage who were pulling truly outrageous things.

Newsweek, Jan. 26, 1987, at 44, col. 3.

The latest attempt to harness peer review came in 1982 when PSROs were redesigned under the name Peer Review Organizations ("PROs"). 42 U.S.C. §1320c (1982); Mellette, supra at 341; Dans, Weiner, & Otter, Peer Review Organizations: Promises and Potential Pitfalls, 313 New Eng. J. Med. 1131 (1985); Gosfield, Hospital Utilization Control by PROs: A Guide Through the Maze, 2 Health Span, Feb. 1985, at 3. The PRO program differs structurally from PSROs in two important respects. PROs are even more centralized because they are organized on a statewide rather than a municipal basis and they are funded through competitive contracts instead of individual grants. Dans, Weiner & Otter, supra at 1132. The process of contract bidding and renewal gives the government substantially greater leverage to focus more scrutiny on costs. For instance, the Alabama PRO is under contract to reduce hospital admissions 10 percent, and the Rhode Island PRO must eliminate 187 pacemaker implants over two years. N.Y. Times, Sept. 24, 1985 at 12, col. 1; Phillips, Wineberg & Elfenbein, Meeting the Goals of Medicare Prospective Payments, 88 W. Va. L. Rev. 225, 252 (1986).

Despite the greater likelihood of PRO success, however, there are ominous signs of failure once again. According to one report, PROs are disciplining physicians in rural areas who practice more conservative medicine for failing to meet the practice standards of metropolitan areas. Reinhold, Rural Doctors and Patients Fault New Medicare Reviews, N.Y. Times, Mar. 24, 1987 at A1, col. 1. See also Hospitals, April 20, 1988, at 18 ("Quality became the watchword during the second phase of PRO contracts"). However, this emphasis may be more the result of Medicare's new prospective payment system described in the following section than of a weakening of Medicare's cost-containment resolve.

Does it appear that, however managed, peer review will fail to achieve a fundamental change in physician behavior? In order to do so, it must overcome the following endemic flaw: Because peer review operates through standards derived from traditional, established practice, it detects and corrects only aberrant behavior that lies outside of the bell curve of existing utilization patterns. In other words, all that peer review attempts to do is enforce prevailing norms, not change them. Blumstein, The Role of PSROs in Hospital Cost Containment, in Hospital Cost Containment: Selected Notes for Future Policy 461, 472-73 (M. Zubkoff, I. Raskin & R. Hanft, eds. 1978) (peer review "seems to set current practice patterns as the minimum upon which to build"); Congressional Budget Office, supra at 42 ("peer review may alter utilization by patients of physicians whose standards are substantially different from the norm, but such review is unlikely to effect major changes in the standards of physicians as a group").

6. Efforts to implement a 1972 amendment allowing HCFA to limit the amount paid per patient day ("section 223 cost limits") have been struck down by some courts as inconsistent with the overriding statutory requirement of reimbursing all reasonable costs. See Medical Cent. v. Bowen, 839 F.2d 1504 (11th Cir. 1988). If these per diem cost limits were enforced, do you think they would successfully constrain total hospital reimbursement?

Medicare Cost Reports and Appeal Procedures

7. In addition to the problem of *controlling* costs, the government faces the task of *measuring* the costs of treating Medicare patients. Doing so directly is impossible because of the large number of items of overhead and indirect expense that make up a hospital's operation. Therefore, some ratio must be devised to allocate total costs between Medicare and private patients. (What problems would be encountered if the government were to use the ratio of Medicare admissions to total patient admissions?) The ratio of Medicare patient days to total patient days serves adequately for the costs of routine hospital services (room, board, and nursing care), but not for ancillary services (surgery, radiology, pharmacy, laboratory, etc.) because their use varies widely according to age groups. Therefore, for these costs, Medicare allocates total hospital costs using a ratio of Medicare patient charges to charges for all patients, sometimes called the "RCC" formula. This formula must be applied separately to each hospital ancillary department in order to prevent hospitals from manipulating their charge structures to overweight Medicare patients by using disproportionate charge

markups for those services heavily used by Medicare patients (for instance, by having a 100% markup on laboratory testing and only a 25 percent markup on obstetrics care, there being very few pregnant Medicare patients). Still, hospitals are free to engage in this type of pricing manipulation within each ancillary department. See generally 42 C.F.R. §405.43; S. Law, Blue Cross: What Went Wrong? 78-82 (2d ed. 1976).

8. The process of determining total "allowable" hospital costs each year is performed by the fiscal intermediaries. Each hospital completes a lengthy cost report which the intermediary audits. Dissatisfied hospitals may request reconsideration and then appeal to a Provider Reimbursement Review Board (PRRB) before proceeding to court. As *Memorial Hospital* reflects, this is a lengthy process, averaging some four years *before* entering court. Hall, Rate Appeals Under Medicare's New Payment System, 38 U. Fla. L. Rev. 407, 415 (1986). See generally Medicare & Medicaid Guide (CCH) ¶13,510; ABA Report on Medicare Appeal Procedures, Medicare & Medicaid Guide (CCH) ¶30,608; Comment, Medicare Provider Reimbursement Disputes: Mapping the Contorted Borders of Administrative and Judicial Review, 21 Ind. L. Rev. 705 (1988).

9. Various procedural aspects of the cost accounting process are the source of constant litigation in the federal courts. The current major controversies center on:

   a) whether items not claimed in a cost report may be appealed, Bethesda Hospital v. Bowen, 108 S. Ct. 1255 (1988) (yes);
   b) how to allocate the cost of hospital malpractice insurance premiums between Medicare and non-Medicare patients, Bedford County Mem. Hosp. v. Heckler, 769 F.2d 1017 (4th Cir. 1985); and,
   c) how to allocate administrative overhead costs to labor and delivery patients, Community Hosp. v. Heckler, 770 F.2d 1257 (4th Cir. 1985).

10. Determining which hospital services are to be charged to Medicare, in other words, measuring the numerator in the RCC formula, is also a complex process. Individual patient claims denials are reviewable by Social Security Administration administrative law judges. Judicial review may be pursued only for claims greater than $1000 and only after the medical procedure has been performed and reimbursement denied. See Heckler v. Ringer, 466 U.S. 602 (1984). However, there are various inventive ways to circumvent these jurisdictional limitations. See Mathews v. Diaz, 426 U.S. 67 (1976) (administrative exhaustion waived by agency); City of New York v. Heckler, 476 U.S. 467 (1986) (failure to follow normal appeals route

excused by the futility and irreparable injury of strict compliance); Mount Sinai Med. Cent. v. U.S., 13 Ct. Cl. 561 (1987) (jurisdictional limitations do not apply to court of claims review); Bartlett v. Bowen, 816 F.2d 695 (D.C. Cir. 1987) (limits do not apply to constitutional claims); VNA v. Heckler, 711 F.2d 1020 (11th Cir. 1983) (All Writs Act may be invoked in cases of extreme hardship to obtain an injunction preserving the status quo pending full administrative appeals); Rogers, A Way Out of the Social Security Jurisdiction Tangle, 21 Ariz. L. Rev. 689 (1979).

Appeals under Medicare Part B, which are similarly constrained, have proven equally troubling for the courts. See Bowen v. Michigan Acad. of Family Physicians, 476 U.S. 667 (1986) (allowing judicial review of the *method* of determining reimbursement but *not* of the reimbursement determination *amounts*).

See generally Kinney, The Medicare Appeals System for Coverage and Payment Disputes, Admin. Conf. of the U.S., 1986 Recommendations and Reports 339, reprinted in 1 Admin. L.J. 1 (1987); Neeley-Kvarme, Administrative and Judicial Review of Medicare Issues: A Guide Through the Maze, 57 Notre Dame L.J. 1 (1981); Butler, Medicare Appeals Procedures, 70 N.W.U.L. Rev. 139 (1975); Annot., 43 A.L.R. Fed. 484 (1979).

D. Epilogue

Lave & Lave, Medical Care and Its Delivery: An Economic Appraisal*
35 L. & Contemp. Prob. 252-253

Gourmand and Food — A Fable

The people of Gourmand loved good food. They ate in good restaurants, donated money for cooking research, and instructed their government to safeguard all matters having to do with food. Long ago, the food industry had been in total chaos. There were many restaurants, some very small. Anyone could call himself a chef or open a restaurant. In choosing a restaurant, one could never be sure that the meal would be good. A commission of distinguished chefs studied the situation and recommended that no one be allowed to touch food except for qualified chefs. "Food is too important to be left to amateurs," they said. Qualified chefs were licensed by the state with severe penalties for anyone else who engaged in cooking. Certain exceptions were made for food preparation in the home, but a person could serve only his own family. Furthermore, to become a qualified

---

* Copyright © 1970, Duke University School of Law. Reprinted by permission.

chef, a man had to complete at least twenty-one years of training (including four years of college, four years of cooking school, and one year of apprenticeship). All cooking schools had to be first class.

These reforms did succeed in raising the quality of cooking. But a restaurant meal became substantially more expensive. A second commission observed that not everyone could afford to eat out. "No one," they said, "should be denied a good meal because of his income." Furthermore, they argued that chefs should work toward the goal of giving everyone "complete physical and psychological satisfaction." For those people who could not afford to eat out, the government declared that they should be allowed to do so as often as they liked and the government would pay. For others, it was recommended that they organize themselves in groups and pay part of their income into a pool that would undertake to pay the costs incurred by members in dining out. To insure the greatest satisfaction, the groups were set up so that a member could eat out anywhere and as often as he liked, could have as elaborate a meal as he desired, and would have to pay nothing or only a small percentage of the cost. The cost of joining such prepaid dining clubs rose sharply.

Long ago, most restaurants would have one chef to prepare the food. A few restaurants were more elaborate, with chefs specializing in roasting, fish, salads, sauces, and many other things. People rarely went to these elaborate restaurants since they were so expensive. With the establishment of prepaid dining clubs, everyone wanted to eat at these fancy restaurants. At the same time, young chefs in school disdained going to cook in a small restaurant where they would have to cook everything. The pay was higher and it was much more prestigious to specialize and cook at a really fancy restaurant. Soon there were not enough chefs to keep the small restaurants open.

With prepaid clubs and free meals for the poor, many people started eating their three-course meals at the elaborate restaurants. Then they began to increase the number of courses, directing the chef to "serve the best with no thought for the bill." (Recently a 317-course meal was served.)

The costs of eating out rose faster and faster. A new government commission reported as follows: (1) Noting that licensed chefs were being used to peel potatoes and wash lettuce, the commission recommended that these tasks be handed over to licensed dishwashers (whose three years of dishwashing training included cooking courses) or to some new category of personnel. (2) Concluding that many licensed chefs were overworked, the commission recommended that cooking schools be expanded, that the length of training be shortened, and that applicants with lesser qualifications be admitted. (3) The commission also observed that chefs were unhappy because people seemed to be more concerned about the decor and service than about the food. (In a recent taste test, not only could one patron not tell the difference between a 1930 and a 1970 vintage but he also could not distinguish between white and red wines. He explained that he always ordered the 1930 vintage because he knew that only a really good restaurant would stock such an expensive wine.)

The commission agreed that weighty problems faced the nation. They recommended that a national prepayment group be established which everyone must join. They recommended that chefs continue to be paid on the basis of the number of dishes they prepared. They recommended that every Gourmandese be given the right to eat anywhere he chose and as elaborately as he chose and pay nothing.

These recommendations were adopted. Large numbers of people spent all of their time ordering incredibly elaborate meals. Kitchens became marvels of new, expensive equipment. All those who were not consuming restaurant food were in the kitchen preparing it. Since no one in Gourmand did anything except prepare or eat meals, the country collapsed.

II. REGULATORY REFORMS

A. *Medicare Prospective Payment*

Note, Medicare's Prospective Payment System: Can Quality Care Survive?*
69 Iowa 1417 (1984)

The mid-1960's were characterized by the optimistic view that access to high quality health care could be provided for all Americans, regardless of ability to pay. The American people believed that adequate funds were available and that only entitlement was needed. This utopian view led to the passage of the Medicare program in 1965 as an amendment to the Social Security Act. The program's passage was not secured, however, until health care provider opposition had quieted.

During the 1960's providers strongly objected to federal "interference" in the area of health care. Bills similar to Medicare had been defeated, and Congress was concerned that hospitals also would oppose the Medicare program. To counter the anticipated hostility, Congress chose to promise retrospective cost-based reimbursement for inpatient services provided under Medicare. Retrospective reimbursement on the basis of "reasonable cost" essentially means that

---

* Reprinted with permission.

payment is open-ended; providers are reimbursed for costs incurred in rendering care. Thus, hospitals participating in the Medicare program basically received a guarantee that they would recoup the reasonable cost for all inpatient services they chose to provide. Moreover, participating hospitals could generate additional revenue in the form of depreciation payments and an " 'allowance in lieu of specific recognition of other costs in providing and improving services.' "

While Congress' retrospective payment approach drew widespread participation in the Medicare program, this "reasonable cost" methodology ultimately proved wholly unreasonable. Instead of encouraging hospitals to contain costs, retrospective reimbursement created incentives to expand services and raise prices, and fostered a belief in "spare-no-expense" medicine. Medicare expenditures for inpatient services quickly surpassed original estimates of program costs. Program spending increased from about $3 billion in 1967 to over $37 billion in 1983. Although a number of factors contributed to this tremendous growth, retrospective reimbursement primarily was responsible. Recognition of that fact, coupled with the worsening plight of the federal budget, combined to create a political demand for reform of Medicare's repayment system. . . .

On December 27, 1982, Secretary Richard S. Schweiker of HHS . . . proposed a prospective payment system. Under the proposal, hospitals are paid a fixed amount that is based on the principal diagnosis of each Medicare discharge — the diagnosis chiefly responsible for the admission. The Secretary's report was fairly well received, and in April 1983 the President signed the Social Security Amendments of 1983.[31] These Amendments provide that the prospective payment plan replace the retrospective reimbursement system . . . effective with hospital cost reporting periods beginning on or after October 1, 1983.[33]

The new prospective plan differs from reasonable cost reimbursement in significant respects. Instead of paying hospitals after the fact for costs incurred in caring for Medicare beneficiaries, the new system pays hospitals prospectively determined rates that vary in accordance with the diagnosis of each discharged beneficiary. Because beneficiaries may be charged only for deductibles, coinsurance amounts, and noncovered services, hospitals are at risk for operating costs that

---

31. Pub. L. No. 98-21, 97 Stat. 65 (1983) [42 U.S.C. §1395ww(d)]; see 48 Fed. Reg. 39,752, 39,753-54 (1983) (discussing history of interim final rule that implements the Social Security Amendments of 1983).

33. Pub. L. No. 98-21, §604, 97 Stat. 65, 168 (1983); *see also* 48 Fed. Reg. 39,752, 39,817 (1983) (to be codified at 42 C.F.R. §[412]). The following Medicare participating hospitals and hospital units are exempt from the statute's coverage: long-term, rehabilitation, psychiatric, and children's hospitals; and distinct psychiatric and rehabilitation units of acute care hospitals.

run above the fixed payment rate. A hospital that keeps its costs below the payment rate, however, is allowed to keep the difference. . . .

I. The Mechanics of Medicare's New Prospective Payment System

Under Medicare's new payment system, hospitals are paid a fixed, prospectively determined amount for each Medicare discharge. Using a classification system called diagnosis-related groups (DRGs), Medicare patients are categorized into fairly homogeneous groups based on resource consumption. The classification system was developed by researchers at Yale University and is based on a nationwide sample of over 1.4 million discharge records taken from 332 hospitals. The researchers classified the cases according to principal diagnosis, age, sex, procedures performed, discharge status, and any secondary diagnoses. This process resulted in the development of 470 DRG categories. Each Medicare discharge is assigned to one of these DRGs and the hospital is reimbursed according to the applicable DRG-specific payment rate, adjusted to reflect cost differences between urban hospitals and rural hospitals, and area wage variations. . . .

To calculate the DRG-specific rates, the Health Care Financing Administration (HCFA) established weighting factors for . . . the 470 groups.[66] These weights reflect the relative cost, across all hospitals, of treating patients within a particular DRG. For each discharged beneficiary the payment rate is the product of the applicable DRG weight and a standardized amount. . . .

HCFA predicts that the full impact of prospective payment includes the following positive features: strengthened supply and demand forces in the health care delivery system; better identification of the product being purchased because payment is linked to diagnosis; development of the federal government as a prudent buyer of health services; and a reduced rate of inflation in hospital costs. . . .

The structure chosen to monitor the impact of prospective payment is the peer review organization (PRO). Created by the Peer Review Improvement Act of 1982, PROs replace an earlier system of federally mandated medical review, the professional standards review organizations (PSROs). . . .

The function of the PROs is to review the appropriateness of hospital admissions, discharges, transfers, and lengths of patient stays. In addition, each PRO is responsible for assessing the quality of

---

66. 48 Fed. Reg. 39,752, 39,760 (1983). For example, a craniotomy case might be 3.5 times the cost of the average Medicare case. The DRG weight (3.5 in this example) is used to adjust the cost of the average Medicare discharge to obtain the prospective payment rate for cases within specific DRGs.

hospital services provided and the validity of diagnostic and procedural data furnished by participating hospitals located within the PRO's review area. Thus, PROs provide a mechanism for evaluating the quality and cost of medical services furnished under prospective payment. . . .

NOTES

Diagnosis Related Groups

1. Jack Wood, a prominent health care lawyer, describes DRGs as health care's second "mega event" (the first being the enactment of Medicare). DRGs were first used in New Jersey as the basis for state regulation of hospital rates charged to all payers, and they have now spread to several other state hospital rate-regulation systems and form the basis for reimbursement under several state Medicaid systems. Also, Blue Cross/Blue Shield plans around the country have implemented the DRG method in their private reimbursement. Some policy analysts predict that DRGs will provide the catalyst for a comprehensive national health insurance. Monroe & Dunham, Slouching Toward National Health Insurance: The New Health Care Politics, 2 Yale J. Reg. 262 (1985).

The rapidly expanding body of literature discussing DRG reimbursement crosses many disciplines. The leading discussions in the legal literature are cited throughout these notes and in Section II.B below. See also Office of Technology Assessment, Medicare's Prospective Payment System (1986); P. Grimaldi & J. Micheletti, Prospective Payment: The Definitive Guide to Reimbursement (1985); P. Grimaldi & J. Micheletti, Diagnosis Related Groups: A Practitioner's Guide (1983).

2. The table below provides a sampling of DRGs for respiratory illnesses. Each patient is assigned to one DRG based on the patient's age, principle diagnosis, and condition. To illustrate, an adult pneumonia patient with a complicating condition ("cc") will be assigned to DRG 89 and given a weight somewhat higher than one. DRGs 90 and 91 apply to less difficult or younger pneumonia patients and have a weight less than one. Notice that not every single diagnosis receives a separate group. For example, all surgical respiratory cases are lumped into either "major" cases or "other" (75 and 76); bronchitis and asthma are treated together (96-98). The legislation calls for DRG weights to be recalibrated only every 4 years. 97 Stat. 157.

3. The ultimate reimbursement amount is the product of the DRG weight and the hospital's standardized payment rate. This rate is roughly the same for all hospitals, approximately $3000 (it varies

TABLE 8.1

DRG	Title	Relative Weights	Geometric Mean Los	Outlier Threshold
75	Major chest [surgery]	2.9600	11.9	39
76	Other resp system [surgery] w cc	2.2936	10.4	37
77	Other resp system [surgery] w/o cc	1.0910	4.8	32
78	Pulmonary embolism	1.4386	8.9	36
79	Respiratory infections & inflammations age >17 with cc	1.8426	9.3	36
80	Respiratory infections & inflammations age >17 w/o cc	1.1360	7.1	34
81	Respiratory infections & inflammations age 0-17	1.1032	6.1	33
82	Respiratory neoplasms	1.2022	6.6	34
83	Major chest trauma with cc	.9878	6.5	33
84	Major chest trauma w/o cc	.4903	3.9	31
85	Pleural effusion with cc	1.1409	6.8	34
86	Pleural effusion w/o cc	.7229	4.6	32
87	Pulmonary edema & respiratory failure	1.4326	6.0	33
88	Chronic obstructive pulmonary disease	1.0150	6.1	33
89	Simple pneumonia & pleurisy age >17 with cc	1.2034	7.2	34
90	Simple pneumonia & pleurisy age >17 w/o cc	.7806	5.7	32
91	Simple pneumonia & pleurisy age 0-17	.7357	4.7	32
92	Interstitial lung disease with cc	1.2148	6.9	34
93	Interstitial lung disease w/o cc	.7892	5.2	32
94	Pneumothorax with cc	1.3275	7.4	34
95	Pneumothorax w/o cc	.6583	4.8	32
96	Bronchitis & asthma age >17 with cc	.9739	6.0	33
97	Bronchitis & asthma age >17 w/o cc	.6824	4.7	27
98	Bronchitis & asthma age 0-17	.9036	6.2	33
99	Respiratory signs & symptoms with cc	.8401	4.4	31
100	Respiratory signs & symptoms w/o cc	.5122	2.8	20
101	Other respiratory system diagnoses with cc	.9808	5.2	32
102	Other respiratory system diagnoses w/o cc	.5607	3.5	30
103	Heart transplant	13.4829	26.5	54

* Source: 54 Fed. Reg. 19697 (1989).

according to prevailing wages and other adjustment factors). A single DRG-weighted rate is the only payment a hospital receives for each patient, regardless of the number of secondary diagnoses or the expense of treatment, unless the patient is classified as an "outlier," one whose costs of treatment lie far outside a specified normal range. The size of the additional outlier payment varies with the patient's length of stay and is designed to cover only the marginal costs of extended treatment. 42 C.F.R. §§412.80-84.

4. "Both the government and the industry have been astonished by the rapid rate of change in hospital operations since the enactment of prospective payment legislation." Iglehart, Early Experience with Prospective Payment of Hospitals, 314 New Eng. J. Med. 1460, 1461 (1986). Based on first year statistics, PPS has worked phenomenally well. 1984 hospital inflation was cut by more than half, to 4.5 percent, and occupancy rates stood at 66.6 percent, the lowest level since the AHA began keeping statistics in 1963. Average lengths of stay plummeted by 21 percent. Hospital employment also showed an unprecedented decline. AHA, 1984 Hospital Statistics; Philipps, Wineberg & Elfenbein, Meeting the Goals of Medicare Prospective Payments, 88 W. Va. L. Rev. 225, 227, 231 (1986); Sloan, Morrisey & Valvona, Effects of the Medicare Prospective Payment System on Hospital Cost Containment: An Early Appraisal, 66 Milbank Q. 191 (1988); DesHarnais, et al., The Early Effects of Prospective Payment, 24 Inquiry 7 (1987).

5. The standardized hospital rate is subject to adjustment each year. This annual rate adjustment provides a convenient tool for continuously ratcheting down Medicare outlays, almost like a form of Chinese finger torture: the more economizing effort hospitals exert in response to the incentives of prospective payment, the more leeway Medicare will have each year to tighten up the standardized rate. DRGs thus have the prospect of not only halting future increases in spending (relative to inflation) but also gradually eliminating the system's built-up fat.

6. Another of the system's advantages is its apparent simplicity. Complex cost accounting procedures are no longer necessary to calculate the amount of reimbursement: computer programs simply assign individual patients to their respective categories based on the objective criteria of diagnosis and age. Of course, there are complexities in the initial process of setting the hospital rate and the weights for the categories, but Congress shielded these complexities by precluding review of the DRG weighting process. In addition, HCFA has sharply limited review of individual hospital rates. Hall, Rate Appeals Under Medicare's New Payment System: Reflections on the Meaning of "Prospectivity," 38 U. Fla. L. Rev. 407, 410 (1986). Query, then, whether the system's simplicity is deceptively purchased at the cost of accuracy and fairness.

II. Regulatory Reforms 723

Concerning the validity of these and other hospital appeal restrictions, see Georgetown Univ. Hosp. v. Bowen, 862 F.2d 323 (D.C. Cir. 1988) (striking restriction on retroactive corrections); Springdale Mem. Hosp. Assoc. v. Bowen, 828 F.2d 491 (8th Cir. 1987) (contra); Hall supra (criticizing both results); HCFA Ruling No. 89-1, Medicare & Medicaid Guide (CCH) ¶37,614 (acquiescing in the *Georgetown* position); Thallner, Prospective Payment System: Preclusion of Review of Hospital Base Year Cost Calculations, 6 J. Leg. Med. 509 (1985).

The review of individual coverage determinations under PPS (that is, which particular patient admissions are covered by Medicare) is performed by entities known as Peer Review Organizations (see 711 supra). Their implementation has also proven troublesome. AHA v. Bowen, 834 F.2d 1037 (D.C. Cir. 1987) (formal rulemaking proceeding not required for regulations and directives implementing PRO review process); Jost, Administrative Law Issues Involving the Medicare Utilization and Quality Control PRO Program, 30 Ohio St. L.J., 1 (1989); Mellette, The Changing Focus of Peer Review Under Medicare, 20 U. Rich. L. Rev. 315, 347-353 (1986); Marfino, Prospective Payment Systems: Rights of Review of Medicare Beneficiaries, 34 Med. Tr. Tech. Q. 297 (1988).

Reimbursement of Capital Costs and Physician Fees

7. It is critical to observe that DRGs cover only operating expenses for acute-care general hospitals. Excluded are (a) capital costs, (b) long-term facilities (nursing homes, home health agencies), (c) specialty hospitals (rehabilitation, tuberculosis, psychiatric etc.), and (d) physician payments. Medicare still pays these services separately based on the conventional cost or charge formulas.

8. The DRG legislation contemplates its expansion to cover capital costs by October 1991. Consider the potential problems in so doing. If the standardized hospital rate included an add-on for the *national* average capital cost per patient, how would this affect newer hospitals or hospitals that have made major capital expenditures recently? If prospective capital rates were individualized to each hospital's situation, how would this affect older hospitals with low capital costs whose assets are wearing out? Initial administrative proposals to phase in a capital cost add-on over 7 to 10 years have been stymied by opposition from the hospital industry. See Grace & Mitchell, Regulation of Health Care Costs: The Implications of PPS, 2 U. Fla. J.L. Pub. Poly. 125 (1989).

9. What difficulties would be encountered in extending DRGs to physician services? Consider the following explanation by the former head of HCFA:

> In view of the generally successful change in Medicare's hospital-payment system, many wonder why we cannot repeat the accomplishment with

respect to Medicare payment of physicians. The answer is simple: Paying physicians is far more complicated. When developing a hospital-payment system for Medicare, one must handle 11 million admissions to 7000 hospitals for 475 diagnosis-related groups. Those numbers pale in comparison to Medicare's 350 million claims from 500,000 physicians for 7000 different procedure codes. Moreover, whereas hospitals can average their gains and losses under a prospective payment system across many cases, physicians' smaller caseloads and greater specialization make such averaging much more risky for them. These differences mean that improving the way Medicare pays physicians will be vastly more difficult, both analytically and administratively.

Roper, Perspectives on Physician-Payment Reform, 319 New Eng. J. Med. 865 (1988). Congress has abandoned any effort toward physician DRGs as a result of these design difficulties, as well as tremendous AMA opposition. See generally, Mitchell, Physician DRGs, 313 New Eng. J. Med. 670 (1985); Secretary's Report to Congress on DRG-Based Physician Payments for Inpatient Hospital Services, Sept. 4, 1987, reprinted in Medicare & Medicaid Guide (CCH) ¶36,625; DHHS Report to Congress, Medicare Physician Payment, Medicare & Medicaid Guide ¶38,218 (Oct. 1989); and the Annual Reports of the Physician Payment Review Commission.

10. Instead of physician DRGs, the federal government has recently adopted a modified form of fee-for-service reimbursement that employs a "relative value scale" 42 U.S.C. §1395w-4. An RVS attempts to achieve some degree of parity in the amount that physicians charge for various services by measuring the relative costs of each service according to the time, mental effort, and technical skill required, as well as differences in the costs of malpractice premiums and specialty training. Hsiao et al., Estimating Physicians' Work for a Resource-Based Relative-Value Scale, 319 New Eng. J. Med. 835 (1988). This initial study indicates, for instance, that "the average family practitioner could receive 60 percent more revenue from Medicare, whereas the average ophthalmologist could lose 40 percent of current revenues." Hsiao et al., Results and Policy Implications of the Resource-Based Relative-Value Study, 319 New Eng. J. Med. 881 (1988).

Commenting on this study, William Roper, former HCFA Administrator, contends:

> A fee schedule based on a relative-value scale, no matter how carefully constructed, cannot be expected to address the growth in the volume and intensity of services. Whatever their merits, fee-for-service systems do not provide physicians with incentives to control this growth. At best, a revamped fee schedule may send physicians "better" signals, rewarding those who provide cognitive services as opposed to those who perform procedures. In the long run, . . . this may improve the mix of services provided to Medicare beneficiaries, . . . reduce perceived

II. Regulatory Reforms 725

inequities in payment and establish fairer relative prices — a goal I support. . . . [But], to be clear, a relative-value scale cannot do for physicians what diagnosis-related groups did for hospitals. The question facing the HCFA and the Congress is one I asked at a hearing on physician payment:

> Is it worth investing the lion's share of our analytic, administrative, and political resources to substitute one fee-for-service payment system for another, leaving Medicare's most important issue — increased volume and intensity — untouched?

Roper supra, 319 New Eng. J. Med. at 866-867. For further discussion and debate on relative value scales, see The Physician Payment Review Commission Report to Congress, 261 J.A.M.A. 2382 (1989), and the several articles collected at 260 J.A.M.A. 2347-2444 (1988).

11. In response to these concerns, Congress, in adopting an RVS fee schedule, included certain complex measures to control the volume of physician services. Briefly, DHHS and the Physician Payment Review Commission (PPRC) are to recommend to Congress each year a "volume performance standard," which sets a target for that year's Medicare spending on doctors' services. If actual expenditures exceed this amount, then the following year, Congress will adjust downward (relative to inflation) the "conversion factor" that is used to convert the relative value scores to an actual payment amount. Both the setting of the volume performance standard and the adjustment of the conversion factor are decisions left to Congress each year and are therefore subject to various political and lobbying forces. However, if Congress fails to act, the statute contains default provisions that compel DHHS to lower total physician reimbursement (relative to inflation) in graduated amounts each year beginning at ½ percent and increasing to 2 percent annually by 1993. The maximum reductions are capped at graduated amounts that increase to 3 percent by 1996. 42 U.S.C. §1395w-4 (f); see Ginsburg, LeRoy & Hammons, Medicare Physician Payment Reform, 9 Health Affairs 178 (Spring 1990).

> Many regard this new payment system as one of the most sweeping reforms of the U.S. health care system since the enactment of Medicare over a quarter century ago. . . . Its underlying concept is that by basing fee updates on how expenditure growth compares to a performance standard, the medical profession is given a collective incentive to foster approaches to cost containment. While these incentives are not intended to influence the decisions of individual practitioners directly, they do provide a reason for physicians to become more involved in efforts to contain medical costs. Approaches that medical organizations can pursue include developing and disseminating practice guidelines, expanding continuing education, and providing both technical and po-

litical support to carriers and Peer Review Organizations (PROs) in their utilization review activities.

PPRC 1990 Annual Report to Congress 27. We will have to await actual experience under this system to determine how aggressively Congress actually decides to tighten the screws.

On physician payment reform generally, see Iglehart, Payment of Physicians Under Medicare, 318 New Eng. J. Med. 863 (1988); 8 Health Affairs, No. 1 (Spring 1989) (symposium on physician payment policy); Glaser, The Politics of Paying American Physicians, 9 Health Affairs 129 (Fall 1989).

Prospective Payment for Medicare Inpatient Hospital Services — Final Rule
49 Fed. Reg. 301-304 (1984)

Objectives of the Prospective Payment System

The prospective payment system is designed to alter . . . past incentives by providing hospitals with a fixed set of payment rates for each type of discharge. Prospective rates represent a set of prices with characteristics similar to the prices a hospital would face in a more conventional market. Therefore, each hospital will know the amount it will be paid per discharge and that the payment rate will remain unchanged regardless of its own operating cost experience. Setting payment rates prospectively places hospitals at risk in terms of the management of their operations and the use of their resources. A hospital that spends, on the average, more than it is paid to treat Medicare beneficiaries, will lose money. Conversely, as in any normal industry, a hospital that spends less than it is paid will make money. . . .

Reductions in cost per admission can be achieved in several ways, such as —

- Reducing length-of-stay by —
  — Better scheduling of tests and procedures;
  — Improved discharge planning; and
  — More careful review of the need for hospitalization.
- More careful examination of the number, mix, and quality of services furnished during a patient's stay in order to —
  — Reduce unnecessary utilization of ancillary services;
  — Ensure appropriate and cost-effective assignment of personnel; and
  — Reduce waste of supplies and other resources; and
- More careful examination of the prices a hospital pays for the resource inputs into the production of hospital services, including supplies, equipment, and personnel. . . .

II. Regulatory Reforms

In addition to improving the ratio of costs to revenues by reducing cost per case, a hospital could attempt to improve its revenues by increasing admissions. Whereas cost and charge-based reimbursement gave the hospital an incentive to keep occupancy rates high by increasing either admissions or lengths-of-stay, only admissions increases produce or increase revenue under DRG payment. Every new admission generates new revenue (in the amount of the DRG price) and new costs. In general, a hospital benefits from any admission for which the revenue for that patient exceeds the marginal cost of furnishing services to that patient, even if the hospital's average cost for treating a patient in that DRG equals or exceeds the DRG payment rate. As a result, hospitals may adopt a variety of "marketing" strategies to increase their admissions, including —

- Public relations campaigns designed to influence patient choice;
- Recruitment of physicians; and
- Expansion, adoption, or specialization of services.

These strategies may be called "competitive" in that they are designed to increase admissions by attracting patients from other hospitals.

In addition to adopting competitive strategies such as those discussed above, some hospitals may turn to noncompetitive means to increase admissions and lower per-case-costs. There has been extensive concern that this incentive could result in an increase in inappropriate admissions. For example, physicians or staff might be encouraged (directly or indirectly) to hospitalize marginally ill patients and to discharge and readmit patients at a later date for deferrable procedures that might otherwise be performed as part of a single stay. This strategy is both easy for physicians to implement and difficult for third-party payors to control.

Enthoven & Noll, Prospective Payment: Will It Solve Medicare's Financial Problem?*
1 Issues in Science and Technology 101 (1984)

To solve Medicare's financial problem, the government must bring the growth in outlays approximately into line with the growth in the economy as a whole. The Prospective Payment System is unlikely to come close to achieving this goal. It works on too small a part of the problem. While it might reduce the growth in reported real cost per Medicare case, it seems sure to suffer leakages that will offset a

---

* Copyright © 1984, National Academy of Sciences. Reprinted by permission.

substantial part of the savings. There is a good chance that PPS will have practically no effect on total expenditures. It might even make things worse. . . .

Four important things can be said about these prices. First, they are administered, not market, prices. Competition will not drive them down. A low-cost hospital cannot compete for patients by offering a lower price.

Second, they are crude approximations of average cost per case, not estimates of marginal cost. (The marginal cost of a case is the increase in a hospital's total annual cost associated with the care of an additional case.) Because hospitals have high fixed costs and produce numerous joint products, such as patient care and research, average costs are usually above marginal costs by widely varying and unknown amounts. For example, if a case is treated with the use of a great deal of expensive capital equipment, such as a CT scanner, the treatment of an additional case is likely to cost the hospital less than the average expense for that type of case, where the average includes a share of the fixed cost of the equipment.

Third, these are not prices calculated by a cost-conscious purchaser to elicit from suppliers exactly the desired number and quality of services at minimum cost. In many cases, Medicare under PPS will pay more than necessary; in other cases, less.

Fourth, within many of the 468 diagnostic categories, the actual cost per case varies widely. Susan Horn of The Johns Hopkins University, a leading researcher in this field, found that DRGs explained between 21 and 53 percent of the variance in hospital charges, depending on the hospital. In one example involving DRG 405, lymphoma or leukemia in children, in a particular hospital, she found that the range of lowest to highest charge was from $747 to $233,122. . . .

The source of our pessimism about the effectiveness of the Prospective Payment System is that its structure creates incentives for cost increases that could be substantial. For example, it creates obvious incentives to hospitals to increase net revenue by increasing admissions, by unbundling services so as to shift costs to other parts of the Medicare program, and by diagnosing and even treating patients so as to place them in the most highly reimbursed diagnostic category. Furthermore, the assumed behavior of the medical system under PPS ignores some important elements of the economic context in which hospitals operate. These are major shortcomings that deserve careful attention.

Consider the incentives to increase admissions. Because the cost of an additional patient is usually less than the average cost on which payments are based, hospitals will be able to increase net revenue by increasing admissions. Because reimbursement within a diagnostic

II. Regulatory Reforms

category is based on a fixed price per case, payment is independent of case severity; thus hospitals are rewarded for increasing admissions of low-severity cases. For example, persons suffering from trauma are more likely to be held overnight for observation rather than be dismissed. Breast biopsies that could be performed on outpatients will more likely be performed on inpatients: under DRG 262, the payment is calculated on the basis of a mean stay of three days. For patients with multiple diagnoses or in need of multiple procedures, the system creates an incentive to treat each in a separate admission, rather than to treat them all at once; doing joint replacements one at a time, for example. When multiple diagnoses are unrelated and do not demand immediate attention, such a practice will not appear abnormal. Even when diagnoses are related, practice styles and cases vary sufficiently that a small change in the fraction that are treated separately is unlikely to be detected.

The Prospective Payment System also creates powerful incentives for hospitals to refer elsewhere those cases that are particularly severe and costly, a practice known as "dumping." This makes one admission into two. Severe cases can cost many times the average cost within a diagnostic category, so that a hospital can enhance its financial position by dumping very ill patients onto government or teaching hospitals that are less free to refuse them on grounds that they are not equipped to handle such cases. . . .

Another factor that can be expected to undermine the financial benefits of the Prospective Payment System is the incentive it creates to shift costs to other parts of the Medicare program. To thwart this, PPS requires that all services to inpatients except physicians' services be covered by the DRG price. But there are many ways to "unbundle" inpatient services. As health economist Judith Lave of the University of Pittsburgh has pointed out, a hospital and its medical staff can perform the diagnostic workups before admission and charge the cost to Medicare's Supplementary Medical Insurance. In addition, more recovery and monitoring services can take place in skilled nursing facilities or with nursing care at home. These services also are paid by Medicare. Thus unbundled services will be reimbursed twice, once in the DRG price and again in the cost-reimbursement or fee-for-service payments at both ends of the hospital stay. This is ironic because outpatient diagnostic workups and home nursing are generally thought to reduce real costs of care. . . .

Still another source of financial problems in PPS lies in the definitions of the Diagnosis Related Groups. Assignment to a DRG is based on the principal diagnosis: "the condition established after study to be chiefly responsible for occasioning the admission of the patient to the hospital." All other diagnoses are secondary no matter how severe. The hospital is not supposed to select the most resource-intensive diagnosis and designate it as the principal DRG; however, properly identifying the principal diagnosis has never before been freighted with financial significance. Moreover, for patients with multiple medical problems, the principal diagnosis can be a rather metaphysical concept. Consequently, the classifications of diagnosis in hospital discharge records have often been arbitrary, inaccurate, and incomplete. For example, a 1977 study found that about one-third of hospital discharge records had an incorrect principal diagnosis, and a quarter had the wrong principal procedure. There were conflicting opinions as to what constituted the "principal" or "primary" diagnosis, and many secondary diagnoses were omitted because they were of no consequence to the hospital. . . .

The likely result of making diagnosis classification financially consequential is "DRG creep"; that is, a trend toward categorization in more profitable diagnoses. For the first time, classifying a resource-intensive diagnosis as secondary could be regarded by a hospital and its staff as a "mistake." Indeed, a new consulting industry is emerging to tell hospitals how to report cases for the best reimbursement. In some instances, the new importance of classification may gradually influence patterns of treatment. . . .

In other cases, DRG creep will result from more aggressive discovery and reporting of secondary diagnoses, complications, or co-morbidities that simply were not reported before. For example, an average urban hospital in 1984 will be paid $3,070 for an appendectomy without a complicated principal diagnosis for a patient under 70 without complications or co-morbidities (DRG 167). But if the surgeon finds and reports one of a list of complications of the principal diagnosis, some of which are not very severe, the case becomes an appendectomy with complicated principal diagnosis (DRG 165), and the hospital is paid $4,584. This creates quite an incentive to identify and report minor complications. . . .

Another source of problems is that, as we noted earlier, most hospitals will receive DRG payments that are well above the marginal cost of a patient. Hence, a hospital has an incentive to admit more patients. One time-honored way to do this is to attract more doctors by providing more services and facilities to their patients. Under PPS, hospitals cannot compete for Medicare patients by cutting prices; however, they can compete by offering more services. Meanwhile, some high-cost hospitals are likely to economize, cutting costs to the DRG price, but others — those having on average more severely ill patients — will cry for help. Thus, for most hospitals, costs will converge to the DRG price, while a few will be in trouble even though they provide essential services efficiently. . . .

Hospitals with costs above those allowed under prospective payment will thereby shift unpaid costs to insured private patients. The outcome of this process will depend a great deal on the response of employers. Employers may shift to health providers chosen on the basis of negotiated prices and limit employee choices to those providers. Alternatively, they may limit their financial contributions to employee health insurance and give employees a choice of Health Maintenance Organizations and other competitive medical plans. If so, they will bring pressure on hospitals to control costs and therefore will avoid becoming the victims of the cost shift. But if they remain with traditional open-ended, free-choice-of-provider insurance, they will be the victims of a substantial cost shift. Indeed, hospitals can shift costs by simply raising charges, even before they make accounting adjustments to justify it.

The government is not exactly unaffected by this shift in costs. Private health insurance is largely a tax-free fringe benefit that in 1983 cost the government about $30 billion. As a result, a $100 increase in health care outlays by employers in lieu of $100 in salary means about a $40 revenue loss for federal and state governments. Consequently, to the extent that prospective payment causes cost shifting, a major share of the cost reduction in Medicare will reappear in the federal deficit through reduced tax revenues. . . .

Hall, Institutional Control of Physician Behavior: Legal Barriers to Health Care Cost Containment*
137 U. Penn. L. Rev. 431, 438, 449, 475-476, 479-480, 483, 488, 499-502, 528-536 (1988)

A singular fact characterizes . . . prospective payment. [It] is aimed at health care institutions rather than physicians. The DRG payment system applies only to hospitals. Medicare continues to pay physicians on a fee-for-service basis. . . . This fact presents an extraordinary anomaly. Physicians, not institutions, control the vast bulk of health care expenditures. Doctors determine when, how long, how intensively, and in what environment to treat patients. They order the laboratory tests, x-rays, pharmaceuticals, and surgery that determine the short-term institutional costs of treatment and that ultimately create the long-term demand for capital resources and insurance coverage. Although difficult to quantify with precision, informed estimates place 70 to 90 percent of health care expenditures within the control of practitioners. In order for health care cost containment to succeed, then, it is necessary for those institutions that employ, retain

---

* Reprinted with permission.

or house doctors to implement new managerial control techniques that alter treatment behavior. . . .

Hospitals, HMOs, and other health care institutions might respond to cost containment pressures by: (1) dictating the details of treatment, (2) motivating physicians with financial incentives to practice more conservatively, or (3) restructuring their relationship with the medical staff to subordinate physicians to institutional constraints. Directing treatment runs afoul of laws prohibiting various forms of interference with the practice of medicine. Sharing the profits generated from treatment reductions violates a recent federal statute and may constitute prohibited fee splitting. Restructuring hospitals is inhibited by laws requiring an open, independent, and self-governing medical staff. The task at hand is to evaluate these laws against the dual demands of sound medical practice and cost containment policy.

II. Interference with the Practice of Medicine

The most direct method for reducing health care costs is to issue specific treatment instructions or restrictions. . . . Administrative controls such as these strike directly at the profession's most sensitive nerve, the preservation of clinical autonomy. Bureaucratic control is the antithesis of the collegial values inherent in professionalism. Eliot Freidson, a pioneering medical sociologist, discovered in a study of an HMO that "any effort at arbitrary quota-setting was resisted almost automatically by virtually everyone because it constituted an attack on freedom of judgment and practice." . . .

Physician resistance to interference is warranted, to a degree. Most medical practice does not lend itself to lock-step directives from either lay or professional sources because of the intensely judgmental, individualistic, uncertain, and humane nature of health care. Thus, "efficiency protocols . . . can only be medically sound if they allow considerable room for clinical freedom." As the argument is frequently put: "One cannot practice good medicine by committee or cookbook or computer. A person or group reviewing summaries of information cannot possibly appreciate all the clinical factors that make each situation different — and it is these judgments that make medicine such a complex, demanding profession." . . .

Inevitably, then, treatment directives have only a limited potential for bringing medical decisionmaking within the arena of cost containment. Detailed standards are capable of covering only a very limited part of the medical treatment terrain, and it is impossible for both theoretical and practical reasons to impose on physicians a new treatment philosophy. They must be allowed to evolve their own practice styles. To precipitate and sustain this process, it is necessary to supplement general treatment guidelines with an intervention that

II. Regulatory Reforms

maintains continuing influence on discrete treatment decisions, an intervention that alters more fundamentally the basic incentives that influence physician behavior.

III. Financial Incentives and the Fee Splitting Prohibitions

The intervention with the best prospect for reconciling physician autonomy with cost control is structuring financial incentives to reward conservative treatment.[194] We have learned that preserving physician autonomy, both on a collective and an individual level, is a social and a practical necessity for effective physician control. Only the exercise of professional judgment and discretion in each case will permit the individualization of patient care that is required to maintain humane service. What is needed, then, is some form of decentralized influence that preserves complete autonomy by internalizing cost consciousness at the bedside level. Health care can only be transformed by altering the process by which doctors make day-to-day treatment decisions. . . . Consequently, the control strategy that will work best is to influence physicians to change their practice styles, to acquire a new treatment philosophy, through a motivational force that orients them toward a more conservative end of the acceptable range of variation in medical practice. . . .

The most effective motivational force is likely to be financial incentive. If fee-for-service or cost-based reimbursement is seen as the source of health care's excesses, reversing financial incentives to reward physicians for less rather than more treatment can be expected to change practice styles across the board. Structuring financial rewards can be a powerful control technique because this is a single

---

194. [For example,] hospitals have [ ] instituted efficiency bonus plans . . . in response to the Medicare DRG reimbursement method. The plan that has received the most attention was that implemented for a brief time by the Paracelsus Corporation chain of hospitals in California. . . . The Paracelsus DRG incentive plan paid each member of the medical staff a percentage of the profits the hospital earns from that physician's Medicare patients. U.S. General Accounting Office, Physician Incentive Payments by Hospitals Could Lead to Abuse, Report to the Chairman, Subcommittee on Health, House Committee on Ways and Means 14 (1986). For purposes of computing the profit margin, Paracelsus considered its costs to be 70 or 75 percent of its charges. The bonus percentage escalated from 10 to 20 percent as the profit margin increased.

An incentive plan proposed by another hospital works as follows. Each physician has an "efficiency index" that is determined by debits and credits earned for each patient treated. Debits and credits are awarded according to whether the patient is discharged within the mean length of stay and whether ancillary service use is below the norm for that patient's condition. Each physician's index then determines her share of the hospital cost savings, to be paid only upon the physician's retirement or death. Only physicians with a certain level of admissions are eligible to participate. See Tatge, Illinois Hospital Awaits IRS Ruling on Prototype Physician Incentive Plan, 14 Modern Health Care, June 1984, at 23, 23-24.

intervention that has a continuing, decentralized influence on the universe of individual treatment decisions. . . .

Institutional cost containment techniques that rely on financial incentives must contend with . . . [a] new federal statute, part of the Omnibus Budget Reconciliation Act of 1986 ("OBRA 1986"), [that] allows the Department of Health and Human Services to assess civil monetary penalties of up to $2000 against a hospital that "makes a payment, directly or indirectly, to a physician as an inducement to reduce or limit services provided with respect to [Medicare or Medicaid patients] who . . . are under the direct care of the physician."[209] This prohibition of efficiency incentives is scheduled to extend to HMOs as well beginning April 1, [1991]. . . .

It is difficult to imagine more precipitous and poorly conceived legislation. . . . This bludgeoning of physician incentive plans entirely loses sight of Congress' established reimbursement policy that allows hospitals to profit based on their ability to reduce services. The insights of Professors Havighurst and Blumstein, who convincingly explained the inevitable tendency of quality concerns to undermine governmental cost containment programs, have been proven correct once again: "A policy . . . in which a taboo surrounds any concession to the reality of limited resources is bound to be rich in posturing and assertion" and impoverished in effect.

Any reimbursement policy will have the potential to induce some form of abusive behavior. Traditional fee-for-service reimbursement suffers from the costs of overutilization, the harms of unnecessary treatment, and the distortions of rewarding self-referrals. We trust professional ethics to hold these inflationary incentives in check, but ethics, coupled with peer pressure, the threat of malpractice liability, and competitive business forces, serve even more strongly to constrain health care providers from responding to deflationary pressures with excessive cuts in quality. . . .

In sum, the government failed to see clearly through the medical profession's vitriolic barrage to the observation made recently by the prestigious Institute of Medicine: "All compensation systems [ ] . . . present some undesirable incentives for providing too many services, or too few. No system will work without some degree of integrity, decency, and ethical commitment on the part of professionals. Inevitably, we must presume some underlying professionalism that will constrain the operation of unadulterated self-interest." Ironically, doctors were successful in convincing Congress that they lack this "professionalism" sufficient to "constrain the operation of unadulterated self-interest." . . .

---

209. 42 U.S.C. §1320a-7a(b)(2) (West Supp. 1988). The penalty also extends to doctors who receive such payments.

IV. Organizational Reform of Medical Institutions. . . .

D. Hospital Reorganization and the Autonomous Medical Staff

1. Demise of the Traditional Medical Staff

Many management techniques envision nontraditional medical staff structures as alternatives to the independent, open, self-governing model that currently prevails. For instance, hospital management may have to assume control of the credentialing process in order to implement efficiency screening. Separating the medical staff into an independent entity that forms a joint venture with the hospital in order to create financial incentives for more economical care also entails a departure from the traditional model. Finally, to give hospitals greater control over the details of practice, many commentators envision hospitals that will no longer consist of two separate lines of authority — one with control over financial matters and one with control over clinical matters. The two would be merged into a single, hierarchical bureaucracy, similar to European hospitals. In short, this radical proposal calls for the outright demise of the self-governing medical staff.

2. Institutionalization of the Medical Staff

Physicians can be expected to show intense opposition to full-scale bureaucratization of the hospital. . . . [State hospital licensure statutes] preserve medical staff autonomy completely by ensuring that the staff has exclusive or substantial control over vital aspects of hospital operations. Critically, the medical staff has the self-perpetuating power to determine its own membership.[365] This legislated power over its own destiny gives the medical staff effective veto power over attempts to reformulate hospital structure. Physicians can frustrate the hospitals' unilateral attempts to choose medical staff members contrary to physician desires, and they can prevent hospitals from independently changing their staff from an open to a closed model, or from independent practitioners to employees.

To the extent that state laws do not explicitly promote medical staff self-governance, the same effect is accomplished through the JCAH accreditation standards, which are thoroughly enmeshed in the public regulatory process. JCAH standards decree an organized med-

---

365. See, e.g., Cal. Health & Safety Code §32128 (West Supp. 1988) (stating that the medical staff "shall be self-governing with respect to the professional work performed in the hospital"); Fla. Admin. Code Ann. r. 10D-28.156(4) (1986) ("No action on appointment . . . or dismissal shall be taken without prior referral to the organized medical staff for their recommendation. . . .").

ical staff whose bylaws "establish a framework for self-governance." Notably the medical staff must have substantial authority over membership selection: it alone conducts the credentialing process that is the basis for determining admitting and treating privileges. . . .

Cementing the JCAH medical staff model into the law is poor public policy. Mandating a single institutional structure blocks organizational innovation in response to new environmental forces. As Clark Havighurst has convincingly argued, "how a hospital is internally organized and run should be a managerial issue, not a legal one." What the optimal hospital structure is and how the institution will be transformed if public and private barriers are removed should be left to the future. If the forces of this new era are applied to an unbending structure, they will either be deflected or the structure will shatter.

V. Conclusion

. . . The principal reason our nation's emerging health care policy is in shambles is that policymakers have ignored the law's institutionalization of physician autonomy. Contemporary reimbursement policy assigns to institutions the broad responsibility of leading the revolution in health care cost containment. . . . However, the law frustrates institutional control at every turn. . . . By this critique, I do not mean to accuse physicians or lawmakers of calculated manipulation of the law to pursue evil ends. I mean only to register the undeniable fact that the law acts as a force against reform because it is naturally contoured to fit the shape of traditional medical relationships. The connection between the law and physicians' interests is an organic one, not a conspiratorial one. Nevertheless, the blunt fact remains that our health care cost containment policy is doomed to failure, or at least to mediocrity, in the current legal environment.

NOTES

Will DRGs Help?

1. "It's too soon to tell whether the softening of the hospital business is a pause to catch breath in the twenty-year marathon of escalating costs, or whether a new era of efficiency is at hand." J. Califano, America's Health Care Revolution 122 (1986). Recent health care inflation statistics suggest the pessimistic view:

> Despite implementation of [PPS], Medicare's share of the Nation's hospital bill continues to rise, from 26 percent in 1981 to 29 percent

II. Regulatory Reforms

in 1985. In 1985 alone, Medicare expenditures for hospital services rose 10.1 percent. . . .

8 Health Care Fin. Rev. 1, 7 (1986).

There has been a substantial increase in Medicare inpatient operating costs per case from the first year to the third year of PPS, . . . [estimated] in excess of 10 percent per year.

ProPAC Release, Jan. 19, 1988.

Health care expenditures increased 8.4 percent from 1985 to 1986, . . . much faster than the increase in overall inflation (1.1 percent). . . . After adjusting for overall inflation and population growth, expenditures for health care increased 6.3 percent during 1986, a rate substantially above the rate occurring in the period from 1980 to 1985. . . . These data suggest that the overall rate of increase in health care spending has not been slowed significantly by recent cost-containment initiatives.

Anderson & Erickson, National Medical Care Spending, 6 Health Affairs, Fall 1987, at 96, 98, 103. See also ProPac, Medicare Prospective Payment and the American Health Care System, Report to Congress (June 1988), reprinted in Medicare & Medicaid Guide (CCH), Rep. No. 560, Extra Edition; Russell & Manning, The Effect of Prospective Payment on Medicare Expenditures, 320 New Eng. J. Med. 439 (1989) (PPS will save 20 percent accumulated over six years).

2. Further problems with DRGs have been reported:

"DRG creep" really exists — and it's costing Medicare millions of dollars annually, according to two recent reports by HHS Inspector General (IG) Richard Kusserow. . . . Kusserow found that about half the patients assigned to [DRGs 82 and 88, respiratory neoplasms and chronic pulmonary disease] should have been assigned to less-expensive DRGs or shouldn't have been admitted at all. . . . This could represent as much as $34 million a year in overpayments to PPS hospitals.

Hospitals, April 20, 1986.

Another report found:

In New Jersey, a study found that 26.4 percent of the patients had been misclassified. . . . One of the most publicized examples was the softball player who had injured his finger. He had to be hospitalized for 2 days so that the bone in his finger could be repaired with a metal pin. The DRG category assigned to this patient was "fracture with major surgery," usually reserved for serious cases such as total hip replacement. While the patient's actual charges would have been less than $1000, the DRG classification resulted in a bill for $5000.

P. Feldstein, Health Care Economics 296 (2d ed. 1982). See also Hsiao et al., Accuracy of Diagnostic Coding for Medicare Patients Under the Prospective Payment System, 318 New Eng. J. Med. 352 (1988) (finding a 20 percent error rate); Horn et al., Misclassification Problems in Diagnosis-Related Groups, 314 New Eng. J. Med. 484 (1986); Medicare & Medicaid Guide (CCH) ¶37,072 (1988) (10 percent of Medicare hospital admissions under DRGs are unnecessary); Verville, Medicare Rate Setting and its Problems, 6 J. Leg. Med. 85 (1985).

3. Although the jury may still be out on the success of DRGs in controlling *inpatient hospital* costs, DRGs are manifestly unable to limit the growth in spending on *outpatient* and *physician* services. Indeed, the effect is the opposite. Through the "unbundling" technique described by Enthoven and Noll, DRGs have greatly accelerated the increase in nonhospital expenditures. "Between 1975 and 1987, Medicare spending on physicians' services per beneficiary increased at a compound annual rate of 15 percent. . . . Over the next 10 years, . . . Medicare spending for physicians' services will probably triple." Roper, Perspectives on Physician-Payment Reform, 319 New Eng. J. Med. 863, 864 (1988). These increases "appear to have overwhelmed many of the gains made in the inpatient setting." ProPac 1988 Report to Congress supra, at 101.

Mariner, Prospective Payment for Hospital Services: Social Responsibility and the Limits of Legal Standards*
17 Cumb. L. Rev. 379 (1987)

. . . Criticisms of the DRG prospective payment system fall into three categories:

1. DRGs may restrict access to important health care services;
2. DRGs may compromise the quality of care;
3. DRGs may impede the development and use of beneficial new biomedical technologies.

Criticisms of the prospective payment system generally take the form of attacks on its incentives to place economic reward, or profit, above satisfactory quality of care and to avoid providing services to expensive patients. The underlying concern here seems to be that DRGs cannot or do not serve the important social goals of maintaining

---

* Wendy K. Mariner is Associate Professor of Health Law at Boston University Schools of Public Health and Medicine.
Reprinted with permission of the Cumberland Law Review.

II. Regulatory Reforms

and improving the quality of care, providing adequate care to persons in need, and maintaining and improving access to essential services.

Why is there so much concern and debate about the potential adverse effects of DRGs on the quality and availability of care? Why do we care whether some people may not get an adequate quality of service or perhaps none at all? The answer lies in the fact that, in spite of our efforts to force health care into an industrial model of efficiency, most of us still consider health care as something quite different from ordinary commercial goods. Health care is special. . . .

B. Will DRGs Compromise the Quality of Care?

. . . DRGs obviously create incentives to reduce the level and type of services provided in the hospital such that the costs of providing services will be no more (and preferably far less) than the amount of the DRG payments received. Because there is no corresponding mechanism in the prospective payment system that determines how services are to be allocated and provided, the only incentive created is that of doing less. Less is more — more profit. No one would dispute the fact that more is not always better, and that the cost reimbursement system probably encouraged doing some unnecessary procedures, which even may have exposed patients to unjustifiable risks. To the extent that DRGs correct that type of practice, they are laudable.

The problem is that DRGs do not offer any criteria for deciding what is necessary and what is unnecessary. After they have eliminated any unnecessary procedures, they still reward doing less. How do we know how much less is still good enough? An initial concern is the fact that DRGs are based on an early 1980s conception of medical practice and disease categories. We have partly enshrined the status quo.

There are several ways that hospitals and physicians could respond to DRGs by doing less in a manner that compromises any reasonable definition of the quality of care. An obvious example is discharging patients before they are truly medically stable or in a condition to care for themselves. This is a key concern because DRGs are based so heavily on average hospital costs per bed-day, which means that a hospital that discharges a patient after three days, when the DRG for that patient's condition effectively pays for five days, makes money.

Similarly, DRGs provide incentives to reduce or omit certain diagnostic procedures or particular kinds of treatment, especially those that are costly to provide. They may do so either by omitting them entirely, which may result in a failure to diagnose a serious illness in a patient, or in a failure to treat an illness effectively. While diagnostic procedures can be redundant in some cases, they are critical in others.

Alternatively, a hospital may shift the performance of these services to an outpatient facility, thereby preserving what it perceives to be the appropriate level of quality, but at the same time shifting the costs of services to nongovernment sources. A stronger adverse alternative is that of closing down entire services within a hospital — those that are determined to cost more than DRG revenues provide. The effect on the quality of care depends to some degree on the needs of the patient population and whether such services are available elsewhere. If every hospital finds that certain services are simply cost-inefficient under DRGs, a widespread unavailability will have serious adverse consequences for the quality of care.

A related possibility is that of hospitals opting to expand nonmedical ancillary services which are only marginally related to the quality of care, but which are demonstrably profitable under DRGs. The corollary is that of dropping the kind of services that have little measurable effect on efficiency or profitability, such as patient support services.

DRGs may also offer disincentives for hospitals to acquire equipment that is either expensive to purchase or likely to increase the cost of patient care on an ongoing basis, such as nuclear magnetic resonance imaging. The amount of money available for the purchase of new equipment has been deliberately and strictly limited by Congress, which attributed the increase in medical expenditures in part to the introduction of high technology in hospital care.

Another disincentive to acquiring new technology lies in the time lag between equipment purchase and new DRG category payment adjustments or recalibrations. Recalibration adjusts the amount of payment for one DRG relative to another, not the overall amount payable to the hospital. It is intended to reflect the differences in the cost of caring for different types of medical conditions. The initial calculation is based on 1983 data; that is, it based the cost of care on the expenditures made with respect to particular DRG categories as medicine was practiced in 1983. Although medicine as a whole is not dramatically different from its 1983 state, there are enough differences in the cost and use of certain kinds of equipment to make 1983 figures an imperfect proxy for the current cost of treating particular conditions. Therefore, it seems likely that the cost basis for future payments will be understated for certain DRGs. If a hospital will not receive payment for the cost of equipment or its use until several years after it is acquired, and then perhaps receive only a fraction of that cost, there is a real disincentive to purchase the equipment.

The short-term effect of such disincentives may be minimal. There are sufficient noneconomic incentives to acquire high technology equipment from competition to attract patients by offering the most modern facilities, and from physician motivation to work with the best and latest equipment. Physicians also have economic incentives to press for more technology because their compensation increases with the degree of technology employed. Nonetheless, financially pressed hospitals will ultimately have to resist such pressures. If prospective payment for physicians' services is introduced, physicians may face the same disincentives as hospitals.

Physician Incentives

The quality issue is largely a function of the fact that DRGs create a conflict of interest for physicians. Although physicians traditionally have acted as advocates for their patients, their ability to do so has hinged primarily on the fact that the basis for calculating their compensation was consistent with the provision of services for patients. The incentives operated in the same direction. Under DRGs, physicians will face incentives not to provide additional services. . . . [These] conflicts of interest may arise out of salary and profit-sharing arrangements. If a physician's income depends upon the profitability of the hospital, the economic incentives to do less . . . are not necessarily known to patients. Some have argued that physicians have an obligation to disclose to their patients any financial interests they have in the hospital; but this does not resolve the conflict. First, it is hard to imagine that physicians will readily disclose financial ties when they are reluctant to discuss treatment alternatives with patients. Secondly, it creates an odd new quasi-adversarial relationship between physician and patient, undermining the trust that patients may have that their physicians have their best interests in mind. Few patients would feel comfortable knowing that recommendations for their treatment are being strongly influenced by the cost of the alternatives. . . .

It seems unlikely that physicians would advise their patients adequately of the alternative that they do not feel they can afford. We may find something like the phenomenon of British physicians, who, constrained by the National Health Service in the number of patients who could have hemodialysis, reportedly began to restrict the medical criteria of suitability for dialysis in order to accommodate the limitations. The difference is, of course, that in the United Kingdom, the government made the decision about how many patients it could fund on dialysis by limiting the overall budget, while under DRGs there is no externally imposed limit within which the physician must operate. Instead, the physician is supposed to weigh the benefits against the cost in order to determine whether the treatment is the most efficient therapy. Yet this calculus easily transforms itself into an assessment of whether the individual patient is worth the benefit. Physicians may then be making judgments about the social worth and merit of individuals that may have nothing to do with the patient's responsiveness to a particular form of therapy. . . .

C. Will DRGs Restrict Access to Care?

Perhaps the earliest and most forceful criticism of DRGs was the charge that they create disincentives for hospitals to admit and care for seriously ill patients whose conditions are expensive to treat — more expensive than the payment provided by the relevant DRG. Although the DRGs do include adjustments and different categories for complications and coexistent disease conditions, they do not really deal with severity of illness. . . .

Among clinicians, [i]ndigent patients are perceived to be sicker or to require more services and resources than persons with the same medical condition who have more income and education. They may defer seeking health care, especially preventive care, until they suffer severe illness, thereby entering the hospital in worse condition than other patients. Their nutritional status may compromise the rapidity or effectiveness of treatment. In addition, poor persons are more likely to be overweight, which increases the time and expense required to treat many surgical and medical problems. . . .

Does the law provide any counterincentives to restricting access to care? Does it require that care be made available or distributed in any particular way? Are there any rights to care that could be enforced against restrictive action? . . .

Dolenc & Dougherty, DRGs: The Counterrevolution in Financing Health Care*
15 Hastings Cent. Rep. 19 (1985)

Some hospitals — because of their locations, the demographics of nearby populations, traditional specializations and services, and a sense of institutional mission — treat sicker-than-average patients. . . . [Low income patients, for instance,] will typically enter hospitals with a poorer overall state of health than the relatively affluent. If so, they will . . . cost more to treat. . . . This will create a strong economic incentive to avoid providing medical services to the poor. . . . This needn't occur by literally turning persons away at hospital doors. The poor can be excluded by closing hospital emergency rooms in their neighborhoods, [a]nd inner-city hospitals can move to the suburbs. . . .

* Danielle A. Dolenc is a medical student at the University of California, San Diego. Charles J. Dougherty is Chairman of the Philosophy Department at Creighton University, Omaha, Neb.

II. Regulatory Reforms

Rural hospitals are also in immediate financial danger. While large urban hospitals may be able to consolidate or eliminate services to "manage case-mix," a rural hospital is often the sole local provider and must maintain a full line of service areas. . . . Under prospective payments, small, and even large, free-standing hospitals will be more and more inclined to seek the economic shelter and capital power of the for-profit chains, to shore up their finances. . . . Prospective payment will likely hasten the advent of complete proprietary corporate control over the distribution of American health care. . . . As the DRG-fueled demand for efficiency accelerates, the patient will more and more come to be regarded as a product. Even if this were the only price exacted by the DRGs, it would be too high.

NOTES

Will DRGs Hurt?

1. Contrast the preceding critics with Philipps & Wineberg, Medicare Prospective Payment: A Quiet Revolution, 87 W. Va. L. Rev. 13, 28 (1984): "Although Congress enacted [PPS] as a reaction to rapid inflation in the health care industry, it was equally concerned with maintaining quality health care. Detailed description of PPS reveals that each aspect of the system has been carefully crafted to encourage economically efficient behavior without impairing the quality of care." See also L. Russell, Medicare's New Hospital Payment System: Is It Working? (1989) (PPS provides substantial savings without compromising quality). DesHarnais et al., The Early Effects of the Prospective Payment System on Inpatient Utilization and the Quality of Care, 24 Inquiry 7 (1987) ("We found no evidence that the quality of care deteriorated in 1984 for Medicare patients"); Sloan et al., Hospital Care for the "Self-Pay" Patient, 13 J. Health Pol. Poly. & L. 83 (1988) ("no evidence that PPS reduced hospitals' willingness to treat uninsured patients"); Sloan, Morrisey & Valvona, Case Shifting and the Medicare Prospective Payment System, 78 Am. J. Pub. Health 553 (1988) (same); ProPac, Medicare Prospective Payment and the American Health Care System, Report to Congress (June 1988) at 4, reprinted in Medicare & Medicaid Guide (CCH), Rep. No. 560, Extra Edition ("ProPac's analyses of the effect of PPS on the quality of and access to care for Medicare beneficiaries have not identified systemic problems."); Special Report on Premature Discharges, Medicare & Medicaid Guide (CCH) ¶36,836 (1988) (fewer than one percent of all Medicare discharges are premature).

2. Senator John Heinz, Chairman of the Senate Select Committee on Aging, is Capitol Hill's leading critic of DRGs. His committee hearings have demonstrated that Medicare patients are in fact being

discharged "quicker and sicker." Philipps, Wineberg & Elfenbein supra, 88 W. Va. L. Rev. at 235; Quality of Care Under Medicare's Prospective Payment System, Sen. Hearing No. 195, 99th Cong. 1st Sess. (1985); Out "Sooner and Sicker": Myth or Medicare Crisis?, H.R. Hearings No. 591, 99th Cong., 2d Sess. (1986); Examination of Quality of Care Under Medicare's Prospective Payment System, Sen. Hearing No. 895, 99th Cong., 2d Sess. (1986). But is it necessarily wrong that a patient not be allowed to remain in the hospital for the full period of recuperation, as long as there are no systemic effects on quality of care? A recent study by the DHHS Office of Inspector General indicates that truly abusive incidents are not systemic. However, another recent study concluded that "since the implementation of PPS, hospitals have . . . shifted much of the rehabilitation burden [for patients with hip fracture] to nursing homes, . . . [such that] the overall quality of care for these patients may have deteriorated." Fitzgerald et al., The Care of Elderly Patients with Hip Fracture, 319 New Eng. J. Med. 1392 (1988). Another found that 1.8 percent of Medicare discharges are premature and 3 percent occur without adequate discharge planning. "The percentages are seemingly low, but when extrapolated onto the 11 million annual Medicare admissions, [t]he Committee finds a strong basis for [concern]." House Committee on Government Operations, Quicker and Sicker: Substandard Treatment of Medicare Patients, H.R. Rep. No. 101-387 (1989), reprinted in Medicare & Medicaid Guide (CCH) ¶38,287.

3. "At least part of the [premature discharge] problem appears to stem from simple ignorance. When the DRGs and their respective weights were first published, the average LOS [length of stay] for each DRG was also published. Some hospital administrators have taken this average figure as a maximum. . . . It is reported that in some instances when the average DRG days are up, patients have been told they must leave the hospital because 'their Medicare coverage has run out.' These are obviously abuses of the system, but they are not the result of defects inherent to PPS/DRG itself. . . . The remedy is not to change the system; it is to better inform the system's participants about how it works." 88 W. Va. L. Rev. at 236.

HCFA has attempted this remedy by requiring that all Medicare patients be given upon admission a written statement of their rights to protest a discharge decision. Kinney, Making Hard Choices Under the Medicare Prospective Payment System, 19 Ind. L. Rev. 1151, 1193-1195 (1986). In addition, patients are given a two-day grace period after written notice of discharge, during which they may remain in the hospital and protest the decision to the PRO. 42 C.F.R. §412.42(c)(3); Wilson, How to Appeal Medicare Hospital Coverage Denials Under the DRG System, Clearinghouse Rev. Summer 1986, at 434. For additional reference to the PRO appeal process, see 711 and 723 supra.

II. Regulatory Reforms

4. Confirming the wide variation in costs of treating cases within individual DRGs and the uneven impact of these variations on certain classes of hospitals, see GAO Report, Refinement of Diagnosis Related Groups Needed to Insure Payment Equity (1988), reprinted in Medicare & Medicaid Guide (CCH) ¶37,085. Reluctantly, HCFA has begun to make an adjustment for the special circumstances of sole community hospitals and "disproportionate share" hospitals (those that receive a large number of poor and elderly patients). See Redbud Hosp. Dist. v. Heckler, Medicare & Medicaid Guide (CCH) ¶¶34,085, 34,669 (N.D. Cal. 1984, 1985); Kinney, supra, 19 Ind. L. Rev. at 1187-1189. Researchers are investigating ways to bring greater refinements to DRGs generally by introducing a severity-of-illness adjustment. See Mariner, supra, 17 Cumb. L. Rev. at 391 n.30; Jencks, Refining Case-Mix Adjustment, 317 New Eng. J. Med. 679 (1987); Comment, Diagnosis Related Groups and the Price of Cost Containment, 2 J. Contemp. Health L. & Poly. 305, 320-325 (1986).

5. The effect of DRGs on technology acquisition and medical innovation may be more complex than the Mariner article suggests. While limited reimbursement will surely retard some technology investment, the DRG system will encourage other innovations, perhaps excessively. One such instance relates to a procedure known as P.T.C.A. (percutaneous transluminal coronary angioplasty) or "balloon angioplasty," an alternative to bypass surgery that involves inserting a balloon into an artery and inflating it to clear blockage. The DRG system initially reimbursed this relatively inexpensive procedure as if it were complex surgery, prompting a hospital gold rush of sorts on establishing P.T.C.A. programs. The problem is that P.T.C.A. may not be appropriate in all circumstances; some arteries reocclude, requiring repetition of the procedure. HCFA has since created a new DRG to reimburse this procedure more accurately.

In general, what are the likely effects of DRGs on innovations that are (a) operating as opposed to capital-cost intensive, (b) cost-decreasing as opposed to cost-increasing, or (c) cost-decreasing in the long term versus the short term? See Anderson & Steinberg, To Buy or Not To Buy: Technology Acquisition under Prospective Payment, 311 New Eng. J. Med. 182 (1984); Garrison & Wilensky, Cost Containment and Incentives for Technology, 5 Health Affairs, Summer 1986, at 46; Mehlman, Health Care Cost Containment and Medical Technology: A Critique of Waste Theory, 36 Case West. Res. L. Rev. 778 (1986); Sloan, Morrisey & Valvona, Medicare Prospective Payment and the Use of Medical Technologies in Hospitals, 26 Med. Care, No. 8 (1988).

6. The thorniest dilemma that DRGs and other cost containment measures present is the ethical bind they impose on practicing physicians. Is it morally correct for a doctor to be influenced by the inevitable resource constraints placed on hospitals or on society at

large, if, as a result of third-party reimbursement, the doctor's patients do not face the same constraints? Aspects of this dilemma will plague us throughout this chapter. For now, consider the following hypothetical (but very real) problem:

> Lakeview Hospital's medical director, Jared Lapin, M.D., . . . analyzed a lengthy computer report that matched, for each physician, the revenue the hospital received with the costs incurred for treating patients in each of the DRGs in one month. While studying the fifteen DRGs under Major Diagnostic Category number 14 (Pregnancy, Childbirth, and the Puerperium), [he] noticed that, . . . across all deliveries, the costs of treating Dr. Weiner's patients exceeded the revenue received from the DRG rates. But the total cost incurred in providing care to the other obstetricians' patients was considerably below revenue and hence the hospital was able to earn a "profit." . . . The reason for Dr. Weiner's comparatively poor overall "financial performance" . . . was that he performed many fewer cesarians than did his colleagues . . . Dr. Lapin countered that "it's in all our interests to look out for the financial health of the hospital. And since it is unclear which of the two approaches benefits the patient more, I urge you to reconsider the way you handle these cases."
>
> Was it ethical for Dr. Lapin to approach Dr. Weiner if there was no indication he was delivering poor quality care? How should financial considerations, both those related to the hospital and society at large, be weighed against physician judgment?

Wasserman, The Doctor, The Patient and the DRG, 13 Hastings Cent. Rep., Nov. 1983, at 23. See also Veatch, DRGs and the Ethical Reallocation of Resources, 16 Hastings Cent. Rep., June 1986, at 32; Capron, Containing Health Care Costs: Ethical and Legal Implications of Changes in the Methods of Paying Physicians, 36 Case West. Res. L. Rev. 708 (1986); Morreim, Cost Containment: Issues of Moral Conflict and Justice for Physicians, 6 Theor. Med. 257 (1985); Begley, Prospective Payment and Medical Ethics, 12 J. Med. & Philo. 107 (1987); Symposium, 19 Hastings Cen. Rep. (Jan./Feb. 1989).

7. DRGs are not the government's final word. Dr. William L. Roper, former head of HCFA, was quoted as follows:

> Over the long term, this administered price system is going to collapse of its own weight. I am angry over the terrible complexity of the system, . . . but I don't think the solution is further fine-tuning of a terribly flawed system. The answer is a new system, based on private health plan options.

New York Times, Nov. 23, 1987, at 10, col. 3. This new system would use vouchers to allow patients to select among competing HMOs, a system like that described in Section III.B. See Roper, Balancing Efficiency and Quality — Toward Market-Based Health Care,

3 Notre Dame J. L. Ethics & Pub. Pol. 169 (1988); Dobson, et al., The Future of Medicare Policy Reform, Health Care Fin. Rev., 1986 Supp., at 1.

B. *The Malpractice Implications of Cost Containment*

Wickline v. State
239 Cal. Rptr. 810 (Cal. App. 1986), *review dismissed,*
741 P.2d 613 (Cal. 1987)

ROWEN, ASSOCIATE JUSTICE. [Lois Wickline, who was treated under California's Medicaid program (known as "Medi-Cal"), sued the State, but not her physician, for negligently causing her premature discharge from the hospital, resulting in complications that eventually necessitated amputation of her right leg. Wickline alleged that her premature discharge was the fault of Medi-Cal's erroneous withholding of its authorization for her continued hospitalization.] This is an appeal from a judgment for plaintiff entered after a trial by jury. For the reasons discussed below, we reverse the judgment.

Principally, this matter concerns itself with the legal responsibility that a third party payor, in this case, the State of California, has for harm caused to a patient when a cost containment program is applied in a manner which is alleged to have affected the implementation of the treating physician's medical judgment. . . .

I

Responding to concerns about the escalating cost of health care, public and private payors have in recent years experimented with a variety of cost containment mechanisms. We deal here with one of those programs: The prospective utilization review process.

At the outset, this court recognizes that this case appears to be the first attempt to tie a health care payor into the medical malpractice causation chain and that it, therefore, deals with issues of profound importance to the health care community and to the general public. For those reasons we have permitted the filing of amicus curiae briefs in support of each of the respective parties in the matter to assure that due consideration is given to the broader issues raised before this court by this case. . . .

Early cost containment programs utilized the retrospective utilization review process. In that system the third party payor reviewed the patient's chart after the fact to determine whether the treatment provided was medically necessary. If, in the judgment of the utilization reviewer, it was not, the health care provider's claim for payment was denied.

In the cost containment program in issue in this case, prospective utilization review, authority for the rendering of health care services must be obtained before medical care is rendered. Its purpose is to promote the well recognized public interest in controlling health care costs by reducing unnecessary services while still intending to assure that appropriate medical and hospital services are provided to the patient in need. However, such a cost containment strategy creates new and added pressures on the quality assurance portion of the utilization review mechanism. The stakes, the risks at issue, are much higher when a prospective cost containment review process is utilized than when a retrospective review process is used.

A mistaken conclusion about medical necessity following retrospective review will result in the wrongful withholding of payment. An erroneous decision in a prospective review process, on the other hand, in practical consequences, results in the withholding of necessary care, potentially leading to a patient's permanent disability or death.

II

Though somewhat in dispute, the facts in this case are not particularly complicated. In 1976, Wickline, a married woman in her mid-40's, with a limited education, was being treated by Dr. Stanley Z. Daniels (Dr. Daniels), a physician engaged in a general family practice, for problems associated with her back and legs. Failing to respond to the physical therapy type of treatment he prescribed, Dr. Daniels had Wickline admitted to Van Nuys Community Hospital (Van Nuys or Hospital) in October 1976 and brought in another physician, Dr. Gerald E. Polonsky (Dr. Polonsky), a specialist in peripheral vascular surgery, to do a consultation examination. Peripheral vascular surgery concerns itself with surgery on any vessel of the body, exclusive of the heart.

Dr. Polonsky examined plaintiff and diagnosed her condition as arteriosclerosis obliterans with occlusion of the abdominal aorta, more generally referred to as Leriche's Syndrome. . . .

According to Dr. Polonsky, the only treatment for Leriche's Syndrome is surgical. In Wickline's case her disease was so far advanced that Dr. Polonsky concluded that it was necessary to remove a part of the plaintiff's artery and insert a synthetic (Teflon) graft in its place.

After agreeing to the operation, Wickline was discharged home to await approval of her doctor's diagnosis and authorization from Medi-Cal for the recommended surgical procedure and attendant acute care hospitalization. It is conceded that at all times in issue in this case, the plaintiff was eligible for medical benefits under California's medical assistance program, the "Medi-Cal Act," which is more com-

II. Regulatory Reforms

monly referred to as Medi-Cal. (Welf. & Inst. Code, §§14000 et seq., 14000.4.)

As required, Dr. Daniels submitted a treatment authorization request to Medi-Cal, sometimes referred to as form "161," "MC-161" or "TAR." In response to Dr. Daniels' request, Medi-Cal authorized the surgical procedure and 10 days of hospitalization for that treatment.

On January 6, 1977, plaintiff was admitted to Van Nuys by Dr. Daniels. On January 7, 1977, Dr. Polonsky performed a surgical procedure in which a part of plaintiff's artery was removed and a synthetic artery was inserted to replace it. Dr. Polonsky characterized that procedure as "a very major surgery."

Later that same day Dr. Polonsky was notified that Wickline was experiencing circulatory problems in her right leg. He concluded that a clot had formed in the graft. As a result, Wickline was taken back into surgery, the incision in her right groin was reopened, the clot removed and the graft was resewn. Wickline's recovery subsequent to the two January 7th operations were characterized as "stormy." She had a lot of pain, some spasm in the vessels in the lower leg and she experienced hallucinating episodes. On January 12, 1977, Wickline was returned to the operating room where Dr. Polonsky performed a lumbar sympathectomy.

A lumbar sympathectomy is a major operation in which a section of the chain of nerves that lie on each side of the spinal column is removed. The procedure causes the blood vessels in the patient's lower extremity to become paralyzed in a wide open position and was done in an attempt to relieve the spasms which Wickline was experiencing in those vessels. Spasms stop the outflow of blood from the vessels causing the blood to back up into the graft. Failure to relieve such spasms can cause clotting.

Dr. Polonsky was assisted in all three surgeries by Dr. Leonard Kovner (Dr. Kovner), a board certified specialist in the field of general surgery and the chief of surgery at Van Nuys. Dr. Daniels was present for the initial graft surgery on January 7, 1977, and for the right lumbar sympathectomy operation on January 12, 1977.

Wickline was scheduled to be discharged on January 16, 1977, which would mean that she would actually leave the hospital sometime before 1 p.m. on January 17, 1977. On or about January 16, 1977, Dr. Polonsky concluded that "it was medically necessary" that plaintiff remain in the hospital for an additional eight days beyond her then scheduled discharge date. Drs. Kovner and Daniels concurred in Dr. Polonsky's opinion.

Dr. Polonsky cited many reasons for his feeling that it was medically necessary for plaintiff to remain in an acute care hospital for an additional eight days, such as the danger of infection and/or clotting. His principal reason, however, was that he felt that he was going to be able to save both of Wickline's legs and wanted her to remain in the hospital where he could observe her and be immediately available, along with the hospital staff, to treat her if an emergency should occur.

In order to secure an extension of Wickline's hospital stay, it was necessary to complete and present to Medi-Cal a form called "Request for Extension of Stay in Hospital," commonly referred to as an "MC-180" or "180." . . .

At Van Nuys, Patricia N. Spears (Spears), an employee of the hospital and a registered nurse, had the responsibility for completing 180 forms. In this case, as requested by Dr. Polonsky, Spears filled out Wickline's 180 form and then presented it to Dr. Daniels, as plaintiff's attending physician, to sign, which he did, in compliance with Dr. Polonsky's recommendation. All of the physicians who testified agreed that the 180 form prepared by Spears was complete, accurate and adequate for all purposes in issue in this matter.

Doris A. Futerman (Futerman), a registered nurse, was, at that time, employed by Medi-Cal as a Health Care Service Nurse, commonly referred to as an "on-site nurse." . . .

Futerman, after reviewing Wickline's 180 form, felt that she could not approve the requested eight-day extension of acute care hospitalization. While conceding that the information provided might justify some additional time beyond the scheduled discharge date, nothing in Wickline's case, in Futerman's opinion, would have warranted the entire eight additional days requested and, for those reasons, she telephoned the Medi-Cal Consultant. She reached Dr. William S. Glassman (Dr. Glassman), one of the Medi-Cal Consultants on duty at the time in Medi-Cal's Los Angeles office. The Medi-Cal Consultant selection occurred randomly. As was the practice, whichever Medi-Cal Consultant was available at the moment took the next call that came into the office. . . .

After speaking with Futerman on the telephone, Dr. Glassman rejected Wickline's treating physician's request for an eight-day hospital extension and, instead, authorized an additional four days of hospital stay beyond the originally scheduled discharge date. . . .

After review of Wickline's 180 form, Dr. Glassman testified that the factors that led him to authorize four days, rather than the requested eight days, was that there was no information about the patient's temperature which he, thereupon, assumed was normal; nothing was mentioned about the patient's diet, which he then presumed was not a problem; nor was there any information about Wickline's bowel function, which Dr. Glassman then presumed was functioning satisfactorily. Further, the fact that the 180 form noted

II. Regulatory Reforms

that Wickline was able to ambulate with help and that whirlpool treatments were to begin that day caused Dr. Glassman to presume that the patient was progressing satisfactorily and was not seriously or critically ill. . . .

In essence, respondent argues, Dr. Glassman based his decision on signs and symptoms such as temperature, diet and bowel movements, which were basically irrelevant to the plaintiff's circulatory condition for which she was being treated and did not concern himself with those symptoms and signs which an ordinary prudent physician would consider to be pertinent with regard to the type of medical condition presented by Wickline.

Complying with the limited extension of time authorized by Medi-Cal, Wickline was discharged from Van Nuys on January 21, 1977. Drs. Polonsky and Daniels each wrote discharge orders. At the time of her discharge, each of plaintiff's three treating physicians were aware that the Medi-Cal Consultant had approved only four of the requested eight-day hospital stay extension. While all three doctors were aware that they could attempt to obtain a further extension of Wickline's hospital stay by telephoning the Medi-Cal Consultant to request such an extension, none of them did so. . . .

At trial, Dr. Polonsky testified that in the time that had passed since the first extension request had been communicated to Medi-Cal, on January 16th or 17th, and the time of her scheduled discharge on January 21, 1977, Wickline's condition had neither deteriorated nor become critical. In Dr. Polonsky's opinion no new symptom had presented itself and no additional factors had occurred since the original request was made to have formed the basis for a change in the Medi-Cal Consultant's attitude regarding Wickline's situation. In addition, he stated that at the time of Wickline's discharge it did not appear that her leg was in any danger.

Dr. Polonsky testified that at the time in issue he felt that Medi-Cal Consultants had the State's interest more in mind than the patient's welfare and that that belief influenced his decision not to request a second extension of Wickline's hospital stay. In addition, he felt that Medi-Cal had the power to tell him, as a treating doctor, when a patient must be discharged from the hospital. Therefore, while still of the subjective, non-communicated, opinion that Wickline was seriously ill and that the danger to her was not over, Dr. Polonsky discharged her from the hospital on January 21, 1977. He testified that had Wickline's condition, in his medical judgment, been critical or in a deteriorating condition on January 21, he would have made some effort to keep her in the hospital beyond that day even if denied authority by Medi-Cal and even if he had to pay her hospital bill himself. . . .

All of the medical witnesses who testified at trial agreed that Dr. Polonsky was acting within the standards of practice of the medical community in discharging Wickline on January 21, 1977. . . .

Wickline testified that in the first few days after she arrived home she started feeling pain in her right leg and the leg started to lose color. In the next few days the pain got worse and the right leg took on a whitish, statue-like marble appearance. Wickline assumed she was experiencing normal recovery symptoms and did not communicate with any of her physicians. Finally, when "the pain got so great and the color started changing from looking like a statue to getting a grayish color," her husband called Dr. Kovner. It was Wickline's memory that this occurred about the third day after her discharge from the hospital and that Dr. Kovner advised Mr. Wickline to give extra pain medicine to the plaintiff.

Thereafter, gradually over the next few days, the plaintiff's leg "kept getting grayer and then it got bluish." The extra medication allegedly prescribed by Dr. Kovner over the telephone did not relieve the pain Wickline was experiencing. She testified that "by then the pain was just excruciating, where no pain medicine helped whatsoever." Finally, Wickline instructed her husband to call Dr. Kovner again and this time Dr. Kovner ordered plaintiff back into the hospital. Wickline returned to Van Nuys that same evening, January 30, 1977, nine days after her last discharge therefrom. . . .

Attempts to save Wickline's leg through the utilization of anticoagulants, antibiotics, strict bed rest, pain medication and warm water whirlpool baths to the lower extremity proved unsuccessful. On February 8, 1977, Dr. Polonsky amputated Wickline's leg below the knee because had he not done so "she would have died." The condition did not, however, heal after the first operation and on February 17, 1977, the doctors went back and amputated Wickline's leg above the knee. . . .

In Dr. Polonsky's opinion, to a reasonable medical certainty, had Wickline remained in the hospital for the eight additional days, as originally requested by him and her other treating doctors, she would not have suffered the loss of her leg. . . .

Dr. Polonsky testified that in his medical opinion, the Medi-Cal Consultant's rejection of the requested eight-day extension of acute care hospitalization and his authorization of a four-day extension in its place did not conform to the usual medical standards as they existed in 1977. He stated that, in accordance with those standards, a physician would not be permitted to make decisions regarding the care of a patient without either first seeing the patient, reviewing the patient's chart or discussing the patient's condition with her treating physician or physicians. . . .

II. Regulatory Reforms

III

From the facts thus presented, appellant takes the position that it was not negligent as a matter of law. Appellant contends that the decision to discharge was made by each of the plaintiff's three doctors, was based upon the prevailing standards of practice, and was justified by her condition at the time of her discharge. It argues that Medi-Cal had no part in the plaintiff's hospital discharge and therefore was not liable even if the decision to do so was erroneously made by her doctors. . . .

As to the principal issue before this court, i.e., who bears responsibility for allowing a patient to be discharged from the hospital, her treating physicians or the health care payor, each side's medical expert witnesses agreed that, in accordance with the standards of medical practice as it existed in January 1977, it was for the patient's treating physician to decide the course of treatment that was medically necessary to treat the ailment. It was also that physician's responsibility to determine whether or not acute care hospitalization was required and for how long. Finally, it was agreed that the patient's physician is in a better position than the Medi-Cal Consultant to determine the number of days medically necessary for any required hospital care. The decision to discharge is, therefore, the responsibility of the patient's own treating doctor.

Dr. Kaufman testified that if, on January 21, the date of the plaintiff's discharge from Van Nuys, any one of her three treating doctors had decided that in his medical judgment it was necessary to keep Wickline in the hospital for a longer period of time, they, or any of them, should have filed another request for extension of stay in the hospital, that Medi-Cal would expect those physicians to make such a request if they felt it was indicated, and upon receipt of such a request further consideration of an additional extension of hospital time would have been given.

Title 22 of the California Administrative Code section 51110, provided, in pertinent part, at the relevant time in issue here, that: "The determination of need for acute care shall be made in accordance with the usual standards of medical practice in the community."

The patient who requires treatment and who is harmed when care which should have been provided is not provided should recover for the injuries suffered from all those responsible for the deprivation of such care, including, when appropriate, health care payors. Third party payors of health care services can be held legally accountable when medically inappropriate decisions result from defects in the design or implementation of cost containment mechanisms as, for example, when appeals made on a patient's behalf for medical or hospital care are arbitrarily ignored or unreasonably disregarded or overridden. However, the physician who complies without protest with the limitations imposed by a third party payor, when his medical judgment dictates otherwise, cannot avoid his ultimate responsibility for his patient's care. He cannot point to the health care payor as the liability scapegoat when the consequences of his own determinative medical decisions go sour.

There is little doubt that Dr. Polonsky was intimidated by the Medi-Cal program but he was not paralyzed by Dr. Glassman's response nor rendered powerless to act appropriately if other action was required under the circumstances. If, in his medical judgment, it was in his patient's best interest that she remain in the acute care hospital setting for an additional four days beyond the extended time period originally authorized by Medi-Cal, Dr. Polonsky should have made some effort to keep Wickline there. He himself acknowledged that responsibility to his patient. It was his medical judgment, however, that Wickline could be discharged when she was. All the plaintiff's treating physicians concurred and all the doctors who testified at trial, for either plaintiff or defendant, agreed that Dr. Polonsky's medical decision to discharge Wickline met the standard of care applicable at the time. Medi-Cal was not a party to that medical decision and therefore cannot be held to share in the harm resulting if such decision was negligently made.

In addition thereto, while Medi-Cal played a part in the scenario before us in that it was the resource for the funds to pay for the treatment sought, and its input regarding the nature and length of hospital care to be provided was of paramount importance, Medi-Cal did not override the medical judgment of Wickline's treating physicians at the time of her discharge. It was given no opportunity to do so. Therefore, there can be no viable cause of action against it for the consequences of that discharge decision. . . .

V

This court appreciates that what is at issue here is the effect of cost containment programs upon the professional judgment of physicians to prescribe hospital treatment for patients requiring the same. While we recognize, realistically, that cost consciousness has become a permanent feature of the health care system, it is essential that cost limitation programs not be permitted to corrupt medical judgment. We have concluded, from the facts in issue here, that in this case it did not.

For the reasons expressed herein, this court finds that appellant is not liable for respondent's injuries as a matter of law. That makes unnecessary any discussion of the other contentions of the parties.

The judgment is reversed.

FEINERMAN, P.J., and HASTINGS, J., concur.

II. Regulatory Reforms

NOTES

Economic Malpractice

1. Although *Wickline* does not squarely confront the issue, it is the case that comes closest to addressing the extent to which emerging cost containment policy conflicts with established malpractice law. As physicians decline to perform procedures for cost reasons that were once considered necessary, will they be exposed to liability or will legal standards shift to accommodate the new constraints? This dilemma is one of the most important issues that will confront health care tort law in the coming decade. What does *Wickline* suggest? See Morreim, Cost Containment and the Standard of Medical Care, 75 Cal. L. Rev. 1719 (1987) (*Wickline* prohibits cost considerations in treatment decisions); Hall, The Malpractice Standard Under Health Care Cost Containment; 17 L. Med. & Health Care 347 (Winter 1989) (arguing that *Wickline* is fundamentally ambivalent).

For a sampling of the burgeoning literature on this topic, see in addition Bovbjerg, The Medical Malpractice Standard of Care: HMOs and Customary Practice, 1975 Duke L.J. 1375; Blumstein, Rationing Medical Resources: A Constitutional, Legal, and Policy Analysis, 59 Tex. L. Rev. 1345 (1981); Rosenblatt, Rationing "Normal" Health Care: The Hidden Legal Issues, 59 Tex. L. Rev. 1401 (1981); Schuck, Malpractice Liability and the Rationing of Care, 59 Tex. L. Rev. 1421 (1981); Kapp, Legal and Ethical Implications of Health Care Reimbursement by Diagnosis Related Groups, 12 L. Med. & Health Care 245 (1984); Note, Rethinking Medical Malpractice Law in Light of Medicare Cost-Cutting, 98 Harv. L. Rev. 1004 (1985); Marsh, Health Care Cost Containment and the Duty to Treat, 6 J. Leg. Med. 157 (1985); Macaulay, Health Care Cost Containment and Medical Malpractice: On a Collision Course, 21 Suffolk L. Rev. 91, 103-104 (1987); Note, Reexamining the Physician's Duty of Care in Response to Medicare's Prospective Payment System, 62 Wash. L. Rev. 791 (1987); Furrow, Medical Malpractice and Cost Containment: Tightening the Screws, 36 Case W. Res. L. Rev. 985 (1986).

2. Addressing the issue of "economic malpractice" from a theoretical perspective, there are two important questions: do the existing standards of care in fact conflict with cost-sensitive treatment standards; and, if so, are the existing standards so codified in the law that they are incapable of evolving. On the first point, recognize that professional standards of care are not nearly so monolithic as malpractice law often suggests. John Wennberg is the most prominent among the medical epidemiologists who have demonstrated phenomenal variations in local practice patterns. Through a technique known as "small area analysis," he and his associates have documented variations among New England communities of six-fold in the rate of

tonsillectomies and four-fold in the rate of hysterectomies. Wennberg, McPherson, & Caper, Will Payment Based on Diagnosis-Related Groups Control Hospital Costs?, 311 New Eng. J. Med. 295 (1984); Wennberg & Gittelsohn, Variations in Medical Care Among Small Areas, 246 Sci. Am. 120 (April 1982). Equally egregious variations have been documented for other medical procedures, including a 17-fold variation in test ordering within a single hospital. Studies are collected and discussed in Paul-Shaheen, Clark & Williams, Small Area Analysis: A Review and Analysis of the North American Literature, 12 J. Health Pol. Poly. & L. 741 (1987). Does this phenomenon account for the fact in *Wickline* that the court found no negligent premature discharge on the part of the doctors even though her stay was extended only half of the recommended eight days? Is this phenomenon also captured by the "respectable minority" rule discussed at 363 supra?

3. One scholar has argued, by extension from the "similar locality rule," that the standard of care is capable of evolving to accommodate the economic constraints of different practice environments. Thus, for instance, we might apply a different standard of care to HMOs than to university medical centers, much as we now apply different standards to small, rural practitioners than to metropolitan specialists. Bovbjerg, supra. Would this argument fail to hold in jurisdictions that have adopted the "national" standard of care? See Hall, supra at 350 ("even the national standard . . . enforces only those medical practices that prevail in the 'same or similar circumstances' as the defendant. Recent case law has begun to stress this qualification of the national standard and emphasize its sensitivity to resource constraints").

4. A related, but separate, inquiry is to ask what cost containment might portend for *institutional* liability, in view of the contemplated expansion of institutional oversight of medical care. Consider, for instance, the effect on liability exposure of an internal hospital review mechanism that functions similarly to the Medi-Cal prior authorization system, but the effect of which is to refuse use of the facilities for disapproved procedures, not merely to deny reimbursement. In essence, this is the manner in which many HMOs are structured in that they require medical director approval before hospitalizing a patient or using expensive diagnostic equipment.

C. *Certificate of Need Regulation*

Simpson, Full Circle: The Return of Certificate of Need Regulation of Health Facilities to State Control*
19 Ind. L. Rev. 1025 (1986)

[See article reprinted at p. 612.]

Bovbjerg, Problems and Prospects for Health Planning: The Importance of Incentives, Standards, and Procedures in Certificate of Need*
1978 Utah L. Rev. 83-96, 101

I. *The Rationale for Certificate-of-Need Laws*

Certificate of need singles out investment by institutions, mainly hospitals, for public control. Public assessment of the desirability of new investments is thought necessary because private investment decisions are insufficiently cost conscious. Indeed, it is believed that institutional capacities are overbuilt to the point of waste and unnecessary duplication, with excess capacity going unused. Other producers in our society would be undercut in the marketplace if they raised their costs by investing too heavily in extra production capacity; the threat of losing business to more efficient competitors, who are able to charge lower prices and still make a profit, is a powerful disincentive to "unnecessary" investment.

But health care institutions are different. Several peculiarities of the marketplace for institutional health services allow and encourage providers to indulge in overinvestment that would not occur in more competitive sectors of the economy. The industry is dominated by non-profit institutions, which, lacking shareholders or other residual claimants seeking a profit, have diminished incentive to count costs. Indeed, the "edifice complex" of non-profit organizations is often noted. Large, new, well-equipped facilities add to institutional prestige and administrators' status. Moreover, many communities seek to have their own facilities to provide easy access, to boost local pride, and to attract doctors. Expansive investment decisions are further supported by non-profit hospitals' charitable status, which encourages private philanthropy, and by the attendant indirect subsidies of tax exemption. Further, since 1946 the federal government has directly subsidized private hospital investment through the Hill-Burton program, and governments at all levels have significantly contributed to capacity by building public hospitals. . . .

There would nonetheless be an early limit to hospitals' ability to absorb losses due to overinvestment if there were institutional price competition, that is, if patients left high-priced hospitals (for example, those with too many beds) for lower-priced ones, or if they stayed out of the hospital altogether because of the expense. But, for at least two reasons, price is usually not a factor in hospital competition: First, almost all hospital care is paid for, not by patients, but by third parties, either insurers or government (largely through Medicare and Medicaid). These third-party payers have been unwilling or unable

---

* Reprinted with permission of the Utah Law Review.

to induce hospital cost control by minimizing the price they pay. Indeed, third-party payment is predominantly cost-based reimbursement, including capital costs. Hospitals typically have reasonable assurance of being able to recoup investment costs from third-party payers, which has led to and is evidenced by the growing use of borrowed funds to finance hospital growth. Increasing reliance on debt-financing has lessened even the weak check on overexpansion provided by philanthropic or governmental capital donors. Lenders are more concerned with the availability of third-party revenues than with a demonstration that the proposed facilities or equipment are needed.

Second, most patients are rather insensitive to comparative hospital costs and do not reward an efficient hospital with their patronage. Not only are sick patients often not able or willing to shop around, but third-party payment also plays a role here, reducing the cost consciousness of patients as it does that of hospitals. Since patients pay so little out of pocket at the time of hospitalization (indeed, often less than they would if they were treated outside a hospital), they have little incentive to seek out less expensive, non-overbuilt providers. Moreover, hospitalization decisions, including the choice of hospital, are largely made by physicians rather than by patients. This means that hospitals compete for the patronage of physicians more than for patients; and physicians, who do not face the costs either, prefer well-equipped, modern, and uncrowded facilities.

All these incentives point in the direction of overinvestment and higher costs. These costs are not borne by the institutions or communities responsible for them, but rather by much larger groups through insurance premiums and taxes. Costs increase because the extra capital spending adds extra depreciation and interest charges to hospital expenses, whether or not the extra asset is utilized. Other fixed costs, such as routine maintenance, also rise. Conventional wisdom holds that an empty hospital bed, for example, costs at least fifty percent as much as an occupied one. Moreover, excess assets themselves are thought to generate pressures to utilize them, thus increasing operating costs as well as fixed costs. Obviously, hospitals, in the business of rendering services, prefer their assets to be used and generating income; consequently, subtle (and not-so-subtle) pressures may be put on staff doctors to increase utilization. Doctors themselves, paid on a fee-for-service basis, have little reason to restrain utilization. Health care institutional providers, in short, like individual providers, are thought to be capable of creating their own demand for services in addition to simply responding to patient demand or objective medical needs.

This phenomenon of demand creation is sometimes called "Roemer's law," after the man who first reported that hospital utilization was affected by the number of beds available to be utilized. While Roemer's hypothesis may not be an iron law of health care delivery, it is certainly an important intellectual underpinning for certificate-of-need laws and health planning. Of course, there are limits to the Roemer effect; not every bed that is built can be filled. Quite apart from the extent that supply-induced demand exacerbates the cost problem, unused excess capacity means wasted resources, which planning and certificate-of-need laws are meant to prevent. . . .

II. The Planning Framework and Certificate-of-Need Laws

[A] certificate is . . . a kind of health facilities building permit, without which institutions are not permitted to begin construction or to acquire equipment. . . .

The chief criterion for certificate-of-need review is whether the investment or expenditure is needed. Federal regulations list "need" as a review criterion, as well as compliance with previously prepared plans, themselves primarily concerned with the needs of particular planning areas. Other criteria include financial feasibility and cost of construction. . . . Thus, the central problem for health planning and certificate-of-need review is determining need.

III. Need and Its Determination

The Planning Act and certificate-of-need statutes assume that specific and limited needs can be identified, that plans can be made to assure their being met, and that certificate-of-need reviews can prevent spending beyond needs. For a number of reasons, these assumptions are questionable.

A. The Amorphous Nature of Medical "Need"

Need is a medical concept, largely defined by professionals. It is subjective, rather than objective, and consequently is not a limiting, but an expansive concept. Unlike economic "demand" for goods and services, which reflects both consumers' wants and their resource limitations, medical need reflects what professionals deem desirable, rather than what patients can afford. Professionals decide what is needed according to their concept of what constitutes good care, which tends to be established according to the state of the art — what is medically possible at a given time. Virtually any medical benefit is seen as a need; medical professionals are generally guided by a more-is-better philosophy, which has been characterized as a "technological" or a "quality imperative." This approach is in keeping with the preferred professional role of seeking the best possible services for those being cared for.

Thus, when we as individuals want to know what medical intervention is needed, we ask our doctors. Physicians decide what examinations should be undertaken on an asymptomatic person, what diagnostic measures are needed for a given set of symptoms, what treatment should be given a particular diagnosis, and even when or whether treatment should be stopped. Similarly, the need for facilities and equipment begins with the aggregate needs of the professionals and patients who are to use the facility or equipment; once again, the judgment involved will largely be the expert opinion of physicians. When hospital administrators or boards of directors want to know how many new operating suites to build, they ask the surgeons who will use the suites. When the size and capabilities of a replacement X-Ray machine are at issue, the views of the radiologists are solicited. . . .

Congress presumably did not mean to rely on medical need, the flexible character of which has been a key factor in the growth of demand for care and facilities, to curb that same growth. Rather, the Planning Act embodies a philosophy that rational public planning can successfully define limited needs where medical opinion and the unreliable medical marketplace cannot. A pervasive belief underlying the legislation is that planning is a mechanistic enterprise, a matter of developing and applying technical expertise. The central process of mechanistic planning is the development of objective, numerical standards to rationalize the health facilities system and to determine scientifically the correct health care investments to be made.

The very word "planning" has a comfortable aura of expertise, suggesting precise computations, scientific methodology, and rationality. Although existing planning methodology may be criticized as imperfect, legislators seem to retain their faith in objective planning in the abstract. Thus, the first thing the Planning Act did, after setting forth its findings and purpose, was to require HEW to develop "national guidelines for health planning." Within eighteen months, HEW was to issue "[s]tandards respecting the appropriate supply, distribution, and organization of health resources" and "[a] statement of national health planning goals . . . expressed in quantitative terms." The key question, however, is whether mechanistic planning can meet these objectives. . . .

Unfortunately, this planning ideal is not attainable through mechanistic calculations. The practical difficulties, both methodological and normative, are immense. First, there is little agreement on what constitutes health and less on how it can or should be measured. Health is a very personal matter: A "trick" knee, for example, is a serious health problem for an athlete, but merely an inconvenience for a sedentary lawyer; their views of health are thus different, as is their "need" for a remedial operation. Moreover, efforts to identify and quantify precise states of good and ill health (called "health status" in the jargon) are currently at a very rudimentary level. A number of "health status indices" have been suggested, but there is no theoretical agreement on their relative merits, and little practical application of these efforts can be expected soon. . . .

Even if particular health treatment requirements for a population could be specified, there is no objective way to relate them to particular requirements. Even if it were possible, for example, to develop a reliable figure for the number of knee operations per thousand population needed in a year (assuming that variations in desirability of the operation from person to person could be averaged out), there is no objective way to determine just what this means for resource needs. A knee operation can be accomplished with greater or lesser use of facilities and equipment, for example, either on an inpatient or an outpatient basis. . . .

Considerable effort has been expended in the attempt to formulate public standards of need and methodologies for computing it. As noted above, however, there are no objective standards of need that planners can apply to restructure the system. Planners have therefore sought other, more practical approaches [to defining need]. . . .

The most obvious way to judge future need is to extrapolate from past patterns of growth for the institution or area under consideration. Historically, such projections have been the major quantitative tool of health planners. Simply applied, such methods perpetuate past patterns — including presumably inappropriate growth — but more sophisticated, if potentially arbitrary, adjustments can be made to change future growth. The Hill-Burton formula for hospital bed need is the classic example of a simple version. It projects future hospital utilization by multiplying the projected population for an area by the current rate of hospital usage. The projected future utilization rate is then divided by an occupancy factor (for general hospitals, eighty-five percent). This calculation theoretically gives the number of beds "needed" to accommodate the estimated future population. But this technique is hardly ideal. First, one cannot help indulging a general suspicion that a formula devised for a hospital-building program like Hill-Burton is not an appropriate method for a certificate-of-need program designed to constrain growth. More importantly, this projection simply perpetuates current practice and does not allow for change. Some excess capacity may be adjudged waste because it exceeds the fifteen percent allowance, but the appropriateness of current utilization is not challenged. . . .

Irvington General Hospital v. Department of Health
374 A.2d 49 (N.J. Super. 1977)

[See opinion at 615.]

Clifton Springs Sanitarium Co. v. Axelrod
497 N.Y.S.2d 525 (App. Div. 1985)

[See opinion at 617.]

Florida Medical Center v. Department of Health and Rehabilitative Services
463 So. 2d 380 (Fla. App. 1985)

NIMMONS, JUDGE.

Florida Medical Center (FMC) appeals from a final order of the Department of Health and Rehabilitative Services (HRS) . . . denying FMC's [February 1983] application for a certificate of need (CON) for the acquisition of a nuclear magnetic resonance unit (NMR).[1] FMC is a 400-bed acute care privately owned hospital located in Ft. Lauderdale. As of September 1983, it had 389 physicians on staff, including a radiology staff of nine radiologists and three radiological oncologists. . . .

The [first] reason given [for denial], that placement of such equipment was to be limited to research facilities, was not based upon any rule promulgated by the agency; such reason could not be sustained on the basis that such was "incipient or emerging agency policy," as was found by the hearing officer, because the agency failed to properly establish such non-rule policy.

---

1. A nuclear magnetic resonance scanner and imager [also known as a magnetic resonance imager (MRI)] is medical equipment that looks like a computerized axial tomography scanner (CT scanner) but which works on different principles to obtain an image of portions of the interior of the human body. Utilizing the atomic nuclei of human cells, it aligns and rotates the nuclei by the application of a magnetic field and, once so aligned, applies a radio signal which tips the nuclei and gives them a small amount of extra energy (about one-trillionth of that given in an x-ray) which is radiated back as a radio signal. A radio coil and receiver within the unit pick up this signal and, through computer assistance, translate it into an image which a physician can interpret as normal or abnormal. No radioactivity of any kind is utilized by an NMR device. Instead, the operative force is magnetic. Both CT scanners and NMR scanners are diagnostic tools, not therapeutic measures. They differ significantly, however, in how they operate and what they can see. The CT scanner looks primarily at an alteration of an x-ray beam — it receives a signal from bone, not soft tissue. The NMR scanner receives its signal from soft tissue, not bone. It picks up conditions that CT scanners do not see. In short, the NMR seems to give increased diagnostic ability not only by what it can do, but also by the quality of the picture produced. Some experts believe that the NMR is the most significant diagnostic tool since the development of x-rays. [NMR/MRIs cost $2-3 million installed.]

II. Regulatory Reforms

> To the extent an agency may intend in its final order to rely upon or refer to policy not recorded in rules for discoverable precedents, that policy must be established by expert testimony, documentary opinion, or other evidence appropriate to the nature of the issues involved and the agency must expose and elucidate its reasons for its discretionary action. . . .

Further, the record is clear that FMC was singled out for application of this "research" standard whereas it was not considered (and indeed even rejected as a criterion) by HRS in its favorable consideration of several other applications for similar equipment, including that of a Jacksonville hospital which received approval for an NMR only one week prior to FMC's application. The agency failed to adequately distinguish FMC's application from other such applications so as to justify the application of the "research" standard. Denial on this ground was therefore improper. . . .

Another reason given by the hearing officer and HRS for denial was that not enough is yet known about the effects of such device upon the human physiology. HRS, before and after its denial of FMC's application, has either not addressed the safety factor or has stated that there are no known adverse effects. FMC's was the only application which was denied because not enough was known about NMR's safety. In its granting of a CON for Shands Teaching Hospital in September, 1982, HRS stated: "The advantage [of the NMR] is in greatly improved diagnosis of tumors, stroke, and heart attack with no known adverse effects." In its report on Miami Heart Institute's application, which was granted in November 1982, HRS made no mention of any safety criterion. St. Lukes Hospital in Jacksonville was granted a CON in February 1983 with no discussion of any safety risk. Mount Sinai Medical Center's application was also approved in February, 1983, HRS stating:

> NMR imaging and spectroscopy will serve as an alternative to invasive procedures thereby reducing exploratory surgery and length of stay. NMR imaging entails virtually no radiation exposure to patient, a growing concern in medical care.

As to Jackson Memorial Hospital's certificate granted in June, 1983, HRS had this to say: "The process is non-invasive, uses non-ionizing radiation, uses no contrast agent or radio-nucleides, and uses low power to the advantage of high risk patients. . . . This means greatly improved diagnosis . . . with no known adverse effects." HRS has failed to demonstrate justification for disparate treatment of FMC on the risk issue and none is apparent from the record. The appealed order is therefore vulnerable as to that criterion. . . .

The order of denial also relied upon the alleged lack of financial feasibility. The order found that NMRs had not yet received approval by the Food and Drug Administration and that there would be no Medicare reimbursement until such approval. Neither would private insurance afford reimbursement until such approval. However, in its prior approvals of NMRs, HRS did not rely upon any such policy standard and, in fact, did not even mention the same. HRS has failed in the case at bar to give reasonable justification for this "emerging" policy.

The order appealed is reversed and this cause is remanded with directions to the agency to issue the certificate of need.

Havighurst & McDonough, The Lithotripsy Game in North Carolina: A New Technology Under Regulation and Deregulation*
19 Ind. L. Rev. 989, 992-999 (1986)

I. The Stakes in the Game — Rewards of a New Technology

Every few years, it seems, an expensive new medical technology tests the ability of the health care system to assess its efficacy, safety, and cost-effectiveness and to allocate resources so that patients receive optimal treatment at reasonable cost. Resembling in this respect earlier diagnostic imaging technologies, extracorporeal shock wave lithotripsy (ESWL) is a recent technological breakthrough that has captured the attention of health planners and policymakers. This noninvasive procedure, which employs equipment costing up to $2.7 million per installed unit, is revolutionizing the treatment of urinary stones.[2]

ESWL appears to be a highly desirable technology from every standpoint. Not only does it achieve excellent results with lower complication rates than invasive therapies, but even given the high

---

* Clark C. Havighurst is William Neal Reynolds Professor of Law, Duke University. Robert S. McDonough is B.A., 1982, B.S., 1982, University of Texas at Austin; J.D. Candidate, Duke University School of Law, 1987; M.A.P.P.S. Candidate, Duke Institute of Policy Sciences and Public Affairs, 1988; M.D. Candidate, Duke University School of Medicine, 1988.
Reprinted with permission of the Indiana Law Review.

2. In ESWL, electrohydraulic shock waves shatter kidney stones into small fragments so that they can be passed naturally by the patient. Chaussy & Schmiedt, Shock Wave Treatment for Stones in the Upper Urinary Tract, 10 Urologic Clinics N. Am. 743 (1983). Prior to the procedure, the patient is anesthetized to keep him pain-free and immobilized while shocks are administered. Finlayson & Thomas, Extracorporeal Shock-Wave Lithotripsy, 101 Annals Internal Med. 387, 388 (1984). The patient is then placed into a tub of water over a shock-wave generator. A two-axis x-ray system is used to locate the stone and the shock-wave generator is adjusted so that the shockwaves are focused on the stone. Approximately 1300 shocks are administered during the average one-hour procedure.

II. Regulatory Reforms

cost of "lithotripters," it may cost less per treatment than the surgical procedures it replaces.[4] Margaret Heckler, Secretary of Health and Human Services, called attention to both the medical benefits and the cost savings of ESWL when she announced the approval of the first lithotripter by the Food and Drug Administration (FDA) in 1984.

Although there is virtually no question that ESWL is highly efficacious and extremely safe, it has created significant problems for the health care system. In particular, early and widespread recognition of the potential benefits of ESWL put intense and sudden pressure on those processes that society has installed to evaluate medical technology and to guide the health care system's development. State certificate-of-need (CON) regulators were put in the position of being able to award very big prizes to a very few. Entrepreneurial urologists and hospitals, playing for large stakes, pushed the regulatory system very hard. In cases where the regulators stood firm, they were in the potentially awkward position of giving the winners valuable monopolistic franchises and depriving the losers of patients and significant income. Where the regulatory system gave way, the possibility of overinvestment in duplicative facilities raised the specter of excessive costs, overuse of ESWL, and neglect of alternative therapies when they might be medically indicated.[8] Although ESWL is a striking development in itself, much of its interest for policymakers lies in the lessons it teaches about the overall health care system and its ability to allocate resources and accommodate technological change.

ESWL has had a particularly significant impact on urologic practice in North Carolina. That state lies in the center of the so-called "stone belt," an area of the country where urinary stones are particularly common. North Carolina urologists are thus heavily committed to the treatment of urinary stones, devoting an estimated fifteen to twenty percent of their professional work to this condition. Hospitals, too, obtain significant income from urinary stone patients, and this business has been widely shared by all hospitals. ESWL thus posed an economic threat to both urologists and hospitals in North Carolina. If treatment of stones in the kidney and upper urinary tract

---

4. The primary cost saving of ESWL comes from a reduction in the length of hospital stay. FDA Approves Lithotripter for Kidney Stone Shattering, 253 J.A.M.A. 620 (1985) [hereinafter FDA Approves Lithotripter]. An uncomplicated surgical lithotomy requires an average stay of one to three weeks. Castaneda-Zuniga, Nephrostolithotomy: Percutaneous Techniques for Urinary Calculus Removal, 134 Am. J. Radiology 721, 724 (1982). The newer technique of percutaneous nephrolithotomy requires four to eight days of hospitalization. *Id.* ESWL patients currently remain in the hospital only three days on average, and it is anticipated that ESWL will eventually be performed on an outpatient basis. FDA Approves Lithotripter, supra, at 620-21.

8. See, e.g., Freifeld, The Rush to Crush, Forbes, March 11, 1985, at 170, 171 (stating that in Chicago, health planners had succumbed to provider pressures in approving more lithotripters than were necessary).

were suddenly concentrated in a small number of lithotripsy centers, the impact on the providers losing that business would be substantial. . . .

II. The CON Game — Winner Take All

State CON laws were intended to contain costs and make the development of the health care system more rational by requiring prior state approval before major capital expenditures could be made and new health services could be introduced. Because prevention of duplication is a key regulatory goal, these laws create a powerful incentive for providers to put any promising new technology, tried or untried, in place as quickly as possible; once CON approval is obtained, there is a strong regulatory barrier to entry by competitors until the market expands enough to support a second facility without appreciable harm to the first. Even if the first mover purchases costly first-generation equipment, it will be protected against competition from a later applicant offering to provide the same service for less. The convoluted rationale for protecting inefficient providers from price competition in this way is not addressed here, but it is notable that one effect of this form of regulation is to encourage early investment by relieving the proponent of the concern that his investment will be devalued when more efficient technology becomes available. . . .

North Carolina providers began jockeying for CON's soon after the announcement of plans for introducing the lithotripter into the United States from Europe, where it was first developed. [Four were approved in short order]. . . .

A fifth lithotripter slipped into the state through a crack in the regulatory defenses. A CON application by physician-owned Piedmont Urinary Stone Center, Inc. (Piedmont) . . . was denied because only one service was deemed necessary in the Winston-Salem/Greensboro area and the CON agency preferred that such a service be associated with an academic institution. Piedmont then proposed, however, to install a lithotripter in an outpatient facility unconnected with a hospital and successfully applied to the CON agency for a ruling that the CON statute did not apply to capital investments in major medical equipment to be installed in physicians' offices. Although the legislature quickly moved to close this loophole by extending CON regulation to lithotripters "regardless of ownership or location," Piedmont's plans were unaffected, and its lithotripter is currently operating in Winston-Salem. . . .

Although the CON regulators stood firm against exceeding a total of five lithotripters in the state, certain powerful interests were unhappy with the outcome of the CON process, which resulted in inconvenience for citizens in the western part of the state and left one prestigious institution (Duke) barred from charging for the use of a lithotripter already in place. Several legislators took up the cause of Duke and St. Joseph's Hospital in Asheville and explored the possibility of legislation that would bypass the CON agency. Because North Carolina, unlike some states, does not allow "special legislation" favoring named private interests, it was necessary to write the exception in generic terms that bespoke a plausible legislative objective. In about two days' time, a bill was written and passed by the House of Representatives defining conditions for exemption that only Duke and St. Joseph's could meet. . . .

The North Carolina experience reveals once again the political dimensions and debatable premises of CON regulation. Despite numerous objective studies of the question, CON regulation has never been shown to control health care costs. Indeed, substantial evidence suggests that CON laws were put in place not primarily to control costs but to protect the most powerful existing institutions against competitors skimming profitable business and to legitimize rapidly rising costs in the eyes of an increasingly concerned public.

NOTES

The Failure of CON Regulation

1. Certificate of Need laws, previously discussed in Chapter 7.IV, present a heavy-handed, regulatory approach to health care cost containment: they require new and existing hospitals to justify the need for all major capital expenditures. As such, "[c]ertificate-of-need laws establish entry controls which are similar in intent and impact to the certificate-of-public-convenience-and-necessity device widely employed in public utility and common carrier regulation." Havighurst, Regulation of Health Facilities and Services by "Certificate of Need," 59 Va. L. Rev. 1143, 1153 (1973). Yet CON laws have performed miserably in containing health care expenditures; they have "had either essentially no impact on hospital costs or a cost-increasing effect. No statistically controlled studies have reached the opposite conclusion." A. Enthoven, Health Plan 102 (1980). See Ashby, The Impact of Hospital Regulatory Programs on Per Capita Costs, Utilization, and Capital Investment, 21 Inquiry 45 (1984); Congressional Budget Office, Health Planning: Issues for Reauthorization 19-30, 57-64 (1982); Steinwald & Sloan, Regulatory Approaches to Hospital Cost Containment: A Synthesis of Empirical Research, in A New Approach to the Economics of Health Care 274 (M. Olsen ed. 1981); Sloan & Steinwald, Effects of Regulation on Hospital Costs and Input Use, 23 J. L. & Econ. 81 (1980); D. Salkever & T. Bice, Hospital

Certificate-of-Need Controls: Impact on Investment, Costs, and Use (1979).

2. One reason for the failure of CON is the law's limited scope. CON addresses primarily capital investment, not operating expenses. Thus, "evaluation studies show that [some] CON programs slow the increase in numbers of beds; but the funds saved are simply moved to new services and equipment, so that there is no perceptible effect on overall hospital costs." H. Aaron & W. Schwartz, The Painful Prescription: Rationing Hospital Care at 5 (1984). Moreover, CON laws constrain only expenditures, not charges. In the latter respect, certificate of need programs constitute incomplete public utility regulation. Most such regulation imposes price controls in addition to entry controls. Indeed, price control would seem essential since restricting entry tends to create monopoly power. One court relied on this effect of conferring state sanctioned monopolies without controlling for monopolistic abuse to support its holding that the original North Carolina CON statute was unconstitutional. In re Certificate of Need for Ashton Park Hospital, 193 S.E.2d 729 (N.C. 1973). All other courts to consider the issue, though, have upheld the constitutionality of CON regulation. E.g., State of North Carolina ex rel. Morrow v. Califano, 445 F. Supp. 532 (E.D.N.C. 1977), *aff'd mem.*, 435 U.S. 962 (1978).

3. "[T]he prevention of all duplication would achieve only modest, one-time savings," which would not affect the subsequent rate of increases in cost. H. Aaron & W. Schwartz, The Painful Prescription, note 2, at 116. Why is this so? Consider, for example, whether, after the development of X-rays, CAT scans, and now MRIs, there will be a "need" for "PETs": positive emission tomographers. "They are remarkable medical detectives that reveal all sorts of information about chemical activity, show what parts of the brain you use when you move an arm or leg or think, and diagnose certain kinds of heart and brain disease and cancer. But PETs have expensive taste. They need to be near a cyclotron. The combined cost of the PET and the cyclotron approaches $5 million; cyclotrons cost at least $1000 per hour to run. . . . [An individual] PET scan could . . . cost $7000 to $10,000." J. Califano, America's Health Care Revolution 103 (1986).

Would a "proton beam accelerator" pass the CON review criteria?

> It is a vision of the future that medical scientists have had for more than 40 years: Inside a space-age hospital room, a team of doctors activate an atomic accelerator. . . . In a few seconds, the proton beam kills cells in a cancerous tumor, leaving nearby healthy cells untouched. Now, this vision is no longer so far away. Last month, scientists at the Fermi National Accelerator Laboratory here unveiled the first proton beam accelerator built for hospital use. When the machine is ready for operation next year at Loma Linda University Medical Center near Los

II. Regulatory Reforms

Angeles, many believe it will prove itself a major breakthrough in the war on cancer.

Others, however, think the proton accelerator is a white elephant. They complain that its untested medical benefits and enormous price make it the ultimate example of medical technology run amok. Some doctors say proton therapy will prove useless in the treatment of most cancers. It is unquestionably the most expensive piece of medical equipment ever built. The cost — $40 million, including the special building needed to house the machine — dwarfs the cost of the next most expensive medical device. . . . At this stage, Loma Linda officials say they can't even begin to guess what patients will be charged for treatment on the machine.

Nevertheless, the device does have wide support. Proton therapy for cancer is believed to have a number of advantages over chemotherapy, conventional radiation and surgery. . . . Loma Linda is sure there will be enough patient demand for its machine. [At] Harvard, . . . [p]atients typically have a two-month wait for its machine, says Herman Suit, the chairman of Harvard Medical School's department of radiation medicine. "There's no excess capacity," he says.

Wall Street Journal, March 17, 1989, at A1.

4. Lithotripters illustrate how quickly the medical profession pushes new innovations to their limits and beyond:

Not only the number of ESWL devices [lithotripters] in the United States but the medical indications for their use have increased considerably over time. . . . The use of ESWL was first restricted to single small kidney stones, presumably ones that would have required surgery. . . . During the three years of ESWL experience in the United States, the indications for its use have been extended in three directions. First, ESWL has been tried on lower urinary stones. . . . Second, ESWL, in combination with other techniques, has been extended to treating more difficult stones. . . . Third, ESWL is being used to treat small stones that formerly would have been treated, at least initially, with fluids and analgesics rather than with surgery. . . . For these patients ESWL substitutes not for surgery, but for much less expensive (and possibly more painful and time consuming) medical regimens.

Power, The Adoption and Use of Extracorporeal Shock Wave Lithotripsy by Hospitals in the United States, 3 Intl. J. Tech. Assess. in Health Care 397, 401-403 (1987). Does this example suggest another version of Roemer's law?

5. How is an agency to "take into account all of the factors set out in [the CON statute]" as required by *Irvington* when those factors are as diverse (and opposed) as quality and cost? Consider:

Most CON programs . . . have one stated goal: the promotion of equal access to quality health care at reasonable cost. The problem is that this single, seemingly unimpeachable goal is in reality three goals that

> compete and are often mutually irreconcilable: quality, accessibility, and cost control. How these three goals are interpreted and implemented varies directly with who is doing the interpreting and for what purpose. Health care providers, for example, tend to perceive need from the quality side of the spectrum. . . . Consumers, while also oriented to issues of quality, tend to view accessibility as a major goal of CON. . . . As for the regulators, there can be little doubt that CON has one essential purpose: to keep costs down.

Medicine in the Public Interest, Certificate of Need: An Expanding Regulatory Concept (1978). In a similar vein, see Payton & Powsner, Regulation Through the Looking Glass: Hospitals, Blue Cross, and Certificate-of-Need, 79 Mich. L. Rev. 203 (1980):

> This is the story of the forgotten origins of hospital certificate-of-need. . . . [CON] was not designed to be a cost containment program. CON was invented in the 1950s when [i]nsurance commissioners in several states threatened to use their power over Blue Cross rates to institute hospital cost containment measures; regional planning and hospital construction controls were put forth by the hospital and public health establishments as an alternative . . . [they hoped] would educate the public to the increasing quality and expense of good hospital care and thereby lead to public acceptance of rising costs.

See also Havighurst, Developing Noninstitutional Health Services: The Role of Certificate-of-Need Regulation, in Cost, Quality and Access in Health Care: New Roles for Health Planning in a Competitive Environment (F. Sloan et al. eds. 1988).

6. When CON laws were first adopted, the CAT scanner was one of the primary examples cited of a technology much in need of centralized planning. Ironically, the capital expenditure threshold for CON review of equipment purchases has risen to the extent that CAT scanners no longer require approval. See 614 supra. A greater irony is that the CON laws have proven inadequate for controlling even far more expensive technological devices. As the facts of *Florida Medical Center* illustrate, the lithotripsy game has been played out in a similar fashion for MRI scanners. See also Hospitals, April 20, 1987, p. 124 ("Mount Sinai's diagnostic imaging department sounds like the '12 Days of Christmas': five nuclear medicine cameras, four MRIs, three mammography machines, two regular [CAT] scanners, and PET"); Hospitals, Nov. 5, 1987, at 59 ("Sooner or later, the excess capital spending for MR[Is] will merit a discussion on '60 Minutes' ").

7. "Perhaps the chief source of discouragement about health planning is the complexity of the task. Among the factors relevant in the planning effort are [the nature of existing facilities and their service areas, population size and characteristics, and current use patterns.] Even this list fails to convey the difficulty of projecting

changes in population, technology, . . . and patterns of utilization. . . . The complexity is such that the agencies themselves lack confidence in their ability to make hard-and-fast judgments, and the result is a lack of firm standards for decision making. In such circumstances, the pressures of politics necessarily become dominant." Havighurst supra, 59 Va. L. Rev. 1202-1204. See D. Altman, R. Greene & H. Sapolsky, Health Planning and Regulation: The Decision-Making Process (1981).

"The cost of applying for a CON [consultants, attorneys fees, etc.] can be considerable, exceeding $100,000 for major projects. If litigation is required, the cost may reach $350,000. . . . The enormous expenditure of time and money by both administrative agencies and health care providers in complying with the CON process substantially reduces any savings that might be attributable to it. For all its promise, CON review has resulted in the elimination of few projects. Of over 20,000 CON applications reviewed throughout the country between 1979 and 1981, only ten percent were ultimately disapproved. DHHS Report to Congress, Hospital Capital Expenses 124-125 (1986)." Comment, Certificate of Need for Health Care Facilities: A Time for Re-examination, 7 Pace L. Rev. 491, 509, 528 (1987).

The Anticompetitive Effects of CON Regulation

8. CON disputes frequently lead to allegations that the losing applicant was the victim of a conspiracy among regulators and opposing hospitals. These brouhahas tend to result in epic litigation. See, for instance,

- a) Huron Valley Hosp., Inc. v. City of Pontiac, 666 F.2d 1029 (6th Cir. 1981) (reinstating antitrust complaint of frustrated CON applicant); ibid., 792 F.2d 563 (6th Cir. 1986) (reinstating civil rights complaint); ibid., 849 F.2d 262 (6th Cir. 1988) (affirming dismissal of civil rights conspiracy theory); ibid., 887 F.2d 710 (6th Cir. 1989) (dismissing remaining civil rights claims).
- b) Hospital Build. Co. v. Trustees of Rex Hosp., 425 U.S. 738 (1976) (reinstating antitrust complaint of frustrated CON applicant); ibid., 691 F.2d 678 (4th Cir. 1982) (reversing $7.3 million verdict in favor of applicant); ibid., 791 F.2d 288 (4th Cir. 1986) (sustaining jury verdict against applicant).

9. Apart from whether the maneuverings of various CON actors are valid under the antitrust laws, it is clear that, at its core, the regulation itself has an anticompetitive effect. Like other public utility regulation of natural monopolies, the intent of CON is to replace

competition with comprehensive state planning. Moreover, existing competitors are naturally favored because they are in a better position to propose the least expensive project and the one in which regulators have the most confidence. "The inability of new entrants to obtain certificates of need is not attributable solely to political factors, for the mechanics of this form of regulation alone make displacement of an established provider difficult. . . . Thus, an existing provider, which can offer to replace old facilities even at a different location, has almost a license in perpetuity." Havighurst supra, 59 Va. L. Rev. at 1187. For additional discussion of CON and competition, see Oregon Eye Assocs. v. SHPDA, 732 P.2d 41 (Or. App. 1987) (CON isn't necessarily inconsistent with competition); J. Gelman, Competition and Health Planning (1982); Havighurst, Deregulating and Health Care Industry (1982) (proposing reforms to CON to make it a better vehicle for enhancing competition); Lynk, Antitrust Analysis and Hospital Certificate of Need Policy, 32 Antitrust Bull. 61 (1987).

10. Because the CON laws displace competition, there has been extensive discussion of the extent to which certificate of need preempts or impliedly repeals antitrust law. See National Gerimedical Hosp. v. Blue Cross, 452 U.S. 378 (1981) (no blanket preemption, but there may be limited preemption with respect to specific planning activities); *Rex Hosp.* supra, 691 F.2d 678 (4th Cir. 1982) (partial preemption, to extent planning activities are in good faith). See also State v. P.I.A. Asheville, 740 F.2d 274 (4th Cir. 1984), *cert. denied*, 471 U.S. 1003 (1985); Groner, Hospital Mergers, Health Planning, and the Antitrust Law: A Principled Approach to Implied Repeal, 7 J. Leg. Med. 471 (1986); Note, Antitrust and Certificate of Need: A Doubtful Prognosis, 69 Iowa L. Rev. 1451 (1984); Havighurst, Health Planning and Antitrust Law: The Implied Amendment Doctrine and the Rex Hospital Case, 14 N.C. Cent. L. Rev. 45 (1983). While the federal repeal of CON may moot this debate to some extent, the persistence of state CON laws gives it continuing relevance under the guise of state action analysis. E.g., General Hosps. of Humana v. Baptist Med. Sys., 1986-1 Trade Cases ¶66,996 (E.D. Ark. 1986) (CON process immune under state action doctrine).

11. In addition to the citations in these notes, the following sources are valuable references on various aspects of CON regulation. Cost, Quality and Access in Health Care: New Roles for Health Planning in a Competitive Environment (F. Sloan et al. eds. 1988); Hyman, Health Regulation: Certificate of Need and Section 1122 (1977) (health planning theory); Curran, Present at the Creation: Health Planning and the Inevitable Reorganization, 1 Health Care Mgt. Rev. 34 (1976) (historical account); C. Havighurst, Regulating Health Facilities Construction (1972) (well-regarded conference proceedings); Brown, Common Sense Meets Implementation: Certificate of Need Regulation in the States, 8 J. Health Pol. Poly. & L. 480

(1981) (overview of CON failures); Institute of Medicine, Health Planning in the United States: Selected Policy Issues (1981).

D. Public Utility Regulation: Hospital Rate Setting and the British and Canadian Systems

Hospitals as Public Utilities

"Some argue that the remedy for the ineffectiveness of [certificate of need] controls is more rigorous regulation, a comprehensive system with firm ceilings on total health services spending. In effect, the government would control the whole health services industry in detail, including the budget of every hospital and the fees of every doctor. Under such controls, health services would resemble a nationalized industry. . . . Some people think of medical care as a kind of public utility. It does respond to a vital need, and many people think of it as inherently a monopoly — or at least as unsuitable for competitive private enterprise. As a consequence, we are now in the process of accepting the public-utility model of health care regulation." A. Enthoven, Health Plan xxi, 1 (1980).

" '[W]hether we like it or not, whether good or bad, the health care industry, especially the hospital component, is already extensively controlled by both federal and state governments. Few, if any, other industries have been subject to so much piecemeal and uncoordinated regulation. Hardly any aspect of hospital operation, from the width of the corridors and the number of fire extinguishers to the method of cost finding in accounting and the overtime pay of the orderly, escapes the scrutiny of some public officials.' . . . The question then, no longer is whether we will have regulation but rather how much we will have. Can we anticipate public utility status or total government control and/or operation?" Corley, Hospitals as a Public Utility: or "Work with Us Now or Work for Us Later," 2 J. Health Pol. Poly. & L. 304 (1978). See also Priest, Possible Adaptation of Public Utility Concepts in the Health Care Field, 35 L. & Contemp. Prob. 839 (1970).

Schramm, State Hospital Cost Containment: An Analysis of Legislative Initiatives*
19 Ind. L. Rev. 919, 924-926 (1986)

C. Primer on State Hospital Regulation

Modern state efforts at regulating the hospital industry began in the late 1960's. In several states, controlling hospital cost inflation

---

* Former Director, Johns Hopkins Center for Hospital and Finance Management;

emerged as a matter for public concern and eventual legislation because of the public cost of care for the poor. In New York, . . . the state established a program to supervise budgets of all hospitals, attempting to reduce spending for all payers, including Medicaid. The second state to establish a hospital cost containment program was Maryland, where . . . trustees of the state's hospitals petitioned the legislature for an agency that would reduce hospital spending for all payers and distribute the expense of delivering care to the poor among all patients by establishing a uniform rate.

In these two programs the seeds of the hospital regulation movement were planted. In both, the state stepped in to protect both the citizens who ultimately pay for care and the hospital system from financial insolvency related to uncompensated care. In each instance, the system of budget discipline imposed on the hospital was prospective payment for all care provided over a given period. Also, in both states all payers for care were made to pay the same price, thus allowing the costs of care provided to the poor to be redistributed over the entire patient population.

Shortly after the New York and Maryland legislatures established their programs, four other states initiated prospective hospital cost-containment programs. Three of these states, Connecticut, Massachusetts, and New Jersey were in the northeast, where state legislatures had created substantial Medicaid programs in the mid-sixties. [The fourth state was Washington.] Because of the balanced budget requirements of state constitutions and recession-connected declines in tax revenues, these states were interested in reducing hospital cost inflation from a budgetary perspective. . . .

Because of varying delays in collecting necessary financial information, all six states began regulating hospital rates at virtually the same time. Examination of the regulatory period from 1976 to the present has consistently shown statistically significant reductions in the rate of hospital cost inflation in the regulated states. It is these data that in part account for the growing interest in hospital regulation at the state level.

D. *State Activity to Date and its Classification*

After nearly fifteen years, there are now several types of formal state-level initiatives to control hospital costs. The most extensive, typified by the first six states, is the regulation of total hospital revenues and the rates that all payers in the state are charged for care. In

---

Former Vice Chairman, Maryland Health Services Cost Review Commission.
Reprinted with permission.

II. Regulatory Reforms

1983, Maine, West Virginia, and Wisconsin enacted statutes similar to those in effect in the original six states.

A second group of states are those that supervise hospital rates but do not have authority to set them. For example, in Florida, a public body exists to collect hospital price information and to disclose it publicly. A third type of statute [exemplified in California and Arizona] merely requires reporting of information on hospital prices to a state agency, which in turn may publish the information. While it is still too early to judge the latter two types of efforts, ample evidence suggests that cost-containment programs are effective in direct proportion to the amount of government power vested in the regulating agency. . . .

As a result of the success of various state efforts at containing hospital cost inflation, . . . a second wave of state initiatives directed at regulating hospital revenues appears to be breaking out in legislatures across the land. In 1983, three states enacted mandatory hospital rate-setting legislation. In 1984, at least ten legislatures considered similar proposals.* It has been suggested that in the next few years over half of the states will have adopted such measures.

P. Feldstein, Health Care Economics**
288-301 (2d ed. 1983)

Rate regulators must be able to reimburse hospitals while making adjustments for the many ways in which they may differ, including size, products, and efficiency, and they must be able to determine the rate at which hospital input prices are rising. . . . Unless the rate regulators are able to distinguish the sources of cost differences among hospitals and estimate the amount of those differences, the rates that are established may reward some hospitals unfairly while penalizing others. . . . The task of rate regulators is not easy; unless they are extremely accurate in accounting for differences among hospitals and in estimating increases in hospital input prices, the consequences of their actions will be different from what they intended. . . .

The general approach of the proposals offered for prospective reimbursement are discussed below. Within each of these broad classifications considerable variation in rate setting and administration is possible.

---

* [Eds. Note: Two of these states adopted mandatory rate setting in 1987. Kinney, Coordinating Rate Setting and Planning in States with Mandatory Hospital Rate Regulation, 8 J. Leg. Med. 397, 399 n.5 (1987).]

** Paul Feldstein is a Professor at the School of Public Health and Department of Economics, University of Michigan.

Copyright © 1983. Reprinted by permission of John Wiley & Sons, Inc.

Budget Review on a Prospective Basis

Hospitals favor the budget review approach for determining hospital reimbursement. This approach assumes that it is impossible to separate out differences in products, size, and efficiency among hospitals. A representative of the rate-setting agency would review each hospital's budget for the reasonableness of its cost increases. . . . Critics of this approach maintain that it poses no risk for the hospital, and therefore is unlikely to result in cost savings, . . . since it can receive a pass-through for legitimate costs such as wage increases. . . .

If the prospective rate for a hospital is set too tightly, then the hospital might take actions to enable it to live within that rate without necessarily increasing efficiency. Some payment unit or units must be chosen to which the prospective rates apply: examples are the total budget, department budgets, the patient day, the admission, or specific services. In each case the hospital might take action to lower its costs without increasing efficiency. If the entire budget is determined prospectively, for example, the hospital can reduce costs by decreasing its volume of services or lowering quality. If reimbursed on a per admission basis, it can admit less complex and costly cases. . . .

Establishing Reimbursement Levels Based on a Hospital's Performance Relative to Other Hospitals

The second basic approach to establishing hospital reimbursement rates is to base the rate upon the particular classification in which a hospital is grouped. . . . The difficulty is in properly determining each hospital's classification. Critics of this approach, primarily hospital administrators, claim that it is not possible to develop adequate classifications for each hospital. Hospitals vary so greatly in the services and quality of care they provide, and in their case mix of patients, that three or four major groupings will not reflect the differences among them. . . .

A major weakness of the method that pays hospitals on the basis of a group average is that it never penalizes hospitals that keep their costs in line with their group average. . . . If low-cost hospitals are not motivated to become even more efficient by the possibility of earning incentive payments, the average level of efficiency within each group may not change significantly over time. . . .

Setting a Maximum Rate of Increase in Total Hospital Expenditures

In the third basic method of hospital reimbursement, the regulatory authority determines prospectively a maximum allowable rate of increase in community hospital expenditures. . . . The advantage of this approach is that it is relatively simple and straightforward to apply. . . . However, its main disadvantage is that it allows an equal percentage increase both to hospitals that are costly or inefficient and those that have kept their costs down. . . .

[T]he method used to establish the percentage increase is either a result of negotiations with the hospital associations (it may be arbitrarily determined) or it is related to inflation in the general economy. Hospital associations have maintained that hospital input prices rather than an economywide measure of inflation should determine the rate of hospital cost inflation.

NOTES

Hospital Rate Regulation

1. "The most recent findings concerning the effectiveness of [hospital] rate regulation programs . . . indicated that seven of the nine mandatory rate setting programs had statistically significant reductions in hospital expenditures per adjusted patient day. The rate of increase of hospital expenses per adjusted patient day fell two to five percentage points annually as a result of the programs. Since the . . . savings compound each year, . . . the estimated cumulative effect . . . for [a] five-year period was a savings of $7.6 billion. However, due to substantial increases in length of stay, the savings were reduced by half. This increase in length of stay is said to be due to the inherent incentives in the original rate setting methodologies to increase the number of patient days per admission." Arizona House of Representatives, Health Care Cost Containment: A Briefing Paper (June 1984). The latest statistics continue to reflect at least a modest (3 to 4 percent) annual savings from hospital rate regulation. Schramm, Renn, & Biles, Controlling Hospital Cost Inflation: New Perspectives On State Rate Setting, Health Affairs 22 (Fall 1986). Do these statistics present a compelling case? Consider the following less charitable review of the evidence:

> Briefly, the evidence suggests that, where they have been tried, rate-setting programs have generally constrained per diem or per admission hospital costs; there is less evidence that per capita hospital costs have been constrained, and no direct evidence that total health care costs have been constrained. [T]here is good reason to question the applicability of the evidence to most of the states currently without rate regulation. [T]he states that have tried rate-setting are not representative of the entire country, much less the remaining unregulated states. Most

are in the Northeast corridor. They continue to be among the states with the highest hospital costs in the country.

Eby & Cohodes, What Do We Know About Rate-Setting?, 10 J. Health Pol. Poly. & L. 299, 301, 307, 309 (1985).

3. For a sampling of the litigation produced by rate setting programs, see Griffin Hosp. v. Commission on Hospitals and Health Care, 512 A.2d 199 (Conn. 1986) (largely unsuccessful challenge to accuracy and procedure of rate setting); Prince George's Doctors' Hosp. v. Health Servs. Cost Review Comm., 486 A.2d 744 (Md. 1985) (unsuccessful challenge to accuracy of rates); Brooklyn Hosp. v. Axelrod, 467 N.Y.S.2d 687 (1983) (same); Riverside Gen. Hosp. v. New Jersey Hosp. Rate Setting Commn., 487 A.2d 714 (N.J. 1985) (successful challenge).

4. The materials immediately following study the British and Canadian health care systems as two examples of health care regulated as a public utility. In particular, the British system demonstrates that it is at least possible for a regulatory model to make deep cuts in health care expenditures while at the same time providing comprehensive health care coverage for all members of the public. As you read these materials, notice that the British system for financing *hospital* care is structurally the same as a mandatory total budget approach to hospital rate regulation: each hospital must live within a fixed annual government budget. Conceivably, the regulatory aspects of the British system could be severed from its insurance function and transplanted to the United States: states could strictly limit the total annual amount each private hospital may receive from either public or private patients. Indeed, one proposal for a national health insurance during the Carter era was a revenue cap for each geographic area, apportioned among area hospitals. See Furrow, Johnson, Jost & Schwartz, Health Law 443 (1987).

However, despite the cultural similarities of our two countries, it is naive to assume that the British system could be so easily cloned. As you read the following excerpts, consider what specific barriers and complications might be presented by differences between our two countries'

- political structures,
- cultural attitudes,
- historical settings,
- demographic distributions,
- hospital industries,
- medical professions,
- and legal systems.

H. Aaron & W. Schwartz, The Painful Prescription: Rationing Hospital Care*
12-21, 25, 28, 53-56, 97-99, 121 (1984)

. . . The problem that all developed nations face is how to alter the behavior of providers and patients so that expenditures are curtailed on care that, in some sense, is worth less than it costs. The British have addressed this question directly. For several reasons they have been able to hold expenditures on medical care well below those in the United States and other industrial nations [through its National Health Service ("NHS"), a government owned and operated system of hospitals and clinics that provides comprehensive health care for all citizens.] . . .

The American health care system costs much more than the British system — nearly three times as much per capita.

The difference between health expenditures in Britain and those in the United States somewhat exaggerates the discrepancy between health care in the two countries. Doctors and nurses are paid more in the United States than in Britain, and the difference is even wider than that in average wages. But even if one assumes that none of the extra pay U.S. doctors and nurses receive reflects differences in quality, and if one excludes expenditures on research and administration that do not contribute directly to patient care in the short run, the United States still spends about twice as much on hospital care.

Although Britain spends much less than the United States, . . . crude indicators of health status put Britain abreast or slightly ahead of the United States. Life expectancy at birth for men was 70.2 years in Britain in 1979 and 69.9 years in the United States: British baby girls born in 1979 could expect to live 76.2 years, and their American counterparts about 1 year more. During the first year of life babies born in 1979 died at the rate of 12.9 per thousand in Britain and 13.1 per thousand in the United States.

Such measures do not mean that the British health care system is better or worse than the U.S. system, because much health care affects the quality of life, not its duration. Furthermore, genetic and environmental factors have a strong effect on life expectancy. But these data do show that the large differences in per capita average medical expenditures between the two countries are not associated with large differences in life expectancy.

---

* Reprinted with permission.

How the National Health Service Works

Any health care system must solve two problems — how to ensure that patients are seen by the right health care providers, and how to pay for the services that providers render. The way the British system deals with these two issues differs sharply from the American approach. . . .

The National Health Service is supported by government funds except for modest exceptions. Seventy-five percent of these funds come from general revenues. Another 20 percent come from earmarked involuntary contributions by each person covered under the NHS and from charges imposed for drugs, eyeglasses, and a few other items. And 5 percent come from other sources. About 60 percent of the British population is exempt from these charges for drugs and other items.

Government provides health care through three channels that are administered by different government agencies. First, primary care is provided by general practitioners, who are employed by the NHS and who receive an income based on the number of patients they have. . . .

Second, institutional care is provided through the system of hospitals and nursing homes of various kinds, organized in England in 192 districts and 14 regions. Such agencies allocate two-thirds of NHS expenditures. Scotland, Northern Ireland, and Wales each have separate health services and receive their budgets from the House of Commons.

Third, nonhospital community care is provided by district nurses and health visitors, all under the administrative control of local authorities. The local authority is also responsible for social services, ambulance services, domestic help for the sick, and for the provision of some accommodation for the elderly who are not infirm enough to need a hospital bed. These services are financed by local authority budgets that are supported in part by local taxes and in part by payments from the central government. . . .

Each British resident enrolls with one of approximately 27,000 general practitioners (GPs). Patients may choose any doctor who has an opening and may switch when they wish, but few exercise this option. A visit to a GP is normally the first point of contact with the health care system during any spell of illness. In the past, patients commonly stopped by to visit their GPs unannounced, but GPs are now trying to encourage their patients to make specific appointments. An office visit is likely to be brief, averaging six minutes. GPs carried an average of 2,200 patients in 1981. If the patient is too ill to leave home, the GP will often make a house call. The GP may decide to prescribe medication or send specimens to hospital laboratories for analysis, but in most cases he cannot order complicated tests or admit patients to a hospital.

If the GP finds indications of an illness that requires more extensive testing or treatment than he can provide from his office, he will refer the patient to a consultant — a specialist, in American parlance. Nearly all specialists who see patients through the NHS are employed by regional health authorities on a salaried basis. The GP may write a letter to the consultant or telephone him. If the case is urgent, a call is likely to be made and the patient will be seen immediately. Otherwise, he may have to wait several weeks or even months for an appointment.

Patients on the waiting list are classified as urgent or nonurgent. Urgent cases are supposed to be admitted within one month and nonurgent cases within one year, but these standards are not met. According to one correspondent, there are no objective definitions of which kinds of illness merit admission without delay; rather the distinction between such cases and others depends on the medical judgment of individual doctors and the availability of beds. The definitions of who should be on the waiting list vary from time to time and place to place. For example, the criteria used for listing cases for immediate admission or for classifying them as urgent or nonurgent grew more exacting when a strike of hospital workers slowed admissions to a trickle and relaxed after the strike ended.

Waiting lists for admission to British hospitals are long. One-third of all admitted patients were on waiting lists for three months or more, 6 percent for one year or more. In March 1982 the waiting lists had 625,000 names. Nearly all the people on these lists were waiting for surgery, much of it elective in that delay does not threaten the patient's life.

The size of these waiting lists clearly shows a demand for health care greater than supply. . . . Evidence is abundant that waiting times for specific treatments such as orthopedic surgery are very long, stretching into years in some regions. . . .

Budget Setting

In the British system, . . . expenditures of all hospitals are limited by fixed budgets set by the national government. . . .

How do spending limits get set in Britain? Although the procedure is largely "top down," it is tightly constrained by spending levels in previous years. Each budget is formulated in the shadow of a published multiyear plan endorsed by the government. The British Treasury, which performs functions like those of the U.S. Office of Management and Budget, sets spending targets based on the previous year's outlays and anticipated inflation. It also determines whether the NHS will receive an increment for real growth in expenditures and, if so, how large it will be. The Treasury goes through similar exercises for other segments of public expenditure, and the full budget is ultimately modified and approved by the cabinet before being submitted to the House of Commons. In practice, party discipline assures that the House of Commons will not change the budget significantly.

The resulting health appropriation is a global projection for the National Health Service. Thus the secretary of state for health and social services, the cabinet officer responsible for health and the NHS, retains some discretion in allocating expenditures among the fourteen health regions.

Even the best-laid plans must sometimes be changed. When prices rise faster than anticipated, no adjustment is made in the current year and each jurisdiction must absorb the higher costs. If any geographic entity overspends its budget, the excess is subtracted from its allocation for the next period. A second adjustment is made to account for movement of patients across jurisdictional boundaries. Each region is reimbursed an amount equal to its net "imports" multiplied by the average cost of patient care. The arrangement compensates for patients who generate average costs but is inadequate for patients who leave their districts to get costly specialized care.

The effect of this system is roughly as follows. A hospital is likely to get a budget, adjusted for inflation, that is equal to that of the preceding year unless it can make a persuasive case for a specific additional outlay. If the cost of supplies or wages happens to rise more rapidly than the price index used by the health authorities for adjusting budgets, the hospital administrators and staff must find ways to cut back. Maintenance is an early casualty of restrictions on spending for current operations, with painting cycles, for example, sometimes stretching to decades. Long-term budget control depends on strictly enforced limits on the hiring of physicians, nurses, and other staff. Backlogs of requests for new equipment and replacement of old equipment grow — one piece of radiological equipment in a distinguished London hospital is approaching its golden anniversary. The larger or more experimental the new expenditure, the more likely that the decision about it will be made at a higher jurisdiction, such as the region. A decision on whether to build a new hospital, for example, will fall in this category.

Because the total budget is fixed nationally, one locality can gain only at the expense of another. . . .

Regional Inequalities

British health planners have tried to equalize expenditures among the regions. When the NHS began, parts of Britain had a number

II. Regulatory Reforms 783

of new or endowed hospitals and an ample supply of physicians, but many other areas were much less fortunate. To improve the distribution of physicians, the NHS provided bonuses for general practitioners who set up practice in underserved areas. But until 1976 it made little progress in reducing the inequality of expenditure on hospital services across regions. In 1975 per capita spending in the highest-spending region was 39 percent higher than in the lowest-spending one, even after adjusting for the flow of patients across boundaries. Because pay scales in Britain are uniform (except for distinction awards), unlike those in the United States, they did not contribute to the disparities. In any event, even in the mid-1970s this difference was nearly as great as when the NHS began. . . .

[B]oosting outlays in low-spending regions has been slowed by an aversion to cutting real outlays in high-spending regions.

Some regional and subregional planners have tried to carry the policy of equalization from the fourteen regions to their districts. But a lack of information on movement of patients and other data makes it difficult to apply. Furthermore, the goal of creating national or regional centers of excellence and the inappropriateness of offering complex care in sparsely populated places make equalization among the many, small districts undesirable. . . . The problem is how to balance conflicting goals: achieving equality of access against achieving efficiencies of scale and providing the high-technology, high-quality care and scientific advance that depend on concentration of resources. . . .

[A] British patient ordinarily has no direct access to a specialist through the NHS. Usually, he must first see a general practitioner. Only if his GP feels that the patient should see a consultant can he readily do so. Such sequential referral predated the NHS. British patients are reported to be using hospital emergency rooms increasingly to provide primary care. In emergency cases, waiting for hospital admission is rare.

By contrast, in the United States patients may see any doctor with whom they can get an appointment. Many physicians who provide primary care, such as routine checkups and examinations, also have specialist training. This difference between access to specialists in the United States and in Britain expresses national customs and attitudes about doctor-patient relations. British physicians, many of whom have studied or practiced in the United States, repeatedly told us that they think British patients are more likely than their American counterparts to accept a doctor's judgment as final. Part of the difference may come from a kind of New World prometheanism — American patients seem unwilling to acknowledge that there may be no effective therapy for certain illnesses.

Whatever the explanation, the British patient is clearly part of a structured social and medical care system, bound by custom and by a long-term dependency on his GP and conditioned to accept the authority of prestigious consultants. In contrast, the American patient is likely to see different doctors for different problems and more frequently to regard doctors as technicians who are periodically called on to repair his physical machinery, to be dropped if they are unable to solve the current problem or to be sued if they botched the last one. . . .

The structure of governance within the hospital and the district also furthers the achievement of budget goals. The British hospital is a quasi-feudal enterprise, ruled largely by a peerage of senior physicians (consultants) who usually work only at one hospital and derive most or all of their income from salary. Each has junior physicians assigned to him, and each has a variable number of beds to which he can admit patients. British consultants are responsible, directly or indirectly, for the disposition of almost all the hospital's resources. The typical British hospital administrator, unlike his U.S. counterpart, has little power or authority within his institution. Thus consultants, whose personal salaries and positions are unaffected directly by budgetary vicissitudes, must parcel out the meager rations allotted through the health district. They have every incentive to do so amicably, for they are part of a select medical club whose members must work together, usually for the rest of their professional lives. That each has only a limited personal economic stake in the outcome of the allocations facilitates such cooperation. . . .

Differences Between U.S. and British Use of Technology

Three therapeutic procedures are provided at essentially the same level in Britain as in the United States.

1. All patients with hemophilia obtain high-quality treatment, including adequate supplies of the required clotting factors.
2. Megavoltage radiotherapy appears to be readily available in England to virtually all patients with cancer who can benefit from it.
3. Bone marrow transplantation is carried out with the same frequency per capita in Britain as in the United States.

Many other services are clearly rationed in Britain when compared with levels of consumption in the United States.

1. The British carry out only half as many x-ray examinations per capita as Americans do, and they use only half as much film per examination.

II. Regulatory Reforms

2. The overall rate of treatment of chronic renal failure in Britain is less than half of that in the United States. Kidneys are transplanted at a comparable rate, but dialysis is carried out at a rate less than one-third of that in the United States.
3. Total parenteral nutrition is undertaken only about one-fourth as often in Britain as in the United States.
4. Great Britain has only one-sixth the CT scanning capability of the United States. Many major teaching hospitals lack a facility.
5. The British hospital system has only one-fifth to one-tenth as many intensive care beds, relative to population, as does the United States. Most hospitals have few intensive care beds or none at all.
6. The rate of coronary artery surgery in Britain is only 10 percent that of the United States. Even if the rate in the United States is excessive, the British could perform six or seven times more bypass procedures than at present, with probable benefit to patients. . . .

Factors That Seem to Influence Resource Allocation

A set of general principles can be extracted from the representative technologies we have examined. Some reflect the influence of administrative arrangements on the allocation process. Others are an expression of society's value judgments or of attempts to make the most efficient use of resources.

Age

If all other factors were held constant, we would expect less rationing of health care for children than for adults. Aggregate data support this prediction. Health expenditures per child in Britain are 119 percent of expenditures per prime age adult, whereas in the United States they are only 37 percent as much.

These results are hardly surprising. Adults respond to sick children with strong emotions. Furthermore, care that saves a child's life or improves its quality yields benefits much longer than those same resources used on an older person.

The responsibilities of prime age adults as parents and earners sometimes override these considerations, but such offsetting factors seldom apply to the elderly. The low incidence of chronic dialysis among the elderly with renal failure dramatizes such discrimination. The limitation of resources allocated to the treatment of terminal illness is another expression of this bias.

Dread Disease

Some diseases, depending on the culture and the historical moment, inspire more fear than others. Currently, the prime example is cancer. One might expect that such diseases would receive a disproportionate share of the available resources.

Such appears to be the case. Megavoltage radiotherapy is made available to all who can benefit from it, even if the expectation is palliation rather than cure. Moreover, cancer chemotherapy is provided to all in whom there is hope of prolonging life by as much as several years or an expectation of significant palliation of symptoms.

Visibility of Illness

People do not like visible misery. They are made uncomfortable if they must watch severe and untreated suffering. The bleeding joints, swelling, and disabilities of hemophilia are likely to stir more feeling in bystanders than the silent pain of angina pectoris. It is thus not surprising that more support is allocated to clotting factors for hemophiliacs than to bypass surgery for angina patients, as is indeed the case in Britain.

Advocacy

Organized advocates can try to use political pressure, publicity, or charity to obtain facilities and personnel for a particular service. Oddly enough, we found little evidence that advocacy plays an important role in shaping allocation decisions in Britain. Other than bone marrow transplantation, we have found no service significantly increased by the efforts of pressure groups. We suspect that in this regard the United States will prove to be quite different.

Aggregate Cost

A service that is costly relative to the benefit it yields may still be provided if the total cost for all patients is fairly small. It may simply not be seen as worthwhile to enforce the general principles of rationing when the total cost of a program seems negligible. The full-scale treatment of hemophilia in Britain may be an example. Only about seventy-five new cases of hemophilia are diagnosed each year in Britain. At an annual cost of $10,000 to $20,000 each, this small number of patients appears to be exempted from rationing. It seems less likely that the same would be true if there were 25,000 new patients every year.

II. Regulatory Reforms

Need for Capital Funds

The use of new technology can be controlled much more easily if it requires a large capital outlay than if it depends only on funds from the hospital's operating budget. A vivid contrast is provided by outlays on CT scanners as opposed to expenditures for total parenteral nutrition. Only about $10 million a year is committed to CT scanners, which have been installed in only a few hospitals, even though they could make an important contribution in any facility with more than 200 beds. By contrast, the benefit of total parenteral nutrition to most of the patients receiving it has not been well documented. But Britain spends as much on the service as on CT scanning. At least part of the reason, we surmise, is that total parenteral nutrition requires no appreciable capital outlay and can be allocated, case by case, at the discretion of individual physicians.

Costs of Alternative Modes of Care

Our observations support the notion that a given therapy will be provided in larger quantity if the costs of not treating the patient exceed the costs of active intervention. This thesis gains compelling support from a comparison of coronary bypass surgery with hip replacement. The costs of each operation are similar, as are the ages of the patients, but hip replacements are done with far greater frequency. As we noted earlier, the much higher cost of caring for disabled patients with hip disease than for patients with angina seems likely to be the main determinant of the difference. . . .

Decisions on Resource Allocation

Overall budget limits require someone or some group to decide who gets what kind of care. Within the British hospital this decision is made on a collegial basis by consultants, subject to peer pressure, and by district and regional planning officials, not all of whom are doctors. As we have pointed out earlier, the fact that consultants are salaried and enjoy lifetime tenure purges negotiations among them of personal material considerations. Decisions have personal consequences only as far as the physician's ability to pursue his work is influenced by the availability of beds, staff, and equipment. That concern is obviously important, but removing the issue of income makes the decisionmaking process easier. Our discussions with British physicians and administrators suggest that optimal use of resources in the interests of patient welfare is usually the central focus.

The situation in the United States is quite different. Unlike hospital administrators in Britain, who have little to say about policy, the administrators and the boards of trustees in U.S. hospitals have great power. Although they cannot make day-to-day decisions, they help set policy and also resolve disputes among the medical staff. Given budget limits, they would influence current expenditures as well as both capital outlays and the size and composition of staff, a function carried out largely by higher administrative authorities in Britain.

Under budget limits the importance of hospital administrators would be further heightened because of the incentives to physicians created by the fee-for-service system. In contrast to the British physician, most American doctors have a direct financial stake in decisions that bear on the number of patients they can admit and the diagnostic procedures and treatments they can perform. The desire of physicians to admit and practice as they think best will create conflicts with administrators charged with living under fiscal constraints. . . .

Conclusions

At least seven features of the British health care system have facilitated the imposition of budget limits and made them stick. First, the National Health Service is organized within a parliamentary democracy marked by party discipline; the House of Commons does not usually reverse policies set by the cabinet. Second, the principle of public ownership and management of important sectors of the British economy is widely accepted, particularly for health care services. Third, a reservoir of goodwill exists for the NHS because of its origins in wartime adversity and its assurance of care to even the poorest people. Fourth, sequential referral of patients — from general practitioner to consultant — creates a mechanism not present in the United States, which allows the trusted family doctor to screen out cases not deemed medically suitable for complex care. Fifth, the residue of class structure in Britain increases the ability of physicians to persuade patients that aggressive treatment is inappropriate and increases the willingness of patients to accept such bleak news. Sixth, the British are less driven than Americans by the "don't just stand there, do something" attitude toward disease. Finally, hospital governance by salaried consultants provides a notably effective instrument for encouraging the quiet enforcement of budget limits.

D. Green, Challenge to the NHS
94-96 (1986)

There is a lingering feeling that sordid consideration of cost should have nothing to do with medical care. But the cost of care is always a factor which cannot be escaped, whether we like it or not. The only question is *who* decides. . . . Under the NHS, such decisions are usually taken by doctors and administrators with the patient wholly or partially excluded. A striking example is access to kidney machines which is rationed by putting a "use-value" on people's lives. If you are over 55 or have diabetes or a bad heart, or no dependents, or are not well known, it is likely that you will score a low "use-value" and be allowed to die. Such rationing is an inevitable result of government decisions to allocate fixed annual sums for health care. . . .

From the first days of the NHS in 1948, resources have been allocated to health according to criteria unrelated to either medical demand or medical "need" — sometimes cut in an effort to control inflation, or perhaps raised when the economy was booming, or cut in order to spend more on defence or housing or social services. . . . The general result in Britain has been that very much less has been spent on health care than would otherwise have been the case. And this is reflected in the evidence that, of all the industrialized nations, Britain is one of the lowest spenders on health as a proportion of GNP.

Daniels, Why Saying No to Patients in the United States is So Hard: Cost Containment, Justice, and Provider Autonomy*
314 New Eng. J. Med. 1380 (1986)

Rationing in Great Britain takes place under two constraints that do not operate at all in the United States. First, although the British say no to some beneficial care, they nevertheless provide universal access to high-quality health care. In contrast, over 10 percent of the population in the United States lacks insurance, and racial differences in access and health status persist. Second, saying no takes place within a regionally centralized budget. Decisions about introducing new procedures involve weighing the net benefits of alternatives within a closed system. When a procedure is rationed, it is clear which resources are available for alternative uses. When a procedure is widely used, it is clear which resources are unavailable for other uses. No such closed system constrains American decisions about the dissemination of technological advances.

These two constraints are crucial to justifying British rationing. The British practitioner who follows standard practice within the system does not order the more elaborate x-ray diagnosis that might be typical in the United States, possibly even despite the knowledge that additional information would be useful. Denying care can be justified as follows: Though the patient might benefit from the extra

---

* Reprinted with permission.

service, ordering it would be unfair to other patients in the system. The system provides equitable access to a full array of services that are fairly allocated according to professional judgments about which needs are most important. The salve of this rationale may not be what the practitioner uses to ease his or her qualms about denying beneficial treatment, but it is available. . . .

Saying No in the United States

Cost-containment measures in the United States reward institutions, and in some cases practitioners, for delivering treatment at a lower cost. Hospitals that deliver treatment for less than the DRG rate pocket the difference. Hospital administrators therefore scrutinize the decisions of physicians to use resources, pressuring some to deny beneficial care. Many cannot always act in their patients' best interests, and they fear worse effects if DRGs are extended to physicians' charges.

When economic incentives to physicians lead them to deny beneficial care, there is a direct threat to what may be called the ethic of agency. In general, granting physicians considerable autonomy in clinical decision making is necessary if they are to be effective as agents pursuing their patients' interests. The ethic of agency constrains this autonomy in ways that protect the patient, requiring that clinical decisions be competent, respectful of the patient's autonomy, respectful of the other rights of the patient (e.g., confidentiality), free from consideration of the physician's interests, and uninfluenced by judgments about the patient's worth. Incentives that reward physicians for denying beneficial care clearly risk violating the fourth-mentioned constraint, which, like the fifth, is intended to keep clinical decisions pure — that is, aimed at the patient's best interest.

American physicians face a problem even when the only incentive for denying beneficial care is the hospital's, not theirs personally. For example, how can they justify sending a Medicare patient home earlier than advisable? Can they, like their British peers, claim that justice requires them to say no and that therefore they do no wrong to their patients?

American physicians cannot make this appeal to the justice of saying no. They have no assurance that the resources they save will be put to better use elsewhere in the health care system. Reducing a Medicare expenditure may mean only that there is less pressure on public budgets in general, and thus more opportunity to invest the savings in weapons.

Some Consequences

Saying no to beneficial treatments or procedures in the United States is morally hard, because providers cannot appeal to the justice of their denial. In ideally just arrangements, and even in the British system, rationing beneficial care is nevertheless fair to all patients in general. Cost-containment measures in our system carry with them no such justification.

Enthoven & Kronick, A Consumer-Choice Health Plan for the 1990s*
320 New Eng. J. Med. 94, 100 (1989)

What about the Canadian system as a model for the United States? In Canada's federal-provincial system, the federal government makes a substantial per capita payment to each province's health insurance plan, provided the province publicly administers universal, comprehensive coverage for hospital and physicians' services and meets certain other conditions. The provinces finance hospital care through prospective global budgets, determined on a historical basis, with annual increases for inflation, increases in workload, and approved new programs. Physicians are paid on a fee-for-service basis, according to a fee schedule negotiated between each province and its medical association. . . .

It is hard to imagine a process of incremental change by which the Canadian model would be re-created in the United States. But any fair appraisal of the Canadian model would have to acknowledge some major strengths and achievements. Canada has universal coverage at a 1985 cost of 8.6 percent of the gross national product, as compared with 10.6 percent in the United States. Its share of the gross national product has apparently stabilized, whereas ours is accelerating. Canadians have much less paperwork because there is a single insurer for everyone — the provincial government — to whom the physicians send their bills. Fee-for-service payment gives the doctors an incentive to deliver services, whereas hospital expenditures are capped by global prospective budgets. Thus, Canadian doctors have a financial interest in hospital productivity, because their receipts for services to inpatients are directly related to the number of patients hospitals can serve within their limited budgets.

Would the Canadian system be a good model for the United States? The answer is very uncertain. The Canadian system is locked into the fee-for-service model, with no built-in forces of the market or other forces to lead its providers to organize the system for optimal quality and efficiency. . . . Nor does it motivate doctors to avoid providing services of little or no marginal benefit to the patient. We do not know how much of Canada's lower rate of expense is the

* Reprinted with permission.

result of greater efficiency and how much the result of the denial of access to technology that would be beneficial.

Serious questions can be raised about the capability of the American federal and state governments to manage the whole health care system with a tolerable level of competence. The Canadians have a parliamentary system that is less vulnerable than our own to the pressures of special-interest groups. They have a stronger tradition of civil service. And the provinces operate on a smaller scale and with much more cultural homogeneity than many of our larger states.

But the key problem is that an attempt to enact a system like the Canadian one, involving a virtually complete government takeover of health care financing, would represent far too radical a change to be politically feasible in this country. . . . Any serious attempt to reproduce the Canadian model would provide the intense and concerted opposition of powerful groups. Providers would resist the notion of government as the sole source of payment. Health insurance companies, HMOs, other intermediaries, and administrators would resist the threat to put them out of business. Millions of relatively well-to-do Americans would fear that "socialized medicine" would deprive them of access to high-quality care and advanced technology. Although some might support it (big business, eager to unload its heavy liabilities, or the millions badly served by the present system), we would expect a firestorm of opposition. We see no evidence that the American people are sufficiently fed up to consider taking such a leap.

NOTES

Foreign Health Care Systems

1. For additional reading on the British National Health Service, see C. Ham, Health Policy in Britain (2d ed. 1985); R. Brown, Reorganizing the National Health Service (1979).

Prime Minister Thatcher has proposed sweeping reorganization of the NHS in a fashion that would make it much more privitized by removing hospitals from the direct control of regional and district health authorities and instead requiring those authorities to purchase health care services in the private marketplace. N.Y. Times, Feb. 1, 1989, at 1. If this proposal is implemented, it would not change the essential feature of the system for purposes of our study, namely, annual budget caps for defined population groups.

2. The Canadian system, also known as "Medicare," is garnering mounting attention in U.S. health policy circles because it appears more adaptable to American society than the British system. However, it has generated some of the same criticisms as the NHS: "In all of

Canada, there are 11 hospitals where open-heart surgery can be performed. In the United States there are 793. . . . In Vancouver, patients must wait . . . two years to four years for corneal transplants. . . . In Quebec, many patients wait six months for angiograms, and [8 to 9] months for coronary artery bypass surgery." Editorial, American Medical News, April 14, 1989, at 31. For additional readings on Canada, see Evans et al., Controlling Health Expenditures — The Canadian Reality, 320 New Eng. J. Med. 571 (1989); Barer et al., Fee Controls as Cost Control: Tales from the Frozen North, 66 Milbank Q. 1 (1988); Iglehart, Canada's Health Care System, 315 New Eng. J. Med. 202, 778, 1623 (1986); R. Evans, Strained Mercy: The Economics of Canadian Health Care (1984).

For analyses of national health care funding systems in other industrialized nations, see Raffel, Comparative Health Systems: Descriptive Analyses of Fourteen National Health Systems (1984); National Strategies for Health Care Organization: A World Overview (1985); Able-Smith, Who is the Odd Man Out?: The Experience of Western Europe in Containing the Costs of Health Care, 63 Milbank Mem. Fund Q. 1 (1985).

3. Apart from the question of whether the British or Canadian systems might succeed here, these materials raise the larger problem of the inevitable effects of *any* system capable of doing more than eliminating wholly unnecessary care. Success in health care cost containment forces us to grapple with the problem of rationing health care, that is, allocating limited resources among competing uses. Consider whether the British system purchases its remarkable cost containment success at too great a sacrifice to the quality of its health care. Is it appropriate to force patients to wait many months to receive relief from painful and disabling conditions that are not life-threatening? To withhold kidney dialysis from elderly patients who are otherwise healthy? To severely limit the availability of new technology?

The problem of health care rationing is pursued in the following sections, which focus on three sets of questions:

(1) At what level is rationing occurring?

— *macro* allocation of global resources among competing *societal* needs;
— *intermediate* allocation of health care resources among competing *treatment* needs;
— *micro* allocation of individual hospital budgets to *particular* patients.

(2) Who is making the rationing decision — patients, providers, or payers?

(3) What are the criteria for rationing?

E. Rationing Organ Transplants and Other Health Care Resources

Thurow, Learning to Say "No"*
311 New Eng. J. Med. 1569 (1984)

Public and private expenditures on health care rose from 5 to 11 per cent of the gross national product between 1960 and 1983. Although there is no magic formula for determining a precise limit on what a country can afford to spend for health care, there is a limit. Every dollar spent on health care is a dollar that cannot be spent on something else. No set of expenditures can rise faster than the gross national product forever. At some point, health-care expenditures must slow down to the rate of growth of the gross national product. . . .

It is traditional medical practice in the United States to employ treatments until they yield no additional payoffs, but with the development of more and more expensive techniques and devices that can slightly improve a diagnosis or marginally prolong life, the expenditures that have to be made before this traditional stopping point is reached have grown to almost unlimited levels. To some extent this may be caused by the use of unproved or useless techniques, but to an even greater extent it is caused by employing expensive techniques for which the expected benefits are simply very small relative to the costs.

These new medical techniques require a shift in standard medical practice. Instead of stopping treatments when all benefits cease to exist, physicians must stop treatments when marginal benefits are equal to marginal costs. But where lies the point at which marginal costs equal marginal benefits? And who is to make this ethical decision — the patient, the doctor, some third-party payer? And how do we as a society decide that we cannot afford a medical treatment that may marginally benefit someone?

Ethically, most Americans are simultaneously egalitarians and capitalists. None of us wants to die because we cannot afford to buy medical care, and as egalitarians few of us want to see others die because they cannot afford to buy medical care. As capitalists, Americans believe that individuals should be allowed to spend their money on whatever they wish, including health care.

This set of beliefs leads to an explosive chain reaction. A new expensive treatment is developed. In accordance with capitalistic principles, the wealthy are allowed to buy the treatment privately regardless of its medical effectiveness. Persons with a moderate or low

---

* Reprinted with permission.

II. Regulatory Reforms

income who cannot privately afford the treatment want it. They demand it. Being egalitarians, Americans do not have the political ability to say "no" to any person dying from a treatable disease. Ways are found to provide the treatment through private or public health insurance. Being egalitarians, we have to give the treatment to everyone or deny it to everyone; being capitalists, we cannot deny it to those who can afford it. But since resources are limited, we cannot afford to give it to everyone either.

In the summer of 1983 such a situation arose with respect to heart transplantations in Massachusetts. To save money, regulatory authorities were preventing Massachusetts hospitals from performing such transplantations. Some Massachusetts citizens were able to afford to fly to California to receive a transplant; others were not able to do so but needed a transplant just as much. The media and the public essentially wheeled those needing treatment up on the State House steps and dared the public authorities to let them die for want of treatment. Not surprisingly, the authorities relented. They altered rules and regulations to pay for California heart transplantations and quickly began allowing at least one Massachusetts hospital to perform the procedure.

I do not pretend to know whether the costs and benefits of heart transplantations have reached the point where any hospital with the technical capacity should or should not be allowed to perform them, but I do know that this is the wrong way to make the decision. . . .

Our basic problem is that somehow we are going to have to learn to say "no." . . .

If you are an egalitarian when it comes to medical care, and I confess that I am, what is the answer? One answer is that third-party payers can write rules and regulations concerning what they will and will not pay for and can prohibit their clients from buying services that are not allowed under the private or public insurance systems. This is essentially how the British have kept health-care spending at half the American level.

Such a procedure works, but it works clumsily, since no set of rules can be adjusted to the nuances of individual medical problems. It will be far better if American doctors begin to build up a social ethic and behavioral practices that help them decide when medicine is bad medicine — not simply because it has absolutely no payoff or because it hurts the patient — but also because the costs are not justified by the marginal benefits. To do this we are going to have to develop and disseminate better information on the cost effectiveness of alternative medical techniques for treating different ailments. Some small fraction of what we now spend on health care could be better spent to determine the limits of health-care expenditures under different circumstances.

The medical profession now has professional norms concerning what constitutes bad medical practice. Those norms have to be expanded to include cases in which high costs are not justified by minor expected benefits. If such norms are developed and then legally defended against malpractice suits, it just may be possible to build up a system of doctor-imposed cost controls that will be much more flexible than any system of cost controls imposed by third-party payers could be. But if the medical profession fails to do this, sooner or later the United States will move to a system of third-party controls. Something will have to be done.

As a society, how much are we willing to spend (sacrifice) to prolong life? The easy answer is any amount, but that answer is neither true nor feasible. Like it or not, Americans are going to have to come to some social consensus concerning the trade-off between costs of medical services and the life-extending benefits that result.

Health-care costs are being treated as if they were largely an economic problem, but they are not. To be solved, they will have to be treated as an ethical problem.

Levinsky, The Doctor's Master*
311 New Eng. J. Med. 1573 (1984)

There is increasing pressure on doctors to serve two masters. Physicians in practice are being enjoined to consider society's needs as well as each patient's needs in deciding what type and amount of medical care to deliver. Not surprisingly, many government leaders and health planners take this position. More remarkably, important elements of the medical profession are promoting this view.

I would argue the contrary, that physicians are required to do everything that they believe may benefit each patient without regard to costs or other societal considerations. In caring for an individual patient, the doctor must act solely as that patient's advocate, against the apparent interests of society as a whole, if necessary. An analogy can be drawn with the role of a lawyer defending a client against a criminal charge. The attorney is obligated to use all ethical means to defend the client, regardless of the cost of prolonged legal proceedings or even of the possibility that a guilty person may be acquitted through skillful advocacy. Similarly, in the practice of medicine, physicians are obligated to do all that they can for their patients without regard to any costs to society.

Society benefits if it expects its medical practitioners to follow

---

* Reprinted with permission.

II. Regulatory Reforms

this principle. As Fried[1] has eloquently argued, in any decent, advanced society there are rights in health care, in that "one is entitled to be treated decently, humanely, personally and honestly in the course of medical care. . . ." In such a just society "the physician who withholds care that it is in his power to give because he judges it is wasteful to provide it to a particular person breaks faith with his patient." A similar position has been stated by Hiatt[2]: "A physician or other provider must do all that is permitted on behalf of his patient. . . . The patient and the physician want no less, and society should settle for no less." A just society must have a group of professionals whose sole responsibility as health-care practitioners is to their patients as individuals.

The issue is not whether physicians must do everything technically possible for each patient. Rather it is that they should decide how much to do according to what they believe best for that patient, without regard for what is best for society or what it costs. I do not argue, as some have, that doctors are obligated to prolong life under all circumstances or that they are required to use their expertise to confer technological immortality on dehumanized bodies. Actual practice is infinitely complex and varied. Caring and experienced doctors will differ about what to do in individual cases. In my opinion, ethical physicians may discontinue life-extending treatment if their decisions are based solely on what they and the patient or his or her surrogate believe to be the patient's best interests. (The legal issues surrounding such decisions are beyond the scope of this paper.) They are not entitled to discontinue treatment on the basis of other considerations, such as cost. This distinction may become blurred if physicians are pressed to balance the needs of their patients with societal needs. The practitioner may make decisions for economic reasons but rationalize them as in the best interest of the individual patient. This phenomenon may be occurring in Britain, where physicians "seem to seek medical justification for decisions forced on them by resource limits. Doctors gradually redefine standards of care so that they can escape the constant recognition that financial limits compel them to do less than their best." . . .

None of the foregoing implies that in caring for individual patients doctors should disregard the escalating cost of medical care. Physicians can help control costs by choosing the most economical ways to deliver optimal care to their patients. They can use the least expensive setting, ambulatory or inpatient, in which first-class care can be given. They

---

1. Fried C. Rights and health care — beyond equity and efficiency. N. Engl. J. Med. 1975; 293:241-5.

2. Hiatt H.H.: Protecting the medical commons: who is responsible? N. Engl. J. Med. 1975; 293:235-41.

can eliminate redundant or useless diagnostic procedures ordered because of habit, deficient knowledge, personal financial gain, or the practice of "defensive medicine" to avoid malpractice judgments.

However, it is society, not the individual practitioner, that must make the decision to limit the availability of effective but expensive types of medical care. Heart and liver transplantation are current cases in point. These are extraordinarily expensive procedures that may prolong a life of "good quality" for some people. Society, through its elected officials, is entitled to decide that the resources required for such programs are better used for other purposes. However, a physician who thinks that his or her patient may benefit from a transplant must make that patient aware of this opinion and assist the patient in obtaining the organ.

The continuous increase in the costs of medical care is a difficult social issue. However, it is not self-evident that expenditures for health care should be limited to any arbitrary percentage of the gross national product, such as the current 11 per cent figure. Moreover, if physicians and others make concerted and effective attempts to eliminate healthcare expenditures that do not truly benefit patients, it is not a given fact that the proportion of the national wealth devoted to health care will increase indefinitely. It certainly is not self-evident that resources saved by limiting health care will be allocated to other equally worthy programs, such as preventive medicine, health maintenance, or improved nutrition and housing for the needy. . . .

Through its democratic processes, American society may well choose to ration medical resources. In that event, physicians as citizens and experts will have a key role in implementing the decision. Their advice will be needed in allocating limited resources to provide the greatest good for the greatest number. As experience in other countries has shown, it may be difficult for doctors to separate their role as citizens and expert advisors from their role in the practice of medicine as unyielding advocates for the health needs of their individual patients. They must strive relentlessly to do so. When practicing medicine, doctors cannot serve two masters. It is to the advantage both of our society and of the individuals it comprises that physicians retain their historic single-mindedness. The doctor's master must be the patient.

Eisenberg, Doctors' Decisions and the Cost of Medical Care*
82 (1986)

A rebuttal [to the physician's objection to considering costs in making treatment decisions] can be found in a scenario first described

* Copyright © 1986, Health Administration Press. Reprinted with permission.

in 1833 by a mathematical amateur named William Forster Lloyd. Hardin has recounted this scenario and entitled it "the tragedy of the commons." It takes place in a common pasture that is used by a number of herdsmen. As a rational being, each herdsman seeks to maximize his personal gain. He asks himself, "What is the value to me of adding another animal to my herd?" He concludes that the only sensible course is to add another animal, and he does so. But so do all the other herdsmen, and soon thereafter, each adds another animal, followed by even more. The commons becomes overcrowded with animals and there is insufficient grass for grazing. As Hardin describes the dilemma, each man is locked into a system that compels him to increase his herd without limit, in a world that is limited. Each pursued his own best interest in a society that believes in the freedom of the commons, but freedom of the commons brings ruin to all.

Somers first drew a parallel from the "tragedy of the commons" to health care several years ago, and the analogy is all the more fitting today. As the resources available for medical services are increasingly limited, the dilemma of the individual practitioner will become even more important. As the individual responsible for optimizing the patient's health, the physician would like to be able to use resources as if they were unlimited except by the patient's own resources and values. However, as a responsible member of society, the physician will want to strive for efficiency in the use of medical services. This goal of equity and efficiency suggests that the marginal yield for society should be the same for all medical services in order to ensure efficient allocation of resources. Of course, this allocation will depend on how society defines its values and, therefore, its utilities for medical services, their cost, and their outcomes.

Havighurst & Blumstein, Coping with Quality Cost Trade-Offs in Medical Care: The Role of PSROs*
70 N.W. L. Rev. 6, 6-7, 12, 16-18 (1975)

The health policy debate suffers from the reluctance of the debaters to face up to one central reality — namely, that high-quality medical care, which all endorse in general terms, can cost a great deal more than we ought to pay. For example, those advocates who emphasize that "health care is a right" are slow to concede that, like other "rights," it cannot be made absolute (in the sense of meeting, at no charge, every colorable need with the finest technology and personnel) without distorting society's priorities. Others, who worry about those priorities, hesitate to contend openly that, except for

---

* Reprinted by special permission of Northwestern University, School of Law.

some disadvantaged groups, spending in pursuit of "quality" in medical care may already be too high. In other words, in health policy debates perhaps more than anywhere else, the inevitable trade-off between benefits and costs is practically unmentionable. A policy dialogue in which a taboo surrounds any concession to the reality of limited resources is bound to be rich in posturing and assertion and, more seriously, is likely to produce programs whose marginal benefits are not worth their costs. . . .

The Trade-off Problem: The Benefits of Medical Care

It is a common mistake to think of medical care simply as the difference between life and death and therefore as a necessity which would be consumed at the same level whatever price is charged, except for the falling away of those whose demand is curtailed by impoverishment. While some medical care is clearly of this essential life-and-death character, most of it is not, consisting instead of a variety of interventions of widely varying benefits to patients. . . . Thus, for example, a 95 percent certain diagnosis might be made 97 percent certain by additional laboratory tests or X-rays costing, say, $200 and 99 percent certain by spending an additional $800 on inpatient diagnostic measures. While a person of means might well tell his doctor to spend the $1000, an uninsured person of average income and adequate savings might rationally choose to forgo one or both increments of certainty, depending on the magnitude of the consequences of not knowing for sure. Similarly, the benefit/cost ratio of extra hospital days, follow-up visits to the physician, annual physical exams, preventive screening, and even some widely accepted therapies can be extremely troublesome. . . .

Another way of understanding the allocative issue in health care is through the graphic conceptualization in Figure 1. The "benefits" curve in Figure 1a illustrates heuristically a possible set of relationships between the benefits of health care and the inputs necessary to obtain them. At low input levels, the curve rises steeply, showing large returns (measured in dollars on the vertical axis) from each unit of input. The leveling off of the curve reveals that smaller and smaller health returns are obtained from further increases in inputs. The curve is completely level after point x, illustrating the concept of "unnecessary care" — namely, that which returns no net health benefit at all to the patient. The curve declines after point y, to show that some medical care is positively harmful.

A policy maker seeking to allocate societal resources optimally must attempt to equate marginal benefits and marginal costs so that "the last dollar's worth of resources devoted to health care increase[s] human satisfaction by exactly the same amount as the same dollar's

II. Regulatory Reforms

worth devoted to other goals." In Figure 1a, a straight line portrays the dollar cost of the inputs on the horizontal axis. The *slope* (rate of increase) of this line is the critical feature and is reflected in the dotted parallel line, which allows the decision maker to find the point of tangency (*0*), where the benefits curve is rising at exactly the same rate as the cost line. After this point, the increase in benefits obtainable by adding more inputs is no longer as great as the cost of those inputs, that is, marginal benefits do not at least equal marginal cost. I_0 then represents the optimal quantity of inputs and C_0 the optimal level of expenditures. Beyond these points, added inputs and expenditures, though productive of greater health, are inappropriate because greater benefits can be gained by employing resources in nonhealth uses.

The portion of the benefits curve between *o* and *x* is identified as the "quality/cost no man's land," signifying care which may seem warranted as long as the decision maker — public or private, as the case may be — does not consider the true cost of providing it. Such care, when provided, is an artifact not of benefit/cost calculations (which would contraindicate it) but of the distortions introduced by physician control of demand and the health care financing system

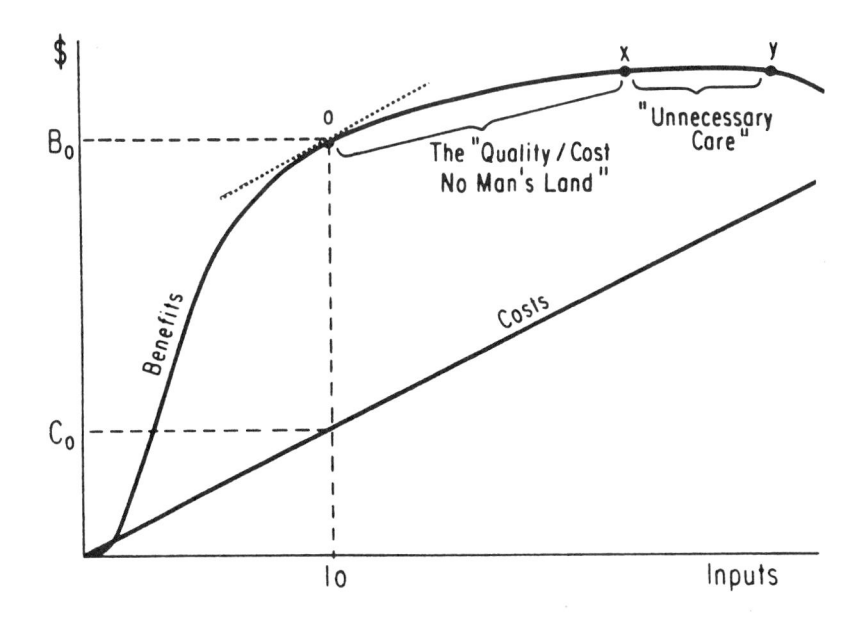

Figure 1a.
The Optimal Level of Health Care Spending

and of the inability or unwillingness of public decision makers or providers to impose limits on the provision of care falling in this range. The curve is of course drawn in such a way as to make the "quality/cost no man's land" look very large in relative terms.

There is no way of knowing how much of the care possible above point o in Figure 1a is in fact being rendered, but Figure 1b illustrates the potential for distortion introduced by third-party payment, which causes social and private costs to diverge. The "private costs" curve portrays the costs visible to private decision makers under a 20 percent coinsurance requirement (SC = 5 × PC), and the slope of this line is used to find point p, the amount of benefits sought by rational, subsidized consumers. I_0I_p indicates the additional inputs consumed as a result of the implicit subsidies, and the points on the vertical axis reveal the benefit/cost relationships; $PC_1PC_2 < B_1B_2$, showing that the additional care makes sense from the standpoint of private decision makers; $B_1B_2 < SC_1SC_2$, showing that the extra care is a poor social investment. The vertical axis also provides a striking illustration of the importance of viewing the benefits of health care in marginal rather than aggregate terms since the benefits of spending at the level SC_1 are very large (B_1), while the benefits of increasing spending to the level of SC_2 are small (B_1B_2).

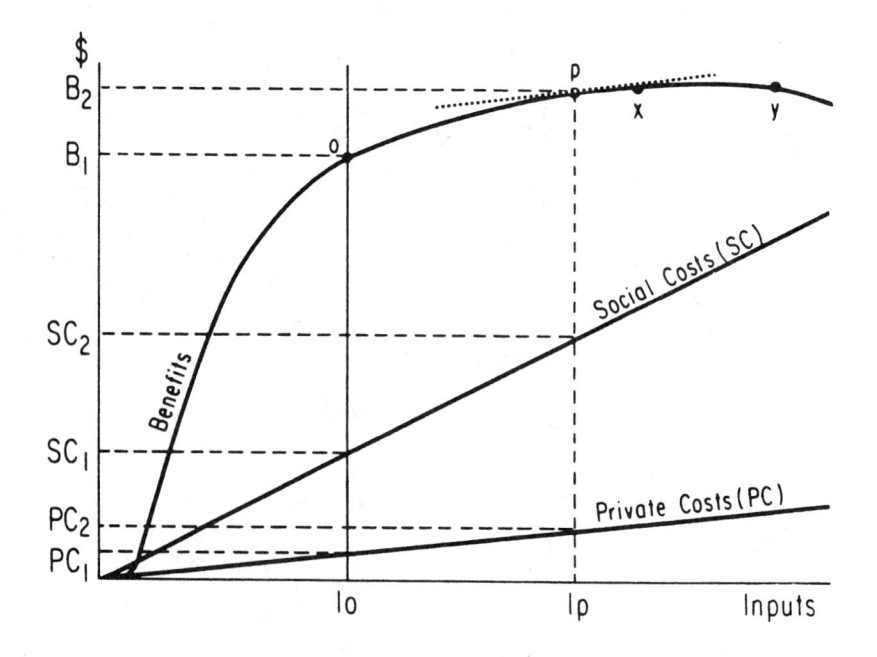

Figure 1b.
The Distortion Introduced by the Divergence of Private and Social Costs

Weinstein & Stason, Foundations of Cost-Effectiveness Analysis for Health and Medical Practice*
296 New Eng. J. Med. 716 (1977)

It is now almost universally believed that . . . we, as a nation, will have to think very carefully about how to allocate the resources we are willing to make available for health care. . . .

. . . To facilitate these critical allocation decisions, the best current information on both the efficacy of medical practices and their costs must be made available to decision makers in a systematic fashion that will allow them to make valid comparisons among alternative uses of resources. To implement the conclusions from such comparisons, incentives must be offered to providers and patients alike, to adopt cost-effective health practices.

In this context, increasingly frequent studies have been sought to guide present and future decisions by systematic analysis. These efforts, based on such approaches as benefit-cost analysis, cost-effectiveness analysis and decision analysis, attempt to use existing information in a given area of health care to develop criteria for allocating resources. Such approaches have potential value both for allocation decisions within a categorical health problem and across diseases or health problems. If these approaches were to become widely understood and accepted by the key decision makers in the health-care sector, including the physician, important health benefits or cost savings might be realized. The purpose of this paper is to describe the basic foundations of the methods of cost-effectiveness analysis in the allocation of health-care resources. . . .

General Analytic Approaches

Cost-effectiveness analysis and benefit-cost (or cost-benefit) analysis are two related, but quite different, approaches to the assessment of health practices. Confusion frequently exists between the two approaches, and many analyses that are technically cost-effectiveness analyses are often labeled "cost-benefit" analyses, and vice versa. The key distinction is that a benefit-cost analysis must value all outcomes in economic (e.g., dollar) terms, including lives or years of life and morbidity, whereas a cost-effectiveness analysis serves to place priorities on alternative expenditures without requiring that the dollar value of life and health be assessed.

---

* This paper by Milton C. Weinstein and William B. Stason, both from the Center for the Analysis of Health Practices, Harvard School of Public Health, is reprinted with the permission of the New England Journal of Medicine. Copyright © 1977 by the Massachusetts Medical Society.

The underlying premise of cost-effectiveness analysis in health problems is that, for any given level of resources available, society (or the decision-making jurisdiction involved) wishes to maximize the total aggregate health benefits conferred. Alternatively, for a given health-benefit goal, the objective is to minimize the cost of achieving it. In either formulation, the analytical methodology is the same. First of all, health benefits and health-resource costs must each be expressed in terms of some common unit of measurement. Health-resource costs are inevitably measured in dollars. Health benefits, or health effectiveness, may be expressed in a variety of ways, the most common being either lives or life years, or some variant of them. The use of "quality-adjusted life years" has the advantage of incorporating changes in survival and morbidity in a single measure that reflects tradeoffs between them. The ratio of costs to benefits, expressed as cost per year of life saved or cost per quality-adjusted year of life saved, becomes the cost-effectiveness measure. Alternative programs or services are then ranked, from the lowest value of this cost-per-effectiveness ratio to the highest, and selected from the top until available resources are exhausted. The point on the priority list at which the available resources are exhausted, or at which society is no longer willing to pay the price for the benefits achieved, becomes society's cutoff level of permissible cost per unit effectiveness. For example, the level of blood pressure at which antihypertensive treatment is recommended might be based on the corresponding cost-effectiveness cutoff level. Application of this procedure ensures that the maximum possible expected health benefit is realized, subject to whatever resource constraint is in effect.

Benefit-cost analysis has been applied in many health contexts ranging from mobile coronary-care units to venereal-disease control programs. To value life years and quality of life in dollars, the traditional approach is to use the annual earnings of a worker as a measure of the value of a productive year of life. The value of time lost from work is similarly calculated. The rationale is that society, including the individual in question, would lose potential consumption of goods and services in proportion to lost productivity. Critics of the lost-earnings approach have argued that it fails to take into account many subjective values associated with health and life that are not captured by earnings alone. Some favor, as alternatives, the assessment of individual willingness to pay to reduce the probabilities of death and disease or the imputation of the added wages that workers in hazardous jobs require as compensation for their risks. Once benefits and costs have been somehow expressed in dollar terms, net benefits are derived as the difference between the two: if the results are positive, the argument goes, the program or practice should be undertaken, and if negative it should not.

II. Regulatory Reforms

The major disadvantage of the benefit-cost framework is the requirement that human lives and quality of life be valued in dollars. Many decision makers find this point difficult, and do not trust analyses that depend on such valuations. Cost-effectiveness analysis, on the other hand, requires only that health outcomes be expressed in commensurate units (e.g., quality-adjusted life years), generally involving tradeoffs more palatable to physicians. An advantage of the benefit-cost framework is that it leads to a positive or negative (or zero) number for each program or practice evaluated, and therefore, does not require knowledge of a cost-effectiveness cutoff level to decide whether a particular practice should be undertaken. Finally, a limitation of both approaches is that the benefits and costs to individual members of society need to be aggregated. If the equitable distribution of benefits and costs across individuals or groups are of concern, a single cost-effectiveness measure will not do. However, as economists are wont to argue, over large numbers of programs and practices the inequities are likely to even themselves out and, with some exceptions, may reasonably be ignored. . . .

Elements of Cost-Effectiveness Analysis. . . .

Net Health Effectiveness

The basic quantitative measure of health effectiveness is the increase in expected number of life years. Given a schedule of age-specific mortality probabilities with and without the program or practice in question, it is a straightforward matter of life-table analysis to compute life expectancies with and without the program or practice, the difference being the expected net increase in life years (ΔY).

It has become more and more evident, however, that the effects of health practices on the quality of life occupy an equally prominent role in the objective of providers and consumers of health care. On the one hand, concern over the often highly subjective side effects of medications must somehow be factored into the analysis. On the other hand, the quality-of-life-improving effects of an operation are frequently more important considerations than its effect on longevity. A year of life of a patient on renal hemodialysis or of one who has chronic disability from a severe cerebrovascular accident must surely be counted differently from a completely healthy year.

Although still controversial, methods for explicitly incorporating quality-of-life concerns into formal cost-effectiveness analyses are becoming more widely used and accepted. The general approach that has been used is to derive some measure like "quality-adjusted life years" to express the total health effect in common units. The first approaches to this problem fall under the rubric of "health-status indexes." A health-status index is essentially a weighting scheme: each definable health status, ranging from death to coma to varying degrees of disability and discomfort to full health, and accounting for age differences, is assigned a weight from zero to one, and the number of years spent at a given health status, Y_s, is multiplied by the corresponding weight, λ_s, to yield a number, $\lambda_s Y_s$, that might be thought of as an equivalent number of years with full health — a number of quality-adjusted life years (QALYs). The source of these weights is ultimately subjective, and can be thought of as reflecting answers to either of the following questions: "Taking into account your age, pain and suffering, immobility, and lost earnings, what fraction, P, of a year of life would you be willing to give up to be completely healthy for the remaining fraction of a year instead of your present level of health status for the full year?" Or "Taking into account these same factors, what probability, P, of death would you be willing to accept so that, if you survived, you would have full health rather than your present health status for the rest of your life?" In both cases, an answer of P near 1.0 would imply that the health status is nearly as bad as death; an answer near 0.0 would imply a mild or negligible level of disability. The weight, λ_s, above would correspond to 1–P.

Clearly, different people would answer these questions differently. In a cost-effectiveness analysis at the societal level, it is therefore essential that a range of possible weights be used to reflect the spectrum of individual values. . . .

Discounting Future Costs and Health Benefits: Present-Value Analysis

Rarely do all costs and benefits occur at the same time. It is therefore necessary to combine present and future costs, as well as present and future benefits, in comparable units. One simple way would be to add up all dollar costs, regardless of when they are incurred, and all benefits, regardless of when they occur. This procedure, however, ignores the fact that a dollar in 1977 is worth more than it will be in 1978 or 2077. Present-value analysis is a widely accepted method of weighting future dollars by a discount factor to make them comparable to present dollars. For consistency, the same discount factor should be applied to future health benefits (i.e., quality-adjusted life years) as well. . . .

On the health-benefit side, the use of discounting requires more justification. For programs involving screening for disease, where the life years saved are far in the future, it matters a great deal whether expected benefits are discounted. Without discounting, a program that saves one quality-adjusted life year 40 years hence at a present-value cost of $10,000 would have a cost-effectiveness ratio of $10,000 per QALY. With discounting at 5 per cent per year, the present value of that future QALY is reduced to $1/(1.05)$ or about 0.14, and the ratio becomes $70,000 per QALY, a remarkable difference in the implied priority of the program in the range of possible alternative uses of health resources.

The reason for discounting future life years is not that life years can, in any sense, be invested to yield more life years as dollars can be invested to yield more dollars. Nor is it necessary to assume that life years in the future are less valuable than life years today in any absolute utilitarian sense. Rather, the reason for discounting future life years is precisely that they are being valued relative to dollars and, since a dollar in the future is discounted relative to a present dollar, so must a life year in the future be discounted relative to a present dollar. . . .

Conclusions on the Value and Application of Cost-effectiveness Analysis in Health Care

The principal value of formal cost-effectiveness analysis in health care is that it forces one to be explicit about the beliefs and values that underlie allocation decisions. Opposing points of view can be clarified in terms of specific disagreements over assumptions, probability estimates or value tradeoffs.

Cost-effectiveness analysis often takes the societal point of view and is therefore directed at decision makers who act as agents for society as a whole. Nevertheless, the basic analytic framework should be useful to a variety of decision makers, who may include in the definitions of cost and benefit whatever elements they perceive to be within their domain. Such concepts as quality-adjusted life years, discounting and sensitivity analysis are equally applicable to analyses directed at physicians, hospitals and insurance programs. Moreover, as we as a nation move toward the creation of institutions that take on more of the societal perspective (e.g., national health insurance, health-systems agencies and health-maintenance organizations), the importance and value of cost-effectiveness analysis will increase even more.

[Selected] REFERENCES

1. Hiatt, H. H.: Protecting the Medical Commons: Who is Responsible? N. Engl. J. Med. 293:235-241, 1975. . . .
4. Neuhauser, D., Lewicki, A. M.: What Do We Gain from the Sixth Stool Guaiac?, N. Engl. J. Med. 293:226-228, 1975.

5. Acton, J. P.: Evaluating Public Programs to Save Lives: The Case of Heart Attacks (Rand Corporation Report R-950-RC). Santa Monica, California, Rand Corporation, 1973.
6. Bunker, J. P., Mosteller, C. F., Barnes, B. A.: Costs, Risks, and Benefits of Surgery. New York, Oxford University Press, 1977.
7. Zeckhauser, R.: Procedures for Valuing Lives. Public Policy 23:419-464, 1975. . . .
10. Rice, D. P.: Estimating the Cost of Illness. Am. J. Public Health 57:424-440, 1967.

NOTES

The Ethics and Economics of Health Care Rationing

1. Where on the quality/cost graph in the Havighurst and Blumstein article would you represent the British system? Defensive medicine? Unnecessary surgery?

2. Havighurst and Blumstein's analysis is helpful in understanding in an abstract way what the goal of appropriate health care rationing is, but their model does not answer the critical questions of implementation that are addressed in the New England Journal of Medicine excerpts (and further below): who should decide, according to what criteria, and based on what evidence? Weinstein and Stason's analysis is helpful in answering the third question; they set forth a structured and mathematically oriented technique for measuring the costs and benefits of alternative treatment modalities. Which method — cost-benefit or cost-effectiveness analysis — is best suited to resolving the global tradeoff issues that Havighurst and Blumstein raise? Does cost-benefit analysis unfairly deny care to the elderly since their greatly decreased earning power results in a devaluation of the benefits of treatment? See Avorn, Benefit and Cost Analysis in Geriatric Care, 310 New Eng. J. Med. 1294 (1984) (arguing yes).

3. Health policy analysts frequently observe that there is a critical shortage of information of the type that Weinstein and Stason seek because very few medical procedures have been subjected to the controlled clinical trials necessary to produce reliable cost effectiveness information. In no small part, the medical profession is responsible for this information gap. For example, the federal government decided to dismantle an effort to judge the effectiveness of various medical procedures in part because of AMA opposition grounded on the fear that such an endeavor would threaten the autonomy of professional medical judgment. See Sun, Fishing for a Forum on Health Policy, 219 Science 37 (1983); Blumenthal, Federal Policy Toward Health Care Technology: The Case of the National Center, 61 Milbank Mem. Fund Q. 584, 600 (1983).

II. Regulatory Reforms

However, researchers and protocol setters are beginning to employ cost-effectiveness analysis more frequently. For example, it has been estimated recently that the cost of administering Pap smears, which detect cervical cancer, is $12,000 per additional year of life expectancy for testing every three years and $930,000 per year of life for annual testing. Which would you choose if you were a patient paying out of pocket? If you were a gynecologist? As a Medicare bureaucrat? See N.Y. Times, Jan. 7, 1988, col. 1, p. 10 (gynecologists and oncologists compromise by recommending testing every three years after a series of negative one-year exams). HCFA recently proposed to begin using cost-effectiveness analysis (to a limited extent) in deciding whether to pay for new medical technologies. 54 Fed. Reg. 4302, 4308-4309 (1989). See generally Doubilet, Weinstein & McNeil, Use and Misuse of the Term "Cost Effective" in Medicine, 314 New Eng. J. Med. 253 (1986); Neuhauser & Stason, Cost-effective Clinical Decision Making, in The Physician and Cost Control 133 (E. Carels, D. Neuhauser & W. Stason eds. 1980); Costs, Risks and Benefits of Surgery (J. Bunker, B. Barnes & F. Mosteller eds. 1977).

The federal government has given a large boost to assessing the effectiveness and outcomes of various medical procedures by establishing a new Agency for Health Care Policy and Research within the Public Health Service, with appropriations starting at $50 million and increasing to $185 million by 1994. This agency will develop treatment- and condition-specific practice guidelines based on its research findings. 42 U.S.C. §299 et seq. For a discussion of these developments and their effect on malpractice liability, see generally Hall, The Effect of Medical Practice Policies on Malpractice Litigation, forthcoming, L. & Contemp. Prob.; Kinney & Wilder, Medical Standard Setting in the Current Malpractice Environment, 22 U. Calif. Davis L. Rev. 421 (1989); Havighurst, Practice Guidelines for Medical Care: The Policy Rationale, forthcoming, St. Louis U. L. Rev. An excellent series of essays discussing clinical policies and clinical decision making, all authored by David Eddy, runs periodically in J.A.M.A. beginning with vol. 263, no. 2 (1990).

4. For another argument that physicians breach their fiduciary responsibility to patients by treating with costs in mind, see Veatch, Physicians and Cost-Containment: The Ethical Conflict, 30 Jurimetrics (Summer 1990). If physicians became health care rationers (as Professor Thurow would like) and began to take economic costs as well as medical costs into consideration in making their treatment decisions, what would their obligations be under informed consent principles? Would doctors be required to tell patients of each time they decided to forgo a specific medical procedure on account of cost constraints, or would it be enough that the patient were generally aware that the doctor is employing a rough cost/benefit analysis? Suppose, for in-

stance, that an HMO physician, without telling the patient, declines to recommend an expensive diagnostic procedure (an MRI scan, for example) in order to confirm a diagnosis of which she is already fairly certain. Which informed consent theory might apply to such a situation? What sort of disclosure would the theory require: disclosure at the time of joining the HMO of the general resource constraints and financial incentives for physicians or specific disclosure at the point of each treatment decision?

5. One-third of Medicare's budget is spent on medical treatment that is provided during the patient's last year of life. Daniel Callahan, a prominent medical philosopher, has provocatively proposed that, once a patient reaches a certain, advanced age (say, 84), Medicare should deny funding for expensive procedures such as by-pass surgery or hip replacements. Setting Limits: Medical Goals in an Aging Society (1987). Do you agree? See also Battin, Age Rationing and the Just Distribution of Health Care: Is There a Duty to Die? 97 Ethics 317 (1987); T. Smeeding, Should Medical Care be Rationed by Age? (1987).

6. "A rationing plan advocated by an Oregon MD-legislator to rank Medicaid health benefits based on cost and effectiveness is spreading across the country. Officials in Arizona, Alaska, Colorado, Kentucky, and Vermont are talking about the plan. Recently, Alameda County [Cal.] officials began placing priorities on medical services for poor people . . . The president of the Oregon Senate . . . started the movement by introducing legislation to ration health services. . . . Under his bill, consumers and health care providers would define an adequate level of health care for the Medicaid population. After the legislature approved these priorities, the state would contract with managed care systems to provide services." Am. Med. News, May 5, 1989, at 1. "Priority has been given to prenatal care, disease prevention and the treatment of acute and chronic disease. . . . Services that improve the quality of life for the elderly, like treatment for bunions and home nursing, rank higher than measures to delay death in cases of terminal illness. Most organ transplants, infertility services, plastic surgery [etc.] . . . are given low priority." Gross, What Medical Care the Poor Can Have: Lists are Drawn Up, N.Y. Times, March 27, 1989, at 1.

7. A related controversy surrounds research support for development of a totally implantable artificial heart. The few patients who have used this device have died after a few months of agonizing setbacks. The National Institute of Health announced in mid-1988 that it would cease all funding for this project in favor of developing a more promising "simpler artificial device, the left ventricular assist, which helps but does not replace a diseased heart." N.Y. Times, May 20, 1988, at 7. However, Senators Kennedy and Hatch (who represent

II. Regulatory Reforms

states with medical institutions that receive the bulk of the research funds) threatened the agency with funding disruption unless it reinstated the $22 million artificial heart research program, which it did.

For discussion generally of how we go about assessing new medical technology, see 54 Fed. Reg. 4302 (1989) (description of the process used in making Medicare coverage decisions for new technologies); Havighurst, Applying Antitrust Law to Collaboration in the Production of Information: The Case of Medical Technology Assessment, 51 L. & Contemp. Prob. 341 (1988); Mehlman, Health Care Cost Containment and Medical Technology: A Critique of Waste Theory, 36 Case West. Res. L. Rev. 778 (1986); Mehlman, Rationing Expensive Life-Saving Medical Treatments, 1985 Wisc. L. Rev. 7 (1985).

8. It is impossible to overemphasize the importance of health care rationing issues. As the following materials demonstrate, we are already squarely confronted with serious rationing problems in the context of deciding how to allocate a limited supply of transplantable organs. As cost containment strategies such as DRGs become more successful and more widespread, rationing problems will proliferate across the spectrum of diagnostic and therapeutic procedures. Other aspects of this, perhaps the most perplexing health care policy issue of our times, are explored in Sections II.A and III.B. For a sampling of the rapidly expanding multidisciplinary literature, see (in addition to the sources cited at 807 and elsewhere in these notes) R. Blank, Rationing Medicine (1988); G. Calabresi & P. Bobbitt, Tragic Choices (1978); Hiatt, America's Health in the Balance (1987); Blumstein, Rationing Medical Resources: A Constitutional, Legal, and Policy Analysis, 59 Tex. L. Rev. 1345 (1981); 60 Tex. L. Rev. 899 (1982); Moskop, The Moral Limits of Federal Funding for Kidney Disease, Hastings Center Report, April 1987, at 11; Rosenblatt, Rationing "Normal" Health Care: The Hidden Legal Issues, 59 Texas L. Rev. 1401 (1981); 60 Texas L. Rev. 919 (1982).

Besharov & Silver, Rationing Access to Advanced Medical Techniques*
8 J. Leg. Med. 507 (1987)

Introduction

Explicit rationing of medical care, that is, the deliberate denial of treatment for some individuals who might benefit therefrom, may

---

* Douglas J. Besharov is Resident Scholar at the American Enterprise Institute for Public Policy Research and Adjunct Professor of Law at Georgetown and American Universities. . . . When this article was written, Jessica Dunsay Silver was a Visiting Fellow at the American Enterprise Institute for Public Policy Research, on leave from the Department of Justice, Civil Rights Division.

Copyright © Shugar Publishing, reproduced with permission.

seem totally alien to our expectations about access to health care. Until now, explicit rationing of medical care has been avoided, except when natural scarcity places an *unalterable* limit on availability. However, rising health care costs and the federal budget deficit have forced the government to consider rationing some health care because it costs too much.

While there is much informal or "hidden" rationing in health care, this article focuses on the explicit, formal methods of rationing that might be used to determine access to advanced medical techniques. It describes the various means by which such rationing might be accomplished, illustrating each by an actual example of its use, and then it examines the ethical and legal concerns that are raised.

To illustrate the currency of these issues, this article concentrates on the example of rationing of heart transplants. This focus is chosen for several reasons. Heart transplantation is currently an area of explicit and severe rationing because of the natural scarcity of donor organs. In addition, patient selection criteria are publicly known, and, therefore, easier to identify and analyze. Moreover, the federal government seems to be deliberately rationing heart transplants. Finally, the rationing criteria established for heart transplants will set an important precedent for future decisions about access to advanced medical techniques.

I. Reluctance to Ration: The Kidney Dialysis Experience

Perhaps the best known recent example of explicit rationing involved kidney dialysis. In the 1960s and early 1970s, the high cost of kidney dialysis (approximately $12-15,000 per year) placed the procedure out of the reach of many patients.[2] Demand, however, still outstripped the limited facilities and staff available, and hospitals were forced to ration. Many applied medical and/or social worth criteria, including age, medical suitability, mental acuity, family involvement, criminal record, economic status, employment record, availability of transportation, willingness to cooperate in the treatment regimen, likelihood of vocational rehabilitation, psychiatric status, marital status, educational background, occupation, and future potential.[3]

At the Seattle Artificial Kidney Center, an anonymous screening committee was set up to choose patients. The committee was composed of a physician, a lawyer, a housewife, a businessman, a labor leader,

---

2. Note, *Scarce Medical Resources*, 69 Colum. L. Rev. 620, 637 (1969).

3. Evans, *Health Care Technology and the Inevitability of Resource Allocation and Rationing Decisions*, 249 J.A.M.A. 2208, 2209 (1983).

II. Regulatory Reforms

a state government official, and a minister. One lay member reported his experience:

> The choices were hard . . . I remember voting against a young woman who was a known prostitute. I found I couldn't vote for her, rather than another candidate, a young wife and mother. I also voted against a young man who, until he learned he had renal failure, had been a ne'er-do-well, a real playboy. He promised he would reform his character, go back to school, and so on, if only he were selected for treatment. But I felt I'd lived long enough to know that a person like that won't really do what he was promising at the time.[5]

One writer saw in its deliberations "a disturbing picture . . . of the Seattle committee measuring persons in accordance with its own middle-class suburban value system. . . . The Pacific Northwest is no place for a Henry David Thoreau with bad kidneys.[6] The committee came to be known as the "God squad."

The Los Angeles County — USC Medical Center took a different approach. It used a lottery to select dialysis patients. Initial screening on the basis of medical and other criteria placed a prospective patient into either an optimal or an alternate group. Candidates were chosen at random from the optimal group. When that group was exhausted, patients were selected from the group of alternates.

Congress turned its attention to the shortage of kidney dialysis during consideration of the Social Security Amendments of 1972. It found a medical technology that could save lives, but that was available to only a small percentage of those needing it. Senator Hartke articulated the fundamental question that faced our elected representatives: "How do we explain that the difference between life and death is a matter of dollars?"

Not surprisingly, Congress rejected rationing. It chose to solve the shortage by simply expanding Medicare coverage to pay for kidney dialysis for virtually everyone in need. The ease with which it did so was undoubtedly influenced by the then rapid growth in federal tax receipts.

Unrestricted access to kidney dialysis was assured at a high price. Although original cost estimates ranged from $100,000 to $250,000 per year, they were overtaken by political and medical realities. In 1965, there were only 300 dialysis patients; in 1969, the number was still under 1,000. But by 1972, the number grew to 10,000. The End-Stage Renal Disease dialysis program now covers 78,000 patients, at an annual cost of over $1.5 billion.

---

5. R. Fox & J. Swazey, The Courage to Fail, 232 (1974).

6. Sanders & Dukeminier, *Medical Advance and Legal Lag: Hemodialysis and Kidney Transplantation*, 15 UCLA L. Rev. 357, 378 (1968).

II. No More "Easy" Solutions: Current Budgetary Realities

The development of advanced medical techniques has been welcomed by society as a means of lengthening and improving the quality of life. As the kidney dialysis experience demonstrates, it has been assumed that costs alone should not bar access to needed medical care. The result has been to keep sicker people alive, for longer periods of time — at ever greater cost. . . .

It has been estimated that each year hundreds, and perhaps thousands, of new technologies are developed. Many are very expensive. For example, magnetic resonance imaging (MRI), the new imaging device, costs between $800,000 and $2 million per unit. A lithotriper, a device used to dissolve kidney stones without surgery, can cost between $600,000 and $1.5 million. The total price for coronary artery by-pass surgery, neo-natal intensive care, and kidney dialysis all number in the billions of dollars. Some of these new technologies save money in patient care costs, and so pay for themselves. Others do not. In any event, it has been estimated that new technology has accounted for a 50 percent increase in per diem costs of hospital care.

III. The Cost of One New Technology: Heart Transplants

The improved ability to transplant hearts illustrates the present dilemma over costs. Successful heart transplantation is a recent medical miracle. As recently as the early 1970s, less than 25 percent of all heart transplant patients survived more than five years. But the improvements in surgical techniques and the use of cyclosporine, the anti-rejection drug, have raised five year survival rates to over 40 percent. In 1984, 346 heart transplants were performed. In 1986, the last year for which data are available, 1,368 were performed. Heart transplants cost between $57,000 and $110,000 each, and the average cost is $95,000.

In November of 1979, the federal government authorized Medicare payment for heart transplants at Stanford University on a temporary basis pending the development of final criteria for establishing coverage. In June, 1980, just seven months later, Medicare coverage was discontinued in an apparent effort to avoid the massive costs involved. The Secretary of Health and Human Services (HHS) announced, at that time, that Medicare would evaluate not only the safety and efficacy of new technologies, but also their "social consequences," before "financing their wide distribution." Thereafter, HHS contracted with the Battelle Institute to conduct a massive technology assessment, which was not completed until late 1984.

II. Regulatory Reforms

The Battelle study revealed how expensive a heart transplant program could become. According to the Battelle Institute study, each year, over 84,000 Medicare beneficiaries of all ages die of heart ailments when they might be kept alive by a transplant. For the whole population, the number is about 272,000. . . .

. . . Even if only 8,500 transplants are performed for Medicare recipients each year, [the maximum number of donated hearts currently available] and each transplant costs a conservatively estimated $80,000, the annual bill for heart transplants would be over $680 million . . . This does not include annual follow-up costs of six to twelve thousand dollars for each patient, costs which increase geometrically each additional year of the program.

At a not too distant date, it will be possible to perform many more transplants, as more donor, artificial, and animal hearts become available. If only half of those needing a new heart were given one, the price would be over $3 billion for Medicare beneficiaries alone. If the kidney dialysis experience were repeated, and coverage were extended to the whole population, the cost would be over $10 billion annually.

These staggering numbers help explain why federal health officials were so hesitant to extend Medicare coverage to heart transplants. Medicare officials realized that once they began funding heart transplants, there would be immense pressure to extend coverage to everyone in need. The simple truth is that, in deciding who gets a new treatment, the line will be drawn where the money stops.

IV. *Expanding Medicare to Cover Heart Transplants*

In mid-1986, federal officials bowed to professional and political pressure. On October 17, 1986, they announced that Medicare would soon begin to cover heart transplants. On April 6, 1987, the HCFA issued a ruling that formally extended Medicare coverage to heart transplants. Coverage was extended retroactively to October 17, 1986.

In its "summary and final expenditure estimate," HCFA projected that Medicare would cover 98 heart transplants in fiscal year 1988, with an increase in federal expenditures of $10 million. By 1990, the cost would be an estimated $20 million.

How are these estimates to be reconciled with the results of the Battelle study? The answer is that in the ruling Medicare did not extend Medicare coverage to all potential transplant recipients.

First, a patient must receive disability benefits for 29 months before even qualifying for Medicare benefits. However, by statute, this is not a requirement for kidney dialysis and kidney transplant patients. This limits the number of potential recipients in two ways: (1) many patients needing a new heart simply die before their 29-

month waiting period ends, and, (2) those that have been on disability long enough tend to be older, and many of them will be disqualified because of their age.

Second, the HCFA ruling sharply limits coverage in two ways. Patient selection criteria were established that substantially shrank the pool of eligible patients. . . .

The HCFA ruling also rations heart transplants by restricting the number of hospitals that can qualify for Medicare reimbursement. It imposes minimum standards for experience, commitment of resources and professional expertise, success, and patient selection. . . .

Under these strict criteria, Medicare officials have estimated that only 10 medical centers will qualify for heart transplant funding. The HCFA acknowledged that these criteria both limit the number of facilities approved for reimbursement and preclude some patients from receiving heart transplants. In fact, the cost saving was estimated to be about $25 million in 1990, or half the program's total cost. HCFA stated that, in adopting the criteria, it "did not propose to assure an even geographic distribution" of facilities and stated that it recognized "the hardship that this may place on some transplant recipients and their families." Despite this, HCFA maintained that the criteria would ensure a successful clinical outcome and that "the issue of geographic access will diminish over time as more centers gain the necessary experience to meet the criteria." Thus, those patients whose financial status precludes them from traveling to a qualified facility must wait until their local hospital meets these criteria.

By adopting these limitations on eligibility, Medicare officials obtained an easily enforced limit on the number of transplants. Without acknowledging it, Medicare officials have opted for rationing — to limit costs of this advanced medical technology.

V. *Rationing Advanced Medical Techniques.* . . .

From now on, with each new medical technique that emerges, society must answer two related questions: (1) Will this technique be made available to all, regardless of cost? and, (2) If not, how will it be distributed?

The first question, of course, is one of the macroallocation of resources between health and other programs, and among health programs. In answering it, society must examine the effect of allocation on anonymous "statistical lives." The second inquiry is one of microallocation, or rationing. Here society is forced to examine the effect of its decisions — often matters of life and death — on identified individuals. Unfortunately, those who advocate rationing often underestimate the moral, practical, and legal obstacles.

A. Let the Market Do Its Work

A market system rations based on ability and willingness to pay. Ordinarily, the market determines access to most goods and services. If people want something enough, they will pay its market price. The advantages of a market economy, to all citizens, outweigh the fact that many cannot afford to pay the market price for some things and, therefore, must do without them, no matter how badly they are desired.

While financial ability is accepted as the means of distributing most goods, society has generally taken a different approach to medical care. There was public outrage in 1985 when the *Washington Post* reported that rich foreign nationals were receiving a disproportionate percentage of kidney transplants in the Washington, D.C. area. The foreign nationals' ability to pay more for a transplant than that provided by private insurance or public funds made them more valuable, and therefore more attractive, patients.

The report of the President's Commission for the Study of Ethical Problems in Medicine and Behavioral Research reflected a widely accepted belief that society has an ethical obligation to ensure equitable access to health care for all. It asserted: "[A]ll citizens should be able to secure an adequate level of care without excessive burdens."

With the enactment of Medicare and Medicaid, the federal government rejected a purely market approach to providing medical care. It decided that American society was rich enough and humane enough to make provision for the medical needs of the elderly and the poor. . . .

. . . [E]ven if routine medical care were distributed on the basis of ability to pay, society might well reject that method when the patient's life is at stake. Furthermore, it will be difficult to deny Medicare coverage of transplants for people who could return to healthy, productive lives while continuing to provide, for example, kidney dialysis treatments for elderly, comatose patients, as is now the case.

Assuming that society decides that ability to pay or the possession of private insurance should not alone decide who gets access to advanced medical techniques, what else is there that does not open the floodgates to additional and uncontrolled spending? This takes us to the next form of rationing — putative medical criteria.

B. Establish Strict Medical Criteria

Once it is concluded that rationing is necessary, reliance on medical criteria is, perhaps, the most acceptable approach. It is certainly the most rational — selecting patients for treatment by deciding who can benefit most therefrom. Moreover, it corresponds with public perceptions of how medical treatment decisions are made.

But the issue is more complicated if, as with heart transplants, there are more who can benefit than there are available hearts. Physicians are then asked to choose who has the greatest chance of survival.

Medical selection standards are currently being used to ration heart transplants. Generally, patients who can pay for a transplant (or who have insurance or Medicare or Medicaid that will pay) are deemed eligible if they have a critical medical need for a transplant, that is, they have less than a 25 percent likelihood of surviving more than six months. Most often, they are invalids for whom no other treatment is expected to be successful. But since there are more who qualify even under these strict criteria, further screening is necessary.

When HHS invited transplant centers to participate in the Battelle study, it published suggested eligibility criteria developed by the National Heart, Lung, and Blood Institute. The criteria illustrate the kinds of complex, subjective factors involved in an honest assessment of medical eligibility.

The guidelines are presented to demonstrate that there is no magic line that separates those whose condition justifies a transplant and those whose do not. Although the criteria vary somewhat, the six participating hospitals generally followed these criteria, which can be summarized as follows:

1. Advancing age, beyond the age (usually 50 or 55) at which the "individual begins to have diminished capacity to withstand postoperative complications."
2. Comorbid conditions, including severe pulmonary hypertension, severe liver or kidney dysfunction, active systemic infection, recent pulmonary infarction, insulin-requiring diabetes mellitus, significant peripheral or cerebrovascular disease, acute peptic ulcers, or any other systemic disease "likely to limit or preclude survival and rehabilitation after transplantation."
3. History of a behavior pattern (including drug or alcohol addiction) or psychiatric illness "likely to interfere significantly with compliance with a disciplined medical regimen."
4. "Absence of adequate external psychosocial supports for either short or long term."

Physicians undoubtedly would describe all of these criteria as medical. That is, they are designed to produce a successful clinical outcome. For example, some of the "comorbid conditions" are considered disqualifying because a patient who has one of these conditions may be unable to survive a transplant or the use of immunosuppressive drugs, which are necessary to avoid rejection of the transplant. Similarly, behavioral history and external psychosocial supports are considered relevant to the patient's ability to adapt to the necessary alterations of lifestyle, including adherence to a strict diet, medication regimen, and other restrictions. . . .

[T]he vague and undefined nature of these criteria afford the decision maker wide discretion to act in accordance with personal values. That may be true even though facially valid criteria are being applied. For example, the transplant policy of one Washington, D.C. hospital, after outlining a set of explicit "clinical factors," goes on to state that such factors are "unique to each case" and that it is difficult to form and adhere to any set of explicit rules concerning them.

Some of these criteria may be valid as threshold qualifications. For example, an alcoholic derelict may have no prospect of adopting the necessary post-operative regimen. However, when the criteria are employed as relative qualifications (who has the optimum external supports), the result may be to favor the patient whose lifestyle reflects that of the decisionmaker. . . .

C. The Egalitarian Approach — Use a Queue or a Lottery

Assuming that X dollars are available for a particular medical treatment and that basic medical suitability is established (recognizing that even this is an ambiguous concept), access could be determined by random selection. Under a lottery, after a pool of those needing treatment is developed, final selection is done by the luck of the draw. The draft lotteries of the not so distant past provide an apt picture of how a lottery might be approached. As need be, the names of winners could be pulled from the wicker basket or the bouncing ping-pong balls.

Lotteries expose the arbitrariness of random decision making processes, and it is not surprising that research uncovered only one example of a medical lottery, the Los Angeles procedures for determining access to kidney dialysis described earlier.

A queue has received more serious consideration. The Massachusetts Task Force on Organ Transplantation, for example, recommended a queue system because "it most closely approximates the randomness of a straight lottery, without having [the] obviousness of making equity the only value being promoted."[70] In the manner of a bread line, advanced medical techniques could be rationed on the

---

70. Department of Public Health, Commonwealth of Massachusetts, Report of the Massachusetts Task Force on Organ Transplantation 81 (1984) (hereinafter Massachusetts Task Force Report).

basis of "first come, first served." A waiting list could be established, then published, so that people know where they stand in line, much as is done for many public housing projects.

Rationing by queue takes place in Britain, where many patients must wait considerable periods of time — even years — for many surgical procedures. After being referred for treatment, patients are added to a waiting list, and then must wait their turn in the queue for treatment, although exceptions are made for emergencies. . . .

. . . [B]oth lotteries and queues can produce results that are most charitably described as anomalous. They can award a new heart to a 65-year-old person but deny one to an individual who is 45 years old. At the extreme, they can award a new heart to a convicted murderer while letting the mother of five children or a research scientist die. Remember the mini-uproar when the first Swedish artificial heart was implanted in a tax dodger. Such results might well offend notions of fairness and efficiency,[76] and could be seen as a "capitulation to irrationality."[77]

Certainly, a lottery or a queue system that would deny a new heart to the President of the United States would be unacceptable. It has been suggested that some "escape valve" from the queue be permitted for an individual expected to make a contribution that he or she alone can make and that is "related to a concern which society values more than the life of one man."

It is likely that an egalitarian approach would add utilitarian considerations to the process. For example, the Massachusetts Task Force, although proposing a queue to avoid using "conscious, value-laden, social worth selection criteria" of the sort employed by the Seattle Artificial Kidney Center, nevertheless described the purpose of the initial medical screening as offering "transplantation to those who can benefit the most from it in terms of probability of living for a significant period of time with a reasonable prospect for rehabilitation." Thus, it is clear that even a random system may employ social worth criteria.

The problem lies in deciding who, besides the President, should get a new heart. What, then, can be said about such explicitly utilitarian rationing?

---

76. Annas, The Prostitute, the Playboy, and the Poet: Rationing Schemes for Organ Transplantation, 75 Am. J. Pub. Health 187, 188 (1985).

77. Bayer, Justice and Health Care in an Era of Cost Containment, 9 Soc. Responsibility 37, 39 (1983).

D. The Utilitarian Approach — Determine the Social Worth of Providing Treatment

A utilitarian rationing scheme would explicitly employ the kinds of social worth criteria that are an implicit element in many medical criteria. Social worth criteria could be used to measure the value to society of saving an individual's life. Considerations could include the patient's occupation, marital status and family size, religious/moral attributes, intelligence, economic status, and educational background.

It seems highly unlikely that evaluation of social worth by any of these criteria would be considered an acceptable basis for rationing. Principles of equality reject the notion of evaluating the relative worth of individuals. Even if such evaluations were acceptable, consensus would be achieved only at the extremes — preferring a research scientist over a mass-murderer. Otherwise, there would be no general agreement on the importance of any of these criteria. Such an approach would be reminiscent of the workings of the Seattle "God squad." . . .

Conclusion

Society has not yet been forced to adopt widespread rationing of medical care. The climate, however, is changing. With federal budget reductions, programs which, in the past, have been allowed to grow indiscriminately, will be faced with the need to cut expenditures. Assuming, for the purposes of discussion, that existing benefits will not be reduced sufficiently to pay for the provision of advanced medical technologies, this article has described the various ways in which access to them might be rationed.

Before adopting such ethically troubling schemes to decide who should live and who should die, society should sharply reconsider the open-ended and largely unquestioning way in which other medical services are provided — a practice that creates the financial pressure to ration advanced technology. The overuse of heart bypass operations has led them to be called the hysterectomies of the 1980s. Similarly, it seems impossible to justify denying heart transplants for people who could return to healthy, productive lives while continuing to use limited Medicare funds, for example, to pay for dialysis treatments of elderly, comatose patients, as is now the case. That Medicare coverage for even minor medical procedures, like bunion removals, is not based on the patient's ability to pay only magnifies the inequities of current reimbursement policies.

Asking such questions about the relative merit of different health care benefits is not for the faint of heart. It is many times more difficult to take away benefits from current recipients — and the industry groups that serve them — than it is to refuse to give a new benefit, however needed, to an amorphous group of potential beneficiaries. Entering this political and ethical thicket will require government leaders to show common sense and courage, two commodities in short supply these days. But it is worth a try. After all, heart transplants are only one of the many expensive new medical techniques that do not save money — only lives.

Ellis v. Patterson
859 F.2d 52 (8th Cir. 1988)

Brandy Ellis brought this suit in order to get a determination that the Arkansas Medicaid plan must pay for her liver transplant. The District Court denied her relief, holding that Congress left to the states the choice of whether to include organ transplants in their Medicaid plans. . . .

Brandy Ellis is a ten-month-old baby girl who suffers from a fatal liver condition, biliary atresia. If she receives a liver transplant, she has a 90 percent chance to live an active and normal life for the next five years. If she does not, then, in the opinion of her physician, Brandy Ellis will die in less than two months. The tragic facts of her medical condition are not in dispute.

Brandy was evaluated at the University of Nebraska Medical Center and determined to be a medically appropriate candidate for a liver transplant. However, before the University will add her to the list of patients waiting for livers to become available, it requires either a $110,000 deposit, or assurance of sufficient insurance to cover the procedure.

Plaintiff receives Supplemental Security Income as a disabled child, and is therefore entitled to Medicaid from the Arkansas Department of Human Services. However, the Department does not now provide for the funding of liver transplants under its Medicaid program (though, as we have noted, it has announced its intention to do so). A local fund drive raised only $3,000, and plaintiff has no health insurance other than Medicaid. Thus, unless the Department provides assurance of adequate insurance, the University of Nebraska Medical Center will not place Brandy Ellis on the waiting list for a liver transplant. . . .

Title XIX of the Social Security Act, 42 U.S.C. §1396 et seq., better known as Medicaid, is a federal-state cooperative program designed to provide medical assistance to indigents. Under the program, the states devise their own medical-assistance plans, which are funded in part by the federal government. A state is not required to participate in Medicaid, but once it elects to do so, it must establish a state plan that comports with federal statutory and regulatory requirements. 42 U.S.C. §1396a.

II. Regulatory Reforms

Section 1396d(a)(1)-(5) requires participating states to provide inpatient hospital services; out-patient hospital services, other laboratory and x-ray services, skilled nursing facilities, and physicians' services. Relying on language in Beal v. Doe, 432 U.S. 438 (1977),[5] courts have held that Medicaid must fund these services whenever they are "medically necessary." See, e.g., Pinneke v. Preisser, 623 F.2d 546, 548 n.2 (8th Cir. 1980); Lee v. Page, No. 86-1081 CIV-J-14 (M.D. Fla. 1986); Allen v. Mansour, 681 F. Supp. 1232 (E.D. Mich. 1986); Simpson v. Wilson, 480 F. Supp. 97, 101 (D. Vt. 1979). The extent of medical assistance provided by the state for each service must be "sufficient in amount, duration, and scope to reasonably achieve its purpose." 42 C.F.R. §440.230(b). In addition, "[t]he Medicaid agency may not arbitrarily deny or reduce the amount, duration, or scope of a required service . . . to an otherwise eligible recipient solely because of the diagnosis, type of illness, or condition." Id. at §440.230(c).

The plaintiff contends that because the State of Arkansas must, in general, provide necessary in-patient services and cannot discriminate among Medicaid recipients on the basis of their diagnoses or illnesses, the State must fund organ transplants, including the liver transplant she desperately needs. To do otherwise would be to deny her a medically necessary service on the basis of her illness. In support of her position she notes this Court has held that "a state plan absolutely excluding the only available treatment . . . for a particular condition must be considered an arbitrary denial of benefits based solely on the 'diagnosis, type of illness, or condition.'" Pinneke v. Preisser, supra at 549. This Court has also held that states may restrict the medical assistance they offer based on the degree of medical need, but not on the type of medical disorder. Hodgson v. Board of County Comm'rs, 614 F.2d 601, 610-11 (8th Cir. 1980). One court has modified a state's Medicaid plan to cover liver transplants after applying these principles. In Lee v. Page, supra, the Court rejected the state's fiscal arguments and ruled that Florida Medicaid must fund liver transplants where medically necessary.

This line of analysis is appropriate in the usual case where a state denies a necessary medical service to a Medicaid recipient based on that person's diagnosis. However, as the State aptly observes, organ transplants are a special situation. In 1985 and again in 1987 Congress

---

5. The Court stated

[a]lthough serious statutory questions might be presented if a state Medicaid plan excluded necessary medical treatment from its coverage, it is hardly inconsistent with the objectives of the Act for a State to refuse to fund *unnecessary* — though perhaps desirable — medical services.

Id. at 444-45 (emphasis in original).

amended the Medicaid statute to add a section governing payments for organ transplants. 42 U.S.C. §1396b(i).[6] The statute itself can be read as merely laying out additional standards the states must meet to receive federal funds for organ transplants, but the legislative history of the provision reveals that Congress intended the states to have discretion whether to include organ transplants in their Medicaid plans. . . . Allowing the states some discretion in the funding of medical procedures is, after all, consistent with the policy behind the Medicaid Act: federal appropriations are "[f]or the purpose of enabling each State, *as far as practicable under the conditions in such State,*" to furnish medical assistance to the needy. 42 U.S.C. §1396. Other limitations on medically necessary services, such as the number of physician visits, Curtis v. Taylor, 625 F.2d 645 (5th Cir. 1980), or in-hospital days, Charleston Memorial Hosp. v. Conrad, 693 F.2d 324 (4th Cir. 1982), have been permitted as reasonable. And we think plaintiff's position that all organ transplants (including hearts and lungs) must be covered by Medicaid is unrealistic. Surely Congress did not intend to require the states to provide funds for exotic surgeries which, while they might be the individual patient's only hope for survival, would also have a small chance of success and carry an enormous price tag. Medicaid was not designed to fund risky, unproven procedures, but to provide the largest number of necessary medical services to the greatest number of needy people. Thus, we hold the State of Arkansas is not required to fund organ transplants under Medicaid, and that it may choose which kinds of organ transplants, if any, to cover. . . .

This holding (on which we agree with the District Court) does not end Brandy Ellis's case, however. The situation has changed dramatically since plaintiff filed her suit. The State has now decided to modify its Medicaid plan to provide funding for some additional organ transplants, including liver transplants. We expect the State will proceed with the formulation, approval, and adoption of the announced plan with all practicable speed. Counsel so stated at oral argument. But we cannot assume that the plan adopted will be adequate in practice to provide a Medicaid recipient with an organ

---

6. 42 U.S.C. §1396b(i) provides in pertinent part:

>Payment under the preceding provisions of this section shall not be made —
> (1) for organ transplant procedures unless the State plan provides for written standards respecting the coverage of such procedures and unless such standards provide that —
>   (A) similarly situated individuals are treated alike; and
>   (B) any restriction on the facilities or practitioners which may provide such procedures is consistent with the accessibility of high quality care to individuals eligible for the procedures under the State plan . . .
>
>Nothing in paragraph (1) shall be construed as permitting a State to provide services under its plan under this subchapter that are not reasonable in amount, duration, and scope to achieve their purpose.

transplant. For example, a ceiling on transplant funding so low as to prevent a patient from getting on a hospital waiting list — let alone actually pay for the surgery — would in fact deprive her of a transplant. To deny services arbitrarily and unreasonably to an otherwise eligible Medicaid recipient in this manner would be impermissible. See Montoya v. Johnston, 654 F. Supp. 511, 514 (W.D. Tex. 1987). There are some medical procedures, such as transplants, which Medicaid participation does not obligate the states to provide. However, once these optional services are undertaken, they must be reasonably funded. See, e.g., Montoya, supra; Meyers v. Reagan, 776 F.2d 241 (8th Cir. 1985). Thus, we remand this case to the District Court with directions to review the modified plan when it comes out and to ascertain whether it actually makes possible the transplants which it is intended to provide. The plan must, in the words of Section 1396b(i), be sufficient to provide services reasonable in amount, scope, and duration to achieve their purpose. . . .

The judgment of the District Court is accordingly vacated, and the case is remanded for further proceedings consistent with this opinion.

NOTES

The Rationing of Organ Transplants

1. The number of heart and other organ transplants performed annually has skyrocketed since the 1983 introduction of cyclosporin, the highly effective immune-reaction suppressing drug. Surgeons now perform 1800 heart transplants each year, 1200 liver, 9000 kidney, and 1500 bone marrow. Chapter 9.II.A.2 discusses new strategies for greatly increasing organ donations. If these strategies prove effective, the number of transplants could take another quantum leap.

Liver transplants cost about $250,000 each, heart and bone marrow transplants $100,000, and kidney transplants $30,000. Cyclosporin is expensive and must be taken for the remainder of the patient's life, at an annual cost of about $6000. See Roberts, The Economics of Organ Transplants, 25 Jurimetrics 256 (1985). Because cyclosporin suppresses the body's immune system, it leads to multiple infections, which are usually treated with expensive antibiotics. The cost of follow-up care for the 19 liver transplantations funded in Oregon from 1985 to 1987 was $24,000 per year, yet only 9 of these patients survived to 1988. Welch & Larson, Dealing with Limited Resources, 319 New Eng. J. Med. 171 (1988).

Where, if anywhere, should we set a limit on such expenditures? Imagine that you are in charge of allocating limited government health care funds between (1) a large expansion in low-cost prenatal care, which would help decrease the high costs of caring for premature births, and (2) a few expensive organ transplants. Would you fund a liver transplant for a patient whose recovery is only 50 percent certain? For a patient with only partial liver disfunction whose life is not at stake? For an alcoholic? Would you support lung transplants for cigarette smokers? Heart transplants for overeaters?

2. Ellis v. Patterson and the dilemma over whether to limit funding for organ transplants highlight the major problem that confronts rationers of health care: statistical vs. identifiable lives. While it is easy to observe in the abstract that it is more cost effective to spend on preventative, primary care that will lower the incidence of disease and injury than to spend on high-cost and high-technology interventions for those who are ill, it is very difficult effectively to sentence identifiable persons to suffering or death in favor of a statistical lowering of disease in unidentifiable persons. "To many, it seems morally more important to help identifiable individuals than to do what we perceive will only statistically avert some harm to people whose identity we do not yet know." P. Menzel, Medical Costs, Moral Choices at 159 (1983). See also Havighurst, Blumstein & Bovbjerg, Strategies in Underwriting the Costs of Catastrophic Disease, 40 L. & Comtemp. Prob. 122 (1976); Blumstein, Rationing Medical Resources: A Constitutional, Legal, and Policy Analysis, 59 Tex. L. Rev. 1345 (1981).

3. Besharov's & Silver's article addresses two levels of the rationing decision for heart transplants: (i) the "macro" decision of whether to fund the procedure at all, and if so, (ii) the "micro" decision of who receives priority in allocating the limited supply of transplantable organs. Addressing the first issue, consider the following: "[An] analysis compar[ing] the costs and outcome of heart transplantation with those of conventional care for congestive heart failure yield[ed] a figure of $23,000 [to $33,700] per added year of life. . . . By comparison, in 1984 dollars, coronary-artery bypass grafting cost about $10,000 per added year of life, [and] hemodialysis for [kidney failure] about $32,000. . . . Treatment of [AIDS] costs about $140,000 per case." Casscells, Heart Transplantation: Recent Policy Developments, 315 New Eng. J. Med. 1365, 1366 (1986). See also Centerwall, Cost-Benefit Analysis and Heart Transplantation, 304 New Eng. J. Med. 901 (1981) (impossible to obtain an accurate quantification of costs and benefits).

Considering the micro-level issue, should the decision be based purely on maximizing medical benefit (in terms of the probability of life-years saved), or should other factors be considered (such as who is in the most desperate need or who has been on the list the longest). To focus your thinking on this difficult issue, consider whether you would prefer a heart-transplant patient whose chance of survival would increase from 70 to 100 percent over one whose chances would increase from 20 to 40 percent.

II. Regulatory Reforms

4. The federal government has contracted with the United Network for Organ Sharing ("UNOS") to develop a national organ allocation system. Hospitals are required to adhere to UNOS policies in order to participate in Medicare and Medicaid.

> UNOS has developed point systems for the allocation of hearts and livers as well as kidneys. . . . The UNOS point system for cadaveric kidneys . . . requires that [they] be offered to patients on the local waiting list . . . in descending order [of point totals]. Points are assigned according to time on the waiting list (maximum 10 points); quality of [tissue compatibility] . . . for a maximum of [22 points]; medical urgency, which is usually not granted if dialysis is feasible (maximum of 10 points); and logistical score, based on ease and rapidity of performance of the transplant (maximum of 6 points). . . . [These] criteria, [ ] are not value-free or value-neutral. The vigorous debate about how much weight each criterion should have is . . . to a great extent ethical. Some factors, such as quality of [tissue compatibility] and logistical score, focus on the chance of successful outcome; [ ] medical urgency . . . focus[es] on patient need . . . ; and time on the waiting list introduces a nonmedical factor. . . . The points assigned to these various factors thus reflect value judgments about the relative importance of patient need, probability of success, and time of waiting.

Childress, Ethical Criteria for Procuring and Distributing Organs for Transplantation, 14 J. Health Pol. Poly. & L. 87, 104-105 (1989).

Is it wise policy to impose uniform organ allocation criteria on all hospitals? To delegate these crucial decisions to a private agency? Does the UNOS point system preclude a hospital from honoring an individual's decision to donate an organ to a specified individual such as a friend or family member? See Blumstein, Federal Organ Transplantation Policy: A Time for Reassessment?, 22 U.C. Davis L. Rev. 451, 487 (1989) (criticizing federal policy and noting this unresolved conflict between state and federal law).

5. Ellis v. Patterson outlines the law respecting the obligation of Medicaid (the federally financed program for the poor) to fund organ transplants. The furthest extension of the "medically necessary" standard crafted from the Supreme Court's Beal v. Doe dictum is a group of cases that require Medicaid to fund sex change operations. Rush v. Parham, 625 F.2d 1150 (5th Cir. 1980); Pinneke v. Preisser, 623 F.2d 546 (8th Cir. 1980). See also 686 supra.

Ellis stands apart from a number of other decisions that have unambiguously mandated Medicaid funding for liver transplant surgery. In Lee v. Page, No. 86-1081-Civ-J14 (M.D. Fla. Dec. 19, 1986), the court held that "there is no basis in the law for Florida to determine that this procedure is not medically necessary by comparing the costs and benefits of liver transplantation with other services." The *Montoya* decision, which *Ellis* discusses, declared invalid a $50,000 cap on Medicaid transplant funding. A third court has invalidated a liver transplant policy that required former alcoholics to document a two-year period of abstinence. Allen v. Mansour, 681 F. Supp. 1232 (E.D. Mich. 1986). See also DiDomenico v. Employers Cooperative Indus. Trust, No. F87-322 (N.D. Ind., Nov. 24, 1987) (ordering private insurer to cover liver transplant); National Health Law Program, Medicaid Transplant Litigation Proliferates, 21 Clearinghouse Rev. 20 (1987) (collecting cases); Havighurst & King, Liver Transplantation in Massachusetts: Public Policymaking in Morality Play, 19 Ind. L. Rev. 955 (1986).

As *Ellis* quotes in footnote 6, in order for state Medicaid programs to receive federal support for organ transplants, the state must adopt a plan providing "written standards . . . that similarly situated individuals are treated alike. 42 U.S.C. 1396(i)(1)(A)." In Todd v. Sorrell, 841 F.2d 87 (4th Cir. 1988), the court held that the plaintiff's liver condition was close enough to those described in the state plan that coverage was required by this nondiscrimination standard. Is *any* discrimination among the types of transplants covered allowed in view of the prohibition of handicapped discrimination contained in §504 of the Rehabilitation Act of 1974? See Chapter 6.II.B; Merrikan and Overcast, Patient Selection for Heart Transplantation: When is a Discriminating Choice Discrimination?, 10 J. Health Pol. Poly. & L. 7 (1985).

6. A few state legislatures have bitten the bullet and refused Medicaid funding for the more costly adult organ transplants, in favor of beefing up primary and preventative care programs such as prenatal care. Oregon and Arizona were the first to take this step, and Virginia has also recently restricted transplant funding. (Oregon subsequently qualified its decision by agreeing to reinstate funding if sufficient private support could be raised, but it has not yet been seen whether this will occur.) See BioLaw, at U:848, U:881, U:931 (1988).

7. For additional discussion of the selection criteria for individual transplant recipients and the role of federal policy, see Report of the Massachusetts Task Force on Organ Transplantation, reprinted in 13 L. Med. & Health Care 8 (1985); Annas, The Prostitute, The Playboy, and the Poet: Rationing Schemes for Organ Transplantation, 75 Am. J. Pub. Health 187 (Feb. 1985); Annas, Allocation of Artificial Hearts in the Year 2002, 3 Am. J.L. & Med. 59 (1977); Blumstein, Government's Role in Organ Transplantation Policy, 14 J. Health Pol. Poly. & L. 5 (1989); Childress, Some Moral Connections Between Organ Procurement and Organ Distribution, 3 J. Contemp. Health L. & Poly. 85, 94 (1987); Note, Due Process in the Allocation of Scarce Life-saving Medical Resources, 84 Yale L.J. 1734 (1975).

On transplant funding issues generally, see Cotton & Sandler, The Regulation of Organ Procurement and Transplantation, 7 J.

Leg. Med. 55 (1986); Cowan et al., Human Organ Transplantation: Societal, Medical-Legal, Regulatory, and Reimbursement Issues (1987) (extensive bibliography); Schuck, Government Funding for Organ Transplants, 14 J. Health Pol. Poly. & L. 169 (1989).

III. COMPETITIVE REFORMS

A. The Role of Competition in the Health Care Sector

A. Enthoven, Health Plan*
3, 12, 93-95, 111-113 (1980)

The fundamental strategic choice for public policy on health care costs is competition or regulation. . . .

The choice between competition and regulation is a choice about the role of government. In the strategy of competition the government takes a much simpler and less intrusive role than in the regulatory approach. It seeks to set the basic framework of rules and incentives in such a way that the market (that is, the interaction of people making transactions in their own best interests) will produce the desired result. In the regulatory approach applied to health care, the government takes on a much more complex and demanding role, a role in which, in my view, it is bound to fail. In the regulatory approach government would leave today's cost-increasing incentives in place and then try to stop them from having their natural effect by direct detailed controls such as telling doctors how much they can charge for each service. In this approach direct controls are intended to substitute for rational economic incentives. In my view, the regulatory approach is like trying to make water run uphill, whereas in the competitive market approach the government is merely trying to channel the stream in its downhill course.

Procompetitive regulation is likely to be much simpler and more effective than direct controls on prices, capacity, and use of services, which act in opposition to the financial incentives. For in this case the basic incentives are pointing people in about the right direction. The regulators are attempting merely to modify the behavior of the regulated at the margin. . . .

On the other hand, under the regulatory approach, the regulators are attempting to make regulated entities behave in ways that are directly opposed to their financial interests, possibly even threatening

* Copyright © 1980, Addison-Wesley Publishing Co., Inc., Reading, Massachusetts. Reprinted by permission.

their survival. Therefore, the incentive to attempt to bend, fight, or evade the regulations is much stronger. . . .

Regulation often raises costs to consumers. Regulators become responsible for the economic survival of the regulated. If they let a regulated entity fail, they will be blamed for denying society a needed service and for causing a loss of jobs. So they cannot force the regulated to sustain losses or even to live with less than some target rate of return on investment. So cost increases have to be "passed through" to consumers, and price controls become cost reimbursement, with all of its cost-increasing incentives.

Regulators are often "captured" by the regulated. They must get their information about the regulated industry from the regulated. The regulated firms hire high-priced lawyers and lobbyists who exert a constant pressure in their favor. The consumer interest in lower prices or better service is too diffused to allow for an effectively organized counterpressure. The formal procedures of regulation also make it very costly and time-consuming. This is especially true if there are many entities to be regulated, with many special circumstances to be considered, as is the case with physicians and hospitals. All this helps explain why, for example, for many years, intrastate air travel, beyond the reach of the Civil Aeronautics Board, cost about half as much as interstate flights of the same length. Similarly, Interstate Commerce Commission regulation of trucking has added billions of dollars to the costs to customers.

Competition, on the other hand, sets up an inexorable force for cost reduction. If company B can make a product of equal quality to company A's, but for less cost, it can sell it for a lower price and take the business away from company A. If company A cannot match the cost reduction, it will lose profits in the short run and risk being driven out of business in the long run. Survival demands that it cut costs. It has no regulators to appeal to for protection. . . .

Competition rewards innovation and often channels it in socially desirable directions. Fortunes are made on new products and services, so innovations that lead to better services or reduced costs are encouraged. Firms that do not match their competitors' innovations often do not survive.

Market economies are the most effective in improving productivity and raising living standards. There are good reasons for this. People accept efficiency-improving changes such as closing unneeded plants or hospitals produced by impersonal market forces in the private sector. The people directly affected may not like them, but there is not much they can do about them. In the long run the whole economy benefits. But when such changes are imposed by government, those who would be harmed resist them, usually successfully, through legal and political action. . . .

III. Competitive Reforms

In market systems producers and consumers adapt continuously and gradually to changing conditions, even in anticipation of future events. The expectation of higher gasoline prices in the future motivates people to buy cars with good mileage now. In regulatory systems the rules themselves create vested interests which make the rules very difficult to change. These factors make for great rigidity in regulated industries, in contrast to flexible adaptation in markets.

Government often responds to well-focused producer interests; competitive markets respond systematically, if imperfectly, to consumer interests. Voters base their choices on issues of decisive personal importance, on their pocketbooks if they see their livelihoods at stake. People specialize in production and diversify in consumption. To a dairy farmer, a rise in coffee prices is a minor irritant, but an increase in the price of milk (supported by government) is a "make-or-break" issue. People are therefore much more likely to pressure their representatives about the issues that affect their livelihoods than on their interests as consumers, and their companies and unions provide natural organizations for doing so. In competitive markets companies get their revenues from satisfied customers who have alternative choices. So in product and pricing decisions, business must seek to serve the desires of consumers. Thus the choice between a regulated and a competitive market system of health care services is a choice between service that responds mainly to the interests of providers or to those of consumers.

Regulation depends on coercion, on forcing people to behave in ways they consider opposed to their own best interests. The decentralized competitive market, on the other hand, leaves maximum freedom to individual providers and consumers consistent with achievement of society's purposes. As Charles Schultze put it:

> Relationships in the market are a form of unanimous-consent arrangement. When dealing with each other in a buy-sell transaction, individuals can act voluntarily on the basis of mutual advantage. . . . Market-like arrangements not only minimize the need for coercion as a means of organizing society; they also reduce the need for compassion, patriotism, brotherly love, and cultural solidarity as motivating forces behind social improvement.

The development of these desirable virtues is more likely to be encouraged if we do not place too heavy a burden on people who practice them. Moreover, the market encourages the pluralism and diversity that is valued by the American people. The regulatory approach works on the basis of uniform numerical standards. . . .

A patient's needs, preferences, and lifestyle are important. Consider a woman who likes to ski and ride horseback and who has a partially detached retina in one eye. One ophthalmologist believes in an operation that does a minimum amount of "welding" (photocoagulation) and would minimize her loss of vision. Although that might satisfy the physician's criterion of technical excellence, it does not allow the woman to resume her athletic pursuits safely. Another ophthalmologist might propose to coagulate a complete circle around her retina. In this case the patient would lose some vision, but would have more of a guarantee that the retina will not detach again, and she could ski and ride again.

Patients suffering from severe angina pectoris (chest pain thought to be due to a lack of oxygen supply to the heart) pose another therapeutic dilemma. One doctor may recommend heart surgery; another, treatment with drugs such as nitroglycerine. For most such patients, there is no consensus among physicians today as to which is the better treatment.

What is "best" in a particular case will depend on the values and needs of the patient, the skills of the doctor, and the other resources available. The quality of the outcome depends a great deal on how the patient feels about it. What is an annoyance for one patient may mean the inability to keep a job for another with the same condition. . . .

Fuchs, Who Shall Live? Health, Economics and Social Choice
4-5 (1974)

The economic point of view is rooted in three fundamental observations about the world. The first is that resources are scarce in relation to human wants. . . . Some advances in technology (e.g., automated laboratories) make it possible to carry out current activities with fewer resources, but others open up new demands (e.g., for renal dialysis or organ transplants) that put further strains on resources. . . .

The second observation is that resources have alternative uses. . . . If we want more hospitals, we can get them only at the expense of more housing, or factories, or something else that could use the same land, capital, and labor.

Finally, economists note that people do indeed have different wants, and that there is significant variation in the relative importance that people attach to them. The oft-heard statement, "Health is the most important goal," does not accurately describe human behavior. Everyday in manifold ways (such as overeating or smoking) we make choices that . . . place a higher value on satisfying other wants.

Given these three conditions, the basic economic problem is how to allocate scarce resources so as to best satisfy human wants. This point of view may be contrasted with two others: . . . the *romantic* and the *monotechnic*. The romantic point of view fails to recognize the scarcity of resources relative to wants. . . . [It] confus[es] the real world with the Garden of Eden. . . . The monotechnic point of view, frequently found among physicians, . . . fails to recognize the multiplicity of human wants and the diversity of individual preferences.

NOTES

The Case in Favor of Competition

1. The case in favor of competition can take on a moral cast:

[E]ven if [economic regulation] should succeed in imposing effective controls, it would do so at the expense of important values. . . . Regulation's chief tendency is [ ] toward narrowing consumers' range of choice, enforcing a false consensus, and obscuring the wide variations that exist in both consumer preferences and medical practice. [I]t would seem more appropriate in a pluralistic society to widen opportunities for consumer choice under meaningful cost constraints.

C. Havighurst, Deregulating the Health Care Industry 49-50 (1982).

2. The case against regulation is bolstered by one estimate that places the cost of health care "bureaucracy" at $77.7 billion annually! Himmelstein, Cost Without Benefit: Administrative Waste in U.S. Health Care, 314 New Eng. J. Med. 441 (1986).

Rosenblatt, Health Care, Markets, and Democratic Values*
34 Vand. L. Rev. 1067 (1981)

I. Introduction

Proposals to restructure the health care industry by increasing market competition currently have much political and academic momentum. Whether such proposals will work necessarily depends in part upon the criteria for success that are applied. Viewed from the market perspective, the question is whether procompetitive reforms will achieve their stated goals of containing costs, increasing efficiency, and enhancing consumer sovereignty over health care decisions. From

---

* Professor of Law, Rutgers University Law School — Camden, B.A., 1966, Harvard College; M.Sc. (Econ.), 1967, London School of Economics; J.D., 1971, Yale University.
Copyright © 1981, Vanderbilt Law Review. Reprinted by permission.

a broader perspective, other questions are also of concern: whether increased competition in health care will actually improve people's health, and whether the operations and effects of health care competition are consistent with important values such as individual dignity, democracy, and equality. These questions need to be seriously addressed, if not finally answered, before the federal and state governments embark on a policy of widespread market reform. . . .

The purpose of this Article is to articulate the major problems with the currently popular market perspective. The Article does not suggest that either the traditional fee-for-service system, which delegates an enormous amount of unaccountable power to the medical profession, or the compromised and limited efforts at government regulation, is markedly superior. Nor does it suggest that there is an easily available fourth perspective to help define and organize the complex task of necessary reform. This Article does contend, however, that a fourth perspective is both desirable and is beginning to be developed, at least in a preliminary form. This perspective recognizes the inadequacy of both professional norms and individual income as the primary means of organizing and distributing health care, and attempts to build a democratic social process to make what are inevitably social as well as individual decisions about health care delivery.

II. *The Market Approach to Health Care Delivery: An Overview.* . . .

1. *Individual Competition*

Those market advocates who follow the individual model focus almost exclusively on the health care consumer. From this perspective, the commodity being purchased is a service such as a particular diagnostic test or surgical procedure. The important transactions are the consumer's choice of physician, and the decision whether to follow the physician's advice or perhaps seek a second opinion. To make these decisions economically rational ones, the market proponents recommend tax policies that would induce consumers to limit their health insurance to catastrophic or major risks. Under this model, most of the patient's health care costs — up to ten, fifteen, or even twenty percent of annual income — would be paid for out of current assets. According to the market advocates, this cost-sharing would make patients highly conscious of the relative costs and benefits of treatment and would lead to consumer pressure on hospitals and doctors to operate more efficiently, without requiring other major changes in the financing or organization of health care. The model of reducing insurance and imposing heavy costs on individual patients generally is not viewed as including the poor, whose lack of funds

III. Competitive Reforms

would make their choices coerced rather than rational. Instead, proponents of the individual competition model usually favor — though without extensive discussion — some form of subsidy for low income persons to enable them to have the same purchasing power as persons with average or median income. . . .

2. *Entrepreneurial Competition*

Some market advocates accept many of the premises of individual competition but take a more complex view of both the commodity that is or should be sold and the difficulty of promoting efficient health care delivery. One of these advocates, Professor Clark Havighurst, believes that health transactions not only involve particular medical services, but also have a brokering or "middleman" function. Havighurst suggests that the patient needs an "expert intermediary" to help him make efficient choices in the complex world of health care. While an individual physician facing a cost-conscious patient might play this role, the current system of reimbursing doctors for particular services rendered creates a powerful economic incentive for doctors to provide services of doubtful medical benefit, and thereby to fail as expert intermediaries dedicated to efficiency.

Havighurst would change the physicians' financial incentives through a system of entrepreneurial competition. He argues that more efficient providers may be able to supply necessary health care to a given population at a cost of ten to forty percent less than the existing fee-for-service system. Furthermore, he believes that "[n]o more than a fraction of these savings . . . would have to be shared with consumers to induce their enrollment in the plan." The balance could be divided between insurance companies or other entrepreneurs and the participating physicians. Thus, under Havighurst's model, the present system of insurance payments to doctors and hospitals who often provide services of dubious medical benefit would be replaced by a price competitive system that rewards those who provide only necessary services in the most efficient manner possible. To create and maintain this type of entrepreneurial market, Havighurst would give insurance companies and health plan entrepreneurs great latitude in designing benefit packages and provider arrangements, which would allow them to appeal to a wide range of provider interests and consumer tastes and incomes. His approach would entail two principal legal changes: (1) tax incentives to allow employees to choose among competing plans and keep part of their premium savings; and (2) increased antitrust enforcement to prevent physician and hospital resistance to entrepreneurial influence.

To the extent that Havighurst relies on cost-sharing to stimulate consumer cost-consciousness, he would apparently exempt low income persons, who would be given "more comprehensive coverage" on a subsidized basis, without any or with less cost-sharing. Havighurst also believes, however, that market competition and the profit motive actually will provide advantages for the poor, since "[p]rofit-seekers are less fastidious . . . and could be expected to create opportunities for those physicians who might be attracted into deprived-area practice by the right offer. . . ."

The various models of market competition share the general theory that price competition in some form will reduce unnecessary and inefficiently provided services. They differ, however, on the complexity of the mechanisms that should be employed to instill this competition. The individual model focuses on the competition that operates at the level of the individual patient and physician. The entrepreneurial model relies on profitmaking middlemen to translate consumer demand for lower premiums into provider arrangements that will lower costs. . . .

IV. Market Competition and Health Care: The Human and Social Issues

A. Introduction

Market advocates attempt to structure the patient's relationship to health care as an economic transaction, namely, as an exchange of a commodity for money in a competitive market setting. A primary justification for increasing market competition in health care is to promote efficiency in the use and delivery of services. Some proponents argue that market competition also has value in its own right as a uniquely legitimate method of defining and promoting efficiency. It is argued that collective social decisions, however made, are inherently coercive and inevitably inefficient. Market mechanisms are said to promote only the value of individual liberty, which enables consumers to express their own preferences by their economic "votes"; otherwise, these mechanisms are considered to be value-neutral.

Despite its considerable superficial appeal, this position is misguided. The distribution of health services through competitive markets promotes at least three major and related nonneutral values. First, in a competitive market individuals are encouraged to make decisions about health care primarily from an economic perspective, as opposed to a broader, more realistic view. Second, individuals also are encouraged to perceive health care choices and health itself as an individual matter, rather than as a matter based upon a close interrelationship between individual decisions and social patterns concerning nutrition, work, environmental quality, economic opportunity, and many other factors. Last, in a competitive market, individuals in their role as citizens or government officials are encouraged to believe that the proper goal of most government policy is to encourage voluntary market transactions. As a result, issues of equality become confined to the special and limited sphere of redistributing purchasing power, the purpose of which is to permit deserving low income persons to participate in the free market. This part of the . . . Article argues that in addition to inhibiting desirable improvements in efficiency, these three aspects of the market approach generally will have a negative effect on people's health. . . .

B. Markets, Health, and Whole Individuals

1. The Nature of the Problem

Health can be understood rather simply as the absence of disease and death, and health care as a "curative defence" against both. When this is the accepted criterion, a particular medical procedure can be evaluated in terms of whether it contributes to reduced morbidity and mortality — disease and death respectively. Health care, however, also must be understood as a caring rather than purely a curative activity, the goal of which is to reduce pain and anxiety and increase the patient's sense of self-determination and quality of life. . . . From this perspective, a central need of health care reform is not more refined quantitative cost-benefit analyses, but rather a restructuring of the patient-provider relationship that ideally could increase the sense of self-determination and satisfaction for both.

The market advocates recognize that much of modern health care has both a caring and a curing function. While conceding that caring services are of "undeniable value," the market advocates also argue that this value is very difficult to measure in quantitative or statistical terms. Because of our inability to measure the benefit generated by caring services, Enthoven argues that "we cannot give a clear answer to the question of whether or not we are getting much health improvement for [the] large increases in [health] spending." In other words, although the market advocates in theory recognize the importance and value of caring services, as a practical matter these benefits are excluded from the cost-benefit analysis. The rationale for this de facto exclusion is that since the benefits of many types of health care are not clear in curative or statistical terms, they are best treated as matters of individual consumption to be paid for out of patients' own current assets, instead of from collective funds such as government programs or insurance. . . .

Enthoven uses the example of the terminal patient who may not desire life-prolonging treatment as a case in support of his thesis. Under current financing arrangements, most insurance policies would cover the expenses of such care, assuming these costs did not exceed some stated dollar or service limit. In these circumstances, the decision whether to prolong life would be made on quality of life grounds, without consideration of monetary cost to the patient. A market approach presumably would add the factor of economic cost in some form to the decision. Havighurst, for example, advocates the marketing of cheaper insurance policies that would exclude one or another form of costly care for catastrophic illnesses. As Enthoven suggests, the consumer would be permitted in such a market to opt for greater financial risk in return for more cash to expend on immediate consumption. It is more likely, however, that the vast majority of patients faced with the decision whether to incur a $25,000 liability for continued treatment, for example, would not feel that their capacity for self-determination had been expanded, nor would they be consoled by the knowledge that they had exercised their self-determination in the prior choice of premium.

2. *Childbirth, Heart Disease, and Problems in Market Approach Application*

Despite the market advocates' claims that price competition gives more power to the consumer as a whole human being, their analyses inevitably reduce consumer choice to a forced acceptance of narrowly defined risk or efficiency in the face of economic constraint. In addition, the unequal impact of that constraint, which results from substantial income inequality, and the pressures to transfer even this degree of choice to an insurance company or health plan, further restricts the consumer's already diminished capacity for choice. Enthoven's discussions of childbirth and heart disease most clearly reveal these reductionist features of the market approach, and for that reason they will be examined in detail here.

Enthoven has suggested that market competition would improve efficiency in childbirth services in two ways: (1) it would reduce the use of electronic fetal monitoring (EFM) — an electronic process for measuring both the fetal heart rate and uterine contractions during labor — and (2) it would concentrate hospital care for childbirth in large centers. In either case, his argument relies on oversimplified cost-benefit criteria. In the case of electronic monitoring, Enthoven compares the average cost per delivery — from thirty-five to seventy dollars — with newborn mortality rates in various "risk groups" and concludes that for the majority of births, the newborn mortality rate benefits probably do not justify the EFM costs. Similarly, on the issue of the volume of childbirths performed in hospitals, Enthoven relies on a study which claims that the concentration of births in large centers reduces costs per admission by fifty percent, presumably through spreading capital and labor costs over a larger number of cases, and also that it increases quality by "maintain[ing] the proficiency of the specialized personnel." In both cases, using the simple criteria of cost

III. Competitive Reforms

and benefit alone seriously distorts the issues, which in turn undermines the possibility of increased consumer self-determination.

From the perspective of the patient as a whole person, the issue whether and under what circumstances electronic monitoring should be used requires more complex, patient-centered judgments than are required in a comparison between unit costs and newborn mortality rates. At a minimum, these judgments should include the following three considerations: (1) an understanding of the childbirth process; (2) a comprehension of the advantages and limits of electronic monitoring, specifically its positive and negative effect not only on the woman's physical and mental condition, but also on her relationship to professional as well as lay care-givers; and (3) an awareness of the implications of EFM for other types of intervention such as Caesarean section operations and their attendant risks. Furthermore, it can be argued convincingly that these considerations are relevant to both the caring, quality of life model of health and the reduction in morbidity and mortality rates model. In childbirth, the pregnant woman's own subjective feelings can have a significant influence on the length of labor and other factors relating to successful delivery. Indeed, such psychosomatic reactions are typical in all areas of health care, with the exception of extreme life and death emergencies. . . .

C. Markets, Health, and Social Context

The preceding subsection argues that the market approach to health care tends to discount the caring relationship element of health and distorts the concepts of cost and benefit. A reluctance to examine and respond to the social causes of illness and unhealthy behavior, except through imposing negative economic incentives on individuals, causes part of this distortion. The market advocates' strong preference for individual negative incentives affects their approach in another context as well.

Most market advocates recognize and indeed stress that additional expenditures for health services to individuals, at least in industrial societies, yield few measurable benefits in terms of actual health indicators such as mortality and morbidity. The argument is then made that most health care is not a life and death matter at all; rather, it is a consumption choice much like any other that should be subject to the usual constraints of price competition and income inequality. The point also is made that society as a whole probably would obtain more health benefits for health dollars if the latter were spent on nutrition, environmental quality, and workplace safety, rather than on costly, inefficient, and often ineffective individual health services.

The central problem with this contention is that the same pro-market arguments currently used in the area of health care are also being advanced to reduce substantially nutrition programs for low income people, environmental regulation, and regulation of occupational health and safety. Cost-benefit analysis, it turns out, is not contained easily. For example, scholars in the academic literature, industry in litigation, and now the Reagan Administration make the argument that costs should not be incurred to improve workplace health and safety unless they can be justified by health benefits that are measurable in terms of morbidity and mortality. . . .

V. The Market, Social Class, and the Assault on the Unitary Ideal

A question of great importance about the market approach to health care delivery is how it will affect people with low incomes. By their very nature, markets respond to those consumer preferences that are expressed with money, and people with the least money, therefore, tend to have their preferences given the least attention. Market advocates are aware that some number of low income people could not afford to pay for services or insurance in a competitive health care market. Consequently, they usually propose the simple solution of income transfers — typically effected through a voucher for medical care — that would be sufficient to purchase "basic or necessary" services. . . .

Despite this apparently benign intention of the market advocates, there are strong reasons to believe that poor and low income persons will suffer grievously. A society that embraces a market approach to most of its daily economic life, including the socially sensitive area of health care, is unlikely to redistribute adequate purchasing power to people in economic need. Whether it is theoretically possible for a market society to be strongly egalitarian as well need not be definitively resolved; it is sufficient to note the major reasons why the market perspective is often inconsistent with egalitarian redistribution. First, such a society, or the dominant groups within it, are likely to have a strong belief that the income distribution produced by the market is just. Moreover, they are likely to see unequal economic rewards as necessary incentives for socially desirable qualities such as hard work, risk taking, and entrepreneurial initiative. Income redistribution — even in the form of in-kind vouchers for medical care — probably will be viewed as threatening work incentives and efficient allocation of resources. The result is likely to be policies that bear harshly particularly on the "near-poor" or "working poor," that is, persons who are able and willing to work, but whose earnings place them substantially below the median income. These workers do not fall within the traditional categories of people who are excused from the workforce such as the aged, disabled, and single parents with young children, nor are they usually so destitute that they need government assistance for survival. Income supplementation for them will tend to be viewed both as unnecessary and as threatening to the fragile work incentives at the lower end of the wage scale. Indeed, this view appears to lie behind much of the Reagan Administration's initial budget proposals.

Langwell & Moore, A Synthesis of Research on Competition in the Financing and Delivery of Health Services
5-11 (Oct. 1982)

In the health services market, the conditions necessary for the existence of a competitive market are not fully met. Basic conditions affecting market structure which have been discussed extensively in the literature are:

- Uncertainty with respect to the occurrence of illness and the efficacy of treatment which has led to the development of extensive insurance;
- The complexity and rapid technological change in medical services which has led consumers to delegate much decision-making to providers; and
- Societal commitment to the concept that access to essential health services should be guaranteed to all and has resulted in tax subsidies and public insurance programs for the poor and elderly. . . .

All of these factors create imperfections in the structure and the conduct of the market for health services. The major issues of concern for the purposes of this review are:

- Inadequate consumer information;
- Tax treatment of health insurance and medical expenses;
- Health insurance and reimbursement policies;
- Professional control of the industry;
- Nonprofit components of the market; and
- Constraints on consumer choices.

Each of these issues are discussed in the sections which follow.
Inadequate consumer information: Informed choice by *some* consumers is a precondition to the successful operation of the competitive market. Indeed, this view has been accepted by a wide range of

researchers and policymakers. Davis states, "The nature of health care is such that the consumer knows very little about the medical services he or she is buying — possibly less than about any other service purchased." . . .

Weisbrod (1978) suggests that, while rising levels of education are making patients more skillful as consumers of medical care, advances in the state of knowledge have continually expanded the ability of professionals to diagnose and treat. As a result, the patient/consumer is continually uncertain as to whether some new development has made his/her knowledge obsolete. Weisbrod also suggests that consumers are generally informed "rather poorly" about the quality of care being purchased — even when the consumer *is* informed with respect to appropriate care. Providing consumers with additional information on price will not lead to "better" choices if consumers are poorly informed on quality. . . .

In summary, there is nearly complete agreement among researchers and policymakers that consumers are ignorant of the appropriateness of *some* types of services and of the quality of *some* types of medical services. Disagreement on the extent and the implications of this ignorance exists, however. If consumer ignorance is extensive, then it is unlikely that a competitive market for health services can exist. On the other hand, if some consumers are relatively well informed about a relatively large share of medical services, that portion of the market for health services may operate competitively, in the absence of other barriers.

Public policy has been based upon an assumption that consumers *are* ignorant and that regulation, rather than the provision of more information, has been the government's preferred remedy. Consequently, the market for medical services has in place several constraints which act to ensure that consumers' choices are limited:

- Licensure of physicians and of other types of providers, with unlicensed providers forbidden to provide services; and
- Requirements that certain types of medical care cannot be directly purchased by a consumer (e.g., prescription drugs) but, instead, must be ordered by an intermediary.

These regulations, in turn, have an impact on the market for health services and on its performance. . . .

Professional control of the market: It has been suggested that physicians control a major portion of total health care expenditures. Although individual patients make an initial decision to visit the physician, the physician then takes "control" of the patient's subsequent demand for health services at least insofar as it is related to the reason for the initial visit. The consumer lacks the necessary

III. Competitive Reforms

medical knowledge to diagnose, treat, or to judge the quality of care offered. Thus, responsibility for much medical decisionmaking is delegated to the physician. M. Feldstein (1973) characterizes this as an "agency relationship," where the physician acts as purchasing agent for the patient.

The legal and institutional structure of the market for health services reinforces the patient's need to delegate authority to the physician. Even if the patient has adequate knowledge to permit self-diagnosis and treatment, he/she could not legally order many diagnostic tests and prescription drugs, nor could the patient be admitted to the hospital without a physician's order. . . .

It also has been suggested by some researchers that individual physicians are able to create demand for their services. The importance of this issue for policy formulation is substantial. If physicians can create demand for their services, then policies designed to increase competition among physicians and other providers would merely cause physicians to generate new patient demand. More efficient production of services, and reduced expenditures and utilization, would not necessarily result.

The source of this power to generate demand derives from patient ignorance and willingness to delegate decisionmaking to the physician. In addition, the presence of substantial insurance coverage for health services causes patients to have little incentive to become sufficiently informed to monitor the physician's decisions on their behalf.

NOTES

The Case Against Competition

1. The two types of competitive reforms outlined by Rosenblatt are relatively pure or "raw" forms of competition. The first would essentially prohibit all insurance except for catastrophic coverage, forcing consumers to evaluate the costs and benefits of each discrete item of medical care. The second competitive model would allow comprehensive insurance, but would require the typical consumer to pay some or all of the premium out of pocket, forcing a decision among a wide variety of coverage, quality, and cost options. See also Kalb, Controlling Health Care Costs by Controlling Technology: A Private Contractual Approach, 99 Yale L.J. 1109 (1990) ("beneficiaries should have the option to select a coverage plan that excludes wasteful technologies in return for a lower premium"). An excluded portion of Rosenblatt's article reviews a variation of the second model that offers a more refined or structured form of competition wherein the cost and coverage requirements of available insurance options would be confined to a more restricted range. This "managed competition"

model is discussed in the following section. Another helpful outline and analysis of these three approaches is found in McClure, Implementing a Competitive Medical Care System through Public Policy, 7 J. Health Pol. Poly. & L. 2 (1982).

A mild form of the second model actually exists in "flexible benefit programs" or "cafeteria plans" that allow employees to pocket the savings generated by choosing less expensive insurance, or even *no* insurance. The federal civil service has followed this approach for a number of years, and it is now used by over 800 major private employers. Hospitals, May 5, 1988, at 56; March 20, 1987, at 92.

2. Are the health care market conditions that are incompatible with competition inherent or remediable? Consider: "The noncompetitiveness of the market in question is neither accidental nor the result of revealed consumer preferences. . . . [It] is the result . . . of careful nurturing by organized providers, who have adamantly demanded that third parties not act as purchasing agents for their subscribers." C. Havighurst supra at 115.

In response, Professor Jost argues:

> The ability of consumers to make useful judgments about the quality of medical care through their own search and experience is quite limited. Much medical care is terribly complex. . . . In many markets the careful search by a comparatively small number of purchasers may protect the less careful consumers, as providers will gear the quality of the product to satisfy these picky marginal consumers. . . . In markets that sell individualized services, such as the health care market, this strategy is much less useful. Sellers can discriminate, offering . . . lower quality products to consumers less likely to search. . . .
>
> Recent scholarship urging reliance on the market to assure health care quality has noted the emerging role of insurers, employers and other agents as sources of health care quality information. . . . But, while these developments will no doubt result in the generation of additional information for consumers, it is doubtful that they will substantially solve the information problems facing consumers. The primary interest of employers and insurers continues to be cost containment, not quality assurance. . . . Moreover, most insurers and employers lack not only the interest but also the capacity for assembling and disseminating information on quality of providers. The cost of creating quality assessment mechanisms is considerable. Given the public-good nature of quality information [which means that once produced, it is available to all, without the users bearing the full cost to produce the information], it is likely that any individual insurer or employer that assembled such information would face a substantial free rider problem.

Jost, The Necessary and Proper Role of Regulation to Assure the Quality of Health Care, 25 Hous. L. Rev. 525, 560-561, 565-567 (1988). See also Mechanic, Consumer Choice Among Health Insurance

III. Competitive Reforms

Options, 8 Health Affairs 138 (Spring 1989) ("a truly competitive marketplace will require that consumers receive information on a broader range of dimensions than now available, in forms that are easily understood and that facilitate comparison").

For further discussion of health care market defects, see Cohodes, Where you Stand Depends on Where you Sit: Musings on the Regulation/Competition Dialogue, 7 J. Health Pol. Poly. & L. 54 (1982); Ginzberg, The Grand Illusion of Competition in Health Care, 249 J.A.M.A. 1857 (1983); Havighurst, Competition in Health Services: Overview, Issues and Answers, 34 Vand. L. Rev. 1117 (1981).

3. Do you agree with the following response to Rosenblatt?:

> Perhaps the ultimate stumbling block in implementing a policy of encouraging price competition and consumer choice is an unarticulated but overriding sense that willingness to pay, which is in part a function of ability to pay, should have no place in determining consumption of health services. This egalitarian impulse, because it is not articulated, explained, or justified, is difficult to confine to the areas where valid social justice issues are indeed present. . . . To insist on total equality throughout the medical care spectrum is to defy the reality of differences in people's tastes and preferences, to give the poor medical benefits when they would much rather have other things, and to carry symbolism very far.

C. Havighurst, Deregulating the Health Care Industry 97-98 (1982).

4. Discussing some of the same themes sounded in the Rosenblatt piece are Dunham, Morone & White, Restoring Medical Markets: Implications for the Poor, 7 J. Health, Pol. Poly. & L. 488 (1982); Kinzer, The Decline and Fall of Deregulation, 318 New Eng. J. Med. 112 (1988); Menzel, Economic Competition in Health Care: A Moral Assessment, 12 J. Med. & Philo. 63 (1987). A particularly well-stated argument is made in Vladeck, The Market v. Regulation: The Case for Regulation, 59 Milbank Mem. Fund Q. 209 (1981):

> The current argument for greater competition in the health care sector is based on the initial assumption that health care markets are distorted because of the wide prevalence of insurance. . . . But the advocates of increased competition seldom go the further step: inquire just why it is that there is so much health insurance around. . . . Consumers have sought the kinds of health insurance they have, not because they wish to act irrationally in the aggregate economic sense, but precisely because they don't wish to be forced to make rational trade-offs when they are confronted with medical care consumption decisions. No matter how we draw our curves or shape our abstract arguments, the elemental fact is that medical care is about living and dying, something considered by many to be of a rather different character from the purchase of tomatoes. The primary characteristic of most consumers of medical care

most of the time is that they are scared. They are scared of dying, or disfigurement, or permanent disability; and these are serious matters. It is hardly fair to expect any of us to make rational decisions about matters of such import. As a society, we may be prepared to pay a substantial economic premium to insulate people from having to make such decisions.

5. If health care policy makers tire of the interminable disagreement among theorists on the competition versus regulation question, they can now begin to turn to actual evidence thanks to the increasing efforts of empiricists. The Rand Corporation recently completed an extensive controlled study of the effects of placing patients under varying degrees of financial responsibility for their care. The results reveal that cost-sharing indeed has a striking effect on utilization: "A catastrophic insurance plan [one that requires the patient to pay 95 percent of the first $1000] reduces expenditures 31 percent relative to zero out-of-pocket price." For most patients, the various insurance plans caused no discernible differences in health status. But the lowest income participants under the cost sharing plans scored noticeably worse on several measures of health status than did low income participants under the free plan. Manning et al., Health Insurance and the Demand for Medical Care: Evidence from a Randomized Experiment, 77 Am. Eco. Rev. 251 (1987). Another recent study reported that most patients who paid more out of pocket scored *better* on most health measures and had *less* anxiety about their health, possibly because they were required to take more responsibility for maintaining their own health. Keeler et al., Effects of Cost Sharing on Physiological Health, Health Practices, and Worry, 22 Health Servs. Res. 279 (1987).

Concerning the effects of competition on providers, a recent study found an 11 percent decrease in costs over three years at California hospitals in highly competitive markets as compared with low competition hospitals. Melnick & Zwanziger, Hospital Behavior Under Competition and Cost-Containment Policies, 260 J.A.M.A. 2669 (1988). The authors concluded that "pro-competition policies are having dramatic and potentially far-reaching effects, . . . leading to increased competition based on price." However, other studies have found no price restraint resulting from the competitive effects of HMOs. 10 J. Health Pol. Poly. & L., No. 4 (Winter 1986) (symposium). See generally Wooley & Frech, How Hospitals Compete: A Review of the Literature, 2 U. Fla. J.L. & Pub. Poly. 57 (1989).

6. The following additional materials provide ready access to the large body of literature generated by the competition/regulation debate. Federal Trade Commission, Competition in the Health Care Sector (1978); Symposium, Market-Oriented Approaches to Achieving

Health Policy Goals, 34 Vand. L. Rev., May 1981; Market Reforms in Health Care (J. Meyer ed. 1983); Competition in the Health Care Sector: Past, Present, and Future (W. Greenberg ed. 1978); Symposium, Competition in the Health Care Sector: Ten Years Later, 13 J. Health Pol. Poly. & L. 223-364 (W. Greenberg ed. 1988); Symposium, 7 Health Affairs (Summer 1988); Incentives vs. Controls in Health Policy (J. Meyer ed. 1985); Havighurst, The Changing Locus of Decision Making in the Health Care Sector, 11 J. Health Pol. Poly. & L., 697 (1986); Greaney, Competitive Reform in Health Care: The Vulnerable Revolution, 5 Yale J. Reg. 179 (1988); Pauly, A Primer on Competition in Medical Markets, in Health Care in America (Frech & Zeckhauser eds. 1988).

7. Whether competition works or does not, whether it is good or bad, it is undeniably on the rise throughout the health care delivery system. Oversupply of hospital beds and increasing numbers of physicians are creating intense competition for patients within (and between) these two sectors, as evidenced by the dramatic increase in health care advertising and marketing and the rise of alternative health care institutions such as ambulatory surgery clinics and freestanding emergency centers. Likewise, there is intense price competition within the health insurance industry, evidenced by the rise of HMOs and PPOs (discussed in the following sections) and the impetus for large employers to self insure. See generally, Alpert & McCarthy, Beyond *Goldfarb:* Applying Traditional Antitrust Analysis to Changing Health Markets, 29 Antitrust Bull. 165 (1984).

B. Health Maintenance Organizations

Mayer & Mayer, HMOs: Origins and Development*
312 New Eng. J. Med 590 (1985)

Health maintenance organizations (HMOs) were first developed on a large scale around the turn of the 19th century, but were not then known as HMOs. These earliest forms were called prepaid group practices, and most of them originated in the American Northwest. They came about largely as a result of the opening up of the West by the railroads and were a part of the industrial development that followed.

Probably the first example of such a prepaid group practice was the Western Clinic in Tacoma, Washington. Turn-of-the-century Tacoma was the lumber capital of the world, and mill owners and their employees sought to lock in medical services through prepaid con-

---

* Reprinted with permission.

tracts, wherein doctors would deliver whatever health care services were needed for a set fee every month. The Western Clinic had begun in 1906 as a fee-for-service partnership between Drs. Thomas Curran and James Yocum. Around 1910 they became pioneers in the field of prepaid medicine when they entered into their first contract with the lumber industry at a cost of 50¢ per member per month. . . .

In 1937, the first urban precursor of HMOs, Group Health Association of Washington, D.C., was begun. . . .

Initially, the District of Columbia insurance commissioner claimed authority over Group Health and forbade its operation, but Group Health challenged that decision in court and won. The trial resulted in an important legal precedent that Group Health and other prepaid group practice programs did not constitute medical insurance.

Then the District of Columbia Medical Society went to work to oppose Group Health. It impeded recruitment of physicians for the Group Health staff, limited access to hospitals for physicians in Group Health, and threatened expulsion from the medical society for those who already belonged to hospital staffs.

Group Health took the District of Columbia Medical Society to court. After four years of what has been characterized as one of the bitterest battles in the history of modern American medicine, the U.S. Supreme Court decided in favor of Group Health.* The District of Columbia Medical Society was indicted by a grand jury for restraint of trade by blocking the development of Group Health, and organized medicine was once again facing charges of antitrust violations. . . .

Depending on who does the counting, there were between 28 and 39 prepaid group practices in operation in the United States in 1970. . . .

Thus, although prepaid group practices enjoyed legal acceptance and member satisfaction, their use remained limited. For most Americans, no such plan was available. In fact, most Americans did not even know what a prepaid group practice plan was, let alone how to find, join, or use one. But big changes were in store for the early 1970s, and they were largely due to the endeavors of one man, Dr. Paul Ellwood, who has been almost single-handedly responsible for the rapid growth in HMOs that began a little over a decade ago and continues today.

As the executive director of the American Rehabilitation Institute, Ellwood concluded that the existing fee-for-service system created "perverse incentives," which rewarded physicians and institutions for treating illness and then withdrew those rewards when health was

---

* [Eds. Note: See AMA v. United States, 317 U.S. 519 (1943) (sustaining criminal indictment under antitrust laws for the boycott against Group Health).]

III. Competitive Reforms

restored. Such a system discouraged preventive health care as well as rehabilitative care. Ellwood believed that the health care system could be made more functional if it were restructured and incorporated genuine incentives to promote health.

When Ellwood sought to construct a more functional system, he found that it already existed in prepaid group practices. He saw that Kaiser-Permanente and similar groups were providing good care to large populations at reasonable cost. He set about trying to convince the federal government of the inherent logic in supporting and stimulating the growth of such a system. . . .

. . . One additional contribution by Ellwood secured his reputation as the modern-day father of the HMO concept. To avoid the traditional negative response to prepaid group practice, he wanted to describe his program in a manner that was unique, plus both politically neutral and medically nebulous. It was for this reason that he coined the term "health maintenance organization."

HMOs were to be enthusiastically embraced in the next two years. Nixon's 1971 Health Message to Congress made them the keystone of the entire national health policy. They were to receive redirected funding until the passage of HMO legislation. This expression of government interest and the venture capital it foreshadowed led to an explosive growth in HMO development. During this period $26 million in redirected funds were allocated in support of 155 HMO projects. A goal was established to make the HMO option available to 90 per cent of the population through 1700 programs.

But substantial legislation could not be passed in spite of numerous bills submitted to Congress. Those two years (1971 and 1972) allowed opponents of HMOs to weaken the administration's commitment. Ultimately, the Health Maintenance Act of 1973 was laden with stipulations and limitations that restricted HMO development. Since the act provided funds for two to three years of study, planning, and development, its effects were not apparent until 1975 or 1976. The restrictive nature of the legislation is apparent from the number of HMOs that were developed thereafter.

The initial optimism of 1970 led to the establishment of 166 HMOs with 5.8 million enrollees in 1975, up from 33 HMOs in 1970. By 1977 there were only 183 plans in operation, with 6.85 million people enrolled. The efforts of a group of HMO advocates eventually altered the restrictive nature of government policy through the amendments of 1976 and 1978, resulting in a more workable law. By 1979 there were 224 plans and an additional 2 million members.

There are now about 323 HMOs in the United States, which serve 15 million members. They have grown by 10 per cent annually since 1980, and in 1983 they grew by 15.3 per cent; by 1993, membership is expected to approach 50 million. Of the nation's 38 major metropolitan areas, 37 have at least one HMO, and most have several.

Health Maintenance Organization Act
42 U.S.C. §300e et seq.

§300e. Requirements of health maintenance organizations.

(a) For purposes of this subchapter, the term "health maintenance organization" means a[n entity] which . . . is organized and operated in the manner prescribed [in this section].

(b) A health maintenance organization shall provide, without limitations as to time or cost . . . , health services to its members in the following manner:

(1) Each member is to be provided basic health services for a basic health services payment which is . . .

(B) fixed without regard to the frequency, extent, or kind of health service . . . actually furnished; . . .

(C) is fixed under a community rating system; and

(D) may be supplemented by additional nominal payments . . . , except that such payments may not be required where they serve . . . as a barrier to the delivery of health services. . . .

(c) Each health maintenance organization shall . . .

(2) assume full financial risk on a prospective basis for the provision of basic health services . . . ;

(3) enroll persons who are broadly representative of the various age, social, and income groups within the area it serves . . . ; [and]

(4) not expel or refuse to re-enroll any member because of his health status or his requirements for health services.

["Basic health services" is defined as a comprehensive range of inpatient and outpatient services, including mental health, well-child care, annual checkups and other preventive measures. See 42 C.F.R. §110.102 et seq. The Act then provides for grants and loans to HMOs that meet these qualifications.]

§300e-9. Employees' health benefits plan. . . .

(a) [E]ach employer which . . . employ[s] an average number of employees of not less than 25 shall include in any health benefits plan . . . offered to such employees . . . the option of membership in qualified health maintenance organizations [in the area]. . . .

(c) [T]he employer . . . shall make a contribution [to the HMO premium] in an amount which does not financially discriminate against an employee who enrolls in such organization. . . . [A] contribution does not financially discriminate if the employer's . . . method of determining the contributions on behalf of all employees is reasonable and is designed to assure employees a fair choice among health benefits plans.

§300e-10. Restrictive State laws and practices.

In the case of any entity —

(1) which cannot do business as a health maintenance organization [because state law]

(A) requires as a condition to doing business in that State that a medical society approve the furnishing of services by the entity,

(B) requires that physicians constitute all or a percentage of its governing body,

(C) requires that all physicians or a percentage of physicians in the locale participate or be permitted to participate in the provision of services for the entity,

(D) requires that the entity meet requirements for insurers of health care services . . . respecting initial capitalization and establishment of financial reserves against insolvency, or

(E) imposes requirements which would prohibit the entity from complying with the requirements of this title, and

(2) . . . which is a qualified health maintenance organization for purposes of section 300e-9 of this title,

such requirements shall not apply to that entity so as to prevent it from operating as a health maintenance organization in accordance with section 300e of this title.

Havighurst, Health Maintenance Organizations and the Health Planners*
1978 Utah L. Rev. 123, 130-136

II. HMOs and Competition. . . .

A. Perceptions of HMOs

Despite the attractiveness of HMOs as part of a competitive strategy to bring some order out of chaos in health services, the wide

---

* Professor of Law and Director, Program on Legal Issues in Health Care, Duke University. J.D., 1958, Northwestern University.
Reprinted with permission.

support that the HMO idea has attracted, including the enactment of the federal HMO Act, does not signify equivalent support for the idea of competition. Indeed, HMO supporters fall into two distinct camps, with widely varying perceptions of the HMO and its role. The first camp, typified by proponents of the HMO Act, values HMOs as a model health care system, providing a large population with comprehensive services of good quality and plowing savings from efficiency in resource use back into improved accessibility, better care, and more extensive services. Under this view, heavy subsidies are deemed appropriate to help create large multi-service HMOs. The HMO Act makes such subsidies available, but only for HMOs meeting very substantial requirements and restrictions designed to foster those aspects of HMOs thought to be desirable and to minimize potential bad aspects. To those who hold this view, the HMO model is a promising way to improve the quality of care and to extend more health care to people, particularly those whose health needs have not been well served. Government support for HMOs is also embraced as a means of restructuring the health care delivery system along more rational lines. It is fair to say that, for this group of observers, the challenges of improving quality and meeting previously neglected health needs have long been paramount, and the problem of containing the total volume of health services and their cost to the nation has been of only secondary concern.

The other camp of HMO supporters responds to all of the positive quality and access benefits of the HMO, but sees as the cardinal virtue its cost consciousness and its consequent potential for restoring effective price competition, as well as quality competition, in the market for health services. These observers view such competition as supplying a needed brake on the health care system's capacity to consume, without considered justification, an ever-increasing share of the nation's resources. They anticipate that fee-for-service providers, facing the active price competition which could be supplied by HMOs would, in due course, be induced to cooperate in keeping health insurance premiums competitive by curtailing over-utilization of resources. Supporters of HMOs as a new competitive force do not seek to obtain subsidies for them so much as to obtain freedom of entry and a market test from which might emerge a mixed system of fee-for-service providers and HMOs of many kinds, some emphasizing comprehensiveness and high quality and others offering somewhat lower quality, but adequate, care at less cost. Even imperfect market competition among delivery systems is seen as the best available way to steer a safe course between the Scylla of unnecessary care, over-utilization, and extravagance, which too often characterize fee-for-service medicine, and the Charybdis of inadequate care, which might occur in an excessively cost conscious HMO. Holders of this view of

III. Competitive Reforms 853

HMOs and the health policy problem are simultaneously dubious that governmental or professionally imposed controls can approach a proper balance between the cost and the value of health services consumed by Americans. . . .

C. Federal HMO Policy: Competition Slighted

The HMO Act of 1973 was supposed to provide a major impetus for the HMO idea. Although the HMO concept came into prominence as a policy initiative as early as 1970, it was not until late 1973 that Congress enacted legislation designed to advance it materially. That law turned out to be something of a "white elephant," however, since the requirements to qualify for the Act's benefits were quite extensive, creating high costs and uncertainties that set back or aborted many HMO initiatives already underway. Long delays in writing implementing regulations created additional problems. Some observers have felt that the federal act was, on balance, a step backward since it interrupted what had been promising private initiatives and favorable developments in the states.

The HMO Act was amended in 1976 to make HMOs more competitive with the existing system. It was recognized that the idealistic regulatory requirements included in the original enactment had hampered HMO development, and the stated intention of the amendments was to improve HMOs' prospects. Nevertheless, extensive qualification requirements were retained, and federal law still seems to embrace the HMO more as a model system than as a feature of a rejuvenated market for medical services. The most likely reason that the amendments did so little is that the changes were made primarily to benefit the large, well established HMOs which lobbied intensively for the changes. Congress made only a limited effort to minimize the problems of those prospective HMOs that could come into being only if nonrestrictive policies were adopted and the costs and risks of entry into the market were reduced.

That increased competition flowing from relative ease of market entry by HMOs has not been high on Congress' list of priorities is also revealed by the provisions of the HMO Act dealing with "dual choice." The 1976 amendments actually cut back substantially on the original law's chief contribution to competition, namely the obligation of certain employers to offer the HMO option (dual choice) to their employees. Only relatively large employers are now subject to the dual choice requirement; thus HMOs serving only a small service area have less chance of being offered to employees. Moreover, labor unions are now permitted to decline the employer's offer of an HMO option, thereby precluding individual employees from exercising the choice for themselves. Competitive opportunities were thus actually reduced by the amendments out of regard for the complaints of employers who did not want the trouble of offering a choice and for unions wishing either to maintain total control over their members' fringe benefits or to protect their own health plans from competition.

Unfortunately, the dual choice provisions have, from the beginning, reflected a congressional notion that it is the opportunity to choose an HMO meeting federal requirements that is important, not competition. The dual choice provisions require employers to offer one HMO of each of two types: a prepaid group practice HMO and an IPA [Individual Practice Association]. A second qualified HMO of the prepaid group practice variety has no right to be offered, and HMOs not meeting all the demanding federal requirements have no improved chances of being offered as a result of the law. The implication of the dual choice provisions is therefore that one HMO of each type is sufficient in congress' view and that more HMOs would be superfluous. Yet it is elementary that two or three competitors in a market may not be enough to insure meaningful competition. Especially in the health care sector, with its traditional toleration of explicit or tacit agreements to divide markets and to avoid competition in other ways, the introduction of one independent HMO and a medical-society-dominated IPA promises only small improvement compared to what more intense competition might bring.

NOTES

The Development of HMOs

1. An HMO is an entity, typically a group of doctors, that provides a comprehensive range of medical services to its members for a fixed, periodic premium paid in advance. This is known as the "capitation" form of prospective payment: the HMO receives a fixed sum for each person enrolled. The most critical respect in which HMOs differ from traditional reimbursement is that the costs of treatment are internalized to the provider rather than being borne by a third-party. (In what other ways are HMOs fundamentally different from conventional reimbursement?) By combining treatment and insurance functions in one entity, HMOs bring cost consciousness to bear at the critical point of the treatment decision. In contrast with the present system that pays doctors the most for the sickest patients, capitation rewards doctors for maintaining their patients' health.

This revolutionary change in incentives has the prospect for producing a dramatic change in physician behavior: "First, because the organization receives a fixed amount not based on the kind or amount of service provided to a particular individual, the financial incentive is to provide care in the most economical way possible. . . .

III. Competitive Reforms

Second, by combining a comprehensive range of health services, the HMO will have the inducement and opportunity to choose the most efficient form of treatment for its patients." S. Law, Blue Cross: What Went Wrong? 107 (2d ed. 1976).

It is believed that the improved performance of HMOs will have spillover effects on the health care delivery system as a whole by confronting both the traditional insurance industry and the medical profession with superior competition. Thus visionaries embrace HMO competition as the solution to the deficiencies in both the quality and the cost of health care. This has not yet occurred, in part because the medical profession's historical antagonism toward prepaid group practice has only partially abated. See Hull, Physicians Organize to Stop HMOs From Altering Practice of Medicine, Wall Street Journal, June 23, 1986, p.23, col. 4.

2. There are two basic types of HMOs: the group model, in which physicians practice together in the same setting, typically as salaried employees, and the individual practice association ("IPA") model, a contractual association of a larger number of doctors who maintain their practices in their individual offices and typically are paid on a fee-for-service basis. There are several variations of these basic forms so that the full list of HMO models is somewhat longer. For instance, some practicing physicians are owners rather than employees of their practice groups, and some IPAs are composed of a network of clinics rather than solo practitioners. See generally Luft, Health Maintenance Organizations: Dimensions of Performance 4-6 (1981); Shouldice & Shouldice, Medical Group Practice and Health Maintenance Organizations 12-17 (1978).

How successful an HMO is depends in part on how it transfers the efficiency incentives of capitation to its physicians. Realize that while *external* payments to an HMO *institution* are structured on a capitation basis, there is wide variation in the *internal* financial arrangements that HMOs strike with their individual *doctors*. Within group models, employed doctors receive salary; owners receive profit distributions. IPAs usually continue to pay their doctors on a fee-for-service basis supplemented with bonus systems to reward economy. Typically, an IPA will withhold a percentage of a physician's payments to offset any excessive hospitalization charges attributed to that physician's practice patterns or to pay the physician as a bonus if the withheld funds are not needed. Welch, The New Structure of Individual Practice Associations: 12 J. Health Pol. Poly. & L. 723 (1987). Which of these financial incentives do you think is strongest? Is any too strong? In 1986, Congress banned the payment of efficiency bonuses to hospital physicians, but exempted HMOs pending further study of the effects. See 734 supra.

3. HMOs of all types have in fact demonstrated impressive re-

ductions in unnecessary hospitalization, largely by substituting outpatient for hospital care. For HMOs, the average annual rate of hospitalization per 1000 people is 300-400 days, in contrast with a rate of 800-900 days for traditional medicine. See Taylor & Kagay, The HMO Report Card: A Closer Look, 5 Health Affairs, Spring 1986, at 81. Paradoxically, though, despite these impressive reductions in unnecessary treatment, HMOs have not succeeded in significantly lowering the *overall costs* of health insurance. See Hospitals, March 20, 1989, at 82 ("Only one-third of 1,600 employers surveyed . . . in 1988 reported that HMOs have helped reduce their health insurance costs"); Monahan & Willis, Special Legal Status for HMOs, 18 Stetson L. Rev. 352, 386 (1989) ("It is rather clear that . . . [employers] are not overly impressed with HMO performance to date").

Professor Havighurst's analysis of the obstacles created by the federal HMO Act helps to explain this anomaly. Primarily, because HMOs have been forced to engage in community rating rather than experience rating, they have not been able to offer lower premiums to employee groups with superior health status. Moreover, even if HMOs were permitted to lower their premiums, they have little incentive to do so since the federal law, until 1988, required employers to contribute equal dollar amounts to both conventional insurance and HMOs. See Monahan & Willis, supra. Therefore, to date HMOs have engaged largely in only quality or service competition, attempting to attract more subscribers by turning their savings into more comprehensive coverage. This has led to the irony that an institution with tremendous potential to restrain the abuses of excessive insurance has been used primarily to extend insurance coverage even more.

An additional defect of the HMO Act is that "the burden is on the HMO to enforce the [dual choice] law by asking the federal government to bring suit against a recalcitrant employer. HMOs are understandably reluctant to antagonize their potential customers." A. Enthoven, Health Plan 74 (1980). See also L. Brown, Politics and Health Maintenance Organizations (1983). Consequently, HMOs have failed to impose significant competitive discipline on the health care industry. Frank & Welch, The Competitive Effects of HMOs: A Review of the Evidence, Inquiry, Summer 1985, at 148; Luft, Maerki & Trauner, The Competitive Effects of Health Maintenance Organizations: Another Look at the Evidence, 10 J. Health Pol. Poly. & L. 625 (1986).

4. Congress sought to address several of the criticisms of the federal HMO Act in a set of 1988 amendments, P.L. 100-517, 102 Stat. 2576. The 1988 amendments allow HMOs to provide up to 10 percent of their services through non-Plan physicians and to charge a "reasonable deductible" for these services. 42 U.S.C. §300e(b)(1). Also, the Act now liberalizes the definition of "community rating"

III. Competitive Reforms   857

to allow HMOs much greater flexibility in adjusting rates according to the health care experiences of different employee groups. Id. at §300e-1(8)(C). Concomitantly, §300e-9(c) (quoted above) replaces the equal contribution requirement with one that allows employers reasonable variation in the amount they contribute to different plans and to different employee groups. However, in a counter measure (championed by then-Senator Quayle), Congress also voted to sunset the dual choice requirement (§300e-9(a)) effective 1995.

5. The federal act does not impose its coverage and organizational provisions on all HMOs; it only sets these requirements as qualifying conditions for the benefits that the Act confers, primarily, eligibility for the dual choice provision and exemption from restrictive state laws. Most of these state laws are artifacts of the medical profession's domination of health insurance. See Section I.B supra. In particular, Blue Cross/Blue Shield enabling acts often prohibit innovative insurance arrangements without the endorsement of local medical societies. See Group Health Assn. v. Moor, 24 F. Supp. 445 (D.D.C. 1938), *aff'd sub nom.* Jordan v. Group Health Association, 107 F.2d 239 (D.C. Cir. 1939); Kissam, Health Maintenance Organizations and the Role of Antitrust Law, 1978 Duke L.J. 487; Developments, The Role of Prepaid Group Practice in Relieving the Medical Care Crisis, 84 Harv. L. Rev. 887 (1971); Comment, Prepayment Health Care Plan Enabling Acts — Are Their Restrictive Features Constitutional? 7 Duq. L. Rev. 125 (1968).

6. Do the organizational variations in HMO forms have any implications for HMOs' *vicarious* responsibility for their doctors' malpractice? Alternatively, could it be argued that HMOs assume a *direct* responsibility for patient care by virtue of their insurance undertaking to provide all necessary treatment? Could one go so far as to argue that HMOs are contractually bound, by virtue of their preventative orientation, to keep subscribers healthy? See Curran & Moseley, The Malpractice Experience of Health Maintenance Organizations, 70 Nw.U.L. Rev. 69 (1975). Will malpractice law evolve to accommodate an HMO standard of care, or will the new incentives to economize run headlong into the entrenched standards of fee-for-service practice? See Section II.B supra.

Are HMOs subject to the same liability for bad faith refusal of coverage as are other insurers? See Rederscheid v. Comprecare, Inc., 667 P.2d 766 (Colo. App. 1983) (yes); Comment, Bad Faith Suits: Are They Applicable to HMOs?, 85 W. Va. L. Rev. 911 (1983).

7. The HMO is the principal example of the various alternative delivery systems ("ADSs") that have flowered during the 1970s and 1980s. PPOs (preferred provider organizations), the second major innovation, are discussed in the following section. Over the next decade, the ready availability through the workplace of conventional,

open-ended health insurance may become a thing of the past. Private employers are so driven to find methods to restrain health insurance premium increases that many employees no longer have the option of a fee-for-service plan with free choice of physician. N.Y. Times, July 27, 1988, at 1.

8. The 1980s have been boom years for HMOs in the public sphere as well as in the private sector. In 1985, Medicare began offering HMO enrollment as an optional method of coverage. Iglehart, Medicare Turns to HMOs, 312 New Eng. J. Med. 132 (1985); Ginsburg & Hackbarth, Alternative Delivery Systems and Medicare, 5 Health Affairs, Spring 1986, at 6; Langwell & Hadley, Capitation and the Medicare Program: History, Issues and Evidence, Health Care Fin. Rev., 1986 Supp., at 9; Rossiter & Langwell, Medicare's Two Systems for Paying Providers, 7 Health Affairs 120 (Summer 1988).

State Medicaid programs are also increasingly turning to HMOs. See Freund & Neuschler, Overview of Medicaid Capitation and Case-Management Initiatives, Health Care Fin. Rev., 1986 Supp., at 21; Perkins, Medicaid Primary Care Case Management Update, 22 Clearinghouse Rev. 348 (1988); 874 infra. CHAMPUS, the military's insurance program, recently awarded what is billed as the largest HMO contract ever. Am. Med. News, Feb. 5, 1988, p. 1. See generally, Gruber et al., From Movement to Industry: The Growth of HMOs, 7 Health Affairs 197 (Summer 1988).

As the following readings demonstrate, the government's entry into prepaid health care has not been without controversy.

Heinz, Medicare and HMOs: A First Look, with Disturbing Findings
Medicare & Medicaid Guide (CCH) ¶36,234 (1987)

Over the last decade, the financing and delivery of health care in the United States has undergone dramatic changes. In an effort to control costs, the Federal government has sought new, more efficient, reimbursement and health delivery systems than traditional fee-for-service medicine. One option that had been encouraged by the government is prepaid health care, with health maintenance organizations (HMOs) being the dominant model.

The Senate Aging Committee began its oversight of the Medicare HMO program in the Spring of 1986. At that time, the risk contract program had been in effect over 15 months, time enough for certain strengths and weaknesses to be apparent. A Federal investigation into International Medical Centers, a Miami-based HMO demonstration project, was prompted by allegations of rapid expansion and profits at Medicare's expense.

III. Competitive Reforms

Newspapers reported in the Fall of 1985 that IMC grossed more than $8 million for the first six months of 1984, with monthly profits on each Medicare patient of nearly 10 times the national average. IMC's practices prompted some to question what other HMOs might be doing — and more broadly, the government's participation in prepaid health care. . . .

The Quality of Medical Care Provided to Medicare Beneficiaries in Some HMOs Is Inadequate.

Unlike fee-for-service medicine, in which physicians have financial incentives to provide more than the necessary level of service, capitated plans such as HMOs have built-in incentives to constrain the use of services. Since the plan receives the same payment regardless of the amount of care provided, it is to the plan's financial benefit to impose limits on care. The dilemma of cost versus quality with HMOs is similar to that under DRGs: if the financial incentives to restrict service are too strong, Medicare beneficiaries may receive inadequate services.

A review of beneficiary and provider complaints to five HCFA regional offices and to senior advocates, revealed that a handful of HMOs — serving 30 percent of Medicare enrollees — generated a large number of serious complaints about impaired access to and poor quality of care. Yet there is little evidence that Federal or state agencies have the will, the resources, and the enforcement mechanisms or legal authority to investigate and, where appropriate, sanction these plans. This finding is confirmed by [a] draft review of 23 Medicare [HMO] plans in six states (not including Florida): "During the course of this inspection, more than 15 percent of beneficiaries complained of inadequate care or withholding of necessary treatment. This was reinforced by [beneficiaries'] friends, legal advocates and senior network members. Some complaints were accompanied by extensive documentation."

Specifically, the Heinz investigation uncovered the following problems with services (or "utilization" of services) as revealed through representative complaints, case histories and other documentation. In the absence of any systematic measure of quality and access, this investigation represents the most accurate picture available.

The Evidence

A number of HMOs employ a variety of tactics to discourage utilization. Sometimes, extraordinary efforts are needed by patients (and their families) to jump the hurdles that [HMO] administrative staff erect to limit care. These range from prolonged delays in scheduling appointments, to providing insufficient phone lines so that it is almost impossible to reach the plan for anything but a clear emergency, to rude and insensitive clerks who intimidate patients from seeking help. The plans also reduce access to services provided by subcontractors, such as pharmacists, by providing slow payment on bills. . . .

Access to care of specialists (both within the plan and outside of the plan) is made so difficult that enrollees resort to finding their own specialists and paying for the care out-of-pocket. Sometimes the delay in obtaining care can be life-threatening. (The GAO also identified this as a major problem with IMC.) . . .

Beneficiaries experience life-threatening delays in obtaining the appropriate diagnostic tests or treatment; in some cases HMO physicians have trivialized the diagnosis, jeopardizing the patient's life. . . .

Case History: A California Medicare beneficiary joined a risk contract HMO because it was close to his home. Subsequent to his enrollment, he became ill and called the clinic for an emergency appointment. He was told to go to a clinic 25 miles away. After going to this clinic, he was then told to go back to the original clinic to make an appointment. Upon arrival at the next clinic he was told to go to a third location to make an appointment. When he arrived at the third clinic, he was told that it would take a week to be seen. He left, went to a private physician, and initiated his disenrollment from the HMO. . . .

S. Law, Blue Cross: What Went Wrong?*
108-109 (2d ed. 1976)

Reversing the financial incentives in the provision of health care would be dangerous to patients. . . . Incentives for economy can also be incentives for no care or inferior care. . . . The danger that HMOs will provide inferior care is particularly acute when the organization is a profit-making one, when the physician's compensation is based on a percentage of profit rather than a fixed salary, . . . when HMO enrollees have no alternative means of obtaining medical care, and when the HMO population is exclusively poor or aged. . . .

HMO proponents see competition as the primary means of controlling the quality of services they render and also as an additional means of reducing health costs. If an HMO serves a captive population, there is no incentive to provide care of decent quality. Competition among HMOs and between HMOs and the private fee-for-service sector are essential if the danger of inferior and inadequate care is to be avoided. . . .

* Reprinted with permission.

III. Competitive Reforms

On a theoretical level, the notion of competing HMOs offering different combinations of services, quality, amenities and price, which consumers could evaluate and select, is attractive. Increased competition is proposed as a means to make the health services industry more responsive to public and consumer preferences. The call for competition recognizes that the delivery of health services involves social choices that are appropriately made by the public, rather than technical medical issues to be resolved by doctors, administrators, or other experts.

Enthoven, Consumer-Choice Health Plan: A National Health Insurance Proposal Based on Regulated Competition in the Private Sector*
298 New Eng. J. Med. 709 (1978)

There is an effective alternative to direct economic regulation. It is to change the financial incentives — i.e., to create a financing framework in which physicians and consumers can benefit from forming and joining organized systems that use health-care resources wisely. In such a system costs can be controlled with freedom of choice that respects each person's preferences. Because the distinctive idea of this proposal is to let consumer preferences guide the reorganization of the health-care delivery system, I have called it "Consumer-Choice Health Plan (CCHP)." Its main ideas are as follows.

Organized Systems with Incentives to Use Resources Wisely

To achieve comprehensive care of good quality for all, at a cost we can afford, we must change the fundamental structure of the system of health-care financing and delivery. Instead of today's fragmented system dominated by the cost-increasing incentives of fee for service, we need a health-care economy made up predominantly, though not exclusively, of competing organized systems. In such systems, physicians would accept responsibility for providing comprehensive health-care services to defined populations, largely for a prospective per capita payment, or some other form of payment that rewards economy in the use of health-care resources. Physicians control the lion's share of health-care expenditures. They are by far the best qualified to make the difficult judgments about need and cost effectiveness. Because of the personal, uncertain, often intangible nature of medical care, physicians' judgment is a far more appropriate

---
* Reprinted with permission.

basis for resource allocation than arbitrary numerical standards are. So it makes sense for physicians to accept the main responsibility for keeping health-care costs within the limits desired by society. I believe that accepting that responsibility is the only way in which the medical profession can maintain its autonomy in the United States.

The government cannot reorganize the health-care economy by direct action. People would resist such changes involuntarily imposed. And nobody can bring about such a change quickly. But the government can change the underlying economic incentives so that consumers and providers of care can benefit from forming and joining organized systems that use resources wisely. The delivery system would then be forced to reorganize itself in response to consumers who are seeking out and choosing what is in their own best interest. CCHP seeks to accomplish this transformation by voluntary changes in a competitive market. . . .

. . . Many types of systems might succeed in such a competition. One is prepaid group practice, in which groups of physicians practicing together accept responsibility for providing comprehensive health-care services to defined populations for a fixed prospective per capita payment, and the individual physicians receive a salary, sometimes augmented by a bonus based on the overall success of the program. Another might be the individual practice association, in which the physicians as a group accept responsibility for providing comprehensive services for a fixed prospective per capita payment. . . .

. . . In such an economy, pure fee-for-service practice would ultimately be reduced to a comparatively small percentage of the total, but it would probably have a secure place, both for specialty services bought by health plans not large enough to have their own full-time specialists and for consumers who preferred to continue to buy their health care and insurance on a fee-for-service third-party reimbursement basis, as most do today, and who would be willing to pay the extra cost above the subsidy level associated with that mode of financing. . . .

Informed Choice among Competing Alternatives

CCHP is designed to assure that all people have a choice among competing alternatives, that they have good information on which to base their choice, and that competition emphasizes quality of benefits and total cost. . . .

[Ed. note. For middle and upper income families, CCHP would replace the tax law's exclusion of employer contributions for insurance premiums with a tax credit equal to 60 percent of the "actuarial cost" (a term described below) of enrolling in a qualified plan that provided basic coverage. In other words, if the average cost of a qualified plan were $1350, anyone who enrolls in such a plan could subtract 60 percent of this amount ($810) from the federal tax they would otherwise pay. They would have to pay the remaining 40 percent out-of-pocket from their taxable income. They could also choose to pay more than the average cost if they wished to enroll in a more expensive plan that provided greater amenities of service or more comprehensive coverage.

Medicare would be changed to give each beneficiary the right to have the government pay 100 percent of the average cost for his actuarial category paid to the qualified plan of his choice. Medicaid would be expanded to cover everyone under the federal poverty guideline and would operate through a "voucher" system that allowed them to purchase a plan of their choice. The face value of the voucher would graduate from 100 percent of the average actuarial cost for a minimum benefits qualified plan to the baseline of 60 percent, depending on the degree of poverty.]

Thus, CCHP would take money now used to subsidize people's choice of more costly systems of care, and use it to raise the floor under the least well covered. It would give people an incentive to seek out systems that provide care economically by letting them keep all the savings. While government assures that people have enough money to join a good plan, above the subsidy-level people would be using their own net after-tax money, which should motivate them to seek value for it. . . .

The Financing System

Actuarial Categories and Costs

The flow of government subsidies to individuals to help them buy health insurance in CCHP would be based on actuarial cost — i.e., the average total costs of covered benefits (insured and out-of-pocket) in the base year, updated each year by a suitable price index, for persons in each actuarial category. For persons not covered by Medicare, the actuarial categories might be the simple and familiar three-part structure of "individual, individual plus one dependent, and individual plus two or more dependents." However, in a competitive situation, this classification might give health plans too strong an incentive to attempt to select preferred risks by design of benefit packages (e.g., good maternity benefits to attract healthy young families), location of facilities, or emphasis in specialty mix (strength in pediatrics, weakness in cardiology). Carried to a logical extreme, such a system could lead to poor care for high-risk persons (though open enrollment — described below — would always assure the right of high-risk persons to join any qualified health plan). So experience might show that a more complex set of actuarial categories is desirable. For example, the three-part structure might be supplemented by special categories for persons 45 to 54 and 55 to 64 years of age. In the limit, one might go to a structure based on individual age (e.g., in 10-year steps) and sex, though I doubt whether this development would be necessary.

Actuarial cost would also reflect location, because there are large regional differentials in health-care costs. The appropriate geographic unit would probably be the state. However, regional differences in real per capita subsidies based on actuarial cost would be phased out over a decade.

The appropriate price index for updating actuarial cost would probably be the "all-services" component of the Consumer Price Index. . . .

In CCHP, premiums would be set by each health plan for each actuarial category and benefit package, on the basis of its own costs and its own judgment of what it can charge in a competitive market. Thus, persons in more costly actuarial categories would pay higher premiums. This step is desirable because we want competing plans to be motivated to serve them and is made socially acceptable by giving such people higher subsidies through tax credits or vouchers.

Rules to Create a Socially Desirable Competition: Criteria for Qualified Health Plans

To qualify to receive tax credits, vouchers or Medicare payments, a health plan would have to operate according to a set of rules intended to create a fair and socially desirable competition based on quality and cost effectiveness . . .

Open Enrollment

Each plan must participate in a periodic government-run open enrollment in which it must accept all enrollees who choose it, without regard to age, sex, race, religion, national origin or, with possible minor exceptions, prior health conditions. Each September, for example, every family would receive an informative booklet published by the administrative agency. The book would give an understandable presentation of the costs, benefits and limitations of each qualified health plan in the area. During October, each head of household would make an election for the coming year, through his employer, welfare office or local office of the administrative agency. This step would greatly enhance competition by giving each person a choice from among competing plans, and it would assure that every person could enroll in a qualified plan. . . .

III. Competitive Reforms

A program to provide meaningful, useful information on the features and merits of alternative health plans would be an essential part of CCHP and a major departure from present practice. To aid consumer choice, each plan would be required to publish total per capita costs, including premiums and out-of-pocket costs. The administrative agency would have authority to review and approve (for accuracy and balance) promotional materials, including presentations to be included in the booklet available to all eligible persons at "open season." The administrative agency would also have authority to review and approve "endorsed options" and contract language so that all options offered would either conform to a standard contract or be able to be described by a standard contract and a manageable number of additions and exclusions. This supervision would force plans to publish their terms in a format that is understandable to consumers and that facilitates direct comparison among plans without forcing the consumer to master and compare a lot of fine print. Uniform financial disclosure would be required — comparable to what the Securities and Exchange Commission requires of public companies. Data on patterns of utilization, availability and accessibility would be required, as is required of HMO's in the HMO Act. . . .

Benefits and Eligibility

Any plan for national health insurance must include definitions of covered benefits and eligible persons. The choices are largely political judgments. The principles of CCHP can be applied to any of a broad range of benefit packages and eligibility criteria, including coverage of essentially every legal resident of the United States. The philosophy of CCHP suggests that, beyond the essentials that must be specified by law, what is included in health benefits plans should be determined by the consumer desires expressed in the marketplace, rather than by provider interests. . . .

Transition

The enactment of CCHP would cause no sudden wrenching upheaval in medical-care delivery or financing. There would be a transition period, of perhaps two years, during which health plans intending to qualify would prepare for the first open enrollment. . . . In the first few years of CCHP, most physicians would continue to practice in their same offices and hospitals and care for the same patients as before.

Gradually, however, competitive economic pressures would have their effect. If capitation or other similar incentive payment systems were effective in reducing cost while maintaining consumer satisfaction, health plans would seek to extend them to more of their participating physicians. Newly trained physicians in specialties in excess supply in a given area would find no health plans interested in signing them up, and they would have to look for work in areas where their services were needed. Primary-care physicians would assume more of the responsibility for the total costs of care of their patients, and specialists whose costs were judged by such primary-care physicians to be excessive would find themselves obliged to negotiate lower fees to retain their referrals. Independent practice associations would tighten utilization controls and more carefully balance the specialty mix of their membership to the needs of their enrolled populations. Prepaid-group-practice HMO's would continue to grow. In short, the competitive market would generate cost controls, but they would be private market controls based on individual and group judgments about cost versus value received and not public controls based on arbitrary numerical standards, insensitive to the quality or value of the services. . . .

The "Consumer-Choice" Issue

Proposals to rely on consumer choice to guide the health-services system are invariably subjected to the attack that consumers are incapable of making intelligent choices in health-care matters. So it seems worthwhile to make clear exactly what is being assumed. Admittedly, the element of ignorance and uncertainty in health care is very large; that is true for physicians and civil servants as well as ordinary consumers. CCHP does not assume that the ordinary consumer is a good judge of what is in his own best interest. Consumers may be ignorant, biased and vulnerable to deception. CCHP merely assumes that, when it comes to choosing a health plan, the ordinary consumer is the best judge of it. The theory of optimum allocation of resources through decentralized markets does not assume that every consumer is perfectly informed and economically rational. Markets can be policed by a minority of well informed rational consumers. And we are seeking merely a good and workable solution, not a theoretical optimum. . . .

Part of the "consumer-choice" issue is resistance to the idea of letting the poor, because of their poverty, choose a less costly health plan that might not meet their medical needs. There is appearance of a conflict here with the principle of CCHP that people must be allowed to benefit from their economizing choices. . . . The problem can be resolved in CCHP by setting the premium vouchers (usable only for health care) at a high enough level to assure access to a plan with adequate benefits — always letting plans that do a better job attract members by offering less cost sharing or more benefits. . . .

Thus CCHP would be a large step toward equalization of health-care purchasing power, without enforcing absolute equality. I believe it would be foolish to reject it on the grounds that it does not reach a hypothetical egalitarian ideal that has never been attained in any society and is surely not supported by the American people today. . . .

The "HMO Underservice" Issue

Some allege that HMO's achieve financial success by underserving their members. . . . The allegations of underservice arose for the Medicaid prepaid health plans, mainly in Southern California. There, a state government was trying to cut costs in a hurry, and accepted unrealistically low bids for Medicaid contracts and enrollment practices that interfered with free choice. The underservice problem arose from the state government's politically motivated purchasing policies, not from the nature of HMO's. If we assure that every family has the purchasing power to buy membership in a good plan, and a free choice among competing plans, organizations that make a practice of underserving members will not last long.

Hellinger, Perspectives on Enthoven's Consumer Choice Health Plan*
19 Inquiry 199 (1982)

The basic assumptions of Enthoven's plan — that ADSs [alternative delivery systems] will evolve, will promote competition, and will eventually lower costs — must be given closer examination than has occurred to date. I raise the following questions in order to examine the soundness of these assumptions.

Question 1: Will alternative delivery systems indeed evolve and promote competition?

In many areas there are no ADSs and all physicians are members of traditional insurance plans based on fee for service. Enthoven assumes that eventually, in a given area, some entrepreneur will plan, organize, and operate an ADS that will successfully compete with the traditional plans in the areas. But as Homans observes, economic theorists have the luxury of assuming the existence of institutions but policy analysts who use economic theory are not so fortunate. If physicians are committed to the fee-for-service practice of medicine and have well-established relationships with their patients, new forms

---
* Reprinted with permission.

of practice will take root slowly and with difficulty; in rural areas, with only a few physicians, new organizations will face even more difficulties. . . .

It is axiomatic that ADSs must be competitive to establish and then retain their membership. Whether ADSs will compete to increase their enrollment, however, is not clear. Organizational theorists argue that HMOs with 20,000 to 30,000 members may view their size as optimal and seek only to maintain their membership. They further argue that an HMO may become increasingly insulated from competition as its members become more familiar with the organization and develop closer ties with its physicians. Such an organization may become less cost conscious and may be restrained only by its desire not to greatly exceed the costs of alternative plans. Evidence exists to support these suggestions. A Federal Trade Commission study indicates that the Health Insurance Plan of Greater New York and the Group Health Association of Washington do not actively attempt to expand their membership through price competition. Both of these plans seem satisfied with their market positions, and both cost about as much as most other health plans in their area. . . .

If ADSs evolve and do compete with existing ADSs and traditional insurers, it is still not certain whether such competition will lower health care costs. Plans that seek to attract new members may compete on the basis of convenience, breadth of coverage, amenities, quality of medical care, and price. Only competition based on price, however, would lead to lower health care costs, and there are some sound reasons for expecting ADSs not to compete on the basis of price.

Suppose an ADS is considering establishing a branch in a suburb where there are only traditional fee-for-service plans. The ADS's costs need be only slightly lower than the available fee-for-service plans to be competitive enough to establish its branch membership. It should not have to lower costs significantly to do so and consequently should be able to avoid the difficult and often disagreeable task (for plan administrators) of attempting to compel its physicians to utilize fewer resources and constrain services. . . .

Question 2: Will ADSs be able to control physician use of resources?

The major problem that plan administrators will face if they attempt to lower costs is controlling physician use of resources. This problem is complex because there are many factors that affect physician use of costly resources and services. Peer pressure and the fear of malpractice suits may create incentives for physicians to order more tests than necessary. Physicians are constrained in their choice of treatment regimen by rulings of utilization review committees, professional standards review organizations, insurance claims advisers, and courts. Such considerations may weigh more heavily than the pleas of a plan administrator to limit the use of resources and services.

This network of physician constraints represents a kind of informal collusion that is difficult to eliminate and that will limit the ability of ADSs to provide health care through innovative and less costly methods. Physician groups are capable, because of professional dominance in the health care field, of dictating acceptable methods of treatment to physicians. Any physician who violates these rules is subject to significant peer pressure and sometimes to legal remedies. These constraints may substantially offset any financial incentives of ADSs. . . .

Further Considerations

. . . The [Enthoven] plan poses some special difficulties for the poor (especially the elderly poor) because many in this group are less educated and may not be capable of making informed decisions. . . .

[I]t would probably be necessary for the government to take action to ensure that each qualified plan provides adequate medical care. This, however, would require continuous and vigilant governmental oversight and the enforcement of a considerable number of detailed regulations. . . .

It is also important not to overload the minimum-benefit package, because every service mandated as a minimum benefit is necessarily placed outside the competitive market place. For example, suppose mental health benefits are not included as a minimum benefit, so that plans that do cover mental health services are more expensive. This creates an incentive for most individuals to purchase a plan that does not cover this service. Those individuals who purchase the less expensive plan (no coverage of mental health) thus have an incentive to minimize the utilization of mental health services because they will have to pay out-of-pocket for this service. Alternatively, suppose mental health benefits were included as a minimum benefit, so that all plans would have to include this service and there would be no incentive for anyone to limit the use of this service. This problem is especially important for relatively discretionary services like mental health care, since there is a significant element of judgment and choice in the decision of many individuals to seek this service. . . . A major concern with requiring government officials to determine which services will be included as minimum benefits is the certain pressure these officials will face to include every type of health care provider (e.g., chiropractors, podiatrists, and all kinds of therapists) and every new and expensive service (e.g., kidney dialysis, heart transplants, and plasmapheresis for rheumatoid arthritics) in the minimum-benefit package. Interest groups and professional associations will be vocal and adamant in their attempts to seek refuge under the umbrella of the minimum-benefit package, because to be excluded from this package would spell economic disaster. . . .

The pressures on government to include new services are proportional to the segment of the prospective population to be included under the program. Enthoven's plan will cover virtually all Americans, and the pressure from people in need of new and costly services will be intense and unending. Indeed, it will be difficult to exclude any group of people suffering from a severe illness, because if government officials decide not to include a service they may be accused of sentencing individuals to death or to lives filled with pain and illness.

Schwartz, The Inevitable Failure of Current Cost-Containment Strategies: Why They Can Provide Only Temporary Relief*
257 J.A.M.A. 220 (1987)

The problem of hospital costs is not simply that they are high, but that they have been rising rapidly and consuming an ever larger fraction of gross national product (GNP). If the fraction of GNP spent on hospital care were relatively constant, the current level might still be criticized but with little sense that a crisis is impending. This distinction between the level of current expenditures and the upward trend in expenditures is critical, but it has not figured in the discussion of policy options such as encouragement to the growth of health maintenance organizations (HMOs). . . . In principle, the attempt to control rising costs can have either of two quite distinct effects. One of these is to lower current baseline expenditures. The other is to restrict the rate at which expenditures are growing, without cutting current outlays. It is possible, of course, that a particular intervention will have both effects, but the more interesting and important possibility is that one of these outcomes will be mistaken for the other. In the long run, only measures that reduce the growth in costs can solve the fundamental problem of a cost spiral.

Why Eliminating "Unnecessary" Care Cannot Provide Long-term Cost Containment

With this vital distinction in mind, let us consider the HMO as an example of a widely promoted approach to limiting expenditures. At any given time, enrollees in HMOs spend less than patients re-

---

* Copyright 1988, American Medical Association. Reprinted by permission.

ceiving fee-for-service care, chiefly because they avoid "unnecessary" admissions and thus use an average of 30 percent fewer hospital days per year than individuals in the fee-for-service sector. . . .

Even if we accept the premise that HMOs eliminate hospital days that have no medical justification, we may not infer that eliminating such care would achieve long-term control of rising costs. Although the average expenditures of HMO enrollees are below those in the fee-for-service sector at any given time, costs in both sectors must rise if they are to provide the full benefits of new technology to their patients. Indeed, a study covering the period 1961 to 1974 showed that fee-for-service and HMO costs rose at approximately the same rate, even though at each point in time the overall costs of HMOs were substantially lower. . . . A more recent study covering the five-year period from 1976 to 1981 also demonstrates that the rate of rise in the two sectors has not been significantly different.

This experience illustrates an important principle: even if all useless care were gradually eliminated, we could anticipate only a temporary respite from rising costs unless the forces sustaining the real rate of change — chiefly technologic innovation and rising input prices — were simultaneously brought under control. . . .

The Underlying Real Rate of Increase and Its Causes

The forces driving hospital costs upward must obviously be the major target of any long-term cost-containment program. Three variables appear to account for most of the current increase in hospital costs: population growth, rising real input prices ("hospital market basket"), and increased intensity of services, caused almost entirely by technologic innovation and diffusion. . . .

Only one element remains readily susceptible to control: the introduction and diffusion of new technology. How much this factor contributes to the growth of hospital costs must be determined by subtracting the contribution of other factors: population growth, rising input prices, and changes in the number of adjusted patient days per capita. The difference — an average of 3.5 percentage points annually from 1977 through 1983 — reflects increased intensity of services, resulting mainly from technologic change. . . .

The Technologic and Fiscal Future

There is good reason to believe that the future rate of technologic change will be at least as great as in the past ten or 15 years. We can thus anticipate serious problems in controlling costs unless we are willing to forgo, at least in part, introduction and diffusion of innovative diagnostic and therapeutic measures. A host of expensive new technologies is now being deployed and an equally promising group is currently being developed. Consider, for example, expensive diagnostic methods such as magnetic resonance imaging (MRI) and spectroscopic examinations of tissues by MRI, positron emission tomography, and laser holography. Therapeutic advances promise to have an even larger impact. Transplantation of organs, the artificial heart, monoclonal antibodies, interventional cardiology, implantable defibrillators, genetic engineering, cochlear implants, and treatments for metastatic tumors (such as interleukin 2) are simply examples of technologies that are likely to add billions to costs if all the benefits they offer are to be exploited.

Although there is hope that future research will lead to the development of technologies that will check the rise in costs, the near or midrange prospects for such an outcome appear to be small. One major reason is the ongoing development of noninvasive diagnostic technologies. Such new devices may provide a unit of service more cheaply than their predecessors, but they can be used on many more patients because the level of risk and pain is negligible. They can thus be employed even when the likelihood of obtaining useful information is small. . . .

Some observers have suggested that eliminating unnecessary laboratory tests and x-ray examinations could make a major contribution to cost-containment efforts. Indeed, within the last year, it has been stated that such ancillary activities "are the most rapidly swelling component of health-care costs." This statement appears to be without foundation. From 1950 to the early 1970s, the use of "little ticket" tests (x-ray examinations, chemical laboratory tests, immunologic studies, etc) did rise dramatically, but since then standard laboratory tests and diagnostic procedures have not been used with increased frequency and have therefore not contributed to rising costs for a given episode of illness. Rather, new procedures and high-technology care have been the major culprits. . . .

. . . If the 6.1 percent reduction in hospital-days that occurred in 1984 were followed by similar reductions over the next four or five years, the underlying rapid growth in costs would be partially offset. Consequently, the share of GNP devoted to hospital care would remain the same or even fall slightly. But by the end of the decade, all of the saving from this policy would be exhausted and the underlying rate of increase in expenditures would become the observed real rate of increase. Even if there were then a slowing in the absolute increase in expenditures (e.g., due to elimination of the useless application of new technology), the rate of increase on the lower base of expenditures would probably remain at about 7 percent; if both useless baseline care and useless novel care were reduced by the same amount, say 20 percent, the rate of change would be about the same as in the past. Long-term control of the rate of increase in expenditures thus requires that we curb the development and diffusion of clinically useful technology. Moreover, for the attenuation achieved in year 1 to be maintained in subsequent years, additional rationing of equal magnitude must be imposed in each successive year. . . .

The mechanisms used for rationing might range from diagnosis related groups and budget caps to the evolution of powerful competitive forces. Whatever the cost-containment strategy, it appears that painful choices lie ahead once we have exhausted the easy savings that can be achieved by eliminating unnecessary hospital care.

NOTES

The Future of HMOs

1. A notorious instance of HMO abuse occurred with the California Medicaid program's experimental use of an HMO option in the early 1970s. See Chavkin & Treseder, California's Prepaid Health Plan Program: Can the Patient be Saved?, 28 Hastings L.J. 685 (1977). "Many of these Medicaid HMOs gave little or no care to enrollees and eventually declared bankruptcy after siphoning off large amounts of their revenue to related for-profit organizations. The administrators of these HMOs apparently felt few compunctions about limiting care to their enrollees." Hellinger supra at 454. An extensive Rand Corporation study found that, while high income enrollees fared better in HMOs, low income enrollees experienced poorer health than fee-for-service patients. Ware et al., Comparison of Health Outcomes at a Health Maintenance Organisation with Those of Fee-for-Service, The Lancet, 1986, Vol. I, at 1017. Also discussing the problems of HMO underservice, particularly in government programs, see National Health Law Program, The Medicare/HMO "Partnership": Some Problems for Beneficiaries, 21 Clearinghouse Rev. 236 (1987); Iglehart, Second Thoughts About HMOs for Medicare Patients, 316 New Eng. J. Med. 1487 (1987); Rosenblatt, Medicaid Primary Care Case Management, The Doctor-Patient Relationship, and the Politics of Privatization, 36 Case W. Res. L. Rev. 915 (1986); Schneider & Stern, Health Maintenance Organizations and the Poor: Problems and Prospects, 70 Nw.U.L. Rev. 90 (1975).

2. Naturally, there is another side to the story. Senator Heinz' report has been sharply criticized for selective presentation of anecdotal evidence. E.g., Iglehart supra, 316 New Eng. J. Med. at 1491. If HMOs systematically produced an inappropriate reduction in the quality of care, one would expect this fact to manifest itself in the malpractice experience of HMOs, but so far HMOs have not suffered

malpractice suits at any greater rate than traditional medicine. See Curran & Moseley supra, 70 Nw.U.L. Rev. 69.

One reason for optimism about the quality of HMO care is that

> [T]here are countervailing pressures against any tendencies to overeconomize. Physicians face the threat of a malpractice suit. . . . Incentives for keeping the subscriber population healthy can be built into the method of rewarding physicians. And competition among pre-paid group practice plans, or between such plans and alternative delivery systems, also limits any potential trend toward unduly low hospitalization rates. Yet the strongest force militating against excessive economizing is the strongly imbued norms of practicing good medicine under conditions of strict professional review.

Developments, The Role of Prepaid Group Practice in Relieving the Medical Care Crisis, 84 Harv. L. Rev. 887, 926 (1971).

3. Enthoven's proposals for "managed competition" among HMOs and other alternative delivery systems have attracted great attention. For a more extensive description of his competing HMO proposal as a basis for a comprehensive national health insurance, see A. Enthoven, Health Plan: The Only Practical Solution to the Soaring Cost of Medical Care (1980). For more recent and less sweeping versions of his proposal, see Enthoven, Managed Competition in Health Care and the Unfinished Agenda, Health Care Fin. Rev., 1986 Supp., at 105. For additional commentary on Enthoven's plan, see Symposium, 7 Health Affairs (Summer 1988); Bovbjerg, Vouchers for Medicare: The Impossible Dream?, in Lessons from the First Twenty Years of Medicare (M. Pauly & W. Kissick eds. 1987); Rushefsky, A Critique of Market Reform in Health Care: The "Consumer-Choice Health Plan," 5 J. Health Pol. Poly. & L. 720 (1981); Lynk, Regulation and Competition: An Examination of the "Consumer Choice Health Plan," 6 J. Health Pol. Poly. & L. 125 (1982); Ginsburg, Competition and Cost Containment, 303 New Eng. J. Med. 1112 (1980). Further development of Hellinger's argument that HMOs will find it difficult to change physicians' practice patterns is contained in Hall, Institutional Control of Physician Behavior: Legal Barriers to Health Care Cost Containment, 137 U. Penn. L. Rev. 431 (1988).

4. Enthoven's plan has found life in several state Medicaid programs. The Arizona Health Care Cost Containment System ("AHCCCS"), the first Medicaid program to rely solely on competing HMOs, has received the most discussion. AHCCCS chooses the lowest cost HMOs through a competitive bidding process. The eligible poor are then allowed to choose among these designated providers and to switch plans during an annual open enrollment period if they are dissatisfied with the care they receive. The still-young Arizona system has experienced difficulties in receiving enough bidders in rural counties, and several of the initially selected HMOs went bankrupt due

to mismanagement and underbidding. See generally Babbitt & Rose, Building a Better Mousetrap: Health Care Reform and the Arizona Program, 3 Yale J. Reg. 243 (1986); Christianson & Hillman, Health Care for the Indigent and Competitive Contracts: the Arizona Experience (1986); McCall et al., Evaluation of AHCCCS, Health Care Fin. Rev., Winter 1985, at 77; Vogel, An Analysis of Structural Incentives in AHCCCS, 5 Health Care Fin. Rev., Summer 1984.

5. The Heinz subcommittee report found that the practices of biased or "adverse" selection forewarned by Hellinger have in fact occurred in Medicare HMOs:

> [T]here are a variety of illegal techniques that an HMO can use to avoid high risk, high cost beneficiaries: 1) pre-enrollment medical screening of the potential enrollee; 2) selective marketing practices [such as targeting specific zip codes for white, middle-class areas]; 3) weeding out high cost beneficiaries once they are enrolled by discouraging utilization . . . , 4) reducing benefits that are attracting high cost patients; and 5) terminating the plan's contract in a specific area where the plan's costs have been too high.

Medicare & Medicaid Guide (CCH) ¶36,234 at 13709.

Rather than policing these abuses, why not design the rates to reimburse HMOs more accurately for their costs? The government could fine-tune payment variations according to the age, health, and geographic location of patients. There are two difficulties, though. One is that a system with sufficient variables to eliminate any incentive for selectivity would be very complex and costly. The second is that, at the extreme, this degree of "experience rating" begins to fade into a form of cost-based reimbursement: HMOs receive what it costs them to treat each patient. See Anderson et al., Paying for HMO Care: Issues and Options in Setting Capitation Rates, 64 Milbank Q. 548 (1986); Gruenberg et al., Pricing Strategies for Capitated Delivery Systems, Health Care Fin. Rev., 1986 Supp., at 35; Luft, Compensating for Biased Selection in Health Insurance, 64 Milbank Q. 566 (1986); Luft & Miller, Patient Selection in a Competitive Health Care System, 7 Health Affairs 97 (Summer 1988).

C. *Preferred Provider Organizations*

Weller, "Free Choice" as a Restraint of Trade in American Health Care Delivery and Insurance*
69 Iowa L. Rev. 1351 (1984)

In 1979 the Federal Trade Commission ruled that the "free choice" ethics of the American Medical Association (AMA) were a

---
* Reprinted with permission.

restraint of trade.[1] The Commission found that the AMA's free choice ethics "impair[ed] competition from alternative providers . . . by discouraging use of innovative arrangements that can deliver services at lower cost."[2] Remarkably, the FTC's ruling has gone virtually unnoticed. As Harvard Professor Paul Starr recently observed, "Seemingly innocuous, . . . [the AMA's 'free choice'] requirement would prevent a group of doctors from offering care to patients at any lower price than their colleagues'. In the name of free choice, it effectively eliminated the possibility of competition and the right of patients to choose among competing physician groups."[3]

This Article explores the implications of the FTC's free choice ruling by first defining two types of free choice. The AMA's "free choice" ethics, ruled inconsistent with antitrust law, is termed "guild 'free choice.'" The other, consistent with antitrust principles, is termed "market 'free choice.'" Specifically, the AMA's free choice ethics, consistent with guild precepts, . . . in substance provided that each public or private health insurer must deal with all members as a guild, and could not split them into competing groups. . . . Market free choice, in turn, means that physicians and other providers can be split into economic entities competing over price. Stated slightly differently, under guild free choice providers can only compete over nonprice factors, while under market free choice providers can compete over price and nonprice factors. . . .

Guild free choice plans can be defined as insurance arrangements that adhere to the AMA's free choice ethics and thus deprive con-

---

1. American Medical Assn., 94 F.T.C. 980, 1015 (1979), *enforced sub nom.* American Medical Assn. v. F.T.C., 638 F.2d 443 (2d Cir. 1980), *aff'd by an equally divided Court*, 455 U.S. 676 (1982). The administrative law judge's Nov. 13, 1978 opinion is reported at 94 F.T.C. 705 (1978). The Commission's Oct. 12, 1979 affirming opinion is reported at 94 F.T.C. 980 (1979).

2. 94 F.T.C. at 1015 (footnote omitted). The full text of the Commission's analysis of the AMA's free choice ethics was short but to the point:

> Respondent's 1971 edition of Opinions and Reports states that in a community where other competent physicians are readily available, a contract to deliver medical services is unethical unless there is a reasonable degree of free choice of physicians. . . . This position, which also traces its origin to the House of Delegates' action of 1927, was reaffirmed in a Judicial Council decision of 1947 . . . and in a 1959 House of Delegates action. . . . The 1932 Minority Report makes clear that the purpose of this provision is primarily the anticompetitive one of suppressing the activities of competitors, not solicitude for the rights of patients. Given this background, it is logical to infer that the ethical restriction has had the effect of impairing competition from alternative providers in the medical service market by discouraging use of innovative arrangements that can deliver services at lower cost. In the absence of mitigating evidence of procompetitive effects, we find the restriction unreasonably restrictive of competition and an unfair method of competition.

Id.

3. P. Starr, The Social Transformation of American Medicine 300 (1982).

sumers of any right or incentive to select providers in part on the basis of price and efficiency. Applying this definition to the present structure of American health care delivery and insurance, guild free choice plans predominate in public and private insurance. Consumers have little or no incentive to choose providers on the basis of price and efficiency, and provider competition is effectively limited to nonprice competition.

Market free choice plans, on the other hand, can be defined as insurance arrangements that permit consumers to choose providers on the basis of price as well as nonprice considerations. There are at least three different types of market free choice plans. First, there are insurance arrangements, such as catastrophic health insurance, that use coinsurance and deductibles to provide consumers with an incentive to choose among all providers in part on the basis of price. This approach basically tinkers with the predominant form of health insurance, and places all the responsibility for selecting providers on consumers at the time they obtain health services. A second type of market free choice plan — McClure's "health care plan," Enthoven's "health plan," and Ellwood's "competitive medical plan" — is any insurance arrangement that provides financial incentives for consumers to choose a distinct and limited group of providers at the time they select their health insurer. . . .

The third form combines the previous two, as represented by preferred provider organizations (PPOs) with limited groups of providers. PPOs generally provide consumers with financial incentives to use one group of providers (the "preferred providers") over another (all other providers). Typically patients have to pay higher deductibles and coinsurance when they use nonpreferred providers. This form provides consumers with price incentives both at the time they select their insurer and at the time they obtain health care services.

Schwartz, The Preferred Provider Organization as an Alternative Delivery System*
6 J. Leg. Med. 149 (1985)

One of the innovative cost containment mechanisms developed by the private sector that is currently receiving much attention is the

* Reprinted with permission. Book review of Attorneys and Physicians Examine Preferred Provider Organizations, edited by Waxman, J. (National Health Lawyers Association, Washington, D.C., 1984); Preferred Provider Organizations: Planning, Structure and Operation, by Cowan, D. H. (Aspen Systems Corp., Rockville, Maryland, 1984); and Preferred Provider Organizations: Their Status, Development and Future, by Barger, S. B.; Hillman, D. G.; and Garland, H. R. (Aspen Systems Corp., Rockville, Maryland 1985).

preferred provider organization (PPO).* Like the health maintenance organization (HMO), the PPO serves as an alternative system for both the delivery and financing of health care.

The PPO Defined

The PPO has been defined as an organization of physicians and hospitals that contracts employers or insurers to provide comprehensive health care services to subscribers on a fee-for-service basis. Generally, a PPO is characterized by an arrangement of selected health care providers, including both physicians and hospitals, offering their services to a pool of participants at discounted fees. The participants are commonly enrolled in the program by their employer or labor union through a group contract with the PPO. The individual enrollee is not locked in to the services of the PPO but retains the freedom to choose a physician or hospital not affiliated with the PPO. If the enrollee so chooses, however, he or she usually will lose the benefit of the discounted fees and may be required to make a copayment or pay a deductible. Therein lies the meaning of "preferred provider."

The PPO is primarily an organization of fee-for-service providers. The fees usually are predetermined through negotiation between the providers and the "payor" (the entity contracting for the services of the providers). This payment structure is the most obvious difference between PPOs and HMOs, since payment in an HMO setting is usually by a periodic, fixed capitation amount.

PPOs are usually sponsored by one or more of a number of entities, including providers, employers, or other payors, entrepreneurs, or insurance companies. The central organization provides a number of services essential to the success of the PPO, including utilization review, quality assurance, rapid payment of provider claims, marketing of the organization to payors and providers, and general administration of plan operation.

What PPOs Offer

Although the characteristics of PPOs will vary with the needs of their organizers, the incentives for entities and individuals to become involved are quite similar. From a hospital's perspective, participation in a PPO enables it to maintain or expand its share of the patient market. In addition, since PPO subscribers are private-pay patients, participation enables a hospital to increase the proportion of private-pay patients in its patient mix. Both of these ends are critical to the

---

* [Ed. Note: Sometimes called Preferred Provider Arrangements ("PPAs").]

financial health of hospitals in light of other cost containment strategies being employed by government and other providers. The major drawback for a hospital participating in a PPO is that it usually will have to accept discounted rates for services.

From a physician's perspective, participation in a PPO should result in an increased patient base. This is an important objective for nearly every practicing physician because of the recent decline in the number of patients per physician. This decrease is the result of many factors, not the least of which is the influx of new physicians into the market. Other characteristics of PPOs which will attract physicians include the fee-for-service payment system and the quick turn-around on claims. As in the case of hospitals, the major drawback for the PPO physician is obvious — the requirement that services be provided at a discount. The stringent utilization review mechanism usually employed in a preferred provider structure also may serve as a disincentive to physicians contemplating participation in a PPO.

The greatest benefits generated by the PPO are conferred upon payors and patients. The payor, whether it be an employer or otherwise, will enjoy a significant reduction in the cost of the health care benefits it underwrites. The patient will enjoy nearly full access to services without being entirely locked in to a particular hospital or a limited roster of physicians, and without having to worry as much about ever-increasing deductibles.

NOTES

Preferred Provider Organizations — State Law Issues

1. PPOs have experienced tremendous growth in the few years since they first emerged in the early 1980s. See Gabel, Ermann, Rice & Lissovoy, The Emergence and Future of PPOs, 11 J. Health Pol. Poly. & L. 305 (1986); Lissovoy, Rice, Gabel & Gelzer, Preferred Provider Organizations One Year Late, 24 Inquiry 127 (1987). The current national tally stands at around 700. Medicare recently announced its intention to use the PPO concept to structure its entire Part B physician reimbursement. N.Y. Times, Oct. 13, 1987, p.1.

2. Although the FTC barred the AMA from enforcing guild free choice principles through professional ethics, many states have codified the free choice ethic in their statutory law. "Virtually every state has some law or administrative regulation that may impede bargaining or restrict an insurer's ability to channel patients to low-cost providers." Greaney, Competitive Reform in Health Care: The Vulnerable Revolution, 5 Yale J. Reg. 179, 187 (1988). For instance, Nevada prohibits health insurance policies from engaging in "unfair discrim-

ination" in the amount paid to different health care providers. Nev. Rev. Stat. §686A.100.

Another state law consideration is the prohibition of referral fees discussed in Chapter 7.III. Can the discount that PPO physicians grant in order to receive more business from an insurance company or employer be characterized as a referral fee? See United Food & Commercial Workers Union v. Kanerk, 2d Civil No. B016194 (Cal. App. 1987) (unpublished) (no, reversing trial court opinion to the contrary).

To overcome these and other inhibitory state laws, many states have adopted PPO "enabling acts." This label may be misleading, however, because these acts frequently contain obstructive provisions that require PPOs to accept "any willing provider" and to limit payment differentials to the 20-25 percent range. One technique for avoiding state law restrictions is for an employer to organize a PPO on a self-insured basis, thereby invoking the federal preemption under ERISA discussed in Chapter 7.II. See generally Rolph, Ginsburg & Hosek, Regulation of Preferred Provider Arrangements, 6 Health Affairs, Fall 1987, at 32; Rand Corporation, State Laws and Regulations Governing PPOs (1986); Comment, Cost v. Quality in the Regulation of Preferred Provider Arrangements, 41 Sw.L.J. 1155 (1988); Elden & Hinden, Legal Issues in Creating PPOs, 1 J.L. & Health 1 (1985); AHA Office of General Counsel, Regulation of Preferred Provider Organizations: A Legal Guide for Hospital Executives (Sept. 1986); Note, ERISA Preemption of State Mandated Provider Laws, 1985 Duke L.J. 1194.

3. Are PPOs potentially liable for the negligence of their member physicians? If so, under what theory? See Note, Preferred Provider Organization Liability for Physician Malpractice, 11 Am J.L. & Med. 345 (1985) (contending that PPOs, unlike hospitals and HMOs, "are at minimal risk of incurring liability").

4. The impetus for the formation of a PPO can come from either consumers or providers. In a consumer-based PPO, an employer or insurance company approaches doctors and hospitals individually and negotiates with each separately the amount of the discount and the other terms of the agreement. More typically, providers take the initiative by jointly agreeing to offer their services as a package to groups of consumers on a discounted basis, along with administrative services such as utilization and quality review. Provider-based PPOs raise the distinct aura of price fixing, which is per se illegal under Section 1 of the Sherman Act, see Chapter 6.I.C, yet it may be necessary for groups of providers to cooperate in order for this potentially pro-competitive activity to succeed. One doctor does not have the capacity to serve all the patients in a large group, and limiting inpatient services to only one hospital may be too restrictive to attract consumer groups in a large market.

Thus, the primary legal concern for PPOs is how to avoid antitrust liability in forming provider-based PPOs. While the following case does not use the term PPO, the arrangement it considers is structurally identical.

Arizona v. Maricopa County Medical Society
457 U.S. 332 (1982)

JUSTICE STEVENS delivered the opinion of the Court.

The question presented is whether §1 of the Sherman Act, 26 Stat. 209, as amended, 15 U.S.C.. §1, has been violated by agreements among competing physicians setting, by majority vote, the maximum fees that they may claim in full payment for health services provided to policyholders of specified insurance plans. The United States Court of Appeals for the Ninth Circuit held that the question could not be answered without evaluating the actual purpose and effect of the agreements at a full trial. 643 F.2d 553 (1980). Because the undisputed facts disclose a violation of the statute, we granted certiorari and now reverse.

I

In October 1978 the State of Arizona filed a civil complaint against two county medical societies and two "foundations for medical care" that the medical societies had organized. The complaint alleged that the defendants were engaged in illegal price-fixing conspiracies. . . . Because the ultimate question presented by the certiorari petition is whether a partial summary judgment should have been entered by the District Court, we must assume that the respondents' version of any disputed issue of fact is correct. We therefore first review the relevant undisputed facts and then identify the factual basis for the respondents' contention that their agreements on fee schedules are not unlawful.

II

The Maricopa Foundation for Medical Care is a nonprofit Arizona corporation composed of licensed doctors of medicine, osteopathy, and podiatry engaged in private practice. Approximately 1,750 doctors, representing about 70 percent of the practitioners in Maricopa County, are members.

The Maricopa Foundation was organized in 1969 for the purpose of promoting fee-for-service medicine and to provide the community with a competitive alternative to existing health insurance plans. The foundation performs three primary activities. It establishes the schedule of maximum fees that participating doctors agree to accept as payment in full for services performed for patients insured under plans approved by the foundation. It reviews the medical necessity and appropriateness of treatment provided by its members to such insured persons. It is authorized to draw checks on insurance company accounts to pay doctors for services performed for covered patients. In performing these functions, the foundation is considered an "insurance administrator" by the Director of the Arizona Department of Insurance. Its participating doctors, however, have no financial interest in the operation of the foundation.

The Pima Foundation for Medical Care, which includes about 400 member doctors, performs similar functions. For the purposes of this litigation, the parties seem to regard the activities of the two foundations as essentially the same. No challenge is made to their peer review or claim administration functions. Nor do the foundations allege that these two activities make it necessary for them to engage in the practice of establishing maximum-fee schedules. . . .

The fee schedules limit the amount that the member doctors may recover for services performed for patients insured under plans approved by the foundations. To obtain this approval the insurers — including self-insured employers as well as insurance companies — agree to pay the doctors' charges up to the scheduled amounts, and in exchange the doctors agree to accept those amounts as payment in full for their services. The doctors are free to charge higher fees to uninsured patients, and they also may charge any patient less than the scheduled maxima. A patient who is insured by a foundation-endorsed plan is guaranteed complete coverage for the full amount of his medical bills only if he is treated by a foundation member. He is free to go to a nonmember physician and is still covered for charges that do not exceed the maximum-fee schedule, but he must pay any excess that the nonmember physician may charge.

The impact of the foundation fee schedules on medical fees and on insurance premiums is a matter of dispute. The State of Arizona contends that the periodic upward revisions of the maximum-fee schedules have the effect of stabilizing and enhancing the level of actual charges by physicians, and that the increasing level of their fees in turn increases insurance premiums. The foundations, on the other hand, argue that the schedules impose a meaningful limit on physicians' charges, and that the advance agreement by the doctors to accept the maxima enables the insurance carriers to limit and to calculate more efficiently the risks they underwrite and therefore serves as an effective cost-containment mechanism that has saved patients and insurers millions of dollars. Although the Attorneys General of 40 different States, as well as the Solicitor General of the United States and certain organizations representing consumers of medical services, have filed amicus curiae briefs supporting the State

III. Competitive Reforms

of Arizona's position on the merits, we must assume that the respondents' view of the genuine issues of fact is correct.

This assumption presents, but does not answer, the question whether the Sherman Act prohibits the competing doctors from adopting, revising, and agreeing to use a maximum-fee schedule in implementation of the insurance plans.

III

The respondents recognize that our decisions establish that price-fixing agreements are unlawful on their face. But they argue that the per se rule does not govern this case because the agreements at issue are horizontal and fix maximum prices, are among members of a profession, are in an industry with which the judiciary has little antitrust experience, and are alleged to have procompetitive justifications. Before we examine each of these arguments, we pause to consider the history and the meaning of the per se rule against price-fixing agreements.

A

Section 1 of the Sherman Act of 1890 literally prohibits every agreement "in restraint of trade." In United States v. Joint Traffic Assn., 171 U.S. 505 (1898), we recognized that Congress could not have intended a literal interpretation of the word "every"; since Standard Oil Co. of New Jersey v. United States, 221 U.S. 1 (1911), we have analyzed most restraints under the so-called "rule of reason." As its name suggests, the rule of reason requires the factfinder to decide whether under all the circumstances of the case the restrictive practice imposes an unreasonable restraint on competition.

The elaborate inquiry into the reasonableness of a challenged business practice entails significant costs. Litigation of the effect or purpose of a practice often is extensive and complex. Judges often lack the expert understanding of industrial market structures and behavior to determine with any confidence a practice's effect on competition. And the result of the process in any given case may provide little uncertainty or guidance about the legality of a practice in another context. [Cit. omitted]

The costs of judging business practices under the rule of reason, however, have been reduced by the recognition of per se rules. Once experience with a particular kind of restraint enables the Court to predict with confidence that the rule of reason will condemn it, it has applied a conclusive presumption that the restraint is unreasonable. As in every rule of general application, the match between the presumed and the actual is imperfect. For the sake of business certainty and litigation efficiency, we have tolerated the invalidation of some agreements that a fullblown inquiry might have proved to be reasonable. . . .

[P]rice-fixing agreements are unlawful per se under the Sherman Act and . . . no showing of so-called competitive abuses or evils which those agreements were designed to eliminate or alleviate may be interposed as a defense." United States v. Socony-Vacuum Oil Co., 310 U.S. 150, 218 (1940). In that case a glut in the spot market for gasoline had prompted the major oil refiners to engage in a concerted effort to purchase and store surplus gasoline in order to maintain stable prices. Absent the agreement, the companies argued, competition was cutthroat and self-defeating. The argument did not carry the day:

> Any combination which tampers with price structures is engaged in an unlawful activity. . . . The Act places all such schemes beyond the pale and protects that vital part of our economy against any degree of interference. . . . Nor has the Act created or authorized the creation of any special exception in favor of the oil industry. Whatever may be its peculiar problems and characteristics, the Sherman Act, so far as price-fixing agreements are concerned, establishes one uniform rule applicable to all industries alike. Id., at 221-222.

The application of the per se rule to maximum-price-fixing agreements in Kiefer-Stewart Co. v. Joseph E. Seagram & Sons, Inc., 340 U.S. 211 (1951), followed ineluctably from Socony-Vacuum: "For such agreements, no less than those to fix minimum prices, cripple the freedom of traders and thereby restrain their ability to sell in accordance with their own judgment. We reaffirm what we said in United States v. Socony-Vacuum Oil Co., 310 U.S. 150, 223 [60 S. Ct. 811, 844, 84 L. Ed. 1129]: "Under the Sherman Act a combination formed for the purpose and with the effect of raising, depressing, fixing, pegging, or stabilizing the price of a commodity in interstate or foreign commerce is illegal per se." 340 U.S., at 213. Over the objection that maximum-price-fixing agreements were not the "economic equivalent" of minimum-price-fixing agreements, Kiefer-Stewart was reaffirmed in Albrecht v. Herald Co., 390 U.S. 145 (1968):

> Maximum and minimum price fixing may have different consequences in many situations. But schemes to fix maximum prices, by substituting the perhaps erroneous judgment of a seller for the forces of the competitive market, may severely intrude upon the ability of buyers to compete and survive in that market. Competition, even in a single product, is not cast in a single mold. Maximum prices may be fixed too low for the dealer to furnish services essential to the value which goods have for the consumer or to furnish services and conveniences which consumers desire and for which they are willing to pay.

III. Competitive Reforms

Maximum price fixing may channel distribution through a few large or specifically advantaged dealers who otherwise would be subject to significant nonprice competition. Moreover, if the actual price charged under a maximum price scheme is nearly always the fixed maximum price, which is increasingly likely as the maximum price approaches the actual cost of the dealer, the scheme tends to acquire all the attributes of an arrangement fixing minimum prices. Id., at 152-153 (footnote omitted).

We have not wavered in our enforcement of the per se rule against price fixing. Indeed, in our most recent price-fixing case we summarily reversed the decision of another Ninth Circuit panel that a horizontal agreement among competitors to fix credit terms does not necessarily contravene the antitrust laws. Catalano, Inc. v. Target Sales, Inc., 446 U.S. 643 (1980).

B

Our decisions foreclose the argument that the agreements at issue escape per se condemnation because they are horizontal and fix maximum prices. *Kiefer-Stewart* and *Albrecht* place horizontal agreements to fix maximum prices on the same legal — even if not economic — footing as agreements to fix minimum or uniform prices. The per se rule "is grounded on faith in price competition as a market force [and not] on a policy of low selling prices at the price of eliminating competition." Rahl, Price Competition and the Price Fixing Rule — Preface and Perspective, 57 N.W.U.L.Rev. 137, 142 (1962). In this case the rule is violated by a price restraint that tends to provide the same economic rewards to all practitioners regardless of their skill, their experience, their training, or their willingness to employ innovative and difficult procedures in individual cases. Such a restraint also may discourage entry into the market and may deter experimentation and new developments by individual entrepreneurs. It may be a masquerade for an agreement to fix uniform prices, or it may in the future take on that character.

Nor does the fact that doctors — rather than nonprofessionals — are the parties to the price-fixing agreements support the respondents' position. In Goldfarb v. Virginia State Bar, 421 U.S. 773, 788, n.17 (1975), we stated that the "public service aspect, and other features of the professions, may require that a particular practice, which could properly be viewed as a violation of the Sherman Act in another context, be treated differently." See National Society of Professional Engineers v. United States, 435 U.S. 679, 696 (1978). The price-fixing agreements in this case, however, are not premised on public service or ethical norms. The respondents do not argue, as did the defendants in Goldfarb and Professional Engineers, that the quality of the professional service that their members provide is enhanced by the price restraint. The respondents' claim for relief from the per se rule is simply that the doctors' agreement not to charge certain insureds more than a fixed price facilitates the successful marketing of an attractive insurance plan. But the claim that the price restraint will make it easier for customers to pay does not distinguish the medical profession from any other provider of goods or services. . . .

The respondents' principal argument is that the per se rule is inapplicable because their agreements are alleged to have procompetitive justifications. The argument indicates a misunderstanding of the per se concept. The anticompetitive potential inherent in all price-fixing agreements justifies their facial invalidation even if procompetitive justifications are offered for some. Those claims of enhanced competition are so unlikely to prove significant in any particular case that we adhere to the rule of law that is justified in its general application. Even when the respondents are given every benefit of the doubt, the limited record in this case is not inconsistent with the presumption that the respondents' agreements will not significantly enhance competition. . . .

It is true that a binding assurance of complete insurance coverage — as well as most of the respondents' potential for lower insurance premiums — can be obtained only if the insurer and the doctor agree in advance on the maximum fee that the doctor will accept as full payment for a particular service. Even if a fee schedule is therefore desirable, it is not necessary that the doctors do the price fixing.[26] The record indicates that the Arizona Comprehensive Medical/Dental Program for Foster Children is administered by the Maricopa Foundation pursuant to a contract under which the maximum-fee schedule is prescribed by a state agency rather than by the doctors. This program and the Blue Shield plan challenged in Group Life & Health Insurance Co. v. Royal Drug Co., 440 U.S. 205 (1979), indicate that insurers are capable not only of fixing maximum reimbursable prices but also of obtaining binding agreements with providers guaranteeing the insured full reimbursement of a participating provider's fee. In light of these examples, it is not surprising that nothing in the record even arguably supports the conclusion that this type of insurance program could not function if the fee schedules were set in a different way.

The most that can be said for having doctors fix the maximum prices is that doctors may be able to do it more efficiently than

---

26. [T]his case [does not] present the question whether an insurer may, consistent with the Sherman Act, fix the fee schedule and enter into bilateral contracts with individual doctors. . . . In an amicus curiae brief, the United States expressed its opinion that such an arrangement would be legal unless the plaintiffs could establish that a conspiracy among providers was at work. . . .

III. Competitive Reforms 887

insurers. The validity of that assumption is far from obvious, but in any event there is no reason to believe that any savings that might accrue from this arrangement would be sufficiently great to affect the competitiveness of these kinds of insurance plans. It is entirely possible that the potential or actual power of the foundations to dictate the terms of such insurance plans may more than offset the theoretical efficiencies upon which the respondents' defense ultimately rests. . . .

IV

Having declined the respondents' invitation to cut back on the per se rule against price fixing, we are left with the respondents' argument that their fee schedules involve price fixing in only a literal sense. For this argument, the respondents rely upon Broadcast Music, Inc. v. Columbia Broadcasting System, Inc., 441 U.S. 1 (1979).

In *Broadcast Music* we were confronted with an antitrust challenge to the marketing of the right to use copyrighted compositions derived from the entire membership of the American Society of Composers, Authors and Publishers (ASCAP). The so-called "blanket license" was entirely different from the product that any one composer was able to sell by himself. Although there was little competition among individual composers for their separate compositions, the blanket-license arrangement did not place any restraint on the right of any individual copyright owner to sell his own compositions separately to any buyer at any price. But a "necessary consequence" of the creation of the blanket license was that its price had to be established. We held that the delegation by the composers to ASCAP of the power to fix the price for the blanket license was not a species of the price-fixing agreements categorically forbidden by the Sherman Act. The record disclosed price fixing only in a "literal sense." Id., at 8.

This case is fundamentally different. Each of the foundations is composed of individual practitioners who compete with one another for patients. Neither the foundations nor the doctors sell insurance, and they derive no profits from the sale of health insurance policies. The members of the foundations sell medical services. Their combination in the form of the foundation does not permit them to sell any different product. Their combination has merely permitted them to sell their services to certain customers at fixed prices and arguably to affect the prevailing market price of medical care.

The foundations are not analogous to partnerships or other joint arrangements in which persons who would otherwise be competitors pool their capital and share the risks of loss as well as the opportunities for profit. In such joint ventures, the partnership is regarded as a single firm competing with other sellers in the market. The agreement under attack is an agreement among hundreds of competing doctors concerning the price at which each will offer his own services to a substantial number of consumers. It is true that some are surgeons, some anesthesiologists, and some psychiatrists, but the doctors do not sell a package of three kinds of services. If a clinic offered complete medical coverage for a flat fee, the cooperating doctors would have the type of partnership arrangement in which a price-fixing agreement among the doctors would be perfectly proper. But the fee agreements disclosed by the record in this case are among independent competing entrepreneurs. They fit squarely into the horizontal price-fixing mold.

The judgment of the Court of Appeals is reversed.

It is so ordered.

JUSTICE BLACKMUN and JUSTICE O'CONNOR took no part in the consideration or decision of this case.

JUSTICE POWELL, with whom THE CHIEF JUSTICE and JUSTICE REHNQUIST join, dissenting.

The medical care plan condemned by the Court today is a comparatively new method of providing insured medical services at predetermined maximum costs. It involves no coercion. Medical insurance companies, physicians, and patients alike are free to participate or not as they choose. On its face, the plan seems to be in the public interest. . . .

III

It is settled law that once an arrangement has been labeled as "price fixing" it is to be condemned per se. But it is equally well settled that this characterization is not to be applied as a talisman to every arrangement that involves a literal fixing of prices. Many lawful contracts, mergers, and partnerships fix prices. But our cases require a more discerning approach. . . . In Broadcast Music, Inc. v. Columbia Broadcasting System, Inc., supra, there was minimum price fixing in the most "literal sense." Id., at 8. We nevertheless agreed, unanimously, that an arrangement by which copyright clearinghouses sold performance rights to their entire libraries on a blanket rather than individual basis did not warrant condemnation on a per se basis. Individual licensing would have allowed competition between copyright owners. But we reasoned that licensing on a blanket basis yielded substantial efficiencies that otherwise could not be realized. Indeed, the blanket license was itself "to some extent, a different product." Id., at 22.

In sum, the fact that a foundation-sponsored health insurance plan literally involves the setting of ceiling prices among competing physicians does not, of itself, justify condemning the plan as per se illegal. Only if it is clear from the record that the agreement among physicians is "so plainly anticompetitive that no elaborate study of [its effects] is needed to establish [its] illegality" may a court properly make a per se judgment. National Society of Professional Engineers v. United States, supra, at 692. . . .

In a complex economy, complex economic arrangements are commonplace. It is unwise for the Court, in a case as novel and important as this one, to make a final judgment in the absence of a complete record and where mandatory inferences create critical issues of fact.

NOTES

PPO Antitrust Liability

1. Medical society "foundation plans," such as those considered in *Maricopa County*, were the product of the medical profession's resistance to the introduction of HMOs in the 1970s. They illustrate the AMA's continuing "strategy of preemption and cooptation [through] professionally sponsored reforms." Havighurst, Professional Restraints on Innovation in Health Care Financing, 1978 Duke L.J. 303. It is therefore not surprising that the Court found these plans to have anticompetitive potential. This ruling is borne out by subsequent developments in Phoenix, where, within three years of the *Maricopa County* decision, the number of PPOs and HMOs increased from one to eighteen.

2. Although PPOs are structurally identical to foundation plans, PPOs are perceived in the climate of the 1980s to be a *pro*competitive innovation in health care financing. Is *Maricopa County* convincingly applied to PPOs nevertheless? Note that, due to recusals, the majority opinion has the support of only four justices.

3. Both the Department of Justice and the FTC, which have enforcement authority over the antitrust laws, have taken a substantially more lenient position with respect to the exercise of their prosecutorial discretion against provider-based PPOs. In a March 22, 1985 speech, J. Paul McGrath, former head of the DOJ Antitrust Division, made the following remarks:

> In business review letters, we repeatedly have stressed the potential procompetitive benefits that may arise from appropriately structured PPOs and similar arrangements. In general, it seems clear that PPOs controlled by insurance companies, third-party administrators, or independent contractors have real procompetitive potential and in most cases pose little risk of anticompetitive harm. Moreover, although PPOs created and controlled by *providers* present somewhat more of an antitrust risk, and thus are subject to somewhat greater scrutiny, we recognize that they too generally provide significant competitive benefits.

Indeed, provider initiative and entrepreneurship are exactly what is needed to inject competition into the market. . . .

But, equally important, we must vigilantly police collective actions by health care providers that are designed only to inhibit competition. Unfortunately, we have witnessed incidents in which health care providers have greeted competitive contracting with cartel activity. . . . Having said that, let me now outline the Division's general approach to analyzing provider-sponsored PPOs. . . .

It is appropriate to analyze provider-sponsored PPOs under principles similar to that applicable to joint ventures generally. Under this analysis, at least three elements must be satisfied for a joint venture among competitors to pass muster under the antitrust law: (1) the horizontal agreements that are part of the venture must be ancillary to a cooperative activity that promotes competition: (2) the collective market share of the participating venturers must not be so large that it forecloses effective competition; and (3) the parties must have no anticompetitive purpose. . . . In short, a PPO of limited size can make a plausible showing that it is an integrated activity enhancing efficiency and competition despite price or other horizontal agreements necessary for and ancillary to its operation.

For the similiar FTC position, see 46 Fed. Reg. 48,982 (1981); Speech by Arthur Lerner, reprinted in D. Cowan, Preferred Provider Organizations 260 (1984).

4. *Maricopa County* suggests three possible avenues for organizing a provider-based PPO so as to avoid a per se price-fixing charge. First, doctors can integrate into a single economic entity, such as an HMO. For instance, Hassan v. Independent Practice Assocs., 698 F. Supp. 679 (E.D. Mich. 1988) held that an IPA's maximum reimbursement schedule does not constitute illegal price fixing.

However, doctors integrating puts them into another antitrust bind. Consider what new antitrust problems would exist if 70 percent of the doctors in Phoenix formed a joint venture. See the discussion of merger law in Chapter 7.VI. On the other hand, what antitrust issues would exist if PPO physicians selectively limited membership to a smaller number of competitors? See the discussion of boycott law in Chapter 6.I.C; Reazin v. Blue Cross & Blue Shield of Kansas, 899 F.2d 1751 (10th Cir. 1990) ($5.4 million verdict sustained in favor of hospital excluded by PPO).

A second way to avoid price fixing, based on the reasoning of the *BMI* case discussed in *Maricopa County*, is for physicians to attempt to form a new product. In *BMI*, the Court used the new product characterization to justify its holding that a "blanket license" for a library of music compositions did not constitute price fixing even though numerous music composers collectively agreed to market their compositions through a joint agency rather than dealing individually with each radio station and night club singer. Why did the Court

III. Competitive Reforms

reject the Foundation plans' argument that the bulk sale of physician services to insurance companies and large employers, coupled with claims processing, quality assurance and utilization review, constitutes a new health care product? What did the Court indicate would suffice to meet the new product test? See Hassan v. Independent Practice Assocs., 698 F. Supp. 679 (E.D. Mich. 1988) (an HMO provides a new "product").

Third, provider-based PPOs might use independent third parties to do their price setting. Indeed, it is through this hybrid structural technique that the Maricopa County Foundation eventually prevailed on remand to the district court. The Foundation revised its bylaws so that the maximum fee schedule is set by a committee composed of consumers and non-Foundation doctors. The Foundation's Board of Trustees selects the initial committee; successor committee members are then elected by subscriber groups from a slate chosen by the incumbent committee. Order of Declaratory Relief, No. Civ. 78-800 (D. Ariz. May 25, 1983) (approving revised bylaws). Is such a committee truly independent? If so, does this matter? Suppose a group of competing doctors agreed with each other to limit their price increases to the consumer price index. Should their lack of control over the CPI make a horizontal price fixing characterization inapplicable?

5. Why might the antitrust risks be greater in the formation of a hospital PPO than a physician PPO?

6. The Department of Justice has caused a considerable stir in the medical profession with several stern public warnings such as the following, delivered May 5, 1989 by the chief of the antitrust division:

> Physicians should be careful that informal discussions do not result in price-fixing agreements. . . . "In the rapidly changing market for high quality, lower-cost health care, the natural inclination of doctors, like other businessmen, to resist discounting is great. The urge of competing doctors within specialty areas, or an array of independentt physicians cutting across many specialties, to get together to discuss 'the situation' is understandable, but fraught with great danger. Such rump sessions are often held under the auspices of a local or *ad hoc* medical society. They can easily turn into discussions about fee levels, agreements to take a 'united front' either to resist certain fee concessions or to engage in a concerted refusal to deal except under specified circumstances."
> . . . The stakes for physicians involved in criminal antitrust investigations are very high. Such doctors risk not only felony conviction, but also imprisonment, fines and license revocation.

Indeed, the DOJ recently initiated criminal grand jury investigations into alleged price-fixing in three separate locations, resulting in indictments against three dentists in Tucson, Arizona. McGinn, U.S.

Won't Let Up on Antitrust Cases, Am. Med. News, March 2, 1990, at 4.

7. Law journals have hashed out provider-based PPO antitrust issues in considerable detail. In addition to the Weller article, see Classen, Provider-Based Preferred Provider Organizations: A Viable Alternative Under Present Federal Antitrust Policies?, 66 N.C.L. Rev. 254 (1988); Costilo & Kazon, Preferred Provider Plans: Avoiding Problems of Horizontal Price-Fixing, 29 Antitrust Bull. 403 (1984); Greaney & Sindelar, Physician-Sponsored Joint Ventures: An Antitrust Analysis of Preferred Provider Organizations, 18 Rutgers L.J. 513 (1987); Walsh & Feller, Provider-Sponsored Alternative Delivery Systems: Reducing Antitrust Liability after Maricopa, 19 U. Rich. L. Rev. 207 (1984).

Barry v. Blue Cross of California
805 F.2d 866 (9th Cir. 1986)

WALLACE, CIRCUIT JUDGE:

Barry and Hassler, two California physicians, appeal from a summary judgment entered in favor of Blue Cross of California (Blue Cross). Their complaint alleges that Blue Cross participated in price-fixing and a group boycott in violation of federal anti-trust law. We have jurisdiction pursuant to 28 U.S.C. §1291, and we affirm.

I

Blue Cross, a nonprofit corporation, offers various forms of medical insurance to residents of California. By statute, at least two-thirds of the members of the Blue Cross governing board must be duly appointed representatives of the public, so that no more than one-third of the board's members can be physicians or representatives of hospitals with which Blue Cross has service contracts. Cal. Ins. Code §11498 (West Supp. 1986). In 1982, California enacted legislation authorizing private insurers to contract with hospitals and health care professionals to provide services for insureds at predetermined prices. Cal. Ins. Code §10133 (West 1972 & Supp. 1986). Blue Cross decided to make such coverage available through an insurance package known as the Prudent Buyer Plan (the Plan).

Blue Cross contracted with physicians and hospitals to provide services at a fixed rate to those who subscribe to the Plan. If a subscriber receives treatment from one of these participating physicians, then Blue Cross pays for ninety percent of the cost of the service, once deductibles are satisfied. If a subscriber elects to use the services of a nonparticipating physician, Blue Cross pays only sixty to seventy percent of the physician's customary fee. Both subscribers

III. Competitive Reforms

and participating physicians are free to deal with any other patient, physician, or insurance company. . . .

Hassler contracted to provide services under the Plan; Barry declined to do so. Barry and Hassler (the two doctors) filed suit in the district court claiming that the Plan resulted in price-fixing and a group boycott in violation of the Sherman Antitrust Act of 1890, 15 U.S.C. (Sherman Act), section 1, and that Blue Cross is a monopolist in violation of Sherman Act, section 2. They also asserted various state law claims. After several months of discovery, the district court granted Blue Cross's motion for summary judgment on all federal claims and dismissed the pendent state law claims. . . .

We consider in turn each of the two doctors' three principal claims: horizontal price-fixing, unlawful vertical restraint of trade, and monopolization.

II

The two doctors allege that the Plan represents a horizontal agreement among competing physicians. If so, the Plan is per se unlawful under section 1 of the Sherman Act because the Plan fixed prices for physician's services. See Arizona v. Maricopa County Medical Society, 457 U.S. 332, 356-57, 102 S. Ct. 2466, 2479, 73 L. Ed. 2d 48 (1982) *(Maricopa)*. To show a horizontal agreement, the two doctors rely on evidence that several thousand physicians signed identical contracts with Blue Cross and that physicians participated in creating the plan. Although their arguments are somewhat confused, we construe them to include two theories of horizontal agreement: (1) that the Plan enables its member physicians to fix prices in a manner similar to the arrangement that the Court found unlawful in *Maricopa;* and (2) that the Plan resulted from conscious parallelism or a tacit conspiracy of physicians.

A

In *Maricopa,* physicians formed an organization to set maximum prices for physician services in Maricopa County, Arizona. 457 U.S. at 339, 341, 102 S. Ct. at 2470, 2471. Although Blue Cross is not an organization of physicians, the two doctors contend that summary judgment should be denied because they have produced sufficient evidence that physicians actually control the Plan.

First, the two doctors point to evidence that Blue Cross obtained advice on the Plan from various physician groups. The record indicates that Blue Cross wanted to test the reaction of physicians before putting the Plan into final form. . . . The record does not indicate that Blue Cross made any changes in the Plan as a result of this or any other information received from physicians. We conclude that this evidence does not permit an inference of physician control of Blue Cross or of the Plan. . . .

B

The other claimed theory of horizontal agreement involves the doctrine of conscious parallelism. Under that doctrine, a tacit agreement is shown if

> [1] knowing that concerted action was contemplated and invited, the [physicians] gave their adherence to the scheme and participated in it. [2] Each [physician] was advised that the others were asked to participate; [and 3] each knew that cooperation was essential to successful operation of the plan.

Interstate Circuit, Inc. v. United States, 306 U.S. 208, 226, 59 S. Ct. 467, 474, 83 L. Ed. 710 (1939). The two doctors argue that because several thousand physicians all signed identical contracts, we should infer a tacit conspiracy among those physicians under the *Interstate Circuit* formula.

Conspiracy cannot be inferred from this evidence, however, because . . . each physician had a good independent reason for joining the Plan (each obtained access to Blue Cross customers), . . . joining the Plan was not against a physician's self-interest, [and] . . . participating physicians did not benefit from having other physicians join. . . .

Because the two doctors have not produced sufficient evidence of a horizontal agreement under any theory, summary judgment was proper on that issue. . . .

III

The two doctors also allege a vertical conspiracy — between Blue Cross at one level and the physicians at another — to engage in unlawful restraints of trade. . . . They contend that under the rule of reason test a court must undertake an elaborate examination of the practice in question, balance its procompetitive and anticompetitive effects, and determine whether a less restrictive alternative is available. Such an examination, they assert, ordinarily can take place only after a trial and extensive fact finding. . . .

Not every practice, however, need be subjected to such an elaborate analysis. . . . Close examination of the vertical agreements in this case reveals that they have no impermissible anticompetitive consequences, but do have procompetitive effects without a less re-

III. Competitive Reforms

strictive alternative being available. Therefore the issue of their validity can be resolved without the need for trial.

First we consider whether the agreements have impermissible anticompetitive effects. The two doctors argue that the Plan has the consequence of boycotting or shutting out nonparticipating physicians by interfering with their access to patients insured by the Plan. We agree. However, every contract between a buyer and seller has precisely the effect of which the two doctors complain. When a buyer contracts with one seller, a second seller no longer has access to the buyer's business to the extent it is covered by the existing contract. This consequence, however, is not unlawful. [Cit. omitted.] The two doctors have confused an agreement to boycott with an agreement to buy and sell services. . . .

Therefore, although the vertical agreements in this case tend to foreclose nonparticipating physicians from doing business with patients insured under the Plan, the agreements do not cause impermissible market distortions. They do not prevent patients from seeing nonparticipating physicians, nor physicians from seeing nonsubscribing patients. Neither do they prevent participating physicians from referring patients to nonparticipating physicians, nor from contracting with other insurance companies. Therefore, the agreements do not have any prohibited anticompetitive effects.

On the other hand, the vertical agreements between Blue Cross and the physicians do have certain procompetitive consequences. By demanding lower prices from participating physicians, Blue Cross injects an element of competition into the market for physician services that otherwise might not be present. The Plan also requires that physicians agree to utilization review — oversight by Blue Cross to see that physicians provide the proper kind and level of care. It therefore offers consumers the added choice of health care services subject to a sort of central "quality control." Blue Cross can only provide assured access to lower cost physicians and utilization review if it has physicians under contract. Therefore, the Plan, with its required vertical agreements with physicians, results in these added elements of competition. . . .

Our conclusion here is supported by a number of decisions in which courts have reviewed and upheld health service plans similar to the one before us. In *Klamath-Lake,* 701 F.2d 1276, an insurer offered a prescription drug benefit available only through a single participating pharmacy. We held that this agreement did not constitute a boycott of pharmacies because the insureds remained free to purchase drugs from other pharmacies, although at higher prices. Id. at 1288; see also *Brillhart,* 768 F.2d at 200-01 (insurer's agreements with physicians to provide services at predetermined prices do not violate antitrust laws); Kartell v. Blue Shield of Massachusetts, Inc., 749 F.2d

922, 930-31 (1st Cir. 1984) (same), *cert. denied,* 471 U.S. 1029, 105 S.Ct. 2040, 85 L. Ed. 2d 322 (1985); *Royal Drug II,* 737 F.2d at 1438-39 (insurer who pays reduced benefits for drugs purchased at nonparticipating pharmacies does not engage in boycott or unlawful vertical price fixing); Proctor v. State Farm Mutual Automobile Insurance Co., 675 F.2d 308, 337-38 (D.C. Cir.) (agreements between insurer and repair shops to provide services to insureds at reduced rates do not violate antitrust laws in absence of unlawful horizontal agreement or conspiracy in restraint of trade), *cert. denied,* 459 U.S. 839, 103 S. Ct. 86, 74 L. Ed. 2d 81 (1982); Sausalito Pharmacy, Inc. v. Blue Shield of California, 544 F. Supp. 230, 235-37 (N.D. Cal.1981) (insurer does not engage in unlawful vertical price-fixing by setting rate at which it will reimburse participating pharmacies), *aff'd per curiam,* 677 F.2d 47 (9th Cir.), *cert. denied,* 459 U.S. 1016, 103 S. Ct. 376, 74 L. Ed. 2d 510 (1982).

The agreement that the Fourth Circuit found unlawful in Virginia Academy of Clinical Psychologists v. Blue Shield of Virginia, 624 F.2d 476 (4th Cir. 1980), *cert. denied,* 450 U.S. 916, 101 S. Ct. 1360, 67 L. Ed. 2d 342 (1981), is distinguishable. In that case, Blue Shield reimbursed for psychologists' services only when billed through a member physician. Psychiatrists, who compete with psychologists, did not face this obstacle because, as medical doctors, they could simply become members of Blue Shield. By contrast, in the present case, Blue Cross does not discriminate against a particular class of medical provider, but instead is willing to purchase services from all physicians on equal terms. Furthermore, the defendant insurer in *Virginia Academy* was found to be controlled by physicians and thus a horizontal conspiracy existed. . . .

IV

The final claim of the two doctors is that Blue Cross has monopolized the market for medical insurance in violation of Sherman Act section 2. To prevail on this claim, they must establish that Blue Cross has a sufficiently large share of a relevant market. . . . Blue Cross insured roughly eight percent of the discharged hospital patients [in California]. If we ignore those patients covered by Medicare, Medi-Cal, and self payment, Blue Cross insured sixteen percent of the remaining patients. Such a market share is far below what we would require for a monopoly. See Forro Precision, Inc. v. International Business Machines Corp., 673 F.2d 1045, 1058 (9th Cir.1982) (a thirty-five percent market share did not permit an inference of monopoly power), *cert. denied,* 471 U.S. 1130, 105 S. Ct. 2664, 86 L. Ed. 2d 280 (1985). Therefore, summary judgment was appropriate on the issue of monopolization.

V

Because the two doctors have not produced sufficient evidence of horizontal conspiracy, because the vertical agreements between Blue Cross and the participating physicians do not unreasonably restrain trade, and because they have produced insufficient evidence of monopoly power, we affirm the district court's judgment in favor of Blue Cross.

Affirmed.

NOTES

Antitrust and the Cost Containment Initiatives of Private Insurers

1. Antitrust attacks on insurance companies have proliferated in recent years because, under pressure from employers and the competition of HMOs, traditional insurers are becoming more aggressive in developing innovative cost containment measures. The citations in *Barry* provide a sampling of these disputes. Some of this litigation has produced startling verdicts. In a case that is as yet unreported, a physician-controlled HMO suffered a $100 million verdict for price-fixing!! Thompson v. Midwest Foundn. Independent Physicians Assoc., 54 Antitrust & Trade Reg. Rep. 492 (S.D. Ohio 1988). See also Reazin v. Blue Cross & Blue Shield of Kansas, 899 F.2d 1751 (10th Cir. 1990) ($5.4 million verdict sustained in favor of hospital excluded by a Blue Cross PPO); Ocean State Physicians Health Plan v. Blue Cross and Blue Shield of Rhode Island, 883 F.2d 1101 (1st. Cir. 1989) (setting aside $3 million award for tortious interference with contract).

For general commentary see Miller, Vertical Restraints and Powerful Health Insurers: Exclusionary Conduct Masquerading as Managed Care? 51 L. & Contemp. Prob. 195 (1988); Steele, Minimizing Antitrust Risks of Blue Cross and Blue Shield Plans, 4 J. Contemp. Health L. & Policy 227 (1988); Rovner, Monopsony Power in Health Care Markets: Must the Big Buyer Beware Hard Bargaining?, 18 Loy. U.L.J. 857 (1987) (collecting cases); Law & Ensminger, Negotiating Physicians' Fees: Individual Patients or Society?, 61 N.Y.U.L. Rev. 1 (1986); Heiter, Antitrust and Third-Party Insurers, 8 Am. J.L. & Med. 251 (1983); Havighurst, Controlling Health Care Costs through Commercial Insurance Companies, 1978 Duke L.J. 728; Kallstrom, Health Care Cost Control by Third Party Payors: Fee Schedules and the Sherman Act, 1978 Duke L.J. 645.

2. Some courts have differed with *Barry* on the possible existence of a horizontal conspiracy by detecting provider PPOs in consumer's

clothing. Consistent with the historical origins of Blue Cross and Blue Shield, see Section I.B supra, a plan in a state where competing providers are allowed to dominate the governing board might be viewed as inherently constituting a conspiracy. See Chapter 6.I.C; Virginia Academy of Clinical Psychologists v. Blue Shield, 624 F.2d 476 (4th Cir. 1980), *cert. denied* 450 U.S. 916 (1981) (section one violation established by Blue Shield's refusal to reimburse psychiatrists directly); Glen Eden Hospital v. Blue Cross and Blue Shield of Michigan, 740 F.2d 423 (6th Cir. 1984) (possible conspiracy); Ratino v. Medical Service, 718 F.2d 1260 (4th Cir. 1983) (same); St. Bernard Gen. Hosp. Inc. v. Hospital Serv. Assn., 712 F.2d 978 (5th Cir. 1983) (same); Hahn v. Oregon Physicians' Service, 868 F.2d 1022 (9th Cir. 1988) (physician-controlled plan not entitled to summary judgment on price-fixing charge).

Also, it is always possible to find that an insurance company has conspired with providers even apart from its internal structure. In Reazin v. Blue Cross & Blue Shield of Kansas, 663 F. Supp. 1360 (D.C. Kan. 1987), the court sustained a $7.8 million verdict arising from the formation of a Blue Cross PPO, based in part on the jury's finding that the excluded hospital was boycotted by the included hospitals and BC/BS.

3. Other courts have differed with *Barry* on whether a Sherman Act section 2 monopolization theory is applicable to Blue Cross/Blue Shield plans, which are often the dominant insurer in a local market. E.g., *Reazin* supra, 663 F. Supp. at 1416 (60 percent market share sufficient to support finding of monopolization). (Sometimes, the technical term "monopsony" is used to describe a *buyer* as opposed to *seller* monopoly.) Nevertheless, most courts have rejected this theory as well, reasoning that possessing a large market share is not necessarily equivalent to possessing dangerous market power if there are no barriers to entry by other firms. The leading decisions to this effect are Kartell v. Blue Shield of Massachusetts, 749 F.2d 922 (1st Cir. 1984), *cert. denied,* 471 U.S. 1029 (1985) (no section 2 violation in limiting amount doctors can charge, despite 74 percent market share). See also Ocean State Physicians Health Plan v. Blue Cross & Blue Shield of Rhode Island, 883 F.2d 1101 (1st Cir. 1989) (no Section 2 violation in Blue Cross' use of a "most favored nation clause" which refused to pay participating physicians any more than they received from competing insurers, even though the Blue Cross leadership "desired to put [competitors] out of business"); Ball Mem. Hosp. v. Mutual Hosp. Ins. Co., 784 F.2d 1325 (7th Cir. 1986) (no violation in restrictive payment policies despite 50-80 percent market share).

4. PPOs and other insurance ventures might seek shelter under the McCarran-Ferguson Act's exemption of the business of insurance from antitrust laws. However, the Supreme Court has narrowly con-

strued this exemption to extend only to insurance's core risk-spreading function and not to the way in which an insurance plan is structured or the way in which claims are paid. See Chapter 7.II; Kimball & Heaney, Emasculation of the McCarran-Ferguson Act: A Study in Judicial Activism, 1985 Utah L. Rev. 1; Anderson, Insurance and Antitrust Law: The McCarran-Ferguson Act and Beyond, 25 Wm. & Mary L. Rev. 81 (1983). Nevertheless, in Health Care Equalization Comm. v. Iowa Medical Society, 851 F.2d 1020 (8th Cir. 1988), the court found the exemption applicable to a BC/BS refusal to reimburse chiropractors.

CHAPTER 9

Medical-Moral Problems in a Changing World

I. INTRODUCTION

Quality, cost, and ethics are the three organizing themes that cut across the multitude of individual topics constituting health care law. This chapter collects together those doctrinal developments that most directly implicate the ethical/moral dimension of medicine, issues focused primarily at the edges of life: procreation and death. The chapter begins at the end, with an examination of how precisely we identify the moment of death and of the relationship of legal concepts of death to the ability to retrieve useful organs for transplanting. We then explore whether patients who are still alive may bring about their death by refusing life-sustaining treatment and whether, if the patient is not competent, anyone else is authorized to make these grave decisions in the patient's stead. Turning to issues of child birth, this chapter sets the legal framework by introducing the concept of reproductive liberty in the context of contraception and sterilization. After attempting to assess abortion at the present juncture in the Supreme Court's evolution, we then study two issues at the cutting edge of bioethics: new reproductive technologies, such as surrogate parenthood, and the duties that pregnant women have to protect their fetuses. The chapter concludes with a discussion of tort actions arising from reproduction.

One of the great difficulties in compiling a set of materials such as these is that the rapid pace of technological advances and the ongoing evolution in social values and mores continually open vast vistas of unchartered territory, just as we are learning to map the past course of the law. Therefore, where possible, these materials attempt to provide a clear indication of where the law is, where it has come from, and where it might be heading — by including the most current cases along with the seminal decisions, and by including some theoretical secondary materials that point in new directions.

A second difficulty of bioethics is mastering its voluminous literature. The number of productive scholars in health care law has increased so prodigiously in recent years that the neophyte bioethicist is best advised to consult treatises and bibliographies for an overview of any aspect of the field. Chapter 1 cites many of these sources directed to health care law generally. Here, we provide citations to those general sources that are most relevant to the bioethics sector. Additional relevant citations to sources that address more specific topics within bioethics are scattered throughout the notes.

The major journals are Bioethics Reporter; Bioethics (an Australian Journal); Hastings Center Report; Issues in Law and Medicine; Journal of Medical Ethics; Journal of Medical Humanities and Bioethics; Journal of Medicine and Philosophy.

Some of the major treatises and monographs are J. Childress & R. Gaare, BioLaw: A Legal and Ethical Reporter on Medicine, Health Care, and Bioengineering; T. Beauchamp & J. Childress, Principles of Biomedical Ethics (2d ed. 1983); J. Glover, Causing Death and Saving Lives (1977); J. Harris, The Value of Life (1985); C. Levine, Taking Sides: Clashing Views on Controversial Bio-ethical Issues (1984); H. Levine, Life Choices (1986); T. Mappes & J. Zembaty, Biomedical Ethics (2d ed. 1986); D. VanDeVeer & T. Regan, Health Care Ethics (1987). There is also a very comprehensive encyclopedia and bibliography of the field. Encyclopedia of Bioethics (W. Reich ed. 1978); L. Walters & T. Kahn, Bibliography of Bioethics (1975-) (annual volumes).

II. TERMINATION OF TREATMENT AND RELATED MATTERS

A. *Defining Death and Harvesting Organs*

1. The Definition of Death

Strachan v. John F. Kennedy Memorial Hospital
538 A.2d 346 (N.J. 1988)

CLIFFORD, J. The pertinent facts may be summarized as follows. At approximately 4:30 P.M. on Friday, April 25, 1980, twenty-year-old Jeffrey Strachan shot himself in the head in an apparent suicide attempt. He was rushed to John F. Kennedy Memorial Hospital (the Hospital), an acute care facility and one of the defendants in this case. At 5:25 that afternoon Dr. Hummel, the emergency room physician, diagnosed Jeffrey as brain dead. The doctor based his conclusion on several factors, including the absence of spontaneous respiration and reflexive movement, as well as the fact that both pupils were dilated and fixed. Dr. Hummel placed Jeffrey on a respirator.

II. Termination of Treatment and Related Matters

Examination later that evening by Dr. Cohen, a neurosurgeon and one of the attending physicians, confirmed that Jeffrey was brain dead. The doctor explained that painful reality to plaintiffs and informed them that nothing could be done to restore brain function.

Because the Hospital is actively involved in organ transplants through its affiliate, the Delaware Valley Transplant Program, Dr. Cohen asked plaintiffs to consider donating Jeffrey's organs. He noted on the medical chart that the staff should proceed to "harvest" Jeffrey's organs if the parents gave their permission (the obvious implication being that there was no doubt about Jeffrey's status: he was dead). Because plaintiffs were uncertain about what to do, they deferred a decision and agreed to return in the morning. Jeffrey was then transferred to the intensive care unit, where he was continued on the life support system in order that the organs would remain in a condition for harvesting should the parents' decision be in favor of donation. Jeffrey's parents were allowed to "visit" him in the intensive care unit.

Plaintiffs returned the next morning, Saturday, April 26. They informed a Dr. Pinsler (whose connection with the hospital is not disclosed in the record) of their decision not to donate any of Jeffrey's organs. They also requested that he be taken off the respirator. Dr. Pinsler advised plaintiffs to "think it over some more." Plaintiffs also discussed their request with Dr. Cohen. When Mr. Strachan asked a nurse when the machine would be turned off, he was informed that the hospital administrator had not given any order for the removal of the machinery, and that the removal could not be effected without such an order. . . .

[D]efendant Pirolli, the hospital administrator, late that same evening . . . called the Hospital's general counsel, Edward Sullivan, for advice. Sullivan suggested that the Hospital obtain plaintiffs' consent for removal of the respirator. He also indicated that the Hospital should run two electroencephalograms (EEGs), twenty-four hours apart, to get a "clear understanding of what the boy's condition is." He suggested to Pirolli that a court order might be obtained as an alternative to a medical decision to turn off the respirator. Another possible solution offered by Sullivan was the convening of a Prognosis Committee to assist the physicians in the decision to pronounce the patient dead.

The results of the two EEGs confirmed that Jeffrey was indeed brain dead. . . . Monday, April 28, 1980 . . . at 4:05 P.M., Dr. Weinstein disconnected the respirator. Dr. Santoro pronounced Jeffrey dead and executed a death certificate, after which Jeffrey's body was turned over to his family for burial.

Plaintiffs thereafter instituted this action against the Hospital [and] administrator Pirolli [alleging that they delayed for two days in turning their son's body over to them in hopes of convincing them to donate his organs. The jury awarded a total verdict of $140,000.]

. . . For more than half a century this state has recognized a quasi property right in the body of a dead person. "[I]t is now the prevailing rule . . . that the right to bury the dead and preserve the remains is a quasi right in property, the infringement of which may be redressed by an action in damages." Spiegel v. Evergreen Cemetery Co., 117 N.J.L. 90, 93, 186 A. 585 (Sup. Ct. 1936). We pause to record our agreement with a commentator's observation about the "somewhat dubious" nature of a property right to the body. Prosser, supra, at 63. "It seems reasonably obvious that such 'property' is something evolved out of thin air to meet the occasion, and that in reality the personal feelings of the survivors are being protected, under a fiction likely to deceive no one but a lawyer." Ibid. The problem may be avoided by recognizing the obvious: the tort contemplates the wrongful infliction of mental distress. Ibid.; see Restatement (Second) of Torts §868 comment a (1977); Annotation, Liability for Withholding Corpse, 48 ALR3d 240, 252-53 (1973). However it may be denominated, the cause of action is firmly in place.

Although the Appellate Division recognized that cause of action as a quasi property right, the majority held that recovery could not be allowed here because Jeffrey was not legally dead until Monday, April 28, at 4:10 P.M., when he was officially pronounced dead, the respirator was turned off, and the death certificate was signed. 209 N.J. Super. at 314, 507 A.2d 718. It was then that Jeffrey's body was turned over to plaintiffs for burial.

Plaintiffs' right of recovery, then, depends on when Jeffrey's death occurred. Jeffrey was pronounced brain dead by the emergency room physician at 5:25 P.M. on Friday. That assessment was confirmed by a neurosurgeon that evening, and again confirmed by other doctors and by the results of additional testing throughout the weekend. The evidence is overwhelming that Jeffrey was deemed brain dead considerably earlier than Monday at 4:10 P.M. when Dr. Santoro pronounced him dead and executed a death certificate. Thus the question comes down to whether our legal definition of death should include brain death.

Traditionally, death was defined as the irreversible cessation of cardiopulmonary function. [ ] This definition, however, came under attack as failing to reflect advances in medical technology. Because cardiac and respiratory activity can be mechanically maintained for some time, definitions of "death" have increasingly focused on the cessation of brain functions. See Comment, Law at the Edge of Life:

Issues of Death and Dying, 7 Hamline L. Rev. 431 (1984). Once the brain is dead, no technology exists to restore its function.

Technological advances have also made possible the performance of organ transplants on a regular basis. For organs to be preserved for transplant, the donor's cardiopulmonary system must continue functioning until the organs can be removed. Under the traditional definition of death, such a donor would be considered as still alive because the heart continues to beat and the lungs continue to perform the respiratory function. In a very real sense, then, a break from the traditional definition of death is a necessary condition to the existence of transplant programs, for otherwise the organ-removal process might be deemed to have "killed" the donor. See Schwartz, Bioethical and Legal Considerations in Increasing the Supply of Transplantable Organs: From UAGA to "Baby Fae," 10 Am. J.L. & Med. 397, 416 (1985).

In response to these concerns, many states have adopted new definitions of death, incorporating brain death. The Uniform Determination of Death Act (UDDA) provides:

§1. [DETERMINATION OF DEATH]
An individual who has sustained either (1) irreversible cessation of circulatory and respiratory functions, or (2) irreversible cessation of all functions of the entire brain, including the brain stem, is dead. A determination of death must be made in accordance with accepted medical standards.

12 U.L.A. 236 (Supp. 1983) (reprinted in President's Commission for the Study of Ethical Problems in Medicine and Biomedical and Behavioral Research, Deciding to Forego Life-Sustaining Treatment at 9 n.7 (1983)). By 1985, thirteen states and the District of Columbia had adopted the UDDA. Bioethical and Legal Considerations, supra, 10 Am. J.L. & Med. at 418. One recent survey estimates that at least thirty states have adopted statutory definitions of death that include cessation of brain function. Law at the Edge, supra, 7 Hamline L. Rev. at 457, Appendix A. In the criminal context, our Appellate Division adopted a definition equating death with brain death. State v. Watson, 191 N.J. Super. 464, 467 A.2d 590, *certif. den.*, 95 N.J. 230, 470 A.2d 443 (1983). Watson held that the defendant was properly convicted under our homicide statute for causing the brain death of his victim. 191 N.J. Super. at 466, 467 A.2d 590.

We therefore conclude that section one of the UDDA provides the appropriate legal definition of death. . . . [Consequently,] there was ample support in the evidence for the jury's conclusion that defendants had "negligently [held] the body of Jeffrey Strachan so as to prevent his proper burial." [The court remanded the case for a retrial on damages because of an error in the jury instructions.]

Harvard Medical School Ad Hoc Committee to Examine the Definition of Brain Death, Report: A Definition of Irreversible Coma*
205 J.A.M.A. 337 (1968)

Our primary purpose is to define irreversible coma as a new criterion for death. There are two reasons why there is need for a definition: (1) Improvements in resuscitative and supportive measures have led to increased efforts to save those who are desperately injured. Sometimes these efforts have only partial success so that the result is an individual whose heart continues to beat but whose brain is irreversibly damaged. The burden is great on patients who suffer permanent loss in intellect, on their families, on the hospitals, and on those in need of hospital beds already occupied by these comatose patients. (2) Obsolete criteria for the definition of death can lead to controversy in obtaining organs for transplantation.

Irreversible coma has many causes, but *we are concerned here only with those comatose individuals who have no discernible central nervous system activity.* If the characteristics can be defined in satisfactory terms, translatable into action — and we believe this is possible — then several problems will either disappear or will become more readily soluble.

More than medical problems are present. There are moral, ethical, religious, and legal issues. Adequate definition here will prepare the way for better insight into all of these matters as well as for better law than is currently applicable.

Characteristics of Irreversible Coma

An organ, brain or other, that no longer functions and has no possibility of functioning again is for all practical purposes dead. Our first problem is to determine the characteristics of a *permanently* nonfunctioning brain.

A patient in this state appears to be in deep coma. The condition can be satisfactorily diagnosed by points 1, 2, and 3 to follow. The

---

* The Ad Hoc Committee included Henry K. Beecher, M.D., chairman; Raymond D. Adams, M.D.; Clifford Barger, M.D.; William J. Curran, J.D., S.M. Hyg.; Derek Denny-Brown, M.D.; Dana L. Farnsworth, M.D.; Jordi Folch-Pi, M.D.; Everett I. Mendelsohn, Ph.D.; John P. Merrill, M.D.; Joseph Murray, M.D.; Ralph Potter, Th. D.; Robert Schwab, M.D.; and William Sweet, M.D. Its report is reprinted here with the permission of the Journal of the American Medical Association. Copyright © 1968 by the American Medical Association.

II. Termination of Treatment and Related Matters

electroencephalogram (point 4) provides confirmatory data, and when available it should be utilized. In situations where for one reason or another electroencephalographic monitoring is not available, the absence of cerebral function has to be determined by purely clinical signs, to be described, or by absence of circulation as judged by standstill of blood in the retinal vessels, or by absence of cardiac activity.

1. *Unreceptivity and Unresponsitivity.* — There is a total unawareness to externally applied stimuli and inner need and complete unresponsiveness — our definition of irreversible coma. Even the most intensely painful stimuli evoke no vocal or other response, not even a groan, withdrawal of a limb, or quickening of respiration.

2. *No Movements or Breathing.* — Observations covering a period of at least one hour by physicians is adequate to satisfy the criteria of no spontaneous muscular movements or spontaneous respiration or response to stimuli such as pain, touch, sound, or light. After the patient is on a mechanical respirator, the total absence of spontaneous breathing may be established by turning off the respirator for three minutes and observing whether there is any effort on the part of the subject to breathe spontaneously. (The respirator may be turned off for this time provided that at the start of the trial period the patient's carbon dioxide tension is within the normal range, and provided also that the patient had been breathing room air for at least 10 minutes prior to the trial.)

3. *No Reflexes.* — Irreversible coma with abolition of central nervous system activity is evidenced in part by the absence of elicitable reflexes. The pupil will be fixed and dilated and will not respond to a direct source of bright light. Since the establishment of a fixed, dilated pupil is clear-cut in clinical practice, there should be no uncertainty as to its presence. Ocular movement (to head turning and to irrigation of the ears with ice water) and blinking are absent. There is no evidence of postural activity (decerebrate or other). Swallowing, yawning, vocalization are in abeyance. Corneal and pharyngeal reflexes are absent.

As a rule the stretch of tendon reflexes cannot be elicited; i.e., tapping the tendons of the biceps, triceps, and pronator muscles, quadriceps and gastrocnemius muscles with the reflex hammer elicits no contraction of the respective muscles. Plantar or noxious stimulation gives no response. . . .

All of the above tests shall be repeated at least 24 hours later with no change.

The validity of such data as indications of irreversible cerebral damage depends on the exclusion of two conditions: hypothermia (temperature below 90 F [32.2 C] or central nervous system depressants, such as barbiturates.

Other Procedures

The patient's condition can be determined only by a physician. When the patient is hopelessly damaged as defined above, the family and all colleagues who have participated in major decisions concerning the patient, and all nurses involved, should be so informed. Death is to be declared and *then* the respirator turned off. The decision to do this and the responsibility for it are to be taken by the physician-in-charge, in consultation with one or more physicians who have been directly involved in the case. It is unsound and undesirable to force the family to make the decision.

Legal Commentary

The legal system of the United States is greatly in need of the kind of analysis and recommendations for medical procedures in cases of irreversible brain damage as described. At present, the law of the United States, in all 50 states and in the federal courts, treats the question of human death as a question of fact to be decided in every case. When any doubt exists, the courts seek medical expert testimony concerning the time of death of the particular individual involved. However, the law makes the assumption that the medical criteria for determination of death are settled and not in doubt among physicians. Furthermore, the law assumes that the traditional method among physicians for determination of death is to ascertain the absence of all vital signs. To this extent, Black's Law Dictionary (fourth edition, 1951) defines death as "The cessation of life; the ceasing to exist; *defined by physicians* as a total stoppage of the circulation of the blood, and a cessation of the animal and vital functions consequent thereupon, such as respiration, pulsation, etc. [italics added]."

In the few modern court decisions involving a definition of death, the courts have used the concept of the total cessation of all vital signs.

In this report, however, we suggest that responsible medical opinion is ready to adopt new criteria for pronouncing death to have occurred in an individual sustaining irreversible coma as a result of permanent brain damage. If this position is adopted by the medical community, it can form the basis for change in the current legal concept of death. No statutory change in the law should be necessary since the law treats this question essentially as one of fact to be determined by physicians. The only circumstance in which it would be necessary that legislation be offered in the various states to define "death" by law would be in the event that great controversy were engendered surrounding the subject and physicians were unable to agree on the new medical criteria.

It is recommended as a part of these procedures that judgment of the existence of these criteria is solely a medical issue. It is suggested that the physician in charge of the patient consult with one or more other physicians directly involved in the case before the patient is declared dead on the basis of these criteria. In this way, the responsibility is shared over a wider range of medical opinion, thus providing an important degree of protection against later questions which might be raised about the particular case. It is further suggested that the decision to declare the person dead, and then to turn off the respirator, be made by physicians not involved in any later effort to transplant organs or tissue from the deceased individual. This is advisable in order to avoid any appearance of self-interest by the physicians involved.

It should be emphasized that we recommend the patient be declared dead before any effort is made to take him off the respirator, if he is then on a respirator. This declaration should not be delayed until he has been taken off the respirator and all artificially stimulated signs have ceased. The reason for this recommendation is that in our judgment it will provide a greater degree of legal protection to those involved. Otherwise, the physicians would be turning off the respirator on a person who is, under the present strict, technical application of law, still alive. . . .

President's Commission for the Study of Ethical Problems in Medicine and Biomedical and Behavioral Research, Defining Death
15-19 (1981)

The Interrelationships of Brain, Heart, and Lung Functions

The brain has three general anatomic divisions: the cerebrum, with its outer shell called the cortex; the cerebellum; and the brainstem, composed of the midbrain, the pons, and the medulla oblongata [Figure 1]. Traditionally, the cerebrum has been referred to as the "higher brain" because it has primary control of consciousness, thought, memory and feeling. The brainstem has been called the "lower brain," since it controls spontaneous, vegetative functions such as swallowing, yawning and sleep-wake cycles. It is important to note that these generalizations are not entirely accurate. Neuroscientists generally agree that such "higher brain" functions as cognition or consciousness probably are not mediated strictly by the cerebral cortex; rather, they probably result from complex interrelations between brainstem and cortex.

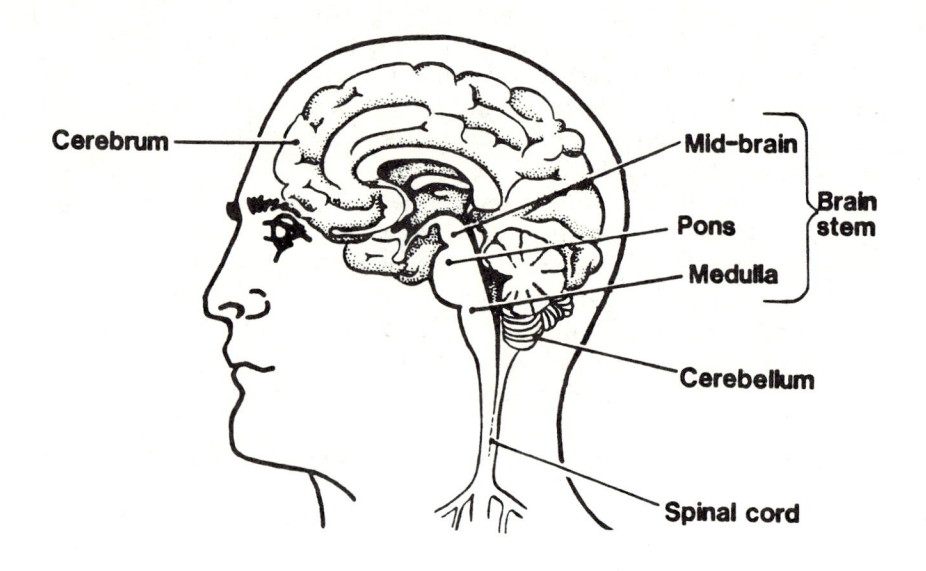

[Figure 1.]

Respiration is controlled in the brainstem, particularly the medulla. Neural impulses originating in the respiratory centers of the medulla stimulate the diaphragm and intercostal muscles, which cause the lungs to fill with air. Ordinarily, these respiratory centers adjust the rate of breathing to maintain the correct levels of carbon dioxide and oxygen. In certain circumstances, such as heavy exercise, sighing, coughing or sneezing, other areas of the brain modulate the activities of the respiratory centers or even briefly take direct control of respiration.

Destruction of the brain's respiratory center stops respiration, which in turn deprives the heart of needed oxygen, causing it too to cease functioning. The traditional signs of life — respiration and heartbeat — disappear: the person is dead. The "vital signs" traditionally used in diagnosing death thus reflect the direct interdependence of respiration, circulation, and the brain.

The artificial respirator and concomitant life-support systems have changed this simple picture. Normally, respiration ceases when the functions of the diaphragm and intercostal muscles are impaired. This results from direct injury to the muscles or (more commonly) because the neural impulses between the brain and these muscles are interrupted. However, an artificial respirator (also called a ventilator) can be used to compensate for the inability of the thoracic muscles to fill the lungs with air. Some of these machines use negative pressure to expand the chest wall (in which case they are called "iron lungs"); others use positive pressure to push air into the lungs. The respirators are equipped with devices to regulate the rate and depth of "breathing," which are normally controlled by the respiratory centers in the medulla. The machines cannot compensate entirely for the defective neural connections since they cannot regulate blood gas levels precisely. But, provided that the lungs themselves have not been extensively damaged, gas exchange can continue and appropriate levels of oxygen and carbon dioxide can be maintained in the circulating blood.

Unlike the respiratory system, which depends on the neural impulses from the brain, the heart can pump blood without external control. Impulses from the brain centers modulate the inherent rate and force of the heartbeat but are not required for the heart to contract at a level of function that is ordinarily adequate. Thus, when artificial respiration provides adequate oxygenation and associated medical treatments regulate essential plasma components and blood pressure, an intact heart will continue to beat, despite loss of brain functions. At present, however, no machine can take over the functions of the heart except for a very limited time and in limited circumstances (e.g., a heart-lung machine used during surgery). Therefore, when a severe injury to the heart or major blood vessels prevents the circulation of the crucial blood supply to the brain, the loss of brain functioning is inevitable because no oxygen reaches the brain.

Loss of Various Brain Functions

The most frequent causes of irreversible loss of functions of the whole brain are: (1) direct trauma to the head, such as from a motor vehicle accident or a gunshot wound, (2) massive spontaneous hemorrhage into the brain as a result of ruptured aneurysm or complications of high blood pressure, and (3) anoxic damage from cardiac or respiratory arrest or severely reduced blood pressure.

Many of these severe injuries to the brain cause an accumulation of fluid and swelling in the brain tissue, a condition called cerebral edema. In severe cases of edema, the pressure within the closed cavity increases until it exceeds the systolic blood pressure, resulting in a total loss of blood flow to both the upper and lower portions of the brain. If deprived of blood flow for at least 10-15 minutes, the brain, including the brainstem, will completely cease functioning.[4] Other pathophysiologic mechanisms also result in a progressive and, ultimately, complete cessation of intracranial circulation.

Once deprived of adequate supplies of oxygen and glucose, brain neurons will irreversibly lose all activity and ability to function. In

---

4. H. A. H. van Till-d'Aulnis de Bourouill. "Diagnosis of Death in Comatose Patients under Resuscitation Treatment: A Critical Review of the Harvard Report," 2 Am. J.L. & Med. 1, 21-22 (1976).

adults, oxygen and/or glucose deprivation for more than a few minutes causes some neuron loss.[5] Thus, even in the absence of direct trauma and edema, brain functions can be lost if circulation to the brain is impaired. If blood flow is cut off, brain tissues completely self-digest (autolyze) over the ensuing days.

When the brain lacks all functions, consciousness is, of course, lost. While some spinal reflexes often persist in such bodies (since circulation to the spine is separate from that of the brain), all reflexes controlled by the brainstem as well as cognitive, affective and integrating functions are absent. Respiration and circulation in these bodies may be generated by a ventilator together with intensive medical management. In adults who have experienced irreversible cessation of the functions of the entire brain, this mechanically generated functioning can continue only a limited time because the heart usually stops beating within two to ten days. (An infant or small child who has lost all brain functions will typically suffer cardiac arrest within several weeks, although respiration and heartbeat can sometimes be maintained even longer.[6])

Less severe injury to the brain can cause mild to profound damage to the cortex, lower cerebral structures, cerebellum, brainstem, or some combination thereof. The cerebrum, especially the cerebral cortex, is more easily injured by loss of blood flow or oxygen than is the brainstem. A 4-6 minute loss of blood flow — caused by, for example, cardiac arrest — typically damages the cerebral cortex permanently, while the relatively more resistant brainstem may continue to function.[7]

When brainstem functions remain, but the major components of the cerebrum are irreversibly destroyed, the patient is in what is usually called a "persistent vegetative state" or "persistent noncognitive state." Such persons may exhibit spontaneous, involuntary movements such as yawns or facial grimaces, their eyes may be open and they may be capable of breathing without assistance. Without higher brain functions, however, any apparent wakefulness does not represent awareness of self or environment (thus, the condition is often described as "awake but unaware"). The case of Karen Ann Quinlan has made

---

5. One exception to this general picture requires brief mention. Certain drugs or low body temperature (hypothermia) can place the neurons in "suspended animation." Under these conditions, the neurons may receive virtually no oxygen or glucose for a significant period of time without sustaining irreversible damage. This effect is being used to try to limit brain injury in patients by giving them barbiturates or reducing temperature; the use of such techniques will, of course, make neurological diagnoses slower or more complicated.

6. Julius Korein, "Brain Death," in J. Cottrell and H. Turndorf (eds.) Anesthesia and Neurosurgery, C. V. Mosby & Co., St. Louis (1980) at 282, 284, 292-293.

7. Ronald E. Cranford and Harmon L. Smith, "Some Critical Distinctions Between Brain Death and Persistent Vegetative State" 6 Ethics in Sci. and Med. 199, 201 (1979).

this condition familiar to the general public. With necessary medical and nursing care — including feeding through intravenous or nasogastric tubes, and antibiotics for recurrent pulmonary infections — such patients can survive months or years, often without a respirator. (The longest survival exceeded 37 years.)

NOTES

Brain Death and the Harvesting of Organs

1. Kansas was the first state to adopt a brain death statute, and its constitutionality was upheld in State v. Schaffer, 574 P.2d 205 (1977). It did so in the context of a murder prosecution, where the defendant had argued that the doctors who removed life support, and not himself, caused the death of the victim. A later case adopting the brain death definition as a matter of common law provides a particularly thorough explanation of the relationship between the definition of death and homicide statutes. People v. Eulo, 482 N.Y.S.2d 436 (1984). At least one decision has declined to change the law in absence of legislative action. State v. Johnson, 395 N.E.2d 369 (Oh. App. 1977).

The definition of death is also relevant to resolving the actual time of death in controversial situations such as homicide investigations and simultaneous death clauses in wills. For a general review, see Coe and Curran, Definition and Time of Death, in Modern Legal Medicine, Psychiatry, and Forensic Science (W. Curran, McGarry & Petty, eds. 1980).

Should the definition of death continue to be left primarily as a medical matter? Should there be only a single concept or time of death? Roger Dworkin argues that the "effort devoted to defining death is wasted at best, counterproductive at worst," because of the variety of contexts in which the issue is relevant, namely: (1) procedural issues such as when the statutes of limitations begin to run for wrongful death actions and murder prosecutions; (2) numerous property and wealth devolution issues such as who died first for purposes of probating the wills of two people with interests in each others' estates; and (3) status relationships such as when remarriage is valid. Consider, for instance, that one accepted departure from the uniform definition of death is the presumption in many states that a person is dead who is missing for more than seven years. Dworkin, Death in Context, 48 Ind. L.J. 623 (1975). See also Bernat, Culver & Gert, On the Definition and Criterion of Death, 94 Ann. Int. Med. 389 (1981) (careful differentiation between the roles of medicine and the law, and among the definition, criterion, and tests of death); Pediatric Brain Death and Organ/Tissue Retrieval (H. Kaufman ed. 1989).

2. The purposefully brief definition of brain death in the Uniform Definition of Death Act (quoted in *Strachan*) has received the endorsement of the ABA, the AMA, and the American Academy of Neurology, among others. The Commissioners' Comment to the Act elaborates to some greater extent. For example:

> "Functioning" is a critical word in the Act. It expresses the idea of *purposeful* activity in all parts of the brain, as distinguished from random activity. In a dead brain, some meaningless cellular processes, detectable by sensitive monitoring equipment, could create legal confusion if the word "activity" were substituted for "functioning."

The full President's Commission report also contains a more extensive discussion of brain death.

3. As the readings make clear, the primary impetus for advancing the time that death is declared is not to relieve the family from years of anguish (since truly brain dead patients will persist for only a few weeks at best), but is to allow for the "harvesting" of organs while the tissue is still healthy. It is now commonplace to surgically remove donated organs while the body is still breathing and the heart pumping. Query whether most family members who assent to organ donation realize this fact. According to one report critical of this practice, "the 'corpse' from which organs are to be removed is commonly capable of reacting sharply as the surgeon makes his first incision. Legs will come up in a protective response, and the muscles in the abdomen will clamp tightly, impeding the operation. Muscle-paralysing drugs have to be given. . . . These are the signs which in a normal operation would indicate to the anaesthetist that the patient was feeling pain and should receive extra anaesthesia." London (Sunday) Times, Dec. 7, 1986, at 1.

4. The proper definition of death may not be as simple and settled a matter as is conventionally thought, and as these readings suggest. A recent survey of 195 medical personnel found that one-third of doctors in charge of identifying brain dead patients were unable to identify the correct legal and medical criteria for death and apply them to two simple cases. Nearly 20 percent believed that death occurs with the loss of *higher* (rather than whole) brain functions, that is, in a patient who is merely in a permanent coma. Youngner et al., "Brain Death" and Organ Retrieval, 261 J.A.M.A. 2205 (1989). Some of this confusion may be due to the Harvard Ad Hoc Committee's choice of the imprecise term "irreversible coma," which fails to distinguish among different states of brain damage:

> The term "irreversible coma" is frequently used with clinically and morally confusing consequences. In retrospect, those who drafted the Harvard Committee criteria for brain death erred in using the term

"irreversible coma" as synonymous with brain death. In a superficial sense, the terminology is correct; brain death is the ultimate "irreversible coma" — there is total destruction of the brain with the deepest possible coma and no possibility of reversibility. Beginning in the 1970s, however, neurological specialists began using the same term to apply to patients in the persistent vegetative state, such as Karen Quinlan.

Cranford, The Persistent Vegetative State: The Medical Reality (Getting the Facts Straight), 18 Hastings Cent. Rep. 27, 28 (March 1988). However, several medical ethicists advocate that we expand the definition of death to include such patients. See Section II.D below.

2. The Procurement of Organs

State v. Powell
497 So. 2d 1188 (Fla. 1986)

OVERTON, JUSTICE.

This is a petition to review a circuit court order finding unconstitutional section 732.9185, Florida Statutes (1983), which authorizes medical examiners to remove corneal tissue from decedents during statutorily required autopsies when such tissue is needed for transplantation. The statute prohibits the removal of the corneal tissue if the next of kin objects, but does not require that the decedent's next of kin be notified of the procedure. . . .

The trial court decided this case by summary judgment. The facts are not in dispute. On June 15, 1983, James White drowned while swimming at the city beach in Dunellon, Florida. Associate Medical Examiner Dr. Thomas Techman, who is an appellant in this cause, performed an autopsy on James' body at Leesburg Community Hospital. On July 11, 1983, Anthony Powell died in a motor vehicle accident in Marion County. Medical Examiner Dr. William H. Shutze, who is also an appellant in this cause, performed an autopsy on Anthony's body. In each instance, under the authority of section 732.9185, the medical examiner removed corneal tissue from the decedent without giving notice to or obtaining consent from the parents of the decedent.

James' and Anthony's parents, who are the appellees in this case, each brought an action claiming damages for the alleged wrongful removal of their sons' corneas and seeking a judgment declaring section 732.9185 unconstitutional. The actions were subsequently consolidated. . . .

In addressing the issue of the statute's constitutionality, we begin with the premise that a person's constitutional rights terminate at death. . . .

The unrebutted evidence in this record establishes that the State of Florida spends approximately $138 million each year to provide its blind with the basic necessities of life. At present, approximately ten percent of Florida's blind citizens are candidates for cornea transplantation, which has become a highly effective procedure for restoring sight to the functionally blind. As advances are made in the field, the number of surgical candidates will increase, thereby raising the demand for suitable corneal tissue. The increasing number of elderly persons in our population has also created a great demand for corneas because corneal blindness often is age-related. Further, an affidavit in the record states: . . . The record reflects that the key to successful corneal transplantation is the availability of high-quality corneal tissue and that corneal tissue removed more than ten hours after death is generally unsuitable for transplantation. The implementation of section 732.9185 in 1977 has, indisputably, increased both the supply and quality of tissue available for transplantation. Statistics show that, in 1976, only 500 corneas were obtained in Florida for transplantation while, in 1985, more than 3,000 persons in Florida had their sight restored through corneal transplantation surgery. . . .

An autopsy is a surgical dissection of the body; it necessarily results in a massive intrusion into the decedent. This record reflects that cornea removal, by comparison, requires an infinitesimally small intrusion which does not affect the decedent's appearance. With or without cornea removal, the decedent's eyes must be capped to maintain a normal appearance. . . .

We conclude that this record clearly establishes that this statute reasonably achieves the permissible legislative objective of providing sight to many of Florida's blind citizens.

We next address the trial court's finding that section 732.9185 deprives appellees of a fundamental property right. All authorities generally agree that the next of kin have no property right in the remains of a decedent. Although, in Dunahoo v. Bess, 146 Fla. 182, 200 So. 541 (1941), this Court held that a surviving husband had a "property right" in his wife's body which would sustain a claim for negligent embalming, id. at 183, 200 So. at 542, we subsequently clarified our position to be consistent with the majority view that the right is limited to "possession of the body . . . for the purpose of burial, sepulture or other lawful disposition," and that interference with this right gives rise to a tort action. . . . The view that the next of kin has no property right but merely a limited right to possess the body for burial purposes is universally accepted by courts and commentators. . . .

Decisions of the United States Supreme Court have clearly established that the loss of a common law right by legislative act does not automatically operate as a deprivation of substantive due process.

Tort actions may be restricted when necessary to obtain a permissible legislative objective. See Duke Power Co. v. Carolina Environmental Study Group, Inc., 438 U.S. 59, 88 n.32, 98 S. Ct. 2620, 2638 n.32, 57 L. Ed. 2d 595 (1978).

Appellees also assert that their right to control the disposition of their decedents' remains is a fundamental right of personal liberty protected against unreasonable governmental intrusion by the due process clause. Appellees argue that, because the statute permits the removal of a decedent's corneas without reference to his family's preferences, it infringes upon a right, characterized as one of religion, family, or privacy, which is fundamental and must be subjected to strict scrutiny. . . . According to appellees, the theme which runs through these [privacy] cases, and which compels the invalidation of section 732.9185, is the protection from governmental interference of the right of free choice in decisions of fundamental importance to the family. We reject appellees' argument. The cases cited recognize only freedom of choice concerning personal matters involved in existing, ongoing relationships among living persons as fundamental or essential to the pursuit of happiness by free persons. We find that the right of the next of kin to a tort claim for interference with burial, established by this Court in *Dunahoo,* does not rise to the constitutional dimension of a fundamental right traditionally protected under either the United States or Florida Constitution. . . .

In conclusion, we hold that section 732.9185 is constitutional because it rationally promotes the permissible state objective of restoring sight to the blind. In so holding, we note that laws regarding the removal of human tissues for transplantation implicate moral, ethical, theological, philosophical, and economic concerns which do not readily lend themselves to analysis within a traditional legal framework. Applying constitutional standards of review to section 732.9185 obscures the fact that at the heart of the issue lies a policy question which calls for a delicate balancing of societal needs and individual concerns more appropriately accomplished by the legislature.

For the reasons expressed, we reverse the trial court's order and remand this cause to the trial court with directions to enter judgment consistent with this opinion.

It is so ordered.

Uniform Anatomical Gift Act*
Commissioners on Uniform State Laws (1968)

An act authorizing the gift of all or part of a human body after death for specified purposes. . . .

* This model act was approved by the Commissioners on Uniform State Laws in

Section 2 [Persons Who May Execute an Anatomical Gift]

(a) Any individual of sound mind and 18 years of age or more may give all or any part of his body for any purposes specified in Section 3, the gift to take effect upon death.

(b) Any of the following persons, in order of priority stated, when persons in prior classes are not available at the time of death, and in the absence of actual notice of contrary indications by the decedent, or actual notice of opposition by a member of the same or a prior class, may give all or any part of the decedent's body for any purpose specified in Section 3:

1) the spouse,
2) an adult son or daughter,
3) either parent,
4) an adult brother or sister,
5) a guardian of the person of the decedent at the time of his death,
6) any other person authorized or under obligation to dispose of the body.

(c) If the donee has actual notice of contrary indications by the decedent, or that a gift by a member of a class is opposed by a member of the same or a prior class, the donee shall not accept the gift. The persons authorized by subsection (b) may make the gift after death or immediately before death.

(d) A gift of all or part of a body authorizes any examination necessary to assure medical acceptability of the gift for the purposes intended.

(e) The rights of the donee created by the gift are paramount to the rights of others except as provided by Section 7(d).

Section 3 [Persons Who May Become Donees, and Purposes for Which Anatomical Gifts May be Made]

The following persons may become donees of gifts of bodies or parts thereof for the purposes stated:

1968 and was subsequently adopted in all 50 states by 1972. 8A U.L.A. 16 (1983). The Commissioners replaced this model act with a substantially amended version in 1987, 8A U.L.A. (Supp.), but we continue to reprint the original version which reflects the statutory wording that still prevails.

1) any hospital, surgeon, or physician, for medical or dental education, research, advancement of medical or dental science, therapy or transplantation; or
2) any accredited medical or dental school, college or university for education, research, advancement of medical or dental science or therapy; or
3) any bank or storage facility, for medical or dental education, research, advancement of medical or dental science, therapy or transplantation; or
4) any specified individual for therapy or transplantation needed by him.

Section 4 *[Manner of Executing Anatomical Gifts]*

(a) A gift of all or part of the body under Section 2(a) may be made by will. . . .

(b) A gift of all or part of the body under Section 2(a) may also be made by document other than a will. The gift becomes effective upon the death of the donor. The document, which may be a card designed to be carried on the person, must be signed by the donor, in the presence of 2 witnesses who must sign the document in his presence. . . .

(c) The gift may be made to a specified donee or without specifying a donee. If the latter, the gift may be accepted by the attending physician as donee upon or following death. If the gift is made to a specified donee who is not available at the time and place of death, the attending physician upon or following death, in the absence of any expressed indication that the donor desired otherwise, may accept the gift as donee. The physician who becomes a donee under this subsection shall not participate in the procedures for removing or transplanting a part. . . .

Section 6 *[Amendment or Revocation of the Gift]*

(a) If the will, card or other document or executed copy thereof, has been delivered to a specified donee, the donor may amend or revoke the gift by:

1) the execution and delivery to the donee of a signed statement, or
2) an oral statement made in the presence of 2 persons and communicated to the donee, or
3) a statement during a terminal illness or injury addressed to an attending physician and communicated to the donee, or
4) a signed card or document found on his person or in his effects.

(b) Any document of gift which has not been delivered to the donee may be revoked by the donor in the manner set out in subsection (a) or by destruction, cancellation, or mutilation of the document and all executed copies thereof.

(c) Any gift made by a will may also be amended or revoked in the manner provided for amendment or revocation of wills, or as provided in subsection (a).

Section 7 [Rights and Duties at Death]

(a) The donee may accept or reject the gift. If the donee accepts a gift of the entire body, he may, subject to the terms of the gift, authorize embalming and the use of the body in funeral services. If the gift is of a part of the body, the donee, upon the death of the donor and prior to embalming, shall cause the part to be removed without unnecessary mutilation. After removal of the part, custody of the remainder of the body vests in the surviving spouse, next of kin or other persons under obligation to dispose of the body.

(b) The time of death shall be determined by a physician who attends the donor at his death, or, if none, the physician who certifies the death. This physician shall not participate in the procedures for removing or transplanting a part.

(c) A person acts in good faith in accord with the terms of this Act, or under the anatomical gift laws of another state [or a foreign country] is not liable for damages in any civil action or subject to prosecution in any criminal proceeding for his act.

(d) The provisions of this Act are subject to the laws of this state prescribing powers and duties with respect to autopsies.

Matas, Arras, Muyskens, Tellis, & Veith, A Proposal For Cadaver Organ Procurement: Routine Removal With Right Of Informed Refusal*
10 Journal of Health Pol. Poly. & L. 231 (1985)

Tremendous progress has been made in the area of organ transplantation in the last twenty years. Transplantation of the kidney, first performed in 1951 and considered an experimental modality throughout the 1960s, has become an accepted treatment method for patients with chronic renal failure. Survival rates of patients who have received kidney transplants, and survival of the transplants themselves, are markedly better than a decade ago. Prospects for the future are even brighter. Cyclosporine, the newly developed immunosuppressive

---

* Reprinted with permission. Copyright © by Duke University Press.

drug, has in recent clinical trials resulted in much better kidney graft survival than had been previously observed. Similar improvements have been reported in the areas of heart, liver, bone marrow, pancreas, and lung transplantation.

Despite these advances, the paucity of donor organs suitable for transplantation remains a major problem and, in consequence, the number of patients awaiting transplantation is increasing steadily. Many studies have demonstrated that the potential pool of donors is large and have documented the many reasons for the low rate of organ retrieval.[1] Although this problem was recognized twenty years ago, it was felt at that time that the rate of organ retrieval would be improved by a combination of (a) brain death legislation, (b) passage of the Uniform Anatomical Gift Act in the United States (Human Tissue Act in the United Kingdom), (c) public acceptance of donor cards, and (d) ongoing public education programs and continued publicity about the successes of transplantation. It is now clear that this combination of measures has not resulted in a marked increase in donors. . . .

Why is there a low rate of organ retrieval?

Two major sources of the low rate of organ retrieval have been documented: (1) failure of hospital personnel to identify potential donors and discuss donation with the families, and (2) failure to obtain consent from families. Although the relative role of each of these factors varies in different studies, solutions to both of these problems must be found if we are to have an effective organ procurement policy. . . .

In the numerous cases in which a donor card has not been signed by the deceased, consent for organ donation must be obtained from the family. As several studies of the process of obtaining familial consent have shown, families — in their turmoil and grief — are stunned when the subject of organ donation is raised. Some become despondent because the discussion of transplantation seems to elim-

---

1. See N. P. Couch, "Supply and Demand in Kidney and Liver Transplantation: A Statistical Survey," Transplantation 4 (1966): 587-595; D. L. Crosby, R. R. West, and H. Davies, "Availability of Cadaveric Kidneys for Transplantation," British Medical Journal 4 (1971): 401-2; J. A. Roloff, J. P. Marshall, and J. P. Reynolds Jr, "Kidney Transplant Donors: Estimate of Availability by Autopsy Survey," Archives of Surgery 103 (1971): 359-62; P. S. Fox et al., "The Cadaver Donor: Logistics of Supply and Demand in an Urban Population," Journal of the American Medical Association 222 (1972): 163-7; M. Friedberg, N. A. Larsen, and S. Larsen, "Potential Sources of Cadaveric Kidneys for Transplantation in a General Hospital," Acta Med Scandinavia 192 (1972): 251-253; H. H. Kaufman et al., "Kidney Donation: Needs and Possibilities," Neurosurgery 5 (1979): 237-244; K. J. Bart et al., "Cadaveric Kidneys for Transplantation: A Paradox of Shortage in the Face of Plenty," Transplantation 31 (1981): 379-82.

inate all vestiges of hope. In the cases most suitable for donation, accidental deaths of young people, families find it difficult to comprehend that someone so young is dead — especially when a heartbeat and normal color have been sustained by a respirator.

One family member wrote of her distress when asked if she would consider donation of her husband's kidneys: "In my state of acute shock, distress and grief, there suddenly came this totally unexpected question — I was astounded and utterly appalled at such a complete lack of feeling. To make such a decision for oneself is hard enough but to be asked to make it on behalf of another, while one is so shocked and grief stricken is both harrowing and cruel. Never could I want any close relative to suffer as I had done in making such an agonizing decision during the worst moment of a lifetime." As this family member stated so well, to be called upon to make a hasty decision in favor of donating organs, when overwhelmed with grief and in need of support, creates a burden too great for most people to bear. No matter what their views in more normal times, they are unable to assume the added burden of deciding for another at this time. . . .

. . . The Uniform Anatomical Gift Act (UAGA) was proposed in 1968 by both the National Bar Association and the National Conference on Uniform State Laws. Over the succeeding years, the law was enacted by all 50 states. The act was designed to provide a favorable legal environment for the use of organs and tissue for transplantation. A major aim of the UAGA was to guarantee that, in those cases in which the deceased had expressed a desire to donate organs for transplantation or to bequeath his or her body to medical authorities for their use, the wishes of the deceased would be given priority over those of the next-of-kin. . . .

Why have these measures had so little effect? We submit that the UAGA only addressed a small part of the problem. The UAGA focuses on the resistance of next-of-kin as the major impediment to donation and prescribes a legal mechanism for overcoming it. At best, this act offers assistance in the relatively small percentage of cases in which a donor card has been signed by the deceased *and* his or her next-of-kin object to donation. In reality, however, despite the legal protection of the UAGA, it is likely in such situations that those involved will accede to the family's wishes. Notwithstanding the ethical force conveyed by a signed donor card, it is exceedingly difficult for nurses and physicians to move the patient to the operating room for organ removal in the face of family opposition. Thus, even in these few cases specifically addressed by the UAGA, the act is likely to be ineffectual. But the larger difficulty is that because next-of-kin resistance has been incorrectly identified as the major impediment to organ retrieval, there has been no attempt to take advantage of the fact that there is strong support for transplantation throughout all segments of society.

Recent poll data clearly show that people have greater hesitancy when contemplating the donation of their own organs than they do when contemplating giving permission for donation of the organs of another family member. In the 1983 Gallup Poll, twice as many respondents (83 percent) claimed they were likely to give permission for donation of a loved one's organs as felt favorable about donating their own after death. The problems, then, lie not with next-of-kin resistance, but with the way (under current policy) familial permission must be obtained and with the lack of a clear mandate from society to physicians to act on its behalf in obtaining life-saving organs for transplantation. . . .

NOTES

Organ Donation Laws

1. An additional development in the legal support of organ procurement has been the passage of state laws authorizing donations through automobile drivers' license applications, both new and renewal. Currently over half the states have such authorizations. The provisions vary considerably, but have two common characteristics: (1) they are voluntary donations on simple forms attached to the application and (2) they refer to the Uniform Anatomical Gift Act in the state for legal support of the donation. The variations in the laws relate to the degree of participation by registry personnel in helping to fill in the cards and supplying witnesses. The simplest laws merely provide a blank card or attachment and leave it to the driver-donee to fill it out and to obtain witnesses. The most successful programs are those where the registry is an active partner in the effort.

2. An important provision in the Uniform Anatomical Gift Act in encouraging physician participation in removal of organs is the tort immunity provided in §7(c). The interpretation of the immunity and its constitutionality were tested in a Wisconsin case where the next of kin, the husband, had authorized the transplant but learned later that the removal had taken place before death and while the wife was on life-support systems. In Williams v. Hofmann, 66 Wis. 2d 145, 223 N.W.2d 844 (1974), the Wisconsin Supreme Court upheld the constitutionality of the provision as providing immunity when the physician acts in good faith in reliance on the next-of-kin consent as in this situation. However, the court also held that the immunity applies only for removal after death in accordance with the Act and does not provide immunity for actions prior to death. A brain-death

statute would probably cover procedures such as in this case, but might leave the surgeons and other personnel open to suit for predeath preparations of the body. It would be necessary for brain death to be declared *prior* to removal of the support systems as in State v. Shaffer, discussed at p. 913. See Luyties, Suggested Revisions to Clarify the Uncertain Impact of Section 7 of the Uniform Anatomical Gift Act on Determination of Death, 11 Ariz. L. Rev. 749 (1969); Comment, Anatomical Transplants: Legal Developments in Wisconsin, 59 Marq. L. Rev. 605 (1976).

3. One commentator has given the following explanation for the failure of the UAGA:

> The reliance on statutory authority for the procurement or donation of organs that persists to this day stems from the common law rule that the previously expressed wishes of the deceased did not bind the person charged with the disposal of the body. This rule, in turn, developed from the common law view that there was no property right in a dead body that one could control through a will or other devise. Thus, at common law, one lacked control over one's body after death. Control rested entirely with the party in rightful possession, generally the spouse or next of kin. . . .
>
> Despite [the UAGA], organ procurement personnel in forty-six states, even given a valid donor instrument, will not remove organs without family approval. [F]ear of liability has been cited by almost every commentator . . . as central to the inefficient use of the UAGA. Physicians and hospitals cite at least two additional reasons for requiring family consent: (1) ethical concerns such as avoiding infliction of further emotional stress on a grieving family . . . ; and (2) the fear of bad publicity. . . . Thus, despite the protection of Sections 2 and 7, the effectiveness of the UAGA has been severely hampered by the defensive mentality pervasive in modern medicine.

Lee, The Organ Supply Dilemma: Acute Responses to a Chronic Shortage, 20 Colum. J.L. & Soc. Prob. 363, 371, 379 (1986).

4. In 1984, Congress passed the National Organ Transplant Act, which established a Task Force on Organ Procurement and Transplantation to study the problems of organ donation. The act also created the Organ Procurement Transplantation Network, a central registry for linking donors with recipients. 42 U.S.C. §273. For the most part, however, this Act continued to leave the substantive law of organ donation to state law. For additional discussion of the federal act and the conventional methods of organ procurement, see Executive Summary of the Report of the National Task Force on Organ Transplantation, reprinted in D. Cowan et al., Human Organ Transplantation (1987); Symposium, Organ Transplantation, 14 J. Health Pol. Poly. & L. (Spring 1989); Blumstein, Federal Organ Transplantation Policy: A Time for Reassessment?, 22 U.C. Davis L. Rev. 451 (1989);

Cotton & Sandler, The Regulation of Organ Procurement and Transplantation, 7 J. Leg. Med. 55 (1986); Schwartz, Bioethical and Legal Considerations in Increasing the Supply of Transplantable Organs: From UAGA to "Baby Fae," 10 Am. J.L. & Med. 397 (1985); Overcast, Evans, Bowen, Hoe & Livak, Problems in the Identification of Potential Organ Donors, 251 J.A.M.A. 1559 (1984). A discussion of liability issues relating to organ transplantation can be found in D. Cowan et al., Human Organ Transplantation (1987). This volume also contains an excellent bibliography on organ transplants and defining death.

5. The failure of the UAGA has forced states and the federal government to turn to a new tactic — required request. In a recent flurry of legislation, more than half the states have required hospitals to personally notify the families of all deceased patients of their option to donate body parts. E.g., Or. Rev. Stat. §97.268; N.Y. Pub. Health Law §4351. Federal law requires the same for hospitals that receive Medicare or Medicaid reimbursement for organ transplants. 42 U.S.C. §1320b-8. Also, the 1988 JCAH Accreditation Manual added a requirement that hospitals adopt "policies and procedures for the identification and referral of organ and tissue donors to organ procurement agencies or tissue banks." See generally 18 Hastings Center Report (April/May 1988). So far, this approach has produced improved, but not dramatic, results.

6. Two early, influential articles proposing even more aggressive strategies for procuring organs are Dukeminier & Sanders, Organ Transplantation: A Proposal for Routine Salvaging of Cadaver Organs, 279 New Eng. J. Med. 413 (1968); Dukeminier, Supplying Organs for Transplantation, 68 Mich. L. Rev. 811 (1970). Each proposes a presumed consent approach to the retrieval of *all* usable organs. Although this approach is widely used in European countries, so far, presumed consent has been implemented here in only two contexts: (1) corneal tissue removal (two more decisions upholding the validity of these statutes are Georgia Lions Eye Bank v. Lavant, 335 S.E.2d 127 (Ga. 1985); Tillman v. Detroit Receiving Hosp., 360 N.W.2d 275 (Mich. App. 1984)); and (2) the unclaimed dead. A few states have adopted provisions that allow the removal of major organs if, after diligent search, no relatives are available and the doctor has no notice that the deceased objected to organ donation. Cal. Health & Safety Code §7151.6; Md. Code Ann. §4-509(a)(2). The drafters of the Uniform Act recently made a similar proposal. 8A U.L.A. 10 (1988 Supp.). Commenting on this tactic, Professor Areen observes that "it may be politically acceptable to harvest organs without express consent from individuals without any available next of kin, but it is certainly ethically troubling to appropriate for public use the body parts of only the most vulnerable citizens." Areen, A Scarcity of Organs, 38 J. Leg. Med. 555, 561 (1988).

7. Aside from your thoughts on policy, do you think it would be constitutional to *require* all deceased persons to donate major organs, regardless of objection? We currently allow medical examiners to order extensive autopsies regardless of familial objection. What additional intrusion is there in removing a few odds and ends while the body is already cut open, as long as the removals are cosmetically masked? See Silver, The Case for a Post-Mortem Organ Draft, 68 B.U.L. Rev. 681 (1988) ("the organ draft [act proposed in this article] would empower the state to conscript every cadaveric organ suitable for transplantation without regard to any contrary wishes expressed by the decedent while he lived or by surviving relatives after he dies," except for bona fide religious objection); Note, 90 Colum. L. Rev. 528 (1990) (nonconsensual removal violates the takings clause if no compensation is paid).

8. A less radical, but still controversial, idea for increasing the supply of transplantable organs is to permit their sale, either by living donors for kidneys and bone marrow, or by families, for the organs of the deceased. See Hansmann, The Economics and Ethics of Markets for Human Organs, 14 J. Health Pol. Poly. & L. 57 (1988) (advocating freedom to sell cadaveric organs, and possibly organs from living donors as well); Note, Sale of Human Organs: Implicating a Privacy Right, 21 Val. U.L. Rev. 741 (1987) (asserting a constitutional right to sell organs); Note, Regulating the Sale of Human Organs, 71 Va. L. Rev. 1015 (1985) (advocating a limited right to sell); Note, The Sale of Human Body Parts, 72 Mich. L. Rev. 1182 (1974).

The federal government and several states have banned organ sales. 42 U.S.C. §274(e); Cal. Penal Code §367f; N.Y. Pub. Health Law §4307. The objections usually raised are: (1) a financial inducement will attract sales from less desirable live donors, possibly creating a risk of hepatitis infection; (2) paying for organs will increase the already high costs of transplantation; (3) the public's moral aversion to treating the body as property could cause a decrease in the supply of organs; and (4) allowing organ purchases will result in scarce, lifesaving resources going to the highest bidder rather than to those with the greatest need. Annas, Life, Liberty and the Pursuit of Organ Sales, 14 Hast. Cent. Rep. 22 (Feb. 1984); Capron, Buying and Selling Human Organs, The Problems, 1 Health Scan 5 (Oct. 1984); Radin, Market-Inalienability, 100 Harv. L. Rev. 1849 (1987). If asked to defend organ sales, how would you respond to each of these objections? Could it be said that we are pursuing a perverse public policy that prohibits voluntary sale of organs at the same time that we are coercing donations through presumed consent and required request statutes?

One proposal for the sale of organs seeks to skirt some of the ethical objections by allowing a "futures market" — one that compensates donors for their advance agreement to supply organs at the time of their death. Cohen, Increasing the Supply of Transplant Organs: The Virtues of a Futures Market, 58 Geo. Wash. L. Rev. 1 (1989). Short of overt cash transactions, how about financially encouraging organ donation by providing an estate or income tax deduction? See Note, Tax Consequences of Transfers of Bodily Parts, 73 Colum. L. Rev. 842 (1973).

Finally, a related issue of current interest is the property right in human tissue used in biotechnology. A recent decision held that a patient could maintain an action for conversion when doctors, without his permission, used tissue from his removed spleen to create an entire line of pharmaceutical products worth millions of dollars. The court reasoned that a person has a property interest in body parts (at least while still alive) and that any public policy objections to this property right must be addressed by legislation. Moore v. Regents, 249 Cal. Rptr. 494 (Cal. App. 1988). See Annas, Whose Waste is it Anyway? The Case of John Moore, 18 Hast. Cent. Rep., No. 5, at 37 (Oct/Nov 1988).

Property rights in body tissue are also at issue in connection with new forms of reproductive technology that are capable of cryopreserving (freeze drying) fertilized human eggs for future use. See Section III.C. See generally, Office of Tech. Assess., Developments in Biotechnology: Ownership of Human Tissues and Cells (1987).

B. The Right to Refuse Life-sustaining Treatment

1. Introduction

Application of the President and Directors of Georgetown College, Inc.
331 F.2d 1000 (D.C. Cir.), *cert. denied*, 377 U.S. 978 (1964)

J. SKELLY WRIGHT, CIRCUIT JUDGE.

Mrs. Jones was brought to the hospital by her husband for emergency care, having lost two thirds of her body's blood supply from a ruptured ulcer. She had no personal physician, and relied solely on the hospital staff. She was a total hospital responsibility. It appeared that the patient, age 25, mother of a seven-month-old child, and her husband were both Jehovah's Witnesses, the teachings of which sect, according to their interpretation, prohibited the injection of blood into the body. When death without blood became imminent, the hospital sought the advice of counsel, who applied to the District Court in the name of the hospital for permission to administer blood. Judge Tamm of the District Court denied the application, and counsel immediately applied to me, as a member of the Court of Appeals, for an appropriate writ. I called the hospital by telephone and spoke with Dr. Westura, Chief Medical Resident, who confirmed the representations made by counsel. I thereupon proceeded with counsel to the hospital, where I spoke to Mr. Jones, the husband of the patient. He advised me that, on religious grounds, he would not approve a blood transfusion for his wife. He said, however, that if the court ordered the transfusion, the responsibility was not his. I advised Mr. Jones to obtain counsel immediately. He thereupon went to the telephone and returned in 10 or 15 minutes to advise that he had taken the matter up with his church and that he had decided that he did not want counsel.

I asked permission of Mr. Jones to see his wife. This he readily granted. Prior to going into the patient's room, I again conferred with Dr. Westura and several other doctors assigned to the case. All confirmed that the patient would die without blood and that there was a better than 50 per cent chance of saving her life with it. Unanimously they strongly recommended it. I then went inside the patient's room. Her appearance confirmed the urgency which had been represented to me. I tried to communicate with her, advising her again as to what the doctors had said. The only audible reply I could hear was "Against my will." It was obvious that the woman was not in a mental condition to make a decision. I was reluctant to press her because of the seriousness of her condition and because I felt that to suggest repeatedly the imminence of death without blood might place a strain on her religious convictions. I asked her whether she would oppose the blood transfusion if the court allowed it. She indicated, as best I could make out, that it would not then be her responsibility.

I returned to the doctors' room where some 10 to 12 doctors were congregated, along with the husband and counsel for the hospital. The President of Georgetown University, Father Bunn, appeared and pleaded with Mr. Jones to authorize the hospital to save his wife's life with a blood transfusion. Mr. Jones replied that the Scriptures say that we should not drink blood, and consequently his religion prohibited transfusions. The doctors explained to Mr. Jones that a blood transfusion is totally different from drinking blood in that the blood physically goes into a different part and through a different process in the body. Mr. Jones was unmoved. I thereupon signed the order allowing the hospital to administer such transfusions as the doctors should determine were necessary to save her life.

This opinion is being written solely in connection with the emergency order authorizing the blood transfusions "to save her life." It should be made clear that no attempt is being made here to determine the merits of the underlying controversy. Actually, the issue on the merits is res nova. Because of the demonstrated imminence of death

II. Termination of Treatment and Related Matters

from loss of blood, signing the order was necessary to maintain the status quo and prevent the issue respecting the rights of the parties in the premises from becoming moot before full consideration was possible. But maintaining the status quo is not the only consideration in determining whether an emergency writ should issue. The likelihood of eventual success on appeal is of primary importance, and thus must be here considered.

Before proceeding with this inquiry, it may be useful to state what this case does not involve. This case does not involve a person who, for religious or other reasons, has refused to seek medical attention. It does not involve a disputed medical judgment or a dangerous or crippling operation. Nor does it involve the delicate question of saving the newborn in preference to the mother. Mrs. Jones sought medical attention and placed on the hospital the legal responsibility for her proper care. In its dilemma, not of its own making, the hospital sought judicial direction.

It has been firmly established that the courts can order compulsory medical treatment of children for any serious illness or injury, e.g., People ex rel. Wallace v. Labrenz, 411 Ill. 618, 104 N.E.2d 769, *cert. denied*, 344 U.S. 824 (1952); Morrison v. State, Mo. App., 252 S.W.2d 97 (1952); Mitchell v. Davis, Tex. Civ. App., 205 S.W.2d 812 (1947), and that adults, sick or well, can be required to submit to compulsory treatment or prophylaxis, at least for contagious diseases, e.g., Jacobson v. Massachusetts, 197 U.S. 11, 25 S. Ct. 358, 49 L. Ed. 643 (1905). And there are no religious exemptions from these orders. These principles were restated by the Supreme Court in Prince v. Massachusetts, 321 U.S. 158, 166-167 (1944): . . . "The right to practice religion freely does not include liberty to expose the community or the child to communicable disease or the latter to ill health or death." [Citations omitted.]

Of course, there is here no sick child or contagious disease. However, the sick child cases may provide persuasive analogies because Mrs. Jones was in extremis and hardly compos mentis at the time in question; she was as little able competently to decide for herself as any child would be. Under the circumstances, it may well be the duty of a court of general jurisdiction, such as the United States District Court for the District of Columbia, to assume the responsibility of guardianship for her, as for a child, at least to the extent of authorizing treatment to save her life. And if, as shown above, a parent has no power to forbid the saving of his child's life, a fortiori the husband of the patient here had no right to order the doctors to treat his wife in a way so that she would die.

The child cases point up another consideration. The patient, 25 years old, was the mother of a seven-month-old child. The state, as parens patriae, will not allow a parent to abandon a child, and so it should not allow this most ultimate of voluntary abandonments. The patient had a responsibility to the community to care for her infant. Thus the people had an interest in preserving the life of this mother.

Apart from the child cases, a second range of factors may be considered. It is suggested that an individual's liberty to control himself and his life extends even to the liberty to end his life. Thus, "in those states where attempted suicide has been made lawful by statute (or the lack of one), the refusal of necessary medical aid (to one's self), whether equal to or less than attempted suicide, must be conceded to be lawful." Cawley, Criminal Liability in Faith Healing, 39 Minn. L. Rev. 48, 68 (1954). And, conversely, it would follow that where attempted suicide is illegal by the common law or by statute, a person may not be allowed to refuse necessary medical assistance when death is likely to ensue without it. Only quibbles about the distinction between misfeasance and nonfeasance, or the specific intent necessary to be guilty of attempted suicide, could be raised against this latter conclusion. If self-homicide is a crime, there is no exception to the law's command for those who believe the crime to be divinely ordained. . . . But whether attempted suicide is a crime is in doubt in some jurisdictions, including the District of Columbia.

The Gordian knot of this suicide question may be cut by the simple fact that Mrs. Jones did not want to die. Her voluntary presence in the hospital as a patient seeking medical help testified to this. Death, to Mrs. Jones, was not a religiously-commanded goal, but an unwanted side effect of a religious scruple. There is no question here of interfering with one whose religious convictions counsel his death, like the Buddhist monks who set themselves afire. Nor are we faced with the question of whether the state should intervene to reweigh the relative values of life and death, after the individual has weighed them for himself and found life wanting. Mrs. Jones wanted to live.

A third set of considerations involved the position of the doctors and the hospital. Mrs. Jones was their responsibility to treat. The hospital doctors had the choice of administering the proper treatment or letting Mrs. Jones die in the hospital bed, thus exposing themselves, and the hospital, to the risk of civil and criminal liability in either case.[18] It is not certain that Mrs. Jones had any authority to put the hospital and its doctors to this impossible choice. The normal principle that an adult patient directs her doctors is based on notions of commercial contract which may have less relevance to life-or-death emergencies. It is not clear just where a patient would derive her

---

18. Whether or not a waiver signed by a patient in extremis would protect the hospital from civil liability, it could not be relied on to prevent criminal prosecution. Death resulting from failure to extend proper medical care, where there is a duty of care, is manslaughter in the District of Columbia. Jones v. United States, 113 U.S. App. D.C. 352, 355, 308 F.2d 307, 310 (1962).

II. Termination of Treatment and Related Matters 931

authority to command her doctor to treat her under limitations which would produce death. . . .

The final, and compelling, reason for granting the emergency writ was that a life hung in the balance. There was no time for research and reflection. Death could have mooted the cause in a matter of minutes, if action were not taken to preserve the status quo. To refuse to act, only to find later that the law required action, was a risk I was unwilling to accept. I determined to act on the side of life.

NOTES

Overview of Treatment Refusal Issues

1. The Georgetown Hospital case is one of the earliest decisions to come squarely to grips with the difficult issues involved in refusing life-sustaining treatment. As such, it received much notoriety in the legal community. It was not until 1976, though, that In re Karen Ann Quinlan, infra at 966, brought these issues to the attention of the general public. The result has been an explosion of legal and ethical interest in the refusal of life-sustaining treatment. The Index to Legal Periodicals lists 85 items under the "Right to Die" heading from 1980 to February 1987. The following bibliographies and treatises provide access to this monumental literature (in addition to the sources cited at p. 902): Society for the Right to Die, Right-to-Die Decisions (1987); The Encyclopedia of Bioethics (1978); C. Cohen, Casebook on the Termination of Life-Sustaining Treatment (1989); G. Trubow, Privacy Law and Practice (1987); Hastings Center, Guidelines on the Termination of Life-Sustaining Treatment (1987); President's Commission for the Study of Ethical Problems in Medicine, Deciding to Forego Life-Sustaining Treatment (1983); A. Buchanan & D. Brock, Deciding for Others (1989); A. Meisel, The Right to Die (1989); B. Brody, Life and Death Decision Making (1988); N. Cantor, Legal Frontiers of Death and Dying (1987); T. Beauchamp & S. Perlin, Ethical Issues in Death & Dying (1977); P. Ramsey, Ethics at the Edges of Life (1978); J. Robertson, The Rights of the Critically Ill (1983); B. Steinbock, Killing and Letting Die (1980); R. Veatch, Life Span (1979); R. Weir, Ethical Issues in Death and Dying (2d ed. 1986); Society for the Right to Die, The Physician and the Hopelessly Ill Patient: Legal, Medical and Ethical Guidelines (1985); Annot., Judicial Power to Order Discontinuance of Life-Sustaining Treatment, 48 A.L.R.4th 67 (1986).

2. We use *Georgetown College* to introduce this section even though *Quinlan* is much more reflective of current law because, as will be seen shortly, most other major cases in this field (indeed, virtually

every case since *Georgetown College*, until 1988) have ultimately been decided in favor of the patient's or family's wish to refuse treatment. Therefore, it is easy to lose sight of why these cases are even controversial. They remain highly controversial not only due to the unsettled ethical issues but also because, as the court observes, health care providers who inappropriately withhold treatment are potentially subject to criminal prosecution. See Annot., Homicide: Physician's Withdrawal of Life Supports from Comatose Patient, 47 A.L.R.4th 18. This risk became reality in Barber v. Superior Court, 195 Cal. Rptr. 484 (Cal. App. 1983) (discussed in Bartling v. Superior Court, infra at p. 947). There, the medical profession was traumatized when murder charges were brought against two doctors for honoring the family's request to remove the feeding tube from a patient in a permanent vegetative state. Although the charges ultimately were dismissed on appeal, this decision to prosecute reflects the sharp divergence of views our society continues to hold on who should control life-and-death medical decisions.

The second reason for beginning with *Georgetown College*, despite its somewhat outdated analysis, is that this decision, written by one of the great jurists of this half-century, is remarkably efficient in identifying and cataloguing most of the issues that we will explore in greater depth in this chapter:

- the importance to society of preserving life
- the application of suicide law and policy to medical decision making
- a patient's competence to refuse treatment
- the authority to control medical decision making for family members, and
- the rights, responsibilities, and liabilities of the medical profession in honoring, or refusing to honor, treatment refusal requests.

3. An important theme that pervades these materials, but one that Judge Wright does not overtly acknowledge, is the proper role of the law in shaping private conduct and decision making in this area. This theme involves two inquiries. First, is this an area where the law should operate at all, or instead one that should be left entirely to the realm of religion, medical ethics, and family prerogative. In other words, should the role of the law be limited simply to clearing the way for private decision making, unfettered by legal concerns of criminal or civil liability? Is it even possible for the law to remain neutral in an area that is this contentious? If so, would Mrs. Jones have received treatment?

If the law is to play a more substantive role — one that actively

II. Termination of Treatment and Related Matters

regulates private conduct by developing a detailed code of rules for when treatment is mandatory and when doctors are prevented from intervening — is the common law the most appropriate vehicle for legal evolution where technology is changing rapidly and where our society may hold widely divergent moral views, or should these issues be left to the legislature? Consider Cruzan v. Harmon, 760 S.W.2d 408, 426 (Mo. 1988), aff'd, — U.S. — (1990):

> Broad policy questions bearing on life and death issues are more properly addressed by representative assemblies. These have vast fact and opinion gathering and synthesizing powers unavailable to courts; the exercise of these powers is particularly appropriate where issues invoke the concerns of medicine, ethics, morality, philosophy, theology and law . . . To the extent that courts continue to invent guidelines on an *ad hoc* basis, legislatures, which have the ability to address the issue comprehensively, will feel no compulsion to act and will avoid making the potentially unpopular choices which issues of this magnitude present.

To the extent you agree with this view that legislatures are *superior* law makers in this field, does this *disqualify* a court from acting when it is presented with a case raising these issues?

4. Judge Wright stressed the temporary and emergency nature of his ruling and referred several times to the need to force treatment in order to avoid mooting the case. Is it not clear, though, that from Mrs. Jones's perspective, the "temporary" order in fact was a final denial of her claim, in other words, an order that effectively mooted *her* legal position? By forcing the treatment she was trying to avoid, the temporary order resulted in alleviating the emergency condition that had created a life-threatening crisis. Put another way, didn't Judge Wright issue an order in the name of avoiding mootness that renders any further litigation unnecessary?

5. Transfusion refusals by adult Jehovah's Witnesses have recurred frequently in the reported cases. Usually, the courts have honored these requests, unless a minor child would be left without support. It is only in this latter respect that *Georgetown College* perhaps continues to reflect prevailing law; the holding has been limited by subsequent decisions to the situation of Mrs. Jones needing to care for her seven-month-old child. Compare In re Osborne, 294 A.2d 372 (D.C. Ct. App. 1972) (refusal of transfusion honored because patient's family was well provided for; *Georgetown College* distinguished); In re Milton, 505 N.E.2d 255 (Ohio 1987) (belief in faith healing respected), with John F. Kennedy Mem. Hosp. v. Heston, 279 A.2d 670 (N.J. 1971) (transfusion forced on pregnant mother (prior to existence of right to abort)), *overruled in part,* In re Conroy, 486 A.2d 1209 (N.J. 1985); Norwood Hospital v. Munoz, Mass. Probate Court (Norfolk Div., 5/11/89) (transfusion ordered where parents' plans for son in event of

mother's death were "vague and inadequate"). Thus, "when courts refuse to allow a competent patient to decline life-sustaining treatment, it is almost always because of the state's interest in protecting innocent third parties who would be harmed by the patient's decision." In re Farrell, 529 A.2d 404, 415 (N.J. 1987). However, even this precedential effect of *G.C.* is beginning to fade. Two recent decisions flatly refused to consider the effect of the mother's death on her children. One ruled that the state's interest in seeing that a child has "the nurturing and support by two parents, [while] important . . . , is not sufficient to override fundamental constitutional rights." Public Health Trust of Dade County v. Wons, 541 So. 2d 96 (Fla. 1989). See also Fosmire v. Nicoleau, 545 N.Y.S.2d 103 (N.Y. 1990) (no basis for state's forcing treatment on mother to benefit child).

2. Patients With Clearly Expressed Wishes

California Natural Death Act
Cal. Health and Safety Code

§7186

The Legislature finds that adult persons have the fundamental right to control the decisions relating to the rendering of their own medical care, including the decision to have life-sustaining procedures withheld or withdrawn in instances of a terminal condition.

The Legislature further finds that modern medical technology has made possible the artificial prolongation of human life beyond natural limits.

The Legislature further finds that, in the interest of protecting individual autonomy, such prolongation of life for persons with a terminal condition may cause loss of patient dignity and unnecessary pain and suffering, while providing nothing medically necessary or beneficial to the patient.

The Legislature further finds that there exists considerable uncertainty in the medical and legal professions as to the legality of terminating the use or application of life-sustaining procedures where the patient has voluntarily and in sound mind evidenced a desire that such procedures be withheld or withdrawn.

In recognition of the dignity and privacy which patients have a right to expect, the Legislature hereby declares that the laws of the State of California shall recognize the right of an adult person to make a written directive instructing his physician to withhold or withdraw life-sustaining procedures in the event of a terminal condition.

II. Termination of Treatment and Related Matters

§7187

The following definitions shall govern the construction of this chapter: . . .

(c) "Life-sustaining procedure" means any medical procedure or intervention which utilizes mechanical or other artificial means to sustain, restore, or supplant a vital function, which, when applied to a qualified patient, would serve only to artificially prolong the moment of death and where, in the judgment of the attending physician, death is imminent whether or not such procedures are utilized. "Life-sustaining procedure" shall not include the administration of medication or the performance of any medical procedure deemed necessary to alleviate pain. . . .

(e) "Qualified patient" means a patient diagnosed and certified in writing to be afflicted with a terminal condition by two physicians, one of whom shall be the attending physician, who have personally examined the patient.

(f) "Terminal condition" means an incurable condition caused by injury, disease, or illness, which, regardless of the application of life-sustaining procedures, would, within reasonable medical judgment, produce death, and where the application of life-sustaining procedures serve only to postpone the moment of death of the patient.

§7188

Any adult person may execute a directive directing the withholding or withdrawal of life-sustaining procedures in a terminal condition. The directive shall be signed by the declarant in the presence of two witnesses not related to the declarant by blood or marriage and who would not be entitled to any portion of the estate of the declarant upon his decease under any will of the declarant or codicil thereto then existing or, at the time of the directive, by operation of law then existing. In addition, a witness to a directive shall not be the attending physician, an employee of the attending physician or a health facility in which the declarant is a patient, or any person who has a claim against any portion of the estate of the declarant upon his decease at the time of the execution of the directive. The directive shall be in the following form:

Directive to Physicians
Directive made this _____ day of _____ (month, year).
  I _____ , being of sound mind, willfully, and voluntarily make known my desire that my life shall not be

artificially prolonged under the circumstances set forth below, do hereby declare:

1. If at any time I should have an incurable injury, disease, or illness certified to be a terminal condition by two physicians, and where the application of life-sustaining procedures would serve only to artificially prolong the moment of my death and where my physician determines that my death is imminent whether or not life-sustaining procedures are utilized, I direct that such procedures be withheld or withdrawn, and that I be permitted to die naturally.

2. In the absence of my ability to give directions regarding the use of such life-sustaining procedures, it is my intention that this directive shall be honored by my family and physician(s) as the final expression of my legal right to refuse medical or surgical treatment and accept the consequences from such refusal.

3. If I have been diagnosed as pregnant and that diagnosis is known to my physician, this directive shall have no force or effect during the course of my pregnancy. . . .

5. This directive shall have no force or effect five years from the date filled in above.

6. I understand the full import of this directive and I am emotionally and mentally competent to make this directive. . . .

Signed _____

[Material omitted]

§7189

(a) A directive may be revoked at any time by the declarant, without regard to his mental state or competency, by any of the following methods:

(1) By being canceled, defaced, obliterated, or burnt, torn, or otherwise destroyed by the declarant or by some person in his presence and by his direction.

(2) By a written revocation of the declarant expressing his intent to revoke, signed and dated by the declarant. . . .

(b) There shall be no criminal or civil liability on the part of any person for failure to act upon a revocation made pursuant to this section unless that person has actual knowledge of the revocation.

§7189.5

A directive shall be effective for five years from the date of execution thereof unless sooner revoked in a manner prescribed in Section 7189. Nothing in this chapter shall be construed to prevent a declarant from reexecuting a directive at any time in accordance

II. Termination of Treatment and Related Matters

with the formalities of Section 7188, including reexecution subsequent to a diagnosis of a terminal condition. If the declarant has executed more than one directive, such time shall be determined from the date of execution of the last directive known to the attending physician. If the declarant becomes comatose or is rendered incapable of communicating with the attending physician, the directive shall remain in effect for the duration of the comatose condition or until such time as the declarant's condition renders him or her able to communicate with the attending physician.

§7190

No physician or health facility which, acting in accordance with the requirements of this chapter, causes the withholding or withdrawal of life-sustaining procedures from a qualified patient, shall be subject to civil liability therefrom. . . .

§7193

Nothing in this chapter shall impair or supersede any legal right or legal responsibility which any person may have to effect the withholding or withdrawal of life-sustaining procedures in any lawful manner. In such respect the provisions of this chapter are cumulative. . . .

§7195

Nothing in this chapter shall be construed to condone, authorize, or approve mercy killing, or to permit any affirmative or deliberate act or omission to end life other than to permit the natural process of dying as provided in this chapter.

NOTES

Living Will Acts and No Code Orders

1. This California statute, enacted in 1976, was the first of the so-called "Living Will" or "Natural Death" acts. Presently, over three dozen states have similar enactments that permit making an advance directive to terminate treatment. In addition, New York and New Jersey case law has authorized the use of living wills even in the absence of legislation. See Gelfand, Living Will Statutes: The First Decade, 1987 Wis. L. Rev. 737 (collecting citations and analyzing variations in the statutory texts); Annot., Living Wills: Validity Construction and Effect, 49 A.L.R.4th 812 (1980). California's statute is

unique in requiring renewal of the living will every five years; in most states, living wills remain in effect until revoked. Also, an omitted portion of the California statute makes directives "conclusive" of the patient's intent only if they are signed *while* the patient is suffering from a terminal illness; otherwise, a directive has only some "weight" in the physician's deliberations. §7191(b). This provision is also unique to California. These provisions explain why Derek Humphrey, the director of the Hemlock Society (which advocates the right to die) has said that the statute "was savaged by opponents and it came out a dog's breakfast." L.A. Times, May 23, 1988, at 1, col. 1.

2. Living will statutes cover only the most obvious instances for refusing life-sustaining treatment: attested, written declarations by lucid adults that, in the event of a terminal illness, they do not want to prolong the dying process with "artificial" or "mechanical" medical interventions, such as respirators or resuscitation, when death is imminent. A law student survey of California doctors revealed that almost half did not consider death to be "imminent" until it will occur in 24 hours or less, and over 80 percent would restrict the time frame to no more than a week. Note, 31 Stan. L. Rev. 913 (1979). To test your understanding of some of the other limitations and ambiguities that plague these statutes, consider whether the California act would apply to the following patients:

- A patient with severe diabetes who refuses insulin;
- A patient with kidney failure who refuses (1) a transplant; (2) dialysis;
- A patient in a permanent vegetative state who needs an appendectomy;
- A patient with terminal cancer who needs open heart surgery to survive for another three months.

Most living will statutes define "terminal illness" to mean a condition that is both incurable *and* "irreversible." Would this definition change your answer with respect to any of these conditions?

3. Most commentators are highly critical of the Living Will Acts' restrictions to terminal illness and imminent death: "If the patient will die shortly with or without life-supporting treatment, there is little reason to [withhold treatment]. Further, if the intent of living will statutes was to permit the 'natural death' of persons who would otherwise linger for years maintained by modern machinery in a vegetative but 'alive' state, then the requirement that death be imminent whether or not treatment is withdrawn nullifies the purpose of such statutes." Gelfand, supra, 1987 Wis. L. Rev. at 741-742. Moreover, living wills may be ineffective even within their limited scope of coverage because physicians are more inclined to rely on

II. Termination of Treatment and Related Matters

the family's instructions or on their own impressions of the patient's desires than on the legal document (much as organ donor cards are ignored, see 921 supra). Zinberg, Decisions for the Dying: An Empirical Study of Physicians' Responses to Advance Directives, 13 Vt. L. Rev. 445 (1989) ("advance directives . . . have not significantly affected physicians' treatment of hopeless patients. Physicians are neither familiar with, nor particularly interested in, the statutes or instruments"); McCrary & Botkin, Hospital Policy on Advance Directives, 262 J.A.M.A. 2411 (1989) (only 4 percent of surveyed hospitals actively inquire whether patients have executed living wills). For a sampling of additional critical commentary, see Marzen, The "Uniform Rights of the Terminally Ill Act": A Critical Analysis, 1 Issues in L. & Med. 441 (1986); Comment, Selecting Medical Treatment: Does Arizona's Living Will Statute Help Enforce Decisions?, 1986 Ariz. Stat. Univ. L.J. 275.

4. As illustrated in the next case, another technique for making an advance treatment refusal directive is the "durable power of attorney" or the "medical power of attorney." Under the common law, all agency relationships cease automatically when the principal becomes incompetent. Therefore, statutes in every state permit the creation of so-called durable powers of attorney that survive incompetence. To resolve the legal uncertainty over whether such powers can extend to personal as well as business matters, a few states have specifically authorized the creation of medical powers of attorney that leave instructions to a specified person for directing the course of medical treatment. See Peters, Advance Medical Directives, 8 J. Leg. Med. 437 (1987); Martyn & Jacobs, Legislating Advance Directives for the Terminally Ill: The Living and Durable Power of Attorney, 63 Neb. L. Rev. 779 (1984); Note, Appointing an Agent to Make Medical Treatment Choices, 84 Colum. L. Rev. 985 (1984); Note, 70 Va. L. Rev. 1269 (1984); In re Peter, 529 A.2d 419 (N.J. 1987) (authorizing use of durable power of attorney for medical decisions even in absence of specific legislation).

5. Another situation in which treatment refusal is relatively uncontroversial is the entry of a "no code" or "DNR" (do not resuscitate) order on the chart of a terminally ill patient. Such orders tell physicians that an extremely debilitated patient (or, more typically, the patient's family) has decided that it would be futile to attempt extraordinary, heroic measures in the event of cardiac arrest. "No-code orders" have been accepted medical practice for decades, to the extent that the JCAH hospital accreditation standards now *require* hospitals to maintain a specific no-code policy. For a description of a well-designed hospital DNR procedure, see Rabkin, Gillerman and Rice, Orders Not to Resuscitate, 295 New Eng. J. Med. 364 (1976).

No-code orders have become such accepted practice that some

physicians consider them a purely medical decision — one that they are free to make without consulting the patient or the family. See "Patients Suffer In Squabble over who Should Die," The Sunday (London) Times, April 23, 1989, at C3 ("Patients with an irreversible disease, for whom death is imminent, may have hospital notes marked. 'In most cases relatives are consulted and occasionally the patient is as well' "). A recent study of 77 seriously ill elderly patients who received CPR found that none survived to leave the hospital (although about one-quarter were successfully resuscitated). Taffet et al., In-Hospital Cardiopulmonary Resuscitation, 260 J.A.M.A. 2069 (1988). In an accompanying article, a respected physician with the George Washington University Medical Center advocated that "no-code" orders should be placed on the charts of elderly, chronically ill patients *without the consent* of the patients or their families, since the treatment is "ineffective," just as physicians routinely exclude other medical treatments without discussion that they have no reason to believe will work. Murphy, Do-Not-Resuscitate Orders: Time for Reappraisal in Long-Term-Care Institutions, 260 J.A.M.A. 2098 (1988). See also Blackhall, Must We Always Use CPR?, 317 New Eng. J. Med. 1281 (1987) ("The principle of autonomy . . . does not allow [patients] to demand nonbeneficial and potentially harmful procedures"). What is the flaw in this argument? Does this give credence to the slippery slope arguments that euthanasia opponents make against permitting any form of treatment refusal? See Section II.D infra.

On DNR orders generally, see Comment, Case of No Consent: The DNR Order as a Medical Decision, 31 St. Louis U.L.J. 699 (1987); Mooney, Deciding not to Resuscitate Hospital Patients: Medical and Legal Perspectives, 1986 U. Ill. L. Rev. 1025; Tomlinson & Brody, Ethics and Communication in Do-Not-Resuscitate Orders, 318 New Eng. J. Med. 43 (1988); Allen, No Code Orders vs. Resuscitation, 26 Wayne St. L. Rev. 139 (1979).

6. Patients have also been allowed without much controversy to refuse deforming medical procedures such as leg amputations, even if gangrene is life-threatening. In re Quackenbush, 383 A.2d 785 (N.J. Super. 1978); Lane v. Candura, 376 N.E.2d 1232 (Mass. App. 1978). See generally Byrn, Compulsory Lifesaving Treatment for the Competent Adult, 44 Ford. L. Rev. 1 (1975).

7. The foregoing well-accepted instances of treatment refusal are all premised on the patient's inevitable imminent demise or the extreme intrusiveness of the treatment, or both. The following two cases implicate the much more controversial question of whether patients who theoretically have the chance to survive may refuse more routine sorts of care. Although the patients in both cases are incapacitated, we treat them as patients with decision-making capacity since they previously made clear expressions of their desires at a time

when they were lucid — either through formal documents, such as living wills and durable powers of attorney, or through explicit conversations that the court takes to be unambiguous.

Bartling v. Superior Court
209 Cal. Rptr. 220 (Cal. App. 2 Dist. 1984)

HASTINGS, ASSOC. JUSTICE. . . . The ruling challenged in this petition is the denial of petitioners' [William Bartling and his wife, Ruth] request for an injunction ordering [respondents Glendale Adventist Medical Center ("Glendale Adventist") and Mr. Bartling's treating physicians] to disconnect Mr. Bartling's ventilator (commonly called a "respirator"), a machine which sustains the patient's breathing. Although petitioners filed an appeal from the Superior Court's order, they also filed the within petition, claiming that the situation was too urgent to await the appeal. Petitioners were unfortunately correct, for Mr. Bartling passed away the afternoon before the hearing on this petition. . . .

At the time of his death, Mr. Bartling was 70-years-old and suffered from emphysema, chronic respiratory failure, arteriosclerosis, an abdominal aneurysm (abnormal ballooning of the main artery passing through the abdomen to the legs), and a malignant tumor of the lung. Mr. Bartling also had a history of what [respondents] term "chronic acute anxiety/depression" and alcoholism.

Mr. Bartling entered Glendale Adventist on April 8, 1984, for treatment of his depression. A routine physical examination, including a chest x-ray, was performed, and a tumor was discovered on Mr. Bartling's lung. A biopsy of the tumor was performed by inserting a needle in the lung, which caused the lung to collapse. Tubes were inserted in Mr. Bartling's chest and through his nasal passage and throat in order to reinflate his lung. Because of his emphysema, the hole made by the biopsy needle did not heal properly and the lung did not reinflate. While Mr. Bartling was being treated with antibiotics to promote healing of the lung, a tracheotomy was performed and he was placed on a ventilator. Mr. Bartling remained on the ventilator until the time of his death, and efforts to "wean" him from the machine were unsuccessful.

On several occasions in April, Mr. Bartling tried to remove the ventilator tubes. To prevent accidental or deliberate disconnection of the ventilator tubes (or any of the other tubes to which he was attached), Mr. Bartling's wrists were placed in "soft restraints." Despite requests from both Mr. and Mrs. Bartling, Glendale Adventist and Mr. Bartling's treating physicians refused to remove the ventilator or the restraints.

In June of this year, petitioners filed a complaint (subsequently amended) in the Superior Court seeking damages for battery (unconsented medical treatment), violation of state and federal constitutional rights, breach of fiduciary duty on the part of Glendale Adventist and Mr. Bartling's treating physicians, intentional infliction of emotional distress, and conspiracy. Petitioners sought an injunction restraining [respondents] from administering any unconsented medical care to Mr. Bartling. This included "forcing Plaintiff to undergo mechanical breathing through the ventilator" and other medical procedures. Attached to the complaint were:

(1) A "living will," signed by Mr. Bartling with an "X" and properly witnessed, which stated in part: "If at such time the situation should arise in which there is no reasonable expectation of my recovery from extreme physical or mental disability, I direct that I be allowed to die and not be kept alive by medications, artificial means or heroic measures."

(2) A declaration from Mr. Bartling in which he stated in part: "While I have no wish to die, I find intolerable the living conditions forced upon me by my deteriorating lungs, heart and blood vessel systems, and find intolerable my being continuously connected to this ventilator, which sustains my every breath and my life for the past six and one-half (6½) weeks. Therefore, I wish this Court to order that the sustaining of my respiration by this mechanical device violates my constitutional right, is contrary to my every wish, and constitutes a battery upon my person. I fully understand that my request to have the ventilator removed and discontinued, which I have frequently made to my wife and to my doctors, will very likely cause respiratory failure and ultimately lead to my death. I am willing to accept that risk rather than to continue the burden of this artificial existence which I find unbearable, degrading and dehumanizing. I also suffer a great deal of pain and discomfort because of being confined to bed, being on this ventilator, and from the other problems which are occurring."

(3) A "Durable Power of Attorney for Health Care,"[2] executed by Mr. Bartling, appointing Mrs. Bartling as his attorney-in-fact. . . .

Despite these strong and unequivocal statements from Mr. Bartling and his family, his treating physicians refused to remove the ventilator and refused to remove the restraints which would allow Mr. Bartling to disconnect the ventilator himself should he choose to do so. . . .

It was the opinion of Mr. Bartling's treating physicians, presented to the trial court by way of declarations, that Mr. Bartling's illness

---

2. The Durable Power of Attorney for Health Care Act (Civ. Code, §§2430-2443), enables a designated proxy to terminate health care if the principal is incompetent.

was not terminal and that he could live for at least a year if he was "weaned" from the ventilator. However, the doctors opined in their declarations that "weaning was unlikely because of his medical and psychological problems that were not under control."

Although they did not challenge his legal competency, the doctors and Glendale Adventist questioned Mr. Bartling's ability to make a meaningful decision because of his vacillation. This opinion was based on the declarations of several nurses who related instances in which the ventilator tube accidentally detached and Mr. Bartling signalled frantically for them to reconnect it. Mr. Bartling also made several statements to his doctors and nurses to the effect that he wanted to live and did not want the ventilator disconnected.

From an ethical standpoint, declarations were submitted to the effect that Glendale Adventist is a Christian hospital devoted to the preservation of life, and it would be unethical for Glendale Adventist's physicians to disconnect life-support systems from patients whom they viewed as having the potential for cognitive, sapient life.

The hospital and doctors also expressed concern about their potential civil and criminal liability should they accede to Mr. Bartling's wishes and disconnect the ventilator.

Before making its ruling on petitioners' request for an injunction, the trial court made several factual findings, including: (1) Mr. Bartling's illnesses were serious but not terminal, and had not been diagnosed as such; (2) although Mr. Bartling was attached to a respirator to facilitate breathing, he was not in a vegetative state and was not comatose; and (3) Mr. Bartling was competent in the legal sense.

The court relied substantially on Matter of Quinlan, 70 N.J. 10, 355 A.2d 647 (1976), which held that life-support systems could be withdrawn from a patient in a comatose, vegetative state should his or her attending physicians conclude that there was no reasonable possibility of the patient ever emerging from that state. The court below concluded that as long as there was some potential for restoring Mr. Bartling to a "cognitive, sapient life," it would not be appropriate to issue an injunction in this case.

We conclude that the trial court was incorrect when it held that the right to have life-support equipment disconnected was limited to comatose, terminally ill patients, or representatives acting on their behalf.

There is no question in our minds that Mr. Bartling was, as the trial court determined, competent in the legal sense to decide whether he wanted to have the ventilator disconnected. The statements made by Mr. Bartling in his declarations and in the other documents executed by him which were submitted to the trial court reflect the fact that Mr. Bartling knew he would die if the ventilator were disconnected but nevertheless preferred death to life sustained by mechanical means. He wanted to live but preferred death to his intolerable life on the ventilator. The fact that Mr. Bartling periodically wavered from this posture because of severe depression or for any other reason does not justify the conclusion of Glendale Adventist and his treating physicians that his capacity to make such a decision was impaired to the point of legal incompetency.

Having resolved the threshold issue of whether or not Mr. Bartling was legally competent, we turn to the major issue in this case: whether the right of Mr. Bartling, as a competent adult, to refuse unwanted medical treatment, is outweighed by the various state and personal interests urged by [respondents]: the preservation of life, the need to protect innocent third parties, the prevention of suicide, and maintaining of the ethics of the medical profession. (Superintendent of Belchertown State School v. Saikewicz, 373 Mass. 728, 370 N.E.2d 417 (1977).)

[Respondents] argue that the interests of the state should prevail. We disagree. In California, "a person of adult years and in sound mind has the right, in the exercise of control over his own body, to determine whether or not to submit to lawful medical treatment." (Cobbs v. Grant, 8 Cal. 3d 229, 242, 104 Cal. Rptr. 505, 502 P.2d 1.) This principle was recently reaffirmed in Barber v. Superior Court, 147 Cal. App. 3d 1006, 195 Cal. Rptr. 484, in which Division Two of this court held that two physicians who were prosecuted for the alleged murder of an incurably ill patient under their care could not be held criminally liable for the patient's death: "In this state a clearly recognized legal right to control one's own medical treatment predated the Natural Death Act. A long line of cases, approved by the Supreme Court in Cobbs v. Grant, . . . have held that where a doctor performs treatment in the absence of an informed consent, there is an actionable battery. The obvious corollary to this principle is that a competent adult patient has the legal right to refuse medical treatment." (147 Cal. App. 3d at p.1015, 195 Cal. Rptr. 484.) (Emphasis added.)[4]

California has also enacted the Natural Death Act (Health & Saf. Code, §7185 et seq.) which provides in part: "The Legislature finds that adult persons have the fundamental right to control the decisions relating to the rendering of their own medical care, including the

---

4. See also Satz v. Perlmutter, 362 So. 2d 160, *aff'd* 379 So. 2d 359 (Fla. 1980) approving the patient's right to have an artificial life sustaining device removed. The court concluded: "[W]e find, and agree with, several cases upholding the right of a competent adult patient to refuse treatment for himself. From this agreement, we reach our conclusion that, because Abe Perlmutter has a right to refuse treatment in the first instance, he has a concomitant right to discontinue it." (362 So. 2d at p.163.) . . .

II. Termination of Treatment and Related Matters 945

decision to have life-sustaining procedures withheld or withdrawn in instances of a terminal condition." The *Barber* court noted that while the Act was specifically addressed to only a limited number of persons, "It is clear from the legislative findings and declaration provided in Health and Safety Code section 7186, that the Legislature recognized such a right to control one's medical treatment, especially in circumstances such as presented here." (147 Cal. App. 3d at p.1015, 195 Cal. Rptr. 484.)[5] . . .

The right of a competent adult patient to refuse medical treatment has its origins in the constitutional right of privacy. This right is specifically guaranteed by the California Constitution (art. I, §1) and has been found to exist in the "penumbra" of rights guaranteed by the Fifth and Ninth Amendments to the United States Constitution. (Griswold v. Connecticut, 381 U.S. 479, 484, 85 S. Ct. 1678, 1681, 14 L. Ed. 2d 510.) "In short, the law recognizes the individual interest in preserving 'the inviolability of the person.'" (Superintendent of Belchertown School v. Saikewicz, supra, 370 N.E.2d 417, 424.) The constitutional right of privacy guarantees to the individual the freedom to choose to reject, or refuse to consent to, intrusions of his bodily integrity.

Balanced against these rights are the interests of the state in the preservation of life, the prevention of suicide, and maintaining the ethical integrity of the medical profession.[6] The most significant of these interests is the preservation of life. This is of prime concern to Glendale Adventist, which submitted a declaration to the effect that it is a Christian, pro-life oriented hospital, the majority of whose

---

5. We agree with the *Barber* court's statement that the Act applies only to a "limited number of persons" (i.e., terminally ill patients). For instance, the Act permits an adult to execute, in advance, a directive for the withholding or withdrawing of life-sustaining procedures in the event he or she later suffers a terminal illness. (Health & Saf. Code, §7188.) The Act provides a form for such a directive, one provision of which says that the patient's physicians, within the preceding 14 days, have diagnosed the patient as being terminally ill. In *Barber*, the court noted that the procedural requirements of the Act were "so cumbersome that it is unlikely that any but a small number of highly educated and motivated patients will be able to effectuate their desires." (147 Cal. App. 3d at p.1015, 195 Cal. Rptr. 484.) In his Declaration attached to the First Amended Complaint, Mr. Bartling stated: "My attorney has explained the provisions of the 'California Natural Death Act'; I understand that I am not a 'qualified patient' under those provisions in that I have not had a written diagnosis of 'terminal illness' submitted to me two weeks ago, or at any time. I do not wish to wait two weeks to become a 'qualified patient' before proceeding with my earnest desire to have the ventilator disconnected."

6. A fourth state interest — the protection of innocent third parties — is not implicated in this case. This interest has been invoked, for example, where the patient attempting to refuse treatment has minor children who would be left without a parent should the treatment not proceed. The leading case in this area is Application of the President & Directors of Georgetown College, Inc., 118 U.S. App. D.C. 80, 331 F.2d 1000, *cert. denied*, 377 U.S. 978, 84 S. Ct. 1883, 12 L. Ed. 2d 746 (1964).

doctors would view disconnecting a life-support system in a case such as this one as inconsistent with the healing orientation of physicians. We do not doubt the sincerity of [respondents'] moral and ethical beliefs, or their sincere belief in the position they have taken in this case.[7] However, if the right of the patient to self-determination as to his own medical treatment is to have any meaning at all, it must be paramount to the interests of the patient's hospital and doctors. The right of a competent adult patient to refuse medical treatment is a constitutionally guaranteed right which must not be abridged. As the court stated in Satz v. Perlmutter, supra, 362 So. 2d 160:

> It is all very convenient to insist on continuing Mr. Perlmutter's life so that there can be no question of foul play, no resulting civil liability and no possible trespass on medical ethics. However, it is quite another matter to do so at the patient's sole expense and against his competent will, thus inflicting never ending physical torture on his body until the inevitable, but artificially suspended, moment of death. Such a course of conduct invades the patient's constitutional right of privacy, removes his freedom of choice and invades his right to self-determination. (362 So. 2d at p. 164.)

Several doctors also expressed the view that disconnecting Mr. Bartling's ventilator would have been tantamount to aiding a suicide. This is not a case, however, where [respondents] would have brought about Mr. Bartling's death by unnatural means by disconnecting the ventilator. Rather, they would merely have hastened his inevitable death by natural causes. (Satz v. Perlmutter, supra, 362 So. 2d 160, 162-163.) Several cases have, to our satisfaction, placed this issue to rest. In Matter of Quinlan, supra, 70 N.J. 10, 355 A.2d 647 (1976), the court stated: "We would see, however, a real distinction between the self-infliction of deadly harm and a self-determination against artificial life-support or radical surgery, for instance, in the face of irreversible, painful and certain imminent death." (355 A.2d at p.665.) And in Superintendent of Belchertown v. Saikewicz, supra, 370 N.E.2d 417, the court succinctly answers this argument as follows:

> The interest in protecting against suicide seems to require little if any discussion. In the case of the competent adult's refusing medical treatment such an act does not necessarily constitute suicide since (1) in refusing treatment the patient may not have the specific intent to die,

---

7. The record in fact shows that real parties attempted to strike a compromise between their position and the wishes of Mr. and Mrs. Bartling by trying to locate another hospital which would accept Mr. Bartling as a patient. This effort was unsuccessful. As real parties point out, none of the medical ethics "experts" who submitted declarations in petitioners' behalf were willing to undertake the care of Mr. Bartling.

II. Termination of Treatment and Related Matters

and (2) even if he did, to the extent that the cause of death was from natural causes the patient did not set the death producing agent in motion with the intent of causing his own death . . . Furthermore, the underlying State interest in this area lies in the prevention of irrational self-destruction. What we consider here is a competent, rational decision to refuse treatment when death is inevitable and the treatment offers no hope of cure or preservation of life. There is no connection between the conduct here in issue and any State concern to prevent suicide. (370 N.E.2d at p.426, fn. 11.)

Aside from their moral and ethical objections, [respondents] have expressed the fear that had they complied with petitioner's wishes they might face criminal and civil liability. As to criminal liability, this was substantially answered in Barber v. Superior Court, supra, 147 Cal. App. 3d 1006, 195 Cal. Rptr. 484. In *Barber* the hospital patient, Clarence Herbert, was in a comatose condition and not likely to recover. He was kept alive by a respirator and intravenous tubes which provided hydration and nourishment. His family drafted a written request to the hospital personnel stating that they wanted "all machines taken off that are sustaining life." The defendant physicians respected these wishes and caused the respirator and other life sustaining equipment to be removed. Prior to the incapacities that led to his comatose condition, Mr. Herbert had expressed to his wife his feeling that he did not want to be kept alive by machines. The defendant doctors were charged with murder and conspiracy to commit murder. Although the appellate court found the actions of the physicians to be intentional and with knowledge the patient would die, based on the same law and reasons we have utilized in this opinion, the court found no criminal liability. Although our present case involves a civil action and factually is distinguishable from *Barber* in that Mr. Bartling was not comatose, we are now satisfied the law as outlined is clear and if Mr. Bartling had lived [respondents] could not have been criminally or civilly liable for carrying out his instructions. Furthermore in future similar situations, parties facing the problems confronting [respondents] here should be free to act according to the patient's instruction without fear of liability and without advance court approval. . . .

Our holding that the court below erred in this case is of little consolation to Mr. Bartling. His death renders moot that portion of the petition which seeks an order compelling the Superior Court to grant the injunction sought. However, petitioners have also requested an award of costs and attorneys' fees under the "private attorney general" theory (Code Civ. Proc., §1021.5). The case is remanded to the Superior Court for a determination as to whether attorneys' fees pursuant to section 1021.5 are appropriate.

Brophy v. New England Sinai Hospital
497 N.E.2d 626 (Mass. 1986)

LIACOS, JUSTICE.

We are asked to decide whether the substituted judgment of a person in a persistent vegetative state that the artificial maintenance of his nutrition and hydration be discontinued shall be honored. The effectuation of the ward's wishes is supported by his wife-guardian and his family, but is opposed by his attending physicians and the defendant hospital. . . .

The Supreme Court of New Jersey has recently restated the dilemma: "As scientific advances make it possible for us to live longer than ever before, even when most of our physical and mental capacities have been irrevocably lost, patients and their families are increasingly asserting a right to die a natural death without undue dependence on medical technology or unnecessarily protracted agony — in short, a right to 'die with dignity.'" Matter of Conroy, supra, 98 N.J. at 343, 486 A.2d 1209.[3] It is in this context that we turn to consider the facts and the law applicable to this appeal.

1. The Facts

a. The Medical Incident and Initial Proceedings

Paul E. Brophy, Sr. (Brophy), was afflicted on March 22, 1983, by the rupture of an aneurysm located at the apex of the basilar artery. Prior to that time, Brophy had been a healthy, robust man, who had been employed by the town of Easton as a fireman and emergency medical technician. He enjoyed deer hunting, fishing, gardening, and performing household chores. . . . Brophy is now in a condition described as a "persistent vegetative state." He is unable to chew or swallow, and is maintained by an artificial device, surgically inserted on December 22, 1983, known as a gastrostomy tube (G-tube) through which he receives nutrition and hydration. On June

---

3. The President's Commission Report reveals that, between 1900 and 1983, the causes and the places of death have changed dramatically. Death caused by communicable disease has declined sharply; most deaths now are caused by heart disease, cancer, and cerebrovascular disease or illness — "illnesses that occur later in life and that are ordinarily progressive for some years before death." Id. at 16. Institutional settings (hospitals and nursing homes) were the sites of 50 percent of all deaths in 1949, of over 70 percent by 1977, and, by 1983, of over 80 percent. Id. at 17-18. The Commission, thus, has stated: "Once someone realizes that the time and manner of death are substantially under the control of medical science, he or she wants to be protected against decisions that make death too easy and quick as well as from those that make it too agonizing and prolonged." Id. at 23. The Commission notes, also, that "[f]or almost any life-threatening condition, some intervention can now delay the moment of death." Id. at 1.

28, 1983, he was transferred to the New England Sinai Hospital (hospital), where he remains as a patient.

Brophy's wife and family wish the G-tube removed or clamped. When the physicians and hospital refused, litigation was commenced by Brophy's wife in the Probate and Family Court Department. A judge of the Probate Court, after extensive hearings, found that Brophy, now incompetent, would, if competent, decline to receive food and water in this manner, and that Brophy's wife and guardian, Patricia E. Brophy, and his family and relatives agree with this choice. Nevertheless, the judge ordered the continuation of nutrition and hydration by use of the G-tube and enjoined both the hospital and the guardian from removing or clamping the tube. We now set aside the judgment and remand the case for entry of a new judgment. In doing so, we sustain that portion of the judgment which respects the right of the hospital to refuse to remove or clamp the G-tube, but authorize the guardian to remove Brophy from the hospital to the care of other physicians who will honor Brophy's wishes.

b. The Medical Facts. . . .

Apart from the extreme injury to his brain, Brophy's other organs are functioning relatively well. The judge found that he is not terminally ill, nor is he in danger of imminent death from any other medical cause. It appears that he may live in a persistent vegetative state for several years, although a nonaggressive treatment plan will probably shorten his life. . . .

Brophy shows no signs or symptoms of discomfort as a result of the use of the G-tube. The judge found that utilization of the G-tube is not "painful, uncomfortable, burdensome, unusual, hazardous, invasive or intrusive," even in relation to a conscious patient.

Removal of the G-tube likely would create various effects resulting from the lack of hydration and nutrition, leading ultimately to death. The judge found that death by dehydration is extremely painful and uncomfortable for a human being.[20] . . .

The judge found on the basis of ample evidence which no one disputes, that Brophy's judgment would be to decline the provision of food and water and to terminate his life. . . .[22]

---

20. The judge concluded that the possibility that Brophy would experience a painful death "cannot be ruled out." This finding apparently was based on the testimony of Brophy's attending physician and seems inconsistent with the judge's findings as to the nature of Brophy's persistent vegetative state. The American Academy of Neurology, as amicus, claims in its brief that patients in a persistent vegetative state, like Brophy, do not experience pain and suffering. . . .

22. About ten years ago, discussing Karen Ann Quinlan, Brophy stated to his wife, "I don't ever want to be on a life-support system. No way do I want to live like

2. The Law

. . . The right of a patient to refuse medical treatment arises both from the common law and the unwritten and penumbral constitutional right to privacy. . . .

The right of self-determination and individual autonomy has its roots deep in our history. John Stuart Mill stated the concept succinctly: "[T]he only purpose for which power can be rightfully exercised over any member of a civilized community, against his will, is to prevent harm to others. His own good, either physical or moral, is not a sufficient warrant. He cannot rightfully be compelled to do or forbear because it will be better for him to do so, because it will make him happier, because, in the opinion of others, to do so would be wise, or even right." Mill, On Liberty, in 43 Great Books of the Western World 271. . . .

It is in recognition of these fundamental principles of individual autonomy that we sought, in *Saikewicz* [infra at 972], to shift the emphasis away from a paternalistic view of what is "best" for a patient toward a reaffirmation that the basic question is what decision will comport with the will of the person involved, whether that person be competent or incompetent. . . .

Accepting that Brophy's substituted judgment would be to discontinue providing nutrients through the G-tube, we are left only with the question whether the Commonwealth's interests require that his judgment be overridden. It is natural to begin with the most significant interest in this case, the interest in the preservation of life.

The concern for the preservation of the life of the patient normally involves an interest in the prolongation of life. Thus, the State's interest in preserving life is very high when "human life [can] be saved where the affliction is curable." *Saikewicz,* supra, 373 Mass. at 742, 370 N.E.2d 417. That interest wanes when the underlying affliction is incurable and would "soon cause death regardless of any medical treatment." Commissioner of Correction v. Myers, supra, 379 Mass. at 262, 399 N.E.2d 452. The calculus shifts when the issue is not "whether, but when, for how long, and at what cost to the individual that life may be briefly extended." Id.

---

that; that is not living." He had a favorite saying: "When your ticket is punched, it is punched." Approximately five to six years ago, he helped to rescue from a burning truck a man who received extensive burns and who died a few months later. He tossed the commendation he received for bravery in the trash and said, "I should have been five minutes later. It would have been all over for him." He also said to his brother regarding that incident, "If I'm ever like that, just shoot me, pull the plug." About one week prior to his illness, in discussing a local teenager who had been put on a life support system he said, "No way, don't ever let that happen to me, no way." Within twelve hours after being transported to Goddard Hospital following the rupture of the aneurysm, he stated to one of his daughters, "If I can't sit up to kiss one of my beautiful daughters, I may as well be six feet under."

II. Termination of Treatment and Related Matters

When we balance the State's interest in prolonging a patient's life against the rights of the patient to reject such prolongation, we must recognize that the State's interest in life encompasses a broader interest than mere corporeal existence. In certain, thankfully rare, circumstances the burden of maintaining the corporeal existence degrades the very humanity it was meant to serve. The law recognizes the individual's right to preserve his humanity, even if to preserve his humanity means to allow the natural processes of a disease or affliction to bring about a death with dignity. In stating this, we make no judgment based on our own view of the value of Brophy's life, since we do not approve of an analysis of State interests which focuses on Brophy's quality of life. The judge correctly disavowed pronouncing judgment that Brophy's life is not worth preserving. . . .

In this case, the State's concern for the preservation of the life of the patient is implicated. Here, Brophy is not terminally ill nor in danger of imminent death from any underlying physical illness. It is true, however, that his life expectancy has been shortened by his physical affliction. While the judge found that continued use of the G-tube is not a highly invasive or intrusive procedure and may not subject him to pain or suffering, he is left helpless and in a condition which Brophy has indicated he would consider to be degrading and without human dignity. In making this finding, it is clear that the judge failed to consider that Brophy's judgment would be that being maintained by use of the G-tube is indeed intrusive. Additionally, in our view, the maintenance of Brophy for a period of several years, is intrusive treatment as a matter of law. . . .

A few States have decided cases with fact patterns similar to the one at hand. The leading case is the New Jersey Supreme Court decision in Matter of Conroy, supra. In that case the court would have refused to force a patient who had less than a year to live to endure the pain of a nasogastric tube used to supply nutrition and hydration, rejected the distinction between active or passive treatment, and stated that "the primary focus should be the patient's desires and experience of pain and enjoyment — not the type of treatment involved." 486 A.2d at 1209. In rejecting this distinction, the New Jersey Supreme Court overturned the appellate division, which had held that, because provision of nutrition and hydration through a nasogastric tube was "ordinary" care, the patient must be maintained by the nasogastric tube. The recent California case of Bouvia v. Superior Court for Los Angeles County, 179 Cal. App. 3d 1127, 225 Cal. Rptr. 297 (1986) . . . upheld the right of the patient, who was fully competent but hopelessly quadriplegic and in continual pain, to end the use of a feeding tube which had been inserted against her will. An intermediate court of appeals decision in Florida similarly authorized the cessation of artificial feeding by use of a nasogastric tube. Corbett v. D'Alessandro, 487 So. 2d 368 (Fla. App. 1986) ("we see no reason to differentiate between the multitude of artificial devices that may be available to prolong the moment of death").

The New Jersey Supreme Court has stated that the State's interest in preserving life "generally gives way to the patient's much stronger personal interest in directing the course of his own life." Matter of Conroy, supra, 98 N.J. at 350, 486 A.2d 1209. The New Jersey Supreme Court [refused to] consider the fact that a nasogastric tube is less invasive than hemodialysis or a respirator. The court concluded that the individual's interest in bodily integrity, which is weighed against competing State interests, is a constant value to be considered. . . . Although we have recognized that the invasiveness of the treatment sought to be terminated is an important factor to be considered in balancing the individual's and the State's interests, [ ] we agree with the New Jersey court's view that "the primary focus should be the patient's desires and experience of pain and enjoyment — not the type of treatment involved." Matter of Conroy, supra, 98 N.J. at 369, 486 A.2d 1209. In *Saikewicz*, we spoke with approval of the distinction made by medical ethicists between extraordinary and ordinary care. The New Jersey Supreme Court in Matter of Quinlan, 70 N.J. 10, 355 A.2d 647 (1976), had considered the distinction to have significance at that time in the medical community. We recognize that, more recently, such a distinction has been criticized. See, e.g., Matter of Conroy, citing President's Commission Report at 84-88.

While we believe that the distinction between extraordinary and ordinary care is a factor to be considered, the use of such a distinction as the sole, or major, factor of decision tends, in a case such as this, to create a distinction without meaning. Additionally, to state that the maintenance of nutrition and hydration by the use of the existing G-tube is only ordinary is to ignore the total circumstances of Brophy's situation. He cannot swallow. The judge found that Brophy may be maintained by the use of the G-tube for "several years," the longest recorded survival by such means extending for thirty-seven years. Clearly, to be maintained by such artificial means over an extended period is not only intrusive but extraordinary. . . .

Just as the distinction between extraordinary and ordinary arguably obscures the real issue, so, too, the distinction between withholding and withdrawing treatment has no moral significance. "Moreover, from a policy standpoint, it might well be unwise to forbid persons from discontinuing a treatment under circumstances in which the treatment could permissibly be withheld. Such a rule could discourage families and doctors from even attempting certain types of care and could thereby force them into hasty and premature decisions to allow a patient to die." Matter of Conroy, supra at 370, 486 A.2d 1209. . . .

Thus, we conclude that the State's interest in the preservation of life does not overcome Brophy's right to discontinue treatment. Nor do we consider his death to be against the State's interest in the prevention of suicide. "[D]eclining life-sustaining medical treatment may not properly be viewed as an attempt to commit suicide. Refusing medical intervention merely allows the disease to take its natural course; if death were eventually to occur, it would be the result, primarily, of the underlying disease, and not the result of a self-inflicted injury." Matter of Conroy, 98 N.J. 321, 350-351, 486 A.2d 1209 (1985). . . .

We now turn to consider briefly the position of the defendant hospital. . . . There is nothing in *Saikewicz* and its progeny which would justify compelling medical professionals, in a case such as this, to take active measures which are contrary to their view of their ethical duty toward their patients. See Brandt v. St. Vincent Infirmary, 287 Ark. 431, 701 S.W.2d 103, 106-107 (1985). There is substantial disagreement in the medical community over the appropriate medical action. It would be particularly inappropriate to force the hospital, which is willing to assist in a transfer of the patient, to take affirmative steps to end the provision of nutrition and hydration to him. A patient's right to refuse medical treatment does not warrant such an unnecessary intrusion upon the hospital's ethical integrity in this case.

Conclusion. Accordingly, we uphold that portion of the judgment which pertains to the hospital, but set aside that portion of the judgment which enjoins the guardian from authorizing a facility to remove or clamp Brophy's G-tube. A new judgment is to be entered ordering the hospital to assist the guardian in transferring the ward to a suitable facility, or to his home, where his wishes may be effectuated, and authorizing the guardian to order such measures as she may deem necessary and appropriate in the circumstances.

So ordered.

NOLAN, JUSTICE (dissenting).

The court today has rendered an opinion which affronts logic, ethics, and the dignity of the human person.

As to logic, the court has built its entire case on an outrageously erroneous premise, i.e., food and liquids are medical treatment. The issue is not whether the tube should be inserted but whether food should be given through the tube. The process of feeding is simply not medical treatment and is not invasive, as that word is used in this context. Food and water are basic human needs. They are not medicines and feeding them to a patient is just not medical treatment. Because of this faulty premise, the court's conclusions must inevitably fall under the weight of logic.

In the forum of ethics, despite the opinion's high-blown language to the contrary, the court today has indorsed euthanasia and suicide.

Suicide is direct self-destruction and is intrinsically evil. No set of circumstances can make it moral. Paul Brophy will die as a direct result of the cessation of feeding. The ethical principle of double effect is totally inapplicable here. This death by dehydration and starvation has been approved by the court. He will not die from the aneurysm which precipitated loss of consciousness, the surgery which was performed, the brain damage that followed or the insertion of the G-tube. He will die as a direct result of the refusal to feed him. He will starve to death, and the court approves this death. See Bannon, Rx: Death by Dehydration, 12 Human Life Rev., 70 (No. 3, 1986). . . .

The withdrawal of the provision of food and water is a particularly difficult, painful and gruesome death;[2] . . . Such a process would not be very far from euthanasia, and the natural question is: Why not use more humane methods of euthanasia if that is what we indorse? The State has an interest in maintaining the public integrity of the symbols of life; apparent euthanasia, and an apparently painful and difficult method of euthanasia, is contrary to that interest.

Moreover, until this case, it was clear that the State's interest in life was to be balanced against the individual's right to privacy and bodily integrity. . . . Today, however, the majority essentially equate the right to privacy-bodily integrity with a right to choose or refuse all bodily invasions. Thus, if an individual's choice would be to refuse treatment or care, it is not important that that treatment or care is minimally invasive. . . .

In upholding a substituted judgment decision to refuse nutrition and hydration, this court and the California and New Jersey courts have not been willing to take the final step and rule directly that the right to privacy and bodily integrity entails a (limited) right to die. Cf. Bouvia v. Superior Court for Los Angeles County, supra, 225 Cal. Rptr. at 307-308 (Compton, J., concurring). Massachusetts law has not heretofore acknowledged a right to die emanating from the

---

2. Removal of the G tube would likely create various effects from the lack of hydration and nutrition, leading ultimately to death. Brophy's mouth would dry out and become caked or coated with thick material. His lips would become parched and cracked. His tongue would swell, and might crack. His eyes would recede back into their orbits and his cheeks would become hollow. The lining of his nose might crack and cause his nose to bleed. His skin would hang loose on his body and become dry and scaly. His urine would become highly concentrated, leading to burning of the bladder. The lining of his stomach would dry out and he would experience dry heaves and vomiting. His body temperature would become very high. His brain cells would dry out, causing convulsions. His respiratory tract would dry out, and the thick secretions that would result could plug his lungs and cause death. At some point within five days to three weeks his major organs, including his lungs, heart, and brain, would give out and he would die. The judge found that death by dehydration is extremely painful and uncomfortable for a human being. The judge could not rule out the possibility that Paul Brophy could experience pain in such a scenario. Paul Brophy's attending physician described death by dehydration as cruel and violent.

right to privacy, but now, in essence, it does. Under *Saikewicz* and its progeny, the invasiveness of the procedure sought to be terminated was an important factor to be considered in assessing the strength of the State's interest in preserving life against the individual's rights. For all intents and purposes, this element has been eliminated and the *Saikewicz* "balancing test" is all but chimerical once it has been discerned what the individual's choice would be. . . .

Here it is clear that the continued use of a G-tube presents few risks, no surgery, no pain or discomfort, and is minimally invasive; it is hardly more invasive than letting air into the room so that a patient can breathe. While what degree of invasiveness is involved in a particular medical regimen may present issues of difficult line-drawing, this is not such a case.

Second, it appears that the majority have refused to overrule *Saikewicz* directly and to rule in favor of a constitutional right to die, so as to avoid the obvious conflict with the law against suicide. The State has an interest in the prevention of suicide. The underlying State interest in this area is the prevention of irrational self-destruction. . . . Here, Brophy is not terminally ill, and death is not imminent. [T]he judge specifically found that . . . "Brophy's decision, if he were competent to make it, would be primarily based upon the present quality of life possible for him, and would not be based upon the burdens imposed upon him by receiving food and water through a G tube, which burdens are relatively minimal. . . ." Where treatment is burdensome and invasive, no such specific intent is normally at issue because, whether or not the patient seeks to die, the patient primarily seeks to end invasive or burdensome treatment. . . . If nutrition and hydration are terminated, it is not the illness which causes the death but the decision (and act in accordance therewith) that the illness makes life not worth living. . . .

[Two other Justices of the seven-member court joined this dissent.]

NOTES

Suicide and the Refusal of Nutrition and Hydration

1. In trying to sort out whether treatment refusal constitutes suicide, it is helpful to consider three separate categories of cases:

1) patients who refuse treatment because the *treatment itself* is burdensome, demeaning, or contrary to religious principles, such as leg amputations or Jehovah's Witness blood transfusions;
2) patients who do not object to the nature of treatment per se other than that they no longer wish to live because the

illness being treated is burdensome and demeaning, such as Mr. Brophy or a terminal cancer patient; and

3) patients who are simply seizing on the fortuitous need for treatment in order to fulfill a wish to die that exists independently of the illness that requires treatment.

A classic example of the first category is Dax Cowart, who was blinded and severely disfigured by third-degree burns over two-thirds of his body. Burn treatment, which involves repeated immersions into a disinfectant bath, is excruciatingly painful, but effective. Throughout his 14 months of hospitalization, family members and medical personnel ignored Mr. Cowart's repeated demands that he be allowed to die. In subsequent interviews, Mr. Cowart states that he is now enjoying life and is glad to be alive, but he still objects to having been forced to undergo the burn therapy. See Areen et al., Law, Science & Medicine 1112-1117 (1984); L. Kliever, Dax's Case: Essays in Medical Ethics and Human Meaning (1989).

Does Mr. Bartling's past alcoholism and present "severe depression" suggest that he might fall into the third category?

Once patients are placed in one of these three categories, then can the validity of the treatment refusals be adequately distinguished using a specific intent test, that is, asking whether they intended to bring about their death? Be careful to differentiate between intent and motivation. For instance, can it not be said, even of the religiously-motivated Jehovah's Witness, that a specific intent to die exists in deliberately choosing an action that will certainly lead to death? Wouldn't we say that a religious fanatic who dies from a hunger strike has committed a form of suicide?

Is it any more helpful to employ a causation test, that is, to ask whether death results from the underlying illness rather than from the treatment refusal? Obviously, the fact that a terminally ill patient is soon to die does not change the fact that the patient's putting a gun to his head causes his own death. If the patient yanks the ventilator plug out of the wall, or has someone do it for him, why is the causation issue any different? See generally R. Weir, Ethical Issues in Death and Dying, "Part 6: Suicide" (2d ed. 1986) (collecting various essays); M. Battin & D. Mayo, Suicide: The Ethical Issues (1980) (same).

2. Perhaps it advances clearer analysis simply to recognize that not all suicide is condemned by the law. As the *Bartling* majority and the *Brophy* dissent state, the policy of suicide law is to prevent "irrational" self-destruction. For example, we do not condemn the sacrifice of a parent who jumps in front of a speeding train to save a child's life or the heroism of a captain who goes down with his ship. See Mayo, The Concept of Rational Suicide, 11 J. Med. & Philo. 143

(1986). What test for prohibited suicide would this reasoning generate? The author of Comment, Suicidal Competence and the Patient's Right to Refuse Lifesaving Treatment, Cal. L. Rev. 707, 753-754 (1987) suggests the following:

> Suicidal intent is not a sufficient reason to deny a patient the right to refuse treatment. [C]ourts should not use analytically rigid distinctions to evade making such determinations. Rather, . . . courts should be guided by two considerations:
> 1) Whether the patient's refusal is a reflective, settled decision, consistent with the patient's general way of life or religious or philosophical convictions; or alternatively, a hasty decision made in reaction to a sudden personal catastrophe, temporary severe depression, or a mental impairment due to pain, disease, or the side effects of medication.
> 2) Whether the patient's probable future life will be so diminished in quality that a reasonable person could conclude that it is not worth living; or alternatively, the patient's life could be valuable and fulfilling, thus raising doubt about whether the patient appreciates the prospects she is renouncing.

See also Smith, All's Well That Ends Well: Toward a Policy of Assisted Rational Suicide or Merely Enlightened Self-Determination?, 22 U.C. Davis L. Rev. 275, 357 (1989) ("The major focus of all inquiry into actions previously classified as suicide or euthanasia [sh]ould be simply: Did the individual in question, exercising her powers of rational thinking, exercise an act of enlightened self-determination or autonomy?"). How would these standards govern a patient who refuses treatment in order to protect his family from the emotional burdens involved in continued care? The financial burdens?

The related line of argument over whether the law should go further and allow active euthanasia, that is, overt mercy killing at the patient's request through means other than treatment withdrawal, is pursued below in Section II.D.

3. An excellent illustration of the dilemma over the definition of suicide is presented by the case of Elizabeth Bouvia, a bright, young woman who suffers from severe cerebral palsy and arthritis. These conditions have rendered her a quadriplegic suffering from constant pain and unable to care for herself, but they do not in any way threaten her immediate life expectancy of several dozen years. In 1983, Bouvia suffered a series of emotional setbacks when her husband left her and her physical deterioration forced her to drop out of school and become dependent on family members for feeding and virtually every daily need. Despondent, she admitted herself to Riverside Hospital in California as a psychiatric patient, with the apparent intent of starving herself to death using the assistance of pain relief and other comfort care provided by the public hospital.

In the first, unappealed decision, the trial court ruled that "a severely handicapped, mentally competent person who is otherwise physically healthy and not terminally ill [does not have] the right to end her life with the assistance of society." Bouvia v. County of Riverside, No. 159780 (Cal., Riverside County, Super. Ct., Dec. 16, 1983), reprinted in 1 Issues in Law & Med. 485 (1986). Following this decision, Bouvia left the hospital but did not carry out her planned starvation. However, two years later her condition deteriorated further to the extent that she was physically unable to eat enough to sustain her health, so she entered a second hospital where she was force-fed through a nasogastric tube. The second lawsuit sought to have this feeding tube removed.

The court of appeals upheld Bouvia's right to take charge of her own food intake, even if this meant the hastening of her death:

> At bench the trial court concluded that with sufficient feeding petitioner could live an additional 15 to 20 years; therefore, the preservation of petitioner's life for that period outweighed her right to decide. In so holding the trial court mistakenly attached undue importance to the *amount of time* possibly available to petitioner, and failed to give equal weight and consideration for the *quality* of that life. . . . In Elizabeth Bouvia's view, the quality of her life has been diminished to the point of hopelessness, uselessness, unenjoyability and frustration. She, as the patient, lying helplessly in bed, unable to care for herself, may consider her existence meaningless. . . .
>
> [Respondents] assert that what petitioner really wants is to "commit suicide" by starvation at their facility. The trial court in its statement of decisions said: "It is fairly clear from the evidence . . . [that petitioner] has formed an intent to die . . . [and] has purposefully engaged in a selective rejection of medical treatment and nutritional intake to accomplish her objective and accept only treatment which gives her some degree of comfort pending her demise. . . ."
>
> Overlooking the fact that a desire to terminate one's life is probably the ultimate exercise of one's right to privacy, we find no substantial evidence to support the court's conclusion. Even if petitioner had the specific intent to commit suicide in 1983, while at Riverside, she did not carry out that plan. Then she apparently had the ability without artificial aids, to consume sufficient nutrients to sustain herself, now she does not. . . . As a consequence of her changed condition, it is clear she has now merely resigned herself to accept an earlier death, if necessary, rather than live by feedings forced upon her by means of a nasogastric tube. Her decision to allow nature to take its course is not equivalent to an election to commit suicide. . . .
>
> Moreover, the trial court seriously erred by basing its decision on the "motives" behind Elizabeth Bouvia's decision to exercise her rights. If a right exists, it matters not what "motivates" its exercise. We find nothing in the law to suggest the right to refuse medical treatment may be exercised only if the patient's *motives* meet someone else's approval.

It certainly is not illegal or immoral to prefer a natural, albeit sooner, death than a drugged life attached to a mechanical device.

Bouvia v. Superior Court, 225 Cal. Rptr. 297, 304-305 (Cal. App. 1986). As of this writing, Elizabeth Bouvia is still alive.

4. Another area of the law that considers the validity of forced treatment to prevent suicide is the law of involuntary commitment for psychiatric treatment. State statutes uniformly authorize involuntary hospitalization of mentally ill persons who are a "danger to *themselves* or others." The law in some states goes further and allows psychiatric hospitals to forcibly medicate dangerous patients with "psychotropic" (that is, mind-altering) drugs. Again, one justification is protection of patients from themselves. See Rogers v. Okin, 738 F.2d 1 (1st Cir. 1984); U.S. v. Charters, 863 F.2d 302 (4th Cir. 1988). Thus, even when only the patient's own welfare is at stake, *mental* health law *denies* the right to refuse treatment. Right-to-die courts and commentators seldom recognize or attempt to reconcile this apparent inconsistency between lifesaving psychiatric and lifesaving medical treatment.

One possible rationale for this discrepancy is the presumed incompetence of mental patients. However, as most courts have recognized, mental illness and decisional incompetence are not coextensive. Just because patients might suffer a mental illness does not mean they are incapable of rationally deciding how and whether that illness should be treated. It is for this reason that several recent decisions have prohibited forced psychotropic medication absent an "emergency" situation. Jarvis v. Levine, 418 N.W.2d 139 (Minn. 1988); State v. Gerhardstein, 416 N.W.2d 710 (Wisc. 1987); Rivers v. Katz, 504 N.Y.S.2d 74 (1986); Rogers v. Commissioner of Dept. of Mental Health, 458 N.E.2d 308 (Mass. 1986). However, the law still authorizes forced hospitalization and forced chemical or physical restraint in order to protect the patient's life or physical health. See generally Clayton, From *Rogers* to *Rivers:* The Rights of the Mentally Ill to Refuse Medication, 13 Am. J.L. & Med. 7 (1987).

5. Following *Brophy* and the supporting cases it cites, several other state supreme courts have allowed the withdrawal of nutrition and hydration from comatose patients. In re Grant, 747 P.2d 445 (Wash. 1987); Rasmussen v. Fleming, 741 P.2d 674 (Ariz. 1987); In re Jobes, 529 A.2d 434 (N.J. 1987); In re Gardner, 534 A.2d 947 (Me. 1987). In one case, the court permitted even a sapient patient to order the removal of a feeding tube, a 34-year-old stroke victim paralyzed from the neck down. See Ross v. Hilltop Rehabilitation Hosp., 676 F. Supp. 1528 (D. Colo. 1987). Another decision somewhat more restrictively allowed feeding tube withdrawal only for terminally ill patients. In re Estate of Longeway, 549 N.E.2d 292 (Ill. 1989).

Demonstrating the rapid evolution of medical ethics in this field, the AMA Council on Ethical and Judicial Affairs has issued a statement supporting the right to refuse nutrition and hydration. For other approving authority, see Hastings Center, Guidelines on the Termination of Life-Sustaining Treatment (1987); J. Lynn, By No Extraordinary Means: The Choice to Forgo Life-Sustaining Food and Water (1986); Lynn & Childress, Must Patients Always be Given Food and Water?, 13 Hastings Cent. Rep. at 17 (No. 5 1983); Steinbrook & Lo, Artificial Feeding — Solid Ground, Not a Slippery Slope, 318 New Eng. J. Med. 286 (1988).

However, the *Brophy* dissent demonstrates that these views are not uniformly held in our society:

> Early this year, a New England Journal of Medicine article described "an emerging medical, ethical and legal consensus" on the situations in which life-prolonging artificial feeding can be withheld from hopelessly ill or permanently unconscious patients. . . . That emerging consensus, however, is no longer so clear. The recent events disquieting the right-to-die supporters and heartening the right-to-life side include: (1) A [4-3] Missouri Supreme Court decision rejecting efforts by the parents of Nancy Cruzan, a 31-year-old hopelessly comatose woman, to end the artificial feeding that's kept her alive since a January 1983 auto accident. . . . [2] A [5-2] decision last month by the New York Court of Appeals . . . ordering continued artificial feeding of Mary O'Connor, a 77-year-old mentally incompetent hospital patient, despite testimony by her two daughters and a family friend that over the years she often said she never wanted to be kept alive that way. . . . It's the New York appeals court ruling that particularly threatens to overshadow many of the right-to-die gains.

Wall St. J., Nov. 11, 1988 at B1. The *O'Connor* decision, which is excerpted in the following section at 988, is based on the lack of clear evidence of the patient's desires, but *Cruzan* goes more to the nature of the treatment itself. The gist of the Missouri court's reasoning is captured in its opening salvo that "we are asked to allow the medical profession to make Nancy die by starvation and dehydration" and is continued in its opining, contrary to all medical testimony, that "common sense tells us that food and water do not treat an illness, they maintain a life." 760 S.W.2d at 412, 423.

What role do living will acts play in the analysis of feeding tube withdrawals, given that most exclude the refusal of nutrition and hydration from the scope of permissible treatment refusals? One court has ruled that these restrictions do not preclude a common law rule allowing feeding tube refusal since the living will act is not intended to be a patient's exclusive remedy. Rasmussen v. Fleming, 741 P.2d 674 (Ariz. 1987). A second court has narrowly construed the act's exclusion of hydration and nutrition as applying only to natural methods of feeding, such as by spoon or straw. McConnell v. Beverly Enterprises, 553 A.2d 596 (Conn. 1989). A third court has held that a statutory preclusion of the right to refuse nutrition and hydration is unconstitutional. Corbett v. D'Alessandro, 498 So. 2d 368 (Fla. App. 1986).

Oklahoma is the first state to enact a statute addressing feeding tube withdrawal in detail. It specifically authorizes the refusal of nutrition and hydration, but only when death due to the underlying illness is "imminent" and treatment withdrawal will not "result in death from dehydration or starvation." Okla. Stat. Ann., tit. 63, §3080.4.

For additional commentary arguing against the withdrawal of feeding tubes, see Bopp, Nutrition and Hydration for Patients: The Constitutional Aspects, 4 Issues in L. & Med. 3 (1988); May et al., Feeding and Hydrating the Permanently Unconscious and other Vulnerable Persons, 3 Issues in L. & Med. 203 (1987); Comment, Hold on Courts: May a Comatose Patient be Denied Food and Water, 31 St. Louis U.L. Rev. 749 (1987).

The Balancing Test and the Constitutional Right of Privacy

6. Although right-to-die decisions still continue to pay lip service to the four-factor balancing test, the *Brophy* dissent questions the extent to which courts actually are engaging in a sensitive evaluation of the state's competing interests in life preservation. Absent situations such as *Georgetown College* where a treatment refusal will directly harm a third party, is it possible to conceive of *any* case in which the countervailing factors will outweigh a lucid patient's interest in self-determination? Now that refusal of artificial feeding is allowed, the intrusiveness or extraordinariness of the treatment does not seem to matter. Recent influential decisions have also disavowed any reliance on the patient's life expectancy or prognosis for recovery: "The privacy that we accord medical decisions does not vary with the patient's condition or prognosis. The patient's medical condition is generally relevant only to determine whether the patient is competent. . . ." In re Peter, 529 A.2d 419, 423 (N.J. 1987). Given this state of the case law, is it permissible for an otherwise totally healthy person to refuse to eat anymore simply out of empathy for the plight of starving Ethiopians? Because he or she didn't (or did) make law review? See generally Peters, The State's Interest in the Preservation of Life, S. Oh. St. L.J. 891 (1989).

What type of legal standard do you think works best in this area of law: a case-by-case balancing approach, or a more certain rule, subject to defined exceptions?

7. Most right-to-die decisions are founded on a constitutional privacy interest in controlling medical treatment. Is it advisable to elevate these cases to constitutional stature? See Capron, Borrowed Lessons: The Role of Ethical Distinctions in Framing Law on Life-Sustaining Treatment, 1984 Ariz. St. L.J. 647 (suggesting no). To do so, courts must overcome two analytical barriers: (1) finding that forced treatment by private hospitals and doctors constitutes state action; and (2) finding that the constitutional privacy interest established in cases such as Roe v. Wade and Griswold v. Connecticut, discussed in sections III.A and III.B below, extends beyond the arena of procreational liberty. As a matter of *federal* constitutional law, both of these findings are problematic at best. Nevertheless, the decisions that have constitutionalized right-to-die law gloss over these complications. While state courts are of course free to reach differing interpretations under their own constitutions, it is seldom evident that these decisions are restricted to state constitutional law.

It is difficult to find state action in a private hospital's or physician's decision to treat. See 476 supra. The fact that a court might refuse to enforce a patient's (or family's) objection hardly converts the treatment itself to state action. See Blum v. Yaretsky, 457 U.S. 991 (1982) (no state action implicated by a private nursing home's decision to discharge a patient despite ratification by Medicaid program) ("a State normally can be held responsible for a private decision only when it has exercised [such] coercive power . . . that the choice must in law be deemed to be that of the State"). A case for state action possibly exists only where the state does more than refuse to intervene, but uses criminal or civil liability to effectively force the doctor to treat.

Even where state action does exist, a federal constitutional claim is questionable on the merits given the current Supreme Court's restrictive approach to the privacy interest. See Chapters 6.II.D and 9.III.B; Bowers v. Hardwick, 478 U.S. 186 (1986) (no privacy interest in homosexual conduct, in part because there is "no connection between family, marriage, or procreation on the one hand and homosexual activity on the other"). The only *federal* decision to generalize the privacy interest beyond matters of family and procreation to cover decisions that fundamentally affect one's body generally is Gray v. Romeo, 697 F. Supp. 580 (D.R.I. 1988). But see Cruzan v. Harmon, 760 S.W.2d 408, 418 (Mo. 1988), reprinted infra at 995 ("we carry grave doubts as to the applicability of privacy rights to decisions to terminate the provision of food and water"). The Supreme Court may resolve this uncertainty if it issues an opinion on the merits in the *Cruzan* case, in which it has just granted certiorari. 57 U.S.L.W. 3852 (1989). See generally, Delgado, Euthanasia Reconsidered: The Choice of Death As an Aspect of the Right of Privacy, 17 Ariz. L.

Rev. 474 (1975); Hufstedler, The Directions and Misdirections of a Constitutional Right to Privacy, 26 Rec. Assn. B. City N.Y. 546 (1971).

Provider Responsibility for Humane Treatment Withdrawal

8. Is the aspect of the *Brophy* decision that allows the hospital to avoid the responsibility of treatment withdrawal consistent with the law of abandonment? What should a hospital do where no other willing provider can be located (which apparently was the dilemma the hospital faced in the original *Bouvia* decision)? See Annas, When Suicide Prevention Becomes Brutality: The Case of Elizabeth Bouvia, 14 Hastings Cent. Rep. 20 (April 1984) (hospital is stuck).

As *Bartling* reflects, *Brophy* is in the minority on this issue. For other decisions that prevent a hospital from transferring a patient who wants to die, see In re Requena, 517 A.2d 869, 886 (N.J. 1986); In re Jobes, 529 A.2d 434 (N.J. 1987); Bouvia v. Superior Court, 225 Cal. Rptr. 297, 306 (Cal. App. 1986). However, another California decision more recently refused to compel a physician against his moral objection to withdraw treatment because the hospital had not yet attempted to transfer the patient to a willing provider. It refused to rule on the result if no transfer could be made, opining that the issue is "too profound for gratuitous discussion in dictum." Conservatorship of Morrison, 253 Cal. Rptr. 530 (Cal. App. 1988).

Does a religious hospital have a greater right to refuse participation in a nontreatment decision? See Note, When Ethics Collide: Enforcement of Institutional Policies of Non-Participation in the Termination of Life-Sustaining Treatment, 41 Rutgers L. Rev. 399 (1988) (arguing "yes").

9. Treatment refusal cases do not arise only in hospitals. They are equally frequent in nursing homes, and occasionally occur outside of institutions altogether. In all three situations, the question repeatedly arises whether it is necessary to obtain judicial approval in every case before honoring a patient's (or family's) wishes. The New Jersey Supreme Court provided the following guidance in the widely noted opinion In re Farrell, 529 A.2d 404, 415 (N.J. 1987):

> A competent patient's right to exercise his or her choice to refuse life-sustaining treatment does not vary depending on whether the patient is in a medical institution or at home. . . . [However, the questions of whether a patient is competent, informed, and free of coercion] are more easily resolved when the patient is in a hospital, nursing home, or other institution, because in those settings the patient is observed by more people. To protect the patient who is at home, we require that two non-attending physicians examine the patient to confirm that he or she is competent and is fully informed about his or her prognosis, the medical alternatives available, the risks involved, and the likely

outcome if medical treatment is disconnected. [Fn. 8: "The procedure we hereby establish . . . is likewise applicable to patients in hospitals and nursing homes."]

Judicial review of a competent patient's refusal of life-sustaining treatment is generally not appropriate. . . . Unfortunately, fears of civil and criminal liability have often forced family members or doctors to seek judicial intervention before they help a patient effectuate his or her decision to withdraw treatment. . . . In light of this, we specifically hold that no civil or criminal liability will be incurred by any person who, in good faith reliance on the procedures established in this opinion, withdraws life-sustaining treatment at the request of an informed and competent patient who has undergone the required independent medical examination described above.

10. Mr. Bartling's "frantic signalling" to reconnect the ventilator when it accidentally disconnected is properly viewed by the court as not indicating a change in heart because it is a natural instinctive reaction to the discomfort of suffocation. For a thoughtful discussion of humane medical techniques for discontinuing treatment that avoid such incidents, see Schneiderman & Spragg, Ethical Decisions in Discontinuing Mechanical Ventilation, 318 New Eng. J. Med. 984 (1988). The Georgia Supreme Court has ruled, in the case of a fully-competent quadriplegic dependent on a ventilator, that "the right to have a sedative (a medication that in no way causes or accelerates death) administered before the ventilator is disconnected is a part of his right to control his medical treatment." Georgia v. McAfee, 385 S.E.2d 651 (Ga. 1989).

Damages for Ignoring Treatment Refusals

11. Given the clarity of Mr. Bartling's wishes and the settled nature of California law under the previous *Barber* opinion, why did the hospital insist on a court order before honoring the patient's wishes? Religious scruples may be the answer, but it may also be that the hospital's attorneys viewed the legal risks, however minimal, as existing only on the side of withdrawing treatment. To counter hospitals' persistent risk aversion, right-to-die advocates have adopted the strategy followed in *Bartling* of suing noncompliant hospitals and doctors for battery damages in addition to seeking an order discontinuing treatment.

A battery cause of action would appear to be open and shut: informed consent law prohibits treatment without consent regardless of the doctor's opinion as to the medical benefits. Indeed, two cases have explicitly refused to dismiss damages complaints in right-to-die cases. Estate of Leach v. Shapiro, 469 N.E.2d 1047 (Oh. App. 1984);

Holmes v. Silver Cross Hosp., 340 F. Supp. 125 (N.D. Ill. 1972). However, a subsequent decision in the *Bartling* litigation held that the law at the time of his treatment was too unsettled to form the basis for a duty in tort. Bartling v. Glendale Adventist Med. Cent. (Bartling II), 184 Cal. Rptr. 360 (Cal. App. 1986). See also Foster v. Tourtellotte, 704 F.2d 1109 (9th Cir. 1983) (denying attorney fees for the same reason); McVey v. Englewood Hosp. Assoc., 524 A.2d 450 (N.J. App. 1987) (no clear duty arises without "documentation" of comatose patient's prior wishes). If a patient fails to object to treatment because the doctor does not disclose that this option exists, does the patient have an action for breach of the duty of informed consent? Iafelice v. Luchs, 501 A.2d 1040 (N.J. Super. 1985) (no), *aff'd on other grounds*, 534 A.2d 417 (N.J. App. Div. 1987).

12. If a cause of action for battery is sustained, the patient (or the patient's estate) still faces the problem of making a case for compensatory damages. As explored at more length in Section III.E, the law has difficulty in conceiving that a patient is worse off by being kept alive. Reflecting this attitude, no right-to-die action for compensatory battery damages has yet succeeded in this country. In particular, when the *Leach* supra was tried on remand, it resulted in a directed verdict for the defendants based on the lack of sufficient evidence of damages. New York Times, Sept. 19, 1985. Recall, though, that in Strachan v. John F. Kennedy Mem. Hosp., supra at 902, the patient's *family* recovered a substantial verdict against a hospital for *mental anguish* resulting from a delay in removing life-support from their already brain-dead son. Also, a *Canadian* court has awarded a Jehovah's Witness $20,000 in damages for mental anguish after she was given a blood transfusion contrary to instructions contained on a medical alert card in her possession at the time of an automobile accident. Malette v. Shulman, 88 Dominion Rep. Srvc. 48,795 (Ont. 1987). Consider also the validity of other possible measures of damages such as punitive damages and the costs of extended medical treatment borne by uninsured patients. At least one court has rebuffed a nursing home's claim for payment after the patient's family requested that life support be discontinued. Grace Plaza v. Elbaum, No. 19068/88 (N.Y. Sup. Ct., Nassau Co.) (Jan. 9, 1990). Finally, in both the *Bartling* and *Bouvia* cases, courts have established the right to recover substantial attorneys fees. Bartling v. Glendale Adventist Med. Cent., 228 Cal. Rptr. 847 (Cal. App. 1986); Bouvia v. Glenchur, 241 Cal. Rptr. 239 (Cal. App. 1987). See generally Miller, Right-to-Die Damage Actions: Developments in the Law, 65 Denver U.L. Rev. 181 (1988); Pedrick, The Right to Disconnect: Judgment in a Hypothetical Case, 22 Ariz. St. L.J. — (forthcoming, Spring 1990); Oddi, The Tort of Interference with the Right to Die: The Wrongful Living Cause of

Action, 75 Geo. L.J. 625 (1986); Comment, Damage Actions for Nonconsensual Life-sustaining Medical Treatment, 30 St. L. Univ. L.J. 895 (1986); Annot., 58 A.L.R.4th 222.

3. Patients Without Clearly Expressed Wishes

In re Karen Ann Quinlan
355 A.2d 647 (N.J. 1976)

HUGHES, CHIEF JUSTICE. The central figure in this tragic case is Karen Ann Quinlan, a New Jersey resident. At the age of 22, she lies in a debilitated and allegedly moribund state at Saint Clare's Hospital in Denville, New Jersey. The litigation has to do, in final analysis, with her life, — its continuance or cessation, — and the responsibilities, rights and duties, with regard to any fateful decision concerning it, of her family, her guardian, her doctors, the hospital, the State through its law enforcement authorities, and finally the courts of justice. . . . [A]ppealing to the power of equity, and relying on claimed constitutional rights of free exercise of religion, of privacy and of protection against cruel and unusual punishment, Karen Quinlan's father sought judicial authority to withdraw the life-sustaining mechanisms temporarily preserving his daughter's life, and his appointment as guardian of her person to that end. His request was opposed by her doctors, the hospital, the Morris County Prosecutor, the State of New Jersey, and her guardian ad litem.

The Factual Base

An understanding of the issues in their basic perspective suggests a brief review of the factual base developed in the testimony and documented in greater detail in the opinion of the trial judge. In re Quinlan, 137 N.J. Super. 227 (Ch. Div. 1975).

On the night of April 15, 1975, for reasons still unclear, Karen Quinlan ceased breathing for at least two 15 minute periods. She received some ineffectual mouth-to-mouth resuscitation from friends. She was taken by ambulance to Newton Memorial Hospital. There she had a temperature of 100 degrees, her pupils were unreactive and she was unresponsive even to deep pain. . . .

Dr. Morse and other expert physicians who examined her characterized Karen as being in a "chronic persistent vegetative state." Dr. Fred Plum, one of such expert witnesses, defined this as a "subject who remains with the capacity to maintain the vegetative parts of neurological function but who . . . no longer has any cognitive function."

II. Termination of Treatment and Related Matters

Dr. Morse, as well as the several other medical and neurological experts who testified in this case, believed with certainty that Karen Quinlan is not "brain dead." They identified the Ad Hoc Committee of Harvard Medical School report as the ordinary medical standard for determining brain death, and all of them were satisfied that Karen met none of the criteria specified in that report and was therefore not "brain dead" within its contemplation.

Because Karen's neurological condition affects her respiratory ability (the respirator system being a brain stem function) she requires a respirator to assist her breathing. From the time of her admission to Saint Clare's Hospital Karen has been assisted by a MA-1 respirator, a sophisticated machine which delivers a given volume of air at a certain rate and periodically provides a "sigh" volume, a relatively large measured volume of air designed to purge the lungs of excretions. Attempts to "wean" her from the respirator were unsuccessful and have been abandoned.

The experts believe that Karen cannot now survive without the assistance of the respirator; that exactly how long she would live without it is unknown; that the strong likelihood is that death would follow soon after its removal, and that removal would also risk further brain damage and would curtail the assistance the respirator presently provides in warding off infection.

It seemed to be the consensus not only of the treating physicians but also of the several qualified experts who testified in the case, that removal from the respirator would not conform to medical practices, standards and traditions. . . .

From all of this evidence, and including the whole testimonial record, several basic findings in the physical area are mandated. Severe brain and associated damage, albeit of uncertain etiology, has left Karen in a chronic and persistent vegetative state. No form of treatment which can cure or improve that condition is known or available. As nearly as may be determined, considering the guarded area of remote uncertainties characteristic of most medical science predictions, she can *never* be restored to cognitive or sapient life. Even with regard to the vegetative level and improvement therein (if such it may be called) the prognosis is extremely poor and the extent unknown if it should in fact occur.

She is debilitated and moribund and although fairly stable at the time of argument before us (no new information having been filed in the meanwhile in expansion of the record), no physician risked the opinion that she could live more than a year and indeed she may die much earlier. Excellent medical and nursing care so far has been able to ward off the constant threat of infection, to which she is peculiarly susceptible because of the respirator, the tracheal tube and other incidents of care in her vulnerable condition. Her life accordingly is sustained by the respirator and tubal feeding, and removal from the respirator would cause her death soon, although the time cannot be stated with more precision. . . .

This brings us to a consideration of the constitutional and legal issues underlying the foregoing determinations. . . .

III. The Right of Privacy

It is the issue of the constitutional right of privacy that has given us most concern, in the exceptional circumstances of this case. Here a loving parent, qua parent and raising the rights of his incompetent and profoundly damaged daughter, probably irreversibly doomed to no more than a biologically vegetative remnant of life, is before the court. He seeks authorization to abandon specialized technological procedures which can only maintain for a time a body having no potential for resumption or continuance of other than a "vegetative" existence.

We have no doubt, in these unhappy circumstances, that if Karen were herself miraculously lucid for an interval (not altering the existing prognosis of the condition to which she would soon return) and perceptive of her irreversible condition, she could effectively decide upon discontinuance of the life-support apparatus, even if it meant the prospect of natural death. . . . We perceive no thread of logic distinguishing between such a choice on Karen's part and a similar choice which, under the evidence in this case, could be made by a competent patient terminally ill, riddled by cancer and suffering great pain; such a patient would not be resuscitated or put on a respirator. . . . and a fortiori would not be kept *against his will* on a respirator. . . .

Our affirmation of Karen's independent right of choice, however, would ordinarily be based upon her competency to assert it. The sad truth, however, is that she is grossly incompetent and we cannot discern her supposed choice based on the testimony of her previous conversations with friends, where such testimony is without sufficient probative weight. 137 N.J. Super. at 260. Nevertheless we have concluded that Karen's right of privacy may be asserted on her behalf by her guardian under the peculiar circumstances here present.

IV. The Medical Factor

Having declared the substantive legal basis upon which plaintiff's rights as representative of Karen must be deemed predicated, we face and respond to the assertion on behalf of defendants that our premise unwarrantably offends prevailing medical standards. . . .

The medical obligation is related to standards and practice prevailing in the profession. The physicians in charge of the case, as

II. Termination of Treatment and Related Matters

noted above, declined to withdraw the respirator. That decision was consistent with the proofs below as to the then existing medical standards and practices.

Under the law as it then stood, Judge Muir was correct in declining to authorize withdrawal of the respirator.

However, in relation to the matter of the declaratory relief sought by plaintiff as representative of Karen's interests, we are required to reevaluate the applicability of the medical standards projected in the court below. The question is whether there is such internal consistency and rationality in the application of such standards as should warrant their constituting an ineluctable bar to the effectuation of substantive relief for plaintiff at the hands of the court. We have concluded not.

In regard to the foregoing it is pertinent that we consider the impact on the standards both of the civil and criminal law as to medical liability and the new technological means of sustaining life irreversibly damaged.

The modern proliferation of substantial malpractice litigation and the less frequent but even more unnerving possibility of criminal sanctions would seem, for it is beyond human nature to suppose otherwise, to have bearing on the practice and standards as they exist. The brooding presence of such possible liability, it was testified here, had no part in the decision of the treating physicians. As did Judge Muir, we afford this testimony full credence. But we cannot believe that the stated factor has not had a strong influence on the standards. . . .

We would hesitate, in this imperfect world, to propose as to physicians that type of immunity which from the early common law has surrounded judges and grand jurors, see, e.g., Grove v. Van Duyn, 44 N.J.L. 654, 656-57 (E. & A. 1882); O'Regan v. Schermerhorn, 25 N.J. Misc. 1, 19-20 (Sup. Ct. 1940), so that they might without fear of personal retaliation perform their judicial duties with independent objectivity.

Nevertheless, there must be a way to free physicians, in the pursuit of their healing vocation, from possible contamination by self-interest or self-protection concerns which would inhibit their independent medical judgments for the well-being of their dying patients. We would hope that this opinion might be serviceable to some degree in ameliorating the professional problems under discussion.

A technique aimed at the underlying difficulty (though in a somewhat broader context) is described by Dr. Karen Teel, a pediatrician and a director of Pediatric Education, who writes in the Baylor Law Review under the title "The Physician's Dilemma: A Doctor's View: What The Law Should Be." Dr. Teel recalls:

> Physicians, by virtue of their responsibility for medical judgments are, partly by choice and partly by default, charged with the responsibility

of making ethical judgments which we are sometimes ill-equipped to make. We are not always morally and legally authorized to make them. The physician is thereby assuming a civil and criminal liability that, as often as not, he does not even realize as a factor in his decision. There is little or no dialogue in this whole process. The physician assumes that his judgment is called for and, in good faith, he acts. Someone must and it has been the physician who has assumed the responsibility and the risk.

I suggest that it would be more appropriate to provide a regular forum for more input and dialogue in individual situations and to allow the responsibility of these judgments to be shared. Many hospitals have established an Ethics Committee composed of physicians, social workers, attorneys, and theologians, . . . which serves to review the individual circumstances of ethical dilemma and which has provided much in the way of assistance and safeguards for patients and their medical caretakers. Generally, the authority of these committees is primarily restricted to the hospital and their official status is more that of an advisory body than of an enforcing body.

The concept of an Ethics Committee which has this kind of organization and is readily accessible to those persons rendering medical care to patients, would be, I think, the most promising direction for further study at this point. . . . [This would allow] some much needed dialogue regarding these issues and [force] the point of exploring all of the options for a particular patient. It diffuses the responsibility for making these judgments. Many physicians, in many circumstances, would welcome this sharing of responsibility. I believe that such an entity could lend itself well to an assumption of a legal status which would allow courses of action not now undertaken because of the concern for liability. [27 Baylor L. Rev. 6, 8-9 (1975)].

The most appealing factor in the technique suggested by Dr. Teel seems to us to be the diffusion of professional responsibility for decision, comparable in a way to the value of multi-judge courts in finally resolving on appeal difficult questions of law. Moreover, such a system would be protective to the hospital as well as the doctor in screening out, so to speak, a case which might be contaminated by less than worthy motivations of family or physician. In the real world and in relationship to the momentous decision contemplated, the value of additional views and diverse knowledge is apparent.

We consider that a practice of applying to a court to confirm such decisions would generally be inappropriate, not only because that would be a gratuitous encroachment upon the medical profession's field of competence, but because it would be impossibly cumbersome. Such a requirement is distinguishable from the judicial overview traditionally required in other matters such as the adjudication and commitment of mental incompetents. This is not to say that in the case of an otherwise justifiable controversy access to the courts would be foreclosed; we speak rather of a general practice and procedure.

II. Termination of Treatment and Related Matters

And although the deliberations and decisions which we describe would be professional in nature they should obviously include at some stage the feelings of the family of an incompetent relative. Decision-making within health care if it is considered as an expression of a primary obligation of the physician, primum non nocere, should be controlled primarily within the patient-doctor-family relationship, as indeed was recognized by Judge Muir in his supplemental opinion of November 12, 1975.

If there could be created not necessarily this particular system but some reasonable counterpart, we would have no doubt that such decisions, thus determined to be in accordance with medical practice and prevailing standards, would be accepted by society and by the courts, at least in cases comparable to that of Karen Quinlan.

The evidence in this case convinces us that the focal point of decision should be the prognosis as to the reasonable possibility of return to cognitive and sapient life, as distinguished from the forced continuance of that biological vegetative existence to which Karen seems to be doomed. . . .

Declaratory Relief

We thus arrive at the formulation of the declaratory relief which we have concluded is appropriate to this case. Some time has passed since Karen's physical and mental condition was described to the Court. At that time her continuing deterioration was plainly projected. Since the record has not been expanded we assume that she is now even more fragile and nearer to death than she was then. Since her present treating physicians may give reconsideration to her present posture in the light of this opinion, and since we are transferring to the plaintiff as guardian the choice of the attending physician and therefore other physicians may be in charge of the case who may take a different view from that of the present attending physicians, we herewith declare the following affirmative relief on behalf of the plaintiff. Upon the concurrence of the guardian and family of Karen, should the responsibile attending physicians conclude that there is no reasonable possibility of Karen's ever emerging from her present comatose condition to a cognitive, sapient state and that the life-support apparatus now being administered to Karen should be discontinued, they shall consult with the hospital "Ethics Committee" or like body of the institution in which Karen is then hospitalized. If that consultative body agrees that there is no reasonable possibility of Karen's ever emerging from her present comatose condition to a cognitive, sapient state, the present life-support system may be withdrawn and said action shall be without any civil or criminal liability therefor on the part of any participant, whether guardian, physician, hospital or others. We herewith specifically so hold. . . .

By the above ruling we do not intend to be understood as implying that a proceeding for judicial declaratory relief is necessarily required for the implementation of comparable decisions in the field of medical practice.

Modified and remanded.

Superintendent of Belchertown State School v. Saikewicz
370 N.E.2d 417 (Mass. 1977)

LIACOS, J. On April 26, 1976, William E. Jones, superintendent of the Belchertown State School (a facility of the Massachusetts Department of Mental Health), and Paul R. Rogers, a staff attorney at the school, petitioned the Probate Court for Hampshire County for the appointment of a guardian of Joseph Saikewicz, a resident of the State school. Simultaneously they filed a motion for the immediate appointment of a guardian ad litem, with authority to make the necessary decisions concerning the care and treatment of Saikewicz, who was suffering with acute myeloblastic monocytic leukemia. The petition alleged that Saikewicz was a mentally retarded person in urgent need of medical treatment and that he was a person with disability incapable of giving informed consent for such treatment.

On May 5, 1976, the probate judge appointed a guardian ad litem. On May 6, 1976, the guardian ad litem filed a report with the court. The guardian ad litem's report indicated that Saikewicz's illness was an incurable one, and that although chemotherapy was the medically indicated course of treatment it would cause Saikewicz significant adverse side effects and discomfort. The guardian ad litem concluded that these factors, as well as the inability of the ward to understand the treatment to which he would be subjected and the fear and pain he would suffer as a result, outweighed the limited prospect of any benefit from such treatment, namely, the possibility of some uncertain but limited extension of life. He therefore recommended "that not treating Mr. Saikewicz would be in his best interests." . . . [The probate judge was uncertain of his authority to rule and of the law on the question, so, after a hearing and lengthy report, he certified the case to the appellate court for decision.]

The judge below found that Joseph Saikewicz, at the time the matter arose, was sixty-seven years old, with an I.Q. of ten and a mental age of approximately two years and eight months. He was profoundly mentally retarded. The record discloses that, apart from his leukemic condition, Saikewicz enjoyed generally good health. He was physically strong and well built, nutritionally nourished, and ambulatory. He was not, however, able to communicate verbally —

II. Termination of Treatment and Related Matters

resorting to gestures and grunts to make his wishes known to others and responding only to gestures or physical contacts. In the course of treatment for various medical conditions arising during Saikewicz's residency at the school, he had been unable to respond intelligibly to inquiries such as whether he was experiencing pain. It was the opinion of a consulting psychologist, not contested by the other experts relied on by the judge below, that Saikewicz was not aware of dangers and was disoriented outside his immediate environment. As a result of his condition, Saikewicz had lived in State institutions since 1923 and had resided at the Belchertown State School since 1928. Two of his sisters, the only members of his family who could be located, were notified of his condition and of the hearing, but they preferred not to attend or otherwise become involved.

On April 19, 1976, Saikewicz was diagnosed as suffering from acute myeloblastic monocytic leukemia. Leukemia is a disease of the blood. It arises when organs of the body produce an excessive number of white blood cells as well as other abnormal cellular structures, in particular undeveloped and immature white cells. Along with these symptoms in the composition of the blood the disease is accompanied by enlargement of the organs which produce the cells, e.g., the spleen, lymph glands, and bone marrow. The disease tends to cause internal bleeding and weakness, and, in the acute form, severe anemia and high susceptibility to infection. Attorneys' Dictionary of Medicine L-37-38 (1977). The particular form of the disease present in this case, acute myeloblastic monocytic leukemia is so defined because the particular cells which increase are the myeloblasts, the youngest form of a cell which at maturity is known as the granulocytes. Id. at M-138. The disease is invariably fatal.

Chemotherapy, as was testified to at the hearing in the Probate Court, involves the administration of drugs over several weeks, the purpose of which is to kill the leukemia cells. This treatment unfortunately affects normal cells as well. One expert testified that the end result, in effect, is to destroy the living vitality of the bone marrow. Because of this effect, the patient becomes very anemic and may bleed or suffer infections — a condition which requires a number of blood transfusions. In this sense, the patient immediately becomes much "sicker" with the commencement of chemotherapy, and there is a possibility that infections during the initial period of severe anemia will prove fatal. Moreover, while most patients survive chemotherapy, remission of the leukemia is achieved in only thirty to fifty per cent of the cases. Remission is meant here as a temporary return to normal as measured by clinical and laboratory means. If remission does occur, it typically lasts for between two and thirteen months although longer periods of remission are possible. Estimates of the effectiveness of chemotherapy are complicated in cases, such as the one presented here, in which the patient's age becomes a factor. According to the medical testimony before the court below, persons over age sixty have more difficulty tolerating chemotherapy and the treatment is likely to be less successful than in younger patients. This prognosis may be compared with the doctors' estimates that, left untreated, a patient in Saikewicz's condition would live for a matter of weeks or, perhaps, several months. According to the testimony, a decision to allow the disease to run its natural course would not result in pain for the patient, and death would probably come without discomfort.

An important facet of the chemotherapy process, to which the judge below directed careful attention, is the problem of serious adverse side effects caused by the treating drugs. Among these side effects are severe nausea, bladder irritation, numbness and tingling of the extremities, and loss of hair. The bladder irritation can be avoided, however, if the patient drinks fluids, and the nausea can be treated by drugs. It was the opinion of the guardian ad litem, as well as the doctors who testified before the probate judge, that most people elect to suffer the side effects of chemotherapy rather than to allow their leukemia to run its natural course. . . .

II

A. . . .

2. There is implicit recognition in the law of the Commonwealth, as elsewhere, that a person has a strong interest in being free from nonconsensual invasion of his bodily integrity. . . .

Of even broader import, but arising from the same regard for human dignity and self-determination, is the unwritten constitutional right of privacy found in the penumbra of specific guaranties of the Bill of Rights. Griswold v. Connecticut, 381 U.S. 479, 484 (1965). As this constitutional guaranty reaches out to protect the freedom of a woman to terminate pregnancy under certain conditions, Roe v. Wade, 410 U.S. 113, 153 (1973), so it encompasses the right of a patient to preserve his or her right to privacy against unwanted infringements of bodily integrity in appropriate circumstances. In re Quinlan, supra at 38-39. In the case of a person incompetent to assert this constitutional right of privacy, it may be asserted by that person's guardian in conformance with the standards and procedures set forth in sections II (B) and II (C) of this opinion. See *Quinlan* at 39.

3. The question when the circumstances are appropriate for the exercise of this privacy right depends on the proper identification of State interests. It is not surprising that courts have, in the course of investigating State interests in various medical contexts and under various formulations of the individual rights involved, reached dif-

II. Termination of Treatment and Related Matters

fering views on the nature and the extent of State interests. We have undertaken a survey of some of the leading cases to help in identifying the range of State interests potentially applicable to cases of medical intervention. . . .

This survey of recent decisions involving the difficult question of the right of an individual to refuse medical intervention or treatment indicates that a relatively concise statement of countervailing State interests may be made. As distilled from the cases, the State has claimed interest in: (1) the preservation of life; (2) the protection of the interests of innocent third parties; (3) the prevention of suicide; and (4) maintaining the ethical integrity of the medical profession. . . .

Applying the considerations discussed in this subsection to the decision made by the probate judge in the circumstances of the case before us, we are satisfied that his decision was consistent with a proper balancing of applicable State and individual interests. Two of the four categories of State interests that we have identified, the protection of third parties and the prevention of suicide, are inapplicable to this case. The third, involving the protection of the ethical integrity of the medical profession was satisfied on two grounds. The probate judge's decision was in accord with the testimony of the attending physicians of the patient. The decision is in accord with the generally accepted views of the medical profession, as set forth in this opinion. The fourth State interest — the preservation of life — has been viewed with proper regard for the heavy physical and emotional burdens on the patient if a vigorous regimen of drug therapy were to be imposed to effect a brief and uncertain delay in the natural process of death. To be balanced against these State interests was the individual's interest in the freedom to choose to reject, or refuse to consent to, intrusions of his bodily integrity and privacy. We cannot say that the facts of this case required a result contrary to that reached by the probate judge with regard to the right of any person, competent or incompetent, to be spared the deleterious consequences of life-prolonging treatment. We therefore turn to consider the unique considerations arising in this case by virtue of the patient's inability to appreciate his predicament and articulate his desires. . . .

B

The "best interests" of an incompetent person are not necessarily served by imposing on such persons results not mandated as to competent persons similarly situated. It does not advance the interest of the State or the ward to treat the ward as a person of lesser status or dignity than others. To protect the incompetent person within its power, the State must recognize the dignity and worth of such a person and afford to that person the same panoply of rights and choices it recognizes in competent persons. If a competent person faced with death may choose to decline treatment which not only will not cure the person but which substantially may increase suffering in exchange for a possible yet brief prolongation of life, then it cannot be said that it is always in the "best interests" of the ward to require submission to such treatment. Nor do statistical factors indicating that a majority of competent persons similarly situated choose treatment resolve the issue. The significant decisions of life are more complex than statistical determinations. Individual choice is determined not by the vote of the majority but by the complexities of the singular situation viewed from the unique perspective of the person called on to make the decision. To presume that the incompetent person must always be subjected to what many rational and intelligent persons may decline is to downgrade the status of the incompetent person by placing a lesser value on his intrinsic human worth and vitality.

The trend in the law has been to give incompetent persons the same rights as other individuals. Boyd v. Registrars of Voters of Belchertown, 368 Mass. 631 (1975). Recognition of this principle of equality requires understanding that in certain circumstances it may be appropriate for a court to consent to the withholding of treatment from an incompetent individual. This leads us to the question of how the right of an incompetent person to decline treatment might best be exercised so as to give the fullest possible expression to the character and circumstances of that individual.

The problem of decision-making presented in this case is one of first impression before this court, and we know of no decision in other jurisdictions squarely on point. The well publicized decision of the New Jersey Court in In re Quinlan, 70 N.J. 10 (1976), provides a helpful starting point for analysis, however.

Karen Quinlan's situation, however, must be distinguished from that of Joseph Saikewicz. Saikewicz was profoundly mentally retarded. His mental state was a cognitive one but limited in his capacity to comprehend and communicate. Evidence that most people choose to accept the rigors of chemotherapy has no direct bearing on the likely choice that Joseph Saikewicz would have made. Unlike most people, Saikewicz had no capacity to understand his present situation or his prognosis. The guardian ad litem gave expression to this important distinction in coming to grips with this "most troubling aspect" of withholding treatment from Saikewicz: "If he is treated with toxic drugs he will be involuntarily immersed in a state of painful suffering, the reason for which he will never understand. Patients who request treatment know the risks involved and can appreciate the painful side-effects when they arrive. They know the reason for the pain and

II. Termination of Treatment and Related Matters 977

their hope makes it tolerable." To make a worthwhile comparison, one would have to ask whether a majority of people would choose chemotherapy if they were told merely that something outside of their previous experience was going to be done to them, that this something would cause them pain and discomfort, that they would be removed to strange surroundings and possibly restrained for extended periods of time, and that the advantages of this course of action were measured by concepts of time and mortality beyond their ability to comprehend.

To put the above discussion in proper perspective, we realize that an inquiry into what a majority of people would do in circumstances that truly were similar assumes an objective viewpoint not far removed from a "reasonable person" inquiry. While we recognize the value of this kind of indirect evidence, we should make it plain that the primary test is subjective in nature — that is, the goal is to determine with as much accuracy as possible the wants and needs of the individual involved. This may or may not conform to what is thought wise or prudent by most people. The problems of arriving at an accurate substituted judgment in matters of life and death vary greatly in degree, if not in kind, in different circumstances. For example, the responsibility of Karen Quinlan's father to act as she would have wanted could be discharged by drawing on many years of what was apparently an affectionate and close relationship. In contrast, Joseph Saikewicz was profoundly retarded and noncommunicative his entire life, which was spent largely in the highly restrictive atmosphere of an institution. While it may thus be necessary to rely to a greater degree on objective criteria, such as the supposed inability of profoundly retarded persons to conceptualize or fear death, the effort to bring the substituted judgment into step with the values and desires of the affected individual must not, and need not, be abandoned.

The "substituted judgment" standard which we have described commends itself simply because of its straightforward respect for the integrity and autonomy of the individual. We need not, however, ignore the substantial pedigree that accompanies this phrase. The doctrine of substituted judgment had its origin over 150 years ago in the area of the administration of the estate of an incompetent person. . . .

With this historical perspective, we now reiterate the substituted judgment doctrine as we apply it in the instant case. We believe that both the guardian ad litem in his recommendation and the judge in his decision should have attempted (as they did) to ascertain the incompetent person's actual interests and preferences. In short, the decision in cases such as this should be that which would be made by the incompetent person, if that person were competent, but taking into account the present and future incompetency of the individual as one of the factors which would necessarily enter into the decision-making process of the competent person. Having recognized the right of a competent person to make for himself the same decision as the court made in this case, the question is, do the facts on the record support the proposition that Saikewicz himself would have made the decision under the standard set forth. We believe they do.

The two factors considered by the probate judge to weigh in favor of administering chemotherapy were: (1) the fact that most people elect chemotherapy and (2) the chance of a longer life. Both are appropriate indicators of what Saikewicz himself would have wanted, provided that due allowance is taken for this individual's present and future incompetency. We have already discussed the perspective this brings to the fact that most people choose to undergo chemotherapy. With regard to the second factor, the chance of a longer life carries the same weight for Saikewicz as for any other person, the value of life under the law having no relation to intelligence or social position. Intertwined with this consideration is the hope that a cure, temporary or permanent, will be discovered during the period of extra weeks or months potentially made available by chemotherapy. The guardian ad litem investigated this possibility and found no reason to hope for a dramatic breakthrough in the time frame relevant to the decision.

The probate judge identified six factors weighing against administration of chemotherapy. Four of these — Saikewicz's age, the probable side effects of treatment, the low chance of producing remission, and the certainty that treatment will cause immediate suffering — were clearly established by the medical testimony to be considerations that any individual would weigh carefully. A fifth factor — Saikewicz's inability to cooperate with the treatment — introduces those considerations that are unique to this individual and which therefore are essential to the proper exercise of substituted judgment. The judge heard testimony that Saikewicz would have no comprehension of the reasons for the severe disruption of his formerly secure and stable environment occasioned by the chemotherapy. He therefore would experience fear without the understanding from which other patients draw strength. The inability to anticipate and prepare for the severe side effects of the drugs leaves room only for confusion and disorientation. The possibility that such a naturally uncooperative patient would have to be physically restrained to allow the slow intravenous administration of drugs could only compound his pain and fear, as well as possibly jeopardize the ability of his body to withstand the toxic effects of the drugs.

The sixth factor identified by the judge as weighing against chemotherapy was "the quality of life possible for him even if the treatment does bring about remission." To the extent that this formulation equates the value of life with any measure of the quality of life, we firmly reject it. A reading of the entire record clearly reveals, however, the judge's concern that special care be taken to respect the dignity and worth of Saikewicz's life precisely because of his vulnerable position. The judge, as well as all the parties, was keenly aware that the supposed inability of Saikewicz, by virtue of his mental retardation, to appreciate or experience life had no place in the decision before them. Rather than reading the judge's formulation in a manner that demeans the value of the life of one who is mentally retarded, the vague, and perhaps ill-chosen, term "quality of life" should be understood as a reference to the continuing state of pain and disorientation precipitated by the chemotherapy treatment. Viewing the term in this manner, together with the other factors properly considered by the judge, we are satisfied that the decision to withhold treatment from Saikewicz was based on a regard for his actual interests and preferences and that the facts supported this decision.

C

We turn now to a consideration of the procedures appropriate for reaching a decision where a person allegedly incompetent is in a position in which a decision as to the giving or withholding of life-prolonging treatment must be made. . . .

The course of proceedings in such a case is readily determined by reference to the applicable statutes. The first step is to petition the court for the appointment of a guardian (G.L. c. 201, §6A) or a temporary guardian (G.L. c. 201, §14). . . . At the hearing on the appointment of a guardian or temporary guardian, the issues before the court are (1) whether the person involved is mentally retarded within the meaning of the statute (G.L. c. 201, §6A) and (2), if the person is mentally retarded, who shall be appointed guardian. Id. As an aid to the judge in reaching these two decisions, it will often be desirable to appoint a guardian ad litem, sua sponte or on motion, to represent the interests of the person. Moreover, we think it appropriate, and highly desirable, in cases such as the one before us to charge the guardian ad litem with an additional responsibility to be discharged if there is a finding of incompetency. This will be the responsibility of presenting to the judge, after as thorough an investigation as time will permit, all reasonable arguments in favor of administering treatment to prolong the life of the individual involved. This will ensure that all viewpoints and alternatives will be aggressively pursued and examined at the subsequent hearing where it will be determined whether treatment should or should not be allowed. The report of the guardian or temporary guardian will, of course, also be available to the judge at this hearing on the ultimate issue of treatment. Should the probate judge then be satisfied that the incompetent individual would, as determined by the standards previously set forth, have chosen to forgo potentially life-prolonging treatment, the judge shall issue the appropriate order. If the judge is not so persuaded, or finds that the interests of the State require it, then treatment shall be ordered.

Commensurate with the powers of the Probate Court already described, the probate judge may, at any step in these proceedings, avail himself or herself of the additional advice or knowledge of any person or group. We note here that many health care institutions have developed medical ethics committees or panels to consider many of the issues touched on here. Consideration of the findings and advice of such groups as well as the testimony of the attending physicians and other medical experts ordinarily would be of great assistance to a probate judge faced with such a difficult decision. We believe it desirable for a judge to consider such views wherever available and useful to the court. We do not believe, however, that this option should be transformed by us into a required procedure. We take a dim view of any attempt to shift the ultimate decisionmaking responsibility away from the duly established courts of proper jurisdiction to any committee, panel or group, ad hoc or permanent. Thus, we reject the approach adopted by the New Jersey Supreme Court in the *Quinlan* case of entrusting the decision whether to continue artificial life support to the patient's guardian, family, attending doctors, and hospital "ethics committee." 70 N.J. at 55. One rationale for such a delegation was expressed by the lower court judge in the *Quinlan* case, and quoted by the New Jersey Supreme Court: "The nature, extent and duration of care by societal standards is the responsibility of a physician. The morality and conscience of our society places this responsibility in the hands of the physician. What justification is there to remove it from the control of the medical profession and place it in the hands of the courts?" Id. at 44. For its part, the New Jersey Supreme Court concluded that "a practice of applying to a court to confirm such decisions would generally be inappropriate, not only because that would be a gratuitous encroachment upon the medical profession's field of competence, but because it would be impossibly cumbersome. Such a requirement is distinguishable from the judicial overview traditionally required in other matters such as the adjudication and commitment of mental incompetents. This is not to say that in the case of an otherwise justiciable controversy access to the courts would be foreclosed; we speak rather of a general practice and procedure." Id. at 50.

We do not view the judicial resolution of this most difficult and awesome question — whether potentially life-prolonging treatment

II. Termination of Treatment and Related Matters

should be withheld from a person incapable of making his own decision — as constituting a "gratuitous encroachment" on the domain of medical expertise. Rather, such questions of life and death seem to us to require the process of detached but passionate investigation and decision that forms the ideal on which the judicial branch of government was created. Achieving this ideal is our responsibility and that of the lower court, and is not to be entrusted to any other group purporting to represent the "morality and conscience of our society," no matter how highly motivated or impressively constituted.

III

Finding no State interest sufficient to counterbalance a patient's decision to decline life-prolonging medical treatment in the circumstances of this case, we conclude that the patient's right to privacy and self-determination is entitled to enforcement. Because of this conclusion, and in view of the position of equality of an incompetent person in Joseph Saikewicz's position, we conclude that the probate judge acted appropriately in this case. For these reasons we issued our order of July 9, 1976, and responded as we did to the questions of the probate judge.

NOTES

The Role of Doctors, Courts, the Family, and Ethics Committees

1. *Quinlan* illustrates the importance of distinguishing patients who are in a "persistent vegetative state" from those who meet the strict brain-death criteria. If Karen Ann Quinlan had been brain dead, there could have been no objection to terminating life support. Confusion surrounds this point because the terms "comatose" or "irreversible coma" frequently are used imprecisely to describe both situations:

> Patients in a fully developed persistent vegetative state do manifest a variety of normal brain stem functions. The patient's eyes are open at times, and periods of wakefulness and sleep are present. The eyes wander . . . [and] pupils respond normally to light. . . . The patient is also completely unconscious, i.e., unaware of him or herself or the surrounding environment. . . . PVS patients, then, are awake but unaware. These characteristics allow a distinction to be made between comatose patients and [PVS] patients. A coma is a state of sleeplike (eyes-closed) unarousability. . . . Patients in this condition often have impaired cough, gag, and swallowing reflexes. . . .

Cranford, The Persistent Vegetative State: The Medical Reality (Getting the Facts Straight), 18 Hastings Cent. Rep. 27, 28 (March 1988).

2. Karen Ann Quinlan survived almost ten years *after* being removed from her respirator. In a case where everyone expected her to die within a year even *with* treatment and to live only a very short time after treatment withdrawal, what does this say about the medical profession's ability to predict the course of "terminal" conditions, or even the persistence of vegetative states? Consider also a recent report that an 86-year-old stroke victim — who had been diagnosed to be in an irreversible vegetative state and for whom doctors and family members had obtained permission to withdraw feeding tubes — suddenly began talking and eating on her own. "But when asked what she would wish to be done in her case, . . . she replied 'These are difficult decisions,' and lapsed back into sleep." N.Y. Times, April 4, 1989, at A15.

3. The *Quinlan* court's suggestion of resort to an internal hospital committee for advice has been widely followed, leading to two distinct types of committees. A "prognosis committee" is one composed primarily of doctors to determine the purely *medical* issues of the patient's condition and the likely outcomes of various courses of treatment. A prognosis committee may be all the *Quinlan* court had in mind; nevertheless, most major hospitals and many community hospitals also have an "ethics committee" composed of a much broader range of perspectives — ethicists, lawyers, and other community members — to evaluate and advise on the moral/legal dimensions of the medical facts revealed by the prognosis committee. Cranford & Doudera, The Emergency of Institutional Ethics Committees, 1 L. Med. & Health Care 13 (1984).

Ethics committees in turn have spawned a host of new legal issues, such as whether their proceedings are confidential and whether committee members might be liable for an erroneous decision. See R. Macklin & R. Kupfer, Hospital Ethics Committees: Manual for a Training Program (1988); Am. Hosp. Assoc., Legal Issues and Guidance for Hospital Biomedical Ethics Committees (1985); AMA Judicial Council, Guidelines for Ethics Committees in Health Care Institutions, 253 J.A.M.A. 2698 (1985); B. Hosford, Bioethics Committees: The Health Care Provider's Guide (1986); J. Ross, Handbook for Hospital Ethics Committees (1986); Merritt, The Tort Liability of Hospital Ethics Committees, 60 So. Cal. L. Rev. 1239 (1987); Levine, Hospital Ethics Committees: A Guarded Prognosis, 7 Hastings Cent. Rep., no. 6, at 25 (June 1977).

4. The genesis of the *Quinlan* court's suggestion of ethics committee review is Dr. Teel's article in the Baylor Law Review. Do you think the New Jersey Court would have noticed Dr. Teel's views if they had been expressed in a medical journal? Like most modern

courts, the New Jersey Supreme Court still relies heavily on law reviews for medical and scientific information.

5. When appealed to the Massachusetts high court it was generally assumed that the key issue in the *Saikewicz* matter was related to the condition of mental retardation in the person under consideration; i.e., would the "quality of life" of a severely retarded person mean that such a patient would not receive treatment to save his life? For this reason, amicus curiae briefs were filed by retardation advocacy groups. The opinion by Judge Liacos dealt very well with these issues, finding that quality of life in this case relates to "pain and disorientation" rather than to intelligence level. However, the startling result in the *Saikewicz* decision, a unanimous opinion, was its quarrel with the New Jersey Supreme Court over who should decide such matters of life and death for incompetent patients. Judge Liacos, in his last few pages, seems to have interpreted the New Jersey case as a decision to turn over these matters completely to the medical community for handling and resolution. The Massachusetts Court took "a dim view" of such a "shift" in responsibility. Is the court's view of the New Jersey decision correct? Accord, Estate of Longeway, 549 N.E.2d 292 (Ill. 1989).

6. Although it is comforting for all concerned to place a judicial imprimatur on a decision to withdraw treatment from an incapacitated patient, this certainty comes at the expense of several other important values. Requiring judicial approval, as *Saikewicz* seemed to do in all cases, makes an already trying situation even more difficult by forcing the family and physicians into an adversarial posture, it delays resolution of the situation, and it requires the court to issue its decision based on the state of affairs that existed at the time the record was made despite the possibility of rapidly changing facts. See Curran, The *Saikewicz* Decision, 298 New Eng. J. Med. 499 (1978); In re LHR, 321 S.E.2d 716, 720-721 (Ga. 1984). Therefore medical reaction to the *Saikewicz* decision (regarding application in *each instance* to the probate court) was immediate and overwhelmingly disapproving. Legal reaction tended to be related to the parties represented. Hospital attorneys were generally opposed to the decision. Civil rights groups and many academic lawyers were favorable. Probate courts in the state began to receive petitions for appointment of guardians in regard to incompetent persons, unconscious or comatose patients, and children. It was felt by some attorneys that there was an exaggerated reaction in situations where a court petition was unnecessary. A number of articles and papers have been published providing argument for various interpretations of both the *Saikewicz* and *Quinlan* decisions. The pages of one journal largely focused on the debate for over a year. The first offering, by Professor Charles Baron, took the position that the Massachusetts Court did not go *far enough* in spelling out a

truly *adversary process* in such situations. Baron, Assuring "Detached but Passionate Investigation and Decision": The Role of Guardians Ad Litem in *Saikewicz*-type Cases, 4 Am. J.L. & Med. 111 (1978). One of the articles in the series attempted to reconcile the approaches of the New Jersey and Massachusetts highest courts. Annas, Reconciling *Quinlan* and *Saikewicz:* Decision Making for the Terminally Ill Incompetent, 4 Am. J.L. & Med. 367 (1979). Another commentator labelled Baron's view as "legal imperialism" while refering to a medical spokesman's view (Arnold Relman) as "medical paternalism." Buchanan, Medical Paternalism or Legal Imperialism: Not the Only Alternatives for Handling *Saikewicz*-type Cases, 5 Am. J.L. & Med. 97 (1979). Professor Buchanan also rejected Professor Annas' attempt to reconcile the two decisions as unconvincing. Buchanan, a professor of philosophy, found the two cases fundamentally opposed in philosophy and practical application.

7. Some of the heat generated by *Saikewicz* has been dissipated by subsequent developments in Massachusetts case law. For instance, In re Spring, 405 N.E.2d 115 (Mass. 1980), which concerned a senile patient on kidney dialysis, responded to the storm of criticism by taking a step back from *Saikewicz*'s apparent mandate of judicial intervention in every treatment refusal case:

> We in no way disapprove the practice of committee review of decisions by members of a hospital staff. But . . . [w]hen a court is properly presented with the legal question, whether treatment may be withheld, it must decide that question and not delegate it to some private person or group. . . . [We] stress the desirability of expediting such cases. In particular, . . . we impose no duty to present arguments the guardian ad litem does not believe meritorious and no obligation to take appeals as a matter of course.

Elsewhere in its opinion, the court stressed that *Saikewicz* was unique in that the patient there was a ward of the state. Nevertheless, the court ruled that, the case having been presented to the probate judge, the judge must decide himself the need for treatment rather than delegate the decision to the guardian. Compare, In re Dinnerstein, 380 N.E.2d 134 (Mass. App. 1978) (allowing entry of a no-code order for Alzheimer's disease without prior court approval); In re Drabick, 245 Cal. Rptr. 840 (Cal. App. 1988) (conservator may withdraw life support without obtaining court approval).

8. Under the majority, *Quinlan* approach, if the advisory directive to consult an ethics committee is not followed (for instance, because the hospital lacks such a committee), what is there to guard against relatives who are overly eager to read the patient's will and against doctors who lack diligence or scruples? Are such fears realistic? Recent decisions have responded to these concerns by imposing a requirement

that two independent (nontreating) physicians concur with a decision not to treat. In re Farrell, 529 A.2d 404, 415 (N.J. 1987); In re Peter, 529 A.2d 419, 429 (1987); In re Grant, 747 P.2d 445, 456 (Wash. 1987). What principle leads courts to discern in the common law a three-doctor rule? Why not four or two?

> This "three physician rule" seems arbitrary and misguided, since doctors can make *every* other major medical decision with their patients or appropriate surrogate without required consultation. Yet, three is a magical, mystical number that can evoke comfort and signal power. Shakespeare used the number to devastating effect in *Macbeth*, and one can almost see the three doctors at the patient's bedside echoing the words of the first witch: "When shall we three meet again? In thunder, lightning, or in rain?" The court doesn't seem to care, as long as their meeting doesn't take place in the courtroom.

Annas, In Thunder, Lightning, or in Rain: What Three Doctors Can Do, 17 Hastings Cent. Rep. 28, 30 (Oct/Nov 1987). Should courts await statutory guidance, as some state legislatures have provided? See Areen, The Legal Status of Consent Obtained from Families of Adult Patients to Withhold or Withdraw Treatment, 258 J.A.M.A. 229 (1987).

9. The *Quinlan/Saikewicz* debate is usually framed in terms of whether the guardian or the court makes the ultimate treatment decision. But this may be a largely moot point if resort to the court is required in any event to *appoint* a guardian. As the Massachusetts Court reasoned in *Spring* supra, once a case is before the court, it is unrealistic to expect the judge to ignore the substantive merits. Thus, lurking behind these cases is the more important question of whether an incapacitated patient's family may act in the absence of a guardianship appointment. Some courts have said yes:

> In re Jobes, 529 A.2d 434, 448 (N.J. 1987);
> Barber v. Superior Court, 195 Cal. Rptr. 484, 492 (Cal. App. 1983);
> In re Hamlin, 689 P.2d 1372, 1377 (Wash. 1984);

some have said no:

> In re Storar, 438 N.Y.S.2d 266 (1981) (mother not authorized to refuse blood transfusions even though this would be in son's best interests),

and some have ducked the question:

> Rasmussen v. Fleming 741 P.2d 674, 687 (Ariz. 1987) (refusing to decide).

For further discussion of parental authority over medical treatment decisions, see Section II.C. See generally, Comment, The Role of the Family in Medical Decisionmaking for Incompetent Adult Patients, 48 U. Pitt. L. Rev. 539 (1987).

Even in cases where an authorized decision maker already exists at the time when the need for treatment arises, court intervention can result if there is disagreement among the respective parties. Consider the likelihood of a contested decision under a rule like that recently promulgated by the Arizona Supreme Court (which states that it is intended to minimize disputes):

> [The court's] encroachment into the substantive decisions concerning medical treatment should be limited to resolving disputes among the patient's family, the attending physicians, an independent physician, the health care facility, the guardian, and the guardian ad litem.

Rasmussen v. Fleming, 741 P.2d 674, 691 (Ariz. 1987).

Determining Incapacity

10. Determining capacity to consent to medical treatment is not as easy a matter as courts would like, particularly in a class of cases where patients are usually severely debilitated. This may explain why appellate courts are eager to treat capacity as a fact question and why trial courts base the decision on testimony by the attending physician. Where courts do decide the issue, they do not always reach consistent results. Refer back to the *Georgetown College* case, where the Jehovah's Witness patient appeared capable of unequivocally expressing her adamant desire to refuse a blood transfusion, yet the court said "it was obvious that the woman was not in a mental condition to make a decision." Contrast this with the *Bartling* case. What presence of mind should be necessary to make a medical decision? Should this standard be more exacting for life-and-death decisions than for ordinary treatment decisions? The Hastings Center Guidelines on the Termination of Life-Sustaining Treatment 131-133 (1987) offer the following useful explanation:

> There is considerable confusion about capacity. One source of difficulty is the widespread tendency to confuse the notions of "capacity" and "competence." . . . "Competence" and "incompetence" . . . should be restricted to situations in which a formal judicial determination has been made. . . . A person can be legally competent and nonetheless lack the capacity to make a particular treatment decision. Conversely, a person who has been declared legally incompetent for other purposes (such as financial decisions) may still possess the capacity to make a treatment decision. . . .
>
> A second source of confusion is the lack of agreement on the

appropriate standard to use in determining capacity. . . . The key alternatives are: (1) an *outcome standard* in which capacity is judged solely by the content and consequences of the patient's treatment choice; (2) a *status or category standard* in which all patients with certain characteristics (retarded people and minors, for example) are automatically judged to lack decisionmaking capacity; and (3) a *process standard* in which capacity is determined by assessing the patient's exercise of particular abilities in the decisionmaking process.

We believe that the [following] process standard should be used in determining capacity . . . : (a) the ability to comprehend information relevant to the decision; (b) the ability to deliberate about the choices in accordance with personal values and goals; and (c) the ability to communicate (verbally or nonverbally). . . .

The more harmful to the patient his or her choice appears to be, the higher the level of capacity required and the greater the level of certainty the professional should have about the assessment of capacity.

The President's Commission Report on Making Health Care Decisions (1983) provides much the same analysis. A third excellent discussion is Annas & Densberger, Competence to Refuse Medical Treatment: Autonomy vs. Paternalism, 15 Tol. L. Rev. 561 (1984) (advocating as the proper standard "the capacity to understand and appreciate the nature and consequences of one's acts").

Illustrating the application of this standard, one court found that a mental patient with a long-standing belief in faith healing had the capacity to refuse surgery for a malignant tumor, even though she held the delusional fantasy that she was married to a T.V. evangelist she thought would heal her. In re Milton, 505 N.E.2d 255 (Ohio 1987). Annas and Densberger cite Lane v. Candura, 376 N.E.2d 1232 (Mass. 1978), as a model decision, a case involving a 77-year-old patient who refused to have her gangrenous leg amputated. Her physicians thought her without decisionmaking capacity because they considered her decision irrational. The court, however, held that it was enough that Mrs. Candura was capable of appreciating the consequences of her decision. See also In re Quackenbush, 383 A.2d 785 (N.J. Super. 1978) (honoring elderly patient's refusal to amputate gangrenous leg).

More frequently, though, "judgments of competency go beyond . . . straightforward application of legal rules; such judgments reflect societal considerations and societal biases as much as they reflect matters of law and medicine." Roth, Meisel & Lidz, Tests of Competency to Consent to Treatment, 134 Am. J. Psychia. 279, 283 (1977). See, e.g., State Dept. of Human Servs. v. Northern, 563 S.W.2d 197 (Tenn. App. 1978) (ordering amputation against patient's wishes because she refused to consider the possibility that it was necessary to save her life). See generally Appelbaum & Grisso, Assessing Patients' Capacities to Consent to Treatment, 319 New Eng. J. Med. 1635 (1988).

In deciding whether to honor a particular treatment refusal decision, it is perhaps helpful to distinguish between the capacity to make a decision and the determination of when a settled decision has in fact been made. Conceivably, a completely lucid patient may simply be indecisive, or suffering from a transitory period of depression. See Jackson & Younger, Patient Autonomy and "Death with Dignity," 299 New Eng. J. Med. 404 (1979) (detailing six case studies of ambivalent or misapprehended treatment refusals). It would distort the meaning of capacity for these conditions to disqualify a treatment refusal decision. On the other hand, there is good reason to exercise caution in acting precipitously on a life-and-death decision that might have been subject to a change of heart after a short period of time. Without manipulating the legal definition of capacity, then, is it defensible to delay acting on a lucid treatment refusal by requiring a heightened standard for finding that the patient has made a fully informed and settled decision?

In the Matter of Westchester County Medical Center
531 N.E.2d 607 (N.Y. 1988)

WACHTLER, CHIEF JUDGE.

Mary O'Connor is an elderly hospital patient who, as a result of several strokes, is mentally incompetent and unable to obtain food or drink without medical assistance. In this dispute between her daughters and the hospital the question is whether the hospital should be permitted to insert a nasogastric tube to provide her with sustenance or whether, instead, such medical intervention should be precluded and she should be allowed to die because, prior to becoming incompetent, she made several statements to the effect that she did not want to be a burden to anyone and would not want to live or be kept alive by artificial means if she were unable to care for herself. . . .

I

The patient is a 77-year-old widow with two children, Helen and Joan, both of whom are practical nurses. After her husband's death in 1967 she lived alone in her apartment in the New York City area where she was employed in hospital administration. In 1983 she retired from her job after 20 years service.

Over the years a number of her close relatives died of cancer. Her husband died of brain cancer. The last two of her nine brothers died of cancer, one in 1975 and the other in 1977. During their final

II. Termination of Treatment and Related Matters

years she regularly visited them in the hospital and cared for them when they were home. In November 1984, after being informed that her stepmother had died of cancer in Florida, Mrs. O'Connor had an attack of congestive heart failure and was hospitalized. She was released from the hospital in December 1984.

In July of the following year she suffered the first of a series of strokes causing brain damage and related disabilities which rendered her unable to care for herself. She became . . . unresponsive and unable to stand or feed herself. She had to be spoon-fed by others. Her gag reflex was also impaired, as a result of which she experienced difficulty swallowing and thus could eat only pureed foods. In this condition her daughters found that they could no longer care for her at home, and, when she left the hospital in February 1988, she was transferred to the Ruth Taylor Institute (the Institute), a long-term geriatric care facility associated with the Westchester County Medical Center (the hospital). . . .

During the initial part of her stay at the Institute the staff found Mrs. O'Connor was cooperative, capable of sitting in a chair and interacting with her surroundings. However, in June her condition deteriorated. She became "stuperous, virtually not responsive" and developed a fever. On June 20, 1988, she was transferred from the Institute to the hospital.

At the hospital it was determined that she was suffering from dehydration, sepsis and probably pneumonia. The hospital staff also found that she had lost her gag reflex, making it impossible for her to swallow food or liquids without medical assistance. She showed marked improvement after receiving fluids, limited nourishment and antibiotics intravenously. Within a few days she became alert, able to follow simple commands and respond verbally to simple questions. However her inability to swallow persisted and her physician, Dr. Sivak, determined that a nasogastric tube should be used to provide more substantial nourishment. When Mrs. O'Connor's daughters objected to this procedure, the matter was brought before the hospital's ethics committee which found that it would be inappropriate to withhold this treatment under the circumstances.

On July 15, the hospital commenced this proceeding by order to show cause seeking court authorization to use the nasogastric tube, claiming that without this relief Mrs. O'Connor would die of thirst and starvation within a few weeks. . . .

The treating physician, Dr. Sivak, testified that Mrs. O'Connor was suffering from multiinfarct dementia as a result of the strokes. This condition substantially impaired her cognitive ability but she was not in a coma or vegetative state. She was conscious, and capable of responding to simple questions or requests sometimes by squeezing the questioner's hand and sometimes verbally. She was also able to respond to noxious stimuli, such as a needle prick, and in fact was sensitive to "even minimal discomfort", although she was not experiencing pain in her present condition. When asked how she felt she usually responded "fine", "all right" or "ok." The treating physician also testified that her mental awareness had improved at the hospital and that she might become more alert in the future. In fact during the latest examination conducted that morning, in response to the doctor's request she had attempted to sit up and had been able to roll over on her side so that he could examine her lungs. However, Dr. Sivak stated that she is unable to comprehend complex questions, such as those dealing with her medical treatment, and doubted that she would ever regain significant mental capacity because the brain damage was substantial and irreparable. . . .

The doctor stated that death from starvation and especially thirst, was a painful way to die and that Mrs. O'Connor would, therefore, experience extreme, intense discomfort since she is conscious, alert, capable of feeling pain, and sensitive to even mild discomfort.

The respondents' expert Dr. Wasserman, a neurologist, agreed essentially with Dr. Sivak's evaluation and prognosis. In his opinion, however, Mrs. O'Connor would not experience pain if permitted to die of thirst and starvation. Because of the extensive brain damage she had suffered, the doctor did not "think she would react as you or I would under the circumstances" but would simply become more lethargic, unresponsive and would ultimately die. If she experienced pain he believed she could be given pain killers to alleviate it. He conceded, however, that he could not be "medically certain" that she would not suffer because he had never had a patient, or heard of one, dying after being deprived of food and water. Thus he candidly admitted: "I guess we don't know." . . .

Mrs. O'Connor's daughter Helen testified that her mother informed her on several occasions that if she became ill and was unable to care for herself she would not want her life to be sustained artificially. The first discussion occurred after her husband was hospitalized with cancer in 1967. At that time Mrs. O'Connor said that she never wanted to be in a similar situation and that she would not want to go on living if she could not "take care of herself and make her own decisions." The last discussion occurred after Mrs. O'Connor's stepmother died of cancer and Mrs. O'Connor was hospitalized for a heart attack: "My mother said that she was very glad to be home, very glad to be out of the hospital and hope[d] she would never have to be back in one again and would never want any sort of intervention any sort of life support systems to maintain or prolong her life." Mrs. O'Connor's other daughter, Joan, essentially adopted her sister's testimony. She described her mother's statements on this subject as less solemn pronouncements: "It was brought up when we were together,

II. Termination of Treatment and Related Matters

at times when in conversations you start something, you know, maybe the news was on and maybe that was the topic that was brought up and that's how it came about."

However, [ ] these witnesses also agreed that Mrs. O'Connor had never discussed providing food or water with medical assistance, nor had she ever said that she would adhere to her view and decline medical treatment "by artificial means" if that would produce a painful death. When Helen was asked what choice her mother would make under those circumstances she admitted that she did not know. Her sister Joan agreed, noting that this had never been discussed, "unfortunately, no." . . .

The trial court denied the hospital's petition . . . concluding that Mrs. O'Connor's "past expressions plainly covered any form of life-prolonging treatment." The Appellate Division affirmed noting that requiring greater specificity would impose an undue burden on those seeking to avoid life-prolonging treatment.

II

It has long been the common-law rule in this State that a person has the right to decline medical treatment, even life-saving treatment, absent an overriding State interest (Schloendorff v. Society of N.Y. Hosp., 211 N.Y. 125, 129-130, 105 N.E. 92). In 1981, we held, in two companion cases, that a hospital or medical facility must respect this right even when a patient becomes incompetent, if while competent, the patient stated that he or she did not want certain procedures to be employed under specified circumstances (Matter of Storar and Matter of Eichner v. Dillon, 52 N.Y.2d 363, 438 N.Y.S.2d 266, 420 N.E.2d 64). In *Storar,* involving a retarded adult suffering from terminal cancer, who needed blood transfusions to keep him from bleeding to death, we declined to direct termination of the treatment because it was impossible to determine what his wish would have been were he competent and it would be improper for a court to substitute its judgment for the unascertainable wish of the patient. Commencing on this latter principle in a subsequent case we noted that the right to decline treatment is personal and, under existing law in this State, could not be exercised by a third party when the patient is unable to do so (People v. Eulo, 63 N.Y.2d 341, 482 N.Y.S.2d 436, 472 N.E.2d 286).[2]

---

2. The status of the law on this point has since been changed to some extent by legislation. The Legislature has now authorized third parties to issue do not resuscitate orders for incompetent patients under certain circumstances (Public Health Law art. 29-B). More recently the Legislature enacted a statute permitting individuals to create "springing powers of attorney," which come into effect when another designated person determines that the maker has become incompetent. . . . There is therefore no longer

In contrast to the patient in *Storar*, the patient in *Eichner* had been competent and capable of expressing his will before he was silenced by illness. In those circumstances, we concluded that it would be appropriate for the court to intervene and direct the termination of artificial life supports, in accordance with the patient's wishes, because it was established by "clear and convincing evidence" that the patient would have so directed if he were competent and able to communicate (52 N.Y.2d, at 379, 438 N.Y.S.2d 266, 420 N.E.2d 64, supra; see also, Matter of Delio v. Westchester County Med. Center, 129 A.D.2d 1, 516 N.Y.S.2d 677; Addington v. Texas, 441 U.S. 418, 424, 99 S. Ct. 1804, 1808, 60 L. Ed. 2d 323. We selected the "clear and convincing evidence" standard in *Eichner* because it " 'impress[es] the factfinder with the importance of the decision' . . . and it 'forbids relief whenever the evidence is loose, equivocal or contradictory' " (Matter of Storar, supra, 52 N.Y.2d at 379, 438 N.Y.S.2d 266, 420 N.E.2d 64). Nothing less than unequivocal proof will suffice when the decision to terminate life supports is at issue.

In *Eichner*, we had no difficulty finding "clear and convincing" evidence of the patient's wishes. Brother Fox, the patient in *Eichner*, was a member of a religious order who had conscientiously discussed his moral and personal views concerning the use of a respirator on persons in a vegetative state. The conclusion that "he carefully reflected on the subject . . . [was] supported by his religious beliefs and [was] not inconsistent with his life of unselfish religious devotion." (Id., at 379-380, 438 N.Y.S.2d 266, 420 N.E.2d 64.) Further, his expressions were "solemn pronouncements and not casual remarks made at some social gathering, nor c[ould] it be said that he was too young to realize or feel the consequences of his statements." . . .

III

At the outset, since the inquiry in New York is limited to ascertaining and then effectuating the patient's expressed wishes, our focus must always be on what the patient would say if asked today whether the treatment in issue should be terminated. However, we can never be completely certain of the answer to our question, since the inquiry assumes that the patient is no longer able to express his or her wishes. . . .

But the existence of these problems does not lead inevitably to the conclusion that we should abandon the inquiry entirely and adopt as guideposts the objective factors used in the so-called "substituted judgment" approach (see, Brophy v. New England Sinai Hosp., 398

---

any reason in principle why those wishing to appoint another to express their specific or general desires with respect to medical treatment, in the event they become incompetent, may not do so formally. . . .

Mass. 417, 429-440, 497 N.E.2d 626). That approach remains unacceptable because it is inconsistent with our fundamental commitment to the notion that no person or court should substitute its judgment as to what would be an acceptable quality of life for another (People v. Eulo, supra, 63 N.Y.2d at 357, 482 N.Y.S.2d 436, 472 N.E.2d 286). Consequently, we adhere to the view that, despite its pitfalls and inevitable uncertainties, the inquiry must always be narrowed to the patient's expressed intent, with every effort made to minimize the opportunity for error. . . .

. . . [T]he "clear and convincing" evidence standard requires proof sufficient to persuade the trier of fact that the patient held a firm and settled commitment to the termination of life supports under the circumstances like those presented. . . . The ideal situation is one in which the patient's wishes were expressed in some form of a writing, perhaps a "living will," while he or she was still competent. . . .

Although Mrs. O'Connor's statements about her desire to decline life-saving treatments were repeated over a number of years, there is nothing, other than speculation, to persuade the fact finder that her expressions were more than immediate reactions to the unsettling experience of seeing or hearing of another's unnecessarily prolonged death. Her comments — that she would never want to lose her dignity before she passed away, that nature should be permitted to take its course, that it is "monstrous" to use life-support machinery — are, in fact, no different than those that many of us might make after witnessing an agonizing death. Similarly, her statements to the effect that she would not want to be a burden to anyone are the type of statements that older people frequently, almost invariably make. If such statements were routinely held to be clear and convincing proof of a general intent to decline all medical treatment once incompetency sets in, few nursing home patients would ever receive life-sustaining medical treatment in the future. The aged and infirm would be placed at grave risk if the law uniformly but unrealistically treated the expression of such sentiments as a calm and deliberate resolve to decline all life-sustaining medical assistance once the speaker is silenced by mental disability. That Mrs. O'Connor made similar statements over a long period of time, does not, by itself, transform them from the type of comments that are often made casually into the type of statements that demonstrate a seriousness of purpose necessary to satisfy the "clear and convincing evidence" standard.

We do not mean to suggest that, to be effective, a patient's expressed desire to decline treatment must specify a precise condition and a particular treatment, . . . but another element to be considered [is] . . . whether her pronouncement made on some previous occasion bears relevance to her present condition.

Thus, it is appropriate for us to consider the circumstances in which Mrs. O'Connor made the statements and to compare them with those which presently prevail.

Her statements with respect to declining artificial means of life support were generally prompted by her experience with persons suffering terminal illnesses, particularly cancer. However, Mrs. O'Connor does not have a terminal illness, except in the sense that she is aged and infirm. Neither is she in a coma nor vegetative state. She is awake and conscious; she can feel pain, responds to simple commands, can carry on limited conversations, and is not experiencing any pain. She is simply an elderly person who as a result of several strokes suffers certain disabilities, including an inability to feed herself or eat in a normal manner. She is in a stable condition and if properly nourished will remain in that condition unless some other medical problem arises. Because of her age and general physical condition, her life expectancy is not great. But that is true of many nursing home patients. The key thing that sets her apart — though there are likely thousands like her — is her inability to eat or obtain nourishment without medical assistance. . . .

In sum, on this record it cannot be said that Mrs. O'Connor elected to d[i]e under circumstances such as these. Even her daughters, who undoubtedly know her wishes better than anyone, are earnestly trying to carry them out, and whose motives we believe to be of the highest and most loving kind, candidly admit that they do not know what she would do, or what she would want done under these circumstances.

Accordingly the order of the Appellate Division should be reversed, the petition granted and counterclaim dismissed, without costs.

HANCOCK, JUDGE (concurring).

I concur in the result reached by the majority and with its application of the *Storar* rule (Matter of Storar, 52 N.Y.2d 363, 438 N.Y.S.2d 266, 420 N.E.2d 64) to the facts of this case. In my view, however, there are serious deficiencies in *Storar*, making it particularly unrealistic and unsatisfactory for deciding cases involving circumstances more extreme than those presented here. I believe that a critical need exists for a change in the present New York rule — either through legislative action or judicial decision. . . .

. . . I am quite confident that I would reach the same decision in this case under whatever reasonable standards might be adopted to replace our present rule, whether they constituted the "substituted judgment rule," "best interests analysis," "balancing of competing interests," or some combination thereof. . . . The particular circumstances here — e.g., the patient is neither terminal, comatose nor vegetative; she is awake, responsive and experiencing no pain; and the prescribed procedure is relatively simple and routine — would weigh heavily in favor of continuing the medically assisted feeding under any of the approaches adopted by other state courts or recommended in the pertinent literature.

But there are, I believe, several reasons why the present New York rule — requiring a factual finding of the patient's actual intent and precluding the exercise of judgment, in her best interests and on her behalf, by her physician and family, a court or guardian — is unrealistic, often unfair or inhumane and, if applied literally, totally unworkable.

The rule posits, as the only basis for judicial relief, the court's finding by clear and convincing proof of a fact which is inherently unknowable: what the incompetent patient would actually have intended at the time of the impending life-support decision. . . .

At best, the finding of "actual intent" required by the rule must be based on nothing more than a calculated guess as to what the incompetent patient would have thought if she were competent. But even if a wise and well-founded guess were assumed to be enough to constitute proof that is clear and convincing, the fact finder could still never satisfy the rule because it insists upon a finding of actual present intent. There is simply no way of excluding the possibility that the patient has had a change of mind so that her past statements do not indicate her present wishes (cf., Dresser, Life, Death, and Incompetent Patients: Conceptual Infirmities and Hidden Values in the Law, 28 Ariz. L. Rev. 373, 379 ["people experiencing various life events, including set-backs in their physical and mental functioning, may revise their goals, values, and definitions of personal well-being"]). . . .

I believe that a more flexible rule, and one which does not circumscribe so narrowly the limits of legal conduct, is required. Only such a rule, in my opinion, can be applied satisfactorily — and with wisdom and sensitivity — by decision makers in legal proceedings, and by hospitals and physicians who must daily face the exigencies of making life-support determinations in cases involving the terminally ill. . . .

Cruzan v. Director, Missouri Department of Health
— U.S. — (1990), U.S. LEXIS 3301

CHIEF JUSTICE REHNQUIST delivered the opinion of the Court.

On the night of January 11, 1983, Nancy Cruzan lost control of her car as she traveled down Elm Road in Jasper County, Missouri. The vehicle overturned, and Cruzan was discovered lying face down in a ditch without detectable respiratory or cardiac function. Paramedics were able to restore her breathing and heartbeat at the accident site, and she was transported to a hospital in an unconscious state. An attending neurosurgeon diagnosed her as having sustained probable cerebral contusions compounded by significant anoxia (lack of oxygen). The Missouri trial court in this case found that permanent brain damage generally results after 6 minutes in an anoxic state; it was estimated that Cruzan was deprived of oxygen from 12 to 14 minutes. She remained in a coma for approximately three weeks and then progressed to an unconscious state in which she was able to orally ingest some nutrition. In order to ease feeding and further recovery, surgeons implanted a gastrostomy feeding and hydration tube in Cruzan with the consent of her then husband. Subsequent rehabilitative efforts proved unavailing. She now lies in a Missouri state hospital in what is commonly referred to as a persistent vegetative state: generally, a condition in which a person exhibits motor reflexes but evinces no indications of significant cognitive function. The State of Missouri is bearing the cost of her care.

After it had become apparent that Nancy Cruzan had virtually no chance of regaining her mental faculties her parents asked hospital employees to terminate the artificial nutrition and hydration procedures. All agree that such a removal would cause her death. The employees refused to honor the request without court approval. The parents then sought and received authorization from the state trial court for termination. The court found that . . . Nancy's "expressed thoughts at age twenty-five in somewhat serious conversation with a housemate friend that if sick or injured she would not wish to continue her life unless she could live at least halfway normally suggests that given her present condition she would not wish to continue on with her nutrition and hydration."

The Supreme Court of Missouri reversed by a divided vote. The court recognized a right to refuse treatment embodied in the common-law doctrine of informed consent, but expressed skepticism about the application of that doctrine in the circumstances of this case. Cruzan v. Harmon, 760 S.W.2d 408, 416-417 (Mo. 1988) (en banc). . . . The court found that Cruzan's statements to her roommate regarding her desire to live or die under certain conditions were "unreliable for the purpose of determining her intent," id., at 424, "and thus insufficient to support the co-guardians' claim to exercise substituted judgment on Nancy's behalf." Id., at 426. It rejected the argument that Cruzan's parents were entitled to order the termination of her medical treatment, concluding that "no person can assume that choice for an incompetent in the absence of the formalities required under Missouri's Living Will statutes or the clear and convincing, inherently reliable evidence absent here." Id., at 425. . . .

We granted certiorari to consider the question of whether Cruzan has a right under the United States Constitution which would require the hospital to withdraw life-sustaining treatment from her under these circumstances. . . .

II. Termination of Treatment and Related Matters

In the *Quinlan* case, . . . [the court] concluded that the "only practical way" to prevent the loss of Karen's privacy right due to her incompetence was to allow her guardian and family to decide "whether she would exercise it in these circumstances." After *Quinlan*, however, most courts have based a right to refuse treatment either solely on the common-law right to informed consent or on both the common-law right and a constitutional privacy right. . . . For instance, in In re Conroy, 98 N.J. 321, 486 A.2d 1209 (1985), the same court that decided *Quinlan* considered whether a nasogastric feeding tube could be removed from an 84-year-old incompetent nursing-home resident suffering irreversible mental and physical ailments. While recognizing that a federal right of privacy might apply in the case, the court . . . decided to base its decision on the common-law right to self-determination and informed consent. . . .

As these [and other extensively-discussed] cases demonstrate, the common-law doctrine of informed consent is viewed as generally encompassing the right of a competent individual to refuse medical treatment. Beyond that, these decisions demonstrate both similarity and diversity in their approach to decision of what all agree is a perplexing question with unusually strong moral and ethical overtones. State courts have available to them for decision a number of sources — state constitutions, statutes, and common law — which are not available to us. In this Court, the question is simply and starkly whether the United States Constitution prohibits Missouri from choosing the rule of decision which it did. This is the first case in which we have been squarely presented with the issue of whether the United States Constitution grants what is in common parlance referred to as a "right to die." We follow the judicious counsel of our decision in Twin City Bank v. Nebeker, 167 U.S. 196, 202 (1897), where we said that in deciding "a question of such magnitude and importance . . . it is the [better] part of wisdom not to attempt, by any general statement, to cover every possible phase of the subject."

The Fourteenth Amendment provides that no State shall "deprive any person of life, liberty, or property, without due process of law." The principle that a competent person has a constitutionally protected liberty interest in refusing unwanted medical treatment may be inferred from our prior decisions. In Jacobson v. Massachusetts, 197 U.S. 11, 24-30 (1905), for instance, the Court balanced an individual's liberty interest in declining an unwanted smallpox vaccine against the State's interest in preventing disease. Decisions prior to the incorporation of the Fourth Amendment into the Fourteenth Amendment analyzed searches and seizures involving the body under the Due Process Clause and were thought to implicate substantial liberty interests. See, e.g., Breithaupt v. Abrams, 352 U.S. 432, 439 (1957) ("As against the right of an individual that his person be held inviolable . . . must be set the interests of society . . .").

Just this Term, in the course of holding that a State's procedures for administering antipsychotic medication to prisoners were sufficient to satisfy due process concerns, we recognized that prisoners possess "a significant liberty interest in avoiding the unwanted administration of antipsychotic drugs under the Due Process Clause of the Fourteenth Amendment." Washington v. Harper, — U.S. —, — (1990) (slip op., at 9); see also id., at — (slip op., at 17) ("The forcible injection of medication into a nonconsenting person's body represents a substantial interference with that person's liberty"). . . .

But determining that a person has a "liberty interest" under the Due Process Clause does not end the inquiry;[7] "whether respondent's constitutional rights have been violated must be determined by balancing his liberty interests against the relevant state interests." Petitioners insist that under the general holdings of our cases, the forced administration of life-sustaining medical treatment, and even of artificially-delivered food and water essential to life, would implicate a competent person's liberty interest. Although we think the logic of the cases discussed above would embrace such a liberty interest, the dramatic consequences involved in refusal of such treatment would inform the inquiry as to whether the deprivation of that interest is constitutionally permissible. But [in] this case, we assume that the United States Constitution would grant a competent person a constitutionally protected right to refuse lifesaving hydration and nutrition.

Petitioners . . . assert that an incompetent person should possess the same right in this respect as . . . a competent person. . . .

The difficulty with petitioners' claim is that in a sense it begs the question: an incompetent person is not able to make an informed and voluntary choice to exercise a hypothetical right to refuse treatment or any other right. Such a "right" must be exercised for her, if at all, by some sort of surrogate. Here, Missouri has in effect recognized that under certain circumstances a surrogate may act for the patient in electing to have hydration and nutrition withdrawn in such a way as to cause death, but it has established a procedural safeguard to assure that the action of the surrogate conforms as best it may to the wishes expressed by the patient while competent. Missouri requires that evidence of the incompetent's wishes as to the withdrawal of treatment be proved by clear and convincing evidence. The question, then, is whether the United States Constitution forbids the establishment of this procedural requirement by the State. We hold that it does not. . . .

. . . The choice between life and death is a deeply personal

---

7. Although many state courts have held that a right to refuse treatment is encompassed by a generalized constitutional right of privacy, we have never so held. We believe this issue is more properly analyzed in terms of a Fourteenth Amendment liberty interest. See Bowers v. Hardwick, 478 U.S. 186, 194-195 (1986).

II. Termination of Treatment and Related Matters

decision of obvious and overwhelming finality. We believe Missouri may legitimately seek to safeguard the personal element of this choice through the imposition of heightened evidentiary requirements. It cannot be disputed that the Due Process Clause protects an interest in life as well as an interest in refusing life-sustaining medical treatment. Not all incompetent patients will have loved ones available to serve as surrogate decisionmakers. And even where family members are present, "[t]here will, of course, be some unfortunate situations in which family members will not act to protect a patient." In re Jobes, 108 N.J. 394, 419, 529 A.2d 434, 477 (1987). A State is entitled to guard against potential abuses in such situations. Similarly, a State is entitled to consider that a judicial proceeding to make a determination regarding an incompetent's wishes may very well not be an adversarial one, with the added guarantee of accurate factfinding that the adversary process brings with it. . . .

In our view, Missouri has permissibly sought to advance these interests through the adoption of a "clear and convincing" standard of proof to govern such proceedings. . . . We think it self-evident that the interests at stake in the instant proceedings are more substantial, both on an individual and societal level, than those involved in a run-of-the-mine civil dispute. . . . An erroneous decision not to terminate results in a maintenance of the status quo; the possibility of subsequent developments such as advancements in medical science, the discovery of new evidence regarding the patient's intent, changes in the law, or simply the unexpected death of the patient despite the administration of life-sustaining treatment, at least create the potential that a wrong decision will eventually be corrected or its impact mitigated. An erroneous decision to withdraw life-sustaining treatment, however, is not susceptible of correction. . . .

The Supreme Court of Missouri held that in this case the testimony adduced at trial did not amount to clear and convincing proof of the patient's desire to have hydration and nutrition withdrawn. In so doing, it reversed a decision of the Missouri trial court which had found that the evidence "suggest[ed]" Nancy Cruzan would not have desired to continue such measures, App. to Pet. for Cert. A98, but which had not adopted the standard of "clear and convincing evidence" enunciated by the Supreme Court. The testimony adduced at trial consisted primarily of Nancy Cruzan's statements made to a housemate about a year before her accident that she would not want to live should she face life as a "vegetable," and other observations to the same effect. The observations did not deal in [explicit] terms with withdrawal of medical treatment or of hydration and nutrition. We cannot say that the Supreme Court of Missouri committed constitutional error in reaching the conclusion that it did.

Petitioners alternatively contend that Missouri must accept the "substituted judgment" of close family members even in the absence of substantial proof that their views reflect the views of the patient. . . . [There is no] doubt . . . in this record but that Nancy Cruzan's mother and father are loving and caring parents. If the State were required by the United States Constitution to repose a right of "substituted judgment" with anyone, the Cruzans would surely qualify. But we do not think the Due Process Clause requires the State to repose judgment on these matters with anyone but the patient herself. Close family members may have a strong feeling — a feeling not at all ignoble or unworthy, but not entirely disinterested, either — that they do not wish to witness the continuation of the life of a loved one which they regard as hopeless, meaningless, and even degrading. But there is no automatic assurance that the view of close family members will necessarily be the same as the patient's would have been had she been confronted with the prospect of her situation while competent. All of the reasons previously discussed for allowing Missouri to require clear and convincing evidence of the patient's wishes lead us to conclude that the State may choose to defer only to those wishes, rather than confide the decision to close family members.[12] . . .

The judgment of the Supreme Court of Missouri is Affirmed.

[JUSTICES O'CONNOR and SCALIA wrote concurring opinions that were more revealing on the critical question that the majority pretermitted: the degree of *substantive* constitutional protection that the due process clause affords the liberty interest in refusing treatment. Justice O'Connor opined that "the refusal of artificially delivered food and water is encompassed within that liberty interest," and that a duty to honor the decisions of a surrogate decisionmaker appointed by the patient "may well be constitutionally required." Justice Scalia, on the other hand, "would have preferred that we announce, clearly and promptly, that the Federal courts have no business in this field . . . [because] the Constitution has nothing to say about the subject."]

JUSTICE BRENNAN, with whom JUSTICE MARSHALL and JUSTICE BLACKMUN join, dissenting. . . .

A grown woman at the time of the accident, Nancy had previously expressed her wish to forgo continuing medical care under circumstances such as these. Her family and her friends are convinced that this is what she would want. A guardian ad litem appointed by the trial court is also convinced that this is what Nancy would want. Yet the Missouri Supreme Court, alone among state courts deciding such a question, has determined that an irreversibly vegetative patient will remain a passive prisoner of medical technology — for Nancy, perhaps for the next 30 years. . . .

---

12. We are not faced in this case with the question of whether a State might be required to defer to the decision of a surrogate if competent and probative evidence established that the patient herself had expressed a desire that the decision to terminate life-sustaining treatment be made for her by that individual.

II. Termination of Treatment and Related Matters

Missouri has no such power to disfavor a choice by Nancy Cruzan to avoid medical treatment, because Missouri has no legitimate interest in providing Nancy with treatment until it is established that this represents her choice. . . . The majority [ ] argues that where, as here, important individual rights are at stake, a clear and convincing evidence standard has long been held to be an appropriate means of enhancing accuracy, citing decisions concerning what process an individual is due before he can be deprived of a liberty interest. In those cases, however, this Court imposed a clear and convincing standard as a constitutional minimum on the basis of its evaluation that one side's interests clearly outweighed the second side's interests and therefore the second side should bear the risk of error. . . . In the cases cited by the majority, the imbalance imposed by a heightened evidentiary standard was not only acceptable but required because the standard was deployed to protect an individual's exercise of a fundamental right, as the majority admits. In contrast, the Missouri court imposed a clear and convincing standard as an obstacle to the exercise of a fundamental right. . . .

In doing so, the court failed to consider statements Nancy had made to family members and a close friend.[19] The court also failed to consider testimony from Nancy's mother and sister that they were certain that Nancy would want to discontinue artificial nutrition and hydration, even after the court found that Nancy's family was loving and without malignant motive. . . . The court did not specifically define what kind of evidence it would consider clear and convincing, but its general discussion suggests that only a living will or equivalently formal directive from the patient when competent would meet this standard.

Too few people execute living wills or equivalently formal directives for such an evidentiary rule to ensure adequately that the wishes of incompetent persons will be honored. . . . The testimony of close friends and family members, on the other hand, may often be the best evidence available of what the patient's choice would be. It is they with whom the patient most likely will have discussed such

---

19. The trial court had relied on the testimony of Athena Comer, a long-time friend, co-worker and a housemate for several months . . . [who] testified that: "Nancy said she would never want to live [in a vegetative state.] . . ." She said "several times" that "she wouldn't want to live that way because if she was going to live, she wanted to be able to live, not to just lay in a bed and not be able to move because you can't do anything for yourself." "[S]he said that she hoped that [all the] people in her family knew that she wouldn't want to live [as a vegetable] because she knew it was usually up to the family whether you lived that way or not." The conversation took place approximately a year before Nancy's accident and was described by Ms. Comer as a "very serious" conversation that continued for approximately half an hour without interruption. . . . [Nancy made similar statements in reference to her sister's stillborn child and her grandmother who had died after a long battle with heart problems.]

questions and they who know the patient best. . . . The rules by which an incompetent person's wishes are determined must represent every effort to determine those wishes . . . as accurately as possible. . . .

I cannot agree with the majority that where it is not possible to determine what choice an incompetent patient would make, a State's role as parens patriae permits the State automatically to make that choice itself. . . . Is there any reason to suppose that a State is more likely to make the choice that the patient would have made than someone who knew the patient intimately? To ask this is to answer it. . . .

A State's inability to discern an incompetent patient's choice still need not mean that a State is rendered powerless to protect that choice. But I would find that the Due Process Clause prohibits a State from doing more than that. A State may ensure that the person who makes the decision on the patient's behalf is the one whom the patient himself would have selected to make that choice for him. And a State may exclude from consideration anyone having improper motives. But a State generally must either repose the choice with the person whom the patient himself would most likely have chosen as proxy or leave the decision to the patient's family.

[JUSTICE STEVENS dissented in a separate opinion, on the grounds that, where a patient's wishes are not known, the State must decide what to do according to a "best interests" standard, which here requires discontinuation of treatment because her comatose condition robs her life of most of its meaning.]

NOTES

Substituted Judgment and Best Interests of the Patient

1. The "substituted judgment" test espoused in *Quinlan* and *Saikewicz* requires for incapacitated patients that we make the treatment decision that the patient would have made if lucid. However, the clarity of patient expressions of preference varies widely along a continuum from formal, advance directives such as living wills and durable powers of attorney to patients like Joseph Saikewicz who have never possessed the capacity to form rational judgments. Patients at the first extreme are unproblematic since they can be treated as if they are competent patients making contemporaneous treatment refusals. Therefore, the primary focus of this section of materials is on patients at the second extreme or those in the middle, whose prior expressions are ambiguous or inexplicit.

New York and Missouri are uniquely demanding in the test they

II. Termination of Treatment and Related Matters   1003

apply to find the necessary settled intent to invoke a substituted-judgment rule. Other states have been willing to consider and enforce more general or informal expressions of opinion. See, e.g., *Brophy*, supra at p. 948 n.22. (The New Jersey Supreme Court has since repudiated dictum in *Quinlan* to the contrary. In re Conroy, 486 A.2d at 647.) Even without such express statements, it is possible for family members to act based on their knowledge of a patient's general value system. New Jersey has the most extensively developed body of precedent describing the circumstances in which its courts are willing to allow the family to decide what the patient would have wanted and the varying tests of validity that apply to comatose patients versus other forms of incapacity.

2. Commenting on the *Westchester County (O'Connor)* decision, George Annas describes "the opinion's most grotesque feature" as its refusal "to acknowledge that all incompetent individuals have constitutional rights. Mrs. O'Connor's body is treated like that of a mollusk which, it seems to be assumed, can neither be harmed or degraded by unconsented to and invasive medical interventions." 18 Hastings Cent. Rep. 32 (Dec. 1988). However, due to Mary O'Connor's physical and mental condition, there was a substantial probability that treatment termination would have caused her considerable pain. Therefore, it is possible to rationalize the court's decision as one that is particularly demanding on the proof standard for a subjective intent to refuse treatment only where such a decision appears objectively unreasonable or unlikely. Does the court's reasoning leave open the possibility of relaxing the standard in cases involving more burdensome forms of treatment? In cases of comatose patients? Once more is known about the physical effects of feeding tube withdrawal?

3. Any pretense of acting based on a patient's actual wishes is impossible for patients like Saikewicz who were never competent and therefore never had an opportunity to express a view on treatment termination or even to develop a general value system. The *Saikewicz* decision has received endless ridicule for the logical contradiction engendered by attempting to apply a subjective, substituted judgment test to such patients. In the words of one court, determining what never-competent patients would have wanted if competent becomes somewhat like asking " 'if it snowed all summer would it then be winter?' " In re Storar and Eichner, 420 N.E.2d 64, 73 (N.Y. 1981).

Professor Ellman offers the following elaboration on this aspect of *Cruzan:* "The Cruzans argue that a patient like Nancy does not lose her right to decide her own medical treatment because she is incapacitated. This is of course true . . . but that observation leads us nowhere, since she is incapable of [deciding]. . . . Where nature has deprived the patient of the capacity to exercise a right, the Constitution cannot restore it. To say that the Constitution protects the right of others to exercise Nancy's right for her will not do where, as here, the right in question is a right *to make a choice*. It stands on the same footing as a claim that Nancy Cruzan's right to vote can be exercised by her family." Ellman, *Cruzan v. Harmon* and the Dangerous Claim that Others Can Exercise an Incapacitated Patient's Right to Die, 29 Jurimetrics 389, 395 (1989).

Nevertheless, even where the wishes of patients are unknown or unknowable, the courts are still forced to decide on some basis whether the patients should be treated. A nondecision is impossible since refusing the family's request is tantamount to an approval of treatment. Therefore, most courts have applied the same objective, "best interests" analysis they customarily use for any decision that must be made on behalf of an incompetent. They ask what most people would want who are in the patient's position.

This understood, the *Saikewicz* analysis is more defensible. It can be read as merely applying the wrong label to the correct test, for, under a best interests test properly applied, it is relevant to consider that "in the patient's same position" means in a state of incompetency where the patient lacks no understanding of the reason for painful and debilitating treatment. Nevertheless, do you think the court adequately evaluated the treatment difficulties created by Joseph Saikewicz's mental retardation? If it is possible the disruptive effects of chemotherapy could have been minimized through sedation?

4. In order to avoid terminological confusion, it is preferrable to apply "substituted judgment" only to patients with some prior expression of preference and reserve "best interests" for patients whose desires are unknown or unknowable. Rasmussen v. Fleming, 741 P.2d 674, 688-689 (Ariz. 1987). Whether one recognizes two branches of a single substituted judgment test or two distinct tests is largely a semantic point, however. One of the most thorough decisions applying the substituted judgment/best interests standard, In re Lucille Boyd, 403 A.2d 744 (D.C. Cir. 1979), offers the following helpful explanation:

> Obviously, in attempting to make such a subjective evaluation, in contrast with an objective, "reasonable person" analysis, the court will be engaging, at best, in approximation; any imputation of a preference to an incompetent person will, to some extent, be fictional. But that inherent limitation does not make the "substituted judgment" analysis less valid than one which purports to be wholly objective, for *any* analysis presupposes the court's judgment as to what a human being would decide for oneself under the circumstances. . . .
>
> With this in mind, we should underscore that inevitably the substituted judgment approach, because of its obvious limitations, will result in a synthesis of (1) factors known to be true about the incompetent (2) other considerations which necessarily suggest themselves when the

court cannot be sure about an incompetent's actual wishes. Thus, in trying to decide what choice the individual would make if competent, the court is not precluded from filling the gaps in its knowledge about the incompetent by taking into account what most persons are likely to do in a similar situation.

This case concerned whether a psychiatric hospital should continue administering psychotropic medication to a practicing Christian Scientist who had repeatedly made her objections to medical treatment clear prior to her incompetence. The court remanded the case to the trial court to reconsider its initial order mandating treatment. What is the correct result?

5. Examples of cases where the substituted judgment/best interests test has resulted in an order of treatment can be found at In re Visbeck, 510 A.2d 125 (N.J. Super. 1986); In re Clark, 510 A.2d 136 (N.J. Super. 1986). In each case the judge ordered the insertion of a feeding tube for a stroke victim with severely diminished mental capacity, yet who had some awareness and sensation. A good contrast to *Saikewicz* is provided by the Massachusetts Court's subsequent decision in *Custody of a Minor*, 379 N.E.2d 1053 (Mass. 1978), where it ordered chemotherapy for a three-year-old leukemia patient with a 50 percent chance of long-term survival, over the objection of parents who preferred nutritional therapy. See also In re Storar, 420 N.E.2d 64 (N.Y. 1981) (blood transfusions ordered for profoundly retarded terminal cancer patient because they "did not involve excessive pain," even though patient found them "disagreeable").

6. Sometimes, the best interests test is framed by asking whether the burdens of treatment outweigh the benefits to the patient. If courts are serious about taking this test literally, how can they ever approve a treatment refusal for a patient in a persistent vegetative state? Since these patients aren't aware of anything, even an infinitesimal chance of recovery statistically outweighs the burdens to the patient of treatment.

Perhaps the best response is to recognize that most patients would also be concerned about the burdens to their families. As one court has noted, "in the case of a comatose individual there is no pain and suffering. [I]t would seem to follow that the direct beneficiary of the request [to terminate treatment] is the family of the patient and that the benefits are financial savings and cessation of the emotional drain occasioned by awaiting the medico-legal death of a loved one." John F. Kennedy Mem. Hosp. v. Bludworth, 432 So. 2d 611, 615 (Fla. App. 1983), *aff'd in part and rev'd in part on other grounds*, 452 So. 2d 921 (Fla. 1984). But doesn't this recognition border dangerously close to allowing the guardian, who is usually a family member, to make a self-interested decision?

Professors Dresser and Robertson comment further on these issues in their article, Quality of Life and Non-Treatment Decisions for Incompetent Patients: A Critique of the Orthodox Approach, 17 L. Med. & Health Care 234, 238 (1989):

> The orthodox judicial approach to non-treatment decisions . . . is too focused on the model of a competent person refusing treatment, even when the case involves a person who is incompetent and unable to choose. . . . [This] approach threatens incompetent patients with undertreatment, because it overlooks the interests they may have in continued life in their diminished state. [F]amilies often have their own interests in being relieved of the distress of seeing their loved ones in a chronic debilitated state. . . . Perhaps [ ] these interests should be influential in the treatment setting. The orthodox approach, however, formally proclaims that they have no role while simultaneously permitting them *sub silentio* to shape non-treatment decisions that may conflict with the patient's current welfare. . . .
>
> An alternative approach . . . is to ask whether treatment actually serves the incompetent patient's existing interests. If treatment cannot succeed in supplying patients with an acceptable quality of life, then external [family] considerations should be permitted to affect the decision. If treatment would serve patient interests but would impose heavy burdens on family or society, the conflict can be faced openly.

Compare Rhoden, Litigating Life and Death, 102 Harv. L. Rev. 375 (1988) (proposing that courts recognize a presumptive right of families to exercise discretion over treatment decisions). In re A.C., — A.2d — (D.C. 1990) ("sometimes family members will rely on their own judgment and predilictions rather than serving as conduits for expressing the patient's wishes. . . . On the other hand, we think it proper for the court to conclude that the patient might consider the views of her family in making a treatment decision").

7. For additional discussion and critique of the substituted judgment test, see Strudler, Self-Determination, Incompetence, and Medical Jurisprudence, 13 J. Med. & Philo. 349 (1988) (arguing that it is permissible to ascribe a right of self-determination to a being who never had capacity for rational choice); Dresser, Life, Death and Incompetent Patients: Conceptual Infirmities and Hidden Values, 28 Ariz. L. Rev. 373 (1986); Ramsey, The *Saikewicz* Precedent: What's Good for an Incompetent Patient?, 8 Hast. Cent. Rep. no. 6, at 36 (Dec. 1978); P. Ramsey, Ethics at the Edges of Life (1978); Welch, Walking in Their Shoes: Paying Respect to Incompetent Patients, 42 Vand. L. Rev. 1617 (1989).

For an early symposium on *Cruzan*, see 20 Hastings Cent. Rep. (Jan/Feb 1990). Much more is sure to follow.

II. Termination of Treatment and Related Matters

4. Severely Deformed Infants

Bowen v. American Hospital Association
476 U.S. 610 (1986)

JUSTICE STEVENS announced the judgment of the Court and delivered an opinion in which JUSTICE MARSHALL, JUSTICE BLACKMUN, and JUSTICE POWELL joined.

This case presents the question whether certain regulations governing the provision of health care to handicapped infants are authorized by §504 of the Rehabilitation Act of 1973. That section provides, in part: "No otherwise qualified handicapped individual . . . shall, solely by reason of his handicap, be excluded from the participation in, be denied the benefits of, or be subjected to discrimination under any program or activity receiving Federal financial assistance." 87 Stat. 394, 29 U.S.C. §794.

I

The American Medical Association, the American Hospital Association, and several other respondents challenge the validity of Final Rules promulgated on January 12, 1984, by the Secretary of the Department of Health and Human Services. These rules establish "Procedures relating to health care for handicapped infants," and in particular require the posting of informational notices, authorize expedited access to records and expedited compliance actions, and command state child protective services agencies to "prevent instances of unlawful medical neglect of handicapped infants." 45 CFR §84.55 (1985).

Although the Final Rules comprise six parts, only the four mandatory components are challenged here. Subsection (b) is entitled "Posting of informational notice" and requires every "recipient health care provider that provides health care services to infants in programs or activities receiving Federal financial assistance" — a group to which we refer generically as "hospitals" — to post an informational notice in one of two approved forms. 45 CFR §84.55(b) (1985). Both forms include a statement that §504 prohibits discrimination on the basis of handicap, and indicate that because of this prohibition "nourishment and medically beneficial treatment (as determined with respect for reasonable medical judgments) should not be withheld from handicapped infants solely on the basis of their present or anticipated mental or physical impairments." 45 CFR §§84.55(b)(3), (4) (1985). The notice's statement of the legal requirement does not distinguish between medical care for which parental consent has been obtained and that for which it has not. The notice must identify the telephone number of the appropriate child protective services agency and, in addition, a toll free number for the Department that is available 24 hours a day. Ibid. Finally, the notice must state that the "identity of callers will be kept confidential" and that federal law prohibits retaliation "against any person who provides information about possible violations." . . .

II

The Final Rules represent the Secretary's ultimate response to an April 9, 1982, incident in which the parents of a Bloomington, Indiana infant with Down's syndrome and other handicaps refused consent to surgery to remove an esophageal obstruction that prevented oral feeding. On April 10, the hospital initiated judicial proceedings to override the parents' decision, but an Indiana trial court, after holding a hearing the same evening, denied the requested relief. On April 12 the court asked the local Child Protection Committee to review its decision. After conducting its own hearing, the Committee found no reason to disagree with the court's ruling. The infant died six days after its birth.

Citing "heightened public concern" in the aftermath of the Bloomington Baby Doe incident, on May 18, 1982, the director of the Department's Office of Civil Rights, in response to a directive from the President, "remind[ed]" health care providers receiving federal financial assistance that newborn infants with handicaps such as Down's syndrome were protected by §504. 47 Fed. Reg. 26027 (1982). . . .

VI

In the immediate aftermath of the Bloomington Baby Doe incident, the Secretary apparently proceeded on the assumption that a hospital's statutory duty to provide treatment to handicapped infants was unaffected by the absence of parental consent. He has since abandoned that view. Thus, the preamble to the Final Rules correctly states that when "a non-treatment decision, no matter how discriminatory, is made by parents, rather than by the hospital, section 504 does not mandate that the hospital unilaterally overrule the parental decision and provide treatment notwithstanding the lack of consent." 49 Fed. Reg. 1631 (1984). A hospital's withholding of treatment when no parental consent has been given cannot violate §504, for without the consent of the parents or a surrogate decisionmaker the infant is neither "otherwise qualified" for treatment nor has he been denied care "solely by reason of his handicap." Indeed, it would almost certainly be a tort as a matter of state law to operate on an infant without parental consent. . . . If, pursuant to its normal practice, a hospital refused to operate on a black child whose parents had withheld their consent to treatment, the hospital's refusal would not be based on the race of the child even if it were assumed that the parents based their decision entirely on a mistaken assumption that the race of the child made the operation inappropriate.

Now that the Secretary has acknowledged that a hospital has no statutory treatment obligation in the absence of parental consent, it has become clear that the Final Rules are not needed to prevent hospitals from denying treatment to handicapped infants. The Solicitor General concedes that the administrative record contains no evidence that hospitals have ever refused treatment authorized either by the infant's parents or by a court order. Even the Secretary never seriously maintained that posted notices, "hotlines," and emergency on-site investigations were necessary to process complaints against hospitals that might refuse treatment requested by parents. . . . In sum, there is nothing in the administrative record to justify the Secretary's belief that "discriminatory withholding of medical care" in violation of §504 provides any support for federal regulation.

Child Abuse and Neglect Prevention and Treatment Regulations
45 C.F.R. §1340.15 (1989)

Services and Treatment for Disabled Infants

(a) *Purpose.* The regulations in this section implement certain provisions of the Child Abuse Amendments of 1984. . . . governing the protection and care of disabled infants with life-threatening conditions.

(b) *Definitions.* (1) . . . The term "medical neglect" includes, but is not limited to, the withholding of medically indicated treatment from a disabled infant with a life-threatening condition.

(2) The term "withholding of medically indicated treatment" means the failure to respond to the infant's life-threatening conditions by providing treatment (including appropriate nutrition, hydration, and medication) which, in the treating physician's (or physicians') reasonable medical judgment, will be most likely to be effective in ameliorating or correcting all such conditions, except that the term does not include the failure to provide treatment (other than appropriate nutrition, hydration, or medication) to an infant, when, in the treating physician's (or physicians') reasonable medical judgment any of the following circumstances apply:

(i) The infant is chronically and irreversibly comatose;

(ii) The provision of such treatment would merely prolong dying, not be effective in ameliorating or correcting all of the infant's life-threatening conditions, or otherwise be futile in terms of the survival of the infant; or

(iii) The provision of such treatment would be virtually futile in terms of the survival of the infant and the treatment itself under such circumstances would be inhumane. . . .

(c) *Eligibility Requirements.* (1) In addition to the other eligibility requirements set forth in this Part, to qualify for a grant under this section, a State must have programs, procedures, or both, in place within the State's child protective service system for the purpose of responding to the reporting of medical neglect, including instances of withholding of medically indicated treatment from disabled infants with life-threatening conditions.

(2) These programs and/or procedures must provide for:

(i) Coordination and consultation with individuals designated by and within appropriate health care facilities;

(ii) Prompt notification by individuals designated by and within appropriate health care facilities of cases of suspected medical neglect (including instances of the withholding of medically indicated treatment from disabled infants with life-threatening conditions); and

(iii) The authority, under State law, for the State child protective service system to pursue any legal remedies, including the authority to initiate legal proceedings in a court of competent jurisdiction, as may be necessary to prevent the withholding of medically indicated treatment from disabled infants with life-threatening conditions.

NOTES

The "Baby Doe" Cases

1. The government's "Baby Doe" regulations invalidated in the principal case prompted a furor of controversy when they were originally issued. The regulations grew out of the Reagan administration's right-to-life concern over what it viewed as a growing practice of infanticide: parents who had failed to detect and abort a Downs Syndrome (severe retardation) child during pregnancy were seizing on the circumstance of a minor, completely correctable medical impairment to avoid the burdens of raising a handicapped child. Although strong reaction to this situation is understandable, the federal regulations provoked attack because (a) they were directed at hospitals

rather than parents, (b) they intruded into an area traditionally the province of states, and (c) they swept far more serious birth defects into their path than Downs Syndrome babies.

On the last point, distinguish what have come to be known as "Baby Jane Doe" babies (after the pseudonym of the infant in a case that arose in New York in 1983, Weber v. Stony Brook Hosp., 469 N.Y.S.2d 63 (1983)). These are children born with spina bifida — an exposed spinal column. Babies with the most severe form of spina bifida have radical congenital defects that prevent them from surviving through childhood, even with treatment. While their precise mental states can vary, it is likely that the most severely afflicted will "never interact with [their] environment or with other people." U.S. v. University Hosp., 729 F.2d 144 (2d Cir. 1984). See Mathieu, The Baby Doe Controversy, 1984 Ariz. St. L.J. 605. In such cases, treatment refusal is far more justifiable because the necessary operations are complex and painful and the medical benefits much less certain, yet the initial "Baby Doe" regulations also compelled aggressive treatment in these cases, contrary to prevailing medical practice as well as in the two following instances: (1) very premature infants, even those with very dim prospects who are born after only five to six months of pregnancy weighing less than three pounds; and (2) anencephalic babies, who are born with most of their brain missing.

2. As the excerpted regulations reveal, the principal case did not end federal involvement in the Baby Doe controversy. Instead, the government shifted to the child abuse laws. See also 42 U.S.C. §§5102, 5103(b)(2). The quoted regulations do not directly bind the states. Instead, they form part of the conditions that are imposed on states for obtaining certain federal funding. Most states attempt to comply with the model federal child abuse laws. See Newman, Baby Doe, Congress and the States: Challenging the Federal Treatment Standard for Infants, 15 Am. J.L. & Med. 1 (1989); Comment, Protection for Handicapped Infants: Decision by Committee Under the Child Abuse Amendments of 1984, 59 U. Colo. L. Rev. 367 (1988). Nevertheless, by placing the Baby Doe issue in the state child neglect system, enforcement is now a matter of local discretion.

3. The child abuse regulations allow parents to refuse treatment for handicapped newborns in three instances: (a) irreversible coma (such as a *Quinlan* situation); (b) terminal illness (as in a classic living will or DNR situation); and (c) where treatment would be "virtually futile" and "inhumane." Interpretive guidelines issued with the regulations explain that these latter terms are intended to cover a situation like that of *Saikewicz*, where death is not "imminent" yet is likely in the "more distant future" regardless of treatment and the treatment is painful. 45 C.F.R. part 1340.

4. Do the substantive provisions of the child abuse regulations differ in any material respect from normal substituted judgment/best interests principles? One commentator argues no, that the rule "is almost entirely symbolic." Murray, The Final, Anticlimactic Rule on Baby Doe, 15 Hastings Cent. Rep. 5, 6 (June 1985). But, the regulations differ from recent adult-patient case law in at least one important respect: they prohibit absolutely the refusal of "appropriate nutrition, hydration, or medication." In any event, the medical community's *perception* of the regulations may be more important than their literal constraint. A recent survey of 500 pediatricians revealed that two-thirds "believed the regulations interfered with parents' right to determine what course of action was in the best interests of their children," and one-third said that the regulations required maximal life-prolonging treatment in cases where such treatment was not in the infant's best interests. Kopelman, Irons & Kopelman, Neonatologists Judge the "Baby Doe" Regulations, 318 New Eng. J. Med. 677 (1988). See also Newman, supra, 15 Am. J.L. & Med. 1 ("The statute, shaped by right-to-life groups and certain medical organizations, calls for aggressive treatment in virtually all cases, regardless of the degree of suffering imposed and the burdens and risks involved") (arguing that states may be precluded by their own constitutions from adopting the federal standards).

A report by the U.S. Commission on Civil Rights, Medical Discrimination Against Children With Disabilities (Sept. 1989), seems to confirm the latter view of the regulations. It advances an extremely conservative reading that, inter alia, observes that treatment must be *both* "virtually futile" *and* "inhumane" to be withheld, suggesting that inhumane care must be rendered even if it has only a slight chance of keeping the infant alive. The committee also maintains that the regulations do not apply to infants in a permanent vegetative state, since the term "irreversibly comatose" designates an even more severe form of brain damage.

5. "In the last few years, doctors have made tremendous advances in the practice of neonatology (the care of newborn babies, [particularly premature infants]). With the aid of sophisticated medical equipment and newly developed techniques, they are able to save babies so small that they fit in an adult's palm. . . . [But] the cost is high — in human as well as financial terms. Although the vast majority of premature babies will live normal lives, others will die after days or weeks of round-the-clock care. And a few will survive with disabilities so severe that their parents will wonder if the technology that saved their babies has become more of a burden than a blessing.

"The most troubling babies are born at the current limit of viability, about 24 weeks old with a weight of about 500 grams (just

over a pound). They bear little resemblance to full-term newborns
. . . [and have at best only] about a 20 percent chance of survival.
. . . [One mother remembers seeing a very premature infant as she
prepared to take her daughter home.] There were more than half a
dozen tubes and wires inserted in various parts of his body, and his
skin was a mottled purple. He was breathing through a special ventilator that made his body shake constantly. . . .

" 'You simply cannot tell early on which babies are going to
make it and which are not,' says Laurence McCullough, a professor
of community medicine at Georgetown. If a baby has no obvious lifethreatening defects that cannot be fixed, doctors almost always begin
treatment . . . because of the so-called 'Baby Doe' rules." Newsweek,
May 16, 1988, at 62, 64-65. Is this a correct interpretation of the
current Baby Does rules? Is it sound policy?

For a gripping personal account of one couple's struggle with
the medical establishment's insensitive refusal to consider the parents'
wishes to cease treating their 1 lb., 12 oz. premature son, see R. &
P. Stinson, The Long Dying of Baby Andrew (1983), excerpted in
244 The Atlantic 64 (July 1979). Although medical attitudes may
differ now, perhaps the pendulum has swung too far in the other
direction. A recent article recounts the collective decision of doctors
at one hospital to refuse a mother's adamant request to mechanically
ventilate her severely brain-damaged infant. Paris, Crone & Reardon,
Physicians' Refusal of Requested Treatment, 322 New Eng. J. Med.
1012 (1990). According to these authors, it is permissible for doctors
"to refuse requested treatments that *they* [think] burdensome and
without benefit" (emphasis added). What is consistent about these two
accounts?

6. Regardless of the uncertainty over the *substantive* impact of
the child abuse amendments, they at least have a definite *procedural*
impact by reinforcing hospitals' duty to notify child protection agencies
of suspected medical neglect of newborns and requiring these agencies
to investigate and prosecute such cases.

7. For a sampling of the voluminous literature on the Baby Doe
controversy, see Huefner, Severely Handicapped Infants with LifeThreatening Conditions: Federal Intrusions into the Decision Not to
Treat, 12 Am. J.L. & Med. 171 (1986); J. Health Pol. Poly. & L.,
Vol. 11, No. 2 (Summer 1986) (symposium); Issues in L. & Med.,
Vol. 1, No. 5 (March 1986) (same); 11 Am. J.L. & Med., No. 1 (1985)
(same); 1984 Ariz. St. L.J. No. 4 (same); R. Weir, Selective Nontreatment of Handicapped Newborns (1984); Rhoden, Treatment
Dilemmas for Imperiled Newborns, 58 So. Cal. L. Rev. 1283
(1985); P. Ramsey, Ethics at the Edges of Life (1978); Robertson,
Involuntary Euthanasia of Defective Newborns, 27 Stan. L. Rev. 213
(1975).

C. Treatment Decisions for Minors and Incompetents

Strunk v. Strunk
445 S.W.2d 145 (Ky. App. 1969)

OSBORNE, JUDGE. The specific question involved upon this appeal is: Does a court of equity have the power to permit a kidney to be removed from an incompetent ward of the state upon petition of his committee, who is also his mother, for the purpose of being transplanted into the body of his brother, who is dying of a fatal kidney disease? We are of the opinion it does.

The facts of the case are as follows: Arthur L. Strunk, 54 years of age, and Ava Strunk, 52 years of age, of Williamstown, Kentucky, are the parents of two sons. Tommy Strunk is 28 years of age, married, an employee of the Penn State Railroad and a part-time student at the University of Cincinnati. Tommy is now suffering from chronic glomerulus nephritis, a fatal kidney disease. He is now being kept alive by frequent treatment on an artificial kidney, a procedure which cannot be continued much longer.

Jerry Strunk is 27 years of age, incompetent, and through proper legal proceedings has been committed to the Frankfort State Hospital and School, which is a state institution maintained for the feebleminded. He has an I.Q. of approximately 35, which corresponds with the mental age of approximately six years. He is further handicapped by a speech defect, which makes it difficult for him to communicate with persons who are not well acquainted with him. When it was determined that Tommy, in order to survive, would have to have a kidney the doctors considered the possibility of using a kidney from a cadaver if and when one became available or one from a live donor if this could be made available. The entire family, his mother, father and a number of collateral relatives were tested. Because of incompatibility of blood type or tissue none were medically acceptable as live donors. As a last resort, Jerry was tested and found to be highly acceptable. This immediately presented the legal problem as to what, if anything, could be done by the family, especially the mother and the father to procure a transplant from Jerry to Tommy. . . .

The Department of Mental Health of this Commonwealth has entered the case as amicus curiae and on the basis of its evaluation of the seriousness of the operation as opposed to the traumatic effect upon Jerry as a result of the loss of Tommy, recommended to the court that Jerry be permitted to undergo the surgery. Its recommendations are as follows: . . .

> Jerry Strunk, a mental defective, has emotions and reactions on a scale comparable to that of a normal person. He identifies with his

II. Termination of Treatment and Related Matters

brother Tom; Tom is his model, his tie with his family. Tom's life is vital to the continuity of Jerry's improvement at Frankfort State Hospital and School. The testimony of the hospital representative reflected the importance to Jerry of his visits with his family and the constant inquiries Jerry made about Tom's coming to see him. Jerry is aware he plays a role in the relief of this tension. We the Department of Mental Health must take all possible steps to prevent the occurrence of any guilt feelings Jerry would have if Tom were to die. . . .

Throughout the legal proceedings, Jerry has been represented by a guardian ad litem, who has continually questioned the power of the state to authorize the removal of an organ from the body of an incompetent who is a ward of the state. We are fully cognizant of the fact that the question before us is unique. Insofar as we have been able to learn, no similar set of facts has come before the highest court of any of the states of this nation or the federal courts. The English courts have apparently taken a broad view of the inherent power of the equity courts with regard to incompetents. Ex parte Whitebread (1816), 2 Mer. 99; 35 E.R. 878, L.C. holds that courts of equity have the inherent power to make provisions for a needy brother out of the estate of an incompetent. This was first followed in this country in New York, In the Matter of Willoughby, a Lunatic, 11 Paige 257 (N.Y. 1844). The inherent rule in these cases is that the chancellor has the power to deal with the estate of the incompetent in the same manner as the incompetent would if he had his faculties. This rule has been extended to cover not only matters of property but also to cover the personal affairs of the incompetent. . . .

The right to act for the incompetent in all cases has become recognized in this country as the doctrine of substituted judgment and is broad enough not only to cover property but also to cover all matters touching on the well-being of the ward. The doctrine has been recognized in American courts since 1844.

"The 'doctrine of substituted judgment,' which apparently found its first expression in the leading English case of Ex parte Whitebread (1816) 2 Mer. 99, 35 Eng. Reprint 878 (Ch.), supra §3(a), was amplified In re Earl of Carysfort (1840) Craig & Ph. 76, 41 Eng. Reprint 418, where the principle was made to apply to one who was not next of kin of the lunatic but a servant of his who was obliged to retire from his service by reason of age and infirmity. The Lord Chancellor permitted the allowance of an annuity out of the income of the estate of the lunatic earl as a retiring pension to the latter's aged personal servant, although no supporting evidence could be found, the court being 'satisfied that the Earl of Carysfort would have approved if he had been capable of acting himself.'" Annot., 24 A.L.R.3d 863 (1969). . . .

The medical practice of transferring tissue from one part of the human body to another (autografting) and from one human being to another (homografting) is rapidly becoming a common clinical practice. . . . It is recognized by all legal and medical authorities that several legal problems can arise as a result of the operative techniques of the transplant procedure. Curran, A Problem of Consent: Kidney Transplantation in Minors, 34 N.Y. University Law Review 891 (1959).

The renal transplant is becoming the most common of the organ transplants. This is because the normal body has two functioning kidneys, one of which it can reasonably do without, thereby making it possible for one person to donate a kidney to another. Testimony in this record shows that there have been over 2500 kidney transplants performed in the United States up to this date. The process can be effected under present techniques with minimal danger to both the donor and the donee. Doctors Hamburger and Crosneir describe the risk to the donor as follows:

> This discussion is limited to renal transplantation, since it is inconceivable that any vital organ other than the kidney might ever be removed from a healthy living donor for transplantation purposes. The immediate operative risk of unilateral nephrectomy in a healthy subject has been calculated as approximately 0.05 per cent. . . . This is an increase in risk equal to that incurred by driving a car for 16 miles every working day (Merrill, 1964). The risks incurred by the donor are therefore very limited, but they are a reality, even if, until now, there have been no reports of complications endangering the life of a donor anywhere in the world. . . .

The circuit court having found that the operative procedures in this instance are to the best interest of Jerry Strunk and this finding having been based upon substantial evidence, we are of the opinion the judgment should be affirmed. We do not deem it significant that this case reached the circuit court by way of appeal as opposed to a direct proceeding in that court.

Judgment affirmed.

HILL, C.J., MILLIKEN and REED, JJ., concur.

NEIKIRK, PALMORE and STEINFELD, JJ., dissent.

STEINFELD, JUDGE (dissenting). Apparently because of my indelible recollection of a government which, to the everlasting shame of its citizens, embarked on a program of genocide and experimentation with human bodies I have been more troubled in reaching a decision in this case than in any other. My sympathies and emotions are torn between a compassion to aid an ailing young man and a duty to fully protect unfortunate members of society.

The opinion of the majority is predicated upon the authority of an equity court to speak for one who cannot speak for himself. However, . . . the authority and duty have been to protect and maintain the ward, to secure that to which he is entitled and preserve that which he has. Ramsey's Ex'r v. Ramsey, 243 Ky. 202, 47 S.W.2d 1059 (1932); Aaronson v. State of New York, 34 Misc. 2d 827, 229 N.Y.S.2d 550, 557 (1962) and Young v. State, 32 Misc. 2d 965, 225 N.Y.S.2d 549 (1962). The wishes of the members of the family or the desires of the guardian to be helpful to the apparent objects of the ward's bounty have not been a criterion. "A curator or guardian cannot dispose of his ward's property by donation, even though authorized to do so by the court on advice of a family meeting, unless a gift by the guardian is authorized by statute." 44 C.J.S. Insane Persons §81, p. 191. . . .

[This] result was reached in In re Bourgeois, 144 La. 501, 80 So. 673 (1919), in which the husband of an incompetent wife sought to change the beneficiary of her insurance policy so that her children would receive the proceeds. Grady v. Dashiell, 24 Wash. 2d 272, 163 P.2d 922 (1945), stands for the proposition that a loan to the ward's adult insolvent son made at a time when it was thought that the ward was incurably insane constituted an improper depletion of the ward's estate.

The majority opinion is predicated upon the finding of the circuit court that there will be psychological benefits to the ward but points out that the incompetent has the mentality of a six-year-old child. It is common knowledge beyond dispute that the loss of a close relative or a friend to a six-year-old child is not of major impact. Opinions concerning psychological trauma are at best most nebulous. Furthermore, there are no guarantees that the transplant will become a surgical success, it being well known that body rejection of transplanted organs is frequent. The life of the incompetent is not in danger, but the surgical procedure advocated creates some peril.

It is written in Prince v. Massachusetts, 321 U.S. 158, 64 S. Ct. 438, 88 L. Ed. 645 (1944), that "Parents may be free to become martyrs themselves. But it does not follow they are free, in identical circumstances, to make martyrs of their children before they have reached the age of full and legal discretion when they can make that choice for themselves." The ability to fully understand and consent is a prerequisite to the donation of a part of the human body. Cf. Bonner v. Moran, 75 U.S. App. D.C. 156, 126 F.2d 121, 139 A.L.R. 1366 (1941), in which a fifteen-year-old infant's consent to removal of a skin patch for the benefit of another was held legally ineffective.

Unquestionably the attitudes and attempts of the committee and members of the family of the two young men whose critical problems now confront us are commendable, natural and beyond reproach. However, they refer us to nothing indicating that they are privileged to authorize the removal of one of the kidneys of the incompetent for the purpose of donation, and they cite no statutory or other authority vesting such right in the courts. The proof shows that less compatible donors are available and that the kidney of a cadaver could be used, although the odds of operational success are not as great in such case as they would be with the fully compatible donor brother.

I am unwilling to hold that the gates should be open to permit the removal of an organ from an incompetent for transplant, at least until such time as it is conclusively demonstrated that it will be of significant benefit to the incompetent. The evidence here does not rise to that pinnacle. To hold that . . . guardians or courts have such awesome power even in the persuasive case before us, could establish legal precedent, the dire result of which we cannot fathom. Regretfully I must say no.

NEIKIRK and PALMORE, JJ., join with me in this dissent.

NOTES

The Respective Authority of Parents and Children

1. *Strunk* raises many important issues. We use it here as an opportunity to generalize the previous discussions of surrogate treatment decisions and apply them to parental authority to make treatment decisions generally for their children. At the outset, we encounter a fundamental uncertainty in the law of medical consent: whether, and under what conditions, a minor has the capacity to consent to medical care for himself. Contract law is quite clear on capacity: it adheres to a prophylactic, bright-line rule that all minors are incompetent to contract. Tort law maintains at least a *presumption* that "most children, even in adolescence, simply are not able to make sound judgments concerning . . . their need for medical treatment," Parham v. J.R., 442 U.S. 584), except in a variety of specialized contexts relating to contraception, contagious diseases, venereal disease, and alcohol and drug abuse where statutes specifically grant minors the right to consent for themselves. Thus, courts sometimes observe that "the general rule is that the consent of the parent is necessary for an operation on a child." Bonner v. Moran, 126 F.2d 121, 122 (D.C. Cir. 1941). It is another question, though, whether tort law goes further and makes this presumption of incapacity absolute, despite a showing that a particular minor is in fact "mature" and therefore fully appreciates the nature and consequences of a treatment decision. (Can you see why the law might not want to do so? Recall that the principal exception to contractual incapacity is for so-called "necessaries" such as food, clothing, and shelter.)

According to "emancipated minor statutes" that exist in most states, parental consent to treatment decisions by minors is not re-

II. Termination of Treatment and Related Matters

quired for minors who are married, have children, or are financially self-supporting and living away from home. It is more controversial whether a related, but distinct, exception to the requirement of parental consent applies to mature minors generally. A few states recognize a "mature minor" doctrine that allows minors to make their own treatment decisions regardless of whether they fit one of the defined categories of emancipation. Also, the U.S. Supreme Court presently (but for how long?) recognizes a constitutional right for mature minors to make abortion decisions without parental approval. However, the mature minor doctrine is much less widely acknowledged outside the abortion context. Only a few states have adopted a "mature minor" statute, Ark. Stat. Ann. §82-363, Miss. Code Ann. §41-41-3(h), or lowered the age of consent below 18, Ala. Code §22-8-4 (14 years); Or. Rev. Stat. §109.640 (15 years).

The context in which the mature minor doctrine has arisen most frequently is as a doctor's defense to a parent's battery suit brought on behalf of a treated minor. These few decisions rule with near unanimity that mature minors are capable of giving valid consent to medical treatment. Younts v. St. Francis Hosp., 469 P.2d 330 (Kan. 1970); Bach v. Long Island Jewish Hosp., 267 N.Y.S.2d 289 (1966). In this respect, at least, tort law is more lenient than contract. It might even be accurate to assert as a general proposition that minors suffer from no legal disability at all in the medical arena, only a heightened proof standard. See Restatement (2d) of Torts §892 A, comment b; National Assoc. of Children's Hospitals, Pediatric Bill of Rights ("Any person, regardless of age, who is of sufficient intelligence to appreciate the nature and the consequences of [beneficial] medical care . . . may effectively consent to such medical care"). The law is not clearer on this point because conflict between child and parent seldom arises.

An important recent decision that cogently explains this area of law is In re. E. G., 549 N.E. 2d 322 (Ill. 1989). This case concerned a 17-year-old woman with leukemia who refused blood transfusions on religious grounds. Avoiding the constitutional dimensions of this question, the court enforced her decision based on the common law right of mature minors to make their own treatment decisions:

> Although the age of majority in Illinois is 18, that age is not an impenetrable barrier that magically precludes a minor from possessing and exercising certain rights normally associated with adulthood. Numerous exceptions are found in this jurisdiction and others which treat minors as adults under specific circumstances. . . . [By statute], a minor 12 years or older may seek medical attention on her own if she believes she has venereal disease or is an alcoholic or drug addict. Similarly, an individual under 18 who is married or pregnant may validly consent to treatment. . . . Also, a minor 16 or older may be declared eman-

cipated under the Emancipation of Mature Minors Act and thereby control his or her own health care decisions. . . .

[T]he mature minor doctrine is not a recent development in the law: "[R]ecognition that minors achieve varying degrees of maturity and responsibility has been part of the common law for well over a century." [Quoting Cardwell v. Bechtol, 724 S.W.2d 739 (Tenn. 1987).]

See generally Holder, Legal Issues in Pediatrics and Adolescent Medicine (1985); Annot., Physician's Treatment of Child Without Parental Consent, 67 A.L.R. 4th (1989); Scherer & Reppucci, Adolescents' Capacities to Provide Voluntary Informed Consent, 12 L. & Hum. Behav. 123 (1988); Holder, Minors' Rights to Consent to Medical Care, 257 J.A.M.A. 3400 (1987); Note, Choosing For Children: Adjudicating Medical Care Disputes Between Parents and the State, 58 N.Y.U.L. Rev. 157 (1983); Ewald, Medical Decision Making for Children: An Analysis of Competing Interests, 25 St. Louis L.J. 689 (1982); Note, Judicial Limitations on Parental Autonomy in Medical Treatment of Minors, 59 Neb. L. Rev. 1093 (1980); Brown & Truitt, The Right of Minors to Medical Treatment, 28 DePaul L. Rev. 289 (Winter 1979); Goldstein, Medical Care for the Child at Risk: State Supervention of Parental Autonomy, 86 Yale L. J. 645 (1977); Bennett, Allocation of Child Medical Care Decision Making Authority: A Suggested Interest Analysis, 62 Va. L. Rev. 285 (1976); Note, The Minor's Right to Consent to Medical Treatment, 48 S. Cal. L. Rev. 1417 (1975); Wilkins, Children's Rights: Removing the Parental Consent Barrier, 1975 Ariz. St. L.J. 31; Wadlington, Minors and Health Care: The Age of Consent, 11 Osgoode Hall L.J. 115 (1973).

2. Although the authority of parents to make treatment decisions is much clearer, the *source* of the law for parental authority is surprisingly obscure: few states have express statutes. Likewise, when one spouse is incapacitated, there is little doubt that the law allows the other spouse to act as the substitute decisionmaker, but few states have explicitly codified this authority. "However, the practice is universal and, given the large number of patients who are mentally incapacitated at some point during their hospitalization, a necessity." M. MacDonald, K. Meyer & B. Essig, Health Care Law 18.05[3][a] (1987). These authors go on to explain:

[T]he legal risks of relying on family consent are negligible if the following circumstances are present, as they are in the majority of cases involving incompetent patients: (1) the decision is in favor of treatment that is medically indicated and is the treatment recommended by the patient's physician; (2) the treatment does not involve the patient's reproductive capacity; (3) no family member is objecting to the decision, and (4) the patient is not objecting. Id.

3. In Parham v. J.R., 442 U.S. 584 (1978), the Supreme Court, stating that "parents cannot always have absolute and unreviewable discretion to decide whether to have a child institutionalized," imposed modest restrictions on the authority of parents to consent to the involuntary hospitalization of their minor children for psychiatric treatment. The Court held that parental decisions to institutionalize their children must be independently reviewed by a medical professional through an informal, nonadversarial proceeding.

4. As developed in the section on informed consent, minors can be treated without parental consent in emergency situations where a delay in obtaining consent would seriously threaten the patient's health.

5. Cases dealing with the power to consent to medical treatment of minors often fail to differentiate between the *sufficiency* and the *necessity* for parental consent. For example, assume a case of an emancipated minor with the power to consent for herself. Does this power override or merely supplement that of the parents? The difference becomes critical if the parents and the children disagree over the need for treatment, as might occur, for example, in the case of a teenager who is reluctant to receive the dental braces her parents insist she needs. The law currently does not deal with this question very clearly. According to one authority, "the answer probably depends on both the nature of the treatment — how invasive it is, how necessary, and the nature of any long term effects it may have on the child — and on the reasons for the child's objection. Lifesaving procedures clearly can be forced, but elective procedures are more problematic." M. MacDonald et al., supra at 18.06[4].

Another unsettled area, one that will begin to take on increasing importance as divorced parents assume joint custody of their children, is whose decision controls in a case where the *parents* disagree over a treatment decision. See Durfee v. Durfee, 87 N.Y.S.2d 275 (1949) (parent with custody decides).

6. Having established parental authority to make treatment decisions for minors generally, the focus then shifts to whether particular treatment decisions are legitimate. For instance, may Jehovah's Witnesses refuse blood transfusions for their children? The courts consistently have answered "no," since, as *Strunk* reveals, parents must decide with their children's, not their own, best interests in mind. In the seminal decision, the Supreme Court held that parents are not free to make martyrs of their children "before they reach the age of full and legal discretion when they can make that choice for themselves." Prince v. Massachusetts (1944), 321 U.S. 158, 170. In the most recent decision of this sort, Walker v. Superior Court, 253 Cal. Rptr. 1 (Cal. 1989), the court allowed the prosecution of Christian Scientist parents for causing the death of their 4 year old daughter

with meningitis. See also Custody of a Minor, 379 N.E.2d 1053 (Mass. 1978), 393 N.E.2d 836 (Mass. 1979) (factors to consider include whether condition is life-threatening and whether the proposed treatment exposes the minor to great risk); In re Phillip B. (1979), 92 Cal. App. 3d 796, 156 Cal. Rptr. 48 (1979) (similar). But see In the Matter of Hofbauer (1979), 419 N.Y.S.2d 936 (1979) (parents allowed to opt for laetrile over chemotherapy for leukemia patient under supervision of a physician).

In contrast, courts typically have shown great reluctance to intervene where the minor's condition is not life threatening. See, e.g., Weber v. Stony Brook Hosp., 469 N.Y.S.2d 63 (1983); In the Interest of D.L.E., 614 P.2d 873 (Colo. 1980); In re Seiferth, 309 N.Y. 80, 127 N.E.2d 820 (1955) (court would not order surgery for 14 year old boy's cleft palate and harelip over religious objections of boy and father, because condition was not life-threatening and success of the procedure demanded the boy's cooperation with physicians and speech therapists); In re Green, 292 A.2d 387 (Pa. 1972). See generally Anno., 52 A.L.R.3d 1118 (1973).

7. *Strunk* has been criticized for confusing the substituted judgment test with the best interests test. The distinction these critics are attempting to draw is between (1) deciding in a purely hypothetical, abstract mode what values and preferences a particular incompetent patient might express if competent, and (2) looking at concrete, objective evidence that indicates what course of action will actually be the most beneficial for that patient. The problem with the first test is that it makes no sense in the case of a person who never has and never will possess a set of values on which to act; therefore, it tends to enforce the guardian's set of values by default.

Although the *Strunk* court framed its analysis in terms of substituted judgment, is it possible to square its decision with a best interests standard? A subsequent case that also authorized an incompetent's donation of a kidney to a sibling provides the following useful explanation:

> The [substituted judgment] doctrine requires that the court "substitute itself as nearly as may be for the incompetent and to act upon the same motives and considerations as would have moved" the incompetent. . . . [It] has been adopted in some jurisdictions and rejected in others. In Texas it has been held that the guardian of the estate of an incompetent lacks the power to make a gift from the estate of the ward, even though the evidence establishes that the ward, if competent, would have made such a gift. . . . It is clear [though] in transplant cases that courts, whether they use the term "substituted judgment" or not, will consider the benefits to the donor as a basis for permitting an incompetent to donate an organ. Although in *Strunk* the Kentucky Court discussed the substituted judgment doctrine in some detail, the

conclusion of the majority there was based on the benefits that the incompetent donor would derive, rather than on the theory that the incompetent would have consented to the transplant if he were competent. We adopt this approach.

Little v. Little, 576 S.W.2d 493 (Tex. App. 1979). See also In re Doe, 481 N.Y.S.2d 932 (App. Div. 1981) (authorizing bone marrow donation to brother of incompetent). But see Lausier v. Pescinski, 226 N.W.2d 180 (Wis. 1975) (refusing donation by retardate); In re Richardson, 284 So. 2d 185 (La. App. 1973) (same). See generally, Robertson, Organ Donations by Incompetents and the Substituted Judgment Doctrine 76 Colum. L. Rev. 48 (1976); 1004 supra.

8. Prior to *Strunk,* the earliest transplant donation cases were single-justice opinions in declaratory judgment actions before the Massachusetts Supreme Judicial Court. These cases were brought to general attention and analyzed in Curran, A Problem of Consent: Kidney Transplantation in Minors, 34 N.Y.U.L. Rev. 891 (1959). The court in each case had allowed the donation to save the life of an identical twin brother. Where the judge thought the child mature enough, he questioned the donor child personally in his chambers and assured himself that the child understood and consented to the procedure. The donations were allowed essentially on the parents' consent, however, and based on testimony that the donor child would "benefit" from the donation in saving or prolonging the life of his very close twin sibling. The Curran paper questioned the validity of the benefit criteria. Later one-justice cases in Massachusetts seem to relieve themselves of both the benefit and the substituted judgment requirements, especially in the more recent bone-marrow transplant requests. For an excellent examination of practices, see Baron, Botsford & Cole, Live Organ and Tissue Transplants from Minor Donors in Massachusetts, 55 B.U.L. Rev. 159 (1975).

Do you think the *Strunk* rationale can be extended to validate the following?

> A baby girl was born Tuesday to a couple who conceived the child to serve as a bone marrow donor for their cancer-stricken [older] daughter . . . as a last resort to save [her] life. . . . The chance that the transplant will cure [the daughter] is reported to be 70 to 80 percent. . . . The baby faces little risk, Dr. Konrad said. The procedure requires the infant to be put under general anesthesia to block pain while a needle is inserted, usually twice, into the hip bone to remove the marrow.

N.Y. Times, April 7, 1990, at 7.

9. "Despite widespread acceptance in the United States, few other nations allow routine use of minors or mentally incompetent persons as organ donors. Judicial decisions of United States courts seem to

be without parallel in any other country. . . . By legislation, Mexico and British Columbia prohibit organ donation by minors and incompetent persons. Restriction on such donations have been enacted by France and Australia. The Council of Europe has recommended that organ donation from wards be forbidden except when the donor, having capacity of understanding, has given consent." R. Adams, Live Organ Donors and Informed Consent, 8 J. Leg. Med. 555, 572 (1987).

D. The Frontiers of Death and Dying

Fletcher, Indicators of Humanhood: A Tentative Profile of Man*
2 Hastings Cent. Rep. no. 5, 1 (1972)

Mark Twain complained that people are always talking about the weather but they never do anything about it. The same is true of the humanhood agenda. In biomedical ethics writers constantly say that we need to explicate humanness or humaneness, what it means to be a truly human being, but they never follow their admission of the need with an actual inventory or profile, no matter how tentatively offered. Yet this is what must be done, or at least attempted.

Synthetic concepts such as *human* and *man* and *person* require operational terms, spelling out the which and what and when. Only in that way can we get down to cases — to normative decisions. There are always some people who prefer to be visceral and affective in their moral choices, with no desire to have any rationale for what they do. But *ethics* is precisely the business of rational, critical reflection (encephalic and not merely visceral) about the problems of the moral agent — in biology and medicine as much as in law, government, education or anything else.

To that end, then, for the purposes of biomedical ethics, I am suggesting a "profile of man" in concrete and discrete terms. As only one man's reflection on man, it will no doubt invite adding and subtracting by others, but this is the road to be followed if we mean business. As a dog is said to "worry" a bone, let me worry out loud and on paper, hoping for some agreement and, at the least, consideration. There is space only to itemize it, not to enlarge upon it, but I have fifteen positive propositions. . . . Let me set them out, in no

---

* This paper by Dr. Joseph Fletcher, Professor of Medical Ethics, University of Virginia School of Medicine, is reprinted with the permission of the Institute of Society, Ethics, and the Life Sciences, publishers of the Hastings Center Report and the author. Copyright © 1972 by the Institute of Society, Ethics, and the Life Sciences.

rank order at all, and as hardly more than a list of criteria or indicators, by simple title.

Positive Human Criteria

Minimal intelligence. Any individual of the species *homo sapiens* who falls below the I.Q. 40-mark in a standard Stanford-Binet test, amplified if you like by other tests, is questionably a person; below the 20-mark, not a person. *Homo* is indeed *sapiens,* in order to be *homo.* The *ratio,* in another turn of speech, is what makes a person of the *vita.* Mere biological life, before minimal intelligence is achieved or after it is lost irretrievably, is without personal status. This has bearing, obviously, on decision making in gynecology, obstetrics and pediatrics, as well as in general surgery and medicine.

Self-awareness. Self-consciousness, as we know, is a quality we watch developing in a baby; we watch it with fascination and glee. Its essential role in personality development is a basic datum of psychology. Its existence or function in animals at or below the primate level is debatable; it is clearly absent in the lower vertebrates, as well as in the nonvertebrates. In psychotherapy non-self-awareness is pathological; in medicine, unconsciousness when it is incorrigible at once poses quality-of-life judgments — for example, in neurosurgical cases of irreversible damage to the brain cortex.

Self-control. If an individual is not only not controllable by others (unless by force) but not controllable by the individual himself or herself, a low level of life is reached about on a par with a paramecium. If the condition cannot be rectified medically, so that means-ends behavior is out of the question, the individual is not a person — not ethically, and certainly not in the eyes of the law — just as a fetus is not legally a person.

A sense of time. Time consciousness. By this is meant clock time or *chronos,* not timeliness or *kairos,* i.e., not the "fulness of time" or the pregnant moment (remember Paul Tillich?). A sense, that is, of the passage of time. A colleague of mine at the University of Virginia, Dr. Thomas Hunter, remarked recently, "Life is the allocation of time." We can disagree legitimately about how relatively important this indicator is, but it is hard to understand why anybody would minimize it or eliminate it as a trait of humanness.

A sense of futurity. How "truly human" is any man who cannot realize there is a time yet to come as well as the present? Subhuman animals do not look forward in time; they live only on what we might call visceral strivings, appetites. Philosophical anthropologies (one recalls William Temple's, for instance) commonly emphasize *purposiveness* as a key to humanness. Chesterton once remarked that we would never ask a puppy what manner of dog it wanted to be when it grows up. The assertion here is that men are typically teleological, although certainly not eschatological.

A sense of the past. Memory. Unlike other animals, men as a species have reached a unique level of neurologic development, particularly the cerebrum and especially its neo-cortex. They are linked to the past by conscious recall — not only, as with subhuman animals, by conditioning and the reactivation of emotions (reactivated, that is, externally rather than autonomously). It is this trait, in particular, that makes man, alone among all species, a cultural instead of an instinctive creature. An existentialist focus on "nowness" truncates the nature of man.

The capability to relate to others. Inter-personal relationships, of the sexual-romantic and friendship kind, are of the greatest importance for the fullness of what we idealize as being truly personal. (Medical piety in the past has always held its professional ethics to be only a one-to-one, physician-patient obligation.) However, there are also the more diffuse and comprehensive social relations of our vocational, economic and political life. Aristotle's characterization of man as a social animal, *zoon politikon,* must surely figure prominently in the inventory. It is true that even insects live in social systems, but the cohesion of all subhuman societies is based on instinct. Man's society is based on culture — that is, on a conscious knowledge of the system and on the exercise in some real measure of either consent or opposition.

Concern for others. Some people may be skeptical about our capacity to care about others (what in Christian ethics is often distinguished from romance and friendship as "neighbor love" or "neighbor concern"). The extent to which this capacity is actually in play is debatable. But whether concern for others is disinterested or inspired by enlightened self-interest it seems plain that a conscious extra-ego orientation is a trait of the species; the absence of this ambience is a clinical indication of psychopathology.

Communication. Utter alienation or disconnection from others, if it is irreparable, is de-humanization. This is not so much a matter of not being disposed to receive and send "messages" as of the inability to do so. This criterion comes into question in patients who cannot hear, speak, feel or see others; it may come about as a result of mental or physical trauma, infection, genetic or congenital disorder, or from psychological causes. Completely and finally *isolated* individuals are subpersonal. The problem is perhaps most familiar in terminal illnesses and the clinical decision-making required.

Control of existence. It is of the nature of man that he is not helplessly subject to the blind workings of physical or physiological nature. He has only finite knowledge, freedom, and initiative, but what he has of it is real and effective. Invincible ignorance and total helplessness are the antithesis of humanness, and to the degree that a man lacks control he is not responsible, and to be irresponsible is to be subpersonal. This item in the agenda applies directly, for example, in psychiatric medicine, especially to severe cases of toxic and degenerative psychosis.

Curiosity. To be without affect, sunk in anomie, is to be not a person. Indifference is inhuman. Man is a learner and a knower as well as a tool maker and user. This raises a question, therefore, about demands to stop some kinds of biomedical inquiry. For example, an A.M.A. committee recently called a halt on *in vitro* reproduction and embryo transplants on the ground that they are dangerous. But dangerous ignorance is more dangerous than dangerous knowledge. It is dehumanizing to impose a moratorium on research. No doubt this issue arises, or will arise, in many other phases of medical education and practice.

Change and changeability. To the extent that an individual is unchangeable or opposed to change he denies the creativity of personal beings. It means not only the fact of biological and physiological change, which goes on as a condition of life, but the capacity and disposition for changing one's mind and conduct as well. Biologically, human beings are developmental: birth, life, health, and death are processes, not events, and are to be understood epigenetically, not episodically. All human existence is on a continuum, a matter of becoming. In this perspective, are we to regard potentials *als ob,* as if they were actual? I think not. The question arises prominently in abortion ethics.

Balance of rationality and feeling. To be "truly human," to be a wholesome *person,* one cannot be either Apollonian or Dionysian. As human beings we are not "coldly" rational or cerebral, nor are we merely creatures of feeling and intuition. It is a matter of being both, in different combinations from one individual to another. To be one rather than the other is to distort the *humanum.*

Idiosyncrasy. The human being is idiomorphous, a distinctive individual. As Helmut Schoeck has shown, even the function of envy in human behavior is entirely consistent with idiosyncrasy. To be a person is to have an identity, to be recognizable and callable by name. It is this criterion which lies behind the fear that to replicate individuals by so-called "cloning" would be to make "carbon copies" of the parent source and thus dehumanize the clone by denying it its individuality. One or two writers have even spoken of a "right" to a "unique genotype," and while such talk is ethically and scientifically questionable it nonetheless reflects a legitimate notion of something essential to an authentic person.

Neo-cortical function. In a way, this is the cardinal indicator, the one all the others are hinged upon. Before cerebration is in play, or with its end, in the absence of the synthesizing function of the cerebral cortex, the *person* is non-existent. Such individuals are objects but not subjects. This is so no matter how many other spontaneous or artificially supported functions persist in the heart, lungs, neurologic and vascular systems. Such non-cerebral processes are not personal. Like the Harvard Medical School's *ad hoc* committee report on "brain death" the recent Kansas statute on defining death requires the absence of *brain* function. So do the guidelines recently adopted by the Italian Council of Ministers. But what is definitive in determining death is the loss of cerebration, not just of any or all brain function. Personal reality depends on cerebration and to be dead "humanly" speaking is to be ex-cerebral, no matter how long the *body* remains alive.

NOTES

Higher Brain Death, Infanticide, and Animal Rights

1. Although full development of Fletcher's analysis is beyond the scope of this book, his profile of human characteristics is included here to evoke two arguments that have been made for extending the law past its present bounds. First, several respected legal and ethical authorities have argued for a "higher brain death" standard that would define death as the permanent loss of consciousness, even though spontaneous breathing and circulation persist. In other words, someone like Karen Ann Quinlan would be considered dead. The argument is made along the lines developed by Fletcher that "a person does not function as a whole unless some higher brain function is present." Veatch, Correspondence, 12 Hastings Cent. Rep., no. 5, at 45 (Oct. 1982). See K. Gervais, Redefining Death (1987); Quinn, The Capacity for Interpersonal Relationships as a Standard for Decisionmaking, 76 Cal. L. Rev. 897 (1988); Smith, Legal Recognition of Neocortical Death, 71 Cornell L. Rev. 850 (1986); Veatch, The Definition of Death: Ethical, Philosophical and Policy Confusion, 315 Ann. N.Y. Acad. Sci. 307 (1978); R. Veatch, Death, Dying and The Biological Revolution (1976).

It might be observed in response that, taking the metaphor literally, even vegetables are alive; in other words, conceding that people in a persistent vegetative state don't fit our concept of a person, they still aren't dead. See Culver & Gert, "The Definition and Criterion of Death," in Philosophy in Medicine (1982). Maybe they've transformed into animals. Stretching this line of reasoning as far as it can go (and beyond), observe that even animals have some rights. See T. Regan, The Case for Animal Rights to Life (1983);

Goodkin, The Evolution of Animal Rights, 18 Colum. Hum. Rgts. L. Rev. 259 (1987); Animals in Research (symposium), J. Med. & Philo. (May 1988).

2. The second extension of Fletcher's analysis is to argue in favor of infanticide, as some have done. E.g., H. Kuhse & P. Singer, Should the Baby Live? The Problem of Handicapped Infants (1985); M. Tooley, Abortion and Infanticide (1983). Again, the argument is that infants during their first few weeks after birth lack the cognitive integration and awareness that characterize humanhood. "Singer defines a person as 'a rational and self-conscious being.' Chimpanzees, whales, dolphins, dogs and cats can make the personhood cut, according to Singer, while newborn infants and retarded humans do not even make the travelling squad." Rice supra, 4 J. Contemp. Health L. & Pol. at 20. However, infants, unlike persistent vegetative patients, have at least the *potential* to become fully human in the near future. But the same is true of fetuses, and, as we will see shortly, the law does not (presently) consider a fetus to be a person.

3. As a review problem, consider an emerging controversy that cuts across a remarkable number of issues raised in this chapter: whether anencephalic newborns should be used as organ donors. Several thousand babies are born each year with a profound birth defect known as anencephaly — missing most of the brain. Many are born alive in the sense that their brain stem is functioning and they can breathe and cry spontaneously for a few days or weeks. The normal medical course is to provide only nutritional and comfort care until all functioning ceases. The result, though, is that possibly salvageable organs deteriorate from the interruptions in respiration during the natural process of dying.

To facilitate harvesting these infants' organs, some hospitals have made efforts, with the parents' approval, to place anencephalic newborns on full life-support until complete brain death occurs, somewhat prolonging the dying process. For instance, Loma Linda University Medical Center, renowned for transplant procedures on children (it is the location of the ill-fated "Baby Fae" baboon heart transplant), instituted a protocol that allowed respirator support to continue for one week. BioLaw p. U:763 (1988) (copy of protocol).

The ethical bind is this: can parents authorize life-support that provides no benefit to their dying infants in order to assist potential organ recipients? The arguments are compelling on both sides. In favor of life-support are the critical shortage of organs for small children and the desperate compulsion of the disheartened parents to allow some good to come from their tragic pregnancy. In one reported case, the parents knowingly chose to carry an anencephalic fetus to term rather than abort, so that the organs could be made available for use by others. New York Times, Dec. 14, 1987, at 18.

On the other hand, one can hardly argue that it is in the infant's best interests to depart from normal clinical routine and prolong the dying process. Also, it is unclear whether organ donations from these infants are actually very beneficial. Loma Linda Hospital suspended its protocol after sustaining six babies without obtaining any usable major organs. New York Times, April 13, 1988, at 4.

One possible resolution of the controversy would be to amend the law to allow immediate organ harvesting at the time of birth. Such a proposal was rejected by the California legislature, though, because it would be tantamount to recognizing a higher-brain definition of death. See generally Moore, Anencephalic Infants as Sources of Transplantable Organs, 30 Jurimetrics 189 (1990); Symposium, Harvesting Cells, Tissues, and Organs from Fetuses and Anencephalic Newborns, 14 J. Med. & Philo. (Feb. 1989); Shewmon, et al., The Use of Anencephalic Infants as Organ Sources: A Critique, 261 J.A.M.A. 1773 (1989); Annas, Anencephalic Newborns as Organ Donors: A Critique, 259 J.A.M.A. 2284 (1988); Anacephalic Infants: A Source of Controversy, 18 Hastings Cent. Rep., no. 5, at 5 (Oct/Nov 1988); Caplan, Should Fetuses or Infants be Utilized as Organ Donors?, 1 Bioethics 119 (1987).

Fletcher, The Courts and Euthanasia*
15 L. Med. & Health Care 223 (1988)

Most of us, I think, supposed that the debate over euthanasia (doing something to end a life that could otherwise continue) had been pretty well settled. For a long time a minority favored it and a majority opposed it — at least in principle, although not always in practice. Recent court decisions, however, have thrown the whole question open again, while public opinion polls reflect a marked increase in tolerance, if not positive approval.[1] What follows is a lay discussion of the issue — not legally or medically professional but still, it is hoped, acceptable intellectually. . . .

In 1954 I published a full-dress defense of what I, groping for

---

* Copyright © 1988. Reprinted with permission, American Society of Law and Medicine, Boston, Massachusetts.

1. About three-quarters of the respondents in recent Gallup and other polls conducted in the U.S., Britain, Holland, France, and Scandinavia favor active euthanasia for irreversibly comatose patients, even when death is not imminent. After the *Conroy* case in New Jersey (1985), a Gallup poll found that 81 percent of Americans approved of stopping treatment so that the patient could die. There was no significant difference between Catholics (77 percent) and Protestants (80 percent). A Roper poll found 52 percent in favor of doctors being allowed by law to end a patient's life if the patient requests it.

the right language, called "voluntary medical euthanasia."[2] It aroused a widespread cry of astonishment, anger, and condemnation from lawyers, physicians, and clergymen. Their feeling (only *feeling* for the most part, not reflection) was that we are morally obliged to do whatever we can to keep all patients alive as long as we can. Yet, amazingly, within a quarter of a century the climate of opinion has come around, if not by 180 degrees then at least by something close to it. . . . [Courts now routinely] tolerate doing something ("pulling the plug") to end the life of a patient if and when death was imminent anyway and the patient preferred to die at once rather than endure further miseries.[4]

For this modulated ideology a new name was coined: "passive euthanasia." In the 1970s and early 1980s it was highly effective. . . . A new idea [took] shape, that it is acceptable to stop treatment and thus let patients die sooner than they otherwise would, if, but only if, it was medically determined that death was near at hand — in short, if the patient was in fact going to die anyway.

Voluntary, active euthanasia was something else. To do something, whether by acts of omission or commission, to end a life that could otherwise continue, with or without medical support, when the patient was not going to die in any case, was generally held to be both immoral and unlawful. The fact that a patient, to say nothing of a proxy, was requesting it — that it was voluntary — was then thought to be irrelevant and immaterial.

Those who analyzed the reasons for this view boiled it down to two things forbidden in conventional wisdom: that such a death was suicide, which as such was condemned; and that it was euthanasia or, in a common pejorative phrase, mercy killing, also as such condemned.

My purpose here is to show that this opposition to rational elective dying is logically and ethically untenable. To choose to die when life could with medical support be continued is properly called suicide, and to help such a patient to end his or her life is indeed euthanasia, yet ethically defensible. Moreover, court discussions on these cases are, whether intentionally or not, equivocal and artful.

Suicide and Euthanasia

We might start with an actual case for the sake of clinical and legal realism. The essence of the question before the court in Patricia Brophy v. New England Sinai Hospital was whether medical treatment

---

2. Fletcher J, Morals and medicine, Princeton: Princeton University Press, 1954, esp. pp. 172-210.

4. For a full account historically, see Humphry D, Wickett A, The right to die: Understanding euthanasia, New York: Harper and Row, 1986.

could be stopped when a patient is permanently impaired neurologically but not terminally ill. . . . In its reasoning the Massachusetts court flatly denied that a request by the patient to stop treatment was suicide. The majority of the justices, without explaining their reasoning in terms of moral or legal philosophy (jurisprudence), simply cited precedents in other court decisions. All of these decisions had denied that removing artificial sustenance or respiration at the patient's request was either suicide or assisting suicide (i.e., euthanasia). In *Bouvia*, by the way, cited by the *Brophy* court, the patient was entirely sapient, was not dependent on artificial support systems, and had a prospect of fifteen to twenty years of life still to come. . . .

These court decisions and others (a total of over twenty in more than a dozen states) all deny that euthanasia and suicide are involved. The nub of the issues at stake is an unexplained and undefended assertion in In re Colyer, a 1975 case in the State of Washington. It has been cited in many subsequent cases, including *Brophy*. Verbatim, it reads: *"A death which occurs after the removal of life support systems is from natural causes, neither set in motion nor intended by the patient"* (my italics).

This opinion is widely held although it is badly contrary to fact. Death in such cases is not due to an "underlying," ultimately fatal disease or disorder; it is due to or a consequence of the patient's decision to die. And when, to instrument the decision, supports are removed, that is helping the patient to die — in a word, euthanasia. . . .

The statement in *Colyer*, repeated again and again in new decisions coming along, is contrary to fact as well as to common sense. It is so completely lacking in both candor and thoughtful reflection, in fact, that we have to wonder what motive lies behind it.

That motive, I submit, comes close to denial, due to the justices' deep-seated repugnance to what they nevertheless find themselves approving because of their humane distaste for futile human misery. They can buttress their decision with legal principles such as privacy and necessity, but it still grates against their traditional, normative sentiments. . . .

The mere terms "suicide" and "euthanasia" are psychologically loaded, evoking moralistic frowns. To ease their discomforts, the courts therefore take refuge in nonsensical and arbitrary statements, trying to hold on to an old way of thinking and talking while having to embrace a new way to meet new realities. . . . The courts are in the position of saying that black is white, spades are not spades, suicide is not suicide. They are trying, it would seem, to keep their skirts clear of an increasingly outworn and outmoded taboo. Their way of keeping clear of the taboo is by illogical and semantic maneuvers, even while they themselves undermine the taboo by their own decisions. . . . Fork-tongued semantics and verbal evasions are counterproductive; the courts' credibility will surely erode if they refuse to call things by their real names much longer. . . .

Poll after poll of public opinion shows a clear and growing majority in favor of the right to choose to die, and to have medical help in doing so. The taboo is simply dying away, as most taboos do sooner or later. The hurdle in the way is a psychological or visceral one, not logical or ethical, as we break through the conventional wisdom. That the taboo has been a double one, against both suicide and euthanasia, has added to the difficulty. But since the two things are coinherent, common sense will put them together. . . .

In order to see the problem as a whole, we need to understand that human initiatives in dying can fall on three different levels. In the relative order of initiative involved, they are: (1) allowing to die, (2) helping to die, and (3) causing to die.

We may allow a patient to die because, as in a living-will declaration, we have exhausted our efforts to fend off the patient's dying and the patient chooses to die without any further medical intervention. Death thus comes about by a "natural" process; the causative agent is solely the pathology. No moral question about choosing to die is posed in these cases. Nature has made the decision.

At the next level of initiative, we may help a patient to die, by some indirect causative action, not the patient's but ours, in response to his or her appeal. We might help by withdrawing support systems such as antibiotics, nasogastric tubes, respirators, or any other stratagem of resuscitative medicine. Death comes in such a case not as a consequence of the disease but as the intended consequence of stopping the treatment. If medical support had not been started in the first place, that would be a different stratagem; but it would be the same thing because the aim or end is the same.

Finally, at the third level, we may directly cause the patient's death. This might be by a lethal dose of something like potassium chloride, or by graduating the dosage of a drug until it lowers respiration to a fatal level, or by any other contrivance directly leading to the patient's death.

Ending a life at the first level is not euthanasia. This is because suicide is a good death induced or contrived by human choice or election. At the second level it is euthanasia, although the courts and some physicians try to deny it. Actions at the third level are clearly and inarguably euthanasia. The point is that at all three levels the end sought is the same, and therefore their moral meaning is the same. Motively, their value or moral significance is identical.

The problem for the courts at the present time lies on the second level, but we should not focus on it so sharply that we lose sight of the whole picture. It is a serious blunder to suppose that because actions at these levels differ descriptively, as to what is done, it follows that they differ morally.

It is of no moral significance if the patient's death is brought about (contrived) only indirectly. If a patient with pulmonary disease dies because we close down the heating system in zero-degree weather, or leave a supply of morphine on the bedside table without careful dosage instructions, we have contrived the patient's death through indirect means. Morally, however, the contrivances are the same as stopping treatment — although not, to be sure, as desirable professionally or socially.

The courts have tried to evade the meaning of what they are doing by arguing that removing life supports is not euthanasia. The patient's death, they say, is not directly caused by withdrawing medical supports. This is to say that only the third level in our scheme of euthanasia modalities is truly euthanasia. Their idea is that directly causing a patient to die — by giving a fatal injection, for example — is morally wrong, but that indirectly causing the patient's death by merely ceasing to prolong life (as on the first and second levels) is not culpable because it is descriptively different. The same retort is in order here: the end or object sought is the same, and therefore the moral significance of the different means is the same.

The courts' moral "reasoning" is based unwittingly on a medieval model called "the rule of double effect." According to this little ploy, we may take actions that foreseeably have both a good and a bad effect, but only (so the argument runs) if we do not desire the bad effect. We must not "intend" the bad effect — in our problem here, the patient's death — and if we do not really want the patient to be dead, then we do not "intend" him or her to be. Here intention has ceased to mean the end or object (plan, aim, design, purpose, goal, or target) and now means preference or first choice (liking, fancy, predilection, favor). Stopping treatment is not euthanasia, on this basis, if you truly wish the patient were not dying. This seems to me to be the theme for another sequel to Alice in Wonderland, but that is exactly where the courts are.

Jurists should be reminded that suicide has been decriminalized in America and Britain, as well as in most of the civilized world. They should then be asked to explain (1) why it is not legal to help people do what they may legally do for themselves, and (2) why, if it is lawful to help patients *in extremis* by indirect means, direct means are not equally lawful. To develop discussions in jurisprudence along these lines would no doubt be worthwhile.

Since they require evidence of the patient's wish to be dead, the decision of the courts should help the "man on the street" pull loose from the taboo and realize that such consent is legally and morally essential for euthanasia — that by definition euthanasia is voluntary.

Many people still confuse euthanasia with the genocide practiced by the Nazis in their concentration camps. Dragging the Hitlerites into the discussion is an unabashed red herring, a false trail. If we allowed euthanasia, the prohibitionists say, we would be no better than the Nazis and soon would be doing mass murders ourselves. In objections of this kind (they are not reasoned arguments), we are dealing with pseudo-pragmatic resistance or so-called "slippery slope" objections arising from what psychologists call "floating anxiety" or unspecific fear.

Such tactics slyly cover up the difference between patients choosing to die, as in euthanasia, and the Schutzstaffel's killing people against their will — the elderly, Jews, Communists, gypsies, handicapped persons, and recidivist criminals. Himmler used the word "euthanasia" (i.e., "good death"), but what he did was diametrically the opposite of euthanasia because it was involuntary, imposed, and cruel. . . .

Doctrinaire and Pragmatic Objections

Current opponents to euthanasia offer two different kinds of objections, and we ought to recognize which is which. Proponents and activists on behalf of euthanasia are certainly well advised to distinguish them. The doctrinaire approach holds that euthanasia is intrinsically and thus morally wrong, *ipso facto*, no matter how much it might help or hurt a patient. The other approach is pragmatic, arguing that the consequences would be bad — at least on balance. It is the second kind of objections that are to be taken seriously; the first kind, which condemn the practice blindly and indiscriminately, are uncritical universal negatives, "damn all" taboos, not open to ethical reasoning or conscientious judgment.

I know of no pragmatic objection that bars euthanasia in all cases. We can find at least a modicum of *laissez-faire* agreement with such objectors, on the ancient principle of *abusus non tollit usum* — abuse does not bar use. This might be called the clinical approach to euthanasia, looking at each case on its own merits, as compared to a dogmatic universalized prohibition.

Generalized objections to or reservations about euthanasia, based on pragmatic rather than dogmatic grounds, seem to fall chiefly under five heads. (1) It undermines the trust people must have in their physicians; to which it can be retorted that treating people against their will also undermines trust. (2) To end the life of a patient would brutalize everybody, including families and the physicians and nurses themselves; to which it can be replied that keeping miserable and subpersonal patients hopelessly alive has the same poisonous effects. (3) Something might come along to save the patient after all; but if this kind of nondecisional gamble based on hope rather than data were to be the practice, it would lead to callous, pointless, and costly consequences, and render medical expertise irrelevant. (4) Euthanasia, it is said, would discourage research aimed at curing or alleviating fatal diseases (cancer, for example); this objection is unacceptably naive in its understanding of the motives behind medical research. (5) Diagnoses and prognoses of terminal illness might be mistaken; to which it can be replied that although physicians are finite and make errors, if the possibility of error was a reason for not acting on medical knowledge, it would subvert medicine itself and give rise to a pervasive distrust of physicians in many nonterminal illnesses as well.

The point is a simple one. Pragmatic objections in any particular case might be found to be valid, and euthanasia would then be contraindicated. It would be a matter of clinical responsibility to use it or not use it, depending upon the foreseeable consequences in each case. What we have to guard against is the simplistic tendency in some people to generalize objections of this kind — to turn them into blanket and undiscriminating taboos. In the forum of ethical discourse we often find that behind such generalized pragmatic objections lie a hidden agenda, some dogmatic and authoritarian condemnation or other, usually but not necessarily religious in nature.

Underlying a lot of resistance to suicide and euthanasia is a kind of ethical vitalism, according to which life itself, the sheer persistence of vital functions, no matter how minimal, is untouchable, taboo, to be accepted without any human initiative. This priority of life as life, over other considerations of human personal integrity and well-being, is often behind the notion that the only legitimate initiatives in dying must be superhuman. Life can end only through God's special providence or through the "natural" death provided by his creation.

In the practical terms of medical decision-making, this all comes down to the question: Is our first-order value to be the quality of a human life or simply its quantity? This basic tension can almost always be detected in juristic reasoning. The judges by and large are caught up — perhaps unconsciously most of the time — in the old notion that an innocent life is sacrosanct. Thus every human initiative in ending a patient's life has to be camouflaged to make it look like nature's or God's doing.

NOTES

Active Euthanasia and the Duty to Die

1. Some additional reasons for prohibiting active but not passive euthanasia are summarized in Case Comment, 73 Geo. L. Rev. 1331, 1341-1343 (1985):

[T]he distinction between killing and letting die should be maintained in the area of medical decision making for several reasons. First, though classifying behavior as an act or an omission does not in itself explain any moral difference between behaviors, fatal actions are more likely to be morally wrong than are fatal omissions. This is usually because of one or more of the following factors: (1) the motives of an agent who acts to cause death are usually worse (for example, self-interest or malice) than those of someone who omits to act and lets another die; . . . (3) the nature and duration of future life denied to a person whose life is ended by another's act is usually much greater than that denied to a dying person whose death comes slightly more quickly due to an omission of treatment. . . .

Third, removing the prohibition of direct killing would threaten our notions of respect for human life. . . . If we introduce rules permitting active killing into our society, it is not implausible that society eventually would move toward involuntary euthanasia of those who are a nuisance and a burden to society (the slippery slope revisited). The argument can be summarized as follows: "Rules against killing in a moral code are not *isolated* moral principles; they are pieces of a web of rules against killing which forms the code. The more thread one removes, the weaker the fabric becomes."

See also, President's Commission, Deciding to Forego Life-Sustaining Treatment 65-73 (1983).

2. In early 1988, the Journal of the American Medical Association precipitated a storm of controversy by printing an anonymous letter from a medical resident that apparently recounted an actual euthanasia of a pain-ridden cancer patient through a lethal injection of morphine. "It's Over Debbie," A Piece of my Mind, 259 J.A.M.A. 272 (1988). The controversy centered more on whether this was an appropriate case for euthanasia than on whether euthanasia generally is permissible. The medical resident was not the patient's primary physician; he appeared to act spontaneously and without much reflection or any consultation; and there was even some question whether the patient was coherent and made an unambiguous plea to die. (On the other hand, there was some question whether the dose of morphine was enough to cause certain death or instead whether death was a calculated risk of the resident's attempt merely to alleviate the patient's pain.) See Letters to Editor and Commentary, 259 J.A.M.A. 2094, 2139 (1988).

3. Although active euthanasia is illegal on the books, the "Law in Action" may be sharply different. In a questionnaire administered recently by the Hemlock Society, 79 of 588 California physicians responding admitted to practicing euthanasia at least once, 29 more than three times. New York Times, Feb. 25, 1988, at A13. Using a rather broad definition of euthanasia (to include mercy killing, "auto-euthanasia," and double suicides), the authors in D. Humphrey & A. Wickett, The Right to Die: Understanding Euthanasia 133 (1986),

report 151 cases of recorded euthanasia between 1920 and 1985. "Slightly more than half of the mercy killings (the taking of a loved one's life to relieve suffering) . . . have occurred in the 1980s, while a quarter of all cases were in 1985 alone. This gives a 300 percent increase from any prior year."

Mercy killings have seldom resulted in criminal conviction, and seldom still have they resulted in imprisonment. When criminal prosecution is pursued, it is usually against family members who euthanize rather than medical professionals. According to one report, "no physician has ever been successfully prosecuted for an act of either omission or commission that led to the death of a seriously ill patient." Glantz, Withholding and Withdrawing Treatment: The Role of the Criminal Law, 15 L. Med. & Health Care 231, 232 (1988).

4. The Netherlands is the one western nation where euthanasia is practiced openly. Dutch physicians reportedly help more than 5000 patients die each year. Intl. Herald Tribune, Nov. 1986, p.1:

> The most radical acceptance of euthanasia in the world is found in the Netherlands. There, a physician who meets strict criteria can give a lethal injection to a dying person who has requested death, and the physician will not be punished. Rather than legalize mercy killing by a bill placed before Parliament — which risks becoming a schismatic political issue — the Dutch, in a series of judicial steps since 1973, have permitted doctors conforming to rules to go unpunished. The hundred-year-old Article 293 of the criminal code says it is a crime for anyone to assist a suicide or take a life, but the Dutch have circumvented the problem by adding, step by step, exemption clauses for the medical profession only. . . .
>
> The Dutch are extremely sensitive to the notion that they have "legalized euthanasia." They hasten to point out that "it goes unpunished," which they argue is different from legalization — a point some observers find moot. They are also sensitive because of the Nazi "euthanasia" atrocities. Semantics aside, their progress toward justified euthanasia shows the willingness of legal authorities to respond to the complexities of the issue. In the 1973 case against Dr. Postma, the judge rejected the defense of "euthanasia," refused to suspend the criminal code, yet went to considerable trouble to spell out conditions under which euthanasia could go unpunished. . . . :
>
> 1. There must be physical or mental suffering which the sufferer finds unbearable.
> 2. The suffering and the desire to die must be lasting (i.e., not temporary).
> 3. The decision to die must be the voluntary decision of an informed patient.
> 4. The person must have a correct and clear understanding of his condition and of other possibilities (the results of this or

that treatment and of no treatment); he must be capable of weighing these options and must have done so.
5. There is no other reasonable (i.e., acceptable for the patient) solution to improve the situation.
6. The [time and manner of] death will not cause avoidable misery to others (i.e., if possible, the next of kin should be informed beforehand).
7. The decision to give aid-in-dying should not be a one-person decision. Consulting another professional (medical doctor, psychologist, social worker, according to the circumstances of the case) is obligatory.
8. A medical doctor must be involved in the decision to prescribe the correct drugs.
9. The decision process and the actual aid must be done with the utmost care.
10. The person receiving aid-in-dying need not be a dying person. Paraplegics can request and get aid-in-dying.

D. Humphrey & A. Wickett, The Right to Die: Understanding Euthanasia 133 170-177 (1986). The Spring 1988 and Spring 1989 volumes of Issues in Law and Medicine (vol. 3, no. 4 and vol. 4, no. 4) contain symposia devoted to euthanasia in the Netherlands.

Whether the Dutch experience has been beneficial for patients overall is subject to some measure of disagreement: "One Dutch physician has reported that *in*voluntary euthanasia has become so rampant and is so overlooked by the courts that elderly patients are afraid to be hospitalized or even to consult doctors. The Netherlands is, therefore, demonstrating the reality, the steepness, and the slipperiness of the 'slippery slope' of legalized euthanasia." Shewmon, Active Voluntary Euthanasia: A Needless Pandora's Box, 3 Issues in L. & Med. 219, 229-230 (1987). For additional readings on the practice of active euthanasia in other cultures, see E. Carmi, Euthanasia (1984); Silving, Euthanasia: A Study in Comparative Criminal Law, 103 U. Pa. L. Rev. 350 (1954).

5. The most recent push to legalize euthanasia in the United States occurred in California where a referendum for a "Humane and Dignified Death Act" proposed by the Hemlock Society garnered several hundred thousand signatures but failed to receive support of a sufficient percentage of registered voters to be placed on the ballot. Am. Med. News, May 20, 1988, at 1. Similar efforts reportedly are under way in three other states. N.Y. Times, May 24, 1989, at A1.

6. Does the case for legalizing euthanasia become stronger in an era of health care rationing? Consider that one-third of Medicare's budget is spent on patients in the last year of life, and almost half of this in the last two months of life. 5 H.C. Fin. Rev. 117 (1984). Margaret Battin argues in "Age Rationing and the Just Distribution of Health Care: Is There a Duty to Die?," 97 Ethics 317 (1987) that

active euthanasia is preferable to the "medical abandonment" the elderly might suffer if cost constraints force a marked reduction in their health care coverage. The Hastings Center Guidelines on the Termination of Life-Sustaining Treatment 125 (1987) provocatively advise that "in deciding whether to receive or forgo various forms of treatment, including life-sustaining treatment, patients may wish to consider what financial burdens the treatment will impose on them and others."

7. The seminal defense of the status quo prohibition of active euthanasia is Kamisar, Some Non-Religious Views Against Proposed Mercy-Killing Legislation, 42 Minn. L. Rev. 969 (1958). See also, T. Beauchamp & J. Childress, Principles of Biomedical Ethics 106 (2d ed. 1983); Potts, Looking for the Exit Door: Killing and Caring in Modern Medicine, 25 Hous. L. Rev. 493 (1988); Shewmon, Active Voluntary Euthanasia: A Needless Pandora's Box, 3 Issues in L. & Med. 219 (1987); Gelfand, Euthanasia and the Terminally Ill Patient, 63 Neb. L. Rev. 741 (1984).

One of the most influential arguments in favor of legalizing euthanasia is Rachels, Active and Passive Euthanasia, 292 New Eng. J. Med. 78 (1975). For additional readings favoring euthanasia, see Model Aid-in-Dying Act, 75 Iowa L. Rev. 125 (1989); H. Kuhse, The Sanctity-of-Life Doctrine in Medicine: A Critique (1987); J. Rachels, The End of Life (1986); D. Humphrey & A. Wickett, The Right to Die: Understanding Euthanasia (1986); Molenda, Active Euthanasia: Can it Be Justified?, 24 Tulsa L.J. 165 (1988); Garbesi, The Law of Assisted Suicide, 3 Issues in L. & Med. 93 (1987); O'Brien, Facilitating Euthanatic, Rational Suicide: Help Me Go Gentle into that Good Night, 31 St. Louis U.L.J. 655 (1987); Note, Voluntary Active Euthanasia for the Terminally Ill and the Constitutional Right to Privacy, 69 Corn. L. Rev. 363 (1984).

An excellent anthology of writings pro and con on euthanasia and suicide is contained in R. Weir, Ethical Issues in Death and Dying (2d ed. 1986). See also Special Supplement, Mercy, Murder & Morality: Perspectives on Euthanasia, 19 Hastings Cent. Rep. (Jan/Feb 1989).

III. ISSUES OF HUMAN BIRTH

A. *Reproductive Rights*

Carey v. Population Services International
431 U.S. 678 (1977)

BRENNAN, JUSTICE. Under New York Ed. Law §6811(8) (McKinney 1972) it is a crime (1) for any person to sell or distribute any

III. Issues of Human Birth 1041

contraceptive of any kind to a minor under the age of 16 years; (2) for anyone other than a licensed pharmacist to distribute contraceptives to persons 16 or over; and (3) for anyone, including licensed pharmacists, to advertise or display contraceptives. . . . [Mail-order distributors of nonmedical contraceptive devices brought an action challenging the constitutionality of this statute. A three-judge district court struck down the statute insofar as it applied to nonprescription contraceptives. This appeal followed.]

II

Although "(t)he Constitution does not explicitly mention any right of privacy," the Court has recognized that one aspect of the "liberty" protected by the Due Process Clause of the Fourteenth Amendment is "a right of personal privacy, or a guarantee of certain areas or zones of privacy." Roe v. Wade, 410 U.S. 113 (1973). This right of personal privacy includes "the interest in independence in making certain kinds of important decisions." Whalen v. Roe, 429 U.S. 589, 599-600 (1977). While the outer limits of this aspect of privacy have not been marked by the Court, it is clear that among the decisions that an individual may make without unjustified government interference are personal decisions "relating to marriage, Loving v. Virginia, 388 U.S. 1, 12 (1967); procreation, Skinner v. Oklahoma ex rel. Williamson, 316 U.S. 535, 541-542 (1942); contraception, Eisenstadt v. Baird, 405 U.S., at 453-454 (White, J., concurring in result); family relationships, Prince v. Massachusetts, 321 U.S. 158, 166 (1944); and child rearing and education, Pierce v. Society of Sisters, 268 U.S. 510, 535 (1925); Meyer v. Nebraska, 262 U.S. 390, 399 (1923)." Roe v. Wade, supra, at 152-153. See also Cleveland Board of Education v. LaFleur, 414 U.S. 632, 639-640 (1974).

The decision whether or not to beget or bear a child is at the very heart of this cluster of constitutionally protected choices. That decision holds a particularly important place in the history of the right of privacy, a right first explicitly recognized in an opinion holding unconstitutional a statute prohibiting the use of contraceptives, Griswold v. Connecticut, supra, and most prominently vindicated in recent years in the contexts of contraception, Griswold v. Connecticut, supra; Eisenstadt v. Baird, 405 U.S. 438 (1972); and abortion, Roe v. Wade, supra; Doe v. Bolton, 410 U.S. 179 (1973); Planned Parenthood of Central Missouri v. Danforth, 428 U.S. 52 (1976). This is understandable, for in a field that by definition concerns the most intimate of human activities and relationships, decisions whether to accomplish or to prevent conception are among the most private and sensitive. "If the right of privacy means anything, it is the right of the individual, married or single, to be free of unwarranted governmental intrusion into matters so fundamentally affecting a person as the decision whether to bear or beget a child." Eisenstadt v. Baird, supra, 405 U.S., at 453. (Emphasis omitted.)

That the constitutionally protected right of privacy extends to an individual's liberty to make choices regarding contraception does not, however, automatically invalidate every state regulation in this area. The business of manufacturing and selling contraceptives may be regulated in ways that do not infringe protected individual choices. And even a burdensome regulation may be validated by a sufficiently compelling state interest. In Roe v. Wade, for example, after determining that the "right of privacy . . . encompass[es] a woman's decision whether or not to terminate her pregnancy," we cautioned that the right is not absolute, and that certain state interests (in that case, "interests in safeguarding health, in maintaining medical standards, and in protecting potential life") may at some point "become sufficiently compelling to sustain regulation of the factors that govern the abortion decision." "Compelling" is of course the key word; where a decision as fundamental as that whether to bear or beget a child is involved, regulations imposing a burden on it may be justified only by compelling state interests, and must be narrowly drawn to express only those interests. With these principles in mind, we turn to the question whether the District Court was correct in holding invalid the provisions of §6811(8) as applied to the distribution of nonprescription contraceptives.

III

We consider first the wider restriction on access to contraceptives created by §6811(8)'s prohibition of the distribution of nonmedical contraceptives to adults except through licensed pharmacists.

Appellants argue that this Court has not accorded a "right of access to contraceptives" the status of a fundamental aspect of personal liberty. They emphasize that Griswold v. Connecticut, struck down a state prohibition of the use of contraceptives, and so had no occasion to discuss laws "regulating their manufacture or sale." Eisenstadt v. Baird, [which extended *Griswold* by striking a ban on the sale of contraceptives to single persons], was decided under the Equal Protection Clause, holding that "whatever the rights of the individual to access to contraceptives may be, the rights must be the same for the unmarried and the married alike." 405 U.S., at 453. Thus appellants argue that neither case should be treated as reflecting upon the State's power to limit or prohibit distribution of contraceptives to any persons, married or unmarried.

The fatal fallacy in this argument is that it overlooks the underlying premise of those decisions that the Constitution protects "the

III. Issues of Human Birth 1043

right of the individual . . . to be free from unwarranted governmental intrusion into . . . the decision whether to bear or beget a child." Id., at 453. *Griswold* did state that by "forbidding the use of contraceptives rather than regulating their manufacture or sale," the Connecticut statute there had "a maximum destructive impact" on privacy rights. 381 U.S., at 485. This intrusion into "the sacred precincts of marital bedrooms" made that statute particularly "repulsive." But subsequent decisions have made clear that the constitutional protection of individual autonomy in matters of childbearing is not dependent on that element. Eisenstadt v. Baird, holding that the protection is not limited to married couples, characterized the protected right as the "decision whether to bear or beget a child." 405 U.S., at 453. Similarly, Roe v. Wade, held that the Constitution protects "a woman's decision whether or not to terminate her pregnancy." 410 U.S., at 153. See also Whalen v. Roe, supra, 429 U.S., at 599-600 and n.26. These decisions put *Griswold* in proper perspective. *Griswold* may no longer be read as holding only that a State may not prohibit a married couple's use of contraceptives. Read in light of its progeny, the teaching of *Griswold* is that the Constitution protects individual decisions in matters of childbearing from unjustified intrusion by the State.

Restrictions on the distribution of contraceptives clearly burden the freedom to make such decisions. A total prohibition against sale of contraceptives, for example, would intrude upon individual decisions in matters of procreation and contraception as harshly as a direct ban on their use. Indeed, in practice, a prohibition against all sales, since more easily and less offensively enforced, might have an even more devastating effect upon the freedom to choose contraception. Cf. Poe v. Ullman, 367 U.S. 497 (1961).

An instructive analogy is found in decisions after Roe v. Wade, supra, that held unconstitutional statutes that did not prohibit abortions outright but limited in a variety of ways a woman's access to them. Doe v. Bolton, 410 U.S. 179 (1973); Planned Parenthood of Central Missouri v. Danforth, 428 U.S. 52 (1976). See also Bigelow v. Virginia, 421 U.S. 809 (1975). The significance of these cases is that they establish that the same test must be applied to state regulations that burden an individual's right to decide to prevent conception or terminate pregnancy by substantially limiting access to the means of effectuating that decision as is applied to state statutes that prohibit the decision entirely. Both types of regulation "may be justified only by a 'compelling state interest' . . . and . . . must be narrowly drawn to express only the legitimate state interests at stake." Roe v. Wade, supra, 410 U.S., at 155.[5] This is so not because there

5. Contrary to the suggestion advanced in Mr. JUSTICE POWELL's opinion, we do

is an independent fundamental "right of access to contraceptives," but because such access is essential to exercise of the constitutionally protected right of decision in matters of childbearing that is the underlying foundation of the holdings in *Griswold,* Eisenstadt v. Baird, and Roe v. Wade.

Limiting the distribution of nonprescription contraceptives to licensed pharmacists clearly imposes a significant burden on the right of the individuals to use contraceptives if they choose to do so. The burden is, of course, not as great as that under a total ban on distribution. Nevertheless, the restriction of distribution channels to a small fraction of the total number of possible retail outlets renders contraceptive devices considerably less accessible to the public, reduces the opportunity for privacy of selection and purchase, and lessens the possibility of price competition. . . .

There remains the inquiry whether the provision serves a compelling state interest. Clearly "interests . . . in maintaining medical standards, and in protecting potential life," Roe v. Wade, 410 U.S., at 154, cannot be invoked to justify this statute. Insofar as §6811(8) applies to nonhazardous contraceptives,[8] it bears no relation to the State's interest in protecting health. . . .

[The Court then struck down on first amendment grounds the prohibition of contraceptive advertising.]

[Addressing the ban on contraceptive sales to minors, Justice Brennan reasoned that "state restrictions inhibiting privacy rights of minors are valid only if they serve 'any significant state interest . . . that is not present in the case of an adult,' " a less rigorous test "than the 'compelling state interest' test applied to restrictions on the privacy rights of adults." He then found that the "state's policy against promiscuous sexual intercourse among the young" was not sufficient to meet this test. Relying on the abortion decisions discussed in Section II.B of this book, he observed that "since the State may not impose a blanket prohibition, or even a blanket requirement of parental consent, on the choice of a minor to terminate her pregnancy, the constitutionality of a blanket prohibition of the distribution of contraceptives to minors is a fortiori foreclosed." Moreover, Justice Brennan thought that " 'it would be plainly unreasonable to assume that (the State) has prescribed pregnancy and the birth of an unwanted child (or the physical and psychological dangers of an abortion) as punishment for fornication.' "]

---

not hold that state regulation must meet this standard "whenever it implicates sexual freedom," or "affect(s) adult sexual relations," but only when it "burden(s) an individual's right to decide to prevent conception or terminate pregnancy by substantially limiting access to the means of effectuating that decision." . . .

8. We have taken judicial notice that "not all contraceptives are potentially dangerous." Eisenstadt v. Baird, 405 U.S., 438, 451, and n.9 (1972).

[The sale-to-minors portion of Justice Brennan's opinion garnered the votes of only four Justices. Three others concurred in the result, though, based on the more limited reasoning that (1) the state had failed to prove any link between contraceptives and increased sexual activity, (2) the contraception ban infringed the privacy interests of teenage married females, and (3) the ban precluded parents who wanted to do so from giving contraceptives to their children.]

NOTES

Birth Control and Population Control

1. For commentary on *Carey*, see Benson, Carey v. Population Services International: An Extension of the Right of Privacy, 5 Ohio N.L. Rev. 167 (1978): Herbst, Juvenile Privacy: A Minor's Right of Access to Contraceptives, 6 Fordham Urb. L.J. 371 (1978): Note, Minor's Right of Privacy: Limitations on State Action After *Danforth* and *Carey*, 77 Colum. L. Rev. 1216 (1977).

2. Is the state also precluded from *mandating* birth control, or are the interests of the state in avoiding overpopulation compelling enough to limit the size of families? For various perspectives, see Marsden, Human Rights and Population Growth: A Feminist Perspective, 3 Intl. J. Health Serv. 567 (1973); Young, Alverson, and Young, Court-Ordered Contraception, 55 A.B.A.J. 223 (1969) (suggesting court-ordered insertion of intrauterine contraceptive device after juvenile has second illegitimate child). For adverse reactions to this proposal, see Note, Court-Ordered Contraception: A Reasonable Alternative To Institutionalization for Juvenile Unwed Mothers, 1970 Wis. L. Rev. 899; Note, Court-Ordered Contraception in California, 23 Hastings L. Rev. 1505 (1972); Note, Legal Analysis and Population Control: The Problem of Coercion, 84 Harv. L. Rev. 1856 (1971).

Consider the language in Justice Goldberg's concurring opinion in *Griswold*, which speaks directly to the constitutional objections that coercive birth control methods raise: ". . . Surely the Government, absent a showing of a compelling subordinating state interest, could not decree that all husbands and wives must be sterilized after two children have been born to them. . . . Yet, if upon a showing of a slender basis of rationality, a law outlawing voluntary birth control by married persons is valid, then, by the same reasoning, a law requiring compulsory birth control would also seem to be valid. In my view, however, both types of law would unjustifiably intrude upon rights of marital privacy which are constitutionally protected." 381 U.S. 479, 496-497 (1965). Does Justice Goldberg's analogy adequately take into consideration the disparate rationales for each type of regulation?

More subtle problems are raised when governmental action is not overtly coercive, but merely seeks to encourage reproductive restraint by structuring government benefit or taxation programs to discriminate against large families. In Dandridge v. Williams, 397 U.S. 471 (1970), the Supreme Court upheld a Maryland regulation limiting payments under the state's Aid for Dependent Children program (AFDC) to no more than $240 or $250 per family. As a result of the regulation, AFDC payments equaling a calculated subsistence standard went only to families with fewer than five or six children. 397 U.S. at 509-510, n.2 (Marshall, J., dissenting). The Court did not answer plaintiffs' contentions that the regulation infringed parents' rights "to freedom of choice concerning procreation and reproduction and to marital privacy." Brief for Appellees at 31. See Note, Legal Analysis and Population Control: The Problem of Coercion, supra, at 1856-1858.

3. Do parents have a constitutional right to be consulted (or informed) when professional clinics offer contraceptive advice or services to minor children living with parents? In Doe v. Irwin, 615 F.2d 1162 (6th Cir. 1980), the court held that there was no such parental right and reversed the district court's finding that a state-funded family planning center's practice of distributing contraceptives to unemancipated minors without parental notice or consultation violated the parent's constitutional right to oversee the care, custody, and nurturing of their children. See also M. S. v. Wermers, 557 F.2d 170 (8th Cir. 1977), where the court held that when a minor challenges a parental consultation requirement, it is not appropriate to appoint the child's parents as guardians ad litem or to notify them that the action is pending. See Comment, Minors' Right to Litigate Privacy Interests Without Parental Notice, 1978 Wash. L.Q. 431 (1978); Note, Parental Consent Requirements and Privacy Rights of Minors: The Contraception Controversy, 88 Harv. L. Rev. 1001 (1975).

4. Family planning counseling for minors may raise special problems of medical ethics for physicians and other health care personnel. How Do You Manage the Teenage Patient Who Comes to You for Contraception?, 24 Intl. J. Fertility 78 (1979). For other medical literature on the subject, see Rozenbaum, Teenagers and Contraception, 16 Intl. J. Gynecology & Obstetrics, 564 (1978-1979). Freeman, Adolescent Contraceptive Use: Current Status of Practice and Research, 53 Obstetrics & Gynecology 388 (March 1979). There are also continuing religious and philosophical objections to artificial birth control measures. See Barrett, Politics of Birth Control, 43 U.S. Catholic 46 (1978); Friedman, Interference with Human Life: Some Jurisprudential Reflections, 70 Col. L. Rev. 1058 (1970).

5. Although individuals make the final decisions about fertility regulation, there are also policy decisions concerning the contraceptive

field which must be made in the interest of the public as a whole. The Food and Drug Administration is the federal agency responsible for protecting contraceptive users through its regulatory activities concerning safety, research, and user education. Most of the FDA's efforts have been directed at the potential side effects and long term health hazards of the use of oral contraceptives and intrauterine devices.

B. Abortion Regulation and Funding

Webster v. Reproductive Health Services
— U.S. —, 109 S. Ct. 3040 (1989)

REHNQUIST, C.J.

This appeal concerns the constitutionality of a Missouri statute regulating the performance of abortions. The United States Court of Appeals for the Eighth Circuit struck down several provisions of the statute on the ground that they violated this Court's decision in Roe v. Wade, 410 U.S. 113 (1973), and cases following it. We . . . now reverse. . . .

II

Decision of this case requires us to address [two] sections of the Missouri Act [two other sections are omitted]: . . . (b) the prohibition on the use of public facilities or employees to perform abortions; . . . and (d) the requirement that physicians conduct viability tests prior to performing abortions. We address these seriatim. . . .

[Only Justices White and Kennedy joined the remainder of the opinion. The concurring opinions of Justices O'Connor and Scalia are excerpted below.]

B

Section 188.210 provides that "[i]t shall be unlawful for any public employee within the scope of his employment to perform or assist an abortion, not necessary to save the life of the mother," while §188.215 makes it "unlawful for any public facility to be used for the purpose of performing or assisting an abortion not necessary to save the life of the mother." The Court of Appeals held that these provisions contravened this Court's abortion decisions. 851 F.2d, at 1082-1083. We take the contrary view.

As we said earlier this Term in DeShaney v. Winnebago County Dept. of Social Services, 489 U.S. —, — (1989) (slip op., at 6), "our cases have recognized that the Due Process Clauses generally confer no affirmative right to governmental aid, even where such aid may be necessary to secure life, liberty, or property interests of which the government itself may not deprive the individual." In Maher v. Roe, supra, the Court upheld a Connecticut welfare regulation under which Medicaid recipients received payments for medical services related to childbirth, but not for nontherapeutic abortions. The Court rejected the claim that this unequal subsidization of childbirth and abortion was impermissible under Roe v. Wade. As the Court put it:

> The Connecticut regulation before us is different in kind from the laws invalidated in our previous abortion decisions. The Connecticut regulation places no obstacles — absolute or otherwise — in the pregnant woman's path to an abortion. An indigent woman who desires an abortion suffers no disadvantage as a consequence of Connecticut's decision to fund childbirth; she continues as before to be dependent on private sources for the service she desires. The State may have made childbirth a more attractive alternative, thereby influencing the woman's decision, but it has imposed no restriction on access to abortions that was not already there. The indigency that may make it difficult — and in some cases, perhaps, impossible — for some women to have abortions is neither created nor in any way affected by the Connecticut regulation. 432 U.S., at 474.

Relying on *Maher*, the Court in Poelker v. Doe, 432 U.S. 519, 521 (1977), held that the city of St. Louis committed "no constitutional violation . . . in electing, as a policy choice, to provide publicly financed hospital services for childbirth without providing corresponding services for nontherapeutic abortions."

More recently, in Harris v. McRae, 448 U.S. 297 (1980), the Court upheld "the most restrictive version of the Hyde Amendment," id., at 325, n.27, which withheld from States federal funds under the Medicaid program to reimburse the costs of abortions, "except where the life of the mother would be endangered if the fetus were carried to term.'" Ibid. (quoting Pub. L. 94-439, §209, 90 Stat. 1434). As in *Maher* and *Poelker*, the Court required only a showing that Congress' authorization of "reimbursement for medically necessary services generally, but not for certain medically necessary abortions" was rationally related to the legitimate governmental goal of encouraging childbirth. 448 U.S., at 325.

The Court of Appeals distinguished these cases on the ground that "[t]o prevent access to a public facility does more than demonstrate a political choice in favor of childbirth; it clearly narrows and in some cases forecloses the availability of abortion to women." 851 F.2d, at 1081. The court reasoned that the ban on the use of public facilities "could prevent a woman's chosen doctor from performing an abortion because of his unprivileged status at other hospitals or because a private hospital adopted a similar anti-abortion stance." Ibid. It also thought that "[s]uch a rule could increase the cost of obtaining an abortion and delay the timing of it as well." Ibid.

We think that this analysis is much like that which we rejected in *Maher, Poelker,* and *McRae*. . . . Having held that the State's refusal to fund abortions does not violate Roe v. Wade, it strains logic to reach a contrary result for the use of public facilities and employees. If the State may "make a value judgment favoring childbirth over abortion and . . . implement that judgment by the allocation of public funds," *Maher,* supra, at 474, surely it may do so through the allocation of other public resources, such as hospitals and medical staff.[8] . . .

D

Section 188.029 of the Missouri Act provides:

Before a physician performs an abortion on a woman he has reason to believe is carrying an unborn child of twenty or more weeks gestational age, the physician shall first determine if the unborn child is viable by using and exercising that degree of care, skill, and proficiency commonly exercised by the ordinarily skillful, careful, and prudent physician engaged in similar practice under the same or similar conditions. In making this determination of viability, the physician shall perform or cause to be performed such medical examinations and tests as are necessary to make a finding of the gestational age, weight, and lung maturity of the unborn child and shall enter such findings and determination of viability in the medical record of the mother.

[T]he parties disagree over the meaning of this statutory provision. . . .

The Court of Appeals read §188.029 as requiring that after 20 weeks "doctors *must* perform tests to find gestational age, fetal weight and lung maturity." 851 F.2d, at 1075, n.5. The court indicated that the tests needed to determine fetal weight at 20 weeks are "unreliable and inaccurate" and would add $125 to $250 to the cost of an abortion. Ibid. It also stated that "amniocentesis, the only method available to determine lung maturity, is contrary to accepted medical practice until 28-30 weeks of gestation, expensive, and imposes significant health risks for both the pregnant woman and the fetus." Ibid. . . .

---

8. A different analysis might apply if a particular State had socialized medicine and all of its hospitals and physicians were publicly funded. This case might also be different if the State barred doctors who performed abortions in private facilities from the use of public facilities for any purpose. See Harris v. McRae, 448 U.S. 297, 317, n.19 (1980).

We think the viability-testing provision makes sense only if the second sentence is read to require only those tests that are useful to making subsidiary findings as to viability. If we construe this provision to require a physician to perform those tests needed to make the three specified findings *in all circumstances,* including when the physician's reasonable professional judgment indicates that the tests would be irrelevant to determining viability or even dangerous to the mother and the fetus, the second sentence of §188.029 would conflict with the first sentence's *requirement* that a physician apply his reasonable professional skill and judgment. It would also be incongruous to read this provision, especially the word "necessary," to require the performance of tests irrelevant to the expressed statutory purpose of determining viability.

The viability-testing provision of the Missouri Act is concerned with promoting the State's interest in potential human life rather than in maternal health. Section 188.029 creates what is essentially a presumption of viability at 20 weeks, which the physician must rebut with tests indicating that the fetus is not viable prior to performing an abortion. It also directs the physician's determination as to viability by specifying consideration, if feasible, of gestational age, fetal weight, and lung capacity. The District Court found that "the medical evidence is uncontradicted that a 20-week fetus is not viable," and that "23½ to 24 weeks gestation is the earliest point in pregnancy where a reasonable possibility of viability exists." 662 F.Supp., at 420. But it also found that there may be a 4-week error in estimating gestational age, id., at 421, which supports testing at 20 weeks.

In Roe v. Wade, the Court recognized that the State has "important and legitimate" interests in protecting maternal health and in the potentiality of human life. 410 U.S., at 162. During the second trimester, the State "may, if it chooses, regulate the abortion procedure in ways that are reasonably related to maternal health." Id., at 164. After viability, when the State's interest in potential human life was held to become compelling, the State "may, if it chooses, regulate, and even proscribe, abortion except where it is necessary, in appropriate medical judgment, for the preservation of the life or health of the mother." Id., at 165.

In Colautti v. Franklin, supra, upon which appellees rely, the Court held that a Pennsylvania statute regulating the standard of care to be used by a physician performing an abortion of a possibly viable fetus was void for vagueness. 439 U.S., at 390-401. But in the course of reaching that conclusion, the Court reaffirmed its earlier statement in Planned Parenthood of Central Missouri v. Danforth, 428 U.S. 52, 64 (1976), that " 'the determination of whether a particular fetus is viable is, and must be, a matter for the judgement of the responsible attending physician.' " 439 U.S., at 396. . . .

III. Issues of Human Birth 1051

To the extent that §188.029 regulates the method for determining viability, it undoubtedly does superimpose state regulation on the medical determination of whether a particular fetus is viable. The Court of Appeals and the District Court thought it unconstitutional for this reason. 851 F.2d, at 1074-1075; 662 F.Supp., at 423. To the extent that the viability tests increase the cost of what are in fact second-trimester abortions, their validity may also be questioned under *Akron*, 462 U.S., at 434-435, where the Court held that a requirement that second trimester abortions must be performed in hospitals was invalid because it substantially increased the expense of those procedures.

We think that the doubt cast upon the Missouri statute by these cases is not so much a flaw in the statute as it is a reflection of the fact that the rigid trimester analysis of the course of a pregnancy enunciated in *Roe* has resulted in subsequent cases like *Colautti* and *Akron* making constitutional law in this area a virtual Procrustean bed. Statutes specifying elements of informed consent to be provided abortion patients, for example, were invalidated if they were thought to "structur[e] . . . the dialogue between the woman and her physician." Thornburgh v. American College of Obstetricians and Gynecologists, 476 U.S. 747, 763 (1986). As the dissenters in *Thornburgh* pointed out, such a statute would have been sustained under any traditional standard of judicial review, id., at 802 (WHITE, J., dissenting), or for any other surgical procedure except abortion. Id., at 783 (BURGER, C.J., dissenting).

Stare decisis is a cornerstone of our legal system, but it has less power in constitutional cases, where, save for constitutional amendments, this Court is the only body able to make needed changes. See United States v. Scott, 437 U.S. 82, 101 (1978). We have not refrained from reconsideration of a prior construction of the Constitution that has proved "unsound in principle and unworkable in practice." Garcia v. San Antonio Metropolitan Transit Authority, 469 U.S. 528, 546 (1985); see Solorio v. United States, 483 U.S. 435, 448-450 (1987); Erie R. Co. v. Tompkins, 304 U.S. 64, 74-78 (1938). We think the *Roe* trimester framework falls into that category.

In the first place, the rigid *Roe* framework is hardly consistent with the notion of a Constitution cast in general terms, as ours is, and usually speaking in general principles, as ours does. The key elements of the *Roe* framework — trimesters and viability — are not found in the text of the Constitution or in any place else one would expect to find a constitutional principle. Since the bounds of the inquiry are essentially indeterminate, the result has been a web of legal rules that have become increasingly intricate, resembling a code of regulations rather than a body of constitutional doctrine. As JUSTICE WHITE has put it, the trimester framework has left this Court to serve as the country's "ex officio medical board with powers to approve or disapprove medical and operative practices and standards throughout the United States." Planned Parenthood of Central Missouri v. Danforth, 428 U.S., at 99 (opinion concurring in part and dissenting in part). Cf. *Garcia,* supra, at 547.

In the second place, we do not see why the State's interest in protecting potential human life should come into existence only at the point of viability, and that there should therefore be a rigid line allowing state regulation after viability but prohibiting it before viability. The dissenters in *Thornburgh,* writing in the context of the *Roe* trimester analysis, would have recognized this fact by positing against the "fundamental right" recognized in *Roe* the State's "compelling interest" in protecting potential human life throughout pregnancy. "[T]he State's interest, if compelling after viability, is equally compelling before viability." *Thornburgh,* 476 U.S., at 795 (WHITE, J., dissenting); see id., at 828 (O'CONNOR, J., dissenting) ("State has compelling interests in ensuring maternal health and in protecting potential human life, and these interests exist 'throughout pregnancy' ") (citation omitted).

The tests that §188.029 requires the physician to perform are designed to determine viability. The State here has chosen viability as the point at which its interest in potential human life must be safeguarded. See Mo. Rev. Stat. §188.030 (1986) ("No abortion of a viable unborn child shall be performed unless necessary to preserve the life or health of the woman"). It is true that the tests in question increase the expense of abortion, and regulate the discretion of the physician in determining the viability of the fetus. Since the tests will undoubtedly show in many cases that the fetus is not viable, the tests will have been performed for what were in fact second-trimester abortions. But we are satisfied that the requirement of these tests permissibly furthers the State's interest in protecting potential human life, and we therefore believe §188.029 to be constitutional.

The dissent takes us to task for our failure to join in a "great issues" debate as to whether the Constitution includes an "unenumerated" general right to privacy as recognized in cases such as Griswold v. Connecticut, 381 U.S. 479 (1965), and *Roe.* But Griswold v. Connecticut, unlike *Roe,* did not purport to adopt a whole framework, complete with detailed rules and distinctions, to govern the cases in which the asserted liberty interest would apply. As such, it was far different from the opinion, if not the holding, of Roe v. Wade, which sought to establish a constitutional framework for judging state regulation of abortion during the entire term of pregnancy. That framework sought to deal with areas of medical practice traditionally subject to state regulation, and it sought to balance once and for all by reference only to the calendar the claims of the State

III. Issues of Human Birth

to protect the fetus as a form of human life against the claims of a woman to decide for herself whether or not to abort a fetus she was carrying. The experience of the Court in applying Roe v. Wade in later cases, see supra, at 20, n.15, suggests to us that there is wisdom in not unnecessarily attempting to elaborate the abstract differences between a "fundamental right" to abortion, as the Court described it in *Akron,* 462 U.S. at 420, n.1, a "limited fundamental constitutional right," which JUSTICE BLACKMUN's dissent today treats *Roe* as having established, post, at 18, or a liberty interest protected by the Due Process Clause, which we believe it to be. The Missouri testing requirement here is reasonably designed to ensure that abortions are not performed where the fetus is viable — an end which all concede is legitimate — and that is sufficient to sustain its constitutionality.

The dissent also accuses us, inter alia, of cowardice and illegitimacy in dealing with "the most politically divisive domestic legal issue of our time." Post, at 23. There is no doubt that our holding today will allow some governmental regulation of abortion that would have been prohibited under the language of cases such as Colautti v. Franklin, 439 U.S. 379 (1979), and Akron v. Akron Center for Reproductive Health, Inc., supra. But the goal of constitutional adjudication is surely not to remove inexorably "politically divisive" issues from the ambit of the legislative process, whereby the people through their elected representatives deal with matters of concern to them. The goal of constitutional adjudication is to hold true the balance between that which the Constitution puts beyond the reach of the democratic process and that which it does not. We think we have done that today. The dissent's suggestion, post, at 1-2, 21-22, that legislative bodies, in a Nation where more than half of our population is women, will treat our decision today as an invitation to enact abortion regulation reminiscent of the dark ages not only misreads our views but does scant justice to those who serve in such bodies and the people who elect them.

III

Both appellants and the United States as Amicus Curiae have urged that we overrule our decision in Roe v. Wade. Brief for Appellants 12-18; Brief for United States as Amicus Curiae 8-24. The facts of the present case, however, differ from those at issue in *Roe.* Here, Missouri has determined that viability is the point at which its interest in potential human life must be safeguarded. In *Roe,* on the other hand, the Texas statute criminalized the performance of *all* abortions, except when the mother's life was at stake. 410 U.S., at 117-118. This case therefore affords us no occasion to revisit the holding of *Roe,* which was that the Texas statute unconstitutionally infringed the right to an abortion derived from the Due Process Clause, id., at 164, and we leave it undisturbed. To the extent indicated in our opinion, we would modify and narrow *Roe* and succeeding cases.

Because none of the challenged provisions of the Missouri Act properly before us conflict with the Constitution, the judgment of the Court of Appeals is

Reversed.

JUSTICE O'CONNOR, concurring in part and concurring in the judgment. . . .

II

In its interpretation of Missouri's "determination of viability" provision, Mo. Rev. Stat. §188.029 (1986), see ante, at 15-23, the plurality has proceeded in a manner unnecessary to deciding the question at hand. . . .

Unlike the plurality, I do not understand these viability testing requirements to conflict with any of the Court's past decisions concerning state regulation of abortion. Therefore, there is no necessity to accept the State's invitation to reexamine the constitutional validity of Roe v. Wade, 410 U.S. 113 (1973). . . . When the constitutional invalidity of a State's abortion statute actually turns on the constitutional validity of Roe v. Wade, there will be time enough to reexamine *Roe.* And to do so carefully.

In assessing §188.029 it is especially important to recognize that appellees did not appeal the District Court's ruling that the first sentence of §188.029 is constitutional. 662 F.Supp., at 420-422. There is, accordingly, no dispute between the parties before us over the constitutionality of the "presumption of viability at 20 weeks," ante, at 17, created by the first sentence of §88.029. . . .

As the plurality properly interprets the second sentence of §188.029, it does nothing more than delineate means by which the unchallenged 20-week presumption of viability may be overcome if those means are useful in doing so and can be prudently employed. Contrary to the plurality's suggestion, see ante, at 19, the District Court did not think the second sentence of §188.029 unconstitutional for this reason. Rather, both the District Court and the Court of Appeals thought the second sentence to be unconstitutional precisely because they interpreted that sentence to impose state regulation on the determination of viability that it does not impose. . . .

It is clear to me that requiring the performance of examinations and tests useful to determining whether a fetus is viable, when viability is possible, and when it would not be medically imprudent to do so, does not impose an undue burden on a woman's abortion decision.

III. Issues of Human Birth

On this ground alone I would reject the suggestion that §188.029 as interpreted is unconstitutional. . . . See Brief for American Association of Prolife Obstetricians and Gynecologists et al. as Amici Curiae 3 ("At twenty weeks gestation, an ultrasound examination to determine gestational age is standard medical practice. It is routinely provided by the plaintiff clinics. An ultrasound examination can effectively provide all three designated findings of sec. 188.029"). . . .

[B]ecause, properly interpreted, §188.029 is not inconsistent with any of this Court's prior precedents, I would reverse the decision of the Court of Appeals. . . .

JUSTICE SCALIA, concurring in part and concurring in the judgment. . . .

The outcome of today's case will doubtless be heralded as a triumph of judicial statesmanship. It is not that, unless it is statesmanlike needlessly to prolong this Court's self-awarded sovereignty over a field where it has little proper business since the answers to most of the cruel questions posed are political and not juridical — a sovereignty which therefore quite properly, but to the great damage of the Court, makes it the object of the sort of organized public pressure that political institutions in a democracy ought to receive. . . .

The real question, then, is whether there are valid reasons to go beyond the most stingy possible holding today. It seems to me there are not only valid but compelling ones. Ordinarily, speaking no more broadly than is absolutely required avoids throwing settled law into confusion; doing so today preserves a chaos that is evident to anyone who can read and count. Alone sufficient to justify a broad holding is the fact that our retaining control, through *Roe*, of what I believe to be, and many of our citizens recognize to be, a political issue, continuously distorts the public perception of the role of this Court. We can now look forward to at least another Term with carts full of mail from the public, and streets full of demonstrators, urging us — their unelected and life-tenured judges who have been awarded those extraordinary, undemocratic characteristics precisely in order that we might follow the law despite the popular will — to follow the popular will. Indeed, I expect we can look forward to even more of that than before, given our indecisive decision today. . . .

It was an arguable question today whether §188.029 of the Missouri law contravened this Court's understanding of Roe v. Wade, and I would have examined *Roe* rather than examining the contravention. Given the Court's newly contracted abstemiousness, what will it take, one must wonder, to permit us to reach that fundamental question? The result of our vote today is that we will not reconsider that prior opinion, even if most of the Justices think it is wrong, unless we have before us a statute that in fact contradicts it — and even then (under our newly discovered "no-broader-than-necessary" requirement) only minor problematical aspects of *Roe* will be reconsidered, unless one expects State legislatures to adopt provisions whose compliance with *Roe* cannot even be argued with a straight face. It thus appears that the mansion of constitutionalized abortion-law, constructed overnight in Roe v. Wade, must be disassembled door-jamb by door-jamb, and never entirely brought down, no matter how wrong it may be.

Of the four courses we might have chosen today — to reaffirm *Roe*, to overrule it explicitly, to overrule it *sub silentio*, or to avoid the question — the last is the least responsible. On the question of the constitutionality of §188.029, I concur in the judgment of the Court and strongly dissent from the manner in which it has been reached.

JUSTICE BLACKMUN, with whom JUSTICE BRENNAN and JUSTICE MARSHALL join, concurring in part and dissenting in part.

Today, Roe v. Wade, 410 U.S. 113 (1973), and the fundamental constitutional right of women to decide whether to terminate a pregnancy, survive but are not secure. Although the Court extricates itself from this case without making a single, even incremental, change in the law of abortion, the plurality and JUSTICE SCALIA would overrule *Roe* (the first silently, the other explicitly) and would return to the States virtually unfettered authority to control the quintessentially intimate, personal, and life-directing decision whether to carry a fetus to term. Although today, no less than yesterday, the Constitution and the decisions of this Court prohibit a State from enacting laws that inhibit women from the meaningful exercise of that right, a plurality of this Court implicitly invites every state legislature to enact more and more restrictive abortion regulations in order to provoke more and more test cases, in the hope that sometime down the line the Court will return the law of procreative freedom to the severe limitations that generally prevailed in this country before January 22, 1973. Never in my memory has a plurality announced a judgment of this Court that so foments disregard for the law and for our standing decisions.

Nor in my memory has a plurality gone about its business in such a deceptive fashion. At every level of its review, from its effort to read the real meaning out of the Missouri statute, to its intended evisceration of precedents and its deafening silence about the constitutional protections that it would jettison, the plurality obscures the portent of its analysis. With feigned restraint, the plurality announces that its analysis leaves *Roe* "undisturbed," albeit "modif[ied] and narrow[ed]." Ante, at 23. But this disclaimer is totally meaningless. The plurality opinion is filled with winks, and nods, and knowing glances to those who would do away with *Roe* explicitly, but turns a

III. Issues of Human Birth

stone face to anyone in search of what the plurality conceives as the scope of a woman's right under the Due Process Clause to terminate a pregnancy free from the coercive and brooding influence of the State. The simple truth is that *Roe* would not survive the plurality's analysis, and that the plurality provides no substitute for *Roe's* protective umbrella.

I fear for the future. I fear for the liberty and equality of the millions of women who have lived and come of age in the 16 years since *Roe* was decided. I fear for the integrity of, and public esteem for, this Court.

I dissent. . . .

I

B

Having set up the conflict between §188.029 and the *Roe* trimester framework, the plurality summarily discards *Roe's* analytic core as " 'unsound in principle and unworkable in practice.' " Ante, at 20, quoting Garcia v. San Antonio Metropolitan Transit Authority, 469 U.S. 528, 546 (1985). This is so, the plurality claims, because the key elements of the framework do not appear in the text of the Constitution, because the framework more closely resembles a regulatory code than a body of constitutional doctrine, and because under the framework the State's interest in potential human life is considered compelling only after viability, when, in fact, that interest is equally compelling throughout pregnancy. Ante, at 21-22. The plurality does not bother to explain these alleged flaws in *Roe*. Bald assertion masquerades as reasoning. The object, quite clearly, is not to persuade, but to prevail.

1

The plurality opinion is far more remarkable for the arguments that it does not advance than for those that it does. The plurality does not even mention, much less join, the true jurisprudential debate underlying this case: whether the Constitution includes an "unenumerated" general right to privacy as recognized in many of our decisions, most notably Griswold v. Connecticut, 381 U.S. 479 (1965), and *Roe*, and, more specifically, whether and to what extent such a right to privacy extends to matters of childbearing and family life, including abortion. See, e.g., Eisenstadt v. Baird, 405 U.S. 438 (1972) (contraception); Loving v. Virginia, 388 U.S. 1 (1967) (marriage); Skinner v. Oklahoma ex re. Williamson, 316 U.S. 535 (1942) (procreation); Pierce v. Society of Sisters, 268 U.S. 510 (1925) (childrearing). These are questions of unsurpassed significance in this Court's interpretation of the Constitution, and mark the battleground upon which this case was fought, by the parties, by the Solicitor General as amicus on behalf of petitioners, and by an unprecedented number of amici. On these grounds, abandoned by the plurality, the Court should decide this case.

But rather than arguing that the text of the Constitution makes no mention of the right to privacy, the plurality complains that the critical elements of the *Roe* framework — trimesters and viability — do not appear in the Constitution and are, therefore, somehow inconsistent with a Constitution cast in general terms. Ante, at 20. Were this a true concern, we would have to abandon most of our constitutional jurisprudence. As the plurality well knows, or should know, the "critical elements" of countless constitutional doctrines nowhere appear in the Constitution's text. . . .

2

The plurality next alleges that the result of the trimester framework has "been a web of legal rules that have become increasingly intricate, resembling a code of regulations rather than a body of constitutional doctrine." Ante, at 20. Again, if this were a true and genuine concern, we would have to abandon vast areas of our constitutional jurisprudence. . . . Are these distinctions any finer, or more "regulatory," than the distinctions we have often drawn in our First Amendment jurisprudence? . . . Our Fourth Amendment jurisprudence recognizes factual distinctions no less intricate. . . . In a recent due process case, THE CHIEF JUSTICE wrote for the Court: "[M]any branches of the law abound in nice distinctions that may be troublesome but have been thought nonetheless necessary: 'I do not think we need trouble ourselves with the thought that my view depends upon differences of degree. The whole law does so as soon as it is civilized.'" Daniels v. Williams, 474 U.S. 327, 334 (1986), quoting Le Roy Fibre Co. v. Chicago, M. & St. P. R. Co., 232 U.S. 340, 354 (1914) (Holmes, J., partially concurring). . . .

For my own part, I remain convinced, as six other Members of this Court 16 years ago were convinced, that the *Roe* framework, and the viability standard in particular, fairly, sensibly, and effectively functions to safeguard the constitutional liberties of pregnant women while recognizing and accommodating the State's interest in potential human life. The viability line reflects the biological facts and truths of fetal development; it marks that threshold moment prior to which a fetus cannot survive separate from the woman and cannot reasonably and objectively be regarded as a subject of rights or interests distinct from, or paramount to, those of the pregnant woman. At the same time, the viability standard takes account of the undeniable fact that as the fetus evolves into its postnatal form, and as it loses its depen-

III. Issues of Human Birth

dence on the uterine environment, the State's interest in the fetus' potential human life, and in fostering a regard for human life in general, becomes compelling. As a practical matter, because viability follows "quickening" — the point at which a woman feels movement in her womb — and because viability occurs no earlier than 23 weeks gestational age, it establishes an easily applicable standard for regulating abortion while providing a pregnant woman ample time to exercise her fundamental right with her responsible physician to terminate her pregnancy.[9] . . .

C

Having contrived an opportunity to reconsider the *Roe* framework, and then having discarded that framework, the plurality finds the testing provision unobjectionable because it "permissibly furthers the State's interest in protecting potential human life." Ante, at 21. This newly minted standard is circular and totally meaningless. Whether a challenged abortion regulation "permissibly furthers" a legitimate state interest is the *question* that courts must answer in abortion cases, not the standard for courts to apply. In keeping with the rest of its opinion, the plurality makes no attempt to explain or to justify its new standard, either in the abstract or as applied in this case. Nor could it. The "permissibly furthers" standard has no independent meaning, and consists of nothing other than what a majority of this Court may believe at any given moment in any given case. The plurality's novel test appears to be nothing more than a dressed-up version of rational-basis review, this Court's most lenient level of scrutiny. One thing is clear, however: were the plurality's "permissibly furthers" standard adopted by the Court, for all practical purposes, *Roe* would be overruled.

The "permissibly furthers" standard completely disregards the

---

9. Notably, neither the plurality nor JUSTICE O'CONNOR advance the now-familiar catch-phrase criticism of the *Roe* framework that because the point of viability will recede with advances in medical technology, *Roe* "is clearly on a collision course with itself." See *Akron*, 462 U.S., at 458 (dissenting opinion). This critique has no medical foundation. As the medical literature and the amicus briefs filed in this case conclusively demonstrate, "there is an 'anatomic threshold' for fetal viability of about 23-24 weeks gestation." Brief for American Medical Association, et al., as Amici Curiae 7. Prior to that time, the crucial organs are not sufficiently mature to provide the mutually sustaining functions that are prerequisite to extrauterine survival, or viability. Moreover, "no technology exists to bridge the development gap between the three-day embryo culture and the 24th week of gestation." Fetal Extrauterine Survivability, Report to the New York State Task Force on Life and Law 10 (1988). Nor does the medical community believe that the development of any such technology is possible in the foreseeable future. Id., at 12. In other words, the threshold of fetal viability is, and will remain, no different from what it was at the time *Roe* was decided. Predictions to the contrary are pure science fiction. See Brief for A Group of American Law Professors as Amici Curiae 23-25.

irreducible minimum of *Roe:* the Court's recognition that a woman has a limited fundamental constitutional right to decide whether to terminate a pregnancy. That right receives no meaningful recognition in the plurality's written opinion. Since, in the plurality's view, the State's interest in potential life is compelling as of the moment of conception, and is therefore served only if abortion is abolished, every hindrance to a woman's ability to obtain an abortion must be "permissible." Indeed, the more severe the hindrance, the more effectively (and permissibly) the State's interest would be furthered. A tax on abortions or a criminal prohibition would both satisfy the plurality's standard. So, for that matter, would a requirement that a pregnant woman memorize and recite today's plurality opinion before seeking an abortion. . . .

It is impossible to read the plurality opinion and especially its final paragraph, without recognizing its implicit invitation to every State to enact more and more restrictive abortion laws, and to assert their interest in potential life as of the moment of conception. All these laws will satisfy the plurality's non-scrutiny, until sometime, a new regime of old dissenters and new appointees will declare what the plurality intends: that *Roe* is no longer good law.[11]

D

Thus, "not with a bang, but a whimper," the plurality discards a landmark case of the last generation, and casts into darkness the hopes and visions of every woman in this country who had come to believe that the Constitution guaranteed her the right to exercise

---

11. The plurality claims that its treatment of *Roe*, and a woman's right to decide whether to terminate a pregnancy, "hold[s] true the balance between that which the Constitution puts beyond the reach of the democratic process and that which it does not." Ante, at 23. This is unadulterated nonsense. The plurality's balance matches a lead weight (the State's allegedly compelling interest in fetal life as of the moment of conception) against a feather (a "liberty interest" of the pregnant woman that the plurality barely mentions, much less describes). The plurality's balance — no balance at all — places nothing, or virtually nothing, beyond the reach of the democratic process.

JUSTICE SCALIA candidly argues that this is all for the best. Post, at 1. I cannot agree. "The very purpose of a Bill of Rights was to withdraw certain subjects from the vicissitudes of political controversy, to place them beyond the reach of majorities and officials and to establish them as legal principles to be applied by the Courts. One's right to life, liberty, and property . . . may not be submitted to vote; they depend on the outcome of no election." West Virginia Board of Education v. Barnette, 319 U.S. 624, 638 (1943). In a Nation that cherishes liberty, the ability of a woman to control the biological operation of her body and to determine with her responsible physician whether or not to carry a fetus to term, must fall within that limited sphere of individual autonomy that lies beyond the will or the power of any transient majority. This Court stands as the ultimate guarantor of that zone of privacy, regardless of the bitter disputes to which our decisions may give rise. In *Roe*, and our numerous cases reaffirming *Roe*, we did no more than discharge our constitutional duty.

some control over her unique ability to bear children. The plurality does so either oblivious or insensitive to the fact that millions of women, and their families, have ordered their lives around the right to reproductive choice, and that this right has become vital to the full participation of women in the economic and political walks of American life. . . .

Of the aspirations and settled understandings of American women, of the inevitable and brutal consequences of what it is doing, the tough-approach plurality utters not a word. This silence is callous. It is also profoundly destructive of this Court as an institution. To overturn a constitutional decision is a rare and grave undertaking. To overturn a constitutional decision that secured a fundamental personal liberty to millions of persons would be unprecedented in our 200 years of constitutional history. . . .

Today's decision involves the most politically divisive domestic legal issue of our time. By refusing to explain or to justify its proposed revolutionary revision in the law of abortion, and by refusing to abide not only by our precedents, but also by our canons for reconsidering those precedents, the plurality invites charges of cowardice and illegitimacy to our door. I cannot say that these would be undeserved.

II

For today, at least, the law of abortion stands undisturbed. For today, the women of this Nation still retain the liberty to control their destinies. But the signs are evident and very ominous, and a chill wind blows.

I dissent.

[JUSTICE STEVENS, opinion concurring in part and dissenting in part is omitted.]

NOTES

Abortion Law in Flux

1. The same day the Court issued its fractured decision in *Webster*, it granted certiorari in three additional abortion cases. Initially, this created the anticipation that the 1989-1990 term would significantly clarify the current status of the law on abortion. However, the case that raised the broadest range of issues concerning the fundamental right to an abortion subsequently was settled by the litigants before it was argued, leaving only the two cases described in note 4 infra that involve narrower issues. These opinions were not available at the time this edition went to press, so students are advised to consult

them in addition to *Webster.* For an early symposium discussing the effect of *Webster,* see 138 U. Penn. L. Rev. 83 (1989).

2. Public interest groups and the media conceived of the issue in *Webster* as whether the Court would overrule Roe v. Wade, but this simplistic characterization fails to capture the important distinction between the two discrete halves of the *Roe* holding: (1) that a woman has a fundamental, constitutionally protected right to an abortion under the privacy doctrine recognized in *Griswold* and *Carey;* and (2) that the proper analysis for accommodating the state's competing interest in the life of the fetus is the "trimester framework." This framework (a) allows only minimal state regulation in the first third of pregnancy when an abortion is medically safer than childbirth, (b) allows only those regulations of the abortion procedure during the second third of pregnancy that reasonably relate to protecting maternal health, and (c) allows a ban on *nontherapeutic* abortions only during the last third of pregnancy, after the fetus is viable outside the womb. Thus, "overruling" *Roe* might mean recognizing no constitutional protection for abortion whatsoever (other than the minimal, rational basis scrutiny that applies to any state law), or it might mean that the degree of protection is substantially lessened from that conferred by the trimester framework.

3. It appears from *Webster* that four justices would overrule *Roe* entirely, giving no special protection to the right to abort, whereas four others would preserve *Roe* intact. Justice O'Connor is thus in the powerful position of being the new consensus builder. Her views therefore take on special significance. From her prior opinions, particularly her dissenting opinion in City of Akron v. Akron Center for Reproductive Health, 462 U.S. 416 (1983), it is clear that *Roe's* trimester framework is dead and that therefore much of the existing abortion jurisprudence will be subject to revision. In *Akron,* Justice O'Connor observed that, as a result of the increasing safety of abortions (which determines the boundary between the first two stages) and the receding date of viability (which marks the beginning of the third stage), "the *Roe* framework . . . is clearly on a collision course with itself." "Sound constitutional theory . . . can[not] accommodate an analytical framework that varies according to the 'stages' of pregnancy, where those stages, and their concomitant standards of review, differ according to the level of medical technology available when a particular challenge to state regulation occurs"). 462 U.S. at 458, 452. See Rhoden, Trimesters and Technology: Revamping Roe v. Wade, 95 Yale L.J. 639 (1986).

On the other hand, Justice O'Connor suggests in *Webster* that she would continue to confer at least some level of heightened constitutional protection, using a standard that prohibits state laws that "unduly burden" the right to seek an abortion. See *Akron* supra, 462

U.S. at 453 ("In my view, this 'unduly burdensome' standard should be applied to the challenged regulations throughout the entire pregnancy without reference to the particular 'stage' of pregnancy involved"). We will have to await future decisions to learn what this standard of review means for the panoply of regulatory approaches that states have devised to restrict abortions.

4. The two cases following *Webster* that will be decided during the 1989-1990 term are Ohio v. Akron Center for Reproductive Health, 854 F.2d 852 (6th Cir. 1988) and Hodgson v. Minnesota, 853 F.2d 1452 (8th Cir. 1988). Each raises the rights of parents to control abortions for their minor children. In the past, the Court has required that statutes calling for parental *consent* to abortions for minors must contain a "judicial bypass" mechanism that allows the minor to demonstrate to a court her maturity to make her own decision or that, independently of her own decision, her best interests require an abortion. See Bellotti v. Baird, 443 U.S. 622 (1979); *Akron* supra. Most statutes have failed to pass muster because the judicial bypass mechanism was found inadequate in design or in implementation. See generally Note, Judicial Consent to Abort: Assessing a Minor's Maturity, 54 G.W.L. Rev. 90 (1985). Following these repeated rejections of parental consent statutes, the states have shifted to mandatory parental *notification* and waiting period requirements as means for overseeing the abortion decisions of minors. By and large, courts so far have treated these statutes with the same scrutiny as parental consent laws. Even *Hodgson*, which upheld Minnesota's parental notification and 48-hour waiting period statute, continued to require an adequate judicial bypass.

Abortion Funding

5. Returning to the one issue that *Webster* clearly did decide — the validity of state refusals to fund or facilitate abortions — the Court left unresolved the latest abortion funding controversy, which centers on federal regulations that withdraw family planning funds from programs that engage in abortion counseling and referral services. The federal funding statute (known as the "Chastity Act") provides that "none of the funds . . . shall be used in programs where abortion is a method of family planning," programs such as many Planned Parenthood Organizations. 42 U.S.C. §300a-6 (1982). Previously, the government had interpreted this statute as prohibiting only the direct use of federal funds for these activities, but in 1988 it stiffened its regulations to preclude funding for organizations that financed these activities from private sources. As a result, two courts have found that these regulations constitute an unconstitutional penalty. Massachusetts v. Secretary of Health and Human Servs., 873

F.2d 1528 (1st Cir. 1989), *aff'd en banc*, 899 F.2d 53 (1st Cir. 1990); Planned Parenthood Federation v. Bowen, 680 F.Supp. 1465 and 687 F.Supp. 540 (D. Colo. 1988). But see New York v. Sullivan, 889 F.2d 401 (2d Cir. 1989) (upholding regulations), *cert. granted*, — U.S. — (1990); Hirt, Why the Government is not Required to Subsidize Abortion Counseling and Referral, 101 Harv. L. Rev. 1895 (1988). Pro-choice advocates have also argued that denying funding based on abortion counseling violates the freedom of speech. Benshoof, The Chastity Act: Government Manipulation of Abortion Information and the First Amendment, 101 Harv. L. Rev. 1916 (1988).

6. State court decisions have sometimes found a *state* constitutional right to Medicaid funding for abortions. See Committee to Defend Reproductive Rights v. Myers, 29 Cal. 3d 252 (1981); Right to Choose v. Byrne, 450 A.2d 925 (N.J. 1982). New Jersey even requires its *private* hospitals to perform abortions, apparently as a matter of state constitutional law. Doe v. Bridgeton Hosp. Assn., 389 A.2d 526 (N.J. Super. 1978). However, under federal law, private hospitals, which are not state actors, presumably are free to decide for themselves not to perform abortions. See Greco v. Orange Mem. Hosp., 513 F.2d 873 (5th Cir. 1975); 20 U.S.C. §1688 ("No provision of [the Civil Rights Act] shall be construed to force or require any individual or hospital . . . to perform or pay for an abortion"). Query, though, whether the "quasi-public facility" theory used in staff privileges cases, see Chapter 6.I.B, could be brought to bear on this issue. In one instructive case, the court held that a Catholic hospital "can prohibit staff from performing sterilization procedures or abortions in the hospital, but cannot require staff to [refrain from performing these services elsewhere] as a condition of employment or extension of privileges." Watkins v. Mercy Med. Cent., 364 F.Supp. 799, 803 (D. Idaho 1973), *aff'd* 520 F.2d 894 (9th Cir. 1975). See also Regan, Constitutional Rights of Catholic Hospitals, 54 Hosp. Prog. 66 (1973).

Consider also the rights of individual health care practitioners (as opposed to facilities) to refuse to participate in abortions. Following *Roe*, Congress and many state legislatures moved quickly to enact so-called "conscience clause" statutes that protect physicians, nurses, and other medical personnel from retaliatory measures for refusing to participate in abortions. See 42 U.S.C. §300a-7 (known as the "Church Amendment"); N.Y. Civ. Rights Law §79i; Wyo. Stat. §35-6-106; Davis, Defining the Employment Rights of Medical Personnel Within the Parameters of Personal Conscience, 3 Det. Col. L. Rev. 847 (1986) (survey of provisions).

Other Abortion Issues

7. The *law* on abortion does not differentiate among the various possible nontherapeutic reasons that a woman might want to end a

pregnancy, but surely these reasons have at least *moral* significance. Should potential parents engage in "eugenic abortion," that is, abortions to avoid defective children? If so, which defects? See Rhoden, Trimesters and Technology: Revamping Roe v. Wade, 95 Yale L.J. 639, 684-691 (1986). Should abortion be used for sex selection? Note, Sex-Selection Abortion: A Constitutional Analysis, 56 Ind. L.J. 281 (1981). If so, how about using abortion to select other characteristics such as size, hair color, personality, etc., at a time when genetic science has progressed further? Should abortion be used purely as a means of after-the-fact birth control? See Thompson, A Defense of Abortion, 1 Phil. & Pub. Aff. 47 (1971) (mounting a defense of abortion, but suggesting that abortion merely as birth control exceeds ethical bounds). In order to eliminate multiple births? Obstetricians have recently developed the ability to selectively reduce the number of fetuses in multifetal pregnancies. For a discussion of the clinical and ethical issues, see Evans et al., Selective First-Trimester Termination in Octuplet and Quadruplet Pregnancies, 71 Obstetrics & Gynecology 289 (1988); Berkowitz et al., Selective Reduction of Multifetal Pregnancies in the First Trimester, 318 New Eng. J. Med. 1043 (1988); Price, Selective Reduction and Feticide: The Parameters of Abortion, 1988 Crim. L. Rev. 199 (1988).

8. It had long been thought that Planned Parenthood of Missouri v. Danforth, 428 U.S. 52 (1976), eliminated any question about whether putative fathers have an interest in blocking an abortion. There, the Court invalidated a requirement that the spouse consent to a woman's abortion unless necessary to save her life. The Court reasoned that "the State cannot delegate to a spouse a veto power which the state itself is absolutely and totally prohibited from exercising. [W]hen the wife and the husband disagree on this decision, the view of only one of the two marriage partners can prevail. Inasmuch as it is the woman who physically bears the child and who is the more directly and immediately affected by the pregnancy, as between the two, the balance weighs in her favor." Recently, however, a scattering of trial courts have intervened to protect the father's interest, suggesting that, by virtue of the common law, spouses/mates retain a *privately* enforceable interest in the decision to abort their offspring. See Moss, "Fathers' Rights" Sought, A.B.A.J. (July 1, 1988); N.Y. Times, April 14, 1988, at 10; April 22, 1988 at 11; BioLaw, at U:863 (1988). These courts have distinguished *Danforth* on the basis that, unlike the explicit statutory enactment at issue there, the private enforcement of common law rights and obligations does not implicate state action and therefore does not create a constitutional issue. But see New York Times Co. v. Sullivan, 376 U.S. 254, 265 (1964) ("It matters not that the law has been applied in a civil action and that it is common law only"). However, the only decisions to reach an appellate court were reversed. Conn v. Conn, 526 N.E.2d

958 (Ind. App. 1988); Coleman v. Coleman, 471 A.2d 1115 (Md. App. 1984) (husband constitutionally prohibited from enjoining wife's abortion). See generally Levy, Abortion and the Dissenting Parent: A Dialogue, 90 Ethics 162 (1980): Annot., 62 A.L.R.3d 1097 (1975).

It is a separate question whether the courts will sustain a state spousal notification (as opposed to consent) requirement. So far, they have not. Eubanks v. Brown, 604 F.Supp. 141 (W.D. Ky. 1984).

9. Of particular relevance to health care law courses are statutes that regulate the process of informed consent to abortions. The *Roe* progeny have invalidated attempts to dictate the specifics of what doctors must disclose to their patients — scripts that are usually blatant attempts to discourage the procedure. See *Akron* supra (striking requirement that woman be informed, inter alia, that "the unborn child is a human life from the moment of conception"). An outgrowth of this case law is language that seems to give constitutional protection to the physician's discretion in such matters, leading to the criticism that it converts abortion into more of a physician's right than a patient's right. See Appleton, Doctors, Patients and the Constitution: A Theoretical Analysis of the Physician's Role in "Private" Reproductive Decisions, 63 Wash. U.L.Q. 183 (1985); Jipping, Informed Consent to Abortion: A Refinement, 38 Case W. Res. L. Rev. 329 (1988).

10. One of the conundrums created by the receding date of fetal viability is what to do if a legal abortion results in a live birth. Previously, methods of abortion such as "D & E" ("dilation and evacuation" by suction) and saline amniocentesis (injecting the womb with a salt solution that triggers expulsion), ensured the destruction of the fetus. New methods of abortion that simply induce premature labor, coupled with recent advances in neonatal intensive care, create the possibility of preserving the life of a significant number of second-trimester aborted fetuses. Does a pregnant woman have the right to insist not only on ending the pregnancy but also causing the death of the fetus? The Baby Doe analysis in section II.B.4 would suggest no, unless the fetus' condition is so precarious that eventual survival is unlikely. For an excellent discussion of these issues, see Rhoden, The New Neonatal Dilemma: Live Births From Late Abortions, 72 Geo. L.J. 1451 (1984).

11. A number of state legislatures have prohibited the use of fetal remains in medical research. E.g., Ariz. Rev. Stat. Ann. §36-2302; Ark. Stat. Ann. §82-438. However, fetal tissue potentially has tremendous medical benefit in the treatment of Parkinson's disease, diabetes, and bone marrow disease, as well as in providing valuable information about fetal development and the formation of birth defects. Assuming abortions are performed for family planning reasons and not simply to produce fetal tissue, what is the ethical or public

III. Issues of Human Birth   1067

policy rationale for preventing these valuable uses of the remains? In Margaret S. v. Edwards, 794 F.2d 994 (5th Cir. 1986), the court struck down Louisiana's fetal tissue statute, finding that it served no rational purpose, interfered with the decision to abort, and was unconstitutionally vague.

On the federal level, although research on fetal tissue is legal, there has been tremendous controversy over whether federal funding agencies such as the NIH should support such research. A panel of experts convened to study the question recommended that no bar to funding be imposed, but the present administration continues to refuse any funding. Biolaw, U:1299 (March 1989); N.Y. Times, Nov. 2, 1989. A related issue concerns whether the sale of fetal tissue should be permitted, either by the aborting woman or by others. See Note, Evolving Conceptualizations of Property: A Proposal to De-Commercialize the Value of Fetal Tissue, 99 Yale L.J. 169 (1989) (opposing a commercial property interest in fetal tissue); Note, Commercialization in Fetal-Tissue Transplantation: Steering Medical Progress to Ethical Cures, 68 Tex. L. Rev. 213 (1989) (same, but proposing to allow biotechnology companies that process fetal tissue to earn a profit).

See generally, Robertson, Fetal Tissue Transplants, 66 Wash. U.L.Q. 443 (1988); Symposium on Fetal Tissue Transplantation, id; Robertson, Rights, Symbolism and Public Policy in Fetal Tissue Transplants, Hastings Cent. Rep., Dec. 1988, at 5; Comment, State Prohibition of Fetal Experimentation and the Fundamental Right of Privacy, 88 Colum. L. Rev. 1057 (1988); Terry, "Alas! Poor Yorick," I Knew Him *Ex Utero:* The Regulation of Embryo and Fetal Experimentation and Disposal in England and the United States, 39 Vand. L. Rev. 419 (1986); Note, Embryo Transplant, Parental Conflict, and Reproductive Freedom: A Prospective Analysis of Issue Arguments Created by Forthcoming Technology, 15 Hofstra L. Rev. 609 (1987).

C. *New Reproductive Technologies*

C. M. v. C. C.
377 A.2d 821 (N.J. Super. 1977)

TESTA, J. C. C., Temporarily Assigned. This is a case of first impression, presenting a unique factual situation with no reported legal precedents directly on point, in this or any other jurisdiction.

C. C. had a child who was conceived through the use of sperm donated by C. M. C. C. testified that she had been discussing with C. M. the possibility of having a child by artificial insemination, inquiring of him whether she should ask one of his friends to supply the sperm. C. M. suggested that he provide it and C. C. agreed to his suggestion. C. M. testified he and C. C. had been seeing each other for some time and were contemplating marriage. She wanted a child and wanted him to be the father, but did not want to have intercourse with him before their marriage. Therefore, he agreed to provide the sperm.

After the decision to have the child was made, the testimony of both parties are substantially the same. C. C. and C. M. went to a doctor who referred them to a sperm bank. The doctor at the sperm bank refused to allow its facilities to be used. However, C. C. learned, as a result of her conversation with the doctor, of a procedure for artificial insemination using a glass syringe and a glass jar.

Over a period of several months, C. C. went to C. M.'s apartment where they attempted the artificial insemination. C. M. would stay in one room while C. C. went to another room to attempt to inseminate herself with semen provided by C. M. After several attempts over a period of several months, C. C. did conceive a child.

C. M. testified that until C. C. was about three months pregnant, he assumed he would act toward the child in the same manner as most fathers act toward their children. C. C. denies this, testifying that C. M. was to be only a visitor in her home — much as any of her other friends. In either case, at that point the relationship between C. M. and C. C. broke off. This present application is a request by C. M. for visitation rights to the baby. His request is strenuously opposed by C. C.

A natural father is entitled to visitation rights with respect to his illegitimate children. See R v. F, 113 N.J. Super. 396 (Cty. Ct. 1971). The key issue in this case is whether C. M. is the natural father of the child or whether he should be considered not to be such because the sperm used to conceive was transferred to C. C. by other than natural means. C. C. does not dispute that the sperm used to conceive the child was provided by C. M.

The question of who is the father of a child conceived by artificial insemination has been addressed by a few courts in the United States and has been addressed by authorities in the field of family law. In most cases the donor is unknown, and the issue involves whether the husband of the mother is, in fact, the father. In Strnad v. Strnad, 190 Misc. 786, 78 N.Y.S.2d 390 (Sup. Ct. 1948), the New York court considered a situation where a woman was artifically inseminated by a third-party donor with the consent of her husband. The court held that the husband was entitled to visitation, also holding that the child had been "potentially or semi-adopted by the defendant." The husband was "entitled to the same rights as that acquired by a foster parent who has formally adopted a child, if not the same rights as those to which a natural parent under the circumstances would be

III. Issues of Human Birth   1069

entitled." It was the court's opinion that if the mother was artificially inseminated with the consent of the husband, the child would not be illegitimate.

In 1963 a New York court considered the case of Gursky v. Gursky, 39 Misc. 2d 1083, 242 N.Y.S.2d 406 (Sup. Ct. 1963). In that case an annulment was granted by the trial court because the husband was unable to consummate the marriage. When the couple had discovered the husband's infirmity, they decided that the wife should be artificially inseminated with the semen of a third-party donor. Both husband and wife signed the proper consent for the procedure. The husband agreed to pay all expenses and signed a contract for waiver of liability as well as for the medical and/or surgical treatments. As a result of using the procedure a child was born. The birth certificate listed the wife as mother and the husband as father. The issue raised in the appellate court was whether the child was legitimate.

The court discussed the *Strnad* case, but noting that the child had not been legally adopted, held that "the court's conclusion that the child was legitimate cannot logically be sustained." The court also quoted from an unreported case which said, "[w]here the precise issue of legitimacy has been squarely presented for determination, it has been held that heterologous artificial insemination by a third-party donor with or without the consent of the husband, constitutes adultery on the part of the mother and, that a child so conceived is not a child born in wedlock and is therefore illegitimate (Doornbos v. Doornbos, No. 54 S. 1498 [Superior Court, Cook Co., December 13, 1954]." The court in *Gursky* concluded (242 N.Y.S.2d at 410-411) that "the child in the instant case, which was indisputably the offspring of artificial insemination by a third-party donor with the consent of the mother's husband, is not the legitimate 'issue' of the husband." However, the court held that in light of the husband's consent to the procedure, he was obligated to support the child, basing its decision on theories of implied contract and equitable estoppel.

A California court considered a similar situation in People v. Sorenson, 68 Cal. 2d 280, 66 Cal. Rptr. 7, 437 P. 2d 495 (Sup. Ct. 1968). In that case a sterile husband and his wife consented to her artificial insemination, resulting in the birth of a child. For the following four years they lived together in a normal family relationship. When the husband and wife were divorced the wife stated that she wanted no child support from her husband. However, under the divorce decree "the court retained jurisdiction regarding the possible support obligation of plaintiff in regard to a minor child born to defendant." Later, when the wife became ill and unable to work, she applied for public assistance, which was given to her until she was able to resume work. Although the district attorney demanded child support, her former husband did not support the child. A municipal court found him to be in violation of the state's Penal Code and placed him on probation on condition that he make certain monthly payments for support.

In reaching a decision, the court noted that the determinative factor was whether the relationship of father and child existed. It stated: ". . . a child conceived through heterologous artificial insemination does not have a 'natural father,' as that term is commonly used. The anonymous donor of the sperm cannot be considered the 'natural father,' as he is no more responsible for the use made of his sperm than is the donor of blood or a kidney. . . . With the use of frozen semen, the donor may even be dead at the time the semen is used. [66 Cal. Rptr. at 10, 437 P.2d at 498]" At footnote 2, the court notes that there are two types of artificial insemination — one is with the husband's semen, and the other with that of a third-party donor. "Only the latter raises legal problems of fatherhood and legitimacy." *Sorenson,* supra, 66 Cal. Rptr. at 10, 437 P.2d at 498. The court stated that one who actively participated and consented to his wife's artificial insemination knew the legal responsibility of fatherhood and criminal responsibility for nonsupport. The court went on to state that "One who consents to the production of a child cannot create a temporary relation to be assumed and disclaimed at will, but the arrangement must be of such character as to impose an obligation of supporting those for whose existence he is directly responsible. As noted by the trial court, it is safe to assume that without defendant's active participation and consent, the child would not have been procreated. [66 Cal. Rptr. at 11, 437 P.2d at 498]" The court decided that the question of legitimacy of the child was properly left to the legislature, but noted that it was sufficient to find that the husband was the "lawful father" of the child to establish the responsibility to support. It held that the husband was the "lawful father."

A slightly different issue was addressed by a court in Adoption of Anonymous, 74 Misc. 2d 99, 345 N.Y.S.2d 430 (Sup. Ct. 1973). In that case the husband consented to artificial insemination of the wife and was listed as father on the birth certificate. The couple later separated and were divorced. Both the separation agreement and the divorce decree referred to the child as the "daughter" or "child" of the couple. Support and visitation were awarded and the husband faithfully supported and visited the child. When the wife later remarried, her second husband wanted to adopt the child. The proposed adoption was opposed by the first husband. The second husband argued that consent of the first should not be required as he was not the "parent" of the child.

The court in Adoption of Anonymous, as did the court in People

v. Sorenson, supra, differentiates between artificial insemination using a husband's semen and that using the semen of a third-party donor. The first situation, it notes (345 N.Y.S.2d at 430-431) "creates no legal problems since the child is considered the natural child of the husband and wife." The court concluded that *Gursky,* supra was not persuasive. It noted that New York had a "strong policy in favor of legitimacy" and held "that a child born of consensual [artificial insemination by a donor] during a valid marriage is a legitimate child entitled to the rights and privileges of a naturally conceived child of the same marriage." The court went on to hold that the first husband's consent was required for the adoption.

It is clear that the situation in the case at bar is different from that directly addressed in these cases. There is no married couple. There is no anonymous donor. Rather, we have a woman who chooses to have a baby and a man who chooses to provide the needed sperm, who are not married to each other and who choose a method of conception other than sexual intercourse. If the conception took place by intercourse, there would be no question that the "donor" would be the father. The issue becomes whether a man is any less a father because he provides the semen by a method different from that normally used.

In the cases above, there are at least three people involved in the conception of the child — a woman, her husband and an anonymous donor. The cases mention a second possible situation — where a woman is artificially inseminated by her husband's own sperm. As we noted above, the courts in both People v. Sorenson and the Adoption of Anonymous stated that in the latter situation no legal issue was raised. In that situation the husband is clearly the father of the child.

The case at bar is more analogous to the second situation. In the first, there is competition over whether the husband or donor has the legal responsibility of fatherhood. The donor is unknown. In the second, there is no such competition. The husband and donor are the same person — and dictum, at least, tells us that there would be no question that such husband-donor would be the father.

Certain principles discussed in the earlier cases do shed some light on the instant case. In 1963 the court in *Gursky,* although refusing to label a child born of heterologous artificial insemination legitimate, did find that a husband consenting to his wife's insemination was obligated to support the child. In *Sorenson,* the California court held (66 Cal. Rptr. at 11, 437 P.2d at 499) that a husband who consented to a child's birth through artificial insemination, "cannot create a temporary relation to be assumed and disclaimed at will, but the arrangements must be of such character to impose an obligation of supporting those for whose existence he is directly responsible."

The courts have consistently shown a policy favoring the requirement that a child be provided with a father as well as a mother. In a situation where there is an anonymous donor the courts have required that the person who consents to the use of sperm, not his own, be responsible for fathering the child.

In this case there is a known man who is the donor. There is no husband. If the couple had been married and the husband's sperm was used artificially, he would be considered the father. If a woman conceives a child by intercourse, the "donor" who is not married to the mother is no less a father than the man who is married to the mother. Likewise, if an unmarried woman conceives a child through artificial insemination from semen from a known man, that man cannot be considered to be less a father because he is not married to the woman.

When a husband consents to his wife's artificial insemination from an anonymous donor, he takes upon himself the responsibilities of fatherhood. By donating his semen anonymously, the donor impliedly gives it without taking on such responsibilities for its use. But here C. C. received semen from C. M., who was a friend — someone she had known for at least two years. The court finds that the evidence supports C. M.'s contention that he and C. C. had a long-standing dating relationship and he fully intended to assume the responsibilities of parenthood. There was no one else who was in a position to take upon himself the responsibilities of fatherhood when the child was conceived. The evidence does not adequately support C. C.'s contention, as argued by her attorney in his brief and stated in her testimony, that C. M. waived his parental rights.

It is in a child's best interests to have two parents whenever possible. The court takes no position as to the propriety of the use of artificial insemination between unmarried persons, but must be concerned with the best interests of the child in granting custody or visitation, and for such consideration will not make any distinction between a child conceived naturally or artificially. See DiBiano v. DiBiano, 105 N.J. Super. 415, 419 (App. Div. 1969); Sheehan v. Sheehan, 51 N.J. Super. 276 (App. Div. 1958). In this situation, a man wants to take upon himself the responsibility of being a father to a child he is responsible for helping to conceive. The evidence does not support C. C.'s argument that he is unfit. The evidence demonstrates that C. M. attempted to establish a relationship with the child but was thwarted in his attempts by C. C. Contrary to C. C.'s argument, C. M. has shown a genuine interest in the child; he is a teacher and educationally able to aid his development, and is financially capable of contributing to his support. C. M.'s consent and active participation in the procedure leading to conception should place upon him the responsibilities of fatherhood. The court will not

III. Issues of Human Birth

deny him the privileges of fatherhood. His motion for the right of visitation is granted. The court reserves the right to hold a hearing as to the period and manner of visitation on behalf of C. M.

Inasmuch as the court has found C. M. to be the natural father, the court must consider support and maintenance of the child and payment of any expenses incurred in his birth. Proper application shall be made by the parties to effect the above.

NOTES

Artificial Insemination and In Vitro Fertilization

1. An estimated 10,000 children are born each year through artificial insemination. Wadlington, Artificial Conception: The Challenge for Family Law, 69 Va. L. Rev. 465, 472 (1983). In one notorious case, a lesbian couple consisting of one biological female and one transsexual female agreed to artificial insemination of the fertile partner. When they broke up, the court ordered the transsexual to provide child support, citing the strength of the best-interests-of-the-child principle. Karin T. vs. Michael T., 484 N.Y.S.2d 780 (Fam. Ct. 1985).

The principal case is unique in dealing with the rights of the donor in artificial insemination. Most third party donors seek anonymity and confidentiality. As artificial insemination becomes more popular, recordkeeping requirements may threaten this status. Could a child born through artificial insemination insist on obtaining records of the donor's identity as in adoption cases? See Shaman, Legal Aspects of Artificial Insemination, 18 J. Fam. L. 331 (1980). See also the Uniform Parentage Act §5, Note 3 infra, which calls for sealed records only to be opened with a court order for "good cause." See also a subsequent decision involving the same parties as in the principal case, in which the court required the mother to list the semen donor's name on the birth certificate, C. M. v. C. C., 407 A.2d 849 (N.J. Juv. Dom. Rel. Ct. 1979).

2. Artificial insemination (AI) can be provided in one of three ways: (1) with the sperm of the husband donor (AIH), (2) with the sperm of a third party donor (AID), and (3) with the combined sperm from both the husband and a third party (AIC). The latter is used in cases of low fertility and may resolve many emotional and legal questions since there is no way to determine the identity of the sperm. See Wadlington, Artificial Insemination: The Dangers of a Poorly Kept Secret, 64 Nw. U.L. Rev. 777 (1970); Guttmacher, Artificial Insemination, 18 De Paul L. Rev. 566 (1969).

3. Over half the states have adopted statutes which generally prohibit the use of artificial insemination by an unmarried woman,

require the written consent of both the husband and the wife, and consider the child legitimate. What will be the status of such acts in the light of *Griswold* and *Roe?*

The Uniform Parentage Act §5 addresses some of the basic issues, but leaves many unanswered:

> (a) If, under the supervision of a licensed physician and with the consent of her husband, a wife is inseminated artificially with semen donated by a man not her husband, the husband is treated in law as if he were the natural father of a child thereby conceived. The husband's consent must be in writing and signed by him and his wife. The physician shall certify their signatures and the date of the insemination, and file the husband's consent with the [State Department of Health], where it shall be kept confidential and in a sealed file. However, the physician's failure to do so does not affect the father and child relationship. All papers and records pertaining to the insemination, whether part of the permanent record of a court or of a file held by the supervising physician or elsewhere, are subject to inspection only upon an order of the court for good cause shown.
>
> (b) The donor of semen provided to a licensed physician for use in artificial insemination of a married woman other than the donor's wife is treated in law as if he were not the natural father of a child thereby conceived.

What effect would such a statute have on the outcome of a case where the couple is not married and does not act "under the supervision of a licensed physician"? In one such case, the court granted the sperm donor parental and visitation rights because the statutory conditions were not fully satisfied. Jordan C. v. Mary K., 224 Cal. Rptr. 530 (Cal. App. 1986). However, in another case, the court held that the statute precludes parental rights and responsibilities for a donor, even if the woman is unmarried and inseminates without medical assistance; yet, the court went on to hold, this statutory effect unconstitutionally invades the privacy interest of a donor who claims that the mother agreed with him that he could assume parental status. McIntyre v. Crouch, 780 P.2d 239 (Or. App. 1989).

Aside from such statutory constraints, do you think that an unmarried male companion who consents to the sperm donation from a third party (as opposed to his own sperm donation, as in the principal case) should have paternal rights and responsibilities? The law uniformly answers "no." Why should the male companion's marital status matter, if it does not matter for true, genetic offspring? If the law were otherwise, consider the difficulties it would face in differentiating paternity in AID cases where the companion is only a weekend houseguest, or is only a good friend rather than a sexual partner.

4. In addition to the issues of adultery, legitimacy, support, and

visitation rights, consider also the possible civil and criminal actions that might be brought against a physician or attorney recommending the procedure. Might rape be alleged if the procedure is performed by force or fraud upon an unwilling patient? Cases are collected in Note, 25 A.L.R.3d 1103 (1969). Will a physician be liable for genetically defective semen? For a revealing discussion of the lack of donor screening see Currie-Cohen et al., Current Practice of Artificial Insemination by Donor in the United States, 300 New Eng. J. Med. 585 (1978).

5. Sperm banks are another recent development which raise similar questions. While most state statutes do not allow this, does an unmarried woman have a right to conceive through the use of a sperm bank? One has been established solely for the sperm of Nobel Prize winners. Consider also the moral issues involved in the production of an Orwellian test tube society which allows conception and childbearing only by the selected few favored people (positive eugenics). It should also be noted that both moral and practical problems might arise with the possibility of incest occurring due to a policy of not identifying the sperm donor. Cases have already been reported. See Hoffer, The Legal Limbo of AID — Artificial Insemination by Donor, 47 Mod. Med. no. 11, 27 (Nov. 1979); HEW, Report of Ethics Advisory Board: HEW Support of Research Involving Human in vitro Fertilization and Embryo Transfer (May 4, 1979).

6. Religious attitudes may also affect the law in this area. See Lombard, Civil Law and Ecclesiastical Views, 2 Suffolk U.L. Rev. 137 (1968); Ryan, Noble, and Friedman, The Religious Viewpoints, in Symposium on Artificial Insemination, 7 Syracuse L. Rev. 99 (1955); Dedek, Contemporary Ethics (1975); Van Allen, Artificial Insemination (AIH); A Contemporary Re-analysis, 1970 Homiletic & Pastoral Rev. 363; Häring, Manipulation: Ethical Boundaries of Medical Behavioral and Genetic Manipulation (1975); Annas, Artificial Insemination: Beyond the Best Interests of the Donor, 9 Hastings Cent. Rep. 14 (Aug. 1979); Kass, "Making Babies" Revisited, 1979 Pub. Interest 32; Walters, Human in Vitro Fertilization: A Review of the Ethical Literature, 9 Hastings Center Rep. 23 (Aug. 1979).

7. Frozen embryos present even more mind-boggling issues:

> With her conception occurring in a petrie dish, the birth of Louise Brown in 1978 launched a powerful new technology for treating infertility and exercising control over the earliest stages of human development. Since that birth, in vitro fertilization (IVF) technology has spread rapidly throughout the world. More than 140 programs exist in the United States, and more than 5000 IVF children have been born worldwide. . . .
>
> The IVF procedure works by removing one or more eggs from the ovary, inseminating them in a glass dish with partner's sperm, and

after 48-72 hours transferring the cleaving embryos to the egg source's uterus. In the best programs a pregnancy will result in twenty to twenty-five percent of the attempts.

A central feature of the IVF approach is stimulation of the ovaries to produce multiple eggs. Administration of hormones at set times in the menstrual cycle spurs follicular development and leads to the recovery of multiple eggs (as many as 6 or 8) just before ovulation. By increasing the number of eggs that are inseminated, superovulation enables several embryos to be transferred to the uterus, which greatly increases the chance of pregnancy occurring.

Yet superovulation presents a dilemma at the same time that it enhances the possibility of pregnancy. Transfer of more than three or four embryos to the uterus greatly increases the risk of multiple pregnancy, which presents severe risks for the mother and offspring. Yet discarding all embryos beyond the number (three or four) that can be safely transferred is objectionable to some people, and not permitted in most programs. . . .

Cryopreservation of embryos poses a solution to this problem. The ability to store excess embryos allows the optimum number to be transferred while preserving the others for use in a later cycle. By avoiding discard of those embryos that are too numerous to transfer at one time, all eggs can be recovered and inseminated, thus maximizing the number of embryos for transfer. . . . Successful pregnancies have been reported after freeze-thawing of human embryos in the United States, Great Britain, Australia, France and the Netherlands. A growing number of programs are now offering cryopreservation on an experimental basis.

Freezing technology will also increase the reach and impact of IVF technology in other ways. The ability to maintain the embryo outside the body for long or indefinite periods will facilitate such novel means of family formation as egg and embryo donation and gestational surrogacy. It will also increase the ability to select embryos for transfer on genetic grounds, by preserving them during a period of embryo examination and biopsy. Selection of embryos on genetic grounds will also facilitate gene therapy on embryos and greater control over the genetic characteristics of offspring. Eventually persons at risk of loss of ovarian function, fearful of future sterility or age-related birth defects, may bank embryos to insure against those contingencies. Grobstein speculates that in the more distant future cryopreserved embryos may play a role in space exploration and migration to distant planets. . . .

Given patient demand, many IVF programs are likely to incorporate human embryo freezing into infertility practice. The result will be that thousands of embryos will be stored for varying periods across the country in IVF clinics and embryo banks. In time an entire industry devoted to embryo banking with regionalized storage facilities and even international transport of embryos, as now occurs in the cattle and sheep industry, might emerge.

Robertson, Decisional Authority over Embryos and Control of IVF Technology, 28 Jurimetrics 285 (1988). The extent to which this new

III. Issues of Human Birth   1077

technology can be carried is illustrated by a South African woman who gave birth to her own grandchildren — triplets nonetheless — after agreeing to act as a surrogate for her daughter unable to bear children. N.Y. Times, April 9, 1987, at 1.

Consider also a divorced couple in Tennessee who could not agree over who controls their frozen embryos. Their previous attempt at insemination had failed and she wanted to try again, whereas he objected to further attempts. The trial court sided with the wife, reasoning that the embryos "are human beings . . . not property" and that "human life begins at the moment of conception." Accordingly, he found that the "best interests of the children" dictated that "they be made available for implantation to assure their opportunity for live birth." Davis v. Davis, Fifth Jud. Ct., No. E-14496 (Sept. 21, 1989). An appeal is certain to follow. Commenting on this decision, Professor Annas observes that "if these embryos really were children, people, or human beings it would not be lawful to conduct deadly experiments on them, such as freezing. . . . Every national commission worldwide that has examined the status of the human embryo to date has placed it in [a] third category: neither people nor products, but nonetheless entities of unique symbolic value that deserve society's respect and protection." Annas, A French Homunculus in a Tennessee Court, Hastings Cent. Rep., Nov/Dec. 1989, at 20, 21. See also, in the same issue, Robertson, Resolving Disputes over the Disposition of Frozen Embryos.

8. As is evident from the Robertson excerpt above, artificial insemination is only the tip of the new reproductive technology iceberg. Consider the dizzying host of legal/ethical issues raised by the ability to donate eggs as well as sperms and to gestate these various combinations in donor wombs. For example, what is the status of a child born from an embryo that is formed when a couple fertilizes the wife's egg with a donor sperm in vitro and implants the embryo in a surrogate womb? (No one knows.) Within the realm of imagination exists the possibility of ectogenesis, the extracorporeal gestation of human beings.

To get some handle on this tremendously fertile area for legal analysis, it helps to think of the issues as clustering into two categories: (1) family law issues, which tend to center on the status consequences of engaging in new forms of reproduction, issues such as who the legal parents are, who has custody and visitation rights, and who bears the responsibility of support; and (2) constitutional/regulatory issues, such as whether the new technology and practices pose any harm, whether they should be allowed, and whether their restriction poses constitutional problems. An excellent analysis of IVF technology that looks at the first cluster of issues is Wadlington, Artificial Conception: The Challenge for Family Law, 69 Va. L. Rev. 465 (1983). Robertson's work provides the most thorough analysis of the second

© 1987 reprinted by permission of Doug Marlette and the Atlanta Constitution.

group of issues. See also Robertson, Embryos, Families and Procreative Liberty: The Legal Structure of the New Reproduction, 59 S. Cal. L. Rev. 939 (1986).

9. Recent additions to this burgeoning literature include S. Fishel & E. Symonds, In Vitro Fertilization: Past, Present, Future (1986); Robertson, Technology and Motherhood: Legal and Ethical Issues in Human Egg Donation, 39 Case W. Res. L. Rev. (1989); Seibel, A New Era in Reproductive Technology: In Vitro Fertilization, Gamete Intrafallopian Transfer, and Donated Gametes and Embryos, 318 New Eng. J. Med. 828 (1988); Special Project, Legal Rights and Issues Surrounding Conception, Pregnancy, and Birth, 39 Vand. L. Rev. 597 (1986); Annas, Making Babies Without Sex, 74 Am. J. Pub. Health 1415 (1984). For access to earlier articles, see G. McNabb, Ethical and Legal Aspects of Human in Vitro Fertilization: A Select Annotated Bibliography (1984).

In the Matter of Baby M
537 A.2d 1227 (N.J. 1988)

WILENTZ, C. J., writing for a unanimous Court. In this matter the Court is asked to determine the validity of a contract that purports to provide a new way of bringing children into a family. For a fee

III. Issues of Human Birth

of $10,000, a woman agrees to be artificially inseminated with the semen of another woman's husband; she is to conceive a child, carry it to term, and after its birth surrender it to the natural father and his wife. The intent of the contract is that the child's natural mother will thereafter be forever separated from her child. The wife is to adopt the child, and she and the natural father are to be regarded as its parents for all purposes. The contract providing for this is called a "surrogacy contract," the natural mother inappropriately called the "surrogate mother."

We invalidate the surrogacy contract because it conflicts with the law and public policy of this State. While we recognize the depth of the yearning of infertile couples to have their own children, we find the payment of money to a "surrogate" mother illegal, perhaps criminal, and potentially degrading to women. . . .

I. Facts

In February 1985, William Stern and Mary Beth Whitehead entered into a surrogacy contract. It recited that Stern's wife, Elizabeth, was infertile, that they wanted a child, and that Mrs. Whitehead was willing to provide that child as the mother with Mr. Stern as the father.

The contract provided that through artificial insemination using Mr. Stern's sperm, Mrs. Whitehead would become pregnant, carry the child to term, bear it, deliver it to the Sterns, and thereafter do whatever was necessary to terminate her maternal rights so that Mrs. Stern could thereafter adopt the child. . . .

Mr. Stern, on his part, agreed to attempt the artificial insemination and to pay Mrs. Whitehead $10,000 after the child's birth, on its delivery to him. In a separate contract, Mr. Stern agreed to pay $7,500 to the Infertility Center of New York ("ICNY"). The Center's advertising campaigns solicit surrogate mothers and encourage infertile couples to consider surrogacy. ICNY arranged for the surrogacy contract by bringing the parties together, explaining the process to them, furnishing the contractual form, and providing legal counsel.

The history of the parties' involvement in this arrangement suggests their good faith. William and Elizabeth Stern were married in July 1974, having met at the University of Michigan, where both were Ph.D. candidates. Due to financial considerations and Mrs. Stern's pursuit of a medical degree and residency, they decided to defer starting a family until 1981. Before then, however, Mrs. Stern learned that she might have multiple sclerosis and that the disease in some cases renders pregnancy a serious health risk. Her anxiety appears to have exceeded the actual risk, which current medical authorities assess as minimal. Nonetheless that anxiety was evidently quite real,

Mrs. Stern fearing that pregnancy might precipitate blindness, paraplegia, or other forms of debilitation. Based on the perceived risk, the Sterns decided to forego having their own children. The decision had a special significance for Mr. Stern. Most of his family had been destroyed in the Holocaust. As the family's only survivor, he very much wanted to continue his bloodline.

Initially the Sterns considered adoption, but were discouraged by the substantial delay apparently involved and by the potential problem they saw arising from their age and their differing religious backgrounds. They were most eager for some other means to start a family. . . .

On February 6, 1985, Mr. Stern and Mr. and Mrs. Whitehead executed the surrogate parenting agreement. After several artificial inseminations over a period of months, Mrs. Whitehead became pregnant. The pregnancy was uneventful and on March 27, 1986, Baby M was born.

Not wishing anyone at the hospital to be aware of the surrogacy arrangement, Mr. and Mrs. Whitehead appeared to all as the proud parents of a healthy female child. Her birth certificate indicated her name to be Sara Elizabeth Whitehead and her father to be Richard Whitehead. In accordance with Mrs. Whitehead's request, the Sterns visited the hospital unobtrusively to see the newborn child.

Mrs. Whitehead realized, almost from the moment of birth, that she could not part with this child. She had felt a bond with it even during pregnancy. Some indication of the attachment was conveyed to the Sterns at the hospital when they told Mrs. Whitehead what they were going to name the baby. She apparently broke into tears and indicated that she did not know if she could give up the child. She talked about how the baby looked like her other daughter, and made it clear that she was experiencing great difficulty with the decision.

Nonetheless, Mrs. Whitehead was, for the moment, true to her word. Despite powerful inclinations to the contrary, she turned her child over to the Sterns on March 30 at the Whiteheads' home.

The Sterns were thrilled with their new child. They had planned extensively for its arrival, far beyond the practical furnishing of a room for her. It was a time of joyful celebration — not just for them but for their friends as well. The Sterns looked forward to raising their daughter, whom they named Melissa. While aware by then that Mrs. Whitehead was undergoing an emotional crisis, they were as yet not cognizant of the depth of that crisis and its implications for their newly-enlarged family.

Later in the evening of March 30, Mrs. Whitehead became deeply disturbed, disconsolate, stricken with unbearable sadness. She had to have her child. She could not eat, sleep, or concentrate on anything

III. Issues of Human Birth

other than her need for her baby. The next day she went to the Sterns' home and told them how much she was suffering.

The depth of Mrs. Whitehead's despair surprised and frightened the Sterns. She told them that she could not live without her baby, that she must have her, even if only for one week, that thereafter she would surrender her child. The Sterns, concerned that Mrs. Whitehead might indeed commit suicide, not wanting under any circumstances to risk that, and in any event believing that Mrs. Whitehead would keep her word, turned the child over to her. . . .

[W]hen it became apparent that Mrs. Whitehead [w]ould not return the child to Mr. Stern, [he obtained an *ex parte* order to relinquish custody]. [T]he process server, aided by the police, in the presence of the Sterns, entered Mrs. Whitehead's home to execute the order. Mr. Whitehead fled with the child, who had been handed to him through a window while those who came to enforce the order were thrown off balance by a dispute over the child's current name.

The Whiteheads immediately fled to Florida. . . . For the next three months, the[y] lived at roughly twenty hotels, motels, and homes in order to avoid apprehension. From time to time Mrs. Whitehead would call Mr. Stern to discuss the matter; the conversations . . . show an escalating dispute about rights, morality, and power, accompanied by threats of Mrs. Whitehead to kill herself, to kill the child, and falsely to accuse Mr. Stern of sexually molesting Mrs. Whitehead's other daughter.

Eventually, the Sterns discovered where the Whiteheads were staying . . . and obtained an order requiring the[m] to turn over the child. Police in Florida enforced the order, forcibly removing the child from her grandparents' home. . . .

The trial court concluded that the various statutes governing this matter, including those concerning adoption, termination of parental rights, and payment of money in connection with adoptions, do not apply to surrogacy contracts. It reasoned that because the Legislature did not have surrogacy contracts in mind when it passed those laws, those laws were therefore irrelevant. Thus, assuming it was writing on a clean slate, the trial court analyzed the interests involved and the power of the court to accommodate them. It then held that surrogacy contracts are valid and should be enforced and furthermore that Mr. Stern's rights under the surrogacy contract were constitutionally protected. 525 A.2d 1128. . . .

II. Invalidity and Unenforceability of Surrogacy Contract

We have concluded that this surrogacy contract is invalid. Our conclusion has two bases: direct conflict with existing statutes and conflict with the public policies of this State, as expressed in its statutory and decisional law.

One of the surrogacy contract's basic purposes, to achieve the adoption of a child through private placement, though permitted in New Jersey "is very much disfavored." Sees v. Baber, 74 N.J. 201, 217, 377 A.2d 628 (1977). Its use of money for this purpose — and we have no doubt whatsoever that the money is being paid to obtain an adoption and not, as the Sterns argue, for the personal services of Mary Beth Whitehead — is illegal and perhaps criminal. N.J.S.A. 9:3-54. In addition to the inducement of money, there is the coercion of contract: the natural mother's irrevocable agreement, prior to birth, even prior to conception, to surrender the child to the adoptive couple. Such an agreement is totally unenforceable in private placement adoption. See 74 N.J. at 212-14, 377 A.2d 628. Even where the adoption is through an approved agency, the formal agreement to surrender occurs only after birth (as we read N.J.S.A. 9:2-16 and -17, and similar statutes), and then, by regulation, only after the birth mother has been counseled. N.J.A.C. 10:121A-5.2(a). Integral to these invalid provisions of the surrogacy contract is the related agreement, equally invalid, on the part of the natural mother to cooperate with, and not to contest, proceedings to terminate her parental rights, as well as her contractual concession, in aid of the adoption, that the child's best interests would be served by awarding custody to the natural father and his wife — all of this before she has even conceived, and, in some cases, before she has the slightest idea of what the natural father and adoptive mother are like.

The foregoing provisions not only directly conflict with New Jersey statutes, but also offend long-established State policies. These critical terms, which are at the heart of the contract, are invalid and unenforceable; the conclusion therefore follows, without more, that the entire contract is unenforceable.

A. Conflict with Statutory Provisions

The surrogacy contract conflicts with: (1) laws prohibiting the use of money in connection with adoptions; (2) laws requiring proof of parental unfitness or abandonment before termination of parental rights is ordered or an adoption is granted; and (3) laws that make surrender of custody and consent to adoption revocable in private placement adoptions.

(1) Our law prohibits paying or accepting money in connection with any placement of a child for adoption. N.J.S.A. 9:3-54a. Violation is a high misdemeanor. Excepted are fees of an approved agency (which must be a non-profit entity) and certain expenses in connection with childbirth.

III. Issues of Human Birth

Considerable care was taken in this case to structure the surrogacy arrangement so as not to violate this prohibition. [T]he money paid to Mrs. Whitehead was stated to be . . . "compensation for services and expenses and in no way . . . a fee for termination of parental rights or a payment in exchange for consent to surrender a child for adoption." . . . Nevertheless, it seems clear that the money was paid and accepted in connection with an adoption.

The surrogacy agreement requires Mrs. Whitehead to surrender Baby M for the purposes of adoption. The agreement notes that Mr. and Mrs. Stern wanted to have a child, and provides that the child be "placed" with Mrs. Stern in the event Mr. Stern dies before the child is born. The payment of the $10,000 occurs only on surrender of custody of the child and "completion of the duties and obligations" of Mrs. Whitehead, including termination of her parental rights to facilitate adoption by Mrs. Stern. As for the contention that the Sterns are paying only for services and not for an adoption, we need note only that they would pay nothing in the event the child died before the fourth month of pregnancy, and only $1,000 if the child were stillborn, even though the "services" had been fully rendered. . . .

The evils inherent in baby bartering are loathsome for a myriad of reasons. The child is sold without regard for whether the purchasers will be suitable parents. N. Baker, Baby Selling: The Scandal of Black Market Adoption 7 (1978). The natural mother does not receive the benefit of counseling and guidance to assist her in making a decision that may affect her for a lifetime. In fact, the monetary incentive to sell her child may, depending on her financial circumstances, make her decision less voluntary. . . .

(2) The termination of Mrs. Whitehead's parental rights, called for by the surrogacy contract and actually ordered by the court fails to comply with the stringent requirements of New Jersey law. . . . In order to terminate parental rights under the private placement adoption statute, there must be a finding of "intentional abandonment or a very substantial neglect of parental duties without a reasonable expectation of a reversal of that conduct in the future." . . . As the trial court recognized, without a valid termination there can be no adoption. This requirement applies to all adoptions, whether they be private placements, ibid., or agency adoptions, N.J.S.A. 9:3-46a, -47c. . . . Since the termination was invalid, it follows, as noted above, that adoption of Melissa by Mrs. Stern could not properly be granted.

(3) The provision in the surrogacy contract stating that Mary Beth Whitehead agrees to "surrender custody . . . and terminate all parental rights" contains no clause giving her a right to rescind. It is intended to be an irrevocable consent to surrender the child for adoption — in other words, an irrevocable commitment by Mrs.

Whitehead to turn Baby M over to the Sterns and thereafter to allow termination of her parental rights. . . . Such a provision, however, making irrevocable the natural mother's consent to surrender custody of her child in a private placement adoption, clearly conflicts with New Jersey law. . . .

B. Public Policy Considerations

The surrogacy contract's invalidity, resulting from its direct conflict with the above statutory provisions, is further underlined when its goals and means are measured against New Jersey's public policy. The contract's basic premise, that the natural parents can decide in advance of birth which one is to have custody of the child, bears no relationship to the settled law that the child's best interests shall determine custody. . . .

The surrogacy contract guarantees permanent separation of the child from one of its natural parents. Our policy, however, has long been that to the extent possible, children should remain with and be brought up by both of their natural parents. . . . This is not simply some theoretical ideal that in practice has no meaning. The impact of failure to follow that policy is nowhere better shown than in the results of this surrogacy contract. A child, instead of starting off its life with as much peace and security as possible, finds itself immediately in a tug-of-war between contending mother and father.

The surrogacy contract violates the policy of this State that the rights of natural parents are equal concerning their child, the father's right no greater than the mother's. . . . The whole purpose and effect of the surrogacy contract was to give the father the exclusive right to the child by destroying the rights of the mother. . . .

Under the contract, the natural mother is irrevocably committed before she knows the strength of her bond with her child. She never makes a totally voluntary, informed decision, for quite clearly any decision prior to the baby's birth is, in the most important sense, uninformed, and any decision after that, compelled by a pre-existing contractual commitment, the threat of a lawsuit, and the inducement of a $10,000 payment, is less than totally voluntary. Her interests are of little concern to those who controlled this transaction. . . .

Worst of all, however, is the contract's total disregard of the best interests of the child. There is not the slightest suggestion that any inquiry will be made at any time to determine the fitness of the Sterns as custodial parents, of Mrs. Stern as an adoptive parent, their superiority to Mrs. Whitehead, or the effect on the child of not living with her natural mother. This is the sale of a child, or, at the very least, the sale of a mother's right to her child, the only mitigating factor being that one of the purchasers is the father. Almost every evil that prompted the prohibition of the payment of money in connection with adoptions exists here.

The differences between an adoption and a surrogacy contract should be noted, since it is asserted that the use of money in connection with surrogacy does not pose the risks found where money buys an adoption. Katz, "Surrogate Motherhood and the Baby-Selling Laws," 20 Colum. J.L. & Soc. Probs. 1 (1986). . . .

The main difference, that the plight of the unwanted pregnancy is unintended while the situation of the surrogate mother is voluntary and intended, is really not significant. Initially, it produces stronger reactions of sympathy for the mother whose pregnancy was unwanted than for the surrogate mother, who "went into this with her eyes wide open." On reflection, however, it appears that the essential evil is the same, taking advantage of a woman's circumstances (the unwanted pregnancy or the need for money) in order to take away her child, the difference being one of degree.

In the scheme contemplated by the surrogacy contract in this case, a middle man, propelled by profit, promotes the sale. Whatever idealism may have motivated any of the participants, the profit motive predominates, permeates, and ultimately governs the transaction. . . .

Intimated, but disputed, is the assertion that surrogacy will be used for the benefit of the rich at the expense of the poor. See, e.g., Radin, "Market Inalienability," 100 Harv. L. Rev. 1849, 1930 (1987). In response it is noted that the Sterns are not rich and the Whiteheads not poor. Nevertheless, it is clear to us that it is unlikely that surrogate mothers will be as proportionately numerous among those women in the top twenty percent income bracket as among those in the bottom twenty percent. Ibid. Put differently, we doubt that infertile couples in the low-income bracket will find upper income surrogates. . . .

The point is made that Mrs. Whitehead agreed to the surrogacy arrangement, supposedly fully understanding the consequences. Putting aside the issue of how compelling her need for money may have been, and how significant her understanding of the consequences, we suggest that her consent is irrelevant. There are, in a civilized society, some things that money cannot buy. In America, we decided long ago that merely because conduct purchased by money was "voluntary" did not mean that it was good or beyond regulation and prohibition. West Coast Hotel Co. v. Parrish, 300 U.S. 379, 57 S. Ct. 578, 81 L. Ed. 703 (1937). Employers can no longer buy labor at the lowest price they can bargain for, even though that labor is "voluntary," 29 U.S.C. §206 (1982), or buy women's labor for less money than paid to men for the same job, 29 U.S.C. §206(d), or purchase the agreement of children to perform oppressive labor, 29 U.S.C. §212, or purchase the agreement of workers to subject themselves to unsafe or unhealthful working conditions, 29 U.S.C. §651 to 678. (Occupational Health and Safety Act of 1970). There are, in short, values that society deems more important than granting to wealth whatever it can buy, be it labor, love, or life. . . .

The surrogacy contract creates, it is based upon, principles that are directly contrary to the objectives of our laws. It guarantees the separation of a child from its mother; it looks to adoption regardless of suitability; it totally ignores the child; it takes the child from the mother regardless of her wishes and her maternal fitness; and it does all of this, it accomplishes all of its goals, through the use of money.

Beyond that is the potential degradation of some women that may result from this arrangement. In many cases, of course, surrogacy may bring satisfaction, not only to the infertile couple, but to the surrogate mother herself. The fact, however, that many women may not perceive surrogacy negatively but rather see it as an opportunity does not diminish its potential for devastation to other women.

In sum, the harmful consequences of this surrogacy arrangement appear to us all too palpable. In New Jersey the surrogate mother's agreement to sell her child is void.[11] Its irrevocability infects the entire contract, as does the money that purports to buy it. . . .

---

11. Michigan courts have also found that these arrangements conflict with various aspects of their law. See Doe v. Kelley, 106 Mich. App. 169, 307 N.W.2d 438 (1981), *cert. den.*, 459 U.S. 1183 (1983) (application of sections of Michigan Adoption Law prohibiting the exchange of money to surrogacy is constitutional); Syrkowski v. Appleyard, 122 Mich. App. 506, 333 N.W.2d 90 (1983) (court held it lacked jurisdiction to issue an "order of filiation" because surrogacy arrangements were not governed by Michigan's Paternity Act), *rev'd*, 420 Mich. 367, 362 N.W.2d 211 (1985) (court decided Paternity Act should be applied but did not reach the merits of the claim). . . .

The Supreme Court of Kentucky has taken a somewhat different approach to surrogacy arrangements. In Surrogate Parenting Assocs. v. Commonwealth ex. rel. Armstrong, 704 S.W.2d 209 (Ky. 1986), the court held that the "fundamental differences" between surrogate arrangements and baby selling placed the surrogate parenting agreement beyond the reach of Kentucky's baby-selling statute. Id. at 211. The rationale for this determination was that unlike the normal adoption situation, the surrogacy agreement is entered into before conception and is not directed at avoiding the consequences of an unwanted pregnancy. Id. at 211-12.

Concomitant with this pro-surrogacy conclusion, however, the court held that a "surrogate" mother has the right to void the contract if she changes her mind during pregnancy or immediately after birth. Id. at 212-13. The court relied on statutes providing that consent to adoption or to the termination of parental rights prior to five days after the birth of the child is invalid, and concluded that consent before conception must also be unenforceable. Id. at 212-13. . . .

In contrast to the law in the United States, the law in the United Kingdom concerning surrogate parenting is fairly well-settled. Parliament passed the Surrogacy Arrangements Act, 1985, ch. 49, which made initiating or taking part in any negotiations with a view to making or arranging a surrogacy contract a criminal offense. The criminal sanction, however, does not apply to the "surrogate" mother or to the natural father, but rather applies to other persons engaged in arranging surrogacy contracts on a commercial basis. Since 1978, English courts have held surrogacy agreements unenforceable as against public policy, such agreements being deemed arrangements for the purchase and sale of children. A. v. C., [1985] F.L.R. 445, 449 (Fam. & C.A. 1978). It should be noted, however, that certain surrogacy arrangements, i.e., those

IV. Constitutional Issues

Both parties argue that the Constitutions — state and federal — mandate approval of their basic claims. The source of their constitutional arguments is essentially the same: the right of privacy, the right to procreate, the right to the companionship of one's child, those rights flowing either directly from the fourteenth amendment or by its incorporation of the Bill of Rights, or from the ninth amendment, or through the penumbra surrounding all of the Bill of Rights. They are the rights of personal intimacy, of marriage, of sex, of family, of procreation. . . . The right asserted by the Sterns is the right of procreation; that asserted by Mary Beth Whitehead is the right to the companionship of her child. We find that the right of procreation does not extend as far as claimed by the Sterns. . . . The right to procreate very simply is the right to have natural children, whether through sexual intercourse or artificial insemination. It is no more than that. Mr. Stern has not been deprived of that right. Through artificial insemination of Mrs. Whitehead, Baby M is his child. The custody, care, companionship, and nurturing that follow birth are not parts of the right to procreation; they are rights that may also be constitutionally protected, but that involve many considerations other than the right of procreation. . . .

Mrs. Whitehead, on the other hand, asserts a claim that falls within the scope of a recognized fundamental interest protected by the Constitution. As a mother, she claims the right to the companionship of her child. This is a fundamental interest, constitutionally protected. Furthermore, it was taken away from her by the action of the court below. Whether that action under these circumstances would constitute a constitutional deprivation, however, we need not and do not decide. By virtue of our decision Mrs. Whitehead's constitutional complaint — that her parental rights have been unconstitutionally terminated — is moot. . . .

Conclusion

This case affords some insight into a new reproductive arrangement: the artificial insemination of a surrogate mother. The unfortunate events that have unfolded illustrate that its unregulated use can bring suffering to all involved. Potential victims include the surrogate mother and her family, the natural father and his wife, and most importantly, the child. Although surrogacy has apparently provided positive results for some infertile couples, it can also, as this

---

arranged without brokers and revocable by the natural mother are not prohibited under current law in the United Kingdom.

case demonstrates, cause suffering to participants, here essentially innocent and well-intended.

We have found that our present laws do not permit the surrogacy contract used in this case. Nowhere, however, do we find any legal prohibition against surrogacy when the surrogate mother volunteers, without any payment, to act as a surrogate and is given the right to change her mind and to assert her parental rights. Moreover, the Legislature remains free to deal with the most sensitive issue as it sees fit, subject only to constitutional constraints.

If the Legislature decides to address surrogacy, consideration of this case will highlight many of its potential harms. We do not underestimate the difficulties of legislation on this subject. In addition to the inevitable confrontation with the ethical and moral issues involved, there is the question of the wisdom and effectiveness of regulating a matter so private, yet of such public interest. Legislative consideration of surrogacy may also provide the opportunity to begin to focus on the overall implications of the new reproductive biotechnology — in vitro fertilization, preservation of sperm and eggs, embryo implantation and the like. The problem is how to enjoy the benefits of the technology — especially for infertile couples — while minimizing the risk of abuse. The problem can be addressed only when society decides what its value and objectives are in this troubling, yet promising, area.

The judgment is affirmed in part, reversed in part, and remanded for further proceedings consistent with this opinion.

Robertson, Embryos, Families, and Procreative Liberty: The Legal Structure of the New Reproduction*
59 S. Cal. L. Rev. 939, 945-946, 1013-1015, 1021-1024 (1986)

Infertility, a perennial human problem, is increasing in the United States. . . . In 1983 more than one in eight American married couples had failed to conceive after one year of trying.** . . .

---

* © 1986 John A. Robertson. Reprinted by permission.

John A. Robertson is Baker and Botts Professor of Law, University of Texas at Austin.

** The rising rate of infertility can be explained by changes in sexual behavior, work roles, and postponement of marriage and childbearing. Changing work roles and the availability of contraception have led many women to postpone childbearing. Deferring childbirth allows age-related endogenous biologic factors to reduce the ability to conceive. It also gives infectious, occupational, and environmental factors a longer time to exert their cumulative effect on infertility. Changing sexual practices among the middle class is also a key factor. A trend to earlier first intercourse and multiple sexual partners has increased the frequency of sexually transmitted disease, which in

Although there is a demographically significant trend in the United States toward voluntary childlessness, cultural norms supporting reproduction remain very powerful. The inability to beget, bear, and rear children is a great loss for many infertile men and women. Infertility often implicates the most fundamental feelings about self and one's relation to the natural order, and may leave persons feeling handicapped or defective in an area central to personal identity and fulfillment. Infertile couples often experience, and may suffer enormously from, isolation, guilt, marital strife, and intense assaults on feelings of self-worth. Not surprisingly, they are ready to seek medical assistance and use techniques such as IVF [and surrogacy] that offer the hope of fertility. . . .

The baby boom generation's inability to reproduce has thus increased professional interest in the field, and spawned technical advances that are likely to increase demand for IVF and its donor-assisted variations. A strong demand for infertility treatments is likely to continue. Thus, demographic change and the continued evolution of sexual, work, and family roles converge to place noncoital, external conception and its collaborative variations on the public agenda. . . .

. . . Restrictions on paying surrogate fees and on enforcing surrogate contracts would infringe the procreative liberty of the couple providing the embryo. Unless the couple can hire a surrogate to bring the embryo to term, the couple will never be able to rear a child of their blood. The couple's reproductive experience will be limited to gene transfer without rearing (through gamete or embryo donation), or rearing without gene transfer (through adoption).

Such an interference with procreative liberty requires a justification beyond the prevention of symbolic harm or elevation of a particular morality of reproduction. Since the transfer of an embryo to a woman not providing the ovum does not physically damage the child, the main concerns with surrogacy are the psychosocial impact on offspring of rearing by a nongestating couple, the effect on the surrogate, and the symbolic meaning of hiring wombs for gestation. . . .

Harm to the surrogate is a real possibility, but it may not be sufficient ground for overriding contractual commitments. Although a surrogate may be able to think of the gestating fetus as the couple's, as pregnancy continues and birth approaches, she is likely to begin regarding it as "hers." Relinquishing the child at birth may be extremely difficult, and could lead to grief, depression and the need for counselling. Yet preventing informed women from playing such

---

turn leads to the pelvic inflammatory disease that often causes infertility. Widespread use of the intrauterine device by nulliparous women has also increased pelvic inflammatory disease. [Extracted from omitted material by Professor Robertson.]

partial procreative roles denies them the freedom to decide how best to fulfill their own procreative needs. If they are willing to undergo those risks, it may be unfairly paternalistic to prevent them from doing so.

Beyond the potential harm to offspring and the surrogate, many people find a woman's detached and instrumental attitude toward her gestating capacity distasteful. Site of our gestation and the most intimate bond of all, the womb, is fraught with symbolic significance. Surrogate gestation appears to treat the body as a reproductive machine and the child as an instrument to selfish ends. In doing so, surrogate gestation denigrates a concept of motherhood that posits a sacred, natural bond between biological mother and child. Such meanings run deep and are of great significance. Yet they are symbolic concerns, and symbolic concerns do not generally justify infringement of reproductive liberty.

An analysis finding surrogate contracts to be constitutionally protected suggests that the allocation of rearing rights and duties in surrogate contracts should be given legal effect. Allowing a surrogate gestator to violate the agreement and abort or retain custody of the child at birth overlooks the impact of nonenforcement on the ability of couples to procreate through such contracts. Refusing to enforce a surrogate contract as against public policy would infringe the couple's procreative liberty as much as an outright ban. Without the assurance of an enforceable contract, couples will be leery of entrusting their embryos to surrogates, and will be deprived of this solution to their infertility.

One solution to the contract enforcement problem is to distinguish damages from specific performance as a remedy for the surrogate's breach of contract. Procreative liberty requires that the contract be honored, but it does not require that it be enforced by specific performance. If a surrogate is not enjoined from aborting, she can be ordered to pay damages to the couple for the loss that they have suffered. Similarly, in lieu of specific performance, damages can be awarded when the surrogate refuses to relinquish the child at birth.

However, the case for specific performance of the promise to relinquish the child is strong in the case of a surrogate gestator. The surrogate received the couple's embryo on condition that she relinquish it to them at birth. Assuming all parties are fit parents, it is unclear why her wish to rear should override her promise to honor the genetic bond. The surrogate would never have had the embryo to bear if she had not agreed to return a child nine months later. As "trustee" of the embryo for the couple, she should be obligated to transfer custody at birth. . . .

A similar analysis applies to paying surrogates for their services, a prospect that has raised considerable controversy. Payment is thought

III. Issues of Human Birth 1091

to exploit the surrogate's financial need and to be illegal under laws prohibiting "baby-selling."

A ban on paying surrogates would interfere with the procreative liberty of the person engaging the surrogate and possibly the surrogate as well. The burdens of gestation are so great that few unrelated women will choose to gestate the embryo of another for altruism alone. A woman in need will thus not be able to reproduce unless she can pay a gestator to bear "her" child and return it to her for rearing.

Assuming that altruistic surrogacy is permitted, are there additional harms, when surrogates are paid, that would justify this interference with a couple's procreative choice? "Baby-selling" laws prohibit fees for adoption in order to protect the child from unfit parents and the mother from exploitation and coercion. But these concerns do not apply to surrogate gestators who freely choose this reproductive role before pregnancy occurs, uninfluenced by the stigma of illegitimacy or the financial burdens of single parenthood. An acceptable system of paid surrogacy must assure that the surrogate is fully informed, has independent legal counsel, and has made a deliberative choice.

There is also a fear that surrogates will be drawn primarily from poorer groups, who will serve the rich with their bodies as well as their housekeeping and childrearing services. Indeed, money is likely to be a prime motive in the decision of women to serve as surrogates, but other factors are reported to play a role. It is not apparent that only poor women will select that occupation, much less that the operation of a labor market in this area is more unjust than labor markets in other areas.

A more basic concern is the acceptability of women freely choosing to "rent" their uteri to others as a source of income. The idea of paying women to gestate for nine months, with all the attendant physical and psychological complications of pregnancy and birth, followed by transfer of the child to another, is discomforting. Part of the discomfort arises from witnessing another person risking life and limb for money, just as witnessing the backbreaking labor of manual workers' discomforts.[288]

Discomfort also arises from the symbolic devaluation of the ma-

---

288. The role of money in leading people to engage in physical labors, including highly risky ones, is accepted in numerous ways. In fact, many occupations can be characterized as the slow sale of one's body, health, and vitality over time. Consider the slow erosion of the bodies of miners, petrochemical workers, and professional athletes in the course of their work. Indeed, the Internal Revenue Code gives professional sports team owners the right to depreciate the players, a recognition of the way that their bodies are used in their work. Pregnancy is a unique physical experience, but many kinds of work also involve strenuous, physical labor.

ternal bond that payment signifies. A widespread and perhaps dominant moral sensibility recoils at transforming the mystery of birth into a commercial transaction.[289] The surrogate is literally renting her womb to another couple. She is willing to alienate "her" child and forsake the sacred maternal bond for money. Banning the practice is a way to show that the community supports the importance of the mother-child bond.

The goal is a laudable one. However, the surrogate and couple engaging her are likely to see matters differently. They would probably rate their desire to procreate or to assist others to do so to be more important than the need to maintain this symbol of the maternal-child bond. If the contract implications of procreative liberty are recognized and the interests of the parties or offspring are not tangibly harmed, gestator salaries should remain a matter of individual choice, and should not be prohibited by state law. . . .

Beyond fears of harm to embryo, offspring, family or collaborators is a more generalized concern that technologizing conception demeans human dignity and exploits women, and may lead down a slippery slope to complete genetic and technical control of humans.

A powerful image of these fears is Huxley's description in Brave New World of state hatcheries where babies with predetermined characteristics are decanted from bottles with pre-assigned social roles. [B]ut a host of factors independent of noncoital conception would have to coalesce to bring about that dystopia. Such a hypothetical possibility does not justify denying married couples safe and effective infertility treatments now. Generalized fears about technology often reflect symbolic, moral, or religious concerns and thus are not constitutional grounds for government action in the public sphere. But they do caution us to use noncoital technology safely and reasonably, taking steps to avert the most likely kinds of harm. A privately-derived ethic is necessary, even if a public one is not constitutionally available.

NOTES

Surrogate Motherhood

1. "In the nine months after the *Baby M* trial court's decision was handed down, 70 bills addressing surrogacy were reportedly introduced in 27 states. . . . The bills in a minority of jurisdictions would ban surrogacy (paid, unpaid, or both), and bills pending in at least six states would allow the surrogate mother to revoke her consent

---

289. George Annas has articulated this idea in several contexts. See, e.g., Annas, Redefining Parenthood and Protecting Embryos: Why We Need New Laws, 14 Hastings Center Rep., Oct. 1984, at 50, 50-62.

III. Issues of Human Birth

to surrendering the child and renouncing her parental rights." Andrews, The Aftermath of Baby M: Proposed State Laws on Surrogate Motherhood, Hast. Cent. Rep. (Oct/Nov 1987) at 31. See also Note, Surrogate Motherhood Legislation: A Sensible Starting Point, 20 Ind. L. Rev. 879 (1987); Flaherty, Enforcement of Surrogate Mother Contracts: Case Law, the Uniform Acts, and State and Federal Legislation, 36 Clev. St. L. Rev. 223 (1988). The latter approach (revocable consent) "may eventually be adopted by a larger number of states, since it appears to appeal to both opponents and supporters of surrogacy." Mayo, Medical Decision Making During a Surrogate Pregnancy, 25 Hous. L. Rev. 599, 603 n.9 (1988). See also, Comment, Model Human Reproductive Technologies and Surrogacy Act, 72 Iowa L. Rev. 943 (1987) (recommending strict procedural safeguards for surrogacy contracts that require each couple to petition the court, and allowing surrogate mother to revoke decision three days after birth); Capron, Alternative Birth Technologies: Legislative Challenges, 20 U.C. Davis L. Rev. 679 (1987); Charo, Legislative Approaches to Surrogate Motherhood, 16 L. Med. & Health Care 96 (1988); Developments, Surrogate Parenthood Contracts After Baby "M," 24 Wilamette L. Rev. 1053 (1988) (proposing model statute); Parental Guidance Suggested: A Proposal for Regulating Surrogate Parenthood, 22 Col. J.L. & Soc. Prob. 115 (1989) (same).

Louisiana has passed a law declaring surrogacy contracts unenforceable. La. Rev. Stat. Ann. §9:2713. Michigan became the first state to outlaw commercial surrogacy by making it a misdemeanor to participate in such a contract and a felony to assist in the formation of the contract. Maximum punishment is $50,000 and five years imprisonment. Mich. Stat. Ann. §722.851. A subsequent attorney general opinion interpreted this statute narrowly to apply only to contracts where the payment is contingent on relinquishing custody of the child, not to contracts where the surrogate is free to change her mind. As so construed, a state trial court upheld the statute's constitutionality. N.Y. Times, Sept. 20, 1988, at 9.

"What we're seeing now," said Prof. James B. Boskey, a family law expert and professor at Seton Hall Law School, "is an emotional outburst of hasty legislation in response to perceived political pressures. It's classic first-stage American politics: Ban it now! That's quick and easy. Then, in a year or two, comes the next stage, a more sophisticated, complex approach to regulate human behavior, where appropriate, because laws can't forbid it as we've seen with drugs, Prohibition and abortions." Malcolm, Steps to Control Surrogate Births Stir Debate Anew, N.Y. Times, June 26, 1988, at 1. Perhaps signalling the start of this second phase, in 1989 the Nevada Assembly became the first legislature to pass a bill explicitly legalizing surrogate motherhood. It requires proof that the intended mother is infertile and requires all parties to undergo counseling and psychological exams. Am. Med. News, June 9, 1989, at 2.

2. Despite the absence of a valid surrogacy contract or an adoption, the *Baby M* court treated Mr. Stern as Melissa's legal (and natural) father, even though Mr. Whitehead was present and consented to his wife's artificial insemination. Is this consistent with the AID precedents discussed above? What if Mr. Stern had also been infertile and they had used donated sperm? See "A Custody Case With Extra Tangles," N.Y. Times, Jan. 26, 1989, at A7 (recounting custody dispute that resulted from surrogate birth where insemination was by fourth-party sperm donor).

On remand in the *Baby M* case, the Superior Court found that it would be in Melissa's best interests to award custody to Mr. Stern, but the court also granted frequent, unsupervised visitation rights to Mrs. Whitehead (whose last name is now Gould as a result of a subsequent divorce and remarriage). 542 A.2d 52 (1988). Does this outcome resolve the "tug-of-war" concern that so influenced the court's determination of public policy?

3. If you think surrogacy should be legal, does your endorsement extend to parents who simply want to avoid the inconvenience of pregnancy? What level of perceived medical risk is required to make surrogacy ethically appropriate: A serious medical complication during a previous childbirth? Excessive morning sickness with previous pregnancies?

4. A portion of the Baby M surrogacy contract, reprinted as an appendix to the case, required Mrs. Whitehead to:

— not abort unless necessary for her health,
— undergo amniocentesis to detect genetic defects,
— undergo an abortion in the event of a defective fetus,
— not smoke, drink alcohol, take illegal drugs, or take any medications without her physician's approval, and
— adhere to all medical instructions.

The validity and enforcement of these particular aspects of a surrogacy agreement (assuming the agreement's basic validity) are among the more intriguing issues created by surrogacy arrangements. Would you support specific enforcement of these terms if the doctor ordered confinement to bed for five months in order to avoid premature labor? For further discussion, see Mayo, Medical Decision Making During a Surrogate Pregnancy, 25 Hous. L. Rev. 599 (1988) ("This article proposes to make specific performance of the abortion provisions impossible to obtain and specific performance of the medical care provisions no more obtainable than would otherwise be the case if there were no surrogate contract at all"); Note, Rumpelstiltskin Revisited: The Inalienable Rights of Surrogate Mothers, 99 Harv. L.

Rev. 1936 (1986) (specific performance of agreement not to abort is unconstitutional). Further aspects of maternal health during pregnancy are explored in the next section.

5. Professor Robertson introduced and developed his arguments in favor of a positive procreational right in an earlier article, Procreative Liberty and the Control of Conception, Pregnancy, and Childbirth, 69 Va. L. Rev. 405 (1983). There, he observed that "because reproductive control involves issues affecting population growth, sexual behavior, the role of women in society, and technological manipulation of life, it is likely to be a political and moral battleground for the rest of the century." Id. at 408. See also Robertson, Procreative Liberty and the State's Burden of Proof in Regulating Noncoital Reproduction, 16 L. Med. & Health Care 18 (1988); Ikemoto, Providing Protection for Collaborative, Noncoital Reproduction: The Right of Intimate Association, 40 Rutgers L. Rev. 1273 (1988); Comment, Prohibiting Payments to Surrogate Mothers: Love's Labor Lost and the Constitutional Right of Privacy, 20 J. Marsh. L. Rev. 715 (1987). For a critique of Robertson's position, see Hollinger, From Coitus to Commerce: Legal and Social Consequences of Noncoital Reproduction, 18 J. Law Reform 866 (1985).

The surrogate motherhood controversy has generated profuse commentary in legal, medical, philosophical and popular journals. Writings up to the *Baby M* decision are collected in K. Bach, Research Guide: Surrogate Motherhood (1987). For a sampling of subsequent discussion, in addition to the sources cited above, see M. Field, Surrogate Motherhood (1988); Symposium, 18 Seton Hall L. Rev. 827 (1989); Symposium, 16 L. Med. & Health Care (1988); Colloquy: *In re Baby M,* 76 Geo. L.J. 1717 (1988) (collection of essays); Annot. 77 A.L.R.4th 70 (1990); Feinerman, A Comparative Look at Surrogacy, 76 Geo. L.J. 1837 (most European and British Commonwealth countries to consider the issue have banned surrogacy).

D. *Maternal-Fetal Conflict*

Robertson, Procreative Liberty and the Control of Conception, Pregnancy, and Childbirth*
69 Va. L. Rev. 405, 437-446 (1983)

III. *Managing the Pregnancy*

A. **Maternal-Fetal Conflicts**

Procreation involves a woman in bearing and giving birth as well as in conceiving. Full freedom in procreation includes a woman's

---

* Reprinted by permission of the Virginia Law Review and Fred B. Rothman & Co.

freedom to make the myriad decisions she faces in gestating and giving birth to the child — decisions about work, recreation, and medical care. The pregnant woman's choices may, however, adversely affect the fetus, causing it to die in utero, to be stillborn, or to be born damaged. To analyze the maternal-fetal conflicts that arise in the course of pregnancy, one must first distinguish the question of procreation from the question of managing the pregnancy.

The maternal-fetal conflicts that arise in managing pregnancy do not involve the woman's right *to* procreate, but rather her right to bodily integrity *in the course of* procreating. Whereas restrictions on conception would prevent a woman from using her physiological capacity to reproduce, restrictions on her conduct during pregnancy only affect how she will behave in carrying the child to term. A woman is free not to conceive or, even though her actions destroy the fetus, to terminate the pregnancy altogether up to the point of viability, and she can terminate the pregnancy beyond the point of viability if its continuation threatens her life or health. Conflicts over management of the pregnancy arise only after she has decided to become or remain pregnant. Once she decides to forgo abortion and the state chooses to protect the fetus, the woman loses the liberty to act in ways that would adversely affect the fetus. . . .

The mother has, if she conceives and chooses not to abort, a legal and moral duty to bring the child into the world as healthy as is reasonably possible. She has a duty to avoid actions or omissions that will damage the fetus and child, just as she has a duty to protect the child's welfare once it is born until she transfers this duty to another. In terms of fetal rights, a fetus has no right to be conceived — or, once conceived, to be carried to viability. But once the mother decides not to terminate the pregnancy, the viable fetus acquires rights to have the mother conduct her life in ways that will not injure it.

This preference for fetal interests over maternal freedom during pregnancy is rooted in an enduring criminal law tradition and in a relatively recent tenet of tort law. In Anglo-American criminal law, a person who performs an act before a fetus' birth that results in its death after birth commits homicide. Although a prenatal act that causes a fetus to die in utero or to be stillborn is not homicide, it has traditionally been punished separately as feticide or perhaps as abortion. The fetus' mother is as much subject to liability under these doctrines as anyone else, although she can be punished for killing the fetus in utero only after viability.

The mother might also be convicted of child abuse if her actions during pregnancy, such as drug and alcohol use, caused an injury to her fetus that lasted after its birth. The only appellate case to address

III. Issues of Human Birth

this issue, People v. Reyes,[100] involved a mother addicted to heroin during pregnancy who gave birth to a child congenitally addicted to heroin. The California appeals court reversed her conviction for child abuse on the ground that the statute's proscription of abuse to a "child" was not intended to include the unborn. This interpretation of the statute is erroneous, for it overlooks the fact that the abused child here is not the fetus, but the child who has been born and is suffering from injuries occurring before its birth. There is nothing in the history or wording of the statute that requires the abusive conduct to occur after birth, as long as the child who suffers from the prenatal injuries is born before the action is brought. Indeed, to limit the statute to postnatal actions would be inconsistent with California homicide law, which imposes liability for prenatal actions that cause death postnatally.

Like the criminal law tradition, tort law now requires a person to avoid action that will harm a fetus. The history of this development in tort law has been amply described elsewhere,[103] so a brief review will suffice here. For some fifty years after Judge, later Justice, Holmes' decision in Dietrich v. Northampton,[104] American courts denied recovery in tort to children who were born alive but injured by a defendant's prenatal conduct. With Bonbrest v. Kotz[105] in 1946, however, the tide began to turn, and now all American jurisdictions recognize a cause of action for prenatal (and, in some cases, preconception) conduct that causes death or injury to a child born alive. Damages can be awarded for injuries caused by prenatal actions prior to viability or prior even to conception when it is reasonably foreseeable that a child might be born who will suffer from these actions. . . .

Recovery in prenatal injury cases rests on a claim that but for the defendant's prenatal negligence, the child would have been born healthy. The issue is quite different from that in a "wrongful life" case, in which a plaintiff claims that bringing a handicapped child into the world, when there is no possibility that the child could have been born healthy, causes that child a compensable injury. The courts have generally been unsympathetic to "wrongful life" claims because it is difficult to see how a child has been wronged by being born handicapped when the only alternative was for it not to be born at all. In a prenatal injury case, however, the child's claim is not that

---

100. 75 Cal. App. 3d 214, 141 Cal. Rptr. 912 (1977).

103. Horace Robertson has written perhaps the best article on this topic. Robertson, Toward Rational Boundaries of Tort Liability for Injury to the Unborn: Prenatal Injuries, Preconception Injuries and Wrongful Life, 1978 Duke L.J. 1401.

104. 138 Mass. 14 (1884).

105. 65 F.Supp. 138 (D.D.C. 1946).

defendant wronged him by causing him to be born when defendant knew the child was defective, but that defendant engaged in conduct that caused the child to be damaged when otherwise the child would have been born healthy. . . .

In Grodin v. Grodin,[113] the only reported case on this issue, the court recognized the possibility of maternal liability for prenatal conduct. A child born with tooth discoloration caused by his mother's taking tetracycline during pregnancy sued his mother for negligence in failing "to seek proper prenatal care." The negligent actions that the complaint alleged included the mother's failure to seek a pregnancy test when her symptoms suggested pregnancy and her failure to inform the doctor who finally diagnosed pregnancy that she was taking a drug that might be contraindicated for pregnant women.[114] . . .

B. Prohibition of Behavior Dangerous to the Fetus

There is no question that a state could prohibit actions by a pregnant woman that might reasonably be thought to kill a viable fetus in utero or cause it to be born in a damaged state. Laws that prohibited pregnant women from obtaining or using alcohol, tobacco, or drugs likely to damage the fetus would be constitutional, even if these laws applied only to pregnant women. Because there is no fundamental right to use psychoactive substances, the state would not have to show a compelling interest in order to restrict their use by pregnant women. A statute forbidding pregnant women the use of alcohol or tobacco in order to minimize risks to their fetuses would pass the courts' "rational basis" test.

Similarly, states could amend or interpret child abuse, feticide, or abortion laws to include a wide range of behavior by pregnant women that is likely to cause harm to their unborn children. Under such statutes, it would be possible to punish a woman who refused to take a necessary medication (as, for example, a diabetic mother who failed to take insulin) or who knowingly exposed herself to teratogenic substances or environments.

---

113. 102 Mich. App. 396, 301 N.W.2d 869 (1980) [reversing trial court dismissal of action].

114. The history of this case is instructive because it illustrates one of the situations in which a child might bring suit against its parents. The child originally filed suit against the physician alone for his injury. During discovery the physician claimed that he had warned the mother to stop taking tetracycline. To guard against the possibility that the jury might ascribe the child's injury to the mother and refuse to award damages, the attorney advised amending the complaint to include the mother as a defendant, because a homeowner's policy insured the mother against tort liability. But for the existence of a homeowner's insurance policy with broad coverage, the suit against the mother would not have been filed. Telephone interview with John Kunkel, plaintiff's attorney (Oct. 15, 1982) (copy on file with the Virginia Law Review Association).

Many other state regulations seeking to protect fetuses against injurious maternal behavior would also be valid. For example, statutes excluding pregnant women from workplaces inimical to fetal health and those requiring women to take certain medications or tests to assure their health or that of the fetus would be valid.

C. In Utero Fetal Therapy

A significant medical development potentially affecting a woman's freedom during pregnancy is the prenatal diagnosis and treatment of fetal defects. Until recently, prenatal diagnosis offered only the option of abortion to women whose fetuses were discovered to have severe defects. Now some conditions can be treated in utero by administering drugs to the mother or by intervening surgically through fetoscopy. . . .

. . . A mother's refusal of therapy in these situations could be the basis for civil suit or criminal prosecution if it resulted in death or injury to the fetus, just as a parent's refusal of necessary medical care for a child can now be the basis for civil or criminal liability. The fact that the mother must undergo surgery as part of the fetal therapy procedure would be no defense if the procedure did not present an undue risk to her life or health.[119] She waived her right to resist bodily intrusions made for the sake of the fetus when she chose to continue the pregnancy.

The more difficult question would be whether the therapy could be directly imposed on her against her will. Would her interest in bodily integrity override the unborn child's interest in life and health? Bodily intrusions for the sake of another are highly disfavored, but are not unknown to the law. If the risk to the mother is slight and the benefit to the child is great, there are precedents that would authorize a court to order treatment against the mother's will. In Raleigh Fitkin-Paul Morgan Memorial Hospital v. Anderson,[124] the New Jersey Supreme Court ordered blood transfusions against the wishes of a Jehovah's Witness whose severe hemorrhaging threatened her life and that of her eight-month-old fetus. More recently, the Georgia Supreme Court ordered that a cesarean section be performed on a full-term woman who refused it on religious grounds and who had complete placenta previa, a condition almost certain to cause her death and the death of the fetus.[125]

---

119. Robertson, The Right to Procreate and In Utero Fetal Therapy, 3 J. Legal Med. 333, 345-349 (1982).

124. 42 N.J. 421, 201 A.2d 537, *cert. denied*, 377 U.S. 985 (1964).

125. Jefferson v. Griffin Spalding County Hosp., 247 Ga. 86, 274 S.E.2d 457 (1981).

These cases allow direct bodily intrusions to benefit a viable, full-term fetus when the risks that the intervention poses to the mother are reasonable. Although these cases involved saving both the fetus and the mother's life, they lay the foundation for requiring a pregnant woman to permit in utero fetal therapy essential to the health or survival of a viable fetus, so long as the therapy does not pose substantial threats to her life or health.[126] For example, a court could probably order medication or intrauterine transfusions for Rh incompatibility, because these procedures pose relatively small health risks and may be essential for the unborn child to survive and to be healthy. A mentally ill pregnant woman whose conduct threatened a viable fetus could probably be civilly committed to protect the unborn child.[127] Perhaps a pregnant teenager who became anorectic could be force-fed if she were in the third trimester and the danger to the fetus were clearly established. In utero surgery performed through fetoscopy could also be ordered, once its safety and efficacy for the fetus is established, because fetoscopy does not carry high risks to the mother.

The hardest case in this area will arise with procedures that subject the mother to substantial risk. For example, extrauterine fetal surgery and cesarean section require the mother to submit to general anesthesia and major surgery, and may thus bring her interests into conflict with those of her fetus. . . . The outcomes in cases of this sort will vary with the medical circumstances. It is conceivable, however, that a court would judge the health risks to the mother of a cesarean section under general anesthesia to be insufficient to prevent the state from preferring the interests of the fetus and ordering the surgery. . . .

In re A.C.
— A.2d — (D.C. 1990)

TERRY, ASSOC. J. . . .

I

This case came before the trial court when George Washington University Hospital petitioned the emergency judge in chambers for

---

126. *Roe* permits the state to prefer the interests of the viable fetus over the mother's autonomy to abort except where abortion is "necessary for the preservation of the life or health of the mother." Roe v. Wade, 410 U.S. 113, 165 (1973).

127. See Soloff, Jewell & Roth, Civil Commitment and the Rights of the Unborn, 136 Am. J. Psychiatry 114 (1979), for a description of a case in which a schizophrenic woman, seven months pregnant, was civilly committed to protect the unborn child.

III. Issues of Human Birth

declaratory relief as to how it should treat its patient, A.C., who was close to death from cancer and was twenty-six and one-half weeks pregnant with a viable fetus. After a hearing lasting approximately three hours, which was held at the hospital (though not in A.C.'s room), the court ordered that a caesarean section be performed on A.C. to deliver the fetus. Counsel for A.C. immediately sought a stay in this court, which was unanimously denied by a hastily assembled division of three judges. In re *A.C.*, 533 A.2d 611 (D.C. 1987). The caesarean was performed, and a baby girl, L.M.C., was delivered. Tragically, the child died within two and one-half hours, and the mother died two days later.

Counsel for A.C. now maintain that A.C. was competent and that she made an informed choice not to have the caesarean performed. Given this view of the facts, they argue that it was error for the trial court to weigh the state's interest in preserving the potential life of a viable fetus against A.C.'s interest in having her decision respected. They argue further that, even if the substituted judgment procedure had been followed, the evidence would necessarily show that A.C. would not have wanted the caesarean section. Under either analysis, according to these arguments, the trial court erred in subordinating A.C.'s right to bodily integrity in favor of the state's interest in potential life. . . .

II

[A.C. had suffered from cancer for 14 years. During a period of remission, she married and conceived a child. At twenty-five weeks in her pregnancy, her doctors found a terminal, inoperable tumor in her lung. She decided to continue with her pregnancy and to receive palliative treatment, apparently with the desire to extend her life at least to the twenty-eighth week of pregnancy, when the prognosis for the fetus would be much better if intervention were necessary. However, as her condition worsened during her twenty-sixth week, her stated desire to have the baby became more equivocal. Her mother opposed the operation, but her husband "was too distraught to testify and uttered only a few words at the hearing."]

After hearing this testimony and the arguments of counsel, the trial court made oral findings of fact. It found, first, that A.C. would probably die, according to uncontroverted medical testimony, "within the next twenty-four to forty-eight hours"; second, that A.C. was "pregnant with a twenty-six and a half week viable fetus who, based upon uncontroverted medical testimony, has approximately a fifty to sixty percent chance to survive if a caesarean section is performed as soon as possible"; third, that because the fetus was viable, "the state has [an] important and legitimate interest in protecting the potentiality of human life"; and fourth, that there had been some testimony that the operation "may very well hasten the death of [A.C.]," but that there had also been testimony that delay would greatly increase the risk to the fetus and that "the prognosis is not great for the fetus to be delivered post-mortem. . . ." Most significantly, the court found:

> The court is of the view that it does not clearly know what [A.C.'s] present views are with respect to the issue of whether or not the child should live or die. She's presently unconscious. As late as Friday of last week, she wanted the baby to live. As late as yesterday, she did not know for sure.

Having made these findings of fact and conclusions of law, and expressly relying on In re Madyun, 114 Daily Wash. L. Rptr. 2233 (D.C. Super. Ct. July 26, 1986),[5] the court ordered that a caesarean section be performed to deliver A.C.'s child. . . .

[After the judge's order was communicated to A.C. by her doctors, she at first agreed to the operation, but shortly later she refused. Although she appeared lucid, her doctors differed in their opinions as to whether she had reached a truly competent and informed decision one way or the other.] After hearing this new evidence, the court found that it was "still not clear what her intent is" and again ordered that a caesarean section be performed. . . . The operation took place, but the baby lived for only a few hours, and A.C. succumbed to cancer two days later. . . .

IV . . .

A. Informed Consent and Bodily Integrity

A number of learned articles have been written about the propriety or impropriety of court-ordered caesarean sections. E.g., Johnsen, The Creation of Fetal Rights: Conflicts with Women's Constitutional Rights to Liberty, Privacy, and Equal Protection, 95 Yale L.J. 599 (1986); Kolder, Gallagher & Parsons, Court-Ordered Obstetrical Interventions, 316 New Eng. J. Med. 1192 (1987) (hereafter *Obstetrical Interventions*); Rhoden, The Judge in the Delivery Room: The Emergence of Court-Ordered Caesareans, 74 Cal. L. Rev. 1951 (1986); Robertson, Procreative Liberty and the Control of Conception, Pregnancy, and Childbirth, 69 Va. L. Rev. 405 (1983). Commentators have also considered how medical decisions for incompetent persons which may involve some detriment or harm to them should be made. E.g., Pollock, Life and Death Decisions: Who Makes

---

5. *Madyun* was affirmed by this court in an unreported order. See also note 28, infra. [The opinion is attached as an appendix to the dissent.]

III. Issues of Human Birth

Them and by What Standards?, 41 Rutgers L. Rev. 505, 518-540 (1989); Robertson, Organ Donations by Incompetents and the Substituted Judgment Doctrine, 76 Colum. L. Rev. 48 (1976). These and other articles demonstrate the complexity of medical intervention cases, which become more complex with the steady advance of medical technology. From a recent national survey, it appears that over the five years preceding the survey there were thirty-six attempts to override maternal refusals of proposed medical treatment, and that in fifteen instances where court orders were sought to authorize caesarean interventions, thirteen such orders were granted. *Obstetrical Interventions,* supra, 316 New Eng. J. Med. at 1192-1193. Compare Goldberg, Medical Choices During Pregnancy: Whose Decision Is It Anyway?, 41 Rutgers L. Rev. 591, 609 (1989) (finding twelve such cases). Nevertheless, there is only one published decision from an appellate court that deals with the question of when, or even whether, a court may order a caesarean section: Jefferson v. Griffin Spalding County Hospital Authority, 247 Ga. 86, 274 S.E.2d 457 (1981).

Jefferson is of limited relevance, if any at all, to the present case. In *Jefferson* there was a competent refusal by the mother to undergo the proposed surgery, but the evidence showed that performance of the caesarean was in the medical interests of both the mother and the fetus.[7] . . .

[O]ur analysis of this case begins with the tenet common to all medical treatment cases: that any person has the right to make an informed choice, if competent to do so, to accept or forego medical treatment. . . .

[C]ourts do not compel one person to permit a significant intrusion upon his or her bodily integrity for the benefit of another person's health. See, e.g., Bonner v. Moran, 75 U.S. App. D.C. 156, 157, 126 F.2d 121, 122 (1941) (parental consent required for skin graft from fifteen-year-old for benefit of cousin who had been severely burned); McFall v. Shimp, 10 Pa. D. & C. 3d 90 (Allegheny County Ct. 1978). In *McFall* the court refused to order Shimp to donate bone marrow which was necessary to save the life of his cousin, McFall:

> The common law has consistently held to a rule which provides that one human being is under no legal compulsion to give aid or to take action to save another human being or to rescue. . . . For our

---

7. Because the patient in *Jefferson* had a placenta previa which blocked the birth canal, doctors estimated that without caesarean intervention there was a ninety-nine percent chance that her full-term fetus would perish and a fifty percent chance that the mother would die as well. The mother was unquestionably competent to make her own treatment decisions, but refused a caesarean because of her religious beliefs. A trial court gave custody of the fetus to the state human resources officials and ordered a caesarean section; the Georgia Supreme Court denied the parents' motion for a stay. [Nevertheless, the mother went into hiding, and both she and the child survived without the operation.]

law to *compel* defendant to submit to an intrusion of his body would change every concept and principle upon which our society is founded. To do so would defeat the sanctity of the individual, and would impose a rule which would know no limits, and one could not imagine where the line would be drawn.

Id. at 91 (emphasis in original). Even though Shimp's refusal would mean death for McFall, the court would not order Shimp to allow his body to be invaded. It has been suggested that fetal cases are different because a woman who "has chosen to lend her body to bring [a] child into the world" has an enhanced duty to assure the welfare of the fetus, sufficient even to require her to undergo caesarean surgery. Robertson, *Procreative Liberty*, supra, 69 Va. L. Rev. at 456. Surely, however, a fetus cannot have rights in this respect superior to those of a person who has already been born.[8] . . .

In those rare cases in which a patient's right to decide her own course of treatment has been judicially overridden, courts have usually acted to vindicate the state's interest in protecting third parties, even if in fetal state. See Jefferson v. Griffin Spalding County Hospital Authority, supra (ordering that caesarean section be performed on a woman in her thirty-ninth week of pregnancy to save both the mother and the fetus); Raleigh Fitkin-Paul Morgan Memorial Hospital v. Anderson, 42 N.J. 421, 201 A.2d 537 (ordering blood transfusions over the objection of a Jehovah's Witness, in her thirty-second week of pregnancy, to save her life and that of the fetus), *cert. denied*, 377 U.S. 985 (1964); In re Jamaica Hospital, 128 Misc. 2d 1006, 491 N.Y.S.2d 898 (Sup. Ct. 1985) (ordering the transfusion of blood to a Jehovah's Witness eighteen weeks pregnant, who objected on religious grounds, and finding that the state's interest in the not-yet-viable fetus outweighed the patient's interests); Crouse Irving Memorial Hospital, Inc. v. Paddock, 127 Misc. 2d 101, 485 N.Y.S.2d 443 (Sup. Ct. 1985) (ordering transfusions as necessary over religious objections to save the mother and a fetus that was to be prematurely delivered); cf. In re President & Directors of Georgetown College, Inc., supra, 118 U.S. App. D.C. at 88, 831 F.2d at 1008 (ordering a transfusion, inter alia, because of a mother's parental duty to her living minor children). But see Taft v. Taft, 388 Mass. 331, 446

8. There are also practical consequences to consider. What if A.C. had refused to comply with a court order that she submit to a caesarean? Under the circumstances, she obviously could not have been held in civil contempt and imprisoned or required to pay a daily fine until compliance. Cf. United States v. United Mine Workers, 330 U.S. 258, 304-306 (1947); *D.D.* v. *M.T.*, 550 A.2d 37, 43 (D.C. 1988). Enforcement could be accomplished only through physical force or its equivalent. A.C. would have to be fastened with restraints to the operating table, or perhaps involuntarily rendered unconscious by forcibly injecting her with an anesthetic, and then subjected to unwanted major surgery. Such actions would surely give one pause in a civilized society, especially when A.C. had done no wrong. Cf. Rochin v. California, 342 U.S. 165, 169 (1952).

N.E.2d 395 (1983) (vacating an order which required a woman in her fourth month of pregnancy to undergo a "purse-string" operation, on the ground that there were no compelling circumstances to justify overriding her religious objections and her constitutional right of privacy). . . .

. . . We hold, however, that without a competent refusal from A.C. to go forward with the surgery, and without a finding through substituted judgment that A.C. would not have consented to the surgery, it was error for the trial court to proceed to a balancing analysis, weighing the rights of A.C. against the interests of the state.

There are two additional arguments against overriding A.C.'s objections to caesarean surgery. First, as the American Public Health Association cogently states in its amicus curiae brief:

> Rather than protecting the health of women and children, court-ordered caesareans erode the element of trust that permits a pregnant woman to communicate to her physician — without fear of reprisal — all information relevant to her proper diagnosis and treatment. An even more serious consequence of court-ordered intervention is that it drives women at high risk of complications during pregnancy and childbirth out of the health care system to avoid coerced treatment.[16]

Second, and even more compellingly, any judicial proceeding in a case such as this will ordinarily take place — like the one before us here — under time constraints so pressing that it is difficult or impossible for the mother to communicate adequately with counsel, or for counsel to organize an effective factual and legal presentation in defense of her liberty and privacy interests and bodily integrity. Any intrusion implicating such basic values ought not to be lightly undertaken when the mother not only is precluded from conducting pre-trial discovery (to which she would be entitled as a matter of course in any controversy over even a modest amount of money) but also is in no position to prepare meaningfully for trial. . . . Gallagher, Prenatal Invasions and Interventions: What's Wrong with Fetal Rights, 10 Harv. Women's L.J. 9, 49 (1987).

In this case A.C.'s court-appointed attorney was unable even to meet with his client before the hearing. By the time the case was heard, A.C.'s condition did not allow her to be present, nor was it reasonably possible for the judge to hear from her directly. The factual record, moreover, was significantly flawed because A.C.'s med-

---

16. In at least one case, a woman whose objection to a caesarean delivery had been overridden by a court went into hiding and gave birth to her child vaginally. See Rhoden, supra, 74 Cal. L. Rev. at 1959-1960. In another case, "a 16-year-old pregnant girl in Wisconsin has been held in secure detention for the sake of her fetus because she tended to be on the run and to lack motivation or ability to seek prenatal care." *Obstetrical Interventions*, supra, 316 New Eng. J. Med. at 1195.

ical records were not before the court and because Dr. Jeffrey Moscow, the physician who had been treating A.C. for many years, was not even contacted and hence did not testify.[17] . . .

C. The Trial Court's Ruling

We reiterate that we cannot find the facts in this or any other case. That is the function of trial judges, who can view the witnesses and discern from their demeanor and testimony, rather than a cold written record, what the facts are. In this case there is an understandable paucity of factual findings, which necessarily limits our review. The trial court, faced with an issue affecting life and death, was forced to make a decision with almost no time for deliberation. Nevertheless, . . . the court did not go on, as it should have done, to make a finding as to what A.C. would have chosen to do if she were competent. Instead, the court undertook to balance the state's and L.M.C.'s interests in surgical intervention against A.C.'s perceived interest in not having the caesarean performed.

After A.C. was informed of the court's decision, she consented to the caesarean; moments later, however, she withdrew her consent. The trial court did not then make a finding as to whether A.C. was competent to make the medical decision or whether she had made an informed decision one way or the other. Nor did the court then make a substituted judgment for A.C. Instead, the court said that it was "still not clear what her intent is" and again ordered the caesarean.

It is that order which we must now set aside. What a trial court must do in a case such as this is to determine, if possible, whether the patient is capable of making an informed decision about the course of her medical treatment. If she is, and if she makes such a decision, her wishes will control in virtually all cases. If the court finds that the patient is incapable of making an informed consent (and thus incompetent), then the court must make a substituted judgment. This means that the court must ascertain as best it can what the patient would do if faced with the particular treatment question. Again, in virtually all cases the decision of the patient, albeit discerned through the mechanism of substituted judgment, will control. We do not quite foreclose the possibility that a conflicting state interest may be so compelling that the patient's wishes must yield,

---

17. In an affidavit filed after the hearing, Dr. Moscow said that if he had been notified of the proceedings, he would have come to the hospital immediately and would have testified that a caesarean section was medically inadvisable *both for A.C. and for the fetus.* Dr. Moscow also viewed the hospital's handling of A.C.'s case as deficient in several other significant respects. In these circumstances we think it unfortunate that Dr. Moscow was not called by representatives of the hospital and made available to the court when the hospital decided to seek judicial guidance.

III. Issues of Human Birth

but we anticipate that such cases will be extremely rare and truly exceptional. This is not such a case.

Having said that, we go no further. We need not decide whether, or in what circumstances, the state's interests can ever prevail over the interests of a pregnant patient.[23] We emphasize, nevertheless, that it would be an extraordinary case indeed in which a court might ever be justified in overriding the patient's wishes and authorizing a major surgical procedure such as a caesarean section.[10] . . .

. . . If the substituted judgment procedure were to be followed, there is evidence going both ways as to what decision A.C. would have made, and we see no point in requiring the court now to make that determination when it can have no practical effect on either A.C. or L.M.C.

Accordingly, we vacate the order of the trial court and remand the case for such further proceedings as may be appropriate.

BELSON, ASSOCIATE JUDGE, concurring in part and dissenting in part: I agree with much of the majority opinion, but I disagree with its ultimate ruling that the trial court's order must be set aside, and with the narrow view it takes of the state's interest in preserving life and the unborn child's interest in life. . . . I would hold that in those instances, fortunately rare, in which the viable unborn child's interest in living and the state's parallel interest in protecting human life come into conflict with the mother's decision to forgo a procedure such as a caesarean section, a balancing should be struck in which the unborn child's and the state's interest are entitled to substantial weight.

It was acknowledged in Roe v. Wade, 410 U.S. 113 (1973), that the state's interest in potential human life becomes compelling at the

---

23. In particular, we stress that nothing in this opinion should be read as either approving or disapproving the holding in In re Madyun, supra. There are substantial factual differences between *Madyun* and the present case. In this case, for instance, the medical interests of the mother and the fetus were in sharp conflict; what was good for one would have been harmful to the other. In *Madyun*, however, there was no real conflict between the interests of mother and fetus; on the contrary, there was strong evidence that the proposed caesarean would be beneficial to both. Moreover, in *Madyun* the pregnancy was at full term, and Mrs. Madyun had been in labor for two and a half days; in this case, however, A.C. was barely two-thirds of the way through her pregnancy, and there were no signs of labor. If another *Madyun*-type case ever comes before this court, its result may well depend on facts that we cannot now foresee. For that reason (among others), we defer until another day any discussion of whether *Madyun* was rightly or wrongly decided.

10. In the present case we are dealing with a caesarean section, which is plainly a major surgical procedure. Our discussion of the circumstances, if any, in which the patient's wishes may be overridden presupposes a major bodily invasion. We express no opinion with regard to the circumstances, if any, in which lesser invasions might be permitted, or where the line should be drawn between "major" and "minor" surgery.

point of viability. Even before viability, the state has an "important and legitimate interest in protecting the potentiality of human life." Id. at 162. When approximately the third trimester of pregnancy is reached (roughly the time of viability, although with advances in medical science the time of viability is being reached sooner and sooner), the state's interest becomes sufficiently compelling to justify what otherwise would be unduly burdensome state interference with the woman's constitutionally protected privacy interest. Beal v. Doe, 432 U.S. 438, 446 (1977). Once that stage is reached, the state "may, if it chooses, regulate, and even proscribe, abortion except where it is necessary, in appropriate medical judgment, for the preservation of the life or health of the mother." *Roe,* supra, 410 U.S. at 165. In addressing this issue, it is important to emphasize, as does the majority opinion, that this case is not about abortion, majority opinion at 22 n.9; we are not discussing whether a woman has the legal right to terminate her pregnancy in its early stages. Rather, we are dealing with the situation that exists when a woman has carried an unborn child to viability. When the unborn child reaches the state of viability, the child becomes a party whose interests must be considered. See, King, The Juridical Status of the Fetus: A Proposal for Legal Protection of the Unborn, 77 Mich. L. Rev. 1647, 1687 (1979) (viability, not birth, the determinative moment in development for purpose of determining when fetus is entitled to legal protection). This view is consistent with the decision of the only appellate court which has heretofore considered this issue. In Jefferson v. Griffin Spalding County Hosp. Auth., 247 Ga. 86, 274 S.E.2d 457 (1981), the Supreme Court of Georgia denied a stay of an order authorizing a hospital to perform a caesarean section to which the mother did not consent. Concurring, Presiding Justice Hill described the way in which the outcome was reached in the following language:

> In denying the stay of the trial court's order and thereby clearing the way for immediate reexamination by sonogram and probably for surgery, we weighed the right of the mother to practice her religion and to refuse surgery on herself, against her unborn child's right to live. We found in favor of her child's right to live.

Id. at 460.

The balancing test should be applied in instances in which women become pregnant and carry an unborn child to the point of viability. This is not an unreasonable classification because, I submit, a woman who carries a child to viability is in fact a member of a unique category of persons. Her circumstances differ fundamentally from those of other potential patients for medical procedures that will aid another person, for example, a potential donor of bone marrow for transplant.

This is so because she has undertaken to bear another human being, and has carried an unborn child to viability. Another unique feature of the situation we address arises from the singular nature of the dependency of the unborn child upon the mother. A woman carrying a viable unborn child is not in the same category as a relative, friend, or stranger called upon to donate bone marrow or an organ for transplant. Rather, the expectant mother has placed herself in a special class of persons who are bringing another person into existence, and upon whom that other person's life is totally dependent. Also, uniquely, the viable unborn child is literally captive within the mother's body. No other potential beneficiary of a surgical procedure on another is in that position.

For all of these reasons, . . . I cannot agree that in cases where a viable unborn child is in the picture, it would be extremely rare, within that universe, to require that the mother accede to the vital needs of the viable unborn child.[8] . . .

For the reasons stated above, I would affirm.

NOTES

Fetal Rights

1. Forced C-sections are at the cutting edge of bioethics. The A.C. court's approach is far from a settled analysis; indeed, this is the first case ever to present any in-depth thought on these issues. The clash between optimal fetal development and basic lifestyle choices such as whether to smoke, what to eat, and how to conduct childbirth is likely to arise with much greater frequency in the future due to rapid advances of medical science on three fronts: (1) understanding the fetal developmental process; (2) refining diagnostic techniques that detect fetal problems; and (3) developing modes of surgical and medical intervention that allow in utero therapy.

2. The Kolder study described by the court also found:

> Among 21 cases in which court orders were sought, the orders were obtained in 86 percent; in 88 percent of those cases, the orders were received within six hours. Eighty-one percent of the women involved were black, Asian, or Hispanic, 44 percent were unmarried, and 24

---

8. To the contrary, it appears that a majority of courts faced with this issue have found that the state's compelling interest in protection of the unborn child should prevail. See Noble-Allgire, Court-Ordered Cesarean Sections, 10 J. Legal Med. 211, 236 (1989). I add that in mapping this uncharted area of the law, we can draw lines, and a line I would draw would be to preclude the use of physical force to perform an operation. The force of the court order itself as well as the use of the contempt power would, I think, be adequate in most cases. See id. at 243.

percent did not speak English as their primary language. All the women were treated in a teaching-hospital clinic or were receiving public assistance. . . . Forty-six percent of the heads of fellowship programs in maternal-fetal medicine thought that women who refused medical advice and thereby endangered the life of the fetus should be detained.

Kolder, Gallagher & Parsons, Court-Ordered Obstetrical Interventions, 316 New Eng. J. Med. 1192 (1987). These authors also found that one quarter of the respondents thought that home birth should be outlawed. Id. at 1194.

3. In a surprising number of the reported cases, such as the principal case and *Jefferson*, described in footnote 7, the doctors' predictions of the need for fetal intervention proved completely wrong. "In at least five other cases, women naturally delivered healthy babies after doctors assured judges of the medical necessity for a Caesarean." Jost, Mother versus Child, A.B.A.J., April 1989, at 84, 86.

The acknowledged "limitations and fallibility" of medical knowledge played strongly in the American College of Obstetrics and Gynecology adopting a policy statement that doctors "should refrain from performing procedures unwanted by the pregnant woman," and that "the use of judicial authority to implement treatment regimens in order to protect the fetus violates the pregnant woman's autonomy." N.Y. Times. Nov. 23, 1987, at 1; ACOG Committee on Ethics Opin. No. 55 (Oct. 1987).

4. Could the *A.C.* dissent have found support in the fact that many living will statutes, including the California law at p. 934 supra, restrict their application to pregnant women? See Note, Pregnancy Clauses in Living Will Statutes, 87 Colum. L. Rev. 1280 (1987) (contending such restrictions are unconstitutional); Comment, A Time to be Born and a Time to Die, 20 Ind. L. Rev. 859 (1987).

5. "A frighteningly high number of babies are being exposed to cocaine or other illegal drugs in the womb, according to data from 36 hospitals around the country. . . . The survey found that at least 11 percent of women in the hospitals studied had used illegal drugs in pregnancy. Experts said the data suggested that 375,000 newborns a year nationwide faced the possibility of health damage from their mothers' drug abuse." New York Times, Aug. 30, 1988, at 1.

Child abuse statutes have sometimes been invoked to authorize detention orders for pregnant women whose lifestyle is endangering the fetus. The Kolder article supra describes one case in Wisconsin. See footnote 16. In another, "California authorities jailed a woman [heroin addict] whose baby was born brain-dead, on charges that she took drugs during pregnancy and 'willfully disregarded' doctors' instructions. A judge dismissed those charges, but a bill to allow such prosecutions was immediately introduced in the California legislature."

316 New Eng. J. Med. 1195-1196. See also, Robertson & Schulman, Pregnancy and Prenatal Harm to Offspring, 18 Hastings Cent. Rep. 23, 29 (Aug. 1987) ("A Baltimore court in 1984 ordered a pregnant drug abuser committed for the last two months of pregnancy"); Churchville, "D.C. Judge Jails Woman as Protection for Fetus," Wash. Post, July 23, 1988, at A1 ("I'm going to keep her locked up until the baby is born because she's tested positive for cocaine . . . and I'll be darned if I'm going to have a baby born that way").

The California courts have refused to construe their child abuse statutes to cover drug addiction during pregnancy, but other states differ. See In re Ruiz, 500 N.E.2d 935 (Ohio App. 1986); In re Baby X, 293 N.W.2d 736 (Mich. Ct. App. 1980); Mass. Gen. Laws Ann. ch. 119, §51A (West Supp. 1985). Still, child abuse statutes generally do not provide clear authority to intervene *during pregnancy*, as opposed to taking custody of the child after birth. In one case, though, the court suggested that an order "to follow an intensive prenatal and neonatal treatment program monitored by both the probation officer and by a supervising physician" might be appropriate for a woman convicted of child endangerment for insisting on strict adherence to a macrobiotic diet. People v. Pointer, 199 Cal. Rptr. 357 (Cal. App. 1984). A Florida prosecutor discovered an even more innovative tactic; he obtained a conviction against a drug-abusing pregnant woman on the charge of "delivering drugs to a minor." N.Y. Times, July 14, 1989, at A10.

6. On the extraordinary question of whether a child injured by its mother's conduct during pregnancy may maintain a tort action against its mother for damages, the recent decision in Stallman v. Youngquist, 531 N.E.2d 355 (Ill. 1988) reached the opposite conclusion from the *Grodin* case discussed by Robertson. In *Stallman*, Lindsay Stallman (by her father) sued her mother on account of prenatal injuries Lindsay suffered in a car accident while her mother was driving to a restaurant when she was five months pregnant. Avoiding the question of parental immunity (which many courts have abandoned), the Illinois Court refused to recognize a cause of action by a fetus for unintentional injuries caused by its mother:

> It is clear that the recognition of a legal right to begin life with a sound mind and body on the part of a fetus which is assertable after birth against its mother would have serious ramifications for all women and their families, and for the way in which society views women and women's reproductive abilities. The recognition of such a right by a fetus would necessitate the recognition of a legal duty on the part of the woman who is the mother; a legal duty, as opposed to a moral duty, to effectuate the best prenatal environment possible. . . . Any action which negatively impacted on fetal development would be a breach of the pregnant woman's duty to her developing fetus. Mother

and child would be legal adversaries from the moment of conception until birth. . . .

The relationship between a pregnant woman and her fetus is unlike the relationship between any other plaintiff and defendant. No other plaintiff depends exclusively on any other defendant for everything necessary for life itself. No other defendant must go through biological changes of the most profound type, possibly at the risk of her own life, in order to bring forth an adversary into the world. It is, after all, the whole life of the pregnant woman which impacts on the development of the fetus. As opposed to the third-party defendant, it is the mother's every waking and sleeping moment which, for better or worse, shapes the prenatal environment which forms the world for the developing fetus.

Id. at 359-360.

7. "A study [at one hospital] revealed that out of 18 pregnant [AIDS]-infected women who received their test results in time to get an abortion, only three actually chose to end their pregnancies." Biolaw at U:1064 (1988). Could these women be forced to undergo an abortion?

8. Should a brain dead pregnant woman be kept on life support in order to save the fetus? Who should decide? These questions are raised by the medical case reported in Field et al., Maternal Brain Death During Pregnancy, 260 J.A.M.A. 816 (1988), where the patient was maintained in a brain-dead state for nine weeks at a cost of $217,784 before delivery of an infant weighing about 3 pounds.

9. Maternal-fetal conflict is perhaps the most extensively analyzed bioethics topic of the last couple of years. In addition to the sources cited in the principal materials, see S. Elias & G. Annas, Reproductive Genetics and the Law (1987); Nelson & Milliken, Compelled Medical Treatment of Pregnant Women, J.A.M.A. 259 (1988); Note, The Criminalization of Maternal Conduct During Pregnancy, 64 Ind. L.J. 357 (1989); Note, In re A.C.: Foreshadowing the Unfortunate Expansion of Court-ordered Caesarean Sections, 74 Iowa L. Rev. 287 (1988); Singer, Maternal Smoking and Fetal Injury, 21 Health & Hosp. L. 153 (1988); Robertson & Schulman, Pregnancy and Prenatal Harm to Offspring: The Case of Mothers with PKU, Hastings Cent. Rep., Aug. 1987, at 23; Johnsen, A New Threat to Pregnant Women's Autonomy, 17 Hastings Cent. Rep. 33 (Aug. 1987); Rusk, Prenatal Caretaking: Limits of State Intervention With and Without *Roe*, 39 U. Fla. L. Rev. 55 (1987); Sherman, Keeping Baby Safe From Mom, Natl. L.J., Oct. 3, 1988, at 1; Comment, Maternal Substance Abuse: The Need to Provide Legal Protection for the Fetus, 60 S. Cal. L. Rev. 1209 (1987); Note, Fetal Surgery: A Developing Legal Dilemma, 31 St. Louis U.L.J. 775 (1987); Comment, Maternal Liability: Courts Strive to Keep Doors Open to Fetal Protection, 20 J. Marsh. L. Rev.

747 (1987); Special Project, Legal Rights and Issues Surrounding Conception, Pregnancy, and Birth, 39 Vand. L. Rev. 597 (1986); Blank, Emerging Notions of Women's Rights and Responsibilities During Gestation, 7 J. Leg. Med. 441 (1986); Dougherty, The Right to Begin Life with Sound Body and Mind: Fetal Patients and Conflicts with Their Mothers, 65 U. Det. L. Rev. 89 (1987); Myers, Abuse and Neglect of the Unborn, 23 Duq. L. Rev. 1 (1984); Note, A Maternal Duty to Protect Fetal Health?, 58 Ind. L.J. 531 (1983); Annas, Forced Cesarean Sections: The Most Unkindest Cut of All, 12 Hastings Cent. Rep. 16 (No. 3, 1982). For a British view, see Fortin, Legal Protection for the Unborn Child, 51 Mod. L. Rev. 54 (1988).

E. Tort Actions Arising from Procreation: Wrongful Life, Wrongful Birth, and Wrongful Conception.

Curlender v. Bio-Science Laboratories
165 Cal. Rptr. 477 (Cal. App. 1980)

JEFFERSON, PRESIDING JUSTICE. . . . Th[is] appeal presents an issue of first impression in California: What remedy, if any, is available in this state to a severely impaired child — genetically defective — born as the result of defendants' negligence in conducting certain genetic tests of the child's parents — tests which, if properly done, would have disclosed the high probability that the actual, catastrophic result would occur?

I

. . . [P]laintiff Shauna alleged that on January 15, 1977, her parents, Phillis and Hyam Curlender, retained defendant laboratories to administer certain tests designed to reveal whether either of the parents were carriers of genes which would result in the conception and birth of a child with Tay-Sachs disease, medically defined as "amaurotic familial idiocy."[4] The tests on plaintiff's parents were

---

4. Schmidt's Attorneys' Dictionary of Medicine (1980). There the disease is more particularly described as "(a) familial (hereditary) disease affecting children of various ages, from four months to 12 years. It is characterized by partial or complete loss of vision, mental underdevelopment, softness of the muscles, convulsions, etc. Known as Tay-Sachs disease, cerebromacular degeneration, and Batten-Mayou's disease."

Tay-Sachs is a "fatal progressive degenerative disease of the nervous system which primarily affects the Eastern European Jewish population and their progeny. Only in the circumstance where both parents are carriers will there be a great likelihood of the presence of the disease in the offspring. In 1969, a relatively simple test to reveal carriers was developed, requiring only a blood sample. Parents-to-be, if individually

performed on January 21, 1977, and, it was alleged, due to defendants' negligence, "incorrect and inaccurate" information was disseminated to plaintiff's parents concerning their status as carriers.

The complaint did not allege the date of plaintiff's birth, so we do not know whether the parents relied upon the test results in conceiving plaintiff, or, as parents-to-be when the tests were made, relied upon the results in failing to avail themselves of amniocentesis and an abortion.[6] In any event, on May 10, 1978, plaintiff's parents were informed that plaintiff had Tay-Sachs disease.

As the result of the disease, plaintiff Shauna suffers from "mental retardation, susceptibility to other diseases, convulsions, sluggishness, apathy, failure to fix objects with her eyes, inability to take an interest in her surroundings, loss of motor reactions, inability to sit up or hold her head up, loss of weight, muscle atrophy, blindness, pseudobulper palsy, inability to feed orally, decerebrate rigidity and gross physical deformity." It was alleged that Shauna's life expectancy is estimated to be four years. The complaint also contained allegations that plaintiff suffers "pain, physical and emotional distress, fear, anxiety, despair, loss of enjoyment of life, and frustration. . . ." The complaint sought costs of plaintiff's care as damages and also damages for emotional distress and the deprivation of "72.6 years of her life."

II

Defendants successfully argued below that plaintiff Shauna, in essence, was seeking damages for negligence which resulted in her birth; the action was thus termed one for "wrongful life," a cause of action which when brought by the infant so born, has almost universally been barred in various factual contexts by courts in jurisdictions other than California, and has been rejected in this state insofar as damages were sought for an illegitimate birth by the infant so born. (Stills v. Gratton (1976) 55 Cal. App. 3d 698, 127 Cal. Rptr. 652.)

The term "wrongful life" has to date served as an umbrella for causes of action based upon any distinguishable factual situations; this has led to some confusion in its use. For purposes of our discussion,

---

tested and found both to be carriers, could then agree to a second test. Such second test (known as amniocentesis) involved the drawing and testing of amniotic fluid from the sac in which the unborn child rests within the mother. With the information that their child would be born suffering from this fatal disease, parents could make an informed, although difficult, decision as to whether to continue or terminate the pregnancy." (Howard v. Lecher (1977), 42 N.Y.2d 109, 114, 397 N.Y.S.2d 363, 366, 366 N.E.2d 64, 67 (dissent).)

6. An abortion undertaken to prevent birth of a genetically defective child is term[ed] "eugenic" while one to prevent harm to the mother-to-be is termed "therapeutic." (Speck v. Finegold (Pa. 1979) 408 A.2d 496, 499, fn. 4.)

III. Issues of Human Birth   1115

the term "wrongful life" will be confined to those causes of action *brought by the infant*. . . . [For a discussion of t]he decisional law concerning *parental* causes of action, . . . see "Tort Liability for Wrongful Birth," 83 A.L.R.3d 15, 29, and an excellent analysis in Speck v. Finegold, supra, footnote 6, of the case law that has developed in the last 50 years. . . .

A major (and much cited) opinion considering a claim for damages by an impaired infant plaintiff and his parents is Gleitman v. Cosgrove (1967) 49 N.J. 22, 227 A.2d 689, from the New Jersey Supreme Court. The Gleitmans brought a malpractice action against Mrs. Gleitman's physician for damages because the Gleitman child, Jeffrey, had been born with serious impairments of sight, speech, and hearing. Mrs. Gleitman had contracted rubella (measles) during the first trimester of pregnancy (the first three months). Defendant was made aware of this fact, but failed to inform the mother-to-be of any potentially harmful consequences to her child; Mrs. Gleitman was assured by him that such consequences would not occur, although it was common medical knowledge that rubella, contracted during early pregnancy, often causes the type of defects suffered by Jeffrey, who was also mentally retarded.

The majority of the *Gleitman* court barred recovery by either the parents or the child on two grounds: (1) the perceived impossibility of computing damages and (2) public policy. With respect to the computation of damages, the court explained that "[t]he normal measure of damages in tort actions is compensatory. Damages are measured by comparing the condition plaintiff would have been in, had the defendants not been negligent, with plaintiff's impaired condition as a result of the negligence. The infant plaintiff would have us measure the difference between his life with defects against the utter void of nonexistence, but it is impossible to make such a determination. This Court cannot weigh the value of life with impairments against the nonexistence of life itself. By asserting that he should not have been born, the infant plaintiff makes it logically impossible for a court to measure his alleged damages because of the impossibility of making the comparison required by compensatory remedies." . . .

A vastly different view was expressed by a dissenting opinion in *Gleitman*. It was there declared that the majority "permits a wrong with serious consequential injury to go wholly undressed. That provides no deterrent to professional irresponsibility and is neither just nor compatible with expanding principles of liability in the field of torts." As to the impossibility of computing damages, reference was made to a statement by the United States Supreme Court in Story Parchment Co. v. Paterson Co. (1931) 282 U.S. 555, 563, that difficulties encountered in computing damages cannot be permitted to justify a denial of liability. However, the reasoning and result in *Gleitman*'s majority opinion have been, in the main, followed (albeit blindly in our opinion) in other jurisdictions. (See Stewart v. Long Island College Hospital (1968) 58 Misc.2d 432, 296 N.Y.S.2d 41 and Dumer v. St. Michael's Hospital (1975) 69 Wis.2d 766, 233 N.W.2d 372.) It has also been analyzed and criticized. (See Note, 55 Minn. L. Rev. 58 (1971).) . . .

The Roe v. Wade case played a rather substantial part in the partial retreat from the *Gleitman* holding by the New Jersey Supreme Court majority in Berman v. Allan (1979) 80 N.J. 421, 404 A.2d 8. The Bermans, parents and child, brought suit for medical malpractice. Mrs. Berman had become pregnant in her late thirties, a circumstance involving a substantial risk that the child would be born with Down's syndrome (mongolism), one of the major characteristics of which is mental retardation. Sharon Berman, the child, was so afflicted. Amniocentesis by that time a well established technique for discerning birth defects in utero had not been suggested to the Bermans. The majority in the *Berman* court held that the *parents* had stated a cause of action, and that they could recover damages for emotional distress, but that lifetime support for Sharon could not be awarded.

But the *Berman* court rejected the concept that the infant Sharon possessed an independent cause of action. . . . Here, the majority chose to rely on public policy considerations. The *Berman* court considered that Sharon had not suffered any damage cognizable at law by being brought into existence. It was explained that "[o]ne of the most deeply held beliefs of our society is that life whether experienced with or without a major physical handicap is more precious than non-life. . . . Sharon, by virtue of her birth, will be able to love and be loved and to experience happiness and pleasure emotions which are truly the essence of life and which are far more valuable than the suffering she may endure. To rule otherwise would require us to disavow the basic assumption upon which our society is based. This we cannot do." . . .

The dissenting opinion in *Berman* expressed the cogent observation that, as for the child, "[a]n adequate comprehension of the infant's claims under these circumstances starts with the realization that the infant has come into this world and is here, encumbered by an injury attributable to the malpractice of the doctors." . . .

In Park v. Chessin (1977) 60 A.D. 80, 400 N.Y.S.2d 110, an intermediate New York appellate court . . . gave both the parents and child causes of action, that "decisional law must keep pace with expanding technological, economic and social change. Inherent in the abolition of the statutory ban on abortion . . . is a public policy consideration which gives potential parents the right, within certain statutory and case law limitations, *not* to have a child. This right extends to instances in which it can be determined with reasonable medical certainty that the child would be born deformed. *The breach of this right may also be said to be tortious to the fundamental right of a child to be born as a whole, functional human being."* [Emphasis added]. . . . But this view of the law also had a short life span. This decision was reviewed in Becker v. Schwartz (1978), 46 N.Y.2d 401, 413 N.Y.S.2d 895, 386 N.E.2d 807 (as a companion case) and overruled. . . . The court particularly rejected the idea that a child may expect life without deformity: "There is no precedent for recognition at the Appellate Division of 'the fundamental right of a child to be born as a whole, functional human being'. . . ."

The high court in Pennsylvania issued an exhaustive opinion in 1979 concerning the various aspects of the "wrongful-life" problem. The case was Speck v. Finegold, 408 A.2d 496, a malpractice suit by parents and child occasioned by the birth of the child with neurofibromatosis, a seriously crippling condition already evidenced in the child's siblings. Overruling the trial court, *Speck* recognized the parents' cause of action but not that of the infant plaintiff.

We quote at length from the *Speck* court's opinion: . . . "Whether it is better to have never been born at all rather than to have been born with serious mental defects is a mystery more properly left to the philosophers and theologians, a mystery which would lead us into the field of metaphysics, beyond the realm of our understanding or ability to solve." . . .

Other jurisdictions, following the lead of the New Jersey and New York cases, have rejected the concept of an infant's cause of action for "wrongful life." . . .

III

From our analysis and study, we conclude that certain general observations are appropriate concerning the decisional law in this country to date with respect to the "wrongful life" problem. . . . The decisional law of other jurisdictions . . . ha[s] progressed from a stance of barring all recovery to a recognition that, at least, the parents of such a child may state a cause of action founded on negligence. . . .

Another factor of substantial proportions in "wrongful-life" litigation is the dramatic increase, in the last few decades, of the medical knowledge and skill needed to avoid genetic disaster. As the author of the article in ["Father and Mother Know Best: Defining the Liability of Physicians for Inadequate Genetic Counseling" (1978) 87 Yale Law Journal 1488] points out: "Genetic defects represent an increasingly large part of the overall national health care burden." (87 Yale Law Journal 1496). The writer concluded that the law indeed has an appropriate function in encouraging adequate and careful medical practice in the field of genetic counseling, observing that "[t]ort law, a well-recognized means of regulating the practice of medicine, can be used both to establish and to limit the duty of physicians to fulfill this (genetic counseling) function." . . .

The circumstance that the birth and injury have come hand in hand has caused other courts to deal with the problem by barring recovery. The reality of the "wrongful-life" concept is that such a plaintiff both *exists* and *suffers,* due to the negligence of others. It is neither necessary nor just to retreat into meditation on the mysteries of life. We need not be concerned with the fact that had defendants not been negligent, the plaintiff might not have come into existence at all. The certainty of genetic impairment is no longer a mystery. In addition, a reverent appreciation of life compels recognition that plaintiff, however impaired she may be, has come into existence as a living person with certain rights.

One of the fears expressed in the decisional law is that, once it is determined that such infants have rights cognizable at law, nothing would prevent such a plaintiff from bringing suit against its own parents for allowing plaintiff to be born. In our view, [i]f a case arose where, despite due care by the medical profession in transmitting the necessary warnings, parents made a conscious choice to proceed with a pregnancy, with full knowledge that a seriously impaired infant would be born, . . . we see no sound public policy which should protect those parents from being answerable for the pain, suffering and misery which they have wrought upon their offspring. . . .

We have concluded that it is clearly consistent with the applicable principles of the statutory and decisional tort law in this state to recognize a cause of action stated by plaintiff against the defendants. To do otherwise would negate and run counter to the course of tort law so nobly chartered and enunciated in the landmark cases [citations omitted].

The extent of recovery, however, is subject to certain limitations due to the nature of the tort involved. While ordinarily a defendant is liable for all consequences flowing from the injury, it is appropriate in the case before us to tailor the elements of recovery, taking into account particular circumstances involved.

The complaint seeks damages based upon an actuarial life expectancy of plaintiff of more than 70 years — the life expectancy if plaintiff had been born without the Tay-Sachs disease. The complaint sets forth that plaintiff's actual life expectancy, because of the disease, is only four years. We reject as untenable the claim that plaintiff is entitled to damages as if plaintiff had been born without defects and would have had a normal life expectancy. Plaintiff's right to damages must be considered on the basis of plaintiff's mental and physical condition at birth and her expected condition during the short life span (four years according to the complaint) anticipated for one with her impaired condition. In similar fashion, we reject the notion that a "wrongful-life" cause of action involves any attempted evaluation of a claimed right *not* to be born. In essence, we construe the "wrongful-life" cause of action by the defective child as the right of such child to recover damages for the pain and suffering to be endured during the limited life span available to such a child and any special pecuniary loss resulting from the impaired condition. . . .

Turpin v. Sortini
643 P.2d 954 (Cal. 1981)

KAUS, JUSTICE. This case presents the question of whether a child born with an hereditary affliction may maintain a tort action against a medical care provider who — before the child's conception — negligently failed to advise the child's parents of the possibility of the hereditary condition, depriving them of the opportunity to choose not to conceive the child. Although the overwhelming majority of decisions in other jurisdictions recognize the right of the parents to maintain an action under these circumstances, the out-of-state cases have uniformly denied the child's right to bring what has been commonly termed a "wrongful life" action. In Curlender v. Bio-Science Laboratories however, the Court of Appeal concluded that under California common law tort principles, an afflicted child could maintain such an action and could "recover damages for the pain and suffering to be endured during the limited life span available to such a child and any special pecuniary loss resulting from the impaired condition," including the costs of medical care to the extent such costs were not recovered by the child's parents. In the case at bar, a different panel of the Court of Appeal disagreed with the conclusion in *Curlender* and affirmed a trial court judgment dismissing the child's cause of action on demurrer. We granted a hearing to resolve the conflict.

I

The allegations of the complaint disclose the following facts. On September 24, 1976, James and Donna Turpin, acting on the advice of their pediatrician, brought their first — and at that time their only — daughter, Hope, to the Leon S. Peters Rehabilitation Center at the Fresno Community Hospital for evaluation of a possible hearing defect. Hope was examined and tested by Adam J. Sortini, a licensed professional specializing in the diagnosis and treatment of speech and hearing defects.

The complaint alleges that Sortini and other persons at the hospital negligently examined, tested and evaluated Hope and incorrectly advised her pediatrician that her hearing was within normal limits when, in reality, she was "stone deaf" as a result of an hereditary ailment. Hope's parents did not learn of her condition until October 15, 1977 when it was diagnosed by other specialists. According to the complaint, the nature of the condition is such that there is a "reasonable degree of medical probability" that the hearing defect would be inherited by any offspring of James and Donna. The complaint further alleges that in December 1976, before learning of Hope's true condition and relying on defendants' diagnosis, James and Donna conceived a second child, Joy. The complaint avers that had the Turpins known of Hope's hereditary deafness they would not have conceived Joy. Joy was born August 23, 1977, and suffers from the same total deafness as Hope.

On the basis of these facts, James, Donna, Hope and Joy filed a complaint setting forth four causes of action against defendants Sortini, the hospital, the rehabilitation center and various Does. The first cause of action, brought on behalf of Hope, seeks damages for the harm Hope has allegedly suffered as a result of the delay in the diagnosis of her condition. The second cause of action — the only cause before us on this appeal — was brought on behalf of Joy and seeks (1) general damages for being "deprived of the fundamental right of a child to be born as a whole, functional human being without total deafness" and (2) special damages for the "extraordinary expenses for specialized teaching, training and hearing equipment" which she will incur during her lifetime as a result of her hearing impairment. [T]he court entered a judgment dismissing the action as to Joy. As noted, Joy's action is the only matter before us on this appeal.

II

Although this is the first case in which we have faced the question of potential tort liability in a "wrongful life" or "wrongful birth" context,[4] there is no dearth of authority in this area.[5] In recent years,

---

4. While courts and commentators have not always been consistent in their terminology, "wrongful life" has generally referred to actions brought on behalf of children, and "wrongful birth" to actions brought by parents. Some authorities have broken these categories down further (see Comment, "Wrongful Life": The Right Not to be Born (1980) 54 Tulane L.Rev. 480, 483-485), but in this opinion we will follow the general usage: "wrongful life" for all actions brought by children and "wrongful birth" for all actions brought by parents.

5. The subject has also proved a popular topic for legal commentators. (See, e.g., Capron, Tort Liability and Genetic Counseling (1979) 79 Colum. L. Rev. 618; Note, Father and Mother Know Best: Defining the Liability of Physicians for Inadequate

III. Issues of Human Birth

many courts in other jurisdictions have confronted similar claims brought by both parents and children against medical professionals whose negligence had allegedly proximately caused the birth of hereditarily afflicted children. The overwhelming majority of the recent cases have permitted parents to recover at least some elements of damage in such actions. [Citations omitted] At the same time, the out-of-state authorities have uniformly rejected the children's own claims for general damages [citations omitted]. . . .

IV

Plaintiff, of course, relies heavily — indeed exclusively — on the *Curlender* decision in support of her action in this case. . . . Joy's complaint . . . assert[s] that as a result of defendants' negligence she was "deprived of the fundamental right of a child to be born as a whole, functional human being without total deafness. . . ." While the *Curlender* decision did not embrace this approach to "injury" completely — refusing to permit the plaintiff to recover for a reduced lifespan — it too maintained that the proper point of reference for measuring defendant's liability was simply plaintiff's condition after birth, insisting that "[w]e need not be concerned with the fact that had defendants not been negligent, the plaintiff might not have come into existence at all", and rejecting "the notion that a 'wrongful life' cause of action involves any attempted evaluation of a claimed right not to be born."

The basic fallacy of the *Curlender* analysis is that it ignores the essential nature of the defendants' alleged wrong and obscures . . . the obvious tragic fact [ ] that plaintiff never had a chance "to be born as a whole, functional human being without total deafness"; if defendants had performed their jobs properly, she would not have been born with hearing intact, but — according to the complaint — would not have been born at all.

A plaintiff's remedy in tort is compensatory in nature and damages are generally intended not to punish a negligent defendant but to restore an injured person as nearly as possible to the position he or she would have been in had the wrong not been done. Because nothing defendants could have done would have given plaintiff an unimpaired life, it appears inconsistent with basic tort principles to view the injury for which defendants are legally responsible solely by reference to plaintiff's present condition without taking into consid-

---

Genetic Counseling (1978) 87 Yale L.J. 1488; Comment, "Wrongful Life": The Right Not to be Born (1980) 54 Tulane L. Rev. 480; Note, A Reassessment of "Wrongful Life" and "Wrongful Birth" (1980) 1980 Wis. L. Rev. 782; Kelley, Wrongful Life, Wrongful Birth and Justice in Tort Law (1979) 4 Wash. U.L.Q. 919.)

eration the fact that if defendants had not been negligent she would not have been born at all. . . .

In this case, in which the plaintiff's only affliction is deafness, it seems quite unlikely that a jury would ever conclude that life with such a condition is worse than not being born at all. Other wrongful life cases, however, have involved children with much more serious, debilitating and painful conditions, and the academic literature refers to still other, extremely severe hereditary diseases. Considering the short life span of many of these children and their frequently very limited ability to perceive or enjoy the benefits of life, we cannot assert with confidence that in every situation there would be a societal consensus that life is preferable to never having been born at all.

We believe, however, that there is a profound qualitative difference between the difficulties faced by a jury in assessing general damages in a normal personal injury or wrongful death action, and the task before a jury in assessing general damages in a wrongful life case. . . . In this context, a rational, nonspeculative determination of a specific monetary award in accordance with normal tort principles appears to be outside the realm of human competence. . . .

While it thus seems doubtful that a child's claim for general damages should properly be denied on the rationale that the value of impaired life, as a matter of law, always exceeds the value of nonlife, we believe that the out-of-state decisions are on sounder grounds in holding that — with respect to the child's claim for pain and suffering or other general damages — recovery should be denied because (1) it is simply impossible to determine in any rational or reasoned fashion whether the plaintiff has in fact suffered an injury in being born impaired rather than not being born, and (2) even if it were possible to overcome the first hurdle, it would be impossible to assess general damages in any fair, nonspeculative manner. . . .

V

Although we have determined that the trial court properly rejected plaintiff's claim for general damages, we conclude that her claim for the "extraordinary expenses for specialized teaching, training and hearing equipment" that she will incur during her lifetime because of her deafness stands on a different footing.[11]

As we have already noted, in the corresponding "wrongful birth" actions parents have regularly been permitted to recover the medical

---

11. As noted, in a separate cause of action Joy's parents seek to recover, inter alia, for the medical expenses which they will incur on Joy's behalf during her minority. Since both Joy and her parents obviously cannot both recover the same expenses, Joy's separate claim applies as a practical matter only to medical expenses to be incurred after the age of majority.

expenses incurred on behalf of such a child. [Citations omitted] In authorizing this recovery by the parents, courts have recognized (1) that these are expenses that would not have been incurred "but for" the defendants' negligence and (2) that they are the kind of pecuniary losses which are readily ascertainable and regularly awarded as damages in professional malpractice actions.

Although the parents and child cannot, of course, both recover for the same medical expenses, we believe it would be illogical and anomalous to permit only parents, and not the child, to recover for the cost of the child's own medical care. If such a distinction were established, the afflicted child's receipt of necessary medical expenses might well depend on the wholly fortuitous circumstance of whether the parents are available to sue and recover such damages or whether the medical expenses are incurred at a time when the parents remain legally responsible for providing such care.

Realistically, a defendant's negligence in failing to diagnose an hereditary ailment places a significant medical and financial burden on the whole family unit. Unlike the child's claim for general damages, the damage here is both certain and readily measurable. Furthermore, in many instances these expenses will be vital not only to the child's well-being but to his or her very survival. . . .

VI

In sum, we conclude that while a plaintiff-child in a wrongful life action may not recover general damages for being born impaired as opposed to not being born at all, the child — like his or her parents — may recover special damages for the extraordinary expenses necessary to treat the hereditary ailment.

The judgment is reversed and the case is remanded to the trial court for further proceedings consistent with this opinion.

NOTES

Negligent Genetic Screening and Failed Sterilizations

1. Genetic screening and counseling mistakes are likely to assume increasing importance in coming years. "The last several decades have brought dramatic improvements in medicine's ability to predict and diagnose genetic and congenital disease. The first prenatal diagnosis of a chromosome defect occurred as recently as 1967, followed the next year by the successful detection of an inborn error of metabolism. Currently, some 200 metabolic and chromosomal disorders can be diagnosed prenatally, and with the rapid development of powerful DNA probes, it may soon be possible to detect all of the 3000 known

single-gene defects in humans." Botkin, The Legal Concept of Wrongful Life, 259 J.A.M.A. 1541 (1988). Moreover, far-reaching genetic mapping projects are likely to increase exponentially our current knowledge of gene defects.

2. The decision that most influenced the extension of Roe v. Wade to recognize the parents' cause of action for wrongful birth of a deformed infant is Becker v. Schwartz, 386 N.E.2d 807 (N.Y. 1978), discussed in *Curlender*. All courts since have agreed, except Azzolino v. Dingfelder, 337 S.E.2d 528 (N.C. 1985) (dismissing action by parents of Downs Syndrome child which alleged that doctor failed to advise of availability of genetic counseling and screening tests), and Wilson v. Kuenzi, 721 S.W.2d 741 (Mo. 1988) (rejecting action because of the inherent unreliability of the mother's testifying after the fact that she would have obtained an abortion). Also, a few legislatures have outlawed the parents' action. S.D. Codified Laws §21-55-1; Minn. Stat. §145.424; Pa. Cons. Stat. §8305. Given the significance of Roe v. Wade in this area, are these statutes unconstitutional? Hickman v. Group Health Plan, 396 N.W.2d 10 (Minn. 1986) (statute prohibiting wrongful life and birth actions held constitutional); Note, Wrongful Birth Actions: The Case Against Legislative Curtailment, 100 Harv. L. Rev. 2017 (1987) (contra).

Otherwise, the parents' wrongful birth action has been accepted almost uniformly, although damages are usually limited to the "extraordinary" expenses of raising a deformed child, which excludes mental anguish and the ordinary expenses of child care. See Lininger v. Eisenbaum, 764 P.2d 1202 (Colo. 1988); Haymon v. Wilkerson, 535 A.2d 880 (D.C. Ct. App. 1987). Is this limitation consistent with the theory of the action and with general tort theory, or is this simply a compromise position? Compare Robak v. U.S., 658 F.2d 471 (7th Cir. 1981) (allowing recovery under Virginia law of full expenses of child rearing); James G. v. Caserta, 332 S.E.2d 872 (W.Va. 1985) (allowing recovery for parents' mental distress and loss of consortium associated with Downs syndrome child); Gallagher v. Duke University Hosp., 852 F.2d 773 (4th Cir. 1988) (similar).

After the *Becker* decision was handed down, it became known that the Beckers' child had been adopted during the proceedings. N.Y. Times, January 17, 1979, at 23. What are the damages in a wrongful birth action when the natural parents will not bear the cost of the child's care? For specific commentary regarding the *Becker* case, see Curran, Tay-Sachs Disease, Wrongful Life, and Preventative Malpractice, 67 Am. J. Pub. Health 568 (May 1977); Curran, Genetic Counseling and Wrongful Life, 68 Am. J. Pub. Health 501 (1978).

3. What do you think of the idea *Curlender* endorsed of allowing defective children to sue their parents for deciding to conceive or for failing to abort? "In evident response to this suggestion, . . . the

[California] Legislature enacted section 43.6 of the Civil Code . . . reliev[ing] the parents of any liability in this situation." *Turpin*, 182 Cal. Rptr. at 342.

4. Most courts still continue to reject any "wrongful life" recovery by the deformed child. E.g., Lininger v. Eisenbaum supra; Ellis v. Sherman, 515 A.2d 1327 (Pa. 1986); Goldberg v. Ruskin, 499 N.E.2d 406 (Ill. 1986). The only other jurisdictions to allow wrongful life suits are Procanik v. Cillo, 478 A.2d 755 (N.J. 1984); Harbeson v. Park-Davis Inc., 656 P.2d 483 (Wash. 1983); Pitre v. Opelousas Gen. Hosp., 530 So. 2d 1151 (La. 1988); Annot., 78 A.L.R.4th — (1990). Like *Turpin*, however, these cases limit damages to the extraordinary medical expenses not borne by parents. No court has gone as far as *Curlender*. With this damages limitation intact, is there really that much at stake in the wrongful life/wrongful birth distinction? Is there any conceivable rationale for distinguishing between the parents' action and the child's action for medical expenses?

One possible distinction that has bothered some courts is the notion of privity that sometimes surfaces in tort law. As explored more fully at 524 supra, some courts limit malpractice actions to the confines of the doctor/patient relationship. In the present context of genetic counseling, the patient is the parent, not the fetus, so some courts have balked at finding that the doctor owes it any duty. In response to this line of thought, the *Turpin* court reasoned: "In this case, although the Turpins' older daughter Hope, and not Joy, was defendants' immediate patient, it was reasonably foreseeable that Hope's parents and their potential offspring would be directly affected by defendants' negligent failure to discover that Hope suffered from an hereditary [hearing defect]. . . . In cases involving contagious diseases, doctors have frequently been found to owe a duty of care to a patient's immediate family." 182 Cal. Rptr. at 343 & n.7. See also Gallagher v. Duke Univ., 638 F. Supp. 979 (D.C.N.C. 1986).

5. Actions for a failed sterilization have generated much the same analysis as negligent genetic screening suits. Courts have had no difficulty in allowing recovery for the medical expenses and suffering incident to the health complications of an unexpected pregnancy, particularly in cases of failed *therapeutic* sterilizations. E.g., Goforth v. Porter Med. Assoc., 755 P.2d 678 (Ok. 1988); C.S. v. Nielson, 767 P.2d 504 (Utah 1988). But the courts balk where the parents' only complaint is having to raise a normal, healthy child. In such cases, "there are three views:

1) The no recovery rule: the parent may not recover the costs of rearing [a healthy] child;
2) the full recovery rule: the parent may recover the full costs of rearing the child; and

3) the "benefits" rule: the parent may recover the costs of rearing the child, less the benefits the parent will receive from a normal, healthy child."

Byrd v. Wesley Med. Cent., 699 P.2d 459 (Kan. 1985). The full recovery rule has little support. The majority of courts have followed the no recovery rule, e.g., Morris v. Sanchez, 746 P.2d 184 (Okla. 1987), while only a minority have allowed juries to consider whether the burdens outweigh the benefits, e.g., University of Arizona v. Superior Court, 667 P.2d 1294 (Az. 1983).

Until recently, the only decision that approached a full recovery rule was Custodio v. Bauer, 59 Cal. Rptr. 463 (Cal. App. 1967):

> The mental suffering attendant to the unexpected pregnancy because of the complications which may or may not result, the complications that do result, and the delivery of a child are all foreseeable consequences of the failure of the operation. . . . Where the mother survives without casualty there is still some loss. She must spread her society, comfort, care, protection and support over a larger group. If this change in the family status can be measured economically it should be as compensable as the former losses. [T]he compensation is not for the so-called unwanted child or "emotional bastard" but to replenish the family exchequer so that the new arrival will not deprive the other members of the family of what was planned as their just share of the family income.

Is this an accurate depiction of the typical family's response to an unexpected birth (question intended nonrhetorically)? *Custodio* was joined by Marciniak v. Lundborg, 450 N.W.2d 243 (Wis. 1990), which held that parents who suffer a negligent sterilization operation may recover the costs of raising a healthy child. The court rejected any offset for the emotional (or financial) benefits of having the child, observing that "it was precisely to avoid that 'benefit' that the parents went to the physician in the first place." Yet the court rejected the argument that "the refusal of the [parents] to abort the unplanned child or give it up for adoption should be considered as a failure . . . to mitigate their damages." See generally Note, Judicial Limitations on Damages Recoverable for the Wrongful Birth of a Healthy Infant, 68 Va. L. Rev. 1311 (1982); 27 A.L.R.3d 906 (1969); 74 A.L.R.4th 798 (1989).

6. For further discussion of these issues, see President's Commission, Screening and Counseling for Genetic Conditions (1983); Bopp et al., The "Rights" and "Wrongs" of Wrongful Birth and Wrongful Life, 27 Duq. L. Rev. 461 (1989); Steinbok, The Logical Case for Wrongful Life, 16 Hastings Cent. Rep. 15 (1986); Special Project, Legal Rights and Issues Surrounding Conception, Pregnancy, and Birth, 39 Vand. L. Rev. 597 (1986); Currier, The Judicial System's

III. Issues of Human Birth

Wrongful Conception of Wrongful Life, 6 West. New Eng. L. Rev. 493 (1983); Sonnenburg, A Preference for Nonexistence: Wrongful Life and a Proposed Tort of Genetic Malpractice, 55 S. Cal. L. Rev. 477 (1982); Minott & Zurzolo, Wrongful Life: A Misconceived Tort, 15 U.C. Davis L. Rev. 447 (1981); Note, Wrongful Birth Damages: Mandate and Mishandling by Judicial Fiat, 13 Val. U.L. Rev. 127 (1978); Note, Civil Liability Arising From "Wrongful Birth" Following Unsuccessful Sterilization Operation, 4 Am. J.L. & Med. 131 (1978); Carey, Physician's Liability for Pre-Conception Torts, 54 Notre Dame L. Rev. 696 (1979); Clark, Wrongful Conception: A New Kind of Medical Malpractice? 12 Fam. L.Q. 259 (1979); Note, Medical Malpractice: Wrongful Birth, 13 Akron L. Rev. 390 (1979); 83 A.L.R.3d 15 (1978).

Social and ethical aspects of genetic screening are considered in Riccardi et al., Genetic Counseling as Part of Hospital Care, 68 Am. J. Pub. Health 652 (1978); Schneiderman et al., Psychological Aspects of a Tay-Sachs Screening Clinic, 135 Am. J. Psychia. 1101 (1978); Fletcher, Ethics and Amniocentesis for Fetal Sex Identification, 10 Hastings Center Rep. 15 (Fall 1980).

CHAPTER 10

Public Health Regulation and the AIDS Epidemic

I. PUBLIC HEALTH REGULATORY POLICY: ISSUES OF INDIVIDUAL FREEDOM AND COMPULSION

Jacobson v. Massachusetts
197 U.S. 11 (1904)

[The case involved the validity under the U.S. Constitution of the Massachusetts law requiring vaccination against smallpox. The defendant refused to be vaccinated and was prosecuted criminally for violation of the law and of regulations of the Board of Health of Cambridge. The defendant was found guilty of the violation and appealed to the Massachusetts Supreme Judicial Court which upheld the conviction. In an appeal to the U.S. Supreme Court, the defendant argued that the compulsory vaccination was in violation of the Preamble to the U.S. Constitution and tended to subvert and defeat the purposes of the Constitution as set out in the Preamble. He also argued that the compulsory vaccination was in violation of the spirit of the Constitution.]

HARLAN, J.

The authority of the State to enact this statute is to be referred to what is commonly called the police power — a power which the State did not surrender when becoming a member of the Union under the Constitution. Although this court has refrained from any attempt to define the limits of that power, yet it has distinctly recognized the authority of a State to enact quarantine laws and "health laws of every description;" indeed, all laws that relate to matters completely within its territory and which do not by their necessary operation affect the people of other States. According to settled principles the police power of a State must be held to embrace, at least, such reasonable regulations established directly by legislative enactment as will protect the public health and the public safety. Gibbons v. Ogden, 9 Wheat. 1, 203; Railroad Company v. Husen, 95 U.S. 465, 470; Beer Company v. Massachusetts, 97 U.S. 25; New Orleans Gas Co. v. Louisiana Light Co., 115 U.S. 650, 661; Lawton v. Steele, 152 U.S. 133. It is equally true that the State may invest local bodies called into existence for purposes of local administration with authority in some appropriate way to safeguard the public health and the public safety. The mode or manner in which those results are to be accomplished is within the discretion of the State, subject, of course, so far as Federal power is concerned, only to the condition that no rule prescribed by a State, nor any regulation adopted by a local governmental agency acting under the sanction of state legislation, shall contravene the Constitution of the United States or infringe any right granted or secured by that instrument. A local enactment or regulation, even if based on the acknowledged police powers of a State, must always yield in case of conflict with the exercise by the General Government of any power it possesses under the Constitution, or with any right which that instrument gives or secures. Gibbons v. Ogden, 9 Wheat. 1, 210; Sinnot v. Davenport, 22 How. 227, 243; Missouri, Kansas & Texas Ry. Co. v. Haber, 169 U.S. 613, 626.

We come, then, to inquire whether any right given, or secured by the Constitution, is invaded by the statute as interpreted by the state court. The defendant insists that his liberty is invaded when the State subjects him to fine or imprisonment for neglecting or refusing to submit to vaccination; that a compulsory vaccination law is unreasonable, arbitrary and oppressive, and, therefore, hostile to the inherent right of every freeman to care for his own body and health in such way as to him seems best; and that the execution of such a law against one who objects to vaccination, no matter for what reason, is nothing short of an assault upon his person. But the liberty secured by the Constitution of the United States to every person within its jurisdiction does not import an absolute right in each person to be, at all times and in all circumstances, wholly freed from restraint. There are manifold restraints to which every person is necessarily subject for the common good. On any other basis organized society could not exist with safety to its members. Society based on the rule that each one is a law unto himself would soon be confronted with disorder and anarchy. Real liberty for all could not exist under the operation of a principle which recognizes the right of each individual person to use his own, whether in respect of his person or his property, regardless of the injury that may be done to others. This court has more than once recognized it as a fundamental principle that "persons and property are subjected to all kinds of restraints and burdens, in order to secure the general comfort, health, and prosperity of the State; of the perfect right of the legislature to do which no question ever was, or upon acknowledged general principles ever can be made, so far as natural persons are concerned." Railroad Co. v. Husen, 95 U.S. 465, 471; Missouri, Kansas & Texas Ry. Co. v. Haber, 169 U.S. 613, 628, 629; Thorpe v. Rutland & Burlington R.R., 27 Vermont, 140, 148. In Crowley v. Christensen, 137 U.S. 86, 89, we said: "The possession and enjoyment of all rights are subject to such reasonable

I. Public Health Regulatory Policy

conditions as may be deemed by the governing authority of the country essential to the safety, health, peace, good order and morals of the community. Even liberty itself, the greatest of all rights, is not unrestricted license to act according to one's own will. It is only freedom from restraint under conditions essential to the equal enjoyment of the same right by others. It is then liberty regulated by law." In the constitution of Massachusetts adopted in 1780 it was laid down as a fundamental principle of the social compact that the whole people covenants with each citizen, and each citizen with the whole people, that all shall be governed by certain laws for "the common good," and that government is instituted "for the common good, for the protection, safety, prosperity and happiness of the people, and not for the profit, honor or private interests of any one man, family or class of men." The good and welfare of the Commonwealth, of which the legislature is primarily the judge, is the basis on which the police power rests in Massachusetts. Commonwealth v. Alger, 7 Cush. 53, 84.

Applying these principles to the present case, it is to be observed that the legislature of Massachusetts required the inhabitants of a city or town to be vaccinated only when, in the opinion of the Board of Health, that was necessary for the public health or the public safety. The authority to determine for all what ought to be done in such an emergency must have been lodged somewhere or in some body; and surely it was appropriate for the legislature to refer that question, in the first instance, to a Board of Health, composed of persons residing in the locality affected and appointed, presumably, because of their fitness to determine such questions. To invest such a body with authority over such matters was not an unusual nor an unreasonable or arbitrary requirement. Upon the principle of self-defense, of paramount necessity, a community has the right to protect itself against an epidemic of disease which threatens the safety of its members. It is to be observed that when the regulation in question was adopted, smallpox, according to the recitals in the regulation adopted by the Board of Health, was prevalent to some extent in the city of Cambridge and the disease was increasing. If such was the situation — and nothing is asserted or appears in the record to the contrary — if we are to attach any value whatever to the knowledge which, it is safe to affirm, is common to all civilized peoples touching smallpox and the methods most usually employed to eradicate that disease, it cannot be adjudged that the present regulation of the Board of Health was not necessary in order to protect the public health and secure the public safety. Smallpox being prevalent and increasing at Cambridge, the court would usurp the functions of another branch of government if it adjudged, as matter of law, that the mode adopted under the sanction of the State, to protect the people at large, was arbitrary and not justified by the necessities of the case. We say necessities of the case, because it might be that an acknowledged power of a local community to protect itself against an epidemic threatening the safety of all, might be exercised in particular circumstances and in reference to particular persons in such an arbitrary, unreasonable manner, or might go so far beyond what was reasonably required for the safety of the public, as to authorize or compel the courts to interfere for the protection of such persons.... There is, of course, a sphere within which the individual may assert the supremacy of his own will and rightfully dispute the authority of any human government, especially of any free government existing under a written constitution, to interfere with the exercise of that will. But it is equally true that in every well-ordered society charged with the duty of conserving the safety of its members the rights of the individual in respect of his liberty may at times, under the pressure of great dangers, be subjected to such restraint, to be enforced by reasonable regulations, as the safety of the general public may demand. An American citizen, arriving at an American port on a vessel in which, during the voyage, there had been cases of yellow fever or Asiatic cholera, although apparently free from disease himself, may yet, in some circumstances, be held in quarantine against his will on board of such vessel or in a quarantine station, until it be ascertained by inspection, conducted with due diligence, that the danger of the spread of the disease among the community at large has disappeared.

Whatever may be thought of the expediency of this statute, it cannot be affirmed to be, beyond question, in palpable conflict with the Constitution. Nor, in view of the methods employed to stamp out the disease of smallpox, can anyone confidently assert that the means prescribed by the State to that end has no real or substantial relation to the protection of the public health and the public safety. Such an assertion would not be consistent with the experience of this and other countries whose authorities have dealt with the disease of smallpox.[1] . . .

---

1. "State-supported facilities for vaccination began in England in 1808 with the National Vaccine Establishment. In 1840 vaccination fees were made payable out of the rates. The first compulsory act was passed in 1853, the guardians of the poor being entrusted with the carrying out of the law; in 1854 the public vaccinations under one year of age were 408,825 as against an average of 180,960 for several years before. In 1867 a new Act was passed, rather to remove some technical difficulties than to enlarge the scope of the former Act; and in 1871 the Act was passed which compelled the boards of guardians to appoint vaccination officers. The guardians also appoint a public vaccinator, who must be duly qualified to practice medicine, and whose duty it is to vaccinate (for a fee of one shilling and sixpence) any child resident within his district brought to him for that purpose, to examine the same a week after, to give a certificate, and to certify to the vaccination officer the fact of vaccination or of insusceptibility.... Vaccination was made compulsory in Bavaria in 1807, and subsequently in the following countries: Denmark (1810), Sweden (1814), Würtemburg,

I. Public Health Regulatory Policy

The defendant offered to prove that vaccination "quite often" caused serious and permanent injury to the health of the person vaccinated; that the operation "occasionally" resulted in death; that it was "impossible" to tell "in any particular case" what the results of vaccination would be or whether it would injure the health or result in death; that "quite often" one's blood is in a certain condition of impurity when it is not prudent or safe to vaccinate him; that there is no practical test by which to determine "with any degree of certainty" whether one's blood is in such condition of impurity as to render vaccination necessarily unsafe or dangerous; that vaccine matter is "quite often" impure and dangerous to be used, but whether impure or not cannot be ascertained by any known practical test; that the defendant refused to submit to vaccination for the reason that he had, "when a child," been caused great and extreme suffering for a long period by a disease produced by vaccination; and that he had witnessed a similar result of vaccination not only in the case of his son, but in the cases of others.

These offers, in effect, invited the court and jury to go over the whole ground gone over by the legislature when it enacted the statute in question. The legislature assumed that some children, by reason of their condition at the time, might not be fit subjects of vaccination; and it is suggested — and we will not say without reason — that such is the case with some adults. But the defendant did not offer to prove that, by reason of his then condition, he was in fact not a fit subject of vaccination at the time he was informed of the requirement of the regulation adopted by the Board of Health. It is entirely consistent with his offer of proof that, after reaching full age he had become, so far as medical skill could discover, and when informed of the regulation of the Board of Health was, a fit subject of vaccination, and that the vaccine matter to be used in his case was such as any medical practitioner of good standing would regard as proper to be

---

Hesse, and other German states (1818), Prussia (1835), Roumania (1874), Hungary (1876), and Servia (1881). It is compulsory by cantonal law in ten out of the twenty-two Swiss cantons; an attempt to pass a federal compulsory law was defeated by a plebiscite in 1881. In the following countries there is no compulsory law, but Government facilities and compulsion on various classes more or less directly under Government control, such as soldiers, state employés, apprentices, school pupils, etc.: France, Italy, Spain, Portugal, Belgium, Norway, Austria, Turkey.... Vaccination has been compulsory in South Australia since 1872, in Victoria since 1874, and in Western Australia since 1878. In Tasmania a compulsory Act was passed in 1882. In New South Wales there is no compulsion, but free facilities for vaccination. Compulsion was adopted at Calcutta in 1880, and since then at eighty other towns of Bengal, at Madras in 1884, and at Bombay and elsewhere in the presidency a few years earlier. Revaccination was made compulsory in Denmark in 1871, and in Roumania in 1874; in Holland it was enacted for all school pupils in 1872. The various laws and administrative orders which had been for many years in force as to vaccination and revaccination in the several German states were consolidated in an imperial statute of 1874." 24 Encyclopaedia Britannica (1894), Vaccination.

used. The matured opinions of medical men everywhere, and the experience of mankind, as all must know, negative the suggestion that it is not possible in any case to determine whether vaccination is safe. Was defendant exempted from the operation of the statute simply because of his dread of the same evil results experienced by him when a child and had observed in the cases of his son and other children? Could he reasonably claim such an exemption because "quite often" or "occasionally" injury had resulted from vaccination, or because it was impossible, in the opinion of some, by any practical test, to determine with absolute certainty whether a particular person could be safely vaccinated?

It seems to the court that an affirmative answer to these questions would practically strip the legislative department of its function to care for the public health and the public safety when endangered by epidemics of disease. Such an answer would mean that compulsory vaccination could not, in any conceivable case, be legally enforced in a community, even at the command of the legislature, however widespread the epidemic of smallpox, and however deep and universal was the belief of the community and of its medical advisers, that a system of general vaccination was vital to the safety of all.

We are not prepared to hold that a minority, residing or remaining in any city or town where smallpox is prevalent, and enjoying the general protection afforded by an organized local government, may thus defy the will of its constituted authorities, acting in good faith for all, under the legislative sanction of the State. . . .

We now decide only that the statute covers the present case, and that nothing clearly appears that would justify this court in holding it to be unconstitutional and inoperative in its application to the plaintiff in error.

The judgment of the court below must be affirmed.

It is so ordered.

MR. JUSTICE BREWER and MR. JUSTICE PECKHAM dissent.

Dowell v. City of Tulsa
273 P.2d 859 (Okla. 1954), *cert. denied*, 348 U.S. 912 (1955)

BLACKBIRD, J. Plaintiffs in error commenced the present action, as plaintiffs, to enjoin defendants in error, as defendants, from enforcing and/or complying with Ordinance No. 6565, passed by the Board of Commissioners of the City of Tulsa, on March 3, 1953, authorizing fluoridation of said city's water supply by its Water Department and Commissioner of Waterworks and Sewerage. The purpose of such fluoridation, as indicated in the ordinance, was "to aid in the control of dental caries" (tooth decay), and by reason of the

I. Public Health Regulatory Policy

emergency therein declared to exist for "preservation of the public peace, health and safety," it was provided by Section 4 thereof that the ordinance would become effective upon its passage, approval and publication.

The parties appear here in the same order as they appeared in the trial court, and they will be referred to by their trial designations.

Plaintiffs are individual taxpayers of the city. Their effort to enjoin the enforcement of the Ordinance was based upon the alleged ground that it is invalid. The only alleged reasons for such invalidity which they apparently urged are that (1) the ordinance constitutes an "unwarranted exercise of police power" in violation of the Fourteenth Amendment of the U.S. Constitution; (2) that it is an exercise of power beyond that delegated to the city by the State Legislature; (3) it violates the U.S. Constitution's First Amendment concerning freedom of religion; and (4) it violates Title 63 O.S. 1951 §196 forbidding the manufacture and sale of "food" to which "fluorine compounds" have been added as the term "food" is defined in Section 183 to include "articles of food, meat, drink . . . beverage. . . ."

After a trial at which plaintiffs introduced no evidence, but entered into a stipulation with defendants as to certain facts, the court made specific findings against plaintiffs on all the issues above described and entered judgment denying them the injunction. From said judgment they have lodged this appeal.

With apparent reference to (1) and (3) above, plaintiffs contend under the first two propositions formulated in their briefs that our State Legislature has never established a policy of attempting to regulate or control any disease except those that are "contagious, infectious or dangerous"; and that it could not constitutionally do so. In denying the first part of this contention, defendants point to various statutes enacted by the Oklahoma Legislature, particularly sections appearing under Title 63 O.S. 1951, which they say plainly show that its policy in matters of public health and welfare has never been confined to seeking control, regulation and prevention of contagious, infectious, or dangerous diseases. Among these are provisions for safeguards pertaining to bedding and the germicidal treatment of secondhand materials, Section 51 et seq.; provisions requiring the injection of "nitrate of silver or other proven antiseptic" into the eyes of newborn infants, for their protection against "Inflammation of the eyes . . ." (ophthalma neonatorum), Sections 71-77, incl.; those pertaining to the regulation of milk production and marketing, Section 295 et seq.; and of hotels, etc., Section 331 et seq.; to the regulation of bakeries and other foodstuff factories, Section 151; to the regulation of bottling works, Section 27 et seq.; to the Section 296.2, specifying the vitamin and mineral requirement for flour; and to the statutes creating the State Board of Health, Tit. 63 O.S. 1951 §1.1, and creating in the State Health Department a division to be known as the " 'Division of Preventive Dentistry,' " Tit. 63 O.S. 1951 §41. In fact, it was apparently in conformity with the provisions of the latter section that said State Department made its study of the fluoridation of public water supplies for controlling dental caries and promulgated certain rules and recommendations, or a policy to govern it in assisting municipalities considering such projects. A written statement of these was introduced in evidence as Defendants' Exhibit 3, and the parties' stipulation of facts as well as Ordinance No. 6565 shows that these recommendations were considered and were to be followed in the fluoridation of the water supply contemplated in the ordinance in accord with certain rules, standards and prerequisites (unnecessary here to set forth) prescribed by the State Board.

In view of the broad terms in which our Legislature has spoken on the subject, we cannot believe that it has intended to restrict its enactment of measures designed to promote the public health and welfare to those designed to prevent the spread of infectious, contagious or dangerous diseases. We think the mere reading of the statutes herein cited and others enacted by our Legislature is sufficient to show that it has not so restricted its policy, and that it has chosen to make many minimum requirements with reference to food, lodging and a myriad of subjects connected with the public health and/or welfare that have no direct connection with or relation to infectious, contagious or dangerous diseases.

The next question then is: Recognizing that such a thing is not against public policy as declared by our Legislature, can the police power delegated to a city by the Legislature be exercised to the extent of what in practical analysis amounts to a compulsory measure requiring people of the city to use or pay for water that is fluoridated in order to control a physical characteristic or weakness which is not an infectious, contagious or dangerous disease? Plaintiffs say that it cannot — that under the guarantees of freedom contained in the 1st and 14th Amendments to the U.S. Constitution the citizens of Tulsa have a right to be furnished city water not "medicated" or treated with fluorides. We do not agree.

The tests by which such matters are to be governed in two of the cases quoting or expressing them in verbage most favorable to plaintiffs are Lawton v. Steele, 152 U.S. 133, 14 S. Ct. 499, 501, 38 L. Ed. 385, and Bowes v. City of Aberdeen, 58 Wash. 535, 542, 109 P.369, 372, 30 L.R.A., N.S., 709. In the first of these it is said:

> To justify the state in thus interposing its authority in behalf of the public, it must appear — First, that the interests of the public generally, as distinguished from those of a particular class, require such interference; and, second, that the means are reasonably necessary for

I. Public Health Regulatory Policy

the accomplishment of the purpose, and not unduly oppressive upon individuals.

In the Washington case, it was said:

" 'The questions which present themselves in the examination of a safety or health measure are: Does a danger exist? Is it of sufficient magnitude? Does it concern the public? Does the proposed measure tend to remove it? Is the restraint or requirement in proportion to the danger? Is it possible to secure the object sought without impairing essential rights and principles? Does the choice of a particular measure show that some other interest than safety or health was the actual motive of the Legislature?' " In suggesting negative answers to the above-quoted questions when propounded about Ordinance 6565, it seems to be plaintiffs' position that (1) since it is not contended that Tulsa's water is not pure, or that unless treated with fluorides it will tend to spread contagious disease or that an epidemic of an infectious or dangerous disease is threatened or imminent unless said water is so treated, the exercise of the police power to the extent of interfering with Tulsa citizens' freedom to purchase and use its water without such treatment cannot be justified; that (2) since the only direct evidence on the matter went no further than showing that drinking fluoridated water reduces caries in the lower-age group of minor persons, such treatment could not be justified as a measure to improve the health or welfare of the public generally; (3) that the evidence tended to show that the same object could be attained by leaving to individuals the treatment of their own drinking water with fluorides on an individual and voluntary basis, as could be attained by requiring the wholesale treatment of the City's entire water supply and therefore that the latter is not "reasonably necessary" to attain that end, thus belying the Ordinance's announced representation or misrepresentation that it is necessary to preservation of the public health and safety. We do not find any of these arguments tenable for the reasons hereinafter set forth. While most of the reported cases that have arisen in the past involved the so-called "purity" or "purification" of municipal water supplies and the regulations upheld with reference thereto were designed to prevent contamination or pollution with consequent epidemics or spread of disease, notice Annotations, 6 A.L.R. 228, and 8 A.L.R. 673; 23 A.L.R. 228; 72 A.L.R. 673, we think the weight of well-reasoned modern precedent sustains the right of municipalities to adopt such reasonable and undiscriminating measures to improve their water supplies as are necessary to protect and improve the public health, even though no epidemic is imminent and no contagious disease or virus is directly involved. See Blue v. Beach, 155 Ind. 121, 56 N.E. 89, 50 L.R.A. 64; and the Annotations thereto, at 80 Am. St. Rep. 212; 25 Am. Jur., "Health," Secs. 21 and 25, inclusive; 56 Am. Jur., "Water Works," Sec. 76. Where such necessity is established, the Courts, especially in recent years, have adopted a liberal view of the health measures promulgated and sought to be enforced. See McQuillin, Municipal Corporations (3d Ed.), Vol. 7, Sec. 24-224. As said in 11 Am. Jur., "Constitutional Law," Sec. 271, at page 1023:

> The protection of the public health and safety is the basis of much valid regulation over persons. This broad field includes not only legislation relating to the prevention and curtailment of disease through quarantine, when not in conflict with Federal regulations on the subject, vaccination, and segregation in special hospitals of persons suffering from contagious and infectious illnesses, but also measures relating to eugenics and the maintenance of a healthy, normal, and socially sound populace.

As knowledge in both the medical and dental fields has increased, the subject of health in both of these spheres has become more important, and modern experience shows that private convenience and individual freedom of action are required to yield to the public good in instances where formerly there was observed no necessity for legislative interference. . . . [Citations omitted.] Plaintiffs concede, as they must, that municipalities may chlorinate their water supply, Commonwealth v. Town of Hudson, 315 Mass. 335, 52 N.E.2d 566; McQuillin Municipal Corporations (3d Ed.), Vol. 7, Sec. 24.265 and though they contend, under one proposition, that a city's treatment of its water supply with fluorides is the unlicensed practice of medicine, dentistry and pharmacy under our Statutes, they here argue that such treatment must be distinguished from treatment with chlorides, because the latter will kill germs, purify water and accordingly aid in the prevention and spread of disease, whereas fluorides will not. We think that if the putting of chlorides in public water supplies will in fact promote the public health, the distinction sought to be drawn by plaintiffs is immaterial. To us it seems ridiculous and of no consequence in considering the public health phase of the case that the substance to be added to the water may be classed as a mineral rather than a drug, antiseptic or germ killer; just as it is of little, if any, consequence whether fluoridation accomplishes its beneficial result to the public health by killing germs in the water, or by hardening the teeth or building up immunity in them to the bacteria that causes caries or tooth decay. If the latter, there can be no distinction on principle between it and compulsory vaccination or inoculation, which, for many years, has been well-established as a valid exercise of police power. See Blue v. Beach and other authorities cited, supra, as well as the Annotations at 93 A.L.R. 1434. See also De Aryan v. Butler, 119 Cal. App. 2d 674, 260 P.2d 98 in which some of the same

I. Public Health Regulatory Policy

arguments made here were made and rejected concerning the fluoridation of the water supply of the City of San Diego, California. While the evidence in the present case did not purport to establish fluoridation as a remedy or prevention for any specific contagious disease, it did show, without contradiction, that it will materially reduce the incidence of caries in youth. The relation of dental hygiene to the health of the body generally is now so well recognized as to warrant judicial notice. Accordingly, we hold that in establishing the fluoridation prescribed by Ordinance 6565, as effective to reduce dental caries, the evidence also sufficiently established it as a health measure to be a proper subject for exercise of the police power possessed by the City of Tulsa.

We now come to plaintiffs' argument that fluoridation of Tulsa's water supply cannot be justified as a *public* health measure because the evidence went no further than establishing it as an aid to the prevention of caries in persons under sixteen years of age, and tended to show that consumption of such water is of no benefit to older persons. The evidence did not reveal what proportion of Tulsa's population is under sixteen years of age, but under our view this was not necessary. When it is borne in mind that the children and youth of today are the adult citizens of tomorrow, and that this one segment of the population unquestionably benefitted by the drinking of fluoridated water now, will in a few years comprise all or a very large percentage of Tulsa's population; and it is further realized that reducing the incidence of dental caries in children will also benefit their parents, the fallacy of plaintiff's argument is manifest. . . .

Since the filing of the original briefs in the present case, an Ohio Court has reached similar conclusions on the same questions involved herein and similar ones in the Case of Kraus v. City of Cleveland, Ohio Com. Pl., 116 N.E.2d 779.

As no ground for reversal has been found in any of the arguments advanced by plaintiffs, the judgment of the trial court is hereby affirmed.

Addington v. Texas
441 U.S. 418 (1979)

[The appellant had a long history of temporary commitments as mentally ill (seven occasions between 1969 and 1975) to various Texas mental hospitals. In December 1975, appellant was arrested on charges of assault and threats against his mother. His mother filed a petition for indefinite commitment. A trial was held before a jury to determine whether the appellant was mentally ill and in need of treatment for his welfare and protection, or for the protection of others. The trial lasted six days. The appellant was found mentally ill and subject to commitment under the law based upon "clear, unequivocal and convincing evidence." The Supreme Court of Texas upheld the commitment and the applicable standard of proof.]

BURGER, C.J. The question in this case is what standard of proof is required by the Fourteenth Amendment to the Constitution in a civil proceeding brought under state law to commit an individual involuntarily for an indefinite period to a state mental hospital.

A

This Court repeatedly has recognized that civil commitment for any purpose constitutes a significant deprivation of liberty that requires due process protection. See, e.g., Jackson v. Indiana, 406 U.S. 715 (1972); Humphrey v. Cady, 405 U.S. 504 (1972); In re Gault, 387 U.S. 1 (1967); Specht v. Patterson, 386 U.S. 605 (1967). Moreover, it is indisputable that involuntary commitment to a mental hospital after a finding of probable dangerousness to self or others can engender adverse social consequences to the individual. Whether we label this phenomena "stigma" or choose to call it something else is less important than that we recognize that it can occur and that it can have a very significant impact on the individual.

The state has a legitimate interest under its *parens patriae* powers in providing care to its citizens who are unable because of emotional disorders to care for themselves; the state also has authority under its police power to protect the community from the dangerous tendencies of some who are mentally ill. Under the Texas Mental Health Code, however, the State has no interest in confining individuals involuntarily if they are not mentally ill or if they do not pose some danger to themselves or others. Since the preponderance standard creates the risk of increasing the number of individuals erroneously committed, it is at least unclear to what extent, if any, the state's interests are furthered by using a preponderance standard in such commitment proceedings.

The expanding concern of society with problems of mental disorders is reflected in the fact that in recent years many states have enacted statutes designed to protect the rights of the mentally ill. However, only one state by statute permits involuntary commitment by a mere preponderance of the evidence, Miss. Code Ann. §41-21-75 (1978 Supp.), and Texas is the only state where a court has concluded that the preponderance-of-the-evidence standard satisfies due process. We attribute this not to any lack of concern in those states, but rather to a belief that the varying standards tend to produce comparable results. As we noted earlier, however, standards of proof

I. Public Health Regulatory Policy

are important for their symbolic meaning as well as for their practical effect. . . .

B

Appellant urges the Court to hold that due process requires use of the criminal law's standard of proof — "beyond a reasonable doubt." . . .

There are significant reasons why different standards of proof are called for in civil commitment proceedings as opposed to criminal prosecutions. In a civil commitment state power is not exercised in a punitive sense. . . .

In addition, the "beyond a reasonable doubt" standard historically has been reserved for criminal cases. This unique standard of proof, not prescribed or defined in the Constitution, is regarded as a critical part of the "moral force of the criminal law," In re Winship, 397 U.S., at 364, and we should hesitate to apply it too broadly or casually in noncriminal cases. . . .

The heavy standard applied in criminal cases manifests our concern that the risk of error to the individual must be minimized even at the risk that some who are guilty might go free. Patterson v. New York, 432 U.S. 197, 208 (1977). The full force of that idea does not apply to a civil commitment. It may be true that an erroneous commitment is sometimes as undesirable as an erroneous conviction, 5 J. Wigmore, Evidence §1400 (Chadbourn rev. 1974). However, even though an erroneous confinement should be avoided in the first instance, the layers of professional review and observation of the patient's condition, and the concern of family and friends generally will provide continuous opportunities for an erroneous commitment to be corrected. Moreover, it is not true that the release of a genuinely mentally ill person is no worse for the individual than the failure to convict the guilty. One who is suffering from a debilitating mental illness and in need of treatment is neither wholly at liberty nor free of stigma. See Chodoff, The Case for Involuntary Hospitalization of the Mentally Ill, 133 Am. J. Psychiatry 496, 498 (1976); Schwartz, Myers, & Astrachan, Psychiatric Labeling and the Rehabilitation of the Mental Patient, 31 Arch. Gen. Psychiatry 329, 334 (1974). It cannot be said, therefore, that it is much better for a mentally ill person to "go free" than for a mentally normal person to be committed.

The subtleties and nuances of psychiatric diagnosis render certainties virtually beyond reach in most situations. The reasonable-doubt standard of criminal law functions in its realm because there the standard is addressed to specific, knowable facts. Psychiatric diagnosis, in contrast, is to a large extent based on medical "impressions" drawn from subjective analysis and filtered through the experience of the diagnostician. This process often makes it very difficult for the expert physician to offer definite conclusions about any particular patient. Within the medical discipline, the traditional standard for "factfinding" is a "reasonable medical certainty." If a trained psychiatrist has difficulty with the categorical "beyond a reasonable doubt" standard, the untrained lay juror — or indeed even a trained judge — who is required to rely upon expert opinion could be forced by the criminal law standard of proof to reject commitment for many patients desperately in need of institutionalized psychiatric care. See ibid. Such "freedom" for a mentally ill person would be purchased at a high price. . . .

C . . .

We have concluded that the reasonable-doubt standard is inappropriate in civil commitment proceedings because, given the uncertainties of psychiatric diagnosis, it may impose a burden the state cannot meet and thereby erect an unreasonable barrier to needed medical treatment. Similarly, we conclude that use of the term "unequivocal" is not constitutionally required, although the states are free to use that standard. To meet due process demands, the standard has to inform the factfinder that the proof must be greater than the preponderance-of-the-evidence standard applicable to other categories of civil cases.

We noted earlier that the trial court employed the standard of "clear, unequivocal and convincing" evidence in appellant's commitment hearing before a jury. That instruction was constitutionally adequate. However, determination of the precise burden equal to or greater than the "clear and convincing" standard which we hold is required to meet due process guarantees is a matter of state law which we leave to the Texas Supreme Court. Accordingly, we remand the case for further proceedings not inconsistent with this opinion.

Vacated and remanded.

NOTES

Public Health Regulatory Programs: Disease Prevention and Compulsory Treatment

1. The three decisions reprinted in this section illustrate quite well the broad sweep of compulsory powers in health authorities to take action to prevent disease and to provide health-care treatment. In all of these areas, there have been vigorous efforts to stop en-

forcement of these compulsory measures. As the *Jacobson* case indicates, opposition to compulsory measures in the health field go back at least 200 years in the history of the United States. For a historical review of public health regulatory policy, especially in regard to smallpox vaccination and public campaigns of opposition, see MacLeod, Law, Medicine and Public Opinion: The Resistance to Compulsory Health Legislation, 1870-1907, 1967 Pub. Law 107, 189. See also Miller, The Adoption of Inoculation for Smallpox in England and France (1957). For a review of legal support for compulsory measures, see Hershey, Compulsory Personal Health Measure Legislation, 84 Pub. Health Reps. 341 (1969). See also G. Rosen, History of Public Health (1958); Brockington, Public Health in the Nineteenth Century (1965). More recently, see Burris, Rationality Review and the Politics of Public Health.

2. Compulsory vaccination against smallpox was the beginning of the successful campaigns against infectious diseases afflicting adults and children. Later programs were targeted at early vaccination of children prior to attending public school. Vaccinations were made a prerequisite to school attendance. In another classic decision, the U.S. Supreme Court held that religious objection by parents to vaccination under the First Amendment's protection of religious freedom would not justify avoiding vaccination of children. See Prince v. Commonwealth, 321 U.S. 158 at 166-167 (1943), where the Court ruled, "The right to practice religion freely does not include liberty to expose the community or the child to communicable diseases or the latter to ill health or death." On religious objection to health measures generally, see Note, Compulsory Medical Treatment and the Free Exercise of Religion, 42 Ind. L. Rev. (1967).

3. Various religious sects and conservative political groups still object to preventive measures like vaccination or to medical treatment for themselves or their children. See Cude v. State, 377 S.W.2d 816 (Ark. 1964), where a parent had kept his eight children out of school for varying periods of years because of his refusal to have them vaccinated. Some of the children were in their teens and had not attended schools at all. One of the children was twelve at the time of the case and had attended school only to second grade. The Supreme Court of Arkansas in a split decision upheld the constitutionality of an order turning the children over to the Child Welfare Division of the State Welfare Department in order to have them vaccinated so they could attend school. The order provided that the children would be returned to the parents immediately after the vaccination if the parents would accept them. Otherwise, the order provided that the children would be put up for adoption. The Court refused to accept a fine as an adequate remedy since the parents had been fined on three previous occasions and had not complied with

the law. The court said that the desired result was to benefit the children and to get them into school. The dissenting opinion took strong exception to the holding. Associate Justice Jim Johnson said, "In the absence of legislation to the contrary, I, as a judge, am not willing now or ever to say as a matter of law that the failure to comply with a simple regulation of school administrative authorities constitutes such neglect of children so as to warrant the state administering the cruel and unusual punishment of depriving such children of their natural parents and depriving the natural parents of their children. . . . History reveals that once a door is open to an administrative agency that door is not easily closed. Whose children under what pretext will be taken next? Will they be kept forever?" 237 Ark. at 937-938, 377 S.W.2d at 821-822. Justice Johnson did not have long to wait. Two years later the same court was asked to rule on whether the Cude case applied to a child of parents of a fundamentalist religious sect opposed to fluoridation but who attended an unapproved parochial school run by the same sect. The court held that it did. Justice Johnson again dissented, citing with frustrated pride his dissent in Cude. Mannus v. State, S.W.2d 206 (Ark. 1966).

4. Has the acceptance of vaccination by nearly all of the population and the virtual elimination of many infectious diseases made it unnecessary to make these vaccinations compulsory? Should "an occasional rebel" be allowed to refuse vaccination? In 1959, North Carolina became the first state to require children to be vaccinated against poliomyelitis. The statute added an exception for children of parents who object on religious grounds to the vaccination, but the parents must be members of a recognized religious group whose teachings are contrary to medical vaccination or treatment. Many other states have added such religious exceptions to their laws on compulsory health measures. See Beauchamp, Public Health and Individual Liberty, 1 Ann. Rev. of Public Health 121 (1980). See also T. Christoffel, Health and the Law Ch. 5 (1982).

5. The compulsory fluoridation of water supplies has been opposed by numerous religious groups and conservative political organizations. Only one court has upheld a constitutional attack on the validity of the fluoridation laws. McGurren v. Fargo, 66 N.W.2d 207 (N.D. 1954). See Strong, Liberty, Religion and Fluoridation, 8 Santa Clara L. Rev. 37 (1967). Opposition groups have been successful in local referenda campaigns to have fluoridation removed from local water supplies. See Mueller, Fluoridation Attitude Change, 58 Am. J. Pub. Health 1876 (1968). Why has there been so much less public objection to compulsory food supplements (iodized salt, vitamins in cereals, etc.) and to the food additive laws? See Turner, The Chemical Feast (1970). See generally, Hayes, Food and Drug Regulation after 75 Years, 246 J. Amer. Med. Assoc. 1223 (1981). Several conservative political

groups have also fought against most of the federal environmental health legislation enacted in the past 20 years, including the Clean Water Act. Are objections to these regulatory programs different from the objections to compulsory vaccination or treatment?

6. The *Addington* case in the Supreme Court represented a high-water mark in efforts to raise the standard of proof for compulsory hospitalization of the mentally ill. In large measure, the laws on commitment of the mentally ill came full circle in some 200 years in the United States. The nineteenth century laws were essentially modeled after criminal procedures. The person who was believed to be mentally ill was "arrested" and "charged" with being "insane" and at large and was "committed" to a mental institution, usually for life. On any escape, the patient was hunted down like a criminal and returned to the institution in chains. In the middle years of the twentieth century, the laws concerning mental illness were largely decriminalized, and compulsory hospitalization was made considerably easier as an administrative action without judicial intervention. This was the case all over the world. The primary model for the less formal, nonjudicial hospitalization legislation was the British Mental Health Act of 1959. The movement away from the informal system back to a much more structured, judicially sanctioned review procedure for compulsory hospitalization began in the 1970s and continued into the 1980s. Changes to a more formal system have even been enacted in Great Britain. See the Mental Health Amendments Act of 1982. For a review of the British legislation, see L. Gostin, Mental Health Services — Law and Practice (1986) (annual supplements). For an international survey of legislation concerning hospitalization of the mentally ill, see W. Curran & T. Harding, The Law and Mental Health: Harmonizing Objectives, World Health Organization, Geneva (1978).

For a recent state supreme court ruling applying the "clear and convincing" evidence requirement to both the diagnosis of mental illness and the requirement of dangerousness, see In re Kottle, 433 N.W.2d 881 (Minn. 1988). A similar ruling was made in the Colorado Supreme Court. See Colorado v. Stevens, 761 P.2d 768 (Colo. 1988). See generally Mills, Civil Commitment of the Mentally Ill: An Overview, 484 Annals of Am. Ac. Pol. and Social Science 28 (1986); Wexler, The Structure of Civil Commitment: Patterns, Pressures, and Interactions in Mental Health Legislation, 7 Law and Human Beh. 1 (1983).

Are the legal requirements for compulsory treatment of alcoholics or persons dependent on drugs different from those for persons who are mentally ill? Are the requirements of dangerousness potential the same for any required residential commitment? See discussion of these issues at 1174-1175 later in this chapter.

7. When compulsory treatment measures are applied as in compulsory vaccination, the person who is vaccinated may suffer an adverse reaction of very serious proportions. Informed consent issues and assumption of risk are not primary considerations, since the exposure is mandatory. Many lawsuits have been brought against manufacturers and against health care providers alleging negligence or seeking recovery on a warranty basis under product liability laws. In many of these cases, substantial damages have been awarded. See Reyes v. Wyeth Lab., 498 F.2d 1264 (5th Cir. 1973); Stahlheber v. American Cyanamid Co., 451 S.W.2d 48 (Mo. 1972). See also Cunningham v. Pfizer, 532 P.2d 1377 (Okla. 1974).

Most of the pharmaceutical companies producing vaccines have withdrawn from the field because of lawsuit vulnerability and the inability to obtain insurance coverage at an affordable and reasonable premium. After many years of effort in the U.S. Congress, legislation was enacted in 1986 to protect (at least to some degree) the few remaining manufacturers of vaccines and to provide a no-fault compensation system for children who receive an adverse reaction from a vaccine that is mandated by law in the state where the child resides. North Carolina has also adopted a no-fault compensation system for adverse reactions to mandated childhood vaccinations. The federal and state legislation is described in Chapter 5 at page 426. See also Mariner and Clark, Confronting the Immunization Problem: Proposals for Reform, 76 Am. J. Pub. Health 703 (1986); Franklin & Mais, Tort Law and Mass Immunization Programs: Lessons from the Polio and Flu Episodes, 65 Cal. L. Rev. 754 (1977).

The effort to provide a massive, nationwide immunization program for an influenza epidemic that never struck the United States also produced its own problems of serious adverse reactions in Guillain-Barre Syndrome. See In re Swine Flu Immunization Products Liability Litigation, reprinted in Chapter 4 at page 245. See also a historical review and analysis of the decision to adopt a national immunization program to combat the potential epidemic of swine flu. R. Neustadt & H. Fineberg, The Swine Flu Affair: Decision-Making on a Slippery Disease (1978).

II. DISEASE AND ACCIDENT PREVENTION: ISSUES OF QUARANTINE, PROHIBITION, SURVEILLANCE AND TREATMENT

Ex Parte Company and Irwin
106 Ohio St. 50 (1922)

[The petitioners brought writs of habeas corpus for release from custody at the Women's Detention Home in the City of Akron. Both women were arrested without warrant and charged with unlawful solicitation for purposes of prostitution. After dismissal of the criminal charges, however, the women were held in the detention home on the order of the Commissioner of Health of Akron and placed in quarantine under the State Sanitary Code, having been found infected with gonorrhea. They were to be held for a sufficient period of time as to render them non-infectious from the disease, estimated to be about two months in duration.]

CLARK, J. . . . Quarantine in the sense herein used means detention to the point of preserving the infected person from contact with others. The power to so quarantine in [a] proper case and reasonable way is not open to question. It is exercised by the state and the subdivisions of the state daily. The protection of the health and lives of the public is paramount, and those who by conduct and association contract such disease as makes them a menace to the health and morals of the community must submit to such regulation as will protect the public.

"It appears that petitioner was originally taken into custody without a warrant, and, basing his argument upon such arbitrary action, counsel draws a lurid picture of what might result from maladministration of the law by those charged with the duty of enforcing it. The fact that the authority so delegated may, in a given case, be abused, is no legal reason for denying the power to quarantine summarily in a case where grounds therefor concededly exist. . . . Assuming the action of the police officer arbitrary and unjustified, she is not restrained of her liberty by reason thereof, but on account of a disease with which she was subsequently found to be afflicted, and in the ascertainment of which fact there appears to have been no arbitrary or unlawful action taken." . . .

It is our conclusion that the provisions of sections 1232, 1234, 1235 and 1236, General Code, creating a state department of health, a public health council, and authorizing such public health council "to make and amend sanitary regulations to be of general application throughout the state," and to provide for the certification, publication and enforcement of such regulations, are lawful and valid exercise of legislative power.

Writs refused; petitioners are remanded to the respondent, the commissioner of health of the city of Akron, Ohio, and the petitions are dismissed.

Judgment for respondent.

Reynolds v. McNichols
488 F.2d 1378 (10th Cir. 1973)

[The plaintiff was a prostitute with several previous arrests. She had been ordered to report to the Department of Health and Hospitals of the City of Denver and had been found to have gonorrhea on at least one occasion. She was arrested again in June, 1972, in a hotel room with a man not her husband and was charged with solicitation and prostitution. Thereafter, she was detained in jail, but was given a choice under Ordinance 735 of the City of Denver of being detained in jail for a further 48 hours during which period she would be tested for venereal disease and treated therefor, if necessary, or of simply being treated immediately with penicillin without a blood test and then would be released from jail.]

MCWILLIAMS, CIRCUIT JUDGE.

The legislative intent behind enactment of Ordinance 735 was to attempt to bring under control, and lessen, the incidence of venereal disease in Denver by determining and treating the source of such infection. The evidence before the trial court showed, incidentally, that the incidence of venereal disease had reached virtually epidemic proportions. . . .

Plaintiff's constitutional argument is summarized as follows: (1) The ordinance authorizes involuntary detention, without bond, involuntary examination and involuntary treatment, all in violation of her Fourth Amendment right to be secure in her person; (2) the ordinance does not spell out adequate guidelines as to the class of persons who can be compelled to submit to examination and treatment; (3) the current practice whereby a person, though initially detained in jail, is nonetheless eligible for immediate release if he or she submits to the injection of penicillin, even though there be no examination to indicate the presence of gonorrhea, results in an unconstitutional coercion of the person thus detained whereby one submits to an invasion of her right to be secure in her person in exchange for immediate release; (4) the injection of penicillin without first determining the presence of gonorrhea is contrary to accepted medical practice; and (5) the ordinance is applied only to females and not to males. In our view, none of these arguments stands up under scrutiny.

The principal thrust of the ordinance is aimed at bringing under control the *source* of communicable venereal disease. To that end, the city authorities are empowered to examine and treat those reasonably suspected of having an infectious venereal disease. It is not illogical or unreasonable, and on the contrary it is reasonable, to suspect that known prostitutes are a prime source of infectious venereal disease. Prostitution and venereal disease are no strangers.

In the instant case, the plaintiff freely admits, and the record amply supports her admission, that for some two and one-half years she was a prostitute operating in the Denver area and the fact that she was a prostitute was known to the local police. And in our view the fact that the plaintiff was a prostitute is of crucial significance.

II. Disease and Accident Prevention 1149

Finally, on at least one occasion, plaintiff was found to be infected with gonorrhea. Let us now examine the authorities.

Involuntary detention, for a limited period of time, of a person reasonably suspected of having a venereal disease for the purpose of permitting an examination of the person thus detained to determine the presence of a venereal disease and providing further for the treatment of such disease, if present, has been upheld by numerous state courts when challenged on a wide variety of constitutional grounds as a valid exercise of the police power designed to protect the public health [Citations omitted.] . . .

The aforesaid proposition would also appear to be in accord with the rationale of such cases as Jacobson v. Massachusetts, 197 U.S. 11, 25 S. Ct. 358, 49 L. Ed. 643 (1905), and Compagnie Francaise v. State Board of Health, 186 U.S. 380, 22 S. Ct. 811, 46 L. Ed. 1209 (1902), the former being concerned with compulsory smallpox vaccinations and the latter with a statute quarantining persons suspected of having infectious disease and precluding others from entry into the quarantined area. These two cases were concerned with, among other things, the interaction between the police power and the Fourteenth Amendment. Nor in our view is the proposition set forth above foreclosed by Camara v. Municipal Court of City and County of San Francisco, 387 U.S. 523, 87 S. Ct. 1727, 18 L. Ed. 2d 930 (1967). It is true that in *Camara* the Supreme Court struck down on Fourth Amendment grounds a municipal ordinance of San Francisco which authorized under certain conditions a warrantless inspection of an apartment building under the city's housing code. At the same time, however, the Court stated that nothing in the opinion was intended to foreclose "prompt inspections, even without a warrant, that the law has traditionally upheld in emergency situations," and cited with approval both Jacobson v. Massachusetts, supra, and Compagnie Francaise v. Board of Health, supra.

Under the authorities above cited, we conclude, as did the trial court, that the provisions of Ordinance No. 735 authorizing limited detention in jail without bond for the purpose of examination and treatment for a venereal disease of one reasonably suspected of having a venereal disease by virtue of the fact that she has been arrested and charged with solicitation and prostitution is a valid exercise of the police power. It would seem to follow that the milder provisions of the ordinance providing for a walk-in order of one reasonably suspected of having a venereal disease for the purpose of involuntary examination and treatment are also valid under the police power, and we so hold.

We now turn to the plaintiff's contention that the ordinance has been unconstitutionally applied to her. As above indicated, the evidence was that as a matter of practice a person detained in jail under the provisions of Ordinance 735 was given a choice between staying in jail while the examination was being conducted, or submitting to an immediate injection of penicillin, without examination, in which latter event the person would be eligible for immediate release. According to the record, there was no particular risk involved in the taking of a penicillin shot, nor was there any injurious effect from the injection of one who did not in fact have gonorrhea. On this state of the record, we find no unconstitutional coercion of the plaintiff. The provisions of the ordinance permitting limited detention for involuntary examination and treatment of a venereal disease being in themselves constitutional, the fact that the city provides a less onerous alternative, which the plaintiff in this case elected to follow, does not violate any constitutional right of the plaintiff.

Similarly, the claim that the ordinance was enforced only against females, and not males, is, under the circumstances of this case, insufficient to invoke the equal protection provision of the Fourteenth Amendment. The trial court indicated that it was of the view that the equal protection argument was not properly within the issues raised by the pleadings in the case and accordingly did not consider it. In any event, in our view plaintiff's suggestion that she was unconstitutionally dealt with by the city authorities is under the circumstances unavailing.

In regard to her equal protection argument, the fact that on the two occasions when plaintiff was arrested in a hotel room the plaintiff's customer was not himself arrested and detained for examination is not significant. From the record before us, there is nothing to indicate that plaintiff did in fact have sex relations with either of her male companions, though evidence of solicitation was obvious. Such being the case, there was no reason to examine plaintiff's male companions.

Be that as it may, as above indicated, the ordinance is aimed at the primary source of venereal disease and the plaintiff, being the prostitute, was the potential source, not her would-be customer. Plaintiff's argument in this regard would perhaps carry more weight if she had shown that male prostitutes were dealt with differently than female prostitutes. There is nothing in the record to show that such is the case. In fact, there is nothing in the record to indicate that male prostitution is as yet the vogue in Denver.

Judgment affirmed.

LEWIS, CHIEF JUDGE (concurring):

I concur but consider it appropriate to emphasize or reemphasize the limited posture of the case within which the issues are both presented to the court and determined by our decision.

This is not a medical practice case. As a consequence we do not consider and certainly do not determine that the giving of a curative drug for a venereal disease not diagnosed as existent is acceptable medical practice. Nor do we, in holding that the subject ordinance is neither unconstitutional on its face nor unconstitutionally applied to appellant, hold that the ordinance is constitutional *in toto*. A statute is not unconstitutional on its face if objectionable features are clearly severable or if its contained language can be reasonably interpreted to project a constitutionally accepted standard.

In the case at bar we are concerned only with the self-imposed plight of a prostitute and the admitted occupational hazard of venereal disease to her and through her to the community. We do not hold that a vagrant is similarly situated nor are we required, at this time, to spell out the limitations, if any, that the word "suspicion" may have as a legal standard. Sufficient cause existed in this case for the authorities to consider appellant to be a probable health hazard to the community.

NOTES

Public Health Regulatory Measures Regarding Sexually Transmitted Diseases: From Quarantine to Treatment

1. In earlier centuries, the victims of disease who were believed to be dangerous to the public through some human contact (which then included most of the known afflictions of humans) were banished from the community and abandoned, beyond the campfire, the village, or the wall of the city. In urbanized areas in the Middle Ages, the practice of "quarantine" began. Voyagers were held on board ship; the local afflicted were confined to their homes. As hospitals and detention houses were developed, they were utilized for disease quarantine when other quarters were not available. With no available treatment, quarantine for a temporary period until the person recovered and was no longer infectious, or until death, was the most humane alternative.

In the nineteenth century and the early twentieth century, quarantine and isolation were the most common means of disease control. "Quarantine" was designed for longer periods of confinement until infectiousness had passed. "Isolation" was a brief, immediate action taken in a hospital or at home to allow care and attention to the sick person until other measures were needed. Over the years, the terms have been used interchangeably in regulatory procedures and in court actions.

2. The application of quarantine has deep roots in international health regulation. In earlier centuries, the only way to help to prevent or control contagious diseases entering national territory was to stop persons and goods at the border. The first work of the American federal health authorities after the American Revolution and inde-

pendence was to set up quarantine stations at ports of entry and to develop hospitals for merchant marine personnel, citizens of the United States, who were nevertheless confined and isolated on entry (or reentry) to the country if they were ill or showed signs of contagious disease. (The obvious nature of a disease that is shown by a rash on the skin was the most easily detected on observation at the ports, as shown in the 1863 decision, Evans v. People, the case which opens Chapter 4 of this text at page 201. In that case, the disease was erysipelas, a condition clearly evident due to a distinctive skin eruption called "St. Anthony's Fire.") The quarantine work of the federal officers led to the establishment of a network of federal "marine hospitals" that still exists today and to the development of the United States Public Health Service. For a historical review of the development of international health regulation, see Hobson, World Health and History (1963). For a comprehensive historical analysis of the sweep of diseases and plagues from ancient times, see a wonderfully enlightening and exciting review by a leading American historian, W. McNeill, Plagues and Peoples (1976). For a legal review of federal activities, see Edelman, International Travel and Our National Quarantine System, 37 Temple L.Q. 28 (1963). For an explanation of international efforts, see Shubber, World Health and WHO, chapter in Legal Issues in Medicine (McLean ed. 1981); Gutteridge, The World Health Organization: Its Scope and Achievements, 37 Temple L.Q. 1 (1963).

3. For venereal diseases (now referred to mainly as sexually transmitted diseases), the use of quarantine was readily adapted from its application to other infectious conditions. Quarantine was used extensively against the syphilis epidemic which hit Europe in the late fifteenth century. The vast and devastating outbreak was blamed on the voyages of Columbus to the New World with the disease coming to Europe in the loins of the European sailors who visited the West Indies islands and had sexual intercourse with the West Indian population.

Most of the venereal diseases did not disappear, as did so many other infectious diseases, after the discovery of bacteria and the development of vaccines. The venereal diseases continue to infect millions of people around the world. For an examination of efforts to control these diseases, see A. Brandt, No Magic Bullet: A Social History of Venereal Disease in the United States Since 1880 (1985).

4. The American courts were quite deferential to the public health regulatory policies of earlier years and found quarantine of known and suspected cases of venereal disease to be a legitimate application of the government's police powers. Little was said about treatment, but when available it was assumed that the treatment would be given during the confinement; voluntarily if possible, forcibly if

necessary. See People ex rel Baker v. Stauty, 54 N.E.2d 441 (Ill. 1944); Ex parte Shepard, 195 P. 1077 (Cal. App. 1921); Jew Ho v. Williamson, 103 F.10 (C.C.N.D. Cal. 1900).

5. Quarantine, isolation, and forcible treatment are still a part of the statutory powers of state and local health departments across the United States in the efforts to prevent, control, and treat sexually transmitted diseases. Vigorous enforcement of control measures followed the development of highly effective treatment during and after World War II. The practice of "contact tracing" was employed by health department epidemiology personnel in order to reach the known sexual partners of persons who were infected. The contact would be made by the trained health department workers and treatment services would be made available at public clinics free of charge. The new contact was not told of the identity of the person who was infected. In most situations, the infected person gave names of persons who were at risk for the disease on a voluntary basis with an assurance of confidentiality. However, health department personnel can (and do) use threats of a court order, isolation, or quarantine to gain cooperation, especially to get infected persons into treatment on an out-patient basis at public clinics. Programs of disease reporting, contact tracing, and diagnostic testing are described later in this chapter. See particularly the article by Judson and Vernon at 1228. See also Washington, Treatment of Sexually Transmitted Diseases: New Additions to an Old Tradition, 4 Rev. Infect. Dis. (Supp. 2) S727 (1982); Henderson, Control of Sexually Transmitted Diseases in the United States — A Federal Perspective, 53 Brit. J. Ven. Dis. 211 (1977). See generally R. Noble, Sexually Transmitted Diseases: Guide to Diagnosis and Therapy (3d ed. 1984); Sexually Transmitted Diseases (K. Holmes, R. Mårdh, P. Sparling & P. Wiesner eds. 1984).

Air Line Pilots Association v. Quesada
276 F.2d 892 (2d Cir. 1960)

LUMBARD, CHIEF JUDGE.

On December 1, 1959 the defendant, Elwood R. Quesada, Administrator of the Federal Aviation Agency, promulgated a regulation which provides:

> No individual who has reached his 60th birthday shall be utilized or serve as a pilot on any aircraft while engaged in air carrier operations.[1]

This regulation took effect on March 15, 1960.

1. 14 C.F.R. §40.260(b). . . .

The plaintiffs, thirty-five individual pilots, their collective bargaining representative, Air Line Pilots Association, and its president, brought the suit in January 1960 for a declaratory judgment that the regulation was null and void and for an injunction against its threatened application. . . .

The Federal Aviation Act was passed by Congress for the purpose of centralizing in a single authority — indeed, in one administrator — the power to frame rules for the safe and efficient use of the nation's airspace. . . .

. . . Pursuant to this statutory authority the Administrator and his medical staff in the fall of 1958 began a study concerning the aging process and the diseases and physiological deterioration that accompany it in an effort to determine whether a maximum age should be set for service by commercial pilots. The Administrator took counsel with various experts in aviation medicine and safety and, among other things, determined the practices followed by five foreign air lines with respect to a mandatory retirement age. Finally, in June 1959 the Administrator published a proposed regulation in substance the same as that ultimately prescribed. In accordance with the rulemaking requirements of §4 of the Administrative Procedure Act, 5 U.S.C.A. §1003, opportunity was afforded for the submission of written data and briefs. About one hundred comments, including those of the plaintiff association, were received. A large majority favored the regulation. No hearing was held since the Administrator determined, as he was entitled to under the rulemaking provisions of the Administrative Procedure Act, that a hearing would not "serve a useful purpose" and that it was not "necessary in the public interest." . . .

. . . The immediate impetus to the legislation was a series of major air crashes culminating in the midair collision of two large airlines over the Grand Canyon in 1956 with the loss of 128 lives. Congress believed there was a need for a more streamlined and efficient means for safety rule-making in place of the system of divided duties and responsibilities existing under the Civil Aeronautics Act, 49 U.S.C.A. §401 et seq. . . .

Plaintiffs assert that the age sixty limitation is arbitrary and discriminatory and without relation to any requirements of safety. For purposes of judicial review, such an argument must mean that the Administrator had no reasonable basis for his exercise of judgment. . . . [Citations omitted.] Surely this is not the fact in the case before us as there is considerable support for the Administrator's action. The Administrator found that the number of commercial pilots over sixty years of age has until recent years been very few but is increasing rapidly; that older pilots because of their seniority under collective bargaining agreements often fly the newest, largest, and fastest planes;

II. Disease and Accident Prevention

that available medical studies show that sudden incapacitation due to heart attacks or strokes become more frequent as men approach age sixty and present medical knowledge is such that it is impossible to predict with accuracy those individuals most likely to suffer attacks; that a number of foreign air carriers contacted had mandatory retirement ages of sixty or less; and that numerous aviation safety experts advocated establishing a maximum age of sixty or younger. In spite of these considerations, plaintiffs ask us to weigh other arguments against the establishment of a maximum age and to hold that the Administrator's action was unreasonable. It is not the business of courts to substitute their untutored judgment for the expert knowledge of those who are given authority to implement the general directives of Congress. The Administrator is an expert in his field; this is the very reason he was given the responsibility for the issuance of air safety regulations. We can only ask whether the regulation is reasonable in relation to the standards prescribed in the statute and the facts before the Administrator. Of that there can be no doubt in this case.

Nor is the regulation discriminatory because it applies only to the piloting of commercial aircraft, and does not restrict pilots with respect to other planes. The Administrator did not act unreasonably in placing greater limitations on the certificates of pilots flying planes carrying large numbers of passengers who have no opportunity to select a pilot of their own choice. The Federal Aviation Act contemplates just such distinctions between the regulations governing "air commerce" and those governing other air transportation. See §601(b), 49 U.S.C.A. §1421(b).

The preliminary injunction was properly denied. The order is affirmed.

NOTES

Prohibitions and Affirmative Safety Actions as Regulatory Policy for Accident Prevention

1. The *Air Line Pilots* case is an example of the early efforts of the then newly established Federal Aviation Agency (and the Federal Air Surgeon, its chief medical officer, who was transferred to the new agency from the U.S. Public Health Service) to provide greater safety in commercial air travel. The Court exhibited considerable deference to the expertise of the Administrator, newly in office, but known for his long experience as chief operational executive of Pan American Airways. The Court also observed, however, the fact that the Administrator had consulted experts in aviation medicine and safety and followed rule-making procedures.

Was the complete prohibition of flying by pilots after reaching 60 years of age the only rational approach available? Would a program of surveillance and regular physical examination be adequate to assure safe operation? Should the Administrator produce statistical data showing actual airliner crashes due to physical or mental disability of pilots over 60? Compare, for example, the approach here with the attitude of courts and legislature to the proof of dangerousness potential in the mentally ill as a basis for compulsory hospitalization and treatment.

2. Another example of accident prevention regulatory policy is the required or forced application of safety precautions. The enumeration of examples would take up pages of space from safety caps on aspirin bottles to safety glass in automobiles, to requiring that pleasure boat owners take a course in safety and the rules of the sea before being licensed to operate a powerboat. A large majority of mandated safety precautions are passive; that is, they require no affirmative action of the person involved. Much of the opposition to safety measures has come in relation to more affirmative requirements, especially to crash helmets for motorcyclists and seatbelt restraints for motor vehicles. The courts have upheld the legislation. See State v. Albertson, 470 P.2d 300 (Idaho 1970); Simon v. Sargent, 346 F. Supp. 277 (D. Mass. 1972). Cases challenging automobile seatbelt laws have received a similar review and have been found justified in the interest of personal safety. See the excellent opinion of the Illinois Supreme Court in People v. Kolrig, 498 N.E.2d 1158 (Ill. 1986). See also a California decision upholding a requirement of a seat restraint designed for small children. People v. Thomas, 206 Cal. Rptr. 84 (Cal. App. 1984). Opposition to mandatory seatbelt and crash helmet laws has been more successful before the legislature and in referenda petitions. See generally Warner, Bags, Buckles and Belts: The Debate over Mandatory Passive Restraints in Automobiles, 8 J. Health Pol. Poly. & L. 1 (1983). Studies have shown increases in highway deaths and injury after repeals. See Watson, Zador & Wilks, The Repeal of Helmet Use Laws and Increased Motorcyclist Mortality in the United States, 1975-1978, 70 Am. J. Pub. Health 579 (1980); McSwain & Lummis, Impact of Motorcycle Helmet Law Repeal, 1 Amer. Assoc. for Auto. Med. Q.J. 29 (1979). See also Societal Risk Assessment: How Safe is Safe Enough? in Gen. Motors Res. Lab. Symposium (Schwing & Albers eds. 1980). On scientific methods of risk assessment, see Risk and Decision Making: Perspectives and Research (National Academy of Sciences) (1982).

Grossman v. Baumgartner
271 N.Y.S.2d 195 (N.Y. 1966)

FULD, JUDGE.

Whether the prohibition against tattooing, provided by New York

II. Disease and Accident Prevention

City's Health Code, constitutes an impairment of constitutional right, is the question we are here called upon to resolve.

The Health Code of New York City, in section 181.15, recites that it "shall be unlawful for any person to tattoo a human being, except . . . for medical purposes by [one] licensed . . . to practice medicine or osteopathy." Each of the plaintiffs was engaged in the business of tattooing in Coney Island for some years before the provision became effective in 1961. They seek a judgment (1) declaring that the section is unconstitutional and (2) enjoining the defendants, the Board of Health and the Department of Health, from enforcing it.

At the time of the trial, the plaintiff Grossman was a laborer, the plaintiff Funk, a roofer. The former testified in detail about the manner in which he had operated his tattooing parlor six days a week, all year round, from noon to midnight, in compliance with the then applicable rules of the Board of Health, until he was forced out of business by the new Health Code provision. He had, he noted, used a sterilizer and sterilized the dyes (which were employed) in pyrex baby bottles; he admitted that he wore no gloves and that the tattooing at times resulted in some bleeding.

The evidence offered on behalf of the defendants strongly supported the conclusion that there was a connection between tattooing and serum hepatitis, that those tattooed, despite all precautions taken by the tattooer, were subjected to a far greater risk of contracting hepatitis than those not tattooed.

In the case before us, there is no warrant for the charge that the Board of Health acted arbitrarily or capriciously or that the regulation under attack was unreasonable. A review of the evidence given by the defendants' witnesses thoroughly demonstrates the compelling medical necessity for section 181.15 of the Health Code. Not only was a connection shown between tattooing and hepatitis but the proof convincingly established that rigorous regulation would be ineffective. The police power is exceedingly broad, and the courts will not substitute their judgment of a public health problem for that of eminently qualified physicians in the field of public health. . . .

Thus, the Assistant Commissioner of the City's Health Department, in charge of its inspection service, testified that in 1959 several cases of hepatitis, one resulting in death, had been traced to tattooing. Although the health authorities initially believed that it would be possible to adopt stringent regulations which would permit tattooing without danger to the public, supervision of the tattoo parlors to assure proper sterilization was found to be a practical impossibility and dangerous and unsanitary conditions continued to prevail. Persuaded that "the threat of hepatitis [from tattooing] was too imminent . . . too dangerous and too deadly" to permit it to depend on regulatory measures to assure proper sterilization, the board enacted the challenged prohibitory section. The director of the Health Department's bureau of preventable diseases also testified that there was a direct causal connection between tattooing and the disease. It was his opinion, based on a statistical analysis, that those who were tattooed ran a risk of contracting hepatitis "seven times as great" as those not tattooed and that "the tattoo industry, from a public health point of view . . . [was] not regulatable" in New York City. Other witnesses — a dermatologist, a psychiatrist and a public health expert — furnished additional confirmation for this view: all of them agreed that tattooing was a health hazard that could be controlled only by prohibition.

Despite this testimony, the trial court concluded, in essence, that there was no justification for abandoning regulation in favor of prohibition and declared the Health Code provision unconstitutional. The Appellate Division reversed with the comment that "[t]he record shows, to our minds conclusively, that the prohibition of lay tattooing was an advisable procedure for the security of life and health". We agree with this determination.

The order appealed from should be affirmed, without costs.

NOTES

Prohibitions and Abatement of Public Nuisances and Other Hazards Dangerous to the Public Health

1. Along with disease control and quarantine, the abatement of nuisances dangerous to the public health was a major activity of state and local health departments in America and in Europe in the eighteenth and nineteenth centuries and throughout the earlier decades of the current century. Legislation to regulate and prohibit public health nuisances was enacted as early as 1692 in the Provinces of South Carolina and the Massachusetts Bay Colony. These early provisions dealt with the location of slaughterhouses for animals, with the maintenance of swine on private properties, and with the control of noxious weeds. Blackstone in 1765 provided an early and characteristically broad definition of a public nuisance as "whatever unlawfully annoys or does damage to another." 3 Blackstone's Commentaries 5 (Sp. Ed., Legal Classics Library, 1983).

Powers to abate public nuisances have been exercised by health authorities, by local police, and by state attorneys general. For early analysis in the public health field, see J. Tobey, Public Health Law (3d ed. 1947) Chapter XIII. See also Parker & Worthington, The Law of Public Health and Safety (1892). Revocation of business licenses for violations of health and safety regulations establishing the existence of a nuisance were early remedies recognized by the courts. An interesting early case involved an action by the federal government

II. Disease and Accident Prevention

itself to enjoin operation of a particularly unpleasant and odorific fish-processing factory nearby, of all things, a disease quarantine station. See U.S. v. Luce, 141 F.385 (Del. 1905).

2. The most common action against a public nuisance, including those dangerous (or discomforting) to health, has been abatement by court injunction. When brought by a private party, damages could also be obtained for previous harm. When a public authority sought a court order to abate a nuisance, the court, when convinced of the existence of the nuisance, would generally not order the problem corrected in a specific way, but would allow the wrongdoer to select an effective method. This practice of the courts often created severe and frustrating problems for health authorities that were forced to bring violators to court time and again to obtain adequate compliance with health department regulations. In emergency situations, the health authorities could take immediate action and could destroy or burn dangerous substances that were clearly creating serious health hazards. Notice was required to the owners or operators, but summary action would not violate due process of law requirements. A court hearing after the fact could, of course, challenge the health authority's basis for taking emergency abatement steps. Lawton v. State, 152 U.S. 136 (1894).

In more modern times, the control of public health nuisances has evolved into a highly technical operation handled by federal and state environmental health agencies. Similar problems can occur, however, when business establishments resist enforcement measures. See particularly F. Grad, Environmental Law: Sources and Problems (3d ed. 1985); T. Schoenbaum, Environmental Policy and Law (1983).

3. The *Grossman* case has received little notice in the textbooks, but it is an interesting modern example of the prohibition of an entire industry or business in a particular location because of its hazard to public health. The highest court in New York State had little trouble finding the policy to close all of the tattoo establishments on Coney Island, a recreational beach resort that attracted thousands of people from the New York City area, to be justified in the interest of preventing the spread of hepatitis B and other blood-borne diseases. The health department did not take action under general nuisance provisions. It acted directly under a provision in the newly adopted City Sanitary Code which outlawed tattooing of the human body except for medical purposes. This new Code was a model for the development of new general public health codes in the early 1960s, having been prepared by the Columbia University Law School's legislative drafting group under Professor Frank Grad. See Grad and Baumgartner, A New Health Code for New York City, 49 Am. J. Pub. Health 1313 (1959); Mantel, New Horizons for Local Legislation: The New York City Health Code, 10 Brooklyn Barrister 216 (1959).

On the drafting of state and local health regulations in this period, see Curran, The Architecture of Public Health Statutes and Administrative Regulations, 79 Pub. Health Reps. 747 (1964); Curran, The Preparation of State and Local Health Regulations, 59 Am. J. Pub. Health 314 (1959).

As in the *Air Line Pilots* case at 1153 in this chapter, the compelling issues of strategy and policy for the court and the public authorities in the *Grossman* case revolved around whether surveillance and regular inspection could satisfy the public interest in disease control. In the *Grossman* case, unlike the *Air Line Pilots* litigation, the health authorities were able to point to actual cases of disease contact due to tattooing. Does informed consent to the tattooing present any effective defense to a personal lawsuit against a tattoo establishment for a hepatitis infection caused by an unclean tattoo needle?

It must be admitted that the artistic tattooing of the human body in small-business "tattoo parlors" on Coney Island (and on the waterfronts of other cities around the world) has little "social utility" in the eyes of the more conservative elements of well-to-do communities. Does this attitude have an influence on the development of the public regulatory policy found in the New York Sanitary Code? Are tattoo parlors considered to be in the same class as houses of prostitution, bookstores selling pornographic books and allowing private showings of pornographic films? Gay bars and bathhouses? See the examination of these issues later in this chapter at 1263-1266.

III. DRUG AND ALCOHOL ABUSE AND DEPENDENCE: REGULATORY POLICIES, TREATMENT, AND REHABILITATION

Whalen v. Roe
429 U.S. 589 S. Ct. (1977)*

Mr. Justice Stevens delivered the opinion of the Court.

The constitutional question presented is whether the State of New York may record, in a centralized computer file, the names and addresses of all persons who have obtained, pursuant to a doctor's prescription, certain drugs for which there is both a lawful and an unlawful market.

The District Court enjoined enforcement of the portions of the New York State Controlled Substances Act of 1972 which require such recording on the ground that they violate appellees' constitu-

---

* Numerous footnotes are omitted.

III. Drug and Alcohol Abuse and Dependence

tionally protected rights of privacy. We noted probable jurisdiction of the appeal by the Commissioner of Health, 424 U.S. 907, and now reverse.

Many drugs have both legitimate and illegitimate uses. In response to a concern that such drugs were being diverted into unlawful channels, in 1970 the New York Legislature created a special commission to evaluate the State's drug-control laws. The commission found the existing laws deficient in several respects. There was no effective way to prevent the use of stolen or revised prescriptions, to prevent unscrupulous pharmacists from repeatedly refilling prescriptions, to prevent users from obtaining prescriptions from more than one doctor, or to prevent doctors from overprescribing, either by authorizing an excessive amount in one prescription or by giving one patient multiple prescriptions. In drafting new legislation to correct such defects, the commission consulted with enforcement officials in California and Illinois where central reporting systems were being used effectively.

The new New York statute classified potentially harmful drugs in five schedules.[7] Drugs, such as heroin, which are highly abused and have no recognized medical use, are in Schedule I; they cannot be prescribed. Schedules II through V include drugs which have a progressively lower potential for abuse but also have a recognized medical use. Our concern is limited to Schedule II, which includes the most dangerous of the legitimate drugs.[8]

With an exception for emergencies, the Act requires that all prescriptions for Schedule II drugs be prepared by the physician in triplicate on an official form. The completed form identifies the prescribing physician; the dispensing pharmacy; the drug and dosage; and the name, address, and age of the patient. One copy of the form is retained by the physician, the second by the pharmacist, and the third is forwarded to the New York State Department of Health in Albany. A prescription made on an official form may not exceed a 30-day supply, and may not be refilled.

The District Court found that about 100,000 Schedule II prescription forms are delivered to a receiving room at the Department of Health in Albany each month. They are sorted, coded, and logged and then taken to another room where the data on the forms is recorded on magnetic tapes for processing by a computer. Thereafter,

---

7. These five schedules conform in all material aspects with the drug schedules in the Federal Comprehensive Drug Abuse Prevention and Control Act of 1970. 21 U.S.C. §801 et seq.

8. These include opium and opium derivatives, cocaine, methadone, amphetamines, and methaqualone. Pub. Health Law §3306. These drugs have accepted uses in the amelioration of pain and in the treatment of epilepsy, narcolepsy, hyperkinesia, schizoaffective disorders, and migraine headaches.

the forms are returned to the receiving room to be retained in a vault for a five-year period and then destroyed as required by the statute.

A few days before the Act became effective, this litigation was commenced by a group of patients regularly receiving prescriptions for Schedule II drugs, by doctors who prescribe such drugs, and by two associations of physicians. After various preliminary proceedings, a three-judge District Court conducted a one-day trial. Appellees offered evidence tending to prove that persons in need of treatment with Schedule II drugs will from time to time decline such treatment because of their fear that the misuse of the computerized data will cause them to be stigmatized as "drug addicts."

The District Court held that "the doctor-patient relationship is one of the zones of privacy accorded constitutional protection" and that the patient-identification provisions of the Act invaded this zone with "a needlessly broad sweep," and enjoined enforcement of the provisions of the Act which deal with the reporting of patients' names and addresses.

I

The District Court found that the State had been unable to demonstrate the necessity for the patient-identification requirement on the basis of its experience during the first 20 months of administration of the new statute. . . .

State legislation which has some effect on individual liberty or privacy may not be held unconstitutional simply because a court finds it unnecessary, in whole or in part. For we have frequently recognized that individual States have broad latitude in experimenting with possible solutions to problems of vital local concern.

The New York statute challenged in this case represents a considered attempt to deal with such a problem. It is manifestly the product of an orderly and rational legislative decision. It was recommended by a specially appointed commission which held extensive hearings on the proposed legislation, and drew on experience with similar programs in other States. There surely was nothing unreasonable in the assumption that the patient-identification requirement might aid in the enforcement of laws designed to minimize the misuse of dangerous drugs. For the requirement could reasonably be expected to have a deterrent effect on potential violators as well as to aid in the detection or investigation of specific instances of apparent abuse. At the very least, it would seem clear that the State's vital interest in controlling the distribution of dangerous drugs would support a decision to experiment with new techniques for control. For if an experiment fails — if in this case experience teaches that the patient-

III. Drug and Alcohol Abuse and Dependence

identification requirement results in the foolish expenditure of funds to acquire a mountain of useless information — the legislative process remains available to terminate the unwise experiment. It follows that the legislature's enactment of the patient-identification requirement was a reasonable exercise of New York's broad police powers. The District Court's finding that the necessity for the requirement had not been proved is not, therefore, a sufficient reason for holding the statutory requirement unconstitutional.

II

Appellees contend that the statute invades a constitutionally protected "zone of privacy." The cases sometimes characterized as protecting "privacy" have in fact involved at least two different kinds of interests. One is the individual interest in avoiding disclosure of personal matters, and another is the interest in independence in making certain kinds of important decisions. Appellees argue that both of these interests are impaired by this statute. The mere existence in readily available form of the information about patients' use of Schedule II drugs creates a genuine concern that the information will become publicly known and that it will adversely affect their reputations. This concern makes some patients reluctant to use, and some doctors reluctant to prescribe, such drugs even when their use is medically indicated. It follows, they argue, that the making of decisions about matters vital to the care of their health is inevitably affected by the statute. Thus, the statute threatens to impair both their interest in the nondisclosure of private information and also their interest in making important decisions independently.

We are persuaded, however, that the New York program does not, on its face, pose a sufficiently grievous threat to either interest to establish a constitutional violation.

Public disclosure of patient information can come about in three ways. Health Department employees may violate the statute by failing, either deliberately or negligently, to maintain proper security. A patient or a doctor may be accused of a violation and the stored data may be offered in evidence in a judicial proceeding. Or, thirdly, a doctor, a pharmacist, or the patient may voluntarily reveal information on a prescription form.

The third possibility existed under the prior law and is entirely unrelated to the existence of the computerized data bank. Neither of the other two possibilities provides a proper ground for attacking the statute as invalid on its face. There is no support in the record, or in the experience of the two States that New York has emulated, for an assumption that the security provisions of the statute will be administered improperly. And the remote possibility that judicial supervision of the evidentiary use of particular items of stored information will provide inadequate protection against unwarranted disclosures is surely not a sufficient reason for invalidating the entire patient-identification program.

Even without public disclosure, it is, of course, true that private information must be disclosed to the authorized employees of the New York Department of Health. Such disclosures, however, are not significantly different from those that were required under the prior law. Nor are they meaningfully distinguishable from a host of other unpleasant invasions of privacy that are associated with many facets of health care. Unquestionably, some individuals' concern for their own privacy may lead them to avoid or to postpone needed medical attention. Nevertheless, disclosures of private medical information to doctors, to hospital personnel, to insurance companies, and to public health agencies are often an essential part of modern medical practice even when the disclosure may reflect unfavorably on the character of the patient. Requiring such disclosures to representatives of the State having responsibility for the health of the community, does not automatically amount to an impermissible invasion of privacy.

Appellees also argue, however, that even if unwarranted disclosures do not actually occur, the knowledge that the information is readily available in a computerized file creates a genuine concern that causes some persons to decline needed medication. The record supports the conclusion that some use of Schedule II drugs has been discouraged by that concern; it also is clear, however, that about 100,000 prescriptions for such drugs were being filled each month prior to the entry of the District Court's injunction. Clearly, therefore, the statute did not deprive the public of access to the drugs.

Nor can it be said that any individual has been deprived of the right to decide independently, with the advice of his physician, to acquire and to use needed medication. Although the State no doubt could prohibit entirely the use of particular Schedule II drugs, it has not done so. This case is therefore unlike those in which the Court held that a total prohibition of certain conduct was an impermissible deprivation of liberty. Nor does the State require access to these drugs to be conditioned on the consent of any state official or other third party. Within dosage limits which appellees do not challenge, the decision to prescribe, or to use, is left entirely to the physician and the patient.

We hold that neither the immediate nor the threatened impact of the patient-identification requirements in the New York State Controlled Substances Act of 1972 on either the reputation or the independence of patients for whom Schedule II drugs are medically indicated is sufficient to constitute an invasion of any right or liberty protected by the Fourteenth Amendment.

III

The appellee doctors argue separately that the statute impairs their right to practice medicine free of unwarranted state interference. If the doctors' claim has any reference to the impact of the 1972 statute on their own procedures, it is clearly frivolous. For even the prior statute required the doctor to prepare a written prescription identifying the name and address of the patient and the dosage of the prescribed drug. To the extent that their claim has reference to the possibility that the patients' concern about disclosure may induce them to refuse needed medication, the doctors' claim is derivative from, and therefore no stronger than, the patients'. Our rejection of their claim therefore disposes of the doctors' as well. . . .

Reversed.

Curran, Arif & Jayasuriya, Guidelines for Assessing and Revising National Legislation on Treatment of Drug and Alcohol-Dependent Persons*
38 Int. Digest of Health Legis. (Supp. 1) 3 (1987)

[The following is an excerpt from a longer report prepared for the World Health Organization.]

2. *Role of Legislation in the Treatment of Drug- and Alcohol-dependent Persons*

2.1 Introduction

These Guidelines are intended to help Member States to evaluate and improve their legislation in this field. The approaches suggested here, as already pointed out, are based on practical experience and have proved successful in the prevention and treatment of drug and alcohol dependence and the rehabilitation of dependent persons. It is realized, however, that differences in tradition and culture, religious beliefs, available facilities, and manpower resources, as well as budgetary constraints, make it necessary to suggest different approaches to improving the relevant national services.

2.2 Advantages of Legislative Support

A treatment programme for drug or alcohol dependence gains appreciably by being supported by effective national legislation which

---

* This excerpt by Prof. Curran (one of the editors), Dr. A.E. Arif, Senior Medical Officer in Charge of the Drug Dependence Program, W.H.O., and Mr. D. C. Jayasuriya, Consultant Attorney, W.H.O., is reprinted by permission of the World Health Organization.

helps to achieve for it the national priority that these extremely serious public health problems demand. The advantages of such support may be summarized as follows:

1. The legislative position is clarified and authority given to develop, coordinate, supervise, and evaluate clinical services for drug and alcohol dependence programmes.
2. Budgetary support is provided specifically for treatment programmes in these fields.
3. The reluctance of treatment personnel to deal with drug- and alcohol-dependent patients is overcome.
4. Compliance with international obligations to provide treatment in this field, particularly in regard to drug dependence, under the 1961 Single Convention on Narcotic Drugs and the 1971 Convention on Psychotropic Substances, is assured.
5. The national strategy for the treatment of drug and alcohol dependence is integrated with national strategic planning for public health.

2.3 Policy-making and Symbolic Roles of Legislation

National legislation constitutes a public endorsement of the goals and methods of programmes for dealing with serious public health problems. Great attention is currently being given throughout the world to drug and alcohol abuse and dependence, thus providing a great opportunity to seek more effective and more comprehensive national legislation in these fields.

Closely related to the public policy role of new and improved legislation is the symbolic role of legislative endorsement by the national legislature.

In organized society, laws adopted and promulgated by a properly constituted legislative body provide guidance as to what is expected in relations between people. In most languages, there is a close relationship between what is "right", in a morally or culturally accepted sense, and what is "right" in terms of "legitimacy" or "law", even though many laws are, in fact, morally neutral. Nevertheless, law seen as enacted for the public good is highly symbolic of "rightness" and "legitimacy".

In this symbolic sense, it is important for those interested in changes in public attitudes and practices in the drug and alcohol fields to seek legislative reform. The *content* of that reform is the subject-matter of this publication, but its *symbolic value* lies in achieving the reform or change desired through legislative endorsement of the *new philosophy* of the treatment programme.

2.4 Treatment Objectives and Law Enforcement

It would be a dangerous mistake in determining national policy on the treatment of drug and alcohol dependence to dismiss the importance of prevention and control through law enforcement programmes. "Supply side" issues such as availability and number, transport and sale, and agricultural policies discouraging the production and distribution of illegal substances of dependence, will continue to be of great significance in any comprehensive attack on these problems. Law enforcement, backed by appropriate penalties, is necessary to deal with the profitable business of producing, distributing, and supplying such substances to the public.

Some degree of "decriminalization", however, and especially the avoidance of very severe criminal penalties for clearly dependent, sick persons, can help to encourage such persons to seek early treatment and rehabilitation. It is not advisable, however, to try to achieve the complete decriminalization of all conduct related to trafficking in and profiting from the illicit distribution of dangerous drugs. It is also necessary to use law enforcement measures to protect the public from conduct such as dangerous driving, violent assaults, and theft by persons heavily under the influence of alcohol or illicit drugs.

2.5 Establishment of Goals and Priorities

Whenever a campaign to change the legislation is begun, certain precautions must be observed in working with national parliamentary bodies and with the media (newspapers, television, etc.) interested in proposals for new or revised legislation.

It must be realized, in particular, that the resources and manpower available in the mental health and public health systems will rarely be enough to provide services for everyone who may need or seek help. The problems of drug and alcohol abuse and dependence are too great and too widespread for all the demands to be met. This means that it must be made clear to both the legislative bodies concerned and the media that the programme will need to select "target groups" on which the limited treatment and rehabilitation resources will be focused.

It must also be remembered that at present no simple, inexpensive, highly effective treatment exists which can guarantee success and long-term recovery for large numbers of substance-dependent persons, nor is one likely in the foreseeable future. There is a great temptation to promise therapeutic results in the mental health field as a whole that cannot, in fact, be achieved. As a result, in some countries, there have been adverse reactions against legislation which has not fulfilled unrealistic expectations, and drug and alcohol dependence treatment programmes can suffer from such reactions.

Provided that these two facts are remembered, it should be possible to lay down clear priorities and to establish realistic goals for treatment programmes.

2.6 Integration with Community-based Services

The integration of many treatment services for drug and alcohol dependence with community health services may be advisable in many countries. Such community-based services may well be associated with other local primary health care services. For this reason, treatment programmes will often be under the authority of the Ministry of Health, although they may be coordinated by a National Board for Drug and/or Alcohol Control.

The legislative approach to drug and alcohol treatment programmes should also be developed in harmony with overall community health objectives and the trend away from the concentration of mental health resources in large, impersonal hospitals and excessive reliance on highly trained professionals. Drug and alcohol dependence treatment services have been developed in many countries at the local level, using alternative, much less expensive types of personnel and other resources. Such services can easily be brought into line with WHO's emphasis on Health for All by the Year 2000 through primary health care, since it has long been recognized that dependence is not a purely medical problem and that the traditional medical approach alone cannot provide an adequate framework for successful treatment or prevention.

The adoption by WHO's Member States of the goal of Health for All by the Year 2000 through primary health care has led to changes in the way that the physician-patient relationship is perceived, since this goal cannot be achieved by the efforts of the medical profession alone. The community itself has an equally important part to play, and the health system should educate and motivate people to assume responsibility for their own health. This approach has been reflected in the targets for the WHO programme on prevention and control of alcohol and drug abuse, which have been adopted by the World Health Assembly for the Eighth General Programme of Work covering the period 1990-1995.

3. Legislative Strategy

3.1 Introduction

The content of legislation on the treatment of drug- and alcohol-dependent persons will be discussed in subsequent chapters under a number of headings. To begin with, however, some general issues of legislative strategy and philosophy will be dealt with. In general terms, such legislation should:

a) serve as a rallying point for *enlightened and organized legislative support,* including provision of the budgetary allocations necessary to establish and continue a treatment programme and for appropriate manpower and other resources;
b) establish a *philosophy of comprehensive treatment* in which use is made of all available resources, public and private, in a variety of settings, and of the most modern methods of treatment and rehabilitation;
c) designate a specific *authority* to conduct, supervise, and coordinate *comprehensive treatment services* for drug and alcohol dependence;
d) lay down *definitions and procedures* for treatment programmes, including both voluntary and various types of compulsory services, as well as for diversion from the criminal justice system;
e) ensure *equitable nondiscriminatory access* to treatment services located close to patients' own communities;
f) protect the *human and civil rights* of patients, and their dignity and privacy, and ensure the confidentiality of all information on those seeking and receiving treatment;
g) authorize the *delegation* of further *regulatory authority* to the agency responsible for the operation of the treatment programme in order to ensure that it is modified and improved in line with new demands on it and to take account of technical and scientific advances in the field; and
h) provide for the *evaluation* of the results achieved by the programme and for a system of *periodic reporting* back to the legislature on its progress.

3.4 Combined or Separate Legislation for Drugs and Alcohol

As indicated in the survey of legislation on the treatment of drug and alcohol dependence, most of the countries covered had separate legislation on drugs and alcohol. Of the 43 countries surveyed, only five had legislation containing provisions governing the treatment of both forms of substance dependence. More recently, however, treatment and other services have been combined under a single administrative agency or commission in Sweden, several provinces of Canada, and several states of the USA.

More countries had specialized legislation on the treatment of drug dependence (28 of 43) than for that of alcohol dependence.

The reason for this difference is clearly the existence of treaty obligations under the 1961 Single Convention on Narcotic Drugs, as amended in 1972, and the 1971 International Convention on Psychotropic Substances, which came into force in 1976. Both these Conventions call for the establishment of programmes for the treatment and rehabilitation of drug-dependent persons.

In contrast, the introduction of specialized legislation on the treatment of alcohol dependence is not aided by such formal requirements in international agreements. Furthermore, the much lower percentage of countries worldwide with such specialized legislation is the consequence of the fact that very few national laws on the subject exist in the Eastern Mediterranean and South-East Asia Regions of WHO. Successful specialized treatment programmes for alcohol dependence aided by special legislation are, however, in operation in several countries, notably in Scandinavia, the USSR, Poland, and Hungary. Some of these countries have enacted specialized legislation on the treatment of alcohol dependence, but not of drug dependence.

The decision as to the need for separate, specialized legislation in these fields is left to individual Member States. For ease of presentation, however, and to avoid repetition, both types of dependence will be considered together in what follows.

A number of arguments have, however, been put forward in support of at least a limited combined approach. The WHO Expert Committee on Mental Health first used the term "combined approach" is its 1960 report, in which it suggested that such an approach would be most effective in research and perhaps also in treatment and community education, but less effective in control and law enforcement. Subsequently, the combined approach has received further support as more data have been produced indicating that, in many substance-dependent groups, drug abuse not uncommonly leads to alcohol abuse and vice versa, and ultimately to dependence. Patient identification techniques and dependence profiles have also often been found to have features in common. Control programmes which make some drugs of dependence much more difficult or expensive to obtain often drive dependent persons to replace them by other more readily available drugs or alcohol, thus putting different pressures on treatment services. In contrast, in some countries where, on religious grounds, government efforts may be directed particularly against any type of alcohol use, some sections of the population, at least, may not be as strongly opposed to certain drugs, especially those available across the counter in local pharmacies.

In terms of legislation, a combined approach will ensure the coordinated administration of both programmes and encourage cooperation in prevention, control, treatment, and rehabilitation in both fields without requiring all treatment centres and personnel to deal with all dependent persons alike or even in the same locations or centres. It may well be possible to cover both drug and alcohol dependence in areas such as strategic planning, research, epidemiology, and community education.

A combined approach also has the advantage of bringing together those involved in fighting both forms of substance abuse and of avoiding or discouraging divisiveness. This is particularly valuable at the highest levels as, for example, in a national coordinating and policymaking board. It is also important that a comprehensive approach to community education and treatment should be adopted in the primary health care services for drug and alcohol dependence.

Oliphant, Drug Programs with Specifics That Don't Match Goals*
Boston Globe, July 28, 1989, at 11

WASHINGTON — It is emotionally and politically helpful to portray drug dealers as vermin feeding off the weakness and illness of the young.

It is more useful to see them as largely rational, evil people who have responded rationally to the lurches of federal law enforcement policy in the 1980s. That policy, rivaled only by Prohibition 60 years ago in its uselessness, is not about to be reversed by President Bush. The mindless pursuit of the chimera of interdiction will continue at the expense of the education of potential addicts and the treatment of actual ones.

The just-announced prime target of drug czar William Bennett for his program due in September — crack cocaine — was the result of the Reagan-Bush policy that gutted treatment and education to pay for real-life "Miami Vice" raids.

On Monday, Senate Judiciary Committee chairman Joseph Biden will offer some tenets for a more sensible program in a speech here, focusing in part on the government's inability to live up to the promise of the "drug war" statute in 1988 with adequate funds. His fellow Democrats, though, must share the responsibility for spending but $500 million of the $2.7 billion authorized for new efforts last year.

The priorities are the greater evil. As a recent paper for the 20th Century Fund explained, money for drug law enforcement more than doubled from 1981 to 1986, consuming 90 percent of the jump in drug-control spending. After inflation, money for programs to cut demand was cut nearly 40 percent.

---

* This column by Thomas Oliphant is reprinted with permission of the author and the Boston Globe Newspaper.

What happened in the criminal world was simple. With a high federal presence at the borders, smugglers shifted to a smaller product (cocaine) from huge bales of marijuana (this country's second-largest cash crop); at the street level, crack was developed as a way to market the drug in dose levels suitable to a more impoverished market with vastly higher profits, thus creating employment for a new army of street dealers and messengers. A kilo of cocaine that cost $60,000 to import in 1980 cost $10,000 eight years later.

Meanwhile, in a besieged city such as New York — with 200,000 intravenous drug users and 500,000 serious cocaine abusers — there are no more than 35,000 slots for free treatment of addicts, and most of those dish out methadone to heroin addicts. The prospects for major change are limited without a change in government policy, which does not appear likely.

The latest symptom of a floundering government was the administration's attention to a fiscally preposterous idea — the public sale of $4 billion in "drug war bonds" to pay for the administration's initiatives as well as additional federal prisons. Supported by a citizens group and several congressional Republicans, the idea got brief encouragement from Bennett before the White House said that backdoor financing will not be used for the new drug program.

The Democrats, however, have not had much better luck. Biden recommended to House and Senate colleagues this month that Congress take the dramatic step of fully funding the 1988 law — thus busting the current budget agreement's spending ceilings that will enable the administration and Congress to limp through the coming fiscal year. His argument — that the agreement has no deficit-reduction significance as it is, and what better program to bust it with than the fight against illegal drugs — got a sympathetic hearing from Democrats tired of playing nickel-and-dime incrementalism with huge national challenges; however, the leadership's commitment to putting off serious budget work until next year proved stronger than the lure of offering a comprehensive drug program this year.

The result, though, is almost certain to be one more example of a drug program whose specifics don't match its goals, whose continuing emphasis on Prohibition-era assaults on supply masks a near-willful misunderstanding of the nature and costs of addiction.

NOTES

Strategies for Treatment and Regulatory Programs for Drug and Alcohol Problems

1. The excerpts from the *W.H.O. Guidelines* reprinted above provide an indication of the philosophy behind the document. In the

remainder of the report, suggestions are made for statutory and regulatory provisions on administration of the programs and on standards and procedures for treatment facilities, professional services, voluntary treatment, restrictive or compulsory treatment, emergency care and detoxification, and out-patient community services. There are provisions for diverting or transferring criminal offenders from the courts and prisons to drug and alcohol treatment programs. There are also extensive provisions regarding protection of personal rights.

2. In the legislation of most countries, the eligibility of patients for treatment is governed by statutory definitions of "drug dependence" and "alcohol dependence." These are the more accepted scientific terms, but the statutes of many countries still use terms such as "drug addict" or "alcoholic." The coverage of the terms is essentially similar. The definitions in the drug field usually contain three elements: (1) diagnostic criteria, (2) behavioral aspects, and (3) linkages to national drug law enforcement programs. When the procedure relates to compulsory restraint and residential treatment, the behavioral aspect will usually contain a requirement that the person is known to be dangerous to others or to himself or herself because of the loss of control over drug use. Reference is also often made to criminal behavior related to the drug dependence.

The diagnostic criteria for drug dependency should correspond to the International Classification of Diseases, Ninth Series. There will be a Tenth Series in 1990 or 1991. In 1984, an expert committee at W.H.O. recommended that the definition of "drug dependence" in the ICD-10 should bring together all diagnoses under one heading of drug dependence or syndrome with a group of subdivisions in terms of severity. It is suggested that distinctions between physical and psychological dependence be abandoned in favor of a single dependency status known as "socio-psycho-biological syndrome." See Nomenclature and Classification of Drug and Alcohol Related Problems; A W.H.O. Memorandum, 59 Bull. W.H.O. 225 (1981).

3. As indicated in the excerpt from the *Guidelines,* most countries have separate programs of treatment for drug dependence and alcohol dependence. The survey referred to in the *Guidelines* is an international review of legislation throughout the member states of W.H.O.; a total of 42 countries and one territory (Hong Kong) provided legislation to the survey. In most countries, each form of dependence is dealt with in national legislation (with national and sub-national legislation in countries with federal systems), but some countries were found to concentrate in one area. Alcohol dependence is the subject of legislation in Bulgaria and the Soviet Union, for example, with no drug dependence treatment legislation, while the opposite prevails in several other countries (such as Burma and Thailand). In the United States, the federal-level efforts in this field are separate for drugs and alcohol.

There are also separate federal agencies in the United States concerned with education, treatment, and research: the National Institute of Drug Abuse and the National Institute of Alcohol Abuse and Alcoholism. Currently, the state agencies administering programs for drug and alcohol treatment are combined in most of the 50 American states. The only other industrialized countries where combined programs are authorized by legislation are Sweden and Switzerland. See Porter, A. Arif & W. Curran, The Law and Treatment of Drug- and Alcohol-Dependent Persons (W.H.O., Geneva, 1986). For an earlier international survey of treatment legislation for mental illness as well as for drug and alcohol dependence, see W. Curran & T. Harding, The Law and Mental Health: Harmonizing Objectives (W.H.O. Geneva, 1978).

4. For more detailed examination of methods of drug dependence treatment and rehabilitation in the United States, see O'Brien & Woody, Drug Abuse Treatment Programs, in Modern Legal Medicine, Psychiatry and Forensic Science (W. Curran, A. McGarry & C. Petty eds. 1980); Jaffe, Drug Addiction and Drug Abuse, in Goodman and Gilman's, The Pharmacological Basis of Therapeutics (Goodman, Gilman, Rall & Murad, eds. 1985). See also Drug Abuse Treatment and the Criminal Justice System (N.I.D.A. Res. Mon. Series, 1977). For a review and analysis of the cost-benefit of drug abuse and dependence treatment, see Quantitative Explorations in Drug Abuse Policy (I. Leveson ed. 1980). See also Mezochow, Miller et al, The Impact of Cost Containment on Alcohol and Drug Treatment, 38 Hosp. and Comm. Psychia. 357 (1987).

There is now a certification system for medical specialists in drug and alcohol treatment. It was begun in the mid-1980s and granted its first certificates in 1986. It was organized by the American Medical Society on Alcohol and Other Drug Dependencies. The certification is not associated with the American Board of Medical Specialists. The most useful and current review of state-level programs for drug and alcohol treatment can be found in two annual reports produced jointly by N.I.D.A. and N.I.A.A.A. See National Directory of Drug Abuse and Alcoholism Treatment and Prevention Programs (D.H.H.S. Pub., annual); State Resources and Services for Alcohol and Drug Problems (D.H.H.S. Pub., annual).

5. Requirements for civil commitment of drug-dependent persons have received attention in the American courts. As in the field of mental illness, the states differ on requirements for proof of dependence and dangerousness. California has required proof beyond reasonable doubt. See Gilmore v. People, 129 Cal. Rptr. 388 (Cal. App. 1976). In New York, the standard of preponderance of the evidence has been upheld. See People v. Fuller, 248 N.E.2d 17 (N.Y.2d 1969). The U.S. Supreme Court has not reviewed the issue directly, but see

Marshall v. U.S., 414 U.S. 417 (1974). Would the standard of proof for civil commitment of the mentally ill in Addington v. Texas, at 1139 of this chapter, apply to drug addiction treatment? See Abramovsky, Civil Commitment of the Non-Criminal Narcotic Addict: Parens Patriae; A Valid Exercise of a State's Police Power; or an Unconscionable Disregard of Individual Liberty?, 38 U. Pitt. L. Rev. 477 (1977). See also Morgan, The Development of Drug Legislation: Economic Crisis and Social Control, 8 J. Drug Issues 53 (1978). For a general examination of treatment programs, see Ray & Ksir, Drugs, Society and Human Behavior (1987). See also Drug Abuse and Drug Abuse Research, A Report to Congress (N.I.D.A. 1987).

6. In most countries, alcohol-related treatment has a quite different history from drug dependence treatment. In the United States, as in most other countries where alcoholic beverages were available legally, the criminal system has traditionally dealt with the "drunk and disorderly person." Private programs for alcohol addiction treatment (such as "drying out" residential programs) predated specialized public programs in most states. Specialized treatment was developed in the United States in the 1960s and 1970s as the laws concerning public drunkenness were "decriminalized" across the country. The development of modern programs of alcohol-dependence treatment in the states was encouraged by the Uniform Alcoholism and Detoxification Act of the National Conference of Commissioners on Uniform State Laws. The Act was based primarily on work done at the Columbia University Law School's Legislative Drafting Fund. For a report on this work at Columbia, see F. Grad, Goldberg & Shapiro, Alcoholism and the Law (1971).

For the history of alcoholism and alcoholism treatment programs in the United States, see J. Blocker, American Temperance Movements (1989); O. Ray & O. Ksir, Drugs, Society and Human Behavior (1987); Alcohol and Public Policy (Moore & Gerstein eds. 1981). For earlier classic reviews of the field, see M. Chafetz & H. Demone, Alcoholism and Society (1962); E. Jellineck, The Disease Concept of Alcoholism (1960).

7. As mentioned in Note 4 above, there is now a certification system for medical specialists in alcohol and drug treatment. See also Mendelson & Mello, Studies in Alcohol: Past, Present and Future, 50 J. Studies on Alcoh. 293 (1989); Galanter, Blume & Bissell, Physicians in Alcoholism: A Study of Current Status and Future Needs, 4 Alcoh. Clin. and Exper. Res. 389 (1983). The two major resource books on state-level programs for alcohol abuse and alcoholism treatment, jointly produced annually by N.I.A.A.A. and N.I.D.A., were also described in Note 4 above. See also R. O'Brien & M. Chafetz, The Encyclopedia of Alcoholism (1982); E. Pattison & E. Kaufman, Encyclopedic Handbook of Alcoholism (1982). For a review of basic and clinical research

in the field, see J. Mendelson & N. Mello, Alcohol: Use and Abuse in America (1985). For a comprehensive review of research studies on prevention and treatment, see Moskowitz, The Primary Prevention of Alcohol Problems: A Critical Review of the Literature, 50 J. Studies on Alcoh. 54 (1989).

8. The national policy in the United States regarding drug control is found in a landmark piece of legislation, the Comprehensive Drug Abuse Prevention and Control Act of 1970, Public Law 91-513; 21 U.S. Code §801.966 et seq. The law provides for regulation of what are called "controlled substances" in a series of schedules subject to change over time as more is learned about the drugs and their qualities. There are five schedules, each with its own criteria in regard to abuse potential and dependency. Schedule 1 covers drugs not permitted for legitimate use in medical practice. Schedule 2 covers the most dangerous prescriptive drugs such as morphine. Schedule 3 covers the less dangerous prescriptive drugs. Schedule 4 covers chloral hydrate and meprobamate. Schedule 5 contains low-level dangerous compounds such as cough medicines. Across the schedules, there are essentially four types of drugs: narcotics (heroin and morphine), hallucinogens (LSD, mescaline, and marihuana), depressants (barbiturates), and stimulants (amphetamines). The 1970 legislation deemphasized the federal role in the operation of treatment facilities and called for support (by financial grants) for local community treatment. The Federal Narcotic Addict Rehabilitation Act was left intact by the 1970 law. The state legislatures have adapted very similar drug control legislation based upon the Uniform Controlled Substances Act. Physicians are required to have a specific license to prescribe controlled substances. See particularly Zinberg & Dickstein, Prescribing Controlled Substances: Physicians' Rights and Responsibilities, chapter in Modern Legal Medicine, Psychiatry and Forensic Science (W. Curran, A. McGarry & C. Petty eds. 1980).

9. The history of the 1970 legislation on drug control is contained in a useful text by the lawyers who worked on the legislation. See H. Bogomolny, M. Sonnenreich & A. Roccograndi, Handbook of the 1970 Federal Drug Act (1970). In the same period, a national commission produced important research findings and recommendations. See Drug Abuse in America: Problems in Perspective, Report of the National Commission on Marihuana and Drug Abuse (1973). See also Legal Aspects of Drug Dependence (R. Bonnie & M. Sonnenreich eds. 1975).

10. In the middle 1970s, federal activities in the drug abuse field were concentrated into two agencies: the Federal Drug Enforcement Administration (D.E.A.) and the National Institute of Drug Abuse (N.I.D.A.). These agencies continue to be the primary agencies in the field, along with a National Coordinator or "Drug Czar" who

works directly with the Office of the President. The D.E.A. is charged with enforcement of federal laws on drug control and illicit drug traffic. The N.I.D.A. is the federal agency concerned with scientific research and the support of education, rehabilitation, and treatment programs at the federal and state levels. N.I.D.A. produces a highly useful series of research monographs on various subjects related to drug abuse and dependency. See, for example, Public Health Issues and Drug Abuse Research (N.I.D.A., Res. Mon. Series, 1981). The later federal legislation in the field has tended to concentrate on issues of drug control law enforcement. From 1970 to 1987 the percentage of federal spending on drug treatment fell from 56 percent of the total federal budget allocated to the drug abuse field to 23.7 percent. See the Anti-Drug Abuse Act of 1988, Public Law 100-690, 21 U.S. Code 1501. That legislation set as its goal a "drug-free America" by 1995. See generally Bakalar & Grinspoon, Drug Control in a Free Society (1984); Tenim, Taking Your Medicine: Drug Regulation in the United States (1980); Handbook of Drug Abuse (DuPont, Goldstein & O'Donnell eds., N.I.D.A. Res. Mon. Series, 1979).

The national policies on drug abuse control and treatment have changed, often quite profoundly, over the decades of this century and from one federal administration to another. The vagaries of national policy on drugs over the years are traced quite well in R. Musto, The American Disease: Origins of Narcotic Control (Expanded Edition, 1987). The change from the Carter Administration to that of President Reagan is described, in part, as follows:

> For Ronald Reagan and his wife, to be against drugs was as natural a reaction as tolerance would be for some of the young Carter supporters who had battled against draconian laws and scare tactics in the 1960s. Influential elements on each side had a vision of America where every person could achieve his or her maximum potential, but one saw drugs as helping people enhance life, while the other saw ultimate personal achievement only reduced by drug use. Each side translated its vision for the nation into a political movement that profoundly affected elected representatives, laws, and policy regarding drugs. . . .
>
> In 1985 the appearance in several areas of the United States of "crack," a smokable form of cocaine, created a wave of fear that resulted in enormous media and public attention to the drug problem. . . .
>
> The intimate association of AIDS with drug users who share contaminated needles adds to the general and powerful disapproval of drug users, for they promote the spread of AIDS into the rest of the community. The specter of AIDS in fact has scared some casual as well as some habitual needle users into quitting intravenous drug use. Some have switched to smoking crack, and others have entered methadone or drug-free treatment programs.
>
> This growing intolerance now resembles in many ways the intolerance early in this century, which was associated with a reduction in

drug use until the 1960s. Perhaps the explosion of fear regarding cocaine will lead the broad anti-drug effort as it apparently did in the first decade of this century.

Id. at 273-275.

The editorial article by Oliphant paints a picture of the political environment in Washington and the continued emphasis on law enforcement and harsh punishment. In the strategy debates on control measures, as indicated in the book by Musto, the arguments go back and forth between "supply issues" and "demand issues." The efforts to interdict supply are described graphically in the Oliphant editorial. On the demand side, the current national strategy seems to be directing efforts at punishment of middle-level suppliers as well as users. There is also some support of treatment programs (at quite low levels of financial assistance) as a further means of reducing demand.

11. There has been for many decades an international effort to control illegal drug trafficking and to encourage national efforts in education, research, treatment, and rehabilitation. The basis of the effort at the current time lies in two international treaties signed by the great majority of nations of the world: The Single Convention on Narcotic Drugs of 1961 and the International Convention on Psychotropic Substances of 1971. There are also several international treaties related to special geographic regions, such as the South American Regional Agreement on Narcotics and Psychotropic Substances, which became operative in 1977. Activities under the treaties are carried out by specialized United Nations agencies, particularly the U.N. Fund for Drug Abuse Control, the U.N. Division of Narcotic Drugs, and the International Narcotics Control Board. The World Health Organization cooperates with all of these agencies, acting as an expert medical review and consultation source on matters of classification of controlled substances and on the development of treatment methods. There are several important publications of W.H.O. on drug and alcohol policy. See, for example, D. Jayasuriya, I. Arif, A. Khan and R. Gulbinat, Drug Abuse: Guidelines for National Policy Formulation, Implementation and Evaluation (W.H.O., Geneva, 1987); Archibald, Narcotic and Psychotropic Drug Problems: International Collaboration on Health Aspects (W.H.O., Geneva, 1986); B. Rexed, Guidelines for the Control of Narcotic and Psychotropic Substances in the Context of the International Treaties (W.H.O., Geneva, 1984). See also Jayasuriya, The Regulation of Drug Abuse in Developing Countries, 31 Int. Digest Health Legis. 705 (1980). Further references to publications of the World Health Organization related to treatment and rehabilitation of drug and alcohol dependent persons will be found later in this chapter.

12. The dangerous or addictive drug field is changing constantly

as further scientific research and field investigation indicate changes in drug use and drug effects in the United States and in other parts of the world. Until the middle and late 1980s, cocaine and "crack" cocaine received surprisingly little attention in the scientific research literature. There has been a substantial increase in publications in recent years. See State Resources and Services for Alcohol and Drug Problems (D.H.H.S., Report of N.I.D.A. and N.I.A.A.A., 1989); Harruff, Francisco et al., Cocaine and Homicide in Memphis and Shelby County: An Epidemic of Violence, 33 J. For. Sci. 1231 (1989); Gradman, Cardiac Effects of Cocaine: A Review, 61 Yale J. Bio. Med. 137 (1988); Smart, "Crack" Cocaine Use in Canada: A New Epidemic?, 127 Am. J. Epidem. 1315 (1988). See also Adverse Health Consequences of Cocaine Abuse (A. Arif ed., W.H.O. Geneva, 1987). See generally R. O'Brien & S. Cohen, Encyclopedia of Drug Abuse (1980).

National Treasury Employees Union v. Von Raab
— U.S. —, 109 S. Ct. 1384 (1989)

JUSTICE KENNEDY delivered the opinion of the Court.

We granted certiorari to decide whether it violates the Fourth Amendment for the United States Customs Service to require a urinalysis test from employees who seek transfer or promotion to certain positions.

I

A

The United States Customs Service, a bureau of the Department of the Treasury, is the federal agency responsible for processing persons, carriers, cargo, and mail into the United States, collecting revenue from imports, and enforcing customs and related laws. See Customs USA, Fiscal Year 1985, p.4. An important responsibility of the Service is the interdiction and seizure of contraband, including illegal drugs. Ibid. In 1987 alone, Customs agents seized drugs with a retail value of nearly 9 billion dollars. See Customs USA, Fiscal Year 1987, p.40. In the routine discharge of their duties, many Customs employees have direct contact with those who traffic in drugs for profit. Drug import operations, often directed by sophisticated criminal syndicates, United States v. Mendenhall, 446 U.S. 544, 561-562, 100 S. Ct. 1870, 1880-1881, 64 L. Ed. 2d 497 (1980) (Powell, J., concurring), may be effected by violence or its threat. As a necessary response, many Customs operatives carry and use firearms in connection with their official duties. App. 109.

In December 1985, respondent, the Commissioner of Customs,

established a Drug Screening Task Force to explore the possibility of implementing a drug screening program within the Service. Id., at 11. After extensive research and consultation with experts in the field, the Task Force concluded "that drug screening through urinalysis is technologically reliable, valid and accurate." Ibid. Citing this conclusion, the Commissioner announced his intention to require drug tests of employees who applied for, or occupied, certain positions within the Service. Id., at 10-11. The Commissioner stated his belief that "Customs is largely drug-free," but noted also that "unfortunately no segment of society is immune from the threat of illegal drug use." Id., at 10. Drug interdiction has become the agency's primary enforcement mission, and the Commissioner stressed that "there is no room in the Customs Service for those who break the laws prohibiting the possession and use of illegal drugs." Ibid.

In May 1986, the Commissioner announced implementation of the drug-testing program. Drug tests were made a condition of placement or employment for positions that meet one or more of three criteria. The first is direct involvement in drug interdiction or enforcement of related laws, an activity the Commissioner deemed fraught with obvious dangers to the mission of the agency and the lives of customs agents. Id., at 17, 113. The second criterion is a requirement that the incumbent carry firearms, as the Commissioner concluded that "[p]ublic safety demands that employees who carry deadly arms and are prepared to make instant life or death decisions be drug free." Id., at 113. The third criterion is a requirement for the incumbent to handle "classified" material, which the Commissioner determined might fall into the hands of smugglers if accessible to employees who, by reason of their own illegal drug use, are susceptible to bribery or blackmail. Id., at 114.

After an employee qualifies for a position covered by the Customs testing program, the Service advises him by letter that his final selection is contingent upon successful completion of drug screening. An independent contractor contacts the employee to fix the time and place for collecting the sample. On reporting for the test, the employee must produce photographic identification and remove any outer garments, such as a coat or a jacket, and personal belongings. The employee may produce the sample behind a partition, or in the privacy of a bathroom stall if he so chooses. To ensure against adulteration of the specimen, or substitution of a sample from another person, a monitor of the same sex as the employee remains close at hand to listen for the normal sounds of urination. Dye is added to the toilet water to prevent the employee from using the water to adulterate the sample. . . .

Customs employees who test positive for drugs and who can offer no satisfactory explanation are subject to dismissal from the Service.

III. Drug and Alcohol Abuse and Dependence   1181

Test results may not, however, be turned over to any other agency, including criminal prosecutors, without the employee's written consent.

B

Petitioners, a union of federal employees and a union official, commenced this suit in the United States District Court for the Eastern District of Louisiana on behalf of current Customs Service employees who seek covered positions. Petitioners alleged that the Customs Service drug-testing program violated, inter alia, the Fourth Amendment. The District Court agreed. 649 F. Supp. 380 (1986). The court acknowledged "the legitimate governmental interest in a drug-free work place and work force," but concluded that "the drug testing plan constitutes an overly intrusive policy of searches and seizures without probable cause or reasonable suspicion, in violation of legitimate expectations of privacy." Id., at 387. The court enjoined the drug testing program, and ordered the Customs Service not to require drug tests of any applicants for covered positions.

A divided panel of the United States Court of Appeals for the Fifth Circuit vacated the injunction. 816 F.2d 170 (1987). The court agreed with petitioners that the drug screening program, by requiring an employee to produce a urine sample for chemical testing, effects a search within the meaning of the Fourth Amendment. The court held further that the searches required by the Commissioner's directive are reasonable under the Fourth Amendment. It first noted that "[t]he Service has attempted to minimize the intrusiveness of the search" by not requiring visual observation of the act of urination and by affording notice to the employee that he will be tested. Id., at 177. The court also considered it significant that the program limits discretion in determining which employees are to be tested, ibid., and noted that the tests are an aspect of the employment relationship. Id., at 178.

The court further found that the Government has a strong interest in detecting drug use among employees who meet the criteria of the Customs program. It reasoned that drug use by covered employees casts substantial doubt on their ability to discharge their duties honestly and vigorously, undermining public confidence in the integrity of the Service and concomitantly impairing the Service's efforts to enforce the drug laws. Id., at 178. Illicit drug users, the court found, are susceptible to bribery and blackmail, may be tempted to divert for their own use portions of any drug shipments they interdict, and may, if required to carry firearms, "endanger the safety of their fellow agents, as well as their own, when their performance is impaired by drug use." Ibid. "Considering the nature and responsibilities of the jobs for which applicants are being considered at Customs and the limited scope of the search," the court stated, "the exaction of consent as a condition of assignment to the new job is not unreasonable." Id., at 179.

The dissenting judge concluded that the Customs program is not an effective method for achieving the Service's goals. He argued principally that an employee "given a five day notification of a test date need only abstain from drug use to prevent being identified as a user." Id., at 184. He noted also that persons already employed in sensitive positions are not subject to the test. Ibid. Because he did not believe the Customs program can achieve its purposes, the dissenting judge found it unreasonable under the Fourth Amendment.

We granted certiorari. 485 U.S. — , 108 S. Ct. 1072, 99 L. Ed. 2d 232 (1988). We now affirm so much of the judgment of the court of appeals as upheld the testing of employees directly involved in drug interdiction or required to carry firearms. We vacate the judgment to the extent it upheld the testing of applicants for positions requiring the incumbent to handle classified materials, and remand for further proceedings.

II

In Skinner v. Railway Labor Executives Assn., — U.S. — , — - — , 109 S. Ct. 1402, 1412-1413, — L. Ed. 2d — , decided today, we hold that federal regulations requiring employees of private railroads to produce urine samples for chemical testing implicate the Fourth Amendment, as those tests invade reasonable expectations of privacy. Our earlier cases have settled that the Fourth Amendment protects individuals from unreasonable searches conducted by the Government, even when the Government acts as an employer, O'Connor v. Ortega, 480 U.S. 709, 717, 107 S. Ct. 1492, 1498, 94 L. Ed. 2d 714 (1987) (plurality opinion); see id., at 731, 107 S. Ct., at 1505 (SCALIA, J., concurring in judgment), and, in view of our holding in *Railway Labor Executives* that urine tests are searches, it follows that the Customs Service's drug testing program must meet the reasonableness requirement of the Fourth Amendment.

While we have often emphasized, and reiterate today, that a search must be supported, as a general matter, by a warrant issued upon probable cause, see, e.g., Griffin v. Wisconsin, 483 U.S. 868, — , 107 S. Ct. 3164, 3167, 97 L. Ed. 2d 709 (1987); United States v. Karo, 468 U.S. 705, 717, 104 S. Ct. 3296, 3304, 82 L. Ed. 2d 530 (1984), our decision in *Railway Labor Executives* reaffirms the longstanding principle that neither a warrant nor probable cause, nor, indeed, any measure of individualized suspicion, is an indispensable component of reasonableness in every circumstance. Ante, at 1413-

1416. See also New Jersey v. T.L.O., 469 U.S. 325, 342, n.8, 105 S. Ct. 733, 743, n.8, 83 L. Ed. 2d 720 (1985); United States v. Martinez-Fuerte, 428 U.S. 543, 556-561, 96 S. Ct. 3074, 3082-3085, 49 L. Ed. 2d 1116 (1976). As we note in *Railway Labor Executives,* our cases establish that where a Fourth Amendment intrusion serves special governmental needs, beyond the normal need for law enforcement, it is necessary to balance the individual's privacy expectations against the Government's interests to determine whether it is impractical to require a warrant or some level of individualized suspicion in the particular context. Ante, at 1413-1414.

It is clear that the Customs Service's drug testing program is not designed to serve the ordinary needs of law enforcement. Test results may not be used in a criminal prosecution of the employee without the employee's consent. The purposes of the program are to deter drug use among those eligible for promotion to sensitive positions within the Service and to prevent the promotion of drug users to those positions. These substantial interests, no less than the Government's concern for safe rail transportation at issue in *Railway Labor Executives,* present a special need that may justify departure from the ordinary warrant and probable cause requirements.

A

Petitioners do not contend that a warrant is required by the balance of privacy and governmental interests in this context, nor could any such contention withstand scrutiny. We have recognized before that requiring the Government to procure a warrant for every work-related intrusion "would conflict with 'the common-sense realization that government offices could not function if every employment decision became a constitutional matter.' " O'Connor v. Ortega, supra, 480 U.S., at 722, 107 S. Ct., at 1500, quoting Connick v. Myers, 461 U.S. 138, 143, 103 S. Ct. 1684, 1688, 75 L. Ed. 2d 708 (1983). See also id., 480 U.S., at 732, 107 S. Ct., at 1506 (SCALIA, J., concurring in judgment); New Jersey v. T.L.O., supra, 469 U.S., at 340, 105 S. Ct., at 742 (noting that "[t]he warrant requirement . . . is unsuited to the school environment: requiring a teacher to obtain a warrant before searching a child suspected of an infraction of school rules (or of the criminal law) would unduly interfere with the maintenance of the swift and informal disciplinary procedures needed in the schools"). Even if Customs Service employees are more likely to be familiar with the procedures required to obtain a warrant than most other Government workers, requiring a warrant in this context would serve only to divert valuable agency resources from the Service's primary mission. The Customs Service has been entrusted with pressing responsibilities, and its mission would be compromised if it were required to seek search warrants in connection with routine, yet sensitive, employment decisions.

Furthermore, a warrant would provide little or nothing in the way of additional protection of personal privacy. A warrant serves primarily to advise the citizen that an intrusion is authorized by law and limited in its permissible scope and to interpose a neutral magistrate between the citizen and the law enforcement officer "engaged in the often competitive enterprise of ferreting out crime." Johnson v. United States, 333 U.S. 10, 14, 68 S. Ct. 367, 369, 92 L. Ed. 436 (1948). But in the present context, "the circumstances justifying toxicological testing and the permissible limits of such intrusions are defined narrowly and specifically . . . , and doubtless are well known to covered employees." Ante, at 1415. Under the Customs program, every employee who seeks a transfer to a covered position knows that he must take a drug test, and is likewise aware of the procedures the Service must follow in administering the test. A covered employee is simply not subject "to the discretion of the official in the field." Camara v. Municipal Court, 387 U.S. 523, 532, 87 S. Ct. 1727, 1732, 18 L. Ed. 2d 930 (1967). The process becomes automatic when the employee elects to apply for, and thereafter pursue, a covered position. Because the Service does not make a discretionary determination to search based on a judgment that certain conditions are present, there are simply "no special facts for a neutral magistrate to evaluate." South Dakota v. Opperman, 428 U.S. 364, 383, 96 S. Ct. 3092, 3104, 49 L. Ed. 2d 1000 (1976) (POWELL, J., concurring).

B

Even where it is reasonable to dispense with the warrant requirement in the particular circumstances, a search ordinarily must be based on probable cause. . . .

Our precedents have settled that, in certain limited circumstances, the Government's need to discover such latent or hidden conditions, or to prevent their development, is sufficiently compelling to justify the intrusion on privacy entailed by conducting such searches without any measure of individualized suspicion. E.g., ante, at 1416-1417. We think the Government's need to conduct the suspicionless searches required by the Customs program outweighs the privacy interests of employees engaged directly in drug interdiction, and of those who otherwise are required to carry firearms.

The Customs Service is our Nation's first line of defense against one of the greatest problems affecting the health and welfare of our population. We have adverted before to "the veritable national crisis in law enforcement caused by smuggling of illicit narcotics." United States v. Montoya de Hernandez, 473 U.S. 531, 538, 105 S. Ct. 3304,

III. Drug and Alcohol Abuse and Dependence

3309, 87 L. Ed. 2d 381 (1985). See also Florida v. Royer, 460 U.S. 491, 513, 103 S. Ct. 1319, 1332, 75 L. Ed. 2d 229 (BLACKMUN, J., dissenting). Our cases also reflect the traffickers' seemingly inexhaustible repertoire of deceptive practices and elaborate schemes for importing narcotics, e.g., United States v. Montoya de Hernandez, supra, 473 U.S., at 538-539, 105 S. Ct., at 3309-3310; United States v. Ramsey, 431 U.S. 606, 608-609, 97 S. Ct. 1972, 1974-1975, 52 L. Ed. 2d 617 (1977). The record in this case confirms that, through the adroit selection of source locations, smuggling routes, and increasingly elaborate methods of concealment, drug traffickers have managed to bring into this country increasingly large quantities of illegal drugs. App. 111. The record also indicates, and it is well known, that drug smugglers do not hesitate to use violence to protect their lucrative trade and avoid apprehension. Id., at 109. . . .

It is readily apparent that the Government has a compelling interest in ensuring that front-line interdiction personnel are physically fit, and have unimpeachable integrity and judgment. Indeed, the Government's interest here is at least as important as its interest in searching travelers entering the country. We have long held that travelers seeking to enter the country may be stopped and required to submit to a routine search without probable cause, or even founded suspicion, "because of national self protection reasonably requiring one entering the country to identify himself as entitled to come in, and his belongings as effects which may be lawfully brought in." Carroll v. United States, 267 U.S. 132, 154, 45 S. Ct. 280, 285, 69 L. Ed. 543 (1925). See also United States v. Montoya de Hernandez, supra, 473 U.S., at 538, 105 S. Ct., at 3308; United States v. Ramsey, supra, 431 U.S., at 617-619, 97 S. Ct., at 1979-1980. This national interest in self protection could be irreparably damaged if those charged with safeguarding it were, because of their own drug use, unsympathetic to their mission of interdicting narcotics. A drug user's indifference to the Service's basic mission or, even worse, his active complicity with the malefactors, can facilitate importation of sizable drug shipments or block apprehension of dangerous criminals. The public interest demands effective measures to bar drug users from positions directly involving the interdiction of illegal drugs.

The public interest likewise demands effective measures to prevent the promotion of drug users to positions that require the incumbent to carry a firearm, even if the incumbent is not engaged directly in the interdiction of drugs. Customs employees who may use deadly force plainly "discharge duties fraught with such risks of injury to others that even a momentary lapse of attention can have disastrous consequences." Ante, at 1419. We agree with the Government that the public should not bear the risk that employees who may suffer from impaired perception and judgment will be promoted to positions where they may need to employ deadly force. Indeed, ensuring against the creation of this dangerous risk will itself further Fourth Amendment values, as the use of deadly force may violate the Fourth Amendment in certain circumstances. . . .

Against these valid public interests we must weigh the interference with individual liberty that results from requiring these classes of employees to undergo a urine test. The interference with individual privacy that results from the collection of a urine sample for subsequent chemical analysis could be substantial in some circumstances. Ante, at 1418. We have recognized, however, that the "operational realities of the workplace" may render entirely reasonable certain work-related intrusions by supervisors and co-workers that might be viewed as unreasonable in other contexts. See O'Connor v. Ortega, 480 U.S., at 717, 107 S. Ct., at 1498; id., at 732, 107 S. Ct., at 1506 (SCALIA, J., concurring in judgment). While these operational realities will rarely affect an employee's expectations of privacy with respect to searches of his person, or of personal effects that the employee may bring to the workplace, id., at 716, 725, 107 S. Ct., at 1498, 1502, it is plain that certain forms of public employment may diminish privacy expectations even with respect to such personal searches. Employees of the United States Mint, for example, should expect to be subject to certain routine personal searches when they leave the workplace every day. Similarly, those who join our military or intelligence services may not only be required to give what in other contexts might be viewed as extraordinary assurances of trustworthiness and probity, but also may expect intrusive inquiries into their physical fitness for those special positions. . . .

We think Customs employees who are directly involved in the interdiction of illegal drugs or who are required to carry firearms in the line of duty likewise have a diminished expectation of privacy in respect to the intrusions occasioned by a urine test. Unlike most private citizens or government employees in general, employees involved in drug interdiction reasonably should expect effective inquiry into their fitness and probity. Much the same is true of employees who are required to carry firearms. Because successful performance of their duties depends uniquely on their judgment and dexterity, these employees cannot reasonably expect to keep from the Service personal information that bears directly on their fitness. . . . While reasonable tests designed to elicit this information doubtless infringe some privacy expectations, we do not believe these expectations outweigh the Government's compelling interests in safety and in the integrity of our borders.

Without disparaging the importance of the governmental interests that support the suspicionless searches of these employees, petitioners nevertheless contend that the Service's drug testing program is un-

III. Drug and Alcohol Abuse and Dependence

reasonable in two particulars. First, petitioners argue that the program is unjustified because it is not based on a belief that testing will reveal any drug use by covered employees. In pressing this argument, petitioners point out that the Service's testing scheme was not implemented in response to any perceived drug problem among Customs employees, and that the program actually has not led to the discovery of a significant number of drug users. Brief for Petitioners 37, 44; Tr. of Oral Arg. 11-12, 20-21. Counsel for petitioners informed us at oral argument that no more than 5 employees out of 3,600 have tested positive for drugs. Id., at 11. Second, petitioners contend that the Service's scheme is not a "sufficiently productive mechanism to justify [its] intrusion upon Fourth Amendment interests," Delaware v. Prouse, 440 U.S., at 648, 658-659, 99 S. Ct. at 1391, 1398-1399, because illegal drug users can avoid detection with ease by temporary abstinence or by surreptitious adulteration of their urine specimens. Brief for Petitioners 46-47. These contentions are unpersuasive.

Petitioners' first contention evinces an unduly narrow view of the context in which the Service's testing program was implemented. Petitioners do not dispute, nor can there be doubt, that drug abuse is one of the most serious problems confronting our society today. There is little reason to believe that American workplaces are immune from this pervasive social problem, as is amply illustrated by our decision in *Railway Labor Executives.* See also Masino v. United States, 589 F.2d 1048, 1050, 218 Ct. Cl. 531 (1978) (describing marijuana use by two Customs Inspectors). Detecting drug impairment on the part of employees can be a difficult task, especially where, as here, it is not feasible to subject employees and their work-product to the kind of day-to-day scrutiny that is the norm in more traditional office environments. Indeed, the almost unique mission of the Service gives the Government a compelling interest in ensuring that many of these covered employees do not use drugs even off-duty, for such use creates risks of bribery and blackmail against which the Government is entitled to guard. In light of the extraordinary safety and national security hazards that would attend the promotion of drug users to positions that require the carrying of firearms or the interdiction of controlled substances, the Service's policy of deterring drug users from seeking such promotions cannot be deemed unreasonable.

The mere circumstance that all but a few of the employees tested are entirely innocent of wrongdoing does not impugn the program's validity. . . .

We think petitioners' second argument — that the Service's testing program is ineffective because employees may attempt to deceive the test by a brief abstention before the test date, or by adulterating their urine specimens — overstates the case. As the Court of Appeals noted, addicts may be unable to abstain even for a limited period of time, or may be unaware of the "fade-away effect" of certain drugs. 816 F.2d, at 180. More importantly, the avoidance techniques suggested by petitioners are fraught with uncertainty and risks for those employees who venture to attempt them. A particular employee's pattern of elimination for a given drug cannot be predicted with perfect accuracy, and, in any event, this information is not likely to be known or available to the employee. Petitioners' own expert indicated below that the time it takes for particular drugs to become undetectable in urine can vary widely depending on the individual, and may extend for as long as 22 days. App. 66. See also ante, at 1420 (noting Court of Appeals' reliance on certain academic literature that indicates that the testing of urine can discover drug use " 'for . . . weeks after the ingestion of the drug' "). Thus; contrary to petitioners' suggestion, no employee reasonably can expect to deceive the test by the simple expedient of abstaining after the test date is assigned. Nor can he expect attempts at adulteration to succeed, in view of the precautions taken by the sample collector to ensure the integrity of the sample. In all the circumstances, we are persuaded that the program bears a close and substantial relation to the Service's goal of deterring drug users from seeking promotion to sensitive positions.

In sum, we believe the Government has demonstrated that its compelling interests in safeguarding our borders and the public safety outweigh the privacy expectations of employees who seek to be promoted to positions that directly involve the interdiction of illegal drugs or that require the incumbent to carry a firearm. We hold that the testing of these employees is reasonable under the Fourth Amendment.

C

We are unable, on the present record, to assess the reasonableness of the Government's testing program insofar as it covers employees who are required "to handle classified material." App. 17. We readily agree that the Government has a compelling interest in protecting truly sensitive information from those who, "under compulsion of circumstances or for other reasons, . . . might compromise [such] information." Department of the Navy v. Egan, 484 U.S. 518, —, 108 S. Ct. 818, 824, 98 L. Ed. 2d 918 (1988). See also United States v. Robel, 389 U.S. 258, 267, 88 S. Ct. 419, 425, 19 L. Ed. 2d 508 (1967) ("We have recognized that, while the Constitution protects against invasions of individual rights, it does not withdraw from the Government the power to safeguard its vital interests. . . . The Government can deny access to its secrets to those who would use such information to harm the Nation"). We also agree that employees who seek promotions to positions where they would handle sensitive

III. Drug and Alcohol Abuse and Dependence 1189

information can be required to submit to a urine test under the Service's screening program, especially if the positions covered under this category require background investigations, medical examinations, or other intrusions that may be expected to diminish their expectations of privacy in respect of a urinalysis test. . . .

It is not clear, however, whether the category defined by the Service's testing directive encompasses only those Customs employees likely to gain access to sensitive information. Employees who are tested under the Service's scheme include those holding such diverse positions as "Accountant," "Accounting Technician," "Animal Caretaker," "Attorney (All)," "Baggage Clerk," "Co-op Student (All)," "Electric Equipment Repairer," "Mail Clerk/Assistant," and "Messenger." App. 42-43. We assume these positions were selected for coverage under the Service's testing program by reason of the incumbent's access to "classified" information, as it is not clear that they would fall under either of the two categories we have already considered. Yet it is not evident that those occupying these positions are likely to gain access to sensitive information, and this apparent discrepancy raises in our minds the question whether the Service has defined this category of employees more broadly than necessary to meet the purposes of the Commissioner's directive.

We cannot resolve this ambiguity on the basis of the record before us, and we think it is appropriate to remand the case to the court of appeals for such proceedings as may be necessary to clarify the scope of this category of employees subject to testing. Upon remand the court of appeals should examine the criteria used by the Service in determining what materials are classified and in deciding whom to test under this rubric. In assessing the reasonableness of requiring tests of these employees, the court should also consider pertinent information bearing upon the employees' privacy expectations, as well as the supervision to which these employees are already subject.

III

Where the Government requires its employees to produce urine samples to be analyzed for evidence of illegal drug use, the collection and subsequent chemical analysis of such samples are searches that must meet the reasonableness requirement of the Fourth Amendment. Because the testing program adopted by the Customs Service is not designed to serve the ordinary needs of law enforcement, we have balanced the public interest in the Service's testing program against the privacy concerns implicated by the tests, without reference to our usual presumption in favor of the procedures specified in the Warrant Clause, to assess whether the tests required by Customs are reasonable.

We hold that the suspicionless testing of employees who apply for promotion to positions directly involving the interdiction of illegal drugs, or to positions which require the incumbent to carry a firearm, is reasonable. The Government's compelling interests in preventing the promotion of drug users to positions where they might endanger the integrity of our Nation's borders or the life of the citizenry outweigh the privacy interests of those who seek promotion to these positions, who enjoy a diminished expectation of privacy by virtue of the special, and obvious, physical and ethical demands of those positions. We do not decide whether testing those who apply for promotion to positions where they would handle "classified" information is reasonable because we find the record inadequate for this purpose.

The judgment of the Court of Appeals for the Fifth Circuit is affirmed in part and vacated in part, and the case is remanded for further proceedings consistent with this opinion.

It is so ordered.

JUSTICE MARSHALL, with whom JUSTICE BRENNAN joins, dissenting.

JUSTICE SCALIA, with whom JUSTICE STEVENS joins, dissenting.

NOTES

Drug Testing Programs in Government Agencies and in Private Workplaces

1. The emphasis in programs of control, prevention, and treatment of abuse and dependence swings rapidly from one period to another, from one federal administration to another, as was indicated earlier in this chapter. One of the activities that has received much more emphasis in recent years is periodic and random drug testing of employees in government and private industry. A Gallup survey in 1988 of 1000 companies in the United States indicated that 28 percent of the larger companies (over 5000 employees) used some type of drug testing of employees periodically. Among the companies not utilizing testing programs, 14 percent indicated they were planning to initiate testing within the year. Gallup Organization, Drug Testing At Work: A Survey of American Organizations (1988). Another survey produced similar responses from American industry. A survey of the Fortune 500 companies found that over 25 percent required drug testing of new job applicants, current employees, or both. See Lacayo, Putting Them to the Test, Time Magazine, October 12, 1985, p.61.

2. In government workplaces, drug testing programs have been installed in recent years from local communities, to state agencies, to the federal level. In municipalities and state agencies, the efforts have been concentrated on law enforcement, licensing, and fire-fighting departments. Two important court cases, however, involved such

III. Drug and Alcohol Abuse and Dependence   1191

diverse activities as horse racing, Shoemaker v. Handel, 619 F. Supp. 1089 (D.N.J. 1985), and nuclear power plants, Rushton v. Nebraska Pub. Power Dist., 653 F. Supp. 1510 (D. Neb. 1987). In most of the programs, an effort is made to stress the *sensitivity* of the work (in terms of protecting the community or of the magnitude of the financial issues involved) or the *exemplary nature* of the work (in terms of setting an example for other government agencies or the public). Do these distinctions matter? Is there any way to predict the impact of any particular employee's decision making or other activity; generally, or on any given day? The federal government certainly does not seem to be making its policy in any selective manner. President Reagan issued an Executive Order on September 15, 1986, requiring all federal agencies to introduce programs to achieve a "drug-free workplace" throughout the federal government. Executive Order, No. 12564, 51 Fed. Reg. 32, 889 (1986). The program includes authority to install compulsory drug testing for all new job applicants and for current employees, at least when there is suspicion of drug use. It was declared that persons who use illegal drugs would no longer be considered "suitable" for federal employment. In November of 1986, further guidelines were adopted despite doubts in several federal agencies about their constitutionality. Williams, Reagan Drug Testing Plan to Start Despite Court Rulings Opposing It, N.Y. Times, Nov. 29, 1986, p.1. The Executive Order did make efforts to meet objections to drug testing procedures that had been brought out in earlier court cases. The testing must be done in a manner to assure individual privacy unless the agency has reason to believe that the person would alter or replace the specimen. In the agencies themselves, the Order returns again to issues of sensitivity of particular activities. Although the plan is sweeping in regard to its general policy, it leaves implementation to individual agency heads based upon the agency's "mission" and the danger to the public health, safety, or national security that would result from failure of its employees to carry out their responsibilities.

3. There have been numerous other court challenges to the federal government's drug testing programs based upon the Executive Order of President Reagan. The program of the Department of Transportation has been brought into court by different parties in at least 22 cases. See Cushman, Opposition is Slowing Drug Testing Programs for Transportation Workers, N.Y. Times, Aug. 21, 1989, p.A15. These cases involve several agencies, most of them regulatory and law enforcement in character, such as the U.S. Coast Guard, the Federal Aviation Administration, the Federal Railway Administration, the Federal Highway Administration, and the Urban Mass Transportation Administration. Most recently the Department's comprehensive mandatory and suspicionless drug testing was held reasonable

and consistent with the Fourth Amendment. American Fed. Gov. Employees v. Skinner, 885 F.2d 884 (D.C. Cir. 1989).

4. There are other aspects of the governmental anti-drug programs beyond testing for evidence of current use. What significance should be given to previous illegal use of drugs? Should the government apply its "exemplary" criterion to prior conduct? The issue was brought into public focus when Federal Judge Douglas Ginsburg, after admitting that he had smoked marihuana some years earlier while on the faculty at Harvard Law School, withdrew from consideration for appointment to the United States Supreme Court. Should all applicants for appointment to the federal judicial bench be asked about prior illegal drug use? All applicants for appointment to the federal government as attorneys? As law enforcement or Secret Service personnel? Should answers in the affirmative automatically bar the applicant from appointment? How widespread should a policy of questioning and non-appointment be in the federal establishment? See Willard, Toward a Drug-Free Work Place, 34 Fed. Bar News & J. 74 (1987).

5. Drug testing programs are very expensive to install and to operate. When accompanied by an "employee assistance program," that is, a program of counseling and referrals for treatment, the costs are even greater. In addition to a general policy of a "drug-free workplace," are there clear benefits to industry and government in testing and seeking to prevent drug abuse on the job? Drug abuse and alcohol abuse are claimed to account for between $60 and $100 billion annually in productivity loss annually in the United States. There are other costs in increased health insurance premiums, workers' compensation, employee theft, and employee morale problems. See Economic Costs to Society of Alcohol and Drug Abuse and Mental Illness, D.H.H.S. Pub. No. (ADM) 86-1477 (1986). There are also issues of employer legal liability in tort for injuries to third parties by reckless or negligent employees who were under the influence of alcohol or other drugs at the time of the injury. See, for example, Otis Engineering Co. v. Clark, 668 S.W.2d 307 (Tex. 1983).

Hon v. Stroh Brewery Co.
835 F.2d 510 (3d Cir. 1988)

Stapleton, Circuit Judge.

In this product liability, diversity action, appellant Nancy Hon seeks recovery for the death of her husband, William. The district court entered summary judgment for appellee Stroh Brewery Company (Stroh). See Hon v. Stroh Brewery Co., 665 F. Supp. 1140 (M.D. Pa. 1987). Because we find that triable issues of fact exist, we will reverse.

III. Drug and Alcohol Abuse and Dependence

I

It is undisputed that William Hon died from pancreatitis at the age of 26. Prior to contracting this disease, Mr. Hon had been in excellent health. Mrs. Hon claims that her husband's pancreatitis resulted from his consumption of alcohol.

The record contains evidence of Mr. Hon's drinking habits only for the six years immediately preceding his death. During that time, according to the evidence tendered by Mrs. Hon, Mr. Hon's alcohol consumption consisted mainly of Old Milwaukee Beer and Old Milwaukee Light Beer, both of which are manufactured by Stroh. He may also have consumed other brands of beer from time to time and only occasionally drank hard liquor. Mr. Hon consumed beer at the rate of two to three cans per night on an average of four nights per week. Mr. Hon never gave a reason for preferring Old Milwaukee other than its taste. In particular, he never indicated that he was in any way influenced by Stroh's advertisements for its beer. . . .

In response to Stroh's summary judgment motion, Mrs. Hon introduced an affidavit of Dr. Harry Plotnick, a toxicologist and pharmacologist.[1] In his affidavit, Dr. Plotnick expresses his opinion that Mr. Hon's drinking caused his pancreatitis.[2] Dr. Plotnick then goes on to state several other opinions, which may be summarized as follows: (1) the understanding shared by members of the public is that excessive *and* prolonged use of alcoholic beverages is likely to result in disease, principally of the liver; (2) Mr. Hon's case was not

---

1. Dr. Plotnick is a registered pharmacist with a Ph.D. in toxicology. Since 1977, he has been engaged in the private practice of law in a general civil practice. Since Stroh did not challenge Dr. Plotnick's expertise for purposes of the motion of summary judgment, we assume *arguendo* that he is an expert qualified to testify on all of the matters set forth in his affidavit.

2. In pertinent part Dr. Plotnick's affidavit states:

Based on my review of these records, it is my professional opinion, based upon a reasonable degree of scientific certainty, that the death of William Hon from pancreatitis, complicated with hepatic disease and gastric ulcerations, was the direct result of the ingestion by the decedent of alcohol-containing beverages over a prolonged period of time. The patient history data contained in the medical records reviewed suggests that Mr. Hon's consumption of alcoholic beverages would be considered moderate. It is this moderate consumption of alcohol for a prolonged period of time which resulted in the alcoholic pancreatitis to which Mr. Hon succumbed.

Members of the public generally believe that the excessive and prolonged use of alcohol results in the development of disease. In my experience, laymen consider liver disease to be the principal or sole malady associated with such excessive and prolonged use of alcoholic beverages. Such is not the case, however, as clearly demonstrated by the case of Mr. Hon. His use of alcohol appears to have been prolonged, but was not, in my view, excessive. Additionally, Mr. Hon died as a result of pancreatitis, not hepatic disease. The general public's concept of alcohol-related disease is archaic. Medical science has clearly established that liver, pancreatic, gastrointestinal, and neurological disease are the result of either excessive or prolonged consumption of alcoholic beverages.

within the risk thus appreciated by the public both because (a) his use was prolonged but not excessive and (b) his disease was of the pancreas; and (3) the public's understanding is "archaic" because medical science has now established that *either* excessive *or* prolonged, even though moderate, use of alcohol may result in diseases of many kinds, including pancreatic disease.

Mrs. Hon also filed an affidavit of Dr. Jack Marks, a medical doctor, which states that "small amounts of alcohol taken for a relatively brief period of time are occasionally lethal." Dr. Marks relies in part on medical literature reporting that "no threshold of toxicity can be established with ethanol consumption." App. at 188a-189a.

Finally, Mrs. Hon tendered television advertising boards showing commercials that have been aired to promote Old Milwaukee beer. See App. at 173a-184a. Mrs. Hon offered these advertising boards to show that Stroh has attempted to cultivate a belief among the consuming public that moderate consumption of its product is safe. . . .

The district court granted summary judgment to Stroh because it concluded "as a matter of law that [Mr. Hon] knew or should have known that the amount of beer that he consumed was potentially lethal." 665 F. Supp. at 1146. It erred in reaching this conclusion. On the record before the district court, a trier of fact could properly find that while the amount of beer consumed by Mr. Hon was potentially lethal, that fact was known neither to him nor to the consuming public. For this reason, we conclude that there is a material dispute of fact as to whether Stroh's beer without a warning is safe for its intended purpose and, accordingly, that summary judgment was inappropriate.

Dr. Marks' and Dr. Plotnick's affidavits provide evidence tending to show that beer in the quantity and manner Mr. Hon consumed it can have fatal consequences. Nothing in the record suggests that Mr. Hon was aware of this fact, however. Moreover, Dr. Plotnick's affidavit tends to show that the general public is unaware that consumption at this level and in this manner can have any serious adverse effects. There is no evidence in the record that the public appreciates any hazard that may be associated with this kind of consumption.

In addition, we conclude that the story boards of Stroh's commercials provide additional evidence from which a jury could conclude that the general public is unaware of the hazard that allegedly led to Mr. Hon's death.[4] If a jury finds that Stroh's marketing of its

---

4. Stroh maintains that its advertisements are irrelevant in this case because there is no evidence that Mr. Hon relied on these advertisements. We disagree. Where the duty to warn is at issue, the appropriate standard looks to the effect of warnings or nullifying advertisements on the general public, as well as on the individual plaintiff.

III. Drug and Alcohol Abuse and Dependence

product has effectively taught the consuming public that consumption of beer on the order of eight to twelve cans of beer per week can be a part of the "good life" and is properly associated with healthy, robust activities, this conclusion would be an important consideration for the jury in determining whether an express warning was necessary to make Old Milwaukee beer safe for its intended purpose. Cf. Baldino v. Castagna, 505 Pa. 239, 478 A.2d 807, 810 (1984) (jury may consider whether a manufacturer has nullified warning that has been given by its promotion of the product); Incollingo v. Ewing, 444 Pa. 263, 282 A.2d 206, 220 (1971) ("Action designed to stimulate the use of a potentially dangerous product must be considered in testing the adequacy of a warning as to when and how the product should *not* be used. . . ."). Based on this evidence we believe there is a material dispute of fact as to whether the sale of Stroh's beer products with no warning was safe for its intended purpose.

It is true, as Stroh stresses, that Mrs. Hon cites no case holding a brewer strictly liable for a failure to warn. We find this fact neither surprising nor at odds with our analysis, however. So far as we have been able to ascertain, there is no case in which the plaintiff allegedly consumed beer in the quantity and manner reflected in this record. The fact that such a case has not been litigated is explainable on either of two grounds. It may be, as Mrs. Hon contends, that consumers are unaware of the risk created by the consumption of beer in this manner. On the other hand, it may be, as Stroh's answer indicates it will attempt to prove, that Mr. Hon's quantity and manner of beer consumption poses no significant risk of bodily injury. In this context, the absence of authority for Mrs. Hon's position provides no persuasive reason to depart from the analysis suggested by the Pennsylvania authorities we have discussed above.

III

We will vacate the summary judgment granted to Stroh and remand the case to the district court for further proceedings consistent with this opinion.

NOTES

Consumer Warnings and Product Labels for Alcoholic Beverages, Drugs, and Tobacco

1. The *Hon* case was the first American decision by a higher court allowing a claim to reach a jury against a manufacturer of alcoholic beverages on a theory of failure to warn of the severely adverse effects of alcohol consumption. As the defendant beer com-

pany argued in the *Hon* litigation, other courts have denied a duty to warn because the dangers of drinking alcoholic beverages is "open and obvious." Under these conditions, the Restatement of Torts, Second, §402A requirement of a warning to the consumer of the inherent danger of the product is not applicable. See the leading cases, Garrison v. Heublein, 673 F.2d 189 (7th Cir. 1982); Abernathy v. Shenley Ind., 556 F.2d 242 (4th Cir. 1977).

2. Most of the research on the dangers of alcohol consumption has dealt with long-term drinking in substantial quantities. When the drinking is heavy and prolonged, there is no doubt of the extremely damaging results to internal organs and the brain. Moderate drinking, however, has been found not only *not* lethal or highly damaging, but often of general benefit to the individual (as compared to total abstinence) in matters such as the development of heart disease and mental distress. These findings are broad in nature over population groups, of course; results differ with individuals. On the effects of moderate alcohol consumption, see Neuropsychology of Alcoholism: Implications for Diagnosis and Treatment (Parsons, Butters & Nathan eds. 1986); Mendelson & Mello, Alcohol: Use and Abuse in America (1985); Biomedical Processes and the Consequences of Alcohol Use (D.H.H.S. Alcohol and Health Mon. Series, 1982). See also Guralnick & Kaplan, Predictions of Healthy Aging: Prospective Evidence from the Alameda County Study, 79 J. Pub. Health 703 (1989). However, also see Harper, Kril and Daly, Does a "Moderate" Alcohol Intake Damage the Brain?, 51 J. Neurol. Neurosurg. and Psychia. 909 (1988); Willett, Stampfer et al, Moderate Alcohol Consumption and the Risk of Breast Cancer, 316 N. Engl. J. Med. 1174 (1987).

3. The Federal Congress, after much consideration and compromise, has adopted legislation requiring a "warning label" on alcoholic beverages, effective on November 16, 1989. See Alcoholic Beverage Labeling Act of 1988, Pub. L. No. 100-690, Title VIII. What should such labels say? Should they warn against the adverse health effects of all drinking? Should they warn only of "excessive drinking"? Should warnings be specific for particular health risks or diseases? Should the labeling be limited to warnings relating to safety, such as the dangers of drinking and then operating motor vehicles, power boats, or airplanes? The wording adopted by the Congress is as follows:

GOVERNMENT WARNING

(1) According to the Surgeon General, women should not drink alcoholic beverages during pregnancy because of the risk of birth defects.
(2) Consumption of alcoholic beverages impairs your ability to drive a car or operate machinery and may cause health problems.

Final regulations governing various aspects of instructions to the alcoholic drug industry regarding placement of the label, legibility, type size, and so forth have now been adopted by the Bureau of Alcohol, Tobacco and Firearms of the Treasury Department. See 55 C.F.R. 5414, Feb. 14, 1990.

The federal legislation specifically prohibits the states from enacting any statement on alcoholic beverage labels other than the required statement set out above.

4. Most of the attention to warnings to the public (in publicly supported media) in recent years has concerned dangers from drinking and then operating motor vehicles or boats. (On the forensic science aspects of relating impaired driving capacity to alcohol consumption, see Chapter 3 at 106.)

As indicated in the labeling adopted by Congress, one of the areas in which alcoholic beverage warning labels may be most needed is in providing women with information on the extreme damage that can result to the growing fetus during pregnancy when the mother drinks excessively. This information may not be "open and obvious." See particularly E. Abel, Fetal Alcohol Syndrome (1987); E. Quilligan & N. Kretchmer, Fetal and Maternal Medicine (1980). See also Rosett, A Clinical Perspective on the Fetal Alcohol Syndrome, 4 Alcoh. Clin. and Exp. Res. 118 (1980); Clarren & Smith, Fetal Alcohol Syndrome, 298 New Eng. J. Med. 1063 (1978). The danger is greatest, of course, when the mother is an alcoholic and has considerable difficulty stopping drinking when she is pregnant. See also Alcohol and Women (N.I.A.A.A. Res. Mon. Series, 1980); Dalgren & Willander, Are Special Treatment Facilities for Female Alcoholics Needed?, 50 J. Studies Alcoh. 293 (1989) (a Swedish study).

5. The classic example of label warnings is the prescription drug field. Under the regulatory policy of the Federal Food and Drug Administration, each prescription drug carries a package-insert label with quite elaborate information on the methods of administering the drug, conditions for which the drug is recommended, as well as warnings about contra-indications for use and about known dangers and side-effects. The package inserts have considerable, although not totally controlling influence over the proper standard of accepted patient care related to the drug. See cases and commentary in Chapter 5, at 269-278.

Physicians did not, however, always accept this warning label system as universally as they seem to do today. In the 1960s, Dr. Walter Modell, a professor of pharmacology at Cornell Medical College, attacked the informational labels as "package stuffers" that were designed to stifle the clinical judgment of physicians. He wrote a series of articles on what he insisted was censorship on the part of the FDA. See for example, Modell, How to Stuff a Stuffer and Cook a Wolf, 8 Med. Tribune 1 (1967). See also Modell, Editorial: FDA Censorship, 8 Clin. Pharm. & Ther. 359 (1967).

In the prescription drug field, the courts have quite uniformly accepted the package-insert warnings to physicians as meeting the drug manufacturers' legal obligation. The physician is expected to be a "learned intermediary" between the company and the patient in protecting the patient and in providing direct information about the drug to the patient. The retail pharmacist is also a source of advice for drug consumers. On the learned intermediary role, see Kirk v. Michael Reese Hosp. and Med. Center at 427 of Chapter 5. There are exceptions to the practice of addressing warnings only to physicians as in the direct information on oral contraceptives, and in special situations such as public vaccination programs. See Reyes v. Wyeth Laboratories, 498 F.2d 1264 (5th Cir. 1974) *cert. denied*, 419 U.S. 1096 (1974). On oral contraceptives, see Pharmaceutical Man. Asso. v. F.D.A., 484 F. Supp. 1179 (1980).

6. The more apt comparison, of course, for the development of warning labels on alcoholic beverages is the warning label on packages of cigarettes and other tobacco products. The labels currently on cigarette packages warn of a variety of fatal and disabling conditions resulting from smoking. There is no identified threshold of "moderate smoking" that is not dangerous to health. Nearly all campaigns against smoking have targets of complete abstinence. There can be considerable personal gain in better health and more favorable long-term predictions of life expectancy from stopping smoking, even in people who have smoked regularly and excessively for many years. For a statistical review, see Osler, Colditz, & Kelly, The Economic Costs of Smoking and the Benefits of Quitting (1984).

Cigarette and cigar smoking has been in considerable decline in the United States since the first strong case was made against tobacco in the Surgeon General's Report in 1965. Up to 1965, more than half of American men and about one-third of American women smoked. By the mid-1980s, only about 25 percent (or less) of men smoked while about 29 percent of women still smoked. The bad news, however, was that the remaining smokers are much more apt to smoke excessively (25 or more cigarettes per day). These statistics prompted Surgeon General Koop in Congressional testimony in 1988 to assert that cigarette smoking was equally addictive as heroin. See also Reducing the Health Consequences of Smoking: 25 Years of Progress, Report of the Surgeon General, D.H.H.S. Pub. No. (PHS) (CDC) 89-3411, Wash. D.C. (1989).

The American tobacco companies at first fought against the warning labels, but do not now seem as publicly opposed. This change in attitude seems due to the benefit achieved in avoidance of further product liability suits and some evidence that the warnings alone are not a significant factor either in stopping smoking or in prevention of the development of the habit in young people. See Dixon, Product Liability §8.09 (1982). See also Garner, Cigarette Dependency and Civil Liability, 53 S. Cal. L. Rev. 1423 (1980).

7. Anti-smoking campaigns have been much less successful in European countries. Both the European Community and the European Regional Office of the World Health Organization have been increasing their efforts to combat smoking. This campaign includes encouraging countries to require health warnings on tobacco product packages. See Roemer, Legislative Strategies for a Smoke-free Europe, Regional Office for Europe, W.H.O., Copenhagen (1988).

IV. THE AIDS EPIDEMIC: ISSUES OF TRADITIONAL PUBLIC HEALTH REGULATION IN A NEW ERA OF PUBLIC POLICY AND HUMAN RIGHTS

U.S. Centers for Disease Control, Update: Acquired Immunodeficiency Syndrome — United States, 1981-1988*
38 Morb. and Mort. Wkly Rep. 231 (1989)

In 1988, state and local health departments reported 32,311 persons (28,432 men, 3296 women, and 583 children [<13 years of age]) diagnosed with illnesses that meet the CDC case definition for acquired immunodeficiency syndrome (AIDS) in the United States and its territories. Excluding U.S. territories, these persons represent an annual incidence rate of 13.7 AIDS cases per 100,000 population: 31.2 cases per 100,000 men, 3.2 cases per 100,000 women, and 1.3 cases per 100,000 children. During this period, blacks and Hispanics had the highest annual incidence rates per 100,000 population (34.9 and 28.9, respectively), followed by whites (9.6), Asians/Pacific Islanders (5.4), and American Indians/Alaskan Natives (2.2).

As of December 31, 1988, a total of 82,764 AIDS cases had been reported to CDC. The number of AIDS cases reported each year continues to increase; however, the rate of increase has steadily declined, except in 1987, when the revision of the case definition resulted in an abrupt increase in reported cases (Figure 1).

Impact of the 1987 revision of the AIDS case definition. In September 1987, the CDC AIDS case definition was revised for persons with laboratory evidence of human immunodeficiency virus (HIV) infection (e.g., positive HIV-antibody test) to include a broader spectrum of diseases characteristically found in persons with HIV infection and

---

* This update summary of data on the AIDS epidemic by the Centers for Disease Control, U.S. Public Health Service, is reprinted by permission of the Massachusetts Medical Society and the Centers for Disease Control. (Technical references to the Editorial Note have been omitted.)

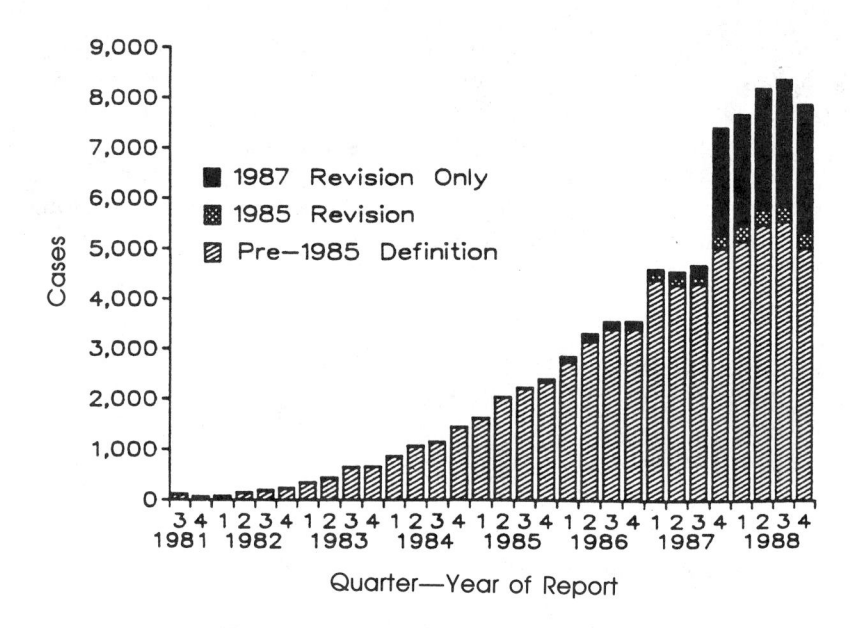

Figure 1.
AIDS cases, by quarter of report and case definition — United States, 1981-1988

the presumptive diagnosis of selected diseases. The revision has markedly affected the distribution of reported cases. Of the 40,836 cases reported between September 1987 and December 1988, 11,966 (29 percent) met only the 1987 revision. Of these persons, 3949 (33 percent) had a presumptive diagnosis of *Pneumocystis carinii* pneumonia, 3904 (33 percent) had HIV wasting syndrome, 1781 (15 percent) had HIV dementia, 1639 (14 percent) had a presumptive diagnosis of esophageal candidiasis, and 737 (6 percent) had extrapulmonary tuberculosis (658 definitively diagnosed and 79 presumptively diagnosed). Compared with patients with illnesses meeting the pre-1985 or the 1985 case definitions, a higher proportion of patients reported since September 1987 with illnesses meeting only the 1987 case definition were female (15 percent compared with 9 percent), black or Hispanic (34 percent and 21 percent, respectively, compared with 26 percent and 14 percent, respectively), or heterosexual intravenous-drug users (IVDUs) (35 percent compared with 18 percent). A lower proportion of those meeting only the 1987 case definition had a history of male homosexual/bisexual activity without IV-drug use (41 percent compared with 63 percent).

Geographic distribution. AIDS cases have been reported from all 50 states, the District of Columbia, and four U.S. territories. Annual incidence rates by state for 1988 varied from 0.6 cases per 100,000

IV. The AIDS Epidemic 1201

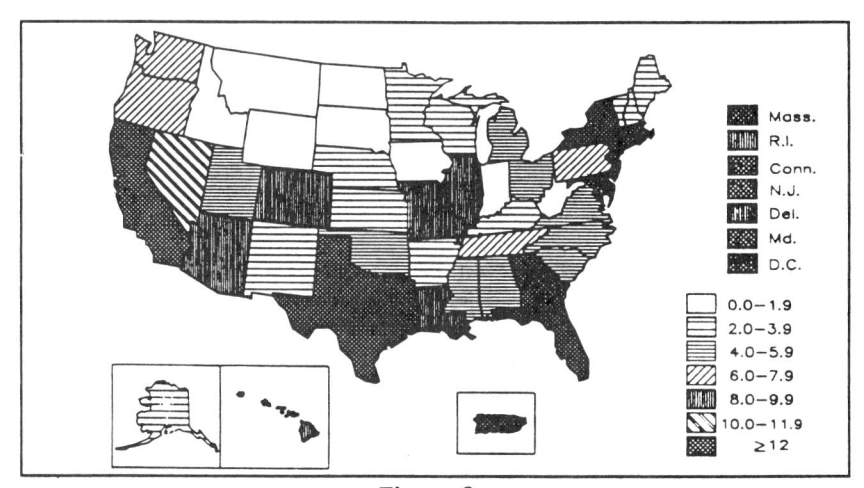

Figure 2.
AIDS incidence rates per 100,000 population — United States, 1988

persons in North Dakota to 38.9 per 100,000 in New York (Figure 2).

The geographic distribution of AIDS cases has shifted over time. Before 1984, the Mid-Atlantic region of the United States (New Jersey, New York, and Pennsylvania) reported 54 percent of all AIDS cases (52 percent of men and 73 percent of women with AIDS). In 1988, the Mid-Atlantic region reported only 32 percent of all AIDS cases (29 percent of men and 50 percent of women with AIDS) (Figure 3). Before 1984, 47 percent of all male patients with histories of homosexual/bisexual activity were reported from the Mid-Atlantic region; in 1988, 21 percent of these men were reported from the Mid-Atlantic region. The proportion who had histories of IV-drug use without homosexual activity from this region also decreased, from 85 percent to 59 percent. The proportion of all cases from all other regions increased during this period, except for the Pacific† region, which remained stable. Increases were greatest in the East North Central, South Atlantic, and West South Central regions.†

Men. Of the 82,764 AIDS cases reported to CDC as of December 31, 1988, 74,435 (90 percent) were in males $\geq$ 13 years of age. The mean age at the time of diagnosis was 37.0 years. A total of 61.0 percent were white (non-Hispanic); 23.7 percent, black (non-Hispanic); 14.5 percent, Hispanic; 0.6 percent, Asian/Pacific Islander; and 0.1

---

† The Pacific region consists of Alaska, California, Hawaii, Oregon, and Washington. The East North Central region consists of Illinois, Indiana, Michigan, Ohio, and Wisconsin. The South Atlantic region consists of Delaware, District of Columbia, Florida, Georgia, Maryland, North Carolina, South Carolina, Virginia, and West Virginia. The West South Central region consists of Arkansas, Louisiana, Oklahoma, and Texas.

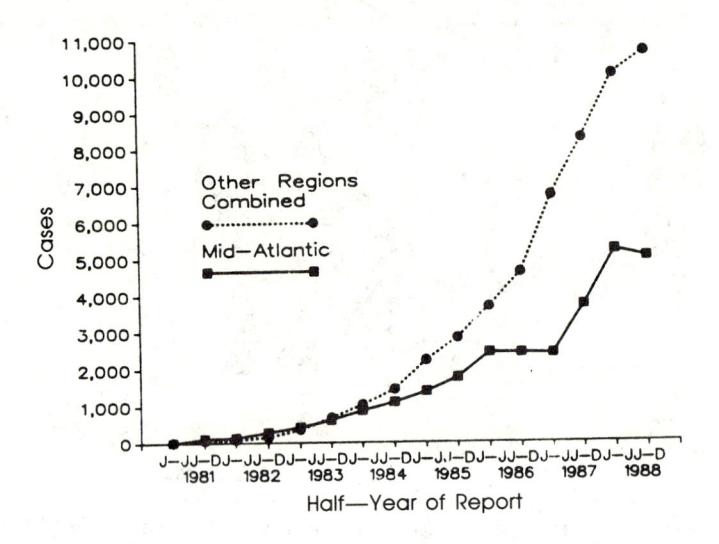

Figure 3.
AIDS cases, by region and date of report — United States, 1981-1988

percent, American Indian/Alaskan Native. This distribution has remained stable over time, except for a decrease in the proportion of men who were white (from 64 percent in 1987 to 57 percent in 1988) and an increase in the proportion that was black and Hispanic (from 22 percent and 12 percent, respectively, in 1987 to 25 percent and 16 percent in 1988), reflecting the 1987 revision of the case definition. The cumulative incidence of AIDS between 1981 and 1988 was 3.0 times higher among black men and 2.8 times higher among Hispanic men than among white men.

Sixty-eight percent of men with AIDS had histories of homosexual/bisexual activity without IV-drug use, 17 percent had IV-drug use without homosexual/bisexual activity, and 8 percent had both homosexual activity and IV-drug use. Another 2 percent had histories of blood transfusion, 1 percent had hemophilia or other coagulation disorder, 1 percent had sex partners at increased risk for or known to be infected with HIV, 1 percent were born in countries with predominantly heterosexual transmission of HIV, and 3 percent had undetermined means of exposure to HIV. This distribution has remained stable, except for a decrease in the proportion of men with histories of homosexual/bisexual activity without IV-drug use (from 70 percent of those reported in 1987 to 63 percent of those reported in 1988) and an increase in the proportion with histories of IV-drug use and no homosexual/bisexual activity (from 14 percent in 1987 to 20 percent in 1988), again partially reflecting the 1987 revision of the case definition. This trend was most evident in the Mid-Atlantic region, where the proportion of homosexual/bisexual men without IV-drug use decreased from 54 percent to 46 percent and the proportion of heterosexual IVDUs increased from 34 percent to 41 percent. In addition, the proportion of all men with AIDS born in countries with predominantly heterosexual transmission of HIV decreased from 4 percent before 1984 to 1 percent in 1988. Black and Hispanic men with AIDS were more likely to have had histories of IV-drug use and less likely to have had histories of homosexual activity than white men. . . .

Women. As of December 31, 1988, 6983 AIDS cases have been reported among females ≥ 13 years of age, constituting 8 percent of all AIDS cases. This proportion increased from 8 percent of reported cases in 1987 to 10 percent of reported cases in 1988. The mean age at diagnosis was 35.7 years; 51.6 percent were black; 27.9 percent, white; 19.5 percent, Hispanic; 0.6 percent, Asian/Pacific Islander; and 0.2 percent, American Indian/Alaskan Native. This distribution has been relatively stable. The cumulative incidence of AIDS between 1981 and 1988 was 13.6 times higher among black women and 10.2 times higher among Hispanic women than among white women.

Among women with AIDS, 52 percent had histories of IV-drug use, 18 percent had sex partners with histories of IV-drug use, 7 percent had sex partners otherwise at increased risk for or known to be infected with HIV, 11 percent had histories of blood transfusion, 4 percent were born in countries with predominantly heterosexual transmission of HIV, and 8 percent had undetermined means of exposure. The proportion of women with AIDS who had sex partners at increased risk for HIV rose from 15 percent before 1984 to 26 percent in 1988, and the proportion born in countries with predominantly heterosexual transmission decreased from 11 percent to 3 percent. Black and Hispanic women with AIDS were more likely than white women to have had histories of IV-drug use or histories of sex with IVDUs. . . .

Children. As of December 31, 1988, 1346 AIDS patients <13 years of age had been reported to CDC. Of these, 55 percent were male. Eighty-two percent of pediatric patients were <5 years of age at diagnosis, and 40 percent were <1 year of age. Racial distribution among pediatric patients was similar to that among women with AIDS: 52.5 percent were black; 23.9 percent, white; 22.9 percent, Hispanic; 0.5 percent, Asian/Pacific Islander; and 0.2 percent, American Indian/Alaskan Native. Among pediatric patients, 78 percent are presumed to have acquired HIV infection perinatally from their mothers, 13 percent from blood transfusion, and 6 percent from blood products used to treat hemophilia. Four percent had undetermined means of exposure to HIV. Of those infected from their mothers, maternal risk factors included IV-drug use (54 percent), sex with an IVDU (19 percent), sex with a man otherwise at increased risk for or infected with HIV (7 percent), birth in a country with predominantly heterosexual transmission (11 percent), and transfusion (2 percent). The mothers' risk factors were not reported in 7 percent. The proportion of perinatally infected children whose mothers had sex partners at increased risk for or infected with HIV (including IVDUs) rose from 11 percent of all pediatric cases before 1985 to 21 percent in 1988; the proportion of those whose mothers were born in countries with predominantly heterosexual transmission decreased from 22 percent to 7 percent. Black and Hispanic pediatric patients were more likely to have had mothers with histories of IV-drug use or of sex with IVDUs than were white children. . . .

Patients with no identified risk factor. AIDS patients initially reported as having undetermined means of exposure to HIV are investigated by local or state health officials for a possible means of exposure. Overall, 2706 (3 percent) reported AIDS cases fall into this category; this percentage has remained stable, except for an increase to 5 percent in 1988. This greater proportion of patients with no identified risk factor in the most recent reporting periods reflects the large number of cases still under investigation. Of all AIDS patients initially reported to CDC with undetermined means of exposure, 83 percent have been reclassified into a known exposure category when follow-up information was obtained. Therefore, many of the persons reported in 1988 with no identified risk factor will be reclassified after additional information becomes available.

In general, patients with no identified risk factor are not characteristic of the U.S. population: 79 percent are male, 39 percent are white (compared with 80 percent of the U.S. population), and 90 percent are 20-59 years of age (compared with 54 percent of the U.S. population). Of the 2706 patients currently listed as having undetermined means of exposure, investigations were not completed for 11 percent due to death, 4 percent due to refusal to be interviewed, and 2 percent due to loss to follow-up. Of the remaining 2231 patients, 1892 are under investigation, and 339 had no risk factor identified after investigation. Among the latter, many had histories of a sexually transmitted disease other than AIDS and/or reported sexual contact with prostitutes and may have been at increased risk for HIV infection because of sexual activity. Investigations have revealed no evidence of new modes of transmission of HIV.

Mortality. Fifty-six percent of all AIDS patients (56 percent of adults/adolescents and 55 percent of children) and 85 percent of those diagnosed before 1986 are reported to have died. The actual case-fatality rate is higher due to incomplete reporting of deaths. In 1987, HIV infection/AIDS ranked 15th among leading causes of death in the United States and seventh among all causes of years of

TABLE 1. Adult and pediatric AIDS patients,* by exposure category, race/ethnic group, and sex — United States, 1981-1988

Category	Total	Homosexual, non-IVDU†	IVDU	Homosexual and IVDU	Heterosexual contact — Sex with IVDU	Heterosexual contact — Sex with person at risk (non-IVDU)	Transfusion recipient	Coagulation disorder	Other risk factor	NIR§
White										
Adult, Male	45,359	81	5	8	<1	<1	2	1	<1	2
Adult, Female	1,948	—	40	—	12	13	26	1	<1	8
Pediatric	321	—	22¶	—	10**	8††	29	19	9	3
Black										
Adult, Male	17,618	45	34	8	1	<1	1	<1	5	4
Adult, Female	3,604	—	58	—	17	5	4	<1	8	7
Pediatric	707	—	47¶	—	15**	4††	5		23	5
Hispanic										
Adult, Male	10,773	48	37	8	<1	<1	1	1	<1	5
Adult, Female	1,360	—	54	—	29	5	5	<1	<1	7
Pediatric	308	—	50¶	—	21**	4††	11	4	6	4
Asian/Pacific Islander										
Adult, Male	440	82	2	2	<1	<1	6	2	<1	6
Adult, Female	42	—	19	—	10	19	36	<1	<1	17
Pediatric	6§§									
American Indian/ Alaskan Native										
Adult, Male	75	61	9	17	<1	<1	1	4	<1	7
Adult, Female	12§§									
Pediatric	2§§									

* Adult = person ≥ 13 years old; pediatric = person < 13 years old.
† Intravenous-drug user.
§ NIR = no identified risk factor.
¶ Mother with history of IV-drug use.
** Mother with history of sex with IVDU.
†† Mother with history of sex with person at risk for HIV (other than IVDU).
§§ Small numbers make calculations of percentages of limited value.

potential life lost. Deaths occurring in 1987 among persons with AIDS that were reported to CDC represented 9 percent of all deaths among persons 25-34 years of age and 7 percent of all deaths among persons 35-44 years of age.

Reported by: Local, state, and territorial health departments. AIDS Program, Center for Infectious Diseases, CDC.

Editorial Note: National surveillance of AIDS encompasses severe diseases thought to be highly specific for HIV infection. CDC first outlined a surveillance case definition in 1982, which was modified in 1983. As knowledge about HIV infection increased, other severe and commonly occurring manifestations of HIV infection were included in the case definition in 1985 and again in 1987. Additions included disseminated histoplasmosis, chronic isosporiasis, and certain non-Hodgkins lymphomas (1985 revision) and extrapulmonary tuberculosis, HIV encephalopathy, HIV wasting syndrome, multiple or recurrent bacterial infections (in children only), and presumptively diagnosed *Pneumocystis carinii* pneumonia and esophageal candidiasis (1987 revision). In both instances, the revision applied to patients with laboratory evidence (e.g., positive antibody test) for HIV infection. The number of AIDS cases increased 3 to 4 percent as a result of the 1985 revision. The 1987 revision has had an even greater effect. Studies in selected groups and areas suggest that the number of cases may increase as much as 22 percent among homosexual men and persons with hemophilia and even more among pediatric patients. Therefore, the increase in the number of cases reported in 1987 and 1988 reflect, at least in part, the revision of the case definition. The long-term effects of the revised case definition on surveillance trends are not clear-cut because 1) HIV testing and the revised case definition are not used uniformly in all populations, 2) diagnostic practices for specific AIDS-indicator diseases may be changing, and 3) some patients with illnesses initially meeting only the 1987 case definition may eventually develop illnesses meeting the previous case definition.

AIDS incidence is highest in the most populous metropolitan areas in the United States. Standard metropolitan statistical areas (SMSAs) with >1 million residents comprise 41 percent of the U.S. population but accounted for 75 percent of U.S. AIDS cases between 1981 and December 1988. This distribution of cases, however, is changing, as reflected in the decrease in the proportion of cases reported from the Mid-Atlantic region. The proportion of AIDS cases from SMSAs with ≤500,000 population increased from 12 percent before 1986 to 19 percent in 1988. Such findings are important in the development of prevention strategies and suggest that HIV prevention activities should be conducted in areas with smaller populations, as well as in large metropolitan areas.

Blacks and Hispanics continue to be disproportionately represented among AIDS patients, particularly among those who were IVDUs or sex partners or children of IVDUs. In 1988, the annual incidence rate of AIDS cases associated with IV-drug use was 11.5 times higher among blacks and 8.8 times higher among Hispanics than among whites. This difference was even more dramatic in the Northeast. Although the racial/ethnic distribution of IVDUs in the United States is unknown, a 1982 National Institute on Drug Abuse survey of drug-abuse treatment centers suggests that a disproportionate number of IVDUs attending treatment clinics in high AIDS-incidence areas were black or Hispanic. Furthermore, HIV seroprevalence rates are higher among black and Hispanic IVDUs than among white IVDUs, except on the West Coast. These findings emphasize the need for community-based HIV prevention programs in areas with a high prevalence of drug use, especially among minorities. These programs should include HIV educational programs and counseling and testing facilities in drug-treatment centers, sexually transmitted disease clinics, tuberculosis clinics, jails and prisons, and health-care facilities.

Rothman, Public Policy and Risk Assessment in the AIDS Epidemic (1987)*

Conference on AIDS: Public Policy Dimensions (J. Griggs ed., United Hospital Fund of N.Y., 1987)

AIDS and the Unknown

AIDS has many unique and unprecedented features. Too young to remember the summer scares about polio in the early 1950s, not to mention the deep concern about tuberculosis in earlier decades, no one under the age of 45 in the United States has any firsthand experience with a deadly and transmissible disease. Nevertheless, this is hardly the first time that policy decisions must be made when the number of unknowns is high and the potential injury significant. In the debate about appropriate responses to AIDS, as in many other controversies, the dispute comes down to judgments of how far one will allow potential negative consequences to determine social policy. What is the appropriate degree of risk tolerance as against risk aversion? Are policy decisions to be made on the basis of the best-case or the worst-case scenario? Are all the many unknowns to be put in the favorable or unfavorable outcome column?

* This article by Professor David J. Rothman of Columbia University, College of Physicians and Surgeons, Center for the Study of Society and Medicine, is reprinted by permission of the United Hospital Fund of New York.
 References appear at the end of the article.

Although the literature on risk analysis is substantial — with findings available on how individuals will balance future losses against immediate gains, or sacrifice small gains to minimize the possibility of greater losses — we know very little about how one or another public issue ends up in the risk-maximizing or risk-minimizing category (Covello 1983). In some areas, public policy tends to adopt apocalyptic thinking and do everything possible to avoid a negative outcome, even if the probability of that outcome is judged to be quite low. In other instances, apocalyptic thinking seems very foreign to policy considerations and day-to-day decisions are made with little regard for potential disaster.

Before attempting to analyze where AIDS fits into this framework, let us briefly examine one or two other cases, for they will demonstrate that no obvious reasons determine how distinctions are made. The commonsense notion, for example, that the greater the possible risk, the more likely that apocalyptic visions will abound and that everything possible will be done to avert the disaster, turns out not to be a useful predictor of policy directions.

Apocalyptic Thinking

There are two classic instances in which apocalyptic thinking dominates much, although certainly not all, policy consideration. The most obvious one is nuclear war; the other is nuclear energy. In both cases, debate and decision-making are in deep dialogue with the possibility of catastrophe. Those who would block the development of nuclear energy, for example, point to the potential failure of plant safety mechanisms and insist that the benefits of nuclear power are far outweighed by the risks, even if the risks are relatively low. They repeatedly cite the 1979 incident at the Three Mile Island nuclear facility near Harrisburg, Pennsylvania; indeed, it is not difficult to imagine how much more heated their rhetoric would be had even one or two deaths occurred there. In any event, when it comes to issues involving nuclear power, the debate is often framed in apocalyptic terms.

Yet, there are other potential disasters that could be almost as devastating as what would follow from nuclear power plant failures that do not raise such specters. The injuries that would follow from the collapse of a dam are not necessarily fewer than those that would result from the malfunction of a nuclear power plant, but the public concern about regulation of dam safety or the location of dams in areas with a high likelihood of earthquakes certainly does not rise to the level evoked by nuclear energy. Somehow, death from drowning is not perceived to be as terrifying as death from radiation.

So too, significant health damage from pesticides is probably more real and extensive at the moment than damage from nuclear power plants, but, by comparison, the level of agitation is low. And, to cite examples from the area of drugs and medical innovations, it is clear that apocalyptic visions are not allowed to keep new therapies out of the marketplace. We do not, as a matter of course, test all drugs for safety to the children of the users, although we have no way of knowing when we may be creating a second diethylstilbestrol (DES) incident. By the same token, no restrictions are being placed on *in vitro* fertilization programs, despite the imaginable possibility of some grave defect in the children or grandchildren of those born from test tube procedures. In brief, the willingness to maximize an unknown risk is not spread evenly among policy debates; the gravity of the risk is not by itself determinative of the public response. At times, we are prepared to run the risk of danger to gain benefits; at other times, we are not, and where an issue will appear on this scale is not easily predicted.

Apocalyptic Thinking and Public Health

From this perspective, let us move directly into the field of public health. Here, one finds a tradition of maximizing the degree of risk and taking all measures that seem necessary to counter it. Public health practitioners generally tend to act upon apocalyptic visions, to treat unknowns as unfavorable outcomes. When in doubt, they assume that the risks are maximal and they will recommend doing everything possible to avert them.

The Great Swine Flu Disaster of 1976

The example that best demonstrates this mind-set in action is the 1976 swine flu incident (Neustadt and Feinberg 1977). After some American soldiers were diagnosed as harboring an influenza virus that was antigenically related to the influenza virus of the 1918-1919 epidemic, the Centers for Disease Control (CDC) had to confront the question of the likelihood of the spread of the disease to the general population, and to determine what precautionary steps, if any, should be taken. The CDC's subsequent decision to recommend vaccinating the entire population of the United States clearly reflected the triumph of apocalyptic thinking.

At the time, there was no consensus among public health experts on the likelihood of a swine flu epidemic. A significant body of opinion held that the CDC should do nothing. However, this group lost out in the debate precisely because it could not demonstrate that the epidemic would *not* occur. The burden of proof fell on those who would minimize the potential risk; they had to prove conclusively that the disaster would not happen. In other words, the operating assumption was that those who predicted disaster were right until proven wrong. As long as no one could conclusively demonstrate that the untoward event would *not* take place, health policy assumed that it *would* occur, and moved to counteract it. When risks cannot be ruled out, they must be ruled in. In the field of public health, a virus or its carrier is guilty until proven innocent.

In the end, of course, the swine flu epidemic did not materialize, but a number of vaccine recipients developed Guillain-Barré syndrome. The effects of the vaccination policy were costly not only in terms of energy and fiscal resources but also in actual harm done. Thus, it must be remembered that acting on the worst-possible-case scenario is not a neutral decision or without costs of its own. The actions taken can and often do have important negative consequences.

The Case of Hepatitis B in the Classroom

Another example of the public health readiness to maximize risks — and one that is even more immediately relevant to the AIDS controversy — involved a consideration of the threat that hepatitis B carriers posed to their classmates and teachers in New York public schools (Rothman and Rothman 1984). A 1975 consent decree called for the return to the community of some 5,400 severely and profoundly retarded residents at the Willowbrook State School on Staten Island. Hepatitis B had been endemic at the institution, so endemic, in fact, that pediatrician-researcher Dr. Saul Krugman felt justified in purposefully injecting the virus into new arrivals in order to study the etiology of the disease. Not surprisingly, about 40 of those residents released to the community, and who subsequently attended public schools, were hepatitis B carriers.

After an incident in September 1977, in which a Staten Island teacher of the retarded came down with hepatitis (at first thought to be hepatitis B but which turned out to be hepatitis A), the Board of Education and the Department of Health became concerned about the possibility of contagion. The Department of Health sent two staff members to observe the carriers in their classrooms and they reported an epidemiological nightmare: the carriers hugged, kissed, drooled over, and shared food and drink with their susceptible classmates. After convening a task force of hepatitis B researchers and other public health professionals, the Department of Health recommended segregating the carriers in their own classrooms, on the grounds that the risk of contagion was great. One new case of hepatitis B was one case too many, and, given the risks of the spread of disease, the carriers had to be isolated from day-to-day contact with susceptible students. Upon receiving this recommendation, the Board of Education went a step beyond the Department of Health's advice and summarily expelled the carriers from the schools.

Civil Liberties Versus Public Health

Since the Willowbrook deinstitutionalization effort had been spearheaded and supervised by a group of civil libertarian lawyers, the Board of Education's action was immediately contested. Attorneys for the ex-Willowbrook residents moved to enjoin the expulsion, and the federal courtroom became the setting for a fascinating and revealing conflict between a public health outlook and a civil libertarian point of view.

The public health representatives argued that, because the carriers were so likely to transmit hepatitis B through blood or saliva contact with susceptible persons, it was appropriate to adopt preventive measures such as carrier segregation. Since no one could demonstrate that the carriers would not seed the classrooms with the hepatitis B virus, the carriers had to be isolated. The civil libertarians, on the other hand, insisted that the students could not be penalized in advance of any demonstrable evidence of contagion. They maintained that, since there was no documented case of any student in a classroom with a carrier contracting hepatitis B, the carriers should not be deprived of their right to an education in the least restrictive setting. The carriers were, according to the civil libertarian view, innocent until proven guilty, and predictions of dangerousness were not dispositive.

After hearing this dispute, the court ruled in favor of the civil libertarians: Judges are not in the habit of penalizing anyone without proof of guilt. The conflict did not end there, however; the Department of Health next tested the blood of all the classmates of the carriers and discovered that six of them had antibodies to the hepatitis B virus, a finding that the Department of Health presented as evidence of contagion and a justification for isolation. The civil libertarian attorneys countered that, since this was the first time that the classmates had been tested, there was no way of knowing whether the change in antibody status had occurred before the carriers entered the classrooms, or was the result of contact in some other, nonclassroom setting. Again, there was a difference in the evidence that a public health specialist found conclusive, as compared to an attorney. The public health professional is trained to act on suspicion; the civil libertarian lawyer represents a tradition in which suspicions are not enough. Not surprisingly, the court adopted the civil libertarian perspective: It was unwilling to penalize anyone — whether a carrier or an accused felon — without firm evidence; it wanted a smoking gun, not a statistical probability.

A Ruling with Relevance to AIDS

One final consideration led the court to rule against the Board of Education and the Department of Health, a consideration that also has direct relevance to the AIDS issue. The Department of Health offered recommendations for policy toward mentally retarded hepatitis B carriers but not toward any other group of carriers. Its proposals did not affect hepatitis B carriers who might be surgeons or dentists or gays or persons of Chinese origin or dialysis patients, all groups with abnormally high percentages of carriers. In fact, it was the reluctance of the Department of Health to write a general code about hepatitis B carriers that kept it in a posture of recommending actions but not promulgating binding regulations, and the court took this distinction very seriously. It appeared that the retarded were being singled out for special, discriminatory treatment. If this were not so, then why had the Department of Health failed to follow its own established procedures and issued a binding and general administrative ruling?

Apocalyptic Thinking and AIDS

Judged against the background of the swine flu and hepatitis B incidents, one would have anticipated that both the societal and public health responses to the AIDS crisis would be quintessentially apocalyptic. The disease is deadly; it makes hepatitis B seem trivial by comparison. The groups most affected, male gays and intravenous (IV) drug users, are stigmatized and considered socially deviant. Indeed, among the gays, it is thought that the most sexually active or "promiscuous" are at greatest risk and disproportionately affected. Here, then, is a disease that victims seem to bring on themselves, and hence any risk that they pose to others might well be defined as too great. Some proponents of such a position argue that the moral culpability of the victims, their blameworthiness, justifies measures that would protect others from the possibility of contagion; others in this camp avoid moral judgments but fault the AIDS victims for not adopting safer sexual or drug habits. In either case, the thinking goes, "the rest of us" should not run the risk of danger because "they" behaved badly or imprudently. Thus, if ever incentives existed to put all the unknowns into the dismal outcome column, for considering the risks to be maximal rather than minimal, surely AIDS is that case.

Predictably, there are groups that have adopted and urged this very approach, and segments of the media have encouraged and supported it. Even among those not prone to define gays as blameworthy or culpable, the risk of contagion seems to justify an exclusionary response. Some of the parents who have wanted to remove AIDS-afflicted students and teachers — and even those who only test positive for AIDS virus antibodies — from their children's classrooms are not responding to AIDS hysteria so much as to the lessons of good health care that have been learned over the years. These parents have been trained to believe that lice is sufficient grounds for keeping a child out of school and that youngsters with sore throats should be kept home so as to minimize contagion. Without belaboring the point, American society tends to be obsessive in matters of health. So how unreasonable would it be to conclude that, if saccharine can be banned because megadoses fed to mice proved to be carcinogenic, then, in a crisis situation, surely a student with AIDS can be excluded from a classroom?

Notions of Catastrophe Have Not Dominated

Despite the seeming likelihood of apocalyptic thinking, the extent to which the AIDS threat has been met with reasoned, sane, and non-exclusionary responses is remarkable. Had someone 20 years ago described an epidemic like AIDS and predicted the public response, surely findings would have been in the direction of massive hysteria and extraordinary sanctions. However, to date, apocalyptic thinking has not marked the general reaction, although, with little difficulty, one could sketch an apocalyptic ending to this epidemic. In fact, several leading AIDS researchers, including Harvard University's William Haseltine and Myron Essex, have begun to draw this very picture. "The dire predictions of those who have cried doom ever since AIDS appeared," Essex told the New York Times Magazine, "haven't been far off the mark" (Hunt 1986). Haseltine informed a Senate subcommittee that "for every case of reported AIDS in the United States there are about 100 or more carriers . . . Once infected, infected for life. . . . We see a wave of devastating disease approaching" (Hunt). To date, however, notions of impending catastrophe have not been the dominant theme of scientists' statements.

By the same token, many of the leading daily newspapers and weekly magazines have been educative, not inflammatory, in their editorials and news coverage of AIDS, and have taken the minimal-risk side in policy arguments. The editorial page of the New York Times (1985), for example, has more consistently adopted a civil libertarian stance on AIDS matters than on the rights of the homeless or the mentally ill. Nor have the public health professionals been as unanimous or aggressive in this case, as they have been in others, in staking out a guilty-until-proven-innocent position. The posture of the New York City Department of Health regarding AIDS, for example, is far more risk tolerant than it was with hepatitis B.

The Situation Is Volatile

To be sure, the situation is volatile and hysteria can be contagious. Incidents of rank discrimination have certainly occurred; one would probably want to include on this side of the ledger the recent attempts to shut down a few bathhouses, not to mention hearings held in the state of Texas on the right to quarantine persons with AIDS. Generally, though, in the conflict between a public health "guilty-till-proven-innocent" stance and the civil libertarian "innocent-until-proven-guilty" attitude, the AIDS victims and potential victims have been spared many imaginable sanctions and reprisals. Compulsory testing for HTLV-III/LAV* antibodies or the virus is not the rule, outside the armed forces at least, and boards of health are not carrying out massive screening efforts. Neither universities in general nor medical schools in particular are revising application procedures to screen out gays; neither are they asking students to take blood tests. Attempts by insurance companies to discriminate against gays are being contested, with some success. Calling for the massive segregation or quarantine of people with AIDS has so far been a fringe effort. Schoolchildren with AIDS appear more often than not to be able to keep their places in classrooms. All of this suggests that what needs explaining most is why, to date, the civil libertarian perspective, rather than the traditional public health one, has dominated.

The Role of Politics

Some of the answer may rest in politics. By happenstance, the majority of people with AIDS live in the two states with the highest number of electoral votes, California and New York. So, Congressional pressure for earmarking funds for AIDS research, and the administration's approval, however grudging and inadequate, points to the importance of not alienating a large bloc of voters. By the same token, people with AIDS cluster in the two cities and states whose political leaders have been relatively enlightened on gay rights in general and, now, on AIDS in particular. Gays are a much stronger political force than, for example, the retarded, and hence AIDS victims are being dealt with in ways that the hepatitis B carriers were not.

There is no doubt that part of the reason for the more tolerant response to people with AIDS reflects the continuing strength in the 1980s of a minority rights orientation. Following the civil rights agitation of the 1960s, the gays won their place as a minority group, and penalizing them is often viewed on a par with penalizing women, blacks, or the mentally handicapped. In a very real way, the court victory that the hepatitis B carriers won in 1978 works to the benefit of AIDS victims in 1986, making it all the more likely that measures that claim to be advancing the public health will be judged by civil

The Role of Health Care Professionals

The part that physicians and other health care professionals have played in reassuring the public should not be minimized. They have explained that the virus does not appear to be easily transmitted — one physician has called it a "pathogenic weakling" (Osborn 1986) — and that, absent intimate and sustained contact, the risks of contagion are very low. Perhaps their stance would have been different had even a handful of health professionals not in known risk groups succumbed to the disease in the course of diagnosing it or treating it. Standard precautions in handling blood, however, have proved completely efficacious for health care workers, and research findings have been able to demonstrate why this is so. Still, in and of itself, this message might not have been heard, and the fright around AIDS could have been so great as to render the public incapable of grasping the information.

It is also possible that public health professionals have learned some lessons from past actions. The head of the New York City Department of Health through 1985, David Sencer, headed the CDC during the swine flu scare, and the criticism leveled at him in that affair may have influenced him to adopt a very different strategy with regard to AIDS. So too, the Department of Health may have learned something from the hepatitis B litigation and decided this time to proceed more cautiously.

A Court Test of AIDS Public Health Policy

That disputes about AIDS frequently end up in the courtroom has helped ensure an equitable response, as evidenced by the New York Supreme Court decision, in February 1986, on the rights of students with AIDS to attend public school (District 27 Community School Board v. The Board of Education of the City of New York; Supreme Court, Queens County; 11 February 1986; Index No. 14940/85). In the fall of 1985, the New York City Board of Education adopted a policy that children with AIDS would not be automatically excluded from the schools; instead, each case would be reviewed individually. The review that followed permitted the admission of a child with AIDS to a Queens County school, whereupon two local community school boards and the parent of a public school child went to court to obtain a permanent injunction against the admission of pupils with AIDS. A five-week trial ensued, attracting wide press coverage. Many of those who participated in the proceedings, noting the ways in which the issues were framed and considering the asides and questions of the judge, predicted that the court would grant the injunction.

To the contrary, however, the judge upheld the child's admission to school, and his decision in many ways echoed the federal court's findings in the Willowbrook case. Again, uncertainty was not allowed to become the basis for penalties. According to the ruling by Judge Harold Hyman, "Although this court certainly empathizes with the fears and concerns of parents . . . at the same time it is duty bound to objectively evaluate the issue of automatic exclusion according to the evidence gathered and not be influenced by unsubstantiated fears of catastrophe." Again, the court would not allow one group to be singled out for what seemed to be discriminatory action: "It is difficult to conceive of a rational justification imposing a discriminatory burden on known [AIDS] carriers . . . while untested and unidentified carriers still remain in the classroom where they pose the same theoretical (though undocumented) risks of transmitting the virus to normal children." In the end, the courts are not likely to allow sanctions to be imposed on vulnerable groups because they pose a "theoretical" risk.

Quarantine: Inappropriate and Ineffective

It may be, too, that circumspection has outbalanced panic because, in truth, there is really very little that can be done on a grand scale to prevent the spread of AIDS. The traditional mechanisms by which early modern communities combatted the spread of epidemics are irrelevant. It makes no sense to talk of sealing one's borders to keep out gays, IV drug users, or AIDS patients in particular. The other major weapon, quarantine, is equally ineffective. On the one hand, it is probably too late; on the other, the logistics of quarantining no fewer than one million people are truly daunting.

Moreover, exploring the history of plagues and epidemics reveals a record of the failure of quarantines. In seventeenth-century Tuscany, for example, there were constant struggles between the authorities and the townspeople over such orders, and the authorities generally lost. They would appoint watchmen to make certain that the co-residents of a plague victim did not leave their quarters, and the residents would then proceed to bribe the watchmen and sneak out at night. So, too, disputes over the costs involved in maintaining the quarantine were bitter. Every family confined was a family that had to be fed, and the towns vigorously protested the expense (Cipolla 1980; Defoe [1722] 1984).

The historical precedents suggest only a few of the problems that would face any contemporary effort to quarantine (Mills et al. 1986). Imagine trying to select those who would be forced into an encampment: Would the gays be expected to identify themselves? Would there be hearings in cases of a protest of misidentification? Imagine keeping people inside the encampment: Would it have barbed wire? Imagine trying to care for those in the encampment: Would the food be prison fare? Would the inmates be expected to keep internal order? Even so brief an exercise makes clear how utterly fantastic notions of quarantine are.

Conclusion

None of this is to suggest that the story is over or that less extreme, but nevertheless important, discriminatory measures are unlikely. The possibility that gays will be deprived of the opportunity to purchase life or health insurance is strong, and so is the potential for job discrimination. If, as is expected, the number of AIDS cases climbs — with the number of new cases in 1986 equaling the total of all previous cases — then the possibilities for discrimination in jobs, housing, and even in access to health care services will be greater. And if female-to-male transmission becomes frequent, the public — and public health — attitude could change markedly.

Aware of all that may happen, however, it still remains impressive that, thus far, civil liberties concerns have been more influential than traditional public health orientations, and that the representatives of public health, the media, and a large segment of the public have been more sensitive to civil liberties issues in this crisis than in others. Not that the conflict between the two orientations is, in theory, any less severe. Rather, the initial responses have tilted more to the civil liberties side.

In this same spirit, we have allowed the existing data, not the possibility of catastrophic events, to set the basis for policy: Children with AIDS are being allowed in public classrooms. In fact, a poll of adult Americans, conducted by the Gallup Organization in March 1986, indicated not only that 98 percent of the respondents were aware of AIDS but also that two-thirds of them would permit their children to attend school with an AIDS-afflicted student (New York Times 1986). Although it is possible that all that we have seen so far is the sore throat before the flu strikes, fears of catastrophe have not become the foundation for public policy or, by and large, other reactions. In sum, apocalyptic visions have not carried the day, a fact that is one more astonishing feature of this astonishing epidemic.

REFERENCES

1. Cipolla, C. M. 1980. Faith, reason, and the plague in 17th century Tuscany. Trans. M. Kittel. Ithaca, NY: Cornell University Press.

2. Covello, V. 1983. The perception of technological risks: A literature review. Technological Forecasting and Social Change 23:285-97.
3. Defoe, D. [1722] 1984. A journal of the plague year. Reprint. New York: New American Library.
4. Hunt, M. 1986. Teaming up against AIDS. New York Times Magazine, 2 March, 42, 81-82.
5. Mills, M., C. B. Wofsy, and J. Mills. 1986. The acquired immunodeficiency syndrome: Infection control and public health law. New England Journal of Medicine 314:931-36.
6. Neustadt, R., and H. Feinberg. 1977. The epidemic that never was: Policy making and the swine flu scare. In Influenza in America 1918-1976: History, science, and politics, ed. J. Osborn. Canton, MA: Neale Watson Academic Publications.
7. New York Times. 1985. AIDS and the new apartheid. Editorial. 7 October.
8. New York Times. 1986. Poll finds support for pupils with AIDS. 17 April.
9. Osborn, J. E. 1986. The AIDS epidemic: Multidisciplinary trouble. New England Journal of Medicine 314:779-82.
10. Rothman, D. J., and S. M. Rothman. 1984. The Willowbrook wars: A decade of struggle for social justice. New York: Harper & Row, Chap. 11.

National Research Council, Recommendations on IV Drug Use and AIDS*

Summary of the Report on AIDS: Sexual Behavior and Intravenous Drug Use 16-18 (Turner, Miller & Moses eds. 1989)

IV. Drug Use and AIDS

Since AIDS was first recognized, there has been growing appreciation of the critical role played by IV drug use in the spread of HIV infection. As of November 14, 1988, 20,752 cases of AIDS — approximately one quarter of all cases — had been diagnosed in individuals who reported using IV drugs.

The main factor in the spread of infection by this group is the practice of sharing injection equipment, which acts as a vector for HIV-contaminated blood. Sharing occurs for a variety of economic, cultural, and practical reasons, but whatever the individual causes of

* This excerpt is taken from the Summary of the Report on AIDS: Sexual Behavior and Intravenous Drug Use 16-18 (Turner, Miller & Moses eds.: National Research Council, National Academy Press, Wash. D.C. 1989). It is reprinted with permission of the National Research Council.

the behavior, almost all IV drug users report "needle-sharing"[10] at some time during their drug-use "careers."

HIV infection among IV drug users also poses a threat to their sexual partners and offspring, as well as to persons with whom they share injection equipment. Nearly 70 percent of the reported cases of heterosexually acquired AIDS in the United States have been associated with IV drug use, and almost 75 percent of pediatric AIDS cases have been diagnosed in cities with high seroprevalence rates among IV drug users. These data, combined with the potential (through needle-sharing) for the rapid spread of HIV infection among IV drug users, define a problem whose solution requires both immediate action and long-term research. The current state of knowledge suggests that there will be no immediate resolution to the problem of IV drug use itself; nevertheless, existing research provides a basis for establishing programs to slow the spread of HIV infection among those who inject drugs.

Obviously, primary prevention of drug use could be an extremely effective prevention strategy for drug-associated HIV transmission. Relying on primary prevention *alone* is not realistic, however, given the uneven record of past efforts to control drug use and the threat of a continued epidemic of HIV transmission in the United States among persons who inject drugs, their sexual partners, and their children. The committee recommends that the nation adopt a three-pronged strategy to control the spread of AIDS through IV drug use.

First, drug treatment programs should be available to all who desire treatment. Several studies conducted prior to the advent of AIDS show that treatment can reduce IV drug use. Moreover, studies conducted during the AIDS era have shown that entering and remaining in drug treatment programs are factors associated with significant reductions in the rates of HIV infection among IV drug users.

Second, the committee concludes that, regardless of the availability of treatment opportunities, a substantial number of people in the United States will continue to inject drugs, at least in the short run. Consequently, the committee also recommends expanding programs for "safer injection" (including sterile needle and syringe exchanges and the promotion of injection equipment sterilization using bleach). None of the current studies on safer injection programs has shown increased IV drug use. Indeed, it appears that safer injection programs may indirectly encourage IV drug users to seek treatment. Furthermore, although results are still preliminary, many studies in-

---

10. This practice includes the sharing of needles, syringes, and various other paraphernalia used for dissolving drugs and straining impurities.

dicate that such programs do reduce the risk of HIV transmission among IV drug users. Finally, action should also be taken to provide a better understanding of the effects of these programs. The committee recommends that well-designed, staged trials of sterile needle programs, such as those requested in the 1986 Institute of Medicine/National Academy of Sciences report Confronting AIDS, be implemented.

Thus, the committee believes it is necessary to establish better data collection systems to monitor current AIDS prevention efforts for IV drug users. The quality of existing data on IV drug use is not adequate to answer the difficult questions AIDS poses. Assessing the scope of the problems associated with HIV transmission among IV drug users is difficult when neither the number of IV drug users nor the seroprevalence rate is known with any certainty. Current estimates rely on data that were collected for other purposes and that were acquired through efforts intended to measure only crude trends.

In sum, the committee recommends that the appropriate governmental authorities take immediate action to

1. provide drug treatment upon request for IV drug users throughout the country;
2. sustain and expand current programs that provide for "safer injection" to reach all current IV drug users in the nation on a continuing basis and with appropriate research evaluation; and
3. establish data collection systems for monitoring present AIDS prevention efforts for IV drug users.

The IV drug-using population is also at risk of acquiring and spreading HIV infection through unprotected sexual behaviors. Little is known about the sexual, contraceptive, and childbearing practices of IV drug users, although early studies indicate that more risk-reducing change has occurred in injection practices than in sexual behaviors. The committee recommends that high priority be given to studies of the sexual and procreative behavior of IV drug users, including methods to reduce sexual and perinatal (mother-infant) transmission of HIV.

Although the committee urges that more basic behavioral research be undertaken to improve understanding of risk-associated behaviors and how to change them, it also finds that the implementation of intervention programs cannot wait upon the findings of such research. The severity of the AIDS epidemic demands innovative approaches to prevent the spread of infection among IV drug users, with special attention to collecting good evaluation data. Reaching and serving IV drug users will require innovative methods and additional resources.[11] Slowing the spread of HIV infection in this country depends on the ability to find new ways to reach and influence this population. Planned variations of intervention strategies, accompanied by sound evaluation measures, will enable a determination of which kinds of programs are most successful in facilitating change in risky behaviors in this population.

NOTES

The New Epidemic: AIDS Issues in Public Policy and Disease Control

1. The background data on the spread of AIDS in the United States over the decade of the 1980s is necessary for any examination of public policy issues and for the establishment of regulatory efforts to deal with the disease and its impact. The Centers for Disease Control of the U.S. Public Health Service currently perform the key role in surveillance of the progress of the epidemic. The main source of general information on AIDS and all other epidemiological matters in the United States is found in the weekly publication from which the first article was taken, The Morbidity and Mortality Weekly Report. There are also more specialized weekly and monthly publications, The HIV/AIDS Surveillance Reports, Centers for Disease Control, National AIDS Clearinghouse, Rockville, MD. Information collected by state-level public health agencies is sent to the Centers for Disease Control and becomes part of the national statistics.

2. On an international level, the disease is tracked by a special unit of the World Health Organization in Geneva. The W.H.O.'s Global Program on AIDS was established in a formal manner in February 1987, although work had been going on in surveillance of the disease since 1983. The Global Program has three goals: prevention of new HIV infection, establishing health care for those sick and infected, and harnessing international and national efforts to find new strategies for controlling spread of the disease. The Program is directly attached to the Office of the Director-General of W.H.O. It has seven major units: national program support; surveillance, forecasting, and assessment; health promotion; social and behavioral research; biomedical research; epidemiological support and research; and a management unit.

3. The spread of the disease throughout the world has earned

---

11. For example, some AIDS intervention programs use mobile vans and cadres of "outreach workers" — who can go into "shooting galleries" and other places in which drug use occurs — which have proven helpful in serving people who have not been reached by other services or agencies.

it the title of the great pandemic of the 1980s. As many as 100 million people may be infected with HIV by 1991. There are still some parts of the world where the disease is less prevalent and where national efforts are still being made to keep the pandemic out of the country by controls on immigration, tourism, and travel by domestic citizens. This is particularly true in the Western Pacific Region of W.H.O. In the American hemisphere, there were 89,834 full-blown AIDS cases diagnosed by October of 1988. A publication of the Pan American Health Organization, a regional office of W.H.O., released in mid-1989, provides a review of the disease and national control programs in North and South America. Five countries (the United States, Brazil, Canada, Haiti, and Mexico) accounted for 96 percent of all of the AIDS cases in the hemisphere. See AIDS: Profile of an Epidemic, Pan Amer. Health Org., Scientific Pub. No. 514 (Wash. D.C. 1989).

4. The Rothman article provides a very useful perspective on the AIDS epidemic in the United States in comparison to earlier infectious diseases. Also, the Rothman article points out that public policy regarding control of the disease has not yielded to panic or what he calls "notions of catastrophe." The state governments and the state legislatures have generally taken the advice of their state public health departments and have moved with caution in applying *any* kind of compulsory measure. The earliest nationwide survey of state legislative activity, a survey commissioned by the U.S. Public Health Service, reached similar conclusions to those identified in the Rothman paper. See W. Curran, L. Gostin & M. Clark, Acquired Immunodeficiency Syndrome: Legal, Regulatory and Policy Analysis (D.H.H.S., Wash., D.C. 1986). See also Gostin & Curran, Legal Control Measures for AIDS: Reporting Requirements, Surveillance, Quarantine, and Regulation of Public Meeting Places, 77 Amer. J. Pub. Health 214 (1987). For a history of the development of public policy, see Fox, AIDS and the American Health Polity: The History and Prospects of a Crisis of Authority, 64 Milbank Q. (Supp. 1) 7 (1986). See also Black, The Plague Years: A Chronicle of AIDS, the Epidemic of Our Times (1986).

5. Legislative activity in the states has been very extensive. For a comprehensive, state-by-state review, see Gostin, Public Health Strategies for Confronting AIDS: Legislative and Regulatory Policy in the United States, 261 J.A.M.A. 1621 (1989). As indicated earlier, most state legislatures acted upon the advice (most of it very good) of their own state public health authorities. Traditional public health disease control systems were allowed to operate largely without new legislation on compulsory measures. In California and New York, vocal and active AIDS-patient groups fought, along with civil rights organizations, to prevent over-reaction in such areas as compulsory diagnostic

testing and quarantine. See Symposium, AIDS: Public Health and Civil Liberties, Hastings Cent. Rep., Special Supplement (Dec. 1986). Over a period of years, the state legislative activity has been tracked in a series of publications by the George Washington University Intergovernmental Health Policy Project. See AIDS: A Public Health Challenge: State Issues, Policies and Programs, 3 vol., George Wash. U., Wash., D.C. (1987) (and annual updates).

6. The National Research Council Report on IV Drug Use calls attention to one of the most serious public policy issues for the early 1990s. During the earlier years of the 1980s, the primary source of infection and spread of the disease was the male homosexual and bisexual community. Educational programs and prompt measures of treatment for sick victims of AIDS in this community were quite successful and the infection rate among persons in these high-risk groups was reduced considerably. See particularly Becker & Joseph, AIDS and Behavior Change to Reduce Risk: A Review, 78 Am. J. Pub. Health 394 (1988). See also Winkelstein, Samuel et al., The San Francisco Men's Health Study: III. Reduction in Human Immunodeficiency Virus Transmission Among Homosexual/Bisexual Men, 1982-86, 76 Am. J. Pub. Health 685 (1987). Currently, however, the spread of the disease by IV drug users is the most serious problem, especially in the larger cities where IV drug use is most common. Needle sharing is the most dangerous and most frequent mode of transfer of the disease through the bloodstream. See Magura, Grossman et al., Determinants of Needle Sharing Among Intravenous Drug Users, 79 Am. J. Pub. Health 459 (1989). The latest surveys indicate that the drugs used most frequently are cocaine mixed with heroin. Injection of heroin alone is decreasing significantly. About one-half of all needle sharing occurs in communal "shooting galleries," but a large segment of users share only in small groups with known associates. See Ginsberg, Intravenous Drug Abusers and HIV Infections: Consequences of Their Actions, 14 La. Med. & Health Care 268 (1986). For a collection of articles, see AIDS and IV Drug Abusers (Gala, Lewis & Baker eds. 1988).

7. The type of recommendation in the National Research Council Report for greater availability of clean needles, including programs of wide distribution free of charge in high-risk communities, has drawn considerable criticism from drug-control law enforcement officials and from political and religious leaders in minority (black and hispanic) neighborhoods. In terms of public policy, the issues are very difficult to resolve, particularly in an era of political conservatism and reluctance to increase governmental spending programs for drug treatment. See two conflicting views, Bennett, AIDS: Education and Public Policy, 7 St. Louis L. Rev. 1 (1988); Brown, AIDS: The Public Policy Imperative, 7 St. Louis L. Rev. 11 (1988). The most well

known of the needle distribution programs in a high-risk drug user population is that in Amsterdam, the Netherlands. See a description and evaluation, Needle Sharing Among Intravenous Drug Abusers: National and International Perspectives, Battjes and Pickens eds. (N.I.D.A. Res. Mon. Series 1988).

V. THE AIDS EPIDEMIC: ISSUES OF DISCRIMINATION, CONFIDENTIALITY, AND DISEASE CONTROL

World Health Organization, Resolution on Avoidance of Discrimination in Relation to HIV-Infected People and People with AIDS*
39 Intl. Dig. Health Legis. 761 (1988)

[After an extensive preamble, the following resolution was adopted by the WHO's World Assembly (representing all member states) and sent to all member states.]

Strongly convinced that respect for the human rights and dignity of HIV-infected people and people with AIDS, and of members of population groups, is vital to the success of national AIDS prevention and control programmes and of the global strategy;

1. Urges Member States, particularly in devising and carrying out national programmes for the prevention and control of HIV infection and AIDS:

(1) to foster a spirit of understanding and compassion for HIV-infected people and people with AIDS through information, education and social support programmes;

(2) to protect the human rights and dignity of HIV-infected people and people with AIDS, and of members of population groups, and to avoid discriminatory action against and stigmatization of them in the provision of services, employment and travel;

(3) to ensure the confidentiality of HIV testing and to promote the availability of confidential counselling and other support services to HIV-infected people and people with AIDS;

(4) to include in any reports to WHO on national AIDS strategies information on measures being taken to protect the

---

* This Resolution (41st World Health Assembly, Res. No. 41.24 (1988)) is reprinted from the International Digest of Health Legislation with permission of the Digest and the World Health Organization, Geneva, Switzerland.

human rights and dignity of HIV-infected people and people with AIDS;

2. Calls on all governmental, nongovernmental and international organizations and voluntary bodies engaged in AIDS control programmes to ensure that their programmes take fully into account the health needs of all people as well as the health needs and dignity of HIV-infected people and people with AIDS;

3. Requests the Director-General:

(1) to take all measures necessary to advocate the need to protect the human rights and dignity of HIV-infected people and people with AIDS, and of members of population groups;

(2) to collaborate with all relevant governmental, nongovernmental and international organizations and voluntary bodies in emphasizing the importance to the global strategy for the prevention and control of AIDS of avoiding discrimination against HIV-infected people and people with AIDS;

(3) to stress to Member States and to all others concerned the dangers to the health of everyone of discriminatory action against and stigmatization of HIV-infected people and people with AIDS, and members of population groups, by continuing to provide accurate information on AIDS and guidance on its prevention and control;

(4) to report annually to the Health Assembly through the Executive Board on the implementation of this resolution.

W.H.O. Regional Office for Europe, Report on International Consultation on Health Legislation and Ethics in the Field of AIDS and HIV Infection*
(1988)

I. Notification and Reporting Systems

This is a key area which required immediate action after the beginning of the epidemic in 1981 — with cases being reported in many countries, their incidence rising rapidly, the disease being fatal and its epidemiological nature and extent a matter of speculation. Governments in the European Region have therefore reacted very quickly in setting out arrangements for the notification and reporting of AIDS.

About two-thirds of the European countries have taken measures to classify AIDS as a "notifiable disease".

The passing of measures concerning the notification of confirmed

---

* This excerpt from the above-entitled report is reprinted by permission of the European Office of the World Health Organization, Copenhagen, Denmark.

AIDS cases encountered relatively minor difficulties. More serious controversy was aroused when measures were passed which required further notification on the basis of seropositivity. Thirteen countries notify seropositivity in addition to AIDS.

In a few countries, six at present, the reporting of AIDS cases is part of a monitoring system based on voluntary reporting (Belgium, Ireland, the Netherlands, Portugal, Spain and the United Kingdom).

It is interesting to note that since 1987 two countries have moved from voluntary reporting towards a compulsory system: the Federal Republic of Germany and Switzerland.

At the very early stages of the epidemic there was clearly in many countries a hesitation to classify AIDS as a venereal disease. The two countries, Iceland and Sweden, who, then classified AIDS as a venereal disease maintain their stand. Since then Romania has also taken this stand.

The safeguarding of confidentiality is a shared preoccupation in European countries. Twenty-seven Member States reported that they have adopted specific safeguards. It is noteworthy that some have passed regulations which make provision for a special form of notification for AIDS cases, different from the one normally used for other communicable diseases. The intention was to produce a new type of form that would better safeguard confidentiality concerning the identity of the person, while still enabling the medical officer concerned to follow up the case.

II. Follow-up Procedures

By "follow-up procedures" we mean: tracing contacts, duties of patients, counselling of seropositives and measures against unsocial behaviour.

The measures vary from country to country depending on factors which characterize these societies and, in particular, their administrative traditions and cultural conditions. There is a striking difference in the attitudes of different countries. Some countries, such as Austria, Finland, Norway, Romania, Sweden, and the USSR, insist on a whole range of procedures which have traditionally been applied for sexually-transmitted diseases.

As one might expect in a situation where a frightening disease of epidemic proportion threatens with no known control measures, the handling of confirmed AIDS cases has been approached in a drastic manner. In some exceptional circumstances the law even foresees a variety of coercive measures, such as obligatory removal to a hospital, confinement in isolation and penalties for wilful spread of the disease.

Systematic counselling of seropositive people is increasing; in a

V. Issues of Discrimination, Confidentiality, and Disease Control

few countries, such as Austria, there have been important items of legislation providing for the appropriation of funds to subsidise AIDS psychosocial counselling programmes. Roughly two thirds of the countries have such systematic counselling.

III. Preventive Measures

It is generally agreed that the best preventive action is the exchange of high-quality information and efficient health education strategies. A host of measures geared at supporting or creating an appropriate programme of information for the public have been taken by many of the Member States. In some countries where restrictions on the advertising of contraceptives have existed (France and Belgium), these have recently been waived.

Steps have recently been taken to systematically propose premarital testing and testing for pregnant women on a voluntary basis; particularly in Bulgaria, Greece, Iceland, Norway, Spain and Sweden.

There are also important items of legislation providing for the appropriation of funds to subsidize and create so-called alternative testing sites which enable testing without any charge and with strict confidentiality. Eleven countries specifically refer to this.

Preventive measures concerning the screening of high risk groups has been a controversial subject and the last WHO Regional Committee for Europe urged caution in that field, where stringent measures could be counterproductive.

In fact, there is clearly a growing demand for designing measures to protect seropositive individuals from discrimination with regard to job applications, renting apartments, health insurance, and to prevent their becoming victims of potentially ill-informed communities, such as in schools and at work places.

IV. General Considerations

A striking feature of legislation on AIDS in Europe is the true diversity of situations in the various Member States, in spite of similar epidemiological characteristics and the common threat of the spread of the virus.

For instance, the Netherlands and Sweden are two countries where one might expect to find some similarities in policy attitudes and legislative approach in the public health field.

In the Netherlands, the Government did not feel the necessity to introduce specific legislation on AIDS, and has thus maintained a stand characterized by a voluntary reporting system and accompanied by specific measures such as the safeguarding of confidentiality, measures for the counselling on seropositives, and the creation of alternative testing sites.

In contrast, Sweden has undertaken a broad range of measures covering the main problem areas and, since 1983, has declared AIDS a notifiable disease; HIV-infection must also be reported. Norway, which also made AIDS cases notifiable in 1983, waited until mid-1986 to make HIV-infection notifiable. A similar move away from voluntary reporting to compulsory reporting in the Federal Republic of Germany and in Switzerland, both in September 1987, might well indicate a trend to take a stronger line.

It is interesting to note that, since August 1983, Norway has produced no fewer than 31 circulars specifying various measures and precautions to prevent infection. While other countries did not go beyond the initial measures enforced a couple of years ago with regard to the most urgent areas of concern, e.g. the protection of blood and other donated items. Other countries have also recorded a rise in legislative activities; for example France passed 22 texts (be it law, decree, order or circular) between 1983 and 1987. There is [a] growing trend for governments to use circulars to take action on measures which would in other cases warrant more advanced instruments as well as relevant public involvement.

In some countries, such as Bulgaria, Hungary and the USSR, legislation has aimed at more stringent proposals including mandatory screening of high-risk groups, while in others the value of many of these initiatives is questioned.

Judson & Vernon, The Impact of AIDS on State and Local Health Departments: Issues and a Few Answers*
78 Am. J. Pub. Health 387 (1988)

The many [AIDS] activities to impact on [the] Denver Public Health [Department] have included:

- Extensive studies of the epidemiology of human immunodeficiency virus (HIV) in Denver which built upon prior long-term studies of HBV (hepatitis B virus) in homosexual men and the remarkable level of mutual trust and commitment which they engendered;
- Surveillance of all AIDS cases in Colorado which was initiated prior to funding in 1982 and carried on with funding after 1983;

* This excerpt from the article by Franklyn N. Hudson of the City of Denver Health Department and Thomas M. Vernon, Commissioner of the Colorado State Department of Health is reprinted by permission of the American Journal of Public Health. (References in the original article are omitted.)

V. Issues of Discrimination, Confidentiality, and Disease Control   1229

- Direct care to more than 30 per cent of all Colorado AIDS patients and medical consultation on an additional 20 per cent;
- Enactment in early 1986 of one of the first regulations in the nation to provide for regular inspections of bathhouses for gay men (and similar establishments) to assure that patrons were warned of the risk of AIDS and that defined unsafe sexual acts were not permitted;
- Development in 1985 and 1986, without additional tax payer support, of a clinic in Denver Public Health dedicated to the care and treatment of patients with AIDS virus infections including zidovudine and intravenous pump therapy;
- In 1985, successful competition for and deployment of a Centers for Disease Control AIDS Prevention Demonstration Project;
- Provision of 65 per cent of all HIV testing and counseling performed in Colorado through a dedicated testing clinic, the sexually transmitted diseases (STD) clinic, and a substance abuse treatment center;
- Establishment early on of a cordial and productive working and funding relationship with the independent Colorado AIDS Project;
- Close collaboration with the Colorado Department of Health (CDH) on AIDS control efforts, including development of AIDS control regulations and laws.

Because the Colorado Department of Health and its STD/AIDS Control Program do not directly provide patient care or clinical research, the CDH was not heavily impacted by AIDS until the availability of HIV antibody detection tests in the spring of 1985. Since then the CDH has been extensively involved through its implementation of HIV testing and counseling sites and educational programs throughout the state. In addition, much effort was expended by the CDH with the collaboration of Denver Public Health and other health leaders to pass one of the first two regulations in the nation requiring the reporting of all HIV infections by name to the CDH and local health departments. Subsequently, similar collaboration occurred in developing more comprehensive AIDS control legislation and in implementing one of the first HIV contact tracing programs.

With this background in mind, we will discuss in greater detail some of the AIDS issues and problems affecting state and local health departments.

AIDS Control Regulations and Legislation

The availability in early 1985 of a simple, inexpensive, and accurate screening test for HIV infections, coupled with geometric increases in the number of new AIDS cases, demanded that public health departments everywhere address the AIDS epidemic as a first priority. In a March 25, 1985 presidential letter to members of the American Venereal Disease Association, one of us (Judson) commented on the obvious need for more proactive control efforts which would include specific AIDS legislation.

> I am most concerned about the lack of movement towards an organized HTLV-III control program. At this point it seems that control measures, such as the new ELISA HTLV-III antibody tests, are being directed exclusively at preventing transfusion acquired infections, which represent less than 2 percent of all infections. Are we guilty of taking an ostrich approach to the most deadly STD threat in recent history? The realities of imperfect diagnostic tests and fears about confidentiality should not drive us to the sidelines to observe the natural history of this epidemic. In my mind, the consequences to gay men and other high risk groups of doing nothing are far worse than the consequences of an active program which at least considers the use of traditional public health disease control measures. These might include serologic screening of high risk individuals for HTLV-III, compulsory reporting of test results for entry into restricted access registers, contact tracing and cluster interviews, and legal restrictions on the sexual activities of seropositive individuals who continue to expose others to infection without warning. For years, each of these measures has been practiced to control infectious syphilis, 60-70 percent of which now occurs in gay men. The goal for the near term is to better understand the epidemiology of sexually transmitted HTLV-III infections and to contain further spread of the virus. The longer term goal is to use registers to quickly and efficiently recall seropositive individuals for effective antivirals, and seronegative individuals for retesting and administration of protective vaccines.
>
> No matter what form control programs may take, their success will depend upon the active participation and support of gay organizations and the gay community at large. This support understandably will be weak until we are able to convince the general public that there is virtually no risk of contracting AIDS through nonsexual contact with HTLV-III positive men, and until we are able to assure gay men that their confidentiality will be protected.

The foregoing excerpt proved to be a gross underestimate of the difficulties we would encounter in passing responsible and effective AIDS control legislation in Colorado. Mainly, it failed to anticipate the intensity and persistence of the opposition to reporting HIV infections by name which would come from a small, well organized group of gay men who claimed to represent the "gay community." Debate over civil rights issues began with the first mention of AIDS control legislation.

In 1985, with the Director of the Colorado Department of Health

V. Issues of Discrimination, Confidentiality, and Disease Control 1231

STD/AIDS Control Section and the Assistant Director of the Denver Disease Control Service, we proposed a more comprehensive AIDS control program which addressed the following problems and principles:

- Public Health must not apply a lesser standard of control to AIDS than to syphilis and other STDs, since AIDS was spreading far more rapidly, was far more deadly, and could only be averted through prevention.
- Existing STD and general communicable disease control regulations and laws were often out of date, were overly broad (in the case of quarantine provisions), or were not clearly applicable to AIDS.
- AIDS case reports are inadequate to monitor the course of the HIV epidemic. AIDS cases occurred an average of more than five years after infection and were outnumbered by undetected HIV infections by 30-50 to one. More accurate knowledge of HIV antibody prevalence with a means to correct for multiple positive results from a single person would assist in better understanding of the epidemic.
- Approximately 10-20 percent of individuals who voluntarily are tested for HIV do not return for their test results and therefore do not receive the all-important counseling. Much benefit could come from locating such individuals, and providing counseling in the field.
- Persons at risk of HIV infection have an ethical responsibility to be tested and, if positive, to notify all unsuspecting partners in unsafe sex or needle sharing activities. When an infected individual is unwilling or unable to notify partners of exposure, the health care provider and/or public health authorities are obligated to assume this responsibility through traditional or innovative methods of partner notification.
- To achieve the full public health benefit of these principles, confidential reporting by name and locating information of all persons testing positive for HIV antibody is indicated.
- To obtain full participation of individuals at risk for HIV infection in the essential testing and counseling programs, public health records containing individual identifier data must receive near absolute legal protections against unauthorized disclosure.
- Mechanisms incorporating appeal rights and confidentiality protections must be developed to restrict the behavior of the occasional HIV-infected person who, after appropriate and intensive counseling, continues to expose others.
- Behaviors at high risk of transmitting HIV were continuing to occur in certain establishments such as bathhouses for gay men,

adult bookstores, bars, and shooting galleries for intravenous drugs. Public health leaders bear responsibility for protecting the public from exposure to HIV by promoting measures which would either regulate or close such establishments.

To these ends, two board of health regulations and one state statute have since been passed and are reviewed, because each was among the first of its kind in the United States.

State Board of Health HIV Reporting Regulations

Within eight months of the Food and Drug Administration's approval of the ELISA (enzyme-linked immunosorbent assay) test for HIV antibody, the Colorado State Board of Health in November 1985 unanimously voted to amend Colorado's communicable disease reporting regulations by adding positive ELISA and Western Blot antibody tests and virus cultures to its list of over 50 infectious disease diagnostic tests the results of which must be reported by clinical laboratories to the state and local health departments of Colorado. Colorado, along with most other states, has used reporting by clinical laboratories as a component of communicable disease surveillance systems for many years. Laboratory reporting of serologic tests for syphilis has made a critical contribution to syphilis control, both in promoting direct public health intervention and in reducing the administrative burden of repeated and duplicate tests on the same individual.

In adopting the amendment, the Board of Health accepted four purposes for making the HIV antibody tests reportable:

1) to alert responsible health agencies to the presence of persons likely to be infected with a highly dangerous virus;

2) to allow responsible health agencies to ensure that such persons are properly counseled as to the significance of their laboratory test, and as to what they need to do to prevent further transmission of the virus;

3) to allow responsible health agencies to monitor the occurrence and spread of infection with this virus in the population of Colorado; and

4) to allow responsible health agencies to recall persons with likely or proven HTLV-III infection when specific antiviral treatment becomes available.

The Board of Health also restated principles of confidentiality of these reports as follows:

> All information with personal identifiers collected according to the communicable disease reporting rules is held by local and state health departments as confidential information and is not released to anyone

V. Issues of Discrimination, Confidentiality, and Disease Control

without specific written permission of the person tested, as provided in Board of Health rules. Thus the information is not available to insurance companies or employers without permission from the person tested.

In the debate over the regulations, there were two salient issues:

First, would large numbers of individuals who might benefit from testing be driven underground by the reporting requirement? At the time of adopting the regulation there was no definitive answer to this question but, consistent with previous testing policy, it was made clear that proof of identification would not be requested of individuals who came for testing, thus offering the de facto option of using a pseudonym. Results gained since November 1985 have been encouraging and are noted in the following section. Perhaps 20 percent of individuals have used a pseudonym, but at least some of them at the same time offered a correct address and/or telephone number.

The second concern was whether outside pressure on confidentiality protections would lead to breaches. The precautions taken to date including sophisticated physical security may have been superfluous. Even telephone inquiries from employers, family members, or other groups have been rare to nonexistent, and there has been no inappropriate disclosure of confidential public health reports by public health agencies or employees.

Rules and Regulations to Minimize Transmission of the AIDS Virus in Certain Establishments within the City and County of Denver

Following three months of heated discussions and public hearings, the Rules and Regulations were approved and adopted by the Board of Health and Hospitals of the City and County of Denver on February 10, 1986. During the discussions, bathhouses for gay men were the central focus and it became apparent that the bathhouses symbolized at once sexual liberation for gay men and the risk behavior which had produced the AIDS epidemic. This created an unwanted confrontation between bathhouse owners, certain gay rights activists, and the American Civil Liberties Union (ACLU) of Colorado on the one side, and Denver Public Health, the Board of Health and Hospitals, and certain gay rights activists on the other side. The ACLU argued that the City and County of Denver had no authority to regulate the sexual activities of consenting adults anywhere, no matter how deadly the AIDS epidemic might be. Denver Public Health and the Board of Health and Hospitals argued that the City and County of Denver had both legal and moral obligations to control the AIDS epidemic by preventing new cases, particularly within licensed establishments open to the public. They argued further that while adults were consenting to sexual contact, they probably were not consenting to infection with a deadly virus. It was the goal of Denver Public Health to strike a compromise in which the social functions of the bathhouses were maintained while unsafe sex was largely regulated out. Because Denver Public Health had been screening regularly for gonorrhea and syphilis in the bathhouses since 1975, we also were aware of the unique potential for on-site AIDS prevention through access to a population with demonstrated high-risk behavior. Following are the abbreviated regulations:

Definitions

"Unsafe sexual activities" means sexual activities which are likely to result in the transmission of the HTLV-III virus through the exchange of body fluids, i.e., anal intercourse without the use of a condom lubricated with nonoxynol-9 ointment, fellatio and analingus.

"Regulated Establishment" means an establishment licensed to do business in the City and County of Denver where public health officials have reason to believe that unsafe sexual activities take place, including, but not limited to bathhouses, adult book stores, adult movie theaters, hot tub and spa establishments, and massage parlors.

Duty of Owner or Operator

The person in charge of a regulated establishment must take reasonable steps to prohibit unsafe sexual activities in the establishment, including the following:

Signs — Regulated establishments must post signs in prominent locations in every room, describing the risks and methods of transmission of the HTLV-III virus and listing unsafe sexual activities.

Monitoring and Expulsion — The person in charge of a regulated establishment must monitor the premises with sufficient frequency to assure compliance with these regulations. Any patrons who engage in unsafe sexual activities must be immediately expelled.

Prevention Information — The person in charge of a regulated establishment shall make available to each patron of the facility a pamphlet containing AIDS prevention information.

Inspection Requirements

Observation — All activity or recreational areas in regulated establishments shall have an observation window or opening which permits complete viewing of the interior of the area at all times.

Summary Closure — If the Manager of Health and Hospitals finds that a regulated establishment poses an imminent threat to the health and safety of its patrons due to repeated violations of these Rules and Regulations, the Manager may order summary closure of the establishment, for a period not to exceed 10 days, pending further investigation.

Within five months, the largest of Denver's three bathhouses closed for reasons unrelated to the regulations. A second bathhouse closed shortly thereafter, only to reopen in the same facility under a different name and, we are told, without liability insurance. Inspectors from Denver Public Health have continued to make unannounced weekly visits to each bathhouse to ascertain compliance with AIDS control and other health regulations. For the most part, bathhouse managements have been cooperative. Inspections of certain adult bookstores and bars have been less regular, but through other sources it is believed that unsafe sexual activities occur there only rarely.

Although we have no methods to quantitate the extent to which the regulations have reduced HIV transmission in these establishments, we feel certain that the overall effect has been positive for Colorado's AIDS control program. The biggest threat to the continued existence of the bathhouses comes from declining customer interest and the increasing threat of liability suits.

Colorado Revised Statutes, Title 25, Article 4, Part 14; HIV Infection and Acquired Immune Deficiency Syndrome

By the fall of 1986, the reporting requirements for positive HIV antibody tests by clinical laboratories had been instituted, and there was neither evidence of significant fall-off in numbers of gay and bisexual men tested nor any serious challenge to the confidentiality of public health records. Nevertheless, with the sponsorship of a thoughtful moderate legislator, the Department of Health proposed legislation to the 1987 Colorado General Assembly which would achieve three goals: First, and most important, was to strengthen the statutory protections of the reports to public health agencies which were required by the State Board of Health regulations. Second, was to codify in law the responsibilities of the Department of Health for educational efforts to slow the AIDS epidemic. Third, was to modify the overly broad existing authority of the Department of Health for dealing with recalcitrant individuals. This older legislation, adopted in 1947, read: "To establish, maintain, and enforce isolation and quarantine, and . . . to exercise such physical control over property and the persons of the people within the state as the department may find necessary for the protection of the public health."

The 1987 legislation, introduced as House Bill 1177, spawned a long and occasionally contentious debate, but one which served to educate members of the Legislature and the general public on the difficult social and policy issues of the AIDS epidemic. The debate on confidentiality protections of the public health reports was converted by the ACLU and a well organized group of gay men to a test of confidential versus anonymous testing. ACLU of Colorado was following national and local policy which opposed name reportability of HIV infections in any form. Nonetheless, an initial House Committee vote requiring anonymous testing was overwhelmingly rejected by the entire House. We believe the final result to be among the strongest protections of confidentiality for HIV disease and test reports in the nation. Among other particulars, the reports to public health may not be released, shared or made public "upon subpoena, search warrant, discovery proceedings, or otherwise . . ." Strong penalties are applied to anyone releasing information or breaching confidentiality requirements.

The component of the bill addressing educational efforts produced little controversy, but the third component dealing with procedures for placement of restrictive measures on recalcitrant persons was complex, with committees in both the House and the Senate spending considerable time on legal safeguards. The final product includes requirements that all reasonable efforts be made to obtain the voluntary cooperation of an individual; that the burden of proof be on the health department to show by clear and convincing evidence that grounds exist for measures taken; that the sequence of measures directed at the recalcitrant person be applied serially and not be more restrictive than necessary to protect the public health; a right of refusal to comply with any health department order; a right for any individual to appeal an order to a court; closed and confidential court hearings as well as transcripts or records; and a right to have an attorney appear on the individual's behalf in any hearing. We believe that these limitations on the antiquated quarantine isolation law of 1947 are eminently sensible.

Although the legislative process has been frustrating, it has resulted in public education about communicable disease control in general and AIDS control in particular. An important outcome appears to be broad public understanding that Colorado's AIDS control programs protect both an individual's confidentiality and the public's health, and that public health agencies in Colorado are acting vigorously and responsibly. . . .

Public Fear Reactions to AIDS and to AIDS Control Efforts

Public health efforts to control the AIDS epidemic often are caught in a cross fire of fears epitomized by two small, vocal groups

V. Issues of Discrimination, Confidentiality, and Disease Control   1237

of individuals within our communities. On the one side are heterosexual parents of school children who have unsupported fears of HIV contagion in the schools, while on the other side are gay men (usually educated and White) who have unsupported fears that AIDS control efforts will become a weapon for discrimination. Neither side seems able to overcome its fears except through an impossible guarantee that the perceived risks will be reduced to zero. Parents may fail to place in perspective a reality in which vehicular accidents, voluntary and involuntary exposure to tobacco smoke, and alcohol present greater risks to their children than does infection with the AIDS virus through casual contact. In like manner, gay men may fail to place in perspective an historical reality in which the threats to their own rights to life, liberty, and pursuit of happiness are greater from contracting the AIDS virus, and from other life-style related risks, than they are from public health AIDS prevention actions. Paradoxically, education is touted by some gay community leaders as a cure for societal fears of AIDS, but not as a cure for their own fears of responsible and confidential HIV testing.

One would have hoped that irrational fears would be eased by the reality of the situation: intensive study of an epidemic which is now over six years old and in which there have been no documented instances of casual contagion in schools and, at least in Colorado, no human rights violations from public health actions. That this is not the case has been attributed to the nature of the fears which reside in areas over which individuals feel they lack control and in which there is much that is unknown. Whatever the psychodynamics, public health must not let political influence born out of unsupported fears interfere with responsible AIDS control policy. . . .

NOTES

AIDS Control Programs at the National, State, and Local Levels

1. There are often conflicting goals of public policy in AIDS prevention and control. Efforts have been made to reconcile the main conflict between identifying HIV-infected persons (for purposes of tracking the disease and providing counseling and treatment) and preventing improper and punitive discrimination against AIDS patients and HIV-positive persons. The fact that the disease is not easily contracted helped to encourage support for antidiscrimination in employment, housing, schooling, and general health care. As indicated in the W.H.O. resolution, antidiscrimination policies have had the support of international and national public health authorities. In the United States, a recommendation for legislation preventing improper

discrimination came from the Presidential Commission on the AIDS Epidemic appointed by President Reagan. In a chapter of the Report of the Commission with recommendations on legal and ethical issues, a firm national policy of antidiscrimination against both AIDS patients and HIV-infected persons was given first priority. See the Report of the Presidential Commission on the HIV Epidemic (U.S. Gov. Pub. 1988-0-214-701-QL3, 1988) pp. 119 et seq. The recommendation did not receive strong support from the Reagan Administration. As indicated later in this chapter, however, considerable progress has been achieved at the state level. See Gebbie, The President's Commission on AIDS: What Did It Do?, 79 Am. J. Pub. Health 868 (1989).

2. The Report from the European Office of W.H.O. illustrates different approaches in several European countries in dealing with AIDS in relation to traditional methods of public health regulation of infectious diseases. The range of approaches in Europe is actually more varied than in the American states, due largely to the greater diversity in political and social orientation. Also, the United States Public Health Service and the Centers for Disease Control have been unifying forces in developing and implementing policies of AIDS prevention and control at the state level in America.

3. The article by Judson and Vernon describes the earliest American public health program that applied the more traditional public health regulatory policies to the AIDS epidemic, particularly in the reporting of HIV-infected cases to the health departments. These programs are often followed by efforts to notify sexual and drug partners of infected persons of the personal risk to which they have potentially been exposed. As indicated in the Gostin article, cited in this chapter at 1222, the number of states requiring reporting of HIV-infection has been increasing rapidly in recent years. Such a policy has received greater support from leading public health figures, even in New York and California, along with support for more diagnostic testing so that the infection can be tracked more accurately. See Lambert, With Few Tested, AIDS Debate Erupts, New York Times, Sunday, July 23, 1989, at 28. For a review of another approach at the local level in the United States, see Konigsberg & Barrera, Local Public Health Perspectives on the AIDS Epidemic, 12 Nova L. Rev. 1141 (1988) (reviewing regulatory efforts at the local and state levels in Florida). For a review of an antidiscrimination program in California by the head of the AIDS Discrimination Unit in the Los Angeles City Attorney's Office, see Schulman, AIDS Discrimination: Its Nature, Meaning and Function, 12 Nova L. Rev. 1113 (1988).

4. The major objections among public health authorities to widespread diagnostic testing have related to the low yield of positive cases among low-risk populations. The cost of such programs can be quite high and can drive high-risk populations to resist the programs

V. Issues of Discrimination, Confidentiality, and Disease Control

and go "underground." See for example, Confronting AIDS: Directions for Public Health, Health Care, and Research (Institute of Medicine, Wash. D.C., 1986). See also Gostin, Curran and Clark, The Case Against Casefinding in Controlling AIDS: Testing, Screening and Reporting, 12 Am. J. L. & Med. 7 (1987); Cleary, Barry et al, Compulsory Premarital Screening for the Human Immunodeficiency Virus, 258 J.A.M.A. 1757 (1987). The State of Illinois, the first to adopt a premarital test requirement, repealed that law in September 1989.

Support for both voluntary and compulsory diagnostic testing has been greatly undermined by the absence of an effective follow-up program of care and treatment. As was indicated earlier in this chapter in regard to control of sexually transmitted diseases, programs of partner notification, sexual contact tracing, and compulsory treatment measures could be justified legally only when the disease was not only dangerously infectious, but easily and effectively treated. As yet, no such fully effective treatment exists for AIDS or HIV infection. However, the more recent research studies (indicating that AZT not only delays serious symptoms and prolongs life in AIDS cases, but may also delay the onset of symptoms in HIV-infected persons) could lead to more aggressive regulatory efforts.

5. The problems with developing treatment programs for AIDS and HIV infection were aggravated by the high price of the only known active drug, azidothymidine (AZT). Drug prices have been reduced due to public pressure, but also because of the expectation that many more patients with asymptomatic conditions will be placed on drug treatment. There is currently a federal subsidy of $30 million for the treatment of uninsured AIDS patients. The federal program of Medicaid covers about 40 percent of all health care for AIDS patients. Persons with a diagnosed case of AIDS (in accordance with the CDC definition) are now immediately classified as "disabled" under the federal Disability Insurance Program and Supplementary Social Security. However, they must meet other eligibility requirements such as a sufficient work history to accumulate income benefits.

6. The federal government operates a number of programs related to the AIDS epidemic. The National Institutes of Health (NIH) in 16 different scientific institutes supported some $1.6 billion in AIDS and HIV research in the 1989 federal budget. The NIH made some 600 financial grants to scientists in 1989 studying aspects of the epidemic and seeking to develop vaccines and therapeutic drugs.

The Centers for Disease Control, as indicated earlier, are active in epidemiological surveillance of the disease and in public information and education programs. In 1989, the CDC spent almost $60 million in its special program of surveillance of HIV seropositivity in patients (new admissions and newborn infants) in a national sample of 42 selected hospitals across the country. The Health Resources and Services Administration with an AIDS-related budget of $149 million conducted and made financial grants for programs of health care services to AIDS patients including demonstration projects in 21 cities.

The Alcohol, Drug Abuse, and Mental Health Administration, with a budget for AIDS programs of $352 million in 1989, conducted research in relation to spread of the disease among intravenous drug abusers, and provided education and training of personnel for counseling, treatment, and rehabilitation programs related to AIDS. At the National Institute of Drug Abuse, mentioned earlier in this chapter, some 40 percent of the 1989 budget was allocated to AIDS-related activities.

The Federal Food and Drug Administration is one of the most important regulatory agencies active in the AIDS field since it regulates the blood banks all over the country and has national authority over evaluation and licensing of all drugs and vaccines developed to cope with the disease. The U.S. Public Health Service also manages the National AIDS Program Office, an agency for overall coordination of AIDS activities.

See generally Winkenwerder, Kessler & Stolec, Federal Spending for Illness Caused by the Human Immunodeficiency Virus, 320 New Engl. J. Med. 1598 (1989). For statistical data over a period of years, see Scitovsky & Rice, Estimates of the Direct and Indirect Costs of the AIDS Syndrome in the United States, 1985, 1986, and 1991, 102 Pub. Health Rep. 5 (1987). For a general review of the costs of caring for AIDS patients, see Fox & Thomas, AIDS Cost Analysis and Social Policy, 15 L. Med. & Health Care 186 (1988).

New York Public Health Law Concerning AIDS Diagnostic Testing, Informed Consent, Confidentiality, and Disclosure Provisions
N.Y. Public Health Law §2781 et seq. (1989)

§2781. HIV Related Testing

1. Except as provided in section three thousand one hundred twenty-one of the civil practice law and rules, or unless otherwise specifically authorized or required by a state or federal law, no person shall order the performance of an HIV related test without first receiving the written, informed consent of the subject of the test who has capacity to consent or, when the subject lacks capacity to consent, of a person authorized pursuant to law to consent to health care for such individual. A physician or other person authorized pursuant to law to order the performance of an HIV related test shall certify, in the order for the performance of an HIV related test, that informed

V. Issues of Discrimination, Confidentiality, and Disease Control 1241

consent required by this section has been received prior to ordering such test by a laboratory or other facility.

2. Informed consent to an HIV related test shall consist of a statement signed by the subject of the test who has capacity to consent or, when the subject lacks capacity to consent, by a person authorized pursuant to law to consent to health care for the subject which includes at least the following:

(a) an explanation of the test, including its purpose, the meaning of its results, and the benefits of early diagnosis and medical intervention; and

(b) an explanation of the procedures to be followed, including that the test is voluntary, that consent may be withdrawn at any time, and a statement advising the subject that anonymous testing is available; and

(c) an explanation of the confidentiality protections afforded confidential HIV related information under this article, including the circumstances under which and classes of persons to whom disclosure of such information may be required, authorized or permitted under this article or in accordance with other provisions of law or regulation.

3. Prior to the execution of a written informed consent, a person ordering the performance of an HIV related test shall provide to the subject of an HIV related test or, if the subject lacks capacity to consent, to a person authorized pursuant to law to consent to health care for the subject, an explanation of the nature of AIDS and HIV related illness, information about discrimination problems that disclosure of the test result could cause and legal protections against such discrimination, and information about behavior known to pose risks for transmission and contraction of HIV infection.

4. A person authorized pursuant to law to order the performance of an HIV related test shall provide to the person seeking such test an opportunity to remain anonymous and to provide written, informed consent through use of a coded system with no linking of individual identity to the test request or results. A health care provider who is not authorized by the commissioner to provide HIV related tests on an anonymous basis shall refer a person who requests an anonymous test to a test site which does provide anonymous testing. The provisions of this subdivision shall not apply to a health care provider ordering the performance of an HIV related test on an individual proposed for insurance coverage.

5. At the time of communicating the test result to the subject of the test, a person ordering the performance of an HIV related test shall provide the subject of the test or, if the subject lacks capacity to consent, the person authorized pursuant to law to consent to health care for the subject with counseling or referrals for counseling: (a)

for coping with the emotional consequences of learning the result; (b) regarding the discrimination problems that disclosure of the result could cause; (c) for behavior change to prevent transmission or contraction of HIV infection; (d) to inform such person of available medical treatments; and (e) regarding the test subject's need to notify his or her contacts.

6. The provisions of this section shall not apply to the performance of an HIV related test:

(a) by a health care provider or health facility in relation to the procuring, processing, distributing or use of a human body or a human body part, including organs, tissues, eyes, bones, arteries, blood, semen, or other body fluids, for use in medical research or therapy, or for transplantation to individuals provided, however, that where the test results are communicated to the subject, post-test counseling, as described in subdivision five of this section, shall nonetheless be required; or

(b) for the purpose of research if the testing is performed in a manner by which the identity of the test subject is not known and may not be retrieved by the researcher; or

(c) on a deceased person, when such test is conducted to determine the cause of death or for epidemiological purposes.

§2782. *Confidentiality and Disclosure*

1. No person who obtains confidential HIV related information in the course of providing any health or social service or pursuant to a release of confidential HIV related information may disclose or be compelled to disclose such information, except to the following:

(a) the protected individual or, when the protected individual lacks capacity to consent, a person authorized pursuant to law to consent to health care for the individual;

(b) any person to whom disclosure is authorized pursuant to a release of confidential HIV related information;

(c) an agent or employee of a health facility or health care provider if (1) the agent or employee is permitted to access medical records, (2) the health facility or health care provider itself is authorized to obtain the HIV related information, and (3) the agent or employee provides health care to the protected individual, or maintains or processes medical records for billing or reimbursement;

(d) a health care provider or health facility when knowledge of the HIV related information is necessary to provide appropriate care or treatment to the protected individual or a child of the individual;

(e) a health facility or health care provider, in relation to the procurement, processing, distributing or use of a human body or a human body part, including organs, tissues, eyes, bones, arteries,

V. Issues of Discrimination, Confidentiality, and Disease Control

blood, semen, or other body fluids, for use in medical education, research, therapy, or for transplantation to individuals;

(f) health facility staff committees or accreditation or oversight review organizations authorized to access medical records; provided that such committees or organizations may only disclose confidential HIV related information: (1) back to the facility or provider of a health or social service; (2) to carry out the monitoring, evaluation, or service review for which it was obtained; or (3) to a federal, state or local government agency for the purposes of and subject to the conditions provided in subdivision six of this section;

(g) a federal, state, county or local health officer when such disclosure is mandated by federal or state law;

(h) an authorized agency in connection with foster care or adoption of a child. Such agency shall be authorized to redisclose such information only pursuant to this article or in accordance with the provisions of section three hundred seventy-three-a of the social services law;

(i) third party reimbursers or their agents to the extent necessary to reimburse health care providers for health services; provided that, where necessary, an otherwise appropriate authorization for such disclosure has been secured by the provider;

(j) an insurance institution, for other than the purpose set forth in paragraph (i) of this subdivision, provided the insurance institution secures a dated and written authorization that indicates that health care providers, health facilities, insurance institutions, and other persons are authorized to disclose information about the protected individual, the nature of the information to be disclosed, the purposes for which the information is to be disclosed and which is signed by: (1) the protected individual; (2) if the protected individual lacks the capacity to consent, such other person authorized pursuant to law to consent for such individual; or (3) if the protected individual is deceased, the beneficiary or claimant for benefits under an insurance policy, a health services plan, or an employee welfare benefit plan as defined in 29 U.S.C. 1002(1), covering such protected individual;

(k) any person to whom disclosure is ordered by a court of competent jurisdiction pursuant to section twenty-seven hundred eighty-five of this article;

(*l*) an employee or agent of the division of parole, in accordance with paragraph (a) of subdivision two of section twenty-seven hundred eighty-six of this article, to the extent the employee or agent is authorized to access records containing such information in order to carry out the division's functions, powers and duties with respect to the protected individual, pursuant to section two hundred fifty-nine-a of the executive law;

(m) an employee or agent of the division of probation, in

accordance with paragraph (a) of subdivision two of section twenty-seven hundred eighty-six of this article, to the extent the employee or agent is authorized to access records containing such information in order to carry out the division's functions, powers and duties with respect to the protected individual, pursuant to article twelve of the executive law;

(n) a medical director of a local correctional facility as defined in section forty of the correction law, in accordance with paragraph (a) of subdivision two of section twenty-seven hundred eighty-six of this article, to the extent the medical director is authorized to access records containing such information in order to carry out his or her functions, powers and duties with respect to the protected individual; or

(o) an employee or agent of the commission of correction, in accordance with paragraph (a) of subdivision two of section twenty-seven hundred eighty-six of this article, to the extent the employee or agent is authorized to access records containing such information in order to carry out the commission's functions, powers and duties with respect to the protected individual, pursuant to article three of the correction law.

2. A state, county or local health officer may disclose confidential HIV related information when:

(a) disclosure is specifically authorized or required by federal or state law; or

(b) disclosure is made pursuant to a release of confidential HIV related information; or

(c) disclosure is requested by a physician pursuant to subdivision four of this section; or

(d) disclosure is authorized by court order pursuant to the provisions of section twenty-seven hundred eighty-five of this article.

3. No person to whom confidential HIV related information has been disclosed pursuant to this article shall disclose the information to another person except as authorized by this article, provided, however, that the provisions of this subdivision shall not apply to the protected individual or a natural person who is authorized pursuant to law to consent to health care for the protected individual.

4. (a) A physician may disclose confidential HIV related information under the following conditions:

(1) disclosure is made to a contact or to a public health officer for the purpose of making the disclosure to said contact; and

(2) the physician reasonably believes disclosure is medically appropriate and there is a significant risk of infection to the contact; and

(3) the physician has counseled the protected individual

V. Issues of Discrimination, Confidentiality, and Disease Control 1245

regarding the need to notify the contact, and the physician reasonably believes the protected individual will not inform the contact; and

(4) the physician has informed the protected individual of his or her intent to make such disclosure to a contact and has given the protected individual the opportunity to express a preference as to whether disclosure should be made by the physician directly or to a public health officer for the purpose of said disclosure. If the protected individual expresses a preference for disclosure by a public health officer or by the physician, the physician shall honor such preference.

(b) When making such disclosures to the contact, the physician or public health officer shall provide or make referrals for the provision of the appropriate medical advice and counseling for coping with the emotional consequences of learning the information and for changing behavior to prevent transmission or contraction of HIV infection. The physician or public health officer shall not disclose the identity of the protected individual or the identity of any other contact. A physician or public health officer making a notification pursuant to this subdivision shall make such disclosure in person, except where circumstances reasonably prevent doing so.

(c) A physician shall have no obligation to identify or locate any contact.

(d) A physician may, upon the consent of a parent or guardian, disclose confidential HIV related information to a state, county, or local health officer for the purpose of reviewing the medical history of a child to determine the fitness of the child to attend school.

(e) A physician may disclose confidential HIV related information pertaining to a protected individual to a person (known to the physician) authorized pursuant to law to consent to health care for a protected individual when the physician reasonably believes that: (1) disclosure is medically necessary in order to provide timely care and treatment for the protected individual; and (2) after appropriate counseling as to the need for such disclosure, the protected individual will not inform a person authorized by law to consent to health care; provided, however, that the physician shall not make such disclosure if, in the judgment of the physician: (A) the disclosure would not be in the best interest of the protected individual; or (B) the protected individual is authorized pursuant to law to consent to such care and treatment. Any decision or action by a physician under this paragraph, and the basis therefor, shall be recorded in the protected individual's medical record.

5. (a) Whenever disclosure of confidential HIV related information is made pursuant to this article, except for disclosures made pursuant

to paragraph (a) of subdivision one of this section or paragraph (a) or (e) of subdivision four of this section, such disclosure shall be accompanied or followed by a statement in writing which includes the following or substantially similar language: "This information has been disclosed to you from confidential records which are protected by state law. State law prohibits you from making any further disclosure of this information without the specific written consent of the person to whom it pertains, or as otherwise permitted by law. Any unauthorized further disclosure in violation of state law may result in a fine or jail sentence or both. A general authorization for the release of medical or other information is NOT sufficient authorization for further disclosure." An oral disclosure shall be accompanied or followed by such a notice within ten days.

(b) Except for disclosures made pursuant to paragraph (c) of subdivision one of this section, or to persons reviewing information or records in the ordinary course of ensuring that a health facility is in compliance with applicable quality of care standards or any other authorized program evaluation, program monitoring or service review, or to governmental agents requiring information necessary for payments to be made on behalf of patients or clients pursuant to contract or in accordance to law, a notation of all such disclosures shall be placed in the medical record of a protected individual, who shall be informed of such disclosures upon request; provided, however, that for disclosures made to insurance institutions such a notation need only be entered at the time the disclosure is first made.

6. (a) The provisions of this subdivision shall apply where a provider of a health or social service possesses confidential HIV related information relating to individuals who are recipients of the service, and a federal, state or local government agency supervises or monitors the provider or administers the program under which the service is provided.

(b) Confidential HIV related information relating to a recipient of such service may be disclosed in accordance with regulations promulgated pursuant to paragraph (a) of subdivision two of section twenty-seven hundred eighty-six of this article to an authorized employee or agent of such provider or government agency, when reasonably necessary for such supervision, monitoring, administration, or provision of such service. The term "authorized employee or agent", as used in this subdivision shall only include any employee or agent who would, in the ordinary course of business of the provider or government agency, have access to records relating to the care of, treatment of, or provision of a health or social service to the protected individual.

7. Nothing in this section shall limit a person's or agency's

V. Issues of Discrimination, Confidentiality, and Disease Control 1247

responsibility or authority to report, investigate, or redisclose, child protective and adult protective services information in accordance with title six of article six and titles one and two of article nine-B of the social services law, or to provide or monitor the provision of child and adult protective or preventive services.

8. Confidential HIV related information shall be recorded in the medical record of the protected individual. The provisions of this section shall not prohibit the listing of acquired immune deficiency syndrome, HIV related illness or HIV infection in a certificate of death, autopsy report or related documents prepared pursuant to article forty-one of this chapter or other applicable laws, ordinances, rules or regulations relating to the documentation of cause of death, nor shall this section be construed to modify any laws, ordinances, rules or regulations relative to access to death certificates, autopsy reports or such other related documents. Under no circumstances shall confidential HIV related information be disclosable pursuant to article six of the public officers law.

§2783. Penalties; Immunities

1. Any person who shall:
  (a) perform, or permit or procure the performance of, an HIV related test in violation of section twenty-seven hundred eighty-one of this article; or
  (b) disclose, or compel another person to disclose, or procure the disclosure of, confidential HIV related information in violation of section twenty-seven hundred eighty-two of this article; shall be subject to a civil penalty not to exceed five thousand dollars for each occurrence. Such penalty may be recovered in the same manner as the penalty provided in section twelve of this chapter.

2. Any person who willfully commits an act enumerated in subdivision one of this section shall be guilty of a misdemeanor and subject to the penalties provided in section twelve-b of this chapter.

3. There shall be no criminal sanction or civil liability on the part of, and no cause of action for damages shall arise against any physician or his or her employer, or health facility or health care provider with which the physician is associated, solely on account of:
  (a) the failure to disclose confidential HIV related information to a contact or person authorized pursuant to law to consent to health care for a protected individual; or
  (b) the disclosure of confidential HIV related information to a contact or person authorized pursuant to law to consent to health care for a protected individual, when carried out in good faith and without malice, and in compliance with this article; or
  (c) the disclosure of confidential HIV related information to

any person, agency, or officer authorized to receive such information, when carried out in good faith and without malice, and in compliance with the provisions of this article.

4. Any cause of action to recover damages based on a failure to provide information, explanations, or counseling prior to the execution of a written informed consent, or based on a lack of informed consent in the ordering or performance of an HIV related test in violation of this article shall be governed by the provisions of section two thousand eight hundred five-d of this chapter.

§2784. Applicability to Insurance Institutions and Insurance Support Organizations

Except for disclosure to third party reimbursers and insurance institutions pursuant to paragraphs (i) and (j) of subdivision one of section twenty-seven hundred eighty-two of this article and except for disclosures pursuant to section twenty-seven hundred eighty-five of this article, the provisions of this article shall not apply to insurance institutions and insurance support organizations, except that health care providers associated with or under contract to a health maintenance organization or other medical services plan shall be subject to the provisions of this article.

§2785. Court Authorization for Disclosure of Confidential HIV Related Information

1. Notwithstanding any other provision of law, no court shall issue an order for the disclosure of confidential HIV related information, except a court of record of competent jurisdiction in accordance with the provisions of this section.

2. A court may grant an order for disclosure of confidential HIV related information upon an application showing: (a) a compelling need for disclosure of the information for the adjudication of a criminal or civil proceeding; (b) a clear and imminent danger to an individual whose life or health may unknowingly be at significant risk as a result of contact with the individual to whom the information pertains; (c) upon application of a state, county or local health officer, a clear and imminent danger to the public health; or (d) that the applicant is lawfully entitled to the disclosure and the disclosure is consistent with the provisions of this article.

3. Upon receiving an application for an order authorizing disclosure pursuant to this section, the court shall enter an order directing that all pleadings, papers, affidavits, judgments, orders of the court, briefs and memoranda of law which are part of the application or

V. Issues of Discrimination, Confidentiality, and Disease Control 1249

the decision thereon, be sealed and not made available to any person, except to the extent necessary to conduct any proceedings in connection with the determination of whether to grant or deny the application, including any appeal. Such an order shall further direct that all subsequent proceedings in connection with the application shall be conducted in camera, and where appropriate to prevent the unauthorized disclosure of confidential HIV related information, that any pleadings, papers, affidavits, judgments, orders of the court, briefs and memoranda of law which are part of the application or the decision thereon not state the name of the individual concerning whom confidential HIV related information is sought.

4. (a) The individual concerning whom confidential HIV related information is sought and any person holding records concerning confidential HIV related information from whom disclosure is sought shall be given adequate notice of such application in a manner which will not disclose to any other person the identity of the individual, and shall be afforded an opportunity to file a written response to the application, or to appear in person for the limited purpose of providing evidence on the statutory criteria for the issuance of an order pursuant to this section.

(b) The court may grant an order without such notice and opportunity to be heard, where an ex parte application by a public health officer shows that a clear and imminent danger to an individual whose life or health may unknowingly be at risk requires an immediate order.

(c) Service of a subpoena shall not be subject to this subdivision.

5. In assessing compelling need and clear and imminent danger, the court shall provide written findings of fact, including scientific or medical findings, citing specific evidence in the record which supports each finding, and shall weigh the need for disclosure against the privacy interest of the protected individual and the public interest which may be disserved by disclosure which deters future testing or treatment or which may lead to discrimination.

6. An order authorizing disclosure of confidential HIV related information shall:

(a) limit disclosure to that information which is necessary to fulfill the purpose for which the order is granted; and

(b) limit disclosure to those persons whose need for the information is the basis for the order, and specifically prohibit redisclosure by such persons to any other persons, whether or not they are parties to the action; and

(c) to the extent possible consistent with this section, conform to the provisions of this article; and

(d) include such other measures as the court deems necessary to limit any disclosures not authorized by its order.

NOTES

Statutory Provisions on Major Legal Issues in the AIDS Epidemic

1. The New York statutes reprinted above are an example of aggressive legislative efforts to deal with some of the most serious legal issues presented by the AIDS epidemic. The statutes are not necessarily representative of other state actions. The states that took the early lead in protecting confidentiality with special statutes on AIDS were California, Massachusetts, Hawaii, Kentucky, and Maine. Later statutes, such as those above, and also those in Florida, provide much more detail on allowable disclosure of otherwise confidential information on AIDS and HIV infection. The earlier statutes allowed very little exception to the policy of nondisclosure, even for necessary medical and public health purposes.

The enactment of this type of statute was not provoked by widespread breaches of confidentiality in public health agencies; on the contrary, confidentiality has been traditionally protected very well in these programs. The highest degree of confidentiality has been accorded information on sexually transmitted diseases. Several states have added AIDS and HIV infection to their lists of sexually transmitted diseases, in part in order to provide the highest level of confidentiality protection. The statutes on sexually transmitted disease control have usually been adopted in more recent times than the laws on other communicable diseases, and they generally contain more up-to-date provisions on protecting the civil rights of persons involved.

The AIDS epidemic has led to calls for the redrafting and restructuring of the public health regulatory statutes in the states. See Gostin, The Future of Communicable Disease Control: Toward a New Concept in Public Health Law, 64 Milbank Q. (Supp. 1) 79 (1986). See also Mills, Wofsky & Mills, The Acquired Immunodeficiency Syndrome, Infection Control, and Public Health Law, 314 New Eng. J. Med. 931 (1986).

Although confidentiality protection has been very good in public health agencies, there have been instances of breach of confidentiality, including information given to and published by newspapers, from employers, property owners, school authorities, and, in some instances, hospitals. The most flagrant situations have related to school children. Publicity in newspapers and among school authorities and parent groups has resulted in retaliation against school children and their families. See Sotto, Undoing a Lesson of Fear in the Classroom: The Legal Recourse of AIDS-linked Children, 193 U. Pa. L. Rev. 193 (1986); Schwartz & Schaffer, AIDS in the Classroom, 14 Hofstra L. Rev. 163 (1985). See also Heaney, The Constitutional Right of In-

V. Issues of Discrimination, Confidentiality, and Disease Control

formational Privacy: Does It Protect Children Suffering from AIDS?, 14 Fordham Urban Law J. 927 (1985-1986). On confidentiality issues in public health agencies, see Assoc. State and Terr. Health Officials, AIDS Confidentiality and Discrimination, Guide to Public Health Practices (Wash. D.C. 1987).

2. The New York statutes also deal with voluntary diagnostic testing. As examples of greater sophistication in the state legislatures in the late 1980s, the laws are intended to encourage voluntary testing by controlling the systems of testing and by assuring individuals of informed consent before testing, of adequate counseling before and after the tests, and by protecting the confidentiality of test results. It was public fears about these aspects of testing that slowed down and often prevented testing in earlier years. The most successful of the early testing programs were those developed by the blood banks. These were anonymous testing sites where the person seeking the test was not required to give a name and was tested only on a random numbering basis. These programs were developed to avoid HIV-seropositive persons coming to blood banks to donate in order to find out their own serostatus. This type of system still provides the best opportunity for confidential testing. In clinics for the treating of sexually transmitted diseases and in drug abuse treatment programs, these anonymous testing centers for AIDS and HIV infection have often been used as referral sources when clinic patients have refused to allow diagnostic testing by the clinics themselves. See, for example, Bayer, HIV Screening: An Ethical Framework for Evaluating Proposed Programs, 256 J.A.M.A. 1768 (1986). See also Closen, AIDS: Testing Democracy — Irrational Responses to the Public Health Crisis and the Need for Privacy in Serological Testing, 19 J. Mar. Law Rev. 361 (1986).

3. One of the most interesting ethical and legal aspects of the effort to encourage more active programs of diagnostic testing for HIV seropositivity has been the requirement of pre- and post-test counseling. Such a requirement is now contained in virtually all programs. It is required also in federally supported research projects where diagnostic testing is a part of the experimental project design. This service is the only new ethical or legal provision that was not already a part of other types of public health disease control programs in past years. As noted earlier, this counseling requirement can also be found in the statutes on AIDS testing in Europe.

The inclusion of a personal counseling component in AIDS testing began with the blood banks in the United States in the spring of 1986 when the blood bank officials began conducting extensive "lookback programs" of contact with persons who had received transfusions with blood found later to have been contaminated with the AIDS virus. These people, nearly all symptom-free, were receiving this information in great shock, since they had no warning of such news. These people were not involved in a diagnostic testing program. The blood banks developed a counseling program for these people; the idea struck a responsive chord and personal counseling stayed on as a part of later developed diagnostic testing efforts.

School Board of Nassau County v. Arline
408 U.S. 273 S. Ct. (1987)

[See opinion at p. 528.]

Chalk v. United States District Court
840 F.2d 701 (9th Cir. 1988)

[See opinion at p. 532.]

NOTES

AIDS Discrimination and Legal Remedies

1. The notes that follow the *Arline* and *Chalk* cases in Chapter 6 describe well the issues in determining whether AIDS and HIV infection are covered as handicaps under Section 504 of the federal Rehabilitation Act of 1973. The development of national policy on preventing improper discrimination against AIDS patients and HIV seropositive persons was not greatly helped during the Reagan Administration, when there was resistance to establishing a clear policy under Section 504. There is still considerable resistance in Congress to a broadly applicable nondiscrimination position. For a review of the problems in this area during the Reagan Administration, see Brown, AIDS: The Public Policy Imperative, 7 St. Louis U. Pub. Law Rev. 11 (1988). See also R. Shilts, And the Band Played On: Politics, People and the AIDS Epidemic (1987). The Presidential Commission on the HIV Epidemic, noted earlier in this chapter, also called attention to the lack of a clear national policy against improper discrimination, not only regarding coverage of the Rehabilitation Act, but on other aspects of discrimination. There is no doubt but that, particularly in the earlier years of the 1980s, public fears of the spread of the disease did cause widespread discrimination which acted against the development of the more traditional programs of public health surveillance and control of the disease. See Matthews & Neslund, The Initial Impact of AIDS on Public Health Law in the United States, 257 J.A.M.A. 258 (1987).

2. The applicability of the federal Rehabilitation Act is relatively narrow. The Congress is currently reviewing the Americans with Disabilities Act. The state governments have actually moved more quickly and broadly in developing antidiscrimination policies than the federal level. Forty-five states and the District of Columbia have their own handicap statutes. The great majority of these have already declared AIDS and HIV infection covered under these laws. There are also more general antidiscrimination laws in most states related to public accommodations and private housing. Some 20 states and the District of Columbia have enacted AIDS-specific statutes, either as independent new provisions or as amendments to existing legislation. The Presidential Commission viewed this situation as a confusing patchwork approach and called for a more uniform national enforcement program. See also Inst. of Medicine, Confronting AIDS: Directions for Public Health, Health Care, and Research (Wash. D.C. 1986). On state government policy, see Nat. Governors' Association Policy Position on AIDS (1987). For listing of state-level agencies dealing with discrimination against AIDS patients and HIV-infected persons, see Resources Guide, vol. 3, AIDS: A Public Health Problem, State Issues, Policies and Programs (Intergov. Health Policy Project, Georgetown Univ., 1987, with supplements). For general issues on discrimination, see Parmet, AIDS and the Limitations of Discrimination Law, 15 L. Med. & Health Care 61 (1987). For an analysis of enforcement methods on the national, state, and local levels, see a review by the attorney who headed the AIDS Discrimination Unit of the Los Angeles City District Attorney's Office, the nation's first such unit in the office of a local prosecutor, Schulman, AIDS Discrimination: Its Nature, Meaning and Function, 12 Nova L. Rev. 1113 (1988).

Glover v. Eastern Nebraska Community Office of Retardation
686 F.2d 243 (D. Neb. 1988)

STROM, CHIEF JUDGE.

This matter is before the Court for determination after trial to the Court. Jurisdiction of this Court is pursuant to 28 U.S.C. §1331. Pursuant to Fed. R. Civ. P. 52, the Court sets forth the following findings of fact and conclusions of law.

The controversy in this case surrounds the Chronic Infectious Disease Policy No. 8.85 (the policy) adopted by the governing board of defendant Eastern Nebraska Human Services Agency (ENHSA) which requires certain employees to submit to mandatory testing for tuberculosis (TB), hepatitis B (HBV), and human immunodeficiency virus (HIV). The policy also contains a reporting requirement for employees who know or suspect they have any of the diseases and a disclosure requirement for employees who are hospitalized or receiving treatment for any of the diseases. This Court issued a temporary restraining order on December 7, 1987, restraining all testing for HIV and the reporting and disclosure requirements for all of the specified diseases. A revised policy was adopted on January 20, 1988, and it is the subject of this action.[1]

The plaintiffs in this class action suit consist of Patricia Ann Glover, Michael R. Macrander, Susan I. Davidson, Mary St. George, Rebecca A. Demuth, Timothy Sikora, Daphne Holmes, Shawne A. Kinsman, and Daniel B. Champ, on behalf of themselves and all other persons similarly situated.

The defendants in this action are: the Eastern Nebraska Community Office of Retardation (ENCOR); the Eastern Nebraska Human Services Agency (ENHSA); the members of the governing board of ENHSA, Michael Albert, Donald Claasen, Ronald Hineline, Ray Lind and Hilton Rogers; the Executive Director of ENHSA, Ray Christianson; and the Executive Director of ENCOR, Donald Moray.

The policy in question requires employees in certain identified positions to submit to mandatory testing for tuberculosis (TB), the hepatitis B virus (HBV) and the human immunodeficiency virus (HIV or the AIDS virus), or be subjected to discipline for refusal to test.

The testing requirement will be applied annually if recommended by the agency's medical consultant to employees in the identified positions, and ENHSA reserves the right under the policy to require employees testing positive for TB, HBV or HIV to be tested more frequently than annually.

The policy also requires employees in the identified positions who know or suspect that they have a chronic infectious disease, as identified in the policy, to inform the ENCOR employee relations officer immediately. Failure to inform will result in disciplinary action which may include termination. [The reporting requirement, Policy, Par. III(a).]

The policy requires employees in the identified positions hospitalized or receiving treatment for a chronic infectious disease, as identified in the policy, to submit the medical records relating to treatment for the disease to the ENCOR employee relations officer, if requested. [The disclosure requirement, Policy, Par. III(b).] Curtis Starks, the affirmative action director and employee relations officer at ENHSA, will have responsibility for notifying ENCOR employees in the identified positions of positive test results.

---

1. The plaintiffs have not challenged the policy as to tuberculosis, thus that disease is not at issue here.

V. Issues of Discrimination, Confidentiality, and Disease Control 1255

The Eastern Nebraska Community Office of Retardation (EN-COR), a sub agency of the Eastern Nebraska Human Services Agency (ENHSA) is a community based program which provides residential, vocational and other specialized services for the mentally retarded. ENCOR serves approximately six hundred clients who are mentally retarded, ranging from the mild to the profound level of retardation. ENCOR's client based foundation respects the individual rights of its clients, and the agency works diligently to insure that these rights are upheld on behalf of these clients. ENCOR's philosophy recognizes the dignity of risk, thus permitting its clients to live life with all its inherent risks, as they live in a community setting.

In this regard, ENCOR staff members receive training in numerous areas. For example, the staff members are taught behavior management skills and passive defense skills to enable them to deal with violent and/or aggressive clients in a nonabusive manner. Violent and aggressive behavior by the clients does exist at ENCOR. The evidence in this case shows numerous incidents involving biting, scratching, throwing of objects, hitting, violent outbursts, and pinching by the clients. . . .

In July of 1987, ENCOR's concern with AIDS became more acute when it learned that two clients from the Omaha Manor facility, a private facility that had recently closed, who were transferred to the Beatrice State Development Center, tested positive for the AIDS virus. Even though these clients were eventually found to not have the virus, the intense concern had taken root at ENCOR.

In September of 1987, an ENCOR employee, unrelated to the Omaha Manor incident, died from AIDS. At this point, the ENHSA governing board instructed Executive Director Donald Moray to develop a policy for mandatory AIDS testing of employees. The original policy was announced and challenged by the ENCOR employees. After this Court restrained the policy, and pending the trial on the merits, the policy was reviewed and some aspects were changed. The new policy, effective January 20, 1988, states that the persons holding or applying for the following titles must undergo testing: home teacher, residential associate, residential assistant, vocational program manager, vocational production manager, registered nurse, and licensed practical nurse. The policy also states that new positions may be added to the list. The rationale behind testing staff members in the identified positions is that these positions involve extensive contact with clients. The evidence in this case, however, shows that staff members who hold non-test positions have also been the recipients of bites and scratches from ENCOR clients.

The evidence shows that the ENCOR staff member who died from AIDS was involved in numerous incidents where he was bitten, scratched, pinched, kicked and hit by clients. When this staff member died from AIDS, however, ENCOR did not follow up on the clients involved in any of these incidents, nor did they notify these clients or their guardians that ENCOR believed they were potentially at risk of contracting the AIDS virus because of the contact with this staff member.

There is some evidence of sexual abuse of clients at ENCOR. These incidents, however, are not limited to staff/client contacts, of which there are few reported incidents. The testimony of the ENCOR staff members, Executive Director Moray, and Deputy Director Brinker are all in agreement and establish that there is not a sexual abuse problem at ENCOR.

The State of Nebraska is a low prevalence area for the AIDS virus, that is, the amount of the disease in the State is low. As such, the predictive value of a positive result in any individual test is low, because the few positive test results that occur will contain some false positives. Thus, the percentage of false positives in a low prevalence community will be much higher than in a high prevalence community.

The medically indicated reasons for HIV testing are: (a) as an adjunct to the medical workup of a patient who may be infected, (b) for epidemiological purposes to establish the level of infection in a community, and (c) as a device used in conjunction with counseling those in high risk groups to stimulate them to change their high-risk behaviors. Testing in isolation as provided in ENCOR's policy does not serve these purposes. . . .

In short, the evidence in this case establishes that the risk of transmission of the HIV virus at ENCOR is minuscule at best and will have little, if any, effect in preventing the spread of HIV or in protecting the clients. Further, from a medical viewpoint, this policy is not necessary to protect clients from any medical risks. . . .

There was testimony in this case that there can be no guarantee that the ENCOR clients could not possibly contract the AIDS virus, and thus the policy is necessary because of the devastating consequences of the disease. This overly cautious, "better to be safe than sorry" approach, however, is impermissible as it infringes on the constitutional rights of the staff members to be free from unreasonable searches and seizures.

In addition, the mandatory testing of staff members is not an effective way to prevent the spread of the disease. This policy simply ignores the current state of medical knowledge which establishes that the AIDS virus is not contracted by casual contact. The defendants are simply asking that this Court approve their policy because it is better to be safe than sorry. Donald Moray, the Executive Director of ENCOR, stated that his paramount concern was to "protect clients at all cost." This approach is impermissible for "at all cost" in this case includes the violation of the plaintiffs' constitutional rights.

V. Issues of Discrimination, Confidentiality, and Disease Control   1257

The Court is convinced that the evidence, considered in its entirety, leads to the conclusion that the policy was prompted by concerns about the AIDS virus, formulated with little or erroneous medical knowledge, and is a constitutionally impermissible reaction to a devastating disease with no known cure. The risk of transmission of the disease from the staff to the clients at ENCOR is minuscule, trivial, extremely low, extraordinarily low, theoretical, and approaches zero. Such a risk does not justify the implementation of such a sweeping policy which ignores and violates the staff members' constitutional rights.

Likewise, the mandatory testing of staff members for HBV is not justified at its inception. There is no evidence in this case that the clients are at risk of contracting HBV from staff members. Even if there were evidence of such a risk, the policy would not be justified as other measures exist to promote ENCOR's interests in protecting its clients. Specifically, ENCOR could administer the HBV immunization to its clients, and be prepared to administer the hepatitis B immune globulin to an unimmunized client who was exposed to the disease. In addition, unlike testing, these measures are effective in preventing the spread of HBV and protecting the health of ENCOR's clients.

Accordingly, a separate order will be issued this date in conformity with this opinion enjoining the defendant from implementing ENHSA policy 8.85, the chronic infectious disease policy, in regard to hepatitis B and human immunodeficiency virus.

NOTES

Mandatory Screening for HIV Infections; Obligations of Health Care Providers to Treat AIDS Patients and HIV-Infected Persons

1. The only other court review of a mandatory testing program in an American workplace involved the Foreign Service of the U.S. State Department. In that case, the Federal District Court for the District of Columbia upheld the testing in the special circumstances of the program. See Local 1812, American Fed. of Gov. Employees v. Department of State, 662 F. Supp. 50 (D.D.C. 1987). In the Foreign Service, new appointees and current employees are tested for HIV infection. The justification put forward by the State Department was that the Foreign Service Officers are in sensitive positions and are often assigned to posts where adequate medical services are not available. The HIV infection, because of its effects upon the immune system, could place the individual in a vulnerable condition to contract various illnesses in these more remote postings. All new applicants

who test positive would not be accepted to the Foreign Service. For current employees, no job loss would be occasioned by a positive test result, but there would be no posting to selected countries. The Court found the plan reasonable in that there was no punitive action or loss of benefits for current employees.

2. What would be the legal justification for installing mandatory testing or screening in most workplaces? In large population groups? Do the U.S. Supreme Court decisions on drug testing in workplaces reviewed earlier in this chapter provide support for HIV testing or screening? (By "testing" we usually mean small-scale diagnostic programs on selected groups or individuals at high risk; by "screening" we usually mean widespread examinations across population groups where the risk is low or largely undetermined.)

3. Mandatory screening in large population groups in the United States is currently limited to the U.S. military, other federal agencies such as the State Department and the Peace Corps, and in a few states to premarital screening for HIV. In several states, prison populations are routinely screened. In a few states, prostitutes and sex offenders are tested in the court systems, usually after conviction. A few states also require testing in public drug treatment programs.

4. In hospital settings where patients with AIDS are treated, how can confidentiality concerning the diagnosis be ensured? Should confidentiality requirements prevent the setting up of specialized units to treat AIDS patients? In situations where HIV-infected persons are treated for independent medical or dental conditions, do the healthcare providers involved have a right to know of the seropositivity of the patient? See Hagen, Meyer & Pauker, Routine Preoperative Screening for HIV: Does the Risk to the Surgeon Outweigh the Risk to the Patient?, 259 J.A.M.A. 1357 (1988). See also Richardson, Lochner et al, Physician Attitudes and Experience Regarding Care of Patients with Acquired Immunodeficiency Syndrome (AIDS) and Related Disorders (ARC), 26 Med. Care 675 (1987).

5. On the other side of the coin from the issues presented above is the obligation, ethical and legal, of health care providers to care for patients with AIDS and HIV infection. The American Medical Association and the American Dental Association have taken the position that there is an ethical obligation of care in such situations. Is there a legal obligation to treat such patients on the part of legally licensed health care professionals? See Annas, Not Saints but Healers: The Legal Duties of Health Care Professionals in the AIDS Epidemic, 78 Am. J. Pub. Health 844 (1988); Dickens, Legal Rights and Duties in the AIDS Epidemic, 239 Science 580 (1988); Fox, The Politics of Physicians' Responsibility in Epidemics, A Note on History, Hasting Cent. Rep. (AIDS Supp) 1 (April, May 1988). On the ethical aspects of the responsibility, see Peterson, AIDS: The Ethical Dilemma for

V. Issues of Discrimination, Confidentiality, and Disease Control 1259

Surgeons, 17 L. Med. & Health Care 139 (1989); Emanuel, Do Physicians Have an Obligation to Treat Patients with AIDS?, 318 New Eng. J. Med. 1686 (1988).

There has been some attempt to force physicians and dentists to treat AIDS patients by arguing that the office of the practitioner is a public accommodation and thus subject to statutory obligations of nondiscrimination in services. See Hurwitz v. New York City Commn. on Human Rights, 535 N.Y.S.2d 1007 (N.Y. Sup. Ct. 1988). See also issues of discrimination, particularly concerning access to needed health care, under the federal Rehabilitation Act of 1973 in Chapter 6 at page 536.

Rasmussen v. South Florida Blood Service
500 So. 2d 533 (Fla. 1987)

BARKETT, JUSTICE.

We have for review South Florida Blood Service, Inc. v. Rasmussen, 467 So. 2d 798 (Fla. 3d DCA 1985). In that decision, the district court certified the following as a question of great public importance:

> Do the privacy interests of volunteer blood donors and a blood service's and society's interest in maintaining a strong volunteer blood donation system outweigh a plaintiff's interest in discovering the names and addresses of the blood donors in the hope that further discovery will provide some evidence that he contracted AIDS from transfusions necessitated by injuries which are the subject of his suit?

Id. at 805 n.13. We have jurisdiction. Art. V, §3(b)(4), Fla. Const. We answer the question in the affirmative.

On May 24, 1982, petitioner, Donald Rasmussen, was sitting on a park bench when he was struck by an automobile. He sued the driver and alleged owner of the automobile for personal injuries he sustained in the accident. While hospitalized as a result of his injuries, Rasmussen received fifty-one units of blood via transfusion. In July of 1983, he was diagnosed as having "Acquired Immune Deficiency Syndrome" (AIDS) and died of that disease one year later. In an attempt to prove that the source of his AIDS was the necessary medical treatment he received because of injuries sustained in the accident, Rasmussen served respondent, South Florida Blood Service (Blood Service), with a subpoena duces tecum requesting "any and all records, documents and other material indicating the names and addresses of the [51] blood donors." (South Florida Blood Service is not a party to the underlying personal injury litigation, and there has been no allegation of negligence on the part of the Blood Service.)

The Blood Service moved the trial court to either quash the subpoena or issue a protective order barring disclosure. That court denied the motion and ordered the Blood Service to disclose the subpoenaed information. On certiorari review, the Third District Court of Appeal, applying the balancing test that courts have traditionally performed under the Florida discovery rules, concluded that the requested material should not be discovered. Although we agree with respondent's contention that Rasmussen's blood donors' rights of privacy are protected by state and federal constitutions, we need not engage in the stricter scrutiny mandated by constitutional analysis. We find that the interests involved here are adequately protected under our discovery rules and approve the decision of the district court. . . .

As the district court recognized, petitioner needs more than just the names and addresses of the donors. His interest is in establishing that one or more of the donors has AIDS or is in a high risk group. Petitioner argues that his inquiry *may* never go beyond comparing the donors' names against a list of known AIDS victims,[8] or against other public records (e.g., conviction records in order to determine whether any of the donors is a known drug user). He contends that because a limited inquiry *may* reveal the information he seeks, with no invasion of privacy, the donors' privacy rights are not yet at issue. We find this argument disingenuous. As we have already noted, the discovery rules allow a trial judge upon good cause shown to set conditions under which discovery will be given. Fla. R. Civ. P. 1.280(c). Some method could be formulated to verify the Blood Service's report that none of the donors is a known AIDS victim while preserving the confidentiality of the donors' identities. However, the subpoena in question gives petitioner access to the names and addresses of the blood donors with no restrictions on their use. There is nothing to prohibit petitioner from conducting an investigation without the knowledge of the persons in question. We cannot ignore, therefore, the consequences of disclosure to nonparties, including the possibility that a donor's coworkers, friends, employers, and others may be queried as to the donor's sexual preferences, drug use, or general life-style. . . .

. . . We wish to emphasize that although the importance of protecting the privacy of donor information does not depend on the special stigma associated with AIDS, public response[9] to the disease

---

8. South Florida Blood Service has stated that none of Rasmussen's fifty-one donors appears in lists of identified AIDS victims. We agree with petitioner, however, that he should not have to rely on the Blood Service's statement.

9. Social hostility to the disease has been extended to individuals associated with the disease, however tangentially, even though they do not in fact have AIDS. See,

V. Issues of Discrimination, Confidentiality, and Disease Control 1261

does make this a more critical matter. By the very nature of this case, disclosure of donor identities is "disclosure in a damaging context." See *Lora*, 74 F.R.D. at 580. We conclude, therefore, that the disclosure sought here implicates constitutionally protected privacy interests. . . .

. . . Society has a vital interest in maintaining a strong volunteer blood supply, a task that has become more difficult with the emergence of AIDS. The donor population has been reduced by the necessary exclusion of potential blood donors through AIDS screening and testing procedures[10] as well as by the unnecessary reduction in the donor population as a result of the widespread fear that donation itself can transmit the disease.[11] In light of this, it is clearly "in the public interest to discourage any serious disincentive to volunteer blood donation." *Rasmussen*, 467 So. 2d at 804. Because there is little doubt that the prospect of inquiry into one's private life and potential association with AIDS will deter blood donation, we conclude that society's interest in a strong and healthy blood supply will be furthered by the denial of discovery in this case. . . .

Accordingly, we approve the decision of the Third District.

It is so ordered.

NOTES

Confidentiality in the Blood Banks; Legal Liability for Blood Contaminated with HIV

1. Since the beginning of the AIDS epidemic, the blood banks have been at the center of the storm. Because the virus is blood-borne, spread of the infection has come from blood transfusions and the transplantation of human organs and tissue. Among the first

---

e.g., N.Y. City Commission on Human Rights, Gay and Lesbian Discrimination Documentation Project (1984).

10. On March 2, 1985, a serologic test which detects the presence of AIDS antibodies (the "HTLV-III antibody test") was licensed by the FDC, and is now being implemented in blood centers across the nation. Testing data indicates that, for a blood center collecting 100,000 units of blood annually, use of the HTLV-III test could result in discarding 610 units of blood annually and deferring 220 donors. Council of Community of Blood Centers Newsletter (March 4, 1985) at 3.

11. This fear prompted the Surgeon General to distribute the following to newspapers across the nation: "There is no way that a donor can contract AIDS or any other disease by giving a pint of blood. Despite the known safety of donating blood, some people are afraid to give. In fact, blood donations are down from a year ago, and there is evidence that some previous donors are staying away from blood drives because they are afraid they will get AIDS." Public Health Service, Department of Health and Human Services, Donate Blood Regularly (December 1984).

objectives of the national strategy to combat the disease was the protection of the blood-bank supplies. (See the article by Gostin on legislative strategy earlier in this chapter.) Over 12 million units of blood are transfused in the United States each year. About half of the blood banks are operated by the American Red Cross while the remainder are associated with the American Association of Blood Banks or the Council of Community Blood Centers. All of the blood banks are nonprofit organizations.

By late 1982, it was known that the infection was being passed by blood transfusions. Efforts were made to discourage high-risk persons from giving blood. After the availability of an accurate test for the existence of HIV antibodies in blood, the Federal Food and Drug Administration required all blood banks to screen each unit of blood and to discard all contaminated blood supplies. The FDA also imposed further requirements in regard to record-keeping and protection of donor confidentiality. Many state legislatures have also enacted further statutory and regulatory controls over blood banks operating in their states.

2. The American blood banks have a serious commitment to confidentiality. Without assurance of such protection, the voluntary donor system could fail. The *Rasmussen* case, both in the federal court and in the Florida courts, received considerable attention in the blood banks of the country. There was strong support for the outcome throughout the litigation that confidentiality would be respected.

The *Rasmussen* case involved blood transfusions done before development of the accurate HIV antibody screening techniques. How much assurance could the blood bank give that its later investigations would identify whether or not the petitioner in *Rasmussen* had received HIV-contaminated blood?

After the installation of the ELISA test, there can still be false positives and false negatives. The false negatives are, of course, the source of further potential for HIV infection. The bulk of the cases of a false negative are due to the fact that HIV antibodies had not as yet developed in an infected person. Efforts to screen such donations must depend on the social background data questionnaire required of all donors. In this way, the blood banks seek to eliminate potentially high-risk donations.

3. The protection afforded in the *Rasmussen* case set the tone for public policy in the blood banking system. The Florida Supreme Court did, however, use a "balancing test" of the interests of the parties in protection of confidentiality versus disclosure under evidentiary discovery practices. The implication of these practices is that a trial judge in other situations may find the balance to swing in the direction of disclosure, at least of a limited nature. A court in Texas

has done just that. In Tarrant County Hospital District v. Hughes, 734 S.W.2d 675 (Tex. App. 1987), the court examined the *Rasmussen* case and concluded that on balance, a limited disclosure without direct contact with donors was allowable and would not compromise the basic confidentiality of the blood bank system.

4. Several hundred lawsuits have been brought against blood banks across the country alleging liability for contracting HIV infection from contaminated blood. All but a few have failed to convince a jury of negligence. Nearly all of the claims have involved infection before development of the HIV antibody tests mentioned earlier. Allegations of negligence usually fail because of the fact that the contamination could not be detected before the development and installation of the ELISA test in late 1985. Early on, the plaintiffs' lawyers in these tragic situations sought to have liability imposed without fault on a warranty basis. Most of these claims have been dismissed because nearly all jurisdictions, with the exception of New Jersey, Vermont, and the District of Columbia, have enacted "shield laws" to block suits against blood banks and hospitals. These statutes declare the making available and the transfusion of blood and blood products and the transplantation of body tissues and organs to be a *service* and not a sale carrying a sales warranty. These statutes were enacted during the 1960s and 1970s largely in reaction to vulnerability to claims of liability for contamination with hepatitis B. The courts have had no trouble in finding these statutes to cover the contamination with the AIDS virus. The constitutionality of the "shield laws" has also been upheld in several AIDS-related cases. See, for example, McKee v. Cutter Laboratories, 866 F.2d 219 (6th Cir. 1989), dealing with the Kentucky statute. An attempt to find a strict liability warranty in the District of Columbia has also failed, even though the District has no statutory "shield law." See a comprehensive review of the subject, Kozup v. Georgetown University, 663 F. Supp. 1048 (1987).

City of New York v. New St. Mark's Baths
13 Misc. 2d 911 (S. Ct. N.Y. 1986)

[The Health Department of the City of New York acted under an emergency resolution added to the State Sanitary Code authorizing local health authorities to close any facilities in which "high-risk sexual activity takes place." Such facilities were declared to constitute "a public nuisance dangerous to the public health." The Health Department, under this authority, moved to close the New St. Mark's Baths as a public nuisance. The State Commissioner of Health and the Attorney General of New York moved to intervene as plaintiffs to defend the validity of the State regulation.]

WALLACH, J. The City has submitted ample supporting proof that high risk sexual activity has been taking place at St. Mark's on a continuous and regular basis. Following numerous on-site visits by City inspectors, over 14 separate days, these investigators have submitted affidavits describing 49 acts of high risk sexual activity (consisting of 41 acts of fellatio involving 70 persons and 8 acts of anal intercourse involving 16 persons). This evidence of high risk sexual activity, all occurring either in public areas of St. Mark's or in enclosed cubicles left visible to the observer without intrusion therein, demonstrates the inadequacy of self-regulatory procedures by the St. Mark's attendant staff, and the futility of any less intrusive solution to the problem other than closure. . . .

To be sure, defendants and the intervening patrons challenge the soundness of the scientific judgments upon which the Health Council regulation is based, citing, inter alia, the observation of the City's former Commissioner of Health in a memorandum dated October 22, 1985 that "closure of bathhouses will contribute little if anything to the control of AIDS." (For a vigorous medical opinion to the contrary from a specialist in this field see letter of Stephen S. Calazza, M.D., dated Jan. 24, 1985.) Defendants particularly assail the regulation's inclusion of fellatio as a high risk sexual activity and argue that enforced use of prophylactic sheaths would be a more appropriate regulatory response. They go further and argue that facilities such as St. Mark's, which attempts to educate its patrons with written materials, signed pledges, and posted notices as to the advisability of safe sexual practices, provide a positive force in combatting AIDS, and a valuable communication link between public health authorities and the homosexual community. While these arguments and proposals may have varying degrees of merit, they overlook a fundamental principle of applicable law: "It is not for the courts to determine which scientific view is correct in ruling upon whether the police power has been properly exercised. 'The judicial function is exhausted with the discovery that the relation between means and end is not wholly vain and fanciful, an illusory pretense' (Williams v. Mayor of Baltimore, 289 U.S. 36, 42)" (Chiropractic Assn. v. Hilleboe, 12 N.Y.2d 109, 114). Justification for plaintiffs' application here more than meets that test.

Clearly, plaintiff Department of Health had discretion to pursue the remedy of civil injunctive relief. Defendants have no valid due process objection, inasmuch as they have been afforded a complete right to be heard in the course of litigating this application.

Accordingly, defendants' motion to dismiss the complaint is in all respects denied.

NOTES

Public Health Regulatory Measures: Bathhouses, Gay Bars, and Other Establishments

1. The *St. Mark's* case has been the most closely watched legal action involving high-risk establishments related to the AIDS epidemic. There is a similar public health code provision in Georgia prohibiting the operation of bathhouses where high-risk sexual conduct is being carried on. New York has also moved against some gay bars, notably The Mine Shaft in New York City, and ordered them closed as public nuisances. Actions have also been successful against adult bookstores with private booths where sexual contacts can take place. See Rabin, The AIDS Epidemic and Gay Bathhouses: A Constitutional Analysis, 10 J. Health Pol. Poly. & L. 729 (1986); Gostin & Curran, Control Measures for AIDS: Reporting Requirements, Surveillance, Quarantine, and Public Meeting Places, 77 Am. J. Pub. Health 214 (1987); Collier, Preventing the Spread of AIDS by Restricting Sexual Contact in Gay Bathhouses, A Constitutional Analysis, 15 Golden Gate L. Rev. 301 (1985).

2. According to earlier court decisions, there should be no great trouble in finding legal authority to close establishments where there is an acknowledged high risk of contracting infectious diseases and the activity is extremely difficult, if not impossible, to control by other means. The classic case of Grossman v. Baumgarter, earlier in this chapter at 1156, provided the support for such actions. The enforcement of a nuisance abatement is particularly justified when the activity or business does not have a great deal of social value as in tattoo parlors, bathhouses, and adult bookstores with private booths. There is more difficulty in closing taverns and drinking bars or cafes where social activity and drinking may take place along with some sexual involvement. However, when a drinking establishment becomes "open and notorious" as a meeting place primarily for prostitution and sexual contact on the premises, there are grounds for removal of the liquor license as well as for closure as a public nuisance.

3. In San Francisco early in the epidemic, the head of the health department was reluctant to move to close bathhouses and gay bars because of the possible breakdown of good relations and cooperation from the large community of gay people in the area. The health department was then seeking cooperation in public education to change dangerous sexual practices and to encourage voluntary testing and the development of home treatment programs. Later, action was taken against some bathhouses. Was the health department correct in this strategy? Should such a strategy be adopted in other cities? Should the reluctance also extend to avoiding nuisance abatement in

"shooting galleries" for IV drug needle sharing? For an examination of the strategy in San Francisco and the later effort to close bathhouses, see Collier, cited in Note 1 above. See also the important data from population samples of gay and bisexual men in San Francisco over this period of time indicating considerable success in public education and the reduction by 60 percent or more in high-risk sexual practices. Winkelstein, Samuel et al, The San Francisco Men's Health Study: III. Reduction in HIV Transmission Among Homosexual/Bisexual Men, 1982-1986, 76 Am. J. Pub. Health 685 (1987). On strategies for changing sexual behavior and increasing personal responsibility in the AIDS epidemic and in IV drug use, see Beauchamp, Morality and the Health of the Body Politic, Hastings Cent. Rep., Spec. Supp., p.30 (1986); McCusker, Stoddard et al., Effects of Antibody Test Knowledge on Subsequent Sexual Behavior in a Cohort of Homosexually Active Men, 78 Am. J. Pub. Health 462 (1988); Friedman, Des Jarlais et al, AIDS and Self-Organization Among Intravenous Drug Users, 22 J. Addict. 201 (1987); Raymond, Combatting a Deadly Combination: Intravenous Drug Abuse, Acquired Immunodeficiency Syndrome, 259 J.A.M.A. 329 (1988).

Cordero v. Coughlin
607 F. Supp. 9 (D.C.N.Y. 1984)

OWEN, District Judge.

Plaintiffs are inmates in various New York State prisons who suffer from Acquired Immune Deficiency Syndrome ("AIDS"). Proceeding under 42 U.S.C. §1983, they allege that the policies and practices of the prison officials in segregating them from the general inmate population, and the consequent lack of social, recreational and rehabilitative opportunities, violate their rights under the First, Eighth and Fourteenth Amendments to the Constitution, and under the New York law governing the administration of a correctional facility.

The undisputed facts as set forward in the pleadings and affidavits before me reveal that plaintiffs' situations are indeed grim. They suffer from an incurable, fatal disease, both the genesis and transmission of which is poorly understood. They are therefore greatly feared by fellow inmates and, apparently, ostracized. The papers before me, however, reveal no breach of any duty by defendants. On the contrary, they give the clear impression that defendants are doing their best to cope with an extraordinarily difficult problem involving issues of correctional management, security and health care provision. Each of the constitutional bases asserted for plaintiffs' claims fails as a clear matter of law.

The Equal Protection Clause requires that similarly situated peo-

V. Issues of Discrimination, Confidentiality, and Disease Control 1267

ple be treated equally. Because AIDS victims are not similarly situated to other prisoners the Equal Protection Clause simply does not apply here. Francis v. Immigration and Naturalization Service, 532 F.2d 268, 272-33 (2d Cir. 1976). Even assuming that the Equal Protection Clause does apply, AIDS victims are not a "suspect class" and therefore as long as there is a legitimate government end and the means used are rationally related to that end, the Equal Protection Clause is not violated. Massachusetts Board of Retirement v. Murgia, 427 U.S. 307, 96 S. Ct. 2562, 49 L. Ed. 2d 520 (1976). Here, the state sets forth its objective: to protect both the AIDS victims and other prisoners from the tensions and harm that could result from the fears of other inmates. The existence of such fears, whether realistic or not, has not been contradicted. Certainly the separation of these inmates therefore bears a rational relation to this objective, at least until some better system is developed, and it is undisputed that defendants are changing their programs as they work to improve their ability to cope with the needs of prisoners with AIDS. It is clear therefore that as a matter of law defendants must prevail on the equal protection claim.

Plaintiffs next claim that they have been denied such liberty as is guaranteed by the Fourteenth Amendment of the Constitution. The Supreme Court itself has stated, however, that "the transfer of an inmate to less amenable and more restrictive quarters for nonpunitive reasons is well within the terms of confinement ordinarily contemplated by a prison sentence." Hewitt v. Helms, 459 U.S. 460, 103 S. Ct. 864 at 869-70, 74 L. Ed. 2d 675. To argue otherwise would be to "draw from the due process clause more than it can provide." Id. at 869. Prison officials have broad discretion and incarcerated individuals retain "only a narrow range of protected liberty interests." Id.

Furthermore, under applicable New York law, there is no requirement of a hearing before prison officials may act. Id. at 871. 7 NYCRR, parts 250-300. A decision such as is involved here is clearly one of discretion, and as a matter of law plaintiffs' due process rights have not been violated.

Plaintiffs also assert that their Eighth Amendment rights to be free of cruel and unusual punishment have been violated. However, the degree of Eighth Amendment scrutiny afforded an inmate is limited to ensuring that they receive "adequate food, clothing, shelter, sanitation, medical care and personal safety." Wolfish v. Levi, 573 F.2d 118, 125 (2d Cir. 1978). Here, plaintiffs make no assertion that they have been deprived of the above cited necessities. As Justice Rehnquist has stated: "I know of nothing in the Eighth Amendment which requires that [inmates] be housed in a manner most pleasing to them or considered even by most knowledgeable penal authorities to be likely to avoid psychological confrontations, psychological depression, and the like." Atiyeh v. Capps, 449 U.S. 1312, 1315-16, 101 S. Ct. 829, 831, 66 L. Ed. 2d 785. Plaintiffs here have alleged no facts which could entitle them to relief under the Eighth Amendment.

Plaintiffs last constitutional claim is that they have been denied their rights to privacy, free expression and free association in violation of the First Amendment. However, First Amendment rights are limited by "[t]he fact of [a prisoner's] confinement and the needs of the penal institution. . . ." Jones v. North Carolina Prisoners' Labor Union, Inc., 433 U.S. 119, 125, 97 S. Ct. 2532, 2537, 53 L. Ed. 2d 629 (1977). Obviously, in a case such as this, defendants cannot be compelled to provide plaintiffs with the identical privileges available to the other inmates. There is therefore no basis for relief under the First Amendment on the circumstances of this case.

Finally, plaintiffs have asserted claims under New York law. However, Pennhurst State School & Hospital v. Halderman, 465 U.S. 89, 104 S. Ct. 900, 907-11, 79 L. Ed. 2d 67 (1984) precludes a federal court from awarding injunctive and declaratory relief solely on the basis that defendants violated requirements of state law. The state law claims are therefore dismissed.

Defendants' motion for summary judgment is granted. Plaintiffs' motion is denied.

Submit order and judgment accordingly.

NOTES

The AIDS Epidemic in the American Criminal Justice System

1. The *Cordero* case illustrates the application of accepted constitutional principles in the courts that prison authorities have considerable discretion in classification and placement of inmates. Similar suits have been brought in other courts by AIDS prisoners and the result has been essentially similar. Most importantly, another federal court upheld the decision of the Oklahoma prison authorities to segregate in a separate part of the facility those inmates who were seropositive for HIV and who had no symptoms of AIDS. See Powell v. Department of Corr. 647 F. Supp. 968 (N.D. Okla. 1986). See also Doe v. Coughlin, 125 A.D.2d 783, 509 NYS.2d 209 (N.Y. Sup. Ct. 1986) (prison authorities refusal to allow family conjugal visits to AIDS patients upheld).

2. Several courts have dismissed attempts by inmates to force prison authorities to test prisoner populations for AIDS. See, for example, La Rocca v. Dalsheim, 120 Misc. 2d 697, 467 N.Y.S.2d 302 (N.Y. Sup. Ct. 1983). On the other hand, testing of all prisoners for HIV followed by segregation of those who are found seropositive is

now operational in the federal prisons and at least 14 states. (See the Gostin article surveying state legislation earlier in this chapter.) See also Lambrou, AIDS behind Bars: Prison Responses and Judicial Deference, 62 Temple L. Rev. 327 (1989). For guidelines prepared for federal and state correctional administrators, see AIDS in Correctional Facilities: Issues and Options, Nat. Inst. of Justice, U.S. Dept. of Justice, Wash. D.C. (2d ed. 1987).

3. There are several states that provide criminal penalties for the intentional transmission of HIV to another person without consent in sexual intercourse. Most of these provisions are added to existing statutes providing similar penalties for intentional transmission of other sexually transmitted diseases. There have also been criminal prosecutions against persons with AIDS or HIV infection for allegedly attempting to infect other persons by biting them or spitting upon them. See a collection of articles on AIDS and criminal law issues, Symposium, 10 J. Legal Med. 103 et seq. (1989). For a discussion of the use of the criminal law as an enforcement mechanism for public health control of the AIDS epidemic, see Schultz, AIDS: Public Health and the Criminal Law, 7 St. Louis U. Pub. L. Rev. 65 (1988). See also Field & Sullivan, AIDS and the Criminal Law, 15 L. Med. & Health Care 46 (1987).

Table of Cases

Principal cases appear in italics.

Abernathy v. Shenley Ind., 1196
Abouna v. Foothills Provincial Gen. Hosp., 486
A. C., In re, 1100
Addington v. Texas, 168, *1139*, 1175
Aden v. Younger, 565
Aetna Life Ins. Co. v. Lavoie, 687
"Agent Orange," In re — Product Liability Litigation, 234
Agnew v. Parks, 524
AHA v. Bowen, 723
AHA v. NLRB, 660
AHA v. Schweiker, 553
Air Line Pilots Assn. v. Quesada, 1153
Ake v. Oklahoma, 158
Akron v. Akron Cent. for Reproductive Health, Inc., 1062
Alexander v. Alexander, 154
Alexander v. Gosner, 320
Alexander v. Mt. Carmel Med. Cent., 210
Allen v. Mansour, 828
Allison v. Davies, 206
American Council of Life Ins. v. District of Columbia, 539
American Enka Corp. v. Sutton, 206
American Fedn. of Gov. Employees v. Skinner, 1192
American Med. Assn. v. F.T.C., 510
American Med. Assn. v. Weinberger, 687, 710
Anderson v. Somberg, 283
Andrews v. Ballard, 560
Andrews v. State, 148
Anonymous v. Hospital, 379
Appeal of Behavior Science Inst., 620
Applebaum v. Board of Directors, 476
Archie v. Racine, 558-559
Arizona v. Maricopa County Med. Soc., 507, 881
Arizona v. Youngblood, 144
Armstrong v. Board of Directors, 483
Ascherman v. San Francisco Med. Soc., 485
Association of Am. Physicians and Surgeons v. Weinberger, 687, 711
Austin v. McNamara, 516
Azzolino v. Dingfelder, 1124

"Baby Girls," In re, 154
Baby M, In the Matter of, 1078, 1094
Baby X, In re, 1111
Back v. Long Island Jewish Hosp., 1019
Backus v. Baptist Med. Cent., 663
Baerman v. Reisinger, 212
Baker v. Chastain, 292
Ball Mem. Hosp. v. Mutual Hosp. Ins. Co., 898
Barber v. Superior Court, 932, 985
Barefoot v. Estelle, 160, 207
Barnette v. Patenza, 379
Barrows v. Northwestern Mem. Hosp., 477
Barry v. Blue Cross of California, 892
Bartlett v. Bowen, 715
Bartling v. Glendale Adventist Med. Center, 965
Bartling v. Superior Court, 941
Bartron v. Coddington County, 584
Beal v. Doe, 559
Becker v. Schwartz, 1124
Bedford County Mem. Hosp. v. Heckler, 714
Beeck v. Tucson Gen. Hosp., 336
Bell v. Hart, 209, 276
Bellardini v. Krikorian, 234
Bellotti v. Baird, 1063
Belmar v. Cipolla, 484
Benedictine Sisters Benevolent Assn. v. Petterson, 621
Benson, Carey v. Population Serv. Intl., 1045
Berbarian v. Lancaster Osteopathic Hosp., 476
Berman v. Valley Hosp., 484
Berry v. State, 90, 92
Bethesda Hosp. v. Bowen, 714
Bio-Medical Applications v. Department of Health & Rehab. Serv., 620
Bird v. Pritchard, 379
Bivens v. Detroit Osteopathic Hosp., 277
Blair v. Eblen, 379
Blood v. Lea, 228, *449*
Blum v. Yaretsky, 476, 962
Board of Curators v. Horowitz, 486

Table of Cases

Board of Med. Quality Assur. v. Andrews, 465
Bolt v. Halifax Hosp. Med. Cent., 500
Bonner v. Moran, 1018
Bordie v. State Bd. of Med. Examiners, 466
Boulware v. State Dept. of Human Resources, 619
Bouvia v. County of Riverside, 958
Bouvia v. Glenchur, 965
Bouvia v. Superior Court, 959, 963
Bowen v. American Hosp. Assn., 1007
Bowen v. Michigan Acad. of Family Physicians, 715
Bowers v. Hardwick, 565, 962
Bowland v. Municipal Court, 464, 465
Boyd, In re, 1004
Boyd v. Albert Einstein Med. Cent., 348
Brady v. Maryland, 144
Bredice v. Doctor's Hosp., 516
Bricker v. Sceva Speare Mem. Hosp., 477
Brooklyn Hosp. v. Axelrod, 778
Brophy v. New England Sinai Hosp., 948
Brown v. Rogers, 206
Burke v. Tower East Restaurant, 206
Burns v. Wannemaker, 299
Byrd v. Wesley Med. Cent., 1126

Calderon v. Sharky, 217
California v. Trombetta, 144
Campbell v. Pitt County Mem. Hosp. Inc., 320
Canfield v. Spear, 664
Canterbury v. Spence, 304, 318, 320
Carey v. Population Serv. Intl., 1040
Carle Foundn. v. United States, 640
Carrao v. Health Care Serv. Corp., 686
Carswell v. Peachford Hosp., 613
Carver v. Orange County, 217
Caspito v. Heckler, 623
Cedars-Sinai Med. Cent. v. Cedars-Sinai Housestaff, 659
Central Gen. Hosp. v. Lukash, 103
Certificate of Need for Ashton Park Hosp., In re, 768
Chalk v. United States Dist. Court, 432, 1252
Chandler v. Hospital Auth., 524
Charter Med. v. HCA Health Serv., 619
Charter Southland Hosp. v. Hospital Corp. of America, 619
Children's Hosp. v. Whitcomb, 600
Childs v. Weis, 525
Chumbler v. McClure, 363
Ciaccio v. Housemann, 277
City of New York v. Heckler, 714
City of New York v. New St. Mark's Baths, 1263

Clark, In re, 1005
Clifton Springs Sanitarium Co. v. Axelrod, 617, 762
C. M. v. C. C., 1067, 1073
Cobbs v. Grant, 304, 306, 316, 318, 320
Coleman v. Coleman, 1066
Coleman v. Commonwealth, 90
Coleman v. Garrison, 299
Collins v. Associated Pathologists, Ltd., 511
Colorado v. Stevens, 1145
Committee to Defend Reproductive Rights v. Myers, 1064
Commonwealth v. Beausoleil, 144
Commonwealth v. Gomes, 129
Commonwealth v. Noxon, 103
Community Care Cents. v. Missouri Health Facilities Review Comm., 621
Community Hosp. v. Heckler, 714
Company and Irwin, Ex Parte, 1146
Conn v. Conn, 1065
Connecticut State Med. Board v. Connecticut Bd. of Exam. of Podiatry, 465
Conroy, In re, 933, 1003
Cook v. Ochsner Foundation Hosp., 553
Cooper v. Faroyth County Hosp. Auth., 510
Cooper Med. Cent. v. Boyd, 554
Coppolino v. State, 114
Corbett v. D'Alessandro, 961
Cordero v. Coughlin, 1266
Cornfield v. Tangen, 210
Cowan v. Myers, 711
Cox v. Haworth, 320
Cruzan v. Director, Missouri Dept. of Health, 933, 962, *995*
C. S. v. Nielson, 1125
Cude v. State, 1143
Cunningham v. Chas. Pfizer & Co., 374, 1146
Curlender v. Bio-Science Labs., 1113
Custodio v. Bauer, 1126
Custody of a Minor, In re, 1005, 1022

Dallas v. Burlington Northern Inc., 229
Dandridge v. Williams, 1046
D'Angelis v. Zakato, 363
Daniels v. Bloomquist, 205
Darling v. Charleston Community Mem. Hosp., 321
Davidson v. Youngstown Hosp. Assn., 477
Davila v. Bodelson, 379
Davis v. Davis, 1077
Dawson v. Whaland, 600
Dean v. Chapman, 102

Table of Cases

De Falco v. Long Island College Hosp., 210
Denver Pub. Co. v. Dreyfus, 102
Department of Health & Rehab. Serv. v. Johnson & Johnson Home Health Care, 619
Desai v. St. Barnabas Med. Cent., 484
DeShaney v. Winnebago County Dept. of Soc. Serv., 558
Deutsch v. Skein, 293
Dick v. Geist, 664
Dickson v. Minnesota Mut. Life Ins., 205
Di Domenico v. Employers Cooperative Indus. Trust, 828
Diggs v. Harris Hosp., 476, 663
Dinnerstein, In re, 984
D.L.E., In the interest of, 1022
Dodds v. Stellar, 379
Doe v. Bolton, 465
Doe v. Bridgeton Hosp. Assn., 1064
Doe v. Centinela, 537
Doe v. Coughlin, 1268
Doe v. Irwin, 1046
Doe v. St. Joseph's Hosp., 476, 663
Doe, In re, 1023
Dooley v. Barberton Citizens Hosp., 510
Dowd v. Calabrese, 114
Dowell v. City of Tulsa, 1134
Downtown Hosp. Assn. v. Tennessee State Bd. of Equalization, 638
Dr. Allison, Dentist, Inc. v. Allison, 593
Drobick, In re, 984
Duldulao v. St. Mary of Nazareth Hosp. Cent., 661
Durfee v. Durfee, 1021

Eastern Kentucky Welfare Rights Org. v. Simon, 638
Edwards v. State, 155
E. G., In re, 1019
Elam v. College Park Hosp., 334
Ellis v. McDaniel, 664
Ellis v. Patterson, 822
Ellis v. Sherman, 1125
Equitable Life Assur. Soc. of the U.S. v. Bomar, 205
Esquivel v. Nancarrow, 206
Estelle v. Smith, 168
Etheridge v. Med. Cent. Hosps., 441
Eubanks v. Brown, 1066
Eubanks v. Farrier, 515
Evans v. Hayme, 455
Evans v. People, 201
Ezekial v. Winkley, 478

Fabian v. Matzko, 551
Fall v. White, 363, 375

Farrel, In re, 934, 963, 985
Fein v. Permanente Med. Group, 440
Ferlito v. Cecola, 299
Finger Lakes HSA v. St. Joseph's Hosp., 619
Finnegan v. Fall River Gas Works Co., 232
Fiorentino v. Wenger, 320
Florida Med. Center v. Department of Health & Rehab Serv., 762
Flowers v. District of Columbia, 379
Ford v. Wainwright, 158
Foster v. Georgia Bd. of Chiropractic Examiners, 464
Foster v. Mobile County Hosp., 482
Foster v. Tourtellotte, 965
Frazier v. Board of Trustees, 538
Friedman v. Delaware County Mem. Hosp., 499
Friedman v. Rogers, 470
Fritz v. Huntington Hosp., 482
Frye v. United States, 103, 129, *169*
F.T.C. v. Indiana Fedn. of Dentists, 501, 507, 510
Furlong v. Long Island College Hosp., 501

Gallagher v. Detroit Macomb Hosp. Assn., 515
Gallagher v. Duke Univ. Hosp., 1124, 1125
Garcia v. Texas State Bd. of Med. Examiners, 597
Gardener, In re, 959
Garrison v. Heublein, 1196
Garvey v. O'Donoghue, 278
Gates v. Jensen, 348
General Hosp. of Humana v. Baptist Med. Sys., 772
Gensemer v. Williams, 206
Georgetown Univ. Hosp. v. Bowen, 723
Georgia v. McAfee, 964
Georgia Lions Eye Bank v. Lavant, 925
Gianetti v. Norwalk Hosp., 476
Gibson v. Berryhill, 470
Gideon v. Johns-Manville Sales Corp., 229
Gill v. Mercy Hosp., 485
Gilmore v. People, 1174
Glen Eden Hosp. v. Blue Cross & Blue Shield of Michigan, 898
Glover v. Eastern Nebraska Commun. Office of Retardation, 1253
Goforth v. Porter Med. Assn., 1125
Goldberg v. Ruskin, 1125
Goldfarb v. Virginia State Bar, 507
Golob v. Buckingham Hotel, 15
Gonzales v. Nork, 334
Goodman v. Sullivan, 711

1274   Table of Cases

Grace Plaza v. Ellbaum, 965
Grad v. Kaasa, 99
Graham v. Police & Fireman's Ins. Assn., 205
Grand Prairie Hosp. Auth. v. Dallas County Appraisal Dist., 639
Granite State Ins. Co. v. Martin, 206
Grant, In re, 959, 985
Gray v. Romero, 962
Greco v. Orange Mem. Hosp., 1064
Green, In re, 1022
Gridley v. Johnson, 276
Griffin Hosp. v. Commission on Hosp. & Health Care, 778
Griswold v. Connecticut, 962
Grossman v. Baumgartner, 1156, 1265
Group Health Assn. v. Moor, 857
Group Life and Health Ins. Co. v. Royal Drug Co., 599
Guardano v. Long Is. Plastic Surg. Group, 453
Guerrero v. Copper Queen Hosp., 551

Hahn v. Oregon Physicians' Serv., 898
Hamil v. Bashline, 525
Hamlin, In re, 985
Hanley v. Town of Rainelle, 206
Hansbrough v. Kasyak, 267
Harbeson v. Park-Davis Inc., 1125
Harding Hosp. Inc. v. United States, 633
Hardy v. Brantley, 266
Harrell v. Total Health Care Inc., 356
Harris v. Groth, 348
Harris v. McRae, 559
Hartz v. Bensinger, 566
Harvey v. Raleigh Police Dept., 85
Hassan v. Independent Practice Assn., 890, 891
Hayes v. Shelby Mem. Hosp., 663
Hayman v. City of Galveston, 476, 483
Hayman v. Wilkerson, 1124
HCSC-Laundry v. United States, 642
Health Care Equal. Comm. v. Iowa Med. Socy., 899
Health Care & Retirement Corp., In re, 620
Health Coordinat. Council v. Gen. Hosp. of Humana, 619
Health Ins. Assn. of America v. Corcoran, 540
Heckler v. Ringer, 714
Heiting v. Heiting, 205
Helling v. Carey, 347
Helling v. Carey and Laughlin, 341
Henning v. Thomas, 223
Herald Co. v. Murray, 102
Herrera v. Roessing, 299
Hickman v. Group Health Plan, 1124

Hicks v. Arkansas State Med. Bd., 464
Hicks v. United States, 282
Highland Park v. State, 639
Hill v. Highland Park Gen. Hosp., 466
Hill v. Ohio County, 550
Hinson v. Cameron, 662
Hi-Plains Hosp. v. United States, 641
Hiser v. Randolph, 526
Hobson v. McLean Hosp. Corp., 661
Hodgson v. Minnesota, 1063
Hofbauer, In the Matter of, 1022
Hoffman v. Garden City Hosp., 477
Hoffman v. Tracy, 103
Holmes v. Hoemako Hosp., 484
Holmes v. Silver Cross Hosp., 965
Holt v. City of Statesville, 206
Home Health Care v. Heckler, 711
Hon v. Stroh Brewery Co., 1192
Hopp v. Lepp, 306
Hospital Build. Co. v. Trustees of Rex Hosp., 771
Hospital Corp. of America, In re, 695
Hospital Corp. of America v. Federal Trade Comm., 645
Hottentot v. Mid-Maine Med. Cent., 477
Hoven v. Kelble, 341
Hughes v. Blue Cross of North. Calif., 687
Hulit v. St. Vincent's Hosp., 478
Humana Hosp. Desert Valley v. Superior Court, 515
Hurd v. State, 191
Hurley v. Eddingfield, 518
Huron Valley Hosp. v. Mich. State Health Fac. Comm., 620
Huron Valley Hosp., Inc. v. City of Pontiac, 771
Hurwitz v. New York City Commn. on Human Rights, 1259
Hutton v. Craighead, 370

Iafelice v. Luchs, 965
Irdell Digestive Disease Clinic v. Petrozza, 664
Irvington General Hosp. v. Department of Health, 615, 762

Jackson v. Kelly, 385
Jackson v. Power, 329
Jacobs v. Painter, 305
Jacobson v. Massachusetts, 1129
James G. v. Caserta, 1124
Janus v. Hackensack Hosp., 212
Jarvis v. Levine, 959
Jefferson Parish Hosp. Dist. v. Hyde, 511, 651
Jeffries v. Marzano, 234

Table of Cases

Jew Ho v. Williamson, 1153
JIGC Nursing Home Co. v. Bowen, 710
Jobes, In re, 959, 963, 985
John C. Lincoln Hosp. v. Sup. Court, 515
John F. Kennedy Mem. Hosp. v. Bludworth, 1005
John F. Kennedy Mem. Hosp. v. Heston, 933
Johnson v. Misericordia Community Hosp., 326
Jones v. Bloom, 276
Jones v. Harrisburg Polyclinic Hosp., 292
Jones v. United States, 168
Jordan v. Group Health Assn., 857
Jordan C. v. Mary K., 1074
Joyner v. Alton Ochsner Med. Foundn., 551
Jurek v. Texas, 166

Kaczanowski v. Medical Cent. Hosp., 499
Karen Ann Quinlan, In re, 931, 966
Karin T. v. Michael T., 1073
Karlin v. Weinberg, 663
Karp v. Cooley, 306, 373
Karpinski v. Ingrasci, 663
Kartell v. Blue Shield of Massachusetts, 898
Katsetos v. Nolan, 212
Kealohapauole v. Shimoda, 89, 90
Kentucky Central Life Ins. Co. v. Fannin, 205
King v. Coe, 267
King v. Tanner, 154
Kirk v. Michael Reese Hosp. and Med. Cent., 427
Klarfeld v. Salsbury, 515
Koefoot v. American College of Surgeons, 511
Kompare v. Stein, 102
Kottle, In re, 1145
Krame v. St. Anthony Hosp. Sys., 320
Kreuzer v. American Academy of Periodontology, 511
Kuntzelman v. Black, 91

Lakeside Community Hosp. v. Levenson, 477
Landros v. Flood, 357
Lane v. Candura, 940, 987
Largey v. Rothman, 305
LaRocca v. Dalsheim, 1268
Lausier v. Pescinski, 1023
Lawton v. State, 1159
Leach v. Drummond Med. Group, 527
Leach, Estate of v. Shapiro, 964

Lee v. Page, 827
Lemmon v. State Bd. of Med. Examiners, 566
LHR, In re, 983
Life & Casualty Ins. Co. of Tennessee v. Rivera, 205
Limmer v. Samaritan Health Serv., 483
Lindsey v. United States, 194
Lineberry v. Schull, 217
Lininger v. Eisenbaum, 1124, 1125
Little v. Little, 1023
Local 1812, Am. Fedn. of Gov. Employees v. Department of State, 1257
Lockshin v. Blue Cross of Northeast Ohio, 686
Logan v. Greenwich Hosp. Assn., 308
Longeway, Estate of, 959, 983
Lou R., Matter of, 234
Lundgren v. Eustermann, 267
Lyons v. Grether, 525, 527

Maben v. Rankin, 379
McConnell v. Beverly Enters., 961
McGuire v. Sifers, 378
McGurren v. Fargo, 1144
Machuca, In re, 470
McIntyre v. Crouch, 1074
McKee v. Cutter Labs., 1263
McKellips v. St. Francis Hosp., 278
McKenna v. Cedars of Lebanon Hosp., 384
MacKey v. Greenview Hosp. Inc., 379
McMahon v. Young, 228, 229
McQuary v. Bel Air Convalescent Home, 662
McVey v. Englewood Hosp. Assn., 965
Madden v. Kaiser Foundn. Hosps., 442
Magee, In re, 470
Mahanna v. Hirsch, 267
Maher v. Rose, 559
Maimon v. Sisters of the Third Order, 476
Malette v. Shulman, 965
Manchester Health Center v. NLRB, 660
Mannus v. State, 1144
Marciniak v. Lundborg, 1126
Margaret S. v. Edwards, 1067
Markman v. Kotler, 384
Marshall v. University of Chicago Hosps. and Clinics, 367
Massachusetts v. Secretary of Health & Human Serv., 1063-1064
Mathews v. Diaz, 714
Meadowbrook Nursing Home v. Axelrod, 619
Medical Cent. v. Bowen, 713

Medical Cent. Hosp. v. City of
 Burlington, 638
Medical Socy. v. Toia, 711
*Memorial Hosp./Adair County Health Cent.
 v. Bowen, 703*
Memorial Hosp. of Maricopa
 County, 559
Mercy Med. Cent. v. Winnebago
 County, 524
Metropolitan Life Ins. Co. v.
 Massachusetts, 598
Middlesex Mem. Hosp. v. Town of
 North Haven, 552
Mielke v. Dobrydnio, 206
Miles v. West, 206
Miller v. Indiana Hosp., 509
Miller v. Pate, 59
Milton, In re, 933, 987
Miner v. Walden, 453
Mitchell v. Frank R. Howard Mem.
 Hosp., 501
Mohn v. Hahneman Med. College, 214
Moore v. Board of Trustees of Carson-
 Tahoe Hosp., 326
Moore v. Provident Life and Accident
 Ins. Co., 600
Moore v. Regents, 927
Morelli v. Ehsan, 597
Morganstein v. House, 378
Morris v. Metriyakool, 453
Morris v. Sanchez, 1126
Morrison, Conservatorship of, 963
Mount Sinai Hosp. v. Zorec, 680
Mount Sinai Hosp. v. United
 States, 715
M. S. v. Wermers, 1046
Mueller v. Mueller, 277
Munoz v. Flower Hosp., 476
Myers v. State, 621

*Nanavati v. Burdette Tomlin Memorial
 Hosp., 478*
Nashville Mem. Hosp. v. Brinkley, 476
National Bank of Commerce v. New
 Bedford, 234
National Gerimedical Hosp. v. Blue
 Cross, 772
National Life Ins. & Accident Co. v.
 Whetlock, 205
National Society of Prof. Engineers v.
 United States, 507
*National Treasury Employees Union v. Von
 Raab, 1179*
N.C.A.A. v. Board of Regents, 502
New Hampshire Catholic Charities
 Appeal, 619
New York v. Bowen, 1064
New York Times Co. v. Sullivan, 1065
Nickolls v. Personal Fin. Co., 217

NLRB v. Baptist Hosp. Inc., 660
NLRB v. Beacon Light Christian
 Nursing Home, 659
NLRB v. St. Francis Hosp. of
 Lynwood, 659
NLRB v. Walker County Med.
 Center, 659
Northern Group Servs. v. Auto Owners
 Ins. Co., 600
North Miami Gen. Hosp. v. Goldberg, 338
Norwood Hosp. v. Munoz, 933
Nurse Midwifery Assn. v. Hibbett, 499

Oak Park Manor v. State CON Review
 Bd., 619
Ocean State Physicians Health Plan v.
 Blue Cross & Blue Shield of Rhode
 Island, 897, 898
O'Connor v. Donaldson, 168, 559
Ohio v. Akron Cent. for Reproductive
 Health, 1063
Oltz v. St. Peter's Community
 Hosp., 500, 510
O'Neill v. Montefiore Hosp., 525
Oregon Eye Assn. v. SHPDA, 772
Ornoff v. Kuhn, 210
Ory v. Libersky, 210
Osborne, In re, 933
Otis Engineering Co. v. Clark, 1192
Ouellette v. Mehalic, 305
Ouellette v. Subak, 358

Paravecchio v. Memorial Hosp., 466
Pardazi v. Cullman Med. Center, 663
Parker v. Brown, 517
Parker v. Employers Mut. Liab. Ins.
 Co., 228
Parham v. J.R., 1018, 1021
Parrish v. Lamm, 610
Patrick v. Burget, 385, 519
Payton v. Weaver, 521, 550
Pedroza v. Bryant, 326
Pennsylvania Assn. of State Mental
 Hosp. Physic. v. Commonwealth, 657
People v. Brown, 114, 189
People v. Cox, 103
People v. Eulo, 913
People v. Fierer, 89, 90
People v. Fuller, 1174
People v. Guerra, 189
People v. Hampton, 197
People v. Hughes, 193, 194
People v. John H. Woodbury
 Dermatological Inst., 595
People v. Kelley, 113
People v. Kolrig, 1156
People v. McDonald, 195
People v. Pacific Health Corp., 588

People v. Phillips, 301
People v. Pointer, 1111
People v. Preston, 103
People v. Privitera, 565, 566
People v. Shirley, 192
People v. Thomas, 1156
People v. Walkey, 200
People v. Wesley, 145
People v. Williams, 114
People v. Yoho, 86
People v. Young, 126-137
People ex rel. Baker v. Stauty, 1153
Pepple v. Parkview Mem. Hosp., 477
Peter, In re, 939, 961, 985
Pharmaceutical Socy. v. Lefkowitz, 566
Philip v. Steward, 205
Phillip B., In re, 1022
Pierce v. Ortho Pharmaceutical Corp., 662
Pilot Life Ins. Co. v. Dedeaux, 599, 687
Pinkus v. MacMahon, 464
Pinneke v. Preisser, 827
Pitre v. Opelousas Gen. Hosp., 1125
Planned Parenthood of Cent. Missouri v. Danforth, 302, 1065
Planned Parenthood Fedn. v. Bowen, 1064
Platte County Med. Cent. v. Missouri Health Fac. Rev. Comm., 621
Plemel v. Walter, 144
Pontius v. Children's Hosp., 509
Powell v. Department of Correction, 1268
Pratt v. Stein, 267
Precourt v. Frederick, 364
Priest v. Lindig, 292
Primary Care Physicians Group v. Ledbetter, 622
Prince v. Commonwealth, 1143
Prince v. Massachusetts, 1021
Prince George's Doctor's Hosp. v. Health Servs. Cost Review Comm., 778
Procanik v. Cillo, 1125
Public Citizen v. Young, 248
Public Health Trust of Dade County v. Wons, 934
Pucci v. Rausch, 227

Quackenbush, In re, 940, 987
Quinones v. Public Admin. of County of Kings, 379

Radiology Socy. v. New Jersey State Dept. of Health, 619
Rainis v. Grossman, 300
Ramon v. Farr, 278
Rao v. Board of County Commissioners, 482

Rasmussen v. Fleming, 959, 960, 985, 986, 1004
Rasmussen v. South Florida Blood Serv., 1259
Ratino v. Med. Service, 898
Ratterlee v. Bartlett, 229
Reazin v. Blue Cross & Blue Shield of Kansas, 890, 897, 898
Redbud Hosp. Dist. v. Heckler, 745
Rederscheid v. Comprecare, Inc., 857
Redman v. Sooter, 228
Rehabilitation Assn. of New Eng., Appeal of, 621
Reibl v. Hughes, 306
Reid v. Indiana Osteopathic Med. Center, 357, 550
Requena, In re, 963
Reyes v. Wyeth Lab, 1146, 1198
Reynolds v. McNichols, 1147
Rice v. Renaldo, 527
Richardson, In re, 1023
Richmond County Hosp. Auth. v. Brown, 328
Ricks v. Budge, 526
Right to Choose v. Byrne, 1064
Riley v. Warm Springs State Hosp., 662
Rivers v. Katz, 959
Riverside Gen. Hosp. v. New Jersey Hosp. Rate Setting Comm., 778
Roanoke Mem. Hosp. v. Kenley, 619
Robak v. United States, 1124
Robins v. Katz, 379
Robinson v. Magovern, 651
Rock v. Arkansas, 179
Rock v. State, 188
Roe v. Wade, 962, 1062
Rogers v. Commissioner of Dept. of Mental Health, 959
Rogers v. Meridian Park Hosp., 363
Rogers v. Okin, 959
Rosenberg v. Holy Redeemer Hosp., 477
Ross v. Hilltop Rehab. Hosp., 959
Rozier v. St. Mary's Hosp., 662
Rubino v. Fretios, 304
Ruiz, In re, 1111
Rush v. City of St. Petersburg, 595
Rush v. Parham, 559, 827
Rushton v. Nebraska, 1191

Sacred Heart Hosp. v. United States, 710
St. Bernard Gen. Hosp. Inc. v. Hospital Serv. Assn., 898
St. Francis Regional Med. Center v. Hale, 291, *337*
St. Francis/St. George Hosp. v. Blue Cross, 619

St. John's Med. Staff v. St. John Regional Med. Cent., 485
St. Luke's Hosp. v. United States, 641
St. Paul Elec. Workers Welfare Fund v. Markman, 599
Salgo v. Leland Stanford Univ., 277
Sanderson v. Bryan, 515
Sandow v. Weyerhauser Co., 207
Sarchett v. Blue Shield of Calif., 686
Sarin v. Samaritan Health Cent., 501
Satterwhite v. Texas, 168
Saxton v. Gem County, 552
Schall v. Martin, 168
Schloendorff v. Society of New York Hosps., 304, 314, 319
Schoening v. Grays Harbor Commun. Hosp., 326
School Board of Nassau County v. Arline, 528, 1252
Sears v. Butishauser, 217
Seglin v. Esau, 501
Seiferth, In re, 1022
Shahawy v. Harrison, 517
Share v. Commissioner, 639
Shaw v. Hospital Authority, 483
Sherlock v. Stillwater Clinic, 379
Shilkret v. Annapolis Emergency Hosp., 266
Shoemaker v. Handel, 1191
Shorter v. Drury, 374
SHPA v. Mobile Infirmary Assn., 619
Shumake v. Travelers Ins. Co., 686
Shysard, Ex parte, 1153
Silver v. Castle Mem. Hosp., 477, 485
Silver v. N.Y. Stock Exch., 509
Silverstein v. Gwinnett Hosp. Auth., 483
Simon v. Eastern Kentucky Welfare Rights Org., 553
Simon v. Sargent, 1156
Sioux Valley Hosp. Assn. v. Yankton County, 552
Skelton v. Druid City Hosp. Board, 340
Slater v. Baker and Stapleton, 256
Sloan v. Metropolitan Health Council, 596
Smialek v. Begay, 99, 102
Smith v. Dept. of Ins., 436
Smith v. Horace Williams Co., 12, 211
Smith v. Menet, 261
Snyder v. Holy Cross Hosp., 99
Sosa v. Board of Managers, 483
Sound Health Assn. v. Commnr., 639
Southern Pacific Transp. Co. v. Peralez, 206
Sprowl v. Ward, 361
Spring, In re, 984
Springdale Mem. Hosp. Assn. v. Bowen, 723
Stafford v. Nipp, 277

Stahlheber v. American Cyanamid Co., 1146
Stallman v. Youngquist, 1111
Standard Oil v. Agsalud, 599
Stanley v. Ford Motor Co., 205
Stanturf v. Sysis, 524
Staples v. Glienke, 103
State v. Abortion Information Agency, 598
State v. Albertson, 1156
State v. Black, 197
State v. Carter, 210
State v. Cavallo, 200
State v. Chambers, 96
State v. Chapple, 195
State v. Clawson, 90
State v. Cummings, 206
State v. Gerhardstein, 959
State v. Hall, 198
State v. Hester, 200
State v. Hightower, 229
State v. Hoffman, 465
State v. Johnson, 913
State v. Kim, 74, 195
State v. Kuhwald, 465
State v. Kuntzelman, 91
State v. Lindsey, 194, 198, 199
State v. Lyon, 170
State v. McCoy, 198
State v. Moran, 194
State v. Peterson, 103
State v. P.I.A. Asheville, 772
State v. Poe, 90
State v. Powell, 915
State v. Saldana, 193, 196
State v. Shaffer, 913, 924
State v. Sullivan, 223
State v. Superior Court, 106
State Dept. of Human Serv. v. Northern, 987
State ex rel. Collins v. Superior Court, 113
Stattner v. Caldwell, 102
Steinberg v. Indemnity Ins. Co. of North America, 211
Stern v. Tarrant County Hosp. Dist., 483
Stetina v. Medical Licensing Bd., 464
Stevens v. Smallman, 210
Storar, In re, 985, 1005
Storar & Eichner, In re, 1003
Strachan v. John F. Kennedy Mem. Hosp., 902, 965
Strunk v. Strunk, 1014
Suckle v. Madison Gen. Hosp., 711
Suenram v. Society of Valley Hosp., 565
Sullivan v. O'Connor, 293
Superintendent of Belchertown State School v. Saikewicz, 972

Table of Cases

Suria v. Shiffman, 378
Sutphin v. Platt, 217
Sweasy v. King's Daughters Mem. Hosp., 515
Swine Flu Immuniz., In re — Products Liability Litigat., 217, 245

Taenzler v. Burlington Northern, 228
Tarrant County Hosp. Dist. v. Hughes, 1263
Taylor v. Blue Cross/Blue Shield, 599
Thomas S. v. Morrow, 559
Thompson v. Brett, 364
Thompson v. Carter, 209, 210, *269*
Thompson v. Mayes, 86
Thompson v. Midwest Foundn. Indep. Physicians Assn., 897
Thompson v. Sun City Commun. Hosp., 357, 542
Thornton v. Southwest Detroit Hosp., 550
Thrailkill v. Montgomery Ward & Co., 228
Tillman v. Detroit Receiving Hosp., 925
Todd v. Sorell, 828
Truman v. Thomas, 305, 318, 320
Tunkl v. Regents of Univ. of Calif., 374
Tryon v. Casey, 205, 206
Tulsa Area Hosp. Council v. Oral Roberts Univ., 621
Turpin v. Sortini, 1119

Union Labor Life Ins. Co. v. Perino, 599
United Hosp. Cent. v. Richardson, 621
United States v. Addison, 105
United States v. Baylor Hosp., 539
United States v. Baylor Univ. Med. Center, 527
United States v. Bay State Ambulance & Hosp. Rental Serv., 610
United States v. Bowers, 91
United States v. Carilion Health Serv., 650-652
United States v. Charters, 959
United States v. Downing, 105, *114*, 195
United States v. Grassi, 90
United States v. Greber, 600
United States v. Gwaltney, 143
United States v. Kats, 610
United States v. Kozminki, 166
United States v. Luce, 1159
United States v. Metzger, 114
United States v. National Med. Enters., 649
United States v. Rockford Mem. Corp., 650
United States v. Salerno, 168
United States v. Smith, 195
United States v. Univ. Hosp., 539, 1011
United States, ex rel. DiGiacomo v. Franzen, 69
University of Arizona v. Superior Court, 1126
Utah County v. Intermountain Health Care, Inc., 624

Van Vactor v. Blue Cross Assn., 686
Vasily v. Cole, 453
Vinyard v. King, 662
Virginia Acad. of Clin. Psychol. v. Blue Shield, 898
Visbeck, In re, 1005
V.N.A. v. Heckler, 715

Wagenseller v. Scottsdale Mem. Hosp., 661
Walker v. Pierce, 526
Walker v. Sup. Court, 1021
Wamser v. State, 125
Washington State Nurses Assn. v. Board of Med. Examiners, 466
Watkins v. Mercy Med. Center, 483, 1064
Weatherly v. Miskle, 217
Weaver v. Reagan, 687
Weber v. Reproductive Health Servs., 1047
Weber v. Stony Brook Hosp., 1011, 1022
Weiss v. York Hosp., 489
Weissman v. Blue Cross of Western New York, Inc., 686
Welfare Fund v. Markham, 599
Werner v. Hetrick, 282
West Alleghany Hosp. v. Board of Property Assn., 638
Westchester County Med. Center, in the Matter of, 988
Whalen v. Roe, 566, *1160*
Wickline v. State, 747
Wickline v. State of Calif., 356
Wideman v. Shallowford Commun. Hosp., 554
Wilk v. American Med. Assn., 502
Wilkinson v. Vesey, 304
Williams v. Hofmann, 923
Willman v. Beheler, 664
Wilmington Gen. Hosp. v. Manlove, 518
Wilson v. Keunzi, 1124
Wilson v. Liberty Nat. Life Ins. Co., 205
Wilson v. Stilwell, 217
Withrow v. Larkin, 470
Women's Med. Cent. v. Finely, 619
Wood v. Hilton Head Hosp., 477
Wyatt v. Stickney, 559

Yanktown v. South Dakota Dept. of Health, 619
Ybarra v. Spangard, 292
Younts v. St. Francis Hosp., 1019

Ziegert v. South Chicago Commun. Hosp., 379
Zuckerberg v. Blue Cross & Blue Shield, 686

Index

Abortion
  conscience clauses, 662, 1064
  constitutional issues, 1047
  eugenic abortion, 1065
  genetic counseling, 1113, 1123, 1127
  public funding, 1047, 1063
  spousal rights, 1065
  Tay-Sachs disease, 1113
  viability criteria, 1050, 1052, 1062, 1066
  wrongful life issues, 1113, 1119
Access to treatment, 455. See also Right to treatment
  advanced medical techniques, 811
  AIDS patients, 1252
  DRGs, 742
Acquired immunodeficiency syndrome. See AIDS
Ad Hoc Committee, Harvard Medical School
  definition of death, 906
  legal commentary, 908
Adversarial process science, 361
Adversarial system
  expert witnesses, 64, 65
  forensic experts, 67
Adversary System, 11
AIDS, 527
  access to treatment, 536
  as handicap, 1252
  bathhouses, 1233, 1263, 1265
  black & hispanic patients, 1207, 1273
  children, 1203
  civil liberties issues, 1211
  clearinghouse information, 1221
  comparison with hepatitis B, 1210
  compulsory testing, 1253, 1257, 1266
    hospital patients, 539
  confidentiality, 1224, 1241, 1250
    court disclosures, 1248
    disclosure allowances, 1242-1247
  counseling services, 1251, 1253
  criminal law issues, 1268
  definition, 1199
  diagnostic testing, 1238
  disability insurance, 1239
  discrimination, 536, 1224, 1252, 1266
  disease control programs, 1237
  duty to treat, 527
  duty to warn, 1245
  epidemic (update), 1199
  epidemiological review, 1199-1207
  epidemiology studies, 1228
  ethical issues, 1225, 1251, 1258
  European AIDS legislation, 1225
  federal financing, 1239, 1240
  federal programs, 1239
  gay bars, 1265
  gender differences, 1201-1203
  geographic distribution, 1201
  great pandemic, 1222
  handicap discrimination, 527, 532
  high-risk sexual behavior, 1263, 1265
  history, 1221, 1222
  informed consent requirements, 1240, 1250
  international efforts, 1221
  IV drug use, 1266
  lawyer/physician conflict, 23
  legislation, 1229
  legislative surveys
    American, 1222
    European, 1225
  local health measures, 1228, 1237
  mandatory screening, 1257, 1258, 1266
  needle-exchange programs, 1223
  needle-sharing dangers, 1223, 1266
  notifiable disease, 1225
  pre-marital screening, 1239
  preventive measures, 1227
  prison populations, 1266
  public attitudes, 1236
  public policy issues, 1221
  quarantine, 1216
  racial and ethnic characteristics, 1207
  reportable diseases
    HIV infection, 1230
  right to know, 1258
  right to treatment, 1252, 1258
  risk assessment, 1207
  role of public health professionals, 1215
  standards for control, 1229
  state legislative survey, 1222
  state-level measures, 1228, 1237
  statistical review, 1199
  surveillance measures, 1228, 1234

AIDS (*continued*)
  traditional regulatory measures, 1250
  treatment programs, 1239
  unsafe sexual activities, 1234
  voluntary testing programs, 1241, 1251
  World Health Assembly, 1224
Alcohol abuse
  consumer warning labels, 1196
  fetal alcohol syndrome, 1197
  moderate consumption, 1196
  product liability, 1192, 1195
Alcohol abuse programs
  drinking and driving, 1197
Alcohol dependence treatment
  community-based programs, 1168
  definitions, 1173
  legislative goals, 1165
  legislative history, 1175
  legislative strategies, 1168, 1172
  medical specialization, 1174
  treatment programs, 1165
    combined with drug treatment, 1169, 1173
Alcohol, Drug Abuse, and Mental Health Administration (ADAMHA), 1240
Antitrust laws
  Blue Cross plans, 892
  boycott, 892
  exclusive hospital contracts, 510
  health insurance, 699
  hospital mergers, 644
  hospital peer review, 487
  hospital privileges, 476
  medical care foundations, 881
  medical staff competition, 499
  medical staff conspiracy, 499
  per se violations, 500, 881
  preferred provider organizations, 889
  quality of care, defense, 506
  rule of reason, 502, 506
  shield laws, 516
  state action exemption, 517
Assumption of risk
  malpractice defense, 365, 373
  refusal of treatment, 374
Autopsies
  chief medical examiner, 94
  civil liability, 102
  importance in investigation, 83
  in courtroom, 88
  malpractice, 102
  photography, 88
  psychological, 85
  religious objections, 96, 99
  reports, confidentiality, 102
  videotaped, 90
  wrongfully conducted, 99

"Baby Doe" regulations, 1010
"Baby Fae" transplant case, 1029
Basic science definitions, 31
Bayesian decision theory, 80
Benefit-cost analysis, 803
Bioethics. *See* Medical ethics
Birth control, 1045. *See also* Reproductive rights
Blood banks
  confidentiality, 1259, 1262
  liability issues, 1263
  refusal of transfusions, 927, 933
Blood groupings
  blood stains, 60, 69, 113, 127, 133, 137, 143
  parental testing, 144
  various tests, 143
Blood stains
  blood groupings, 60, 69, 137
  genetic markers, 126, 133, 137
Brain death
  definition, 902, 913, 914
  Harvard Ad Hoc Committee, 906
  humanhood criteria, 1024
  murder charges, 913, 941
  statute, 905, 913
British National Health Service, 779, 788, 789, 792

Canadian Health Service, 792
Case management, 37, 51, 52
Centers for Disease Control, 1199, 1221, 1238, 1239
Certificate of need (CON) programs, 612
  CT scanner, 617
  hospitals, 615, 618
Charitable hospitals, 624, 637
Charitable tax exemption
  basis, 637
  hospitals, 624, 637
Chiropractor, 464, 502, 511
Clinical science definitions, 31
Code of ethics
  forensic sciences, 29
Codes
  interprofessional code for physicians and attorneys, 26
Coma, irreversible. *See* Definition of death
Conflict of interest
  medical practice, 741
Consent, informed. *See* Informed consent
Coroners, 92. *See also* Medical examiners
  duties, 95, 96
Corporate liability, 321
Cost-effectiveness analysis, 803

Index   1283

Critical care
  best-interest test, 1002
  court intervention, 983
  criminal charges, 932, 941
  ethics committees, 970, 982
  euthanasia, 1030, 1036, 1039
  general issues, 931
  guardianship issues, 985, 1000
  humanhood issues, 1024
  incompetent patients, 972, 986
  liability issues
    civil damages, 964
    criminal law, 932, 941
  life-sustaining treatment
    blood transfusions, 927, 933, 955
    right to refuse, 927, 931
  nursing homes, 963
  nutrition needs, 948, 961, 988, 995
  patient wishes, 966
  privacy rights, 961, 968
  prognosis committees, 982
  provider responsibility, 963
  rationing of care for elderly, 1039
  substituted judgement, 972, 1002, 1004, 1005
  suicide issues, 956

Death
  medicolegal investigation, 83
    child abuse, 91
    murder, 83, 91
    suicide, 85
Decision analysis, 39, 803
Definition of death, 902. *See also* Brain death
  brain death, 1028
  EEG test, 903
  Harvard Ad Hoc Committee, 906
  Kansas statute, 913
    constitutionality, 913
  persistent vegetative state, 912
  President's Commission, 909
Dental health regulation, 1134
Diagnosis, 34
  cost-effective clinical decisions, 809
  definitions, 456
  diagnostic certainty, 37, 39
  DRGs, 719, 720, 731, 736
  financial incentives, 37, 733, 796
  glossary of terms, 34
  hypothesis, 37
  insurance coverage, 692
  interview, 45
  medical, 34, 37
  risk, 38
  search for certainty, 37, 800, 841
  technology, 34
  tentative, 51
  testing, 38, 50

  textbooks, 34
  uncertainty, 692, 841
Diagnostic-related groups, 719, 720, 723, 731, 736, 738, 742
  adverse effects, 743
Disability
  definition, 16
Discrimination
  handicap, 527
    AIDS, 532
    otherwise qualified, 528
    tuberculosis, 528
Disease, 16, 37
DNA testing
  paternity, 154
  varieties, 154
DNA typing, 145, 146, 148, 153
  criminal application, 153
  paternity, 153
Do-not-resuscitate code, 939
Drug abuse regulation
  compulsory testing, 1179, 1190
  controlled substances, 1161, 1171
  federal testing programs, 1179, 1190
  IV drug users and AIDS, 1218, 1223
  national policy, 1176
  random testing, 1179
  scheduled drugs, 1161, 1176
Drug dependence treatment
  cocaine, "crack" cocaine, 1179
  commitment standards, 1174
  community-based services, 1168
  definitions, 1173
  employee assistance programs, 1192
  evaluation programs, 1220
  heroin, 1176, 1198
  international efforts, 1178
  IV drug users, 1218
  legislative goals, 1165
  legislative guidelines, 1165, 1173
  legislative strategies, 1168
  marijuana, 1176
  medical specialization, 1174
  methadone treatment, 1172
  morphine, 1176
  "safer injection," 1219
  treatment programs, 1165, 1219
Drug Enforcement Administration, 1176
Durable power of attorney, 939
Duty to die, 1036

Economic malpractice, 357, 755
Emergency care
  definition, 550
  general duty to treat, 550
  patient dumping, 540, 542, 549, 550
Employment law, 652, 661
  conscience clause, on abortion, 662

Employment law (*continued*)
  physician contracts, covenant not to compete, 663
  pregnancy of employee, 663
  whistleblower issues, 662
  wrongful discharge, 661
Environment, 17
Epidemiology, 34, 755
  texts, 34
Euthanasia, 1030, 1036
  physician involvement, 1038
Evidence
  epidemiological
    admissibility, 242
    agent orange, 247
    reliability
    statistical methods, 247
    swine flu immunization, 247
    toxic torts, 247
  medical, 201
    epidemiological studies, 236, 242, 247
    lay opinion and testimony, 201, 204
    mental capacity, 203, 204
    mathematical probability, 69, 71, 72
    reasonable doubt
    quantification, 69
Excessive testing, 37

Family planning
  abortion issues, 1063
  contraceptive use, 1040
  counseling, 1046
  court-ordered contraception, 1045
Fetal alcohol syndrome, 1197
Fetus, rights of
  cesarean sections, 1101, 1109
  fetal abuse, 1109, 1111, 1112
  in utero therapy, 1099
Food and Drug Administration, 277, 1240
Forensic identification
  DNA print, 148, 153
  genetic markers, 126
Forensic medicine, 2
Forensic pathology, 81
Forensic psychiatry, 155
  child custody suits, 168
  competency to stand trial, 158
  "Dr. Death," 167
  expert testimony
    involuntary hospitalization, 168
    predicting dangerousness, 160, 163, 165, 168
    ultimate issues, 159
  insanity defense, 157
  personal injury litigation, 168
  sociopathic personality, 167
  workers' compensation, 168

Forensic sciences, 55
  accuracy, 61
  advocacy system, 65
  blood groupings, 59
  blood stains, 60
  blood tests, 59
  communication, 67, 79
  definition, 55
  Frye test, 103, 105, 119
  laboratory, 56, 61, 63
  nature of, 56
  new scientific tests, 103
  opinions and conclusions, 71
  photography
    gruesomeness, 88
  polygraph tests, 103, 114
  probabilities, 67, 80
    mathematical, 69, 81
  probabilities as proof, 450
  quantification, 81
  references, 58
Forensic Serology
  expert, 133, 143
Forensic Toxicology, 81
  alcohol tests, 112
  succinic acid test, 114

Genetic counseling, 1123, 1127
  Tay-Sachs disease, 1113
Geriatric care, 582. *See also* Nursing homes, Right to Treatment
Global Program on AIDS, 1221
Good Samaritan laws, 336, 380, 383
  emergency care, 381, 384
  statutes, 380-383
Gross national product
  health care services, 668

Hair samples
  analysis, 71, 79
Harvard Medical Practice Study, 414
  adverse events, 415, 417
  economic consequences, 418
  litigation, 418
  risk factors, 416
Health
  right to, 17
Health care
  professionals, 20
Health care access, 455, 567, 742
  DRGs, 742
  medical ethics, 567
  public policy, 567
Health care cost containment, 665, 669, 731
  certificate of need, 756, 757, 762, 767
  duty to treat, 755

Index

economic malpractice, 755, 808
epidemiological analysis, 755
failure of strategies, 870
hospital costs, 673
legal barriers, 731
legislation review, 773
malpractice implications, 747
physician behavior, 631
physicians' fees, 671
public opinion polls, 669
rationing and euthanasia, 1039
"unbundling" hospital costs, 738
Health care delivery systems, 455, 583, 665
AIDS patients, 1258
benefit-cost analysis, 803
consumer-choice plans, 791
CT scanners, 667
deregulation, 845
ethical issues, 808, 809
free choice of services, 671, 875
market forces, 699, 833
patient access, 455
provider access, 455
  freedom of practice, 455
  physician licensure, 455
rationing, 667, 779, 808
regulatory reforms, 665, 829
role of competition, 829, 833, 843
social responsibility, 738
Health care economics, 688, 715, 775
consumer choice plans, 791, 861, 867, 875
fee-for-service system, 689, 698
rationing issues, 808, 832
Health care enterprise, 583. *See also* Health care delivery systems
Health care facilities, 251
regulation, 612, 622
Health care finance, 841, 863. *See also* Health care insurance
Health care foundations, 255
Health care insurance, 673, 678, 697
Blue Cross, 672, 674, 686, 860
Blue Shield, 675, 686
business of, 597
diagnosis, 692
efficiency, 697
employment-based, 573
ERISA, 687
free choice, 698
hospital costs, 673
illness, definition of, 695
medical necessity, 687
Medicare, 701
necessary care, 698
physicians' judgement, 686
private insurance, 684
prospective payment systems, 611
regulatory issues, 597

self-insurance plans, 599, 560
service coverage, 681, 692
third-party payors, 684
uncertainty issues, 696
uninsured coverage, 678
Health care organization, 583. *See also* Health maintenance organizations and Health care delivery systems
Blue Cross/Blue Shield, 583
corporate practice, 584, 591, 593
history, 583, 596
Health care planning, 851
Health care policy, 799, 808, 851
Health law
curriculum, 22
definitions, 9
education, 19
periodicals, 22
terminology, 1
terminology
historical, 1
Health legislation
drug and alcohol treatment, 1165
Health maintenance organizations, 255, 847, 854
capitation fee system, 854
closed panel, 354
financial incentives, 356
future of, 873
gatekeeper function, 353, 354
guarantees of quality care, 354
history, 854
legislation, 850
malpractice liability, 321, 348, 354
medical malpractice, 349
open panel, 354
Health planning, 611
Heart transplant surgery, 814, 828
HIV infection. *See also* AIDS
blood supply issues, 1259
confidentiality, 1259
contagious diseases, 1252
counseling services, 1251
crime of transmission, 1269
discrimination, 536
ethical issues, 1251, 1258
gay men, 1202
  reduced infection, 1266
prison populations, 1266
right to know, 1258
Hospital malpractice, 249, 333
apparent agency, 335
common knowledge, 338
corporate liability
  strict liability, 340
  warranty, 340
emergency services, 329, 335, 336
independent physicians, 325
intermediary corporate providers, 328

Hospital malpractice (continued)
  liability, 261, 321, 325, 333, 336
  monitoring medical staff quality, 321, 326, 334
  moral obligation, 335
  nosocomial infections, 341
  ostensible agency, 335
  reasonable standard, 266
  standards of care
    J.C.A.H. guidelines, 277
  strict liability doctrine, 339, 340
Hospital medical staff, 471
  admission to staff, 471
  antitrust laws, 476
  boycotts, 499, 500
  credentialling process, 501
  direct competition, 499
  disruptive behavior, 479
  excessive quality of care, 484
  failure to cooperate, 479
  hospital bylaws, 485
  judicial review, 475, 482
  peer review, 471
    confidentiality, 512, 515
    immunity, 512, 513, 515
    shield law, 516
  privileges, 471
  procedural issues, 485, 486
  staff bylaws, 485
  utilization criteria, 484
Hospital organization, 253
  chain operation, 648
  mergers, 642, 644, 649
  reorganization plans, 642
  restructure, 642
Hospital regulation
  certificate of need, 612, 615, 618
  duty to provide charitable care, 638
  health planning, 613
  licensure, 612
Hospitals
  certificate-of-need laws, 756, 757, 762, 767
  litigation, 778
  major classifications, 251
  medical staff organization, 735
  merger, 695
  public-utility model, 773
  rate setting, 773, 777
  rationing care, 667
  reorganization, 735
  specialty, 254
Humanhood indicators, 1024
Hypnosis
  restoring memory, 188, 193

Impairment, 16
Informed consent, 15
  alternative treatments, 309
  more hazardous, 308, 310
  assumption of risk by refusal, 306
  basis of liability, 302
  battery, 304
  cancer risks, 305
  consent forms, 315, 369, 370, 372, 374
  consumer choice, 791, 875
  diagrams, disclosure, 307
  duty to warn, 308
  ethical basis, 302
  expression of personal autonomy, 311
  fraudulently obtained, 304
  full disclosure, 311
  informed refusal, 931
  market-theory model, 312
  materiality rule, 304
  medical-consumer choice, 311
  myths, 313, 314
  negligence, 304
  patient autonomy, 311
  professional standard, 305
  proximate causation, 313, 369, 374
  prudent patient rule, 305
  reasonable prudence, 304
  refusal; duty of physician, 305, 318
  remote risk, 364
  risk management alternatives, 313
  scope, 305
  standard of disclosure, 304, 306, 309, 315, 318, 364
  statutory reforms, 370, 374
  therapeutic privilege, 306
Informed refusal to consent, 305, 318
Insurance. See Health insurance
In utero fetal therapy, 1099

J.C.A.H.
  accreditation standards, 485, 510

Kidney dialysis, 812

Laboratory tests, 50
Labor law and relations, 652, 656
  health care industry, 656
  nurses, 661
  peer review, 653
  physicians and dentists' unions, 652
Legal medicine, 3, 7
Liver transplant surgery, 822
Living will legislation
  California, 934
  state legislative survey, 937

Malpractice. See Medical malpractice
Malpractice, hospital. See Hospital malpractice

Index 1287

Malpractice liability
  general theories, 256
Medicaid, 707
  organ transplant surgery, 827
  reimbursement systems, 707
Medical care access. *See* Access to treatment
Medical dictionaries, 33
Medical education, 249
  basic sciences, 31
  clinical science, 31
Medical ethics, 667, 670
  bibliography on death-and-dying issues, 931
  court-ordered cesareans, 1109
  duty to treat AIDS cases, 539
  euthanasia, 1030, 1036
  fetal rights, 1108
  genetic counseling, 1123, 1127
  health care rationing, 808, 809
  mercy killing, 1038
  refusal of life-sustaining treatment, 931, 964
  right to die, 931, 962
  right to treatment, 524, 525
  surrogate mothers, 1088
  textbooks, 901
  wrongful conception, 1113, 1127
Medical evidence. *See also* Evidence, medical
  package inserts, 1197
  probabilities as proof, 450
Medical examiners, 92
  advantage over coroner system, 96
  Model Act, 93
  organ harvesting, 915
  religious objections, 96, 99
  wrongful autopsies, 99
Medical jurisprudence, 3, 4, 6
Medical law, 8
Medical licensure, 455, 463
  discipline, 468
  due process, 470
  patchwork system, 465
  re-testing, 468
  revocation, 468
  supply of physicians, 466
Medical malpractice, 18, 249
  abandonment, 298
  acupuncture, 560
  ad damnum clause, 388, 392
  alternative compensation systems, 390
  alternative dispute resolution, 442
  arbitration, 389, 443, 448, 452
  arbitration clause, 448
  autopsies, 102
  breach of contract, 293, 298
  breach of warranty, 298, 301
  "caps" on recovery, 440
  Common Knowledge Rule, 292
  contingent fee, 387
  contingent fee regulation, 392
  contributory negligence, 378
  current status, 260
  defensive medicine, 386, 808
  economic malpractice, 357, 755
  expert witness, 209, 217
    competency, 221
    locality rule, 217
    standard of care, 220
  faith healer, 300
  fraud, 300
  good samaritans, 386
  grievance mechanisms, 389
  guarantee, 298
  Harvard Practice Study, 414
  health maintenance organizations, 321, 348, 847, 854
  history, 260
  increasing litigation, 261
  informed consent, 387, 388
  insurance premiums, 261
  judicial responses, 439
  jury system, 390
  limitations on awards, 440
  negligence per se, 292
  no-fault plans, 424
    birth injuries, 426
    childhood vaccines, 426
  non-licensed physicians, 300
  nurse's testimony, 209
  patient obligations, 378
  physician-patient relationship, 391
  preferred provider organizations, 321, 354
  qualified immunity, 386
  reasonable prudence rule, 347
  reform movements, 386
  reforms
    A.M.A. plan, 403
    major proposals, 422
    no-fault, 402, 409, 411, 414
    research studies, 422
  res ipsa loquitur, 292, 387
  risk management, 442
  screening panels, 389, 392, 442, 452
  secretary's commission, 261
  six-state study, 392
  standards of care, 262
    evidentiary issues, 276
    locality rule, 267
  sterilization, 299
  strict liability for physicians, 347
  treatment without diagnosis, 1150
  wrongful life, 1115, 1119, 1124
Medical practice
  conflict of interest, 609, 611
  corporate practice, 588, 591, 593
    HMO comparisons, 854

Medical practice (*continued*)
  defensive medicine, 808
  employment contracts
    covenants not to compete, 663
    discrimination, 662
  fee-splitting arrangements, 605, 733
  financial incentives to reduce
      care, 733, 741, 747, 796
  interference with, 732
  "kickback" arrangements, 601
  Medicare fraud, 601, 610
  patient's advocate role, 796
  professional corporations, 596
  profit motive, role of, 624, 631, 632
  referral fee prohibitions, 600, 603, 608
  uncertainty, 37, 800, 841
Medical profession, 249
Medical science
  methods in law, 13
Medical sciences, 31
Medical specialist
  expert testimony, 210, 212, 213
Medical specialties, 250
Medical testimony, 57. *See also* Testimony, medical
Medical witness, 28
Medicare, 701
  appeal procedures, 713
  diagnosis-related groups (DRG), 719, 720
  fiscal intermediaries, 701
  peer review, 709, 711, 712
  pharmacy services, 703
  prospective payment system, 717, 719, 726, 727
  PSRO, 711, 799
  quality of care, 717, 800
  reimbursement systems, 703, 707, 709
    capital costs, 723
  second opinions, 710
  utilization review, 711
Medicine, state, 5
Medicolegal field
  courses, 19
  terminology, 1
Medicolegal relations
  conflict, 23, 25
Medicolegal viewpoints, 10
Mental health regulation, 1139, 1145
  commitment laws, 959
    standards of proof, 1139, 1145, 1174
Model Post-Mortem Examinations Act, 93
Murder
  investigation, 83

Narcoanalysis
  truth and lie detection, 188

Narcotic drug regulation
  failure of policies, 1171
  history, 1176
  national policy, 1176
  1961 Single Convention, 1178
  1971 Psychotropic Drugs Convention, 1178
Narcotic drug treatment
  definitions, 1176
National drug control policy, 1171, 1177
National Institute of Alcohol and Alcohol Abuse, 1174, 1176, 1179
National Institute of Drug Abuse, 1174, 1176, 1179
National Organ Transplant Act, 924
Nurse midwives, 464
Nurses
  expert testimony
    medical standard of care, 209
    nursing standard of care, 209
  malpractice, 209
Nursing homes, 582
  elder abuse, 582
  Medicare/Medicaid requirements, 582

Optometrists, 470
Organizations, Health Maintenance, 255. *See* Health Maintenance Organizations
Organ transplants
  "Baby Fae" case, 1028
  constitutional issues, 913, 915
  corneal tissue, 915
  incompetents, 1014
  minors, 1016, 1018, 1023
  procurement programs, 915
    auto driver's licenses, 923
    informed refusal, 920
  state legislation, 913
Organ transplant surgery, 794, 828
  ethical issues, 827
  rationing systems, 825, 832
Osteopaths, 464, 483, 489

Package inserts, 270, 277, 278, 372, 1197
Pathology, 31. *See also* Forensic pathology
Patient advocates, 581
Patient history, 45
Patient-physician relationship, 524
  Hippocratic Oath, 525
  medical ethics, 525
Patient representatives, 581
Patients' rights, 578
  bill of, 581

Index

patient representatives, 581
Persistent vegetative state, 948, 966, 981, 995, 1028
Pharmacist
  expert witness, 209
Pharmaceutical products
  learned intermediaries, 429, 1198
  package inserts, 1197
Photography
  autopsies, 88
  color, 89
  crime scene, 88
  gruesomeness, 88
    due process violation, 89
Physical examination, 49
Physicians
  expert witness, 210
  patient relationship, 524. *See also* patient physician relationship
Podiatrists, 464
Polygraph test
  admissibility, 170
  diagnostic tool for deception, 114
  lie detector, 178
Population science
  population control issues, 1045
Practice of medicine. *See* Medical practice
  alternative healers, 463
  Chinese medicine, 463, 560
  definition, 459
Preferred provider organizations, 255, 355, 875, 877, 879
  antitrust issues, 889
  Blue Cross/Blue Shield plans, 898
Privacy, right of
  blood banks, 1259
  centralized computer file, 1160
  contraceptive use, 1040, 1042
    minor's rights, 1045
  critical care, 961, 968, 998
  drug prescriptions, 1160
  random drug testing, 1179
  reproductive rights, 1041
Procreative rights
  court-ordered cesareans, 1101, 1109
  fetal rights. *See* Fetus, rights of
  maternal behavior, 1098, 1112
  maternal drug abuse, 1110, 1112
  maternal-fetal conflicts, 1095, 1112
  maternal informed consent, 1102
Products liability litigation
  agent orange, 234
  swine flu, 245
Prognosis, 52
Proof, medical. *See* Evidence, medical
Prospective payment systems, 611
  HMO comparisons, 611
Prostitutes
  quarantine, 1146

Psychiatrists
  expert witness, 206
Psychological profiles, 199
Psychologists
  expert witness, 115, 207, 209, 156
Public health, danger to, 459
Public health regulation. *See also* AIDS
  AIDS control programs, 1237
  AIDS legislation, 1222
  AIDS prevention, 1227
  compulsory treatment, 1139, 1145, 1146, 1147
  controlled substances, 1161
  dangerous premises, 1156
  dental health, 1134
  disease prevention quarantine, 1146, 1151, 1152
  drug abuse, 1160
  drug prescriptions, 1160
  federal regulation, 1152
  fluoridation, 1134, 1144
  hepatitis B, 1157, 1159
  history, 1143, 1151, 1152
  individual freedoms, 1129, 1142, 1143
  infectious diseases, 1129, 1152
  international, 1151
  IV drug use and AIDS, 1223
  local regulation, 1134
  local sanitary codes, 1156, 1159
  mental health, 1139
  modern regulatory systems, 1250
  non-infectious conditions, 1134
  out-of-date legislation, 1231
  parens patriae powers, 1139
  police powers, 1129, 1135, 1149, 1152
  privacy issues, 1179
  public nuisances, 1158
  pure foods and drink, 1135, 1144
  quarantine, 1207
  religious objections, 1143, 1144
  reportable diseases
    AIDS and HIV infection, 1225
  smallpox vaccination, 1129, 1143
  state regulation, 1129, 1228
  surveillance, 1228
    privacy issues, 1160
  swine flu disaster, 120
  swine flu liability, 245
  tattoo parlors, 1156
  vaccine liability issues, 245, 1146
Public policy
  AIDS and IV drug abuse, 1218
  AIDS epidemic issues, 1221, 1223
  drug and alcohol treatment legislation, 1165
  health care policy, 668, 670
  surrogate-mother contracts, 1084
Public safety regulation
  airline pilots, 1153, 1155

Public safety regulation (*continued*)
  crash helmets, 1156
  seat belts, 1156

Quantitative Risk Assessment, 248
Quarantine
  venereal or STD diseases, 1149, 1152

Rape trauma syndrome, 196, 197
Reasonable doubt, 69, 80
  medical evidence quantification, 69
Rehabilitation Act
  AIDS as a handicap, 532, 536, 1252
  contagious diseases, 528, 532, 1252
  tuberculosis as a handicap, 528, 1252
Reproductive rights
  artificial insemination, 1067, 1073
  in vitro fertilization, 1073
  surrogacy contracts, 1078, 1084, 1093, 1094
  surrogate mothers, 1078, 1092
Right to privacy
  health care, 565
Right to treatment, 455, 465, 518. *See also* Access to treatment
  abandonment, 524, 526
  AIDS patients, 527, 536
  constitutional basis, 554, 558
  elderly patients, 582
  indigent patients, 549, 552, 571
  obstetrical care, 554
  patient dumping, 540, 549
  paying patients, 518
  refusal of treatment, 524
  religious issues, 465
  termination of care, 931
  uninsured patients, 540, 574
  women's rights, 465
Risk assessment
  predicting violence, 164
Risk management programs
  alternatives, 313
  informed consent, 320
  reasonable standard, 266

Scientific tests
  admissibility
    Frye test, 105
    general acceptance standard, 105, 106
  alcohol, 106, 112
    HGN test, 112
  chromatography, 114
  duty to preserve evidence, 144
  general acceptance
    alternative tests, 125
    forensic-only techniques, 113

  genetic markers, 126, 144
  polygraph, 114
  reliability, 125
  serological electrophoresis, 126, 129, 133, 137
  validity, 125, 128
  voiceprint, 113
Secretary's Commission on Medical Malpractice, 261
Semen
  analysis, 75
Sexual abuse, 198
Sexually transmitted diseases
  contact tracing, 1153
  history, 1152
  quarantine, 1147, 1152
Standards of Care
  acceptable practice, 266
  average medical care, 262
  choice of treatments, 360
  consultants, 267
  contributory negligence, 378
  defenses, 358
  error of judgement
    biomedical research, 361
    medical care, 358, 360
  fiduciary obligation, 355
  geographic issues, 267
  good medical care, 262, 264, 265, 266
  highest degree of care, 336
  locality rule, 267
  nonphysician experts, 276
  ophthalmology, 342
  package inserts, 270, 277, 278, 372, 1197
  pathologists, 267
  Physician's Desk Reference, 277, 278
  reasonable prudence rule, 347
  reduced standard of care, 336
  schools of medicine, 364
  schools of thought, 363
  substantive issues, 266
  textbooks, 276
Sterilization
  wrongful life, 1123
Substituted judgement, 972, 1002, 1004
Suicidology, 85
Survival, lost chance, 278, 282
  cancer diagnosis, 282
Syndrome, acquired immunodeficiency. *See* AIDS
Syndrome, fetal alcohol, 1197

Termination of treatment. *See also* Critical care and Treatment decisions
  Baby Andrew case, 1013
  best interest test, 1002, 1005

Index

child abuse and neglect, 1009
incompetent patients, 966, 972, 986, 1006
persistent vegetative state, 966, 981, 995
privacy rights, 961, 998
quality of life, 1006
severely deformed infants, 1007
substituted judgement, 972, 1002, 1004
Testimony, expert
  accuracy, 64, 65
  opinion on credibility of witnesses, 194
  psychologist, 115
    eye witnesses' credibility, 114, 195
  quantification, 81
  serial framework, 196
Testimony, medical, 57
  affidavits, 239
  basis of opinion, 223, 233
  content, 223
  expert, 207, 209, 211, 214
    admissibility, 242
    bias, 216, 223
    collateral attack, 207, 211
    compensation, 215, 217, 222
    conflicting testimony, 214
    credibility, 214, 215
    "professional witness," 216, 222
    qualifications, 207, 211, 217
    treating/non-treating physician, 212

medical malpractice
  competency, 221
  opinion, 225
  perjury, 223
  reasonable medical certainty, 227, 248
  reasonable probability standard, 228
Tobacco dependence programs
  consumer-warning labels, 1198
  economic costs, 1198
  prevention, 1198, 1199
Treatment, 51
Treatment decisions
  blood transfusions, 1021
  incompetents, 972, 1014
  kidney transplant, 1014
  minors, 1014
  parental authority, 1018

Uniform Alcoholism and Detoxification Act, 117
Uniform Anatomical Gift Act, 917
Uniform Determination of Death Act, 905, 914

Venereal diseases. *See* Sexually transmitted diseases

Wrongful birth, 1113, 1120
Wrongful conception, 1113, 1124, 1127
Wrongful life, 1113, 1114, 1119
  public policy issues, 1125